# 1996
# Magruder's
# AMERICAN GOVERNMENT

## William A. McClenaghan

The American people have become accustomed to divided government—to a political environment in which one of the major parties holds the presidency and the other party controls Congress. For forty years now, one party (most often, the Republicans) has occupied the White House and the other party (regularly, the Democrats) has had a firm grip on Capitol Hill.

The elections of 1994 renewed the now-familiar pattern of divided government—but with a distinctive twist. Today, the President is a Democrat and the Republicans have a majority of the seats in both houses of Congress.

The American system of government, with its separation of powers and checks and balances, works best when the same party controls its executive and legislative branches. When that is not the case, the relationship between the President and Congress becomes much more difficult and much more confrontational.

Senate Majority Leader
Bob Dole

Speaker of the House
Newt Gingrich

President Bill Clinton

# 1996

# Magruder's
# AMERICAN
# GOVERNMENT

REVISED BY

## William A. McClenaghan

DEPARTMENT OF POLITICAL SCIENCE
OREGON STATE UNIVERSITY

## PRENTICE HALL
### NEEDHAM, MASSACHUSETTS

# AMERICAN GOVERNMENT,

first published in 1917 and revised annually, is an enduring symbol of the author's faith in American ideals and American institutions. The life of Frank Abbott Magruder (1882–1949) was an outstanding example of Americanism at its very best. His career as a teacher, author, and tireless worker in civic and religious undertakings remains an inspiring memory to all who knew him.

## The Magruder's Team

The editors, designers, marketers, managers, electronic publishing specialists, copyeditor, production and manufacturing buyers, page production manager, and advertising and production manager who make up the Magruder's team are listed below.

Laura Asermily

Tom Barber

Leanne Cordischi

Gabriella Della Corte

David Graham

Jeffrey M. Ikler

Linda Johnson

Russell Lappa

David Lippman

Laura Lyon

Jonathan Pollard

Nancy Rogier

Holly Schuster

Virginia Shine

L. Christopher Valente

Samuel S. Wallace

PRENTICE HALL
Simon & Schuster Education Group
A VIACOM COMPANY

ISBN 0-13-413998-4

Printed in the United States of America

1 2 3 4 5 6 7 8 9 03 02 01 00 99 98 97 96

# PROGRAM REVIEWERS AND ADVISORS

Barbara C. Adams — Government Teacher
Coronado High School
Lubbock, Texas

Thomas Bass — Chairman, Political Science Department
University of St. Thomas
Houston, Texas

William J. Bialobrzeski — Political Science Instructor
Southgate Anderson High School
Southgate, Michigan

Connie Hankins — Government Teacher
Miami Carol City High School
Miami, Florida

Melva Ruth Jones — Teacher/Social Studies Department Chair
Lincoln High School
Dallas, Texas

William E. Law — AP Government Teacher
Morse High School
San Diego, California

James I. Malone — Government Teacher
Rancho Buena Vista High School
Vista, California

Dick Parsons — Government Teacher
El Dorado High School
Placerville, California

Ninfa Anita Sepulveda — Social Studies Department Chairperson
S. F. Austin Senior High School
Houston, Texas

Dr. Shelly K. Singer — Divisional Chair, Social Studies/Foreign Language
Larkin High School
Elgin, Illinois

Ellen Stone — Government Teacher
McAllen High School
McAllen, Texas

# PREFACE

*If a nation expects to be ignorant and free, . . .*
*it expects what never was and never will be.*

THOMAS JEFFERSON

THIS IS A BOOK ABOUT GOVERNMENT—and, more particularly, about government in the United States. Over the course of its 25 chapters and more than 800 pages, you will consider the ways in which government in this country is organized, the ways in which it is controlled by the people, the many things that it does, and the various ways in which it does them.

*Magruder's American Government,* 1996, is the latest in a long line of editions of this book. The first one appeared in 1917. Every edition of this book has had one basic purpose: to describe, analyze, and explain the American system of government.

All of the many changes made in each edition of this book illustrate a very important point:

The American system of government is extraordinarily dynamic. Change—growth, adaptation, innovation—is a basic element of its character. While it is true that our government's fundamental principles and its basic structure have remained constant over time, many of its other characteristics have changed. They continue to do so—from year to year and, frequently, from one day to the next, and sometimes remarkably.

To underscore the critical importance of this fact of continuing change, dwell for a moment on the phrase "the American system of government." You will come across it again and again, for it is an apt description of government in the United States. As you will soon discover, that system is a very complex one.

It is complex because it is made up of many different parts, performing many different functions. It is a system because all of its many different parts are interrelated. The whole cannot be understood without a knowledge of its several interacting parts; and those parts cannot be understood without a knowledge of the whole. Given all of this, the vital effects of ongoing change in the system are obvious.

Every effort has been made to see that this book is as accurate, as up-to-date, as readable, and as interesting and usable as possible. The wealth of factual information it contains has been drawn from the most current and reliable of sources. This is not a book on current events, however. It does contain much data and draws many examples from the contemporary scene.

But they are purposefully woven into the context of its primary objective: the description, analysis, and explanation of the American system of government. Another major objective is to provide a basis for understanding how other nations are governed through a careful examination of other political and economic systems.

Textbooks are sometimes criticized as being "too large," "too factual," or "not interpretive enough." *This* textbook includes that material which we believe to be absolutely necessary to a basic knowledge and understanding of the American governmental system. If the book is a "large" one, it is because its subject is a very large *and* a very *important* one.

Every book, regardless of its subject, reflects, to at least some degree, the biases of its author. This book is no exception. We have made a very conscious effort to minimize their appearance and to present a fair and balanced view of government in the United States. But, inevitably, those biases are present. Whenever they appear, they should be examined critically by the reader, of course. One of them is outstandingly obvious: the conviction that the American system of government, despite its imperfections, is in fact and should be government of the people, by the people, and for the people.

One final comment here—from both the original author, the late Frank Abbott Magruder, and the present one: Over the years we have received much valuable help from the many teachers and students who have used this book in classrooms across the nation. Their comments, suggestions, criticisms, and questions have played a large part in the making of each new edition—and they continue to be more than welcome, of course.

WILLIAM A. McCLENAGHAN

*Department of Political Science*
*Oregon State University*
*Corvallis, Oregon*

# TABLE OF CONTENTS

UNIT 1

# UNIT 3

# UNIT 5

# REFERENCE SECTION

## SPECIAL FEATURES

### Debating Key Issues

*Background information and
key arguments on landmark
Supreme Court cases*

### What You Can Do

*Examples of student participation
in government*

# Maps, Charts, Graphs, Diagrams, Tables

## Maps

## Graphs, Charts, Diagrams

# Tables

# Citizenship Charts

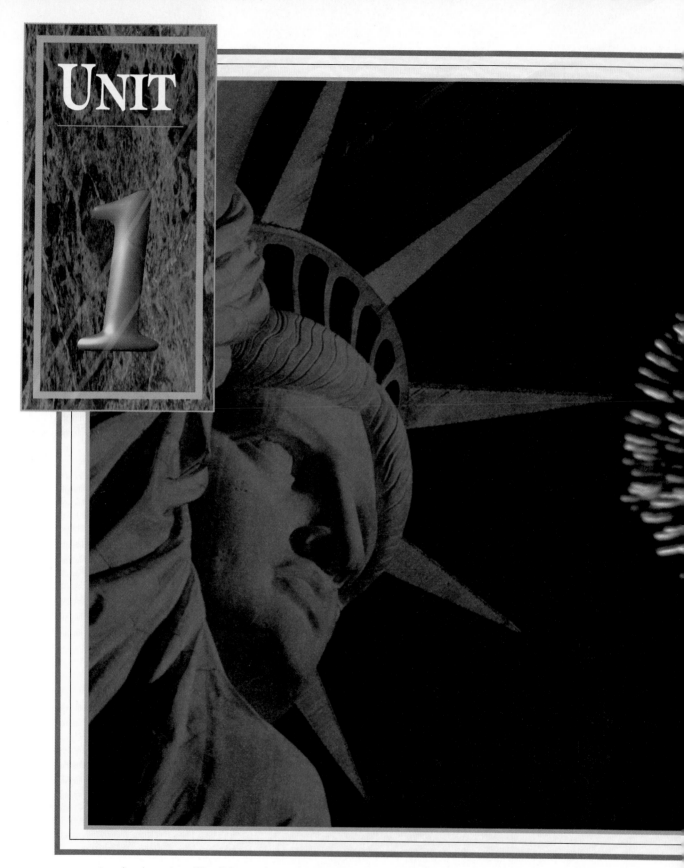

# UNIT

# 1

**An American Tradition**   An explosion of fireworks illuminates the Statue of Liberty during an Independence Day celebration.

# Foundations of American Government

On July 3, 1776, John Adams wrote to his wife, Abigail, his thoughts on how America's Declaration of Independence ought to be observed in the years to come. Adams wrote, "[the day] ought to be solemnized with Pomp and Parade, with Shews, Games, Sports, Guns, Bells, Bonfires and Illuminations from one End of this Continent to the other . . ." A year and a day later, Americans did indeed celebrate the first anniversary of Independence Day in some of the major cities of the 13 States, Philadelphia among them. Beginning at one o'clock in the afternoon, cannons boomed from ships in the river. Parades and banquets were held, accompanied by music and the thunder of musket fire. Bells rang and fireworks rocketed into the sky. Today, Independence Day remains a day of celebration—a day when Americans look back to mark one of the initial steps in the building of American government.

## DID YOU KNOW THAT . . .

- As the Constitutional Convention sat in 1787, a woman was being tried for witchcraft on the north side of Philadelphia.

- Most of those who wrote the Constitution were planters or large-scale farmers, lawyers, or merchants; only a few came from what could be called "modest circumstances."

- Sixteen of the Framers, including James Madison, had no occupation other than "politician."

**CHAPTER**

**1**

# Principles of Government

## Chapter Preview

Hair streaming behind her and the wind in her face, a woman is cruising along on her motorcycle, well within the posted speed limit of 45 miles per hour. She is stopped by a police officer and issued a citation because she is in violation of a State law that requires the wearing of protective helmets. A young father is on the way to the park, his two small children bouncing on the back seat. A police officer pulls him over and gives him a ticket for breaking the law that requires the use of seat belts or car-seats for all occupants of a vehicle.

In recent years, many Americans have questioned the right and responsibility of government to be involved in matters of personal safety. Some fear that the freedom to make many personal choices, even ones that are unhealthy or unsafe, will be eroded. Others disagree. The larger issue is this: What are the roles and the limits of government in a democracy? This chapter is about the purposes of government, its major forms, and the basic concepts of democracy.

### Before you read this chapter:

- **Describe** five ways that government is involved in your life.
- **Predict** what you think is the exact meaning of "democracy."

### As you read, focus on the main objective for each section. Understand:

1. The purposes for which government exists.
2. The major forms of government in the world today.
3. The major concepts of American democracy.

▲ **Popular Patriotism**  Father and child express support for the United States and its government. In a democracy, government cannot exist at all without such support.

# 1 Government and the State

### Find Out:
- What are the four basic characteristics of a state?
- What are the four most influential theories about the origin of the state?
- For what purposes does government exist?

### Key Terms:
government, public policies, state, sovereign

What is government, and why does it exist? One good way to answer those questions is to ask these: What would life be like if there were no government—no police, no public schools, no President, no Congress, no courts? Who would pave the streets? Who would punish those who rob or kill? Who would protect the nation against foreign dangers? Government does those things and much more.

## What Is Government?

**Government** is the institution through which a society makes and enforces its public policies. Government is made up of those people who exercise government's powers, those who have authority and control over other people.

The **public policies** of a government are, in short, all of those things a government decides to do. Here are but a few examples of public policies: imposing an income tax, setting a minimum wage, maintaining large, combat-ready armed forces, protecting the environment.

In the United States and many other countries, the people who exercise the powers of government are legislators, who make public policy in the form of law; executives and administrators, who enforce and administer those laws; and judges, who apply those laws to court cases. In some countries, government is in the hands of religious leaders, or royal families, or tribal chiefs, or soldiers with guns.

Government is among the oldest of all human inventions. Early records of government date back to ancient Egypt and the 6th century, B.C. More than 2,300 years ago, Aristotle observed that "man is by nature a political animal"[1]—a fact that, even then, had been obvious for thousands of years.

## The State

Over the course of human history, the state has emerged as the dominant political unit in the world. The **state** can be defined as a body of people, living in a defined territory, organized politically—that is, under a government—and having the power to make and enforce law without the consent of any higher authority.

There are more than 180 states in the world today. They vary greatly in size, military power, natural resources, economic importance, and in many other ways. Each of them, however, has all four of the characteristics of a state: population, territory, sovereignty, and government.[2]

**Population** Clearly, a state must have people. The size of the population has nothing to do with the existence of a state, however. The smallest state in terms of population is San Marino. Nestled high in the Apennines and bounded on all sides by Italy, it has some 22,000 people. The People's Republic of China is the most populous state. Its population is now well over one billion—one in five of all the world's people are Chinese.

The population of a state may be quite homogeneous—that is, composed of people who are much alike. Or that population may be heterogeneous—that is, made up of people of different races, languages, religions, and customs.

**Territory** Just as a state must have people, so must it have land—territory with known and recognized boundaries. Here, too, San Marino

ranks as the smallest state in the world. It covers only 24 square miles. Russia is now the world's largest state; it stretches across nearly 7 million square miles. (The old Soviet Union covered more than 8 million square miles—nearly one-sixth of all the land surface of the earth.) The total area of the United States is 3,787,425 square miles.

**Sovereignty** Every state is **sovereign**. That is, it has supreme and absolute power within its own territory. Each state can decide its own foreign and domestic policies. It is neither subordinate nor responsible to any other authority.

Thus, as a sovereign state, the United States can determine its form of government. It can frame its economic system and shape its own foreign policies.[3] Sovereignty is the one characteristic that distinguishes the state from all other, lesser political units. For example, the Virgin Islands and Guam are not sovereign; each of them is a territorial possession of the United States.

The States within the United States are not sovereign and so are not states in the international, legal sense. Each State is subordinate to the Constitution of the United States.

The location of sovereignty within a state is of supreme importance. If the people are sovereign, then the government is democratic. If, on the other hand, a single person or a small group holds the power, a dictatorship exists.

**Government** Every state is politically organized. That is, every state has a government. Recall, a government is the institution through which society makes and enforces its public policies. It is the agency through which the state exerts its will and works to accomplish its goals. Government consists of the machinery and the personnel by which the state is ruled.

---

[1]In most of the world's written political record, the words *man* and *men* have been widely used to refer to all of humankind. This text follows that form when presenting excerpts from historical writings or documents and in references to them.

[2]Note that the state is a legal entity. In popular usage, a state is often called a "nation" or a "country." In a strict sense, however, the word *nation* is an ethnic term, referring to races or other large groups of people. The word *country* is a geographic term, referring to a particular place, region, or area of land.

[3]The United States also recognizes the State of Vatican City. The Vatican has a permanent population of some 750 persons, occupies a roughly triangular area of only 109 acres, and is wholly surrounded by the City of Rome. American recognition of the Vatican, which had been withdrawn in 1867, was renewed in 1984.

In this book, *state* printed with a small "s" denotes a state in the family of nations, such as the United States, Great Britain, Mexico, and so on. *State* printed with a capital "S" refers to a State in the American union.

As you will see shortly, governments in the world today take a number of different forms. But whatever form a government takes, it has the authority to make and enforce public policies. That is, it has the power to rule—including the power to use force if necessary to compel people to accept its rule.

## Origins of the State

For centuries, historians, political scientists, philosophers, and others have pondered the question of the origin of the state. What factor or set of circumstances first brought it into being?

Over time, many different answers have been offered, but history provides no conclusive evidence to support any of them. However, four theories have emerged as the most widely accepted explanations for the origin of the state.

**The Force Theory**  Many scholars have long believed that the state was born of force. They hold that one person or group claimed control over an area and forced all within it to submit to that person's or group's rule. When that rule was established, all the basic elements of the state—population, territory, sovereignty, and government—were present.

**The Evolutionary Theory**  Others claim that the state developed naturally out of the early family. They hold that the primitive family, of which one person was the head and thus the "government," was the first stage in political development. Over countless years the original family became a network of related families—a clan. In time the clan became a tribe. When the tribe first turned to agriculture and gave up its nomadic ways, the state was born.

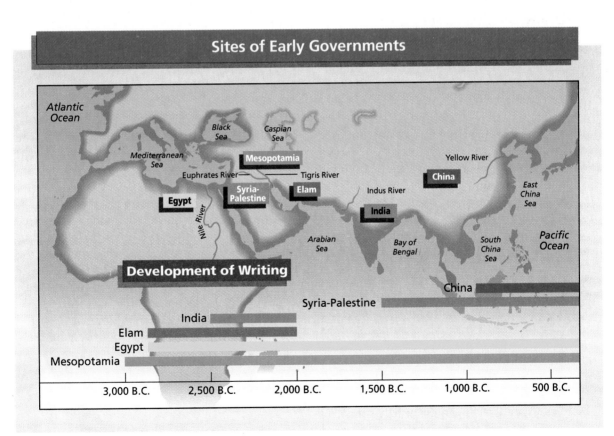

**Sites of Early Governments**

Interpreting Maps: **Multicultural Awareness**  The map shows the areas where the earliest governments are believed to have formed. How would early writing (inset) have played a key part in the development of government?

▲ **Interpreting Political Cartoons** American government was strongly influenced by the social contract theory. How does this cartoon poke fun at that theory?

**The Divine Right Theory**   The theory of divine right was widely accepted in much of the Western world from the 15th through the 18th centuries. It held that the state was created by God and that God had given those of royal birth a "divine right" to rule. The people were bound to obey their ruler as they would God; opposition to "the divine right of kings" was both treason and mortal sin.

Much of the thought upon which present-day democratic government rests was first developed as a challenge to the theory of divine right.

The notion of divine right was not unique to European history. The rulers of many ancient civilizations—including the Chinese, Egyptian, Aztec, and Mayan civilizations—were held to be gods or at least to have been chosen by the gods. The Japanese emperor, the *mikado*, governed by divine right for centuries—in fact, until as recently as 1945.

**The Social Contract Theory**   In terms of the American political system, the most significant of the theories of the origin of the state is that of the "social contract." Philosophers such as John Locke, James Harrington, and Thomas Hobbes in England and Jean Jacques Rousseau in France developed this theory in the 17th and 18th centuries.

Hobbes wrote that in earliest history humans lived in a "state of nature." No government existed; no person was subject to any superior power. That which people could take by force belonged to them. However, all people were similarly free in this state of nature. No authority existed to protect one person from the aggressive or violent actions of another. Thus, individuals were only as safe as their own physical prowess could make them. Human life in the state of nature, wrote Hobbes, was "nasty, brutish, and short."

Human beings overcame their unpleasant condition, says the theory, by agreeing with one another to create a state. By contract, people within a given area agreed to give up to the state as much power as was needed to promote the well-being of all. In the contract—that is, through a constitution—the members of the state created a government to exercise the powers they had granted to the state.

In short, the social contract theory argues that the state arose out of a voluntary act of free people. It holds that the state exists only to serve the will of the people, that they are the sole source of political power, and that they are free to give or to withhold that power as they choose. The great concepts that this theory promoted—popular sovereignty, limited government, and individual rights—were immensely important to the shaping of the American governmental system.[4]

---

[4]The Declaration of Independence (see page 720) laid its justification for revolution on the social contract theory, arguing that the king and his ministers had violated the contract. Thomas Jefferson called the document "pure Locke."

## The Purpose of Government

What does government do? You can find a very meaningful answer to that question in the Preamble to the Constitution of the United States. The American governmental system was created to serve the purposes set out there.

" We the People of the United States, in Order to form a more perfect Union, establish Justice, insure domestic Tranquility, provide for the common defence, promote the general Welfare, and secure the Blessings of Liberty to ourselves and our Posterity, do ordain and establish this Constitution for the United States of America. "

**To Form a More Perfect Union** The United States, which had just won its independence from Great Britain, faced an altogether uncertain future in the postwar 1780s. In 1781 the Articles of Confederation, the nation's first constitution, had created "a firm league of friendship" among the 13 States. But that league soon proved to be neither very firm nor even very friendly. The 1780s were marked by intense rivalries and jealousies among the States; and the government that the Articles had established was powerless to confront the chaos and confusion of the time.

The Constitution of today was written in 1787, and it was adopted by the original States in order to link them, and the American people, more closely together. That Constitution was built in the belief that in union there is strength.

**To Establish Justice** To provide justice is, said Thomas Jefferson, "the most sacred of the duties of government." No purpose, no goal of public policy, can be of greater importance in a democracy.

But what, precisely, is justice? The term is difficult to define, for justice is a concept. Like truth, liberty, good, and other concepts, justice means what people make it mean.

As the concept of justice has developed over time in American thought and practice, it has come to mean this: The law, in both its content and its administration, must be reasonable, fair, and impartial. Those standards of justice have not always been met in this country. We have not attained our professed goal of "equal justice for all." But this, too, must be said: The history of this country can be told largely in terms of our continuing attempts to reach that goal.

"Injustice anywhere," said Martin Luther King, Jr., "is a threat to justice everywhere." You will encounter this idea again and again in this book.

**To Insure Domestic Tranquility** Order is essential to the well-being of any society, and keeping the peace at home has always been a prime function of government.

Most people can only imagine what it would be like to live in a state of anarchy—that is, without government, without law and order. But people do live that way in some parts of the world today. For years now, the government of Lebanon has been too weak to control the actions of several warring religious factions. The street fighting in strife-torn Beirut suggests what life without government is like.

In *The Federalist* No. 51, James Madison observed: "If men were angels no government would be necessary." But Madison, who was perhaps the most thoughtful of the Framers of the Constitution, knew that most human beings fall far short of this standard.

**To Provide for the Common Defense** Defending the nation against foreign enemies has always been one of government's major responsibilities. You can see its importance in this striking fact: Defense is mentioned far more often in the Constitution than any of the other functions of the government it created. The nation's defense and foreign policies are but two sides of the same coin—the security of the United States.

The cold war is now history. It came to an end with the collapse of communism in Eastern Europe and the Soviet Union. That conflict, which lasted for more than 40 years, pitted the United States and its allies in the free world against the Soviet Union and its satellites in the Communist world. For all of those years the world lived with the threat of World War III and nuclear holocaust.

Even with the end of the cold war, the world remains a dangerous place, and the United States must maintain its vigilance and its armed strength. Just a glance at today's newspaper or at one of

National Museum of American Art - Smithsonian.

▲ **Interpreting Political Art** This hand-made quilt hangs in the Smithsonian Institution. What might have been the artist's intent in using multicolored pieces of fabric surrounding the Statue of Liberty?

this evening's television news programs will furnish abundant proof of that fact.

**To Promote the General Welfare** Few people realize the extent to which government acts as the servant of its citizens, yet you can see examples everywhere.

Public schools are a leading illustration of government's work to promote the general welfare. So, too, are government's efforts to protect the quality of the air you breathe, the water you drink, and the food you eat. The list of tasks government performs for your benefit goes on and on.

Some governmental functions that are common in other countries—operating railroads, airlines, and coal mines, for example—are not carried out by government in this country. In general, the services that government provides in the United States are those that benefit all or most people and are not likely to be provided by the voluntary acts of private individuals or groups.

**To Secure the Blessings of Liberty** This nation was founded by those who loved liberty and prized it above all earthly possessions. They believed with Thomas Jefferson that "the God who gave us life gave us liberty at the same time." They subscribed to Benjamin Franklin's maxim: "They that can give up essential liberty to obtain a little temporary safety deserve neither liberty nor safety."

As you will see shortly, the American dedication to freedom for the individual recognizes that liberty cannot be absolute. It is, instead, a relative matter. No person can be free to do whatever he or she pleases—for that behavior would interfere with the freedoms of others. As Clarence Darrow, the great defense lawyer, once said: "You can only be free if I am free."

Both the Federal Constitution and the State constitutions set out many guarantees of rights and liberties for the individual in this country. But that does not mean that those guarantees are so firmly established that they exist forever. To preserve and protect them, each generation must learn and understand them anew, and be willing to stand up for them when necessary. You, too, must agree with Jefferson: "Eternal vigilance is the price of liberty."

## Section 1 Review

**1. Define:** government, public policies, state, sovereign
**2.** What are the four main characteristics of a state?
**3.** For what reason is the location of sovereignty within a state so important?
**4.** What are the four most widely held theories about the origin of the state?
**5.** What are the six purposes of government outlined in the Preamble to the Constitution?

**Critical Thinking**

**6. Recognizing Ideologies** (p. 19) Explain how the language of the Preamble reflects the concept of the social contract.

★

## Campaigning for the Environment

In 1987, a civics class at the Tenakill School in Closter, New Jersey, mounted a campaign to urge their school to stop using polystyrene in the cafeteria. Polystyrene is the soft, lightweight, plastic foam used to make many disposable food containers and trays. The school's group, Kids Against Pollution, attacked the material for two reasons. Polystyrene is nonbiodegradable—that is, it does not readily decay over a few years when disposed of in landfills. In addition, polystyrene gives off toxic fumes when it is burned. The food industry, including many school cafeterias, uses more than one billion pounds of polystyrene each year, mostly for packaging.

With persistence and hard work, the students at the Tenakill School succeeded in their efforts to end polystyrene use in the cafeteria. Their success inspired similar groups in the United States and Europe. In 1988, the students at West Milford High School in New Jersey were also able to ban polystyrene in their school by winning over a reluctant school board and most of their fellow students. Buoyed by their victory, the West Milford group set their sights even higher. They joined a national movement to stop the use of polystyrene containers by the world's largest consumer of the material—McDonald's. The 8,400 McDonald's restaurants across the United States were estimated to use a total of 3.5 billion foam boxes each year, or between 7 to 8 percent of all polystyrene foam products sold in the United States.

Kurtiz Schneid, the leader of the movement in West Milford, and other citizens got involved in this national movement to reduce the use of polystyrene. They demonstrated in front of the United Nations Headquarters in New York to urge a worldwide boycott of McDonald's restaurants. Schneid, dressed as "Ronald McToxic," and his followers spread a message based on the restaurant's advertising slogan: "The planet deserves a break today." Other West Milford residents organized a letter-writing campaign to urge McDonald's to stop using polystyrene.

In November 1990, McDonald's Corp. decided to stop using polystyrene containers for its hamburgers and other sandwiches. This translated into a savings of more than 45 million pounds of the plastic waste a year. Six months later, working with the Environmental Defense Fund, the company launched a major waste-reduction effort including composting and recycling. The fast-food chain aimed to cut its daily generation of garbage by as much as 80 percent; and its efforts have prompted several of its competitors to take a number of similar steps to protect the environment.

## Getting Involved

**1. Identify** a need in your school or community similar to the one addressed by the students in this case.

**2. Formulate** a plan for how you might organize volunteer efforts to help remedy this problem and identify resources that could be used in your plan.

**3. Predict** any problems or objections you might encounter in implementing your plan.

# 2 Forms of Government

**Find Out:**

- What are the characteristics of unitary, federal, and confederate governments?
- How do presidential and parliamentary governments differ?
- How do a dictatorship and a democracy differ?

**Key Terms:**

unitary government, federal government, confederation, presidential government, parliamentary government, dictatorship, democracy, direct democracy, representative democracy

**D**oes the form a government takes, the way in which it is structured, have any importance? Political scientists, historians, and other social commentators have long argued that question. The English poet Alexander Pope weighed in with this couplet in 1733:

❝ For forms of government let fools contest: Whate'er is best adminster'd is best. ❞

Was Pope right? Does it matter what form a government takes? In this section, which focuses on forms of government, you will find some help in framing your own response to those questions.

## Classifying Governments

No two governments are, or ever have been, exactly alike, for governments are the products of human needs and experiences. But all governments can be classified according to one or more of their basic features. Over time, political scientists have developed many bases upon which to classify—and so to describe, compare, and analyze—governments. Three of those classifications are especially important and useful. These are classifications according to: (1) the geographic distribution of governmental power within the state, (2) the relationship between the legislative (lawmaking) and the executive (law-executing) branches of the government, and (3) the number of persons who can take part in the governing process.[5]

## Geographic Distribution of Power

In every system of government the power to govern is located in one or more places, geographically. From this standpoint, three basic forms of government exist: unitary, federal, and confederate governments.

**Unitary Government**   A **unitary government** is often described as a centralized government. It is a government in which all powers held by the government belong to a single, central agency. The central government creates local units of government for its own convenience. Whatever powers those local governments have come only from that central source.

Most governments in the world are unitary in form. Great Britain is an illustration of the type. A single central organ—the Parliament—holds all of the power of the British government. Local governments do exist but solely to relieve Parliament of burdens it could perform only with difficulty and inconvenience. Though hardly likely, Parliament could do away with all agencies of local government at any time.

Be careful not to confuse the unitary form of government with a dictatorship. In the unitary form all of the powers held by the government are concentrated in the central government. But that government might not have *all* power. In Great Britain, for example, the powers held by the government are limited. British government is unitary and, at the same time, democratic.

**Federal Government**   A **federal government** is one in which the powers of government are divided between a central government and several local governments. An authority superior to both the central and local governments makes this division of powers on a geographic basis; and that division cannot be changed by either the local or national level acting alone. Both levels of government act directly on the people through their own sets of laws, officials, and agencies.

---

[5]Note that these classifications are not mutually exclusive. Thus, as you will see, the government of the United States is federal, presidential, and democratic; British government is unitary, parliamentary, and democratic; and so on.

In the United States, for example, the National Government has certain powers and the 50 States have others. This division of powers is set out in the Constitution of the United States. The Constitution stands above both levels of government; and it cannot be changed unless the people, acting through both the National Government and the States, agree to that change.

Australia, Canada, Mexico, Switzerland, Germany, India, and some 20 other states also have federal forms of government today. (Note that the government of each of the 50 States in the American Union is unitary, not federal, in form.)

**Confederate Government** A **confederation** is an alliance of independent states. A central organ—the confederate government—has the power to handle only those matters that the member states have assigned to it. Typically, confederate governments have had limited powers and only in such fields as defense and foreign commerce. Most often, they have not had the power to make laws that apply directly to individuals, at least not without some further action by the member states. A confederate structure makes it possible for the several states to cooperate in matters of common concern and also retain their separate identities.

There is only one confederation in the world today, the Commonwealth of Independent States, a shaky alliance of 11 of the 15 constituent republics that made up the old Soviet Union.

In our own history, the United States under the Articles of Confederation (1781 to 1789) and the Confederate States of America (1861 to 1865) are also examples of the form.

## Relationship Between Legislative and Executive Branches

Viewing governments from the standpoint of the relationship between their legislative and executive agencies yields two basic forms of government: presidential and parliamentary.

**Presidential Government** A **presidential government** features a separation of powers between the executive and legislative branches of the government. The two branches are inde-

**Tribal Council: Multicultural Awareness** Native Americans such as these Apache leaders have governed the internal affairs of their group for centuries. The Iroquois of the 1500s were known for their confederate form of government.

pendent of one another and coequal. The chief executive—president—is chosen independently of the legislature, holds office for a fixed term, and has broad powers not subject to the direct control of the legislative branch. The two branches regularly have several powers with which each can check—block or restrain—actions by the other branch.

Usually, as in the United States, a written constitution provides for the separation of powers between the branches of government.

**Parliamentary Government** In **parliamentary government**, the executive is made up of the prime minister or premier and that official's cabinet. They themselves are members of the legislative branch, the parliament. The prime minister is the leader of the majority party or of a coalition of parties in parliament and is chosen by that body. With parliament's approval, the prime minister selects the members of the cabinet from among the members of parliament. The executive is thus chosen by the legislature, is a part of it, and is subject to its direct control.

The prime minister and the cabinet—often called "the government"—remain in office only as long as their policies and administration have the confidence of a majority in parliament. If parliament defeats the prime minister and cabinet on an important matter—if the government receives a "vote of no confidence"—the

**Legislative and Executive Branches: Two Basic Forms**

▲ **Interpreting Graphs** Compare parliamentary and presidential forms of government. In which form of government is the chief executive both elected from and part of the legislature?

government must resign from office. Then a new government must be formed. Either parliament chooses a new prime minister or, as often happens, all the seats in parliament go before the voters in a general election.

A parliamentary government does not experience one of the major problems of the presidential form—prolonged conflict and sometimes deadlock between the executive and legislative branches. But, notice, that is another way of saying that the checks and balances of presidential government are not a part of the parliamentary system.

The British, most other Europeans, and a majority of all of the other governments in today's world are parliamentary in form.

## The Number Who Can Participate

To most people, the most meaningful of these classifications of governments is the one that depends on the number of persons who can take part in the governing process. Here there are two basic forms to consider: dictatorships and democracies.

**Dictatorship** A **dictatorship** exists where those who rule cannot be held responsible to the will of the people. The government is not accountable for its policies, nor for the ways in which they are carried out. Dictatorship is probably the oldest, and it is certainly the most common, form of government known.[6]

All dictatorships are authoritarian. That is, they are governmental systems in which those in power hold absolute and unchallengeable authority over the people. Modern dictatorships have tended to be totalitarian, as well. That is, they exercise dictatorial (authoritarian) power over nearly every aspect of human affairs. Their power embraces all (the totality of) matters of human concern.

The leading examples of dictatorship in the 20th century have been those in Fascist Italy (from 1922 to 1943), in Nazi Germany (from 1933 to 1945), and in the Soviet Union (from 1917 until the late 1980s), and one that still exists in the People's Republic of China (where the present regime came to power in 1949).

Although they do exist, one-person dictatorships are not at all common today. A few close approaches to such a regime can now be found in Libya, which has been dominated by Muammar al-Qaddafi since 1969, and in some other Arab and African states.

---

[6]The word *dictatorship* comes from the Latin *dictare*, meaning to dictate, issue orders, authoritative commands. *Dictator* was the ancient Roman republic's title for the leader who was given extraordinary powers in times of crisis. Julius Caesar (100–44 B.C.) became the first of the Roman dictators, in 49 B.C.

Dictatorships are sometimes identified as either autocracies or oligarchies. An autocracy is a government in which a single person holds unlimited political power. An oligarchy is a government in which the power to rule is held by a small, usually self-appointed elite.

Most present-day dictatorships are not nearly so monolithic, not nearly so absolutely controlled by a single person or by a very small group as may appear to be the case. Regularly, outward appearances hide the fact that several groups—the army, religious leaders, industrialists, and others—compete for power in the political system.

Dictatorships often present the outward appearance of control by the people. The people often vote in popular elections; but the vote is closely controlled, and ballots usually contain the candidates of but one political party. An elected legislative body often exists, but only to rubber-stamp the policies of the dictatorship.

Typically, dictatorial regimes are militaristic in character. They usually gain power by force. The military holds many of the major posts in the government. After crushing all effective opposition at home, these regimes may turn to foreign aggression to enhance the country's military power and prestige.

**Democracy**  In a **democracy**, supreme political authority rests with the people. The people hold the sovereign power, and government is conducted only by and with the consent of the people.[7]

Abraham Lincoln gave immortality to this definition of democracy in his Gettysburg Address in 1863: "government of the people, by the people, for the people." Nowhere is there a better, more concise statement of the American understanding of democracy.

A democracy can be either direct or indirect in form. A **direct democracy**—also called a pure democracy—exists where the will of the people is translated into public policy (law) directly by the people themselves, in mass meetings. Clearly, such a system can work only in very small communities—where it is possible for the citizenry to meet in some central place, and where, too, the problems of government are few and relatively simple.

Direct democracy does not exist at the national level anywhere in the world today. But the New

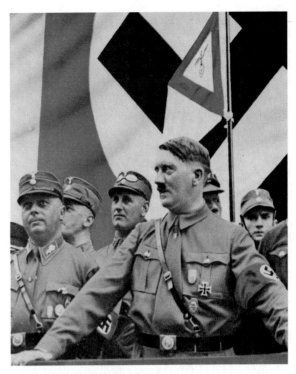

**Absolute Dictator**  Adolf Hitler headed the dictatorship in Nazi Germany from 1933 to 1945.

England town meeting which you will read about in Chapter 24, and the *Landsgemeinde* in a few of the smaller Swiss cantons are excellent examples of direct democracy in action.[8]

Americans are more familiar with the indirect form of democracy—that is, with representative democracy. In a **representative democracy**, a small group of persons chosen by the people to act as their representatives expresses the popular will. These agents of the people are responsible for carrying out the day-to-day conduct of government—the making and executing of laws and so on. They are held accountable to the people for that conduct, especially at periodic elections. At these elections the people have an opportunity to express their approval or disapproval of their representatives by casting ballots

---

[7] The word *democracy* is derived from the Greek words *demos* meaning "the people" and *kratia* meaning "rule" or "authority." The Greek word *demokratia* means "rule by the people."

[8] The *Landsgemeinde*, like the original New England town meeting, is an assembly open to all local citizens qualified to vote. In a more limited sense, lawmaking by initiative petition is also an example of direct democracy; see Chapter 24.

# Global Awareness

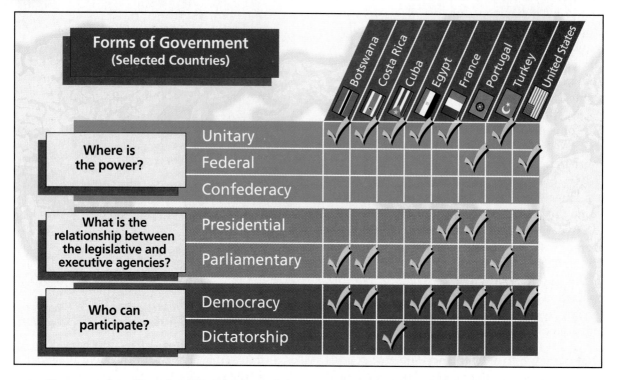

| Forms of Government (Selected Countries) | | Botswana | Costa Rica | Cuba | Egypt | France | Portugal | Turkey | United States |
|---|---|---|---|---|---|---|---|---|---|
| **Where is the power?** | Unitary | ✓ | ✓ | ✓ | ✓ | ✓ | ✓ | | |
| | Federal | | | | | | | ✓ | ✓ |
| | Confederacy | | | | | | | | |
| **What is the relationship between the legislative and executive agencies?** | Presidential | | | | ✓ | ✓ | | | ✓ |
| | Parliamentary | ✓ | ✓ | ✓ | | | ✓ | | |
| **Who can participate?** | Democracy | ✓ | ✓ | | ✓ | ✓ | ✓ | ✓ | ✓ |
| | Dictatorship | | | ✓ | | | | | |

▲ **Interpreting Graphs: Multicultural Awareness**  Different forms of government in several countries are described above. Which two African countries are parliamentary democracies?

for or against them. To put it another way, representative democracy is government by popular consent—government with the consent of the governed.

Some people insist that the United States is more properly called a republic rather than a democracy. They hold that in a republic the sovereign power is held by the electorate—those eligible to vote—and that the political power is exercised by representatives chosen by and held responsible to the electorate. For them, democracy can be defined only in terms of direct democracy. To most Americans, however, the terms *democracy, republic, representative democracy,* and *republican form of government* generally mean the same thing.

Whatever the terms used, remember that in a democracy the people are sovereign. They are the only source for any and all of government's power. In other words, the people rule.

# Section 2 Review

**1. Define**: direct democracy, representative democracy

**2.** (a) What is the basic characteristic of a unitary government? (b) A confederate government? (c) A federal government?

**3.** (a) What is the basic characteristic of a presidential government? (b) A parliamentary government? (c) Which is the most common today?

**4.** (a) What is the basic characteristic of a dictatorial government? (b) A democratic government? (c) Which is the most common today?

## Critical Thinking

**5. Drawing Conclusions** (p. 19) Which combination of governmental forms would best fulfill the purposes of government?

★

# 3 Basic Concepts of Democracy

**Find Out:**

- What are the basic concepts on which American democracy is built?
- How does the operation of American government illustrate these basic concepts?

**Key Terms:**

compromise, anarchy

What do you make of the following assessment of democracy? "No government demands so much from the citizen as Democracy and none gives back so much."[9] What does democratic government demand from you? What does it give you in return? Can you cite any concrete examples in answer to either of these questions? You may find some of those examples as you read this section.

## The Foundations of Democracy

Democracy is not inevitable. It does not exist in the United States simply because Americans regard it as the best of all possible political systems. Nor will it continue to exist for that reason.[10] Rather, democracy exists in this country because the American people believe in its basic concepts. It will continue to exist only for as long as we, the people, continue to subscribe to—and practice—those concepts.

The basic concepts of democracy, as they are understood and applied in the United States, can be described this way:

1. A recognition of the fundamental worth and dignity of every person.

---

[9]James Bryce, *Modern Democracies* (Macmillan, 1921), Vol. II, p. 608.

[10]The late Sir Winston Churchill (1874–1965) once argued for democracy in these terms: "No one pretends that democracy is perfect or all-wise. Indeed, it has been said that democracy is the worst form of government except all of those other forms which have been tried from time to time."

2. A respect for the equality of all persons.
3. A faith in majority rule and an insistence upon minority rights.
4. An acceptance of the necessity of compromise.
5. An insistence upon the widest possible degree of individual freedom.

Of course, these ideas can be worded in other ways. No matter what the wording, however, they form the very minimum that anyone who professes to believe in democracy must agree to. Some people will argue that other concepts belong in such a list—for example, the right of each person to a certain minimum level of economic security. But the point here is that, no matter what else might be included, at least these must be.

These concepts present the American people with a number of problems and challenges. In order to preserve democracy, each generation must develop the skills with which to solve these problems. (You will find a discussion of problem-solving skills on page 19.)

## Fundamental Worth of the Individual

Democracy is firmly based upon a belief in the fundamental importance of the individual. Each individual, no matter what his or her station in life, is a separate and distinct being. Democracy insists that each person's worth and dignity must be recognized and respected by all other individuals, and by society, at all times.

This concept of the dignity and worth of the individual is of overriding importance in democratic thought. Everything a democratic society does must and should be done within the limits of this great concept. American society is constantly striving to fulfill it.

At various times, of course, the welfare of one or a few individuals is subordinated to the interests of the many in a democracy. People can be forced to do certain things whether they want to or not. The examples are many, and they range from paying taxes or registering for the draft to stopping at a stop sign.

When a democratic society forces people to pay a tax or obey traffic signals, it is serving the interests of the many. But the democracy is *not* serving the many simply as the interests of a mass of people who happen to outnumber the few. Rather, it is serving the many who, as individuals, together make up that society.

The distinction here between a single individual and all individuals may be a very fine one. It is, however, critically important to a true understanding of the meaning of democracy.

## Equality of All Persons

Hand-in-hand with the belief in the worth of the individual, democracy stresses the equality of all individuals. It holds, with Jefferson, that "all men are created equal."

Certainly, democracy does *not* insist on an equality of condition for all persons. Thus, it does not claim that all are born with the same mental or physical abilities. Nor does it argue that all persons have a right to an equal share of worldly goods.

Rather, the democratic concept of equality insists that all are entitled to (1) equality of opportunity and (2) equality before the law. That is, the democratic concept of equality holds that no person should be held back for any such arbitrary reasons as those based on race, color, religion, or gender. The concept holds that each person must be free to develop himself or herself as fully as he or she can (or cares to) and that each person should be treated as the equal of all other persons by the law.

We have come a great distance toward reaching the goal of equality for all in this country. But, clearly, we are still a considerable distance from a genuine, universally recognized and respected equality for all.

▲ **Political Equality** Every person in a democratic society, regardless of race, color, religion, or gender, is entitled to live freely and equally and to fulfill his or her potential.

## Majority Rule and Minority Rights

In a democracy, it is the will of the people and not the dictate of the ruling few that determines public policy. But what is the popular will, and how is it determined? How is the democratic society to decide and make public policies? Some standard, some device must exist, by which these crucial questions can be answered. The only satisfactory device democracy knows is that of majority rule. Democracy argues that a majority of the people will be right more often than they will be wrong, and that the majority will also be right more often than will any one person or small group.

Democracy can be described as an experiment—a trial-and-error process—designed to find satisfactory ways to order human relations. Notice that it does *not* say that the majority will always be "right," that it will always arrive at the best of all possible decisions on public matters. In fact, the democratic process—the process of majority rule—does not intend to come up with "right" or "best" answers. Rather, the democratic process searches for satisfactory solutions to public problems.

Of course, democracy insists that the majority's decisions will more often be more, rather than less, satisfactory. Democracy does admit the possibility of mistakes, however—the possibility that "wrong" or less satisfactory answers will sometimes be found. Democracy also recognizes that seldom is any solution to a public problem so satisfactory that it cannot be improved upon. It knows, too, that circumstances can change over time. So, the process of experimentation, of seeking answers to public questions, is really a never-ending one.

Certainly, a democracy cannot work without the principle of majority rule. Unchecked, however, a majority could destroy its opposition and, in the process, destroy democracy as well. Thus, democracy insists upon majority rule restrained by minority rights. The majority must always recognize the right of any minority to become, by fair and lawful means, the majority. The majority must always be willing to listen to a minority's argument, to hear its objections, to bear its criticisms, and to welcome its suggestions. Anything less contradicts the very meaning of democracy.

## Necessity of Compromise

In a democracy, public decision-making must be largely a matter of give-and-take among the various competing interests. It is a matter of **compromise**—the process of blending and adjusting, of reconciling competing views and interests—in order to find the position most acceptable to the largest number.

Compromise is an essential part of the democratic concept for two major reasons. First, remember that democracy puts the individual first and, at the same time, insists that each individual is the equal of all others. In a democratic society made up of many individuals and groups with many different opinions and interests, how can the people make public decisions except by compromise?

Second, few public questions have only two sides. Most can be answered in several ways. As a case in point, take the apparently simple question of how a city should pay for the paving of a public street. Should it charge the costs to those who own property along the street? Or should all of the city's residents pay the costs from the city's general treasury? Or should the city and the adjacent property owners share the costs? What about those who will use the street but do not live in the city? Should they have to pay a toll or buy a license for that use?

Again, the point is that most public policy questions have several possible answers. The fact remains, however, that the democratic society must find some answer.

Remember, compromise is a process, a way of achieving majority agreement. It is never an end in itself. Not all compromises are good, and not all are necessary. Some things—such as the equality of all persons—should never be the subject of any kind of compromise if democracy is to survive.

## Individual Freedom

It should be clear by this point that democracy can thrive only in an atmosphere of individual freedom. But democracy does not and cannot insist on complete freedom for the individual. Absolute freedom can exist only in a state of **anarchy**—in the total absence of government.

## *on Government* VOICES

**Antonia Hernandez,**
president and general
counsel of the Mexican
American Legal Defense
and Educational Fund

### On Multicultural Goals for the 1990s

❝The '90s is a threshold decade. . . . We need to grab control of our destiny. . . . I see a lot of young people in their 30s and 40s who've taken advantage of the educational opportunities. We have lots of leaders. Now it is incumbent upon us to demand our share of power. . . . We need to register and vote, participate from the lowest level to the highest level. Our success will be determined by our willingness to be a part of the solution.❞

Anarchy can only lead, inevitably and quickly, to rule by the strong and ruthless.

Democracy does insist, however, that each individual must be as free to do as he or she pleases as far as the freedom of all will allow. Justice Oliver Wendell Holmes once had this to say about the relative nature of each individual's rights: "The right to swing my fist ends where the other man's nose begins."

Drawing the line between the rights of one individual and those of another is far from easy. But the drawing of that line is a continuous and vitally important function of democratic government. As John F. Kennedy put it: "The rights of every man are diminished when the rights of one man are threatened."

Striking the proper balance between freedom for the individual and the rights of society as a whole is similarly difficult—and vital. Abraham Lincoln once stated democracy's problem in these words:

❝Must a government of necessity be too *strong* for the liberties of its own people, or too *weak* to maintain its own existence?❞

The problem goes to the very heart of democracy. Human beings desire both liberty and authority. Democratic government must work constantly to strike the proper balance between the two. The authority of government must be adequate to the needs of society. But that authority must never be allowed to become so great that it restricts the individual beyond necessity.

Democracy views all rights as vital, but it places its highest value on those necessary to the free exchange of ideas. Several years ago, the President's Committee on Civil Rights made the point:

❝In a free society there is faith in the ability of the people to make sound, rational judgments. But such judgments are possible only when the people have access to all relevant facts and to all prevailing interpretations of the facts. How can such judgments be formed on a sound basis if arguments, viewpoints, or opinions are arbitrarily suppressed? How can the concept of the marketplace of thought in which truth ultimately prevails retain its validity if the thought of certain individuals is denied the right of circulation?❞

You will return to the subject of individual rights later, especially in chapters 19 and 20. You will also return to the other basic democratic concepts throughout this book.

## Section **3** Review

**1. Define:** compromise, anarchy
**2.** What does the text suggest are the basic concepts of democracy?
**3.** For what reasons is compromise an essential part of the democratic process?
**4.** Upon which individual freedoms does democracy place its highest values?

**Critical Thinking**

**5. Formulating Questions** (p. 19) Based on the five concepts of democratic government, write a list of questions you would like to ask the President about democracy in America.

★

## Identify and Clarify the Problem

| SKILL | DEFINITION | Page on which skill is taught |
|---|---|---|
| **Expressing problems clearly** | To succinctly describe a complex situation or body of information | Page 20 |
| **Identifying central issues** | To identify the main ideas in a piece of information | Page 124 |
| **Making comparisons** | To identify how different ideas, objects, historical figures, or situations are alike and/or different | Page 376 |
| **Determining relevance** | To decide if and how events, situations, or items relate to one another | Page 152 |
| **Formulating questions** | To create questions that seek answers to specific objectives and lead to a deeper understanding of an issue | Page 540 |

## Judge Information Related to the Problem

| | | |
|---|---|---|
| **Distinguishing fact from opinion** | To separate those statements that can be proven to be true from those that reflect a personal viewpoint | Page 228 |
| **Checking consistency** | To compare two or more items or ideas and determine whether they agree or disagree with each other | Page 92 |
| **Distinguishing false from accurate images** | To examine a widely held belief about a person, place, or thing and determine whether or not the belief is based in fact | Page 206 |
| **Identifying assumptions** | To recognize unstated beliefs that may underlie a statement, action, or event | Page 480 |
| **Recognizing bias** | To identify a stated or unstated viewpoint or slant that is designed to promote one set of beliefs over another | Page 180 |
| **Recognizing ideologies** | To identify underlying beliefs from actions or statements | Page 600 |

## Draw Conclusions and Solve the Problem

| | | |
|---|---|---|
| **Drawing conclusions** | To find an answer or to form an opinion based on available information | Page 50 |
| **Recognizing cause and effect** | To examine how one event or idea causes other events or ideas to occur | Page 278 |
| **Predicting consequences** | To determine the likely effect of an event or action on the outcome of future events or actions | Page 512 |
| **Identifying alternatives** | To identify one or more methods to achieve a goal or solve a problem; to recognize the possibility of other goals | Page 454 |
| **Testing conclusions** | To examine a conclusion and determine whether or not it is supported by known facts | Page 348 |
| **Demonstrating reasoned judgment** | To present evidence or reasoning that supports a given opinion or statement | Page 568 |

# Expressing Problems Clearly

Expressing problems clearly means succinctly describing a complex situation or body of information. When you express a problem clearly, you have taken the first step toward solving that problem. The table on the previous page includes some of the other critical thinking skills you can use to solve problems.

You have read that "no government demands so much of citizens as democracy." Indeed, your role as a citizen in a democracy will require you to participate in solving many problems. Use the following steps to practice expressing problems clearly.

**1. Analyze the information.** When you are confronted with a problem, you must make yourself familiar with the information involved. Read the sample police report on the right. (a) What is the nature of the complaint made by Citizen A? (b) What is the information given by Citizen B?

**2. Identify the basic concepts involved.** All problems arise out of a specific set of circumstances. However, they often revolve around a general principle, such as fairness. To identify this concept, try to express the problem in terms of what each side wants for itself. (a) What benefit does Citizen A want to achieve for himself by making the complaint? (b) What does Citizen B want?

**3. Identify the function of the supporting details.** In any problem, there are details that are part of the story, but not really part of the overall problem. (a) In the police report below, is it an important part of the problem that Citizen B plays the oboe or that she plays poorly? (b) What other details in this report do not relate to the basic issue of disagreement between Citizen A and Citizen B?

**4. Express the problem clearly.** Now that you have identified the main area of dispute and stripped away the details, you are ready to express the problem clearly. What is a succinct description of the dispute between Citizen A and Citizen B?

## Police Report

Citizen A has lodged a formal complaint about his neighbor, Citizen B. According to Citizen A, Citizen B has been playing her oboe in such a way as to deny Citizen A his peace and quiet. For example, Citizen B regularly practices her oboe near an open window at 6 P.M., when Citizen A and his family are eating dinner. Citizen B also practices on weekend mornings. Citizen A further complains that Citizen B is not a very accomplished oboe player, which makes the annoyance even worse.

Citizen B claims that Citizen A has never tried to work out an agreement by which she could continue practicing at a time more convenient for Citizen A. Instead, Citizen A has made threatening and abusive phone calls. She even suspects that Citizen A is responsible for the destruction of some garden plants, which she found destroyed after a particularly angry phone call from Citizen A. She has no solid evidence to support this accusation, however.

# Chapter-in-Brief

Scan all headings, photographs, charts, and other visuals in the chapter before reading the section summaries below.

## Section 1 Government and the State (pp. 3–8)
Government is the institution through which a society makes and enforces public policies. It is one of humankind's oldest inventions.

The state has emerged as the dominant political unit in the world. A state is a body of people living in a defined area, having a government, and having the power to govern themselves without the consent of any higher authority.

Major theories that seek to explain the origin of the state include (1) the force theory, which holds that the state grew out of the forceful takeover of authority by a person or group; (2) the evolutionary theory, which sees the state as the natural extension of the family system over increasingly large and complex communities; (3) the divine right theory, which says that a god or gods created the state; and (4) the social contract theory, which holds that humans agreed to form states to ensure their own survival.

The social contract theory had the greatest influence on the founders of the United States. The Framers expressed their beliefs in the purposes of government in the Preamble to the Constitution.

## Section 2 Forms of Government (pp. 10–14)
Governments can be classified by one or more of their basic features. These include (1) the geographic distribution of power, (2) the relationship between the legislative and executive branches, and (3) the number of persons who take part in governmental processes.

The geographic distribution of power in a government gives it one of three basic forms: (1) a unitary government, in which all of a government's powers are held by a single central agency; (2) a federal government, in which governmental powers are divided between a central and local governments, and (3) a confederation, which is an alliance of independent states.

Depending on the relationship between the legislative and executive branch, government may take a presidential or parliamentary form. In the presidential form, each branch is independent and coequal. In a parliamentary form, the executive consists of members of the legislative branch.

The number of people who can take part in the governmental process is also a basis by which to classify governments. In a dictatorship, government is not accountable to the people. In a democracy, the people hold supreme political authority, either directly or, more commonly, through elected representatives.

## Section 3 Basic Concepts of Democracy (pp. 15–18)
The basic concepts of democracy in the United States are: (1) a recognition of the worth and dignity of each person; (2) respect for the equality of each person; (3) faith in majority rule and insistence on minority rights; (4) an acceptance of the need to compromise; and (5) an insistence upon the widest possible degree of individual freedom.

To ensure its survival as a democracy, this country must respect and apply these principles. This task requires the society to respect the worth of each person without allowing individual needs to injure the interests of the many. The democracy must ensure equal opportunity and equality for all; it must respect majority rule without allowing the majority to crush the minority; and it must use compromise to reach the most satisfactory decisions without compromising basic principles.

# Chapter Review

## Vocabulary and Key Terms

government (p. 3)
public policies (p. 3)
state (p. 4)
sovereign (p. 4)
unitary government (p. 10)
federal government (p. 10)

confederation (p. 11)
presidential
   government (p. 11)
parliamentary
   government (p.11)
dictatorship (p. 12)

democracy (p. 13)
direct democracy (p. 13)
representative democracy
   (p. 13)
compromise (p. 17)
anarchy (p. 17)

**Matching:** *Review the key terms in the list above. If you are not sure of a term's meaning, look up the term and review its definition. Choose a term from the list above that best matches each description.*

1. a state that has supreme power within its own territory
2. the institution through which society makes and enforces its policies
3. that which a government decides to do
4. an alliance of independent states that expressly delegates limited powers to a central government
5. a form of government that is often totalitarian and authoritarian

**True or False:** *Determine whether each statement is true or false. If it is true, write "true." If it is false, change the underlined word or words to make the statement true.*

1. <u>Compromise</u> can be described as all those things that a government does.
2. <u>Presidential governments</u> do not have to contend with issues of prolonged deadlock and conflict between the executive and legislative branches.
3. A <u>government</u> is a sovereign member of the world community.
4. <u>Democracy</u> comes from Greek words meaning "rule by the people."

**Word Relationships:** *Distinguish between words in each pair.*

1. unitary government/federal government
2. direct democracy/representative democracy
3. dictatorship/anarchy
4. presidential government/parliamentary government

## Main Ideas

### Section 1 (pp. 3–8)

1. What characteristics define a state?
2. Briefly describe the four most widely held theories that attempt to explain the origin of the state.
3. Which theory on the origin of the state was most influential in the founding of the United States?
4. For what reasons do people form governments?

### Section 2 (pp. 10–14)

5. On what three general bases can governments be classified?
6. Name and briefly describe the three forms of government that can result depending on how governmental power is distributed.
7. Name and briefly describe the two forms of government that can result depending on the relationship between the legislative and executive branches.

**8.** Name and briefly describe what forms of government can result depending on the number of people who can participate in the governmental process.

### Section 3 (pp. 15–18)

**9.** Briefly describe the five basic concepts of democracy.

**10.** For what reasons is compromise such an essential part of democracy?

**11.** Describe the relationship between the rights of the individual and the rights of the overall society.

**12.** (a) In what sense must a democratic society provide for the rights of the minority? (b) What obligation does this place upon the majority?

## Critical Thinking

**1.** **Recognizing Ideologies** (p. 19) Consider Martin Luther King, Jr.'s statement that "injustice anywhere is a threat to justice everywhere." (a) What is your understanding of that statement? (b) Why is such a belief necessary in order to maintain a democratic society?

**2.** **Checking Consistency** (p. 19) Review the ideas of Thomas Hobbes regarding the social contract theory and the origin of the state. (a) What is Hobbes's view about the nature of human beings? Explain why you agree or disagree with this view. (b) Given Hobbes's view, do you think it makes sense for people to enter into a contract with other human beings for their mutual protection?

**3.** **Identifying Alternatives** (p. 19) One of the five basic concepts of democracy is majority rule with minority rights. (a) What is the record of the United States in ensuring minority rights? (b) What do you think the United States might do to improve its protection of the rights of the minority?

## Getting Involved

**1.** **Writing Your Opinion** Write your own "social contract" in which you express your feelings about what should be required of members of a political society, and what government should provide the people. Start by creating a chart with two columns. In one column, list the responsibilities of the citizens in your proposed social contract. In the other column, list what you feel government should provide its citizens. Begin your contract with a statement about the need for people to join together for their mutual benefit. Then detail your ideas for the contract. Proofread and revise for corrections. Then, prepare a final copy.

**2.** **Cooperative Activity** Conduct a classroom convention in which you discuss the different classifications of government as described in Section 2. The goal of the convention will be to decide as a class what you consider to be the best possible form of government. Start by creating a chart for each of the three bases of classification: (1) geographic distribution of power; (2) relationship between the legislative and executive; and (3) the number of persons who can take part in the governing process. For each category, discuss the pros and cons of each variation. After you have finished debating, write a profile of your ideal government that explains that government's characteristics.

**3.** **Creating a Poster** Create a poster that illustrates one of the five basic concepts of democracy discussed in Section 3. The poster should contain both words and images to communicate your ideas about how American society can best fulfill the concept you have chosen.

**CHAPTER**

# Origins of American Government

## Chapter Preview

A Russian artist, allowed to travel abroad for the first time in 1991, made this comment about his country, "It's amazing to me that so much freedom could lead to so much *poshlost*." The Russian word *poshlost* is said to be untranslatable, but clearly what the artist meant in this case was "chaos."

Revolutionary changes swept what the world once knew as the Soviet Union and Soviet-dominated Eastern Europe in the late 1980s and early 1990s, and several new nations and governments have emerged from that chaos. Somewhat similarly, the American system of government was created in the late 1780s to bring order out of post-revolutionary chaos. This chapter is about the origins of that system of government, from its beginnings through the adoption of the Constitution.

### Before you read this chapter:

- **Describe** what you think is the most important principle on which a new government should be founded.
- **Predict** some problems the United States would face if it lacked a strong central government.

### As you read, focus on the main objective for each section. Understand:

1. The origins of the American governmental system.
2. The development of that system through the colonial period to the coming of Independence.
3. The Critical Period and the governmental arrangements set up by the Articles of Confederation.
4. The events and the processes involved in the creation and adoption of the Constitution of the United States.

▲ **Our Strength: Diversity** Those who formed the American government crafted a system flexible enough to respond to the needs of the ever-growing and diversifying American population of today.

# 1 Our Political Beginnings

## Find Out:

- What were the basic ideas about government that English colonists brought to America?
- How did governments first develop in the 13 colonies?

## Key Terms:

limited government, representative government, Magna Carta, Petition of Right, English Bill of Rights, charter, bicameral, unicameral

For most Americans, the Fourth of July is the time to celebrate this nation's birthday. Every year, people recall 1776 and the coming of Independence with fireworks and picnics and other festivities.

Of course, the story of the United States begins long before 1776. It starts no later than the mid-1500s when explorers, traders, and settlers first made their way to North America. The French, Dutch, Spanish, Swedes, and others contributed to European domination of the continent—and to the domination of the Native Americans who were here for untold centuries before the Europeans came.

It was the English, however, who came in the largest numbers. And they soon controlled the 13 colonies that stretched some 1,300 miles along the Atlantic seaboard.

## Basic Concepts of Government

The earliest English settlers brought with them the knowledge of a political system—established laws, customs, and practices—that had been developing for centuries. The political system the settlers knew was from 17th-century England, but many ideas that contributed

## Foundations of American Rights

| Rights | Sources of Rights | | | |
|---|---|---|---|---|
| | Magna Carta (1215) | English Bill of Rights (1689) | Virginia Declaration of Rights (1776) | Bill of Rights (1791) |
| Trial by jury | ✔ | ✔ | | ✔ |
| Due process | ✔ | ✔ | | ✔ |
| Private property | ✔ | | | ✔ |
| No unreasonable searches or seizures | | | ✔ | ✔ |
| No cruel punishment | | ✔ | ✔ | ✔ |
| No excessive bail or fines | | ✔ | | ✔ |
| Right to bear arms | | ✔ | | ✔ |
| Right to petition | | ✔ | | ✔ |
| Freedom of speech | | | ✔ | ✔ |
| Freedom of the press | | | ✔ | ✔ |
| Freedom of religion | | | ✔ | ✔ |

▲ **Interpreting Tables: Multicultural Awareness**  Although revolutionary in their day, these rights did not extend to all people. Which group gained the most through these rights?

to it came from other times and places. For example, the concept of the rule of law that influenced English political ideas had its roots in the early river civilizations of Africa and Asia.[1] And the ancient Romans actually occupied much of England, leaving their direct legacy of law, religion, and custom to the people. Most importantly, the English colonists brought three ideas that were to loom large in the shaping of government in the United States.

---

[1]For example, King Hammurabi of Babylonia developed a codified system of laws known as Hammurabi's Code around 1750 B.C. Its 285 laws covered real estate, trade, and business transactions, as well as criminal law. The code distinguished between major and minor offenses, established the state as the authority that would enforce the law, and tried to guarantee social justice. Because of the Babylonians' close contact with the Hebrews, many of their laws became part of the Hebrew law and thus later a part of the Old Testament of the Bible—for example, "An eye for an eye." The English and the English colonists were, of course, familiar with and devoutly attracted to this Biblical concept of the rule of law.

**Ordered Government**  The first English colonists saw the need for an orderly regulation of their relationships with one another—that is, for government. They created local governments, based on those they had known in England. Many of the offices and units of government the early settlers established are still found at the local level today: the offices of sheriff, coroner, assessor, and justice of the peace, the grand jury, counties, townships, and several others.

**Limited Government**  Those first English colonists also brought with them the idea that government is not all-powerful. That is, government is limited in what it may do, and each individual has certain rights that government cannot take away.

The concept of **limited government** described above was deeply rooted in English belief and practice by the time the first English ships reached the Americas. It had been planted there in England with the signing of the Magna Carta in 1215, and it had been developing there for nearly 400 years before Jamestown was settled in 1607.

**Representative Government** The early English settlers also carried another important concept to America: **representative government**. This idea that government should serve the will of the people had also been developing in England for centuries. With it had come a growing insistence that the people should have a voice in deciding what government should and should not do. As with the concept of limited government, this notion of "government of, by, and for the people" found fertile soil in America, and it flourished here.

## Landmark English Documents

These basic notions of ordered government, of limited government, and of representative government can be traced to several landmark documents in English history.

**The Magna Carta** A group of determined barons forced King John to sign the **Magna Carta**—the Great Charter—at Runnymede in 1215. Weary of John's military campaigns and heavy taxes, the barons were seeking protection against arbitrary acts by the king.

The Magna Carta included such fundamental rights as trial by jury and due process of law—protection against the arbitrary taking of life, liberty, or property.

These protections against the absolute power of the king were originally intended only for the privileged classes. Over time, they became the rights of all English people and were incorporated into other documents. The Magna Carta established the principle that the power of the monarchy was not absolute.

**The Petition of Right** The Magna Carta was respected by some monarchs and ignored by others for 400 years. During this time, England's Parliament, a representative body with the power to make laws, slowly grew in influence. In 1628, when Charles I asked Parliament for more money in taxes, Parliament refused until he signed the Petition of Right.

The **Petition of Right** limited the king's power by demanding that the king not imprison political critics without trial by jury; not declare martial law, or rule by the military, during peacetime; nor require people to shelter troops without the homeowner's consent. In addition, the document stated that no man should be:

❝ compelled to make or yield any gift, loan, benevolence, tax, or such like charge, without common consent by act of parliament. ❞

The Petition challenged the idea of the divine right of kings, declaring that even a monarch must obey the law of the land.

**The Bill of Rights** In 1688, after years of revolt and turmoil, Parliament offered the crown to William and Mary of Orange. The events surrounding their ascent to the throne are known in English history as the Glorious Revolution. To prevent abuse of power by William and Mary and all future monarchs, Parliament, in 1689, drew up the Bill of Rights to which William and Mary had to agree.

The **English Bill of Rights** prohibited a standing army in peacetime, except with the consent of Parliament, and required that all parliamentary elections be free. The document also declared

❝ that the pretended power of suspending of laws, or the execution of laws, by regal authority, without consent of Parliament is illegal . . .

that levying money for or to the use of the crown . . . without grant of Parliament . . . is illegal . . .

▲ **Life, Liberty, Property** English philosopher John Locke's argument that these were natural rights rather than privileges heavily influenced 18th-century America.

that it is the right of the subjects to petition the king . . . and that prosecutions for such petitioning are illegal . . . **⟩⟩**

In addition, the English Bill of Rights included such guarantees as the right to a fair and speedy trial, and freedom from excessive bail and from cruel and unusual punishment.

Our nation has built on, changed, and added to those ideas and institutions that settlers brought here from England. Still, much in American government and politics today is based on these early English ideas.

## Government in the Colonies

England's colonies in North America have been described as "13 schools of government." The colonies were the settings in which Americans first began to learn the difficult art of government.[2]

The 13 colonies were established separately, over a span of 125 years. Over that long period, outlying trading posts and isolated farm settlements developed into organized communities. The first colony, Virginia, was founded with the first permanent English settlement in North America at Jamestown in 1607.[3] Georgia was the last to be formed, with the settlement of Savannah in 1733.

Each of the colonies was born out of a particular set of circumstances, and so each had its own character. Virginia was originally organized as a commercial venture. Its first colonists were employees of the Virginia Company, a private trading corporation. Massachusetts was first settled by people who came to North America in search of greater personal and religious freedom. Georgia was founded largely as a haven for debtors—a refuge for the victims of England's harsh poor laws.

But the differences between and among the colonies are really of little importance. Of much greater significance is the fact that all of them were shaped by their English origins. The many similarities among all 13 colonies far outweighed the differences.

Each colony was established on the basis of a **charter**, a written grant of authority from the king.[4] Over time, these instruments of government led to the establishment of three different kinds of colonies: royal, proprietary, and charter.

**Royal Colonies** The royal colonies were subject to the direct control of the Crown. On the eve of the Revolution in 1775, there were eight: New Hampshire, Massachusetts, New York, New Jersey, Virginia, North Carolina, South Carolina, and Georgia.

The Virginia colony was not the quick success its sponsors had promised. So, in 1624, the king revoked the London Company's charter, and Virginia became the first royal colony. Later, as the original charters of other colonies were canceled or withdrawn, they became royal colonies. Georgia was the last to join the list, in 1754.

Over time, a pattern of government emerged for each of the royal colonies. The king named a governor to serve as the colony's chief executive. A council, also named by the king, served as an advisory body to the royal governor. In time, the governor's council became the upper house of the colonial legislature. It also became the highest court in the colony. The lower house of a **bicameral** (two-house) legislature was elected by those property owners qualified

---

[2]The Europeans who came to the Americas brought with them their own views of government, but this does not mean that they brought the idea of government to the Americas. Native Americans had governments. They had political institutions that worked to accomplish the goals of the state; they had political leaders; and they had policies toward other states.

Some Native-American political organizations were very complex. For example, five Native-American groups in present-day New York State—the Seneca, Cayuga, Oneida, Onondaga, and Mohawk—formed a confederation known as the Iroquois League. The League was set up to end conflicts among the groups, but it was so successful as a form of government that it lasted for over 200 years.

[3]St. Augustine, Florida, is the oldest continuously populated European settlement in what is now the United States. St. Augustine was founded by Pedro Menendez in 1565 to establish Spanish authority in the region.

---

[4]Except for Georgia. Its charter was granted by Parliament in 1732.

▲ **Early Colonial Government**    Fiery orator Patrick Henry addresses the Virginia House of Burgesses—the first representative body, or elected legislature, to meet in America.

to vote.[5] It owed much of its influence to the fact that it shared with the governor and his council the power of the purse—that is, the power to tax and the power to spend. The governor, advised by the council, appointed the judges for the colony's courts.

The laws passed by the legislature had to be approved by the governor and the Crown. Royal governors often ruled with a stern hand, following instructions from London. Much of the resentment that finally flared into revolution was fanned by their actions.

**The Proprietary Colonies**    At the time of the Revolution, there were three proprietary colonies: Maryland, Pennsylvania, and Delaware. A proprietor was a person to whom the king had made a grant of land. By charter, that land could be settled and governed much as the proprietor (owner) chose.

In 1632 the king had granted Maryland to Lord Baltimore and in 1681, Pennsylvania to William Penn. In 1682 Penn also acquired Delaware.[6]

The governments of these three colonies were much like those in the royal colonies. The governor, however, was appointed by the proprietor. In Maryland and Delaware, the legislatures were bicameral. In Pennsylvania, the legislature was a **unicameral** (one-house) body. There, the governor's council did not act as one house of the legislature. As in the royal colonies, appeals from the decisions of the proprietary colonies could be carried to the king in London.

---

[5]The Virginia legislature held its first meeting in the church at Jamestown on July 30, 1619, and was the first representative body to meet in the English colonies. It was made up of burgesses—that is, representatives—elected from each settlement in the colony. Virginia called the lower house of its colonial legislature the House of Burgesses; South Carolina, the House of Commons; Massachusetts, the House of Representatives.

[6]New York, New Jersey, North Carolina, South Carolina, and Georgia also began as proprietary colonies. Each of them later became a royal colony.

**The Charter Colonies** Connecticut and Rhode Island were charter colonies. They were based on charters granted in 1662 and 1663, respectively, to the colonists themselves.[7] Thus, they were largely self-governing.

The governors of Connecticut and Rhode Island were elected each year by the white, male property owners in each colony. Although the king's approval was required before the governor could take office, it was not often asked. Laws made by their bicameral legislatures were not subject to the governor's veto nor was the Crown's approval needed. Colonial judges were appointed by the legislature, but appeals could be taken from the colonial courts to the king.

The Connecticut and the Rhode Island charters were so liberal for their time that, with independence, they were kept with only minor changes as State constitutions—until 1818 and 1843, respectively. In fact, many historians say that had Britain allowed the other colonies the same freedom and self-government, the Revolution might never have occurred.

## Section 1 Review

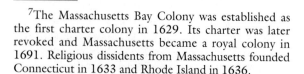

**1. Define:** limited government, representative government, Magna Carta, Petition of Right, English Bill of Rights, charter, bicameral, unicameral
**2.** What major political ideas did the early English settlers bring to America?
**3.** Identify and describe the three types of colonial government in pre-Revolutionary America.

*Critical Thinking*
**4. Making Comparisons** (p. 19) (a) In what ways were the colonial governments similar? (b) How were they different?

★

---

[7]The Massachusetts Bay Colony was established as the first charter colony in 1629. Its charter was later revoked and Massachusetts became a royal colony in 1691. Religious dissidents from Massachusetts founded Connecticut in 1633 and Rhode Island in 1636.

# 2 The Coming of Independence

**Find Out:**

- How did the relationship between the colonies and Great Britain change in the pre-Revolutionary period?
- For what reasons is the Declaration of Independence considered a revolutionary document?
- What was government like in the newly independent United States?

**Key Terms:**

Albany Plan of Union, boycott, constitution, popular sovereignty

"We must all hang together, or assuredly we shall all hang separately." Benjamin Franklin spoke these words on July 4, 1776, as he and the other members of the Second Continental Congress signed the Declaration of Independence. Those who heard him may well have chuckled. But they also may have felt a shiver, for the good doctor's humor carried a deadly serious message.

In this section, you will follow the events that led to the momentous decision to break with Great Britain,[8] and you will also read about the new State governments that were established with the coming of Independence.

## Royal Control

The 13 colonies, which had been separately established, were separately controlled under the king, largely through the Privy Council and the Board of Trade in London. Parliament took little part in the management of the colonies. Although it did become more and more interested in matters of

---

[8]England became Great Britain by the Act of Union with Scotland in 1707.

trade, it left matters of colonial administration almost entirely to the Crown.[9]

Over the century and a half that followed the first settlement at Jamestown, the colonies developed within that framework of royal control. In theory, they were governed in all important matters from London. But London was 3,000 miles away, and it took nearly two months to sail that distance across a peril-filled Atlantic. So, in practice, the colonists became used to a large measure of self-government.

In time, each colonial legislature assumed broad lawmaking powers. Many found the power of the purse to be very effective. They often bent a governor to their will by not voting the money for his salary until he came to terms with them. As one member of New Jersey's Assembly put it: "Let us keep the dogges poore, and we'll make them do as we please."

By the mid-1700s, the relationship between Britain and the colonies had become, in fact if not in form, federal. This means that the central government in London was responsible for colonial defense and for foreign affairs. It also provided a uniform system of money and credit and a common market for colonial trade. Beyond that, the colonies were allowed a fairly wide amount of self-rule. Little was taken from them in direct taxes to pay for the central government. And, the few regulations set by Parliament, mostly about trade, were largely ignored.

This was soon to change. Shortly after George III came to the throne in 1760, Britain began to deal more firmly with the colonies. Restrictive trading acts were expanded and enforced. New taxes were imposed, mostly to support British troops in North America.

Many colonists took strong exception to these moves. They objected to taxes they had had no part in levying. This arrangement, they claimed, was "taxation without representation."

They saw little need for the costly presence of British troops since the French had been defeated and their power broken in the French and Indian War (1754–1763). The colonists considered themselves British subjects loyal to the Crown. They refused, however, to accept Parliament's claim that it had a right to control their own local affairs.

The king's ministers were poorly informed and stubborn. They pushed ahead with their policies, despite the resentments they stirred in America. Within a few years, the colonists were to be forced to a fateful choice: to submit or to revolt.

## Growing Colonial Unity

Long before the 1770s, several attempts had been made to promote cooperation among the colonies.

▲ **The Road to Revolution, 1765–1766**
British enforcement of the Stamp Act led to angry protests against "taxation without representation" in colonial America.

[9]Much of English political history can be told in terms of the centuries-long struggle for supremacy between king and Parliament. That conflict was largely settled by England's Glorious Revolution of 1688, but it did continue on through the American colonial period and into the 19th century. However, Parliament paid little attention to the American colonies until very late in the colonial period.

**Early Attempts**   In 1643 the Massachusetts Bay, Plymouth, New Haven, and Connecticut settlements formed the New England Confederation, a "league of friendship" for defense against the Native Americans. However, as the danger from Native Americans passed and friction among the settlements grew, the confederation lost importance and finally died in 1684. In 1696 William Penn offered an elaborate plan for intercolonial cooperation, largely in trade, defense, and criminal matters. It received little attention and was soon forgotten.

**The Albany Plan**   In 1754 the British Board of Trade called a meeting of seven of the northern colonies at Albany.[10] The main purpose of the meeting was to discuss the problems of colonial trade and the danger of attacks by the French and their Native-American allies. Here, Benjamin Franklin offered what came to be known as the **Albany Plan of Union**.

Franklin proposed the formation of an annual congress of delegates from each of the 13 colonies. That body would have the power to raise military and naval forces, make war and peace with the Native Americans, regulate trade with them, levy taxes, and collect customs duties.

Franklin's plan was ahead of its time. It was agreed to by the Albany meeting, but it was turned down by the colonies and by the Crown. Franklin's plan was to be remembered later, however.

**The Stamp Act Congress**   Britain's harsh tax and trade policies of the 1760s fanned resentment in the colonies. Parliament had passed a number of new laws, among them the Stamp Act of 1765. That law required the use of tax stamps on all legal documents, on certain business agreements, and on newspapers.

The new taxes were widely denounced, in part because the rates were perceived as severe, but largely because they amounted to "taxation without representation." In October of 1765 nine colonies[11] sent delegates to the Stamp Act Congress in New York. They prepared a strong protest, called the Declaration of Rights and Grievances, against the new British policies and sent it to the king. Their actions marked the first time a significant number of the colonies had joined to oppose the British government.

Parliament repealed the Stamp Act, but frictions mounted. New laws were passed and new policies were made to tie the colonies more closely to London. Colonists showed their resentment and anger in wholesale evasion of the laws. Mob violence erupted at several ports, and many colonists supported a **boycott**—a refusal to buy or sell—English goods. On March 3, 1770, British troops in Boston fired on a jeering crowd, killing five, in what came to be known as the Boston Massacre.

Organized resistance was carried on through Committees of Correspondence, which had grown out of a group formed by Samuel Adams in Boston in 1772. Within a year these committees existed throughout the colonies, providing a network for cooperation and the exchange of information among the patriots.

Protests multiplied. The famous Boston Tea Party came on December 16, 1773. A group of men, disguised as Native Americans, boarded three ships in Boston harbor and dumped their cargo into the sea in protest of a new tea monopoly.

## The First Continental Congress

In the spring of 1774, Parliament passed yet another set of laws, this time to punish the colonists for the troubles in Boston and elsewhere. These new laws, denounced in America as the Intolerable Acts, caused the Massachusetts and Virginia assemblies to call a meeting of all the colonies.

Fifty-five delegates, from every colony except Georgia, met in Philadelphia on September 5, 1774. For nearly two months, the members of this First Continental Congress discussed the worsening situation and debated plans for action.

---

[10]Connecticut, Maryland, Massachusetts, New Hampshire, New York, Pennsylvania, and Rhode Island.

[11]All except Georgia, New Hampshire, North Carolina, and Virginia.

They sent a Declaration of Rights, protesting Britain's colonial policies, to George III. The delegates urged each of the colonies to refuse all trade with England until the hated taxes and trade regulations were repealed. The delegates also called for the creation of local committees to enforce that boycott.

The meeting adjourned on October 26, with a call for a second congress the following May. Over the next several months, all the colonial legislatures, including Georgia's, gave their support to the actions of the First Continental Congress.

## The Second Continental Congress

During the fall and winter of 1774–75, the British government continued to refuse to compromise, let alone reverse, its colonial policies. It reacted to the Declaration of Rights as it had to other expressions of colonial discontent—with even stricter and more repressive measures.

The Second Continental Congress met in Philadelphia on May 10, 1775. By then, the Revolution had begun. The "shot heard 'round the world" had been fired. The battles of Lexington and Concord had been fought three weeks earlier, on April 19.

Each of the 13 colonies sent representatives to the Congress. Most of those who had attended the First Continental Congress were again present. Most notable among the newcomers were Benjamin Franklin of Pennsylvania and John Hancock of Massachusetts.

Hancock was chosen president of the Congress.[12] Almost at once, a continental army was organized, and George Washington was appointed its commander in chief. Thomas Jefferson then took Washington's place in the Virginia delegation.

The Second Continental Congress became, by force of circumstance, the nation's first

▲ **Preparing for Victory** George Washington, appointed commander in chief by the Second Continental Congress, plans the next move against British forces.

national government. However, it rested on no constitutional base. It was condemned by the British as an unlawful assembly and a den of traitors. But it was supported by the force of public opinion and practical necessity.

The Second Continental Congress served as the first government of the United States for five fateful years, from the adoption of the Declaration of Independence in July 1776 until the Articles of Confederation went into effect on March 1, 1781. During that time it fought a war, raised armies and a navy, borrowed money, bought supplies, created a monetary system, made treaties with foreign powers, and did those other things that any government would have had to do in the circumstances.

The unicameral Congress exercised both legislative and executive powers. In legislative matters, each colony—later, State—had one vote. Executive functions were handled by committees of delegates.

---

[12]Peyton Randolph, who had also served as president of the First Continental Congress, was originally chosen for the office. He resigned on May 24, however, because the Virginia House of Delegates, of which he was the speaker, had been called into session. Hancock was then elected to succeed him.

Declaration of Independence.

A Declaration by the Representatives of the UNITED STATES [of] AMERICA, in General Congress assembled.

[When] in the course of human events it becomes necessary for one people to [dissolve the] political bands which have connected them with another, and to [assume among] the powers of the earth the separate and equal station to [which the] laws of nature & of nature's god entitle them, a decent respect [to the opinions] of mankind requires that they should declare the causes [which] impel them to the separation.

▲ **"An expression of the American mind"** So Thomas Jefferson (left) described his Declaration of Independence, shown in the author's own hand.

## The Declaration of Independence

On June 7, 1776, Richard Henry Lee of Virginia proposed to the Congress:

❝ *Resolved*, That these United Colonies are, and of right ought to be, free and independent States, that they are absolved from all allegiance to the British Crown, and that all political connection between them and the State of Great Britain is, and ought to be, totally dissolved. ❞

Congress named a committee of five—Benjamin Franklin, John Adams, Roger Sherman, Robert Livingston, and Thomas Jefferson—to prepare a proclamation of independence. Their momentous product, the Declaration of Independence, was almost wholly the work of Jefferson.

On July 2, the final break came. The delegates unanimously agreed to Lee's resolution. Two days later, on July 4, 1776, they adopted the Declaration of Independence and announced it to the world.

The Declaration announces the independence of the United States in its first paragraph. Much of the balance of the document—nearly two-thirds of it—speaks of "the repeated injuries and usurpations" that led the colonists to revolt. At its heart, the Declaration proclaims:

❝ We hold these truths to be self-evident, that all men are created equal, that they are endowed by their Creator with certain unalienable Rights, that among these are Life, Liberty and the pursuit of Happiness. That to secure these rights, Governments are instituted among Men, deriving their just powers from the consent of the governed; That whenever any Form of Government becomes destructive of these ends it is the Right of the People to alter or to abolish it, and to institute new Government, laying its foundations on such principles and organizing its power in such form, as to them shall seem most likely to effect their Safety and Happiness. ❞

With these brave words, the United States of America was born. The 13 colonies became free and independent States. The 56 men who signed the Declaration sealed it with this final sentence:

❝ And for the support of this Declaration, with a firm reliance on the protection of Divine Providence, we mutually pledge to each other, our lives, our Fortunes, and our sacred Honor. ❞

## The First State Governments

In January 1776, New Hampshire adopted a constitution to replace its royal charter. Less than three months later, South Carolina followed suit. Then, on May 10, the Congress urged each of the colonies to adopt:

*❝ such governments as shall, in the opinion of the representatives of the people, best conduce to the happiness and safety of their constituents.❞*

In 1776 and 1777, most of the States adopted written **constitutions**—bodies of fundamental laws setting out the principles, structures, and processes of their governments. Assemblies or conventions were commonly used to draft and then adopt these new documents. Massachusetts set a lasting precedent in the constitution-making process. There, a convention submitted its work to the voters for ratification. The Massachusetts constitution of 1780 is the oldest of the present-day State constitutions. In fact, it is the oldest written constitution in force anywhere in the world today.

## Common Features of New States

The first State constitutions differed, sometimes widely, in detail. Yet they shared many common features.

**Popular Sovereignty** Each of the new constitutions was based on the principle of **popular sovereignty**. This principle insists that government can exist and function *only* with the consent of the governed. It is the people who hold power; it is the people who are sovereign.

**Limited Government** The concept of limited government was a major feature of each document. The powers delegated to government were at best reluctantly granted and hedged with many restrictions.

**Civil Rights and Liberties** Seven of the new documents[13] contained a bill of rights, setting out the "unalienable rights" held by the people. In every State it was made clear that the sovereign people held certain rights that government must at all times respect.

**Separation of Powers and Checks and Balances** The powers granted to the new State governments were purposely divided among three branches: executive, legislative, and judicial. Each branch was given powers with which to check the other branches of government.

The new State constitutions were rather brief documents. For the most part, they were declarations of principle and statements of limitation on governmental power. Memories of the royal governors were fresh and the new State governors were given little real power. Most of the authority that was granted to State government was placed in the legislature. Elective terms of office were made purposely short, seldom more than one or two years. The right to vote was limited to those adult males who could meet property ownership and other rigid qualifications.

Yet with all their shortcomings, these documents would have a large influence on the shaping of a government for the new United States.

## Section 2 Review

**1. Define:** Albany Plan of Union, boycott, constitution, popular sovereignty
**2.** What was the relationship between Britain and the colonies like in the mid-1700s, and how did it change in the 1760s?
**3.** In what ways did the Second Continental Congress serve as the first national government?
**4.** (a) Who wrote the Declaration of Independence? (b) For what reasons are the opening lines of its second paragraph so important?
**5.** List the common features of the first State constitutions.

### Critical Thinking

**6. Recognizing Ideologies** (p. 19) The Second Continental Congress met in violation of the law. (a) What does this say about the colonists' view of governmental authority? (b) How would you respond to such a gathering today?

---

[13]The constitutions of Delaware, Maryland, Massachusetts, New Hampshire, North Carolina, Pennsylvania, and Virginia.

★

# 3 The Critical Period

**Find Out:**

- What were the basic provisions and major weaknesses of the Articles of Confederation?
- For what reasons are the 1780s known as the Critical Period in American history?
- What steps led to the Constitutional Convention in 1787?

**Key Terms:**

ratification, Articles of Confederation

The First and Second Continental Congresses rested on no legal base. They were called in haste to meet an emergency, and they were intended to be temporary. Something more regular and permanent was clearly needed. In this section, you will read about the first attempt to establish a lasting government for the new nation.

## The First National Constitution

Richard Henry Lee's resolution that had led to the Declaration of Independence also called on the Second Continental Congress to propose "a plan of confederation." Off and on, for 17 months, that body considered the problem of uniting the former colonies. Finally, on November 15, 1777, they approved the Articles of Confederation.

The Articles did not go into effect immediately, however. The **ratification**—formal approval—of each of the 13 States was needed first. Eleven States agreed to the document within a year. Delaware added its approval in mid-1779. But Maryland did not ratify until February 27, 1781. The Second Continental Congress then set March 1, 1781, as the date when the Articles were finally to become effective.

The **Articles of Confederation** established "a firm league of friendship" among the States. Each State kept "its sovereignty, freedom, and independence, and every power, jurisdiction, and right . . . not . . . expressly delegated to the United States, in Congress assembled." The States came together "for their common defense, the security of their liberties, and their mutual and general welfare."

**Governmental Structure**  The government set up by the Articles was simple indeed. A Congress was the sole body created. It was unicameral, made up of delegates chosen yearly by the States in whatever way their legislatures might direct. Each State had one vote in the Congress, whatever its population or wealth.

There was no executive or judicial branch. These functions were to be handled by committees of the Congress. Each year the Congress would choose one of its members as its president. That person would be its presiding officer, but not the president of the United States. Civil officers such as postmasters were to be appointed by the Congress.

**Powers of Congress**  Several important powers were given to the Congress. It could make war and peace; send and receive ambassadors; make treaties; borrow money; set up a monetary system; build a navy; raise an army by asking the States for troops; fix uniform standards of weights and measures; and settle disputes among the States.

**State Obligations**  By agreeing to the Articles, the States had pledged to obey the Articles and acts of the Congress; provide the funds and troops requested by the Congress; treat citizens of other States fairly and equally with their own; give full faith and credit to the public acts, records, and judicial proceedings of every other State; surrender fugitives from justice to each other; submit their disputes to Congress for settlement; and allow open travel and trade between and among the States.

Beyond these few obligations, the States retained those powers not explicitly given to the Congress. They, not the Congress, were primarily responsible for protecting life and property and for promoting the general welfare—"the safety and happiness"—of the people.

**Weaknesses** The powers of the Congress appear, at first glance, to have been considerable. Several important powers were missing, however. Their lack, together with other weaknesses, soon proved the Articles inadequate to the needs of the time.

The Congress did not have the power to tax. It could raise money only by borrowing and by asking the States for funds. Borrowing was, at best, a poor source. The Second Continental Congress had borrowed heavily to support the Revolution, and many of those debts had not been paid. And, while the Articles were in force, not one State came close to meeting the financial requests made by the Congress.

Nor did the Congress have the power to regulate trade between the States. This lack of a central mechanism to regulate the young nation's commerce was one of the major factors that led to the adoption of the Constitution, as you will see.

The Congress had no power to make the States obey the Articles of Confederation or the laws it made. Congress could exercise the powers it did have only with the consent of 9 of the 13 State delegations. Finally, the Articles themselves could be changed only with the consent of all 13 of the State legislatures. This procedure proved an impossible task; not one amendment was ever added to the Articles of Confederation.

## The Critical Period, the 1780s

The long Revolutionary War finally ended on October 19, 1781. America's victory was confirmed by the Treaty of Paris in 1783. With peace, however, the new nation's economic and political problems came into sharp focus. The weaknesses of the Articles of Confederation soon surfaced.

With a central government unable to act, the States bickered among themselves and grew increasingly jealous and suspicious of one another. They refused to support the new central government, financially and in almost every other way. Several of them made agreements with foreign governments, even though that was forbidden by the Articles. Most even organized their own military forces. George

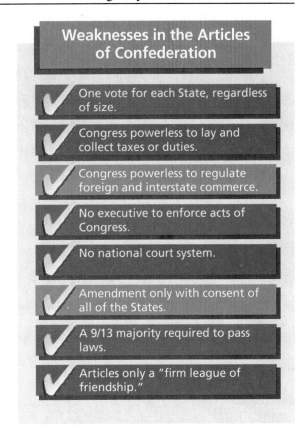

**Weaknesses in the Articles of Confederation**

✓ One vote for each State, regardless of size.

✓ Congress powerless to lay and collect taxes or duties.

✓ Congress powerless to regulate foreign and interstate commerce.

✓ No executive to enforce acts of Congress.

✓ No national court system.

✓ Amendment only with consent of all of the States.

✓ A 9/13 majority required to pass laws.

✓ Articles only a "firm league of friendship."

▲ **Interpreting Charts** The thirst for independence made Americans wary of strong central government. How is this caution reflected in the chart?

Washington complained, "We are one nation today and 13 tomorrow. Who will treat with us on such terms?"

The States taxed each other's goods and even banned some trade. They printed their own money, often with little backing. Economic chaos spread throughout the colonies as prices soared and sound credit vanished. Debts, public and private, went unpaid. Violence broke out in a number of places as a result of the economic chaos. Shays' Rebellion in western Massachusetts in 1786 was only the most spectacular of several incidents.

The Articles had not created a government able to deal with the nation's troubles. Inevitably, demand grew for a stronger, more effective national government. Those who were most threatened by economic and political instability—large property owners, merchants, traders,

**Shays' Rebellion**　To protest the loss of their properties to tax collectors, angry farmers seized courthouses in Massachusetts in 1786.

and other creditors—soon took the lead in efforts to that end. The movement for change began to take concrete form in 1785.

## The Meetings at Mount Vernon and Annapolis

Maryland and Virginia, plagued by bitter trade disputes, took the first step in the movement for change. Ignoring the Congress, the two States agreed to a conference on their trade problems. Representatives from the two States met at Alexandria, Virginia, in March 1785. At George Washington's invitation, they moved their sessions to his home at nearby Mount Vernon. Their negotiations proved so successful that on January 21, 1786, the Virginia Assembly called for "a joint meeting of [all of] the States to recommend a federal plan for regulating commerce."

---

[14]New York, New Jersey, Pennsylvania, Delaware, and Virginia. Although New Hampshire, Massachusetts, Rhode Island, and North Carolina had appointed delegates, none attended the Annapolis meeting.

That joint meeting opened at Annapolis, Maryland, on September 11, 1786. Representatives from only 5 of the 13 States attended.[14] Disappointed, but still hopeful, the Annapolis Convention called for yet another meeting of the States

❝at Philadelphia on the second Monday in May next, to take into consideration the situation of the United States, to devise such further provisions as shall appear to them necessary to render the constitution of the Federal Government adequate to the exigencies of the Union.❞

By mid-February of 1787, seven of the States had named delegates to the Philadelphia meeting. These were Delaware, Georgia, New Hampshire, New Jersey, North Carolina, Pennsylvania, and Virginia. Then, on February 21 the Congress, which had been hesitating, also called upon the States to send delegates to Philadelphia

❝for the sole and express purpose of revising the Articles of Confederation and reporting to Congress and the several legislatures such alterations and provisions therein as shall when agreed to in Congress and confirmed by the States render the [Articles] adequate to the exigencies of Government and the preservation of the Union.❞

That Philadelphia meeting became the Constitutional Convention.

## Section 3 Review

**1. Define:** ratification, Articles of Confederation
**2.** When and by whom were the Articles of Confederation prepared?
**3.** (a) Describe the government set up by the Articles. (b) What powers were given to Congress?
**4.** What were the major weaknesses of the government under the Articles?

**Critical Thinking**

**5. Drawing Conclusions** (p. 19) For what reasons is the period during which the Articles were in force called the Critical Period in American history?

★

# Should Schools Have the Right to Censor Student Newspapers?
## *Hazelwood School District* v. *Kuhlmeier*, 1988

In 1983, the principal of Hazelwood East High School in St. Louis County, Missouri, removed two articles from an upcoming issue of *The Spectrum*, the school's student newspaper. One of the stories to which he objected described three students' experiences with pregnancy; the other discussed the impact of divorce on students at the school. The principal said that those stories were "inappropriate, personal, sensitive, and unsuitable for student readers." The school board later voted to support the principal's action.

Cathy Kuhlmeier and several other students sued the school district, in the United States District Court in St. Louis. They claimed that school officials had violated their 1st and 14th Amendment rights to freedom of expression. The court held that no violation of their constitutional rights had occurred, however. It found that *The Spectrum* could not be considered a "public forum"—that is, not a medium of expression generally open to the public; it was, instead, "an integral part of the school's educational function."

The students appealed that ruling, and the United States Court of Appeals reversed the lower court. The school district then carried the case to the United States Supreme Court.

*Review the following evidence and arguments presented to the U.S. Supreme Court:*

## Arguments for Hazelwood School District

**1.** Students' rights are not violated if educators exercise editorial control over school-sponsored publications, especially when they do so for educational reasons.

**2.** The school newspaper is not a public forum. Therefore, so long as the school remained neutral on controversial matters, the censorship was warranted.

**3.** Educators are responsible for guiding and controlling school-sponsored publications and other creative endeavors when such activities are sanctioned by, and reflect on, the school itself.

## Arguments for Cathy Kuhlmeier

**1.** The students' constitutional rights were violated. Freedom of expression is protected by the Constitution when such expression does not disrupt class work or infringe on the rights of others.

**2.** The school newspaper is a public forum and does not reflect the school's viewpoint. Therefore, the students had the right to express their own opinions to the community.

**3.** An educator's responsibility to instill moral and political values is not meant to stifle free thought and expression. Students should not be forced to limit themselves to state-approved subjects or opinions.

## Getting Involved

**1. Identify** the constitutional grounds on which each side based its arguments.

**2. Debate** the opposing viewpoints presented in the case.

**3. Predict** how you think the Supreme Court ruled in this case and why. Now refer to the Supreme Court Glossary on page 766 to read about the decision. Discuss the impact of the Court's ruling on students' rights of expression in general.

# 4 Creating the Constitution

**Find Out:**

- How was the Constitution written?
- For what reasons were compromises necessary?
- What major compromises were involved?

**Key Terms:**

Framers, Virginia Plan, New Jersey Plan, Connecticut Compromise, Three-Fifths Compromise, Commerce and Slave Trade Compromise

Picture this scene. It's hot—sweltering, in fact. Yet the windows are closed to discourage eavesdroppers. The atmosphere is tense as the men exchange their views. Indeed, some become so angry that they threaten to leave the hall. A few carry out their threats.

This was the scene throughout much of the Philadelphia meeting that began on Friday, May 25, 1787. In this section, you will read about that meeting and its work.

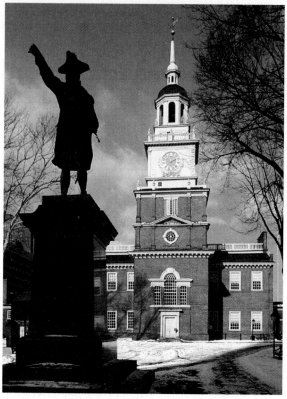

▲ **Seat of Liberty** The Philadelphia Convention met in Independence Hall during the hot summer of 1787. The document crafted by the convention is still regarded as the supreme law of the land today.

## The Framers

Twelve of the 13 States, all but Rhode Island, sent delegates to Philadelphia.[15] In total, 74 delegates were chosen by the legislatures in those 12 states. For a number of reasons, however, only 55 of them actually attended the convention.

Of that 55, this much can be said: Never, before or since, has so remarkable a group been brought together in this country. Thomas Jefferson, who was not among them, later called the delegates "an assembly of demigods."

The group—the **Framers** of the Constitution—included these outstanding personalities: George Washington, James Madison, Edmund Randolph, and George Mason from Virginia; Benjamin Franklin, Gouverneur Morris, Robert Morris, and James Wilson from Pennsylvania; Alexander Hamilton from New York; William Paterson from New Jersey; Elbridge Gerry and Rufus King from Massachusetts; Luther Martin from Maryland; Oliver Ellsworth and Roger Sherman from Connecticut; John Dickinson from Delaware; and John Rutledge and Charles Pinckney from South Carolina.

These were men of wide knowledge and public experience, of wealth and prestige. Many of them had fought in the Revolution; 39 had been members of the Continental Congress or the Congress of the Confederation, or both. Eight had served in constitutional conventions

---

[15]The Rhode Island legislature was controlled by the soft-money forces—mostly debtors and small farmers who were helped by inflation and so were against a stronger central government. The New Hampshire delegation, delayed mostly by lack of funds, did not reach Philadelphia until late July.

in their own States, and seven had been State governors. Eight had signed the Declaration of Independence. Thirty-one of the delegates had attended college in a day when there were but a few colleges in the land, and their number also included two college presidents and three professors. Two were to become Presidents of the United States, and one a Vice President. Seventeen later served in the Senate and 11 in the House of Representatives.

Is it any wonder that the product of such a gathering was described by English statesman William E. Gladstone, nearly a century later, as "the most wonderful work ever struck off at a given time by the brain and purpose of man"?

Remarkably, the average age of the delegates was only 42, and nearly half were only in their 30s. Indeed, most of the real leaders were in that age group—Madison was 36, Gouverneur Morris 35, Randolph 34, and Hamilton 32. At 81, Franklin was the oldest. He was failing, however, and not able to attend many of the meetings. George Washington, at 55, was one of the few older members who played a key role at the meetings.

By and large, the Framers of the Constitution were of a new generation in American politics. Several of the better-known leaders of the Revolutionary period were not in Philadelphia. Patrick Henry said he "smelt a rat" and refused to attend. Samuel Adams, John Hancock, and Richard Henry Lee were not selected as delegates by their States. Thomas Paine was in Paris. So, too, was Thomas Jefferson—as American minister to France. John Adams was our envoy to England and Holland at the time.

## Organization and Procedure

The Framers met in Philadelphia's Independence Hall, probably in the same room in which the Declaration of Independence had been signed 11 years earlier.

They organized immediately on May 25, unanimously electing George Washington president of the convention.[16] Then, and at the second session on Monday, May 28, they adopted several rules of procedure. A majority of the States would be needed to conduct business.

### VOICES on Government

#### On the Task of Writing a Constitution

**"** The [writing of the Constitution] formed a task more difficult than can be well conceived by those who were not concerned in the execution of it. Adding to [the difficulty] the natural diversity of human opinions on all new and complicated subjects, it is impossible to consider the degree of concord which ultimately prevailed as less than a miracle. **"**

**James Madison,** architect of the Constitution and fourth President of the United States

Each State delegation was to have one vote and a majority would carry any proposal.

The convention had drawn much public attention—and speculation. So, to protect themselves from outside pressures, the delegates adopted a rule of secrecy. On the whole, the rule was well kept.

A secretary, William Jackson, kept the convention's *Journal.* That official record, however, was quite sketchy. It was mostly a listing of members present, motions put forth, and votes taken; and it was not always accurate at that.

Fortunately, several delegates kept their own accounts of the proceedings. Most of what is known of the work of the convention

---

[16]Twenty-nine delegates from seven States were present on that first day. The full number of 55 was not reached until August 6, when John Francis Mercer of Maryland arrived. In the meantime, some delegates had departed, and others were absent from time to time. Some 40 members attended most of the daily sessions of the convention.

comes from James Madison's voluminous *Notes*. His brilliance and depth of knowledge led his colleagues to hold him in great respect. Quickly, he became the convention's floor leader. Madison contributed more to the Constitution than did any of the others, and still he was able to keep a close record of its work. Certainly, he deserves the title "Father of the Constitution."

The Framers met on 89 of the 116 days from May 25 through their final meeting on September 17. They did most of their work on the floor of the convention. They handled some matters in committees, but all questions were ultimately settled by the full body.

## The Decision to Write a New Constitution

The Philadelphia Convention was called to recommend revisions in the Articles of Confederation. However, almost at once the delegates agreed that they were, in fact, meeting to create a new government for the United States. On May 30 they adopted this proposal, put by Edmund Randolph of Virginia:

*Resolved*, . . . that a *national* Government ought to be established consisting of a *supreme* Legislative, Executive and Judiciary. 

With this momentous decision, the Framers redefined the purpose of the convention. From that point on, they set about the writing of a new constitution. This new constitution was intended to replace the Articles of Confederation. Their debates were spirited, even bitter. At times the convention seemed near collapse. Once they had passed Governor Randolph's resolution, however, the goal of a majority of the convention never changed.

## The Virginia Plan

No State had more to do with the calling of the convention than Virginia. It was not surprising, then, that its delegates should offer the first plan for a new constitution. On May 29 the Virginia Plan, largely the work of Madison, was presented by Randolph.

The **Virginia Plan** called for a new government with three separate branches: legislative,

executive, and judicial. The legislature—Congress—would be bicameral. Representation in each house was to be based either upon each State's population or upon the amount of money it gave for the support of the central government. The members of the lower house, the House of Representatives, were to be popularly elected in each State. Those of the upper house, the Senate, were to be chosen by the House from lists of persons nominated by the State legislatures.

Congress was to be given all of the powers it held under the Articles. In addition, it was to have the power to legislate "in all cases in which the separate States are incompetent" to act, to veto any State law in conflict with national law, and to use force if necessary to make a State obey national law.

Under the Virginia Plan, Congress would choose a national executive and a national judiciary. Together, these two branches would form a "council of revision." They could veto acts of Congress, but a veto could be overridden by the two houses. The executive would have "a general authority to execute the national laws." The judiciary would "consist of one or more supreme tribunals [courts], and of inferior tribunals."

The Virginia Plan also provided that all State officers should take an oath to support the Union, that each State be guaranteed a republican form of government, and that Congress have the power to admit new States to the Union.

The Virginia Plan, then, called for the creation of a truly national government with greatly expanded powers and, importantly, the power to enforce its decisions.

The Virginia Plan set the agenda for much of the convention's work. But some delegates—especially those from the smaller States of Delaware, Maryland, and New Jersey, and from New York[17]—found it too radical. Soon they

---

[17]The Virginia Plan's major support came from the three largest States: Virginia, Pennsylvania, and Massachusetts. New York was then only the fifth largest. Alexander Hamilton, the convention's most outspoken champion of a stronger central government, was regularly outvoted by his fellow delegates from New York.

developed their counterproposals. On June 15 William Paterson of New Jersey presented the position of the small States.

## The New Jersey Plan

Paterson and his colleagues offered several amendments to the Articles, but not nearly so thorough a revision as that proposed by the Virginia Plan. The **New Jersey Plan** would have kept the unicameral Congress of the Confederation, with each of the States equally represented. To those powers Congress already had would be added closely limited powers to tax and to regulate trade between the States.

The New Jersey Plan also called for a federal executive of more than one person. This plural executive would be chosen by Congress and could be removed by it at the request of a majority of the States' governors. The federal judiciary would be composed of a single supreme tribunal, appointed by the executive.

Among their several differences, the major point of disagreement between the two plans centered on this question: How should the States be represented in Congress? Would it be on the basis of their populations or financial contributions, as in the Virginia Plan? Or would it be on the basis of State equality, as in the Articles and the New Jersey Plan?

For weeks the delegates returned to this conflict. The lines were sharply drawn. Several delegates, on both sides of the issue, threatened to withdraw. Finally, the dispute was settled by one of the key compromises the Framers were to make as they built the Constitution.

## The Connecticut Compromise

The disagreement over representation in Congress was critical. The large States expected to dominate the new government. The small States feared that they would not be able to protect their interests. Tempers flared on both sides. The debate became so intense that Benjamin Franklin was moved to suggest that

ʕʕ henceforth prayers imploring the assistance of Heaven . . . be offered in this Assembly every morning before we proceed to business. ʔʔ

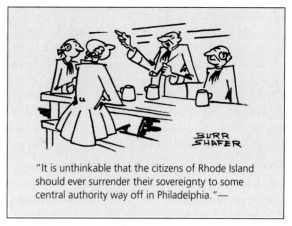

"It is unthinkable that the citizens of Rhode Island should ever surrender their sovereignty to some central authority way off in Philadelphia."—

▲ **Interpreting Political Cartoons** By 1787, Rhode Island had been self-governing for more than 140 years. In light of this, what sense can you make of this cartoon?

The conflict was finally settled by a compromise suggested by the Connecticut delegation. Under the **Connecticut Compromise**, it was agreed that Congress should be composed of two houses. In the smaller Senate, the States would be represented equally. In the House, the representation of each State would be based upon its population.

Thus, by combining basic features of the rival Virginia and New Jersey Plans, the convention's most serious dispute was resolved. The agreement satisfied the smaller States in particular, and it made it possible for them to support the creation of a strong central government.

The Connecticut Compromise was so pivotal to the writing of the Constitution that it has often been called the Great Compromise.

## The Three-Fifths Compromise

Once it had been agreed to base the seats in the House on each State's population, this question arose: Should slaves be counted in the populations of the southern States?

Again debate was fierce. Most delegates from the slave-holding States argued that slaves should be counted. Most of the Northerners took the opposing view. The table on the next page shows the significant percentage of enslaved people among the populations of the southern States.

## Slavery in the United States, 1790

| State | Total Population | Slaves in Population | % Slaves |
|---|---|---|---|
| Connecticut | 237,946 | 2,648 | 1.11 |
| Delaware | 59,096 | 8,837 | 14.95 |
| Georgia | 82,548 | 29,624 | 35.89 |
| Maryland | 319,728 | 103,036 | 32.23 |
| Massachusetts | 475,307 | 0 | 0.00 |
| New Hampshire | 141,885 | 157 | 0.11 |
| New Jersey | 184,139 | 11,423 | 6.20 |
| New York | 340,120 | 21,193 | 6.23 |
| North Carolina | 393,751 | 100,783 | 25.60 |
| Pennsylvania | 434,373 | 3,707 | 0.85 |
| Rhode Island | 68,825 | 958 | 1.39 |
| South Carolina | 249,073 | 107,094 | 43.00 |
| Virginia | 747,600 | 292,627 | 39.14 |

Source: Census Bureau, *Historical Statistics of the United States, Colonial Times to 1970*, Part I, pages 24-36

**Interpreting Tables**   This table shows the slave populations of each State in 1790. Why did the southern States want enslaved people counted in their States' total population?

Finally, the Framers agreed to the **Three-Fifths Compromise**. It provided that all "free persons" should be counted, and so should "three-fifths of all other persons."[18] For the three-fifths won by the Southerners, the Northerners exacted a price. That formula was also to be used in fixing the amount of money to be raised in each State by any direct tax levied by Congress. This unusual compromise disappeared from the Constitution along with slavery itself with the 13th Amendment in 1865. For more than 125 years now, there have been no "all other persons" in this country.

## The Commerce and Slave Trade Compromise

The convention agreed that Congress had to have the power to regulate foreign and interstate trade. To many Southerners, that power carried a real danger, however. They worried that Congress, likely to be controlled by northern commercial interests, would act against the interests of the agricultural South.

They were particularly fearful that Congress would try to pay for the new government out of export duties—and southern tobacco was the major American export of the time. They also feared that Congress would interfere with the slave trade.

Before they would agree to the commerce power, the white Southerners insisted on certain protections. So, according to the **Commerce and Slave Trade Compromise**, Congress was forbidden the power to tax the export of goods from any State. It was also forbidden the power to act on the slave trade for a period of at least 20 years.[19]

## A "Bundle of Compromises"

The convention spent much of its time, said Franklin, "sawing boards to make them fit."

---

[18]Article I, Section 2, Clause 3. For "all other persons" read "slaves."

[19]Article I, Section 9, Clause 1. Congress promptly banned the importation of slaves in 1808, and in 1820 it declared the slave trade to be piracy. The smuggling of the enslaved into this country continued until the outbreak of the Civil War, however.

The Constitution drafted at Philadelphia has often been called a "bundle of compromises." These descriptions are apt, if they are properly understood.

There were differences of opinion among the delegates, certainly. After all, the delegates came from 12 different States which were widely separated in geographic and economic terms. The delegates often reflected the interests of their States. Bringing these interests together did require compromise. Indeed, final decisions on issues such as selection of the President, the treaty-making process, the structure of the national court system, and the amendment process were reached as a result of compromise.

But by no means did all, or even most, of what shaped the document come from compromises. The Framers agreed on many of the basic issues they faced. Thus, nearly all the delegates were convinced that they wanted a new central government. The Framers were also dedicated to the concepts of popular sovereignty and of limited government. None questioned for a moment the wisdom of representative government. The principles of separation of powers and of checks and balances were accepted almost as a matter of course.

## Sources of the Constitution

The Framers were well educated and widely read. They were familiar with the governments of ancient Greece and Rome and those of contemporary Great Britain and Europe. They knew the political writings of their time, of such works as William Blackstone's *Commentaries on the Laws of England*, the Baron de Montesquieu's *The Spirit of the Laws*, Jean Jacques Rousseau's *Social Contract*, John Locke's *Two Treatises of Government*, and many others.

More immediately, the Framers drew on their own experiences. Remember, they were familiar with the Second Continental Congress, the Articles of Confederation, and their own State governments. Much that went into the Constitution came directly, sometimes word for word, from the Articles. A number of provisions were drawn from the several State constitutions, as well.

## The Convention Completes Its Work

For several weeks, through the hot Philadelphia summer, the delegates took up resolution after resolution. Finally, on September 8, a committee was named "to revise the stile of and arrange the articles which had been agreed to" by the convention. That group, the Committee of Stile headed by Gouverneur Morris, put the Constitution in its final form.

Then, on September 17, the convention approved its work and 39 names were placed on the finished document.[20]

Perhaps none of the Framers were completely satisfied with their work. Nevertheless, wise old Benjamin Franklin put into words what many of the Framers must have thought on that final day:

“Sir, I agree with this Constitution with all its faults, if they are such; because I think a general Government necessary for us . . . I doubt . . . whether any Convention we can obtain, may be able to make a better Constitution. For when you assemble a number of men to have the advantage of their joint wisdom, you inevitably assemble with those men, all their prejudices, their passions, their errors of opinion, their local interests, and their selfish views. From such an assembly can a perfect production be expected? It therefore astonishes me, Sir, to find this system approaching so near to perfection as it does . . . ”

On Franklin's motion, the Constitution was signed. Madison tells us that

“ . . . Doctor Franklin, looking toward the President's chair, at the back of which a rising sun happened to be painted, observed to a few members near him, that Painters had found it difficult to distinguish in their art a rising from a setting sun. I have, said he, often and often in the course of the Session . . . looked at that behind the President without being able to tell whether it was rising or setting. But now at length I have the happiness to know that it is a rising and not a setting sun.”

---

[20]Three of the 41 delegates present on that last day refused to sign the proposed Constitution: Edmund Randolph of Virginia, who later did support ratification; Elbridge Gerry of Massachusetts, who later became Vice President under Madison; and George Mason of Virginia, who continued to oppose the Constitution until his death in 1792. George Read of Delaware signed both for himself and for his absent colleague John Dickinson.

▲ **Philadelphia Convention** An artist portrays the gathering that produced our Constitution. The painting highlights Washington's presence, which, though he rarely took part in the debates, was a strong influence on the proceedings.

## Section 4 Review

1. **Define:** Framers, Virginia Plan, New Jersey Plan, Connecticut Compromise, Three-Fifths Compromise, Commerce and Slave Trade Compromise
2. When and where was the Constitution written?
3. (a) Who is known as the "Father of the Constitution"? (b) Why does he have this title?
4. What momentous decision did the Framers make at the beginning of the Convention?
5. In what sense was the Constitution a "bundle of compromises"?
6. From what sources did the Framers draw in writing the Constitution?

### Critical Thinking

7. **Identifying Assumptions** (p. 19) Populations of African Americans serving as slaves were counted at three-fifths of their total to determine congressional representation. What does this fact suggest about the Framers' views on slavery?

★

# 5 Ratifying the Constitution

**Find Out:**
- What were the Anti-Federalists' objections to the ratification of the Constitution?
- How was the Constitution ratified?

**Key Terms:**
Federalists, Anti-Federalists

Today, the Constitution of the United States is the object of extraordinary respect and admiration, both here and abroad. But in 1787 and 1788, it was widely criticized, and in every State there were many who opposed its adoption.

As you will see in this section, the battle over the ratification of the Constitution was not easily decided.

## Ratification

Remember, the Articles of Confederation provided that changes could be made in them only if all of the State legislatures agreed. But the new Constitution was intended to replace, not amend, the Articles. The Framers had seen how crippling the unanimity requirement could be. So, the new Constitution (in Article VII) provided that

❝ The ratification of the conventions of nine States shall be sufficient for the establishment of this Constitution between the States so ratifying the same. ❞

The Congress of the Confederation agreed to this irregular procedure. After a short debate, it sent the new document to the States on September 28, 1787.

**Federalists and Anti-Federalists**   The proposed Constitution was printed, circulated, and debated vigorously. Two groups quickly emerged in each of the States: the **Federalists**, who favored ratification, and the **Anti-Federalists**, who opposed it.

The Federalists were led by many of those who had attended the Philadelphia Convention. Among them, the most active and the most effective were James Madison and Alexander Hamilton. Their opposition was headed by such well-known Revolutionary War figures as Patrick Henry, Richard Henry Lee, John Hancock, and Samuel Adams.

The Federalists stressed the weaknesses of the Articles. They argued that the many difficulties facing the Republic could be overcome only by a new government based on the proposed Constitution.

The Anti-Federalists attacked nearly every part of the new document. Many objected to the ratification process, to the absence of any mention of God, to the denial to the States of a power to print money, and to other features of the Framers' proposals.

Two of the major features of the proposed Constitution drew the heaviest fire, however: (1) the greatly increased powers of the central government and (2) the lack of a bill of rights. The proposed document did not provide for such basic liberties as freedom of speech, press, and religion, nor for the rights of fair trial. Patrick Henry said of the proposed Constitution:

❝ I look upon that paper as the most fatal plan that could possibly be conceived to enslave a free people. ❞

 **Global Awareness**

**A Half Century of Revolution: At Home and Abroad**

| United States | | World |
|---|---|---|
| **1770** Boston Massacre | **1770** | **1770** James Cook lands in Australia |
| **1775** Revolutionary War begins | | **1776** Britisher Adam Smith publishes *Wealth of Nations* |
| **1776** Declaration of Independence | **1780** | |
| **1781** British surrender at Yorktown | | **1784** Russia takes the Crimea from Turkey |
| | | **1788** Freed Africans settle in Freetown, Sierra Leone |
| **1788** Constitution ratified | **1790** | **1791** Haitians revolt against French rule |
| **1789** George Washington elected first President | | |
| **1793** Eli Whitney invents the cotton gin; Escaped slaves legally forced to return | **1800** | **1798–1818** Indian states rebel against British rule |
| | | **1802** Nguyen Anh unites a country and calls it Vietnam |
| **1808** Transportation of Africans to America for slavery prohibited | **1810** | |
| **1812** The United States goes to war against Britain | | **1816–1822** Argentina, Venezuela, and Brazil achieve independence |
| | **1820** | **1821** Mexico gains independence from Spain |
| **1823** Monroe Doctrine ends foreign encroachment of American continent | | |
| **1825** Removal of Native Americans to western territories | **1830** | |

▲ **Interpreting Charts**   Do you think this global turmoil was coincidence, or were the events in various countries connected?

**Success**   The contest for ratification was close in several States, but the Federalists finally won in all of them.

The table below shows that Delaware was the first State to ratify. On June 21, 1788, New Hampshire brought the number of ratifying States to nine. Under Article VII, New Hampshire's ratification should have brought the Constitution into effect, but it did not. Neither Virginia nor New York had yet ratified, and without either of these key states the new government could not hope to succeed.

VIRGINIA   Virginia's ratification followed New Hampshire's by just four days. The brilliant debates in its convention were followed closely throughout the State. The Federalists were led by Madison, the young John Marshall, and Governor Edmund Randolph (even though he had refused to sign the Constitution). Patrick Henry, leading the opposition, was joined by such outstanding Virginians as James Monroe, Richard Henry Lee, and George Mason.

Although George Washington was not a delegate, his strong support for ratification proved vital. With Madison, he was able to get a reluctant

### Steps to a More Perfect Union

| | |
|---|---|
| 1765 | Stamp Act Congress |
| 1770s | Committees of Correspondence |
| 1774 | First Continental Congress |
| 1775–81 | Second Continental Congress |
| 1776 | Declaration of Independence |
| 1781 | Articles of Confederation Adopted |
| 1783 | Treaty of Paris |
| 1785 | Mount Vernon Convention |
| 1786 | Annapolis Convention |
| 1787 | Constitutional Convention |
| 1788 | Ninth State (New Hampshire) ratifies Constitution |
| 1789 | Constitution becomes effective |
| 1790 | Thirteenth State (Rhode Island) ratifies Constitution |

1775–1783 War for Independence

▲ **Interpreting Graphs**   The steps to ratification are illustrated above. If the ninth State ratified the Constitution in 1788, why did it not go into effect until 1789?

### Ratification of the Constitution

| State | Date | Vote |
|---|---|---|
| Delaware | Dec. 7, 1787 | 30-0 |
| Pennsylvania | Dec. 12, 1787 | 46-23 |
| New Jersey | Dec. 19, 1787 | 38-0 |
| Georgia | Jan. 2, 1788 | 26-0 |
| Connecticut | Jan. 9, 1788 | 128-40 |
| Massachusetts | Feb. 6, 1788 | 187-168 |
| Maryland | Apr. 28, 1788 | 63-11 |
| South Carolina | May 23, 1788 | 149-73 |
| New Hampshire | June 21, 1788 | 57-46 |
| Virginia | June 25, 1788 | 89-79 |
| New York | July 26, 1788 | 30-27 |
| North Carolina | Nov. 21, 1789* | 184-77 |
| Rhode Island | May 29, 1790 | 34-32 |

*Second vote; ratification was originally defeated on August 4, 1788, by a vote of 184-84.

▲ **Interpreting Tables**   Virginia's ratification came only after a long struggle. In what other States was ratification won by only a narrow margin?

Jefferson to support the document. Had Jefferson fought as did other Anti-Federalists, Virginia might never have ratified the Constitution.

NEW YORK   A narrow vote in the New York convention brought the number of States to 11. New York ratified only after a long battle. The Anti-Federalists were led by Governor George Clinton and by two of the State's three delegates to the Philadelphia Convention.[21]

---

[21]Robert Yates and John Lansing had quit Philadelphia in July, arguing that the convention had gone beyond its authority. Like many other Anti-Federalist leaders, Governor Clinton later supported the Constitution.

▲ **Defending the Constitution**    Each of the 85 essays in *The Federalist* were signed with the pen name *Publius*. Fifty-one are attributed to Alexander Hamilton (right), eight to John Jay (left) and the rest to James Madison.

The contest in New York gave rise to a remarkable campaign document: *The Federalist.* It was a collection of 85 essays written in support of the Constitution by Alexander Hamilton, James Madison, and John Jay. Those essays were first published as letters to the people in various newspapers of the State and soon were collected in book form. Though written in haste, they remain an excellent commentary on the Constitution, and are among the best political writings in the English language.

## Inauguration of the New Government

On September 13, 1788, with 11 of the 13 States "under the federal roof," the Congress of the Confederation paved the way for its successor. It chose New York as the temporary capital.[22] It set the first Wednesday in January as the date on which the States would choose presidential electors. The first Wednesday in February was set as the date on which those electors would vote, and the first Wednesday in March as the date for the inauguration of the new government.

--------

[22]The District of Columbia did not become the nation's capital until 1800. Congress moved its sessions to Philadelphia in December, 1790. It held its first meeting in the new "federal city," Washington, D.C., on November 17, 1800.

The new Congress convened on March 4, 1789. It met in Federal Hall, on Wall Street in New York City. Because it lacked a quorum, however, it could not count the electoral votes until April 6. Finally, on that day, it found that George Washington had been elected President by a unanimous vote, and John Adams Vice President, with a substantial majority. On April 30, after an historic trip from Mount Vernon to New York, Washington took the oath of office as the first President of the United States.

## Section 5 Review

**1. Define:** Federalist, Anti-Federalist
**2.** (a) How was the Constitution ratified? (b) What was "irregular" about that process?
**3.** The Anti-Federalists centered their opposition to the Constitution on what two main points?

### Critical Thinking

**4. Expressing Problems Clearly** (p. 19) (a) Why might the failure of New York and Virginia to ratify have doomed the Constitution? (b) What did the nation stand to lose by losing those key States?

★

## *Drawing Conclusions*

A conclusion is a judgment based on reason. Drawing a conclusion, therefore, means finding an answer or forming an opinion based on available information. Being able to draw conclusions is an important skill that all citizens need in order to evaluate information and solve problems.

The table below outlines the two major plans put forward at the Constitutional Convention for the legislative branch, as well as the provisions that the Framers finally agreed upon at the Convention. Follow the steps and the information on the table to practice drawing conclusions.

**1. Read and summarize the information on the table.** Before you can draw a conclusion, you must have a firm grasp of the information you are considering. Read down each column of the table and answer the following questions (a) What were the basic features of the Virginia Plan? (b) What were the basic features of the New Jersey

Plan? (c) What was the plan finally adopted by the Convention?

**2. Compare the information in each of the rows of the table.** Read across the rows of the table and ask: (a) In what ways do the three plans differ? (b) In what ways are they similar?

**3. Draw conclusions based on the information in the table.** Comparing the information on the table should raise some questions in your mind. As you answer these questions based on the information in the table, you are drawing conclusions. Answer the following questions: (a) Did both the Virginia and New Jersey plans contribute to the features actually adopted in the Constitution? (b) Which plan, if any, contributed more to the Constitution? (c) What would you expect the proponents of the Virginia Plan to have liked about the Constitution? (d) What about the proponents of the New Jersey Plan?

| | Virginia Plan | New Jersey Plan | Constitution's Provisions |
|---|---|---|---|
| **Number of houses in legislature** | 2 | 1 | 2 |
| **Basis for determining representation in legislature** | each State's population OR amount of each State's financial support for the central government | equal representation for each State | equal representation for each State in upper house; representation by each State's population in lower house |
| **Basis for choosing representatives for legislature** | representatives in lower house chosen by popular vote; representatives in upper house nominated by State legislators and chosen by lower house | elected by State legislatures | representatives in lower house chosen by popular vote in each State; representatives in upper house chosen by State legislatures* |

*17th Amendment provided for popular election of senators.

# Chapter-in-Brief

Scan all headings, photographs, charts, and other visuals in the chapter before reading the section summaries below.

**Section 1 Our Political Beginnings (pp. 25–30)** Europeans began coming to North America in the mid-1500s. While many nations sought to colonize America, the English emerged as the dominant force.

American colonists benefitted from a developing English tradition of ordered, limited, and representative government. This heritage served as the basis of the colonial governments. In turn, these governments helped provide training for the colonists in the art of government.

**Section 2 The Coming of Independence (pp. 30–35)** After 150 years of colonial rule in America, Great Britain began taking a more active role in the colonies in the 1760s. For example, the British increased taxes in the colonies. The colonists resented this "taxation without representation." Twelve of the 13 colonies joined in the First Continental Congress to plan opposition to British policies.

A follow-up to the First Continental Congress met in May of 1775. By that time, the Revolution had begun. The Second Continental Congress became the government of the new United States, and it produced the Declaration of Independence.

The newly formed States now began to write their own constitutions. Portions of these documents would later influence the Constitution of the United States.

**Section 3 The Critical Period (pp. 36–38)** In order to provide a more lasting plan of government, the Second Continental Congress created the Articles of Confederation. The Articles established "a firm league of friendship" among the States. This friendship was not very strong, and bickering among the States soon threatened the new nation. People began to explore new ways to meet the needs of the nation. Ultimately, this movement led to a convention in May 1787, in Philadelphia. This meeting became the Constitutional Convention.

**Section 4 Creating the Constitution (pp. 40–46)** The Philadelphia meeting involved delegates from every State but Rhode Island. The delegates quickly agreed that the nation needed a new government. However, there were many disagreements, as each State sought to protect its own interests.

Among the compromises that made the Constitution possible was the Connecticut Compromise. It led to the creation of the current configuration of Congress. Compromise also helped settle troublesome questions about slavery, the selection of the President, and other issues.

**Section 5 Ratifying the Constitution (pp. 46–49)** The convention created the Constitution; now it was up to the States to accept or reject it. The Constitution was promoted by the Federalists. The Anti-Federalists attacked the document out of fear of the plan's strong central government and because it lacked a bill of rights. One key feature of the debate was the publication of the pro-Constitution *The Federalist*.

The Constitution finally gained the needed support of the States. The new Congress convened in what was then the capital, New York, in March 1789. On April 30, George Washington became the nation's first President.

# Chapter Review

## Vocabulary and Key Terms

limited government (p. 26)
representative government (p. 27)
Magna Carta (p. 27)
Petition of Right (p. 27)
English Bill of Rights (p. 27)
charter (p. 28)
bicameral (p. 28)
unicameral (p. 29)

Albany Plan of Union (p. 32)
boycott (p. 32)
constitution (p. 35)
popular sovereignty (p. 35)
ratification (p. 36)
Articles of Confederation (p. 36)
Framers (p. 40)
Virginia Plan (p. 42)

New Jersey Plan (p. 43)
Connecticut Compromise (p. 43)
Three-Fifths Compromise (p. 44)
Commerce and Slave Trade Compromise (p. 44)
Federalists (p. 47)
Anti-Federalists (p. 47)

**Matching:** *Review the key terms in the list above. If you are not sure of a term's meaning, look up the term and review its definition. Choose a term from the list above that best matches each description.*

1. the written grants that authorized the formation of the colonies
2. the body of fundamental laws that sets out the principles, structures, and processes of government
3. legislative body that has two houses
4. attempted to establish a "firm league of friendship" among the original States
5. enabled the Framers to resolve the dispute over whether or not slaves would be counted among each State's population
6. an agreement that forbade Congress to act against the slave trade for 20 years

**True or False:** *Determine whether each statement is true or false. If it is true, write "true." If it is false, change the underlined word or words to make the statement true.*

1. Pennsylvania's colonial legislature had only one chamber, and so was <u>unicameral</u>.
2. The <u>Virginia Plan</u> outlined the structure of

Congress that was ultimately accepted by the Framers.
3. The <u>Petition of Right</u> represented the earliest expression of the rights of the people of England against abuse from the Crown.
4. The <u>Federalists</u> supported the ratification of the Constitution.
5. The policies of the British in the 1760s led to a <u>ratification</u> of English goods in the colonies.

**Word Relationships:** *Three of the terms in each of the following sets of terms are related. Choose the term that does not belong and explain why it does not belong.*

1. (a) Magna Carta  (b) Albany Plan of Union  (c) English Bill of Rights  (d) Petition of Right
2. (a) Articles of Confederation  (b) Virginia Plan  (c) New Jersey Plan  (d) Connecticut Compromise
3. (a) limited government  (b) popular sovereignty  (c) ratification  (d) representative government
4. (a) Framers  (b) Federalists  (c) Anti-Federalists  (d) boycott

## Main Ideas

### Section 1 (pp. 25–30)

1. What three ideas about government did the colonists take with them from England?
2. What concepts did the colonists derive from the Magna Carta, the Petition of Right, and the English Bill of Rights?
3. (a) How did the colonial governments develop? (b) What shape did they take?

### Section 2 (pp. 30–35)

4. (a) Describe how the British governed the colonies before the 1760s. (b) After the 1760s?
5. What was the colonists' response to the change in British policies in the 1760s?
6. What were the common features of the first State constitutions?

### Section 3 (pp. 36–38)

7. (a) What was the goal of the Articles of Confederation? (b) How well did it succeed?
8. What were the major characteristics of the Articles?
9. How did the nation respond to the shortcomings of the Articles?

### Section 4 (pp. 40–46)

10. (a) Who were the Framers of the Constitution? (b) In what sense did they represent a new generation in American politics?
11. What was the role of compromise in the framing of the Constitution?
12. What were the major areas of agreement at the Constitutional Convention?

### Section 5 (pp. 46–49)

13. (a) Who were the Federalists? (b) What was their argument in favor of the Constitution?
14. What were the main arguments used by the Anti-Federalists?
15. What were their main battlegrounds in the debate over ratification?

## Critical Thinking

1. **Distinguishing False from Accurate Images** (p. 19) What does the fact that the nation needed a stronger central government during the Critical Period suggest about the sense of unity among the States?
2. **Drawing Conclusions** (p. 19) Patrick Henry, a leading patriot during the Revolution, refused to attend the Constitutional Convention, saying ". . . I smell a rat in Philadelphia tending toward monarchy." Why might Henry have felt this way?
3. **Checking Consistency** (p. 19) How does the history of America between the 1600s and 1789 demonstrate that "questions of politics and economics are, in fact, inseparable"?

## Getting Involved

1. **Writing Your Opinion** It is 1789. Write a letter to one of the Framers in which you express your opinion on the Constitution. First, create a list of what you see as the positive aspects of the document. Then, list the negative features. Note any suggestions you have for improvements. Next, write a draft of the letter in which you politely offer your ideas. Revise your letter, making certain that each idea is clearly explained. Proofread your letter and draft a final copy.

2. **Class Debate** Conduct a class debate on the following: *Resolved,* that whenever any form of government becomes destructive of the people's life, liberty, and pursuit of happiness, the people have a right and a duty to abolish it. Select one team to debate in favor of this statement and one team to debate against it. The rest of the class can evaluate each side's presentation.

3. **Creating a Political Cartoon** Draw a political cartoon that illustrates the concept of a constitution. Be sure to consider the ideals and beliefs that helped inspire the Framers. In other words, consider what the Framers hoped to accomplish and the means by which they achieved their goal.

**CHAPTER**

# The Constitution

## Chapter Preview

Why can the NFL legally prohibit the broadcast of some professional football games? Can TV cameras be excluded from courtrooms? Can a State set stricter auto emission standards than those imposed by federal law? Believe it nor not, the answers to these 20th-century questions can be found in the Constitution.

You are probably asking yourself, "What did the Framers of the Constitution know about football, or television, or automobiles?" In fact, nothing. Still, the answers to those questions can be found by examining the Constitution that they drafted in 1787. In this chapter you will examine the nature of the Constitution of the United States, and you will also consider the vital processes by which that extraordinary document has changed and developed over more than 200 years.

### Before you read this chapter:

- **Describe** your reaction to this statement: "In the United States, any citizen can do whatever he or she wants to do."

- **Predict** what might occur if the Constitution no longer met the needs of the people of the United States.

### As you read, focus on the main objective for each section. Understand:

1. The meaning of the basic principles of the American constitutional system in both their historical and current settings.

2. The processes of constitutional change and development by formal amendment.

3. The processes of constitutional change and development by informal amendment.

▲ **"The wise CONSTITUTION** let's truly revere,/It points out the course of our Empire to steer" went the words of a 1787 song about the new Constitution, written in Philadelphia's Independence Hall, shown above.

# 1 The Six Basic Principles

### Find Out:
- What are the six basic principles on which the Constitution of the United States is built?
- How does the American system of separation of powers and checks and balances operate?
- How did the principle of federalism come to be embodied in the Constitution?

### Key Terms:
popular sovereignty, limited government, constitutionalism, rule of law, separation of powers, checks and balances, judicial review, unconstitutional, federalism

Perhaps you have heard the phrase "less is more." Although the Framers of the Constitution probably did not have this exact phrase in mind, the amazing document they created reflects its meaning.

The Constitution of the United States is this nation's fundamental law—in its own terms it is "the supreme law of the land." As such, you might expect the document to fill volumes. The Framers, however, wrote a document of only about 7,000 words that you can read in about half an hour. You will find the text of the Constitution beginning on page 724. As you read it, think about the surprising fact that this brief document has successfully guided this nation through two centuries of tremendous growth and change.

One of the Constitution's strengths is that it does not go into great detail about how the government should be run. Instead, the Constitution is built on six basic principles which are explored in detail in this section. These basic principles are: popular sovereignty, limited government, separation of powers, checks and balances, judicial review, and federalism.

## Popular Sovereignty

In the United States, all political power belongs to the people. The people are sovereign. **Popular sovereignty** means that people are the only source of governmental power. Government can govern only with the consent of the governed.

This principle of popular sovereignty, so boldly stated in the Declaration of Independence, is woven throughout the Constitution. In the Preamble, its opening words, the Constitution declares: "We the People of the United States...do ordain and establish this Constitution for the United States of America."

By creating the Constitution, the sovereign people created the Government of the United States and gave to it certain powers. Through the Constitution and its own fundamental law, each State government received its powers from the people.

## Limited Government

The principle of **limited government** holds that government is *not* all-powerful, that it may do *only* those things that the people have given it the power to do.

In effect, the principle of limited government is the other side of the coin of popular sovereignty. It is that principle stated the other way around: The people are the only source of any and all of government's authority; and government has only that authority the people have given to it.

The concept of limited government can be expressed another way: Government must obey the law. Stated this way, the principle is often called **constitutionalism**—that is, that government must be conducted according to constitutional principles. The concept of limited government is also described as the **rule of law**—that is, government and its officers are always subject to—never above—the law.

In large part, the Constitution is a statement of limited government. Much of it reads as explicit prohibitions of power to government.[1] For example, notice the Constitution's guarantees of freedom of expression. Those great guarantees—of freedom of religion, of speech, of press, of assembly, and of petition—are vital to democratic government. They are set out in the 1st Amendment, which begins with the words: "Congress shall make no law...."

---

[1]See, especially, Article I, Sections 9 and 10; the 1st through the 10th Amendments; and the 13th, 14th, 15th, 19th, 24th, and 26th Amendments.

## Separation of Powers

Recall the brief discussion of the parliamentary and the presidential forms of government in Section 2 of Chapter 1. In a parliamentary system the basic powers of a government—its legislative, executive, and judicial powers—are all gathered in the hands of a single agency. British government is a leading example. In a presidential system, these basic powers are distributed—separated—among three distinct and independent branches of the government as in the United States.

The Constitution distributes the powers of the National Government among the Congress (the legislative branch), the President (the executive branch), and the courts (the judicial branch). This **separation of powers** is clearly set forth in specific places in the Constitution.

Article I, Section 1 declares:

❝All legislative powers herein granted shall be vested in a Congress of the United States...❞

Thus, Congress is the lawmaking branch of the National Government.

Article II, Section 1 declares:

❝The Executive power shall be vested in a President of the United States...❞

Thus, the President is given the law-executing, law-enforcing, law-administering powers of the National Government.

Article III, Section 1 declares:

❝The judicial power of the United States shall be vested in one Supreme Court, and in such inferior courts as the Congress may from time to time ordain and establish.❞

Thus, the federal courts, and most importantly the Supreme Court, interpret and apply the laws of the United States in cases brought before them.

Remember, the Framers of the Constitution intended to create a stronger government for the United States. But they also intended to limit the powers of that government. The doctrine of separation of powers was designed to achieve that end result.

Defending this arrangement, James Madison wrote in *The Federalist* No. 47:

❝The accumulation of all powers, legislative, executive, and judiciary, in the same hands, whether one, a few, or many…may justly be pronounced the very definition of tyranny.❞

## Checks and Balances

The National Government is organized around three separate branches. As you have read, the Constitution gives to each branch its own field of governmental authority: legislative, executive, and judicial.

These three branches are not entirely separated nor completely independent of one another, however. Rather, they are tied together by a complex system of **checks and balances**. This means that each branch is subject to a number of constitutional checks (restraints) by the other branches. In other words, each branch has certain powers with which it can check the operations and balance the power of the other two.

The chart on the next page describes the major features of the check-and-balance arrangement. As you can see, the Congress has the power to make law, but the President may veto, or reject, any act of Congress. In its turn, Congress can override a veto by a two-thirds vote in each house. Congress can refuse to provide funds requested by the President, or the Senate may refuse to approve a treaty or an appointment made by the President.

The chart also shows how the system of checks and balances links the judicial branch to Congress and the executive branch. The President has the power to name all federal judges. Each appointment, however, must be approved by a majority vote in the Senate. At the same time, the courts have the power to determine the constitutionality of acts of Congress and of presidential actions, and to strike down those they find unconstitutional.

Head-on clashes between the branches do not often happen. The check-and-balance system operates all the time, however. And the very fact that it does exist—that each branch has its several checks—affects much of what happens in Washington.

For example, when the President picks someone to serve in some important office in the executive branch—as, say, Secretary of State or Director of the Federal Bureau of Investigation (FBI) or the Central Intelligence Agency (CIA)—the President is quite aware that the Senate must confirm that appointment. So, quite purposely, the President picks someone who will very likely be approved by the Senate. In a similar sense, when Congress makes law, it does so with a careful eye on both the President's veto power and the power of the courts to review its actions.

Spectacular clashes—direct applications of the check-and-balance system—do sometimes occur, of course. The President does veto some acts of Congress. On rare occasion, Congress does override one of those vetoes. Even more rarely, the Senate does reject one of the President's appointees.

But, again, these and other direct confrontations are not common. Congress, the President, and even the courts try to avoid them. The check-and-balance system makes compromise necessary—and compromise is a vital part of democratic government.

Over time, the check-and-balance system has worked quite well. It has done what the Framers intended it to do. It has prevented "an

▲ **"Keeping each other in their proper places"**
In his essay, *The Federalist* No. 51, James Madison used these words to describe the principle of checks and balances, or keeping the branches of government "in their proper places."

## The American System of Checks and Balances

Congress creates lower courts, may remove judges through impeachment; Senate approves or rejects appointment of judges.

Courts may declare acts of Congress to be unconstitutional.

**JUDICIAL BRANCH
THE SUPREME COURT
and other Federal Courts**
"Interprets the law"

Judges, appointed for life, are free from executive control; courts may declare executive actions to be unconstitutional.

**LEGISLATIVE BRANCH
THE CONGRESS**
"Makes the law"

Congress makes laws, creates agencies and programs, appropriates funds to carry out laws and programs, may override veto with two-thirds vote, may remove President through impeachment; Senate approves treaties and presidential appointments.

President may veto legislation, call special sessions, recommend legislation, appeal to the people.

**EXECUTIVE BRANCH
THE PRESIDENT**
"Carries out the law"

President appoints Supreme Court justices and other federal judges.

▲ **Interpreting Charts**　Under the system of checks and balances, each branch of government can check the actions of the others. In what way can the power of the judiciary be checked by the other branches?

unjust combination of the majority." At the same time, it has not very often stalled a close working relationship between the executive and legislative branches.

But that sort of working relationship has been especially evident when the President and a majority in both houses of Congress have been of the same political party. When the other party controls one or both houses, conflicts play a larger than usual part in that relationship.

## Judicial Review

As part of the system of checks and balances, courts have the power of **judicial review**—the power to decide whether what government does is in accord with what the Constitution provides.

More precisely, judicial review may be defined this way: It is the power of a court to determine the constitutionality of a governmental action. In part, then, judicial review is the power to declare **unconstitutional**—to declare illegal, null and void, of no force and effect—a governmental action found to violate some provision in the Constitution. The power of judicial review is held by all federal courts and by most state courts, as well.[2]

The Constitution does not provide for judicial review in so many words. Yet the Framers clearly meant that the federal courts, especially the Supreme Court, should have that power.

In practice, the Supreme Court established the power of judicial review in the landmark case of *Marbury* v. *Madison* in 1803. (See Chapter 18 for a close look at that case.) Since then, the Supreme Court and other federal and State courts have used the power in thousands of cases. Mostly, the courts have upheld challenged governmental actions. That is, in most cases in which the power of judicial review is exercised, the actions of government are found to be constitutional.

That is not always the case, however. To date, the Supreme Court has decided more than 130 cases in which it has found an act or some part of an act of Congress to be unconstitutional. It has struck down several presidential and other executive branch actions as well. The Court has also voided hundreds of actions of the States and their local governments, including more than 1,000 State laws.

## Federalism

As you have read, the American governmental system is federal in form. The powers held by government are distributed on a territorial basis. The National Government holds some of those powers, and others belong to the 50 States.

The principle of **federalism**—the division of power among a central government and several regional governments—came to the Constitution out of both experience and necessity. In Philadelphia, the Framers faced a number of difficult problems, including a major one: How to build a new, stronger, more effective National Government while preserving the existing States and the concept of local self-government.

The colonists had rebelled against the harsh rule of a powerful and distant central government. They had fought for the right to manage their local affairs without the meddling and dictation of the king and his ministers in far-off London. Surely, they would not now agree to another such government.

The Framers found their solution in federalism. In short, they constructed the federal arrangement, with its division of powers, as a compromise. It was an alternative to the system of nearly independent States, loosely tied to one another in the weak Articles of Confederation, and a much feared, too powerful central government. The next chapter explores the federal system at length.

## Section 1 Review

1. **Define:** popular sovereignty, limited government, rule of law, separation of powers, checks and balances, judicial review, unconstitutional, federalism

2. What two factors led the Framers to create a federal system of government?

3. Upon what six basic principles is the Constitution built?

4. What is the principle of constitutionalism?

5. How does the legislative branch check and balance the executive?

6. How does the judicial branch check and balance the Congress?

### Critical Thinking

7. **Drawing Conclusions** (p. 19) The Constitution reflects the Framers' beliefs about people and their need for government. Based on the six basic principles of the Constitution, what can you conclude about the Framers' view of human nature?

---

[2]Generally, the power is held by all courts of record. These are courts that keep a record of their proceedings and have the power to punish for contempt of court. Usually, only the lowest state courts—justice of the peace courts, for example—are not courts of record.

★

# 2 Formally Amending the Constitution

## Find Out:

- How has the Constitution been able to endure more than 200 years of extraordinary change and growth in this country?
- What is the Bill of Rights and why was it added to the Constitution?
- What are the processes by which formal changes can be made in the Constitution?

## Key Terms:

amendment, formal amendment, Bill of Rights

Think about living in a country where there are few good roads, no cars, telephones or televisions, and few cities. There are no factories, few stores, and almost everyone lives and works on a farm. Chances are, living in such a place would represent a big change from the life you live today.

The country described above is the United States—as it was in 1787 when the Constitution was written. Obviously, the needs and concerns of the people at that time were quite different from ours today. Yet the Constitution that those first Americans wrote continues to guide the actions of our government in the 1990s. In fact, it has been in force for more than 200 years—longer than the written constitution of any other nation of the world.[3] It has survived and thrived as the nation changed from a scattered collection of about 4 million people into the far-flung home of over 250 million. The same Constitution has guided the United States through its transformation from a struggling nation on the fringe of survival into the most powerful country on earth.

How has the Constitution endured and kept up with that astounding change? The answer lies in this highly important fact: The Constitution of today *is*, and at the same time *is not*, the document of 1787. Many of its words are the same, and much of their meaning remains the same. But some of its words have been changed, some have been eliminated, and some have been added. And the meanings of many of its provisions have been modified as well.

This process of constitutional change has come about in two basic ways: (1) by formal amendment and (2) by informal amendment. In this section, you will read about the formal process of amending the Constitution.

## Formal Amendment Process

The Framers knew that even the wisest of constitution-makers cannot build for all time. Thus, the Constitution provides for its own **amendment**—that is, for changes in its written words.

Article V sets out two methods for the proposal and two methods for the ratification of constitutional amendments. So, there are four methods of **formal amendment**—changes or additions that become part of the written language of the Constitution itself. The diagram on the next page sets out these four methods.

**First Method**   An amendment may be proposed by a two-thirds vote in each house of Congress and be ratified by three-fourths of the State legislatures. Today, 38 State legislatures must approve an amendment in order to make it a part of the Constitution. Twenty-six of the Constitution's now 27 amendments were adopted in this manner.

**Second Method**   An amendment may be proposed by Congress and then ratified by conventions, called for that purpose, in three-fourths of the States. Only the 21st Amendment, added in 1933, was adopted in this way.[4]

---

[3]The British constitution dates from well before the Norman Conquest of 1066, but it is not a single, written document. Rather, it is an "unwritten constitution," a collection of principles, customs, traditions, and significant parliamentary acts that guide British government and practice. Israel, which has existed only since 1948, is the only other state in the world without a written constitution.

[4]The 21st Amendment repealed the 18th, which had established national prohibition. Conventions were used to ratify the amendment largely because Congress felt that the conventions' popularly elected delegates would be more likely to reflect public opinion on the question of repeal than would State legislators.

## The Formal Amendment Process (Four Methods)

| **1** Proposed by CONGRESS by a 2/3 vote in both houses | **2** Proposed by CONGRESS by a 2/3 vote in both houses | **3** Proposed at a NATIONAL CONVENTION called by Congress when requested by 2/3 (34) of the State legislatures | **4** Proposed at a NATIONAL CONVENTION called by Congress when requested by 2/3 (34) of the State legislatures |
|---|---|---|---|
| Ratified by the State LEGISLATURE in 3/4 (38) of the States | Ratified by CONVENTIONS held in 3/4 (38) of the States | Ratified by the State LEGISLATURE in 3/4 (38) of the States | Ratified by CONVENTIONS held in 3/4 (38) of the States |

▲ **Interpreting Charts**   The four different ways in which amendments may be added to the Constitution are shown here. How does the formal amendment process illustrate federalism?

**Third Method**   An amendment may be proposed by a national convention, called by Congress at the request of two-thirds of the State legislatures—today, 34. And, as you can see in the diagram, it must then be ratified by three-fourths of the State legislatures. To date, Congress has not called such a convention.[5]

**Fourth Method**   An amendment may be proposed by a national convention and ratified by conventions in three-fourths of the States. Remember that the Constitution itself was adopted in much this same way.

The Constitution places only one restriction on the subjects with which a proposed amendment may deal. Article V declares that "no State, without its consent, shall be deprived of its equal suffrage in the Senate."

Note that the formal amendment process emphasizes the federal character of the governmental system. Proposal takes place at the national level and ratification is a State-by-State matter. Also note that when the Constitution is amended, that action represents the expression

of the people's sovereign will—the people have spoken.

When both houses of Congress pass a resolution proposing an amendment, Congress does not send it to the President to be signed or vetoed, though the Constitution would seem to require it.[6] When Congress proposes an amendment, it is not making law (not legislating).

Some criticize the practice of sending proposed amendments to the State legislatures rather than to ratifying conventions, especially because it permits a constitutional change without a clear-cut expression by the people. The critics point out that State legislators, who do the ratifying, are elected to office for a mix of reasons—party membership; name familiarity; incumbency; their stands on such matters as taxes, schools, welfare programs; and a host of other things. They are almost never chosen because of their stand on a proposed amendment to the Federal Constitution. On the other hand, critics claim, the delegates to a ratifying convention would be chosen by the people on the basis of one particular factor: a yes-or-no stand on the proposed amendment.

The Supreme Court has held that a State cannot require an amendment proposed by Congress to be approved by a vote of the people of the State

---

[5]The calling of a convention has been a near thing twice in recent years. Between 1963 and 1969, 33 State legislatures, one short of the necessary two-thirds, sought an amendment to erase the Supreme Court's "one-person, one-vote" decisions; see Chapter 24. Also, between 1975 and 1983, 32 States asked for a convention to propose an amendment that would require that the federal budget be balanced each year, except in time of war or other national emergency.

[6]See Article I, Section 7, Clause 3. This practice of not submitting proposed amendments to the President is an example of the many "informal amendments" to the Constitution, a matter we shall turn to shortly.

## *on Government*

**Susan B. Anthony,** advocate of women's rights, declares her belief in women's equality.

### On the Importance of the 19th Amendment

❝ It may be delayed longer than we think; it may be here sooner than we expect; but the day will come when man will recognize woman as his peer, not only at the fireside but in the councils of the nation. Then, and not until then, will there be the perfect comradeship, the ideal union between the sexes that shall result in the highest development of the race. What this shall be we may not attempt to define, but this we know, that only good can come to the individual or to the nation through the rendering of exact justice. ❞

before it can be ratified by the State legislature. It made that ruling in *Hawke* v. *Smith* in 1920. But a State legislature can call for an advisory vote by the people before it acts, as the Court most recently held in *Kimble* v. *Swackhamer* in 1978.

If a State rejects a proposed amendment, it is not forever bound by that action. It may later reconsider and ratify the proposal. But most constitutional scholars agree that the reverse is not true. Once a State has approved an amendment, that action is final and unchangeable.

More than 10,000 joint resolutions calling for amendments to the Constitution have been proposed in Congress since 1789. Only 33 of them have been sent on to the States. And, of those, only 27 have been finally ratified.[7]

### The 27 Amendments

Congress proposed all of the first 10 amendments in 1789. Each of them arose from the controversy surrounding the ratification of the Constitution itself. Many people, including Thomas Jefferson, had agreed to support the Constitution only on condition that a listing of the basic rights of the people be added to the document immediately. As you can see in the table on the following page, all 10 of these amendments were ratified by the States in 1791.

Collectively, the first 10 amendments are known as the **Bill of Rights**. They set out the great constitutional guarantees of freedom of expression and belief, of freedom and security of the person, and of fair and equal treatment before the law. You will read about the Bill of Rights in detail in Chapters 19 and 20. The 10th Amendment does not deal with civil rights as such. Rather, it spells out the concept of reserved powers in the federal system.

Another cluster of amendments came out of the aftermath of the Civil War. The 13th, 14th, and 15th Amendments are often called the Civil War Amendments. The 13th (1865) ended slavery and prohibits most other forms of "involuntary servitude." The 14th (1868)

---

[7]One of the unratified amendments was offered by Congress in 1789—along with 10 other proposals that became the Bill of Rights in 1791, and another that became the 27th Amendment in 1992. The unratified amendment of 1789 dealt with the distribution of seats in the House of Representatives. A second never-ratified amendment, proposed in 1810, would have voided the citizenship of anyone accepting any foreign title or other honor. Another, in 1861, would have prohibited forever any amendment relating to slavery. A fourth, in 1924, was intended to give Congress the power to regulate

child labor. A fifth one, proclaiming the equal rights of women (ERA), was proposed in 1972; it fell three States short of ratification and died in 1982. An amendment to give the District of Columbia seats in Congress was proposed in 1978; it died in 1985.

Congress can place "a reasonable time limit" on the ratification process, *Dillon* v. *Gloss*, 1921. When Congress proposed the 18th Amendment (in 1917), it set a seven-year deadline for its ratification. It has set a similar deadline for the ratification of each of the amendments (except the 19th) it has proposed since.

## Amendments to the Constitution

| Amendment | Subject | Year | Time Required for Ratification |
|---|---|---|---|
| **1st–10th** | **Bill of Rights** | **1791** | **2 years, 2 months, 20 days** |
| 11th | Immunity of States from certain suits | 1795 | 11 months, 3 days |
| 12th | Changes in Electoral College procedures | 1804 | 6 months, 3 days |
| 13th | Prohibition of slavery | 1865 | 10 months, 3 days |
| 14th | Citizenship, due process, equal protection | 1868 | 2 years, 26 days |
| 15th | No denial of vote because of race, color, previous condition of servitude | 1870 | 11 months, 8 days |
| 16th | Power of Congress to tax incomes | 1913 | 2 years, 6 months, 22 days |
| 17th | Popular election of U.S. Senators | 1913 | 10 months, 26 days |
| 18th | Prohibition of intoxicating liquors | 1919 | 1 year, 2 months, 14 days |
| 19th | Women's suffrage | 1920 | 1 year, 2 months, 14 days |
| 20th | Change of dates for start of presidential, congressional terms | 1933 | 10 months, 21 days |
| 21st | Repeal of Prohibition (18th Amendment) | 1933 | 9 months, 15 days |
| 22nd | Limit on presidential tenure | 1951 | 3 years, 11 months, 3 days |
| 23rd | District of Columbia electoral vote | 1961 | 9 months, 13 days |
| 24th | Ban of tax payment as voter qualification | 1964 | 1 year, 4 months, 9 days |
| 25th | Presidential succession, vice presidential vacancy, and presidential disability | 1967 | 1 year, 7 months, 4 days |
| 26th | Minimum voting age no higher than 18 | 1971 | 3 months, 7 days |
| 27th | Congressional pay | 1992 | 202 years, 7 months, 23 days |

**Interpreting Tables** These 27 amendments have been added to the Constitution since it became effective in 1789. Which amendment was adopted in the shortest time? Which one took the most time to ratify?

defined American citizenship and granted it to former slaves. It also contains the Due Process and Equal Protection clauses, which protect basic civil rights from infringement by the States. The 15th Amendment (1870) forbids restrictions on the right to vote based upon "race, color, or previous condition of servitude."

The table on this page indicates the basic subject matter, the year of adoption, and the time required for the ratification of each of the Constitution's 27 amendments. Among the many things you can learn from the table, note that the most recently adopted amendment, the 27th, was proposed by Congress in 1789 and then languished before the several State legislatures for more than 200 years. It finally became a part of the Constitution in 1992.

The full text of the Constitution, including all of its amendments, is set out on pages 726–742.

## Section 2 Review

1. **Define:** amendment, formal amendment, Bill of Rights
2. Why did the Framers provide for amendment of the Constitution?
3. (a) By what two methods can amendments to the Constitution be proposed? (b) Ratified?

**Critical Thinking**

4. **Demonstrating Reasoned Judgment** (p. 19) Did the Framers make it too hard to amend the Constitution?

★

## Should the Death Penalty Be Declared Unconstitutional?

### *Gregg* v. *Georgia*, 1976

The bullet-ridden bodies of two men were found in a roadside ditch near Atlanta, Georgia, in late 1973. Two days later North Carolina police arrested Troy Gregg and Floyd Allen. They were driving a stolen car, and Gregg was carrying a .25-caliber pistol, later identified as the murder weapon. Allen told Georgia police that Gregg had shot the two men, robbed them, and stolen the car. Gregg was charged with two counts each of murder and armed robbery.

In Georgia, as in most states, capital punishment cases—cases in which the death penalty can be applied—are tried in a two-stage process. In the first stage, a jury must decide a defendant's guilt or innocence. Then, at a second stage, the same jury, acting within very strict guidelines, must decide whether a person should now be put to death. The jury found Gregg guilty on all counts, and it sentenced Gregg to death.

Gregg appealed to the Georgia Supreme Court. Here, his lawyers cited the 8th and 14th amendments, which forbid "cruel and unusual punishment." They also cited *Furman* v. *Georgia*, 1972, in which the U.S. Supreme Court had held that the death penalty, as it was then being applied, was unfair and arbitrary. The State Supreme Court upheld Gregg's sentence, however, and he appealed that ruling to the U.S. Supreme Court.

*Review the following evidence and arguments presented to the United States Supreme Court:*

### Arguments for Troy Leon Gregg

**1.** The death penalty is cruel and unusual punishment, and is unconstitutional.

**2.** The death penalty discriminates against racial minorities and the poor, and so violates the 14th Amendment.

**3.** Because the jury had the discretion to choose the death penalty or life imprisonment, the capital-sentencing decision may have been made in an arbitrary manner.

### Arguments for Georgia

**1.** The Constitution's ban of cruel and unusual punishment is intended to prevent those punishments disproportionate to the crimes involved. Capital punishment for the crime of murder cannot always be viewed as disproportionate.

**2.** In *Furman*, the Supreme Court left open the possibility that States could enact death penalty laws, if those laws included objective, non-discriminatory standards to guide the sentencing decision.

**3.** The Georgia death-penalty statute was based on carefully described standards, including a two-stage trial.

### Getting Involved

**1. Identify** the constitutional grounds upon which each side based its arguments.

**2. Debate** the opposing viewpoints presented in *Gregg* v. *Georgia*.

**3. Predict** how you think the Supreme Court ruled in this case and why. Then refer to the Supreme Court Glossary on page 766 to read about the decision in this case. Discuss the impact that you think the Court's ruling has on the incidence of violent crime in the United States.

# 3 Informal Amendment

**Find Out:**

- For what reasons is the informal amendment process the real key to two centuries of constitutional change and development in this country?
- What are the several means of informal change?

**Key Terms:**

informal amendment, executive agreement

As you read through the Constitution, you will notice that it deals in large part with matters of principle and of basic organization and structure. Most of its sections are brief, even skeletal in nature. Because this is true, it becomes clear that to understand the Constitution and the process of constitutional change, you must understand a key point: There is much in the Constitution that cannot be seen with the naked eye. Much has been put there, not by formal amendment, but by **informal amendment**—the process by which many changes have been made in the Constitution that have not led to changes in the document's written words. These informal amendments are the result of the day-to-day, year-to-year experiences of government under the Constitution.

This highly important process of informal amendment has taken place—and continues to take place—in five basic ways: through (1) the passage of basic legislation by Congress; (2) actions taken by the President; (3) decisions of the Supreme Court; (4) the activities of political parties; and (5) custom. In this section, you will read about these five basic means of informal amendment, and how they have enabled the Constitution to grow and change with the country.

## Basic Legislation

Congress has been a major agent of informal amendment in two ways. First, it has passed many laws to spell out several of the Constitution's brief provisions. That is, Congress has added flesh to the bones of those sections of the Constitution the Framers left purposely skeletal for Congress to add details and meaning as circumstances have required.

Take the structure of the federal court system as an example. In Article III, Section 1, the Constitution provides for "one Supreme Court, and…such inferior courts as the Congress may from time to time ordain and establish." Beginning with the Judiciary Act of 1789, all of the federal courts, except the Supreme Court, have been set up by acts of Congress. Or, similarly, Article II creates only the offices of President and Vice President. The many departments, agencies, and offices in the huge executive branch have been created by acts of Congress.

Second, Congress has added to the Constitution by the way in which it has used many of its powers. For example, the Constitution gives to Congress the expressed power to regulate foreign and interstate commerce.[8] But what is "foreign commerce"? What is "interstate commerce"? What, exactly, does Congress have the power to regulate? The Constitution does not directly answer these questions. In passing thousands of statutes under the Commerce Clause, however, Congress has done much to define the meaning of these words. And, in doing so, it has informally amended—in fact, added a great deal to—the Constitution.

## Executive Action

The manner in which different Presidents have used their powers has also produced a number of important informal amendments. For example, the Constitution states that only Congress can declare war.[9] But the Constitution also makes the President the Commander in Chief of the nation's armed forces.[10] Acting under that authority, several Presidents have made war

---

[8] Article I, Section 8, Clause 3.
[9] Article I, Section 8, Clause 11.
[10] Article II, Section 2, Clause 1.

**Truman Takes Executive Action**   As Commander in Chief of the armed forces, President Truman sent troops to Korea without a formal declaration of war by Congress.

**National Conventions**   The nomination of presidential candidates is a key part of the presidential election process—yet the Constitution says nothing about the matter.

without the benefit of a congressional declaration of war. In fact, Presidents have used the armed forces abroad in combat without such a declaration on no fewer than 200 separate occasions in American history.

Among many other examples is the use of an **executive agreement**—a pact made by the President directly with the head of a foreign state. The principal difference between these executive agreements and treaties is that they need not be approved by the Senate. Executive agreements are as legally binding as treaties, however. Recent Presidents have often used them in the conduct of foreign affairs instead of the more cumbersome treaty-making process outlined in Article II, Section 2 of the Constitution.

## Court Decisions

The nation's courts, most tellingly the United States Supreme Court, interpret and apply the Constitution in many cases they hear. You have already read about several of these instances of constitutional interpretation—that is, informal

amendment—by the Court, such as in *Marbury v. Madison*, 1803. You will encounter many more examples in this text, for the Supreme Court is, as Woodrow Wilson once put it, "a constitutional convention in continuous session."

## Party Practices

The nation's political parties have also been a major source of informal amendment over the course of American political history.

The Constitution makes no mention of political parties. In fact, most of the Framers were opposed to their growth. In his Farewell Address in 1796, George Washington warned the people against what he called "the baneful effect of the spirit of party." Washington feared the divisive effect of party politics. Yet, even as he spoke, parties were developing in this country. They have played a major role in the shaping of government and its processes ever since. There are numerous examples of that point.

Neither the Constitution nor any law provides for the nomination of candidates for the presidency. From the 1830s on, however, the major parties have held national conventions to do just that. The parties have converted the Electoral College, the body that makes the formal selection of the nation's President, from what the Framers intended into a "rubber stamp" for the popular vote in presidential elections. (You will read more about the role of the Electoral College in Chapter 13.) Both houses of Congress are organized and conduct much of their business on the basis of party. The President makes appointments to office with an eye to party politics. In short, government in the United States is in many ways government through party.

## Custom

Unwritten customs may be as strong as written laws, and many customs have developed in our governmental system.

Again, there are many examples. By custom, not because the Constitution says so, the heads of the 14 executive departments make up the Cabinet, an advisory body to the President.

On each of the eight occasions when a President died in office, the Vice President succeeded to that office—most recently in 1963. Yet, the written words of the Constitution did

not provide for this practice until the adoption of the 25th Amendment in 1967. Until then, the Constitution said only that the powers and duties of the Presidency—but *not* the office itself—should be transferred to the Vice President.[11]

Both the strength and the importance of unwritten customs can be seen in the reaction to the rare circumstances in which one of them has not been observed. For nearly 150 years, the "no-third-term tradition" was a closely followed rule in presidential politics. The tradition began in 1796, when George Washington refused to seek another term as President. In 1940, and again in 1944, however, Franklin Roosevelt broke the no-third-term custom. He sought and won a third and then a fourth term in the White House. As a direct result, the 22nd Amendment was added to the Constitution in 1951. So, what had been an unwritten custom, an informal amendment, became a written part of the Constitution itself.

▲ **Unwritten Custom Becomes Formal Amendment** The "no-third-term tradition" was a major issue in the presidential campaign of 1940.

## Section **3** Review

**1. Define:** informal amendment, executive agreement

**2.** Describe the informal amendment process.

**3.** Why is this process of informal amendment important to understanding constitutional change?

**4.** What are the five ways (agents) by which the Constitution has been informally amended?

**Critical Thinking**

**5. Testing Conclusions** (p. 19) When Franklin Roosevelt ran for a third term, he violated the "no-third-term tradition." (a) Do you think that Roosevelt was wrong to violate this informal amendment? (b) What might happen if other informal amendments were also ignored by people in government?

---

[11]Read, carefully, Article II, Section 1, Clause 5, and then Section 1 of the 25th Amendment.

# How to Use Different Sources of Government Information

Information about Federal and State governments is available from many sources. Knowing how to use these sources is important to good citizenship. It is a key skill that enables you to be better informed and better equipped to participate in the democratic process.

For example, suppose you wanted to research how your representatives in Congress stood on the 1990–1991 conflict in the Persian Gulf. You might research speeches they made and votes they cast in the House or Senate. Such information is available from many sources. Follow these steps to practice using different sources of information.

**1. Know what information is available.** Each branch of the Federal Government collects and publishes great quantities of information. State and local governments also gather and distribute much material. In addition, private publishers produce material about government and its activities. Locate the Government Resources Handbook on page 690. This handbook lists just a few of the more popular and widely available sources of information on government and its activities. Have you used any of these resources before?

**2. Know the differences between public and private sources.** Public sources are those published by the Federal Government, a State government, or some other public agency. A private source is one published by a publisher that is not connected to any government agency.

Look in the Government Resources Handbook. (a) Can you find one public and one private source that might include the results of the vote in Congress authorizing the use of force in the Persian Gulf conflict? (b) Can you find one private and one public source that might include a representative's thoughts about the conflict?

**3. Know the differences between primary and secondary sources.** Primary sources are direct, firsthand accounts of an event, such as a court decision, the transcript of a committee debate, or an eyewitness account of an event. Primary sources provide insight into a person's views or attitudes. Secondary sources are secondhand summaries and interpretations of primary sources. Often, secondary sources include the author's opinion and bias. (a) Is the text of a senator's speech a primary or a secondary source? (b) For what kind of information is such a source useful? (c) If you wanted to read an analysis of the actions of Congress during the crisis in the Persian Gulf, would you look for a primary or a secondary source? (d) Can you identify possible sources for these pieces of information in the Government Resources Handbook?

**4. Determine the reliability of your sources.** Each source offers benefits and drawbacks. For example, a primary source gives firsthand information, but might reflect the strong bias of its author. A secondary source might distort the information it summarizes. Public sources might not offer as critical a view of the government as a private source might. A private source might reflect its author's bias. Because each source has benefits and drawbacks, it is always best to check several sources. How might you use all four types of information to complete your research on your representatives in Congress?

# Chapter-in-Brief

Scan all headings, photographs, charts, and other visuals in the chapter before reading the section summaries below.

## Section 1 The Six Basic Principles (pp. 55–59)

The Constitution of the United States is the "supreme law of the land," the nation's fundamental law. It is the framework on which the government is built. The Constitution does not describe in great detail how the government is to work. Rather, the Constitution sets out six basic principles that shape and guide its operations.

1. Popular sovereignty: The people are sovereign; they are the only source for the authority of government.
2. Limited government: Government is not all-powerful; it may do only those things the people have given it the power to do.
3. Separation of powers: Government's legislative, executive, and judicial powers are divided among three independent, coequal branches.
4. Checks and balances: The three branches are tied together through a complex system of checks (restraints) which each can use against the other.
5. Judicial review: The courts have the power to determine the constitutionality of governmental actions.
6. Federalism: The powers of government are distributed on a territorial basis, between the National Government and the several States.

## Section 2 Formally Amending the Constitution (pp. 60–63)

Since 1787, when the Constitution was written, this nation's population has grown from about 4 million people to over 250 million. The nation was then 13 States stretched along the Atlantic seaboard; it now extends across the continent and beyond. How has the Constitution survived such change?

One reason the Constitution has endured is that it contains a built-in mechanism by which it can be adjusted to meet the changing needs of the nation. This is the constitutional amendment process, which includes four formal methods of amending the Constitution. Each of these methods reflects the principle of federalism—amendments may be proposed at the national level, and they can be ratified only at the State level.

The process of amending the Constitution is not easy. More than 10,000 resolutions calling for amendments have been introduced over the years. Only 27 amendments have thus far been added to the Constitution. The first 10 amendments—the Bill of Rights—were all ratified at the same time, in 1791.

## Section 3 Informal Amendment (pp. 65–67)

The Framers wrote much of the Constitution in brief, even outline-like terms. So, the real key to 200 years of constitutional change and development in the United States lies in the informal amendment process, the many changes that have been made in the Constitution but that have not involved changes in its written words.

An almost countless number of informal amendments have been added to the Constitution in five ways: (1) the passage of basic legislation by Congress, (2) actions taken by Presidents, (3) decisions of the Supreme Court, (4) the activities of political parties, and (5) custom.

These informal amendments are the product of the day-to-day, year-to-year experiences of government under the Constitution.

# Chapter Review

## Vocabulary and Key Terms

popular sovereignty (p. 55)
limited government (p.56)
constitutionalism (p. 56)
rule of law (p.56)
separation of powers (p. 56)

checks and balances (p. 57)
judicial review (p. 58)
unconstitutional (p. 59)
federalism (p.59)
amendment (p. 60)

formal amendment (p. 60)
Bill of Rights (p. 62)
informal amendment (p. 65)
executive agreement (p. 66)

**Matching:** *Review the key terms in the list above. If you are not sure of a term's meaning, look up the term and review its definition. Choose a term from the list above that best matches each description.*

1. an example of the judicial branch's check on the legislative branch
2. an official change in the language of the Constitution
3. what a law that violates the Constitution is declared
4. the principle that explains why States hold many powers in the American system of government
5. the principle that divides the executive, legislative, and judicial powers of the government into separate but equal branches

**True or False:** *Determine whether each statement is true or false. If it is true, write "true." If it is false, change the underlined word or words to make the statement true.*

1. Under the principle of <u>popular sovereignty,</u> the National Government has three equal branches.
2. <u>Executive agreement</u> is the process by which the Constitution has been changed and added to during the course of United States history.
3. The first 10 amendments to the United States Constitution are known as the <u>Bill of Rights</u>.

4. <u>Formal amendments</u> have not resulted in changes in the written words of the Constitution.
5. The principle of <u>constitutionalism</u> states that government must be bound by a fundamental law.

**Word Relationships:** *Distinguish between the words in each pair.*

1. limited government/popular sovereignty
2. checks and balances/separation of powers
3. judicial review/unconstitutional
4. rule of law/Bill of Rights

## Main Ideas

### Section 1 (pp. 55–59)

1. How does the Constitution's length and its absence of detail help explain its strength?
2. (a) Who holds the ultimate power in the United States system of government? (b) What two guiding principles of the Constitution serve as the basis for that fact?
3. (a) What are the remaining basic principles upon which the Constitution is built? (b) How do those principles operate in American government?

## Section 2 (pp. 60–63)

**4.** (a) In what ways has the United States changed in its more than 200-year history? (b) How has this change affected the Constitution?

**5.** (a) For what reasons is there a need for the formal amendment of the Constitution? (b) How many times has that process taken place?

**6.** For what reason was the Bill of Rights added to the Constitution?

## Section 3 (pp. 65–67)

**7.** (a) How does an informal amendment differ from a formal amendment? (b) Which is more common?

**8.** For what reason is the process of informal amendment necessary?

**9.** By what major means has the Constitution been informally amended?

## Critical Thinking

**1.** **Drawing Conclusions** (p. 19) The Preamble to the Constitution begins with the words "We the people." This collective "we," however, did not extend far enough to include suffrage and equal rights for women, African Americans, and Native Americans. (a) How has that omission affected the history of the United States? (b) Which, if any, of the 27 amendments to the Constitution affected that situation?

**2.** **Checking Consistency** (p. 19) The concept of majority rule with minority rights, argued in *The Federalist* No. 10 (see page 747), protects the few from the actions of the many. Find examples of both the success and failure of the United States to live up to that concept over its history.

**3.** **Testing Conclusions** (p. 19) The text says that the United States Constitution is a flexible document. Find evidence from the text that you believe supports the validity of that conclusion.

# Getting Involved

**1.** **Writing Your Opinion** You are a newspaper editor in the late 1700s. Alexander Hamilton has just made a statement in which he referred to democracy as "mobocracy." Write an editorial in response to Hamilton's statement. Define the position that you want to take in the editorial. Next, list the arguments you will use. As you revise your editorial, make certain that your arguments are as persuasive as possible. Finally, proofread and make a final copy.

**2.** **Cooperative Activity** Conduct a mini-Constitutional Convention to update the Bill of Rights. Working in small groups, create a chart to organize your revisions and ideas. List the contents of the current Bill of Rights in one column. In the second column, identify which amendments you want to revise. Explain the reasons behind each suggested revision in the third column. As you make your decisions, think about current issues of debate such as gun control and the death penalty, and how they are addressed in the existing Bill of Rights.

**3.** **Class Debate** Hold a debate on the following: *Resolved,* That the Constitution be amended to fix the terms for Supreme Court justices. Select one team to support the proposed amendment and one to oppose it. The rest of the class can evaluate each side's presentation.

**4.** **Gathering Information** (a) Using the Government Resources Handbook beginning on page 690, identify what sources you could use to find the names and addresses of your representatives and senators in Congress. (b) What sources might you use if you wanted to see how often they have voted for/against measures supported by the President?

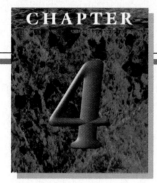

CHAPTER

4

# Federalism

## Chapter Preview

You know that today the American flag is composed of 13 stripes and 50 stars. The stripes represent the 13 original States of the American Union, and the stars stand for the nation's 50 States.

Legend has it that the first Stars and Stripes was sewn by Betsy Ross, in Philadelphia in June of 1776; but there is no credible evidence to support that tale. What is known is that on June 14, 1777, the Second Continental Congress passed this resolution: "*Resolved:* that the flag of the United States be thirteen stripes, alternate red and white; that the union be thirteen stars, white in a blue field. . . ."

Today's 50-star flag was raised for the first time at 12:01 A.M. on July 4, 1960, at Fort McHenry in Baltimore. That flag depicts the subject of this chapter: the American Federal Union.

### Before you read this chapter:

- **Describe** three functions that the Federal Government performs that the States may not.
- **Predict** why the Framers felt it was necessary to divide power between the National and State governments.

### As you read, focus on the main objective for each section. Understand:

1. The division of powers between the National Government and the States.
2. The National Government's obligations to the States.
3. The constitutional provisions that promote cooperation between and among the States.

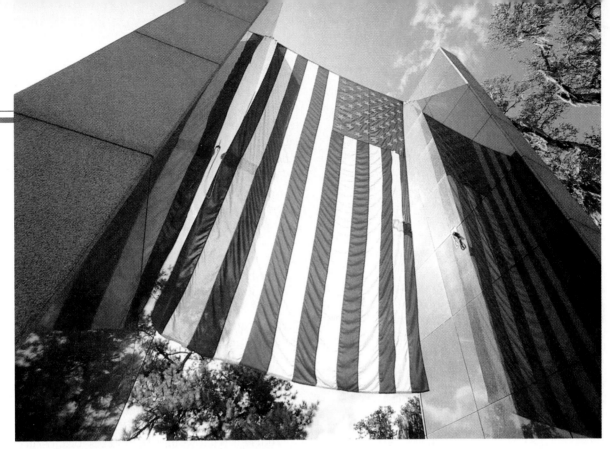

**"That Star-Spangled Banner"** By 1818, with seven new States added to the original thirteen, Congress abandoned its idea of including a stripe for every State. Instead, it enacted that the number of stripes be reduced to the original thirteen.

# 1 Federalism and the Division of Power

**Find Out:**

- What is federalism and why does this country have a federal form of government?
- What are the delegated powers of the National Government? What powers are denied to it?
- What powers belong to the States? To the National Government? What powers are held concurrently by the National Government and the States?
- What role does the Supreme Court play in the federal system?

**Key Terms:**

federalism, division of powers, delegated powers, expressed powers, implied powers, inherent powers, reserved powers, exclusive powers, concurrent powers

When the Framers met at the Philadelphia Convention, they had a complex problem to solve: How could they design a strong, national government with the power to meet the nation's needs and, at the same time, preserve the existing States? The authors of the Constitution were dedicated to the concept of limited government. They believed that to divide governmental power is to restrict it and thus prevent its abuse.

You probably know that according to federal law young men must register for the draft at age 18; most employers must pay their workers at least $4.25 an hour; no one can be denied a job because he or she is African American, Hispanic, or Asian American.

You almost certainly know, too, that according to State law you must have a driver's license in order to drive a car; it is illegal for anyone under 21 to buy beer, wine, or liquor.

These few examples illustrate a complex arrangement: the division of governmental powers in the American federal system. This section will help you to understand that complicated matter.

## Federalism Defined

**Federalism** is a system of government in which a written constitution divides the powers of government on a territorial basis. The division is made between a central, or national, government and several regional or local governments. Each level of government has its own area of powers. Neither level, acting alone, can change the basic division of powers the constitution makes between them. Each level operates through its own agencies and acts directly on the people through its own officials and laws.

The Constitution sets out the basic design of the American federal system. The document provides for a division of powers between the National Government and the States. That **division of powers** was implied in the original Constitution and then spelled out in the 10th Amendment:

❝ The powers not delegated to the United States by the Constitution, nor prohibited by it to the States, are reserved to the States respectively, or to the people. ❞

In effect, federalism produces a dual system of government. It provides for two basic levels of government, each with its own sphere of authority. Each operates over the same people and territory at the same time.

Federalism's major strength is that it allows local actions in matters of local concern and national action in matters of wider concern. Local traditions, needs, and desires vary from one State to another, and federalism allows for this very significant fact.

Illustrations of the point are nearly endless. For example, most forms of gambling are legal in Nevada but are against the law in most other States. New Jersey buses private as well as public school students free of charge, but most States do not. Nebraska is the only State with a one-house, or unicameral, legislature. Only in North Carolina does the governor not have the power to veto acts of the legislature; only North Dakota does not require voter registration.

Federalism allows and encourages local choice in many matters. It also provides for the strength that comes from union. National defense and foreign affairs offer useful illustrations of the point. So, too, do domestic affairs. Take, for example, a natural disaster.

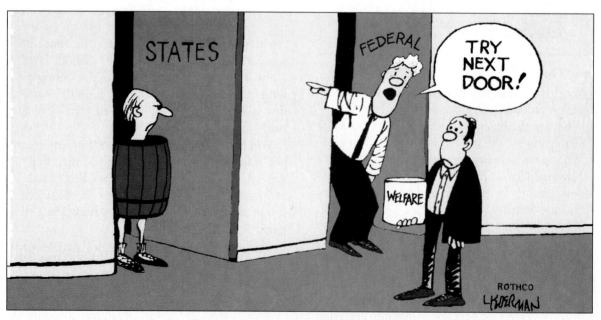

**Interpreting Political Cartoons**    Federalism, like any governmental system, is not without its problems. What particular problem does this cartoon illustrate?

When a flood, drought, winter storm, or other catastrophe hits some State, the resources of the National Government and all of the other States may be mobilized to aid the stricken area.

## The National Government Is One of Delegated Powers

The National Government is a government of **delegated powers**. That is, it has only those powers granted to it in the Constitution. Three distinct types of delegated powers exist: the expressed, the implied, and the inherent powers.

### The Expressed Powers

The **expressed powers** are those delegated to the National Government in so many words—spelled out expressly in the Constitution.

You can find most of the expressed powers in Article I, Section 8. There, in 18 clauses, the Constitution expressly gives 27 powers to Congress. They include the power to lay and collect taxes, to coin money, to regulate foreign and interstate commerce, to raise and maintain armed forces, to declare war, to fix standards of weights and measures, to grant patents and copyrights, and to do many other things.

Note that the Constitution sets out several powers in other places, too. Thus, Article II, Section 2 gives several powers to the President. They include the power to act as commander in chief of the armed forces, to grant reprieves and pardons, to make treaties, and to name major federal officials. Article III grants "the judicial power of the United States" to the Supreme Court and other courts in the federal judiciary. Various amendments to the Constitution also contain several of the expressed powers; for example, the 16th Amendment gives Congress the power to levy an income tax.

### The Implied Powers

The **implied powers** are those that are not expressly stated in the Constitution but are reasonably implied by those powers that are.

The constitutional basis for the implied powers is found in one of the expressed powers. Article I, Section 8, Clause 18 gives to Congress the "necessary and proper" power. The Necessary and Proper Clause says that Congress shall have the power:

> to make all laws which shall be necessary and proper for carrying into execution the foregoing powers, and all other powers vested by this Constitution in the Government of the United States, or in any department or officer thereof.

Through congressional and court interpretation, the words "necessary and proper" have come to mean, in effect, "convenient and expedient." Indeed, the Necessary and Proper Clause is sometimes called the Elastic Clause because, over time, it has been stretched to cover so much.

Here are but a few of the thousands of examples of the exercise of implied powers: Congress has provided for the regulation of labor-management relations, the building of hydroelectric power dams, and the building of a 42,000-mile interstate highway system. It has made federal crimes of such acts as moving stolen goods, gambling devices, and kidnapped persons across State lines. It has prohibited racial discrimination in access to such places as restaurants, theaters, hotels, and motels. Congress has taken these actions, and many more, because the power to do so is reasonably implied by just *one* of the expressed powers: the power to regulate foreign and interstate commerce.[1]

### The Inherent Powers

The **inherent powers** are those that belong to the National Government because it is the national government of a sovereign state in the world community. Although the Constitution does not expressly provide for them, they are powers that national governments have historically possessed. It stands to reason that the Framers intended that the National Government they created would hold these powers.

The inherent powers are few in number. The chief ones include the power to regulate immigration, to deport aliens, to acquire territory, to give diplomatic recognition to other states, and to protect the nation against rebellion or internal subversion.

---

[1]Article I, Section 8, Clause 3. The doctrine of implied powers is treated in greater detail in Chapter 11.

## The Division of Powers Between the National Government and the States

**NATIONAL GOVERNMENT**

**STATE GOVERNMENTS**

Powers Granted

Delegated Powers of the National Government

Concurrent Powers

Reserved Powers of the States

Powers denied the National Government

Powers denied both the National Government and the States

Powers denied the States

Powers Denied

**Interpreting Graphs**   Federalism determines the way that powers are divided between and shared among the National and State governments. Name one concurrent power.

One can argue that most of the inherent powers are implied by one or more of the expressed powers. For example, the power to regulate immigration is suggested by the expressed power to regulate foreign trade. The power to acquire territory can be drawn from the treaty-making power and the several war powers. But the doctrine of inherent powers holds that it is not necessary to go to those lengths to find these powers in the Constitution. In short, these powers exist because the United States exists.

## Powers Denied to the National Government

Although the Constitution delegates certain powers to the National Government, it also denies certain powers to it. The Constitution does so in three distinct ways.

First, the Constitution denies some powers to the National Government in so many words— expressly.[2] Among them are the power to levy

duties on exports; to deny freedom of religion, speech, press, or assembly; to conduct illegal searches or seizures; and to deny to any person a speedy and public trial, or a trial by jury.

Second, several powers are denied to the National Government because of the silence of the Constitution. Recall, the National Government is a government of delegated powers; it has only those powers the Constitution gives to it. Among the many powers not granted to the National Government are these: to create a public school system for the nation, to enact uniform marriage and divorce laws, and to set up units of local government. The Constitution says nothing that would give the National Government the power to do any of these things— expressly, implicitly, or inherently.

Third, some powers are denied to the National Government because the Constitution established a federal system for the United States. Clearly the Constitution does not intend that the National Government should have any power to do those things that would threaten the existence of that system. For example, in the exercise of its power to tax, Congress cannot tax any of the States or their local units in the carrying out of their governmental

_____

[2]Most of the expressed denials of power are found in Article I, Section 9 and in the 1st through the 8th amendments.

functions. If it could, it would have the power to destroy (tax out of existence) one or more, or all, of the States.[3]

## The States Are Governments of Reserved Powers

The Constitution reserves power to each of the States. The **reserved powers** are the powers held by the States in the federal system. They are those powers not given to the National Government and yet, at the same time, are not denied to the States. Read again the words of the Constitution's 10th Amendment set out on page 74.

Thus, any State can forbid persons under 18 to marry without parental consent or those under 21 to buy liquor. A State can require that doctors, lawyers, hairdressers, or plumbers be licensed in order to practice in the State. The State can set up public school systems and units of local government, set the conditions under which it grants divorces, and permit certain forms of gambling and outlaw others.

The sphere of powers held by each State is huge. They can do all of those things just mentioned and much more because the Constitution does not forbid them to do so. At the same time, the National Government can do none of those things because the Constitution does not give it the power to do so. The power to do those things is reserved to the States.

## Powers Denied to the States

As you know, the Constitution denies many powers to the National Government. Similarly, it forbids the States the power to do a great number of things.

The Constitution denies some powers to the States in so many words.[4] For example, no State can enter into any treaty, alliance, or confederation. Nor can a State print or coin money or deprive any person of life, liberty, or property without due process of law.

Some powers are also denied to the States by the existence of the federal system. Thus, no State or local government can tax any of the agencies or functions of the National Government. Remember, too, that each State has its own constitution—and that document also denies many powers to the State.[5]

## The Federal System and Local Governments

Government in the United States is often discussed in terms of three layers: national, State, and local. However convenient this view may be, it is at best misleading. Recall, there are *two* basic levels in the federal system: the National Government and the 50 States.

Governments do exist at the local level all across the country, of course. In fact, there are more than 80,000 units of local government in the United States today. You will take a look at them later in this book; but for now, keep this important point in mind: All of these thousands of local governments are parts—subunits—of the various States.

Each of these local units is located within one of the 50 States. None has an existence apart from its parent State. In its constitution and in its laws, each of the States has created these units. To whatever extent any of these local governments can provide services, regulate activities, collect taxes, or do anything else, they can only because the State has established them and given them the power to do so. In short, as local governments exercise the powers they possess, they are actually exercising State powers. Another way of putting all of this is to remind you of a point that was first made in Chapter 1. Each of the 50 States has a unitary form of government.

---

[3]But note that when a State, or one of its local units, performs a so-called nongovernmental function—for example, operating liquor stores, a bus system, a farmer's market, and so forth—it is liable to federal taxes.

[4]Most of the expressed prohibitions of power to the States and, so, to their local governments are found in Article I, Section 10 and in the 13th, 14th, 15th, 19th, 24th, and 26th amendments.

[5]Study your own State's constitution on this point; as you do, note the significance of the words "or to the people" in the 10th Amendment in the Federal Constitution.

## Governments in the United States

| Type of Government | Number of Governments |
|---|---|
| Federal | 1 |
| State | 50 |
| Local | |
| County | 3,043 |
| Municipality | 19,296 |
| Township | 16,666 |
| School district | 14,556 |
| Other special district | 33,131 |
| **Total** | **86,743** |

*Source:* Bureau of the Census, Census of Governments, 1992. The Census Bureau surveys all units of government in the United States every five years.

**Interpreting Tables**   There are, on average, 1,743 local governments per State in this country. Do any of these local governments have powers other than those granted to them by the States?

## The Exclusive Powers

The **exclusive powers** are those that can be exercised only by the National Government. They include most of the delegated powers.

Some of the delegated powers are also expressly denied to the States—for example, the powers to coin money, make treaties with foreign states, and lay import duties. Thus, these powers belong solely to the National Government.

Some of the powers given to the National Government but not expressly denied to the States are also among the exclusive powers because of the nature of the particular powers involved. For example, the States are not expressly denied the power to regulate interstate commerce. However, if they could do so, trade would be at best chaotic, and at worst impossible. Therefore, States cannot exercise this power.[6]

---

[6]The States cannot regulate interstate commerce as such, but they do affect it. For example, in regulating highway speeds, the States regulate vehicles not only operating wholly within the State, but also those operating from State to State. Generally, the States can affect interstate commerce, but they may not impose an unreasonable burden on it.

## The Concurrent Powers

The **concurrent powers** are those that both the National Government and the States possess and exercise. They include, for example, the power to lay and collect taxes, to define crimes and set punishments for them, and to condemn (take) private property for public use.

The concurrent powers are not held and exercised jointly by the two basic levels of government in this country. Rather, they are held and exercised separately and simultaneously. To rephrase the definition: The concurrent powers are those powers that the Constitution does not grant exclusively to the National Government and that, at the same time, it does not deny to the States.

## The Supreme Law of the Land

The division of powers in the American federal system is a very complicated matter, as the diagram on page 76 shows. Again, it produces a dual system of government, one in which two basic levels of government operate over the same territory and the same people at the same time.

Clearly, such an arrangement is bound to result in conflicts between the two levels, between national law and State law. The Framers anticipated those conflicts—and so, they wrote the Supremacy Clause into the Constitution. Article VI, Section 2 declares

❝This Constitution, and the laws of the United States which shall be made in pursuance thereof, and all treaties made, or which shall be made, under the authority of the United States, shall be the supreme law of the land . . . . ❞

Significantly, Article VI goes on to add:

❝. . . and the judges in every State shall be bound thereby, anything in the constitution or laws of any State to the contrary notwithstanding.❞

The Constitution and the laws and treaties of the United States are "the supreme law of the land." This means that the Constitution stands above all other forms of law in the United

States. Acts of Congress and treaties stand immediately beneath it.[7]

In other words, the Supremacy Clause creates a "ladder of laws" in the United States. The Constitution stands on the topmost rung. Then come the acts of Congress and treaties. Each State's constitution, supreme over all other forms of that State's law, stands beneath all forms of federal law. State statutes are on the next rung. At the base of the ladder are the different forms of local law: city and county charters and ordinances, and so forth.

The Supremacy Clause has been called the "linchpin of the Constitution," for it joins the National Government and the States into a single governmental unit, a federal state.

**The Supreme Court and the Federal System** The Supreme Court is the umpire in the federal system—for one of its chief duties is to apply the Supremacy Clause to the conflicts which that dual system of government inevitably produces.

The Court was first called on to play this role—to settle a clash between a national and a State law—in 1819. The case, *McCulloch* v. *Maryland*, involved the controversial Second Bank of the United States. The Bank had been chartered by Congress in 1816. In 1818 the Maryland legislature, hoping to cripple the bank, placed a tax on all notes issued by its Baltimore branch. James McCulloch, the branch cashier, refused to pay the tax, and the Maryland courts convicted him for that refusal.

The Supreme Court unanimously reversed the Maryland courts, however. Speaking for the Court, Chief Justice John Marshall based the decision squarely on the Constitution's Supremacy Clause:

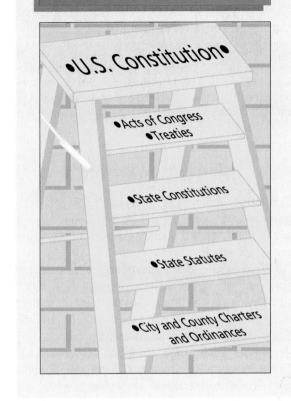

## The Supremacy Clause

- •U.S. Constitution•
- •Acts of Congress
- •Treaties
- •State Constitutions
- •State Statutes
- •City and County Charters and Ordinances

▲ **Interpreting Charts** This "ladder of laws" was created by the Supremacy Clause of the Constitution. Which branch of government decides conflicts between National and State governments?

    ❝ If any one proposition could command the universal assent of mankind we might expect it to be this—that the government of the Union, though limited in its powers, is supreme within its sphere of action . . . . [T]he States have no power to retard, impede, burden, or in any manner control, the operation of the constitutional laws enacted by Congress. ❞[8]

It is impossible to overstate the significance of the Court's function—past and present—as the umpire of the federal system. Had the Court not

---

[7]Acts of Congress and treaties stand on equal planes with one another. Neither can conflict with any provision in the Constitution. In the rare case of conflict between the provisions of an act and those of a treaty, the one more recently adopted takes precedence—as the latest expression of the sovereign people's will. The Supreme Court has regularly held to that position from the first case it decided on the point, *The Head Money Cases,* 1884.

---

[8]The case is also critically important in the development of the constitutional system because, in deciding it, the Court for the first time upheld the doctrine of implied powers. It also held the National Government to be immune from any form of State taxation.

taken this role, the federal system and probably the United States itself could not have survived its early years. Justice Oliver Wendell Holmes once made the point in these words:

"I do not think that the United States would come to an end if we [the Court] lost our power to declare an act of Congress void. I do think the Union would be imperiled if we could not make that declaration as to the laws of the several States."[9]

## Section 1 Review

1. **Define:** federalism, division of powers, delegated power, expressed powers, implied powers, inherent powers, reserved powers, exclusive powers, concurrent powers
2. What is the chief advantage of the federal system?
3. Why is the National Government described as a government of delegated powers and the States as governments of reserved powers?
4. (a) On what three bases are powers denied to the National Government? (b) To the States?
5. What is the "supreme law of the land"?
6. What is the significance of *McCulloch* v. *Maryland* in the development of the federal system?

**Critical Thinking**

7. **Predicting Consequences** (p. 19) The States are denied the power to make treaties. (a) In your opinion, what is the reason for this denial of power? (b) What might happen if States had this power?

---

[9]*Collected Legal Papers* (New York: Harcourt, 1920), pp. 295–296. The Supreme Court first held a State law unconstitutional in a case from Georgia, *Fletcher* v. *Peck,* 1810. The Court found that a Georgia law of 1795, making a grant of land to John Peck, amounted to a contract between the State and Peck. It ruled that the legislature's later repeal of that law violated the Constitution's Contract Clause (Article I, Section 10, Clause 1): "No State shall . . . pass any . . . law impairing the obligations of contracts." Since then, the Court has found more than 1,000 State laws unconstitutional (and has upheld the constitutionality of thousands of others).

## 2 The National Government and the 50 States

**Find Out:**

- What are the obligations of the National Government to the States under the Constitution?
- What kinds of aid does the National Government grant to the States?
- What kinds of aid do the States provide the National Government?

**Key Terms:**

enabling act, act of admission, grants-in-aid program, block grant

Have you ever thought about, analyzed, or really focused on the words "the United States"? The United States is a union of States, the several States joined together, the States united.

The Constitution created and intends to preserve that Union. To that end, as you will see in this section, the Constitution (1) requires the National Government to guarantee certain things to the several States and (2) makes it possible for the National Government to do several things for the States.

### The Nation's Obligations to the States

The Constitution places several obligations on the National Government for the benefit of the States. Most of them are to be found in Article IV.

**Guarantee of a Republican Form of Government** The Constitution requires the National Government to "guarantee to every State in this Union a republican form of government."[10] The Constitution does not define "republican form of government," and the Supreme Court has regularly refused to do so. The term is generally understood to mean a representative government, however.

---

[10]Article IV, Section 4.

The Supreme Court has held that the question of whether or not a State has a republican form of government is a political question. That is, it is one to be decided by the political branches of the government—the President and Congress—and not by the courts.

The leading case here is *Luther* v. *Borden*, 1849. It grew out of Dorr's Rebellion, a revolt led by Thomas W. Dorr against the State of Rhode Island in 1841–1842. Dorr and his followers had written and proclaimed a new constitution for the State.[11] When they tried to put the new document into operation, however, the governor in office under the original constitution declared martial law—temporary rule by military authorities. The governor also called on the Federal Government for help. President John Tyler then took steps to put down the revolt, and it quickly collapsed.

The question of which of the competing governments was the legitimate one was a major issue in *Luther* v. *Borden*. But, again, the Supreme Court refused to decide the matter.

The only extensive use ever made of the republican-form guarantee came in the years immediately following the Civil War. Congress declared that several southern States did not have governments of a republican form. It refused to admit Senators and Representatives from those States until the States had ratified the 13th, 14th, and 15th amendments and broadened their laws to recognize the voting and other rights of African Americans.

**Protection Against Invasion and Domestic Violence**   The National Government must also "protect each of them [States] against invasion; and on application of the legislature, or of the executive (when the legislature cannot be convened), against domestic violence."[12]

Today it is clear that an invasion of any one of the 50 States would be met as an attack on the United States itself. Hence, this constitutional guarantee is now of little, if any, significance.

However, that was not the case in the late 1780s. Then, it was not at all certain that all 13 States would stand together if a foreign power attacked one of them. So, before the 13 States agreed to give up their war-making powers, each demanded an ironclad pledge that an attack on any of them would be met as an attack on all.

The federal system assumes that each of the 50 States will keep the peace within its own borders. Thus, the primary responsibility for curbing insurrection, riot, or other internal disorder rests with the individual States. However, the Constitution does accept the fact that a State might not be able to control some situations. So, it guarantees protection against domestic violence in each of them.

Historically, the use of federal force to restore order within a State has been a rare event. Several instances did occur in the 1960s, however. When racial unrest exploded into violence

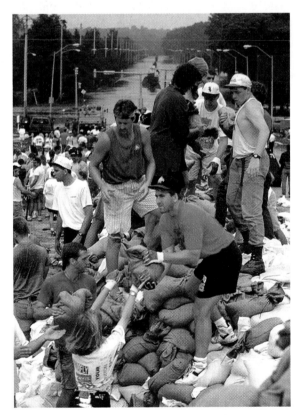

▲ **Federal Aid to the States**   Midwesterners fought devastating floods in 1993. To help the States recover from this "domestic violence," the Federal Government provided a $6.2 billion flood relief package.

---

[11]Rhode Island had not written a new constitution at the time of independence in 1776. Rhode Island's present constitution, which became effective in 1843, came as a direct result of Dorr's rebellion.

[12]Article IV, Section 4.

in Detroit during the "long, hot summer" of 1967, President Lyndon Johnson ordered units of the regular army into the city. He acted at the request of Michigan's Governor George Romney, and only after Detroit's police and firefighters, supported by State Police and National Guard units, could not control riots, arson, and looting in the city. In 1968, again at the request of the governors involved, federal troops were sent into Chicago and Baltimore to help put down the violence that erupted following the assassination of Martin Luther King, Jr.

Normally, a President has sent troops into a State only in answer to a request from its governor or legislature. But when national laws are being broken, national functions interfered with, or national property endangered, a President does not need to wait for such a plea.[13]

The ravages of nature—storms, floods, drought, forest fires, and such—can be more destructive than human violence. Here, too, acting to protect the States against "domestic violence," the Federal Government stands ready to aid stricken areas.

## Respect for Territorial Integrity

The National Government is constitutionally bound to respect the territorial integrity of each of the States. That is, the National Government must recognize the legal existence and the physical boundaries of each State.

The whole scheme of the Constitution imposes this obligation. Several of its provisions do so, as well. For example, Congress must include, in both of its houses, members chosen in each one of the States.[14] Acting alone, Congress cannot create a new State from territory belonging to any one of the existing States. To do so, Congress first must have the consent of the legislature of the State involved.[15] Recall, also, Article V of the Constitution declares that no State can be deprived of its equal representation in the United States Senate without its own consent.

## Admitting New States

Only Congress has the power to admit new States to the Union. The Constitution places only one restriction on that power. A new State cannot be created by taking territory from one or more of the existing States without the consent of the legislature(s) of the State(s) involved.[16]

Congress has admitted 37 States since the original 13 formed the Union. Five States—Vermont, Kentucky, Tennessee, Maine, and West Virginia—were created from parts of already existing States. Texas was an independent republic before admission. California was admitted shortly after being ceded to the United States by Mexico. Each of the other 30 States entered the Union only after a longer period of time, frequently more than 15 years, as an organized territory.

**Admission Procedure** The process of admission is usually simple. The area desiring Statehood first petitions Congress for admission.

[13]President Grover Cleveland ordered federal troops to put an end to rioting in the Chicago railyard during the Pullman Strike in 1894 despite the objections of Governor William Altgeld of Illinois. The Supreme Court upheld his actions in *In re Debs,* 1896. The Court found that rioters had threatened federal property and impeded the flow of the mails and interstate commerce. Thus, more than domestic violence was involved. Since then, several Presidents have acted without a request from the State involved. Most recently, President Dwight Eisenhower did so at Little Rock, Arkansas, in 1957, and President John Kennedy at the University of Mississippi in 1962 and at the University of Alabama in 1963. In each of those instances, the President acted to halt the unlawful obstruction of school integration orders issued by federal courts.

[14]In the House, Article I, Section 2, Clause 1; in the Senate, Article I, Section 3, Clause 1 and the 17th Amendment.
[15]Article IV, Section 3, Clause 1.
[16]Article IV, Section 3, Clause 1. Some argue that this provision was violated with West Virginia's admission in 1863. That State was formed from the 40 western counties that had broken away from Virginia over the issue of secession from the Union. The consent required by the Constitution was given by a minority of the members of the Virginia legislature—those who represented the 40 western counties. Congress accepted their action, holding that they were the only group legally capable of acting as the Virginia legislature at the time.

If and when Congress chooses, it passes an **enabling act**, which directs the framing of a proposed State constitution. A convention prepares the constitution, which is then put to a popular vote in the proposed State. If the voters approve the constitution, it is then submitted to Congress for its consideration. If Congress still agrees to Statehood after reviewing the document, it passes an **act of admission**. If the President signs the act, the new State enters the Union.

The two newest States, Alaska and Hawaii, abbreviated the usual process of gaining admission to the Union. Each adopted a proposed constitution without waiting for an enabling act—Alaska in 1956 and Hawaii in 1950. Both became States in 1959.

**Conditions for Admission**   Before finally admitting a new State, Congress has often established certain conditions. For example, in

1896 Utah was admitted as a State on the condition that its constitution outlaw polygamy— the practice of having more than one spouse at the same time. In the act admitting Alaska to the Union as the 49th State, Congress forever prohibited that State from claiming title to any lands legally held by any Native American.

Each State enters the Union on an equal footing with each of the other States. Thus, although Congress can set certain conditions like those just described, it cannot impose conditions of a political nature on the States. For example, when Oklahoma was admitted to the Union in 1907, Congress said the State could not remove its capital from Guthrie to any other place before 1913. In 1910, however, the Oklahoma legislature moved the State's capital to Oklahoma City. When this step was challenged, the United States Supreme Court held, in *Coyle* v. *Smith*, 1911, that Congress can set conditions for a prospective State's

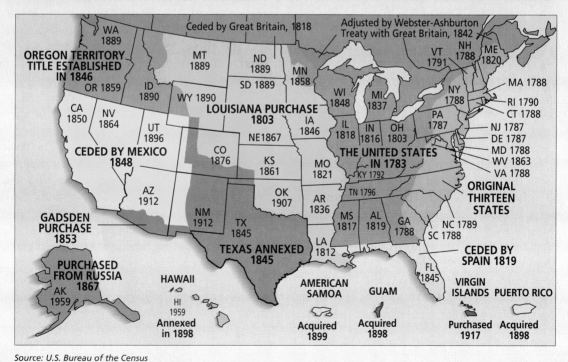

**Territorial Expansion of the United States and Other Acquisitions**

Source: U.S. Bureau of the Census

▲ **Interpreting Maps**   Thirty-seven States have joined the original 13 that formed the United States. Who must sign the act of admission of a new State?

## VOICES *on Government*

### On the Federal Government and Education

**L. Douglas Wilder,** the first elected African American governor in the United States

" ...there's an important federal role in education. I'm not talking about a federal curriculum, or federal regulations dictating what schools should teach. But the federal government has the responsibility to make sure that people are not denied educational opportunities because of their geographic location or their economic status. "

admission. But, held the Court, the conditions cannot be enforced when they compromise the independence of a State to manage its own internal affairs.

Consider one more example here: President William Howard Taft vetoed a resolution to admit Arizona to the Union in 1911 because its proposed constitution provided that members of the State's judiciary could be recalled—removed from office—by popular vote. This provision meant, said Taft, that a judge would have to keep one eye on public opinion rather than leaving both eyes firmly focused onto matters of the law. In response to Taft's concern, Arizona then removed the recall section from the document. In 1912 Congress passed, and the President signed, another act of admission for Arizona. Almost immediately upon admission to the Union, however, the new State amended its new constitution to provide for the recall of judges. That provision remains a valid part of Arizona's constitution today.

## Cooperative Federalism

As you know, federalism produces a dual system of government in the United States. Given this complex arrangement, it should come as no surprise that competition, tensions, and conflicts are a regular part of American federalism. In short, the American governmental system is like a tug-of-war—a continuing power struggle between the National Government and the States.

Keep in mind the central importance of the concept of divided powers in the American governmental system. Add to it this vital point: The American federal arrangement also involves a broad area of shared powers. That is, in addition to the two separate spheres of power held and exercised by the two basic levels of government, there are large and growing areas of cooperation between them.

**Federal Grants-in-Aid** Perhaps the best-known examples of this intergovernmental cooperation are the many federal **grants-in-aid programs**—grants of federal money or other resources to the States and/or their cities, counties, and other local units. These grants provide those levels of government with the funds often needed to carry out many of their functions.

The history of grants-in-aid programs goes back some 200 years—in fact, to the period before the Constitution. In the Northwest Ordinance of 1787, the Congress under the Articles of Confederation provided for the government of the territory beyond the Ohio River. Looking forward to the existence of new States on that frontier, the Congress set aside sections of land for the support of public education in those future States. On through the 19th century, States received grants of federal lands for a number of purposes—schools and colleges, roads and canals, flood control work, and several others. A large number of the major State universities, for example, were founded as land-grant colleges—schools built out of the sale of public lands given to the States by the Morrill Act of 1862.

Congress began to make grants of federal money quite early, too. In 1808 it gave the

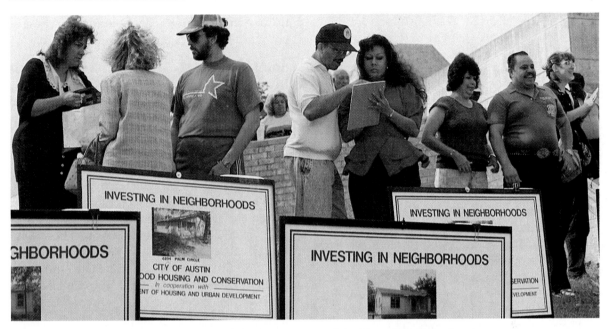

▲ **Cooperative Venture** The best of federalism was at work in this project. Federal and State agencies worked together to provide much-needed fix-up homes for just one dollar.

States $200,000 to support their militia. Cash grants did not come to play a large role until the Depression years of the 1930s, however. Much of the New Deal program aimed at bringing the nation out of its economic crisis was built around cash grants.

Since then, Congress has set up hundreds of grants-in-aid programs. In fact, more than 500 are now in operation. Dozens of programs function in many different areas: in education, mass transit, highway construction, health care, on-the-job training, and many others.

Grants-in-aid are based on the National Government's taxing power. Article I, Section 8, Clause 1 in the Constitution gives Congress that power in order

❝ . . . to pay the debts, and provide for the common defence and general welfare . . . . ❞

Over time, most grants have been both categorical and conditional. That is, Congress has made them for certain closely defined purposes, and it has set certain conditions that the States must meet in order to receive them. Most often, the major "strings" attached to a grant have required a State to (1) use the federal funds only for the purpose specified, (2) make its own contribution, often of an equal amount, sometimes much less, (3) set up an agency and procedures to manage the grant, and (4) obey the federal guidelines for which the aid is given.

In effect, the grants-in-aid process blurs the division-of-powers line in the federal system. It permits the Federal Government to operate in many areas in which it would otherwise have no constitutional authority—for example, public education and mental health programs.

Critics have long made that point in opposition to grant programs. Many also object to the narrowly defined, or categorical, nature of most grants. They insist that those factors give Washington too much control over policy matters that, they claim, should be set at the State and local levels.

**Block Grants** To meet this latter objection, some categorical grants have been combined into larger programs. Congress has converted them into **block grants**. These are grants to State and local governments with more broadly defined purposes and fewer strings attached.

By the early 1980s, federal grants accounted for approximately 25 percent of all State and local governmental expenditures. But, beginning in 1981, the Reagan Administration pushed hard for two major changes here: (1) a sharp cutback in overall grant spending, and (2) the conversion of most grant programs from a categorical to a block-grant format. As a result, federal grant monies now account for less than 20 percent of total State and local spending.

**Revenue Sharing**   A different form of federal money aid, the revenue-sharing program, was in place from 1972 to 1987. Under that arrangement, Congress gave an annual share of the huge federal tax collection to the States and their cities, counties, and townships. Altogether, those "shared revenues" amounted to more than $83 billion over the years the program was in force.

The revenue-sharing program differed from the traditional grants-in-aid approach in a number of ways. Virtually no strings were attached to the money. The "shared revenues" could be spent very largely as the States and their local units chose to spend them.

Needless to say, revenue sharing was quite popular with and strongly supported by many governors, mayors, and other State and local officials. It was opposed by the Reagan Administration, however, and it fell victim to the financial needs of the deficit-ridden Federal Government.

**Other Forms of Federal Aid**   The Federal Government aids the States in several other important ways. Some of the many illustrations are well known—for example, the FBI's extensive help to State and local police. But many forms of aid are not nearly so visible—for example, "lulu payments." These are federal monies that go to local governments in those areas in which there are large federal landholdings. These direct payments are made in lieu of—to take the place of—the property taxes that those local governments cannot collect from the Federal Government.

Among many other examples: The army and the air force equip and train each State's National Guard units. The Census Bureau's data are essen-

tial to State and local school, housing, and transportation officials as they plan for the future.

**State Aid to the National Government**
Intergovernmental cooperation is a two-way street. That is, the States and their local units of government also aid the National Government in many ways. Thus, State and local election officials conduct national elections in each State. These elections are financed with State and local funds and are largely regulated by State laws.

The legal process by which aliens can become citizens, called naturalization, takes place most often in State, not federal, courts. Those who commit federal crimes and are sought by the FBI are often picked up by State and local police officers and then held in local jails. And the examples go on and on.

# Section 2 Review

**1. Define:** enabling act, act of admission, grants-in-aid program, block grant
**2.** (a) For what reason does the Constitution obligate the National Government to protect each State against foreign invasion? (b) Domestic violence?
**3.** In what sense does the Constitution require the National Government to respect the territorial integrity of each State?
**4.** (a) Who has the exclusive power to admit new States? (b) How does that process generally work?
**5.** (a) On what grounds do some people oppose federal grants-in-aid? (b) Support them?
**6.** What was the revenue-sharing program? What became of it?
**7.** In what ways do the States aid the National Government?

**Critical Thinking**

**8. Recognizing Ideologies** (p. 19) If the Framers were alive today, how do you think they would feel about a federal law that required several States to raise the legal drinking age in order to receive federal grants for highway construction?

★

## Should Congress Set a National Drinking Age?
### *South Dakota* v. *Dole*, 1986

Traffic accidents claim the lives of as many as 45,000 people in this country every year. Another 1.8 million Americans are injured, many of them severely, in motor vehicle accidents.

A number of other chilling statistics tell the story of motor vehicle mayhem: Of the more than 20,000 drunk drivers involved in fatal accidents each year, more than 3,000 are under 21 years of age.

Among the many steps, public and private, that have been taken to stem the nation's gruesome traffic toll, Congress passed the National Minimum Drinking Age Act of 1984. That law preempted each State's power to set a legal minimum drinking age. It did so by providing that any State that did not make 21 the legal drinking age would automatically lose tens of millions of dollars (up to 15 percent of its annual share) of federal highway funds.

Most of the 27 States targeted by the new law soon raised the drinking age; but some did not. One of them, South Dakota, sued the Secretary of Transportation, Elizabeth Dole, to prevent enforcement of the statute. South Dakota argued that the law was unconstitutional because its provisions violated Section 2 of the 21st Amendment. The State lost its argument in the federal district court, however, and so appealed to the United States Supreme Court.

*Review the following evidence and arguments presented to the United States Supreme Court:*

### Arguments for Secretary Dole

**1.** Congress passed the law as a proper exercise of its spending power, and it did so to promote the general welfare of the people of the United States.

**2.** The law is also a proper exercise of the commerce power. Its provisions reflect the nation's concern for safe interstate travel. The provision's relation to liquor is only incidental to creating and maintaining safe interstate highways.

**3.** The amount of federal money to be withheld from any State is comparatively small, and any State can forgo that money and set whatever drinking age it chooses.

### Arguments for South Dakota

**1.** Congress compromised the role and the powers of the States when it passed the National Minimum Drinking Age Act.

**2.** The law violates the 21st Amendment, which gives each State complete control over liquor within its borders. A concern for safe travel does not give the Federal Government the power to dictate a minimum drinking age.

**3.** The Federal Government's threat to withhold funds from the States amounts to nothing less than blackmail.

## Getting Involved

**1. Identify** the constitutional grounds on which each side based its arguments in this case.

**2. Debate** the opposing viewpoints presented in this case.

**3. Predict** how the Supreme Court ruled in this case and why. Now turn to page 769 in the Supreme Court Glossary to read the decision. Discuss the effect of the Court's ruling on future struggles between Federal and State governments.

# 3 Interstate Relations

**Find Out:**

■ How do several of the Constitution's provisions promote cooperation between and among the States?

**Key Terms:**

interstate compact, full faith and credit, extradition

You know that conflict among the States was a major reason for the adoption of the Constitution in 1789. The fact that the new document strengthened the hand of the National Government, especially in the field of commerce, lessened many of those interstate frictions. So, too, did several of the Constitution's provisions that deal directly with the States' relationships with one another. This section is concerned with those provisions.

## Interstate Compacts

No State can enter into any treaty, alliance, or confederation. The States may, however, with the consent of Congress, enter into **interstate compacts**—agreements among themselves and with foreign states.[17]

The States made only 26 compacts until 1920. Since then, however, and especially since the mid-1930s, they have been growing in number. New York and New Jersey led the way in 1921 with a compact creating the New York Port Authority to manage and develop the harbor facilities of that great metropolis.

---

[17]Article I, Section 10, Clause 3. The Supreme Court has held that congressional consent is not needed for compacts that do not "tend to increase the political power of the States," *Virginia* v. *Tennessee*, 1893. But it is often difficult to decide whether an agreement is political or nonpolitical. So, most interstate agreements are submitted to Congress as a matter of course.

▲ **Taming the Raging Colorado River**    The Glen Canyon Dam in Arizona is part of an extensive interstate compact that diverts the water of the river to 20 million people. Dams like this provide hydroelectricity for large areas.

Some 200 compacts are now in force, and many involve several States. In fact, all 50 States have joined in two of them: the Compact for the Supervision of Parolees and Probationers and the Compact on Juveniles. These compacts enable States to share important law-enforcement data. Other agreements, many with multi-State membership, cover a widening range of subjects. They include, for example, compacts designed to coordinate the development and conservation of such resources as water, oil, wildlife, and fish; forest fire protection; stream and harbor pollution; tax collections; motor vehicle safety; the licensing of drivers; and the cooperative use of public universities.

## Full Faith and Credit

The Constitution commands

❝Full faith and credit shall be given in each State to the public acts, records, and judicial proceedings of every other State.❞[18]

The words *public acts* refer to the laws of a State. *Records* refers to such documents as birth certificates, marriage licenses, deeds to property, car registrations, and the like. The words *judicial proceedings* relate to the outcome of court actions: judgments for debt, criminal convictions, divorce decrees, and so forth.

Suppose that a person dies in Baltimore and leaves a will disposing of some property in Chicago. The State of Illinois must give **full faith and credit** to—that is, respect the validity of—the proving of that will as a judicial proceeding of the State of Maryland. A person can prove age, place of birth, marital status, title to property, and similar facts by securing the necessary documents from the State where the record was made.

**Exceptions** The Full Faith and Credit Clause is regularly observed and usually operates in a routine way between and among the States. This rule has two exceptions, however. First, it applies only to civil, not criminal, matters. One State cannot enforce another State's criminal

law. Second, full faith and credit need not be given to certain divorces granted by one State to residents of another State.

On the second exception, the key question is always this: Was the person who obtained the divorce in fact a resident of the State that granted it? If so, the divorce will be accorded full faith and credit in other States. If not, then the State granting the divorce did not have the authority to do so and another State can refuse to recognize it.

The matter of interstate "quickie" divorces has been a troublesome one for years. It has been so especially since the Supreme Court's decision in a 1945 case, *Williams* v. *North Carolina*. In that case, a man and a woman had traveled to Nevada, where each wanted to obtain a divorce so they could marry each other. They lived in Las Vegas for six weeks, the minimum period of State residence required by Nevada's divorce law. The couple received their divorces, were married, and then immediately returned to North Carolina. But that State's authorities refused to recognize their Nevada divorces. North Carolina brought the couple to trial and a jury convicted each of them of the crime of bigamous cohabitation—marrying and living together while a previous marriage is still legally in effect.

On appeal, the Supreme Court upheld North Carolina's denial of full faith and credit to the Nevada divorces. It ruled that the couple had not in fact established *bona fide*—good faith, or valid—residence in Nevada. Rather, the Court held that through all of this the couple had remained legal residents of North Carolina. In short, the Court found that Nevada did not have the authority to grant them divorces.

A divorce granted by a State court to a *bona fide* resident of that State must be given full faith and credit in all other States. To become a legal resident of a State, a person must intend to reside there permanently, or at least indefinitely. Clearly, the Williamses had not intended to do so.

The *Williams* case, and later ones, cast dark clouds of doubt over the validity of thousands of other interstate divorces. The later marriages of persons involved in them, and the frequently

---

[18]Article IV, Section 1.

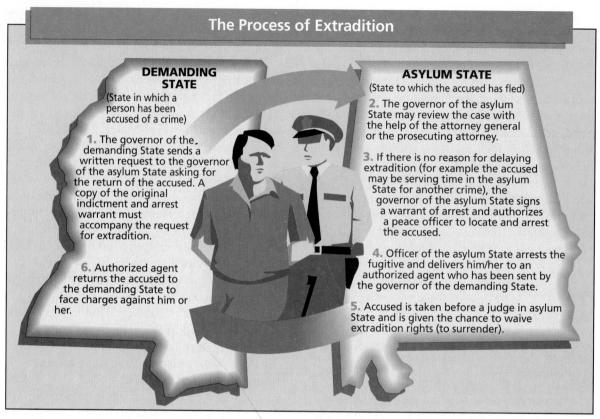

## The Process of Extradition

**DEMANDING STATE**
(State in which a person has been accused of a crime)

**1.** The governor of the demanding State sends a written request to the governor of the asylum State asking for the return of the accused. A copy of the original indictment and arrest warrant must accompany the request for extradition.

**6.** Authorized agent returns the accused to the demanding State to face charges against him or her.

**ASYLUM STATE**
(State to which the accused has fled)

**2.** The governor of the asylum State may review the case with the help of the attorney general or the prosecuting attorney.

**3.** If there is no reason for delaying extradition (for example the accused may be serving time in the asylum State for another crime), the governor of the asylum State signs a warrant of arrest and authorizes a peace officer to locate and arrest the accused.

**4.** Officer of the asylum State arrests the fugitive and delivers him/her to an authorized agent who has been sent by the governor of the demanding State.

**5.** Accused is taken before a judge in asylum State and is given the chance to waive extradition rights (to surrender).

▲ **Interpreting Charts**   When a person charged with a crime flees from one State to another, these steps are taken to bring the accused to face charges. Who is the "executive authority of the State" referred to in the Constitution?

tangled estate problems produced by their deaths, suggest the confused and serious nature of the matter.

## Extradition

### According to the Constitution

❝A person charged in any State with treason, felony, or other crime, who shall flee from justice, and be found in another State, shall, on demand of the executive authority of the State from which he fled, be delivered up, to be removed to the State having jurisdiction of the crime.❞ [19]

---

[19]Article IV, Section 2, Clause 2. Extradition has been carried on between sovereign states for centuries. The word *extradition* is the term popularly used in the United States for what is technically known in the law as interstate rendition.

**Extradition** is a legal process in which a fugitive from justice in a State is returned to that State from another. Extradition is designed to prevent a person from being able to escape justice by fleeing a State. The return of a fugitive from justice in a State is usually a routine matter; governors regularly approve the extradition requests they receive from other States' chief executives. Some of those requests are contested, however—especially in those cases with strong racial or political overtones, and in those increasingly frequent instances of parental kidnapping of children involved in custody disputes as a result of a divorce.

Until just a few years ago, governors could, and on occasion did, refuse to return fugitives. In *Kentucky* v. *Dennison*, 1861, the Supreme Court held that the Constitution did not give the Federal Government any power with which to compel a governor to act in an extradition case. So, for more than a century, the Constitution's word "shall" in the Extradition Clause had to be read as "may."

The Supreme Court overturned that ruling in 1987, however. In *Puerto Rico* v. *Branstad,* a unanimous Court held that the federal courts can indeed order an unwilling governor to extradite a fugitive.

## Privileges and Immunities

The Constitution provides:

“The citizens of each State shall be entitled to all privileges and immunities of citizens of the several States.”[20]

In short, this means that a resident of one State will not be discriminated against unreasonably by another State.

The courts have never handed down a full list of the privileges and immunities of "interstate citizenship." However, here is a partial list: the right to pass through or reside in any other State for the purpose of trade, agriculture, professional pursuits, or otherwise; the right to use the courts; the right to make contracts; the right to buy, own, rent, and sell property; and the right to marry.

Of course, the provision does not mean that a resident of one State need not obey the laws of another State while in that State. Nor does it mean that a State cannot reasonably discriminate against residents of other States. Thus, any State can require that a person live in that State for a certain period of time before he or she can vote or hold any public office. A State can also require a period of residence before it grants a person a license to practice law, medicine, dentistry, and so on.

In another example, the wild fish and game in a State are considered to be the common property of the people of that State. So, a State can require nonresidents to pay higher fees for fishing or hunting licenses than those paid by residents—who pay taxes to provide fish hatcheries,

▲ **Interstate Rights** The right to marry is one of the privileges each State is required to extend to citizens of any other State.

enforce game laws, and so on. By the same token, a State university often charges higher tuition to students from other States than it does to residents.

## Section 3 Review

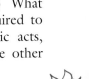

**1. Define:** interstate compacts, full faith and credit, extradition

**2.** What agreements does the Constitution prohibit the States from making?

**3.** (a) For what does the Full Faith and Credit Clause provide? (b) The Extradition Clause? (c) The Privileges and Immunities Clauses?

### Critical Thinking

**4. Predicting Consequences** (p. 19) What might result if each State was not required to give full faith and credit to the public acts, records, and judicial proceedings of the other States?

---

[20]Article IV, Section 2, Clause 1. The provision is reinforced in the 14th Amendment.

## Checking Consistency

Checking consistency means comparing two or more items or ideas and determining whether or not they agree with one another. Being able to check consistency can help you determine if your government is operating the way it was intended to, and if your leaders are living up to the promises they have made. Use the following steps to practice checking the consistency of the actions of your government.

**1. Identify the belief, principle, or rule that applies.** American government is ordered government; it has a clear set of rules that govern its behavior. The overriding statement of beliefs, goals, and principles for American government is the Constitution. Read the excerpts from the Constitution in Column A below. (a) What is the requirement that the Constitution makes in each excerpt? (b) How might you expect a person or organization to act in response to this constitutional requirement?

**2. Note the action taken by the official or governmental body.** Read the statements in Column B, which represent imaginary actions taken by government officials or organizations. For each action taken, answer the following questions. (a) What actions are being taken? (b) What are the likely consequences of this action? (c) What impact will this action have on citizens?

**3. Check for consistency between the action taken and the applicable belief, principle, and rule.** Each statement in Column A relates to the corresponding action in Column B. For each of the three examples, compare the expected or required behavior from Column A with the corresponding action taken in Column B. Ask yourself: (a) Did the action taken live up to your expectations from Column A? (b) If not, in what way is the action inconsistent with the requirement listed in Column A?

| Column A<br>Constitutional Requirement | Column B<br>Government Action |
| --- | --- |
| "Congress shall make no law respecting an establishment of religion, or prohibiting free exercise thereof."<br>—1st Amendment | Congress requires by law any territory wishing to become a State to adopt an official religion. |
| "Full faith and credit shall be given in each State to the public acts, records, and judicial proceedings of every other State."<br>—Article IV, Section 1 | A State requires all residents not married within State borders to obtain a State marriage license in order to be considered legally married. |
| "The judges in every State shall be bound [by the Constitution], anything in the constitution or laws of any State to the contrary notwithstanding."<br>—Article VI, Section 2 | A judge in a State court rules a State law denying residents the right to free speech to be unconstitutional. |

# Chapter-in-Brief

Scan all headings, photographs, charts, and other visuals in the chapter before reading the section summaries below.

## Section 1 Federalism and the Division of Powers (pp. 73–80)
There are two basic levels of government in the American federal system—national and State.

The National Government is one of delegated powers—powers specifically granted by the Constitution itself. The delegated powers are of three types: expressed, implied, and inherent.

The States are governments of reserved powers. That is, the Constitution reserves to the States those powers that the Constitution does not grant to the National Government and does not deny to the States.

The Framers expected conflict between the two basic levels of government, and so made the Constitution the nation's supreme law. The Supreme Court is the umpire in the federal system.

## Section 2 The National Government and the 50 States (pp. 80–86)
The Constitution obligates the National Government to ensure that each State has a republican form of government. Also, the National Government must protect the States against foreign invasion and against domestic violence. Thus, if a State cannot protect itself from internal disorder, the National Government may step in.

The Constitution also requires the National Government to respect the territorial integrity of the States. For example, Congress may not create a new State out of an existing one without the existing State's consent.

Congress has the power to admit new States. Usually, the prospective State petitions Congress, which then passes an enabling act. This act directs the prospective State to draft a constitution. If voters approve of the constitution, and Congress still agrees to Statehood, Congress must then pass an act of admission. With the President's signature, the act creates a new State.

Congress can place conditions on the admission of a prospective State. For example, Congress required Utah to outlaw polygamy before admission. However, Congress cannot make requirements that compromise a State's right to manage its own internal affairs.

The National Government provides financial assistance to the States. Grants-in-aid programs are a major example of this help. Grants take two forms: categorical or block. Block grants generally involve fewer requirements States must satisfy to receive the monies.

States provide numerous services to the National Government, as well. For example, States administer national elections and assist federal law-enforcement efforts.

## Section 3 Interstate Relations (pp. 88–91)
The States cannot enter into treaties, alliances, or confederations. However, they can form interstate compacts—agreements among themselves and with foreign states. These compacts enable States to cooperate on matters of mutual concern.

The Constitution requires each State to give full faith and credit to—respect the validity of—the laws, official records, and court actions of other States. The obligation applies only to civil matters.

The Constitution also requires each State to return fugitives from justice to the State from which they fled.

# Chapter Review

## Vocabulary and Key Terms

federalism (p. 74)
division of powers (p. 74)
delegated powers (p. 75)
expressed powers (p. 75)
implied powers (p. 75)
inherent powers (p. 75)

reserved powers (p. 77)
exclusive powers (p. 78)
concurrent powers (p. 78)
enabling act (p. 83)
act of admission (p. 83)
grants-in-aid program (p. 84)

block grant (p. 85)
interstate compact (p. 88)
full faith and credit (p. 89)
extradition (p. 90)

**Matching:** *Review the key terms in the list above. If you are not sure of a term's meaning, look up the term and review its definition. Choose a term from the list above that best matches each description.*

1. those powers granted by the Constitution to the National Government in so many words
2. congressional measure admitting a United States territory into the Union as a State
3. a type of federal grants-in-aid; monies from which are to be used in a particular but broadly defined area
4. a system of government in which a constitution divides the powers of government on a territorial basis
5. those powers that belong to the National Government because it is the national government of a sovereign state
6. those powers of the National Government that are necessary and proper to the exercise of the expressed powers
7. agreements made by States among themselves and with foreign states

**True or False:** *Determine whether each statement is true or false. If it is true, write "true." If it is false, change the underlined word or words to make the statement true.*

1. <u>Reserved powers</u> are those powers held by the States in the federal system.
2. <u>Delegated powers</u> are those powers granted to the National Government in the Constitution.

3. Some people have questioned whether or not <u>block grants</u> give the federal government too much say in matters of State and local concern.
4. Congress directs an area desiring State-hood to frame a proposed State constitution in an <u>act of admission</u>.
5. Those powers that can only be exercised by the National Government are called <u>exclusive powers</u>.

**Word Relationships:** *Three of the terms in each of the following sets of terms are related. Choose the term that does not belong and explain why it does not belong.*

1. (a) expressed powers (b) division of powers (c) implied powers (d) inherent powers
2. (a) act of admission (b) extradition (c) interstate compact (d) full faith and credit
3. (a) federalism (b) division of powers (c) grants-in-aid program (d) full faith and credit

## Main Ideas

### Section 1 (pp. 73–80)
1. How did the principle of federalism enable the Framers to solve the problems they faced at the Constitutional Convention?
2. Briefly describe the powers of the National Government under the Constitution.
3. Briefly describe the powers of the States under the Constitution.

**4.** What is the role of the Constitution and the Supreme Court in the federal system?

## Section 2 (pp. 80–86)

**5.** According to the Constitution, what must the National Government provide to the States?

**6.** Outline the role of Congress in admitting new States to the Union.

**7.** What is cooperative federalism?

**8.** Give some examples of cooperative federalism at work in the United States.

## Section 3 (pp. 88–91)

**9.** In what two general ways did the Constitution resolve some of the interstate conflicts experienced under the Articles of Confederation?

**10.** What specific provisions does the Constitution include to encourage cooperation among the States?

**11.** Under what circumstances can a State deny another State full faith and credit?

## Critical Thinking

**1. Drawing Conclusions** (p. 19)   For what reason might a governor of a State be reluctant to call for federal troops in the event that violence breaks out in a city in his or her State?

**2. Identifying Central Issues** (p. 19)   (a) Would the United States be better off if there were not as much variety in the laws and customs of different States? (b) Does the fact that different States have different laws lead to unfairness and inequality in the overall legal system?

**3. Determining Relevance** (p. 19)   As you read in this chapter, before a new State can be admitted into the Union, Congress must approve its constitution. Do you think Congress should have this power over the internal affairs and government of a State? Give reasons for your answer.

## Getting Involved

**1. Writing Your Opinion**   Write a letter to a friend, relative, or acquaintance who lives in another State, explaining some of the features that you feel make your State unique among the 50 States. Start by making a list of some of the features of your State that you like and dislike. Consider such factors as the weather, location, the businesses and industries commonly found there, unusual holidays, and the type of people who live there. Also consider the history of the State and any noteworthy current events that have taken place in your State. Next try to identify those features of your State that are not commonly associated with any of the other States. As you write the first draft of your letter, strive to make a convincing argument that your State has a distinct character. Finally, proofread the letter, correct any errors, and make a final copy.

**2. Class Debate**   Hold a debate on one of the following topics: (a) *Resolved,* That the Supreme Court of the United States be denied the power to declare any form of State law unconstitutional; (b) *Resolved,* That grants-in-aid programs undermine the federal system and reduce the power and importance of the States. Choose one team to debate each side of the topic you select. The rest of the class can evaluate each team's presentation.

**3. Gathering Information**   (a) Using the Government Resources Handbook on page 690 of your textbook, identify what sources you could use to find out about a grants-in-aid program recently passed by the National Government. (b) What sources might you consult to find the address of a government agency that could provide information about the grants?

# UNIT

## 2

**Rallying Round Their Candidate**   Government by the people was at work when independent Ross Perot's (left) supporters campaigned vigorously to place him on the ballot in all 50 States.

# Political Behavior: Government by the People

On the morning of November 3, 1948, the day after the presidential election, the *Chicago Tribune* carried this bold headline: "Dewey Defeats Truman." That headline ranks as one of the all-time bloopers in American history—for, in fact, incumbent President Harry Truman defeated Thomas E. Dewey of New York by nearly three million votes.

The next five chapters focus on American politics. In particular, you will read about political parties and the two-party system, the election process and voter behavior, public opinion, the mass media, and interest groups. You will learn that today most of what we know about politics comes from television. Before television, most of what most Americans knew about politics came from newspapers. The news media are usually reliable sources of political information. But, as the *Tribune's* famous miscue should remind you. . . . Read on.

## DID YOU KNOW THAT . . .

- In 1992, at least four presidential candidates were listed on the ballots in all States; voters in Iowa, Tennessee, and Wisconsin chose from among 14 presidential candidacies.

- Television broadcast its first coverage of a presidential election in 1932.

- Young people between the ages of 18 and 21 are statistically the least likely to vote.

# CHAPTER 5

# Political Parties

## Chapter Preview

Do you recognize this name: Andre Marrou? How about Lenora Fulani? James "Bo" Gritz? Each of them was the presidential candidate of a political party in 1992. Mr. Marrou was the Libertarian party nominee; Dr. Fulani headed the New Alliance party's ticket; and Colonel Gritz was the Populist party's candidate.

Political parties are one of the major vehicles of popular participation in the American political system. Except at the local level, nearly every candidate who runs for public office is nominated by a political party. As you will read in this chapter, their nature and function and the roles they play in American politics are a major reason why government in the United States is, in fact, "government by the people."

### Before you read this chapter:

- **Describe** any evidence of the presence of political parties that you have seen in your community.
- **Predict** both the short- and the long-term future of the two-party system in the United States.

### As you read, focus on the main objective for each section. Understand:

1. The nature and functions of parties in American politics.
2. The reasons for the existence of the American two-party system.
3. The evolution of American political parties.
4. The nature and role of minor parties in American politics.
5. The organizational structure and composition of the two major parties.

▲ **Campaign Fever** Without the support of thousands of enthusiastic voters, political parties in the United States would have faded away long ago. Voters rally to the party that best expresses their ideas about the nation's future.

# 1 Parties and What They Do

**Find Out:**
- What is a political party?
- What do political parties do?

**Key Terms:**
political party, major parties, coalition

"Winning isn't everything, it's the only thing." So said legendary football coach Vince Lombardi. Lombardi was talking about his NFL teams. But those words could also be used to describe the Republican and Democratic parties. They, too, are in the business of winning.

In this section, you will look at political parties—what they are and what they do in the American political system.

## What Is a Party?

A **political party** can be defined as a group of persons who seek to control government through the winning of elections and the holding of public office. This definition of a political party is a broad one, and it will fit any political party—including the two major parties in American politics.

Another, more specific definition can be used to describe *most* political parties, both here and abroad: a group of persons, joined together on the basis of certain common principles, who seek to control government in order to bring about the adoption of certain public policies and programs.

But this definition, with its emphasis on principles and public policy positions, will not fit the two **major parties**, the dominant political parties in the United States. The Republican and Democratic parties are not primarily principle- or issue-oriented. They are, instead, *election*-oriented.

In other words, neither the Republicans nor the Democrats can be properly described as a group of like-minded persons who regularly agree with one another on public questions. To illustrate the point, compare the public policy positions taken by various leading Republicans or Democrats. Senators Phil Gramm of Texas and Mark Hatfield of Oregon are both Republicans. Yet they often disagree on important issues and take opposing sides in the Senate. So, too, do such other Republicans as Jesse Helms of North Carolina and William Cohen of Maine, and Orrin Hatch of Utah and Nancy Kassebaum of Kansas. Much the same can be said of many Democrats—for example, Senators Edward Kennedy of Massachusetts and Wendell Ford of Kentucky, or Daniel Moynihan of New York and Sam Nunn of Georgia.

Again, neither of the two major parties is made up of persons who are all of one mind in politics. Instead, each party is a **coalition**—a union of many persons of diverse interests—who have joined together to try to get candidates elected to public office. Each of them includes within its ranks a substantial share of nearly every economic, racial, religious, regional, and ideological grouping that exists in this country.

## What Do Parties Do?

It is clear from American history, and the histories of other people, as well, that political parties are essential to democratic government. Parties are the major mechanisms that develop broad policy and leadership choices and that then present those options to the people.

Political parties are a vital link between the people and their government, between the governed and those who govern. Many argue that they are the principal means by which the will of the people is made known to government and by which government is held accountable to the people.

Parties serve the democratic ideal in another important way. They work to blunt conflict; they are "power brokers." They bring conflicting groups together. They modify and compromise the contending views of different interests and groups, and so help to unify the people.

They soften the impact of extremists at both ends of the political spectrum.

Again, political parties are indispensable to American government. This fact can be underscored by a look at the major functions they perform.

**The Nominating Function** The major function of a political party is to nominate, to name, candidates for public office. That is, the parties select candidates and then present them to the voters.

There must be some way to find—some way to recruit and choose—those candidates. And there must also be some way to gather support (votes) for them. Parties are the best device yet found to do those jobs.

The nominating function is almost exclusively a party function in this country.[1] It is the one particular activity that most clearly sets political parties apart from all of the other groups operating in politics.[2]

**The Informer-Stimulator Function** Parties inform the people and stimulate their interest and participation in public affairs. Other groups also perform this function—in particular, the news media and interest groups.

Parties try to inform and stimulate votes in several ways. Most of all, they campaign for their candidates, take stands on issues, and criticize the candidates and stands of their opponents.

Each party tries to inform the people as it thinks they should be informed—to the party's advantage. It conducts its "educational" process through pamphlets, signs, buttons, and stickers; with advertisements in newspapers and magazines and on radio and television; in speeches, rallies, and conventions; and in many other ways.

Remember, both parties want to win elections, and that consideration has much to do with the positions they take on most issues.

---

[1]The exceptions are in nonpartisan elections and in those rare instances in which an independent candidate enters a partisan contest. Nominations are covered at length in Chapter 7.

[2]Including, most especially, the many kinds of interest groups (special interest organizations) described in Chapter 9.

THE·ADMINISTRATION'S  PROMISES HAVE BEEN KEPT

1896  1900

Gone Democratic.  Gone Republican.

BANK

A run on the Bank  A run to the Bank

THE
AMERICAN FLAG
HAS NOT BEEN PLANTED IN FOREIGN SOIL
TO ACQUIRE MORE TERRITORY
BUT FOR
HUMANITY'S SAKE"

Spanish Rule in Cuba.  American Rule in Cuba.

(McKINLEY, JULY 12, 1900.)

▲ **Winning Republican Votes**   This 1900 campaign poster uses powerful imagery to win Republican votes. What does it say about what the Republican party stood for and what it opposed in that election year?

Both parties try to shape stands that will attract as many voters as possible—and that will, at the same time, offend as few as possible.

**The "Seal of Approval" Function**   A party grants seals of approval, so to speak, to its candidates. It serves, in a sense, as a "bonding agent" to ensure the good performance of its candidates and officeholders. In choosing its candidates, the party tries to see that they are men and women who are both qualified and of good character—or, at least, that they are not unqualified and that they have no serious blemishes on their records. The party also prompts its successful candidates to perform well in office. The democratic process imposes this bonding agent function on a party, whether it really wants to perform it or not. If it fails to do so, both the party and its candidates may suffer the consequences in future elections.

**The Governmental Function**   In several respects, government in the United States can be correctly described as government by party. For example, public officeholders—those who govern—are regularly chosen on the basis of party. Congress and the State legislatures conduct much of their business on a partisan basis. Most appointments to executive offices, both federal and State, are also made on the basis of party—so much so that the party in control of the legislature has some influence on the work it performs.

In yet another sense, parties provide a basis for the conduct of government. Under the system of separation of powers, the party is usually the major agent through which the executive and legislative branches cooperate with one another. For example, a President of one party knows he can usually count on the support of his party members in Congress and so acts accordingly.

Also, remember the discussion of constitutional change by informal amendment in Chapter 3. Political parties have played a large part in that process. As a leading illustration of that fact, the Constitution's cumbersome system of electing the President works principally because political parties reshaped it in its early years and have made it work ever since.

**The Watchdog Function** Parties act as watchdogs over the conduct of the public's business. This is particularly the function of the party out of power. It plays this role as it criticizes the policies and behavior of the party in power.[3] In effect, the party out of power attempts to convince the voters that they should "throw the rascals out," that the "outs" should become the "ins" and the "ins" the "outs." Its attacks tend to make the rascals more careful of their public charge and more responsive to the wishes and concerns of the people. In short, the party out of power plays the important role of "the loyal opposition."

## Section 1 Review

1. **Define:** political party, major parties, coalition
2. What pivotal role do parties play in democratic government?
3. What are the most important functions performed by parties in American politics?

**Critical Thinking**

4. **Identifying Central Issues** (p. 19) Clinton Rossiter once noted, "No America without democracy, no democracy without politics, no politics without parties, no parties without compromise and moderation. . ." Explain your understanding of this statement using information from the section.

---

[3]In American politics the "party in power" is the party that controls the executive branch—i.e., the presidency at the national level, or the governorship at the State level.

# 2 The Two-Party System

**Find Out:**

■ For what reasons does the United States have a two-party system?
■ What are multiparty and one-party systems?
■ What is the nature of party membership?

**Key Terms:**

minor party, two-party system, single-member district, plurality, pluralistic society, consensus, multiparty, one-party system

Do you know who Earl Dodge is? Probably not. Yet, Mr. Dodge was the Prohibition party's candidate for President in 1984, 1988, and 1992; and he is his party's presidential nominee again for 1996.

One of the reasons why Mr. Dodge is not very well known is that he belongs to a **minor party**, one of the less widely supported parties in the political system. The two major parties dominate American politics. That is to say, this country has a **two-party system**. In a typical election, only the Republican or the Democratic party's candidates have a reasonable chance of winning public office.

In this section, you will examine the factors that have produced the American two-party system.

## Reasons for the Two-Party System

In some States, and in many local communities, one of the two major parties may be overwhelmingly dominant, and for a long period of time—as, for example, the Democrats were throughout the South for decades. But, on the whole, and through most of history, the United States has been a two-party nation.

A number of factors help to explain why America has and continues to have a two-party system. No one reason, taken alone, offers a wholly satisfactory explanation for the phenomenon. But, taken together, several do stand as a quite persuasive answer.

**The Historical Basis** The two-party system is rooted in the beginnings of the nation itself. The Framers of the Constitution were opposed to political parties. As you read in Chapter 2, however, the ratification of the Constitution saw the birth of America's first two parties: the Federalists, led by Alexander Hamilton, and the Anti-Federalists, who followed Thomas Jefferson.[4] In short, the American party system began as a two-party system.

**The Force of Tradition** Once established, human institutions are likely to become self-perpetuating—and so it has been with the two-party system. The very fact that the nation began with a two-party system has been a leading reason for its retention, and it has become over time an increasingly important, self-reinforcing reason.

The point can be made this way: Most Americans accept the idea of a two-party system simply because there has always been one. This inbred support for the arrangement is a principal reason why challenges to it have made so little headway in the nation's politics. In other words, America has a two-party system because America has a two-party system.

**The Electoral System** Several features of the American electoral system tend to promote the existence of but two major parties. That is to say, the basic shape, and many of the details, of the election process work in that direction.

---

[4]The Framers hoped to create a unified country; they sought to bring order out of the chaos of the Critical Period of the 1780s. To most of them, parties were "factions," agents of divisiveness and disunity. George Washington reflected this view when, in his Farewell Address in 1796, he warned the new nation against "the baneful effect of the spirit of party." In this light, it is hardly surprising that the Constitution made no provision for political parties. The Framers could not foresee the ways in which the governmental system they set up would develop. Thus, they could not possibly know that two major parties would emerge as prime instruments of government in the United States. Nor could they know that those two major parties would tend to be moderate, to choose middle-of-the-road positions, and so help to unify rather than divide the nation.

### On Political Parties in the 1990s

**Jack F. Kemp,** Secretary of Housing and Urban Development under the Bush administration

❝ Democrats today are beginning to think more in terms of utilizing the private sector and Republicans are now talking about seeking solutions to some of the social and economic problems of poverty. All too long in the past the Democratic Party has simply thought of redistributing wealth, and the Republican Party has had a kind of *laissez-faire* attitude . . . . But I think there are leaders and thinkers in both parties who want to come and find *el otro sendero*, another path. ❞

The single-member district arrangement is among the most prominent of these features. Nearly all of the elections held in this country—from the presidential contest on down to those at the most local of levels—are **single-member district** elections. That is, they are contests in which only one candidate from the district is elected to each office on the ballot. They are winner-take-all elections; the winning candidate is the one who receives a **plurality**—the largest number of votes cast for the office. Note that a plurality need not be a majority, which is more than half of all votes cast.

The single-member district pattern works to discourage minor parties. Because only one winner can come out of each contest, voters usually face only two viable choices: They can vote for the candidate of the party holding the office, or they can vote for the candidate of the party with the best chance of replacing the incumbent. In short, most voters think of a vote for a minor party candidate as a "wasted" one.

Another important aspect of the electoral system works to the same end. Much of American election law is purposely written to discourage non-major party candidates.[5] Or, to put this the other way, American election law is deliberately shaped to preserve, protect, and defend the two-party system. Thus, for example, in most States it is far more difficult for both minor parties and independent groups to nominate their candidates—get them listed on the ballot—than it is for the major parties to do so.

The 1992 presidential election offered a striking illustration of the point. Both George Bush and Bill Clinton were on the ballot in all 50 States and the District of Columbia. But of the dozen or more other serious presidential hopefuls, only two were also listed everywhere: only the independent, Ross Perot, and the Libertarian nominee, Andre Marrou.

To this point, non-major party candidates have been able to make it to the ballot everywhere only five times. Eugene V. Debs of the Socialist party was the first to do so, in 1912. The Socialist party's candidate in 1916, Allan L. Benson, also appeared on the ballots of all of the then 48 States. In 1980 two non-major party candidates were listed everywhere: Ed Clark, the Libertarian party's nominee, and John Anderson, who ran as an independent that year. And in 1988 the New Alliance party's candidate, Lenora Fulani, was on the ballots of all 50 States and the District of Columbia.

In 1992 Dr. Fulani also did far better than minor party nominees usually do: she made it to the ballots of 40 States and the District of Columbia. But the other minor party candidates suffered their usual fate in 1992; most of them

▲ **Minor Parties**    The Prohibition party has worked since 1869 to outlaw the manufacture, sale, or consumption of alcoholic beverages in this country.

were able to gain the ballot in only a handful of the States.

## The American Ideological Consensus

Americans are, on the whole, an ideologically homogeneous people. That is, over time, the American people have shared much the same ideals, the same basic principles, and the same patterns of belief. This is not to say that we are all alike. Clearly, this is not the case. The United States is a **pluralistic society**—one consisting of several distinct cultures and groups. Increasingly, the members of various ethnic, racial, religious, and other social groups compete for and share in the exercise of political power in this country. Still, there is a broad **consensus**—a general agreement among various groups—on fundamental matters.

Nor is this to say that Americans have always agreed with one another in all matters. Far from it. The nation has been deeply divided at times: during the Civil War and in the years of the Great Depression, for example; and over such critical issues as racial discrimination and the war in Vietnam.

However, the nation has not been regularly plagued by sharp cleavages in politics. America has been free of long-standing, bitter disputes based on such factors as economic class, social status, religious beliefs, or national origins.

Those conditions that could produce several strong rival parties simply do not exist in this

---

[5]Nearly all election law in this country is State, not federal, law—a point discussed at length in the next two chapters. But, here, note this very important point: Nearly all of the close to 7,500 State legislators—nearly all of those persons who make State law—are either Democrats or Republicans. Only a handful of minor party members or independents now sit, or have ever sat, in State legislatures.

country, unlike the situation in most other democracies. In short, the realities of American society and politics simply will not permit more than two major parties.

This ideological consensus has had another very important impact on American parties. It has given the nation two major parties that look very much alike. Both tend to be moderate. Both are built on compromise and regularly try to occupy "the middle of the road."

Both parties seek the same prize: the votes of a majority of the voters. To do so, they must woo essentially the same people. Inevitably, each party takes policy stands much like those taken by the other. Often, and for very good reason, the competition between them becomes a struggle between competing political personalities rather than ideas.

## Multiparty Systems

Some critics argue that the American two-party system should be scrapped. They would replace it with a **multiparty** arrangement, a system in which several major and many lesser parties exist. That arrangement exists in most European democracies today.

In the typical multiparty system, the various parties are each based on some particular interest, such as economic class, religious belief, sectional attachment, or political ideology. Those who favor such an arrangement here say that it would be more representative and more responsive to the will of the people. They insist that a multiparty system would give voters a real choice among candidates and policy alternatives.

The practical effect of two of the factors just noted—single-member districts and the American ideological consensus—seems to make such an arrangement impossible, however. Beyond that, a multiparty system tends to produce instability in government. One party is often unable to win the support of a majority of the voters. As a result, the power to govern must be shared by a number of parties, in a coalition. Several of the multiparty nations of Western Europe have long been plagued by governmental crises. They have experienced frequent shifts

in party control as coalitions shift and dissolve. Italy furnishes an almost nightmarish example: It has had a new government on the average of once every nine months since the end of World War II.

## One-Party Systems

In nearly all dictatorships today, only one political party—the party of the ruling clique—is allowed. For all practical purposes, it is quite accurate to say that in those circumstances the resulting **one-party system** is really a "no-party" system.

### How to Discover Your Political Roots

To discover how you have been "socialized to politics," ask yourself the following questions.

**1. Early Political Events** What is the first political event you can remember? How did the adults in your household react?

**2. Family Discussions** Do you talk about politics and public policies at home with your family? How often?

**3. Participation in Your Household** Are any of the adult members of your family politically active? To which of the major parties, if either of them, do the adults in your household belong?

**4. Outside Influences** What other persons have had some influence on your political views? What impact has school had on your views? Television? Newspapers? Other media?

**5. Peer Influence** Are any of your friends interested in politics? If so, do you discuss your views with them? Do they influence your views?

**6. Personal Views** How would you describe your feeling about politics today? Are you a Republican, a Democrat, an independent or in favor of a minor party's policies? Why?

▲ **Interpreting Charts** After studying the various ways to discover your political roots, name one or two other possibilities that are not on the chart.

In quite another sense, several States and many local areas in this country were, and many can still be, described in one-party terms. Until the late 1950s, the Democrats dominated the politics of the South. The Republican party was almost always the winner in New England and in the upper Middle West.

But effective two-party competition has spread fairly rapidly in the past 25 years or so. Democrats have won many offices in every northern State. Republican candidates have become more and more successful throughout the once "Solid South."[6]

## Membership of the Parties

Membership in a party is purely voluntary. A person is a Republican or a Democrat, or belongs to a minor party or is an independent, because that is what he or she chooses to be.[7]

Remember, the two major parties are broadly based. In order to gain more votes than their opponents, they must attract as much support as they possibly can. Each party has always been composed, in greater or lesser degree, of a cross section of the nation's population. Each is made up of Protestants, Catholics, and Jews; whites,

---

[6]Nevertheless, about a third of the States can still be said to have a modified one-party system. That is, one of the major parties regularly wins most elections in those States. Also, while most States have vigorous two-party competition at the Statewide level, within them are many locales dominated by one party.

[7]In most States a person must declare a preference for a particular party in order to vote in that party's primary election. That declaration is usually made as a part of the voter registration process, and it is often said to make one "a registered Republican (or Democrat)." The requirement is only a procedural one, however, and wholly a matter of individual choice.

"And I promise to always be loyal to my party, even if I have to change parties to do it!"

*Dunagin's People by Ralph Dunagin. Reprinted with special permission of NAS, Inc.*

▲ **Interpreting Photos and Political Cartoons**   Political candidates try to attract as much support from as many groups as they can—thus this photo showing Republican George Bush with traditionally Democratic law enforcement officers. How does the cartoon reinforce this concept?

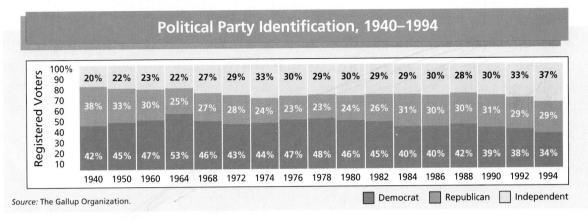

**Political Party Identification, 1940–1994**

| Registered Voters | 1940 | 1950 | 1960 | 1964 | 1968 | 1972 | 1974 | 1976 | 1978 | 1980 | 1982 | 1984 | 1986 | 1988 | 1990 | 1992 | 1994 |
|---|---|---|---|---|---|---|---|---|---|---|---|---|---|---|---|---|---|
| Independent | 20% | 22% | 23% | 22% | 27% | 29% | 33% | 30% | 29% | 30% | 29% | 29% | 30% | 28% | 30% | 33% | 37% |
| Republican | 38% | 33% | 30% | 25% | 27% | 28% | 24% | 23% | 23% | 24% | 26% | 31% | 30% | 30% | 31% | 29% | 29% |
| Democrat | 42% | 45% | 47% | 53% | 46% | 43% | 44% | 47% | 48% | 46% | 45% | 40% | 40% | 42% | 39% | 38% | 34% |

*Source:* The Gallup Organization.

■ Democrat   ■ Republican   □ Independent

▲ **Interpreting Graphs**   This graph shows the percentage of voters who identify with the two major parties, and the percentage of Independents. Which group shows the biggest gain in support between 1940 and 1994?

African Americans, Hispanics, and other minorities; professionals, farmers, and union members. Each numbers the young, the middle-aged, and the elderly; city-dwellers, suburbanites, and rural residents among its members.

It is true that the members of certain segments of the electorate tend to align themselves more solidly with one or the other of the major parties, at least for a time. Thus, in recent decades, African Americans, Catholics and Jews, and union members have voted more often for Democrats. In the same way, white males, Protestants, and the business community have been inclined to back the GOP.[8] Yet, never have all members of any group tied themselves permanently to either party.

Individuals identify themselves with a party for many reasons. Family is almost certainly the most important among them. Studies show that nearly two out of every three Americans follow the party allegiance of their parents.

Major events can also have a decided influence on party choice. Of these, the Civil War and the Depression of the 1930s have been the most significant in American political history.

Economic status also influences party choice, although generalizations are quite risky. Clearly, though, those in higher income groups are more likely to be Republicans, while those with lower incomes tend to be Democrats.

Several other factors also feed into the mix of both party choice and voting behavior—including age, place of residence, level of education, and the work environment. Some of those factors may conflict with one another in the case of any individual—and they often do.

You will read more about the matter of partisan preference and voting behavior in later chapters.

## Section 2 Review

1. **Define:** minor party, two-party system, single-member district, plurality, pluralistic society, consensus
2. What four factors help to explain the existence of America's two-party system?
3. (a) What is a multiparty system? (b) A one-party system?
4. For what reasons does each party represent a cross section of the American population?

**Critical Thinking**

5. **Identifying Alternatives** (p. 19) Imagine that you are a campaign official for one of the two major parties. Think of a slogan that your party's candidate can use to appeal to large numbers of voters.

---

[8]GOP is common shorthand for the Republican party. The initials stand for Grand Old Party, a nickname acquired in the latter part of the last century.

★

## Tackling Politics

**M**easured by age group, the lowest rate of voter turnout in American elections is found in the youngest age bracket—that is, among those who are 18 to 21 years of age. That sad fact was true in 1992, and it has been true in every election since the 26th Amendment was ratified in 1971.

Yet, over time, many young people have discovered that they can play important roles in the political arena. Here are but a few examples.

### Students Take Action

Richard Taylor first got involved in politics at age 14, when he ran a successful campaign to establish a student seat on the Louisiana State Board of Education. Richard and some of his friends had mounted that effort soon after he had been elected governor by the Youth Legislature, at the Louisiana Boys State meeting in Baton Rouge. Three years later, at age 17 and just out of high school, Richard was elected as one of his State's 76 delegates to the 1988 Democratic National Convention in Atlanta. He had to defeat a number of older Democrats, including some elected officials, to win that post.

After Atlanta, Richard worked as a volunteer in the Dukakis campaign in Louisiana. He has urged other young people to become involved in the political process, putting it this way: "It's your future. So why let someone else determine your destiny? You can play a significant role in determining it yourself."

Doris Wart, also from Louisiana, first became interested in politics at age 13, when she visited the Soviet Union. She found the Soviet government and lifestyle oppressive and began to appreciate the American political system. When she got home, she worked for the local Republican party. At 19, she founded a Young Republicans Club at Louisiana State University, and she was elected an alternate delegate to the 1988 Republican National Convention in New Orleans.

Doris sometimes thinks about what it would be like to be the first woman to be elected President. For now, she is active in persuading high school and college students to register and vote; she says her current goal is to become a member of the U.S. House of Representatives.

### Not Just for Future Presidents

Thousands of young people across the country are involved in politics. Steve Densley, an 18-year-old political activist in Utah, says this: "I could have listened to all of the people who told me I was too young to make a difference in politics. But I knew better. Don't let anyone tell you you can't do it, because I've learned . . . that you can."

Johnny Martines, a 17-year-old in Georgia, offers the same advice, and he has directed it to high schoolers all across the country: "Don't worry if you're too young to vote. It's incredible how much one volunteer can do."

## Getting Involved

**1. Identify** an organization involved in national, State, or local politics in which you think you would like to be involved.

**2. Formulate** a plan to become involved in that group and identify those resources that could help you implement that plan.

**3. Predict** what you could accomplish by becoming involved in the work of that organization.

# 3 The Two-Party System in American History

**Find Out:**

- How have political parties developed during the history of this country?
- Which two American political parties have dominated the nation's politics for more than 125 years?

**Key Term:**

electorate

Henry Ford, the great automaker, once said that all history is "bunk." Ford knew a great deal about automobiles and mass production, and much else. But he did not know much about history or its importance.

Listen, instead, to Shakespeare: "The past is prologue." Today is the product of yesterday. You are what you are today because of your history. The more you know about your past, the better prepared you are for today, and for tomorrow.

Much the same can be said about the two-party system in American politics. The more you know about its past, the better you understand its workings today.

In this section, you will take a look at the development of political parties in American history.

## The Nation's First Parties

The beginnings of the American two-party system can be traced to the battle over the ratification of the Constitution. The conflicts of the time, centering on the proper form and role of government in the United States, were not stilled by the adoption of the work of the Framers at the Philadelphia Convention. Rather, those conflicts were carried over into the early years of the Republic, and they led directly to the formation of the nation's first full-blown political parties.

## Political Party Sources

### Political Party Sources

| 🐘 Republican Party | 🐴 Democratic Party |
|---|---|
| 310 First St. SE | 430 So. Capitol St. SE |
| Washington, DC 20003 | Washington, DC 20003 |

### Other Party Organizations

**American Party of the United States** (Founded, 1969)
P.O. Box 597, Provo, Utah 84603

Present-day descendant of the party born with George Wallace's presidential candidacy in 1968.

**The Libertarian Party** (Founded, 1971)
1528 Pennsylvania Ave. SE, Washington, DC 20003

Stresses individual liberty, opposes taxes, foreign involvements, and government intrusion into private lives.

**Prohibition National Committee** (Founded, 1869)
P.O. Box 2635, Denver, Colorado 80201

Sought the presidency in every election since 1869. Advocates a nationwide prohibition of the manufacture, distribution, and sale of alcoholic beverages.

**The Socialist Labor Party** (Founded, 1876)
(In Minnesota: Industrial Government Party)
914 Industrial Ave., Palo Alto CA 94303

Seeks the peaceful abolition of capitalism, backed by an industrial organization.

**The Socialist Party, USA** (Founded, 1901)
516 West 25th St., New York, N.Y. 10001

The most moderate of the several American socialist parties.

**The Socialist Workers Party** (Founded, 1938)
406 West St., New York, N.Y. 10014

Stresses issues of feminism, racism, and economic revolution.

**The Workers World Party** (Founded, 1959)
46 West 21st St., New York, N.Y. 10010

Dedicated to a program of "determined struggle against the bosses, bankers, and landlords."

**The Communist Party USA** (Founded, 1919)
235 West 23rd St., New York, N.Y. 10011

Terms itself "the Party of the American working class." Looks forward to the restructuring of American political and economic systems.

**USA Green Party** (Founded, 1972)
P.O. Box 30208, Kansas City, MO 64112

This party opposes nuclear weapons and promotes environmental concerns with the slogan: "We do not inherit the earth from our parents, we borrow it from our children."

▲ **Interpreting Charts** Only the largest minor parties are shown here. Which party shown has the narrowest political platform?

The Federalist party was the first to appear. It formed around Alexander Hamilton, who served as secretary of the treasury in the new government organized by George Washington. The Federalists were, by and large, the party of "the rich and the well-born." Most of them had supported the Constitution. Now, led by Hamilton, they worked to make a stronger national government a reality. They favored vigorous executive leadership and a set of policies designed to correct the nation's economic ills. The Federalists' program appealed to financial, manufacturing, and commercial interests. To reach their goals, they urged a liberal interpretation of the Constitution.

Thomas Jefferson, the nation's first secretary of state, led the opposition to the Federalists.[9] Jefferson and his followers were more sympathetic to the "common man" than were the Federalists. They favored only a very limited role for the new government created by the Constitution. In their view, Congress should dominate that new government, and its policies should help the nation's small shopkeepers, laborers, farmers, and planters. The Jeffersonians insisted on a strict construction of the provisions of the Constitution.

Jefferson resigned from Washington's cabinet in 1793 to give his time to the organization of his party. Originally, the new party took the name Anti-Federalist. Then it was known as the Jeffersonian Republicans or the Democratic-Republicans. By 1828, it was called the Democratic party.

These two parties first clashed in the elections of 1796. John Adams, the Federalists' candidate to succeed Washington as President, defeated Jefferson by just three votes in the electoral college. Over the next four years, Jefferson and James Madison worked tirelessly to build the Democratic-Republicans. Their efforts paid off in the elections of 1800. Jefferson defeated the incumbent President Adams, and his party also won control of Congress. The Federalists never returned to power.

----

[9] Given his opposition to the rise of parties, President Washington named arch foes Hamilton and Jefferson to his new cabinet to get them to work together—in an unsuccessful attempt to avoid the creation of formally organized and opposing groups.

## The Eras of One-Party Domination

The history of the American party system since 1800 can be divided into four major periods. Through the first three of them, one or the other of the two major parties regularly held the presidency and, usually, both houses of Congress. The nation is now in a fourth period, much of it marked by divided government.

In the first of these periods, from 1800 to 1860, the Democrats won 13 of 15 presidential elections. They lost the office only in the elections of 1840 and 1848. In the second era, from 1860 to 1932, the Republicans won 14 of 18 elections, losing only in 1884, 1892, 1912, and 1916. The third period, from 1932 to 1968, began with the Democrats' return to power and Franklin Roosevelt's first election to the presidency. The Democrats won seven of the nine presidential elections held over those years, losing only in 1952 and 1956. Through the fourth period, which began in 1968, the Republicans have won five of seven presidential elections, and they held the White House until 1993. But the Democrats have controlled both houses of Congress over most of the current period—although they do not do so today.

### The Era of the Democrats, 1800–1860

As you have read, Jefferson's election marked the beginning of a period of Democratic domination that was to last until the Civil War. As the chart on the following page shows, the Federalists, shattered in 1801, had disappeared altogether by 1816.

For a time, through the Era of Good Feeling, the Democratic-Republicans were unopposed in national politics. They had split into factions by the mid-1820s, however. By the time of Andrew Jackson's administration (1829–1837), a potent National Republican (Whig) party had arisen to form a significant challenge to the Democrats. The major issues of the day—conflicts over public lands, the Second Bank of the United States, high tariffs, and slavery—all had made new party alignments inevitable.

The Democrats, led by Jackson, were a coalition of small farmers, debtors, frontier pioneers, and slaveholders. Their main area of political strength lay in the South and West. The years of

Jacksonian democracy saw the coming of universal white male suffrage, a large increase in the number of elective offices around the country, and the spread of the spoils system. (You will read more about the influence of Jacksonian Democracy in Chapter 15.)

The Whig party was led by the widely popular Henry Clay and the great orator, Daniel Webster. A loose coalition of eastern bankers, merchants and industrialists, and southern planters, the Whigs were opposed to the tenets of Jacksonian democracy and dedicated to the high tariff. However, the Whigs' victories were few. As the other major party from the mid-1830s to the 1850s, they were able to elect only two Presidents, both of them war heroes: William Henry Harrison in 1840 and Zachary Taylor in 1848.

By the 1850s the growing crisis over slavery split both major parties. Left leaderless by the deaths of Clay and Webster, the Whigs fell apart. Meanwhile, the Democrats split into two sharply divided camps, North and South. Through the decade the nation drifted toward civil war.

Of the several groupings that arose to compete for supporters during this time, the Republican party was the most successful. Born in 1854, it drew many Whigs and antislavery Democrats. The Republicans nominated their first presidential candidate, John C. Frémont, in 1856 and elected their first President, Abraham Lincoln, in 1860. With those accomplishments, the Republican party became the only party in the history of American politics to make the jump from third-party to major-party status. As you will shortly see, even greater things were in store for the Republican party.

### The Era of the Republicans, 1860–1932

The Civil War signaled the beginning of the second era of one-party domination. For nearly 75 years, the Republicans—supported by business and financial interests, and by farmers, laborers, and newly freed African Americans—dominated the national scene.

The Democrats, crippled by the war, were able to survive mainly through their hold on the "Solid South." For the balance of the century, they slowly rebuilt their electoral base. In all that

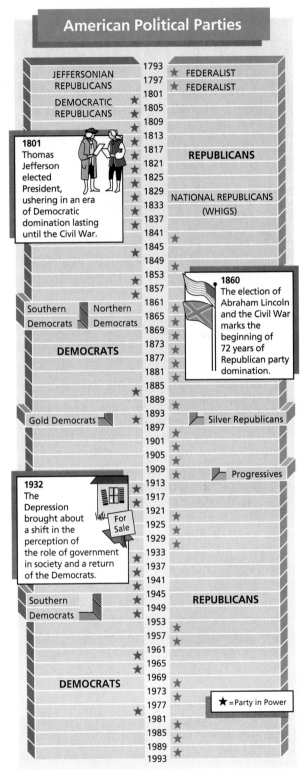

**American Political Parties**

1801 Thomas Jefferson elected President, ushering in an era of Democratic domination lasting until the Civil War.

1860 The election of Abraham Lincoln and the Civil War marks the beginning of 72 years of Republican party domination.

1932 The Depression brought about a shift in the perception of the role of government in society and a return of the Democrats.

★ = Party in Power

▲ **Interpreting Charts**  Three of the four eras of party domination are highlighted here. Which party had the single longest period of control?

▲ **A Voter for FDR**    The holder of this ticket to the Franklin Field ceremonies,
part of the Democratic National Convention at Philadelphia in 1936, helped
nominate President Roosevelt for a second time.

time, they were able to place only one candidate in the White House: Grover Cleveland in 1884 and again in 1892. Those elections marked only short breaks in Republican supremacy, however. Riding the crest of popular acceptance and unprecedented prosperity, the GOP remained the dominant party well into this century.

The election of 1896 was especially critical in the development of the party system. It climaxed years of protest by small business owners, farmers, and the emerging labor unions against big business and financial monopolies and the railroads. The Republicans regained the presidency with William McKinley. In doing so, they were able to gather new support from several segments of the **electorate**—the people eligible to vote. This new strength allowed the Republicans to maintain their role as the dominant party in national politics for another three decades.

The Democrats also made a significant contribution in this election. Although the Democratic nominee, William Jennings Bryan, lost the election, he presented himself as a powerful champion of the "little man"—and so helped to push the nation's party politics back toward the economic arena, and away from the divi-

sions of sectionalism that had plagued the nation for so many years.

The Republicans suffered their worst setback of the era in 1912, when they renominated incumbent President William Howard Taft. Former President Theodore Roosevelt, denied the nomination of his party, left the Republicans to become the candidate of his "Bull Moose" Progressive party. With Republican support divided between Taft and Roosevelt, the Democratic nominee, Woodrow Wilson, was able to capture the presidency. And Wilson managed to keep the office, by a narrow margin, four years later.

But, again, the Democratic successes of 1912 and 1916 proved only a brief interlude. The GOP reasserted its control of the nation's politics by winning each of the next three presidential elections—with Warren Harding in 1920, Calvin Coolidge in 1924, and Herbert Hoover in 1928.

**The Return of the Democrats, 1932 to 1968**    The Great Depression, which began in 1929, had a massive impact on nearly all aspects of American life. Its effect on the American political landscape was considerable indeed. The landmark election of 1932 brought Franklin Roosevelt to the presidency and the Democrats back to power at the national level. Also, and of fundamental importance, that election marked a basic shift in the public's attitude toward the proper place of government in the nation's social and economic life.

Franklin Roosevelt and the Democrats engineered their victory in 1932 with a new electoral base. It was built largely of Southerners, small farmers, organized labor, and big-city political organizations. Roosevelt's revolutionary economic and social welfare programs, which formed the heart of the New Deal of the 1930s, further strengthened that coalition; and it soon brought increasing support from African Americans and other minorities to the Democrats.

President Roosevelt won reelection in 1936. He secured an unprecedented third term in 1940 and yet another term in 1944, each time by heavy majorities. Roosevelt's Vice President, Harry S Truman, completed the fourth term following FDR's death in 1945. Truman was elected to a full term of his own in 1948, when he turned back the GOP challenge led by Governor Thomas E. Dewey.

The Republicans did manage to regain the White House in 1952, and they kept it in 1956. The Republicans were led to victory in both elections by World War II hero Dwight Eisenhower, who both times defeated Democrat Adlai Stevenson.

Like other interludes in the eras of one-party domination, the Republican return to power was short-lived. In 1960 John F. Kennedy recaptured the presidency for the Democrats with a razor-thin plurality over the Republicans' nominee, then Vice President Richard M. Nixon. Lyndon Johnson became President following President Kennedy's assassination in 1963. In 1964, Johnson won by an overwhelming margin over his Republican opponent, Senator Barry Goldwater of Arizona.

**The Start of a New Era** Richard Nixon made a successful return to presidential politics in 1968. In that year's election he defeated Hubert Humphrey, the candidate of a Democratic party torn apart by conflicts over the war in Vietnam, civil rights, and a variety of social welfare issues. The Republican victory came with only a bare plurality over Humphrey and the strong third-party effort of the American Independent party nominee, Governor George Wallace of Alabama.

President Nixon remained in power when he routed the choice of the still-divided Democrats, Senator George McGovern, in 1972. Nixon's role in the Watergate scandal forced him from office in 1974, however. Vice President Gerald Ford then became President, and he filled out the balance of that presidential term. Beset by problems in the economy, by the continuing effects of Watergate, and by his pardon of former President Nixon, Ford lost the presidency to Jimmy Carter and the resurgent Democrats in 1976.

A steadily worsening economy, political fallout from the Iranian hostage crisis, and his own inability to establish himself as an effective President spelled defeat for Mr. Carter in 1980, however. Led by Ronald Reagan, the former governor of California, the Republicans scored an impressive victory that year; and Mr. Reagan won a second term by a landslide in 1984, overwhelming a Democratic ticket headed by former Vice President Walter Mondale.

The GOP kept control of the White House with a third straight win in 1988. Their candidate, George Bush, had served in the vice-presidency through the Reagan years, and he was able to turn back the Democrats and their nominee, Governor Michael Dukakis of Massachusetts.

The Reagan and Bush elections of the 1980s triggered wide-ranging efforts to alter many of the nation's foreign and domestic policies. And these elections led many to the view that a majority of Americans had come to favor more conservative rather than liberal responses to most public policy questions.

President Bush lost his bid for another term in 1992, however. The most recent presidential election was a three-way contest in which the Democrats, led by Bill Clinton, defeated Mr. Bush and also turned back an independent challenge by Texas billionaire Ross Perot.

The years since Richard Nixon's election in 1968 have been marked by divided government. Through most of the period, the Republicans have held the White House while the Democrats have controlled Congress.[10] That situation is exactly reversed today—because the Republicans won control of both houses of Congress in 1994. Even so, the pattern of divided government continues.

This lengthy era of divided government is without precedent. In earlier periods, a newly elected President almost always swept many of his party's candidates into office with him. The Nixon, Reagan, and Bush electoral victories did not carry that kind of coattail effect, however. And, earlier, an incumbent President's party almost never lost its hold on Congress in an off-year election.

## Section **3** Review

**1. Define:** electorate
**2.** (a) Out of what circumstances did the nation's first two parties arise? (b) What were those parties?
**3.** Since 1800 the history of the American party system can be divided into what four eras?
**4.** Much of the present era has been marked by what unusual feature?

### Critical Thinking

**5. Determining Relevance** (p. 19) For years now, presidential and congressional elections have most often resulted in divided government. Does this mean that most voters today favor split control of the White House and Congress? Why might they favor this? What else might it indicate about voters?

★

---

[10]The Democrats held almost uninterrupted control of Congress from 1933 to 1995. Over those years, the Republicans controlled both houses of Congress for only two two-year periods—first, after the congressional elections of 1946 and then after those of 1952. The GOP did win control of the Senate (but not the House) in 1980; the Democrats recaptured the upper chamber in 1986, however.

## **4** The Minor Parties

### Find Out:

- What are the different types of minor parties?
- What is the importance of minor parties?

### Key Terms:

ideological parties, single-issue parties, economic protest parties, splinter parties

Libertarian, Socialist, Prohibition, New Alliance, Communist, American Independent, Socialist Labor, Citizens—these are only some of the several parties whose candidates will seek the presidency in 1996.

You know that none of these parties or their candidates have any real chance of winning. This is not to say that minor parties are unimportant, however. The bright light created by the two major parties too often blinds us to the vital role several minor parties have played in American politics.

In this section, you will read about the place of minor parties in the American political system.

### Minor Parties in the United States

Their number and variety make minor parties difficult to describe and classify. Some have limited their efforts to a particular locale, others to a single State, and some to one region of the country. Still others have tried to woo the entire nation. Most have been short-lived, but a few have existed for decades. And, while most have lived mothlike around the flame of a single idea, some have had a broader, more practical base.

Still, four distinct types of minor parties can be identified:

(1) The **ideological parties**—those based on a particular set of beliefs, a comprehensive view of social, economic, and political matters. Most of these minor parties have been built on some shade of Marxist thought—for example, the Socialist, Socialist Labor, Socialist Worker, and Communist parties. Some

have had a quite different color, however—especially the Libertarian party of today, which emphasizes individualism and calls for doing away with most of government's present functions and programs.

The ideological parties have not often been able to win many votes. But, as a rule, they have been long-lived.

(2) The **single-issue parties**—those concentrating on a single public policy matter. Their names have usually indicated their primary concern—for example, the Free Soil party opposed the spread of slavery in the 1840s and 1850s; the American party, the "Know Nothings," opposed Irish-Catholic immigration in the 1850s; and the Right to Life party, opposed to abortion today.

Most of the single-issue parties have faded into history as events have passed them by, as their themes have failed to attract voters, or as one or both of the major parties have taken their key issues as their own.

(3) The **economic protest parties**—those rooted in periods of economic discontent. Unlike the socialist parties, these groups have not had any clear-cut ideological base. Rather, they have proclaimed their disgust with the major parties, demanded better times, and focused their anger on such real or imagined enemies as the monetary system, "Wall Street bankers," the railroads, or foreign imports. Most often, they have been sectional parties, drawing their strength from the agricultural South and West. Thus, the Greenback party tried to take advantage of agrarian discontent from 1876 through 1884. It appealed to struggling farmers by calling for the free coinage of silver, federal regulation of the railroads, an income tax, and labor legislation. Its descendant, the Populist party of the 1890s, also demanded public ownership of railroads, telephone and telegraph companies, lower tariffs, and the adoption of the initiative and referendum.

Each of these economic protest parties has disappeared as the nation has climbed out of the difficult economic period in which that party was born.

(4) The **splinter parties**—those which have split away from one of the major parties. Most

## Selected American Political Parties Since 1789

| Party | From | To |
|---|---|---|
| **Federalist** | **1790** | **1816** |
| **Anti-Federalist** | **1790** | * |
| **Democratic-Republican** | **1796** | **1828** |
| **Democrat** | **1828** | **Present** |
| **National Republican** | **1828** | **1832** |
| **Whig** | **1836** | **1852** |
| **Republican** | **1856** | **Present** |
| Anti-Masonic | 1832 | * |
| Liberty | 1840 | 1848 |
| Free Soil | 1848 | 1852 |
| American (Know Nothing) | 1856 | * |
| Constitutional Union | 1860 | * |
| Southern Democrat | 1860 | * |
| Prohibition | 1869 | Present |
| Liberal Republican | 1872 | * |
| Greenback | 1876 | 1884 |
| Socialist Labor | 1892 | 1972 |
| Populist | 1892 | 1908 |
| National Democrat | 1896 | * |
| Socialist | 1900 | 1956 |
| Progressive (Bull Moose) | 1912 | * |
| Progressive (La Follette) | 1924 | * |
| Communist | 1928 | 1940 |
| Union | 1936 | * |
| Progressive (H. Wallace) | 1948 | 1952 |
| Socialist Workers | 1948 | Present |
| States' Rights Democrats | 1948 | * |
| Workers World | 1960 | Present |
| American Independent (G. Wallace) | 1968 | Present |
| Communist | 1968 | 1988 |
| Libertarian | 1972 | Present |
| Peoples | 1976 | 1980 |
| U.S. Labor | 1976 | 1984 |
| Socialist | 1980 | Present |
| Citizens | 1980 | Present |
| Populist | 1984 | Present |

**Boldface** entries are major parties; all others are third parties; * Represents parties that were only in existence for one presidential election.
*Note*: The lifespan for many political parties can only be approximated since many existed at the State and local levels before they ran candidates in presidential elections and continued to exist at the State and local levels long after they dropped out of presidential races.

 **Interpreting Tables** This table shows several parties that have tried to challenge the supremacy of the two-party system since 1789. Which of the minor parties has survived the longest?

## The 1912 Presidential Election

| Party and Candidate | Popular Vote | % | Electoral Vote |
|---|---|---|---|
| Democrat—Woodrow Wilson | 6,293,152 | 41.8 | 435 |
| Progressive—Theodore Roosevelt | 4,119,207 | 27.4 | 88 |
| Republican—William H. Taft | 3,486,333 | 23.2 | 8 |
| Socialist—Eugene V. Debs | 900,369 | 6.0 | — |
| Prohibition—Eugene Chafin | 207,972 | 1.4 | — |

▲ **Interpreting Tables**   These figures show that Theodore Roosevelt's Progressives did better than the Republicans in 1912. Why did this pave the way to the election of Woodrow Wilson?

of the more important minor parties in our politics have been of this kind. Among the leading groups that have split away from the Republicans are Theodore Roosevelt's "Bull Moose" Progressive party of 1912, and Robert La Follette's Progressive party of 1924. From the Democrats have come Henry Wallace's Progressive party and the States' Rights (Dixiecrat) party, both of 1948, and George Wallace's American Independent party of 1968.

Most splinter parties have formed around some strong personality—most often one who has failed to win his major party's presidential nomination. They have faded or collapsed when that leader has stepped aside. Thus, the Bull Moose Progressive party passed away when Theodore Roosevelt returned to the Republican fold after the election of 1912. And the American Independent party lost nearly all of its brief strength when Governor George Wallace rejoined the Democrats following his strong showing in the 1968 election.

A few of the minor parties have been successful at the State or local level. Some have elected a few members of Congress and occasionally won some electoral votes in the presidential contest; but, needless to say, none has ever won the presidency.

## The Key Role of Minor Parties

Though most Americans do not support them, minor parties have nonetheless had an impact on American politics and on the major parties. For example, it was a minor party, the Anti-Masons in 1831, that first used a national convention to nominate a presidential candidate. The Whigs and then the Democrats followed suit in 1832. Ever since, the national convention has been the means by which the Democrats and Republicans have picked their presidential tickets.

A strong third-party candidacy can play a decisive role—often a "spoiler role"—in an election. This can be true in national, State, or local politics, and especially where the two major parties compete on roughly equal terms. In such situations, a third party can effectively deny one of the major parties a majority—and an election. The point was dramatically illustrated in the presidential election of 1912. A split in the Republican party and the resulting third-party candidacy of Theodore Roosevelt produced the results shown in the table above. Almost certainly had Theodore Roosevelt not quit the Republican party, Taft would have enjoyed a better showing, and Woodrow Wilson would not have become President.

Historically, however, the most important roles of the minor parties have been those of critic and innovator. Unlike the major parties, the minor parties have been ready, willing, and able to take quite clear-cut stands on the controversial issues of their day. Though such stands rarely lead to any sustained political success for any minor party, these actions have often drawn attention to some issue that the major parties have preferred to ignore or straddle. Over the years, many of the more important issues of American politics were first

## Significant Minor Parties in Presidential Elections, 1880-1992*

| Year | Party and Candidate | Percent of Popular Vote | Electoral Votes |
|---|---|---|---|
| 1880 | Greenback James B. Weaver | 3.72 | — |
| 1888 | Prohibition Clinton B. Fisk | 2.19 | — |
| 1892 | Populist James B. Weaver | 8.50 | 22 |
| | Prohibition John Bidwell | 2.25 | — |
| 1904 | Socialist Eugene V. Debs | 2.98 | — |
| 1908 | Socialist Eugene V. Debs | 2.82 | — |
| 1912 | Progressive (Bull Moose) Theodore Roosevelt | 27.39 | 88 |
| | Socialist Eugene V. Debs | 5.99 | — |
| 1916 | Socialist Allan L. Benson | 3.18 | — |
| 1920 | Socialist Eugene V. Debs | 3.42 | — |
| 1924 | Progressive Robert M. La Follette | 16.56 | 13 |
| 1932 | Socialist Norman M. Thomas | 2.22 | — |
| 1948 | States' Rights (Dixiecrat) Strom Thurmond | 2.40 | 39 |
| | Progressive Henry A. Wallace | 2.38 | — |
| 1968 | American Independent George C. Wallace | 13.53 | 46 |

* Includes all minor parties that polled at least 2% of the popular vote for President. None did so in the years not shown, including each election since 1968.

▲ **Interpreting Tables** The Progressive party is followed closely by the American Independents in terms of high voter appeal. What might have accounted for the success of these parties?

brought to the public's attention by a minor party—for example, the progressive income tax, women's suffrage, railroad and banking regulation, and old-age pensions.

But this very important innovator function of the minor parties has also been a major source of their frustration. When their proposals have gained any real degree of popular support, one and then both of the major parties have taken them over and presented them as their own. After all, when there is a significant pool of votes to be had by supporting some idea, both major parties cannot resist the temptation. The late Norman Thomas, six times the Socialist party's candidate for President, complained that "the major parties are stealing from my platform."

The presidential nominees of 21 minor parties made it to the ballots of at least one State in 1992—and at least that many will likely do so in the 1996 election. In 1992 the more (or at least somewhat) visible minor party presidential campaigns were those of the American Independent, Populist, Libertarian, New Alliance, Prohibition, and Socialist Workers parties. More than 1,000 minor party candidates from a wide variety of minor parties also sought seats in Congress or ran for various State and local offices, as well.

## Section 4 Review

1. **Define:** ideological parties, single-issue parties, economic protest parties, splinter parties
2. What are the major characteristics of the typical minor party in American politics?
3. In what ways have minor parties been important in politics in the United States?
4. Why is the innovator function a source of frustration to minor parties?

**Critical Thinking**

5. **Expressing Problems Clearly** (p. 19) Imagine you are a voter considering casting your ballot for a presidential candidate from a minor party. Explain the benefits and drawbacks of casting your vote that way.

★

# 5 The Organization of Political Parties

## Find Out:

- What factors make both major parties such highly decentralized organizations?
- How are the major parties organized?
- What are the three basic elements of a major party?
- What factors explain the current state of parties and the party system?

## Key Terms:

ward, precinct, split-ticket voting

How strong, how active, how well organized are the Republican and Democratic parties in your community? Contact the county chairperson or another official in one or both of the major parties. They are usually not very difficult to find. For starters, try the telephone directory. You might be surprised by what you discover.

In this section, you will take a look at the overall shape of party organization in the United States; and you will also consider the future of parties and the party system.

## The Reality of Political Parties

You often read of the two major parties in terms that suggest that they are highly organized, close-knit, well-disciplined groups. Even though they may look that way on paper—as in the chart on page 119—neither party is anything of the kind. Rather, both are highly decentralized. They are fragmented, disjointed; and they are often beset by factions and internal squabbling.

In neither party is there a chain of command running from the national through the State to the local level. Each of the State party organizations is only loosely tied to the party's national structure. And local party organizations are often quite independent of their parent State organizations. These various party units usually cooperate with one another, of course—but that is not always the case.

**The Role of the Presidency**   The President's party is usually more solidly united and more cohesively organized than is the opposition. The President is automatically the party leader. He asserts that leadership with a number of weapons, among them the President's access to the media, his popularity, and his power to make appointments to federal office and to dispense other favors.

The other party has no one in an even faintly comparable position. Indeed, in the American party system, there is almost never any one personality in the opposition party who can be called, in fact, its leader. Rather, a number of personalities, frequently in competition with one another, form a more or less loosely identifiable leadership group in the party out of power.[11]

**The Impact of Federalism**   Federalism is a major reason for the decentralized nature of the two major political parties. Remember, the basic goal of the major parties is to gain control of government, and they try to do this by winning elective offices. There are today more than half a million elective offices in the United States—and, in the American federal system, those offices are widely distributed at the national, the State, and the local levels. In short, because the governmental system is decentralized, so, too, are the major parties that serve it.

**The Role of the Nominating Process**   The nominating process is also a major cause of party decentralization. As you recall from Section 1, the nominating process has a central role in the life of political parties. You will read about the selection of candidates at some length in Chapter 7, but, for now, look at two related aspects of that process.

First, candidate selection is an intraparty process. That is, nominations are made within the party. Second, that process can be, and often is, a divisive one. Where there is a fight

---

[11]The party does have a temporary leader for a brief time every fourth year: its presidential candidate, from nomination to election day. A defeated presidential candidate is often called the party's "titular leader"—a leader in title, by custom, but not in fact.

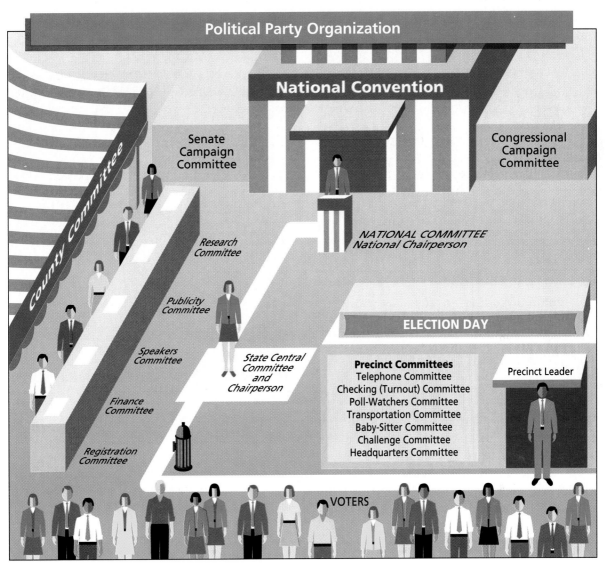

**Political Party Organization**

National Convention

Senate Campaign Committee

Congressional Campaign Committee

County Committee

Research Committee

Publicity Committee

Speakers Committee

Finance Committee

Registration Committee

*NATIONAL COMMITTEE*
*National Chairperson*

State Central Committee and Chairperson

**ELECTION DAY**

**Precinct Committees**
Telephone Committee
Checking (Turnout) Committee
Poll-Watchers Committee
Transportation Committee
Baby-Sitter Committee
Challenge Committee
Headquarters Committee

Precinct Leader

VOTERS

**Interpreting Charts**   This chart shows the complexity of party organization at the national, State, and local levels. What accounts for the highly decentralized structures of the political party system?

over a nomination, that contest pits members of the same party against one another; Republicans fight Republicans, Democrats battle Democrats. In short, the prime function of the major parties—the making of nominations—is also a prime cause of their highly fragmented character.

## National Party Machinery

As the chart above shows, there are four elements in the structure of both major parties at the national level. They are the national convention, the national committee, the national chairperson, and the congressional campaign committees.

**The National Convention**  The national convention is often described as the party's national voice. It meets in the summer of every presidential election year to nominate the party's presidential and vice-presidential candidates. It also performs some other functions, including the adoption of the party's rules and

▲ **Political Workers** At every level of party organization, the work of many individuals is needed to prepare and carry out campaign strategy. Shown here are workers for the Republican (left) and Democratic (right) parties.

the writing of its platform. Beyond that, it has little authority. It has no control over the selection of the party's candidates for other offices nor over the policy stands those nominees take. You will take a longer look at both parties' national nominating conventions in Chapter 13.

**The National Committee** Between conventions, the party's affairs are handled, at least in theory, by the national committee and by the national chairperson.

For years, each party's national committee was composed of a committeeman and a committeewoman chosen by the party organization in each State and several of the territories. Both parties have expanded the committee's membership in recent years, however.

Today, the Republican National Committee (RNC) also seats several of the party's State chairpersons—party leaders from those States that voted for the party's presidential candidate or that elected a Republican to the Senate, a majority of Republicans to the House, or a GOP governor in the preceding election.

The Democratic National Committee (DNC) is an even larger body. In addition to the committeeman and -woman from each State, it now includes each State party's chair- and vice-chairperson, several additional members from the party organizations of the larger States, and 33 at-large members chosen by the DNC itself. Several members of Congress, as well as governors, mayors, and Young Democrats, also have seats.

On paper, the national committee appears to be a powerful organ loaded with many of the party's leading figures. In fact, it does not have a great deal of clout. Most of its work centers on staging the party's national convention every four years.

**The National Chairperson** In each party, the national chairperson heads up the national committee. In form, he or she is chosen to a four-year term by the national committee, at a meeting held right after the national convention. In fact, the choice is made by the just-nominated presidential candidate and is then ratified by the national committee.

Only two women have ever held that top party post. Jean Westwood of Utah chaired the DNC from her party's 1972 convention until early 1973; and Mary Louise Smith of Iowa headed the RNC from 1974 until early 1977. Each lost her post soon after her party lost a presidential election. Ron Brown, the Democrats' National Chairman from 1989 to 1993, is the only African American ever to hold the office in either major party.

The chairperson directs the work of the party's headquarters and its small staff in Washington. In presidential election years, the committee's attention is focused on the national convention and then the campaign. In between, the chairperson and the committee work to strengthen the party and its fortunes—promoting party unity, raising money, recruiting new voters, and otherwise preparing for the next presidential season.

**The Congressional Campaign Committees** As the chart on page 119 shows, each party also has a campaign committee in each house of Congress.[12] These committees work to reelect incumbents and to save the seats given up by retiring party members. The committees also take a hand in some campaigns to unseat incumbents in the other party, at least in those House or Senate races where the chances for success seem to justify such efforts.

In both parties and in both houses, the members of these campaign committees are chosen by their colleagues. They serve for two years—that is, for a term of Congress.

---

[12]In the House, the National Republican Campaign Committee and the Democratic Congressional Campaign Committee; in the Senate, the National Republican Senatorial Campaign Committee and the Democratic Senatorial Campaign Committee.

**Party Leaders** President Clinton endorsed Don Fowler (right) to lead the Democratic National Committee, and the party showed its agreement by voting him chairperson. His Republican counterpart, Haley Barbour (left), was described by *Time* magazine as a "smooth conciliator."

## State and Local Party Machinery

National party organization is largely the product of custom and the rules adopted by national conventions. At the State and local levels, however, party structure is largely set by State law.

**The State Organization**   Look again at the chart on page 119. At the State level, party machinery is built around a State central committee, headed by a State chairperson.

The chairperson may be an important political figure in his or her own right. More often than not, however, the chairperson fronts for the governor, a U.S. senator, or some other powerful leader or group in the politics of the State.

Together, the chairperson and the central committee work to further the party's interests in the State. Most of the time they attempt to do so by building an effective organization and party unity, finding candidates and campaign funds, and so on. Remember, however, both major parties are highly decentralized, fragmented, and sometimes torn by struggles for power. This can complicate the chairperson's and the committee's job.

**Local Organization**   Local party structures vary so widely that they nearly defy even a brief description. Generally, they follow the electoral map of the State, with a party unit for each district in which elective offices are to be filled: congressional and legislative districts, counties, cities and towns, wards, and precincts. A **ward** is a unit into which cities are often divided for the election of city council members. A **precinct** is the smallest unit of election administration—the voters in each precinct report to one polling place. In most larger cities a party's organization is further broken down by residential blocks and sometimes even apartment buildings.

In some places, local party organizations are active year-round, but most often they are inactive except for those few hectic months before an election.

## The Three Elements of the Party

Look at the structure of the two major parties from another angle: the roles of their members, rather than their organizational charts. From this perspective, they are made up of three basic and closely interrelated elements:

1. The party organization: the leaders, the activists, and the hangers-on who control and run the party machinery.
2. The party in the electorate: the party's loyalists who vote the straight party ticket or usually vote for its candidates.
3. The party in government: the party's officeholders at all levels of government.

## The Future of the Major Parties

Political parties have never been very popular in this country. Rather, over time, most Americans have had very mixed feelings about political parties. Most of us have accepted parties as necessary institutions, but, at the same time, people feel that they should be closely watched and controlled. To many, they have seemed little better than necessary evils.

Political parties have been in a period of decline since at least the late 1960s. Their decline has led some analysts to conclude that not only are the parties in serious trouble, the party system itself may be on the point of collapse.

The present, weakened state of the parties can be traced to several factors. They include:

1. A sharp drop in the number of voters willing to identify themselves as Republicans or Democrats, and a growing number who regard themselves as independents.
2. A big increase in **split-ticket voting**—voting for candidates of both parties for different offices at the same election.
3. Various structural changes and reforms—from the introduction of the direct primary in the early 1900s to recent and far-reaching changes in campaign finance laws—that have made the parties more "open" but have also led to greater internal conflict and disorganization.
4. Changes in the technology of campaigning for office—especially the heavy use of television and of such other devices as professional campaign managers and direct-mail advertising. These changes have made candidates much less dependent on party organizations.
5. The growth of single-issue organizations. These groups take sides for or against

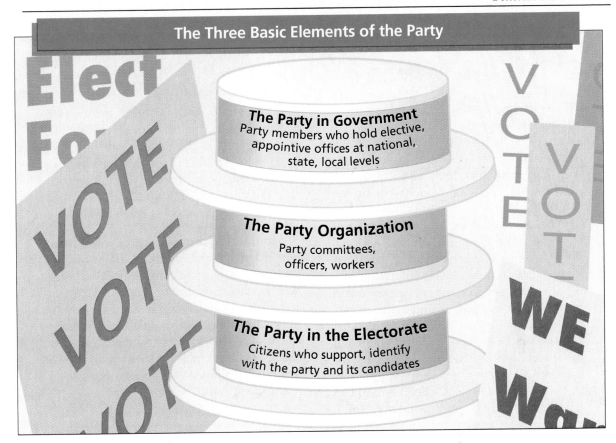

### The Three Basic Elements of the Party

**The Party in Government**
Party members who hold elective, appointive offices at national, state, local levels

**The Party Organization**
Party committees, officers, workers

**The Party in the Electorate**
Citizens who support, identify with the party and its candidates

**Interpreting Graphics** This graphic illustrates the major components of each of the major parties. Which group receives the most attention from the public and the media?

candidates based on their own views in some specific area of public policy. One way such groups are making their presence felt is through political action committees (PACs). PACs raise and distribute money to candidates who will further their goals. Again, PACs have lessened candidates' reliance on party organizations for financial support.

You will look at the matters affecting the condition of the parties in the later chapters. As you do so, remember that political parties are indispensable to democratic government. The major parties have existed longer than have any other party anywhere in the world. And, as you have seen, they perform a number of necessary functions. In short, reports of their passing may be premature—and even farfetched.

## Section 5 Review

1. **Define:** ward, precinct, split-ticket voting
2. What are the main elements of major party organization at the national level?
3. (a) What is the basic shape of party organization at the State level? (b) At the local level?
4. What are the three elements of the parties in terms of the roles of their members?
5. What features have led some observers to predict the collapse of the party system?

**Critical Thinking**

6. **Drawing Conclusions** (p. 19) Based on what you know about parties, their goals, and the American people, why do you think local party organizations vary so widely?

★

# Identifying Central Issues

Identifying central issues means finding the main ideas in a piece of information. Being able to identify central issues enables you to identify quickly the true nature of problems and controversies so that you can begin working on solutions.

Political cartoons are a frequent means of communicating political ideas and information. Cartoons have been a part of the American political scene since colonial days. Today they can be found in most newspapers and in many magazines. Several important characteristics make cartoons different from other kinds of pictures—photographs in books and newspapers or images on television, for example. More often than not, political cartoons are satirical. That is, they are meant to criticize, and they do so with humor. But, a cartoon almost always carries a serious message. In addition, cartoons frequently use caricature. That is, they use purposeful distortions or exaggerations to make a point or to attract attention.

Follow the steps below to practice identifying central issues in a political cartoon.

**1. Examine the cartoon to identify and determine the meaning of the symbols.** Cartoons use pictures and words to symbolize ideas or things. For example, an eagle in a cartoon usually symbolizes the United States. Examine the cartoon on this page. Read any captions or labels. (a) What is the literal meaning of the sentence at the top of the cartoon? (b) What do each of the items in the cartoon represent?

**2. Identify the message or main idea.** Each component of a cartoon generally relates to one basic message or main idea. By pointing out how different objects or events relate to that main idea, the cartoon achieves its comic or ironic effect. For example, look at the cartoon on this page. (a) In what sense is the word *machine* used in the sentence at the top of the cartoon? (b) What is the meaning of the word *machine* as represented by the objects?

**3. Summarize the message or main idea, and identify the central issue of the cartoon.** Any good cartoon makes a point and tries to make the viewer feel a certain way about a topic. (a) What is the cartoonist saying about the politics of yesterday and today? (b) What is the cartoonist saying about PACs, polls, television, and computerized mailings? (c) Is this a positive or negative view of these items?

"In the bad old days, there used to be political machines", ©1984 by Herblock in the Washington Post.

# Chapter-in-Brief

Scan all headings, photographs, charts, and other visuals in the chapter before reading the section summaries below.

## Section 1 Parties and What They Do
**(pp. 99–102)** Political parties are groups of people who join together to elect candidates to public office. Unlike many other parties, the two major parties in the United States do not rest on any common ideological foundation.

Parties serve key functions in the political system: They select and support most candidates, and they help to keep the public informed on important issues, including the actions of the rival party. Parties grant a sort of seal of approval to candidates, thus assuring the public of the candidate's fitness. Indeed, parties are so important that they have even become instrumental in the administration of government.

## Section 2 The Two-Party System (pp. 102–107)
America's two-party system is the result of history and tradition; from its beginning, this nation has had two strong parties.

The American electoral system has several features that enable only two parties to compete. Election laws are written by officials who are usually members of the major parties. These laws tend to make it difficult for minor parties to flourish.

Another cause of the two-party system is that the United States is ideologically homogeneous. Most people have similar feelings about the broad issues of the day. Thus, there is little room or need for more than two parties.

## Section 3 The Two-Party System in American History (pp. 109–114)
The first parties in the United States formed during George Washington's administration. They became a force in the election of 1796. The nation has had strong political parties ever since.

Between 1800 and today, there have been four eras in which one party or the other has dominated national politics. Until recently, the current era was marked by a split in party control of the White House and Congress.

## Section 4 The Minor Parties (pp. 114–117)
Minor parties have enjoyed little success in national politics. However, they have had an impact on the American political system.

Minor parties tend to fall into one of four categories: ideological parties, which are devoted to an overriding set of beliefs; single-issue parties; economic protest parties, which develop during times of economic hardship; and splinter parties—factions of one of the major parties.

The fate of most minor parties is failure. When they are successful, their ideas are often adopted by the major parties.

## Section 5 The Organization of Political Parties (pp. 118–123)
Political parties are not unified groups. National, State, and local branches of each party are only thinly connected. One reason for this is that the goal of electing officials requires different actions at different levels. Also, the act of choosing candidates often results in division within the party.

The national party machinery is generally devoted to trying to fill national offices. Their tasks include organizing the national convention.

State organizations are devoted to looking after the parties' interests in the States. Local organizations vary widely in structure. They tend to be most active at election time.

# Chapter Review

## Vocabulary and Key Terms

political party (p. 99)
major parties (p. 99)
coalition (p. 100)
minor party (p. 102)
two-party system (p. 102)
single-member district
 (p. 103)

plurality (p. 103)
pluralistic society (p. 104)
consensus (p. 104)
multiparty (p. 105)
one-party system (p. 105)
electorate (p. 112)
ideological parties (p. 114)

single-issue parties (p. 115)
economic protest parties
 (p. 115)
splinter parties (p. 115)
ward (p. 122)
precinct (p. 122)
split-ticket voting (p. 122)

**Matching:** *Review the key terms in the list above. If you are not sure of a term's meaning, look up the term and review its definition. Choose a term from the list above that best matches each description.*

1. a group of people who seek to control government by winning elections
2. a minor party that is based primarily on one set of beliefs
3. a general agreement among people
4. an American political party other than the Democrats or Republicans
5. the smallest electoral unit

**True or False:** *Determine whether each statement is true or false. If it is true, write "true." If it is false, change the underlined word or words to make the statement true.*

1. <u>Split-ticket voting</u> involves casting ballots for candidates of different parties in the same election.
2. <u>Economic protest parties</u> generally have no clear-cut ideological base, but are motivated by a demand for "better times."
3. A group of people with different interests who unite together is a <u>consensus</u>.
4. In a <u>single-issue party</u>, only one candidate is elected to each office on the ballot.

5. Candidates in many elections need not get more than half of all votes cast in order to win; a <u>plurality</u> is all that is necessary.

**Word Relationships:** *Three of the terms in each of the following sets of terms are related. Choose the term that does not belong and explain why it does not belong.*

1. (a) ward (b) precinct (c) single-member district (d) electorate
2. (a) single-issue parties (b) major party (c) ideological parties (d) splinter parties
3. (a) two-party system (b) one-party system (c) pluralistic society (d) single-member district

## Main Ideas

### Section 1 (pp. 99–102)

1. What is the purpose of a political party?
2. What does it mean to say that the two major parties are more election-oriented than issue-oriented?
3. What roles do the major parties play in the American political system?

### Section 2 (pp. 102–107)

4. Explain why only two parties successfully compete in the American political system.

**5.** In general, what kind of voters do each of the major parties attract?

**6.** Give reasons for your answer to question number 5.

**7.** Describe the alternatives to the two-party system.

## Section 3 (pp. 109–114)

**8.** When and under what circumstances did political parties first become a part of the American political process?

**9.** Describe the pattern that has characterized the two-party system over the course of American political history.

**10.** What feature makes the current era of one-party domination unusual?

**11.** Describe the differing views about the future of the two major parties.

## Section 4 (pp. 114–117)

**12.** Into what basic categories do most minor parties fall?

**13.** In general, how have the minor parties been able to influence American politics?

**14.** Describe the fate of most minor parties.

## Section 5 (pp. 118–123)

**15.** What factors contribute to the lack of organization of the major political parties?

**16.** Describe the organization of the parties at the national level.

**17.** Describe the organization of the parties at the State and local levels.

## Critical Thinking

**1. Identifying Assumptions** (p. 19) The text refers to the party out of power as the "loyal opposition." (a) What is your understanding of this concept? (b) What does it suggest about the relationship of political parties with each other and the government?

**2. Recognizing Bias** (p. 19) For what reasons do you think that most election laws are written in a way that discourages the success of minor parties?

**3. Identifying Alternatives** (p. 19) What further steps do you think might be taken to limit the role that money plays in American politics?

**4. Predicting Consequences** (p. 19) What do you think would be the consequences if laws were changed to make it easier for candidates from minor parties to get on ballots and receive government funding for their campaigns?

## Getting Involved

**1. Writing Your Opinion** Write a speech to introduce a new political party to the American voting public. Before you begin writing, make a list of the ideals your party will represent. Then make another list of the specific policies and programs you will promote. Use your lists to write a three-part speech. Open your speech with a statement that presents the name of your party and ideals that your new party will pursue. Then present each of your proposed policies and programs. Conclude by encouraging voters to support the new minor party, and explain why you believe their votes will not be "wasted." Proofread and revise the speech to correct errors. Draft a final copy.

**2. Class Debate** Hold a debate on the following topic: *Resolved,* That all political parties have equal opportunity to get on the ballot in all elections. Select teams to debate each side of the topic. The rest of the class can evaluate each of the teams' presentation.

**3. Gathering Information** Suppose you want to find out which of the two major political parties had controlled government in your State during a particular era in history. Use the Government Resources Handbook that begins on page 690 to find some sources you could use to find this information.

**CHAPTER 6**

# Voters and Voter Behavior

## Chapter Preview

Do you, your parents, or your friends believe that you can really make a change in the direction of this country? Do you feel part of the political process? Or do you believe that politics in the United States has been taken over by forces beyond your control? Soon, you will be eligible to vote—but will you? As you will soon see, the record suggests that while *you* may, many of your friends will not—at least not for some time; and it also suggests that some of you will never vote. Yet the success of democracy rests on participation by the people, and, in particular, on the regular and informed exercise of the right to vote.

*Who* has the right to vote in elections in the United States? *How* and *why* do millions of Americans vote? And why do other millions stay away from the polls on election day? The answers to these questions and many others are found in this chapter on voters and voter behavior.

### Before you read this chapter:

■ **Describe** why you do or do not think it is important for every eligible American to exercise his or her right to vote.

**Predict** three factors that affect American voting behavior.

### As you read, focus on the main objective for each section. Understand:

1. The history of voting rights in the United States.
2. The diversity of voter qualifications among the States.
3. The necessity for and effects of civil rights laws on suffrage.
4. Voter turnout and nonvoting in American elections.
5. The factors that affect the way people vote.

▲ **Becoming an Involved Citizen**    Voting in federal, State, and local elections is an important step along the way to becoming a responsible and active participant in the democratic process of government.

# 1 The Constitution and the Right to Vote

### Find Out:

- How did the right to vote evolve in the United States?
- What does the Constitution say about the right to vote?

### Key Terms:

suffrage, franchise, electorate

Try this simple exercise in free association: What is the first word that comes to mind when you read the word *democracy*? Obviously, several thoughts might occur to you. Quite possibly, one that did had something to do with voting or elections—for the right to vote is at the very heart of the democratic process.

In this section, you will see how the right to vote has developed over the course of the nation's history.

## The History of Voting Rights

Because the Framers disagreed on specific requirements, the Constitution left the power to set suffrage qualifications to each State. **Suffrage** means the right to vote. **Franchise** is another term with the same meaning.[1]

When the Constitution went into effect in 1789, the right to vote was everywhere restricted to white male property owners. In fact, probably not one in fifteen adult white males could vote in elections in the different States. Thomas Paine had ridiculed this situation in 1776. In *Common Sense*, he observed that a man whose only property was a jackass would lose his right to vote if the jackass died.

---

[1]Originally, the Constitution had only two suffrage provisions. Article I, Section 2, Clause 1 requires each State to allow anyone qualified to vote for members of "the most numerous branch" of its own legislature to vote as well for members of the national House of Representatives. Article II, Section I, Clause 2 provides that presidential electors be chosen in each State "in such manner as the legislature thereof may direct."

## Extending the Right to Vote

— 1789 —
white male property owners
— 1850 —
nearly all white adult males
— 1870 —
all men over 21
— 1920 —
all men and women over 21
— 1971 —
all men and women over 18

▲ **Interpreting Charts**   The 15th Amendment of 1870 theoretically protected all men from being denied the right to vote because of race or color. In reality, however, what were the voting rights of many African Americans at that time? When did they achieve voting rights in reality?

Asked Paine, "Now tell me, which was the voter, the man or the jackass?"

Today, the size of the American **electorate**—the potential voting population—is truly impressive. More than 190 million people, nearly all citizens who are at least 18 years of age, can qualify to vote. That huge number is a direct result of the legal definition of suffrage. That is, it is the result of those laws that determine who can and cannot vote. The large electorate is also the result of some 200 years of continuing, often bitter, and sometimes violent struggle over the issue of voting rights.

The long history of the development of suffrage since 1789 has been marked by two long-term trends: First, the nation has experienced the gradual elimination of a number of restrictions on the right to vote based on such factors as religious belief, property ownership, tax payment, race, and sex. Second, a significant share of what was originally the States' power over the right to vote has been assumed by the Federal Government.

The growth of the American electorate to its present size and shape has come in five fairly distinct stages—and these two trends have woven through them.

**The Five Stages**   The first stage of the struggle to extend voting rights came in the early part of the 1800s. Religious qualifications, born in colonial days, quickly disappeared. No State has

had a religious test since 1810. Property ownership and tax payment qualifications then began to fall, one by one, among the States. By mid-century, almost all white adult males could vote.

The second major effort to broaden the electorate followed the Civil War. The 15th Amendment, ratified in 1870, was intended to protect any citizen from being denied the right to vote because of race or color. Still, for nearly another century African Americans remained the largest group of disfranchised citizens in the nation's population.

The ratification of the 19th Amendment in 1920—prohibiting the denial of the right to vote because of sex—completed the third expansion of suffrage. Wyoming, while still a territory, had been the first to give women the vote in 1869. By 1920 more than half of the States had followed that lead.

A fourth major extension took place during the 1960s, as federal legislation and court decisions centered on securing to African Americans a full role in the electoral process in all States. With the passing and vigorous enforcement of several civil rights acts, especially the Voting Rights Act of 1965 and its several later extensions, racial equality finally became possible in polling booths throughout the country.[2] The 23rd Amendment, added in 1961, included the voters of the District

---

[2]See pages 138–140.

of Columbia in the presidential electorate. The 24th Amendment, ratified in 1964, eliminated the poll tax (and any other tax) as a condition for voting in any federal election.

The fifth and latest expansion of the electorate came with the adoption of the 26th Amendment in 1971. It provides that no State can set any age above 18 as the minimum age at which a person can qualify to vote.

## The Power to Set Voting Qualifications

The Constitution does not give to the Federal Government the power to set suffrage qualifications. Rather, that matter is reserved to the States. The Constitution does, however, place five restrictions on the States in the use of that power.

1. Any person whom a State allows to vote for members of the "most numerous branch" of its own legislature must also be allowed to vote for representatives and senators in Congress.[3] This restriction is of little real meaning today. With only minor exceptions, each of the States allows the same voters to vote in all elections within the State.

2. No State can deprive any person of the right to vote "on account of race, color, or previous condition of servitude."[4]

3. No State can deprive any person of the right to vote on account of sex.[5]

4. No State can require the payment of any tax as condition for taking part in the nomination or election of any federal officeholder.

That is, no State can levy any tax in connection with any process involved in the selection of the President, the Vice President, or members of Congress.[6]

5. No State can deprive any person who is at least 18 years of age of the right to vote because of age.[7]

Beyond these five restrictions, remember that no State can violate any other provision in the Constitution in the setting of suffrage qualifications—or in anything else that it does. A case decided by the Supreme Court in 1975, *Hill* v. *Stone*, illustrates the point. The Court struck down a section of the Texas constitution that declared that only those persons who owned taxable property could vote in city bond elections. The Court found the drawing of such a distinction for voting purposes—between those who do and those who do not own taxable property—to be an unreasonable classification, prohibited by the 14th Amendment's Equal Protection Clause.

## Section 1 Review

1. **Define:** suffrage, franchise, electorate
2. How large is the American electorate?
3. What two long-term trends have marked the development of the right to vote in the United States?
4. What specific restrictions does the Constitution place upon the States in the setting of suffrage qualifications?

**Critical Thinking**

5. **Recognizing Ideologies** (p. 19) Consider the extent of voting rights in 1789. (a) What do the voting restrictions of that time suggest about the first Americans' views of citizenship? (b) How have those views changed?

★

---

[3]Article I, Section 2, Clause 1; the 17th Amendment extended the "most numerous branch" provision to the election of Senators.

[4]15th Amendment. The phrase "previous condition of servitude" refers to slavery. Note that this amendment does not guarantee the right to vote to African Americans, or to anyone else. Instead, it forbids the States to discriminate against any person on these grounds in the setting of suffrage qualifications.

[5]19th Amendment. Note that this amendment does not guarantee the right to vote to women as such. Technically, it forbids States the power to discriminate against males or females in establishing suffrage qualifications.

[6]24th Amendment.

[7]26th Amendment. Note that this amendment does not prevent any State from allowing persons younger than age 18 to vote. But it does prohibit a State from setting a maximum age for voting.

# 2 Voter Qualifications Among the States

**Find Out:**

■ Who may vote in the United States?
■ How have States restricted voting rights in the past?

**Key Terms:**

registration, literacy, poll tax

Are you eligible to vote? Probably not—at least not yet. But you will be, and fairly soon. In this section, you will see how the States, including yours, determine who is qualified to vote. You will also see how those qualifications have changed over the years.

## Citizenship, Residence, and Age

Today, each State requires all voters to meet qualifications based on at least one of two factors: citizenship and residence.

**Citizenship**    Aliens are generally denied the right to vote in the United States. Still, nothing in the Constitution says that aliens cannot vote, and any State could allow them to do so if it chose.[8]

Only one State now draws any distinction between native-born and naturalized citizens with regard to suffrage. The Minnesota constitution requires a person to have been an American citizen for at least three months before he or she can vote.

In practice, a few aliens do vote—though in what number no one knows. They either wrongly believe that they are citizens or unlawfully pass themselves off as citizens when they report to their polling place.

**Residence**    Most States require that a person live within the State for at least some period of time in order to qualify to vote. The States adopted residence requirements for two reasons: (1) The residence requirement was in part meant to keep a political machine from importing—bribing—enough outsiders to affect the outcome of local elections. The enforcement of residence rules ended that once common practice. (2) Every State has accepted the view that every voter should have at least some time in which to become familiar with the candidates and issues in an election.

For decades, each of the States imposed a comparatively lengthy residence requirement—typically, at least a year in the State, 60 or 90 days in the county, and 30 days in the local ward or precinct.[9]

Residence requirements for voting are not nearly so long today. The details vary, but only slightly, among the 50 States. Nearly half now require voters to have lived in the State for at least 30 days. In several, the period is even shorter—for example, 20 days in Arkansas, Missouri, and Oregon; 15 days in South Dakota; and 10 days in New Hampshire and Oklahoma. Arizona does have a 50-day rule, but it is the only State in which a new resident must wait for more than 30 days to become an eligible voter.[10] Indeed, a growing number of States now require a voter to be a legal resident of the State but attach no time period to that requirement.

Today's much shorter requirements are a direct result of a 1970 law and a 1972 Supreme Court decision. In the Voting Rights Act Amendments of 1970, Congress prohibited any requirement of longer than 30 days for voting in presidential elections.[11] In *Dunn* v. *Blumstein*,

---

[8]At one time about a fourth of the States permitted those aliens who had applied for naturalization to vote. Typically, the western States did so to help attract settlers. Arkansas, the last State in which aliens could vote, adopted a citizenship requirement in 1926. In a few States, local governments can permit noncitizens to vote in local contests—e.g., city council elections—and a handful do.

[9]Recall, the precinct is the basic, smallest unit of election administration; see page 122. The ward is a unit into which cities are often divided for the election of members of the city council.

[10]The Arizona requirement is 50 days for voting in State and local elections and 30 days for presidential elections. The Supreme Court upheld Arizona's residence law in *Burns* v. *Fortson* in 1973, but it also declared that that law "approaches the outer constitutional limit."

[11]The Supreme Court upheld the provision in *Oregon* v. *Mitchell* in 1970, as you will see.

## Political Participation and Awareness in America

| Percentage of Americans who. . . | |
| --- | --- |
| Vote in presidential elections | 50% |
| Vote in congressional elections | 35-40 |
| Know name of congressional representative | 36 |
| Know names of both U.S. senators | 29 |
| Occasionally contact local officials | 28 |
| Vote in local elections | 10-30 |
| Occasionally attend public meetings | 19 |
| Occasionally contact federal or State officials | 16 |
| Know name of State senator | 13 |
| Give money to candidate or party | 13 |
| Know name of State representative | 12 |

Source: Selected polls, including Gallup, *Denver Post* Poll, University of Michigan, and *The New York Times, 1989.*

▲ **Interpreting Tables** Do the percentages shown here seem compatible with the number of citizens eligible to vote based on citizenship, residence, and age qualifications?

1972, the Supreme Court found Tennessee's requirement—at the time, a year in the State and 90 days in the county—unconstitutional. It held such a lengthy requirement to be an unsupportable discrimination against new residents and so in conflict with the 14th Amendment's Equal Protection Clause. The Supreme Court said that "30 days appears to be an ample period of time." Election law and practice among the States quickly accepted that standard.

Nearly every State does prohibit transients—persons living in the State for only a short time—from gaining a legal residence there. Thus, a traveling salesperson, a member of the armed services, or a college student usually cannot vote in a State where he or she has only a temporary physical residence. In several States, however, the courts have held that college students who claim the campus community as their legal residence can vote there.

**Age** The 26th Amendment sets 18 as the cap on the minimum age for voting in any election. Prior to its adoption in 1971, the generally accepted standard was 21 years of age.

In fact, up to 1970 only four States had put the voting age at under 21. Georgia first allowed 18-year-olds to vote in 1943, and then Kentucky did so in 1955. Alaska entered the Union in 1959 with the voting age set at 19, and Hawaii did so later that same year with the age set at 20. Both Alaska and Hawaii set the age above 18 but below 21 to avoid any problems that might be caused by high school students voting in local school-district elections. But, whatever the fears on that score, they have not been borne out by experience under the 26th Amendment.

In a growing number of States, some 17-year-olds can now cast ballots in primary elections. Those States allow anyone whose 18th birthday falls after the primary but before the general election to vote in the primary election—provided that person meets all other qualifications, of course.

One State, Nebraska, has come very close to effectively lowering the voting age to 17 for all elections. There, any person who will be 18 by the Tuesday following the first Monday in November can qualify to vote in any election held during that calendar year.

## Other Qualifications

A few other qualifications, notably registration, are found in several States.

▲ **Interpreting Political Cartoons**  In many parts of the world, the right to vote is still denied, but in America it is guaranteed to every citizen aged 18 and over. What attitude toward this right does the cartoon character portray?

**Registration**  Forty-nine States—all except North Dakota—require that most or all voters be registered to vote. **Registration** is a procedure of voter identification, intended to prevent fraudulent voting.[12] It gives election officials a list of those persons who are qualified to vote in an election. In a few States, the voter registration process is known as enrollment. Most of the States require all voters to register. But in a few—Wisconsin, for example—only those in urban areas must register to vote. Typically, a prospective voter must register his or her name,

age, place of birth, present address, length of residence, and similar facts with some local official—usually a registrar of elections or the county clerk.

Every State except North Dakota now has some form of permanent registration. Typically, a voter remains registered unless or until he or she moves, dies, is convicted of a serious crime, is committed to a mental institution, or fails to vote for a certain number of years or elections.

The registration requirement has become somewhat controversial in recent years. In fact, some people argue that it should be done away with. They view registration as a bar to voter turnout, especially among the poor and the less-educated.

Most people who have studied the problem favor keeping the requirement as a necessary defense against fraud. But they also favor making the process a more convenient one. In short, they see the problem in these terms: Where

---

[12]Several States also use their voter registration to identify voters in terms of their party preference and, hence, their eligibility to take part in closed primaries. In most States voters must be registered in order to vote in any election held within the State, but a few do not impose the requirement for all elections. Wisconsin does not require registration by voters who live in rural areas or in cities with populations of less than 10,000.

is the line between making it so easy to vote that fraud is encouraged and making it so difficult that legitimate voting is discouraged?

In fact, most States have eased the registration process over the last several years, and in 1993 Congress passed a law that requires every State to do so. The new law, dubbed the Motor Voter Law, became effective in 1995. It directs every State to: (1) allow all eligible citizens to register to vote at the same time they apply for or renew a driver's license; (2) provide for voter registration by mail; and (3) make voter registration forms available at the local offices of State employment, welfare, and other social service agencies.

Maine and Wisconsin allow voters to register at any time, up to and including election day. Elsewhere, there is a deadline; a voter must be registered by some date before an election, often 20 or 30 days beforehand.[13] That cutoff gives election officials time to prepare the poll books—the lists of all registered voters in each precinct—for an upcoming election.

**Literacy** Today, no State has a suffrage qualification based on voter **literacy**—a person's ability to read or write.

The literacy requirement could be, and in many places was, used to make sure that a qualified voter had at least some capacity to cast an informed ballot. But it also was used unfairly in many places to prevent or discourage certain groups from voting. The device was used in just that way to keep African Americans from voting for many years in many parts of the South.

Its unfair use finally led Congress to eliminate literacy as a suffrage qualification in the Voting Rights Act Amendments of 1970. The Supreme Court upheld that ban in *Oregon* v. *Mitchell*, 1970:

❝In enacting the literacy ban . . . Congress had before it a long history of discriminatory use of literacy tests to disfranchise voters on account of their race.❞

---

[13]In Minnesota the deadline is 20 days and in Wyoming 30 days before an election; however, in both States any qualified person who misses that deadline can register, and then vote, on election day. Neither Maine nor Wisconsin imposes such deadlines.

## VOICES *on Government*

### Demanding an End to Voting Restrictions

**Martin Luther King, Jr.,** civil rights leader and winner of the Nobel Peace Prize in 1964

❝We can never be satisfied as long as a Negro in Mississippi cannot vote and a Negro in New York believes he has nothing for which to vote. No, we are not satisfied, and we will not be satisfied until justice rolls down like waters and righteousness like a mighty stream. . . . I say to you, my friends, that even though we must face the difficulties of today and tomorrow, I still have a dream. It is a dream deeply rooted in the American dream that one day this nation will rise up and live out the true meaning of its creed—we hold these truths to be self-evident, that all men are created equal.❞

At the time Congress banned literacy tests, 18 States had some form of a literacy requirement. Some required potential voters to prove they had the ability to read; other States the ability to read and write. Still others required the ability to read, write, and "understand" some printed material—usually a passage taken from the State or Federal Constitution. Often, whites were asked simple questions; African Americans were asked questions so complex they would stump even a judge who was familiar with the passage.

Connecticut adopted the first literacy qualifications in 1855. Massachusetts followed in 1857. The actions of these States were aimed at limiting voting by Irish Catholic immigrants. Mississippi adopted a literacy requirement in

1890, and shortly, most of the other southern States followed suit, usually with an "understanding clause."[14]

A number of States outside the South also adopted literacy qualifications of various sorts. Wyoming did so in 1889, California in 1894, Washington in 1896, New Hampshire in 1902, Arizona in 1913, New York in 1921, Oregon in 1924, and Alaska in 1949.

**Tax Payment**   The **poll tax** was a tax payment required by some States before a person was allowed to vote. Property ownership, as proved by the payment of property taxes, was once a common suffrage requirement. That requirement and others that also called for the payment of a tax have now disappeared.

The poll tax was once found throughout the South. Beginning with Florida in 1889, each of the 11 southern States adopted the poll tax as part of an effort to discourage voting by African Americans. The device proved to be of only limited effectiveness, however. That fact, and opposition to the use of the poll tax from within the South as well as elsewhere, led most of those States to abandon it.[15]

The 24th Amendment, ratified in 1964, outlawed the poll tax, or any other tax, as a condition for voting in any federal election. The Supreme Court finally eliminated the poll tax as a qualification for voting in all elections in 1966. In *Harper* v. *Virginia State Board of Elections*, the Court held the Virginia poll tax to be in conflict with the 14th Amendment's Equal Protection Clause. The Court could find no reasonable relationship between the act of voting on the one hand, and the payment of a tax on the other.

**Who May Not Vote**   Clearly, democratic government can exist only where the right to vote is very widely held. Still, every State does purposely deny the vote to certain persons. Thus, none of the 50 States allow people in mental institutions, or any other persons who have been legally found to be mentally incompetent, to vote. Nearly all States also disqualify those who have been convicted of serious crimes. A few States also do not allow anyone dishonorably discharged from the armed forces to vote. In some States, a few groups like duelists, the homeless, or polygamists are also disqualified.

## Section 2 Review

**1. Define:** registration, literacy, poll tax
**2.** On what two bases does each State now set voter qualifications?
**3.** In general, how long must a person be a resident of a place before becoming a qualified voter?
**4.** (a) What is the essential purpose of voter registration? (b) For what reasons do some people urge its elimination?
**5.** For what reasons did Congress decide that literacy cannot be used as a voting qualification anywhere in the United States?
**6.** (a) How was the poll tax used as a voting qualification? (b) What finally became of this device?

**Critical Thinking**

**7. Identifying Alternatives** (p. 19) Imagine that you are a State lawmaker. On what grounds do you feel it is fair to deny someone the right to vote? Make a list of voter qualifications for your State that would meet constitutional standards.

---

[14]A "grandfather clause" was added to the Louisiana constitution in 1895, and Alabama, Georgia, Maryland, North Carolina, Oklahoma, and Virginia soon added them, as well. These clauses stated that any man, or his male descendants, who had voted in the State before the adoption of the 15th Amendment (1870) could become a legal voter without regard to any literacy or taxpaying qualifications. Those qualifications had been aimed at disfranchising African Americans, and the grandfather clauses were designed to enfranchise those white males who were unintentionally disqualified by their failure to meet the literacy or taxpaying requirements. The Supreme Court found the Oklahoma provision, the last to be adopted (in 1910), in conflict with the 15th Amendment in *Guinn* v. *United States* in 1915.

[15]By 1966, the poll tax was still in use only in Alabama, Mississippi, Texas, and Virginia. It had been abolished in North Carolina (1924), Louisiana (1934), Florida (1937), Georgia (1945), South Carolina (1950), Tennessee (1951), and Arkansas (1964).

★

## Should Free Speech Ever Be Suppressed?
### *Feiner v. New York*, 1951

The Free Speech Clause of the 1st Amendment is intended to protect the right of every person to express his or her views without fear of persecution. Does that right extend to those who support unpopular ideas? Does the right mean that police cannot step in when they believe that a speaker's words threaten to incite his or her listeners to violence?

In early 1949, Irving Feiner, a student at Syracuse University in New York, climbed atop a box at a busy street corner in Syracuse and began to speak. He attracted a crowd of about 75 people, and he urged them all to attend a meeting to be held that night by the Young Progressives of America.

The Young Progressives were an off-shoot of the Progressive party, which had split away from the Democrats during the 1948 presidential campaign. The major planks in the Progressives' platform called for repeal of the draft, an end to race-based discrimination, closer ties with the Soviet Union, and greater freedom of political action for the Communist party in this country.

In the course of his speech, Feiner made a number of insulting remarks about President Harry Truman, about the mayor of Syracuse and other local politicians, and about the American Legion. He also urged African Americans in the crowd to fight for equal rights.

According to court records, Feiner's words "stirred up a little excitement." Some pushing and shoving began in the crowd, as well as some angry muttering. After about 20 minutes, two police officers asked Feiner to stop speaking. He refused and they arrested him. Feiner was convicted of disorderly conduct, lost his appeals in the New York courts, and took his case to the U.S. Supreme Court.

*Review the following arguments and evidence presented to the Supreme Court.*

### Arguments for Feiner

**1.** The 1st Amendment guarantees the right to free speech and applies it to the States through the 14th Amendment.
**2.** Police cannot be used as an instrument to suppress unpopular views.
**3.** The ordinary murmurings and objections of an unsympathetic audience cannot be allowed to silence a speaker.

### Arguments for New York

**1.** Neither the 1st nor the 14th Amendment was violated here.
**2.** The police acted not to suppress speech but to preserve public order, which is a legitimate reason for limiting speech.
**3.** The crowd was not merely unsympathetic; it was being moved to violence by Feiner's inflamatory words.

### Getting Involved

**1. Identify** the constitutional grounds on which each side based its arguments.
**2. Debate** the opposing viewpoints presented in this case.
**3. Predict** how you think the Supreme Court ruled in this case and why. Then refer to the Supreme Court Glossary on page 765 to read about the decision. Do you agree with the Court's decision?

# 3 Suffrage and Civil Rights

**Find Out:**
- For what reasons were civil rights laws necessary to secure the right to vote for African Americans?
- What have been the effects of civil rights laws on voting qualifications?

**Key Terms:**
gerrymandering, injunction

How important is the right to vote? For those who do not have it, that right can seem as important as life itself. Indeed, in the Deep South of the 1960s, civil rights workers suffered arrest, beatings, shocks with electric cattle prods, even death—all in the name of the right to vote. Their efforts inspired the nation and led to large-scale federal efforts to secure suffrage for African Americans and other minority groups in the United States.

In this section, you will read about that historic struggle and the landmark federal laws it produced.

## The 15th Amendment

The 15th Amendment was ratified in 1870. It declares that the right to vote cannot be denied to any citizen of the United States because of race, color, or previous condition of servitude. The amendment was plainly intended to ensure that African-American men, nearly all of them former slaves and nearly all of them living in the South, could vote.

The 15th Amendment is not self-executing, however. To make it effective, Congress had to act. Yet for almost 90 years the Federal Government paid little attention to voting rights for African Americans.

Over that period, African Americans were generally and systematically kept from the polls in much of the South. White supremacists employed a number of tactics to that end. Their major weapon was violence; others included more subtle threats and social pressures—for example, firing an African-American man who did try to register or vote, or denying his family credit at local stores.

More formal—"legal"—devices were used, as well. The most effective were the literacy tests. White officials regularly manipulated these tests to disfranchise African-American citizens.

Registration laws served the same end. As written, they applied to all potential voters. In practice, however, they were often administered to keep African Americans from qualifying to vote. Poll taxes, "white primaries," gerrymandering, and several other devices were also used to that end. **Gerrymandering** is the practice of drawing the lines of electoral districts in order to limit the voting strength of a particular group or party.[16]

Led by decisions of the Supreme Court, the lower federal courts began to strike down many of these practices in the 1940s and 1950s. But those courts could act only in suits filed by those who claimed to be victims of discrimination. That case-by-case method was, at best, agonizingly slow.

Finally, Congress was moved to act—very largely in response to the civil rights movement led by Dr. Martin Luther King, Jr. It has passed several civil rights laws since the late 1950s. Those statutes are treated in some detail in Chapter 21. They do contain a number of sections specifically intended to implement the 15th Amendment, however, and those provisions are dealt with here.

---

[16]The Supreme Court outlawed gerrymandering when used for purposes of racial discrimination in a case from Alabama, *Gomillion* v. *Lightfoot,* in 1960. The white primary arose out of the decades-long Democratic domination of the politics of the South. Almost always, only the Democrats nominated candidates for office, and generally in primaries. In several southern States, political parties were defined by law as "private associations." As such, they could exclude members as they chose, and the Democrats regularly refused to admit African Americans. Because only party members could vote in the party's primary, African Americans were then excluded from the critical step in the public election process. The Supreme Court finally outlawed the white primary in a case from Texas, *Smith* v. *Allwright,* 1944.

## The Civil Rights Acts of 1957 and 1960

The first such law passed by Congress, the Civil Rights Act of 1957, set up the United States Civil Rights Commission. One of the Commission's major duties is to inquire into claims of voter discrimination. It reports its findings to Congress and the President and, through the media, to the public. The Act also gave to the attorney general the power to seek **injunctions**—federal court orders—to prevent interference with any person's right to vote in federal elections.

The Civil Rights Act of 1960 added another safeguard. It provided for the appointment of federal voting referees. These officers were to serve anywhere a federal court found voter discrimination. They were given the power to help qualified persons to register and to vote in federal elections.

## The Civil Rights Act of 1964

The Civil Rights Act of 1964 is a much broader measure than either of the two earlier ones. It outlaws discrimination in several areas, and especially in job-related matters. With regard to voting rights, its most important section forbids the use of any registration requirement in an unfair or discriminatory manner.

The 1964 law continued a pattern set in the earlier laws. For example, it relied on judicial action to overcome racial barriers and emphasized the use of federal court orders. These injunctions are backed by the power of the courts to punish for contempt any person who refuses to obey those orders.

Dramatic events in Selma, Alabama, soon pointed up the shortcomings of this approach, however. Dr. King mounted a voter registration drive in that city in early 1965. He and his supporters hoped that they could focus national attention on the issue of African-American voting rights—and they most certainly did. Their registration efforts were met with insults and violence—by local whites, city and county police, and then by State troopers. The nation saw much of the drama on television and was shocked. An outraged President Lyndon Johnson urged

▲ **March on Montgomery, Alabama** Martin Luther King, Jr., led this peaceful protest against voter discrimination in 1965.

Congress to pass new and stronger legislation to ensure the voting rights of African Americans, and Congress acted quickly.

## The Voting Rights Act of 1965 and Its Amendments

The Voting Rights Act of 1965 made the 15th Amendment, at long last, a truly effective part of the Constitution. Unlike its predecessors, this act applies to all elections held anywhere in this country—State and local, as well as federal. The law has now been extended three times, in the Voting Rights Act Amendments of 1970, 1975, and 1982.

The 1965 law directed the attorney general to attack the constitutionality of the remaining State poll tax laws. That provision led directly to *Harper* v. *Virginia State Board of Elections*, in 1966 (see page 136).

The law also suspended the use of any literacy test or similar device in any State or county where less than half of the electorate had been registered or had voted in the 1964 elections. The law authorized the attorney general to appoint voting examiners to serve in any of those States or counties. It also gave these federal officers the power to register voters and otherwise oversee the conduct of elections in those areas. The

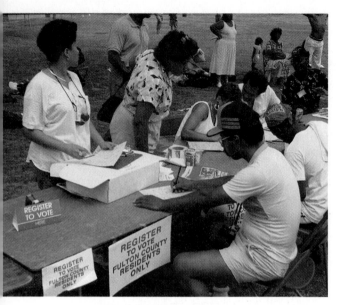

▲ **Civil Rights in Action**   Since the passage of the Voting Rights Act, the number of African-American voters has risen dramatically. Here, residents of Atlanta, Georgia, fill out voter registration forms.

1965 law also declared that no new election laws can go into effect in any of those States unless first approved—given "preclearance"—by the Department of Justice.

Any State or county subject to the voter-examiner and preclearance provisions can be removed from the law's coverage through a "bail-out" process. That relief can come if the State can show the United States District Court in the District of Columbia that it has not applied any of its voting procedures in a discriminatory way for at least the past 10 years.

The voter-examiner and preclearance provisions of the 1965 act applied to six entire States—Alabama, Georgia, Louisiana, Mississippi, South Carolina, and Virginia, and also to 40 North Carolina counties.

The Voting Rights Act was upheld by the Supreme Court in 1966. In *South Carolina* v. *Katzenbach*, the Court ruled that Congress had chosen both "rational and appropriate" means to implement the 15th Amendment.

The 1970 amendments extended the law for another five years. Based on the results of the 1968 elections, several counties in six more States—Alaska, Arizona, California, Idaho, New Mexico, and Oregon—were added to the law's coverage.

The 1970 law also provided that, for five years, no State could use literacy as the basis for any voting requirement. That temporary ban and the law's residence provisions were upheld by the Court in *Oregon* v. *Mitchell* in 1970.

The law was extended again in 1975, this time for seven years. The five-year ban on literacy tests became a permanent one, and the law's voter-examiner and preclearance provisions were broadened. Since 1975 they have also covered any State or county where more than 5 percent of the voting-age population belongs to certain "language minorities." These groups are defined to include all persons of Spanish heritage, Native Americans, Asian Americans, and Alaskan Natives. This addition spread the law's coverage to all of Alaska and Texas and to several counties in 24 other States, as well. In each of these areas, all ballots and official election materials must be printed both in English and in the language of the minority, or minorities, involved.

The 1982 amendments extended the basic features of the Act for another 25 years. In 1992 the law's language-minority provisions were amended: they now apply to any community that has a minority-language population of 10,000 or more persons.

## Section **3** Review

1. **Define:** gerrymandering, injunction
2. (a) Identify the major civil rights laws enacted by Congress over the past 30 years. (b) Describe their voting rights provisions.
3. (a) For what reasons did Congress pass the civil rights laws? (b) What role did Dr. Martin Luther King, Jr., play?
4. What voting rights provision pertains to "language minorities"?

**Critical Thinking**

5. **Drawing Conclusions** (p. 19) Racial prejudice in the United States often took the form of attempts to disfranchise African Americans. For what reasons do you think this was so?

★

# 4 Nonvoting

**Find Out:**
- What is the scope of the nonvoter problem?
- For what reasons do people not vote?

**Key Term:**
political efficacy

You are well aware of the critical link between voting and elections, on the one hand, and democratic government, on the other. Yet, despite the obvious importance of that relationship, there are millions of people in this country who, for one reason or another, do not vote.

The word *idiot* came to our language from the Greek. In ancient Athens, idiots (*idiotes*) were citizens who did not vote or otherwise take part in public life; they were ignorant of public affairs.

There are some quite legitimate reasons for nonvoting, as you will see. But this troubling fact remains: Most of the millions of Americans who could go to the polls but do not do so would have been called idiots in the Greece of 2,000 years ago.

## The Size of the Problem

The table on page 143 lays out the major facts of the nonvoter problem in American elections. Notice that on election day in 1992 there were an estimated 189 million persons of voting age in the United States. But only some 104 million of them—barely 55 percent—actually voted in the presidential election. Some 85 million persons who *might* have voted did not.

In 1992 some 96 million votes were cast in the elections held across the country to fill the 435 seats in the House of Representatives. That means that just about half of the electorate did not vote in the most recent congressional elections. (Notice, too, the even lower rates of turnout in the "off-year" elections, that is, in the congressional elections that are held across the country between the presidential elections.)

## Little-Recognized Aspects of the Problem

Several facets of the nonvoter problem are not very widely known. Take, for example, this striking fact: There are millions of nonvoters *among those who vote*. Look again at the 1992 figures on page 143. Some eight million persons who voted in the last presidential election could also have voted, but did not, for a candidate for a seat in the House of Representatives.

"Nonvoting voters" are not limited to federal elections. In fact, they are much more common in State and local elections. As a general rule, the further down the ballot an office is, the fewer the number of votes that will be cast for it. This phenomenon is sometimes called "ballot fatigue." The expression suggests that many voters exhaust their patience and/or their knowledge as they work their way down the list of offices and measures on the ballot.

Some quick illustrations of the point: More votes are regularly cast in the presidential election than in the gubernatorial election in every State. More votes are generally cast for the governorship than for such other Statewide offices as lieutenant governor or secretary of state. More voters in a county usually vote in the races for Statewide offices than vote in the contests for such county offices as sheriff, county clerk, or district attorney, and so on.

There are other little-recognized facets of the problem, too. Thus, the table on page 143 shows that turnout in congressional elections is consistently higher in presidential years than it is in "off-year elections."

That same pattern holds among the States in terms of the types of elections held; more people vote in general elections than in either primary or special elections.

## Why People Do Not Vote

Why do we have so many nonvoters? Why, even in a presidential election, do nearly half of all those who could vote stay away from the polls?

**"Cannot-Voters"** To begin with, look at another of those little-recognized aspects of the nonvoter problem: Several million persons who are regularly identified as "nonvoters" can be

ROB ROGERS reprinted by permission of UFS, Inc.

### Interpreting Political Cartoons

Nonvoting has many issues at its roots. How is one issue—a lack of confidence in the candidates—conveyed in this cartoon?

more accurately described as "cannot-voters." That is, although it is true that they do not vote, the fact is that they cannot do so. The 1992 data support the point. In that figure of some 85 million who did not vote in the last presidential election, nearly 6 million are resident aliens—and, remember, they are barred from the polls in every State. Another 5 to 6 million citizens were so ill or otherwise physically disabled that they simply could not vote in an election. And an additional 2 or 3 million persons were traveling suddenly and unexpectedly, and so could not vote.

Other groups of cannot-voters include, for example: some 500,000 persons in mental health care facilities or under some other form of legal restraint because of their mental condition; more than a million adults in jails and prisons; and perhaps as many as 100,000 who do not (cannot) vote because of their religious beliefs (for example, those who believe that acts such as voting amount to idolatry).

Racial, religious, and other discrimination still plays a part in voter turnout, too—despite the many recent federal statutes, court decisions, and enforcement actions aimed at eliminating discrimination. An unknown number—but, certainly, more than a million persons—could not vote in 1992 because of (1) the purposeful administration of election laws to keep them from doing

so, and/or (2) "informal" local pressures applied to that same end.

In short, that figure of about 85 million nonvoters in 1992 counts at least 17 million persons who, in fact, really should not be included in that number.

**Actual Nonvoters**   Even so, there are millions of actual nonvoters in the United States. Thus, in 1992 nearly 70 million Americans who could have voted in the presidential election did not.

There are any number of reasons for that behavior. As a leading example: Many deliberately choose not go to the polls. They do not vote because they are convinced that it makes no real difference who wins a certain election. Some are satisfied with the political world as they see it. They believe that, no matter who wins elections, things will continue to go well for themselves and for the country.

But a large number of those who deliberately stay away from the polls do so because they distrust politics and politicians. They have no sense of **political efficacy**. That is, they lack any sense of their own influence or effectiveness in politics. Many of them believe that they have been squeezed out of the political process, that the system that the people should control has been taken over by entrenched politicians, powerful special interests, and the media.

Cumbersome election procedures are another factor here—for example, inconvenient registration requirements, long ballots, and long lines at polling places. Bad weather also tends to discourage turnout. Another possible, though hotly debated, factor is the so-called "time-zone fallout" problem. This refers to the fact that in presidential elections, polls in the East close before polls in the West. Based on the early returns from the East, the news media often predict the outcome of a race before all the voters in the West have gone to the polls. Some people fear that such reports have discouraged western voters from casting their ballots.

But, of all the reasons that may be cited, the chief cause for nonvoting is, purely and simply, a lack of interest. Those who lack sufficient interest, who are indifferent and apathetic, who just cannot be bothered, are usually woefully uninformed. Most often, they do not know even the simplest facts about an upcoming election, let alone the candidates and issues involved in that event.

**Factors Affecting Turnout**  One useful way to get a handle on the problem of nonvoting is to draw a contrast between those persons who tend to go to the polls regularly and those who

do not. There are many differences among them. The people most likely to vote display such characteristics as higher levels of income, education, and occupational status. They are usually well integrated into community life. They tend to be long-time residents who are active in or at least comfortable with their surroundings. They are likely to have a strong sense of party identification, believe that voting is an important act, and are subject to few cross-pressures—contra-

## Voter Turnout, 1952–1994

| Year | Population of Voting Age[a] (in millions) | Votes Cast for President (in millions) | Votes Cast for President (percent) | Votes Cast for U.S. Representatives (in millions) | Votes Cast for U.S. Representatives (percent) |
|---|---|---|---|---|---|
| 1952 | 99.929 | 61.551 | 61.6 | 57.571 | 57.6 |
| 1954 | 102.075 | — | — | 42.580 | 41.7 |
| 1956 | 104.515 | 62.027 | 59.3 | 58.426 | 55.9 |
| 1958 | 106.447 | — | — | 45.818 | 43.0 |
| 1960 | 109.672 | 68.838 | 62.8 | 64.133 | 58.5 |
| 1962 | 112.952 | — | — | 51.267 | 45.4 |
| 1964 | 114.090 | 70.645 | 61.9 | 65.895 | 57.8 |
| 1966 | 116.638 | — | — | 52.908 | 45.4 |
| 1968 | 120.285 | 73.212 | 60.9 | 66.288 | 55.1 |
| 1970 | 124.498 | — | — | 54.173 | 43.5 |
| 1972 | 140.777 | 77.719 | 55.2 | 71.430 | 50.7 |
| 1974 | 146.638 | — | — | 52.495 | 35.9 |
| 1976 | 152.308 | 81.556 | 53.5 | 74.422 | 48.9 |
| 1978 | 158.369 | — | — | 55.332 | 34.9 |
| 1980 | 164.595 | 86.515 | 52.6 | 77.995 | 47.4 |
| 1982 | 169.936 | — | — | 64.514 | 38.0 |
| 1984 | 174.468 | 92.653 | 53.1 | 83.231 | 47.7 |
| 1986 | 178.566 | — | — | 59.619 | 33.4 |
| 1988 | 182.779 | 91.595 | 50.1 | 81.786 | 44.7 |
| 1990 | 186.382 | — | — | 61.506 | 33.0 |
| 1992 | 189.044 | 104.425 | 55.2 | 96.037 | 50.8 |
| 1994 | 193.650 | — | — | 74.942[b] | 38.7[b] |

[a]As estimated by Census Bureau. Population 18 years of age and over since ratification of 26th Amendment in 1971; prior to 1971, 21 years and over in all States, except: 18 years and over in Georgia since 1943 and Kentucky since 1955, 19 years and over in Alaska and 20 and over in Hawaii since 1959. [b]Preliminary.

*Sources: Statistical Abstract*; Committee for the Study of the American Electorate, Clerk of the House of Representatives.

## Voter Turnout, 1992

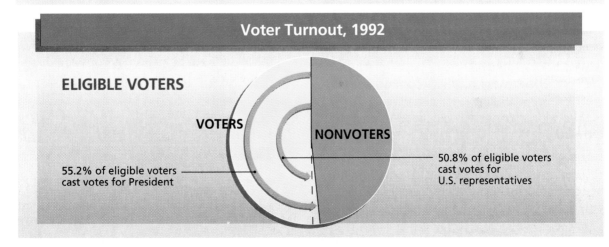

**ELIGIBLE VOTERS**

**VOTERS**

**NONVOTERS**

55.2% of eligible voters cast votes for President

50.8% of eligible voters cast votes for U.S. representatives dictory, competing influences—that would discourage their participation. They also are likely to live in those States and locales where laws, customs, and competition between the parties all work to promote turnout. The opposite characteristics produce a profile of those who are less likely to vote. Nonvoters are likely to be younger than age 35, unmarried, and unskilled. More nonvoters live in the South and in rural, rather than urban or suburban, locales.

A few of the factors are so important that they influence turnout even when they are not supported by, or are in conflict with, other factors. Thus, those persons with a high sense of political efficacy are likely to vote—no matter what their income, education, age, race, and so on. The degree of two-party competition has much the same kind of general, across-the-board effect. It, too, has an extraordinary impact on participation. Thus, the greater the degree of competition between candidates, the higher the rate of voter turnout will be, regardless of other factors.

Despite the greater weight of some factors, however, notice this important point: It is the combined presence of several of them, rather than of one of them alone, that tends to characterize a voter or nonvoter.

## Section 4 Review

**1. Define:** political efficacy
**2.** (a) On average, about what percentage of eligible voters have taken part in presidential elections since 1932? (b) In off-year congressional elections?
**3.** What does "nonvoting by voters" refer to?
**4.** (a) Identify the causes for nonvoting. (b) Which is the major one?
**5.** How does two-party competition affect voter turnout?

### Critical Thinking

**6. Predicting Consequences** (p. 19) What might be the results for the nation if all eligible voters were required to cast ballots?

★

# 5 Voter Behavior

**Find Out:**

- How do sociological and psychological factors work to determine how a person will vote?
- How much does party identification affect voter behavior?

**Key Terms:**

political socialization, party identification, straight-ticket voting, split-ticket voting, independents

As you have just seen, tens of millions of potential voters do not go to the polls in this country. But many millions more do. How do those who do vote behave? What prompts many to vote most often for Republicans and many others to support the Democratic party?

Answers to these questions are not as hard to find as you might think. Voting has been studied more closely than any other form of political participation in the United States.[17] As you are about to see, that research has produced a huge amount of information about why people tend to vote as they do.

## The Study of Voting Behavior

Most of what is known about voter behavior comes from three sources.

1. The results of particular elections. As a quick illustration: The careful study of the returns from areas populated largely by African Americans or Catholics or high-income families will indicate how those groups voted in a given election.

---

[17]Voter behavior has been so widely studied because of (1) the importance of the topic and (2) the almost unlimited amount of data available (innumerable elections in which millions of voters have cast billions of votes over time). Much of the most useful research on voter behavior is done at academic institutions—most notably the Center for Political Studies at the University of Michigan.

## Global Awareness

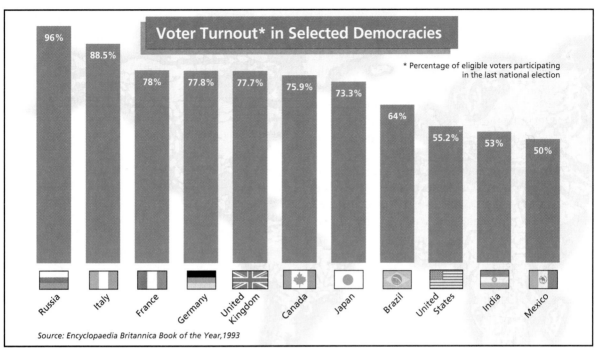

### Voter Turnout* in Selected Democracies

* Percentage of eligible voters participating in the last national election

| Russia | Italy | France | Germany | United Kingdom | Canada | Japan | Brazil | United States | India | Mexico |
|--------|-------|--------|---------|----------------|--------|-------|--------|---------------|-------|--------|
| 96% | 88.5% | 78% | 77.8% | 77.7% | 75.9% | 73.3% | 64% | 55.2% | 53% | 50% |

*Source: Encyclopaedia Britannica Book of the Year, 1993*

**Interpreting Graphs**   Democracy does not ensure high voter turnout. Why might turnout be low in the United States?

2. The field of survey research—polling of scientifically determined cross sections of the population. It is the method by which public opinion is most often identified and measured. The Gallup Poll is perhaps the best known survey research organization today.
3. Studies of **political socialization**—the process by which people gain their political attitudes and opinions. That very complex process begins in early childhood and continues on through each person's life. Political socialization involves all of the experiences and relationships that lead people to see the political world, and to act in it, as they do.

Here you will read about voter behavior—how and why people vote as they do. In Chapter 8, you will turn to the subject of public opinion and take a closer look at the techniques of survey research and the process of political socialization.

**Factors That Influence Voters**   Observers still have much to learn about voter behavior,

but many sociological and psychological factors quite clearly influence the way people vote. Sociology is the study of groups and how people behave within groups. The sociological factors affecting voter behavior are really the many pieces of a voter's social and economic life. Those pieces are of two broad kinds: (1) a voter's personal characteristics—age, race, income, occupation, education, religion, and so on, and (2) a voter's group affiliations—family, co-workers, friends, and the like.

Psychology is the study of the mind and of individual behavior. The psychological factors that influence voter behavior are a voter's perceptions of politics. That is, how the voter sees the parties, the candidates, and the issues in an election.

The differences between these two kinds of influences are not so great as they might seem. In fact, they are closely related and constantly interact with one another. How voters look at parties, candidates, or issues is often shaped by their own social and economic backgrounds.

# The Sociological Factors

From the table on page 147, you can draw a composite picture of the American voter in terms of a number of sociological factors.

But a word of caution here: Do not make too much of any one of these factors. The table reports how voters, identified by a single characteristic, voted in each presidential election from 1964 through 1992. But, remember, each voter possesses several of the characteristics shown in the table.

To make the point, consider these examples: College graduates are more likely to vote Republican. So are persons over 50 years of age. Catholics are more likely to vote for Democrats. So are members of labor unions. How, then, would a 55-year-old college-educated Catholic who belongs to the AFL-CIO vote?

**Income, Occupation**   Voters in the middle- to upper-income brackets are more likely to be Republicans. Voters with lower incomes tend to be Democrats. This pattern has held up over time; in fact, it even showed up in the lopsided elections of 1980, 1984, and 1988: Voters with incomes above $35,000 backed Ronald Reagan, both times, by better than 2 to 1, and they voted for George Bush by a margin of nearly 3 to 2. A majority of those with incomes of less than $15,000 voted for Democrats Jimmy Carter in 1980, Walter Mondale in 1984, and Michael Dukakis in 1988. The same voting patterns were apparent in the presidential election of 1992.

Most often, income and occupation are closely related matters. Professional and business people, and others with higher incomes, tend to vote for Republican candidates. Manual workers, and others from lower income groups, usually vote for Democrats. Thus, with the single exception of 1964, professional and business people have voted heavily Republican in every presidential election in the modern era, including 1992.

**Education**   There is also a close relationship between the level of a voter's education and how he or she votes. College graduates vote for Republicans in higher percentages than do high-school graduates; and high-school graduates vote more often Republican than do those who have only gone through grade school.

**Gender, Age**   Historically, gender has not played a major role in partisan voting behavior. Men have been no more or less likely to favor one party and its candidates than have women. But several studies do suggest this: Men and women do tend to vote in measurably different ways when issues related to war and national defense or to personal rights are prominent in an election.

A "gender gap" has appeared in recent years. Since 1980, women have been noticeably less likely to vote Republican, at least in presidential contests. The table on page 147 shows the point, and so does this: Bill Clinton won 46 percent of the female vote in 1992; George Bush received 38 percent of the votes cast by women and Ross Perot 16.

Younger voters usually have been more likely to be Democrats than Republicans. Older voters are likely to find the GOP and its candidates more attractive. Thus, in every presidential election from 1960 through 1980, the Democrats won a larger percentage of the votes of the under-30 age group than those cast by voters age 50 and over. That long-standing pattern was broken by President Reagan's appeal to younger voters in 1984, and by George Bush in 1988. However, Bill Clinton restored the Democrats' claim to those voters in 1992.

**Religious, Ethnic Background**   A majority of northern Protestants prefer the GOP. Catholics and Jews are much more likely to be Democrats.

Historical factors account for much of this pattern. Most of those who first came from Europe to settle this country were of English stock, and Protestant. The later tides of immigration, from southern and eastern Europe, brought many Catholics and Jews to the United States. Those later immigrants were often treated as minority groups by the largely Protestant establishment. And they most often settled in the larger cities, where local Democratic party organizations helped them to become citizens and voters. From the New Deal period of the

## Voting by Groups in Presidential Elections, 1964–1992 (By Percentage of Votes Reported Cast)

| | 1964 | | 1968 | | | 1972 | | 1976 | | 1980 | | | 1984 | | 1988 | | 1992 | | |
|---|---|---|---|---|---|---|---|---|---|---|---|---|---|---|---|---|---|---|---|
| | **D** | **R** | **D** | **R** | **AIP** | **D** | **R** | **D** | **R** | **D** | **R** | **I** | **D** | **R** | **D** | **R** | **D** | **R** | **I** |
| **National** | 61.3 | 38.7 | 43.0 | 43.4 | 13.6 | 37.5 | 60.7 | 50 | 48 | 41 | 50.7 | 6.6 | 41 | 59 | 46 | 54 | 43.2 | 37.8 | 19 |
| **Sex** | | | | | | | | | | | | | | | | | | | |
| Men | 60 | 40 | 41 | 43 | 16 | 37 | 63 | 53 | 45 | 38 | 53 | 7 | 36 | 64 | 44 | 56 | 41 | 37 | 22 |
| Women | 62 | 38 | 45 | 43 | 12 | 38 | 62 | 48 | 51 | 44 | 49 | 6 | 45 | 55 | 48 | 52 | 46 | 38 | 16 |
| **Race** | | | | | | | | | | | | | | | | | | | |
| White | 59 | 41 | 38 | 47 | 15 | 32 | 68 | 46 | 52 | 36 | 56 | 7 | 34 | 66 | 41 | 59 | 39 | 41 | 20 |
| Nonwhite | 94 | 6 | 85 | 12 | 3 | 87 | 13 | 85 | 15 | 86 | 10 | 2 | 87 | 13 | 82 | 18 | 77 | 11 | 12 |
| **Education** | | | | | | | | | | | | | | | | | | | |
| College | 52 | 48 | 37 | 54 | 9 | 37 | 63 | 42 | 55 | 35 | 53 | 10 | 39 | 61 | 42 | 58 | 43 | 40 | 17 |
| High school | 62 | 38 | 42 | 43 | 15 | 34 | 66 | 54 | 46 | 43 | 51 | 5 | 43 | 57 | 46 | 54 | 40 | 38 | 22 |
| Grade school | 66 | 34 | 52 | 33 | 15 | 49 | 51 | 58 | 41 | 54 | 42 | 3 | 51 | 49 | 55 | 45 | 56 | 28 | 16 |
| **Occupation** | | | | | | | | | | | | | | | | | | | |
| Professional/ business | 54 | 46 | 34 | 56 | 10 | 31 | 69 | 42 | 56 | 33 | 55 | 10 | 34 | 66 | | | | | |
| White-collar | 57 | 43 | 41 | 47 | 12 | 36 | 64 | 50 | 48 | 40 | 51 | 9 | 47 | 53 | NA | NA | NA | NA | NA |
| Manual | 71 | 29 | 50 | 35 | 15 | 43 | 57 | 58 | 41 | 48 | 48 | 5 | 46 | 54 | | | | | |
| Union family members | 73 | 27 | 56 | 29 | 15 | 46 | 54 | 63 | 36 | 50 | 43 | 5 | 52 | 48 | | | | | |
| **Age** | | | | | | | | | | | | | | | | | | | |
| Under 30 | 64 | 36 | 47 | 38 | 15 | 48 | 52 | 53 | 45 | 47 | 41 | 11 | 40 | 60 | 37 | 63 | 40 | 37 | 23 |
| 30–49 | 63 | 37 | 44 | 41 | 15 | 33 | 67 | 48 | 49 | 38 | 52 | 8 | 40 | 60 | 45 | 55 | 42 | 37 | 21 |
| 50 and older | 59 | 41 | 41 | 47 | 12 | 36 | 64 | 52 | 48 | 41 | 54 | 4 | 41 | 59 | 49 | 51 | 46 | 39 | 15 |
| **Religion** | | | | | | | | | | | | | | | | | | | |
| Protestants | 55 | 45 | 35 | 49 | 16 | 30 | 70 | 46 | 53 | 39 | 54 | 6 | 39 | 61 | 42 | 58 | 41 | 41 | 18 |
| Catholics | 76 | 24 | 59 | 33 | 8 | 48 | 52 | 57 | 41 | 46 | 47 | 6 | 39 | 61 | 51 | 49 | 47 | 35 | 18 |
| **Politics** | | | | | | | | | | | | | | | | | | | |
| Republicans | 20 | 80 | 9 | 86 | 5 | 5 | 95 | 9 | 91 | 8 | 86 | 5 | 4 | 96 | 7 | 93 | 7 | 77 | 16 |
| Democrats | 87 | 13 | 74 | 12 | 14 | 67 | 33 | 82 | 18 | 69 | 26 | 4 | 79 | 21 | 85 | 15 | 82 | 8 | 10 |
| Independents | 56 | 44 | 31 | 44 | 25 | 31 | 69 | 38 | 57 | 29 | 55 | 14 | 33 | 67 | 43 | 57 | 39 | 30 | 31 |
| **Region** | | | | | | | | | | | | | | | | | | | |
| East | 68 | 32 | 50 | 43 | 7 | 42 | 58 | 51 | 47 | 43 | 47 | 9 | 46 | 54 | 51 | 49 | 47 | 35 | 18 |
| Midwest | 61 | 39 | 44 | 47 | 9 | 40 | 60 | 48 | 50 | 41 | 51 | 7 | 42 | 58 | 47 | 53 | 44 | 34 | 22 |
| South | 52 | 48 | 31 | 36 | 33 | 29 | 71 | 54 | 45 | 44 | 52 | 3 | 37 | 63 | 40 | 60 | 38 | 45 | 17 |
| West | 60 | 40 | 44 | 49 | 7 | 41 | 59 | 46 | 51 | 35 | 54 | 9 | 40 | 60 | 46 | 54 | 45 | 35 | 20 |

D = Democratic candidate; R = Republican candidate; AIP = American Independent Party candidate (George Wallace, 1968); I = Independent candidate (John B. Anderson, 1980; Ross Perot, 1992). Figures do not add to 100% in some groups because of rounding and/or minor party votes. *Less than 1%.

*Source: The Gallup Organization*

▲ **Interpreting Tables: Multicultural Awareness** Groups have historic loyalties to particular parties. Which racial group has voted largely Democratic since 1964?

1930s on, social welfare programs have strengthened the ties of most minority groups to the Democratic party.

In 1960 John Kennedy became the first Roman Catholic President. His election marked a sharp-er split between Catholic and Protestant voters than that found in any of the other elections covered by the table.

Nonwhites support the Democratic party—consistently and massively. They form the only

# Outcome of Selected Presidential Elections

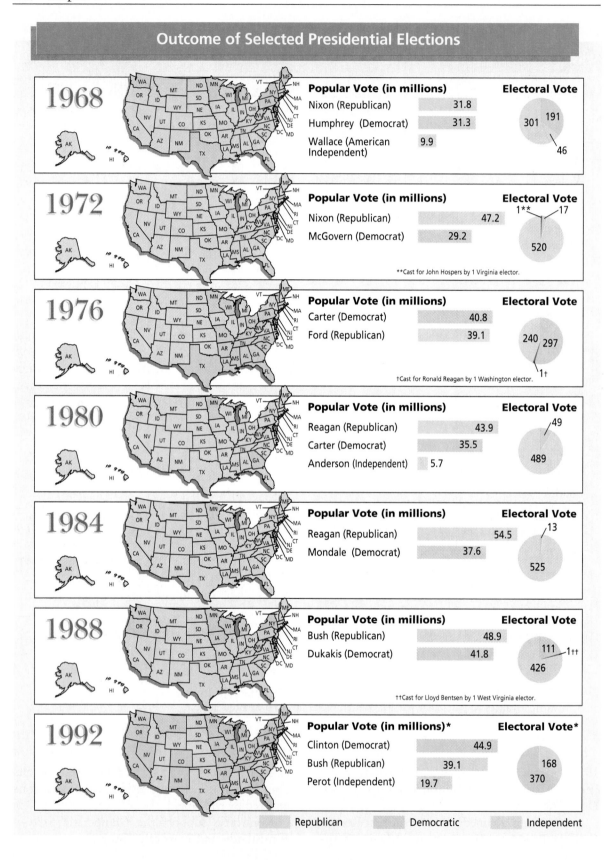

## 1968

**Popular Vote (in millions)**

Nixon (Republican) — 31.8

Humphrey (Democrat) — 31.3

Wallace (American Independent) — 9.9

**Electoral Vote**

301   191

46

## 1972

**Popular Vote (in millions)**

Nixon (Republican) — 47.2

McGovern (Democrat) — 29.2

**Electoral Vote**

1**   17

520

**Cast for John Hospers by 1 Virginia elector.

## 1976

**Popular Vote (in millions)**

Carter (Democrat) — 40.8

Ford (Republican) — 39.1

**Electoral Vote**

240   297

1†

†Cast for Ronald Reagan by 1 Washington elector.

## 1980

**Popular Vote (in millions)**

Reagan (Republican) — 43.9

Carter (Democrat) — 35.5

Anderson (Independent) — 5.7

**Electoral Vote**

49

489

## 1984

**Popular Vote (in millions)**

Reagan (Republican) — 54.5

Mondale (Democrat) — 37.6

**Electoral Vote**

13

525

## 1988

**Popular Vote (in millions)**

Bush (Republican) — 48.9

Dukakis (Democrat) — 41.8

**Electoral Vote**

111   1††

426

††Cast for Lloyd Bentsen by 1 West Virginia elector.

## 1992

**Popular Vote (in millions)***

Clinton (Democrat) — 44.9

Bush (Republican) — 39.1

Perot (Independent) — 19.7

**Electoral Vote***

168

370

Republican          Democratic          Independent

group that has given the Democratic candidate a clear majority in every presidential election since 1952. There are now more than 30 million African Americans, and they make up the single most important racial minority in the country. In the North, African Americans generally voted Republican until the 1930s. They moved away from the party of Abraham Lincoln with the coming of the New Deal, however. The civil rights movement of the 1960s led to greater African-American participation in the South—and there, too, African Americans now vote overwhelmingly Democratic.

There are now more than 23 million Hispanic Americans, people with Spanish-speaking backgrounds. To this point, Hispanics have tended to favor Democratic candidates. But, note, the label "Hispanic" conceals differences among Cuban Americans, who most often vote Republican, and Mexican Americans and Puerto Ricans, who are strongly Democratic. The rate of turnout among Hispanics is comparatively low—just about 30 percent in 1992.

### Geography

Geography—the part of the country, the State, and/or the locale in which a person lives—has an impact on voter behavior.

After the Civil War, the States of the old Confederacy voted so consistently Democratic that the southeast quarter of the nation became known as the Solid South. For more than a hundred years now, most Southerners, regardless of any other factor, have been Democrats. The Solid South has disappeared in terms of presidential elections, but the Democrats still dominate most of the southern political scene.

Over time, the strongest and most consistent support for the Republicans by States can be found in Maine and Vermont in the Northeast and in Kansas, Nebraska, and the Dakotas in the Midwest. Lately, there has been much speculation about voting patterns in the "Sunbelt"—that area stretching from the southeastern States westward to California. Some analysts see the region as a base for increased conservatism and new strength for the Republican party in national politics.

Voters' attitudes also vary in terms of the size of the communities in which they live. In general, the Democrats draw strength from the big cities of the North and East. Many white Democrats have moved from the central cities and taken their political preferences with them, but Republican voters still dominate much of suburban America. Outside the South, voters in the smaller cities and rural areas are likely to be Republicans.

**Family, Other Group Affiliations**  To this point, you have seen the American voter sketched in terms of several broad social and economic characteristics. The picture can also be drawn on the basis of much smaller and more personal groupings, especially such primary groups as family, co-workers, and friends.

Typically, the members of a family vote in strikingly similar ways. Nine out of ten married couples share the same partisan leanings. As many as two out of every three voters follow the political attachments of their parents. Those who work together and circles of friends behave in much the same way; that is, they vote very much alike.

## The Psychological Factors

To understand the voting process, you must look beyond such factors as occupation, education, ethnic background, and place of residence. You must also take into account a number of psychological factors. That is, you must look at the voters' perceptions of politics: how they see and how they react to the parties, the candidates, and the issues in an election.

**Party Identification**  A majority of Americans identify themselves with one or the other of the major parties early in life. Many never change. They support that party with little or no regard for either the candidates or the issues.

The hefty impact of **party identification**—the loyalty of people to a political party—is the single most significant and lasting predictor of how a person will vote. A person who is a Democrat or a Republican will, for that reason, very likely vote for all or most of that party's candidates in an election. The practice of voting for candidates of but one party in an election is called **straight-ticket voting**.

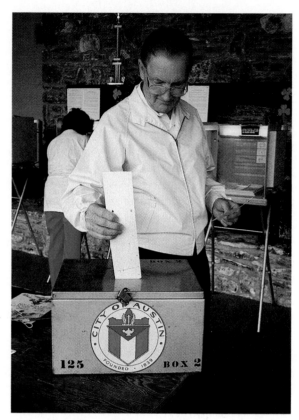

▲ **A Lifelong Responsibility** An eighteen-year old exercises her right to vote (left) as does a veteran of the electoral system (right).

Party identification is, then, a key factor in American politics. Among many other things, it means that each of the major parties can regularly count on the votes of millions of faithful supporters in every election. The Democrats have enjoyed a substantial advantage over the Republicans in this matter for more than 50 years now.

Several signs suggest that, while it remains a major factor, party identification has lost some of its impact in recent years. One of those signs is the weakened condition of the parties themselves. Another is the marked increase in **split-ticket voting**—voting for candidates of both parties at the same election. That practice has increased remarkably since the 1960s.

Another telling sign is the large number of voters who now call themselves **independents**. This term is regularly used to identify those people who have no party affiliation—voters

who are independent of both the Republicans and the Democrats (and of any minor party, as well). But "independent" is a tricky term.[18] Many who claim to be independents actually support one or the other of the major parties quite regularly.

The loose nature of party membership makes it difficult to determine just what proportion of the electorate is independent. The best guesses put the number of independents at some-

---

[18]Notice that the term "independent" is sometimes mistakenly used in ways that suggest that independents form a more or less cohesive group in politics, and one that can be readily compared with Republicans and/or Democrats. (Although the Gallup poll data on pages 107 and 147 do not intend such comparisons, they can be misread to that effect. However, independents in American politics are not only independent of Republicans and Democrats; each of them is also independent of all other independents.

where between a fourth and a third of all the voters today.

Until recently, the typical independent was less concerned, less well informed, and less active in politics than those voters who identified themselves as Republicans or Democrats. That description still fits many independents. A new breed appeared in the 1960s and 1970s, however. Largely because of the political events and personalities of that period, these "new" independents preferred not to join either major party. Still, they are much like the party identifiers—except that they are often young and above average in education, income, and job status.

**Candidates and Issues**    Much of what you have just read about party identification might prompt this question: How does the Republican party ever win a presidential election? A very large part of the answer can be put in these terms: candidates and issues.

Party identification is a long-term factor. Most voters identify with one or the other of the major parties, and over time, they most often support its candidates. But they do not always vote that way. One or more short-term factors can cause them to switch sides in a particular election—or, at least vote a split ticket. Thus, in the 1992 presidential election, 27 percent of those persons who usually vote Republican voted for independent Ross Perot; and 13 percent of those who normally support Democratic candidates also voted for Perot.

The most important of these short-term factors are the candidates and the issues in an election. Clearly, the impressions a candidate makes on the voters can have an impact on how they vote. What image does a candidate project? How is he or she seen in terms of personality, character, style, appearance, past record, abilities, and so on?

Just as clearly, issues can also have a large impact on voter behavior. Their role varies from election to election, however, depending on such things as the emotional content of the issues themselves, the voters' awareness of them, and the ways in which they are presented to the electorate.

Issues have become an increasingly important part of the voter-decision mix in recent years.

▲ **Interpreting Political Cartoons**
Many factors affect voting behavior. At which factor is the cartoonist poking fun?

The tumultuous nature of politics over the past 25 years or so—highlighted by the civil rights movement, the Vietnam War, the Watergate scandal, and ongoing economic problems—is likely responsible for this heightened concern with issues.

# Section **5** Review

**1. Define:** political socialization, party identification, straight-ticket voting, split-ticket voting, independents

**2.** List three of the sociological factors that affect voting behavior.

**3.** Why is it important not to give too much weight to any one of these factors?

**4.** List three of the psychological factors that affect voting behavior.

**5.** What is the most significant, lasting indicator of an individual's voting behavior?

**Critical Thinking**

**6. Determining Relevance** (p. 19) Imagine that in a particular presidential election, the gender gap grew to 20 percent. (a) What would be the most likely explanation for this dramatic change? (b) Would sociological factors or psychological factors more likely be involved?

★

# Determining Relevance

Determining relevance means deciding if and how events, situations, or items relate to or have an effect on one another. Determining relevance between pieces of information is an important skill in understanding relationships in the study of American Government and the political process. By determining whether information is relevant, it is possible to decide which information is important to consider and which information is not essential in the process of solving a problem. Follow the steps below and use the graph and the table to practice determining relevance between different pieces of information. The graph is on the left and gives information about voter registration. The table on the right is titled Elected Officials.

**1. Identify the main idea represented by each piece of information.** Look at the graph and the table shown on this page. Then, answer the following questions: (a) What is the basic idea communicated by the graph? (b) What is the main idea communicated by the table?

**2. Look for connections between the main ideas.** Compare your answers to the questions above about the graph and the table. Answer the following questions: (a) What ideas, concepts, or subjects do the graph and the table share in common with each other? (b) What conclusions can you draw from each one?

**3. Determine the relevance of the two pieces of information.** Once you have identified the similarities and differences between the graph and the table and the information they contain, you are ready to determine if and in what way the information relates. Ask yourself: (a) Does the information in the graph offer any possible explanation for the information in the table? (b) Does the information in the table help explain the graph?

## Political Participation of African Americans in the South

**VOTER REGISTRATION IN ELEVEN SOUTHERN STATES**

(in millions)

| Year | Millions |
|------|----------|
| 1964 | 2.2 |
| 1968 | 3.1 |
| 1972 | 3.65 |
| 1976 | 4.15 |
| 1980 | 4.25 |
| 1984 | 5.6 |
| 1988 | 5.8 |
| 1992 | 6.3 |

**ELECTED OFFICIALS**

| STATE | U.S. Congress | | State Legislature | | City & County Offices | | Courts & Law Enforcement | | Education | | TOTALS | |
|-------|------|------|------|------|------|------|------|------|------|------|------|------|
| | 1970 | 1993 | 1970 | 1993 | 1970 | 1993 | 1970 | 1993 | 1970 | 1993 | 1970 | 1993 |
| Alabama | 0 | 1 | 0 | 22 | 52 | 529 | 27 | 58 | 7 | 89 | 86 | 699 |
| Arkansas | 0 | 0 | 0 | 13 | 14 | 214 | 4 | 51 | 37 | 102 | 55 | 380 |
| Florida | 0 | 3 | 1 | 19 | 31 | 133 | 2 | 28 | 2 | 17 | 36 | 200 |
| Georgia | 0 | 3 | 14 | 40 | 18 | 371 | 1 | 32 | 7 | 99 | 40 | 545 |
| Louisiana | 0 | 2 | 1 | 31 | 34 | 345 | 20 | 104 | 9 | 153 | 64 | 635 |
| Mississippi | 0 | 0 | 1 | 42 | 57 | 495 | 18 | 88 | 5 | 126 | 81 | 751 |
| North Carolina | 0 | 2 | 1 | 26 | 50 | 328 | 1 | 31 | 10 | 81 | 62 | 468 |
| South Carolina | 0 | 1 | 0 | 25 | 32 | 269 | 4 | 15 | 2 | 140 | 38 | 450 |
| Tennessee | 0 | 1 | 8 | 15 | 9 | 104 | 17 | 24 | 4 | 24 | 38 | 168 |
| Texas | 0 | 2 | 3 | 16 | 16 | 323 | 0 | 40 | 10 | 91 | 29 | 472 |
| Virginia | 0 | 1 | 3 | 13 | 27 | 126 | 6 | 15 | 0 | 0 | 36 | 155 |
| **TOTALS** | 0 | 16 | 32 | 262 | 340 | 3,237 | 100 | 486 | 93 | 922 | 565 | 4,923 |

Sources: U.S. Bureau of the Census, Current Population Survey; Joint Center for Political Studies

# Chapter-in-Brief

Scan all headings, photographs, charts, and other visuals in the chapter before reading the section summaries below.

## Section 1 The Constitution and the Right to Vote (pp. 129–131)

The Constitution says very little about the right to vote. For the most part, suffrage qualifications are left to the States.

In this nation's early history, the right to vote was held by a very few, mostly by white male property owners. Over time, the franchise has been extended in two major ways: (1) through the gradual elimination of arbitrary restrictions on the right, and (2) by the Federal Government's assumption of greater authority in suffrage matters. The 15th Amendment forbids denial of the right to vote on grounds of race, the 19th on the basis of gender, the 24th for the failure to pay a tax, and the 26th to those at least age 18.

## Section 2 Voter Qualifications Among the States (pp. 132–136)

Historically, States have set most suffrage restrictions. Today, every State requires that voters be citizens and residents. Residence requirements have been relaxed in recent years—generally to 30 days or less among the States.

Voters must register to vote in every State but one. The registration process has also become less burdensome in recent years.

The use of literacy and tax payment requirements to discourage voting, particularly by African Americans, finally disappeared in the 1960s and 1970s—largely because of new federal civil rights laws and court actions.

## Section 3 Suffrage and Civil Rights (pp. 138–140)

The 15th Amendment was intended to ensure that voting rights would not be denied because of race. For nearly 90 years, however, Congress failed to pass the laws necessary to make the Amendment truly effective. It finally began to do so in response to the Civil Rights Movement in the late 1950s.

Today, the basic statute that protects the right to vote against race-based actions is the Voting Rights Act of 1965. That law has now been extended and expanded three times by Congress, and most recently in 1982.

## Section 4 Nonvoting (pp. 141–144)

At least half of all eligible voters do not vote in most elections in this country. Only 55.2 percent of the electorate voted in the 1992 presidential election. Nonvoting among those who vote is but one of the little recognized aspects of the problem.

Millions of potential voters fail to go to the polls for a variety of reasons, but the chief reason for that behavior is a lack of interest. However, approximately one in every five nonvoters is in fact a "cannot voter."

## Section 5 Voter Behavior (pp. 144–151)

Millions of Americans do vote. Extensive studies of voter behavior show that how they vote is heavily influenced by a number of sociological and psychological factors.

The sociological factors that impact voting include such things as a voter's income, occupation, education, age, gender, and so on, and his/her primary group affiliations—notably, family, friends, and coworkers.

The psychological factors are a voter's perceptions of politics—that is, how he/she sees the parties, candidates, and issues in an election.

# Chapter Review

## Vocabulary and Key Terms

suffrage (p. 129)
franchise (p. 129) .
electorate (p. 130)
registration (p. 134)
literacy (p. 135)

poll tax (p. 136)
gerrymandering (p. 138)
injunction (p. 139)
political efficacy (p. 142)
political socialization (p. 145)

party identification
  (p. 149)
straight-ticket voting
  (p.149)
split-ticket voting (p. 150)
independents (p. 150)

**Matching:** *Review the key terms in the list above. If you are not sure of a term's meaning, look up the term and review its definition. Choose a term from the list above that best matches each description.*

1. the drawing of electoral district lines to the advantage of a party or other group
2. the right to vote
3. the ability to read or write
4. a court order requiring or forbidding some action
5. all the people entitled to vote in a given election

**True or False:** *Determine whether each statement is true or false. If it is true, write "true." If it is false, change the underlined word or words to make the statement true.*

1. Voters who support only those candidates of one party are likely to practice <u>straight-ticket voting</u>.
2. <u>Registration</u> is a now-unconstitutional method of keeping certain people from voting.
3. People who doubt their own ability to influence the political process have little sense of <u>party identification</u>.
4. <u>Political socialization</u> is a complex process by which a person acquires his or her political attitudes.

5. The <u>electorate</u> does not identify with or support one of the two major parties.

**Word Relationships:** *Distinguish between the words in each pair.*

1. registration/poll tax
2. political efficacy/political socialization
3. party identification/independents
4. straight-ticket voting/split-ticket voting

## Main Ideas

### Section 1 (pp. 129–131)
1. What two trends explain the growth in the size of the American electorate?
2. What major events or eras contributed to those trends?
3. (a) At what level of government are voter qualifications set? (b) What restrictions does the Constitution place on the power to set voter qualifications?

### Section 2 (pp. 132–136)
4. (a) On what two factors do each of the States set qualifications to vote? (b) What additional restrictions presently exist in the States?
5. What are some of the suffrage qualifications States used in the past, but no longer use today?

**6.** What was the purpose of literacy tests and poll taxes?

## Section 3 (pp. 138–140)

**7.** What was the purpose of the 15th Amendment?

**8.** For what reasons did the 15th Amendment prove inadequate at protecting the suffrage of many African Americans?

**9.** (a) How did the civil rights movement of the 1950s and 1960s seek to solve the problem of disfranchisement among African Americans? (b) Were these efforts effective?

## Section 4 (pp. 141–144)

**10.** What does it mean to say that the United States has a nonvoter problem?

**11.** (a) Who are the "cannot voters"? (b) What is the significance of their impact on the nonvoter problem?

**12.** What are the major reasons that people do not vote?

## Section 5 (pp. 144–151)

**13.** What are the sociological factors that influence a person's voting decisions?

**14.** What are the psychological factors that influence a person's voting decisions?

**15.** For what reason is it difficult to predict how any one voter will vote based on an analysis of his or her psychological and sociological profile?

## Critical Thinking

**1. Determining Relevance** (p. 19) What relationship, if any, can you see between these two facts: Changes in law and custom in recent years have made it possible for a wider range of citizens to vote. Yet at the same time, smaller percentages of voters take part in elections.

**2. Recognizing Bias** (p. 19) For what reasons do you think that all women were not granted the right to vote by the United States until 1920?

**3. Recognizing Cause and Effect** (p. 19) How would you expect the historical denial of voting rights to African Americans and other minority groups to have influenced the make-up of the Congress and the State legislatures?

## Getting Involved

**1. Writing Your Opinion** Write a letter to a member of Congress about ways to increase voter turnout. Start by setting up a chart with two columns. In one column, brainstorm a list of reasons why you think people do not vote. In the second column, try to come up with solutions to each reason for not voting. Select your three best solutions for increasing voter turnout.

Start your letter by introducing yourself as a concerned citizen and stating the purpose of your letter. Then describe your three ideas to improve voter turnout. For each idea, explain how it addresses a specific cause of low voter turnout. Revise your letter to make sure it is clear and to the point. Then, proofread and make a final copy.

**2. Class Debate** Hold a class debate on the following topic: *Resolved*, That your State should pass a compulsory voting law. Select one team to debate each side of the topic. The rest of the class can evaluate each team's presentation.

**3. Gathering Information** Using the Government Resources Handbook in the Reference Section beginning on page 690, identify what sources you could use to find detailed information about voter turnout in a recent national election.

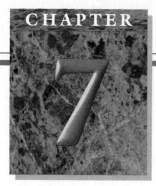

# CHAPTER 7

# The Electoral Process

## Chapter Preview

Twice the Democratic nominee for President in the 1950s, Adlai Stevenson once said this about the process of selecting candidates for an upcoming election: "It's exhausting physically; you burn up yourself, you burn up your ammunition, you burn up your [money]." Stevenson's description makes running for office sound more like war than politics.

The idea that the electoral process is a form of combat is evident in many words that describe it. *Contenders* who are ready to *fight* in the political *arena* are those who throw their hats in the *ring*. Even the word *campaign* has a military origin. This chapter is about running for office—the two basic stages of the electoral process and the very complex role that money plays in the electoral process.

### Before you read this chapter:

- **Describe** two activities that take place during a presidential campaign.
- **Predict** what might occur if running for public office cost less money.

### As you read, focus on the main objective for each section. Understand:

1. The methods by which candidates are nominated to run for public office.
2. The conduct of elections in the United States.
3. The place of money and the regulation of its use in the electoral process.

▲ **Electricity and Excitement**    Perhaps no other political event in America can match the glamour of the national convention. The picture above shows a scene from the 1992 Republican National Convention in Houston.

# 1 The Nominating Process

## Find Out:

- What is the importance of the nominating stage in the electoral process?
- For what reasons did the caucus give way to the convention as the dominant nominating method?
- What are the different forms of the direct primary?
- How are petitions used in the nominating process?

## Key Terms:

nomination, general election, caucus, direct primary, closed primary, open primary, blanket primary, runoff primary

Suppose your teacher stood in front of the class and said: "Here's a $1,000 bill. Who'd like to have it?" You, and everyone else in the room, would promptly say, or at least think: "Me!" Suppose the teacher then said: "Okay, we'll hold an election. The person who wins the most votes gets the money."

What would happen? If the election were held immediately, it is likely that each member of the class would vote for him- or herself. A few might vote for a friend. But, almost certainly, the election would still end in a tie. No one would win the money.

But suppose the teacher said: "We'll hold the election tomorrow." What do you think would happen then? As you think about the answer to that question, you begin to get a sense of the practical importance of the topic of this section: the nominating process—the first step in the process of electing candidates to office.

# The Importance of Nominations

The nominating process is the process of candidate selection. **Nomination**—the naming of those who will seek office—is made in a number of different ways in American politics. Before turning to those several methods, however, consider this significant point: The making of nominations is a critically important matter in the American democratic system.

You have already seen two major illustrations of that point. In Chapter 5, you read about the making of nominations (1) as a prime function of political parties in the United States; and (2) as a leading reason for the decentralized character of the major parties.

The nominating process also has a very real impact on the exercise of the right to vote. In the typical election in this country, voters can make one of only two choices for each office. They can vote for the Republican candidate or they can vote for the Democratic candidate.[1] This is another way of saying that the United States has a two-party system. It is also another way to say that the nominating process is critically important. Those who make nominations place real, very practical limits on the choices that voters can make in an election. In one-party constituencies—those areas where one party regularly wins elections—the nominating process is the only point at which there is usually any real contest for a public office. Once the dominant party has made its nomination, the general election is little more than a formality.

Dictatorial regimes underscore the importance of the nominating process. Many hold **general elections**—regularly scheduled elections at which voters make the final selection of officeholders—much as the United States does. However, the ballots used in those elections usually list only one candidate for each office, and those candidates regularly win with majorities approaching 100 percent.

---

[1]The exception is nonpartisan elections. Other choices are sometimes listed, of course—minor party or independent nominees. But these are not often meaningful alternatives, and most voters choose not to "waste" their votes on candidates who cannot win.

For purposes of description and analysis, the various ways in which nominations are made in this country can be grouped in five broad categories: (1) self-announcement, (2) caucus, (3) convention, (4) direct primary, and (5) petition.

## Self-announcement

Self-announcement is the oldest form of the nominating process in American politics. First used in colonial times, it is still often found at the small-town and rural levels in many parts of the country.

The method is actually quite simple. A person who wants to run for an office simply announces that fact. Modesty or local custom may dictate that someone else make the candidate's announcement, but the process amounts to the same thing.

Self-announcement is sometimes used by someone who failed to win a regular party nomination or by someone unhappy with the party's choice. Note that whenever a write-in candidate appears in an election, the self-announcement process has been used.

Four prominent presidential contenders have made use of the process in recent history: George Wallace, the American Independent party's nominee in 1968, and independent candidates Eugene McCarthy in 1976, John Anderson in 1980, and Ross Perot in 1992.

## The Caucus

As a nominating device, a **caucus** is a group of like-minded persons who meet to select the candidates they will support in an upcoming election.

The first caucus nominations were made toward the end of the colonial period, probably in Boston in the mid-1720s. One of the earliest descriptions of the device can be found in John Adams's diary, in an entry he made in February 1763:

❝This day learned that the Caucus club meets at certain times in the garret of Tom Dawes, the Adjutant of the Boston regiment. He has a large house, and he has a movable partition which he takes down, and the whole club meets in one room. There they smoke tobacco

**Tammany Hall**    Named for a Delaware Native American known for his wisdom, this painting depicts the headquarters of Tammany, a Democratic political organization. The Democratic National Convention was held in the hall in 1868.

until you cannot see from one end of the garret to the other. There they drink flip, I suppose, and they choose a moderator who puts questions to the vote regularly; and selectmen, assessors, collectors, fire-wards, and representatives are regularly chosen before they are chosen in the town. 🙶 [2]

Originally the caucus was a private meeting consisting of a few influential figures. As political parties appeared, they soon took over the device and began to broaden the membership of the caucus.

The coming of independence brought the need to nominate candidates for State offices—for governor, lieutenant governor, and others above the local level. The legislative caucus—a meeting of a party's members in the State legislature—took on the job. At the national level, both the Federalists and the Democratic-Republicans in Congress were, by 1800, choosing their presidential and vice-presidential candidates through the congressional caucus.

The legislative and congressional caucuses were quite practical in their day. Transportation and communication were difficult at best, and legislators regularly came together in a central place. The spread of democracy, especially in the newer States on the frontier, spurred opposition to caucuses, however. More and more, people condemned them for their closed and unrepresentative character.

---

[2]Charles Francis Adams (ed.), *The Works of John Adams* (Boston: Little, Brown, 1856), vol. II, p. 144. The origin of the term *caucus* is not clear. Most authorities suggest that it comes from the word *caulkers*, because the Boston Caucus Club met at times in a room formerly used as a meeting place by caulkers in Boston's shipyards. (Caulkers made ships watertight by filling seams or cracks in the hulls of sailing vessels with tar or oakum.)

Criticism of the caucus reached its peak in the early 1820s. The supporters of three of the leading contenders for the presidency in 1824—Andrew Jackson, Henry Clay, and John Quincy Adams—boycotted the Democratic-Republicans' congressional caucus that year. In fact, Jackson and his supporters made "King Caucus" a leading campaign issue. The other major aspirant, William H. Crawford of Georgia, became the caucus nominee at a meeting attended by fewer than one-third of the Democratic-Republican party's members in Congress.

Crawford ran a poor third in the electoral college balloting in 1824, and the reign of King Caucus at the national level was ended. With its death in presidential politics, the caucus system soon withered at the State and local levels, as well.

The caucus is still used to make local nominations in some places, especially in New England. There, a caucus is open to all members of a party, and it looks only faintly like the original device.

## The Convention

As the caucus method collapsed, the convention system took its place. The first national convention to nominate a presidential candidate was held by a minor party, the Anti-Masons, in Baltimore in 1831. The newly formed Whig party also held a convention later that same year, and the Democrats picked up the practice in 1832. All major party presidential nominees have been chosen by conventions ever since. By the 1840s conventions had become the major means for making nominations at every level in American politics.

On paper, the convention process seems ideally suited to representative government. A party's members meet in a local caucus to pick candidates for local offices and, at the same time, to select delegates to represent them at a county convention.[3] At the county convention, the delegates nominate candidates for county offices and also select delegates to the next rung on the convention ladder, usually the State convention. There, the delegates from the county conventions pick the party's nominees for governor and other State-wide offices. State conventions also send delegates to the party's national convention, where those delegates select its presidential and vice-presidential candidates.

In the theory of the convention system, the will of the party's rank and file membership is passed up through each of its representative levels. Practice soon pointed up the weaknesses of the theory, however, as party bosses found ways to manipulate the process. By playing with the selection of delegates at the local levels, they soon dominated the entire system.

▲ **Campaigning With Ribbons**    These precursors to political lapel buttons promoted Whig Party candidates nominated by convention in the 1840s.

---

[3]The meetings at which delegates to local conventions are chosen are still often called caucuses. Earlier, they were also known as primaries—that is, first meetings. The use of that name gave rise to the term *direct primary*, to distinguish that newer nominating method from the convention process.

The caliber of most conventions, at all levels, declined, especially in the late 1800s. How low some of them fell can be seen in this description of a Cook County (Chicago) convention in 1896:

"Of [723] delegates, those who had been on trial for murder numbered 17; sentenced to the penitentiary for murder or manslaughter and served sentence, 7; served terms in the penitentiary for burglary, 36; served terms in the penitentiary for picking pockets, 2; served terms in the penitentiary for arson, 1; . . . jail-birds identified by detectives, 84; keepers of gambling houses, 7; keepers of houses of ill-fame, 2; convicted of mayhem, 3; ex-prize fighters, 11; poolroom proprietors, 2; saloon keepers, 265; . . . political employees, 148; no occupation, 71; . . . "[4]

By the 1870s, the convention system was under attack as a major source of evil in American politics. And by the 1910s, the direct primary had replaced the convention as the principal nominating method.

Most States now use the direct primary for all or at least most nominations in the State. A few States still use the convention, however—Connecticut, Michigan, Utah, and Virginia, for example, where it is closely regulated by State law. In addition, no adequate substitute for the convention has yet been found for making nominations at the presidential level, as you will read in Chapter 13.

## The Direct Primary

A **direct primary** is an election held within the party to pick the party's candidates for the general election.

Wisconsin adopted the first Statewide direct primary law in 1903, and several other States soon followed its lead. Every State now makes at least some provision for its use.

In most States, State law requires that the major parties use the primary to choose their candidates for the United States Senate and House, for the governorship and all other State offices, and for most local offices, as well. In a few States, however, different combinations of

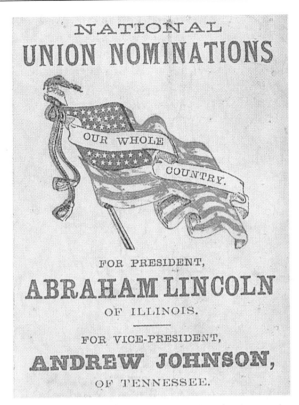

NATIONAL
**UNION NOMINATIONS**

OUR WHOLE
COUNTRY.

FOR PRESIDENT,
**ABRAHAM LINCOLN**
OF ILLINOIS.

FOR VICE-PRESIDENT,
**ANDREW JOHNSON,**
OF TENNESSEE.

▲ **Campaign Ticket: 1864** This election took place before primary laws went into effect. Sometimes tickets such as this one actually were cast as ballots.

convention and primary are used to pick candidates for the top offices. In Michigan, for example, the major parties choose their candidates for the U.S. Senate and House, the governorship, and the State legislature in primaries; their nominees for lieutenant governor, secretary of state, and attorney general are picked by conventions.[5]

Although the primaries are party nominating elections, they are now closely regulated in most States. The State usually sets the dates on which they are held, and it regularly conducts them, too. The State, not the parties, provides polling places and election officials, registration lists and ballots, and otherwise polices the process.

---

[4]R. M. Easley, "The Sine qua Non of Caucus Reform," *Review of Reviews*, September, 1897, p. 322.

[5]In most States, minor parties are required to make their nominations by other, more difficult processes—usually in conventions or by petition. For the significance of this point, see Chapter 5, Section 4.

There are two basic forms of the direct primary in use today: (1) the closed primary and (2) the open primary. The major difference between the two lies in the answer to this question: Who can vote in a party's primary—only qualified voters who are also party members, or any qualified voter?

**The Closed Primary** Thirty-eight States and the District of Columbia now use the **closed primary**—a party nominating election in which only declared party members can vote.[6] The primary is closed to all others.

In most of the closed primary States, party membership is established by registration (see Chapter 6, page 134). When voters appear at the polling places on primary election day, their names are checked against the poll books—the lists of registered voters for each precinct. Each voter is then handed the ballot of the party in which he or she is registered.

In the other closed primary States, voters simply declare their party preference at the polling place. In some of them, that settles the matter; the person may vote in that party's primary. In others, however, that person can be challenged by a party's poll watcher—the person who has been designated by each party to ensure the fairness of the election process at the polls. If that happens, the voter is most often required to take an oath of party loyalty, swearing that he or she has supported that party and its candidates in the past and/or now does so.

**The Open Primary** Although it is the form in which the direct primary first appeared, the open primary is now found in only twelve States (see footnote 6). The **open primary** is a party nominating election in which any qualified voter can take part. It is open to anyone qualified to vote. No one has to declare a party choice at registration or at any other time.

When voters appear at the polling place, they are handed either the ballots of all the parties holding primaries or one large ballot containing the separate ballots of the various parties. Voters then pick the party primary in which they wish to vote.

Washington provides for a different version of the open primary—the so-called **blanket primary**, often called the wide-open primary. There, every voter is handed the same ballot, one listing every contender for every nomination in both parties. Each voter can then vote in one or the other party's primary *or* he or she can vote to nominate a Democrat for one office, a Republican for another, and so on.

Alaska also stages a blanket primary for Democrats and the State's minor parties; but Alaska's Republicans hold a closed primary.

Louisiana has yet another form of the open primary. Its unique "open-election law" provides for what amounts to a combination primary and election. The names of all persons who seek nominations are listed by office on a single primary ballot. A contender who wins more than 50 percent of the primary votes wins the office. In short, the primary in some cases becomes the election. In those contests where there is no majority winner, the two top vote-getters, regardless of party, face off in the general election.

**The Closed vs. the Open Primary** The two basic forms of the primary have excited arguments for decades. Those who favor the closed primary regularly make three arguments for it: (1) it prevents one party from "raiding" the other's primary—in the hope of nominating weaker candidates in the other party; (2) it helps make candidates more responsive to the party, its platform, and its members; and (3) it helps make voters more thoughtful—because they must choose between the parties in order to vote in the primaries.

The critics of the closed primary contend that it (1) compromises the secrecy of the ballot, because it forces voters to make their party preferences known in public, and (2) tends to

---

[6]Every State but Alaska, Hawaii, Idaho, Louisiana, Michigan, Minnesota, Montana, North Dakota, Utah, Vermont, Washington, and Wisconsin. The Supreme Court has held that a State's closed primary law cannot forbid a party to allow independent voters to participate in its primary if the party chooses to do so. In *Tashjian* v. *Republican Party of Connecticut*, 1986, the Court struck down such a State law. Note that the Court did not outlaw the closed primary in this case, nor did it hold that a political party *must* allow independents to vote in its primary.

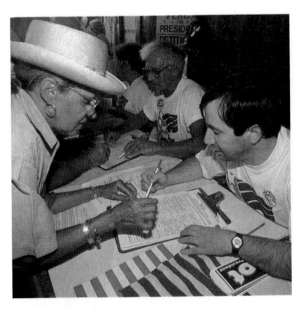

**Getting Their Candidate on the Ballot**
Supporters of Ross Perot for President in 1992 used the petition method to get their candidate on the ballot in all 50 States.

give a party's members the opportunity to participate at the very core of the political process.

**The Presidential Primary**  The presidential primary developed as an offshoot of the direct primary. It is not a nominating device, however. Rather, the presidential primary is an election that is held as a part of the process by which presidential candidates are chosen.

The presidential primary is a very complex device. It is one or both of two things, depending on the State involved. It is a process in which a party's voters elect some or all of a State party organization's delegates to that party's national convention; and/or it is a preference election in which voters can choose—vote their preference—among various contenders for a party's presidential nomination.

Much of what happens in presidential politics in the early months of every fourth year centers on this complicated process. You will read more about it in Chapter 13.

**Nomination by Petition**

One other nominating method is fairly widely used in American politics today—nomination by petition. With this method, candidates for public office are nominated by petitions signed by a certain number of qualified voters in the election district.[10]

Nomination by petition is found most widely at the local level, chiefly for nonpartisan school posts and municipal offices in middle-sized and smaller communities. It is also the process usually required by State law for the nomination of minor party and independent candidates. As noted in Chapter 5, the States frequently make the process of getting on the ballot purposely difficult for those candidates.

The details of the petition process vary widely from State to State, and even from one city to the next. Usually, however, the higher the office and/or the larger the constituency represented by the office, the greater the number of signatures needed for nomination.

## Section 1 Review

**1. Define:** nomination, general election, caucus, direct primary, closed primary, open primary, blanket primary, runoff primary
**2.** In what ways is the nominating process key to the electoral process?
**3.** Which nominating method is the oldest?
**4.** In what ways do conventions seem well suited to democracy?
**5.** What is the difference between an open primary and a closed primary?
**6.** What is a wide-open primary?
**7.** What is a nonpartisan primary?

**Critical Thinking**

**8. Identifying Alternatives** (p. 19) In your opinion, what should be the key purpose of the nominating process? Which of the methods discussed in this section come closest to fulfilling this purpose?

---

[10]The petition device is also used in several other aspects of the electoral process. Thus, it and/or a filing fee is generally the method by which an aspirant's name is placed on the direct primary ballot.

# 2 Elections

**Find Out:**

- For what reasons are the details of the election process so important?
- Where and when do elections take place?
- What is the ballot and what are the many forms it takes?

**Key Terms:**

coattail effect, precinct, polling place, ballot

Most high school students are not old enough to vote. But high school students can serve on local election boards in some parts of the country. First in Hawaii and Oregon and now in several States, 16- and 17-year-olds can become full-fledged members of these official bodies—the panels that administer the elections at which public officeholders are chosen.

Americans hold more elections and vote more often than most people realize. Indeed, Sundays and holidays are about the only days in any year on which people do not go to the polls somewhere in the United States. Americans also elect far more officeholders than most people realize—in fact, more than 500,000 of them.

Obviously, the election of public officials is very serious business. In this section, you will read about the federal and state laws that seek to insure the integrity of this vital process.

## The Administration of Elections

Once candidates have been nominated, they must face their opponents and the voters in the general election—in what H. G. Wells once called democracy's "feast, its great function."

Democratic government cannot succeed unless elections are free, honest, and accurate. Too many people look at the details of the election process as too complicated, too legalistic, too dry and boring, to worry about. But those people miss the vital part those details play in making democracy work. The often lengthy and closely detailed provisions of election law are designed to protect the integrity of that process.

And they often have a very telling effect on the outcome of elections, as well.

You have read several illustrations showing that the details of election law can have real impacts—for example, when you read about voter qualifications and registration in the last chapter. You saw another only a few pages back, when you considered the details of the direct primary.

**The Extent of Federal Control**   Nearly all elections in this country are held to choose the more than 500,000 persons who hold elective offices in the more than 86,000 units of government at the State and local levels. It is quite understandable, then, that most election law in the United States is State law.

There is a body of federal election law, however. The Constitution gives Congress the power to fix "the times, places, and manner of holding elections" of members of Congress.[11] Congress also has the power to set the time for choosing presidential electors, to set the date for casting electoral votes, and to regulate other aspects of the presidential election process.[12]

Congress has set the date for holding congressional elections as the first Tuesday following the first Monday in November of every even-numbered year. It has set the same date every fourth year for the presidential elections.[13]

Congress has required the use of secret ballots and allowed the use of voting machines in federal elections. It has also passed several laws to protect the right to vote in all elections, as you saw in Chapter 6. And it has also prohibited various corrupt practices and regulated the financing of campaigns for federal office, as you will see in the pages ahead.

All other matters relating to national elections, and all of the details involved in choosing the thousands of State and local officials, are dealt with in the laws of the States.

---

[11]Article I, Section 4, Clause 1; 17th Amendment; see Chapter 10, Section 2.

[12]Article II, Section 1, Clause 4; 12th Amendment; see Chapter 13, Section 6.

[13]Congress has made an exception for Alaska, which may, if it chooses, elect its congressional delegation and cast its presidential vote in October. So far, however, Alaska has used the November date.

**When Elections Are Held** Most States hold their elections to fill State offices on the same date Congress has set for national elections—in November of every even-numbered year.[14] Some States do fix other dates for at least some offices. Thus, Louisiana, Mississippi, New Jersey, and Virginia elect the governor, other executive officers, and State legislators in November of the odd-numbered year. City, county, and other local election dates vary from State to State. Where those elections are not held in November, they generally take place in the spring.

**The Coattail Effect** The **coattail effect** occurs when a strong candidate running for an office at the top of the ballot helps attract voters to other candidates on the party's ticket. In effect, the lesser known office seekers "ride the coattails" of the more prestigious personalities. In 1980 and 1984, for example, Ronald Reagan's coattails helped many Republican candidates win office. The coattail effect is usually most apparent in presidential elections. But a popular candidate for senator or governor can have the same kind of pulling power.

There can be a reverse coattail effect, too. It comes when a candidate for high office is less than popular with many voters—for example, Barry Goldwater as the Republican presidential nominee in 1964, and George McGovern for the Democrats in 1972. President Carter's coattails were also of the reverse variety in 1980.

Some have long held that all State and local elections should be held on dates other than those set for federal elections. This, they say, would help make voters pay more attention to State and local candidates and issues and lessen the coattail effects of presidential contests.

## Precincts and Polling Places

A **precinct** is a voting district. Precincts are the basic and smallest geographic units for the conduct of elections. State law regularly restricts

---

[14]The "Tuesday-after-the-first-Monday" formula prevents election day from falling on Sundays—to maintain the principle of separation of church and state—and on the first day of the month, which is often payday and therefore peculiarly subject to campaign pressures.

## VOICES on Government

### On Taking Part in the Electoral Process

❝Our society is a gorgeous mosaic of race and religious faith, of national origin. . . . No one person and no one group possibly can understand the ways and the worries of all. A government that includes all in the process will exclude fewer in the result. Representation . . . will reduce the alienation and frustration that too often characterize our society. Broad-based government is better government.❞

**David N. Dinkins**
former mayor of New York City.

their size, generally to an area with no more than 500 to 1,000 or so qualified voters. A **polling place**—where the voters who live in a precinct actually vote—is located somewhere in or near each precinct.

A precinct election board supervises the polling place and the voting process in each precinct. Typically, the county clerk or county board of elections draws precinct lines, fixes the location of each polling place, and picks the members of the precinct boards.

The precinct board opens and closes the polls at the times set by State law. In most States, the polls are open from 7:00 or 8:00 A.M. to 7:00 or 8:00 P.M. The precinct election board must also see that the ballots and the ballot boxes or voting machines are available. It must make certain that only qualified voters cast ballots in the precinct. Often the board also counts the votes cast in the precinct and then sends the results to the proper place—usually to the county clerk or county board of elections.

Poll watchers, one from each party, are allowed at each polling place. They may challenge any person they believe is not qualified to vote, check to be sure that as many as possible of their own party's supporters do vote, and monitor the whole process, including the counting of the ballots.

## The Ballot

The **ballot** is the device by which a voter registers a choice in an election.[15] It can take a number of different forms.

Each of the States now provides for a secret ballot. That is, each requires that ballots be cast in such manner that others cannot know how a voter has voted.

Voting was a public process through much of the nation's earlier history. Paper ballots were used in some colonial elections, but voting was commonly *viva voce*—by voice. With suffrage limited to the privileged few, many defended oral voting as the only "manly" way in which to participate. Whatever the merits of

---

[15]The word comes from the Italian *ballotta*—"little ball," and reflects the practice of dropping black or white balls into a box to indicate a choice. The term *blackball* comes from the same practice.

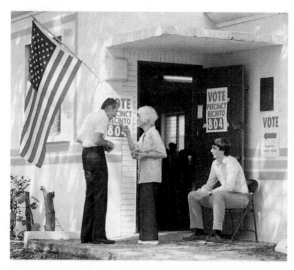

▲ **Election Day**  Citizens wait to cast votes in Coral Gables, Florida. What does the picture indicate about the people living in this particular community?

that view, the expansion of the electorate brought with it a marked increase in intimidation, vote buying, and other corruptions of the voting process.

Paper ballots came into general use by the mid-1800s. The first ones were slips of paper that voters prepared themselves and dropped in the ballot box. Soon candidates and parties began to prepare ballots and hand them to voters to cast—sometimes paying them to do so. Those ballots were often printed on colored paper, and anyone watching could tell for whom voters were voting.

Political machines fought all attempts to make voting a more dependably fair and honest process. The political corruption of the post-Civil War years brought widespread demand for ballot reforms, however.

**The Australian Ballot**  A new voting arrangement was devised in Australia, where it was first used in an election in Victoria in 1856. Its successes there led to its use in other countries. By 1900 nearly all of the States were using it, and it remains the basic form of the ballot today.

The Australian Ballot has four essential features: (1) it is printed at public expense; (2) it lists the names of all candidates in an election; (3) it is given out only at the polls, one to each qualified voter; and (4) it is voted in secret.

Two basic varieties of the Australian ballot have developed over the years. Nearly half the States now use the office-group version; the rest of the States use the party-column ballot.

**The Office-Group Ballot**  The office-group ballot is the original form of the Australian ballot. It is also sometimes called the Massachusetts ballot because of its early (1888) use there. On the office-group ballot, the candidates for each office are grouped together. At first, the names of the candidates were listed in alphabetical order. Most States using the form now rotate the names—so that each candidate will have whatever psychological advantage there may be in having his or her name at the top of the list.

**The Party-Column Ballot**  The party-column ballot is also known as the Indiana ballot, from its early (1889) use in that State. It lists

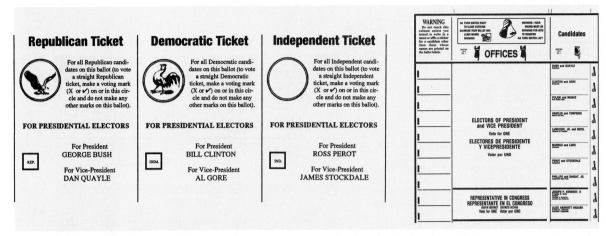

▲ **Presidential Election Ballots**   What two types of ballots are shown in the photograph above?

each party's candidates in a column under the party's name. Often there is a place at the top of each column where, with a single X, the voter can vote for all of that party's candidates.

Professional politicians tend to favor the party-column ballot. It encourages straight-ticket voting, especially if the party has a strong candidate at the head of the ticket. Most students of the political process favor the office-group form because it encourages voter judgment and split-ticket voting.

**Sample Ballots**   Sample ballots, clearly marked as such, are available in most States prior to an election. In some they are mailed to all voters, and they appear in most newspapers. They cannot be cast, but they can help voters prepare for an election.[16]

**The Long and the Short of It**   The ballot in a typical American election is a lengthy one, often and aptly called a "bed-sheet" ballot. It frequently lists so many offices, candidates, and measures that even the most

well-informed voters have a difficult time marking it intelligently.

The long ballot came to American politics in the era of Jacksonian Democracy in the 1830s. Many held the view at the time that the greater the number of elective offices, the more democratic the governmental system. The idea remains widely accepted today.

Generally, the longest ballots are found at the local level, especially among the nation's 3,000-odd counties. In most counties, it is not unusual to find a large number of elected offices listed on ballots—including several commissioners, a clerk, a sheriff, one or more judges, a prosecutor, coroner, treasurer, assessor, surveyor, school superintendent, engineer, sanitarian, and even the proverbial dogcatcher.

Critics of the long ballot do not accept the argument that the more you elect the more democratic you are. They believe that quite the reverse is true; with a smaller number of elected offices to fill, the voter can better know the candidates and their qualifications. Critics also point to "ballot fatigue"—the drop-off in voting that can run as high as 20 to 30 percent at or near the bottom of the typical lengthy ballot.

There seems little, if any, good reason to elect such local officials as clerks, coroners, surveyors, and engineers. Their jobs do not carry basic policy-making responsibilities. Rather, they carry out policies made by others. For good

---

[16]First in Oregon (1907), and now in several States, an official voter's pamphlet is mailed to voters before an election. It lists all candidates and measures that will appear on the ballot. In Oregon each candidate is allowed space to present his or her qualifications and position on the issues, and supporters and opponents of ballot measures are allowed space to present their arguments, as well.

## Before Election Day

**1. Determine whether you are qualified to vote.** To qualify to vote in the United States, you must be

☐ an American citizen,
☐ at least 18 years of age, and
☐ a resident of your State.

**2. Register to vote.** In every State except North Dakota, you must register to vote.

☐ **When?** In most States registration takes place some weeks before election day. To find out the requirements in your locale, call your local election officials or a local civic group such as the League of Women Voters.

☐ **Where?** You can register locally, usually at city hall or the county courthouse. Registration tables or booths are often set up in such places as supermarkets, shopping malls, fire stations, and libraries. Every State now provides for registration by mail and at the offices of various public agencies.

☐ **How?** To register you will need proof of your age such as your birth certificate. Registration forms usually require only such basic information as your full name, address, and date and place of birth. In most closed primary States, those who register to vote may declare a party preference.

 ## On Election Day

**3. Go to your polling place to cast your vote.** In most States each voter receives an official voter registration card that identifies that voter's precinct and polling place. Most local newspapers publish lists of polling places a few days before a primary or general election. In most States the polls are open from 7:00 or 8:00 A.M. to 7:00 or 8:00 P.M.

**4. Check in with election officials at your polling place.** When you arrive, there may be a line of people waiting to vote. When your turn comes, identify yourself to the precinct election board. Your name will be checked against the poll book to be sure that you are entitled to vote. You then will be handed a ballot and directed to a voting booth, or, if your State uses voting machines, you will simply be directed to a booth.

"THERE GO THE KRAVITZES TO VOTE.... WE BETTER GO CANCEL THEM OUT."

**5. Cast your vote.** Depending on State law, you will mark a paper ballot, operate a voting machine, or use a punch card. Read the ballot carefully, and make your choices based on what you know of the candidates and issues in the election. Check to be sure that you have in fact made a selection in every contest in which you want to vote. When you are sure you have completed the ballot, leave the voting booth and hand your ballot to the election judge.

**Congratulations! You have just exercised one of your most important rights as a citizen in a democratic nation!**

government, the rule should be: Elect those who make public policies; appoint those who administer them.

## Voting Machines and Innovations

Thomas Edison took out the first American patent for a voting machine. The community of Lockport, New York, first used his invention in 1892. The use of similar devices has long since spread to the polling places of every State.

Only a handful of States make the use of voting machines mandatory. Most often the machines are used only in some—usually the more populous—areas of a State. All told, however, more than half of all the votes in national elections today are cast on some form of voting machine.

The typical voting machine serves as its own booth. By pulling a lever, the voter encloses himself or herself within a curtain and unlocks the machine. The ballot appears on the face of the machine, and the voter makes his or her choices by pulling down the small levers over the names of the candidates he or she favors. In most States using the party-column ballot, the voter can pull a master lever to vote a straight ticket.

The machine is programmed so that a voter can cast only one vote per contest. Once all levers are in the desired positions, the voter opens the curtain. That action records the votes and, at the same time, clears the machine for the next voter.

The use of voting machines does away with the need for manual vote counting, reduces the number of persons needed to administer elections, and speeds the voting process. It also increases the number of voters who can be handled per precinct, makes ballot mutilation impossible, and minimizes fraud and counting errors.

**Electronic Vote Counting** Electronic data processing (EDP) techniques have been applied to the voting process in recent years—first in California and Oregon and now, to some degree, in more than two-thirds of the States.

The most widely used adaptation of EDP in elections involves punch-card ballots, which are counted by computers. Another involves paper ballots marked with sensitized ink and counted by optical scanners.

**Vote-by-Mail Elections** Some local elections are now conducted with mail-in ballots in a handful of States around the country.

Monterey County, California, held the first vote-by-mail election in 1977. San Diego was the first locality to make large-scale use of the process in 1981. Since then, mail-in ballots have been used in local elections in several other places.

Vote-by-mail elections have stirred a growing controversy. Critics fear that the process threatens the principle of the secret ballot and invites fraud. Its supporters say that it can be as fraud-proof as any other method of voting. They also cite this fact: The process increases voter turnout in local elections and, at the same time, reduces the costs of conducting them.

The use of mail-in ballots has been confined to local-issue elections—except in Oregon and Montana, where State law now allows their use in some local candidate elections.

## Section 2 Review

**1. Define:** coattail effect, precinct, polling place, ballot

**2.** In what ways are the details of the electoral process vital to the success of democratic government?

**3.** For what reason is most election law in this country State rather than federal?

**4.** (a) When are national elections held? (b) When are most State general elections held?

**5.** For what reasons do some people favor separate dates for national and for State and local elections?

**6.** (a) What is the Australian ballot? (b) How do office-group and party-column ballots differ?

**Critical Thinking**

**7. Predicting Consequences** (p. 19) Think about elections in your school for class president and student council. How might these elections be affected if there were no secret ballot?

## Working to Change State Law

Citizens working actively together *can* make a difference. Their participation informs government of their priorities and concerns. Read about how a group of high-school students brought about a change in State law.

### Students Take Action

Dean Neff teaches an American government course at Central High School in Omaha, Nebraska. He and some of his students are largely responsible for allowing most 17-year-olds in Nebraska to vote.

Over the past several years, Neff became more and more convinced that 17-year-olds who would be 18 by the following November—the time when general elections take place—ought to be able to vote in the primary elections in May. It seemed only fair, he felt, to give anyone who could vote in a general election the chance to help choose the candidates for that election.

Neff believed this so firmly that he decided to get involved. That decision turned into a student project in the fall of 1987. A number of high school seniors got deeply involved in research. They discovered that several States recently have allowed 17-year-olds to vote in the primary—including Indiana, Kentucky, Maryland, North and South Carolina, Ohio, Virginia, and West Virginia. Armed with good information and strong commitment, Neff and his students approached their State legislators.

### LR 253 Becomes Law

Senator Carol Prisch of Omaha was so impressed by their presentation that she agreed to support their cause in the 1988 session of Nebraska's legislature. On January 6, 1988, Senator Prisch and three other legislators introduced Legislative Resolution 253, to amend Article VI, Section 1 of Nebraska's constitution. LR 253 was referred to the legislature's Committee on Government, Military, and Veterans Affairs, and the students now became lobbyists. They wrote letters to or called on most of the other members of the legislature, urging them to support the bill. They contacted lawmakers, wrote letters to newspapers, and sought the backing of students and teachers in other schools around the State. Through their efforts they won endorsements from both major political parties and many civic organizations in Nebraska. When the bill finally reached the floor of the legislature on March 25, it was approved by an overwhelming vote, 43 to 3.

Little opposition, none of it organized, emerged after the legislature adjourned. Nebraska voters approved the proposed amendment by a comfortable margin at the general election on November 8, 1988. Students like you made a difference. They changed State law.

### Getting Involved

1. **Identify** a current issue on the State or local level of government similar to the one addressed in this case.
2. **Formulate** a plan for ways that you can get involved and identify resources that could be used in your plan.
3. **Predict** any problems or objections you might encounter in carrying out your plan.

# 3  Money and the Election Process

**Find Out:**
- Why is money an indispensable campaign resource?
- What problems does money pose in the election process?
- How is the use of money regulated in elections today?

**Key Term:**
political action committee

Some believe that this is the golden rule of politics: The person who has the gold rules. That is not true. But this is: Running for public office costs money, and often a lot of it. And that fact creates some of the most difficult problems in American politics. It leaves open the possibility that candidates will try to buy their way into public office. And special interest groups may try to buy favors from those who are in office.

Clearly, government by the people must be protected from these dangers. But how? Parties and candidates must have money. Without it, they cannot campaign or do any of the many things they must do to win elections.

In short, money is an absolutely necessary campaign resource. Yet, the getting and the spending of campaign funds can corrupt the entire political process.

In this section, you will read about the role of money in elections and about the ongoing efforts to regulate campaign finance.

## Campaign Spending Amounts

No one really knows how much money is spent on elections in the United States. Reliable estimates of total spending in recent presidential election years—including nominations and general elections for offices at all levels—are shown in the table on page 174.

The presidential election eats up by far the largest share of campaign dollars: For 1992,

"IF WE RAISE ENOUGH CAMPAIGN FUNDS—

WE MIGHT BE ELECTED TO CONGRESS—

WHERE WE CAN SPEND MOST OF OUR TIME RAISING MORE CAMPAIGN FUNDS"

©1988 by HERBLOCK in the *Washington Post.*

▲ **Interpreting Political Cartoons**  The high cost of running for office is often criticized by the media. What message does the cartoon convey about this issue?

total spending for all of the major and minor party efforts and Ross Perot's bid—for the primaries, conventions, presidential campaign, everything—came to more than $500 million.

Another $500 million was spent in all of the U.S. House and Senate races in 1992—including the more than $27 million spent in a single Senate contest, in California.[17]

Radio and television time, professional campaign managers and consultants, newspaper advertisements, pamphlets, buttons, posters and

---

[17]Principal sources for the data in this section are Herbert E. Alexander, Citizens' Research Foundation; *Congressional Quarterly*; and the Federal Election Commission.

bumper strips, office rent, polls, data processing, mass mailings, travel—these and a host of other items make up the huge sums spent in campaigns. Television is by far the largest item in a typical campaign budget today. A single half hour of network TV time can run as much as $500,000, and a 30-second spot in prime time now runs to at least $150,000. As Will Rogers put it years ago, "You have to be loaded just to get beat."

The total amount spent in particular races varies, of course, and widely. How much depends on many factors: the office involved, the candidate and whether he or she is the incumbent, the opposition, and, not least, the availability of campaign funds.

## Sources of Campaign Funding

In the broadest sense, parties and their candidates draw their money from two sources—private contributors and from the public treasury. Recent campaign finance laws have had a large impact on both of these sources, as you will see.

**Private Givers**    Private givers have always been the major source of campaign funds in American politics. Those givers come in several different shapes and sizes:

| Total Campaign Spending, 1956–1992 (Federal, State, Local) | | | |
|---|---|---|---|
|  | Estimated Spending | Vote Cast for President | Cost per Voter |
| 1956 | 155 million | 62.0 million | 2.50 |
| 1960 | 175 million | 68.8 million | 2.54 |
| 1964 | 200 million | 70.6 million | 2.83 |
| 1968 | 300 million | 73.2 million | 4.10 |
| 1972 | 425 million | 77.7 million | 5.47 |
| 1976 | 540 million | 81.6 million | 6.62 |
| 1980 | 1.2 billion | 86.5 million | 13.87 |
| 1984 | 1.8 billion | 92.6 million | 19.38 |
| 1988 | 3.0 billion | 91.6 million | 32.75 |
| 1992 | 3.5 billion | 104.4 million | 33.52 |

▲ **Interpreting Tables**   What factors might account for the astronomical rise in the cost of campaign spending in recent elections?

1. Small contributors—those who give $5 or $10 or so, and only occasionally. Clearly, democracy would be best served if campaigns were entirely supported by the small contributions of millions of American voters. But only about 10 percent of all persons of voting age ever make such contributions; so, parties and candidates must look to other places for much of their funding.
2. Wealthier persons and families—the so-called "fat cats," who can afford large donations and find it in their best interest to make them.
3. Candidates themselves—both incumbents and challengers, and their families, and, importantly, people who hold and want to keep appointive public offices. Ross Perot spent some $65 million of his own money on his independent bid for the presidency in 1992.
4. Various nonparty groups—especially **political action committees (PACs)**—the political arms of special interest groups that have a major stake in public policy.
5. Temporary organizations—groups formed for the immediate purposes of a campaign, including fund-raising. Hundreds of these short-lived units spring up every two years, and at every level in American politics. Victory '92 (a pro-Bush/Quayle organization) and Women for Choice for Clinton and Gore were but two of the many such groups that raised money in the 1992 presidential contest.

Then, too, parties and their candidates often hold fund-raising events of various sorts. The most common of these social-electioneering affairs are $25-, $100-, or $1,000-a-plate luncheons, dinners, picnics, concerts, receptions, cocktail parties, and rallies. Other commonly used fund-raising events include telethons and direct-mail campaigns.

To these traditional sources, a newer one—public subsidies from federal and/or State treasuries—has lately been added. To this point in time, subsidies have been most important at the presidential level.[18]

---

[18]Public funds for presidential campaigns come from the federal treasury. Several States also have some form of public financing for parties and/or candidates at the State and even the local level.

## The Growth of PACs (Political Action Committees)*

Contributions by PACs
(in millions of dollars)

*Data covers two-year election cycle ending in year noted

Number of PACs

*Source:* Federal Election Commission

▲ **Interpreting Graphs**   Political action committees have become a major source of campaign money over the past 20 years. Why do you think that PACs regularly give far more to incumbents than to challengers?

**Why People Give**   Campaign donations are a form of political participation. Those who make them do so for a number of reasons. Many small contributors give simply because they believe in a party or a candidate. But most of those who give want something in return. They want access to government, and they hope to get it by helping their "friends" win elections. Among the better demonstrations of the point: Some contributors give to both sides in a contest: heads they win and tails they still win.

Some big donors want appointments to public office, and others want to keep the ones they have. Some long for social recognition. For them, dinner at the White House, meeting with a cabinet official, or knowing the governor on a first-name basis may be enough. Organized labor, business, professional, and various other groups have particular policy aims. They want certain laws passed, changed, or repealed, or certain administrative actions taken.[19]

## Regulating Campaign Finance

Congress first began to regulate the use of money in the federal election process in 1907. In that year it became unlawful for any corporation or national bank to make "a money contribution in any election" of candidates for federal office. Since then, Congress has passed several laws to regulate the use of money in presidential and congressional campaigns.

Today, these regulations are found in three detailed laws: the Federal Election Campaign Act (FECA) of 1971, the FECA Amendments of 1974, and the FECA Amendments of 1976.[20]

---

[19]Among those "various other groups" is organized crime, which, although not a PAC, has an obvious stake in public policy and in those who make it. Large-scale operations in narcotics, prostitution, gambling, loan-sharking, and other illegal activities cannot survive without close ties to at least some public officials.

---

[20]The earlier federal laws were loosely drawn, not often obeyed, and almost never enforced. The 1971 law replaced them. The 1974 law marked the major legislative response to the Watergate scandal. The 1976 law was passed in direct response to the Supreme Court's decision in *Buckley* v. *Valeo*, 1976. A number of minor changes were made in these laws in 1980.

Congress does not have the power to regulate the use of money in State and local elections. Every State now regulates at least some aspects of campaign finance. A useful summary of current State campaign finance laws can be found in *The Book of the States,* a biennial publication of the Council of State Governments.

**The Federal Election Commission**    All federal law dealing with campaign finance is administered by the Federal Election Commission. Set up by Congress in 1974, the FEC is an independent agency in the executive branch. Its six members are appointed by the President, with Senate confirmation.[21]

The laws that the commission enforces cover four broad areas. They (1) require the timely disclosure of campaign finance data, (2) place limits on campaign contributions, (3) place limits on campaign expenditures, and (4) provide public funding for several parts of the presidential election process.

**Disclosure Requirements**    Congress first required the reporting of certain campaign finance information in 1910. Today, the disclosure requirements are very detailed. They are intended to spotlight the place of money in federal campaigns. In fact, the reports that candidates must file with the FEC are so comprehensive that nearly all candidates for federal office find that their campaign organizations must include at least one certified public accountant.

---

[21]The clerk of the House of Representatives and the secretary of the Senate also serve on the FEC; they are *ex officio*, nonvoting members of the commission.

▲ **The Expense of Campaigning**  The political action committee funded by the American Association of Retired Persons backed Democrat Bill Clinton in the 1992 presidential election.

No person or group can make a contribution in the name of another. Cash gifts of more than $100 are prohibited. So, too, are contributions from any foreign source. All newspaper, radio, and television ads, circulars, and all other materials promoting a candidate for a federal office must carry the name of the persons or groups that sponsor them.

All contributions to a candidate for federal office must be made through a single campaign committee. Only that committee can spend that candidate's campaign money. All contributions and spending must be closely accounted for by that one committee. Any contribution or loan of more than $200 must be identified by source and by date. So, too, must any spending over $200—by the name of the person or firm to whom payment was made, by date, and by purpose.

Any contribution of more than $5,000 must be reported to the FEC no later than 48 hours after it is received. So, too, must any sum of $1,000 or more received in the last 20 days of a campaign. A cash contribution of more than $100 cannot be accepted under any circumstances.

Any independent committee or person spending more than $250 for a candidate on its own—outside of that candidate's organization—must also file with the FEC. It must report the financial details of its operations and must swear, subject to perjury, that none of its activities was carried on in collusion with that candidate or his or her organization.

Neither corporations nor labor unions can themselves make contributions to federal candidates. But their political action committees can, and do.

**The Role of PACs**    There were only some 600 PACs in 1974. Today, as the graph on page 175 shows, there are more than 4,000—including, for example, COPE (the AFL-CIO's Committee on Political Education), BANKPAC (the American Bankers Association's Political Action Committee), and NEAPAC (the National Education Association's Political Action Committee).

PACs fill their war chests with the voluntary contributions of their members—the executives, stockholders, and employees of a corporation; union members; doctors or dentists or teachers;

## Ten PACs with the Largest Increase in Contributions to Candidates, 1992–1994

| | 1992 Contribution | 1994 Contribution |
|---|---|---|
| United Parcel Service Political Action Committee (UPSPAC) | $439,673 | $1,023,810 |
| American Federation of State, County, & Municipal Employees | $744,283 | $1,118,620 |
| Carpenters Legislative Improvement Committee | $340,454 | $664,700 |
| Nationsbank Corporation PAC | $125,600 | $387,450 |
| Political Action Committee of the American Hospital Association | $249,304 | $466,191 |
| American Association of Anesthesiologists PAC (ASAPAC) | $6,000 | $198,850 |
| NRA Political Victory Fund | $497,292 | $653,626 |
| Machinists Non-Partisan Political League | $626,823 | $782,706 |
| National Committee for an Effective Congress | $323,700 | $459,374 |
| National Air Traffic Controllers Association PAC | $29,850 | $159,720 |

*Source:* Federal Election Commission

**Interpreting Tables**  What issues pending in Congress do you think some of the PACs listed above were interested in influencing?

those who favor or oppose gun control or abortion; and so on. The PACs pool all these small sums into a single, larger fund. Then they distribute their monies to favored candidates. PACs put more than $170 million into the presidential and congressional campaigns of 1988—and millions more into State and local races.

No PAC may give more than $5,000 to any one federal candidate. But there is no overall limit on PAC giving. Each may contribute up to the $5,000 ceiling to as many different candidates as it chooses.[22]

### Limits on Contributions

Congress first began to regulate campaign contributions in 1907, when it outlawed donations by corporations and national banks. A similar ban was first applied to unions in 1943. Individual contributions first became subject to regulation in 1939.

Today, no person can give more than $1,000 to any federal candidate in a primary election, and no more than $1,000 to any federal candidate's general election campaign. Also, no person can give more than $5,000 in any year to a political action committee, or $20,000 to a national party committee. The total of any person's contributions to federal candidates and committees must be limited to no more than $25,000 in any one year.

These limits have been in place since 1974. They have finally curbed the long-standing and substantial impact of the "fat-cats" in federal elections.[23] But remember, the limits do not apply to campaigns of candidates for State and local offices.

### Limits on Expenditures

Congress first began to limit campaign spending in 1925. Most of the spending limitations that are now law apply only to the presidential election process.[24]

---

[22]An independent PAC, one operating on its own, without the approval of or any connection to a candidate, may spend—not contribute to, but spend on its own for a candidate—an unlimited amount. This point is particularly important in terms of presidential campaign financing.

[23]The limits may seem generous; in fact, they are very tight. Before the limits, many wealthy persons made contributions far larger than those amounts. For example, in 1972, W. Clement Stone, a Chicago insurance executive, gave more than $2 million. Furthermore, inflation has had a dramatic impact on these limits. Today, $1,000 will buy less than half of what it did in 1974.

[24]In *Buckley* v. *Valeo*, 1976, the Supreme Court struck down several restrictions that the 1974 FECA Amendments had placed on spending. The Court held each of them to be contrary to the 1st Amendment's guarantees of freedom of expression. In effect, said the Court, in politics "money is speech." The voided provisions (1) limited House and Senate campaign expenditures, (2) limited how much of their own money candidates could put into their own campaigns, and (3) said no person or group (independent committee) could spend more than $1,000 on behalf of a candidate without that candidate's authorization. The Court also struck down limits on presidential campaign spending, except for candidates who accept FEC subsidies.

## Campaign Spending, Major Party Presidential Candidates, 1952–1992

(in millions of dollars)

| | | | | |
|---|---|---|---|---|
| 1952 | $ 6.61 | Eisenhower* | $5.03 | Stevenson |
| 1956 | 7.78 | Eisenhower* | 5.11 | Stevenson |
| 1960 | 10.13 | Nixon | 9.80 | Kennedy* |
| 1964 | 16.03 | Goldwater | 8.76 | Johnson* |
| 1968 | 25.40 | Nixon* | 11.60 | Humphrey |
| 1972 | 61.40 | Nixon* | 30.00 | McGovern |
| 1976 | 21.79 | Ford | 21.80 | Carter* |
| 1980 | 29.19 | Reagan* | 29.35 | Carter |
| 1984 | 40.40 | Reagan* | 40.40 | Mondale |
| 1988 | 46.10 | Bush* | 46.10 | Dukakis |
| 1992 | 55.24 | Bush | 55.24 | Clinton* |

*Indicates winner of presidential election.

*Source*: Adapted from Herbert E. Alexander, *Financing Politics: Money, Elections and Reform* (Washington, D.C.: Congressional Quarterly Press, 3rd ed., 1984), p. 7; 1984, 1988, and 1992 data from Federal Election Commission.

▲ **Interpreting Tables** Why have the two major party candidates spent just about the same amount in each of the last five campaigns?

Those presidential contenders who accept federal campaign subsidies are subject to limits on their campaign spending. These limits apply in both the preconvention primaries and in the general election campaign.[25]

For 1992, no major party contender could spend more than $27.6 million in the preconvention period. After the conventions, the Bush and Clinton campaigns could spend $55.2 million. And each of the major party's national committees could spend no more than $10.3 million in the presidential campaign.

Recall, independent presidential candidate Ross Perot spent his own money on his 1992 campaign. He did not seek or use any federal money—and so his presidential campaign was not subject to any legal spending limit.

## Public Funding of Presidential Campaigns

Congress first began to provide for the public funding of presidential campaigns in the Revenue Act of 1971. It broadened sections

of that law in 1974 and again in 1976.

The 1971 law set up the Presidential Election Campaign Fund. It also provided that each person who files a federal income tax return can give one dollar of his or her tax payment (two dollars on a joint return) to the fund.

As the law now stands, the monies in the fund are to be used to pay for public subsidies for (1) the preconvention campaigns, (2) national conventions, and (3) presidential election campaigns.[26] The FEC administers the public subsidy process.

**Preconvention Period** The presidential primary and caucus campaigns are now supported by the private contributions a candidate raises plus the public money he or she receives from the FEC.

To be eligible for the public funds, a presidential hopeful must first get past a rather complicated barrier. He or she must raise at least $100,000 in contributions from individuals (not organizations). That amount must be gathered in $5,000 lots in each of at least 20 States, with each of those lots built from individual donations of not more than $250. This requirement is meant to discourage hopeless and frivolous candidates.

For each contender who passes that test, the FEC will match the first $250 of each individual's donation to that candidate—up to a total of half of the overall limit on primary spending. Thus, in 1992 the FEC could have given some contenders as much as $13.8 million because the ceiling was $27.6 million for each candidate. The FEC does not match contributions from PACs or other political organizations.

In 1992, all presidential hopefuls, combined, spent about $125 million in the preconvention period—including nearly $43 million in matching funds the FEC gave to two contenders for

---

[25] Through 1992, only one major party aspirant has not accepted federal funds: former Governor John B. Connally of Texas, who sought the Republican presidential nomination in 1980.

---

[26] The Revenue Act of 1971 also tried to stimulate campaign giving. It allowed a federal income-tax payer to take a credit—a subtraction from the total tax due—of up to $50, or $100 on a joint return, for political contributions. However, at President Reagan's urging, Congress eliminated this tax credit when it passed the Tax Reform Act of 1986. Several States allow State income tax credits or deductions for political contributions.

the Republican nod, and seven for the Democrats' prize.

**National Conventions** If a major party applies for the money—and both did in 1976, 1980, 1984, 1988, and 1992—it automatically receives a grant to pay for its national convention. The two parties each got $11 million from the FEC for that purpose in 1992.

**Presidential Campaigns** Every major party presidential nominee automatically qualifies for a public subsidy to cover the costs of the general election campaign. For 1992, the Bush and Clinton campaigns each received $55.2 million from the FEC. A candidate can refuse that money, of course. Should that ever happen, the candidate would be free to raise however much he or she could from private sources.

So far, the nominees of both major parties have taken the public money each time. Because

they did so, each automatically (1) could spend no more than the amount of the subsidy and (2) could not accept campaign funds from any other source.[27]

A minor party candidate can also qualify for public funding, but not automatically. To be eligible, the minor party must either (1) have won at least five percent of the popular vote in the last presidential election or (2) win at least that much of the vote in the election.[28]

No minor party candidate has come even remotely close to winning five percent of the popular vote in any of the five presidential elections in which the subsidy arrangement has been in place. But, over that period (1976 through 1992), two independent candidates have exceeded the five-percent threshold.

John Anderson received 6.6 percent of the popular vote in 1980—and, as a result, he received $4.2 million from the FEC after that election.

And Ross Perot won just over 19 percent of the vote in 1992. But, remember, Mr. Perot did not seek federal subsidy monies nor, in fact, was he qualified to receive them.

---

[27]Two huge loopholes have emerged here. First, recall, independent PACs can spend unlimited sums in any federal campaign; see note 22. Congress did try to limit independent PAC spending in 1974 to no more than $1,000 per candidate; but the Supreme Court declared that restriction unconstitutional on 1st Amendment grounds, *Buckley* v. *Valeo*, 1976.

Second, federal law neither limits nor requires the reporting of so-called "soft money"—funds raised by State and local party organizations for such "party-building activities" as voter registration or get-out-the-vote drives. (Political money raised and spent subject to FEC regulation is known as "hard money.") In both major parties, State and local organizations have found it fairly easy to filter this unregulated money into the party's presidential campaign effort. The soft-money loophole became especially prominent in 1988; both parties exploited it in that campaign and again in 1992.

[28]In the latter case, the public money would be received after the election and could not possibly help the candidate in that election. Again, many provisions of election law are purposely drawn to discourage minor-party efforts.

To this point, three minor party nominees have received FEC money: Sonia Johnson, the Citizens party's presidential candidate in 1984; Lenora Fulani, the New Alliance party's nominee in 1988 and in 1992; and John Hegelin, the Natural Law party's candidate in 1992. In each case, these minor party candidates qualified for the federal funds by meeting the preconvention triggering formula, see page 178; but, of course, they sought and spent the money for their general election campaigns.

## Section **3** Review

1. **Define:** political action committee (PAC)
2. What makes money so important to the election process?
3. Why are campaign finances regulated by law?
4. What are the major sources of campaign contributions in American politics?
5. What is the Federal Election Commission?
6. What four major areas of campaign finance are now covered by federal election laws?

**Critical Thinking**

7. **Distinguishing Fact From Opinion** (p. 19) The text says that "democracy would be best served if campaigns were entirely supported by the small contributions of millions of American voters." Explain why you agree or disagree with this statement.

★

# Recognizing Bias

Recognizing bias means identifying a stated or unstated viewpoint or slant that is designed to promote one set of beliefs over another. As you read and watch political advertising, be on guard for signs of bias. Political advertising might be biased because it does not include all the information the viewer needs to make a good decision. Or, an ad might be biased as a result of a misleading use of statistics or "facts." Follow the steps below to help you identify bias in political advertising.

**1. Watch for overly negative or overly positive ads.** Every ad tries to persuade. But if an ad makes a candidate sound too good or too bad to be true, the ad is probably unbalanced—and biased. (a) What is the overall message of each ad below? (b) Is the message in any of the ads overwhelmingly positive or negative? (c) Do any of the ads present information in a straightforward manner?

**2. Carefully separate fact from opinion.** It might be a fact that candidate X is a scientist. But when an ad calls candidate X a "brilliant scientist," the fact becomes an opinion in disguise. When opinions are presented as facts in this way, it may be a sign of bias. Ask yourself (a) What are the facts presented in the ads below? (b) What are the opinions? (c) Are any opinions reported as facts?

**3. Evaluate the use and accuracy of facts.** Facts and statistics are useful. However, they can also be used unfairly to draw false conclusions. Look at the facts in the ads below. (a) Is there a source given? (b) Can the facts be supported or checked in any way? (c) Are the facts used to support some conclusion? (d) Do the facts actually do so?

**4. Consider what information does not appear.** Recall that bias is designed to promote one view over another. An ad can achieve this effect by leaving out key information. Do any of the ads include information on any rival candidates?

**5. Identify the bias in the advertisements.** Now you are ready to evaluate the ads below. (a) Which of these ads are biased? (b) In what ways do they promote one viewpoint over another?

| A | B | C |
|---|---|---|
| **Do You Know Where Your Senator Is?** | **David Lee Offers Solid Leadership** | **Maria Hernandez For Governor** |
| During the last session, Senator Jones was absent from the Senate floor 30 percent of the time! Don't you think you deserve a full-time Senator, a Senator who cares about the people of the State? Voters, it's time for a change! | As sheriff, Lee has served the people of Green County for 10 years. Five times, voters have elected Lee as their county's chief law enforcement officer. Why not make it six? Reelect Lee for sheriff. | Leading citizen, successful businesswoman, devoted mother—Hernandez offers the qualities and skills we need to recover from the disastrous reign of the Tax and Spend party. A record of accomplishment, a reputation for integrity, a promise of performance—that's Hernandez for governor! |

# Chapter-in-Brief

Scan all headings, photographs, charts, and other visuals in the chapter before reading the section summaries below.

## Section 1 The Nominating Process (pp. 157–165)

The nominating process is critically important to democratic government. This is especially true in a two-party system, where voters usually find only two candidates for each office on the general-election ballot. In one-party areas, the nominating contests are regularly more important than the general election.

Five major nominating methods are used in American politics. They are: (1) self-announcement, (2) the caucus, (3) the delegate convention, (4) the direct primary, and (5) petition.

The direct primary, which developed at the turn of the century in reaction to the boss-dominated convention system, is the most widely used nominating method today. It is an intraparty nominating election. It takes two major forms among the States: (1) the open primary, in which any qualified voter may vote, and (2) the closed primary, where only declared party members may vote. Runoff primaries are widely used in the South. Nonpartisan primaries are often used to pick candidates for nonpartisan offices. Presidential primaries are not nominating devices; they are elections held to allow voters to express candidate preferences and/or to select delegates to the national conventions.

## Section 2 Elections (pp. 166–171)

In the United States, there are more than 500,000 elected offices, most of them at the local level across the country. There is only a limited amount of federal control of the election process. It is highly regulated by State law.

Presidential and congressional elections are held on the Tuesday following the first Monday in November in even-numbered years. Most States hold their general elections at the same time; local elections are generally held then, too, or in the spring. Voting takes place in local precincts and polling places.

Every State now uses the Australian ballot, which is either of the party-column or the office-group type. Long ballots are common in American elections.

Voting machines and electronic vote-counting systems are in wide use among the States. Vote-by-mail elections are being held with increasing frequency at the local level in a number of States.

## Section 3 Money and the Election Process (pp. 173–179)

Money plays a key role in politics and presents serious problems to democratic government.

Most campaign money comes from private sources. Today, the main sources are: (1) small individual contributors, (2) wealthier persons and families, (3) the candidates themselves, (4) nonparty private organizations—special interest groups and their political action committees (PACs), (5) temporary party organizations, and (6) party fund-raising events. The presidential election process is partially subsidized with public funds; so, too, are some State and local campaigns. Most of those persons and groups who make political contributions want something in return.

Federal campaign finance laws are administered by the Federal Election Commission. Those laws apply only to the federal—that is, to presidential and congressional—elections, not to State and local contests. They (1) require timely disclosure of campaign finance data, (2) limit campaign contributions, (3) limit campaign expenditures, and (4) provide public funding for several aspects of the presidential election process.

# Chapter Review

## Vocabulary and Key Terms

nomination (p. 158)
general election (p. 158)
caucus (p. 158)
direct primary (p. 161)
closed primary (p. 162)

open primary (p. 162)
blanket primary (p. 162)
runoff primary (p. 163)
coattail effect (p. 167)
precinct (p. 167)

polling place (p. 167)
ballot (p. 168)
political action
   committee (PAC)
   (p. 174)

**Matching:** *Review the key terms in the list above. If you are not sure of a term's meaning, look up the term and review its definition. Choose a term from the list above that best matches each description.*

1. a group of like-minded persons who meet to choose candidates for office
2. the political arm of a special interest group that seeks to influence the outcome of elections
3. an election held within a political party at which the voters choose candidates who will appear on the ballot in an upcoming general election
4. the phenomenon in which one candidate favorably influences the quantity of the vote cast for other candidates on the ballot from the same party
5. the place where the voters cast their ballots
6. the device by which voters register their choices in an election

**True or False:** *Determine whether each statement is true or false. If it is true, write "true." If it is false, change the underlined word or words to make the statement true.*

1. In a <u>runoff primary</u>, voters must choose between the two top finishers in an earlier primary election.
2. Because of <u>political action committees,</u> candidates of one party can benefit from the popularity of another candidate from their party on the ballot.
3. In a <u>general election</u>, voters must select the persons they want to hold certain public offices.
4. Each <u>precinct</u> has one polling place.
5. One commonly heard criticism of the <u>blanket primary</u> is that it encourages "raiding."

**Word Relationships:** *Distinguish between the words in each pair.*

1. caucus/direct primary
2. nomination/general election
3. precinct/polling place
4. blanket primary/closed primary

## Main Ideas

### Section 1 (pp. 157–165)

1. In what sense does the nominating process have an impact on the voters' right to vote in the American political system?
2. What are the five broad categories that describe the way that most nominations are made?
3. How has the nominating process in American politics changed over the course of American history?
4. Describe the different types of direct primaries that have been used in American politics.

## Section 2 (pp. 166–171)

**5.** What is the overall purpose and importance of election law in the American political process?

**6.** To what extent are States involved in governing elections?

**7.** To what extent is the Federal Government involved in governing elections?

**8.** Describe the basic differences between paper ballots and the other means of casting votes in this country.

## Section 3 (pp. 173–179)

**9.** Briefly describe the role and importance of money in the election process.

**10.** What are the major sources of campaign funding in American politics?

**11.** For what basic reasons do individuals contribute money to political candidates?

**12.** How has the federal government become involved in the regulation of the financing of campaigns?

## Critical Thinking

**1. Drawing Conclusions** (p. 19) Use what you have read in the chapter to make an argument for or against the following statement: The nomination of candidates is more important in the American political system than the election of candidates for office.

**2. Distinguishing Fact from Opinion** (p. 19) (a) Do you agree with the text statement that the election of officials such as clerks and coroners is not necessary in a democratic society? (b) Can you make any argument for the election of such public officials?

**3. Recognizing Cause and Effect** (p. 19) (a) How might the changes in laws regarding contributions to candidates have influenced the growth of PACs? (b) Explain why you would favor or oppose legislation that limited the amount candidates could spend on campaigns.

## Getting Involved

**1. Writing Your Opinion** Write a letter to the governor of your State in which you express your opinion about public financing for election of State and local officials. Before you start your letter, list the reasons why you think your opinion is correct.

Begin your letter by stating your purpose in writing. Then, write one paragraph for each of the reasons for your opinion. Review your first draft, checking to see that each paragraph is as persuasive as possible. Try to address any possible criticisms or questions the reader might have about your argument. Conclude the letter by thanking the governor for considering your ideas. Proofread and correct errors. Then prepare a final copy.

**2. Cooperative Activity** As a class, create an overall plan for elections in your State. Divide the class into three committees: One committee can debate the different methods of nominating candidates and determine the means by which minor parties can get candidates on the ballot. Another committee can decide how elections should be administered, including such questions as what public officials should be elected, what kind of ballot to use, and whether or not to allow voting by mail. The third committee should consider issues of campaign finance, such as limits on contributions, spending, public financing, and the role of PACs. When all three committees are finished, work as a class to organize the results into a single plan.

**3. Create a Political Cartoon** Draw a political cartoon that illustrates the role of money in the election process. Try to focus on some humorous or ironic aspect of the issue. Remember that the cartoon can use a combination of words and pictures to make its point.

# Mass Media and Public Opinion

## Chapter Preview

Did you see much of the last presidential election on television? The beginnings of Ross Perot's candidacy? The Democratic national convention in New York in July of 1992? Were you a witness to Perot's withdrawal from the contest, just as the Democrats were nominating Bill Clinton? The Republican convention in Houston in August, where George Bush was nominated for a second term? Did you read newspaper coverage or see television discussions of the presidential campaign, highlighted by Perot's return to the fray and by the presidential debates? Did you follow the returns on election night? The post-election drama and, finally, President Clinton's inauguration on the 20th of January, 1993?

Television and the other elements of the news media covered the presidential election—both extensively and intensively. But the media do more than merely report events. They also play a large role in shaping the opinions of the American people—a role that you will read about in the pages of this chapter.

### Before you read this chapter:

■ **Describe** how family and friends have an effect on forming your opinions.

■ **Predict** how political campaigning has changed since the development of television.

### As you read, focus on the main objective for each section. Understand:

1. Public opinion and its role in American politics.

2. The means by which opinions are expressed and measured.

3. The impact of the mass media on politics.

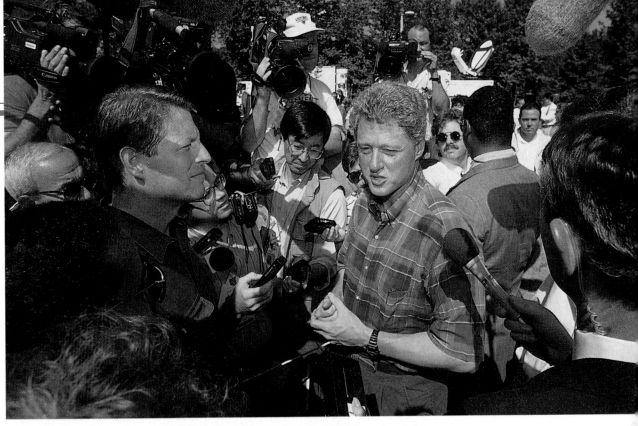

▲ **Media Blitz**   The enormity of the media presence in today's society brings to bear the question: To what extent is American public opinion shaped by the media?

# 1 The Formation of Public Opinion

### Find Out:
- What is public opinion?
- What factors influence the making of public opinion?

### Key Terms
public opinion, opinion leader

**D**o you like broccoli? Blue jeans? Spring vacation? Sports? What about cold weather? Old cars?

You have an opinion on each of those things, of course. In some cases, those opinions may be very strong and very important to you. But each of those opinions is your own view, your private opinion. As you will see, none of them is the kind of opinion discussed in this section—that is, public opinion.

## What Is Public Opinion?

Few terms in American politics are more widely used, and less well understood, than the term *public opinion*. It appears regularly in newspapers and magazines and you hear it frequently on radio and television.

Quite often, the phrase is used in a way that suggests that all or most of the American people hold the same view on some public matter. Thus, time and again, politicians say that "the people" want such and such, television commentators tell us that "the public" favors this or opposes that, and so on.

In fact, there are very few matters in which all or nearly all of "the people" think alike. "The public" holds many different and often conflicting views on nearly every public question.

To understand what public opinion is, you must recognize this important point: Public opinion is a complex collection of the opinions of many different persons. It is the sum total of all of their views. It is *not* the single and undivided view of some mass mind.

## The Political Spectrum

| LEFT | | CENTER | | RIGHT |
|---|---|---|---|---|
| **Radical** Favors extreme change to create an entirely new social system. | **Liberal** Believes that government must take action to change economic, political, and ideological policies that may be unfair. | **Moderate** | **Conservative** Seeks to keep in place the economic, political, and ideological structures of society. | **Reactionary** Favors extreme change to restore society to an earlier state. |

▲ **Interpreting Graphs and Cartoons**  Political opinions are formed throughout a lifetime. The general range, or spectrum, of political opinions are shown here. How does the cartoon reinforce the idea of a political spectrum?

small society

By Brickman

Reprinted with special permission of King Features, Inc.

There are many publics in the United States—in fact, an uncountable number of them. Each public is made up of all those persons who hold the same view on some particular public question. Each group of people with a differing point of view is a separate public with regard to that matter.

To illustrate: All persons who think that Congress should establish a national health insurance program belong to the public that holds that view. All who believe that the President is doing an excellent job as chief executive, or that capital punishment should be abolished, or that prayers should be permitted in the public schools are members of the separate publics with those particular opinions. Clearly, many persons belong to more than one of those publics; but almost certainly only a very few belong to all four of them.

This point is crucial, too: In its proper sense, public opinion includes only those views that relate to matters of public affairs—to politics, to public issues, and to the making of public policies. To be an opinion in the public sense, a view must involve something of general concern, something of interest to a significant portion of the people as a whole.

Of course, the people as a whole are interested in many things—in rock groups and symphony orchestras, the New York Yankees and the Dallas Cowboys, candy bars and green vegetables, and a great deal more. People have opinions on each of these things, views that are sometimes loosely called "public opinion." But, again, in its proper sense, public opinion involves only those views that people hold on such things as parties and candidates, taxes, unemployment, welfare programs, national defense, foreign policy, and so on.

**Definition**  Clearly, public opinion is so complex that it cannot be readily defined. But, for purposes of this book, **public opinion** can be described this way: Those attitudes held by a significant number of persons on matters of government and politics.

As suggested, you can better understand the term in the plural—that is, as public opinions, the opinions of publics. Or, to put it another way, public opinion is made up of expressed group attitudes.

A view must be expressed in order to be an opinion in the public sense. Unless an opinion is expressed in some way, it cannot be known by others. If others cannot know the opinion, it cannot be identified with any public.

## Factors That Shape Public Opinion

No one is born with a set of attitudes about government and politics. Instead, each person learns his or her political opinions, and does so in a lifelong "classroom" and from many different "teachers." In other words, public opinion is formed out of a very complex process, and the factors involved in it are almost without number.

You have already considered much of this—in Chapter 6 with regard to voting behavior. In effect, that extensive look at why people vote as they do amounted to an extensive look at how public opinions form.

There, remember, you read about the process by which each person acquires political opinions—the process of political socialization. That complex process begins in early childhood and continues on through a person's lifetime. It involves all of the experiences and relationships that lead people to see the political world and to act in it as they do.[1]

There are many different agents of political socialization at work in the opinion-shaping process. Again, you looked at these agents at some length in Chapter 6: age, race, income, occupation, residence, group affiliations, and many others. But two of them—the family and education—have such a vital impact that they deserve another look here.

**The Family** Most parents do not think of themselves as agents of political socialization, nor do the other members of most families. They are, nonetheless, and very importantly so.

Children first see the political world from within the family and through the family's eyes. They begin to learn about politics much as they begin to learn about most other things—from what their parents have to say, from the stories that their older brothers and sisters bring home from school, from watching television with the family, and so on.

Most of what smaller children learn in the family setting are not really political opinions. Clearly, toddlers are not concerned with the wisdom of spending billions of dollars on the Star Wars anti-missile defense system or the pros and cons of the monetary policies of the Federal Reserve Board. Children do pick up some basic attitudes, however, and with those attitudes, a basic slant toward such things as authority and rules of behavior, property, neighbors, people of other racial or religious groups, and the like. In short, children lay some important foundations on which they will later build their political opinions.

A large number of scholarly studies report what common sense also suggests. The strong

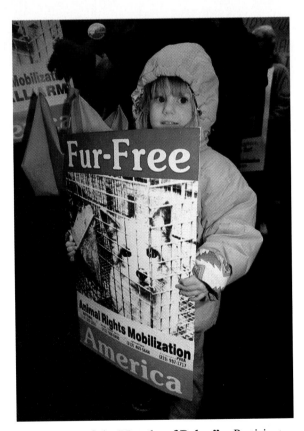

▲ **"Out of the Mouths of Babes"** Participating in public demonstrations—such as this anti-fur protest—helps socialize people to politics at a very early age.

---

[1]The concept of socialization comes from the fields of sociology and psychology. It is used to describe all of the ways in which a society transforms individuals into members of that society.

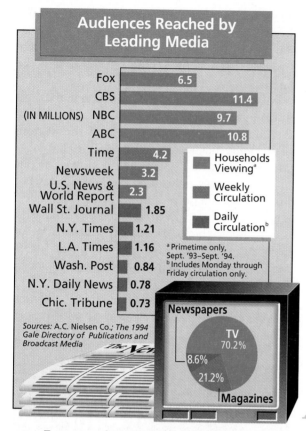

## Audiences Reached by Leading Media

(IN MILLIONS)

Fox — 6.5
CBS — 11.4
NBC — 9.7
ABC — 10.8
Time — 4.2
Newsweek — 3.2
U.S. News & World Report — 2.3
Wall St. Journal — 1.85
N.Y. Times — 1.21
L.A. Times — 1.16
Wash. Post — 0.84
N.Y. Daily News — 0.78
Chic. Tribune — 0.73

- Households Viewing [a]
- Weekly Circulation
- Daily Circulation [b]

[a] Primetime only, Sept. '93–Sept. '94.
[b] Includes Monday through Friday circulation only.

Sources: A.C. Nielsen Co.; The 1994 Gale Directory of Publications and Broadcast Media

Newspapers
TV 70.2%
8.6%
21.2%
Magazines

▲ **Interpreting Graphs** This graph shows the influence of the mass media on the lives of Americans. Why does television reach a larger audience than print media?

influence the family has on the development of political opinions is largely a result of the near monopoly the family has on the child in his or her earliest, most impressionable years. Those studies also show that:

❝The orientations acquired in early childhood tend to be the most intensely and permanently held of all political views. They serve as the base on which all later political learning is built. . . . Adult political behavior is the logical extension of values, knowledge, and identification formed during childhood and youth.❞ [2]

**The Schools** The start of formal schooling marks the first break in the force of family

[2] Richard Dawson, Kenneth Previtt, and Karen Dawson, *Political Socialization*, 2nd ed. (Boston: Little, Brown, 1977), page 48.

influence. For the first time children become regularly involved in activities outside the home.

From the first day, schools teach children the values of the American political system. They purposely work to indoctrinate the young and train them to become "good citizens." Schoolchildren salute the flag, recite the Pledge of Allegiance, and sing patriotic songs. They learn about George Washington, Susan B. Anthony, Martin Luther King, Jr., and other great Americans. From the early grades on, they pick up growing amounts of specific political knowledge, and they begin to form political opinions. In high school, they are often required to take a course in American government and to read books such as this one.

School involves much more than books and classes, of course. It is a complex bundle of experiences and a place where a good deal of informal learning occurs. School is a place where students encounter other students—and find that some of those other persons are like themselves, and some of them are different.

**Opinion Leaders** The views expressed by certain people—opinion leaders—also bear heavily on public opinion. An **opinion leader** is any person who, for any reason, has a more than usual influence on the views of others.

Many opinion leaders hold public office. Some write for newspapers or magazines or broadcast their opinions on radio or television. Others are prominent in business, labor, agriculture, civic organizations, and so on. Many are in professional occupations—doctors, lawyers, teachers, ministers, and the like—and have contact with fairly large numbers of people on a regular basis. Many others are active members of their neighborhood or church, or have leadership roles in their local communities.

Whoever they may be, opinion leaders are persons to whom others listen and from whom others draw ideas and convictions. Whatever their political, economic, or social standing or outlook may be, opinion leaders play a significant role in the formation of public opinion.

**The Mass Media** Obviously the mass media—which includes television, radio, film, books, magazines, and newspapers—have a large influence on the formation of public opinion. Take this as but one indication of that fact: The Census Bureau reports that there is at least one television set in 98 percent of the nation's 96 million households. There are two or more sets in more than 60 million homes and millions more in many other places. Most of those sets are turned on for at least seven hours a day—for a mind-boggling total of a billion hours a day.

**A Mix of Factors** No one factor, by itself, shapes any person's opinion on any matter. Some play a larger role than others, however. Thus, in addition to family and education, occupation and race are usually much more significant than, say, gender or place of residence.

But this is not always the case. On the question of national health insurance, for example, the job a person has—how well-paying it is, whether it includes coverage by a private health-insurance plan, and so on—will almost certainly have a greater impact on that person's view than his or her gender or where he or she happens to live. On the other hand, if the question involves equal pay for women, then gender will almost certainly loom much larger in the opinion-making mix. In short, the relative weight of each of the many factors that influence public opinion depends a great deal on the nature of the particular issue involved.

## Section 1 Review

1. **Define:** public opinion, opinion leader
2. Public opinion includes views on what kinds of matters?
3. What factors shape public opinion?
4. What is political socialization?
5. What makes the family and schools such important agents in the opinion-shaping process?
6. What constitutes the mass media?

### Critical Thinking

7. **Recognizing Ideologies** (p. 19) The text states that schools aim to socialize students so that they become "good citizens." Should this be a function of the educational system?

★

# 2 The Measurement of Public Opinion

**Find Out:**
- How is public opinion measured?
- For what reason is public opinion measured?

**Key Terms:**
mandate, interest group, public opinion poll, straw vote, sample, random sample, quota sample

How many times have you heard this phrase: "According to a recent poll. . ."? Probably more than you can count. It becomes especially common in the months leading up to an important election. If public policy is to be based on public opinion, it has to be possible to find the answers to these questions: What is the content of public opinion on a particular issue? How many people share a given view on that matter? How firmly do they hold that view? That is to say, it must be possible to "measure" public opinion—and, as you will see in this section, it is.

## The Challenge of Measuring Public Opinion

The general content of public opinion on some matter—what different groups of people say they think about it—can be found by consulting the means by which people usually express opinions in American society. Those means are both many and varied. They include voting, lobbying, books, pamphlets, magazine and newspaper articles, editorial comments in the press and on radio and television, paid advertisements, letters to editors and public officials, and so on.

These and other means of expression are the devices through which the general shape of public opinion becomes known. But, usually, the means by which a view is expressed tells little—and often nothing reliable—about the size of the group that holds that opinion or how strongly it is held. In the American political system, these questions are vital ones. To find

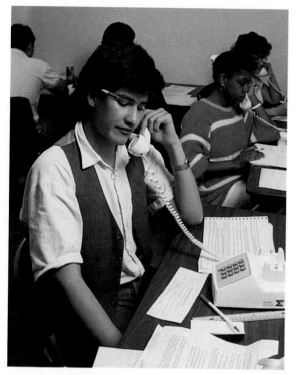

**Measuring Public Opinion by Phone** A telephone poll, conducted at the Texas Democratic headquarters, helps predict support for gubernatorial candidate Ann Richards.

answers to these questions you must make some effort to measure public opinion.

**Measurement Through Elections** In a democracy the voice of the people is supposed to express itself through the ballot box. Election results are very often said to be indicators of public opinion. The votes cast for rival candidates are regularly taken as evidence of the people's approval or rejection of the stands taken by those candidates and their parties. A party and its victorious candidates regularly claim to have received a mandate to carry out their campaign promises. In American politics a **mandate** refers to the instructions or commands a constituency gives to its elected officials.[3]

In fact, however, election results are seldom an accurate measure of public opinion. Voters

make the choices they do in elections for any of several reasons, as you have seen. Very often, those choices have little or nothing to do with the candidates' stands on public questions. Then, too, candidates often disagree with some of the planks of their party's platform. And, as you have also seen, candidates and parties often express their positions in broad, vague terms.

In short, much of what you have read about voting behavior, and about the nature of parties, adds up to this: Elections are, at best, only useful indicators of public opinion. To call the typical election a mandate for much of anything other than a general direction in public policy is to be on very shaky ground.[4]

**Measurement Through Interest Groups** Interest groups are treated at length in the next chapter. For now, remember that **interest groups** are private organizations whose members share certain views and work to shape the making and content of public policy. These organizations are also very aptly known as pressure groups and special interest groups.

Interest groups are a chief means by which public opinion is made known. They present their views—exert their pressures—through their lobbyists, by letters, telephone calls, in political campaigns, and by a number of other methods. In dealing with them, however, public officials often find it difficult to determine two things: How many people does an interest group really represent? And just how strongly do those people hold the views that an organization says they do?

**Measurement Through the Media** Earlier you read some very impressive numbers about television. Those huge numbers help describe the place of the media in the opinion process; and you will read more of those numbers later. But, here, recognize the point that the media are a gauge for assessing public opinion.

---

[3]The term *mandate* comes from the Latin *mandare*—literally, "to place in one's hand or to commit to one's charge."

[4]Initiative and referendum elections, at which voters approve or reject specific measures, are elections in which public opinion is registered much more directly on specific public policy questions. See Chapter 24, Section 1.

The media are frequently described as "mirrors" as well as "molders" of opinion. It is often said that the views expressed in newspaper editorials, syndicated columns, news magazines, television commentaries, and so on, are fairly good indicators of public opinion. The media are *not* very accurate mirrors, as you will soon see.

### Measurement Through Personal Contacts

Most public officials have frequent and wide-ranging contacts in many different forms with large numbers of people. In each of these contacts, they try to read the public's mind. In fact, their jobs demand that they do so.

Members of Congress receive bags of mail, stacks of telegrams, and hundreds of phone calls. Many of them make frequent trips "to keep in touch with the folks back home." Top administration figures are often on the road, selling the President's programs and sensing the people's reactions. Even the President does some of this, with speaking trips to different parts of the country.

Governors, State legislators, mayors, and other officials also have any number of contacts with the public. These officials encounter the public in their offices, in public meetings, at social gatherings, at ball games, and so on.

Can public officials find "the voice of the people" in all of those contacts? Many can and do, and often with surprising accuracy. But some public officials cannot. They fall into an ever-present trap: They find only what they want to find—only those views that support and agree with their own.

### Polls—the Best Measure of Public Opinion

The public's opinions are best measured by public opinion polls. A **public opinion poll** is a device that attempts to collect information about public opinion by asking people questions.[5] The more accurate polls are based on scientific polling techniques.

---

[5]The word *poll* comes from the old Teutonic word *polle*, meaning the top or crown of the head, the part that shows when heads are counted.

Public opinion polls have existed in this country for more than a century. Until the 1930s, however, they were far from scientific. Most earlier polling efforts were of the **straw vote** variety. That is, they were polls that sought to read the public's mind simply by asking the same question of a large number of people. Straw votes are still fairly common. Newspapers often run "clip-out and mail-in" ballots; radio talk shows ask listeners to respond to questions with phone calls; and so on.

The straw-vote technique is highly unreliable, however. It rests on the false assumption that a relatively large number of responses will give a fairly accurate picture of the public's views on a given question. But nothing in the process ensures that those who do respond will in fact represent a reasonably accurate cross section of the total population. The straw vote emphasizes the quantity rather than the quality of the sample to which its question is posed.

The most famous of all straw-polling mishaps took place in 1936. A periodical called the *Literary Digest* mailed postcard ballots to more than 10 million people and received answers from more than 2,376,000 of them. Based on that huge return, the magazine confidently predicted the outcome of the presidential election that year. It said that Governor Alfred Landon, the Republican nominee, would easily defeat incumbent Franklin Roosevelt. Instead, Roosevelt won

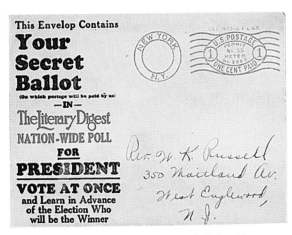

▲ **Choose Your Sample Carefully!** More than two million people responded to this 1936 *Literary Digest* survey. Why do you think the poll was proven to be misleading?

By permission of Mike Luckovich and Creators Syndicate

You did your patriotic duty? You mean you voted ?...

Naw. I responded to a poll....

▲ **Interpreting Political Cartoons**
Public opinion polls are now followed closely by millions of Americans. How does the cartoon convey this as a *negative* phenomenon?

in a landslide. He captured more than 60 percent of the popular vote and carried every State but Maine and Vermont.

The *Digest* had drawn its sample on an altogether faulty basis: from automobile registration lists and from telephone directories. The *Digest* had failed to consider that in the mid-Depression year of 1936, millions of people could not afford to own cars or have private telephones. In short, its poll failed to reach most of the vast pool of the poor and unemployed, millions of blue-collar workers, and most of the ethnic minorities in the country. Those were the very segments of the population from which FDR and the Democrats drew their greatest support.[6]

**Scientific Polling**  Serious efforts to take the public's pulse on a scientific basis date from the mid-1930s. They began with the work of such early pollsters as George Gallup and Elmo Roper. The techniques that they and others have developed since then have reached a highly sophisticated level.

_____

[6]The magazine had predicted the winner of each of the three previous presidential elections, but its failure to do so in 1936 was so colossal that it ceased publication not long thereafter.

There are now more than 1,000 national and regional polling organizations in this country. Many of them do mostly commercial work. That is, they tap the public's preferences on everything from toothpastes and headache remedies to television shows and thousands of other things. However, at least 200 of these polling outfits poll the political preferences of the American people. Among the best known of the national pollsters today are the Gallup Organization (the Gallup Poll) and Louis Harris and Associates (the Harris Survey).

**The Polling Process**  Scientific poll-taking is an extremely complex process that can best be described in five basic steps. In their efforts to discover and report public opinion, pollsters must (1) define the universe to be surveyed; (2) construct a sample; (3) prepare valid questions; (4) select and control the means by which the poll will be taken; and (5) report their findings to the public.

Step 1: DEFINE THE UNIVERSE TO BE SURVEYED. The *universe* is a term that means the whole population that the poll aims to measure, the group whose opinions the poll will seek to discover. That universe can be all voters in Chicago, or every high school student in North Carolina, or all Republicans in New England, or all Democrats in Georgia, or all Catholic women over age 35 in the United States, and so on.

Step 2: CONSTRUCT A REPRESENTATIVE SAMPLE. If a poll's universe is very small—say, the 25 members of a high school class—the best way to find out what that universe thinks about some issue would be to poll every one of them. In most cases, however, it is not possible to interview a complete universe. This is certainly the case in matters of public policy that affect all the people in the nation. There are simply too many people in that universe to talk to. So, the poll-taker must select a **sample**—a representative slice of the total universe.

Most professional pollsters now draw a random sample, also called a probability sample. In a random sample, the poll-taker interviews a certain number of randomly selected people who live in a certain number of randomly selected places. In short, a **random sample** is a sample in which each member of the universe and each geographic area within it have a mathematically equal chance of being included within the sample.

Most major national polls interview just over 1,500 people to represent the universe of the nation's entire adult population—some 190 million people.

How can the views of so few people represent the opinions of so many? The answer to that question lies in the mathematical law of probability. Flip a coin 1,000 times. The law of probability says that, given an honest coin and an honest flip, heads will come up 500 times. Furthermore, the law states that the results of this test will be the same—no matter how often you perform it, and no matter what kind of coin you use. The law of probability is regularly applied in a great many situations: by insurance companies to compute life expectancies, by a food inspector to check the quality of a farmer's truckload of beans, and by others who "play the odds"—including pollsters who draw random samples.

In short, if the sample is of sufficient size and is properly selected at random from the entire universe, the law of probability says that the result will be accurate to within a small and predictable margin of error. Mathematicians tell us that a properly drawn random sample of some 1,500 people will reflect the opinions of all the nation's adult population and will be accurate to within a margin of plus or minus (±) 3 percent.[7]

Some pollsters do use a less complicated, but less reliable, sampling method. They draw a **quota sample**, a sample deliberately constructed to reflect several of the major characteristics of the universe. For example, if 51.3 percent of that overall group is female, 17.5

---

[7]Pollsters acknowledge that it is impossible to construct a sample that would be an absolutely accurate reflection of a large universe—hence, the allowance for error. A margin of ±3 percent means a spread of 6 percentage points, of course. To bring the sampling error down from ± 3 percent to ± 1 percent, the size of the sample would have to be 9,500 people. The time and money needed to interview that big a sample make that a practical impossibility.

## VOICES *on Government*

### On the Value of Public Opinion Polls

**George Gallup,** founder of the Gallup Poll

❝As students, scholars, and the general public gain a better understanding of polls, they will have a greater appreciation of the service polls can perform in a democracy. . . . [M]odern polls are the chief hope of lifting government to a higher level, by showing that the public supports the reforms that will make this possible, by providing a *modus operandi* for testing new ideas. . . . Polls can help make government more efficient and responsive; . . . they can make this a truer democracy. ❞

---

percent of it is African American, and so on, then the sample will be made up of 51.3 percent females, 17.5 percent African Americans, and so on. Of course, most of the people in the sample will belong to more than one of the categories on which it is built. This fact is a major reason why such a sample is less reliable than random samples.

Step 3: PREPARE VALID QUESTIONS. The way in which questions are worded is a very important matter. Wording can affect the reliability of any poll. For example, most people will probably say "yes" to a question put this way: "Should local taxes be reduced?" But many of those same persons will also give the same answer to this question: "Should the city's police force be increased to fight the rising tide of crime in our community?" Yet, expanding the police force almost certainly would require more local tax dollars. Responsible pollsters acknowledge these issues and phrase their questions very carefully. They purposely try not to use "loaded" words, terms that are difficult to understand, and questions that are worded in a way that will tend to shape the answers that are given to them.

Step 4: SELECT AND CONTROL THE POLLING PROCESS. In part, this point relates to how the pollsters communicate with the sample. Most polls are taken face-to-face. That is, the interviewers question the respondents in person. However, pollsters conduct an increasing number of surveys by telephone, and others by mail. Professional pollsters see both advantages and

drawbacks in each of these approaches. They all agree, however, that whichever technique they use to gather information, they must employ the same technique in the questioning of all of the respondents in a sample.

The interview itself is a very sensitive point in the process. The poll-taker's appearance, dress, apparent attitude, or tone of voice in asking questions can influence the replies he or she receives—and thus alter the validity of the poll's results. If the questions are not carefully worded, some of the respondent's replies may be snap judgments or emotional reactions. Others may be of the sort that the person being interviewed thinks "ought" to be given; or they may be answers that the respondent thinks will please—or offend—the interviewer. Thus, polling organizations try to hire and train their interviewing staffs very carefully.

Step 5: REPORT THEIR FINDINGS. Polls, whether scientific or not, try to measure the attitudes of people. To be of any real value, however, someone must analyze and report the results. Scientific polling organizations collect huge amounts of raw data today. In order to handle these data, computers and other electronic hardware have become routine parts of the processes by which pollsters tabulate and then interpret their data, draw their conclusions, and then publish their findings.

## Evaluation of Polls

How good are the polls? On balance, the major national polls are fairly reliable. So, too, are most of the regional surveys around the country. Still, they are far from perfect. Fortunately, most responsible pollsters themselves are quite aware of that fact. Many of them are involved in continuing efforts to refine every aspect of the polling process to acknowledge the limits of their polls.

For example, pollsters know that they have difficulty measuring these qualities of the opinions they report: intensity, stability, and relevance. Intensity is the strength of feeling with which an opinion is held. Stability (or fluidity) is the relative permanence or changeableness of an opinion. Relevance (or salience) is how

### How to Take a Poll

**1. Define the population to be polled.** Decide what group you need to poll in order to find the answer to your question. For example, if you are seeking to learn what percentage of registered voters in Lexington, North Carolina, actually voted, then it would not be sensible to poll anyone who did not register to vote.

**2. Construct a sample.** You may choose to construct either a *random sample*, in which you randomly choose the members of the group to be polled, or a *quota sample*, in which you poll a representative number of people from each subgroup in your survey.

**3. Prepare valid questions.** Try to ask objective questions, questions that can be answered in one word, and questions that do not include terms that are difficult to understand.

**4. Select and control the means by which the poll will be taken.** Decide whether you will conduct an in-person interview, a telephone interview, or a mail interview. Be sure to interview all members of the group in the same manner. Choose interviewers who are careful not to influence the responses by their dress, attitude, or tone of voice.

**5. Report your findings.** Make a table of the results of your poll and then analyze this data to determine the answer to your original question.

▲ **Interpreting Charts** The most important steps to taking a poll are outlined here. Why do you think measuring public opinion is an acceptable part of the democratic process?

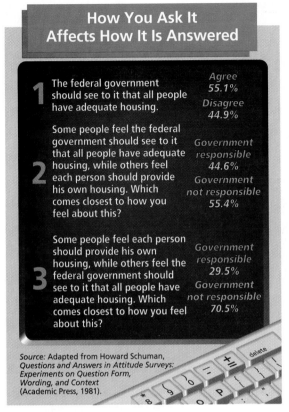

### How You Ask It Affects How It Is Answered

**1** The federal government should see to it that all people have adequate housing.

*Agree* 55.1%
*Disagree* 44.9%

**2** Some people feel the federal government should see to it that all people have adequate housing, while others feel each person should provide his own housing. Which comes closest to how you feel about this?

*Government responsible* 44.6%
*Government not responsible* 55.4%

**3** Some people feel each person should provide his own housing, while others feel the federal government should see to it that all people have adequate housing. Which comes closest to how you feel about this?

*Government responsible* 29.5%
*Government not responsible* 70.5%

*Source: Adapted from Howard Schuman, Questions and Answers in Attitude Surveys: Experiments on Question Form, Wording, and Context (Academic Press, 1981).*

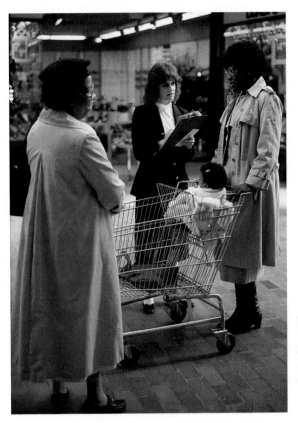

**Interpreting Tables** This table demonstrates the importance of how each question on a poll is worded. Which question above is worded in the least biased manner?

important a particular opinion is to the person who holds it.

Polls and pollsters are sometimes said to shape the opinions they are supposed to measure. Some critics of the polls say that in an election, for example, pollsters often create a "bandwagon effect." That is, some voters, wanting to be with the winner, jump on the bandwagon of the candidate who is ahead in the polls. The charge is most often leveled against those polls that appear as syndicated columns in many newspapers.

In spite of these criticisms, it is clear that scientific polls are the most useful tools there are for the difficult task of measuring public opinion. Though they may not be always or precisely accurate, they do offer reasonably reliable guides to public thought. Moreover, they help to focus attention on public questions and to stimulate discussion of them.

## Limits on the Force of Public Opinion

More than a century ago, Lord Bryce, a very wise Englishman, described government in the United States as "government by public opinion."[8] Clearly, the energy devoted to the measuring of public opinion suggests something of its powerful role in American politics. However, Lord Bryce's opinion is true only if that description is understood to mean that public opinion is the major, but by no means the only, influence on public policy in this country. Its force is tempered by a number of other factors—for example, by interest groups, which you will read about in the next chapter.

Most importantly, however, remember this vital point: Our system of constitutional govern-

[8]James Bryce, *The American Commonwealth* (New York: Macmillan, 1888), vol. 2, page 251.

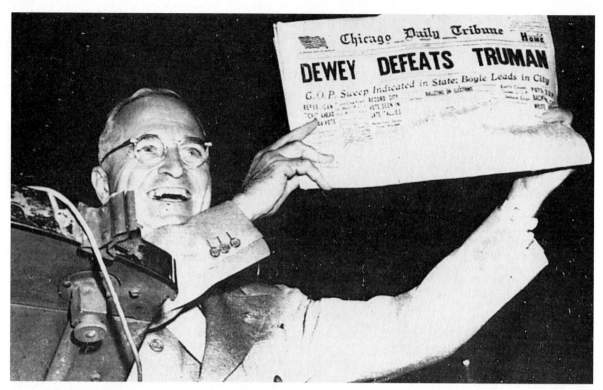

▲ **Poorly Predicted**    An elated Harry Truman holds up a newspaper headline wrongly announcing his defeat in 1948. Pollsters and others had predicted a land-slide victory for Thomas E. Dewey in that election.

ment is not designed to give free and unrestrict-ed play to public opinion—and especially not to majority opinion. In particular, the doctrines of separation of powers and of checks and balances and the constitutional guarantees of civil rights and liberties are intended to protect minority interests against the excesses of majority views and actions.

Finally, note that polls are not elections, or substitutes for elections. It is when faced with a ballot that voters must decide what is important and what is not. Voters must be able to tell the difference between opinions and concrete infor-mation, and should know the difference between personalities and platforms. Democracy is more than a simple measurement of opinion. Democracy is also about making careful choices among leaders and their positions on certain issues, and among the governmental actions that may follow. Ideally, democracy is the thoughtful participation of citizens in the politi-cal process.

## Section 2 Review

1. **Define:** mandate, interest group, public opin-ion poll, straw vote, sample, random sample, quota sample
2. For what reasons is public opinion measured?
3. What device best measures public opinion?
4. What are the other major means of measur-ing public opinion?
5. Why is the wording of questions a criti-cally important fact in the scientific polling process?
6. Name two shortcomings of scientific polling.

**Critical Thinking**

7. **Determining Relevance** (p. 19) What are some good reasons for knowing which candi-date in an upcoming election is ahead in the polls?

★

# Does the Government Have the Power to Restrict the Press?

## New York Times v. United States, 1971

The question of United States involvement in the long war in Vietnam divided the American people more deeply than had any other issue since the Civil War. In the spring of 1971, at the height of popular protests against that war, the *New York Times* and several other newspapers obtained copies of a set of classified Defense Department documents. Those documents, which came to be known as "The Pentagon Papers," were officially titled "History of U.S. Decision-Making Process on Viet Nam Policy."

The documents had been stolen from the Defense Department and then leaked to the press. Among many other things, the Pentagon Papers disclosed a number of instances in which the Johnson Administration had purposely deceived both Congress and the American people with regard to this nation's policies in Southeast Asia.

Acting at the Government's request, the United States district court in New York issued an injunction—a temporary court order—that directed the *New York Times* not to publish the stolen documents. In its arguments for the injunction, the Government claimed that the publication of some of the material in the Pentagon Papers would endanger the security of the United States.

The *New York Times* appealed the district order to the Supreme Court, noting, as it did so, that this case marked the only instance in which the Government of the United States had ever sought to prevent a newspaper from publishing material that was already in its possession.

*Review the following evidence and arguments presented to the United States Supreme Court:*

## Arguments for *New York Times*

**1.** The 1st Amendment's guarantee of freedom of the press protects the newspaper in the publication of these documents.

**2.** One of the few restraints on executive power in matters of national defense is a knowledgeable population. The press must be free to inform the American people.

**3.** The Government has failed to show that publication of the Pentagon Papers would in fact endanger national security.

## Arguments for United States

**1.** The 1st Amendment does not guarantee an absolute freedom of the press, especially when the nation's security is involved.

**2.** The Court must strike a balance between the fundamentally important right to a free press and the equally important duty of the Government to protect the nation.

**3.** To allow the publication of these documents would establish a dangerous precedent for future cases involving national security.

## Getting Involved

**1. Identify** the constitutional grounds on which each side based its arguments in this case.

**2. Debate** the opposing viewpoints in this case.

**3. Predict** how you think the Supreme Court ruled in this case and why. Then refer to page 768 in the Supreme Court Glossary to read about the decision. Discuss the impact of the Court's decision on executive power and executive abuses.

# 3 The Mass Media and Politics

**Find Out:**
- What are the major forms of mass media?
- What is mass media's impact on politics?

**Key Terms:**
medium, mass media, sound bite

How much television do you watch each day? Little or none? Two hours a day? Three hours? More? However much you watch, you no doubt know that your peers spend a great deal of time in front of the tube. Studies show that by the time the average person graduates from high school today, he or she has spent 11,000 hours in classrooms and 15,000 hours watching television.

Television has an extraordinary impact on the lives of everyone in this country. And, as you will see in this section, so do the other elements of the mass media.

## An Overview of the Mass Media

A **medium** is a means of communication; it transmits some kind of information. And media is the plural of medium. The **mass media** include those means of communication that can reach large, widely dispersed audiences—masses of people—simultaneously.

Four major mass media are particularly important in American politics. Ranked in terms of impact, they are television, newspapers, radio, and magazines. Other media—books, films, and audi- and videocassettes, for example—play a lesser role. So, too, do computers—though their communicating capabilities are becoming increasingly important.

The mass media are not a part of government; and, unlike political parties and interest groups, they do not exist primarily to influence government. They are, nonetheless, an important force in politics. Along with entertainment, the media provide people with political information. They do so directly when they report the news—in a newscast or in the news columns of a paper, for example. They also provide a large amount of political information less directly—for example, in radio and television programs, newspaper stories, and magazine articles that deal with such public topics as crime, nuclear power, or the federal deficit. Either way, people acquire most of the information they know about government and politics from the various forms of media.

## Television

Politics and television have gone hand in hand since the new technology first appeared. The first public demonstration of television occurred at the New York World's Fair in 1939. President Franklin Roosevelt opened the fair on camera, and viewers watched him on tiny five- and seven-inch screens. World War II interrupted the development of the new medium, but it began to become generally available in the late 1940s. Television boomed in the 1950s. The first transcontinental broadcast came in 1951, when President Harry Truman, speaking in Washington, addressed the delegates attending the Japanese Peace Treaty Conference in San Francisco.

Today, television is all-pervasive. As you read earlier, there is at least one television set in 98 percent of the nation's 96 million households. In fact, there are more homes in this country with a television set than with indoor plumbing facilities.

The more than 1,400 television stations include more than 1,000 commercial outlets and over 300 public broadcasters. Three major national networks have dominated television from its infancy: the Columbia Broadcasting System (CBS), the American Broadcasting Company (ABC), and the National Broadcasting Company (NBC). Those three giants furnish about 90 percent of the programming of some 700 local stations. That programming accounts for about 65 percent of all television viewing time today.

The major networks' audience share has been declining in recent years, however. The main challenges to their domination have come from three sources: (1) several independent broadcast-

**Global Awareness**

| | U.S.A. | Japan | Bangladesh | Nigeria | Mexico | Italy | Czechoslovakia | Chile | Haiti | Nicaragua |
|---|---|---|---|---|---|---|---|---|---|---|
| Population in millions | 249.2 | 123.5 | 115.6 | 108.5 | 88.6 | 57.1 | 15.7 | 13.2 | 6.5 | 3.9 |
| Number of daily newspapers | 1,657 | 158 | 72 | 31 | 286 | 73 | 30 | 39 | 4 | 3 |
| Circulation per 1000 | 251 | 577 | 9 | — | 119 | 105 | 342 | 67 | 4 | 29 |
| Radios per 1000 | 2,122 | 895 | 41 | 171 | 242 | 794 | 583 | 340 | 42 | 247 |
| Television sets per 1000 | 814 | 610 | 4.4 | 28.6 | 127 | 423 | 410 | 201 | 4.5 | 61.4 |

**Access to Media in Selected Countries**

Source: The World Media Handbook 1992–1994, United Nations

▲ **Interpreting Tables: Multicultural Awareness**   Access to media varies considerably from country to country. From the data on the graph, which country appears to be least influenced by television? Which country sells the most newspapers per thousand people?

ing groups—for example, the Fox Network; (2) cable broadcasters[9]—for example, Turner Broadcasting, and especially its Cable News Network (CNN); and (3) the Public Broadcasting System (PBS) and its more than 300 local stations.

Some of the most highly touted presentations on television—a Super Bowl game, for example, or a debate between the major presidential candidates—are seen by as many as 100 million people. From 15 to 40 million watch the more popular sitcoms. Each of the three major network's nightly news programs draw 12 to 14 mil-

lion viewers. More than 70 million places, including nearly two-thirds of the nation's households, are now hooked up to cable systems.

Television replaced newspapers as the principal source of political information for a majority of the American people in the early 1960s. In fact, television is now the principal source for an estimated 80 percent of the population.

## Newspapers

The first regularly published newspaper in America, the *Boston News-Letter*, appeared in 1704.[10] Other papers soon followed, in Boston

[9]C-SPAN, the Cable-Satellite Public Affairs Network, has begun to attract a significant audience. C-SPAN presents both live and taped coverage of a broad and growing range of public events—including major floor debates and committee hearings in Congress, presidential and other press conferences, and speeches by notable public figures.

[10]The world's first newspaper was almost certainly *Tsing Pao*, a court journal in Beijing. Press historians believe that its first issues, printed from stone blocks, were published some time in the 6th century; its last issue appeared in 1935.

and then in Philadelphia, New York, Annapolis, and elsewhere. By 1775, 35 newspapers were being published in the colonies. All of them were weekly papers, and they were printed on one sheet that was folded to make four pages. The nation's first daily newspaper, the *Philadelphia Evening Post and Daily Advertiser*, began publication in 1783.

Those first papers carried mostly political news and several spurred the colonists to revolution. They carried the news of independence and the text of the Declaration to people throughout the colonies. Thomas Jefferson marked the vital role of the press in the earliest years of the nation when, in 1787, he wrote to a friend:

❝Were it left to me to decide whether we should have a government without newspapers, or newspapers without a government, I should not hesitate a moment to prefer the latter.❞

The 1st Amendment, added to the Constitution in 1791, made the same point with its guarantee of the freedom of the press.

Today, more than 11,000 newspapers are published in the United States—including more than 1,700 dailies, some 570 semiweeklies, more than 8,200 weeklies, and several hundred foreign-language papers. Those publications have a combined circulation of more than 150 million copies per issue. Surveys indicate that some 95 million people, just about half of the nation's adult population, read a newspaper every day; and they spend, on the average, a half-hour doing so.

Contrary to a widespread belief, the number of daily papers in the United States has not declined in recent years. In fact, just about as many dailies are published today as were published 40 years ago. The total circulation of

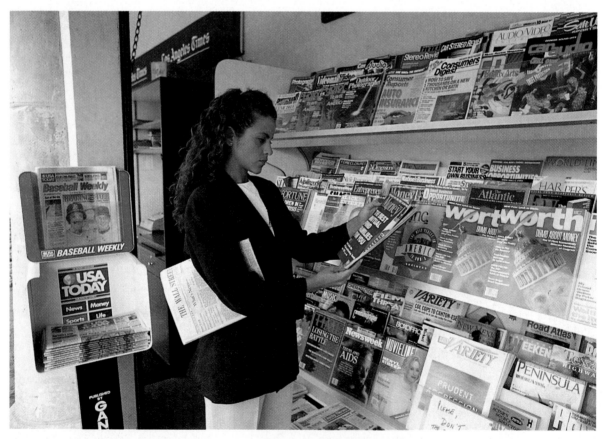

▲ **Something for Everyone** This newsstand in California displays the wide selection of print materials readily available in most American cities. Some 10,000 magazines are published in the United States today.

those papers has gone up about 20 percent in that period—to over 60 million copies today. There has been a marked decline, however, in the number of cities with competing newspapers. Most of the largest cities do have at least two major papers today, but a growing number of other cities do not.

Newspapers rank second only to television as the people's primary source of information about government and politics. Most papers cover stories in much greater depth than television does, and many try to present various points of view in their editorial sections. Those newspapers that have the most substantial reputations and national influence today include the *New York Times,* the *Washington Post,* the *Chicago Tribune,* the *Los Angeles Times,* the *Wall Street Journal,* and the *Christian Science Monitor.*

Most newspapers are local papers. That is, most of their readers live in or near the communities in which they are published. While most papers do carry a substantial amount of national and international news, most focus on their own locales. Advances in telecommunications and computerized operations are working a change in that basic fact, however. Today, each day's editions of the *New York Times,* the *Wall Street Journal,* and the *Christian Science Monitor* are generally available on the day of publication around the country; and *USA Today,* which began publication in the early 1980s, has become a popular national newspaper.

## Radio

Radio as it exists today began in 1920. On November 2nd of that year, station KDKA in Pittsburgh went on the air with presidential election returns. Radio soon became immensely popular. By 1927, 733 commercial stations were on the air, Americans owned more than seven million radio sets, and two national networks were in operation. NBC was established in 1926 and CBS in 1927. The Mutual Broadcasting System was formed in 1934 and ABC in 1943. The advent of networks made it possible for broadcasters to present their programs and advertising messages to millions of people all over the country.

**Radio Survives Television** Use of the air waves is another medium through which the public is bombarded with information. In this country, there are roughly two radio receivers for every person. The disc jockey above is broadcasting from WKGO in San Francisco, California.

By the 1930s, radio had assumed much of the role in American society that television has today. It was a major entertainment medium, and millions planned their daily schedules around their favorite network programs. The networks also provided the nation with dramatic coverage of important events, and radio exposed the American people to national and international politics as never before. President Franklin Roosevelt was the first major public figure to use radio effectively. Author David Halberstam has described the impact of FDR's famous fireside chats:

“He was the first great American radio voice. For most Americans of [that] generation, their first memory of politics would be of sitting by a radio and hearing *that* voice, strong, confident, totally at ease. . . . Most Americans in the previous 160 years had never seen a

President; now almost all of them were hearing him, *in their own homes*. It was literally and figuratively electrifying.**,,** [11]

Many thought that the arrival of television would bring the end of radio as a major medium. But radio has survived, in large part because it is so conveniently available. People can hear music, news, sports, and other radio programs in many places where they cannot watch television—in their cars, at work, in the country, and so on.

Radio remains a major source of news and other political information. The average person hears 20 hours of radio each week. No one knows how many hundreds of millions of radios there are in this country—in homes, offices, cars, backpacks, and a great many other places. Those radios can pick up more than 10,000 stations on the AM and FM dials.

Many AM stations are affiliated with one or another of the national networks. Unlike television, however, most radio programming is local. There are now more than 300 public radio stations, most of them on the FM dial. These noncommercial outlets are part of National Public Radio (NPR), which is radio's counterpart of television's PBS.

In most large cities there is at least one station that broadcasts nothing but news and public affairs programs. In addition, many stations serve the preferences of African-American, Hispanic-American, or other minority audiences.

## Magazines

Several magazines were published in colonial America. Benjamin Franklin began one of the very first, his *General Magazine*, in Philadelphia in 1741. On into the early 1900s, most magazines published in the United States were generally devoted to literature and the social graces. The first political magazines—among them, *Harper's Weekly* and the *Atlantic Monthly*—appeared in the mid-1800s. The progressive reform period in the early years of this century spawned several journals of opinion, including a number that featured articles by the leading muckrakers of the day.[12] For decades before radio and then television, magazines constituted the only national medium.

Some 10,000 magazines are published in the United States today. Most are trade publications—for example, *Veterinary Forum* and the *Automotive Executive*—or periodicals that target some special personal interest, such as *Golf Digest, Teen* and the *American Rifleman*. The top sellers today are *Modern Maturity, TV Guide*, and *Reader's Digest*; they each sell from 15 to 20 million or more copies per issue. Three news magazines, *Time, Newsweek*, and *U.S. News & World Report*, rank in the top 25 periodicals in terms of circulation. They have a combined circulation of nearly 10 million copies a week, and they are important sources of political news and comment. There are several other magazines devoted to public affairs, most of them vehicles of opinion—including the *Nation*, the *New Republic*, and *National Review*.

## The Media's Impact on Politics

Clearly, the media play a significant role in American politics. But just how significant that role is, just how much influence the media have is the subject of long, still unsettled debate.

Whatever its weight, the media's influence can be seen in any number of situations. It is most visible, most often has its greatest weight in two areas: (1) the public agenda and (2) electoral politics.

**The Public Agenda**    The media play a very large role in shaping the public agenda. As they report and comment on events, issues, problems, and personalities, the media determine to a very large extent what public matters the people will think and talk about—and, so, those matters that public policymakers will be concerned

---

[11]David Halberstam, *The Powers That Be* (New York: Knopf, 1979), page 15.

[12]The muckrakers were journalists who exposed wrongdoing in politics, business, and industry. The term was coined by Theodore Roosevelt in 1906 and is derived from the raking of muck—that is, manure and other barnyard debris. The muckrakers set the pattern for what is now called investigative reporting.

about. To put the point another way, the media have the power to focus the public's attention on a particular issue. And they do so by emphasizing some things and ignoring or downplaying others, by featuring certain items on the front page or at the top of the newscast and burying others.

It is not correct to say that the media tell the people *what* to think; but it is clear that they do tell the people what to think *about*. A look at any issue of a daily paper or a quick review of the content of any television news program will demonstrate that point. Remember, people rely on the media for most of the information they receive on public issues.

The mass media also has a direct impact on the nation's leaders. A widely respected authority has identified 11 news organizations that form the "inner ring" of influence in Washington, D.C. They are the three major television networks, CBS, ABC, and NBC; three newspapers, the *New York Times*, the *Washington Post*, and the *Wall Street Journal*; the two leading news wire services, the Associated Press (AP) and United Press International (UPI); and the three major news weeklies, *Time*, *Newsweek*, and *U.S. News & World Report*.[13] CNN has recently joined that select group. Top political figures in and out of government pay close attention to those sources and the President receives a daily digest of the news reports, analyses, and editorial comments broadcast and published by them and by other media.

**Electoral Politics**   You have seen a number of illustrations of the media's importance in electoral politics as you have read this book. Thus, on page 122, you encountered the point that the media, and in particular television, have contributed to a decline in the place of parties in American politics.

---

[13]Stephen Hess, *The Washington Reporters* (Washington, D.C.: The Brookings Institution, 1981).

▲ **Image-Makers**   Political candidates work hard to use the media to their advantage. Above, 1996 presidential hopeful Phil Gramm talks with reporters. Buttons are a "low tech" form of media that have been used by politicians since the early days of the republic.

## the small society
### by Bill Yates

▲ **Interpreting Political Cartoons**　This cartoon pokes fun at the influence of the media on public opinion. How?

Take as an example of that point the fact that television has made candidates far less dependent on party organizations than they once were. Before television, the major parties generally dominated the election process. They recruited most candidates who ran for office, and they ran those candidates' campaigns. The candidates depended on party organizations in order to reach the voters. Now, television allows candidates to appeal directly to the people, without the help of a party organization. Candidates for major office need not be experienced politicians who have worked their way up a party's political ladder over several elections. Today it is not at all unusual for candidates to assemble their own campaign organizations and operate with only loose connections with their political parties.

Recall, too, that in Chapter 6, Section 5 you read that how voters see a candidate—the impressions they have of that candidate's personality, character, abilities, and so on—is one of the major factors that influence voting behavior. Candidates and professional campaign managers are quite aware of this. They know that the kind of "image" a candidate projects in all of the media can have a telling effect on the outcome of an election.

Candidates regularly try to manipulate media coverage to their advantage. Campaign strategists know that almost everything most people know about candidates they learn from television; so they plan campaigns that emphasize television exposure. Such technical considerations as timing, location, lighting, and camera angles loom large, often at the expense of such substantive matters as the issues involved in an election or a candidate's qualifications for public office.

Good campaign managers also know that most television news programs are built out of stories that (1) take no more than a minute or two of air time and (2) show people doing something interesting or exciting. Newscasts seldom feature "talking heads"—speakers who drone on and on about some complex issue. Instead, their stories are usually short, sharply focused **sound bites**—snappy reports that can be aired in 30 or 45 seconds or so. Staged and carefully orchestrated visits to historic sites, factory gates, toxic-waste dumps, football games, and the like have become a standard part of the electoral scene.

## Limits on Media Influence

It is all too easy to overstate the media's role in American politics. A number of built-in factors work to limit the media's impact on the behavior of the American voting public.

For one thing, not very many people follow international, national, or even local political events very closely. Many studies of voting behavior show that in the typical election, only about 10 percent of those who can vote and only about 15 percent of those who do vote are well informed on the many candidates and issues under consideration in that election. In short, only a small part of the public actually takes in and understands much of what the media have to say about public affairs.

Moreover, most of those who do pay some attention to politics are likely to be selective about it. That is, they most often watch, listen to, and read those sources that generally agree with their own viewpoints. They regularly ignore those sources that disagree. Thus, for example, many Democrats do not watch the televised campaign appearances of Republican candidates. Nor do many Republicans read newspaper stories about the campaign efforts of Democratic candidates.

Another important limit on the media's impact on the public can be seen in the content of much of what they carry. This is especially true of radio and television. Most television programs, for example, have little or nothing to do with public affairs.[14] Advertisers who pay the high costs of television air time want to reach the largest possible audiences. So, because most people are far more interested in being entertained than they are in being informed about public issues, few public-affairs programs air in prime time. There are a few exceptions: "60 Minutes" on CBS, "20/20" on ABC, and "Exposé" on NBC, for example. But they are just that—exceptions.

Radio and television mostly "skim" the news. They report only what their news editors judge to be the most important and/or the most interesting stories of the day. Even on the widely watched evening news programs most reports are presented in 60-to 90-second time slots. In short, the broadcast media, or at least most of them, seldom give the kind of in-depth coverage that a good newspaper can supply to the interested reader.

Newspapers are not as hampered as many other media in their ability to cover public affairs. Still, much of the content of most papers is nonpolitical. Newspaper readers are often more interested in the comics, the sports pages, and the social, travel, advertising, and entertainment sections of a paper than they are in its news and editorial pages. Like nearly all of television and radio, newspapers are business ventures dedicated to making a profit. They depend on their advertising revenues, which in turn depend on producing a product with the widest possible appeal.

All of this is not meant to say that in-depth coverage of public affairs is not available in the media. It is, to those who want it and will seek it out. There are a number of good newspapers around the country. In-depth coverage can also be found in several magazines and on a number of radio and television stations, including public broadcast outlets.

Remember, however, there is nothing about democracy that guarantees an alert and informed public. Like voting and other forms of political participation, being an informed citizen does require some effort.

## Section 3 Review

**1. Define:** medium, mass media, sound bite
**2.** What are the four major media in terms of importance to American politics?
**3.** What is the most powerful form of mass media?
**4.** In what two areas does the media have its greatest impact?
**5.** What limits exist on the impact of mass media?

### Critical Thinking

**6. Recognizing Cause and Effect** (p. 19) Which do you think happened first: The public was not interested in public affairs, so television and radio did not air such programming? Or, did television choose not to air public affairs programs, so the public did not develop much interest in such information?

---

[14]At least not directly. A number of popular programs do relate to public affairs in an indirect way, however. Thus, many are "crime shows," and crime is certainly a matter of public concern. Many also carry a political message—for example, that police are hardworking public servants who need the public's support and deserve the public's respect.

★

# Distinguishing False from Accurate Images

Distinguishing false from accurate images means examining a widely held belief about a person, place, thing, or situation and determining whether or not the belief is based in fact. This skill enables you to identify stereotypes or other misleading ideas so you can make your own decisions. As a participant in government, you will encounter both false and accurate images in a number of situations and settings—such as when you read a newspaper or magazine or tune in to the news on television or radio, or when you decide which issue or candidate to support in an election. To practice distinguishing between false and accurate images in the passage below, use the following steps.

**1. Summarize the main message of the presentation.** The first step in evaluating a piece of information is to understand exactly what its main point is. Read the boxed paragraph on this page and answer the following question: What is the main message of the piece?

**2. Look for generalizations and over-statements in the presentation.** General-izations are statements that are presented as being accurate in all cases. Overstatements exaggerate, or enlarge on the truth. Words such as *all, every, none, always,* and *never* often indicate the presence of generalizations or overstatements. People frequently use these techniques to communicate ideas for which they have no hard evidence. In other words, people often use generalizations and overstatements to communicate false images. (a) What indicators of generalizations can you find in the boxed paragraph? (b) In your opinion, does the paragraph include any overstatements? Give support for your answer.

**3. Look for supporting facts or evidence.** People presenting accurate information can back up their statements with evidence—facts such as statistics and direct quotations. Of course, facts can be used in a misleading way, and you must always check facts for accuracy. In general, however, arguments or statements supported by facts are more likely to be accurate than those without facts. (a) What, if any, specific facts are given in the passage below? (b) Based on the use of facts in the passage below, what can you conclude about the accuracy of the passage?

A large percentage of the American people rely on nightly television news programs as their main source of information. Yet many observers have grave concerns about the accuracy and depth of political reporting on television newscasts. These observers say that television news always empha-sizes style over substance. Newscasts typically seem to be devoid of any real content, and the opin-ions expressed never have any real value. News reporters frequently use propaganda techniques to appeal to viewers' emotions rather than to their intellect. As a result of the devastating effects of tele-vision news, the public has stopped reading newspapers. They have become ignorant of politics and have completely lost interest in political contests. Television news, these observers say, is to blame for a catastrophic decline in voter participation.

# Chapter-in-Brief

Scan all headings, photographs, charts, and other visuals in the chapter before reading the section summaries below.

## Section 1 The Formation of Public Opinion (pp. 185–189)

Public opinion is a concept that is both widely used and widely misunderstood. The term does not refer to any opinion shared by all the American people. Nor does public opinion properly include people's views on nonpublic issues. It includes those attitudes held by a significant number of persons on matters of government and politics. In reality, "the public" holds many different and often conflicting views on nearly every public question.

Individuals come by their public opinions through the combined influence of several factors. Children undergo the first, crucial steps of political socialization in the family. Later, in school, students are trained to be "good citizens," a further step in political socialization.

Another factor that influences the acquisition of opinions on public issues is the influence of opinion leaders. The mass media is another force in the formation of public opinions.

## Section 2 The Measurement of Public Opinion (pp. 189–196)

The content of public opinion can be determined to some degree by checking the various means by which the public expresses its opinions.

One vehicle for the expression of public opinions is election returns. However, so many factors influence the behavior of voters that it is impossible to claim that election results are accurate indicators of public opinion.

The activities of interest groups are another public opinion indicator. Yet it is not always possible to determine for whom an interest group is acting, or how strongly the group's members support the group's action. Likewise, the mass media are often regarded as a mirror for public opinion, though in fact they are not very accurate.

Many officials rely on contact with the public to get a feel for public opinion. This method is limited by the extent to which officials are willing to hear views that disagree with their own.

The best way to measure public opinion is by opinion polls. Scientifically designed polls are effective instruments for measuring public opinion.

It is important to measure public opinion, but it is also important to know that public opinion is but one factor shaping public policy.

## Section 3 The Mass Media and Politics (pp. 198–205)

The American public gets information on public issues through the several forms of mass media. Television is the most significant supplier of public information.

Newspapers are another mass medium; before the age of television, they served as the public's primary source of information. Radio and magazines are also major mass media.

The media influence American politics mostly in two areas: (1) The media help set the public agenda, and (2) mass media play a central role in the field of electoral politics. Television especially has influenced the electoral process. It has changed the role of political parties; it has also altered the way candidates present themselves to the public, shifting the emphasis toward style over substance.

The power of the mass media is not all-encompassing. For one thing, people actually absorb little of what the mass media communicate. Many people use the mass media as sources of entertainment rather than information.

# Chapter Review

## Vocabulary and Key Terms

public opinion (p. 186)
opinion leader (p. 188)
mandate (p. 190)
interest group (p. 190)

public opinion poll (p. 191)
straw vote (p. 191)
sample (p. 192)
random sample (p. 192)

quota sample (p. 193)
medium (p. 198)
mass media (p. 198)
sound bite (p. 204)

**Matching:** *Review the key terms in the list above. If you are not sure of a term's meaning, look up the term and review its definition. Choose a term from the list above that best matches each description.*

1. an organization that tries to influence public policy
2. a means of communication
3. a representative slice of the population that a poll aims to evaluate
4. a person who has an unusual amount of influence on the views held by other people
5. news reports that are brief and sharply focused
6. those attitudes held by significant numbers of persons on public issues

**True or False:** *Determine whether each statement is true or false. If it is true, write "true." If it is false, change the underlined word or words to make the statement true.*

1. A <u>public opinion poll</u> aims at measuring the opinions of a group of people by asking them questions.
2. A type of sample that is carefully constructed to reflect the major characteristics of a particular universe is called a <u>random sample</u>.
3. Winners of elections often claim that their victories at the polls represent a <u>mandate</u> to carry out their proposed programs.

4. Any group that tries to influence public policy is an <u>opinion leader</u>.
5. <u>Mass media</u> are those means of communication that can reach large numbers of people.

**Word Relationships:** *Distinguish between words in each pair.*

1. medium/mass media
2. public opinion poll/straw vote
3. public opinion/mandate

## Main Ideas

### Section 1 (pp. 185–189)

1. Why is it incorrect to say that public opinion represents the single, undivided view of the American people?
2. What are the two most important agents of political socialization?
3. What makes the influence of the school and family so powerful in the development of political attitudes?
4. Besides the school and family, what other forces help influence public opinion in American society?

### Section 2 (pp. 189–196)

5. Name four means of measuring public opinion.
6. List the limitations of each of these different means.
7. What is the most reliable means of measuring public opinion?

8. Why is it only partly true to say that government in the United States is "government by public opinion"?

## Section 3 (pp. 198–205)

9. In what two ways do the mass media provide the American people with political information?
10. What is the impact of the mass media on the public agenda?
11. What is the impact of the mass media in electoral politics?
12. What factors limit the impact of the mass media on American politics?

## Critical Thinking

1. **Expressing Problems Clearly** (p. 19) Recall that the text states that schools are key agents of political socialization. What are the key elements of citizenship in American society that you think students ought to learn in school?

2. **Predicting Consequences** (p. 19) Suppose that television stations were required to devote a large percentage of their air time to discussion of public policy issues. What effects would you expect this change to have on the viewing habits of Americans?

3. **Making Comparisons** (p. 19) Compare the advantages and disadvantages of newspapers and television as a means of providing the public with information on important public issues.

4. **Distinguishing False from Accurate Images** (p. 19) In spite of its powerful and important role in American society, television is often criticized for its lack of content on important issues. (a) Considering what you have read in this chapter, do you feel that it is accurate to characterize television as lacking in real content? (b) If so, what do you think is to blame for the quality of television programming?

## Getting Involved

1. **Writing Your Opinion** Write the text to a public service announcement urging people to spend more time educating themselves on public issues. To prepare, write down three reasons why you think people should become more informed on matters of public concern. Also, create a list of ways that people can efficiently educate themselves. As you write your announcement, remember that your purpose is to encourage citizens. State the reasons why you think people should become more involved, and then present your suggestions. Revise your announcement to make sure your ideas are persuasive and encouraging. Correct any errors, then draft a final copy.

2. **Cooperative Activity** Work as a class to publish a school newspaper. First, decide together upon the name for your paper. Then divide the class into four groups. One group will identify, write, and illustrate a story about an issue of national concern to students. A second group will identify, write, and illustrate a story of local concern to all students. A third group will work on a story about a schoolwide issue that is of concern to all students. The fourth group will write an editorial explaining the purpose of the newspaper. Then, the fourth group will collect all the articles, combine them into a single issue, and copy and distribute the paper.

3. **Gathering Information** Use the Government Resources Handbook on page 690 to answer the following questions. (a) What sources might you use if you wanted to find out what public opinion polls predicted for a particular presidential race? (b) What sources might you consult to discover the actual results in that election?

# CHAPTER 9

# Interest Groups

## Chapter Preview

*SURGEON GENERAL'S WARNING: Smoking Causes Lung Cancer, Heart Disease, Emphysema, And May Complicate Pregnancy.* Since 1964, federal law has required that cigarette packages carry this or similar warnings; evidence of health and environmental risks associated with smoking have continued to mount since that time.

For years now, several groups have conducted energetic anti-smoking campaigns. Many of them have worked to achieve laws and other governmental actions intended to discourage or prohibit smoking. Their efforts have been vigorously opposed by the tobacco industry—represented by tobacco farmers and the companies that manufacture cigarettes and other tobacco products. These contending groups typify what this chapter is about: interest groups. These are the private organizations that work to shape public policy.

### Before you read this chapter:

- **Describe** methods an interest group might use to influence public opinion.
- **Predict** some factors that might determine an interest group's success.

### As you read, focus on the main objective for each section. Understand:

1. The nature of interest groups and their role in politics.
2. The several types of interest groups.
3. The means used by interest groups to influence public opinion and public policy.

▲ **United for Their Cause**  These students from Texas School for the Deaf acted as an interest group when they marched on their capital to protest funding cuts that affected their school.

# 1 The Nature of Interest Groups

**Find Out:**

- What are interest groups?
- What are the positive and negative influences of interest groups in American politics?

**Key Terms:**

interest group, public policy, public affairs

Do you belong to an interest group? You may not think so. But, as you read this section, you will almost certainly discover that you do.

## What Is an Interest Group?

Everyone has certain interests that he or she thinks are important. Joining with others who share those interests is both practical and democratic. Organized efforts to protect group inter-

ests are a fundamental part of the democratic process; and the right to do so is protected by the Constitution. Recall, the 1st Amendment guarantees "the right of the people peaceably to assemble, and to petition the government for a redress of grievances."

**Definition**  An **interest group** is a private organization that tries to persuade public officials to respond to the shared attitudes of its members. Interest groups are also called pressure groups or special interests. Committees, clubs, associations, unions, federations, leagues—whatever they call themselves—they seek their ends by attempting to influence the making and the content of public policy. **Public policy** is all those things that a government endeavors to do in order to achieve certain goals. In a democracy, these goals are set by the people.

Because interest groups exist to influence public policy, they operate wherever those policies are made or can be influenced. They function at every level of government—on Capitol Hill and elsewhere in Washington, D.C., in every one of the 50 State capitals, and

## *VOICES on Government*

### On the Lack of Support for Public Interest Groups

**Ralph Nader,** consumer activist and self-described "full-time citizen"

❝ If [people] watch TV 32 hours a week on the average, how much time are they spending watching city hall or watching Congress or watching their community? . . . If people grew up needing to be fulfilled as citizens, needing to feel psychologically that they count, that they could take on city hall, they could stand up and make a difference, then that would become a psychological need that is fulfilled as a form of human happiness. It's important to connect civic activity with human happiness. ❞

in thousands of city halls and county courthouses and other places at the local level all across the country. In short, as diplomat and historian Lord Bryce put it somewhat indelicately more than a century ago: "Where the body is, there will ten vultures be gathered."[1]

Recall, American society is pluralistic. It is not dominated by a single elite but, instead, consists of a great variety of interests. Increasingly, the members of various ethnic, racial, religious, and other social groups compete for and share in the exercise of political power in this country.

### Political Parties and Interest Groups

Interest groups are composed of people who join together for some political purpose. So, too, are political parties. These two types of political organizations necessarily overlap in a number of ways. They differ from one another in three striking ways, however: (1) in the making of nominations, (2) in their primary focus, and (3) in the scope of their interests.[2]

First, parties nominate candidates for public office; interest groups do not. Remember, the making of nominations is a major function of political parties. If an interest group were to nominate candidates, it would, in effect, become a political party.

This is not to say that interest groups do not try to affect the outcomes of primaries and other partisan nominating contests; they often do. However, interest groups do not themselves pick candidates who then run under their labels. It may be widely known that a particular interest group actively supports a candidate, but that candidate seeks votes as a Republican or a Democrat.

The second difference between parties and interest groups is that political parties are chiefly interested in winning elections and controlling government. Interest groups are chiefly concerned with controlling or influencing the *policies* of government. Unlike parties, interest groups do not face the problems involved in trying to appeal to a broad range of people. In short, parties are mostly interested in the *who* and interest groups in the *what* of government.

Finally, political parties are necessarily concerned with the whole range of public affairs, with everything of concern to voters. Interest groups almost always concentrate only on those matters that most directly affect the interests of their members.

Recall, too, that interest groups are private organizations. Unlike parties, they are not accountable to the general public. Their members, not the voters, pass judgment on their performance.

---

[1]James Bryce, *The American Commonwealth* (Chicago: Charles R. Sergel, 1891) American ed., vol. 2, page 153.

[2]Note that this discussion centers on the differences between interest groups and major parties. There are some striking parallels between interest groups and most minor parties—for example, in terms of their scope of interest.

# Interest Groups: Good or Bad?

Do interest groups pose a threat to the well-being of the American political system? Or, on the contrary, are they a valuable part of that system? The argument over the merit of interest groups goes back to the beginnings of the Republic.

Many have long viewed interest groups with deep suspicion. In 1787, James Madison warned the new nation against the dangers of what he called "factions." He made his view of those groups clear in *The Federalist* No. 10, where he defined a faction as

“a number of citizens . . . who are united by some common impulse . . . adverse to the rights of other citizens, or to the permanent and aggregate interests of the community.”[3]

Madison thought that factions were inevitable in human society, however; and he was opposed to any attempt to abolish them. A society could only eliminate factions, he said, by eliminating freedom. Instead, wrote Madison, it was necessary to moderate the violence of factions with a republican remedy—that is, with the governmental system set out in the proposed Constitution. The functional and territorial separations of power in that governmental arrangement would mean, said Madison, that factions would tend to counteract and balance each others' power and none could become a dominating influence.

Nearly 50 years later, Alexis de Tocqueville was deeply impressed by the vast number of organizations he found in the United States. Tocqueville, a Frenchman who toured much of this country in the early 1830s, wrote that

“ In no country in the world has the principle of association been more successfully used, or more unsparingly applied to a multitude of different objects, than in America.”[4]

In a similar vein, he also observed that

“Americans of all ages, all conditions, and all descriptions constantly form associations . . . not only commercial and manufacturing . . . but . . . of a thousand different kinds—religious, moral, serious, futile, extensive or restricted, enormous or diminutive.”[5]

To determine whether interest groups are "good" or "bad," you must weigh, on the one hand, the functions those groups perform in American politics and, on the other, the several criticisms that are often leveled at them.

**Functions**  First among their several valuable functions, interest groups help to stimulate interest in **public affairs,** those events and issues that concern the people at large. They do so mostly by developing and pushing those policies they favor and by opposing those policies they see as threats to their interests.

Second, interest groups represent their members on the basis of shared attitudes rather than on the basis of geography—by what their members think as opposed to where they happen to live. Public officials are elected from districts drawn on maps. But many of the issues that concern and unite people today have less to do with *where* they live than with, say, *how* they make a living. A labor union member who lives in Chicago may have much more in common with someone who does the same kind of work in Seattle than he or she does with someone who owns a business in Chicago or runs a farm in another part of Illinois.

Third, organized interests often provide useful, specialized, and detailed information to government—for example, on civilian employment, price levels, or the sales of new and existing homes. These data are important to the making of public policy, and government officials often cannot obtain them from any other source. This process is a two-way street, however; interest groups frequently get information from public agencies and pass it along to their members.

Interest groups are also vehicles for political participation. They are a means through which like-minded citizens can pool their resources and channel their energies into collective

---

[3]The text of *The Federalist* No. 10 appears in the documents section that begins on page 720.

[4]Alexis de Tocqueville, *Democracy in America*, Henry Reeves, trans. (New York: Schocken Books, 1961), vol. 1, page 216.

[5]*Ibid.*, vol. 2, page 128.

political action. One mother concerned about drunk driving cannot accomplish very much acting alone; but thousands of people joined in an organization like MADD (Mothers Against Drunk Driving) certainly can.

Finally, interest groups add an element to the checks-and-balances feature of the political process. When, for example, one interest group makes an unreasonable or blatantly self-serving demand on government, other interest groups will very likely oppose it. Many interest groups also keep fairly close tabs on the behavior of officials in the government and help to make sure that these officials perform their duties responsibly.

**Criticisms** The "bad" side of interest groups is sometimes all too apparent. Many of these groups push their own special interests which, despite their claims to the contrary, are not always in the best interests of other Americans. Critics often make these more specific charges:

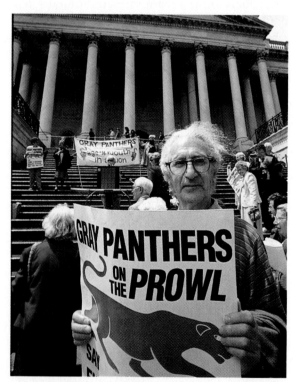

▲ **The Gray Panthers**  As a group of like-minded older Americans, the Gray Panthers have more impact than any one individual would have on calling attention to the special concerns of senior citizens.

First, some interest groups have an influence far out of proportion to their size—or, for that matter, to their importance or contribution to the public good. Thus, the contest over "who gets what, when, and how" is not always a fair fight. The more highly organized and better financed groups often have a decided advantage.

Second, it is sometimes very hard to tell just who or how many people a group really represents. Many groups have titles that suggest that they have thousands—even millions—of dedicated members. Some organizations that call themselves such things as "The American Citizens Committee for . . ." or "People United Against . . ." are, in fact, only "fronts" for a very few persons with very narrow interests.

Third, many groups do not in fact represent the views of all of the people for whom they claim to speak. Very often, both in and out of politics, an organization is dominated by its leaders, by an active minority who conduct its affairs and make its policy decisions.

Finally, some groups use tactics that, if they were to become widespread, would undermine the whole political system. These practices—including bribery and other heavy-handed uses of money, overt threats of revenge, and so on—are not altogether common, but the danger is certainly there.

# Section 1 Review

1. **Define:** interest group, public policy, public affairs
2. Where in the American political system do interest groups operate?
3. What are the three main areas in which political parties and interest groups differ?
4. What are the functions of interest groups in American politics?
5. On what bases are interest groups attacked?

**Critical Thinking**

6. **Distinguishing False from Accurate Images** (p. 19) In what sense do interest groups reflect the representative nature of American democracy?

★

# 2 Types of Interest Groups

**Find Out:**

■ What are the different types of interest groups?

■ On what basis has the largest number of interest groups been founded?

**Key Terms:**

trade association, labor union, public-interest group

"Everything from A to Z." That expression can be very aptly applied to interest groups in this country. These organizations include, among thousands of others, the American Association of Advertising Agencies, the American Association of Retired Persons, the Association on American Indian Affairs, the Amateur Athletic Union of the United States, Zero Population Growth, the Zionist Organization of America, and the American Association of Zoological Parks and Aquariums. As you will see in this section, all of these thousands of organizations can be more or less readily classified and, so, usefully described as interest groups.

## An American Tradition

The United States has often been called "a nation of joiners." Recall what you read about Alexis de Tocqueville's observations in the previous section. Tocqueville's comments, true when he made them, have become even more accurate over time. No one really knows how many associations Americans belong to today. There are thousands upon thousands of them, however—and at every level in society. Each and every one of them, remember, is an interest group whenever it tries to influence the actions of government in order to promote its own goals and special interests.

Interest groups come in all shapes and sizes. They may have thousands or even millions of members, or only a handful. They may be well- or little-known, long-established or new and even temporary, highly structured or quite loose and informal, wealthy or with few resources, and so on. No matter what their characteristics, they are found in every field of human activity in this country.

The largest number of interest groups have been founded on the basis of an economic interest, especially on the bases of business, labor, agricultural, and professional interests. Some groups are grounded in a geographic area, like the South, the Columbia River Basin, or the State of Ohio. Others have been born out of a cause or an idea, such as prohibition of alcohol, environmental protection, or gun control. Still other interest groups exist to promote the welfare of certain groups of people—veterans, senior citizens, a racial minority, the homeless, women, people with disabilities, and so on.

Interest groups often share members. That is, many people belong to a number of them. A car dealer, for example, may be a member of the local Chamber of Commerce, a car dealers' association, the American Legion, a local taxpayers' league, a garden club, a church, the PTA, the American Cancer Society, the National Wildlife Federation, and several other local, regional, or national groups. All of these are, to one degree or another, interest groups, including the church and the garden club, even though the car dealer may never think of them in that light.[6]

Also, many people belong to groups that take conflicting stands on political issues. For example, a program to improve the city's streets may be supported by the local Chamber and the car dealers' association but opposed by the taxpayers' league. The taxpayers' league may endorse a plan to eliminate plantings in traffic islands that has the support of the garden club.

---

[6]Churches often take stands on such public issues as drinking, curfew ordinances, legalized gambling, and so on; and they often try to influence public policy in those matters. Garden clubs often try to persuade cities to do such things as improve public parks, beautify downtown areas, and the like. Not every group to which people belong can properly be called an interest group, of course. But the point here is that many groups that are not often thought to be interest groups in fact are.

## Groups Based on Economic Interests

Most interest groups are formed on economic interests. That is, they are based on the manner in which people make their livings. Among them, the most active, and certainly the most effective, are those representing business, labor, agriculture, and at least certain professional groups.

**Business Groups** Business has long looked to government to promote and protect its interests. Recall that merchants, creditors, and property owners were most responsible for the calling of the Constitutional Convention in 1787. The idea of the protective tariff was fought for and won in the early years of the Republic by business interests. Along with organized labor, they continue to work to maintain it.

The United States Brewers' Association is the oldest organized interest group at work in national politics today. It was born in 1862—when Congress first levied a tax on beer—to assure "the brewing trade that its interests be vigorously prosecuted before the legislative and executive departments."

Hundreds of business groups now operate in Washington, D.C., in the 50 State capitals, and at the local level across the country. The two best-known business organizations today are the National Association of Manufacturers (NAM) and the Chamber of Commerce of the United States. Formed in 1897, NAM now represents some 13,000 firms. It generally speaks for "big business" in public affairs. The Chamber of Commerce was founded in 1912. Over the years, it has become a major voice for the nation's thousands of smaller businesses. It has more than 4,000 local chambers and now counts more than 200,000 business and professional firms and some 5 million individuals among its members. Another major group, the Business Roundtable, has also taken a large role in promoting and defending the business community in recent years. Begun in 1972, the Roundtable is composed of the chief executive officers of 200 of the nation's largest, most prestigious, and most influential corporations.

Most segments of the business community also have their own interest groups, often called trade associations. They number in the hundreds—including the American Trucking Association, the Association of American Railroads, the American Bankers Association, the National Association of Retail Grocers, and many more.

Despite a common impression, business groups do not always present a solid front. In fact, they often disagree, and sometimes fight, among themselves. The trucking industry, for example, does its best to get as much federal aid as possible for highway construction. But the railroads are less than happy with what they see as "special favors" for their competition. At the same time, the railroads see federal taxes on gasoline, oil, tires, and other "highway users fees" as legitimate and necessary sources of federal income. The truckers take quite another view, of course.

**Labor Groups** The strength and the clout of organized labor has ebbed over the past several years. Some 17 million Americans, less than 14 percent of the nation's labor force, belong to labor unions today. A **labor union** is an organization of workers who share the same type of job or who work in the same industry. Labor unions press for policies that will benefit their members. In the 1940s and 1950s as many as a third of all working Americans were union members; and as recently as 1975 union membership accounted for fully a fourth of the labor force. But in spite of recent declines in union membership, labor unions remain a potent force in American politics.

A host of groups represent the interests of organized labor. The largest, in both size and political power, is the AFL-CIO (the American Federation of Labor-Congress of Industrial Organizations). It is now made up of some 100 separate unions, such as the Retail Clerks International Union, the International Association of Machinists and Aerospace Workers, the American Federation of State, County, and Municipal Employees, and the American Federation of Musicians. With all its unions, the AFL-CIO has about 14.5 million members. Each union, like the AFL-CIO itself, is organized on a national, State, and local basis.[7]

There are also a number of independent unions—that is, unions not affiliated with the

AFL-CIO. The largest and most powerful of them include such groups as the United Mine Workers of America, the United Transportation Union, and the International Longshoremen's and Warehousemen's Union.

Organized labor generally speaks with one voice on such social welfare and job-related matters as social security programs, minimum wages, and unemployment. But labor sometimes opposes labor. White-collar and blue-collar workers, for example, do not always share the same economic interests. Then, too, such factors as sectional interests (East-West, North-South, urban-rural, and so on) and production interests (trucks versus railroads versus airplanes, for example) sometimes divide labor's forces.

**Agricultural Groups**  Only about five million people—some two percent of the population—live on farms in this country today. Still, farmers' influence on the government's agricultural policies is and has been enormous. Several powerful associations serve the interests of agriculture. They include several broad-based farm groups and a larger number that represent farmers who raise particular commodities.

The most prominent farm groups are the National Grange, the American Farm Bureau Federation, and the National Farmers Union. The Grange, established in 1867, is the oldest and generally the most conservative of them. Over the years, it has been as much a social as a political organization, concerned about the welfare of farm families. Some 400,000 farm families are now members, and much of the Grange's strength is centered in the Northeast and the Mid-Atlantic States.

The Farm Bureau is the largest and generally the most effective of the three. Formed in 1919, it soon developed a close working relationship with the Department of Agriculture.

---

[7]The AFL was formed in 1886 as a federation of craft unions. A craft union is made up of those workers who have the same craft or skill—for example, a carpenters, plumbers, or electricians union. The growth of mass production industries created a large class of workers not skilled in any particular craft, however. The AFL found it difficult to organize workers in the new mass production industries. Many of its craft unions opposed the admission of unions of unskilled workers to the AFL. After years of bitter fights over craft versus industrial unionism, a group led by John L. Lewis of the United Mine Workers was expelled from the AFL in 1935. They formed the CIO in 1938. The rivalries between these two major national unions eased to the point where a merger, as the AFL-CIO, took place in 1955.

🔺 **Farm Aid**  After such events as this "tractor-cade" down Pennsylvania Avenue dramatized the effects of falling prices and high costs on American farmers (left), a group of popular entertainers sponsored a fundraiser to help farmers meet their expenses (right).

It has some 3.8 million farm-family members and is especially strong in the Midwest. The Farm Bureau generally supports federal programs to promote agriculture. However, it opposes most government regulation and favors the free market economy.

The smaller National Farmers Union draws its strength from smaller and less prosperous farmers. It now has some 250,000 farm-family members, most of them in the upper Midwest and West. The National Farmers Union often calls itself the champion of the dirt farmer and often disagrees with the other two major organizations. It generally favors high levels of federal price supports for crops and livestock and other programs to regulate the production and marketing of commodities.

Another group, the National Farmer's Organization, came to the fore in the 1970s. The NFO calls for efforts to withhold produce from the market in order to raise the prices paid to farmers. It has sponsored "tractor-cades" to Washington and other cities to dramatize the farmers' high-costs/low-prices problems.

Many other groups speak for the producers of specific farm commodities—dairy products, grain, fruit, peanuts, livestock, cotton, wool, corn, soybeans, and so on. For example, three major organizations represent dairy farmers: the Associated Milk Producers, Inc., Mid-American Dairies, and Dairymen, Inc. Then, too, there are the National Association of Wheat Growers, the American Meat Institute, the American Cattlemen's Association, the National Wool Growers Association, the National Cotton Council, and many, many others.

Like business and labor groups, farm organizations sometimes find themselves at odds with one another. Thus, dairy, corn, soybean, and cotton groups compete as each of them tries to influence State laws regulating the production and sale of such products as margarine and yogurt. California and Florida citrus growers, each with their own groups, are sometimes pitted against one another, and so on.

**Professional Groups** The professions—generally defined as those occupations that require extensive and specialized training, such as medicine, law, and teaching—also maintain organizations to protect their interests.

Most professional groups are not nearly so large, well-organized, well-financed, or effective as most business, labor, and farm groups. Three major groups are exceptions, however: the American Medical Association (AMA), the American Bar Association (ABA), and the National Education Association (NEA). Each has a very real impact on public policies—and at every level of government.

There are dozens of less well-known, and less politically active, professional groups—the American Society of Civil Engineers, the American Library Association, the American Political Science Association, and a great many more. Much of their effort centers on such matters as the standards of the profession, the holding of professional meetings, and the publication of scholarly journals. Still, each of them acts in some ways as an interest group, bent on promoting the welfare of the profession and its members.

## The Maze of Other Groups

As you have read, most interest groups are based on economic concerns. But hundreds have been formed for other reasons, and many have a good deal of political clout.

**Groups that Promote Causes** A large number of these other groups exist to promote a cause or an idea. In fact, it would take several pages just to list them here, and so what follows is only a sampling of the more important ones. The National Women's Christian Temperance Union was founded in 1874 and has some 40,000 members today; the NWCTU has long sought the prohibition of alcohol. The American Civil Liberties Union was born in 1920; the ACLU now has some 250,000 members and fights in and out of court to protect civil and political rights. Common Cause dates from 1970 and its membership now exceeds 270,000; it calls itself "the citizen's lobby" and works for major reforms in the political process. The League of Women Voters and its many local leagues and now 120,000 members have since 1920 been dedicated to stimulating participation in and greater knowledge about public affairs.

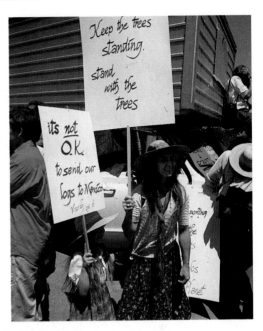

▲ **Conflict of Interest**    Groups that promote causes often find that their causes conflict with other groups' interests. As public sympathy grows for the protection of woodlands and wildlife (right), loggers muster support for protection of their jobs (left).

The list of cause groups goes on and on. Many women's rights groups—such as the National Women's Political Caucus, and several others—carry that banner. Several other groups, including the National Wildlife Federation, the Sierra Club, the Wilderness Society, and Friends of the Earth, are pledged to conservation and environmental protection. The National Right-to-Life Committee, Women Exploited by Abortion, and other groups oppose abortion; they are countered by the National Abortion Rights Action League, Planned Parenthood, and their allies. The National Rifle Association fights gun control legislation; Handgun Control, Inc. works for it. The list is endless.

**Organizations that Promote the Welfare of Certain Groups**    A number of groups seek to promote the welfare of certain segments of the population. Among the best-known and most powerful are the American Legion and the Veterans of Foreign Wars, which work to advance the interests of the country's veterans. Groups like Older Americans, Inc. and the American Association of Retired Persons are very active in such areas as pensions and medical care for senior citizens. Several organizations—notably the National Association for the Advancement of Colored People (NAACP), the National Urban League, and People United to Save Humanity (PUSH)—are closely concerned with public policies of special interest to African Americans. Then, too, there are such organizations as the Japanese American Citizens League, the Mexican-American Legal Defense Fund, and the National Association of Arab Americans. Again, the list goes on and on.

**Religious Organizations**    Many religious organizations also try to influence public policy in several important areas. Thus, many individual Protestants and their local and national churches do so through the National Council of Churches; and many other Protestants belong to such groups as Christian Voice and the Christian Coalition.

Roman Catholics pursue their interests through the National Catholic Welfare Council; and Jewish communicants, through the American Jewish Congress and B'nai B'rith's Anti-Defamation League. Yet again, the list of these organizations is endless.

IN THIS COUNTRY IT'S A GREAT PRIVILEGE TO SAY WHAT YOU PLEASE, EVEN IF NOBODY LISTENS!

WHICH IS ALSO A GREAT PRIVILEGE

Bill Yates

▲ **Interpreting Political Cartoons**    How does this cartoon emphasize the nature of interest groups in the United States?

## Public-Interest Groups

Recall that interest groups are private groups. As you have read, most of them represent some special interest—business, labor, agriculture, veterans, teachers, and so on. They seek public policies of special benefit to their members, and they work against policies that threaten their own interests.

There are some groups, often called public-interest groups, with a broader goal, however. They work for the "public good." That is, a **public-interest group** is an interest group that seeks to institute certain public policies of benefit to all or most people in this country, whether they belong to or support that organization or not.[8]

Unlike most interest groups, public-interest groups focus on the roles that all Americans share. That is, they represent people as citizens, as consumers, as breathers of air, as drinkers of water, and so on.

Public-interest groups have become quite visible over the past 20 years. Among the best-known and most active of them today are Common Cause, of which you read on page 218, and the several organizations that make up Ralph Nader's Public Citizen, Inc. Some have existed for a much longer time—for example, the League of Women Voters. Recall that the League has roots that reach deep into the long history of the women's suffrage movement.

## Section 2 Review

1. **Define:** trade association, labor union, public-interest group
2. At what point does an association become an interest group?
3. On what basis are most interest groups founded?
4. What are the major types of economically based interest groups?
5. What kinds of groups constitute the "maze of other groups"?

### Critical Thinking

6. **Identifying Central Issues** (p. 19) Recall what you have read about interest groups in this section. Interest groups are sometimes criticized for pursuing their interests in spite of the welfare of other people. (a) Is this criticism fair? (b) Explain why you do or do not think a democratic society should tolerate such activities.

---

[8]Of course, nearly all interest groups claim that they work for the "public good." Thus, the NAM says that lower taxes on business will stimulate the economy and so help everyone. The AFL-CIO says the same thing about spending more public dollars for more public works programs. But, as a general rule, most interest groups support or oppose public policies on a much narrower basis: on what they see to be the best interests of their own members.

★

## Should Federal Agencies Be Allowed to Violate the Law?

### Tennessee Valley Authority v. Hill, 1978

In 1967, the Tennessee Valley Authority (TVA) began work on the Tellico Dam and Reservoir Project on a stretch of the Little Tennessee River. The dam and its reservoir were designed primarily for hydroelectric power, flood control, and recreation purposes; the project was also intended to spur economic development in the area around it in eastern Tennessee.

Congress passed the Endangered Species Act in 1973. That law declares that federal agencies cannot engage in any activities that threaten to destroy the natural habitat of any species of life that is in danger of extinction. Acting under the law in late 1975, the secretary of the interior found (a) that the snail darter—a tannish, three-inch species of perch—was close to extinction, (b) that the tiny fish lived only in the section of the Little Tennessee River to be flooded by the Tellico Dam, and (c) that completion of the dam would cause the total destruction of the snail darter's habitat.

Despite the secretary's findings, TVA continued work on the nearly completed Tellico Project. That situation prompted several local residents to sue the agency in the U.S. district court in Tennessee. They lost there, but they took their arguments to the federal court of appeals, and won. TVA then carried the case to the U.S. Supreme Court.

*Review the following arguments and evidence presented to the Supreme Court.*

### Arguments for the Tennessee Valley Authority

**1.** Congress appropriated money for work on the Tellico Project in every year since that work was begun, including each year since passage of the Endangered Species Act. By doing so, Congress made the Tellico Project an exception to the 1973 law.

**2.** TVA is trying to find a new habitat for the snail darter and so should be allowed to complete the dam and its reservoir.

**3.** Congress did not intend that the 1973 law would affect those federal projects already underway and nearing completion.

### Arguments for Hill

**1.** Completion of the Tellico Project would amount to a clear violation of the Endangered Species Act.

**2.** The argument that successive annual appropriations made the project an exception to the 1973 law is flawed. The rules of both houses of Congress declare that the making of an appropriation cannot work a change in the substance of any existing law.

**3.** Congress passed the Endangered Species Act knowing that it would mean that some federal projects already underway would have to be altered, sometimes at great cost.

## Getting Involved

**1. Identify** the grounds upon which each side based its arguments.

**2. Debate** the opposing viewpoints presented in this case.

**3. Predict** how you think the Supreme Court ruled in this case and why. Then refer to page 769 in the Supreme Court glossary to read about the decision. Discuss the factors that you think should be considered in a conflict between technology and wildlife preservation.

# 3 Interest Groups at Work

**Find Out:**

- What is the relationship between interest groups and public opinion?
- What is the role of interest groups in the election process?
- How do interest groups actually apply pressure on the policy-making process?

**Key Terms:**

propaganda, single-interest group, lobbying, grass roots

Interest groups exist to influence public policies—and so they are fairly good illustrations of why it has been said that politics is all about "who gets what, when, and how."[9] As you will

---

[9] The phrase comes from a pioneering study of political behavior, Harold Lasswell, *Politics: Who Gets What, When, How* (New York: McGraw-Hill, 1936).

see in this section, interest groups use a wide range of techniques as they (1) try to influence public opinion, (2) work to affect the outcome of elections, and (3) lobby those who make public policy.

## Interest Groups and Public Opinion

Public opinion is the most significant long-term force in American politics. It is abundantly clear that, over the long run, no public policy can be followed successfully without the support of a goodly portion of the population—and interest groups know this.

Interest groups regularly reach out to the public to accomplish one or all of three major goals:

1. To supply the public with information an organization thinks the people should have. The information is presented to support that group's interests, of course. Thus, Handgun Control, Inc. often runs full-page magazine ads keyed to one fact: the number of Americans who are killed by handguns each year.

2. To build a positive image for a group. Thus, the National Rifle Association frequently

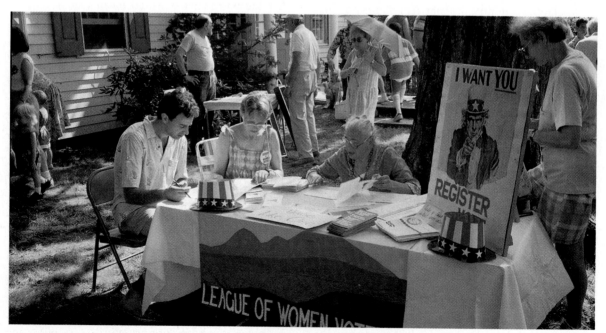

▲ **The League of Women Voters**  Public interest groups exist to respond to the needs of all the people, not just a few. This nonpartisan public-interest group promotes voter registration and dispenses information on election issues.

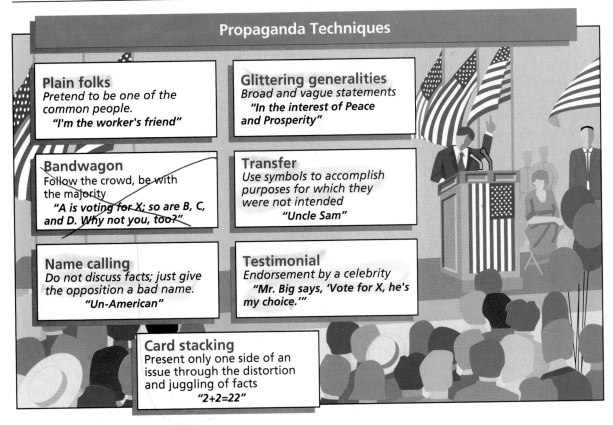

## Propaganda Techniques

**Plain folks**
*Pretend to be one of the common people.*
*"I'm the worker's friend"*

**Glittering generalities**
*Broad and vague statements*
*"In the interest of Peace and Prosperity"*

**Bandwagon**
Follow the crowd, be with the majority
*"A is voting for X; so are B, C, and D. Why not you, too?"*

**Transfer**
*Use symbols to accomplish purposes for which they were not intended*
*"Uncle Sam"*

**Name calling**
*Do not discuss facts; just give the opposition a bad name.*
*"Un-American"*

**Testimonial**
*Endorsement by a celebrity*
*"Mr. Big says, 'Vote for X, he's my choice.'"*

**Card stacking**
Present only one side of an issue through the distortion and juggling of facts
*"2+2=22"*

▲ **Interpreting Charts**   Propaganda is found in every form of mass communication and increases with importance as an issue becomes more controversial. After looking at the chart, list some media where propaganda techniques can be used.

runs ads that feature the NRA's gun-safety programs and the many shooting tournaments it sponsors.

3. To promote a particular public policy. This, of course, is the purpose of most interest groups' efforts.

**Propaganda**   Interest groups try to create the public attitudes they want by using propaganda.[10] **Propaganda** is a technique of persuasion aimed at influencing individual or group behaviors. Its goal is to create a particular popular belief. That belief may be completely true or false, or it may lie somewhere between those extremes. Today, people tend to think of propaganda as a form of lying and deception. As a

technique, however, propaganda is neither moral nor immoral; it is amoral.

Propaganda does not use objective logic. Rather it begins with a conclusion and then brings together any evidence that will support that conclusion and disregards information that will not. Propaganda and objective analysis sometimes agree in their conclusions, but their methods are quite different. In short, propagandists are not teachers interested in determining the truth; rather, they are advertisers, persuaders, and brainwashers who are interested in influencing others.

The development of the mass media in this country encouraged the use of propaganda, first in the field of commercial advertising and then in politics. To be successful, propaganda must almost always be presented in simple, interesting, and credible terms. The major techniques that propagandists use are outlined in the chart on this page.

---

[10]The term comes from the Latin *propagare*—to propagate, to spread, to disseminate. It has been a part of the American political vocabulary since the 1930s.

Talented propagandists almost never attack the logic of some policy they oppose. Instead, they often attack it with name-calling; that is, they paint such labels as "communist," "fascist," "ultraliberal," "ultraconservative," "pie-in-the-sky," or "greedy," and so on. Or they try to discredit the policy or person by card-stacking—that is, presenting only material that will make something appear to be what in fact it is not.

Policies that propagandists support receive labels that will produce favorable reactions—such glittering generalities as "American," "sound," "fair," and "just." Symbols are often used to elicit those reactions, too: Uncle Sam and the flag are favorites. So, too, are testimonials—endorsements, or supporting statements, from well-known television stars, professional athletes, and the like. Both the bandwagon and the plain-folks approaches get heavy use, too.

Propaganda is spread through newspapers, radio, television, movies, billboards, books, magazines, pamphlets, posters, speeches—in fact, through every form of mass communication. The more controversial—or the less popular—a group's position may be, the more necessary the propaganda campaign becomes, because competing groups will likely be conducting campaigns of their own.

## Interest Groups, Parties, and Elections

As you know, interest groups and political parties are very different creatures. They exist in the same environment, however, and their paths often cross.

For their part, interest groups know that political parties play a central role in selecting those people who make public-policy decisions. They are quite aware, too, of the fact that much of government's policy-making machinery is organized by and through parties. So, interest groups try to influence the behavior of political parties—and they do so in a number of ways. Some groups keep close ties with one or the other of the major parties. Most hope to secure the support of both of them, however. Several urge their members to become active in party affairs and try to win posts in party organizations.

As you have seen, campaigns for public office cost money. Interest groups are quite aware of

this fact, too—and they are a major source of campaign funds today. Much of their financial help now goes to parties and their candidates through political action committees (PACs), as you read in Chapter 7.

The number of PACs has grown rapidly in recent years. One particular variety has grown most rapidly, however. These organizations are often called **single-interest groups**. They are PACs that concentrate their efforts on one issue—for example, abortion, gun control, or nuclear power development. They work for or, more often, against a candidate solely on the basis of that candidate's stand on that one issue. For them, all other considerations—the candidate's record on other questions, his or her party identification or political experience, and so on—are of little or no importance.

An interest group's election tactics often have to involve some very finely tuned decisions. The group must consider how its actions on behalf of or against a candidate might affect its overall goal of influencing policy. If, for example, a group supports the Democratic candidate for a seat in the U.S. Senate, it may not want to help that candidate by attacking the Republican nominee in the race—especially if the Republican has some chance of winning. The interest group might also be concerned that another Republican candidate who wins some other office might be offended by attacks on a party colleague, even if he or she agrees with the group's policy aims. Most interest groups try to remember that their first concern is with the making of public policy. Any part they play in the election process is only secondary to that objective. But, notice, single-interest groups do not follow this rule.

## Lobbying

**Lobbying** is usually defined as those activities by which group pressures are brought to bear on legislators and the legislative process. Certainly, it is that, but it is also much more. Realistically, lobbying includes all of the means by which group pressures are brought to bear on all aspects of the public-policy-making process. Lobbying takes place in legislative bodies, of course, and it often has important effects there.

But it is also often directed at administrative agencies, and sometimes even at the courts.

What happens in a legislative body is often of deep concern to several different, and competing, interests. A bill to regulate the sale of firearms, for example, excites the interest of many persons and groups. Those companies that make guns, those that sell them, and those that produce or sell ammunition, targets, scopes, hunting jackets, sleeping bags, and a host of other related products have a clear stake in that bill's contents and its fate. So, too, do law-enforcement agencies, hunters, wildlife conservationists, such groups as the National Rifle Association and the American Civil Liberties Union, and many others.

But public policy is made by much more than the words in a statute. What happens after a law has been passed is often of real concern to organized interests, too. How is a law interpreted and how vigorously is it applied by the agency that enforces it? What attitude do the courts take if the law is challenged on some legal ground? These questions point up the fact that interest groups often have to carry their lobbying efforts beyond the legislative arena—into one and sometimes several agencies in the executive branch and sometimes into the courts, as well.

Nearly all of the more important organized interests in the country—business groups, labor unions, farm organizations, the professions, veterans, churches, and many more—maintain lobbyists in Washington.[11]

**The Work of the Lobbyist** Lobbyists themselves often prefer to be known by some

---

[11]Lobbyists are also stationed in the 50 State capitals, and their number grows whenever the State's legislature is in session. The "lobby" is actually an outer room or main corridor or some other part of a capitol building to which the general public is admitted. The term *lobby-agent* was being used to identify favor-seekers at sessions of the New York State legislature in Albany by the late 1820s. By the 1830s the term had been shortened to *lobbyist* and was in wide use in Washington and elsewhere.

▲ **The Waiting Game** Lobbyists spend many hours waiting to speak with members of Congress and attempting to influence the legislative direction of the nation.

## Taking the Public Pulse

| Question | Response | |
|---|---|---|
| Should laws covering the sale of handguns be more strict, less strict, or kept as they are now? | More strict<br>Less strict<br>Kept as now<br>No opinion | 72%<br>5%<br>22%<br>1% |
| Do you favor/oppose allowing only the police (and some other authorized persons) to possess handguns? | Favor<br>Oppose<br>No opinion | 39%<br>60%<br>1% |

*Source:* Gallup Poll News Service, January 6, 1994

▲ **Interpreting Tables** The table above shows the results of a poll gauging the public's views on laws regulating the sale of handguns and the ownership of those weapons. How might a lobbyist for the National Rifle Association or for Handgun Control, Inc., use this poll data to influence a member of Congress?

other title—"legislative counsel" or "public representative," for example. Whatever they call themselves, their major task is to work for those matters of benefit to their clients and against those that may harm them.

A lobbyist's effectiveness depends in large part on his or her knowledge of the political system. The competent lobbyist is thoroughly familiar with government and its ways, with the facts of current political life, and with the techniques of "polite" persuasion. Some have been members of Congress or the State legislature. They know the "legislative ropes" and have many close contacts among present-day members. Many others are lawyers, former journalists, or men and women who have come into lobbying from the closely related field of public relations.

Lobbyists at work use a number of techniques as they try to persuade legislators and other policy makers to share their points of view. They see that articles, reports, and all sorts of other information favorable to their causes reach those officeholders. Many testify before legislative committees. If the House Committee

on the Judiciary is considering a gun control bill, for example, representatives of all those groups mentioned a moment ago are certain to be invited, or to ask for the opportunity, to present their views. The testimony that lobbyists give is usually "expert," but, of course, it is also couched in terms favorable to the interests they represent.

Most lobbyists also know how to bring "grass-roots" pressures to bear. **Grass roots** means of or from the "common people," the average voter. The groups they speak for can mount campaigns by letter, phone, and telegram from "the folks back home"—and often on short notice. Favorable news stories, magazine articles, advertisements, radio and television appeals, endorsements by noted personalities—these and the many other weapons of publicity are contained within the arsenal of the good lobbyist.

Several interest groups now publish ratings of members of Congress. Those rankings are based on the votes cast on measures that those groups regard as crucial to their interests. Among the most prominent of the many organizations that now compile and publish such ratings are the Americans for Democratic Action (ADA), the American Civil Liberties Union (ACLU), the AFL-CIO's Committee on Political Education (COPE), the American Conservative Union (ACU), the National Tax Limitation Committee (NTLC), and the Chamber of Commerce of the United States.

Each of these groups selects a number of key measures and then rates each member on the basis of his or her votes on those bills. In the usual rating scheme, each senator or representative is given a score, a number that reflects how often he or she voted with the interest group.

Interest groups see to it that the mass media publicize these ratings. They also distribute the ratings to the group's membership. Their ultimate objective is twofold: Either to persuade unfriendly legislators to change their voting behavior or to help bring about their defeat in future elections.

The typical lobbyist of today is a far cry from those of an earlier day—and from many of the ficticious ones still found on television and in novels and the movies. The once fairly common practice of bribery and the heavy-handed use of unethical practices are almost unknown. Most present-day lobbyists work in the open, and their major techniques come under the headings of friendliness, persuasion, and helpfulness.

Lobbyists are ready to do such things as buy lunches and dinners, provide information, write speeches, and prepare bills in proper form. The lunch and dinners are good, the information usually quite accurate, the speeches forceful, and the bills well drawn. Most lobbyists know that if they behaved otherwise—gave false information, for example—they would damage, if not destroy, their credibility and so their overall effectiveness.

Lobbyists work hard to influence committee action, floor debate, and the final vote in a legislative body. If they fail in one house, they carry their fight to the other. If they lose there, too, they may turn to the executive branch[12] and, perhaps to the courts, as well.

**Lobby Regulation** Lobbying abuses do occur now and then, of course. False or misleading testimony, bribery, and other unethical pressures are not common, but they do exist. To try to keep the activities of lobbyists within bounds, Congress passed the Federal Regulation of Lobbying Act in 1946. In addition, each of the States now has a somewhat similar law.

The federal law requires lobbyists to register with the clerk of the house and the secretary of the Senate. More exactly, it requires individuals and groups to register if they collect or spend money for the "principal purpose" of influencing legislation. The Supreme Court narrowed the scope of the law somewhat in 1954. In *United States* v. *Harriss*, the Court upheld the law against 1st Amendment attacks on its constitutionality. But the Court also held that its registration provisions apply only to lobbying efforts aimed at Congress, not to those aimed at the public at large.

The law has proved to be quite inadequate since its passage, and Congress has not seen fit to strengthen it. Its vague phrase "principal purpose" is a huge loophole through which many active groups avoid registration. They do so on the grounds that lobbying is only "incidental" to their main objectives or that their monies are spent for "research" and "public information" rather than on lobbying. Most estimates put the number of people who now earn at least part of their living by lobbying Congress at about 20,000. Yet only some 7,000 persons are registered under the law, and that number includes many multiple filings by persons who lobby for several different groups. The law does have penalties for its violation, but it has no enforcement provisions. Also, it does not apply to lobbying aimed at agencies in the executive branch nor does it cover testifying before congressional committees.

## Section **3** Review

**1. Define:** propaganda, single-interest group, lobbying, grass roots
**2.** For what three reasons do interest groups reach out to the public?
**3.** (a) Identify four of the major techniques of the propagandist. (b) Which technique might involve the endorsement of a celebrity?
**4.** For what reason must interest groups put pressure on government agencies beyond the legislature?
**5.** What are some of the key skills of a good lobbyist?
**6.** (a) What are lobbyists required to do by the Federal Regulation of Lobbying Act of 1946? (b) Why has the law proved to be inadequate?

### Critical Thinking
**7. Formulating Questions** (p. 19) Create a list of five questions you could ask your legislator to determine his or her position on an issue of importance to you.

★

---

[12]Notice that various government agencies often act much like interest groups in their relations with Congress or with a State's legislature—for example, when they seek funds or when they offer testimony for or against a bill in committee.

# Distinguishing Fact from Opinion

Distinguishing fact from opinion means separating those statements that can be proven to be true from those that reflect a particular viewpoint or opinion. Interest groups use both fact and opinion to influence public opinion. So, in order to draw your own conclusions about the issues or policies they support, you need to be able to separate the facts from the opinions when you consider any information these groups put out. The paragraph below is an adaptation from an article published by the American Association of Retired Persons, an interest group serving the needs of senior citizens. Use the following steps to practice distinguishing fact from opinion.

**1. Determine which statements are based on fact.** A fact is something that is true. It can be checked against a reliable source and confirmed. A fact does not include what someone thinks, values, or believes. (a) What information in the paragraph below might qualify as a fact? (b) Does the paragraph include information that you could check against another source? (c) If so, what might constitute a reliable source?

**2. Determine which statements are opinion.** An opinion states a belief or feeling about a subject. Opinions usually cannot be proven. Statements of opinion often begin with phrases such as *I think, I feel, I believe,* and use adjectives such as *best, worst, extraordinary.* Read the paragraph below and answer the following questions: (a) What opinions are expressed in the paragraph? (b) What words or phrases give a signal that the statement is an opinion? (c) Are there any statements in the paragraph that contain both fact and opinion?

**3. Separate facts and opinions when you read.** Well-written material usually contains both facts and opinions, but an opinion is more forceful when facts are given to support it. (a) What facts in the paragraph below support the first sentence? (b) Write down any facts you can find to support this statement: "Higher education has become a necessity for workers."

On average, college students are getting older. In light of this fact, American society ought to change its definition of a college student. A 1988 study of the College Board found that 45 percent of the nation's undergraduate students are at least 25 years old. Studies such as these have led some observers to predict that so-called nontraditional students will become the majority on college campuses within 10 years. The trend is already underway. The City University of New York already has more than 6,000 students over age 65. At the University of Cincinnati students over age 35 make up 14 percent of the student population. The most popular programs are those emphasizing career instruction. With the shift toward a service economy and today's advanced technology, it appears that higher education has become a necessity for workers seeking to upgrade their careers.

Many older students worry that they will not be able to handle the demands of a college education. However, nontraditional students should not feel this way. Research indicates that it is the amount of mental stimulation and not age that determines a person's mental ability.

# Chapter-in-Brief

Scan all headings, photographs, charts, and other visuals in the chapter before reading the section summaries below.

## Section 1 The Nature of Interest Groups (pp. 211–214)
Interest groups are private groups that try to persuade public officials to respond to the shared attitudes of their members. Like political parties, interest groups exist to achieve some political purpose. Unlike the major parties, however, interest groups do not nominate candidates; they do not focus on winning elections; and they are not generally concerned with the broad range of issues with which political parties must contend.

Judgment of interest groups is best achieved by weighing their intended function against some of the frequent criticisms. On one hand, interest groups function to: (1) stimulate interest in public affairs; (2) represent members on the basis of shared attitudes; (3) provide information to governments; (4) serve as a vehicle for participation in the political process; and (5) add an element to the system of checks and balances.

On the other hand, interest groups are often criticized for: (1) having influence out of proportion to their size; (2) being hard to define in terms of the size or nature of their membership; (3) misrepresenting their membership; and (4) occasionally using unethical tactics.

## Section 2 Types of Interest Groups (pp. 215–220)
Interest groups come in all shapes and sizes. Most people belong to several organizations that meet the definition of an interest group, even though those groups may not seem overtly political.

The greatest number of pressure groups exist on the basis of some economic or occupational interest. For example, the business community, labor, and agriculture each have many organizations that serve the peculiar interests of specific professions or industries. Often, the efforts of these groups conflict with one another.

In addition to business, labor, and farm groups, there are many groups devoted to specific political and social causes, to religious interests, and to the welfare of distinct segments of the population.

Most interest groups are private. However, there are groups that work for some aspect of the "public good." These groups are called public-interest groups.

## Section 3 Interest Groups at Work (pp. 222–227)
Interest groups direct their efforts in three main directions. They aim to: (1) influence public opinion, (2) influence elections, and (3) lobby those who make public policy.

Public opinion is the most significant long-term force in American politics. For this reason, interest groups work hard to capture it. Groups court public opinion by supplying the public with information favorable to the group's cause, working to build a positive image for the group, and promoting their policies. Interest groups frequently use propaganda to achieve their goals.

To the extent that they are interested in influencing policy, interest groups are interested in elections. This is especially true of single-interest groups, which seek their narrow aims largely by promoting the election or defeat of candidates. However, most interest groups are cautious when involving themselves in electoral politics that they do not create unfavorable reactions.

Interest groups also influence policy by lobbying, a practice that takes place wherever policy is made or administered. Lobbyists use a variety of means to exert influence. Most rely on ethical practices. Yet enough abuses have taken place that Congress has passed legislation to regulate lobbyists and their actions.

# Chapter Review

## Vocabulary and Key Terms

interest group (p. 211)
public policy (p. 211)
public affairs (p. 213)
trade association (p. 216)

labor union (p. 216)
public-interest group (p. 220)
propaganda (p. 223)
single-interest group (p. 224)

lobbying (p. 224)
grass roots (p. 226)

**Matching:** *Review the key terms in the list above. If you are not sure of a term's meaning, look up the term and review its definition. Choose a term from the list above that best matches each description.*

1. a type of interest group representing the interests of a business group
2. those events and issues of concern to all the people of a society
3. political action committees devoted to one issue
4. an organization that works to influence public policy
5. the means by which group pressures are brought to bear on all aspects of the policy-making process

**True or False:** *Determine whether each statement is true or false. If it is true, write "true." If it is false, change the underlined word or words to make the statement true.*

1. <u>Lobbying</u> is a technique of persuasion aimed at influencing individual or group behaviors.
2. A <u>public-interest group</u> devotes its efforts at defeating or supporting those candidates that support its goals.
3. Interest groups help to stimulate interest in <u>public affairs</u>.
4. As a technique, <u>propaganda</u> is neither moral nor immoral; it is amoral.

**Word Relationships:** *Replace the underlined definition with the correct term from the list above.*

1. Some interest groups put pressure on lawmakers by launching campaigns that rely on <u>the common people, the average voters</u>.
2. Interest groups exist for the purpose of influencing <u>all the things that a government endeavors to do</u>.
3. In many industries workers have formed <u>organizations of those who share the same type of job or who work in the same industry</u>.
4. One type of interest group is <u>an organization devoted to the interests of all the people</u>.

## Main Ideas

### Section 1 (pp. 211–214)

1. For what reason are interest groups sometimes called "pressure groups" or "special interests"?
2. At what levels of government can you find interest groups operating?
3. In what ways are interest groups alike and different from political parties?
4. Summarize the nature of the long debate over the role of interest groups in the American political system.

### Section 2 (pp. 215–220)

5. For what reason has the United States often been called "a nation of joiners"?

**6.** Into what categories do most interest groups fall?

**7.** What is the difference between private and public interest groups?

## Section 3 (pp. 222–227)

**8.** (a) For what reason must interest groups be concerned with public opinion? (b) For what purposes do they appeal to public opinion?

**9.** For what reason is it correct to say that propagandists are not teachers?

**10.** (a) To what extent are most interest groups concerned about elections? (b) What is the exception to this rule?

**11.** (a) At what stage of policy making must lobbyists be involved? (b) Why?

## Critical Thinking

**1. Distinguishing Fact from Opinion** (p. 19) Recall the criticism of interest groups that are discussed on page 214 of this chapter. (a) Which of these criticisms are based on fact? (b) Which are based on opinion?

**2. Demonstrating Reasoned Judgment** (p. 19) The text says that forming interest groups is both practical and democratic. (a) Explain your understanding of this statement. (b) Do you agree or disagree?

**3. Making Comparisons** (p. 19) Consider the discussion of the functions and criticisms of interest groups in Section 1. Based on this information, discuss your opinion about whether or not interest groups are "good" or "bad."

**4. Drawing Conclusions** (p. 19) The text points out that many people belong to several interest groups that often work against one another. What does this suggest about the nature of people's participation in interest groups?

## Getting Involved

**1. Writing Your Opinion** Write a draft of a bill aimed at regulating the influence of interest groups in government. Begin by reviewing some of the criticisms of interest groups discussed in the chapter. For each criticism, suggest a method that might be used to counteract any harmful effects from interest groups. As you make your suggestions, keep in mind the constitutional guarantees of freedom of association and speech. Begin writing your bill with a statement explaining the purpose of the proposed legislation. Then present each of the provisions you have identified for regulating the activities of interest groups. Revise each provision to ensure that it is precise and clear in its language. Review the bill for errors and make corrections. Draft a final copy.

**2. Class Debate** Hold a class debate on the following topic: *Resolved*, That interest groups should not be allowed to donate money to political candidates. Select teams to argue each side of this issue. The rest of the class can evaluate the presentations of each team.

**3. Gathering Information** You are a member of an interest group that is concerned with protecting the nation's coastline against all forms of environmental damage. Turn to the Government Resources Handbook on page 690, and then answer the following questions. (a) Which sources might you use to find the names of the House members whose congressional districts include stretches of coastline? (b) What sources might you seek to find out how those representatives have tended to vote on environmental issues in the past?

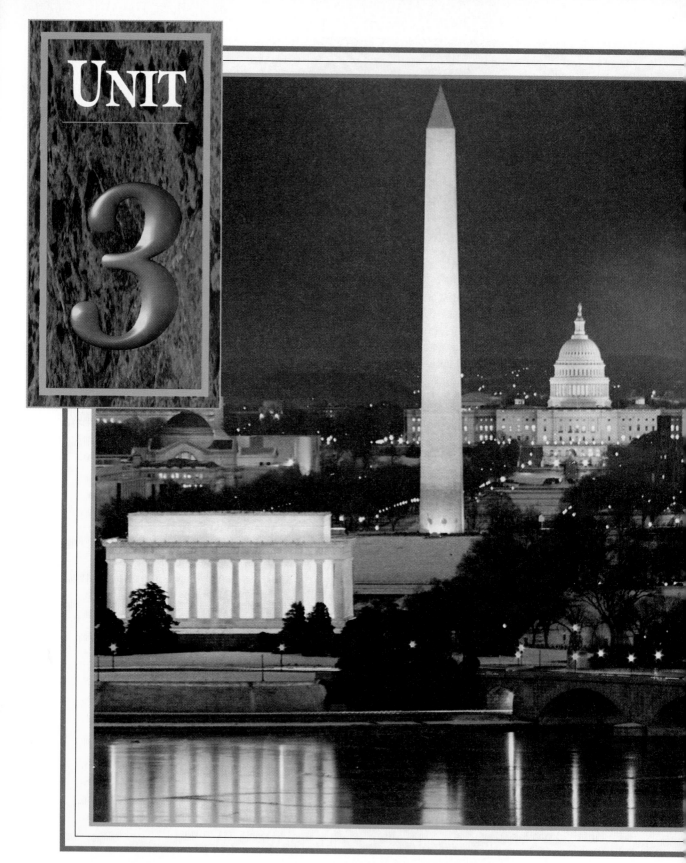

**UNIT**

**3**

**Night View of Washington, D.C.** This photograph of Washington, D.C., displays the grandeur of the Capitol, the Washington Monument, and the Lincoln Memorial.

# The Legislative Branch

In 1847, when Robert C. Winthrop of Massachusetts was chosen to be the new Speaker of the House of Representatives, Winthrop knew that the position entrusted to him was of great importance. In the very first Congress, in fact, the members had voted to pay the Speaker twelve dollars a day—twice the amount of their own wages! And in those days, when senators and representatives had to share boardinghouse rooms in the nation's capital, the Speaker always got a room to himself. John Quincy Adams, on learning that Winthrop had won the post, gave him this advice: "The Speaker of the House of Representatives is next to the President and the Vice President: call upon no one else."

During Winthrop's tenure as Speaker, the 30th Congress enacted 109 bills. Today, Congress enacts approximately 700 bills into law each term. As you will see in this unit, the responsibilities of the nation's legislature are greater than ever.

## DID YOU KNOW THAT . . .

- More than 20,000 persons have served in Congress since 1789. Fewer than 200 of them have been women.

- The record for the longest service in Congress—more than 56 years—is held by the late Carl Hayden (D., Arizona). Mr. Hayden served in the House from 1912 to 1927 and then in the Senate from 1927 to 1969; he left the Senate at age 91.

- The most recent amendment to the Constitution deals with congressional pay—a matter that has been the subject of heated controversy for more than 200 years now.

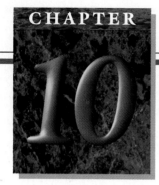

# Congress

## Chapter Preview

Congress has never enjoyed a very high place in public esteem in this country. Its members have often been pictured as overpaid, underworked, and ineffective. Will Rogers was not the first, and far from the last, to make this sort of comment: "Suppose you were an idiot. And suppose you were a Congressman. But I repeat myself." Similar assessments can be found in a good many places today, rather commonly, for example, in editorial cartoons.

This chapter deals with the structure of Congress and with the selection and characteristics of its members. As you read its pages, you will find that the contents do *not* support or agree with the Rogers-like descriptions of Congress and its members. After reading the chapter, you can decide which side you favor.

### Before you read this chapter:

- **Describe** the way that representative government operates in your school or community.
- **Predict** one major difference between the House and the Senate.

### As you read, focus on the main objective for each section. Understand:

1. The place, the role, and the structure of Congress.
2. The structure of the House of Representatives.
3. The structure of the Senate.
4. The general characteristics of members of Congress.

▲ **Leadership in the Senate**   Robert Dole of Kansas (left) is a majority floor leader of the Senate—a strategic post that requires political skills of a high order. He is pictured with Senate colleague Robert C. Byrd of West Virginia.

# 1 The National Legislature

**Find Out:**

- In what way is the lawmaking function central to democracy?
- What does it mean to say that Congress is bicameral?
- What are the terms and sessions of Congress?

**Key Terms:**

term, session, special session

You know that you live in a democracy. And you know, too, that in a democracy the people rule. But what does that really mean? You are one of "the people"—and you know that you do not rule. At least you do not in the hands-on sense. You do not make or enforce laws or collect taxes or decide court cases.

You do not do those and all of the other things that government does because you live in a representative democracy. Here, it is the representatives of the people who do the day-to-day work of government.

Congress stands as a leading example of that fact. It is the legislative branch of the National Government. Its major function is to make law. Congress, then, is charged with the most basic governmental function in a democratic system: that of translating the public will into public policy in the form of law. How profoundly important the Framers thought that function to be can be seen in the fact that the first, and lengthiest, of the articles of the Constitution is devoted to it. Article I, Section 1 reads:

❝All legislative powers herein granted shall be vested in a Congress of the United States, which shall consist of a Senate and House of Representatives.❞

In this section, you will read about some of the important characteristics of Congress—the role and structure of the Senate and the House of Representatives.

# Global Awareness

## Legislative Bodies

| Country | Type of Legislative Body | Size of Legislative Body | How Elected | Term of Office |
|---|---|---|---|---|
| United States | Bicameral (Congress) House of Representatives Senate | 435 members 100 members | Direct popular vote Direct popular vote | 2 years 6 years |
| Costa Rica | Unicameral Legislative Assembly | 57 members | Direct popular vote | 4 years |
| France | Bicameral (Parlement) National Assembly Senate | 577 members 321 members | Direct popular vote Local electoral colleges | 5 years 9 years |
| Israel | Unicameral Knesset | 120 members | Direct popular vote | 4 years |
| Japan | Bicameral (Diet) House of Concillors House of Representatives | 252 members 512 members | Direct popular vote Direct popular vote | 6 years 4 years |
| Saudi Arabia | Unicameral Consultative Council | 60 members | Appointed by the king | Indefinite |
| Denmark | Unicameral Diet | 179 members | 139 directly; 40 allotted to minor parties | 4 years |
| Argentina | Bicameral (National Congress) Senate | 46 members | 2 by each provincial legislature; 2 from Federal District (capital) | 9 years |
| | House of Deputies | 254 members | Direct popular vote | 3 years |

▲ **Interpreting Tables: Multicultural Awareness** A representative government cannot exist without an elected legislative body. Why do you think Saudi Arabia's legislature has an indefinite term of office?

## Bicameralism

As you have just read, the Constitution immediately establishes a bicameral legislature—that is, a legislature made up of two houses. It does so for historical, practical, and theoretical reasons.

Historically, the British Parliament, which the Framers and most other Americans knew quite well, had consisted of two houses since the 1300s. As you may recall from Section 1 of Chapter 2, in 1787 most colonial assemblies and all but two of the new State legislatures were also bicameral.[1]

Practically, the Framers had to create a two-chambered body to settle the conflict between the Virginia and the New Jersey plans at the Philadelphia Convention in 1787. Bicameralism is a reflection of federalism. Each of the States is equally represented in the Senate and in terms of its population in the House.

Theoretically, the Framers favored a bicameral Congress in order that one house might act as a check on the other. A leading constitutional historian reports:

❝Thomas Jefferson, who possessed great faith in 'the voice of the people,' was in France when the Constitution was framed. Upon his return, while taking breakfast with Washington, he opposed the two-body form of legislature, and was disposed to twit Washington about it. At this time Jefferson poured his coffee from his cup into

---

[1] Only Georgia and Pennsylvania had unicameral colonial and then State legislatures. Georgia's legislature became bicameral in 1789 and Pennsylvania's in 1790. Today, only Nebraska (since 1937) has a unicameral legislature.

his saucer. Washington asked him why he did so. 'To cool it,' he answered. 'So,' said Washington, 'we will pour legislation into the Senatorial saucer to cool it.[2]

Some say that the equal representation of the States in the Senate should be scrapped as undemocratic.[3] Those critics often point to the two extremes to make their case. The State with the least population, Alaska, has fewer than 600,000 residents. The largest State, California, has nearly 30 million. Yet each of these States has two senators.

Those who argue against State equality in the Senate ignore a vital fact. The Senate was purposely created as a body in which the States would be represented as coequal members and partners in the Union. Had the States not been equally represented in the Senate, there might never have been a Constitution.

---

[2] Max Farrand, *The Framing of the Constitution* (New Haven: Yale University Press, 1913), page 74.

[3] The prospects for any such change are very slim. Article V of the Constitution says that "no State, without its consent, shall be deprived of its equal suffrage in the Senate."

## Terms and Sessions of Congress

Each **term** of Congress lasts for two years;[4] and each term is numbered consecutively. The first one began on March 4, 1789, and ended on March 4, 1791.

The date for the start of each new term was changed by the 20th Amendment in 1933. It is now "noon on the 3rd day of January" of every odd-numbered year. Thus the term of the 104th Congress began at noon on January 3, 1995, and it will end at noon on January 3, 1997.

There are two **sessions** to each term of Congress—one each year. Section 2 of the 20th Amendment provides that

❝The Congress shall assemble at least once in every year, and such meeting shall begin at noon on the 3d day of January . . . ❞

---

[4] Article I, Section 2, Clause 1 dictates a two-year term for Congress by providing that representatives "shall be chosen . . . every second year."

STILL THE BEST CONGRESSIONAL TERM-LIMITING DEVICE.

▲ **Interpreting Political Cartoons**   Many people think the Constitution should be amended to limit the number of terms any person can serve in the House or Senate. What does this cartoon say about that idea?

Congress adjourns each regular session as it sees fit. Until World War II, a typical session lasted four or five months. Today, however, Congress remains in session through most of each year. Both houses recess for several short periods during a session.

Neither house may adjourn *sine die*—that is, finally, ending a session—without the consent of the other. Article I, Section 5, Clause 4 provides that

❝ Neither House . . . shall, without the consent of the other, adjourn for more than three days, nor to any other place than that in which the two Houses shall be sitting. ❞

Congress can also meet in **special session**—a meeting called by the President to deal with a pressing issue.[5] Only the President may call special sessions and only 26 such sessions have ever been held. President Truman called the last one in 1948, to consider a number of anti-inflation and welfare measures. Of course, the fact that Congress now meets nearly year-round reduces the likelihood of special sessions. That fact also lessens the importance of the President's power to call one.

## Section 1 Review

1. **Define:** term, session, special session
2. What is the basic function of Congress?
3. What are the historical, practical, and theoretical reasons for bicameralism in Congress?
4. Who has the power to call special sessions of Congress? Why has that power lost much of its importance over recent decades?

**Critical Thinking**

5. **Demonstrating Reasoned Judgment** (p. 19) Would Congress be better able to fulfill its basic function of translating the people's will into public policy if it were a unicameral body?

---

[5] Article II, Section 3 provides that the President may "convene both Houses, or either of them," in a special session. The Senate has been called into special session alone on 46 occasions to consider treaties and appointments, but not since 1933. The House has never been called alone.

## 2 The House of Representatives

**Find Out:**

- How are House members chosen and what are their terms and qualifications?
- How and for what reason is the House reapportioned every 10 years?
- What are congressional districts and what is gerrymandering?
- What are the effects of the "one-person, one-vote" rule on the House and on electoral politics in general?

**Key Terms:**

apportion, reapportion, single-member district, at-large, gerrymander

Every other autumn, all across the country, hundreds of men and women seek election to the House of Representatives. Most of them try to attract voters with colorful posters, yard signs, billboards, buttons, and other eye-catching campaign materials. Some of them campaign door to door. And nearly all of them make their "pitches" with radio and television spots and in leaflets and newspaper ads.

In this section, you will discover the general shape of the office that all of those candidates pursue so eagerly.

### Size and Terms

The exact size of the House—today, 435 members—is not fixed by the Constitution. Rather, it is set by Congress. The Constitution provides that the total number of seats shall be **apportioned**—that is, distributed—among the States on the basis of their respective populations.[6]

Each State is guaranteed at least one seat in the House, no matter what its population. Today, seven States—Alaska, Delaware, Montana, North Dakota, South Dakota, Vermont, and Wyoming—have only one representative apiece.

---

[6] Article I, Section 2, Clause 3.

The District of Columbia, Guam, the Virgin Islands, and American Samoa each elect a delegate to represent them in the House; and Puerto Rico chooses a resident commissioner. Those officials are not, however, members of the House of Representatives.

The Constitution provides that "Representatives shall be . . . chosen every second year"—that is, for two-year terms. This rather short term means that, for House members, the next election is always just around the corner—and that fact tends to make them pay close attention to "the folks back home."

There is no constitutional limit on the number of terms representatives may serve.[7]

---

[7] Article I, Section 2, Clause 1. Current efforts to persuade Congress to offer an amendment to limit congressional tenure to 12 years (no more than six terms in the House, two terms in the Senate) mark the strongest attempt yet made to that end.

## Reapportionment

Article I of the Constitution directs Congress to **reapportion**—redistribute—the seats in the House after each decennial census.[8] Until a first census could be taken, the Constitution set the size of the House at 65 seats, and there were that many members in the 1st and 2nd Congresses (1789–1793). The census of 1790 showed a national population of 3,929,214 persons, and in 1792 Congress increased the number of House seats by 41, to 106.

As the nation's population grew, and as the number of States increased, so did the size of the House. It went to 142 seats after the census of 1800, to 186 seats 10 years later, and so on.[9] By 1912, following the census of 1910 and the

---

[8] Article I, Section 2, Clause 3.
[9] Once, following the census of 1840, the size of the House was reduced from 242 to 232 seats.

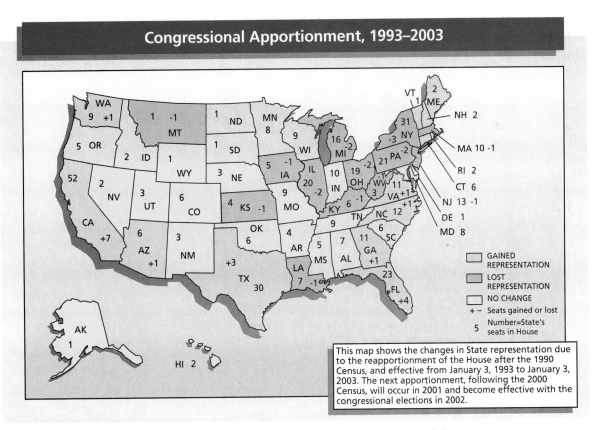

**Congressional Apportionment, 1993–2003**

This map shows the changes in State representation due to the reapportionment of the House after the 1990 Census, and effective from January 3, 1993 to January 3, 2003. The next apportionment, following the 2000 Census, will occur in 2001 and become effective with the congressional elections in 2002.

**Interpreting Maps** Your State is represented by how many members of the House today? Which States gained or lost representation as a result of the last census? Was your State one that changed?

## Off-Year Elections

| Year | Party in Power | House Seats | Senate Seats |
|------|----------------|-------------|--------------|
| 1946 | D | -55 | -12 |
| 1950 | D | -29 | -6 |
| 1954 | R | -18 | -1 |
| 1958 | R | -48 | -13 |
| 1962 | D | -4 | +3 |
| 1966 | D | -47 | -4 |
| 1970 | R | -12 | +2 |
| 1974 | R | -48 | -5 |
| 1978 | D | -15 | -3 |
| 1982 | R | -26 | 0 |
| 1986 | R | -5 | -8 |
| 1990 | R | -9 | -1 |
| 1994 | D | -54 | -8* |

*Includes Senator Richard Shelby of Alabama who switched to the Republican party immediately after the election.

▲ **Interpreting Tables** Which party consistently loses seats in the off-year elections—the party in power, or the party in opposition?

admission of Arizona and New Mexico, the House had grown to 435 seats.

With the census of 1920, Congress found itself in a painfully difficult political position. The House had long since grown too large for effective floor action. But, to reapportion without adding more seats to the House itself meant that some States would lose seats if every State were to be represented by its population.

Congress met the problem by doing nothing. So, despite the Constitution's command, there was no reapportionment on the basis of the 1920 census.

Faced with the 1930 census, Congress moved to avoid repeating its earlier lapse with the Reapportionment Act of 1929. That law, still on the books, sets up what is often called an "automatic reapportionment." It provides for the following:

1. The "permanent" size of the House is 435 members. Of course, that figure is permanent only so long as Congress does not decide to change it. Congress did enlarge the House temporarily in 1959 when Alaska and then Hawaii became States.

2. Following each census, the Census Bureau is to determine the number of seats each State should have.

3. When the Bureau's plan is ready, the President must send it to Congress.

4. If, within 60 days of receiving it, neither house rejects the Census Bureau's plan, it becomes effective.

The scheme set out in the 1929 law has worked quite well through seven reapportionments. The law leaves to Congress its constitutional responsibility to reapportion the House, but it gives to the Census Bureau the mechanical chores (and political "heat") that go with that task. Today each of the 435 seats in the House represents an average of some 595,000 persons.

## Congressional Elections

According to the Constitution, any person whom a State allows to vote for members of "the most numerous branch" of its own legislature is qualified to vote in congressional elections.[10] The Constitution also provides that

❝ The times, places, and manner of holding [congressional] elections . . . shall be prescribed in each State by the legislature thereof; but the Congress may at any time, by law, make or alter such regulations . . . ❞[11]

**Date** Congressional elections are held on the same day in every State. Since 1872 Congress has required that those elections be held on the Tuesday following the first Monday in November of each even-numbered year.[12] Congress has made an exception for Alaska, which may hold its election in October. To date, however, Alaskans have chosen to use the November date. In the same law, Congress directed that representatives be chosen by written or printed ballots. The use of voting machines was sanctioned in 1899.

---

[10] Article I, Section 2, Clause 1.
[11] Article I, Section 4, Clause 1. The Constitution allows only one method for filling a vacancy in the House—by a special election, which may be called only by the governor of the State involved; Article I, Section 2, Clause 4.
[12] On the formula fixing the election date, see page 167.

**Off-Year Elections** Those congressional elections that occur in the nonpresidential years—that is, between presidential elections—are called the off-year elections. The most recent ones were held in 1994, and the next ones will come in 1998.

Quite consistently, the party in power—the party that holds the presidency—loses seats in the off-year elections. The table on page 240 illustrates that point. It sets out the House and Senate seats gained (+) or lost (−) by the President's party in the off-year elections from 1946 through 1994.

**Districts** The 435 members of the House are chosen by the voters in 435 separate congressional districts across the country. Recall that seven States now each have only one seat in the House of Representatives. There are, then, 428 congressional districts within the other 43 States.

The Constitution makes no mention of congressional districts. For more than half a century, Congress allowed each State to decide whether to elect its members by a general ticket system or on a single-member district basis.

Under the **single-member district** arrangement, the voters in each district elect one of the State's representatives from among a field of candidates running for a seat in the House from that district.

Most States quickly set up single-member districts. Several States used the general ticket system, however. Under that arrangement, all of the State's seats were filled from the State **at-large**—that is, from the State as a whole. All the voters could vote for all of that State's representatives.

At-large elections proved grossly unfair. A party with a plurality of the votes in a State, no matter how small, could win all of the State's seats in the House. Congress finally did away with the general ticket system in 1842. Thereafter, all of the seats in the House were to be filled from single-member districts in each State.

The 1842 law made each State legislature responsible for the drawing of any congressional districts within its own State. It also

## Congressional Redistricting in Indiana

Source: Legislative Services Agency, Indianapolis, Indiana; U.S. Bureau of the Census

▲ **Interpreting Maps** State legislatures draw new congressional district lines after each federal census—that is, every ten years. Does it make any real difference which party controls a State's legislature and governorship during that process?

required that each congressional district be made up of "contiguous territory," meaning that it must be all one piece. In 1872 Congress added the command that the districts within each State have "as nearly as practicable an equal number of inhabitants." In 1901 it further directed that all the districts be of "compact territory," meaning that they should cover the smallest possible area.

These requirements of contiguity, population equality, and compactness were often disregarded by State legislatures, and Congress made no real effort to enforce them. The requirements were left out of the Reapportionment Act of 1929, and in 1932 the Supreme Court held (in *Wood v. Broom*) that they had therefore been repealed. Over time, then, and most notably since 1929, the State legislatures have drawn many districts with very peculiar geographic shapes. Moreover, until fairly recently, many districts were also of widely varying populations.

**Gerrymandering** The maps of congressional districts in a number of States show districts shaped much like the letter Y or a dumbbell or other odd form. Those districts have usually

◤ **The Gerrymander!** Gerrymandering takes its name from Governor Elbridge Gerry of Massachusetts, who in 1812 redrew the State's legislative districts to favor the Democratic-Republicans. It is said that the painter Gilbert Stuart added a head, wings, and claws to Essex County on a district map hanging over the desk of a Federalist newspaper editor. "That," he said, "will do for a salamander." "Better say Gerrymander," growled the editor.

been **gerrymandered**. That is, they have been drawn to the advantage of the political party or faction that controls the State legislature.

The practice of gerrymandering can be found in most places where lines are drawn for the election of public officeholders. Most often gerrymandering takes one of two forms. Either the lines are drawn (1) to concentrate the opposition's voters in one or a few districts, thus leaving the other districts comfortably safe for the dominant party; or (2) to spread the opposition as thinly as possible among several districts, limiting the opposition's ability to win anywhere.

For decades, gerrymandering produced congressional districts of widely different populations. State legislatures were responsible for this situation. A number of them regularly drew district lines on a partisan basis. In fact, that remains the case in several States today.

Historically, however, most States were carved up on a rural vs. urban basis—for, until recently, the typical State legislature was dominated by the less-populated, over-represented rural areas of the State.[13]

### *Wesberry* v. *Sanders*, 1964

Suddenly, and quite dramatically, the longstanding patterns of wide population variation in districts and of rural over-representation came to an end in the late 1960s.

These abrupt changes were the direct result of a historic decision by the Supreme Court in 1964. In *Wesberry* v. *Sanders,* the Court held that the population differences among Georgia's congressional districts were so great as to violate the Constitution.

In reaching its landmark decision, the Supreme Court noted that Article I, Section 2 declares that representatives shall be chosen "by the people of the several States" and shall be

---

[13] The pattern of rural overrepresentation in the State legislatures has now all but disappeared as a consequence of the Supreme Court's several "one-person, one-vote" decisions of the 1960s and 1970s. In *Reynolds* v. *Sims,* 1964, the Court held that the seats in both houses of a State's legislature must be apportioned on the basis of population equality.

# CONTEMPORARY AMERICAN REALISM #3

I CALL IT 'REDISTRICTING'

©Steve Magnuson

**▲ Interpreting Political Cartoons** Why would the cartoonist poke fun at the practice of redistricting by drawing a similarity between congressional redistricting maps and abstract art?

"apportioned among the several States . . . according to their respective numbers." These words, the Court held, mean that

❝as nearly as practicable one man's vote in a congressional election is to be worth as much as another's.❞

And, the Court added that

❝While it may not be possible to draw congressional districts with mathematical precision, that is no excuse for ignoring our Constitution's plain objective of making equal representation for equal numbers of people the fundamental goal of the House of Representatives. That is the high standard of justice and common sense which the Founders set for us.❞

The importance of *Wesberry* and the Court's later "one-person, one-vote" decisions cannot be overstated. They have had an extraordinary impact on the makeup of the House, on the content of public policy, and on electoral politics in general. The nation's cities and suburbs now speak with a much larger voice in Congress than ever before. But notice, it is quite possible to draw congressional (or any other) district lines in accord with the "one-person, one vote" rule and, at the same time, to gerrymander them.[14]

---

[14] Except for gerrymandering based on race, a violation of the 14th Amendment's Equal Protection Clause, *Gomillion* v. *Lightfoot,* 1960; see page 138. So-called "majority-minority districts" were carved out by some State legislatures in 1991 and 1992—one or two districts in the State purposefully drawn to include a majority of African American voters and so likely to elect African Americans to Congress. Challenges to these race-based districtings are now on their way to the Supreme Court.

## Qualifications for House Members

According to the Constitution, a member of the House must be at least 25 years of age, must have been a citizen for at least seven years, and must be an inhabitant of the State from which he or she is chosen.[15]

Longstanding custom, not the Constitution, also requires that a representative must live in the district he or she represents. The custom is based on the belief that the legislator should be closely familiar with the locale he or she represents, its people, and its problems. Rarely, then, does a district choose an outsider to represent it.

The Constitution makes the House "the judge of the elections, returns, and qualifications of its own members."[16] Thus, when the right of a member-elect to be seated is challenged, the House has the power to decide the matter. Challenges are rarely successful.

The House may refuse to seat a member-elect by majority vote. It may also "punish its own members for disorderly behavior" by majority vote, and "with the concurrence of two-thirds, expel a member."[17]

Historically, the House viewed its power to judge the qualifications of members-elect as the power to impose additional standards and it did so several times. Thus, in 1900 it refused to seat Brigham H. Roberts of Utah because he was a polygamist—that is, he had more than one wife. In *Powell* v. *McCormack*, 1969, however, the Supreme Court held that the House could not exclude a member-elect who meets the Constitution's standards of age, citizenship, and residence. The House has not excluded anyone since then.

In nearly 200 years, the House has expelled only four members. Three were ousted in 1861 for their "support of rebellion." More recently, Michael Myers (D., Pa.) was expelled in 1980 for corruption. Myers had been caught up in the Abscam probe, an undercover FBI investigation of corruption.[18]

The House has not often punished a member for "disorderly behavior," but such actions are not nearly so rare as expulsions. Most recently, the House voted to "reprimand" Barney Frank (D., Mass.) in 1990 for conduct stemming from his relationship with a male prostitute. Mr. Frank, an avowed homosexual, was subsequently reelected by the voters in his congressional district. The Speaker of the House left Congress under a cloud in 1989. Jim Wright (D., Tex.) resigned his seat after the House Ethics Committee charged him with a number of violations of House rules. Most of those allegations centered around Mr. Wright's financial dealings with individuals and companies with an interest in legislation before the House.

## Section 2 Review

1. **Define:** apportion, reapportion, single-member district, at-large, gerrymander
2. How long is the term of a representative?
3. What are the major provisions of the Reapportionment Act of 1929?
4. Who draws congressional districts?
5. What is the significance of the Supreme Court decision in *Wesberry* v. *Sanders*?
6. What are the constitutional qualifications for membership in the House?
7. What powers does the House have over the elections and qualifications of its members?

**Critical Thinking**

8. **Expressing Problems Clearly** (p. 19) In some cases, courts have found that the drawing of district lines can violate the "one-person, one-vote" standard. Explain how district lines can have this result.

★

---

[15] Article I, Section 2, Clause 2. See also Article I, Section 6, Clause 2.
[16] Article I, Section 5, Clause 1.
[17] Article I, Section 5, Clause 2.

[18] A few members have resigned to avoid almost certain expulsion. The most recent, two New York City Democrats: Mario Biaggi in 1988 and Robert Garcia in 1990. Both had been convicted of federal crimes arising out of their relationships with a defense contractor.

# 3 The Senate

**Find Out:**
- How is the size (number of seats) of the Senate determined?
- What are the terms and qualifications of its members?

**Key Term:**
continuous body

You should not be very much surprised by these facts: Nearly a third of the present members of the Senate once served in the House of Representatives; none of the current members of the House has ever served in the Senate. Indeed, many of the men and women who now serve in the House look forward to the day when, they hope, they will sit in the Senate and, perhaps one day, in the Oval Office.

This section should help you understand why these things are so. Or, to put it another way, as you read this section you will come to see very clearly why the Senate is often called the "upper house."

## Election and Terms

The Senate is a much smaller body than the House. The Constitution states that it "shall be composed of two senators from each State."[19] The first Senate had 22 members when it first met in 1789, and 26 members by the end of the 1st Congress. Like the House of Representatives, the Senate has grown with the country. Today, 100 senators represent the 50 States.

Until the adoption of the 17th Amendment in 1913, senators were chosen by State legislatures. The legislatures were generally expected to choose wealthy, distinguished men to the Senate. From 1914 on, they have been chosen by the people at the regular November elections.[20]

---

[19] Article I, Section 3, Clause 1; 17th Amendment.

## On Being a Woman Senator

" I feel that within my own party, I'm called upon to represent a kind of at-large constituency for the women of America. . . . I hope I'm the first of many. But for now, this is it. Sure, it's a burden when we're talking about issues, where you think you'll do the most good if you have to pick and choose among priorities. And the burden comes from the letters I get from all over the country. People write to me about their concerns as if I were their Congresswoman. . . . It is an enormous responsibility. When you know that you are the first . . . you have a celebrity status, but you also know that you're casting the mold for those who will participate afterward. "

**Barbara Mikulski,**
Democratic senator from Maryland

Each senator is elected from the State at-large. The 17th Amendment declares that all persons whom the State allows to vote for members of "the most numerous branch" of its legislature are qualified to vote for candidates for the United States Senate.

---

[20] Only one senator is elected from a State in any given election, except when the other seat has been vacated by death, resignation, or expulsion. The 17th Amendment gives each State a choice of methods for the filling of a vacancy in the Senate. A State may (1) fill the seat at a special election called by the governor, or (2) allow the governor to appoint someone to serve until the voters fill the vacancy at such a special election or at the next regular (November) election. Most States use the appointment-special election method.

**Early Civil Rights Leader: Multicultural Awareness**  Hiram Rhodes Revels (R., Mississippi), was the first African American to sit in the United States Senate. He served part of one term, 1870–1871.

### How to Write to Your Lawmakers

**1. Choose a method.** You can write to your representative's local address or to their Washington address. Check your telephone directory's blue pages to find local addresses. Letters can be sent to representatives in Washington at the following addresses:

Representative _____
House Office Building
Washington, D.C. 20515

Senator _____
Senate Office Building
Washington, D.C. 20510

**2. Write while your issue is still current.** Don't wait until a bill is out of committee or has passed the House (or Senate).

**3. Be specific.** Identify the bill or issue that prompted you to write, preferably in your first paragraph. Give the bill number or mention its popular title—e.g. the Minimum Wage Bill, the Child Care Bill.

**4. Be brief, but give the reasons for your position.** Avoid these don'ts:
• Don't make threats or promises.
• Don't berate your lawmaker.
• Don't pretend to wield vast political influence.
• Don't try to instruct your lawmaker on every issue.

**Interpreting Charts**  These guidelines were suggested by former Congressman Morris Udall (D., Arizona). After examining the chart, explain why steps 2 and 3 are important.

Senators serve six-year terms—terms three times the length of those for which members of the House are chosen.[21] They may be reelected to any number of terms. The terms are staggered. Only a third of them—33 or 34—expire every two years. The Senate then, can be called a **continuous body**. That is, all its seats are never up for election at the same time.

The six-year term is intended to make senators less subject to the pressures of public opinion and to the pleas of special interests than are their colleagues in the House. The larger size and the geographic scope of their constituencies—the people and interests the senators represent—are designed to have much the same effect. In other words, senators are supposed to be less concerned with the interests of a specific small locality and more focused on the "big picture" of the national interest. Indeed, senators are in general more likely to be regarded as national political leaders than most House members. In addition, senators are more likely to have more power in their State party organizations. This is due partly to the relatively small size of the Senate, to its easier access to the media, and, no doubt, to the larger staffs that senators have at their disposal. Over the past several elections, the Senate has emerged as a prime source of contenders for the presidential nomination in both the Republican and the Democratic parties.

### Qualifications for Senators

A senator must meet a higher level of qualifications than those the Constitution sets for a

[21] Article I, Section 3, Clause 1. See note 7, page 239.

representative. A senator must be at least 30 years of age, must have been a citizen for at least nine years, and must be an inhabitant of the State from which he or she is elected.[22]

The Senate, like the House, judges the qualifications of its members, and it may exclude a member-elect by a majority vote.[23] It may also "punish its members for disorderly behavior" by majority vote and, "with the concurrence of two thirds, expel a member."[24]

Fifteen members of the Senate have been expelled by that body, one in 1797 and 14 during the Civil War. Senator William Blount of Tennessee was expelled in 1797 for conspiring to lead two Native American groups, supported by British warships, in attacks on Spanish Florida and Louisiana. The 14 senators ousted in 1861 and 1862 were all from States of the Confederacy and were expelled for supporting secession. In 1982 Senator

Harrison Williams (D., N.J.) resigned to avoid expulsion by the Senate. He was convicted of bribery in 1981 in a case related to the Abscam probe. Following his trial, the Senate Ethics Committee unanimously recommended that he be expelled.

The punishing of a senator for "disorderly behavior" has also been rare. In one recent case the Senate voted in 1990 to "denounce" one of its members, David Durenberger (R., Minn.), as a result of charges of financial misconduct lodged against him by the Senate Ethics Committee. Among the several counts, the committee found that Senator Durenberger had "knowingly and willfully" tried to avoid the Senate's limits on members' outside income from such sources as speaking fees; he had falsely reported $95,000 in such fees as book royalties. By a vote of 96–0, the Senate formally denounced Durenberger's behavior; it called his conduct "reprehensible" and declared that he had "brought the Senate into dishonor and disrepute." Senator Durenberger chose not to seek reelection to a third term in the Senate in 1994.

---

[22] Article I, Section 3, Clause 3. Under the inhabitant qualification, a senator need not have lived in the State for any prescribed time. Most often, of course, senators have been longtime residents of their States.

[23] Article I, Section 5, Clause 1. As has the House, the Senate has at times refused to seat a member-elect. Presumably, the Court's holding in *Powell* v. *McCormack*, 1969, applies with equal force to the Senate.

[24] Article I, Section 5, Clause 2.

## Major Differences Between the House and the Senate

| House | Senate |
| --- | --- |
| ▪ Larger body (435 members) | ▪ Smaller body (100 members) |
| ▪ Shorter term (2 years) | ▪ Longer term (6 years) |
| ▪ Smaller constituencies (elected from districts within States) | ▪ Larger constituencies (elected from entire State) |
| ▪ Younger membership | ▪ Older membership |
| ▪ Less prestige | ▪ More prestige |
| ▪ Lower visibility in news media | ▪ Higher visibility in news media |

▲ **Interpreting Tables** What effect might the difference in the length of the terms of representatives and senators have on their performance?

## Section 3 Review

1. **Define:** continuous body
2. How many people now serve in the United States Senate?
3. How is that number fixed?
4. What is the term of office for senators?
5. In what way is the Senate a "continuous body"?
6. What are the constitutional qualifications for membership in the Senate?
7. What powers does the Senate have over the election and qualifications of its members?

**Critical Thinking**

8. **Identifying Assumptions** (p. 19) Senators are elected less frequently than House members, and so are supposed to face less political pressure. What does this arrangement suggest about the Constitution's view of political pressure?

★

## Organizing a Food Bank

Many American citizens think of hunger as a problem only in other parts of the world. Unfortunately, however, about 20 million people suffer from hunger in the United States, the world's wealthiest country.

### Costly Cutbacks

During the 1960s and 1970s, Congress appropriated funds to create programs to ease the problems of our country's poor. Among them were Medicaid, Supplemental Security Income (SSI), and Food Stamps. In the early 1980s, however, many programs aimed at fighting poverty and hunger came under attack as being too costly to the American taxpayer, and the government cut back drastically on these programs.

Fortunately, a number of individuals and private organizations picked up where federal programs left off. Sean Fox, from Ethel, Washington, was one of those individuals. At the age of 17, Sean played the leading role in establishing a food bank in Toledo, Washington. Food banks obtain and offer a selection of basic foods to people at no cost. Eligible families may use a food bank for some or all of the food they need. This idea was inspired after he attended a month-long Washington State Governor's School for Leadership. "When I came back," he said, "I wanted to do something."

What Sean did was impress upon his parents and community, civic, and church leaders the need for a food bank in Toledo. Toledo had a high unemployment rate and was the only town in the county that did not have a food bank. Those in need had to drive about 30 miles to another town. Sean felt that the citizens of Toledo should "care for their own."

### A Driving Force

After spearheading the initial organizational efforts, he and his committee worked hard for four months. They formed a corporation, dealt with legal concerns, found a good location, and obtained food. One community leader said, "The effort to form the Toledo Food Bank was probably 25 percent local endeavor and 75 percent Sean's drive, persistence, and unyielding impatience in achieving success . . . [h]e was the driving force in the formation of the food bank."

The food bank was an immediate success. After one year of operation, the Toledo Food Bank aided more than 80 families each month. And in addition to feeling the satisfaction that comes from taking action, Sean was chosen by the U.S. Department of Justice to receive a Young American Medal for outstanding service to his community.

### Getting Involved

**1. Identify** a need in your community similar to the one addressed in this case.

**2. Formulate** a plan for how you might organize volunteer efforts to help remedy this problem and identify resources that could be used in your plan.

**3. Predict** any problems or objections you might encounter in implementing your plan.

# 4 The Members of Congress

## Find Out:

- Who are the members of Congress and what are their personal and political backgrounds?
- What are the several roles members of Congress play in performing their duties?
- What are members of Congress paid—in money and in various other forms of compensation?

## Key Terms:

constituents, oversight function

You have seen help wanted ads in the newspaper—ads that describe jobs to be filled and their pay and so on. But you have never seen one that reads: "Wanted: Members of Congress. . . ." How would an ad like that describe the duties, the pay, and other aspects of the post? This section will enable you to answer that question.

## Personal and Political Backgrounds

Whatever else they may be, the 535 members of Congress are *not* a representative cross section of the American people. Rather, the "average" member is a white male in his mid-50s. The median age of the members of the House is just about 50 and of the Senate, 57.

The composition of both chambers has been changing fairly rapidly over recent years, however. More women now sit in Congress than ever before—49 in the House and eight in the Senate. And a record number of African Americans—39—are also members of Congress today. So, too, are 18 Hispanics and 6 Pacific Islanders. The first African American woman ever elected to the Senate, Carol Moseley Braun (D., Illinois), now sits in that body; and so does the Senate's first full-blooded Native American member. Ben Nighthorse Campbell (D., Colorado). Both were elected in 1992.

Nearly all members are married, a few are divorced, and they have, on the average, two children. Only a few members say they have no religious affiliation. Just about 60 percent are Protestants, a fourth Roman Catholics, and some 8 percent are Jewish.

Well over a third of the members of the House and well over half the senators are lawyers. Most others come from business and banking, education, agriculture, journalism, and public service/politics. Nearly all went to college. More than four out of five have a college degree and a number have several.

Most senators and representatives were born in the States they represent. Only a handful were born outside the United States. Sprinkled among the members of Congress are several millionaires. A surprisingly large number, however, depend on their salaries as their major source of income.

Most members of Congress have had considerable political experience. The average

**First Woman in Congress** Jeannette Rankin (R., Montana) was first elected in 1916. She voted against entering World War I and was the only member of the House to vote against entering World War II.

## The 104th Congress: A Multicultural Profile

| House of Representatives | | Characteristics | Senate | |
|---|---|---|---|---|
| 103rd Congress | 104th Congress | | 103rd Congress | 104th Congress |
| 256 | 204 | Democrats | 56 | 47 |
| 177 | 230 | Republicans | 44 | 53 |
| 2 | 1 | Independents/Other | – | – |
| 47 | 49 | Women | 7 | 8 |
| 388 | 388 | Men | 93 | 92 |
| 376 | 375 | Whites | 96 | 96 |
| 38 | 38 | African Americans | 1 | 1 |
| 17 | 18 | Hispanic Americans | 0 | 0 |
| 4 | 4 | Asian/Pacific Islanders | 2 | 2 |
| 91 | 90 | % college degree | 94 | 93 |
| 42 | 39 | % law degree | 59 | 54 |
| 84 | 83 | % married | 87 | 87 |
| 85 | 83 | % with children | 95 | 93 |
| | | **Years in Chamber** | | |
| 1 | 20 | % with less than 2 years | 2 | 12 |
| 54 | 45 | % with 2-9 years | 39 | 38 |
| 31 | 25 | % with 10-19 years | 39 | 30 |
| 14 | 10 | % with 20 or more years | 20 | 20 |
| | | **Leading Religious Preferences** | | |
| 59.5 | 62 | % Protestant | 59 | 62 |
| 27 | 29 | % Catholic | 24 | 20 |
| 7.6 | 5.5 | % Jewish | 10 | 9 |

Source: USA Today, Congressional Quarterly

▲ **Interpreting Tables: Multicultural Awareness** This graph compares various characteristics of the last Congress with those of the present one. In what areas do you see the largest differences?

senator is serving a second term, and the typical representative has served four terms. Nearly a third of the Senate once sat in the House. Several senators are former governors. A few senators have held cabinet seats or other high posts in the executive branch. The House has a large number of former State legislators and prosecuting attorneys among its members.

Again, Congress is not an accurate cross section of the nation's population. Rather, it is made up of upper-middle-class Americans, who are, on the whole, quite able and hard-working people.

## Duties of the Job

The 535 members of Congress play several closely related and vital roles. Their major job, of course, is to make law. That is, they are (1) legislators. In addition, members of Congress also serve as (2) committee members; (3) representatives of their constituents, the people of their States or districts; (4) servants of their constituents; and (5) politicians. You have read about some aspects of these roles in this and in earlier chapters, and you will consider other facets of them in the next two chapters. For now, consider the following overview of the roles of a member of Congress.

As committee members, representatives and senators serve on those bodies to which proposed laws (bills) are referred in each house. They must screen those proposals and decide which of them will go on to floor consideration—that is, be acted upon by the full membership of their respective chambers.

As another and vital part of their committee work, representatives and senators also exercise the **oversight function**. That is, they check to see that the various agencies in the executive branch are working effectively and are acting in line with the policies that Congress has set by law.

As you have read, members of the Senate and the House are elected to represent their constituents. But what does that really mean? Every senator and representative must cast hundreds of votes during each session of Congress. Many of those votes come on relatively unimportant matters—minor bills and so on. But many votes, including some on matters of organization and procedure, are cast on matters of far-reaching importance.

So, no questions about the lawmaking branch can be more vital than these: How do the people's representatives represent the people? On what basis do they cast their votes?

In broad terms, each lawmaker has four voting options. He or she can vote as a trustee, as a delegate, as a partisan, or as a politico.

**Trustees** These members believe that each question they face must be decided on its merits. Conscience and independent judgment are their guides. Trustees call issues as they see them, regardless of the views held by their constituents or by any of the other groups that seek to influence their decisions.

**Delegates** These members see themselves as the agents of those who elected them. They believe that they should vote the way they think "the folks back home" would want. These members are willing to suppress their own views, ignore those of their party's leaders, and turn a deaf ear to the arguments of colleagues and of special interests from outside their constituencies.

**Partisans** The partisans are those lawmakers who owe their first allegiance to their political party. They feel duty-bound to vote in line with the party platform and the wishes of their party's leaders. Most studies of legislators' voting behavior show that partisanship is the leading factor influencing their votes on most important measures.

**Politicos** Politicos attempt to combine the basic elements of the trustee, delegate, and partisan roles. They try to balance these often conflicting factors: their own views of what is best for their constituents and/or the nation as a whole, the political facts of life, and the peculiar pressures of the moment.

**Other Roles** Representatives and senators also act as servants of their constituents. They do this particularly as they work to help them solve whatever problems they may have with the federal bureaucracy. Many constituents believe members of Congress are in Washington especially to do favors for them. The average member is swamped with constituent requests from the moment he or she takes office. The range of these requests is almost without limit—everything from help in securing a government contract or an appointment to a military academy, to asking for a free sight-seeing tour of Washington or even a personal loan. Consider this job description offered only half-jokingly by former Representative Luther Patrick of Alabama:

“ A Congressman has become an expanded messenger boy, an employment agency, getter-outer of the Navy, Army, Marines, ward heeler, wound healer, trouble shooter, law explainer, bill finder, issue translator, resolution interpreter, controversy oil pourer, gladhand extender, business promoter, convention goer, civil ills skirmisher, veterans' affairs adjuster, ex-serviceman's champion, watchdog for the underdog, sympathizer with the upper dog, namer and kisser of babies, recoverer of lost luggage, soberer of delegates, adjuster for traffic violators, voters straying into Washington and into toils of the law, binder up of broken hearts, financial wet nurse, Good Samaritan, contributor to good causes—there are so many good causes—cornerstone layer, public building and bridge dedicator, ship christener—to be sure he does get in a little flag waving—and a little constitutional hoisting and spread-eagle work, but it is getting harder every day to find time to properly study legislation—the very business we are primarily here to discharge, and that must be done above all things. ”

Most members of Congress know that to deny or fail to respond to these requests would mean to lose votes in the next election. This is a key fact, for all of the roles a member of Congress plays—legislator, committee member, constituent representative, constituent servant, and politician—are related, at least in part, to their efforts to win reelection from the voters of their districts.

## Compensation

The Constitution gives Congress the power to set its own pay and also provide other

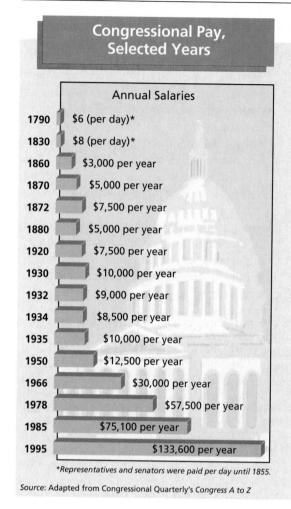

## Congressional Pay, Selected Years

### Annual Salaries

| Year | Salary |
|------|--------|
| 1790 | $6 (per day)* |
| 1830 | $8 (per day)* |
| 1860 | $3,000 per year |
| 1870 | $5,000 per year |
| 1872 | $7,500 per year |
| 1880 | $5,000 per year |
| 1920 | $7,500 per year |
| 1930 | $10,000 per year |
| 1932 | $9,000 per year |
| 1934 | $8,500 per year |
| 1935 | $10,000 per year |
| 1950 | $12,500 per year |
| 1966 | $30,000 per year |
| 1978 | $57,500 per year |
| 1985 | $75,100 per year |
| 1995 | $133,600 per year |

*Representatives and senators were paid per day until 1855.*

Source: Adapted from Congressional Quarterly's *Congress A to Z*

▲ **Interpreting Graphs** Congress sets its own pay. What advantages and disadvantages do you see in this arrangement?

compensations for its members.[25] Today, senators and representatives receive $133,600 a year. (The Speaker of the House is paid $171,500 a year—the same salary Congress has set for the Vice President.)

**Nonsalary Compensation** Each member also receives a number of "fringe benefits," some of which are quite substantial. For example, each member is allowed a tax deduction to help keep up two residences, one in his or her home district and another in Washington. Travel allowances cover the cost of several round trips between the home State and the capital each year.

Members pay only small amounts for life and health insurance and for outpatient care by a medical staff at the Capitol; full medical care can be had, at very low rates, at any military hospital. Also, members contribute to a generous pension plan. The plan is based on one's years in Congress, and it can lead to a yearly pension of $150,000 or more for some long-serving members. Members of Congress are also covered by social security, and they pay the maximum social security taxes on their salaries—now more than $7,000 a year.

Each member also has offices in one of the Senate or House office buildings and allowances for offices in the home State or district. Each is allowed funds for hiring staff and for running those offices. All of a member's official mail is sent postage free under the franking privilege.

There is also free printing and distribution of speeches, newsletters, and other material. Radio and television tapes may also be produced and distributed at very low cost. Each member has free parking, plants for the office, the research help of the Library of Congress, and still more—including the use of several fine restaurants and two first-rate gymnasiums with swimming pools and saunas. All told, the compensation of a typical member of Congress now comes to well over $200,000 a year.[26]

**The Politics of Pay** There are only two real limits on the level of congressional pay. One is the President's veto power. The other and more potent limit is the fear of voter backlash, an angry reaction by constituents at the ballot box. That fear of election-day fallout has always

---

[25] Article I, Section 6, Clause 1. The 27th Amendment, ratified in 1992, says that no increase in members' pay can take effect until after the next congressional election—until, that is, voters have had an opportunity to react to that raise in pay.

[26] For decades, many members of Congress supplemented their salaries with honoraria—speaking fees and similar payments from private sources, mainly special interest groups. Critics long attacked that widespread practice as at least unseemly and, at its worst, a form of legalized bribery. The House finally prohibited its members from accepting honoraria in 1989, and the Senate did so in 1991.

made most members reluctant to vote to raise their own salaries.

Most often, Congress has tried to skirt the troublesome and politically sensitive pay question by providing for such fringe benefits as a special tax break, a liberal pension plan, more office and travel funds, and other perquisites, or "perks"—items of value that are much less apparent to "the folks back home."

The debate over congressional pay is not likely to end soon—at least not as long as the current method of establishing salaries remains in effect. All sides of the issue present reasonable arguments. And clearly, decent salaries—pay in line with the responsibilities of the job—will not automatically bring the most able men and women to Congress, or to any other public office. But certainly, decent salaries can make public service much more appealing to qualified people.

## Privileges of Members

Beyond the matter of their salaries and other compensation, members of Congress enjoy several important privileges. The Constitution commands that senators and representatives

❝shall, in all cases, except treason, felony, and breach of the peace, be privileged from arrest during their attendance at the session of their respective Houses, and in going to, and returning from, the same . . . ❞[27]

The provision dates from English and colonial practice, when the king's officers often harassed legislators on petty grounds. It has been of little importance in our national history, however.[28]

Another much more important privilege is set out in the same place in the Constitution. The Speech and Debate Clause declares

❝. . . for any speech or debate in either House, they shall not be questioned in any other place.❞

The words "any other place" refer to the courts.

The privilege is intended to "throw a cloak of legislative immunity" about members of Congress. The clause protects representatives and senators from suits for libel or slander arising out of their official conduct. The Supreme Court has held that the immunity applies "to things generally done in a session of the House [or Senate] by one of its members in relation to the business before it."[29] The protection goes, then, beyond floor debate, to include work in committees and all other things generally done by members of Congress in relation to congressional business.

The important and necessary goal of this provision of the Constitution is to protect freedom of legislative debate. Clearly, members must not feel restrained in their vigorous discussion of the sometimes contentious issues of the day. However, this provision is not designed to give members unbridled freedom to attack others verbally or in writing. Thus, a member is not free to defame another person in a public speech, an article, a conversation, or otherwise.

## Section 4 Review

**1. Define:** constituents, oversight function
**2.** What are some of the common features found in the backgrounds of members of Congress?
**3.** What are the principal roles that a member of Congress plays?
**4.** (a) Who sets the salary for the members of Congress? (b) How has this fact led to controversy?

**Critical Thinking**

**5. Identifying Central Issues** (p. 19) Former Senator Russell Long (D., La.) once described Congress's power to set its own pay as a "power no good man would want and a power no bad man should have." What do you think he meant by this?

★

---

[27] Article I, Section 6, Clause 1.
[28] The courts have regularly held that the words "breach of the peace" cover all criminal offenses, misdemeanors (minor crimes) as well as felonies. So the protection covers only arrest for civil (noncriminal) offenses while engaged in congressional business.

[29] The leading case is *Kilburn* v. *Thompson*, 1881. The holding has been affirmed many times since. In *Hutchinson* v. *Proxmire*, 1979, however, the Court held that members of Congress may be sued for libel for statements they make in news releases or in newsletters.

# How to Develop Profiles of Your Members of Congress

Who are your senators and who is your representative in Congress? How well do these people represent you and the people of your State and district? These important questions will become even more vital when you become qualified to vote, for casting an informed ballot is a key responsibility for all citizens.

Fortunately, there is no shortage of information about your representatives in Washington, D.C. Follow the steps below to develop a profile of the men and women who represent you in Congress.

**1. Find useful sources of information on your representatives in Congress.** As you know, information about the United States government is available from a wide variety of sources. For example, check the Government Resources Handbook that begins on page 690 of your textbook. (a) Which sources are specifically devoted to the United States Congress? (b) What kinds of information would you be able to find in those sources? (c) What additional sources hold information about Congress?

**2. Check local sources of information.** Local newspapers are an invaluable source of good information about your representatives in Washington. Such sources often include stories about election campaigns and about your representatives.

**3. List the personal backgrounds of your representatives.** Information such as age, birthplace, home, religion, marital status, education, and occupation are available in published sources. In which of the resources listed in the Government Resources Handbook would you most likely find personal background information?

**4. Describe your representatives' political backgrounds.** Political background includes data such as party membership, political experience before serving in Congress, years of service in Congress, and nature of constituency. Research committee assignments, leadership positions, and major bills authored and/or sponsored by your members of Congress. Answer these questions: (a) In which resource(s) would this data be most readily available? (b) In what other sources could you find this information?

**5. Define your representatives' voting records.** It is important to know where your representatives stand on the vital issues of the day. Analyze their positions (votes) on key economic, social, foreign policy, and defense issues. What resource might you use to find this information?

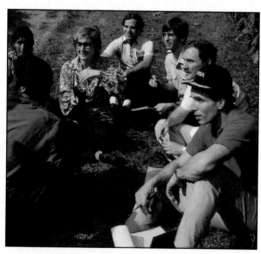

▲ Members of Congress, such as the one shown here (right), have varied personal and political backgrounds.

# Chapter-in-Brief

Scan all headings, photographs, charts, and other visuals in the chapter before reading the section summaries below.

**Section 1 The National Legislature (pp. 235–238)** Because the Framers attached great importance to the legislative branch, they devoted the first and the lengthiest of the articles of the Constitution to it. Article I establishes a bicameral Congress—a two-house body as the national legislature.

Congress is a bicameral body mainly because the Framers (1) were familiar with British, colonial, and early State practice, (2) agreed to the Connecticut Compromise at the Philadelphia Convention, and (3) hoped that one house would act as a check on the other.

A term of Congress extends over two years. There are two regular sessions during each term, one each year. Only the President can call a special session of Congress—but no special sessions have been held in more than 40 years.

**Section 2 The House of Representatives (pp. 238–244)** The House of Representatives is the larger of the two chambers. By law, there are 435 seats (members) in the House. The seats are distributed among the States on the basis of their respective populations.

The Constitution provides for a census to be taken every 10 years, and it directs Congress to reapportion (reallocate) the seats in the House on the basis of each census. Following each of the last seven censuses, Congress has approved the reapportionment plan recommended to it by the Census Bureau. Each State is entitled to at least one seat in the House.

Voters elect members of the House for two-year terms. They are chosen from districts within the States. The State legislatures draw those congressional districts, and they are often gerrymandered. The Supreme Court has held that congressional districts must be drawn in accord with the "one-person, one vote" rule—that is, in terms of population equality.

**Section 3 The Senate (pp. 245–247)** The Constitution provides that each State is to have two senators. Thus, the Senate has 100 members today. Senators serve six-year terms.

The Constitution sets higher qualifications for senators than it does for representatives. Members of the Senate must be at least 30 years of age, unlike 25 years of age for representatives. Also, senators must have been citizens for at least nine (instead of seven) years. Members of both houses must be inhabitants of the States they represent.

**Section 4 The Members of Congress (pp. 249–253)** Members of Congress are not a representative cross section of the American people. Instead, the average member is a white male in his mid-50s. There are only a few women, African Americans, and Hispanic Americans in Congress.

Members of Congress are legislators, of course. They also serve as representatives and servants of their constituents, as committee members, and as politicians. Most members usually adopt one of four styles. They behave and vote as (1) trustees, who base their decisions solely on their best judgments, (2) delegates, who follow the wishes of their constituents, (3) partisans, who feel duty-bound to support their parties' positions, or (4) politicos, who try to balance these roles as situations demand.

# Chapter Review

## Vocabulary and Key Terms

term (p. 237)
session (p. 237)
special session (p. 238)
apportioned (p. 238)

reapportion (p. 239)
single-member district (p. 241)
at-large (p. 241)
gerrymandered (p. 242)

continuous body (p. 246)
constituents (p. 250)
oversight function (p. 250)

**Matching:** *Review the key terms in the list above. If you are not sure of a term's meaning, look up the term and review its definition. Choose a term from the list above that best matches each description.*

1. how you might describe an electoral district that has been drawn by a legislature in a very odd shape
2. what a senator considers every citizen of his or her state
3. what function Congress is performing when it checks on the programs of the executive branch
4. the period of time for which a representative serves in Congress before coming up for reelection
5. what happens to the seats in the House of Representatives every decade

**True or False:** *Determine whether each statement is true or false. If it is true, write "true." If it is false, change the underlined word or words to make the statement true.*

1. The Constitution says that the seats of the House of Representatives must be <u>apportioned</u> among the States based on population.
2. The President has the power to call a <u>session</u> of Congress.
3. A member of Congress represents his or her <u>constituents</u>.
4. Because the entire membership of the Senate is never up for election at the same time, the upper house is called a <u>single-member district</u>.
5. Congress performs its formal legislative work during a <u>special session</u>.

**Word Relationships:** *Distinguish between words in each pair.*

1. at-large/single-member district
2. session/special session
3. apportioned/reapportion

## Main Ideas

### Section 1 (pp. 235–238)

1. What factors explain why the United States Congress is bicameral?
2. How does bicameralism reflect the principle of federalism?
3. How have the terms and sessions of Congress changed over the course of United States history?

### Section 2 (pp. 238–244)

4. For what reasons must Congress be reapportioned every 10 years?
5. In what way has the reapportionment of House seats been used for the political gain of certain groups and parties in the various States?
6. What are the constitutional qualifications that all members of the House must meet?

### Section 3 (pp. 245–247)

7. How does the Senate differ from the House in terms of size and the election of its members?

8. What is the purpose of the differences between the House of Representatives and the Senate?

9. What are the qualifications that all senators must meet?

## Section 4 (pp. 249-253)

10. (a) For what reasons is it untrue to say that the members of Congress represent a cross section of the American people? (b) Describe the typical member.

11. What are the different ways in which members of Congress may view their function?

12. (a) How are members of Congress compensated for their work? (b) What is the controversy surrounding congressional pay?

## Critical Thinking

1. **Identifying Alternatives** (p. 19) In *The Federalist* No. 10, Madison warns that ". . . representatives must be raised to a certain number to guard against the cabals of a few; and that however large it may be, they must be limited to a certain number, in order to guard against the confusion of a multitude." In light of this statement, discuss whether or not you think Congress today—with 535 seats—is too large or too small.

2. **Distinguishing False from Accurate Images** (p. 19) Congress is frequently blamed for many of the problems of the National Government. Yet the text says that the members of Congress are on the whole hard-working and able people. How can you explain the existence of these two opposing viewpoints?

3. **Expressing Problems Clearly** (p. 19) Recall what you have read about the differences between the House and Senate. (a) What are the benefits and drawbacks of having senators serve six-year terms? (b) What might happen if they had shorter or longer terms?

4. **Recognizing Ideologies** (p. 19) The saying "to the victor goes the spoils" has a long tradition in the American political system. (a) What do you think this saying means? (b) How might this saying help explain the practice of gerrymandering?

## Getting Involved

1. **Writing Your Opinion** Write a newspaper editorial about your views on what the qualifications of a member of Congress should be. To start, list the current constitutional qualifications that members must meet. In addition, be sure to consider the standards of behavior discussed in the chapter. Then write down your ideas for any modifications or additions to the list. Begin your first draft with a statement about why firm standards and qualifications are necessary for members of Congress. Then give your own ideas for amending or adding onto the current qualifications. For each idea, explain how you think your idea will make the United States Congress a better institution. Read your draft for clarity and revise. Then proofread and draft a final copy.

2. **Class Debate** Hold a class debate on one of the following topics: (a) *Resolved,* That the minimum age for representatives in the House be 18 years of age; (b) *Resolved,* That no member of either house of Congress be allowed to serve more than 12 years in office. Select one team to debate in favor of the statement and another to argue against it. The rest of the class should evaluate each team's presentation.

3. **Creating a Poster** Consider what you have read in Chapter 10 about the roles of members of Congress. Make a poster that illustrates your idea of what it means to be a member of Congress. You can use a combination of words and images in your poster.

**CHAPTER**

**11**

# Powers of Congress

## Chapter Preview

"If only I had all the money I need. . . . " That thought has occurred to nearly everyone who has ever had to live within a budget, ever had to stretch whatever money was available to cover all the bills that had to be paid. Like many individuals and most businesses, the Federal Government has a budget—a financial plan to guide its operation. Unlike individuals and businesses, however, the Federal Government has the power to acquire all the money it needs, whenever it needs that money.

The Constitution gives to Congress the several powers it needs to finance the government, and a number of other powers as well. This chapter is about the many powers of Congress: (1) its legislative powers, with which it can and does make law, and (2) its nonlegislative powers, with which Congress performs various functions closely related to its role as the lawmaking branch of the National Government.

### Before you read this chapter:

- **Describe** how you or your family creates a budget.
- **Predict** what might happen if Congress were denied the power to borrow money except to reduce the public debt.

### As you read, focus on the main objective for each section. Understand:

1. The scope of the powers of Congress in a governmental system that is both limited and federal in character.
2. The many and important expressed powers of Congress.
3. The nature and extent of the implied powers of Congress.
4. The several nonlegislative powers of Congress.

▲ **When a Member of Congress Talks, the Nation Listens**   Because the work of Congress has such an impact on all aspects of American life, the public pays close attention to what individual members of Congress have to say. Here, Speaker of the House Newt Gingrich (R., Georgia) briefs the press.

# 1 The Scope of Congressional Powers

**Find Out:**

- How does the Constitution and the federal system itself affect the powers that Congress exercises?
- How has the controversy over strict versus liberal construction of the Constitution affected American government?

**Key Terms:**

strict constructionist, liberal constructionist

A typical day in Congress might suggest that there is no limit to what Congress can do. On any given day, the House might consider bills dealing with such varied matters as a reduction in the capital gains tax, the space shuttle program, and the regulation of cable TV. Meanwhile, the Senate might be debating aid to a famine-stricken country, veterans' benefits, and dairy price supports. And the upper house might also be considering the President's nomination of a new Supreme Court justice.

But, as you are well aware, there are very real limits on what Congress can do. Remember that (1) the government in the United States is limited government, and (2) the American system of government is federal in form. In this section you will see how both of those fundamental points work to shape and limit the powers of Congress.

## Congressional Power

The Constitution places many restrictions on Congress, as it does on the Federal Government as a whole. Large areas of power are denied to Congress because of what the Constitution says, what it does not say, and because of the federal system itself.

# *VOICES on Government*

**Norman Y. Mineta,**
Democratic representative
from California

## On Being a Public Servant

❝There is no great secret to performing a public service. There is no magical laundry list of I's to dot or T's to cross before a particular act of selflessness may be officially proclaimed as a public service. But whether you act on your own or in concert with others, there is always one common denominator: the sense of community that says, 'This is my home, and I want to help make it better. I care not only about myself, but about my neighbors, about where I live.'❞

There is much that Congress cannot do. It cannot create a national public school system, require that all persons attend church, set a minimum age for drivers' licenses, or do a great many other things—because the Constitution does not give it the power to do them. Of course, Congress does have the power to do many things. Recall, the Constitution gives it several specific powers, and in three different ways: (1) expressly, in so many words—the expressed powers; (2) by reasonable deduction from the expressed powers—the implied powers; and (3) by creating a National Government for the United States—the inherent powers.

## Strict Versus Liberal Construction

The Framers of the Constitution intended to create a new and stronger National Government. As you know, the ratification of their plan was opposed by many, and that opposition was not stilled by the adoption of the Constitution. Rather, the conflict between the Federalists and the Anti-Federalists continued into the early years of the Republic. Much of that conflict centered on the powers of Congress. Just how broad, in fact, were they?

The **strict constructionists**, led by Thomas Jefferson, continued to argue the Anti-Federalist position from the ratification period: That Congress should be able to exercise only (a) its expressed powers and (b) those implied powers absolutely necessary to carry out those expressed powers. They wanted the States to keep as much power as possible. They agreed with Jefferson that "that government is best which governs least."

The **liberal constructionists**, led by Alexander Hamilton, had led the fight to adopt the

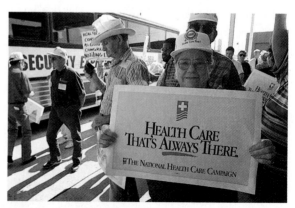

▲ **Interpreting Political Cartoons and Photographs**   Much of the work of Congress affects daily life in this country—for example, the debate over national health care. What does the cartoon say about some members of Congress?

Constitution. Now they favored a liberal inter-pretation of the Constitution, a broad construc-tion of the powers given to Congress. The liberal constructionists won that conflict, as you will see. As a result, the powers of the Federal Government have grown to a point that none of the Framers could have imagined.

Several factors, working together with the lib-eral construction of the Constitution, have been responsible for that marked growth in national power. Wars, economic crises, and other national emergencies have been major causes. Spectacular advances, especially in transportation and com-munication, have also had a real impact on the size and the scope of government. Equally important have been the demands of the people themselves for more and more services from government.

Congress has been led by these and other factors to view its powers in broader and broader terms. Most Presidents have regarded their powers in similar fashion. The Supreme Court has generally taken a like position in its decisions in cases involving the powers of the National Government. Moreover, the American people have generally agreed with a liberal interpretation of the Constitution. This con-sensus has prevailed even though American political history has been marked, and still is, by controversies over the proper limits of national power.

## Section 1 Review

**1.** What two features of the American system of government have an impact on the scope of the powers of Congress?

**2.** (a) What position did the strict constructionists take in the early years under the Constitution? (b) The liberal constructionists? (c) Which group's view prevailed?

### Critical Thinking

**3. Recognizing Cause and Effect** (p. 19) Explain how the growth and change of the nation might have influenced people's views on the expansion of the powers of Congress.

★

## 2 The Expressed Powers

**Find Out:**

- For what purposes was Congress given each of its several expressed powers?
- How does Congress exercise its expressed powers?
- How have the expressed powers granted to Congress changed over time?

**Key Terms:**

direct tax, indirect tax, commerce power, legal tender, bankruptcy, copyright, patent, eminent domain

Most, but not all, of the expressed powers of Congress are found in Article I, Sec-tion 8 of the Constitution. There, in 18 sepa-rate clauses, 27 different powers are explicitly given to Congress.[1]

These grants of power are brief. What they do and do not allow Congress to do often can-not be discovered by merely reading the few words involved. Rather, their meaning is found in the ways in which Congress has exercised its powers since 1789—and, too, in scores of Supreme Court cases arising out of the actions taken by Congress.

As a case in point, take the Commerce Clause. Article I, Section 8, Clause 3 gives to Congress the power

❝To regulate commerce with foreign nations, and among the several States, and with the Indian tribes.❞

Its wording is both brief and broad. Congress and the Court have had to answer hundreds of questions about its scope and content. Here are

---

[1]Several of the expressed powers of Congress are set out elsewhere in the Constitution. Thus, Article IV, Section 3 grants it the power to admit new States to the Union (Clause 1) and to manage and dispose of federal territory and other property (Clause 2). The 16th Amendment gives Congress the power to levy an income tax. The 13th, 14th, 15th, 19th, 24th, and 26th amendments each vest in Congress the "power to enforce" their provisions "by appropriate legislation."

but a few examples: Does "commerce" include persons entering or leaving the country or crossing State lines? Radio and television broadcasts? Air transportation? Does the Commerce Clause give Congress the power to fix a minimum wage? Does it allow Congress to prohibit shipment of certain goods? To regulate banks? To prohibit discrimination?

In answering these and hundreds of other questions on this one brief provision, Congress and the Court have spelled out, and are still spelling out, the meaning of the Commerce Clause.

So it is with most of the other provisions that grant power to Congress.[2] In this section, you will read about these provisions and their evolution over the course of this nation's history.

## The Power to Tax

Article I, Section 8, Clause 1 gives Congress the power

❝ To lay and collect taxes, duties, imposts and excises, to pay the debts, and provide for the common defense and general welfare of the United States . . . ❞

Recall, the Articles of Confederation had not given Congress the power to tax. Without it, the government was impotent; and the lack of that power was a leading cause for the coming of the Constitution.

The Federal Government will take in more than $1.3 trillion in fiscal year 1995, and an even larger sum in fiscal 1996. Over 90 percent of that money will come from the various taxes levied by Congress.

A tax is a charge levied by government on persons or property to meet public needs. But,

notice, taxes are sometimes imposed for other purposes. The protective tariff is perhaps the oldest example of the point. Although it does bring in revenue, its real goal is to "protect" domestic industry against foreign competition by increasing the cost of foreign goods.

Taxes are also sometimes levied to protect the public health and safety. The Federal Government's regulation of narcotics is a case in point. Only those who have a proper federal license may legally manufacture, sell, or deal in those drugs—and licensing is a form of taxation.

But, recall, the power to tax is not unlimited. As with all other powers, it must be used in accord with all other provisions of the Constitution. Thus, Congress cannot lay a tax on church services. Such a tax would violate the 1st Amendment protection of the free exercise of religion.

More specifically, the Constitution places four explicit limitations on the taxing power. First, Congress may tax only for public purposes, not for private benefit. Article I, Section 8, Clause 1 says that taxes may be levied only

❝ to pay the debts, and provide for the common defense and general welfare of the United States . . . ❞

Second, Congress may not tax exports. Article I, Section 9, Clause 5 declares

❝ No duty or tax shall be laid on articles exported from any State. ❞

Thus, customs duties, or tariffs, which are taxes, may be placed only on imports.

Third, direct taxes must be apportioned among the States, according to their populations. Article I, Section 9, Clause 4 declares

❝ No capitation, or other direct tax, shall be laid, unless in proportion to the census or enumeration herein before directed to be taken. ❞

A **direct tax** is one that must be paid by the person on whom it is imposed—for example, a tax on the ownership of land or buildings, or a capitation (head or poll) tax.

An income tax is a direct tax. But, notice, it may be laid without regard to population because of the 16th Amendment:

❝ The Congress shall have power to lay and collect taxes on incomes, from whatever source derived, with-

---

[2]But, notice, a few of the expressed powers are of little importance today. Thus, Congress has the power to grant letters of marque and reprisal, Article I, Section 8, Clause 11; and the States are denied the power to issue them, Article I, Section 10, Clause 1. Letters of marque and reprisal are relics of the past. They are commissions, written grants of power authorizing private persons to fit out vessels to capture and destroy the enemy in time of war. In effect, they authorize a form of legalized piracy. Letters of marque and reprisal are forbidden by international law by the Declaration of Paris, 1856, and the United States honors the rule in practice.

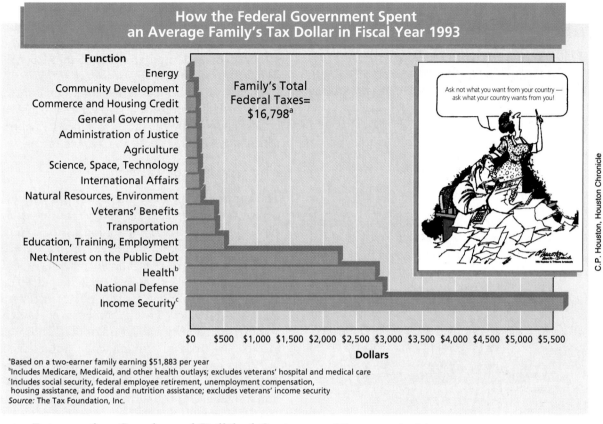

**How the Federal Government Spent an Average Family's Tax Dollar in Fiscal Year 1993**

Family's Total Federal Taxes= $16,798[a]

Ask not what you want from your country — ask what your country wants from you!

C.P. Houston, Houston Chronicle

[a]Based on a two-earner family earning $51,883 per year
[b]Includes Medicare, Medicaid, and other health outlays; excludes veterans' hospital and medical care
[c]Includes social security, federal employee retirement, unemployment compensation, housing assistance, and food and nutrition assistance; excludes veterans' income security
*Source:* The Tax Foundation, Inc.

▲ **Interpreting Graphs and Political Cartoons**   What percent of the average family's taxes was spent on deficit financing (the public debt) in 1993? What does the cartoon say about taxes?

out apportionment among the several States, and without regard to any census or enumeration. 🔊

Finally, Article I, Section 8, Clause 1 provides that

❝all duties, imposts, and excises, shall be uniform throughout the United States.🔊

That is, all indirect taxes must be levied at the same rate in all parts of the country.

Whether a tax is direct or indirect is, in practical terms, decided by Congress and the Supreme Court. As a general rule, however, an **indirect tax** is one first paid by one person but then passed on to another. It is indirectly paid by that second person. Take, for example, the federal tax on cigarettes. It is paid to the Treasury by the tobacco company that makes the cigarettes. But that company then passes the tax on to the person who finally buys the cigarettes.

## The Power to Borrow

Congress has the power "to borrow money on the credit of the United States."[3] That power permits the government to finance projects that cannot be paid for out of current revenues.

There is no constitutional limit on the amount that Congress can borrow. Congress has put a statutory ceiling on the public debt—that is, on the total amount the government has borrowed and not yet repaid, plus accrued interest. But that limit is little more than a political gesture. Congress adjusts the ceiling whenever it needs to borrow beyond that limit.

The Federal Government regularly practices deficit financing. That is, it spends more than it takes in each year, and it borrows to make up the difference. The government's

[3]Article I, Section 8, Clause 2.

# Global Awareness

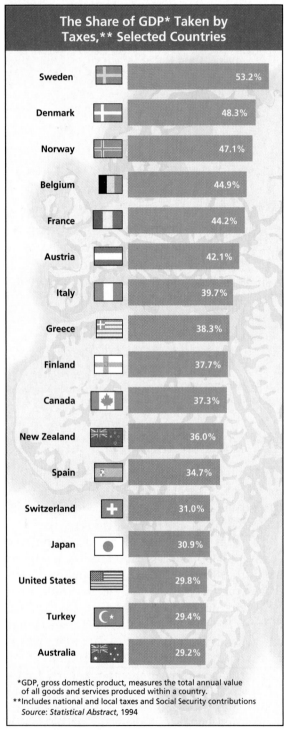

## The Share of GDP* Taken by Taxes,** Selected Countries

| Country | Percentage |
|---|---|
| Sweden | 53.2% |
| Denmark | 48.3% |
| Norway | 47.1% |
| Belgium | 44.9% |
| France | 44.2% |
| Austria | 42.1% |
| Italy | 39.7% |
| Greece | 38.3% |
| Finland | 37.7% |
| Canada | 37.3% |
| New Zealand | 36.0% |
| Spain | 34.7% |
| Switzerland | 31.0% |
| Japan | 30.9% |
| United States | 29.8% |
| Turkey | 29.4% |
| Australia | 29.2% |

*GDP, gross domestic product, measures the total annual value of all goods and services produced within a country.
**Includes national and local taxes and Social Security contributions
*Source: Statistical Abstract, 1994*

▲ **Interpreting Graphs** The U.S. tax rate is much lower than in some other industrialized countries. What factors might account for this?

financial books have not shown a surplus (more income than outgo) in more than 20 years. As a result of this deficit financing, the public debt had risen to more than $4.6 trillion at the beginning of fiscal year 1995.

The power to borrow is absolutely vital to the function of Congress. This power also plays an important role in the field of federal finance, which you will read about in Chapter 16.

## The Commerce Power

The **commerce power**—the power of Congress to regulate interstate and foreign trade—is as vital to the welfare of the nation as the taxing power. As you know, the commerce power played a major role in the formation of the Union. The weak Congress created under the Articles had no power to regulate interstate trade and only very little authority over foreign commerce. The Critical Period of the 1780s was marked by intense commercial rivalries and bickering among the States. High trade barriers and spiteful State laws created chaos and confusion in much of the country.

Consequently, the Framers wrote the Commerce Clause, Article I, Section 8, Clause 3. It gives Congress the power

❝To regulate commerce with foreign nations, and among the several States, and with the Indian tribes.❞

More than any other provision in the Constitution, the Commerce Clause made it possible for a strong Union to be built out of a weak confederation of the States.

The first case to reach the Supreme Court involving the Commerce Clause was *Gibbons* v. *Ogden*, decided in 1824. The case arose out of a clash over the regulation of steam vessels by the State of New York, on the one hand, and the Federal Government, on the other. In 1807 Robert Fulton's steamboat, the *Clermont*, had made its first successful run up the Hudson River, from New York City to Albany. The State legislature then gave Fulton an exclusive, long-term grant to navigate the waters of the State by steamboat. Fulton's monopoly then gave Aaron Ogden a permit for steamboat navigation between New York City and New Jersey.

Thomas Gibbons, operating with a coasting license from the Federal Government, began to carry passengers on a line that competed with Ogden. Ogden sued him, and the New York courts held that Gibbons could not sail by steam in New York waters.

Gibbons appealed that ruling to the Supreme Court. He claimed that the New York grant conflicted with the congressional power to regulate commerce. The Court agreed. It rejected Ogden's argument that "commerce" should be defined narrowly, as simply "traffic" or the mere buying and selling of goods. Instead, it read the Commerce Clause in broad terms. Wrote Chief Justice John Marshall:

**❝**Commerce undoubtedly is traffic, but it is something more—it is intercourse. It describes the commercial intercourse between nations, and parts of nations, in all its branches, and is regulated by prescribing rules for carrying on that intercourse.**❞**

The Court's ruling was widely popular at the time because it dealt a death blow to steamboat monopolies. Freed from restrictive State regulation, steam navigation developed rapidly. Within a few years, the railroads, similarly freed, revolutionized domestic transportation.

Over the decades, the Court's sweeping definition of commerce has brought an extension of federal authority into many areas of American life—a reach of federal power beyond anything the Framers could possibly have imagined.

As another of the many examples of the point, note this: It is on the basis of the commerce power that the Civil Rights Act of 1964 prohibits discrimination in access to or service in hotels, motels, theaters, restaurants, and in other public accommodations on grounds of race, color, religion, or national origin.[4]

Based on the expressed powers to regulate commerce and to tax, Congress and the courts have built nearly all of the implied powers. Most of what the Federal Government does, day to

**Interstate Navigation** This cargo ship on the Delaware River is subject to federal regulation under the Commerce Clause.

day and year to year, it does as the result of legislation passed by Congress in the exercise of these two powers.

The commerce power is not unlimited. It, too, must be used in accord with all other provisions in the Constitution. Thus, Congress could not say that only companies that employ only native-born citizens can do business in more than one State. Such an arbitrary regulation would violate the 5th Amendment's Due Process Clause.

Specifically, the Constitution also places four explicit limitations on the use of the commerce power. First, as you have read, Article I, Section 9, Clause 5 forbids Congress the power to tax exports. Second, Article I, Section 9, Clause 6 prevents Congress from favoring the ports of one State over those of any other in the regulation of trade. Third, the same provision forbids Congress to require that "vessels bound to, or from, one State, be obliged to enter, clear, or pay duties in another." The fourth limitation is the curious "slave trade compromise" found in Article I, Section 9, Clause 1. That clause has been obsolete for more than 180 years now.

---

[4]The Supreme Court considered this use of the commerce power in *Heart of Atlanta Motel, Inc.* v. *United States,* 1964. You will read about this case on page 274 of this chapter.

## The Currency Power

The Constitution gives Congress the power "to coin money [and] regulate the value thereof."[5] The States are forbidden that power.[6]

Until the Revolution, the English money system, built on the shilling and the pound, was in general use in the colonies. With independence, that stable currency system collapsed, however. The Second Continental Congress and then the Congress under the Articles issued paper money. But without sound backing, and with no taxing power behind it, the money was practically worthless. Each of the 13 States also issued its own currency. In several States, this amounted to little more than the State's printing its name on paper and calling it money. Adding to the confusion, people still used English coins, and Spanish money circulated freely in the southern States.

Nearly all the Framers agreed on the need for a single, national system of "hard" money. So the Constitution gave the currency power to Congress, and it all but excluded the States from that field. From 1789 on, among the most important of all of the many tasks performed by the Federal Government has been that of providing the nation with a uniform, stable monetary system.

From the beginning, the United States has issued coins—in gold (until 1933), silver, and other metals. Congress chartered the First Bank of the United States in 1791 and gave it the power to issue bank notes—paper money. But those notes were not legal tender. **Legal tender** is any kind of money that a creditor must by law accept in payment for debts. Congress did not create a national paper currency, and make it legal tender, until 1862.

At first, the new national notes, known as greenbacks, could not be redeemed for gold or silver coin at the Treasury. Their worth fell to less than half of their face value. Then, in 1870, the Supreme Court held their issuance to be unconstitutional. In *Hepburn* v. *Griswold* it said

▲ **Currency Power** State currency, like the banknote issued by Georgia in 1777 (top), was common during the Revolution and then in the Critical Period. Today, only the Federal Government can issue paper money.

"to coin" meant to stamp metal and so the Constitution did not authorize paper money. The Court soon changed its mind, however, in the *Legal Tender Cases* in 1871 and again in *Juliard* v. *Greenman* in 1884. In both cases it held the issuing of paper money as legal tender to be a proper use of the currency power and a power properly implied from the borrowing and the war powers.

## Bankruptcy

Congress has the power "to establish . . . uniform laws on the subject of bankruptcies,

---

[5]Article I, Section 8, Clause 5.
[6]Article I, Section 10, Clause 1 forbids the States the power to coin money, issue bills of credit (paper money), or make anything but gold and silver legal tender.

throughout the United States."[7] A bankrupt individual is one whom a court has found to be insolvent—that is, unable to pay his or her debts in full. **Bankruptcy** is the legal proceeding in which the bankrupt's assets are distributed among those to whom a debt is owed. That proceeding frees the bankrupt from legal responsibility for debts acquired before bankruptcy.

Both the States and the National Government have the power to regulate bankruptcy. It is, then, a concurrent power. In 1898, however, Congress passed a general bankruptcy law, and today that law is so broad that it all but excludes the States from the field. Most bankruptcy cases are heard in the federal district courts; only a very few are handled by State courts today.

## Foreign Relations and War Powers

The Constitution gives Congress several important responsibilities in the country's dealings with foreign states.

**Foreign Relations Powers** The National Government has greater powers in the field of foreign affairs than it has in any other. Congress shares power in this field with the President, who is primarily responsible for the conduct of relations with other nations. Because the States in the Union are not sovereign, they have no standing in international law. The Constitution does not allow them to take part in foreign relations.[8]

Congressional authority in the field of foreign relations comes from two sources: (1) from various expressed powers—including, especially, the several war powers and the power to regulate foreign commerce and (2) from the fact that the United States is a sovereign state in the world community. As the nation's lawmaking body, Congress has the inherent power to act on matters affecting the security of the nation. You will explore this subject at much greater length in Chapter 17.

---

[7]Article I, Section 8, Clause 4.

[8]Article I, Section 10, Clauses 1 and 3.

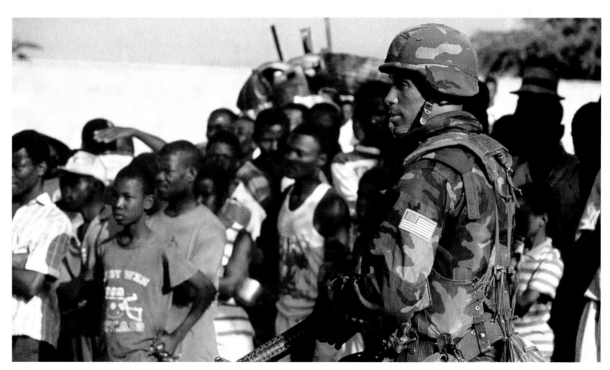

▲ **Show-down in Haiti**  Members of Congress were poised to use their foreign relations powers to block a U.S. invasion of Haiti in late 1994. But military leader Raoul Cédras stepped down, and the invasion became a peacekeeping mission.

**War Powers** Eight of the expressed powers given to Congress in Article I, Section 8 deal with war and national defense.[9] Here, too, Congress shares power with the chief executive. The Constitution makes the President the commander in chief of the nation's armed forces,[10] and, as such, the President dominates the field.

The congressional war powers, however, are extensive and substantial. Only Congress may declare war. It has the power to raise and support armies, to provide and maintain a navy, and to make rules pertaining to governing the land and naval forces. Congress also has the power to provide for "calling forth the militia," and for the organizing, arming, and disciplining of it. And Congress has the power to grant letters of marque and reprisal and make rules concerning captures on land and water.

With the passage of the War Powers Resolution of 1973, Congress claimed the power to restrict the use of American forces in combat in areas where a state of war does not exist; see Chapter 14, Section 3.

## Additional Powers of Congress

The Constitution grants Congress a number of other specific powers.

**Naturalization** Naturalization is the process by which citizens of one country become citizens of another. Article I, Section 8, Clause 4 gives Congress the exclusive power "to establish an uniform rule of naturalization." You will read more about the naturalization process in Chapter 21.

**The Postal Power** Congress has the exclusive power "to establish post offices and post roads."[11] That power covers the authority to protect the mails and to ensure their quick and efficient distribution. Congress is also empowered to prevent the use of the mails for fraud or for the carrying of outlawed materials.

Congress has established a number of crimes based on the postal power. Thus, it is a federal crime for any person to obstruct the mails, to use the mails to commit any fraud, or to use them as a part of any other criminal act.

Articles prohibited by a State's laws, such as firecrackers or switchblade knives, cannot be sent into that State through the mails. A great many other items, including alcoholic beverages, lottery tickets, and obscene materials, are also barred from the mails.

The States cannot interfere with the mails unreasonably. Nor can they require a license for vehicles owned by the Postal Service or tax the gas they use. The States cannot tax the post offices or any other property of the United States Postal Service.

**Copyrights and Patents** Congress has the power

❝ To promote the progress of science and useful arts, by securing, for limited times, to authors and inventors, the exclusive right to their respective writings and discoveries. ❞ [12]

A **copyright** is the exclusive right of an author to reproduce, publish, and sell his or her creative work. That right may be assigned—transferred by contract—to another, as to a publishing firm by mutual agreement between the author and the other party.

Copyrights are registered by the Copyright Office in the Library of Congress. Under present law they are good for the life of the author plus 50 years. They cover a wide range of creative efforts: books, magazines, newspapers, musical compositions and lyrics, dramatic works, paintings, sculptures, cartoons, maps, photographs, motion pictures, sound recordings, and much else.[13]

---

[9]The war powers of Congress are set out in clauses 11 through 16.

[10]Article II, Section 2, Clause 1.

[11]Article I, Section 8, Clause 7. Post roads are all postal routes, including railroads, airways, and waters within the United States, during the time that mail is being carried on them.

[12]Article I, Section 8, Clause 8.

[13]Not all publications can be protected by copyright, however. Thus, the Supreme Court has recently held that such "factual compilations" as telephone directories "lack the requisite originality" for copyright protection, *Feist Publications, Inc.* v. *Rural Telephone Service Co.*, 1991.

William Gropper, *The Senate* (1935).

**Interpreting Political Art** This 1935 painting by artist William Gropper depicts Congress in session. The content of this unit suggests that the work of lawmakers involves heavy responsibilities and hard work. Would Gropper be likely to agree? Why or why not?

A **patent** grants a person the sole right to manufacture, use, or sell "any new and useful art, machine, manufacture, or composition of matter, or any new and useful improvement thereof." A patent is good for a varying number of years—today, 17 years on the patent of an invention. The term of a patent may be extended only by a special act of Congress. The Patent and Trademark Office in the Department of Commerce administers patent laws.[14]

**Weights and Measures** The Constitution gives Congress the power to "fix the standards of weights and measures" throughout the United States.[15] The power reflects the absolute need for and usage of accurate, uniform gauges of time, distance, area, weight, volume, and the like.

In 1838 Congress set the English system of pound, ounce, mile, foot, gallon, quart, and so on, as the legal standards of weights and measures in this country. In 1866 Congress also legalized the use of the metric system.

The National Institute of Standards and Technology in the Commerce Department keeps the original standards for the United States. It is these standards by which all other measures in the United States are tested and corrected.

---

[14]The power to protect trademarks is an implied power, drawn from the commerce power. A trademark is some distinctive word, name, symbol, or device used by a manufacturer or merchant to identify his goods or services and distinguish them from those made or sold by others. A trademark need not be original, merely distinctive. The registration of a trademark carries the right to its exclusive use in interstate commerce for 10 years. The right may be renewed an unlimited number of times.

---

[15]Article I, Section 8, Clause 5.

## The Expressed Powers Vested in Congress by Article I, Section 8 of the Constitution

**Peace Powers**

| | |
|---|---|
| Clause 1. | To lay and collect taxes, duties, imposts and excises. |
| Clause 2. | To borrow money. |
| Clause 3. | To regulate foreign and interstate commerce. |
| Clause 4. | To establish naturalization and bankruptcy laws. |
| Clause 5. | To coin money and regulate its value; to regulate weights and measures. |
| Clause 6. | To punish counterfeiters of federal money and securities. |
| Clause 7. | To establish post offices and post roads. |
| Clause 8. | To grant patents and copyrights. |
| Clause 9. | To create courts inferior to the Supreme Court. |
| Clause 10. | To define and punish piracies and felonies on the high seas, and offenses against the law of nations. |
| Clause 17. | To exercise exclusive jurisdiction over the District of Columbia; to exercise exclusive jurisdiction over forts, dockyards, national parks, federal buildings, and the like. |
| Clause 18. | To make all laws necessary and proper to carry into execution any of the other expressed powers; that is, to exercise implied powers—for example, to define and provide punishment for federal crimes; to improve rivers, harbors, and other waterways; to establish the Federal Reserve System; to fix minimum wages and maximum hours of work. |

**War Powers**

| | |
|---|---|
| Clause 11. | To declare war; to grant letters of marque and reprisal; to make rules concerning captures on land and water. |
| Clause 12. | To raise and support armies. |
| Clause 13. | To provide and maintain a navy. |
| Clause 14. | To make laws governing land and naval forces. |
| Clause 15. | To provide for calling forth the militia to execute federal laws, suppress insurrections, and repel invasions. |
| Clause 16. | To provide for organizing, arming, and disciplining the militia, and for its governing when in the service of the Union. |

▲ **Interpreting Tables**   Why are the commerce and taxing powers of primary importance to the Federal Government?

## Power Over Territories and Other Areas

Congress has the power to acquire, manage, and dispose of various federal areas.[16] That power relates to the District of Columbia and to the several federal territories, including Puerto Rico, Guam, and the Virgin Islands. It also covers hundreds of military and naval installations, arsenals, dockyards, post offices, prison facilities, park and forest preserves, and many other federal holdings throughout the country.

The Federal Government may acquire property by purchase or gift. It may do so, too, through the exercise of **eminent domain**—the inherent power to take private property for public use.[17] Territory may also be acquired from a foreign state based on the power to admit new States, the war powers, and the President's treaty-making power.[18] Under international law, any sovereign state may acquire unclaimed territory by discovery.

## Judicial Powers

As an important part of the principle of checks and balances,

---

[16]Article I, Section 8, Clause 17; Article IV, Section 3, Clause 2.

[17]The 5th Amendment restricts the government's use of the power with these words: "nor shall private property be taken for public use, without just compensation." Each of the State constitutions has a similar provision.

[18]Article IV, Section 3, Clause 1; Article I, Section 8, Clauses 11–16; Article II, Section 2, Clauses 1 and 2.

Congress has several judicial powers. These include the expressed power to create all of the federal courts in the federal judiciary below the Supreme Court and to provide for the organization and composition of the federal judiciary.[19] (You will read more about the federal judiciary in Chapter 18.)Congress also has the power to define federal crimes and provide for the punishment of those who violate federal law.[20]

## Section 2 Review

**1. Define:** direct tax, indirect tax, commerce power, legal tender, bankruptcy, copyright, patent, eminent domain
**2.** Where are the expressed powers of Congress set out in the Constitution?
**3.** (a) What is the purpose of the power to tax? (b) To borrow money?
**4.** For what reason does the Constitution grant the National Government the power to make coins and currency?
**5.** What kind of trade does the Constitution give Congress the power to regulate?
**6.** (a) From what two sources does Congress draw its powers in foreign affairs? (b) With whom does it share power in that field?
**7.** Identify the several war powers that the Constitution gives Congress.

### Critical Thinking

**8. Demonstrating Reasoned Judgment** (p. 19) Explain how Congress' exercise of the expressed powers has reflected the liberal constructionist viewpoint. Cite examples from the text.

---

[19]Article I, Section 8, Clause 9; Article III, Section 1. Also, recall, the President's power to appoint all federal judges is subject to Senate confirmation, Article II, Section 2, Clause 2.

[20]The Constitution mentions only four types of federal crimes: counterfeiting, piracies and felonies committed on the high seas, offenses against the law of nations (in Article I, Section 8, Clauses 6 and 10), and treason (in Article III, Section 3). But Congress has the implied power to define many other offenses and provide for their punishment.

# 3 The Implied Powers

**Find Out:**

■ For what reason did the Framers include the Necessary and Proper Clause in the Constitution?
■ For what reason is *McCulloch* v. *Maryland* one of the most important cases ever decided by the Supreme Court?
■ What impact does the Necessary and Proper Clause have today?

**Key Term:**
Necessary and Proper Clause

As you have just seen, the Constitution grants a number of important expressed powers to Congress. In addition to those powers, recall the Constitution also gives Congress a large number of other vitally important powers—powers that are not specifically mentioned in the document but that are covered in one of its clauses. These are the implied powers.

## The Necessary and Proper Clause

The **Necessary and Proper Clause** is a dramatically important part of the Constitution. It is from that provision that the implied powers flow. The Necessary and Proper Clause, set out in Article I, Section 8, Clause 18, gives to Congress the power

❝To make all laws which shall be necessary and proper for carrying into execution the foregoing powers, and all other powers vested by this Constitution in the Government of the United States, or in any department or officer thereof.❞

Much of the vitality and adaptability of the United States Constitution can be traced directly to this provision—and even more so to the ways both Congress and the Supreme Court have interpreted and applied it over the years. For good reason, the Necessary and Proper Clause has often been called the "Elastic Clause"—for it has been stretched so far and made to cover so much over the years.

## The Battle Over Implied Powers

The Constitution had barely come into force when the meaning of Clause 18 was called into question. In 1790 Alexander Hamilton, as Secretary of the Treasury, urged Congress to set up a national bank. That proposal touched off one of the most important disputes in all of American political history.

The opponents of Hamilton's plan insisted that nowhere did the Constitution give to Congress the power to establish such a bank. As you read in Section 1, these strict constructionists, led by Thomas Jefferson, believed that the new government had only (1) those powers expressly granted to it by the Constitution and (2) those powers absolutely necessary to carrying out those expressed powers.

Hamilton and other liberal constructionists looked to the Necessary and Proper Clause. They said that it gave Congress the power to do anything that was reasonably related to the exercise of the expressed powers. As for the national bank, they argued that it was necessary and proper to the execution of the taxing, borrowing, commerce, and currency powers. Strict constructionists rejected the "implied powers" argument. To do otherwise, they said, would be to give the new government almost unlimited authority and all but destroy the reserved powers of the States.[21]

Reason and practical necessity carried the day for Hamilton and his side. Congress established the Bank of the United States in 1791. Its charter—the act creating it—was to expire in 1811. Over those 20 years, the constitutionality of both the bank and the concept of implied powers went unchallenged in the courts.

*McCulloch* v. *Maryland*, 1819    In 1816 Congress created the Second Bank of the United States. Its charter came only after another hard-fought battle over the extent of the powers of Congress.

Having lost in Congress, opponents of the new bank now tried to persuade several State legislatures to cripple its operations. In 1818 Maryland placed a tax on all notes issued by any bank doing business in the State but not chartered by the State legislature. The tax was aimed directly at the Second Bank's branch in Baltimore. James McCulloch, the bank's cashier, purposely issued notes on which no tax had been paid. The State won a judgment against him in its own courts. Acting for McCulloch, the United States then appealed to the Supreme Court.

Maryland took the strict-construction position before the Supreme Court. It argued that the creation of the bank had been an unconstitutional act. In reply, the United States defended the concept of implied powers, and it also argued that no State could lawfully place a tax on any agency of the Federal Government.

In one of its most important and far-reaching decisions, the Court unanimously reversed the Maryland courts. It held that it was not necessary that the Constitution expressly empower Congress to create a bank. In short, the Court gave sweeping approval to the concept of implied powers.[22]

Chief Justice John Marshall wrote the Court's opinion in the case. For the Court, he said:

"We admit, as all must admit, that the powers of the government are limited, and that its limits are not to be transcended. But we think the sound construction of the Constitution must allow to the national legislature that discretion, with respect to the means by which the powers it confers are to be carried into execution, which will enable that body to perform the high duties assigned to it, in the manner most beneficial to the people. Let the end be legitimate, let it be within the scope of the Constitution, and all means which are appropriate, which are not prohibited, but consist with

---

[21]In 1801 a bill was introduced in Congress to incorporate a company to mine copper. As Vice President, Jefferson ridiculed that measure with this comment: "Congress is authorized to defend the nation. Ships are necessary for defense; copper is necessary for ships; mines necessary for copper; a company necessary to work the mines; and who can doubt this reasoning who has ever played at 'This Is the House that Jack Built'?" While Jefferson himself was President (1801–1809), he and his party were many times forced to reverse their earlier stand. Thus, for example, it was only on the basis of the implied powers doctrine that the Louisiana Purchase in 1803 and the embargo on foreign trade in 1807 could be justified.

[22]The Court also invalidated the Maryland tax. Because, said the Court, "the power to tax involves the power to destroy," no State may tax the United States or any of its agencies or functions.

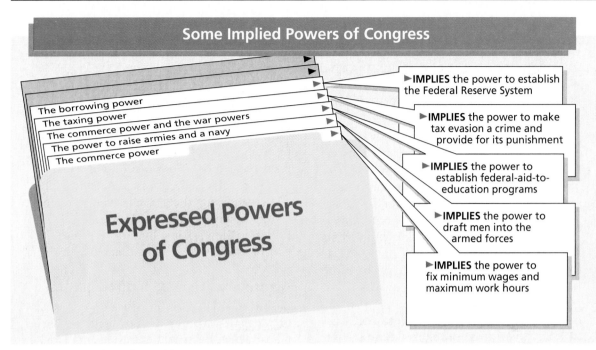

**Some Implied Powers of Congress**

The borrowing power
The taxing power
The commerce power and the war powers
The power to raise armies and a navy
The commerce power

**Expressed Powers of Congress**

►**IMPLIES** the power to establish the Federal Reserve System

►**IMPLIES** the power to make tax evasion a crime and provide for its punishment

►**IMPLIES** the power to establish federal-aid-to-education programs

►**IMPLIES** the power to draft men into the armed forces

►**IMPLIES** the power to fix minimum wages and maximum work hours

▲ **Interpreting Graphics**   The Necessary and Proper Clause gives Congress the expressed power to do those things "necessary and proper" to carry out its other expressed powers. It is from that provision that the implied powers flow.

the letter and spirit of the Constitution, are constitutional.**"**

This broad interpretation of the constitutional powers granted to Congress has become firmly fixed in America's constitutional system. Indeed, it is impossible to see how the United States could have developed as it has under the Constitution without it.

**The Doctrine in Practice**   There are an almost uncountable number of examples of the application of the doctrine of implied powers. Both the way Congress has looked at and used its powers and the supporting decisions of the Supreme Court have made Article I, Section 8, Clause 18 truly the Elastic Clause. Today the words "necessary and proper" really read "convenient and useful." This is most especially true when applied to the power to regulate interstate commerce and the power to tax.

Yet, there is a real limit to how far the doctrine of implied powers can be pushed. Neither Congress nor any other element of the Federal Government has the blanket authority to do anything that may seem desirable or that may

seem to be for the "general welfare" or in the "public interest." As the chart above shows, the basis for any implied power must always be found among the expressed powers. The implied powers are those that may be reasonably drawn from the expressed powers.

## Section 3 Review

**1. Define:** Necessary and Proper Clause
**2.** For what reason is the Necessary and Proper Clause of the Constitution also called the Elastic Clause?
**3.** What is the doctrine of implied powers?
**4.** What is the significance of *McCulloch* v. *Maryland*?
**5.** What is the fundamental limitation on the doctrine of implied powers?

**Critical Thinking**

**6. Predicting Consequences** (p. 19) What might have happened had Jefferson and his supporters won the early debate over implied powers?

★

# Can Discrimination Be Prohibited in Private Facilities?
## *Heart of Atlanta Motel, Inc.* v. *United States*, 1964

The Heart of Atlanta Motel was located two blocks from Peachtree Street, in downtown Atlanta, Georgia. The motel had 216 rooms available to transient guests and could be reached easily from two State highways and two interstate freeways. The motel advertised in various national advertising media, including magazines that circulated nationally. In fact, some 75 percent of its registered guests came from out of State.

Among several other things, the Civil Rights Act of 1964 prohibits discrimination in access to or service in hotels, motels, theaters, restaurants, or any other place of "public accommodation" on grounds of race, sex, color, religion, or national origin.

Before the passage of the Civil Rights Act of 1964, the owner of the Heart of Atlanta Motel had regularly refused to rent rooms to African Americans. In an effort to continue his policy of race-based discrimination, the motel owner filed suit in the federal district court in Atlanta, claiming that the public accommodations provisions of the 1964 law were unconstitutional. He lost in the district court and then took his case to the United States Supreme Court.

*Review the following evidence and arguments presented to the U.S. Supreme Court.*

## Arguments for Heart of Atlanta Motel

**1.** In passing the Civil Rights Act of 1964, Congress exceeded its power to regulate commerce under the Commerce Clause of the Constitution.
**2.** The act violates the 5th Amendment because the motel owner is deprived of the right to operate his business as he wishes, resulting in a deprivation of his liberty and property without due process, and a taking of his property without just compensation.
**3.** By requiring the motel owner to rent rooms to anyone against his will, Congress subjected him to involuntary servitude in violation of the 13th Amendment.

## Arguments for the United States

**1.** The unavailability to African Americans of adequate accommodations interferes significantly with interstate travel, and Congress, under the Commerce Clause, has the power to remove such obstructions.
**2.** The 5th Amendment does not forbid reasonable regulation. Such regulation does not constitute a "taking of liberty" within the meaning of that amendment.
**3.** It is entirely frivolous to claim that forcing a motel owner to obey the act against his will is in violation of the 13th Amendment.

## Getting Involved

**1. Identify** the constitutional grounds on which each side based its arguments in this case.
**2. Debate** the opposing viewpoints presented in this case.
**3. Predict** how you think the Supreme Court ruled in this case and why. Now turn to page 766 in the Supreme Court Glossary to read the decision. What types of businesses, if any, do you think the Federal Government should regulate to prevent race- or sex-based discrimination?

# 4 The Nonlegislative Powers

**Find Out:**

■ For what purposes does the Constitution give several nonlegislative powers to Congress?
■ How does Congress exercise those powers?

**Key Term:**

impeach

As you know, Congress is a legislative body. Its major function, therefore, is to make law. But the Constitution gives it a number of other chores, as well. This section explores those other chores, the nonlegislative powers and duties of Congress.

## Constitutional Amendments

You have read how Congress plays a key role in the process of constitutional amendment.[23] It may propose an amendment to the Constitution by a two-thirds vote in each house—and it has done so 33 times to this point.

Congress may also call a national convention to propose an amendment, but it may do so only if that step has been requested by at least two-thirds of the State legislatures. To this point, no such convention has been called.

In recent years several State legislatures have petitioned Congress in behalf of amendments that would do such things as require that Congress balance the federal budget each year, permit prayers in the public schools, and outlaw abortions. Today, the most vigorous efforts for a convention are being pushed by those who favor an amendment to limit the number of terms that any person might serve in either house of Congress.

## Electoral Duties

The Constitution gives certain electoral duties to Congress, but they are to be exercised only in very unusual circumstances.

▲ **The Power to Impeach**  On February 6, 1974, the House, troubled by the deepening Watergate Scandal, directed its Judiciary Committee "to investigate fully and completely whether sufficient grounds exist for the House . . . to impeach Richard M. Nixon, President of the United States. . . ."

The House of Representatives may be called on to elect a President. If no candidate receives a majority of the electoral votes for President, the House of Representatives, voting by States, must decide the issue. In that situation, it must choose from among the three highest contenders in the electoral college balloting. Each State has but one vote to cast, and a majority of the States is necessary for election.[24]

Similarly, the Senate must choose a Vice President when no candidate wins a majority of the electoral votes for that office. In that situation, the vote is not by States but by individual senators, with a majority of the full Senate necessary for election.[25]

The House of Representatives has had to choose a President only twice: Thomas Jefferson in 1801 and John Quincy Adams in 1825.

---

[24]12th Amendment.

[25] 12th Amendment. Note that these provisions make possible a situation in which the President would be of one party and the Vice President of another. The 12th Amendment also provides that the final, official count of the electoral votes cast for President and for Vice President every four years is to be made by the President of the Senate at a joint session of Congress.

---

[23]Article V; see Chapter 3, Section 2.

The Senate chose Richard M. Johnson as Vice President in 1837.

Remember, too, that the 25th Amendment provides for the filling of a vacancy in the vice presidency. When one occurs, the President nominates a successor, subject to a majority vote in both houses of Congress. That process has been used twice: Gerald Ford was confirmed as Vice President in 1973 and Nelson Rockefeller in 1974.

## Impeachment

The Constitution provides that the President, Vice President, and all civil officers of the United States may "be removed from office on impeachment for, and conviction of, treason, bribery, or other high crimes and misdemeanors."[26] The House has the sole power to **impeach**—bring charges—and the Senate the sole power to judge—sit as a court—in impeachment cases.[27]

The House may impeach by a majority vote. A two-thirds vote of the senators present is needed for conviction. The chief justice must preside over the Senate when a President is tried. The penalty for conviction is removal from office. The Senate may add a prohibition against the person ever holding federal office again. In addition, a person who has been impeached and convicted can also be indicted, tried, convicted, and punished in the regular courts.[28]

---

[26]Article II, Section 4. Military officers are not "civil officers" and may be removed by court-martial. Nor are members of Congress. When the House impeached Senator William Blount of Tennessee in 1798, the Senate refused to try the case on grounds that it had the power to expel one of its own members if it chose to do so. Blount was then expelled. The precedent set in that instance has been followed ever since.

[27]Article I, Section 2, Clause 5; Section 3, Clause 6.

[28]Article I, Section 3, Clause 6 and Clause 7.

[29]All seven persons impeached by the House and then convicted by the Senate were federal judges. Four other federal judges were impeached by the House but later acquitted by the Senate; and two federal judges impeached by the House resigned before the Senate could act in their cases; see Chapter 18, Section 1.

The only other federal officer ever impeached was William W. Bellknap, President Grant's Secretary of War. Bellknap had been accused of accepting bribes and, although he had resigned from office, was impeached by the House in 1876; he was then tried by the Senate and found not guilty.

To date, the House of Representatives has impeached only 16 persons. Of that number, the Senate has convicted seven.[29] Perhaps the most noteworthy impeachment occurred in 1868, when the House impeached President Andrew Johnson. The Senate, however, failed by a single vote to convict him.

A few officeholders have resigned in the face of certain impeachment—most notably Richard Nixon, who resigned the presidency in 1974 after the Watergate scandal. Although the House Judiciary Committee recommended three articles of impeachment against him, the House did not press the matter further after his resignation.

## Executive Powers

The Constitution gives two "executive powers" to the Senate. One of those powers has to do with appointments and the other with treaties made by the President.[30]

All major appointments made by the President must be confirmed by the Senate by majority vote. Each nomination is referred to the appropriate standing committee of the Senate. That committee may then hold hearings to decide whether or not to make a favorable recommendation to full Senate for that appointment. When that committee's recommendation is brought to the floor of the Senate, it may be, but seldom is, considered in executive (secret) session.

The appointment of a cabinet officer or of some other top member of the President's "official family" is rarely turned down by the Senate.[31] But the unwritten rule of "senatorial courtesy" comes into play with the President's appointment of federal officers who serve in the various States—for example, U.S. attorneys and federal marshals. The Senate will turn down such a presidential appointment if it is opposed by a senator of the President's party from the State involved.

The President makes treaties "by and with the advice and consent of the Senate, . . . provided two-thirds of the senators present concur."[32] For a time after the adoption of the Constitution, the President asked the advice of the Senate when a treaty was being prepared. Now the President most often consults the members of the Senate Foreign Relations Committee and other influential senators of both parties.

The Senate may accept or reject a treaty as it stands, or it may offer amendments, reservations, or understandings to it. Treaties are sometimes considered in executive session. Because the House has a hold on the public purse strings, influential members of that body are often consulted in the treaty-making process, too.

## Investigatory Power

Congress has the power to investigate any matter that falls within the scope of its legislative powers. Congress exercises this authority through its standing committees, and subcommittees, and by its special committees; see Chapter 12, Section 2. Congress may choose to conduct investigations for several reasons. Most often, those inquiries are held to (1) gather information useful to Congress in the making of some legislation; (2) oversee the operations of various executive branch agencies; (3) focus public attention on a particular subject; (4) expose the questionable activities of public officials or private persons; and/or (5) promote the particular interests of some members of Congress. Congressional exercise of its investigatory powers has resulted

▲ **Admit the Bearer** Those who wished to attend the history-making impeachment trial of President Andrew Johnson in 1868 had to obtain a ticket to the proceedings and show it at the door in order to be admitted.

in some of the more dramatic moments in American political history.

---

[30]Article II, Section 2, Clause 2.

[31]All told, only 12 of the now more than 600 cabinet appointments have been rejected by the Senate. The first was Roger B. Taney, Andrew Jackson's choice for secretary of the treasury. Two years later President Jackson named Taney to succeed John Marshall as chief justice. The Senate confirmed him, and he served until his death in 1864. The most recent rejection came in 1989 when the Senate refused to approve President Bush's nomination of John Tower as secretary of defense. On the other rejections, see Chapter 14, Section 5.

[32]The Senate's observance of this unwritten rule has a significant impact on the President's exercise of the power of appointment; in effect, some senators virtually dictate certain presidential appointments. The practice is often criticized; those who defend it often argue that a senator is more likely to be better informed about affairs in his/her State than is the President.

[33]Article II, Section 2, Clause 2. It is often said that the Senate "ratifies" a treaty. It does not. The Senate may give or withhold its "advice and consent" to a treaty made by the President. Once the Senate has consented to a treaty, the President then ratifies it by exchanging the "instruments of ratification" with the other party or parties to the agreement.

## Section 4 Review

1. **Define:** impeach
2. What roles does Congress play in the constitutional amendment process?
3. Who makes the choice if the electoral college fails to elect a President?
4. How is a vice-presidential vacancy now filled?
5. (a) Which chamber of Congress has the power to impeach? (b) The power to try those who are impeached?
6. What two "executive powers" are held by the Senate?

### Critical Thinking

7. **Testing Conclusions** (p. 19) Cite examples of the powers with which Congress can check the other two branches of government.

★

# Recognizing Cause and Effect

Recognizing cause and effect means to examine how one event or idea causes other events or ideas to occur. Understanding cause and effect is a key skill in problem solving. If you can see how events or ideas relate to and affect each other, you can see where problems begin. Then, you can begin to formulate solutions. Follow the steps below to practice recognizing cause and effect.

**1. Identify the two parts of a cause-effect relationship.**   A cause is an event or an action that brings about an effect. Writers sometimes indicate a cause-effect relationship by using words such as *so*, *thus*, *because*, and *as a result*. Read statements A through C below and answer the following questions: (a) Which statements contain both a cause and an effect? (b) Which is the cause and which is the effect in each cause-effect statement? (c) What words, if any, indicate the presence of a cause-effect statement?

**2. Remember that an event can have more than one cause and more than one effect.**   Several causes can combine to create one event. In the same way, a single cause can have several effects. Read paragraph D below. (a) Find an example of an effect that has more than one cause. (b) Find an example of a cause that has more than one effect.

**3. Understand that an event can be both a cause and an effect.**   A cause can lead to an effect, which in turn can become the cause of another event. In this way, causes and effects can form a chain of related events. You can diagram such a chain as follows:

- Government borrows to pay for current expenditures. This causes:

- interest rates to rise. This causes:

- fewer people and businesses to borrow money. This causes:

- a drop in purchasing and in the growth of businesses. This causes:

- an economic slump.

Read paragraph D below and draw a diagram of the chain of events formed by causes and effects as shown in the example.

## Statements

**A**  Because the federal budget process was not working well, the Congress, with White House support, voted to approve the Balanced Budget and Emergency Reduction Act of 1985.

**B**  For years, Congress was unable to cure the problem of deficit spending. As a result, Senators Gramm, Rudman, and Hollings opted for what many considered to be radical measures.

**C**  The plan set annual limits on the budget deficit. These limits require that the deficit be cut to zero by 1993.

**D**  Ongoing budget problems and the inability of Congress to come up with any better solutions led Congress to adopt the Gramm-Rudman-Hollings measure. Since its passage many people have criticized the measure. In the long run, the Gramm-Rudman-Hollings approach to budgeting appears to limit Congress's ability to perform some of its critical policy clarification function. It also forces Congress to yield some of its authority to the executive in hopes of resolving our deficit problem. In the end, Congress and the White House will doubtless have to make further cuts in spending as well as raise new revenues.

# Chapter-in-Brief

Scan all headings, photographs, charts, and other visuals in the chapter before reading the section summaries below.

## Section 1 The Scope of Congressional Powers (pp. 259–261)
The Constitution places strict limits on what Congress can and cannot do. However, the Constitution does grant to Congress a number of powers.

The extent of the powers of Congress has long been a subject of debate. Early in the nation's history, this debate was fought between strict constructionists, led by Thomas Jefferson, and liberal constructionists, led by Alexander Hamilton. The liberal constructionists won the early battles. In addition, the viewpoint they represented has been generally supported by Congress, Presidents, the courts, and the American people throughout American history.

## Section 2 The Expressed Powers (pp. 261–271)
The Constitution grants to Congress a large number of specific powers. Most of these expressed powers appear in Article I, Section 8.

The expressed powers are brief and broad, and their full meanings have evolved over time. Congress and the courts have addressed hundreds of questions about the the expressed powers. They have tended to interpret them broadly, thus expanding the powers of Congress.

The Constitution grants Congress the power to tax, to regulate commerce, to coin and borrow money, and to create laws on bankruptcy. The ability of Congress to regulate commerce and to tax have been key to the growth of the nation.

Congress also has extensive powers in the fields of foreign relations and defense.

Other powers of Congress include the power to naturalize citizens, to create a postal system, to govern copyrights and patents, and to set standards for weights and measures. Congress may add and administer new territories. Congress also has certain judicial responsibilities, including the power to establish courts.

## Section 3 The Implied Powers (pp. 271–273)
Besides those powers specifically mentioned in the Constitution, Congress has the power to make laws "necessary and proper" to the execution of any of its expressed powers. The Necessary and Proper Clause is the basis for the implied powers. The extent of the implied powers has long been debated.

A key moment in this debate occurred in 1819, when the Supreme Court decided *McCulloch* v. *Maryland*. In that case, the Court embraced a broad view of implied powers.

## Section 4 The Nonlegislative Powers (pp. 275–277)
Congress has many nonlegislative functions. These include its key role in the process of amending the Constitution. Also, in certain unusual circumstances, the House may be called upon to select a President and the Senate to choose a Vice President.

The House has the power to impeach federal officers, and the Senate to try them. Also, the Senate has the power to confirm or reject major appointments and treaties made by the President. Each House also has a broad power of investigation.

# Chapter Review

## Vocabulary and Key Terms

strict constructionist (p. 260)
liberal constructionist (p. 260)
direct tax (p. 262)
indirect tax (p. 263)
commerce power (p. 264)

legal tender (p. 266)
bankruptcy (p. 267)
copyright (p. 268)
patent (p. 269)

eminent domain (p. 270)
Necessary and Proper
  Clause (p. 271)
impeach (p. 276)

**Matching:** *Review the key terms in the list above. If you are not sure of a term's meaning, look up the term and review its definition. Choose a term from the list above that best matches each description.*

1. the power of a government to take private property for public use
2. a part of the Constitution from which the implied powers flow
3. what a creditor must accept in return for a debt
4. the expressed power by which Congress regulates interstate and foreign trade
5. to formally charge a public official for the purpose of removing him or her from office

**True or False:** *Determine whether each statement is true or false. If it is true, write "true." If it is false, change the underlined word or words to make the statement true.*

1. <u>Bankruptcy</u> is a legal proceeding in which a person who cannot pay his or her debts has his or her assets distributed among the creditors.
2. The <u>commerce power</u> is sometimes referred to as the "Elastic Clause."
3. An example of an <u>indirect tax</u> is the tax on cigarettes, which is passed on to the consumer.
4. An author of a new book would seek a <u>patent</u> on his or her work.

5. A <u>strict constructionist</u> would have approved of the Supreme Court's decision in *McCulloch v. Maryland*.

**Word Relationships:** *Distinguish between the words in each pair.*

1. strict constructionist/liberal constructionist
2. direct tax/indirect tax
3. copyright/patent

## Main Ideas

### Section 1 (pp. 259–261)

1. Describe the several ways in which the Constitution and the American system of government limit the powers of Congress.
2. Describe the basic features of the debate over the proper extent of the Federal Government's power in the early years of the United States.
3. What forces have led to the growth in national power since the first days of the National Government?

### Section 2 (pp. 261–271)

4. What is the significance of the fact that the expressed powers are brief?
5. How did the power to tax and the commerce power address weaknesses in the Articles of Confederation?
6. With whom does Congress share its powers in the areas of foreign policy and war?

## Section 3 (pp. 271–273)

7. What is the relationship between the Necessary and Proper Clause and the implied powers?

8. How has the Necessary and Proper Clause contributed to the vitality of the Constitution over the course of American history?

9. What role did *McCulloch* v. *Maryland* play in the development of the concept of implied powers?

## Section 4 (pp. 275–277)

10. What are the functions that the Constitution gives Congress beyond its basic lawmaking function?

11. How do certain of the nonlegislative powers help preserve the system of checks and balances?

12. In what sense does the practice of "senatorial courtesy" dictate certain presidential appointments?

## Critical Thinking

1. **Demonstrating Reasoned Judgment** (p. 19) The Supreme Court found in *McCulloch* v. *Maryland* that "the power to tax involves the power to destroy." How does this statement explain the constitutional limit on the power of Congress to tax?

2. **Formulating Questions** (p. 19) The American people have long debated the extent of the Necessary and Proper Clause. Write a list of questions that could be applied to any proposed act of Congress to judge whether or not it is necessary and proper.

3. **Recognizing Cause and Effect** (p. 19) Review what you have read in this chapter about the debate over the extent of the powers granted to Congress. How might the short length of the Constitution have influenced the debate over a strict vs. a liberal construction of the Constitution?

## Getting Involved

1. **Writing Your Opinion** The year is 1790. Alexander Hamilton has just made his proposal that Congress set up a national bank. Write a speech in which you argue in favor of either a strict or a liberal interpretation of the Constitution. Before you write, review the facts of the debate between the strict and liberal constructionists. Identify three points that you will use to make your argument. Begin the speech by summarizing the overall debate, explaining why you think it should be of concern to the American people. Then spell out your arguments, devoting one paragraph to each idea. Conclude with a prediction of what will happen if the nation makes the "wrong" decision. Revise your speech to make sure that each paragraph is stated as persuasively as possible. Check for errors, and then make a final draft.

2. **Cooperative Activity** Work as a class to create an illustrated diagram of the powers of Congress. The diagram should clearly show the powers and explain and illustrate their meaning. Begin by dividing the class into three groups. One group should work together to list and define the powers of Congress. Another group should decide on and sketch a design for the diagram. The design should clearly show the organization of the powers of Congress and include suggested illustrations for each of the powers. The third group will actually create the diagram. Some students can draw the illustrations while others construct and letter the diagram itself.

3. **Creating a Political Cartoon** Design and draw a political cartoon that illustrates the concept of the Elastic Clause. Recall that you can use both words and pictures in your cartoon.

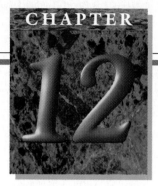

# Congress in Action

## Chapter Preview

Figures run back and forth in the landscape beneath the streets. Subway cars emerge from tunnels to swallow them up, only to deposit them at another location where they start to run again. Who are these people in a perpetual state of motion? They are the senators and representatives who use the maze of subway tunnels beneath Capitol Hill to negotiate the distances between their offices and the House or Senate.

Six office buildings sit adjacent to the Capitol building. In these offices and inside the Capitol building is where most of the complicated legislative work of the country takes place. What happens in this setting? How does Congress perform its lawmaking functions? This chapter answers these questions—by describing Congress in action.

### Before you read this chapter:

- **Describe** any recent action of a congressional committee with which you are familiar.
- **Predict** the percentage of bills introduced in Congress that actually become law.

### As you read, focus on the main objective for each section. Understand:

1. The organizational structure of both houses of Congress.
2. The committee system and the types of committees in both houses of Congress.
3. The legislative process in the House of Representatives.
4. The handling of bills in the Senate and the final stages in the legislative process.

▲ **Grass Roots Campaigning** Representative Richard A. Gephardt (D., Missouri) discusses issues with voters at an informal gathering in the home of a constituent.

# 1 Congress Organizes

### Find Out:

- How do the House and Senate begin new terms?
- What are the contrasts between the roles of the Speaker of the House and the president of the Senate?
- Who are the floor leaders in Congress and where does their power come from?
- How are committee chairmen chosen and what is their role in the legislative process?

### Key Terms:

Speaker of the House, president of the Senate, president *pro tempore*, floor leaders, whip, party caucus, committee chairman, seniority rule

What comes to mind when you hear the word *Congress*? The Capitol? Some particular bill? Those senators and representatives you often see on the evening news. Of course, you know that Congress is much more than that—that it is in fact a very complex enterprise, and much larger than most people realize. Some 37,000 men and women work for the legislative branch; and Congress has appropriated more than $2.4 billion to finance its operations this year.[1]

In this section, you will see how complex Congress is and how it has organized itself to conduct its business.

## Congress Convenes

Congress convenes, begins a new term, every two years—on January 3 of every odd-numbered year, following the general elections in November.

---

[1]More than 19,000 of the men and women who work in the legislative branch have jobs in the House or Senate—in members' offices, as committee staff, or in some part of the administrative organization in one or the other of the two houses. The other 18,000 or so work in the various agencies Congress has over time established within the legislative branch—especially, the Library of Congress, the Government Printing Office, the Congressional Budget Office, and the General Accounting Office.

**Opening Day in the House** When the 435 men and women who have been elected to the House come together at the Capitol to begin a new term, they are, in effect, just so many representatives-elect. Because all 435 of its seats are filled by people elected every two years, the House technically has no sworn members, no rules, and no organization until its opening-day ceremonies are held.

The clerk of the House in the preceding term presides, chairs, at the beginning of the first day's session.[2] The clerk calls the chamber to order and checks the roll of representatives-elect. Those members-to-be then choose a Speaker as their permanent presiding officer. By custom, the Speaker is a long-standing member of the majority party, and election on the floor is only a formality. The majority party's caucus—the conference of party members in the House—has settled the matter beforehand.

The Speaker then takes the oath of office. It is administered by the Dean of the House, the member-elect with the longest record of service in the House of Representatives.[3] With that accomplished, the Speaker swears in the rest of the members as a body. The Democrats take their seats to the right of the center aisle; the Republicans, to the left.

Next, the House elects its clerk, sergeant at arms, doorkeeper, postmaster, and chaplain. These elections are also a formality. The majority party's caucus has already decided who these nonmember officers will be.

Then, the House adopts the rules that will govern its proceedings through the term. The rules of the House have been developing for over 200 years now, and they are contained in a volume of about 400 pages. They are readopted, most often with little or no change, at the beginning of each term.

Finally, members of the 22 permanent committees of the House are appointed by a floor vote, and with that the House is organized.

**Opening Day in the Senate** The Senate is a continuous body. It has been organized without interruption since its first session in 1789. Recall that only one-third of the seats are up for election every two years. From one term to the next, two-thirds of the Senate's membership is carried over. As a result, the Senate does not face large organizational problems at the beginning of a term. Its first-day session is nearly always short and routine, even when the elections have brought a change in the party having the majority of seats. Newly elected and reelected members must be sworn in, vacancies in Senate organization and on committees must be filled, and a few other details attended to.

**The President's State of the Union Message** When the Senate is notified that the House is organized, a joint committee of the two is appointed and instructed

> ❝ to wait upon the President of the United States and inform him that a quorum of each House is assembled and that the Congress is ready to receive any communication he may be pleased to make. ❞

Within a few weeks, the President delivers the annual State of the Union message to a joint session of Congress. The President's speech is a major political event based on this constitutional command:

> ❝ He shall from time to time give to the Congress information of the state of the Union, and recommend to their consideration such measures as he shall judge necessary and expedient . . . ❞ [4]

The members of both houses, together with the members of the cabinet, the justices of the Supreme Court, the foreign diplomatic corps, and other dignitaries assemble in the House chamber to listen.

In his address, the President reports on the state of the nation as he sees it, in both domestic and foreign policy terms. The message is televised live, and it is followed very closely, both here and abroad. In it, the President lays out the broad shape of the policies his administration will follow and the course he has charted

---

[2]The clerk is a nonmember officer, chosen by the House, who serves as that body's chief administrative officer.

[3]Today, Sidney R. Yates (D., Illinois), who was first elected to the House on November 2, 1948.

[4]Article II, Section 3.

for the nation. He also may include specific legislative recommendations.

With the conclusion of the President's speech, the joint session is adjourned, and each house turns to the legislative business before it.

## The Presiding Officers

The Constitution provides for the presiding officers of each house. The Speaker of the House is by far the most important and influential member of the House of Representatives. The Constitution commands that the post be filled by a vote of the House at the beginning of each of its two-year terms. In fact, the Speaker is the leader of the majority party in the House and is chosen by the members of that party.

Although neither the Constitution nor its own rules require it, the House has always chosen the Speaker from among its own members. Usually, the Speaker is a longtime member who has risen in stature and influence through years of service.

Today, Representative Newt Gingrich (R., Georgia) is the Speaker of the House. He was first elected to Congress in 1978 and became Speaker in 1995.[5]

Basically, the great power held by the Speaker arises from this fact: The **Speaker of the House** is both the elected presiding officer of the House *and* the acknowledged leader of its majority party. Speakers are expected to preside in a fair and judicious manner. They are also expected to aid the fortunes of their own parties and their legislative goals.

Nearly all the Speaker's specific powers revolve around two duties: to preside and to keep order. The Speaker presides over all sessions of the House, or appoints a temporary presiding officer. No member may speak until recognized by the Speaker. The Speaker interprets and applies the rules, refers bills to the

[5]Article I, Section 2, Clause 5. Speaker Gingrich is the 50th person to hold the post, and the first Republican to do so in more than forty years. He succeeded Thomas S. Foley (D., Washington). The first Speaker, elected at the first session in 1789, was Frederick A. C. Muhlenburg, a Federalist from Pennsylvania. Sam Rayburn (D., Tex.) held the office for a record 17 years, 62 days in the period from 1940 to 1961.

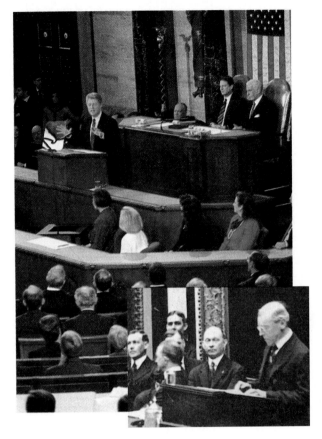

▲ **Presidential Tradition Since 1913**   Every President since Woodrow Wilson (inset) has delivered the State of the Union message to Congress in person. President Clinton delivers his first message in 1993.

standing committees, rules on points of order (questions of procedure raised by members), puts questions to a vote, and decides the outcome of most of the votes taken. The Speaker also names the members of all select and conference committees and signs all bills and resolutions passed by the House.

As a member, the Speaker may debate and vote on any matter before the House. But if he chooses to do so, he must appoint a temporary presiding officer (the Speaker *pro tempore*), and that member then occupies the Speaker's chair. The Speaker does not often vote, and the House rules say that he *must* vote only to break a tie. Notice then, because a tie vote defeats a question, the Speaker can vote to cause a tie and so defeat a proposal.

**An Influential Post**    Speaker of the House Newt Gingrich and his Republican colleagues now control the lower house. The Democrats held a majority of the seats in the house for forty years, 1955–1995.

The Speaker of the House follows the Vice President in the line of succession to the presidency—a considerable testimony to the power and importance of the office.

The **president of the Senate**, the presiding officer in that body, is not a member of the Senate. Instead, the Constitution assigns the office to the Vice President of the United States.[6] Largely for this reason, the president of the Senate occupies a much less powerful chair than the Speaker's in the House. The Vice President does not become the Senate's presiding officer as a direct result of long service in that body. In fact, the president of the Senate is sometimes not even a member of the party with a majority of seats in the upper house.

The president of the Senate does have the usual powers of a presiding officer—to recognize members, put questions to a vote, and so on. However, the Vice President cannot take the floor to speak or debate and may vote *only* to break a tie.

Any influence a Vice President may have in the Senate is largely the result of personal abilities and relationships. Several of the more recent Vice Presidents came to that office from the Senate: Harry Truman, Alben Barkley, Richard Nixon, Lyndon Johnson, Hubert Humphrey, Walter Mondale, Dan Quayle, and now Al Gore. Each of them was able to build at least some power into the position out of that earlier experience.

The Senate does have another presiding officer, the **president *pro tempore***, who serves in the Vice President's absence. The president *pro tem* is elected by the Senate itself and is always a leading member of the majority party. Senator Strom Thurmond (R., South Carolina) became the Senate's president *pro tem* in 1995. Other members of the Senate also preside over the chamber, on a temporary basis. Newly elected senators are regularly given this honor early in their terms.

The president *pro tem* is an important office. But as you will read, it is not the most powerful post to which senators can rise.

## Floor Leaders and Other Party Officers

Congress is a political body. This is so for two leading reasons: (1) because Congress is the nation's central policy-making body and, (2) because of its partisan makeup. Reflecting its political complexion, both houses are organized along party lines. This organization creates some powerful positions.

**The Floor Leaders**    Next to the Speaker, the most important officers in Congress are the majority and minority floor leaders in the House and Senate. They do not hold official positions in either chamber. Rather, they are party officers, picked for their posts by their party colleagues.

The **floor leaders** are legislative strategists. They try to carry out the decisions of their parties' caucuses and steer floor action to their

---

[6]Article I, Section 3, Clause 4.

parties' benefit. All of that calls for political skills of a high order.

The majority leader's post is the more powerful in each house, for the obvious reason that the majority party has more seats—that is, more votes—than the other party has. Together with the presiding officer and the minority leader, the majority leader plans the order of business on the floor.

The two floor leaders in each house are assisted by party whips—a majority whip and a minority whip. They are, in effect, assistant floor leaders. Each of them is chosen by the party caucus, almost always on the floor leader's recommendation. There are a number of assistant whips in the House, and both floor leaders in each house have a paid staff.

The job of a **whip** is to check with party members and advise the floor leader of the number of votes that can be counted on in any particular matter. Whips attempt to see that members of their parties are present for important votes and that they vote with the party leadership. If a member must be absent for some reason, the whip sees that that member is paired with a member of the other party who will also be absent or who agrees not to vote on certain measures. In this way, one nonvote cancels out another.

**The Party Caucus** The **party caucus** is a closed meeting of the members of each party in each house. It meets just before Congress convenes in January and occasionally during a session. In recent years the Republicans have called their caucus in each house the party conference, and the Democrats now use this term in the Senate, too.

The caucus deals mostly with matters of party organization, such as the selection of the party's floor leaders and questions of committee membership. It sometimes takes stands on

**Leadership in 104th Congress, 1995–1997**

**HOUSE**

**Speaker of the House**
Newt Gingrich
(R., Georgia)
Year Elected: 1978

**Majority Floor Leader**
Dick Armey
(R., Texas)
Year Elected: 1984

**Minority Floor Leader**
Dick Gephardt
(D., Missouri)
Year Elected: 1976

**Majority Whip**
Tom DeLay
(R., Texas)
Year Elected: 1984

**Minority Whip**
David Bonior
(D., Michigan)
Year Elected: 1976

**KEY**
Official Presiding Officers
Party Officers

**SENATE**

**President of the Senate**
Albert Gore
(D., Tennessee)
Year Elected: N/A

**President Pro Tempore**
Strom Thurmond
(R., South Carolina)
Year Elected: 1954

**Majority Floor Leader**
Bob Dole
(R., Kansas)
Year Elected: 1968

**Majority Whip**
Trent Lott
(R., Mississippi)
Year Elected: 1988

**Minority Floor Leader**
Tom Daschle
(D., North Dakota)
Year Elected: 1986

**Minority Whip**
Wendell Ford
(D., Kentucky)
Year Elected: 1974

▲ **Interpreting Charts** The chart above shows the organization of congressional leadership and the people currently holding those positions. How can you tell which party holds power in Congress?

# Composition of Congress

## PARTY STRENGTH (at beginning of term)

| House of Representatives—435 Members | | | Senate—100 Members | |
|---|---|---|---|---|
| Democrats | Republicans | | Democrats | Republicans |
| 239 | 192 | †1973–1975* | 56 | 42 |
| 291 | 144 | 1975–1977** | 60 | 37 |
| 292 | 143 | 1977–1979*** | 61 | 38 |
| 276 | 157 | 1979–1981*** | 58 | 41 |
| 243 | 192 | 1981–1983*** | 46 | 53 |
| 269 | 165 | 1983–1985 | 46 | 54 |
| 252 | 182 | 1985–1987 | 47 | 53 |
| 258 | 177 | 1987–1989 | 55 | 45 |
| 259 | 174 | 1989–1991 | 55 | 45 |
| 267 | 167†† | 1991–1993 | 56 | 44 |
| 259 | 175†† | 1993–1995 | 57 | 43 |
| 204 | 230†† | 1995–1997 | 47 | 53 |

**Note: Numbers do not always add to 435 (or 100) due to vacancies.**

*One Independent (Democrat), one Conservative (Republican)

**One Independent (Democrat), one Conservative (Republican), and one seat undecided (New Hampshire)

***One Independent (Democrat)

†One Independent-Democrat

††One Independent

Legend:
- Democrats
- Republicans
- Other

## REPRESENTATION BY STATE, 104th Congress

| State | House (Dem) | House (Rep) | Senate (Dem) | Senate (Rep) |
|---|---|---|---|---|
| Alabama | 4 | 3 | 1 | 1 |
| Alaska | – | 1 | – | 2 |
| Arizona | 1 | 5 | – | 2 |
| Arkansas | 2 | 2 | 2 | – |
| California | 28 | 24 | 2 | – |
| Colorado | 2 | 4 | 1 | 1 |
| Connecticut | 3 | 3 | 2 | – |
| Delaware | – | 1 | 1 | 1 |
| Florida | 8 | 15 | 1 | 1 |
| Georgia | 4 | 7 | 1 | 1 |
| Hawaii | 2 | – | 2 | – |
| Idaho | – | 2 | – | 2 |
| Illinois | 10 | 10 | 2 | – |
| Indiana | 4 | 6 | – | 2 |
| Iowa | – | 5 | 1 | 1 |
| Kansas | – | 4 | – | 2 |
| Kentucky | 1 | 5 | 1 | 1 |
| Louisiana | 4 | 3 | 2 | – |
| Maine | 1 | 1 | – | 2 |
| Maryland | 4 | 4 | 2 | – |
| Massachusetts | 8 | 2 | 2 | – |
| Michigan | 9 | 7 | 1 | 1 |
| Minnesota | 6 | 2 | 1 | 1 |
| Mississippi | 4 | 1 | – | 2 |
| Missouri | 6 | 3 | – | 2 |
| Montana | 1 | – | 1 | 1 |
| Nebraska | – | 3 | 2 | – |
| Nevada | – | 2 | 2 | – |
| New Hampshire | – | 2 | – | 2 |
| New Jersey | 5 | 8 | 2 | – |
| New Mexico | 1 | 2 | 1 | 1 |
| New York | 17 | 14 | 1 | 1 |
| North Carolina | 4 | 8 | – | 2 |
| North Dakota | 1 | – | 2 | – |
| Ohio | 6 | 13 | 1 | 1 |
| Oklahoma | 1 | 5 | – | 2 |
| Oregon | 3 | 2 | – | 2 |
| Pennsylvania | 11 | 10 | – | 2 |
| Rhode Island | 2 | – | 1 | 1 |
| South Carolina | 2 | 4 | 1 | 1 |
| South Dakota | 1 | – | 1 | 1 |
| Tennessee | 4 | 5 | – | 2 |
| Texas | 19 | 11 | 1 | 1 |
| Utah | 1 | 2 | – | 2 |
| Vermont | * | | 1 | 1 |
| Virginia | 6 | 5 | 1 | 1 |
| Washington | 2 | 7 | 1 | 1 |
| West Virginia | 3 | – | 2 | – |
| Wisconsin | 3 | 6 | 2 | – |
| Wyoming | – | 1 | – | 2 |

Legend:
- Democrats
- Republicans
- * Independent

▲ **Interpreting Charts** These charts indicate party strength in Congress over recent years. Have the Republicans controlled either house in recent years?

particular bills, but neither party tries to force its members to follow its caucus decisions, nor can it.[7]

The policy committee, composed of the party's top leadership, acts as an executive committee for the caucus.

In strict fact, that body is known as the policy committee in each party's structure in the Senate and in the Republicans' organization in the House. However, it is called the policy and steering committee by the Democrats in the lower chamber.

## Committee Chairmen

The bulk of the work of Congress, especially in the House, is really done in committee. Thus, each **committee chairman**[8]—those members who head the standing committees in each chamber—also hold strategic posts. The chairman of each of these permanent committees is chosen from the majority party by the majority party caucus. Committee chairmen decide when their committees will meet, which bills they will take up, whether they will hold public hearings, and what witnesses the committee should call. When a committee's bill has been reported to the floor, the chairman usually manages the debate and tries to steer it to final passage.

You will read more about committees, and return to the role of their chairmen, in a moment. But first, you will read about the seniority rule.

---

[7]There are a number of informal groupings of members of Congress who meet to discuss matters of mutual interest. Some are partisan, others bipartisan, and several use the word *caucus* in their titles. These groups include the Congressional Black Caucus, the Democratic Study Group, the House Republican Study Committee, the Northeast-Midwest Congressional Coalition, the Pro-Life Caucus, and the Congressional Hispanic Caucus.

[8]The title *chairman*, rather than *chairperson*, is used here because this is the form used in both houses of Congress, both officially and informally. Only six women have ever chaired a standing committee, and three of them do so today: Senator Nancy Landon Kassebaum (R., Kansas), the only woman ever to chair a Senate committee, and Representatives Nancy Johnson (R., Connecticut) and Jan Meyers (R., Kansas); see pages 292 and 293.

## Seniority Rule

The seniority rule is, in fact, an unwritten custom. It dates from the late 1800s, and is still closely followed in both houses today. The **seniority rule** provides that the most important posts, in both the formal and the party organization in each chamber, will be held by its ranking members—those party members with the longest records of service in Congress.

The rule is applied most strictly to the choice of committee chairmen. The head of each committee is almost always that majority party member who has served the longest time on that committee.

## Criticism of Seniority Rule

Critics of the rule are many, and they do make a strong case. They insist that the seniority system ignores ability and discourages younger members. Critics

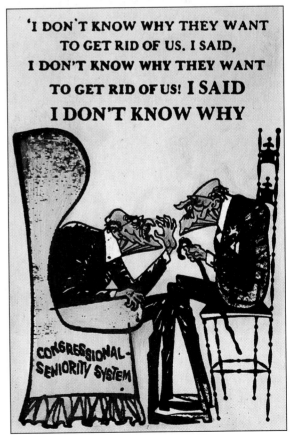

'I DON'T KNOW WHY THEY WANT TO GET RID OF US. I SAID, I DON'T KNOW WHY THEY WANT TO GET RID OF US! I SAID I DON'T KNOW WHY

CONGRESSIONAL SENIORITY SYSTEM

▲ **Interpreting Political Cartoons**
How is the seniority rule, subject to much criticism because it ignores ability, viewed by this cartoonist?

also note that the rule means that a committee head often comes from a "safe" constituency—a State or district in which, election after election, one party regularly wins. With no play of fresh and conflicting forces in those places, critics claim, the chairman of a committee is often out of touch with current public opinion.

Defenders of the seniority rule argue that it ensures that a powerful and experienced member will head each committee, that the rule is easy to apply, and that it very nearly eliminates the possibility of fights within the party.

Opponents of the rule have gained some ground in recent years. Thus, the House Republican Conference (caucus) now picks several GOP members of House committees by secret ballot. House Democrats use secret ballots to choose a committee chairman whenever 20 percent of their caucus requests that procedure. The House Democrats did in fact oust three long-tenured committee chairmen in 1975, one in 1985, two in 1991, and another in 1993.

Whatever the arguments against the rule, there is little chance that it will be eliminated. Those members with the real power to abolish the seniority rule are the ones who benefit most from it.

## Section 1 Review

**1. Define:** Speaker of the House, president *pro tempore*, party caucus
**2.** How does opening day in the House contrast with opening day in the Senate?
**3.** (a) Who presides over the House? (b) How is that officer chosen?
**4.** (a) What is the function of the president of the Senate? (b) How is that officer chosen?
**5.** (a) Who selects the floor leaders in each house? The whips? (b) What are their functions?
**6.** (a) How are committee chairmen chosen? (b) What is the seniority rule?

### Critical Thinking

**7. Making Comparisons** (p. 19) Compare the roles and power of the party officials and presiding officers in both houses of Congress.

★

# 2 Committees in Congress

**Find Out:**
- Why is the committee system necessary?
- What are the different kinds of committees in Congress?
- What is the key role of the House Rules Committee?
- Why is the congressional investigative power important?

**Key Terms:**

standing committee, select committee, joint committee, conference committee

Do you know the phrase "a division of labor"? Roughly explained, it means dividing up the work to be done, assigning the several parts of the overall task to various members of the group.

The House and the Senate are both so large, and the business they each face is so great, that both chambers must rely on a division of labor. That is to say, much of the work that Congress does is in fact done by committees. Indeed, Representative Clem Miller (D., Calif.) once described Congress as "a collection of committees that comes together periodically to approve one another's actions."

As you will see, this section is devoted to the vital role committees play in the work of Congress.

## Standing Committees

In 1789 the House and Senate each adopted the practice of naming a special committee to consider each bill as it was introduced. By 1794 there were more than 300 committees in each chamber. Each house then began to set up permanent groups, known as **standing committees**, to which all similar bills could be sent.

The number of these committees has varied over the years. The graphic on page 291 lists the current 22 standing committees in the

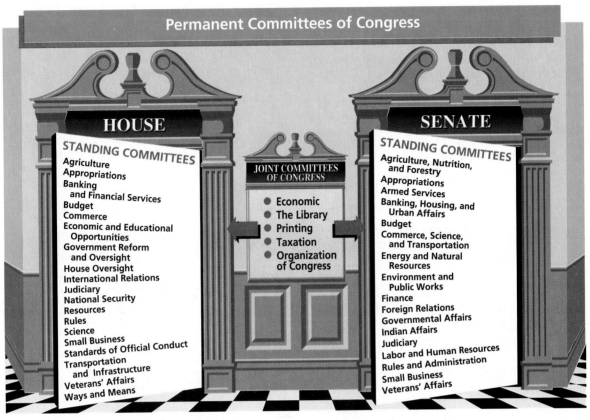

## Permanent Committees of Congress

### HOUSE

**STANDING COMMITTEES**

Agriculture
Appropriations
Banking
   and Financial Services
Budget
Commerce
Economic and Educational
   Opportunities
Government Reform
   and Oversight
House Oversight
International Relations
Judiciary
National Security
Resources
Rules
Science
Small Business
Standards of Official Conduct
Transportation
   and Infrastructure
Veterans' Affairs
Ways and Means

### JOINT COMMITTEES OF CONGRESS

● Economic
● The Library
● Printing
● Taxation
● Organization
   of Congress

### SENATE

**STANDING COMMITTEES**

Agriculture, Nutrition,
   and Forestry
Appropriations
Armed Services
Banking, Housing, and
   Urban Affairs
Budget
Commerce, Science,
   and Transportation
Energy and Natural
   Resources
Environment and
   Public Works
Finance
Foreign Relations
Governmental Affairs
Indian Affairs
Judiciary
Labor and Human Resources
Rules and Administration
Small Business
Veterans' Affairs

▲ **Interpreting Graphics**   Most legislation is considered in standing committees, and party politics shape these committees. Why might a legislator favor participation on one committee over another?

House and 17 in the Senate. Each House committee has from 12 to 60 members, and each Senate committee has from 10 to 29. The rules of the House limit representatives to service on one major committee, and the Senate allows its members to serve on two.

You may also notice from the graphic that most of the standing committees handle bills dealing with particular policy matters, such as veterans' affairs or foreign relations. Three standing committees do not operate as subject-matter bodies, however: in the House the Rules Committee and the Committee on Standards of Official Conduct, and in the Senate the Committee on Rules and Administration.

When a bill is introduced in either house, the Speaker or the president of the Senate refers the measure to the appropriate standing committee. Thus, the Speaker sends all tax measures to the House Ways and Means Committee; in the Sen-

ate tax measures go to the Finance Committee. A bill dealing with, say, enlistments in the armed forces goes to the National Security Committee in the House and to the Armed Services Committee in the Senate, and so on.

Recall that the chairman of each of the standing committees is chosen according to the seniority rule. Indeed, look at the tables on pages 292 and 293 and notice that most committee chairmen have served in Congress for at least 20 years. The seniority rule is also applied closely in each house when it elects the other members of each of its committees.[9]

---

[9]In form, the members of each standing committee are elected by a floor vote at the beginning of each term of Congress. In fact, each party draws up its own committee roster, and those party decisions are then ratified on the floor.

The majority party always holds a majority of the seats on each committee.[10] The other party is well represented, however. Party membership on each committee is more or less in proportion to party strength in each house.

_____

[10]The only exception is the House Committee on Standards of Official Conduct, with six Democrats and six Republicans. Often called the House Ethics Committee, it investigates allegations of misconduct by House members. In the Senate, a six-member bipartisan Select Committee on Ethics plays a similar role.

## The House Rules Committee

The House Committee on Rules is sometimes called the "traffic cop" in the lower house.

So many measures are introduced in the House each term that some sort of screening is necessary. Most bills die in the committees to which they are referred. Still, several hundred bills are reported out every year. So, before most of these bills can reach the floor of the House, they must also clear the Rules Committee.

### House Committee Chairs, 1995

| Position | Name | Age* | Year Elected to House | Party Affiliation and State |
|---|---|---|---|---|
| Agriculture | Pat Roberts | 60 | 1980 | R., Kansas |
| Appropriations | Bob Livingston | 53 | 1977 | R., Louisiana |
| Banking and Financial Services | Jim Leach | 54 | 1976 | R., Iowa |
| Budget | John Kasich | 44 | 1982 | R., Ohio |
| Commerce | Thomas J. Bliley, Jr. | 64 | 1980 | R., Virginia |
| Economic and Educational Opportunities | William Goodling | 69 | 1974 | R., Pennsylvania |
| Government Reform and Oversight | William Clinger | 67 | 1978 | R., Pennsylvania |
| House Oversight | Bill Thomas | 55 | 1978 | R., California |
| International Relations | Benjamin Gilman | 74 | 1972 | R., New York |
| Judiciary | Henry J. Hyde | 72 | 1974 | R., Illinois |
| National Security | Floyd Spence | 68 | 1970 | R., South Carolina |
| Resources | Don Young | 63 | 1973 | R., Alaska |
| Rules | Gerald Solomon | 66 | 1978 | R., New York |
| Science | Bob Walker | 54 | 1976 | R., Pennsylvania |
| Small Business | Jan Meyers | 68 | 1984 | R., Kansas |
| Standards of Official Conduct | Nancy Johnson | 61 | 1982 | R., Kansas |
| Transportation and Infrastructure | Bud Shuster | 64 | 1972 | R., Pennsylvania |
| Veterans' Affairs | Bob Stump | 69 | 1976 | R., Arizona |
| Ways and Means | Bill Archer | 68 | 1970 | R., Texas |

*As of birthdate in 1996.
*Sources: Congressional Directory* and the Clerk of the House.

▲ **Interpreting Tables**   What do their ages, years in the House, and party membership tell you about the post each of these members holds?

## Senate Committee Chairs, 1995

| Position | Name | Age[a] | Year Elected to Senate[b] | Party Affiliation and State |
|---|---|---|---|---|
| Agriculture, Nutrition, and Forestry | Richard Lugar | 64 | 1976 | R., Indiana |
| Appropriations | Mark Hatfield | 74 | 1966 | R., Oregon |
| Armed Services | Strom Thurmond | 94 | 1954 | R., South Carolina |
| Banking, Housing, and Urban Affairs | Alfonse D'Amato | 59 | 1980 | R., New York |
| Budget | Pete Domenici | 75 | 1972 | R., New Mexico |
| Commerce, Science, and Transportation | Larry Pressler | 54 | 1978 (1975) | R., South Dakota |
| Energy and Natural Resources | Frank Murkowski | 62 | 1980 | R., Alaska |
| Environment and Public Works | John Chafee | 74 | 1976 | R., Rhode Island |
| Finance | Bill Roth | 75 | 1970 (1967) | R., Delaware |
| Foreign Relations | Jesse Helms | 75 | 1972 | R., North Carolina |
| Governmental Affairs | Ted Stevens | 73 | 1968 | R., Alaska |
| Indian Affairs | John McCain | 60 | 1986 (1983) | R., Arizona |
| Judiciary | Orrin Hatch | 62 | 1976 | R., Utah |
| Labor and Human Resources | Nancy Kassebaum | 64 | 1978 | R., Kansas |
| Rules and Administration | John Warner | 68 | 1978 | R., Virginia |
| Small Business | Kit Bond | 57 | 1986 | R., Missouri |
| Veterans' Affairs | Alan Simpson | 65 | 1978 | R., Wyoming |

[a] As of birthdate in 1996.
[b] Date in parentheses indicates first year of prior service in House of Representatives.
*Source: Congressional Directory* and Secretary of the Senate.

**Interpreting Tables** How does this table demonstrate the importance of seniority in the United States Senate?

Normally, a bill gets to the floor only if it has been granted a rule—scheduled for floor consideration—by the Rules Committee. The committee decides whether and under what conditions the full House will consider a measure. As you will soon see, this means that the potent 13-member Rules Committee can speed, delay, or even prevent House action on a measure.

In the Senate, where the process is not so closely regulated, the majority floor leader controls the appearance of bills on the floor.

## Select Committees

At times, each house finds need for a **select committee**—a special group set up for some specific purpose and, most often, for a limited time. The Speaker of the House or the president of the Senate appoints the members of these special committees with the advice of the majority and minority leaders. Most select committees are formed to investigate a current matter. The congressional power to investigate is an essential part of the lawmaking function. Congress must decide on the need for new laws and the adequacy of laws it has already passed. And it must exercise its oversight function to ensure that executive agencies are working according to the policies Congress has set by law. Congress sometimes conducts an investigation to focus public attention on some topic.

Most congressional investigations are conducted by standing committees or by their subcommittees. Select committees sometimes perform that work, however. Thus, both houses maintain a Select Committee on Intelligence. These bodies are, in effect, watchdogs; they oversee the day-to-day operations of the Central Intelligence Agency and the other elements of the government's vast intelligence network.

At times, a select committee becomes a spectacularly important body. This happened, for example, to the Senate's Select Committee on Presidential Campaign Activities, popularly known as the Senate Watergate Committee. As the Watergate scandal began to unfold in 1973, the Senate created that committee. Chaired by Senator Sam Ervin (D., N.C.), its job was to investigate "the extent, if any, to which illegal, improper, or unethical activities were engaged in by any persons . . . in the presidential election of 1972." Its sensational hearings fascinated the nation for months.

Two select panels commanded the public's attention through much of 1987: the Senate's Select Committee on Secret Military Assistance to Iran and the Nicaraguan Opposition, and the House Select Committee to Investigate Covert Arms Transactions with Iran. These twin committees, most often called the Iran-Contra Committees, worked closely with one another, probing the Reagan administration's conduct of two highly secret foreign policy initiatives. Their dramatic inquiries focused on the covert sale of arms to the Khomeini regime in Teheran and on clandestine efforts to give military aid to the Contra rebels fighting the Sandanista government in Nicaragua. The Iran initiative was intended, at least in part, as an arms-for-hostages maneuver, and it failed. The Contra aid effort was in part financed with money from the Iranian arms sales, and it was carried out despite an act of Congress prohibiting such aid by the United States.

Most congressional investigations are not nearly so visible, nor are they very often so historic. Their more usual shape can be seen when, for example, the House Committee on Agriculture looks at some problem in the farm price-support system.

## Joint and Conference Committees

A **joint committee** is one composed of members from both houses. You may recall seeing some of these committees listed on the chart on page 291. Some are select committees set up to serve some temporary purpose. Most are permanent groups that serve on a regular basis.

Some joint committees are investigative in nature and issue periodic reports to the House and Senate—for example, the Joint Economic Committee. Most joint committees have housekeeping duties, however—for example, the Joint Committee on Printing and the Joint Committee on the Library of Congress.

Because the standing committees of the two houses often needlessly duplicate one another's work, many have long urged that Congress make much greater use of the joint committee device.

Before a bill may be sent to the President, it must be passed in identical form by each house. Sometimes, the two houses pass differing versions of a measure, and the first house will not agree to the changes the other has made. When this happens a **conference committee**—a temporary, joint body—is created to iron out the differences in the bill. Its job is to produce a compromise bill, one that both houses will accept. You will read more about the strategic role of conference committees later in this chapter.

## Section 2 Review

**1. Define:** joint committee, conference committee
**2.** (a) What is a standing committee? (b) Why are such committees called "subject-matter" committees?
**3.** How are the members of the standing committees chosen?
**4.** What is the role of the Rules Committee?
**5.** What is a select committee?
**6.** For what reason is the investigative power so important to Congress?

**Critical Thinking**

**7. Identifying Central Issues** (p. 19) Woodrow Wilson once noted that "Congress in its committee rooms is Congress at work." Explain what you think is the meaning of this statement.

★

## Should Women Be Drafted?
### *Rostker v. Goldberg*, 1981

Through much of our history, as today, the nation's armed forces have relied on voluntary enlistments to fill their ranks. But the draft—compulsory military service—has a long history in this country. The draft was most recently used to provide men for the armed forces during the war in Vietnam.

In 1971, Robert Goldberg and several other men then subject to the draft challenged the constitutionality of the current draft law, the Military Selective Service Act of 1971. They filed their suit in the federal district court in Pennsylvania, where they claimed that the law was invalid on several grounds. Most importantly, they argued that the law provided for unfair discrimination against men and so violated the 5th Amendment's Due Process Clause. They based their argument on the fact that the law required men but not women to register for the draft and made men but not women liable for involuntary service in the military.

Congress suspended the draft in 1973, and Goldberg and the others saw no point in pursuing their case. The requirement that young men register for the draft was suspended two years later, in 1975.

President Jimmy Carter asked Congress for funds to reinstate the registration requirement in 1980, soon after the Soviet Union's invasion of Afghanistan in late 1979. With that, Goldberg revived the case.

The lower federal court held in Goldberg's favor in 1980. It ruled the gender-based discriminations in the Military Selective Service Act unconstitutional. At that point, the Federal Government, acting on behalf of the Director of the Selective Service System, Bernard Rostker, appealed to the U.S. Supreme Court.

*Review the following evidence and arguments presented to the U.S. Supreme Court.*

### Arguments for Rostker

**1.** The Constitution gives Congress the power "to raise and support armies . . . and maintain a navy."

**2.** The policy of excluding women from the draft is based on military need, not on any traditional view of women's roles in society.

**3.** By both law and military policy, women are excluded from combat; it is therefore logical that they be excluded from the draft.

### Arguments for Goldberg

**1.** The Constitution does not give Congress the power to draw unfair, arbitrary distinctions between men and women.

**2.** Excluding women from the draft perpetuates outdated notions that women are weaker and less able than men.

**3.** The fact that large numbers of women now serve ably in the armed forces refutes the logic of the policy of exclusion.

## Getting Involved

1. **Identify** the constitutional grounds upon which each side based its arguments.

2. **Debate** the opposing viewpoints presented in this case.

3. **Predict** how you think the Supreme Court ruled in this case and why. Then refer to the Supreme Court Glossary on page 768 to read about the decision. Discuss the impact of the Court's decision on the current and future state of gender equality in the United States.

# 3 How a Bill Becomes a Law: The House

## Find Out:

- What is the overall shape of the lawmaking process in both houses?
- What are the several different kinds of measures involved in that process?
- What are the many steps in the lawmaking process in the House of Representatives?

## Key Terms:

bill, joint resolution, concurrent resolution, resolution, rider, discharge petition, subcommittee, Committee of the Whole, quorum

These numbers may surprise you: As many as 10,000 bills—proposed laws—are introduced in the House and Senate during a term of Congress. Fewer than 10 percent ever become law. Where do all those measures come from? Why are so few of them passed? By what process does Congress make law?

In this section, you will see in some detail how the legislative process works in the House. Then, because bills follow a quite similar route in the Senate, the major differences to be found in the upper chamber will be noted.

## Creating and Introducing Bills

Most bills introduced in either house do *not* originate with members of Congress themselves. Instead, most bills—the important as well as the routine—are born somewhere in the executive branch. Business, labor, agriculture, and other pressure groups often draft measures as well. Some bills, or at least the ideas for them, come from private citizens who think "there ought to be a law . . ." And many are born in the standing committees of Congress.

According to the Constitution:

> **"**All bills for raising revenue shall originate in the House of Representatives, but the Senate may propose or concur with amendments as on other bills.**"** [11]

Measures dealing with any other matter may be introduced in either chamber. Only members can introduce bills in the House, and they do so by dropping them into the "hopper" [12]—a box hanging on the edge of the clerk's desk.

---

[11] Article I, Section 7, Clause 1.

[12] Puerto Rico's resident commissioner and the delegates from the District of Columbia, Guam, the Virgin Islands, and American Samoa also may introduce measures in the House. Only a senator may introduce a measure in the upper house. He or she does so by addressing the chair.

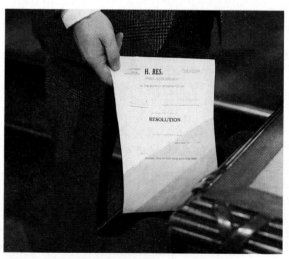

> 101st CONGRESS
> 1st SESSION
>
> # H. R. 4
>
> To amend the Clean Air Act to control hazardous air pollutants.
>
> ---
>
> IN THE HOUSE OF REPRESENTATIVES
>
> JANUARY 3, 1989
>
> Mr. DINGELL introduced the following bill; which was referred to the Committee on Energy and Commerce
>
> ## A BILL
>
> To amend the Clean Air Act to control hazardous air pollutants.
>
> 1   *Be it enacted by the Senate and House of Representa-*
> 2   *tives of the United States of America in Congress assembled,*
> 3   SECTION 1. SHORT TITLE
> 4       This Act may be cited as the "Clean Air Act Amend-

▲ **First Steps to Passage of a Bill**   The hopper is a large box hanging at the edge of the clerk's desk (right). Only a very small number—fewer than 10 percent—of all the bills dropped into the hopper ever become law.

## Types of Bills and Resolutions

The thousands of measures—bills and resolutions— Congress considers at each session take several forms.

**Bills** are proposed laws, or drafts of laws, presented to the House or Senate for enactment. There are two types of bills: public bills and private bills.

Public bills are measures applying to the nation as a whole—for example, a tax measure, an amendment to the copyright laws, or an appropriation of funds for the Navy.

Private bills are those measures that apply to certain persons or places rather than to the nation generally. As an example: Congress recently passed an act to give an Idaho sheep rancher $85,000 for his losses resulting from attacks by grizzly bears, which had been moved from Yellowstone National Park onto nearby public lands on which he grazed his flock.

**Joint resolutions** are little different from bills, and when passed have the force of law. Joint resolutions most often deal with unusual or temporary matters. For example, they may be used to appropriate money for the presidential inauguration ceremonies or correct an error in a statute already passed. Recall that joint resolutions also are used to propose constitutional amendments, and they have been used for territorial annexations.

**Concurrent resolutions** deal with matters in which the House and Senate must act jointly. However, they do not have the force of law and do not require the President's signature. Concurrent resolutions are used most often by Congress to state a position on some matter— for example, in foreign affairs.

**Resolutions** deal with matters concerning either house alone and are taken up only by that house. They are regularly used for such things as the adoption of a new rule of procedure or the amendment of some existing rule. Like concurrent resolutions, a resolution does not have the force of law and is not sent to the President for approval.

A bill or resolution usually deals with a single subject, but sometimes a rider dealing with an unrelated matter is included. A **rider** is a provision not likely to pass on its own merit that is attached to an important measure certain to pass. Its sponsors hope that it will "ride" through the legislative process on the strength of the other measure. Most riders are tacked onto appropriations measures—those in which Congress provides the money to pay for something. In fact, some money bills are hung with so many of them that they are called "Christmas trees." The opponents of those "decorations" and the President are almost always forced to accept them if they want the bill's major provisions to become law.

## The First Reading

The clerk of the House numbers each bill as it is introduced. Thus, H.R. 3410 would be the 3,410th measure introduced in the House during the congressional term.[13] The clerk also gives each bill a short title—a very brief summary of its principal contents.

Having received its number and short title, the bill is then entered in the House *Journal* and in the *Congressional Record* for the day.[14]

With these actions the bill has received its first reading. Each bill that is finally passed in either house is given three readings along the legislative route. In the House, second reading comes during floor consideration if the measure gets that far. Third reading takes place just before the final vote on the measure. Each reading is usually by title only: "H.R. 3410, A bill to provide . . ." However, the more impor-

---

[13]Bills originating in the Senate receive the prefix *S.*—such as S. 210. Resolutions are similarly identified in each house in order of their introduction. Thus, H.J. Res. 12 would be the 12th joint resolution introduced in the House during the term, and, similarly in the Senate, S.J. Res. 19. Concurrent resolutions are identified as H. Con. Res. 16 or S. Con. Res. 4, and simple resolutions as H. Res. 198 or S. Res. 166.

[14]The *Journal* contains the minutes, the official record, of the daily proceedings in the House (Senate). The *Congressional Record* is a voluminous account of the daily proceedings (speeches, debates, other comments, votes, motions, etc.) in each house. The *Record* is not quite a word-for-word account, however. Members have five days in which to make changes in each temporary edition. They often insert speeches that were in fact never made, reconstruct "debates," and revise thoughtless or inaccurate remarks.

# Congressional Record

UNITED STATES OF AMERICA

PROCEEDINGS AND DEBATES OF THE *103ᵈ* CONGRESS, SECOND SESSION

*Vol. 140*　　WASHINGTON, WEDNESDAY, OCTOBER 5, 1994　　*No. 143*

## House of Representatives

The House met at 9:30 a.m.
The Chaplain, Rev. James David Ford, D.D., offered the following prayer:

We are grateful, O God, that Your word to us is a word that challenges and corrects, that gives solace and comfort in every need. We are grateful too for the words of our colleagues and friends...

...stand it. And the American workers fear it. Is it any wonder under NAFTA jobs go to Mexico? Under GATT jobs will go everywhere except America. I do not blame workers.

I will say one thing, I think the Democrat party today is pushing the working people of America away, real far away. But let us tell us like it is.

If GATT is as good for America...

...comply with the laws they impose on others.

Mr. Speaker, let us put an end to Democratic obstructionism by electing a Republican majority for the first time in 40 years.

REPUBLICANS CAN BALANCE THE

▲ The *Congressional Record* This periodical is an account of the daily proceedings on the floor of both the House and the Senate.

---

tant or controversial bills are read in full and taken up line by line, section by section, at second reading.[15]

After first reading, the Speaker refers the bill to the appropriate standing committee—that is, the committee with jurisdiction over the bill's subject matter.

## The Bill in Committee

The standing committees have been described as sieves, sifting out most bills and considering and reporting only those they judge to be worthwhile.

Most bills die in committee. They are pigeonholed[16]—simply put away, never to be acted upon—and most deserve that fate. At times, however, a committee pigeonholes a measure that a majority of the House wishes to consider.

When that happens, the bill can be blasted out of the committee with a **discharge petition**. This device enables members to force a bill that has been in committee 30 days (7 in the Rules Committee) onto the floor for consideration.[17] But this maneuver is not often tried and is seldom successful.

Those bills that a committee, or at least its chairman, does wish to consider are discussed at times chosen by the chairman. Today, most committees do most of their work through their several **subcommittees**—divisions of existing committees formed to address specific issues. There are now some 140 of these committees within committees in the House, and nearly 90 in the Senate. Where an important or controversial bill is involved, a committee, or more often one of its subcommittees, holds public hearings on the measure. Interested persons,

---

[15]All bills introduced are immediately printed and distributed to the members. The three readings, an ancient parliamentary practice, are not very significant today. But they were quite important in the days when some members of Congress could not read.

[16]The term comes from the old-fashioned rolltop desks with pigeonholes into which papers were put and often soon forgotten.

[17]Any member may file a discharge motion. If that motion is signed by a majority (218) of House members, the committee has seven days to report the bill. If it does not, any member who signed the motion may, on the second and fourth Mondays of each month, move that the committee be discharged—relieved—of the bill. If the motion carries, the House considers the bill at once.

special interest groups, and government officials are invited to testify at these information-gathering sessions.[18] If necessary, a committee can force a witness to testify under threat of imprisonment.

Occasionally, a subcommittee will make a junket (trip) to locations affected by a measure. Thus, members of the National Parks, Forests, and Public Lands Subcommittee of the House Committee on Natural Resources may take a firsthand look at a number of national parks. Or, the Water and Power Subcommittee of the Senate Energy and Natural Resources Committee may visit the Pacific Northwest to gather information on a public power bill.

These junkets are made at public expense, and members of Congress are sometimes criticized for taking them. Some junkets deserve criticism. But an on-the-spot investigation often proves to be the best way a committee can inform itself.

When a subcommittee has completed its work on a bill, the measure goes to the full committee. That body may choose one of several courses of action. It may:

1. Report the bill favorably, with a "do pass" recommendation. It is then the chairman's job to steer the bill through debate on the floor.
2. Refuse to report the bill—that is, pigeonhole it. Again, this is the fate suffered by most measures in both houses.
3. Report the bill in amended form. Many bills are changed in committee, and several bills on the same subject may be combined into a single measure.
4. Report the bill with an unfavorable recommendation. This does not often happen. But sometimes a committee feels that the full House should have a chance to consider a bill or does not want to take the responsibility for killing it.

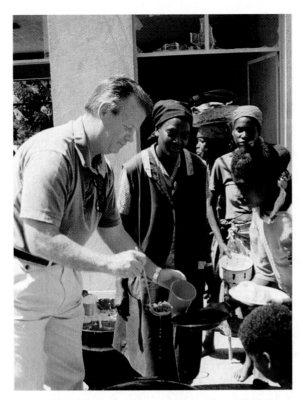

▲ **Trip Abroad**   Representative Tony Hall (D., Ohio) helps feed hungry children in Angola. He visited that war-torn country as chairman of the Congressional Hunger Caucus and Center.

5. Report a committee bill. This is an entirely new bill that the committee has substituted for one or several bills referred to it.

## Rules and Calendars

Before it goes to the floor for consideration, a bill reported by a standing committee is placed on one of several calendars. A calendar is a schedule of the order in which bills will be taken up on the floor. There are five of these calendars in the House:

1. The Calendar of the Committee of the Whole House on the State of the Union, commonly known as the Union Calendar, for all bills having to do with revenues, appropriations, or government property.
2. The House Calendar for all other public bills.
3. The Calendar of the Committee of the Whole House, commonly called the Private Calendar, for all private bills.

---

[18]If necessary, a committee may subpoena witnesses. A subpoena is an order compelling one to appear. Failure to obey a subpoena may lead the House or Senate to pass a resolution citing the offender for contempt of Congress—a federal crime punishable by fine and/or imprisonment.

# VOICES *on Government*

### On the Duties of a Congressman

**Sam Rayburn,** Speaker of the House for nearly 17 years, explains his views on the nation and its lawmakers.

❝I have always dreamed of a country which I should believe this should and will be, and that is one in which the citizenship is an educated and patriotic people, not swayed by passion and prejudice, and a country that shall know no East, no West, no North, no South, but inhabited by a people liberty loving, patriotic, happy and prosperous, with its lawmakers having no other purpose than to write such just laws as shall in the years to come be of service to human kind yet unborn.❞

4. The Consent Calendar for all bills from the Union or House Calendar taken out of order by unanimous consent of the House of Representatives. These are most often minor bills to which there is no opposition.
5. The Discharge Calendar for petitions to discharge bills from committee.

Under the rules of the House, bills are taken from each of these calendars for consideration on a regularly scheduled basis. For example, bills from the Consent Calendar are considered on the first and third Mondays of each month. Measures relating to the District of Columbia are to be taken up on the second and fourth Mondays, and private bills every Friday. On "Calendar Wednesdays" the various committee chairmen may each call up one bill that has cleared their committees.

None of these arrangements is followed too closely, however. What often happens is even more complicated. First, remember that the Rules Committee plays a critical role in the legislative process of the House. It must grant a rule before most bills can in fact reach the floor. That is, before most measures can be taken from a calendar, the Rules Committee must approve that step and set a time for its appearance on the floor.

By not granting a rule for a bill, the Rules Committee can effectively kill it. Or, when the Rules Committee does grant a rule, it may be a special rule—one setting conditions under which the measure will be considered by the members of the House. A special rule regularly sets a time limit on floor debate. It may even prohibit amendments to certain or even to any of the bill's provisions.

Then, too, certain bills are privileged—that is, they may be called up at almost any time, ahead of any other business before the House. The most highly privileged measures include major appropriations (spending) and general revenue (tax) bills, conference committee reports, and special rules from the Rules Committee.

On certain days, usually the first and third Mondays and Tuesdays, the House may suspend its rules. A motion to that effect must be approved by a two-thirds vote of the members present. When that happens, as it sometimes does, the House moves so far away from its established operating procedures that a measure can go through all the many steps necessary to enactment in a single day.

All of these—the calendars, the role of the Rules Committee, and the other complex procedures—have developed over time and for several reasons. In major part, they have developed because of the large size of the House and the sheer number and variety of bills its members introduce. In their own ways, the calendars, rules, and other complex procedures have developed to help members of the House manage their heavy workload. Without such help, no one member could possibly know the contents, let alone the merits, of every bill on which he or she has to vote.

## The Bill on the Floor

If a bill finally reaches the floor, it receives its second reading in the House.

Many bills the House passes are minor ones, with little or no opposition. Most minor bills are called from the Consent Calendar, get their second reading by title only, and are quickly disposed of.

Nearly all the more important measures are dealt with in a much different manner, however. They are considered in the Committee of the Whole, an old parliamentary device for speeding business on the floor.

The **Committee of the Whole** is the House sitting not as itself but as one large committee of itself. Its rules are much less strict than the rules of the House, and floor action moves along at a faster pace. For example, a **quorum**—majority of the full membership, 218—must be present in order for the House to do business. However, only 100 members need be present in the Committee of the Whole.

When the House resolves itself into the Committee of the Whole, the Speaker steps down because the full House of Representatives is no longer in session. Another member presides.

General debate begins, and the bill receives its second reading, section by section. As each section is read, amendments may be offered. Under the five-minute rule supporters and opponents of each amendment have just that long to make their cases. Votes are taken on each section and its amendment as the reading proceeds.

When the bill has been gone through—and many run to dozens and sometimes hundreds of pages—the Committee of the Whole has completed its work. It then rises—that is, dissolves itself. The House is now back in session. The Speaker resumes the chair, and the House formally adopts the committee's work.

**Debate** Its large size has long since forced the House to impose severe limits on floor debate. A rule first adopted in 1841 forbids any member from holding the floor for more than one hour without unanimous consent. Since 1880 the Speaker has had the power to force any member who strays from the subject at hand to give up the floor.

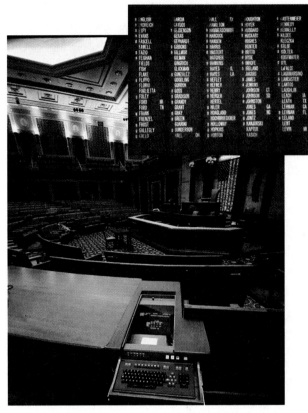

▲ **Recording House Votes** A computerized voting system saves a large amount of time in each session. Progress of the bill on the floor is monitored on a summary board (top).

The majority and minority floor leaders generally decide in advance how they will split the time to be spent on a bill. But at any time, any member may "move the previous question." That is, any member may demand a vote on the issue before the House. If that motion passes, only 40 minutes of further debate are allowed before a vote is taken. This device is the only motion that can be used in the House to close (end) debate, but it can be a very effective one.

**Voting** A bill may be the subject of several votes on the floor. If amendments are offered, as they frequently are, members must vote on each of them. Then, too, a number of procedural motions may be offered—for example, one to table the bill (lay it aside), another for the previous question, and so on. The members must vote on each of these motions. These several other votes can be a better guide to a bill's friends and foes than is the final vote itself. Sometimes, a member votes for a bill that is now certain to pass, even though he or she supported amendments to it that would have scuttled the measure.

The House uses four different methods for the taking of floor votes:

1. Voice votes are the most common. The Speaker calls for the "ayes" and then the "noes," the members answer in chorus, and the Speaker announces the result.
2. If any member thinks the Speaker has erred in judging a voice vote, he or she may demand a standing vote, also known as a division of the House. All in favor, and then all opposed, stand and are counted by the clerk.
3. One-fifth of a quorum (44 members in the House or 20 in the Committee of the Whole) can demand a teller vote. When this procedure is used, the Speaker names two tellers, one from each party. The members pass between them and are counted, for and against. Teller votes are rare today. The practice has been replaced by electronic voting; see below.
4. A roll-call vote, also known as a record vote, may be demanded by one-fifth of the members present.[19]

In 1973, the House installed a computerized voting system for all quorum calls and record votes to replace the roll call by the clerk. Members now vote at any of the 48 stations on the floor by inserting a personalized plastic card in a box and then pushing one of three buttons— "Yea," "Nay," or "Present."[20] A large master board above the Speaker's chair shows instantly how each member has voted. The House rules allow the members 15 minutes to answer quorum calls or cast record votes. Voting ends when the Speaker pushes a button to lock the electronic system, producing a permanent record of the vote at the same time. Under the former roll-call process, it took the clerk up to 45 minutes to call each member's name and record his or her vote. Before 1973, roll calls took up about three months of House floor time each session.

Voting procedures are much the same in the Senate. The upper house uses voice, standing, and roll-call votes, but does not take teller votes or use an electronic voting process. Only six or seven minutes are needed for a roll-call vote in the upper chamber.

## Final Steps

Once a bill has been approved at second reading, it is engrossed—that is, printed in its final form. Then it is read a third time, by title, and a final vote is taken. If the bill is approved at third reading, it is signed by the Speaker. A page—a legislative aide—then carries it to the Senate and places it on the Senate president's desk.

# Section **3** Review

**1. Define:** bill, joint resolution, concurrent resolution, resolution, rider, discharge petition, subcommittee, quorum

**2.** From what main sources do drafts of bills originate?

**3.** (a) Who may introduce a bill in the House? (b) In the Senate?

**4.** What is the purpose of public subcommittee hearings?

**5.** What options does a full committee have when acting on a bill?

**6.** What is the Committee of the Whole?

**7.** What is the role of the Rules Committee?

**Critical Thinking**

**8. Predicting Consequences** (p. 19) What might happen if the House were required to consider each one of the bills introduced by its members?

---

[19]The Constitution (Article I, Section 7, Clause 2) requires a record vote on the question of overriding a presidential veto. No record votes are taken in the Committee of the Whole.

[20]The "Present" button is most often used for a quorum call—a check to make sure that a quorum of the members is in fact present. Otherwise, it is used when a member does not wish to vote on a question but still wants to be recorded as present. A "present" vote is not allowed on some questions—for example, a vote to override a veto.

★

# 4 The Bill in the Senate and the Final Stages

**Find Out:**

- How does the legislative process in the Senate differ from that in the House?
- Why are conference committees sometimes called the "third house"?
- What is a filibuster and how can cloture be imposed?
- What are the options open to the President after both houses have passed a bill?

**Key Terms:**

filibuster, cloture, veto, pocket veto

As you can see in the chart on page 305, the basic steps in the lawmaking process are much the same in the House and the Senate. There are notable differences, however. Given the many similarities, there is no need here to trace a bill step-by-step through the Senate. However, it is important to consider some of the unique characteristics of the Senate's treatment of bills. It is also important to look at what happens to bills once they have passed in each house.

## Introducing the Bill in the Senate

Bills are introduced by senators, who are formally recognized for that purpose. A measure is then given a number and short title, read twice, and referred to committee, where bills are dealt with much as they are in the House.

All in all, the Senate's proceedings are less formal and its rules less strict than those of the much larger House. For example, the Senate has only one calendar for all bills reported out by its committees. Bills are called to the floor at the discretion of the majority floor leader.[21]

---

[21]The Senate does have another, nonlegislative calendar, the Executive Calendar, for treaties and appointments made by the President and awaiting Senate approval or, rarely, rejection. The majority leader controls that schedule, too.

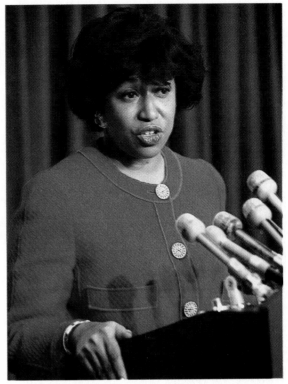

▲ **Overcoming Barriers** Senator Carol Mosely Braun (D., Illinois) was the first African American woman ever elected to the Senate. Since her election in 1992, she's seen many bills passed, including her bill to provide $100 million to rebuild schools.

## The Senate's Rules for Debate

The major differences in House and Senate procedures involve debate. Floor debate is strictly limited in the House, but almost unrestrained in the Senate. Most senators are intensely proud of belonging to what has often been called "the greatest deliberative body in the world."

As a general matter, senators may speak on the floor for as long as they please. There is no rule that they speak only to the measure under consideration. Unlike the House, the Senate's rules do not allow the moving of the previous question.

The Senate's consideration of most bills is brought to a close by unanimous consent agreements. That is, discussion ends and the senators vote at a time previously agreed to by the majority and minority leaders. But if any senator

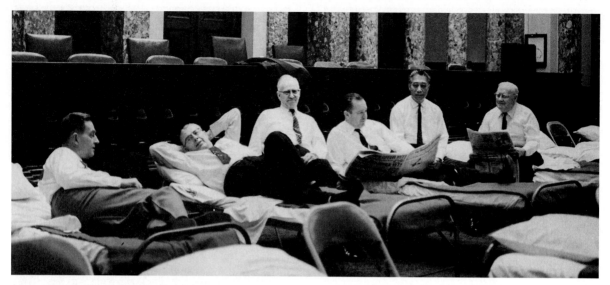

**The Filibuster Rule**   Senators rest on cots set up in the old Supreme Court Chamber during the filibuster that attempted to prevent passage of the Civil Rights Act of 1957.

objects—prevents unanimous consent—the device fails.[22]

The Senate's dedication to freedom of debate is almost unique among modern legislative bodies. That freedom is intended to encourage the fullest possible discussion of matters on the floor. The great latitude it allows, however, can be abused by the filibuster.

**The Filibuster**   Essentially, a **filibuster** is an attempt to "talk a bill to death." It is a stalling tactic, a process in which a minority of senators seeks to delay or prevent Senate action on a measure. The filibusterers try to so monopolize the Senate floor and its time that the Senate must either drop the bill or change it in some manner acceptable to the minority.

Talk—and more talk—is the filibusterers' major weapon. But senators may also use time-killing motions, quorum calls, and other parliamentary maneuvers.

---

[22]The Senate does have a "two-speech rule." Under it, no senator may speak more than twice on a given question on the same legislative day. By recessing—temporarily interrupting—rather than adjourning a day's session, the Senate can prolong a "legislative day" indefinitely. Thus, the two-speech rule does have some limiting effect on the amount of time the Senate spends on some matters on its agenda.

Among the many better known filibusterers, Senator Huey Long (D., La.) spoke for more than 15 hours in 1935. He stalled by reading from the Washington telephone directory and gave his colleagues his recipes for "pot-likker," corn bread, and turnip greens. In 1947, Glen Taylor (D., Idaho) used more than eight hours of floor time talking of his children, Wall Street, baptism, and fishing. The current filibuster record was set by Senator Strom Thurmond (R., S.C.). He held the floor for 24 hours and 18 minutes in an unsuccessful, one-person effort against what later became the Civil Rights Act of 1957.

No later efforts have come close to matching that one. Still, the practice is often used and to great effect in the Senate. Over the past century and more, well over 200 measures have been killed by filibusters. Just the *threat* of a filibuster alone has resulted in the Senate's failure to consider a number of bills and the amending of many more.

The Senate often tries to beat off a filibuster with lengthy, even day-and-night, sessions to wear down the participants. At times, some little-observed rules are quite strictly enforced. Among them are the requirements that senators stand—not sit, lean on their desks, or walk about—as they speak and that they not use "unparliamentary language." But these countermeasures seldom work.

# How Bills Become Laws

The diagram shows the major steps through which a typical bill passes from its introduction, in either the Senate or the House, to final action on it by the President.

Before a bill is sent to the White House, the Senate and the House must pass it in exactly the same form. Note: Most bills never become law.

## House Bill

### COMMITTEE ACTION

Referred to standing committee

Referred to subcommittee for study, hearings, revision, approval

Back to full committee for more hearings and revision. Full committee may approve bill and recommend passage.

Bill goes to Rules Committee to set conditions for debate and amendments on the floor.

Committee may "pigeonhole" a bill or give an unfavorable report (rare).

Bill introduced and passed in the House must then go through the same process in the Senate

Bill introduced and passed in the Senate must then go through the same process in the House

## Senate Bill

### COMMITTEE ACTION

Referred to standing committee

Referred to subcommittee for study, hearings, revision, approval

Back to full committee for more hearings and revision. Full committee may approve bill and recommend passage.

### FLOOR ACTION

Bill is debated, usually amended, then passed or defeated. If passed, it goes to the Senate.

### FLOOR ACTION

Bill is debated, usually amended, then passed or defeated. If passed, it goes to the House.

If House and Senate versions of bill are the same, bill goes directly to the President; if different, to conference committee.

### HOUSE OVERRIDE

Congress may override a veto by a two-thirds majority in both houses. The bill then becomes law without the President's signature.

### ★ ★ CONFERENCE COMMITTEE ★ ★

If the houses cannot agree on the final wording of the bill, both versions go to a conference committee of members from both houses.

### SENATE OVERRIDE

Congress may override a veto by a two-thirds majority in both houses. The bill then becomes law without the President's signature.

### ★ ★ CONGRESS ENACTS BILL ★ ★

Compromise version of bill from conference committee is sent back to both houses for a vote.

### VETO

Bill returns to House

### VETO

Bill returns to Senate

### ★ ★ ★ ★ ★ PRESIDENTIAL ACTION ★ ★ ★ ★ ★

Approved compromise version is sent to the President, who can

either sign it into law or veto it and return it to Congress.

# BILL BECOMES LAW

**The Cloture Rule**  The Senate's real check on the filibuster is its Cloture Rule, Rule XXII in the Standing Rules of the Senate. It was first adopted in 1917, after one of the most notable of all filibusters in Senate history.[23]

Rule XXII provides for **cloture**—that is, limiting debate. The rule is not in regular, continuing force; it can be brought into play only by a special procedure. A vote to invoke the rule must be taken two days after a petition calling for that action has been submitted by at least 16 members of the Senate. If at least 60 senators—three-fifths of the full Senate—then vote for the motion, the rule becomes effective. From that point, no more than another 30 hours of floor time may be spent on the measure. Then it *must* be brought to a final vote.

Invoking the rule is no easy matter. So far, more than 400 attempts have been made to invoke the rule, and only about one-third have succeeded. Many senators hesitate to support cloture motions for two reasons: (1) their dedication to the Senate's tradition of free debate and (2) their practical worry that the frequent use of cloture will undercut the value of the filibuster that they may some day want to use.

## The Conference Committees

If you have ever watched a marathon, you know that no matter how well a runner covers the first 25 miles or so, he or she still has some distance to go in order to finish the race.

So it is for bills in the legislative process. Even those that survive the long route through committees and rules and the floor in both houses still face some important steps before they can finally become law. Some of those final steps can be very difficult ones.

Any measure enacted by Congress *must* have been passed by both houses in identical form. Most often, a bill passed by one house and then approved by the other is not amended in the second chamber. When the House and Senate do pass different versions of the same bill, the first house usually concurs in the other's amendments, and congressional action is completed.

There are times when the House or the Senate will not accept the other's version of a bill. When this happens, the measure is turned over to a conference committee—a temporary joint committee of the two houses. It seeks to iron out the differences and come up with a compromise bill.

The conferees, managers, are named by the respective presiding officers. Mostly, they are leading members of the standing committee that first handled the measure in each house.

Both the House and Senate rules restrict a conference committee to the consideration of those points in a bill on which the two houses disagree. The committee cannot include any new material in its compromise version. In practice, however, the conferees often make changes that were not even considered in either house.

Once the conferees agree, their report—the compromise bill—is submitted to both houses. It must be accepted or rejected without amendment. Only rarely does either house turn down a conference committee's work. This is not surprising, for two major reasons: (1) the powerful membership of the typical conference committee and (2) the fact that its report usually comes in the midst of the rush to adjournment at the end of a congressional session.

The conference committee stage is a most strategic step in the legislative process. A number of major legislative decisions and compromises are often made at that point. Indeed, the late Senator George Norris (R., Nebr.) once quite aptly described conference committees as "the third house of Congress."

---

[23]That filibuster lasted for three weeks, and took place less than two months before the United States entered World War I on April 6, 1917. Because German submarines had renewed their attacks on shipping in the North Atlantic, President Wilson asked Congress for legislation to permit the arming of American merchant vessels. The bill, widely supported in the country, was quickly passed by the House by a vote of 403–12. The measure died in the Senate, however, because twelve senators filibustered it until the end of the congressional term on March 4th. The public was outraged. President Wilson declared: "A little group of willful men, representing no opinion but their own, has rendered the great Government of the United States helpless and contemptible." The Cloture Rule was passed by the Senate at its next session, later that same year.

The Number of Bills That Actually Become Laws*

| | |
|---|---|
| Public Laws | 590 |
| Passed Both Chambers | 667 |
| Passed One Chamber | 1,184 |
| Floor Consideration | 1,201 |
| Reported or Discharged by Committee | 1,405 |
| Referred to or Originated in Committee | 10,178 |
| Bills Introduced | 10,238 |

*Source:* Ilona B. Nickels, Congressional Research Service, Library of Congress, Washington, D.C.
*Statistics represent only measures that can become public law—bills and joint resolutions—and exclude simple and concurrent resolutions and private bills. Figures are for the 102nd Congress.

▲ **Interpreting Graphs**  The left-hand column simplifies the many stages through which a bill must pass before it becomes law. Why do so few bills actually become laws?

## The President Acts

You have followed the long, difficult path of a bill moving through Congress. Still, a measure that survives the legislative process in both houses has yet one more major hurdle to face. The Constitution requires that

❝ Every bill which shall have passed the House of Representatives and the Senate . . . [and] every order, resolution, or vote, to which the concurrence of the Senate and House of Representatives may be necessary (except on a question of adjournment) shall be presented to the President. . . . ❞ [24]

The Constitution presents the President with four options at this point:

1. The President may sign the bill, and it then becomes law.
2. The President may **veto**—refuse to sign—the bill. The measure must then be returned to the house in which it originated, together with the President's objections (a veto message). Although it seldom does, Congress may then pass the bill over the President's veto, by a two-thirds vote of the members present in each house.
3. The President may allow the bill to become law without signing it—by not acting on it within 10 days, not counting Sundays, of receiving it.

4. The fourth option is a variation of the third called the **pocket veto**. If Congress adjourns its session within 10 days of submitting a bill to the President, and the President does not act, the measure dies.

You will read more about the President's veto power and his other legislative powers in Chapter 14.

## Section 4 Review

1. **Define:** filibuster, cloture, veto, pocket veto
2. What is the major difference between floor debate in the Senate and House?
3. (a) What is the Senate's check on the filibuster? (b) How is this procedure invoked?
4. When is a conference committee formed and why is its job so important?
5. Why is a conference committee's report seldom rejected by either house?
6. What four options does the President have on receiving a measure passed by both houses of Congress?

**Critical Thinking**

7. **Drawing Conclusions** (p. 19) (a) If you were the President, under what circumstances might you use a pocket veto? (b) Why might you let a bill become law without signing it?

---

[24]Article I, Section 7, Clauses 2 and 3.

# How to Work in Groups

When people form a group to work together—whether it is the local school committee or the United States Congress—an orderly procedure helps the group to achieve its goals. One set of established rules for conducting a meeting in an orderly manner has been in use for more than three centuries. This set of rules is called parliamentary procedure. *Robert's Rules of Order*, written in 1876 by Major Henry M. Robert, is the most popular guide to parliamentary procedure used in the United States. Use the following steps for parliamentary procedure when working in a group.

**1. Call the meeting to order.** The presiding officer, or chair, officially begins the meeting by calling the group to order. He or she does this when a quorum is present. A quorum is the agreed-upon minimum number of members that must be present in order to conduct business. In most cases, a simple majority constitutes a quorum. Why do you think it is necessary to require a quorum in order to discuss business?

**2. Read and approve the minutes.** The group's secretary keeps a record, called the minutes, of all business matters that the group discusses, the actions proposed, and the actions taken. After the secretary reads the minutes of the previous meeting, the chair asks whether any member wants to make any additions or corrections. Each addition or correction must be voted on. The chair then asks for a vote to approve the minutes. What purpose(s) does the keeping of minutes serve?

**3. Hear committee reports.** Much of the work of large groups, such as Congress, is carried out in committees. Committee reports are handled in much the same way as the reading of the minutes. Why do you think it is advantageous for groups to form committees to perform work?

**4. Discuss unfinished and new business.** Following committee reports, the chair asks if members wish to discuss unfinished business. Then the floor becomes open to new business. In general, the conduct of business is based on the following principles:

- The majority rules.
- The minority will be heard.
- All members have equal rights and responsibilities.
- Only one subject can be debated at a time.
- The presiding officer must remain objective on all matters.

(a) What is the meaning of "floor" as it pertains to parliamentary procedure?
(b) What basic democratic rights are ensured by parliamentary procedure?

**5. Adjourn the meeting.** When the group has no more business to discuss, the chair makes a motion to adjourn. If the motion is seconded, the whole group votes on the measure. What might happen if a member could move for a vote without having the motion seconded?

# Chapter-in-Brief

Scan all headings, photographs, charts, and other visuals in the chapter before reading the section summaries below.

## Section 1 Congress Organizes (pp. 283–290)
Congress convenes each new term on January 3 of every odd-numbered year. Opening day in the House is filled with organizing tasks. A Speaker must be chosen, all members sworn in, rules adopted, and committee and other organization posts filled. The Senate's first day is a much simpler one, for the upper house is a continuous body.

Soon after both chambers are organized, the President delivers the State of the Union message to a joint session.

The Speaker of the House presides over the lower chamber. The Speaker is always a member of the majority party and is the dominant figure in the House. The Constitution makes the Vice President the president of the Senate. The Senate selects an alternate presiding officer, its president *pro tem*.

In both houses, the parties' organizations are headed by floor leaders who are assisted by whips; whips manage their parties' programs on the floor. Each party's caucus is composed of the party's members in that chamber.

## Section 2 Committees in Congress (pp. 290–294)
Congress does much of its work in its committees. Standing committees are the permanent committees in both houses. The Senate has 16 standing committees and the House has 22. Most of them are subject-matter bodies and are dominated by chairpersons chosen under the seniority rule. Both houses may also have select committees, which are special, often temporary bodies. Joint committees, made up of members of both houses, are usually permanent bodies. Conference committees are temporary joint committees formed to iron out the differences in Senate- and House-passed measures.

## Section 3 How a Bill Becomes a Law: The House (pp. 296–302)
Only a member can introduce a bill in either house. Many important measures actually originate elsewhere, however—often in the executive branch. Bills are referred to standing committees, where most die. Those that survive usually receive their closest study in subcommittees.

Bills reported out of committee are placed on a calendar. Also, the Rules Committee must ordinarily approve bills before they can reach the floor. Strict rules govern floor consideration in the House of Representative. Measures that do win House approval are then sent to the Senate.

## Section 4 The Bill in the Senate and the Final Stages (pp. 303–307)
The basic steps in the lawmaking process are much the same in the House and Senate. The Senate's rules are much less strict than those of the House, however.

A key difference lies in debate. Floor debate is strictly limited in the House but largely unrestricted in the Senate. The Senate's dedication to free debate gives rise to the filibuster—the tactic of "talking a bill to death." Senators can end a filibuster by cloture, but senators are often reluctant to do so.

The two houses approve some measures in different form. Before a bill can become law, the differences must be reconciled. Conference committees perform this task. These committees try to forge compromises acceptable to both chambers.

After both houses approve a bill in identical form, it is sent to the President. The President can sign the bill, allow it to become law without his signature, veto it, or, in some cases, apply a pocket veto.

## Vocabulary and Key Terms

| | | |
|---|---|---|
| Speaker of the House (p. 285) | select committee (p. 293) | subcommittee (p. 298) |
| president of the Senate (p. 286) | joint committee (p. 294) | Committee of the Whole |
| president *pro tempore* (p. 286) | conference committee (p. 294) | (p. 301) |
| floor leader (p. 286) | bill (p. 297) | quorum (p. 301) |
| whip (p. 287) | joint resolution (p. 297) | filibuster (p. 304) |
| party caucus (p. 287) | concurrent resolution (p. 297) | cloture (p. 306) |
| committee chairman (p. 289) | resolution (p. 297) | veto (p. 307) |
| seniority rule (p. 289) | rider (p. 297) | pocket veto (p. 307) |
| standing committee (p. 290) | discharge petition (p. 298) | |

**Matching:** *Review the key terms in the list above. If you are not sure of a term's meaning, look up the term and review its meaning. Choose a term from the list above that best matches each description.*

1. selects the party's leaders in each house of Congress
2. can force a committee to bring a bill to the floor of the House or Senate
3. the minimum number of legislators needed to perform official business
4. where a bill goes that has passed each house in different versions
5. a legislative committee created for a limited time and specific purpose

**True or False:** *Determine whether each statement is true or false. If it is true, write "true." If it is false, change the underlined word or words to make the statement true.*

1. A <u>rider</u> is quite similar to a bill, has the force of law, and usually deals with unusual or temporary matters.
2. <u>Floor leaders</u> are party officers selected by their partisan colleagues.
3. When a bill comes before Congress, it is assigned to one of the <u>subcommittees</u>.

4. The President only applies a <u>veto</u> in situations where the Congress has adjourned.
5. It only requires 100 members to form the <u>Committee of the Whole</u> in the House of Representatives.

**Word Relationships:** *Three of the terms in each of the following sets of terms are related. Choose the term that does not belong and explain why it does not belong.*

1. (a) committee chairman (b) seniority rule (c) party caucus (d) resolution
2. (a) filibuster (b) whip (c) cloture (d) discharge petition
3. (a) Speaker of the House (b) president of the Senate (c) president *pro tempore* (d) committee chairman
4. (a) discharge petition (b) resolution (c) bill (d) concurrent resolution

## Main Ideas

### Section 1 (pp. 283–290)

1. (a) What happens at the opening sessions in the House and the Senate? (b) What makes those events different in the two houses?

**2.** What are the functions of the presiding officers in the House and Senate?

**3.** What are the roles of the party officers in the House and Senate?

### Section 2 (pp. 290–294)

**4.** What is the role of the committee in the function of Congress?

**5.** (a) What are the different types of committees? (b) What are their functions?

**6.** (a) What is the role of the Rules Committee in the House? (b) How is that role filled in the Senate?

### Section 3 (pp. 296–302)

**7.** What are the sources of the bills introduced into Congress?

**8.** What are the different types of bills?

**9.** What happens to a bill once it enters the House?

### Section 4 (pp. 303–307)

**10.** For what reasons are the Senate's rules less strict than those of the House?

**11.** (a) What is the unique role of the filibuster in the legislative process of the Senate? (b) For what reason are senators often unwilling to end filibusters?

**12.** What role does the conference committee play in the legislative process?

**13.** After a bill has survived the House, Senate, and conference committee, what might happen to it?

## Critical Thinking

**1. Identifying Assumptions** (p. 19) Consider what you have read about the seniority rule. What assumption about qualifications for leadership underlie the seniority rule?

**2. Predicting Consequences** (p. 19) What do you think would happen to the legislative process in the Senate if the Senate were to no longer allow unlimited debate?

**3. Formulating Questions** (p. 19) Write a list of questions that would enable you to find an answer to this question: Should it be easier or more difficult to override a presidential veto?

## Getting Involved

**1. Writing Your Opinion** You have just been selected as the Speaker of the House. Write a letter to a friend in which you tell of your new job and your expectations for the future. Before you begin writing, list the powers and functions of the Speaker of the House. Review the legislative process in the House, where you will be presiding. Also review the other individuals who will take part in the leadership of the House. Begin your letter with an announcement of your selection. Then describe in order what you see as the most important aspects of your job. Also predict three challenges you might face as Speaker. Conclude your letter by stating what you hope to accomplish as Speaker. Proofread and revise to correct errors. Then draft a final copy.

**2. Class Debate** Hold a class debate on the following topic: *Resolved*, That the seniority rule should be abolished. Select one team to argue in favor of this statement and one to argue against it. The rest of the class should evaluate each team's presentation.

**3. Gathering Information** Using the Government Resources Handbook that begins on page 690, identify sources you could use to find the following information: (a) the subject of a bill recently debated in the Senate; (b) a House member's vote on a measure; (c) the members of a standing committee of Congress.

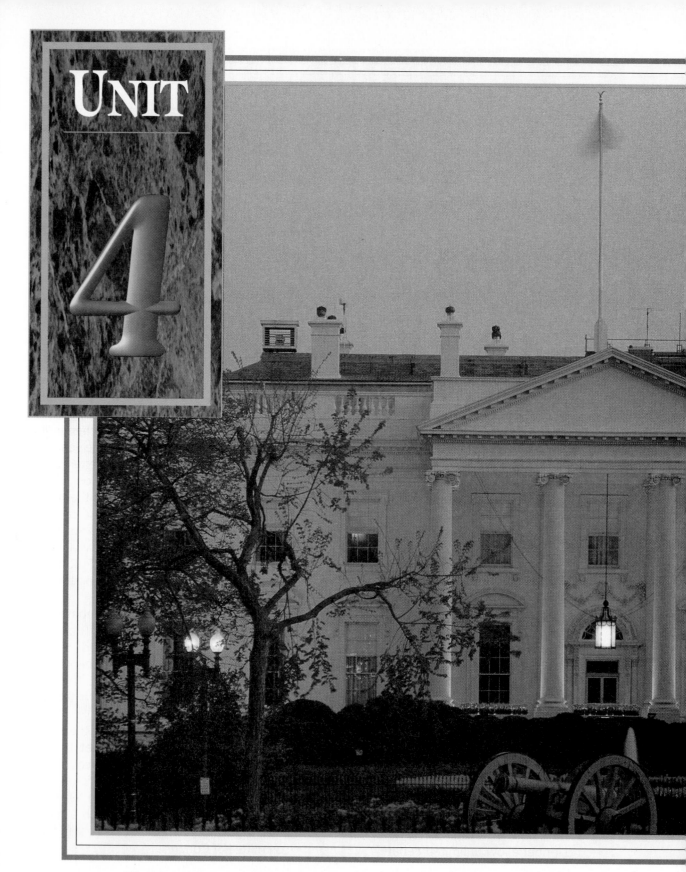

# UNIT 4

**The White House**   In the mid-1800s, any citizen who wished could, at a certain time of day, walk into the White House and shake the President's hand. Today, although the President is not nearly so accessible, he is still the "chief citizen," or representative of the people.

# The Executive Branch

On April 30, 1789, George Washington placed his right hand on a family Bible and his left hand on his heart and swore that he would "preserve, protect, and defend the Constitution of the United States." As he did so—in New York, which was then the nation's temporary capital—he became the first President of the United States.

Over two centuries now, each of President Washington's successors has repeated that ceremony and spoken the Constitution's solemn words. Most Presidents have done so in Washington, D.C., as Thomas Jefferson did for the first time in 1801. Bill Clinton recited the constitutional oath in the nation's capital on January 20, 1993, and so became the 42nd President of the United States. As President, Mr. Clinton holds what is undoubtedly the world's most extraordinary job. You will look at that job, and at the Executive Branch the President heads, throughout the five chapters of this unit.

## DID YOU KNOW THAT . . .

- Fourteen of the nation's now 45 Vice Presidents have become President.
- The Constitution makes no mention of the President's cabinet.
- The Federal Government is the largest single employer in the United States. Its nearly 3 million civilian employees work at more than 2,000 different kinds of jobs; another 1.7 million men and women now serve in the nation's armed forces.

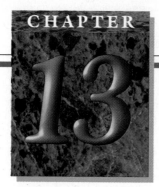
# The Presidency

## Chapter Preview

You are the President of the United States. The Director of the Central Intelligence Agency (the CIA) has just advised you that a country in this hemisphere, headed by a violently anti-American dictator, will soon have the ability to produce nuclear weapons. He also tells you that there is a very strong possibility that this hot-tempered tyrant will use his new-found nuclear muscle to disrupt ongoing peace talks between Israel and its Arab neighbors. What do you, the President, do? What steps do you take to meet this critical situation? What alternatives are available to you?

You are not the President, of course. But Bill Clinton is. And he, like many of his predecessors, has faced situations similar to the one posed here. Read on to learn more.

### Before you read this chapter:

- **Describe** three issues that the President was involved with last week.
- **Predict** what would occur if both the President and Vice President were unable to fulfill their duties.

### As you read, focus on the main objective for each section. Understand:

1. The interrelated roles of the presidency.
2. The process of presidential succession.
3. The qualifications, tenure, and compensation of the office.
4. The roles of primaries, caucuses, and conventions as parts of the nominating process.
5. How the national conventions operate.
6. The presidential campaign and the role of the electoral college.

▲ **"Give Peace a Chance"** Israeli Prime Minister Rabin and Palestine Liberation Organization Chairman Arafat shake hands at an historic White House meeting. An agreement was signed pledging mutual recognition, a step towards lasting peace in the Middle East.

*chief diplomat*

# 1 The President's Job Description

**Find Out:**
- What are the many roles a President must play?
- In what ways are those roles interrelated?
- What are the constitutional guidelines for qualifications and terms?
- What is the President's compensation?

**Key Terms:**
chief of state, chief executive, chief administrator, chief diplomat, commander in chief, chief legislator, chief of party, chief citizen

Thus far, 41 men have served as President of the United States; yet, Bill Clinton is regularly identified as the 42nd President. How can this be so? Do you know who was the youngest person ever to be President? The oldest? Who held the presidency for the longest time? The shortest?

You will find the answers to these questions and much more in this section, which lays out the overall shape of the presidential office.

## The President's Roles

At any given time, of course, only one person is President of the United States. The office, with all of its powers and duties, belongs to that one individual. Whoever that person may be, he—and likely someday she[1]—must fill a number of different roles, and all of them at the same time. The President is, simultaneously, (1) chief of state, (2) chief executive, (3) chief administrator, (4) chief diplomat, (5) commander in chief, (6) chief legislator, (7) party chief, and (8) chief citizen.

---

[1]To this point all of the Presidents have been men, but nothing in the Constitution prevents the election of a woman to that office.

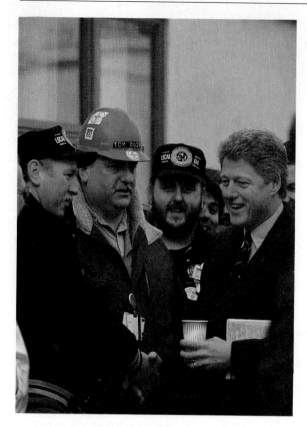

**The President in Action**   To be effective as the nation's chief citizen, President Clinton must stay in touch with all of the people.

CHIEF OF STATE   To begin with, the President is **chief of state**, the ceremonial head of the government of the United States, the symbol of all the people of the nation—in President William Howard Taft's words, "the personal embodiment and representative of their dignity and majesty."

In many countries, the chief of state reigns but does not rule. That is certainly true of the queens of England and of Denmark, the emperor of Japan, the kings of Norway and of Sweden, and the presidents of Italy and of Germany. It is most certainly not true of the President of the United States, who both reigns and rules.

CHIEF EXECUTIVE   The President is the nation's **chief executive**, vested by the Constitution with "the executive power of the United States." As you will see, that power is immensely broad in both domestic and foreign affairs. Indeed, the presidency is often described as "the most powerful office in the world."

CHIEF ADMINISTRATOR   The President is also the **chief administrator** of the Federal Government, heading one of the largest governmental machines the world has known. Today, the President directs an administration that employs nearly three million civilians and spends something on the order of $1.5 trillion a year.

CHIEF DIPLOMAT   The President is also the nation's **chief diplomat**, the main architect of American foreign policy and the nation's chief spokesperson to the rest of the world. "I make foreign policy," President Harry Truman once said— and he did. What the President says and does is carefully followed in this country and abroad.

COMMANDER IN CHIEF   In close concert with the President's role in foreign affairs, the Constitution also makes the President the **commander in chief** of the nation's armed forces. Nearly two million men and women in uniform and all the power in the nation's military arsenal are subject to the President's direct and immediate control.

CHIEF LEGISLATOR   The President is also the nation's **chief legislator**, the main architect of its public policies. It is the President who sets the overall shape of the congressional agenda— initiating, suggesting, requesting, supporting, insisting, and demanding that Congress enact much of the major legislation that it does.

These six presidential roles all come directly from the Constitution. Yet they do not complete the list. The President must fill other vital roles.

CHIEF OF PARTY   The President acts as the **chief of party**—the acknowledged leader of the political party that controls the executive branch. As you know, parties are not mentioned in the Constitution, yet they play a vital role in the function of American government. Thus, much of the real power and influence wielded by the President depends on the manner in which he or she plays this critical role.

CHIEF CITIZEN   The office also automatically makes of its occupant the nation's **chief citizen.** The President is expected to be "the representative of all the people," the one to work for and represent the public interest against the many private interests. "The presidency," said Franklin Roosevelt, "is not merely an administrative office. That is the least of it. It is preeminently a place of moral leadership."

## Interrelated Nature of Presidential Roles

Listing the President's several roles is a very useful way to describe the presidential job. But, remember, the President must play all of these roles simultaneously. None of them can be performed in isolation. The manner in which a President plays any one role can have a powerful effect on his ability to play the others.

As two illustrations, take the experiences of Presidents Lyndon Johnson and Richard Nixon. Each was a strong and a relatively effective President during his first years in office. But the agonizing and increasingly unpopular war in Vietnam persuaded Mr. Johnson not to run for reelection in 1968. In effect, the manner in which he acted as commander in chief during that conflict seriously damaged his effectiveness in the White House.

The many-sided, sordid Watergate scandal and the manner in which he filled the roles of party leader and chief citizen so destroyed Mr. Nixon's presidency that he was forced to leave office in disgrace in 1974.

## Formal Qualifications

The Constitution[2] says that the President must:
1. Be "a natural-born citizen." Under the doctrine of *jus sanguinis* (page 561), it is apparently possible for a person born abroad as an American citizen to become President. Some dispute that view; and the real shape of this requirement cannot be known until someone born a citizen, but born abroad, does in fact become President.[3]
2. Be at least 35 years of age. As the table on the following page shows, John F. Kennedy, at 43, was the youngest person ever to be

**Radio Days**  Each President has reinterpreted his role. President Roosevelt's fireside chats not only gained support for his New Deal program, but also established a personal rapport with the public.

elected to the presidency. Theodore Roosevelt reached it by succession at age 42. Ronald Reagan, who was 69 when he was first elected in 1980, is the oldest man ever elected to the office; and, when he completed his second term eight years later, he was the oldest person ever to hold the office. Bill Clinton was 46 years old when he became President in 1993.
3. Have lived in the United States for at least 14 years.[4]

While these formal qualifications do have some importance, they are really not very difficult to meet. In fact, there are more than 100 million people in this country today who do so.

Clearly, there are other and much more telling informal qualifications for the presidency—as you will see shortly.

---

[2]Article II, Section 1, Clause 5.

[3]Martin Van Buren, who was born December 5, 1782, was the first President actually born in the United States. His seven predecessors were each born before the Revolution. But notice that the Constitution anticipated that situation with these words: "or a citizen of the United States at the time of the adoption of this Constitution."

---

[4]Given Herbert Hoover's election in 1928 and Dwight Eisenhower's in 1952, the 14-year requirement means any 14 years in a person's life. Both Hoover and Eisenhower spent several years before election outside the United States.

## Presidents of the United States

| Name | Party | State[a] | Entered Office | Age on Taking Office | Religion |
|---|---|---|---|---|---|
| George Washington (1732-1799) | Federalist | Virginia | 1789 | 57 | Anglican |
| John Adams (1735-1826) | Federalist | Massachusetts | 1797 | 61 | Unitarian |
| Thomas Jefferson (1743-1826) | Dem-Rep[b] | Virginia | 1801 | 57 | —— |
| James Madison (1751-1836) | Dem-Rep | Virginia | 1809 | 57 | Episcopal |
| James Monroe (1758-1831) | Dem-Rep | Virginia | 1817 | 58 | Episcopal |
| John Q. Adams (1767-1848) | Dem-Rep | Massachusetts | 1767 | 57 | Unitarian |
| Andrew Jackson (1767-1845) | Democrat | Tennessee (SC) | 1829 | 61 | Presbyterian |
| Martin Van Buren (1782-1862) | Democrat | New York | 1837 | 54 | Dutch Reformed |
| William H. Harrison (1773-1841) | Whig | Ohio (VA) | 1841 | 68 | Episcopal |
| John Tyler (1790-1862) | Democrat | Virginia | 1841 | 51 | Episcopal |
| James K. Polk (1795-1849) | Democrat | Tennessee (NC) | 1845 | 49 | Presbyterian |
| Zachary Taylor (1784-1850) | Whig | Louisiana (VA) | 1849 | 64 | Episcopal |
| Millard Fillmore (1800-1874) | Whig | New York | 1850 | 50 | Unitarian |
| Franklin Pierce (1804-1869) | Democrat | New Hampshire | 1853 | 48 | Episcopal |
| James Buchanan (1791-1868) | Democrat | Pennsylvania | 1857 | 65 | Presbyterian |
| Abraham Lincoln (1809-1865) | Republican | Illinois (KY) | 1861 | 52 | —— |
| Andrew Johnson (1808-1875) | Democrat[c] | Tennessee (NC) | 1865 | 56 | —— |
| Ulysses S. Grant (1822-1885) | Republican | Illinois (OH) | 1869 | 46 | Methodist |
| Rutherford B. Hayes (1822-1893) | Republican | Ohio | 1877 | 54 | —— |
| James A. Garfield (1831-1881) | Republican | Ohio | 1881 | 49 | Disciples of Christ |
| Chester A. Arthur (1830-1886) | Republican | New York (VT) | 1881 | 50 | Episcopal |
| Grover Cleveland (1837-1908) | Democrat | New York (NJ) | 1885 | 47 | Presbyterian |
| Benjamin Harrison (1833-1901) | Republican | Indiana (OH) | 1889 | 55 | Presbyterian |
| Grover Cleveland (1837-1908) | Democrat | New York (NJ) | 1893 | 55 | Presbyterian |
| William McKinley (1843-1901) | Republican | Ohio | 1897 | 54 | Methodist |
| Theodore Roosevelt (1858-1919) | Republican | New York | 1901 | 42 | Dutch Reformed |
| William H. Taft (1857-1930) | Republican | Ohio | 1909 | 51 | Unitarian |
| Woodrow Wilson (1856-1924) | Democrat | New Jersey (VA) | 1913 | 56 | Presbyterian |
| Warren G. Harding (1865-1923) | Republican | Ohio | 1921 | 55 | Baptist |
| Calvin Coolidge (1872-1933) | Republican | Massachusetts (VT) | 1923 | 51 | Congregationalist |
| Herbert Hoover (1874-1964) | Republican | California (IA) | 1929 | 54 | Quaker |
| Franklin Roosevelt (1882-1945) | Democrat | New York | 1933 | 51 | Episcopal |
| Harry S Truman (1884-1972) | Democrat | Missouri | 1945 | 60 | Baptist |
| Dwight D. Eisenhower (1890-1969) | Republican | NY-PA (TX) | 1953 | 62 | Presbyterian |
| John F. Kennedy (1917-1963) | Democrat | Massachusetts | 1961 | 43 | Roman Catholic |
| Lyndon B. Johnson (1908-1973) | Democrat | Texas | 1963 | 55 | Disciples of Christ |
| Richard M. Nixon (1913-1994) | Republican | New York (CA) | 1969 | 55 | Quaker |
| Gerald R. Ford (1913-  ) | Republican | Michigan (NE) | 1974 | 61 | Episcopal |
| James E. Carter (1924-  ) | Democrat | Georgia | 1977 | 52 | Baptist |
| Ronald W. Reagan (1911-  ) | Republican | California (IL) | 1981 | 69 | Christian Church |
| George H.W. Bush (1924-  ) | Republican | Texas (MA) | 1989 | 64 | Episcopal |
| William J. Clinton (1946-  ) | Democrat | Arkansas | 1993 | 46 | Baptist |

▲ **Interpreting Tables: Multicultural Awareness** Most Presidents have shared similar backgrounds, although the Constitution sets no qualification regarding the religion, ancestry, or gender of the President. Shown at right are Presidents Andrew Jackson (7th), Theodore Roosevelt (26th), Harry Truman (33rd), and Bill Clinton (42nd).

| Ancestry | Vice President(s) |
|---|---|
| English | John Adams |
| English | Thomas Jefferson |
| Welsh | Aaron Burr/George Clinton |
| English | George Clinton/Elbridge Gerry |
| Scots | Daniel D. Tompkins |
| English | John C. Calhoun |
| Scots-Irish | John C. Calhoun/Martin Van Buren |
| Dutch | Richard M. Johnson |
| English | John Tyler |
| English | . . . . |
| Scots-Irish | George M. Dallas |
| English | Millard Fillmore |
| English | . . . . |
| English | William R. King |
| Scots-Irish | John C. Breckinridge |
| English | Hannibal Hamlin/Andrew Johnson |
| Scots-Irish, English | . . . . |
| English, Scots | Schuyler Colfax/Henry Wilson |
| English | William A. Wheeler |
| English, French | Chester A. Arthur |
| Scots-Irish, English | . . . . |
| Irish, English | Thomas A. Hendricks |
| English, Scots | Levi P. Morton |
| Irish, English | Adlai E. Stevenson |
| Scots-Irish, English | Garret A. Hobart/Theodore Roosevelt |
| Dutch, Scots, English, Huguenot | . . . . /Charles W. Fairbanks |
| English, Scots-Irish | James S. Sherman |
| Scots-Irish | Thomas R. Marshall |
| English, Scots-Irish | Calvin Coolidge |
| English | . . . . /Charles G. Dawes |
| Swiss-German | Charles Curtis |
| Dutch | John N. Garner/Henry A. Wallace/ Harry S Truman |
| Scots-English | . . . . /Alben W. Barkley |
| Swiss-German | Richard M. Nixon |
| Irish | Lyndon B. Johnson |
| English | . . . . /Hubert H. Humphrey |
| English, Scots-Irish | Spiro T. Agnew[d]/Gerald R. Ford[e] |
| English | Nelson A. Rockefeller[f] |
| English | Walter F. Mondale |
| English-Scots-Irish | George H.W. Bush |
| English | J. Danforth Quayle |
| English | Albert Gore, Jr. |

[a]State of residence when elected; if born in another State that State in parentheses.
[b]Democratic-Republican.
[c]Johnson, a War Democrat, was elected Vice President on the coalition Union Party ticket.
[d]Resigned October 10, 1973.
[e]Nominated by Nixon, confirmed by Congress on December 6, 1973.
[f]Nominated by Ford, confirmed by Congress on December 19, 1974.

## The President's Term

The Framers considered a number of different limits on the length of the presidential term. Most of their debate centered on a four-year term, with the President to be eligible for reelection, versus a single six-year or seven-year term. They finally settled on a four-year term.[5] They agreed, as Alexander Hamilton wrote in *The Federalist* No. 71, that that was a long enough period for a President to have gained experience, demonstrated his abilities, and established stable policies.

Until 1951, the Constitution placed no limit on the number of terms a President might serve.

[5]Article II, Section 1, Clause 1.

Several Presidents, beginning with George Washington, refused to seek more than two terms, however. Soon, the "no-third-term tradition" became an unwritten rule in presidential politics.

After Franklin D. Roosevelt broke the tradition by winning a third term in 1940, and then a fourth in 1944, the unwritten custom limiting presidential terms became a part of the written Constitution. The 22nd Amendment, adopted in 1951, reads in part:

❝No person shall be elected to the office of the President more than twice, and no person who has held the office of President, or acted as President, for more than two years of a term to which some other person was elected President shall be elected to the office of the President more than once.❞

## Global Awareness

### Former Professions/Titles of Heads of State, Selected Countries

| Country | Title | Name | Date acquired office | Previous profession/title |
|---------|-------|------|----------------------|---------------------------|
| Philippines | President | Fidel V. Ramos | Inaugurated June 30, 1992 | Defense Minister |
| Saudi Arabia | King | Fahd Ibn Abdul Aziz | Ascended to the throne June 13, 1982 | Crown Prince |
| Nicaragua | President | Violeta Barrios de Chamorro | Inaugurated April 25, 1990 | Newspaper publisher, political activist |
| Japan | Emperor | Akihito | Ascended to the throne November 12, 1990 | Crown Prince |
| Ireland | President | Mary Robinson | Assumed office December 3, 1990 | Lawyer |
| North Korea | President | Kim Jong II | Succeeded to the office July 20, 1994 | Vice President |
| Peru | President | Alberto Fujimori | Inaugurated December 29, 1989 | Agronomist (Agriculturist) |
| China | State President | Jiang Zemin | Assumed office May 27, 1993 | General Secretary, Communist Party |
| Libya | Leader of the Revolution | Muammar al-Qaddafi | Seized power September 1, 1969 | Army officer, Colonel |
| Poland | President | Lech Walesa | Assumed office December 22, 1990 | Leader of Poland's labor union |
| United States | President | Bill Clinton | Inaugurated January 20, 1993 | Governor of Arkansas |

▲ **Interpreting Tables: Multicultural Awareness** The position or the occupation from which a head of state came to his or her current office often suggests something about the political system in that country. What does this table tell you about the governments of Saudi Arabia, Japan, and Libya?

As a general rule, then, each President may now serve a maximum of two full terms—eight years—in office. *But* a President who has succeeded to the office beyond the midpoint in a term to which another person was originally elected could possibly serve for more than eight years. In that circumstance, the President may finish out the predecessor's term and then seek two full terms of his or her own. However, no President may now serve more than 10 years in the office.

Many people, including Presidents Truman, Eisenhower, and Reagan, have called for the repeal of the 22nd Amendment and its limit on presidential service. They argue that it is undemocratic because it places an arbitrary limit on the right of the people to decide who should be President. Some critics also say that the amendment undercuts the authority of a two-term President, especially in the latter part of his second term. Supporters of the amendment defend it as a reasonable safeguard against "executive tyranny."

Several Presidents, most recently Lyndon Johnson and Jimmy Carter, have urged a single six-year term. They, and others, have argued that a single, nonrenewable term would free a President from the pressures of a campaign for a second term, allowing him or her to focus on the pressing duties and/or responsibilities of the office.

## Pay and Benefits

The President's salary is fixed by Congress, and it can neither be increased nor decreased during a term.[6]

The salary was first set at $25,000 a year in 1789. Congress put the figure at its present level—$200,000—in 1969. Since 1949 the

President has also received a $50,000-a-year expense account. This sum is taxable as income and, in effect, it is a part of the President's pay above and beyond the salary.

The Constitution forbids the President "any other emolument from the United States, or any of them." But this clause does not prevent the President from being provided with a great many benefits, including the White House, a magnificent 132-room mansion set on an 18.3-acre estate in the heart of the nation's capital; a sizable suite of offices and a large staff; a yacht, a fleet of automobiles, a lavishly fitted Air Force One, and several other planes and helicopters; Camp David, the resort hideaway in the Catoctin Mountains in Maryland; the finest medical, dental, and other health care available; generous travel and entertainment funds; and many other fringe benefits.

Since 1958 each former President has received a lifetime pension, now $143,800 a year, and each presidential widow is entitled to a pension of $20,000 a year.

## Section 1 Review

**1. Define:** chief of state, chief executive, chief administrator, chief diplomat, commander in chief, chief legislator, chief of party, chief citizen
**2.** (a) What roles must a President play, and (b) how must he fulfill them?
**3.** What are the formal qualifications for the presidency?
**4.** (a) According to the 22nd Amendment, to how many terms may a President be elected? (b) What is the maximum length of time any person may serve as President?
**5.** (a) Who fixes the President's pay? (b) How much is it today?

### Critical Thinking

**6. Distinguishing Fact from Opinion** (p. 19) Admiral George Dewey once said, "The office of President is not such a very difficult one to fill, his duties being mainly to execute the laws of Congress." Do you agree or disagree with this statement? Explain.

---

[6]Article II, Section 1, Clause 7. At Philadelphia, Benjamin Franklin argued that, as money and power might corrupt a man, the President ought to receive nothing beyond his expenses; his suggestion was not put to a vote at the Convention, however. The present salary was set in the first measure passed by Congress in 1969. It was signed by President Johnson on January 17, three days before the new presidential term, President Nixon's first, began.

★

## Should the President's Executive Privilege Be Absolute?
### *United States* v. *Nixon*, 1974

In June 1972, seven men armed with cameras and bugging equipment were arrested inside the Democratic National Committee's offices in the Watergate complex in Washington, D.C. Police soon discovered that five of the burglars worked for the Committee to Re-Elect the President (the 1972 Nixon campaign organization). Both the White House and the President's campaign manager promptly denied any connection with the incident.

The seven men were tried for burglary in federal district court, and all of them were found guilty. Soon afterwards, the presiding judge received a letter from one of the convicted men. The letter spoke of payoffs to the burglars in return for their silence; they had perjured themselves to protect others who were involved in the break-in.

In 1973, a Senate select committee began an investigation, and it became clear that leading members of the Nixon administration were involved in a cover-up of the break-in and in several other illegal operations.

The Senate committee learned that for some time a White House taping system had routinely recorded all the President's conversations with his advisors. A special prosecutor, who had been named by the Justice Department to probe the burgeoning Watergate scandal, subpoenaed the White House tapes. But Mr. Nixon refused to release them, claiming they were protected by executive privilege.

In the ensuing months, as public outrage and pressures for impeachment grew, Mr. Nixon did release nine tapes. Curiously, portions of one of them had been erased. The special prosecutor continued to demand all of the tapes, but the President refused to deliver them. Finally, the prosecutor asked the Supreme Court to compel him to do so.

*Review the following evidence and arguments presented to the U.S. Supreme Court:*

### Arguments for Nixon

**1.** The constitutional scheme of separation of powers grants to the President the privilege of withholding information from the other branches of government.

**2.** The President's power to invoke executive privilege is absolute, and it is vital where high-level communications are involved.

**3.** This dispute should be resolved within the executive branch, not by the courts.

### Arguments for the United States

**1.** The President's power to claim executive privilege has never been held to be an absolute one.

**2.** Executive privilege may not be invoked to deny the courts access to evidence needed in a criminal proceeding.

**3.** This dispute can properly be heard in the federal courts.

### Getting Involved

**1. Identify** the constitutional grounds on which each side based its arguments.

**2. Debate** the opposing viewpoints presented in this case.

**3. Predict** how you think the Supreme Court ruled in this case and why. Then refer to the Supreme Court Glossary on page 769 to read about the decision. What does the Court's decision in this case say about the extent of presidential power?

# 2 Presidential Succession and the Vice Presidency

## Find Out:

- What are the constitutional provisions for succession to the presidency?
- How is presidential disability determined and dealt with?
- What is the status of the vice presidency, in history and today?

## Key Term:

presidential succession

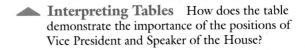

### Presidential Succession

| 1 | Vice President |
|---|---|
| 2 | Speaker of the House |
| 3 | President *pro tempore* of the Senate |
| 4 | Secretary of State |
| 5 | Secretary of the Treasury |
| 6 | Secretary of Defense |
| 7 | Attorney General |
| 8 | Secretary of the Interior |
| 9 | Secretary of Agriculture |
| 10 | Secretary of Commerce |
| 11 | Secretary of Labor |
| 12 | Secretary of Health and Human Services |
| 13 | Secretary of Housing and Urban Development |
| 14 | Secretary of Transportation |
| 15 | Secretary of Energy |
| 16 | Secretary of Education |
| 17 | Secretary of Veterans Affairs |

▲ **Interpreting Tables** How does the table demonstrate the importance of the positions of Vice President and Speaker of the House?

Consider these facts: Forty-five men[7] have served in the vice presidency. Nine of them, one in five, became President by succession. Altogether, 14 Vice Presidents, nearly one in three, later reached the White House—most recently, George Bush. Indeed, five of our last ten Presidents were at some point in their careers Vice President.

Clearly, these facts tell a very significant story. And they point up the importance of the main topics of this section: presidential succession and the vice presidency.

## The Constitution and Succession

If a President dies, or resigns, or is removed from office by impeachment, the Vice President automatically succeeds to the office.

Originally, the Constitution did not provide for the succession of the Vice President, however. Rather, it declared that "the powers and duties" of the office, not the office itself, were to "devolve on the Vice President."[8]

The practice, however, begun by John Tyler

in 1841, had been that should the office become vacant, the Vice President succeeded to it. That informal amendment became a part of the written Constitution with the adoption of the 25th Amendment in 1967. Section 1 of the amendment provides:

"In case of the removal of the President from office or of his death or resignation, the Vice President shall become President."

Congress fixes the order of succession following the Vice President.[9] The present law on the matter is the Presidential Succession Act of 1947. By its terms, the Speaker of the House and then the President *pro tem* of the Senate are next in line. They are followed, in turn, by the secretary of state and then by each of the other 13 heads of the cabinet departments, in order of precedence, as shown on the table at the top of this page.[10]

---

[7]No woman has yet held the office, but nothing in the Constitution bars that possibility. Only one woman has ever run as a major party's vice-presidential nominee: Geraldine Ferraro, the unsuccessful Democratic candidate in 1984.

[8]Article II, Section 1, Clause 6.

---

[9]Article II, Section 1, Clause 6. On removal of the President by impeachment, see Article I, Section 2, Clause 5; Article I, Section 3, Clauses 6 and 7; Article II, Section 4, and Chapter 11, Section 4.

[10]Article II, Section 1, Clause 6.

▲ **The Law of Succession** When Vice President Calvin Coolidge heard of President Harding's death in 1923, his father, a justice of the peace, administered the oath of office, as depicted in this painting.

## Presidential Disability

Before the passage of the 25th Amendment, there were serious gaps in the arrangement for **presidential succession**—the plan by which a vacancy in the presidency would be filled. Neither the Constitution nor Congress had made any provision for deciding when a President was disabled. Nor was there anything to indicate by whom such a decision was to be made.

For nearly 180 years, then, the nation played with fate. President Eisenhower suffered three serious but temporary illnesses while in office: a heart attack in 1955, ileitis in 1956, and a mild stroke in 1957. Two other Presidents were disabled for much longer periods of time. James Garfield lingered for 80 days before he died from an assassin's bullet in 1881. Woodrow Wilson suffered a paralytic stroke in 1919 and was an invalid for the rest of his second term.

He was so ill that he could not meet with his cabinet for seven months after his stroke.

Sections 3 and 4 of the 25th Amendment fill the disability gap, and in detail. The Vice President is to become Acting President if (1) the President informs Congress, in writing, "that he is unable to discharge the powers and duties of his office" or (2) the Vice President and a majority of the members of the cabinet inform Congress, in writing, that the President is so incapacitated.[11]

In either case, the President may resume the powers and duties of the office by informing Congress that no inability exists. However, the

---

[11]The 25th Amendment gives this authority to the Vice President and the cabinet or to "such other body as Congress may by law provide." To date, no "such other body" has been established.

Vice President and a majority of the cabinet may challenge the President on this score. Congress then has 21 days in which to decide the matter.

To this point, the disability provisions of the 25th Amendment have come into play only once and then only for a few hours. On July 13, 1985, surgeons removed a malignant tumor from President Reagan's large intestine. Just before surgery, Mr. Reagan transferred the powers of the presidency to Vice President Bush. He reclaimed those powers immediately after he awoke, seven hours and 54 minutes later.

## The Vice Presidency

"I am Vice President. In this I am nothing, but I may be everything." So said John Adams, the nation's first Vice President. Those words could have been repeated, very appropriately, by each of the 44 Vice Presidents who have followed him in that office.

The Constitution pays little attention to the office. It assigns the Vice President only two formal duties: (1) to preside over the Senate[12] and (2) to help decide the question of presidential disability.[13] Beyond those duties, the Constitution makes the Vice President a "President-in-waiting."

Through much of this nation's history, the vice presidency has been treated as an office of little real consequence and, often, as the butt of jokes. Many Vice Presidents themselves have had a hand in this. John Adams described his post as "the most insignificant office that ever the invention of man contrived or his imagination conceived." Thomas Jefferson, who followed him, found the office "honorable and easy" and "tranquil and unoffending."

Theodore Roosevelt, who had come to the White House from the vice presidency, was annoyed by the tinkling of the prisms of a chandelier in the presidential study. He ordered it removed, saying: "Take it to the office of the Vice President. He doesn't have anything to do.

---

[12]Article I, Section 3, Clause 4; see Chapter 12, Section 1.

[13]25th Amendment, Sections 3 and 4. The 12th Amendment says the Vice President must meet the same qualifications as those set out for the presidency.

### Vice Presidents Who Succeeded to the Presidency

**John Tyler**—on the death (pneumonia) of William Henry Harrison, April 4, 1841.

**Millard Fillmore**—on the death (gastroenteritis) of Zachary Taylor, July 9, 1850.

**Andrew Johnson**—on the death (assassination) of Abraham Lincoln, April 15, 1865.

**Chester A. Arthur**—on the death (assassination) of James A. Garfield, September 19, 1881.

**Theodore Roosevelt**—on the death (assassination) of William McKinley, September 14, 1901.

**Calvin Coolidge**—on the death (undisclosed illness) of Warren G. Harding, August 2, 1923.

**Harry S Truman**—on the death (cerebral hemorrhage) of Franklin D. Roosevelt, April 12, 1945.

**Lyndon B. Johnson**—on the death (assassination) of John F. Kennedy, November 22, 1963.

**Gerald R. Ford**—on the resignation of Richard M. Nixon, August 9, 1974.

**Interpreting Tables** From what you have read, what situation, other than the death or resignation of the President, may lead to a Vice President succeeding to the presidency?

It will keep him awake." The fixture has been in the Vice President's office ever since.

John Nance Garner, who served for two terms as Franklin Roosevelt's Vice President, once said: "The vice presidency isn't worth a warm pitcher of spit." And Alben Barkley, who served during Harry Truman's second term, often told the story of a woman who had two sons. One of them, Barkley said, went away to sea and the other one became Vice President, "and neither of them was ever heard from again."

## Importance of the Office

Despite these and a great many other unkind comments, the office is clearly an important one. Its occupant is literally "only a heartbeat away from the presidency." Remember, eight Presidents have died in office, and one, Richard M. Nixon, was forced to resign. So, clearly, the office has great significance.

Some blame for the low status of the vice presidency in modern times may stem from the way in which the two major parties nominate their candidates for the office. Each convention names the hand-picked choice of its just-nominated presidential candidate. Usually, the presidential candidate picks someone who will "balance the ticket." That is, the presidential candidate chooses a running mate who can improve his electoral chances. In short, fate and the vice presidency do not have a very high priority in the vice-presidential selection process.

The vice presidency has been vacant 18 times thus far—nine times by succession to the presidency, twice by resignation, and seven times by death.[14] Yet, not until 1967 and the 25th Amendment did the Constitution deal with the matter. Section 2 provides:

❝Whenever there is a vacancy in the office of the Vice President, the President shall nominate a Vice President

---

[14]John C. Calhoun resigned to become a senator from South Carolina in 1832. Spiro T. Agnew resigned in 1973, after a conviction for income tax evasion and in the face of charges of corruption dating from his service as a county executive and then governor of Maryland. The seven who died in office were: George Clinton 1812), Elbridge Gerry (1814), William R. King (1853), Henry Wilson (1875), Thomas A. Hendricks (1885), Garret A. Hobart (1899), and James S. Sherman (1912).

▲ **A Heartbeat Away**   Al Gore was serving in the Senate when he became Vice President.

who shall take office upon confirmation by a majority vote of both houses of Congress.❞

The provision was first implemented in 1973, when President Nixon selected and Congress confirmed Gerald Ford to succeed Spiro Agnew as Vice President. It came into play again in 1974, when President Ford named and Congress approved Nelson Rockefeller.

Many have long urged that the Vice President be given a larger role in the executive branch. The more recent Presidents, from Eisenhower to Clinton, have in fact made greater use of their Vice Presidents. Today, Vice President Gore takes part in cabinet meetings, is a member of the National Security Council, and is one of Mr. Clinton's closest advisers. He also performs a variety of political and diplomatic chores for the President.

So far, however, no President has upgraded the Vice President to the role of a true "assistant president." The major reason: Of all the President's official family, only the Vice President is not subject to the ultimate discipline of removal from office by the President. No matter what the circumstances, the President cannot fire the Vice President.

## Section 2 Review

1. **Define:** presidential succession
2. Which amendment states that if the presidency becomes vacant, the Vice President succeeds to that office?
3. Who follows the Vice President in the line of presidential succession?
4. How is presidential disability determined?
5. What official duties does the Constitution grant the Vice President?
6. For what reasons is the vice presidency so lightly regarded?

**Critical Thinking**

7. **Formulating Questions** (p. 19) Imagine you are a politician who has just been offered the vice-presidential nomination. Make a list of questions that will help you decide whether to accept or reject the offer.

★

# 3 Presidential Selection: The Framers' Plan

## Find Out:

- What did the Framers intend the electoral college to be?
- What factors helped transform the presidential selection process?

## Key Terms:

presidential electors, electoral college

In formal terms, the President is chosen according to the provisions of the Constitution.[15] In practice, however, the President is elected through an altogether extraordinary process that is not very well understood by most of the American people. That process is a combination of constitutional provisions, a few State and federal laws, and, in largest measure, a number of practices born of the nation's political parties.

To make sense of that very complex matter, you must first understand the subject of this section: what the Framers had in mind when they designed the presidential election process.

## Original Constitutional Provisions

The Framers of the Constitution gave more time to the method for choosing the President than to any other matter. It was, said James Wilson of Pennsylvania, "the most difficult of all on which we have had to decide." It was difficult largely because most of the Framers were against selecting the President by either of the obvious ways: by Congress or by a direct vote of the people.

Early in the Convention, most of the delegates favored selection by Congress. Later, nearly all delegates came to the view that congressional selection would, as Hamilton said, put the President "too much under the legislative thumb."

Only a few of the Framers favored choosing the President by popular vote. Nearly all agreed that that would lead "to tumult and disorder." Most delegates felt, too, that the people, scattered over so wide an area, could not possibly know enough about the available candidates to make wise, informed choices. George Mason of Virginia spoke for most of his colleagues at the convention: "The extent of the country renders it impossible that the people can have the requisite capacity to judge the respective contentions of the candidates."

After weeks of debate, the Framers finally agreed on a plan first put forward by Hamilton. Under it, the President was to be chosen by a special body of electors. In detail, the plan provided:

1. Each of the several States would have as many **presidential electors** as it has senators and representatives in Congress.
2. These electors would be chosen in each State in a manner the State legislature directed.
3. The electors, meeting in their own States, would each cast two votes—each for a different person for President.
4. The electoral votes from the States would be opened and counted before a joint session of Congress.
5. The person receiving the largest number of electoral votes, provided that total was a majority of all the electors, would become President.
6. The person with the second highest number of electoral votes would become Vice President.
7. If a tie occurred, or if no one received the votes of a majority of the electors, the President would be chosen by the House of Representatives, voting by States.
8. If a tie occurred for the second spot, the Vice President would be chosen by the Senate.[16]

---

[15]The Constitution deals with the process of presidential selection in several places: Article II, Section 1, Clauses 2, 3, and 4, and the 12th, 20th, and 23rd amendments.

[16]Remember, these were the original provisions, in Article II, Sections 2 and 4; they were modified by the 12th Amendment, as you will see. As curious as it may seem today, the electoral college system was one of the few major features of the Constitution to escape widespread criticism in the struggle over the ratification.

The Framers intended the electors to be "the most enlightened and respectable citizens" from each State. They were to be "free agents" who would "deliberate freely" in choosing the persons best qualified to fill the nation's two highest offices.

## The Impact of the Rise of Parties

The original version of the **electoral college** worked as the Framers intended only for as long as George Washington was willing to seek and hold the presidency. He was twice, and unanimously, elected President. That is, in 1789 and again in 1792, each elector cast one of his two ballots for the great Virginian.

Flaws began to appear in the system in 1796, however. By then, political parties had begun to form. John Adams, the Federalist candidate, was elected to the presidency. Thomas Jefferson, an arch-rival and Democratic-Republican, who lost to Adams by just three votes in the electoral balloting, became his Vice President.

**The Election of 1800** The system broke down in the election of 1800. By then there were two well-defined parties: the Federalists, led by Adams and Hamilton, and the Democratic-Republicans, headed by Jefferson. Each of these parties nominated presidential and vice-presidential candidates. They also nominated candidates to serve as presidential electors in the several States. Those elector-candidates were picked with the clear understanding that, if elected, they would then vote for their party's presidential and vice-presidential nominees.

---

### Rating the Presidents

| | |
|---|---|
| **"The Great Presidents"** | George Washington, Thomas Jefferson, Abraham Lincoln, Franklin D. Roosevelt |
| **"The Near Great Presidents"** | Andrew Jackson, Theodore Roosevelt, Woodrow Wilson, Harry Truman |
| **"The Above Average Presidents"** | John Adams, James Madison, James Monroe, John Quincy Adams, James K. Polk, Grover Cleveland, Dwight Eisenhower, John F. Kennedy, Lyndon Johnson |
| **"The Average Presidents"** | Martin Van Buren, Rutherford B. Hayes, Chester A. Arthur, Benjamin Harrison, William McKinley, William Howard Taft, Herbert Hoover, Gerald R. Ford, Jimmy Carter |
| **"The Below Average Presidents"** | John Tyler, Zachary Taylor, Millard Fillmore, Franklin Pierce, James Buchanan, Andrew Johnson, Calvin Coolidge, Richard Nixon |
| **"The Failures"** | Ulysses S. Grant and Warren G. Harding |

▲ **Interpreting Tables and Political Cartoons** This is how a recent survey rated the Presidents. Do you think the passage of time changes such ratings? Why? What value does the cartoon place upon such polls?

Each of the 73 Democratic-Republicans who won posts as electors voted for his party's nominees: Jefferson and Aaron Burr. In doing so, they produced a tie for the presidency. Remember the Constitution gave each elector two votes, each to be cast for a different person, but each to be cast for someone as President. Popular opinion clearly favored Jefferson for the presidency, and the party had intended Burr for the vice presidency. Still, the House of Representatives had to take 36 separate ballots before it finally chose Jefferson.

The spectacular election of 1800 left a lasting imprint on the presidential election process. It marked the introduction of three new elements into the process of selecting a President: (1) party nominations for the presidency and vice presidency, (2) the nomination of candidates for presidential electors pledged to vote for their party's presidential ticket, and (3) the automatic casting of the electoral votes in line with those pledges. Gone forever was the notion that the electors would be "free agents" who would deliberate in the selection of a President to lead the nation.

**The 12th Amendment**  The election of 1800 produced another notable result. The 12th Amendment was added to the Constitution in 1804, to make certain there would never be another such fiasco. The amendment is a lengthy one, but it made only one major change in the electoral college system. It separated the presidential and vice-presidential elections: "The Electors . . . shall name in their ballots the person voted for as President, and in distinct ballots the person voted for as Vice President."[17]

With the appearance of parties, the elections of 1800, and then the 12th Amendment, the constitutional setting was laid for the presidential selection system as it exists today. That system is, indeed, a far cry from what was agreed on in 1787—as you will see in the sections ahead.

---

[17]Not only does the amendment mean there cannot be a tie, it almost certainly guarantees that the President and Vice President will be of the same party.

▲ **Party Impact**  John Adams served as the nation's second President. With his defeat for reelection, the Federalists never again gained control of either the presidency or Congress.

## Section 3 Review

1. **Define:** presidential electors, electoral college
2. (a) Why were most of the Framers opposed to choosing the President by popular vote? (b) To selection by Congress?
3. (a) Outline the original provisions for the electoral college. (b) How did the Framers expect electors to vote?
4. What three events combined to change the intent of the original electoral college system?
5. What major change did the 12th Amendment make in the electoral college system?

**Critical Thinking**

6. **Recognizing Ideologies** (p. 19) The Framers intended the presidential electors to be "the most enlightened and respectable citizens" in each State. What does this suggest about their definition of good citizenship?

★

# 4 Nominating Presidential Candidates Today

**Find Out:**
- What features make the presidential nominating process so complicated?
- What roles do primaries, caucuses, and conventions play in that process?

**Key Terms:**
presidential primary, winner-take-all

The Constitution makes no provision for the nomination of candidates for the presidency. Rather, as you have just seen, the Framers designed a system in which presidential electors would, out of their own knowledge, select the "wisest and best man" as President. But, as you have also seen, the rise of parties altered that system drastically.

In this section, you will examine what emerged from that historic revision of the Framers' original plan: the modern-day presidential nominating process.

## The Role of Conventions

The first method the parties developed to nominate presidential candidates was the congressional caucus. As you read in Chapter 7, that method was regularly used in the elections of 1800 to 1824. But, as you know, its closed character led to its downfall in the mid-1820s. For the election of 1832, both major parties turned to the national convention as their nominating device. It has continued to serve them ever since.

**Extent of Control by Law** As a result of the convention process, the final selection of the President is, for all practical purposes, narrowed to one of two persons: the Republican or the Democratic nominee. Yet in spite of its important role in the American political system, there is almost no legal control over the convention process.

The Constitution is silent on the subject of presidential nominations. There is, as well, almost no statutory law on the matter. The only provisions in federal law have to do with the financing of conventions; see Chapter 7, Section 3. Also, only a very small body of State law deals with a few aspects of convention organization and procedure—for example, the choosing of delegates and the manner in which they may cast their votes, which you will read about in the coming pages. In short, the convention is largely a creation and responsibility of the political parties themselves.

**Convention Arrangements** In both parties the national committee makes the arrangements for the national convention. A year or more before it is held, the committee meets, usually in Washington, D.C., to set the time and place for the convention. Over recent years, the party out of power has held its convention first, sometime in July; the President's party has met a month later, in August.

Where the party holds its convention is a matter of prime importance. There must be an adequate convention hall, sufficient hotel accommodations, plentiful entertainment outlets, and convenient transportation facilities. Political considerations are also key. A city in a doubtful State—one that might vote either way—or in a supportive State is usually picked, in the hope of swaying the election outcome.

Many of the nation's larger cities bid for the honor—and the financial return to local business—of hosting a national convention. For 1996, the Democrats picked Chicago as their meeting place and the Republicans gathered in San Diego.

The Democrats held each of their first six conventions, from 1832 through 1852, in Baltimore. Since 1856—when the Republicans held their first convention in Philadelphia, and the Democrats moved to Cincinnati—the two parties have met in the cities listed in the table on page 331.

**The Apportionment of Delegates** With the date and the location set, the national committee issues its "call" for the convention. That formal announcement names the time and place and also tells the party's organization in each State how many delegates it may send to the national meeting. It is the delegates who will actually cast the votes that will nominate the party's presidential candidate.

Traditionally, both parties give each State organization a number of convention votes based on that State's electoral votes. Over the past several conventions, however, both parties have developed complicated formulas that award bonus delegates to those States that have supported the party's candidates in recent elections.

For 1996, the Republicans' apportionment formula produced a convention of 1,984 delegates, and the Democrats' more complicated plan, 4,295.[18] Given those numbers, it should be fairly clear why neither party's national convention can really be described as "a deliberative body."

**Selection of Delegates**  There are really two campaigns for the presidency every four years. One is the contest between the Republican and the Democratic nominees, of course. The other, earlier and quite different one, takes place within each of the parties: the struggle for convention delegates.

State laws and/or party rules fix the procedures for picking the delegates in each State. That fact is a reflection of federalism, and it has produced a crazy-quilt pattern of presidential primaries, conventions, and caucuses among the 50 States.[19]

---

[18]The conventions of both parties include delegates from the District of Columbia, Puerto Rico, the Virgin Islands, Guam, and American Samoa.

The Democratic convention also includes a number of "superdelegates"—mostly top party officers and Democrats who hold major elective public offices. They are automatically members of their respective State delegations. There were more than 750 superdelegates to the Democrats' 1996 convention; their number included all of the members of the Democratic National Committee, the governors of 19 States, and nearly all of the Democratic members of the House and Senate.

[19]To a very large extent, the GOP leaves the matter of selecting national convention delegates to its State party organizations and to State law.

The Democrats have added several rules in recent years that have in effect nationalized much of the delegate-selection process. Most of these rules are aimed at prompting broader involvement in the choosing of delegates (especially by the young, African Americans, other minority groups, and women) and at making other aspects of convention organization and procedure more democratic.

## National Convention Sites Since 1856

| City | Republicans | Democrats |
|---|---|---|
| Atlanta | | 1988 |
| Atlantic City | | 1964 |
| Baltimore | 1864 | 1860, 1872, 1912 |
| Chicago | 1860, 1868, 1880, 1884, 1888, 1904, 1908, 1912, 1916, 1920, 1932, 1944, 1952, 1960 | 1864, 1884, 1892, 1896, 1932, 1940, 1944, 1952, 1956, 1968, 1996 |
| Cincinnati | 1876 | 1856, 1880 |
| Cleveland | 1924, 1936 | |
| Dallas | 1984 | |
| Detroit | 1980 | |
| Denver | | 1908 |
| Houston | 1992 | 1928 |
| Kansas City, Mo. | 1928, 1976 | 1900 |
| Los Angeles | | 1960 |
| Miami Beach | 1968, 1972 | 1972 |
| Minneapolis | 1892 | |
| New Orleans | 1988 | |
| New York | | 1868, 1924, 1976, 1980, 1992 |
| Philadelphia | 1856, 1872, 1900, 1940, 1948 | 1936, 1948 |
| San Diego | 1996 | |
| St. Louis | 1896 | 1876, 1888, 1904, 1916 |
| San Francisco | 1956, 1964 | 1920, 1984 |

▲ **Interpreting Tables**  Why do you think the Democrats picked Chicago and the Republicans San Diego for their 1996 convention sites?

## Presidential Primaries

More than three-fourths of all the delegates to both conventions now come from States that hold presidential primaries. Several of those primaries are major media events, and serious contenders in both parties must make the best possible showing in most of them.

A **presidential primary** is one or both of two things. Depending on the State, it is a process in which those who vote in a party's primary (1) elect some or all of a State party

## The Path to the White House (selected Presidents)

| President | Highest Previous Public Office |
|---|---|
| John F. Kennedy | U.S. Senator |
| Lyndon B. Johnson | Vice President |
| Richard Nixon | Vice President |
| Gerald Ford | Vice President |
| Jimmy Carter | Governor (Georgia) |
| Ronald Reagan | Governor (California) |
| George Bush | Vice President |
| Bill Clinton | Governor (Arkansas) |

▲ **Interpreting Tables** What public offices seem to be stepping stones to the White House?

organization's delegates to the national convention, and/or (2) express a preference among the various contenders for that party's presidential nomination.

**History** The presidential primary first appeared in the early 1900s. It was part of the reform movement aimed at the boss-dominated convention system. Wisconsin passed the first presidential primary law in 1905, providing for the popular election of national convention delegates. Several States soon followed that lead, and Oregon added the preference feature in 1910.

By 1916 nearly half the States had adopted presidential primary laws. But many States later dropped the device. By 1968 it was found in only 16 States and the District of Columbia.

Efforts to reform the national convention process, especially in the Democratic party, reversed that downward trend in the 1970s, however. For 1992, some form of the presidential primary was in place in 38 of the States[20] and also in the District of Columbia and Puerto Rico.

---

[20]In Alabama, Arkansas, California, Colorado, Connecticut, Florida, Georgia, Idaho, Illinois, Indiana, Kansas, Kentucky, Louisiana, Maryland, Massachusetts, Michigan, Minnesota, Mississippi, Montana, Nebraska, New Hampshire, New Jersey, New Mexico, New York, North Carolina, Ohio, Oregon, Oklahoma, Pennsylvania, Rhode Island, South Carolina, South Dakota, Tennessee, Texas, Washington, West Virginia, Wisconsin. In some of those States, the law permits but does not require a major party to hold a primary.

**Primaries Today** Again, a presidential primary is either or both of two things: a delegate-selection process and/or a candidate preference election. Once that much has been said, however, the device becomes very hard to describe, except on a State-by-State basis.

The difficulty comes largely from two sources: (1) the fact that in each State the details of the delegate-selection process are determined by that State's own law—and those details vary from one State to the next, and (2) the ongoing reform efforts in the Democratic party. Since 1968, when the Democrats were shattered by disputes over Vietnam and civil rights policies, the Democratic National Committee has written and rewritten the party's rules to prompt greater grassroots participation in the delegate-selection process. Those new rules have prompted many changes in most States' election laws.

Even a matter that seems so simple as the date for the primary shows the crazy-quilt pattern of State laws. New Hampshire holds the first of the presidential primaries every four years. For 1992, it scheduled its primary on February 18, and all of the other presidential primaries were set for various dates over the next four months.

Most States prefer an early date, and so the primary schedule has become "front-loaded." Many primaries—and most of the larger States' contests—come in March and early April. For decades, the largest State, California, did hold one of the last primaries, in June. By then, usually, and in both parties, some candidate had won enough delegate support in other States to guarantee victory at the convention. But now, for 1996, California has rescheduled its presidential primary for early March.

Until fairly recently, most primaries were both delegate-selection and preference exercises. Several primaries were also **winner-take-all** contests. That is, the candidate who won the preference vote automatically won the support of all delegates chosen at the primary.

Winner-take-all primaries have all but disappeared, however. The Democratic party rules now prohibit them. Instead the Democrats have a complex "proportional representation" rule. Any aspirant who wins at least 15 percent of the votes cast in a primary gets the number of that State's Democratic convention delegates that corresponds to his or her share of that primary vote. Take, as an example, a State that has 40 convention delegates. If Senator Bob Kerrey won 45 percent of the primary vote, he automatically won the support of at least 18 of the delegates.

Most States had to change their primary laws to account for the Democrats' proportional representation rule—and so in many States, Republican delegates are also chosen on a share-of-the-vote basis. But some States still permit winner-take-all primaries and the Republicans hold them where they can. The Democrats' proportional representation rule had yet another major impact on the shape of these primaries. It led several States—among them both Oregon and Wisconsin, the States that pioneered the presidential primary idea—to give up the popular selection of delegates.

More than half of the presidential primary States now hold only a preference primary. The delegates themselves are chosen later, at party conventions.[21] Most of the preference contests are also "all-candidate" primaries: contests in which all generally recognized contenders for a party's presidential nomination are (must be) listed on that party's preference ballot.

## Evaluation of the Presidential Primary

No one who surveys the presidential primary system needs to be told that it is complicated, nor that it is filled with a number of confusing variations.

Nevertheless, these primaries are vital. Over recent years they have played the major part in deciding the presidential nominating contests in both parties—and especially in the party out of power.

Presidential primaries tend to democratize the delegate-selection process. And, importantly, they

▲ **Campaign '92** Part of the presidential selection process is the winning over of supporters, who may then, in turn, convince other voters to support their candidate.

force would-be nominees to test their candidacies in actual political combat.

Hard-fought contests occur but are not common in the party in power. This tends to be true either because the President (1) is himself seeking reelection or (2) has given his backing to someone he favors for the nomination. In either case the President almost always gets his way.

Both 1976 and 1980 were exceptions to that rule. In 1976 Ronald Reagan made a stiff run at President Ford in the Republican party. Senator Edward Kennedy gave President Carter a real fight in the Democratic party in 1980. But, notice, in the end the incumbent President did win his party's nomination.

For the party out of power, the primaries are often "knock-down, drag-out" battles. Without the unifying force of the President as party leader, the several leaders and factions in the party vie with one another, vigorously, for the presidential nomination. Here, one of the presidential primaries' key functions can be seen: the screening out of the lesser possibilities to the point where only a few contenders for the presidential nomination remain.

The recent explosion in the number of presidential primaries places great demands on

---

[21]In most of these States, the delegates must be picked in line with the results of the preference primary—for example, for the Democrats in 1992, so many delegates for Jerry Brown, so many for Tom Harkin, and so on. In some, however, the preference vote does not govern the choice of the delegates; in those States, the preference primary is often called a "beauty contest."

candidates in terms of time, effort, money, scheduling, and fatigue. They also test the public's endurance. Adlai Stevenson once said, in a day when there were many fewer primaries, "The hardest thing about any political campaign is how to win without proving that you are unworthy of winning."

Many critics think that each of the major parties should hold a single, nationwide presidential primary. Some critics would have both parties nominate their presidential candidates in those contests. They would do away with the conventions, except perhaps to pick vice-presidential nominees or to write platforms.

Other critics see a national primary as the best way for the parties either (1) to select all of their convention delegates or (2) to allow their voters to express their candidate preferences, which would then bind their delegates.

Still other critics favor a series of regional primaries, held at two- or three-week intervals in groups of States across the country.

Hope for any of these plans is dim at best. Each plan would require joint action by Congress, the States, and both major parties.

Beyond that hurdle, recall this point from Chapter 7: However it is conducted, the nominating process can have a very divisive effect on a party; and the primary magnifies that ever-present possibility. In short, neither major party has ever expressed any interest in abandoning its national convention. Both parties see the convention as a device to promote compromise and, out of it, party unity.

## Caucuses and Conventions

In those States that do not hold presidential primaries, delegates to the national conventions are chosen in a system of caucuses and conventions.[22] Here, too, the details of the process are different from State to State. However, it works pretty much as described on pages 158–160.

The party's voters meet in local caucuses, generally at the precinct level. There they choose delegates to a local or district convention where delegates to the State convention are picked. At the State level, and sometimes in the district conventions, delegates to the national convention are chosen.

▲ **Interpreting Political Cartoons** Voters in the New Hampshire primary (above) are the first in the nation to cast their ballots for their preferred presidential candidate. What does the cartoon say about the significance of the Iowa caucus and the New Hampshire primary?

The caucus-convention process is the oldest method for picking national convention delegates. But, notice, in 1992 less than a quarter of all delegates to either party's convention came from those States that still use the caucus-convention process. The Iowa caucuses generally get the most attention, largely because they are now the first delegate-selection event held in every presidential election season.

## Section 4 Review

1. **Define:** presidential primary, winner-take-all
2. (a) To what extent does federal law deal with the national conventions? (b) State law?
3. What effect do the different State laws have upon the nominating process?
4. A presidential primary is one or both of what two things?
5. For what reasons are hard-fought presidential primaries fairly common in the party out of power and rather rare for the President's party?
6. For what reason have the two major parties continued to rely on the national convention to nominate candidates?
7. By what other processes are convention delegates chosen?

### Critical Thinking

8. **Demonstrating Reasoned Judgment** (p. 19) This observation by Adlai Stevenson appears earlier in the section: "The hardest thing about any political campaign is how to win without proving that you are unworthy of winning." What do you think he meant?

★

---

[22] Delegates were chosen, in one or both parties by the caucus-convention method in 17 States in 1992. Both parties chose delegates that way in Alaska, Arizona, Delaware, Hawaii, Iowa, Maine, Missouri, Nevada, North Dakota, Utah, Vermont, Virginia, and Wyoming. The Democrats (but not the Republicans) held caucuses in Idaho, Minnesota, and Washington. In Texas the Democrats selected some of their national convention delegates by caucuses and conventions and some of them in a presidential primary. The caucus-convention process was also used by both parties in Guam, the Virgin Islands, and American Samoa.

# 5 At the National Convention

**Find Out:**
- What are the purposes of the national conventions?
- What takes place at the different sessions?

**Key Terms:**
keynote address, platform

The national conventions have never been very much admired. In fact, they are roundly criticized every four years—by radio and television commentators, newspaper editors, syndicated columnists, late-night talk show hosts, and a great many others.

All of this is nothing new. In 1908 a foreign observer who had just attended both parties' conventions called them "a colossal travesty of popular institutions." He went on to describe the convention participants as: "A greedy crowd of office-holders, or of office-seekers, disguised as delegates of the people . . . "

Despite their many detractors, the conventions do play an important role in the American political system. As you will see in this section, they are held every four years to do three main things: (1) adopt the party's platform, (2) pick its presidential and vice-presidential nominees, and (3) unify the party behind those candidates and for the upcoming campaign.

## The Convention Setting

Each party's national convention meets in a huge auditorium hung with flags, bunting, and various party symbols. Portraits of great figures from the party's past adorn the hall. The front of the hall is dominated by a large platform and the speaker's rostrum. The floor itself is jammed with row upon row of chairs. Standards and placards mark the seating reserved for each State's group of delegates. There are extensive facilities for the army of reporters, commentators, camera operators, technicians, and all their equipment. The galleries seat thousands of people who come from all over the country to see a spectacle H. L. Mencken once described this way:

❝[T]here is something about a national convention that makes it as fascinating as a revival or a hanging. It is vulgar, it is ugly, it is stupid, it is tedious, it's hard upon both the cerebral centers and the gluteus maximus, and yet it is somehow charming. One sits through long sessions wishing heartily that all the delegates were dead and in hell—and then suddenly there comes a show so gaudy and hilarious, so melodramatic and obscene, so unimaginably exhilarating and preposterous that one lives a gorgeous year in an hour.❞

## The Opening Session

Each party's convention generally runs four days, with one and sometimes two sessions held each day. The order of business is much the same in both conventions.

The opening session is very largely devoted to two matters: organizing the convention and delivering rousing speeches. The delegates are called to order by the chairperson of the party's national committee. The "Star Spangled Banner" is sung, the official call is read, prayer is offered, and the temporary roll of delegates is called. The national chairperson and party dignitaries make welcoming speeches.

▲ **Keynote Speaker** At the 1992 Democratic Convention, the honor of making this mood-setting speech went to Barbara Jordan, former U.S. Representative from Texas.

The chairperson then announces a slate of temporary officers for the convention—all of them picked by the national committee. The delegates promptly elect them.

The **keynote address** is almost always the high point of the first session. That speech is usually delivered by one of the party's most dynamic orators. It is intended to spur the delegates and set the tone for the convention and the campaign to come. The keynoter's remarks, and nearly all of the many other speeches made during the convention, follow a predictable pattern: They glorify the party, its leaders, and its programs, condemn the opposition, urge party unity, and predict a smashing victory for November.

The opening session winds down with the routine election of the convention's standing committees. There are four major committees at every convention: rules and order of business, permanent organization, credentials, and platform and resolutions. Each State delegation now has two of its members, a man and a woman, on each of them.

## The Second and Third Sessions

The next two or three, and sometimes four, sessions of the convention are given over to more speeches by leading party figures and to committee reports.

Typically, the committee on rules and order of business reports first. It regularly recommends the adoption of the rules of the last convention, with perhaps a few changes. Its report, which also presents an agenda for the rest of the convention, is generally accepted with little or no dissent.

The credentials committee prepares the permanent roll of delegates entitled to seats and votes in the convention. Occasionally, there are disputes over the right of particular delegates and even whole delegations to be seated, and the credentials committee must decide those disputes. Its decisions may be appealed, but the floor almost always adopts its report unchanged.

The committee on permanent organization nominates a slate of permanent convention officers. Their selection, and especially the naming of the permanent chairperson, can be a major test of strength within the party. Those officers run the remaining sessions of the convention.

The report of the committee on platform and resolutions, in the form of a proposed platform, usually reaches the floor by the third session.

The party's platform emerges from a draft drawn up by the party's leadership before the convention meets. Its more controversial planks often prompt heated disputes within the committee, and those struggles may spill over to the convention floor.

Platform-writing is a fine art. A **platform** is supposed to be a basic statement of the party's principles and its stands on major policy matters. It is also a campaign statement, aimed at appealing to as many people and winning as many votes as possible. So, both parties tend to produce somewhat generalized comments on many of the hard questions of the day. Neither wishes to alienate large blocks of voters but, necessarily, both end up alienating some voters because of stands on controversial issues.

Some party platforms are regularly criticized for their apparent blandness. Listen to Senator Barry Goldwater, the Republicans' presidential nominee in 1964: "Platforms are written to be ignored and forgotten . . . Like Jell-O shimmering on a dessert plate, there is usually little substance and nothing you can get your teeth into."

Still, the platforms are important. They usually do set out a number of hard and fast policy positions advocated by the two parties. At the same time, they reflect the compromise nature of both American politics and the two major parties.

## The Final Sessions

By its fourth, sometimes fifth session, the convention at last comes to its chief task: the nomination of the party's candidate for the presidency.

The names of any number of contenders may be offered to the delegates.[23] For each con-

**Republican National Convention**　In a tradition called "the greatest political show on earth," a 1992 delegate unabashedly shows her loyalty to the Grand Old Party.

tender, a nominating speech and then several seconding speeches are made. They are lavish hymns of praise, extolling the virtues of "The person who. . . " The "who" is well known before the nominator begins to speak, but tradition has it that the speaker only hint at that person's name until the very end of the speech. Its final announcement sets off a lengthy, wild, noisy demonstration on the floor of the convention hall. These "spontaneous" demonstrations—supposed to show widespread and enthusiastic support for the aspirant—are carefully planned, of course.

After all the nominating speeches and their seconds have been made, the balloting finally begins. The secretary calls the names of the States alphabetically, and each State chairperson announces the vote of his or her delegation or may pass. Each complete roll call is known as a ballot. Balloting goes on until a candidate achieves a majority of the delegates' votes and is thus nominated.

Most often, the results of the first ballot produce a choice. In the 23 conventions held by each party between 1900 and 1988, the Republicans have made a first ballot nomination 19 times and the Democrats, 18 times.[24]

Once the convention has chosen the presidential nominee, the choice of a running mate often comes as an anticlimax. The vice-presidential nominee is almost invariably the choice of the just-nominated presidential candidate; see Section 2.

With its candidates named, the convention comes to the last major item on its agenda: the presidential candidate's acceptance speech. And, as that speech comes to an end, the delegates—all of them superpatriots of the party—nearly tear the convention hall apart in wild celebration.

## Whom Does the Party Nominate?

If an incumbent President wants another term, the convention's choice of a nominee is easy. The President is almost certain to get the nomination, and usually with no real opposition from within the party. Indeed, in this century, each time the incumbent has sought the nomination, he has received it. The President's advantages are immense: the majesty and publicity of the office and close control of the party's machinery.[25]

When the President is not in the field, up to a dozen or so contenders surface in the preconvention period. At most, two or three of them may survive to contest the prize at the convention.

Who among them will win the nomination? The record argues this answer: the one who is, in the jargon of politics, the most available—the one who is the most electable. Conventions want to pick candidates who can win, candidates with the broadest possible appeal within the party and to the electorate.

Most presidential candidates have come to their nominations with substantial and well-known records in public office. But those records have to be free of controversies that could have antagonized important elements within the party or among the voting public. Generally, presidential candidates have served in elective office, where they have shown vote-getting ability. Seldom does a candidate step from the business world or from the military directly into the role of candidate, as did Wendell Willkie in 1940 or Dwight Eisenhower in 1952.

Historically, the governorships of larger States have produced the largest number of presidential candidacies. Eleven of the 20 men nominated by the two major parties between 1900 and 1956 were either then serving or had once served as a governor. Note that governors can claim experience as chief executives of a government.

For a time, however, the Senate became the prime source. In the four elections from 1960 through 1972, each major party nominee had been a senator. None had ever been a governor.

But the old pattern has been restored. Jimmy Carter, the former governor of Georgia, was nominated by the Democrats in 1976 and 1980. Ronald Reagan, former governor of California, was the GOP choice in 1980 and again in 1984. The Democrats nominated the governor of Massachusetts, Michael Dukakis, in 1988, and they picked Governor Bill Clinton of Arkansas in 1992.

With a few exceptions, notably Democrats Alfred E. Smith in 1928, John F. Kennedy in 1960, and Michael Dukakis in 1988, most leading contenders for presidential nominations have been Protestants. Most have also come from the larger and doubtful States. Thus, candidates from such pivotal States as New York, Ohio, Illinois, and California are usually more available than those from smaller States. But television has reshaped this matter over the past

---

[24]A convention can become deadlocked—that is, find itself unable to make a choice between the top two, or sometimes three, contenders for the nomination. In that event, a "dark horse" (someone who did not appear to be a likely choice before the convention) may finally be nominated. The most spectacular deadlock occurred at the Democratic convention in New York in 1924. The convention took 123 separate ballots, over a period of nine days, before John W. Davis became the party's candidate.

[25]In fact, only four sitting Presidents have ever been denied nomination: John Tyler, by the Whigs in 1844; Millard Fillmore, by the Whigs in 1852; Franklin Pierce, by the Democrats in 1856; and Chester Arthur, by the Republicans in 1884.

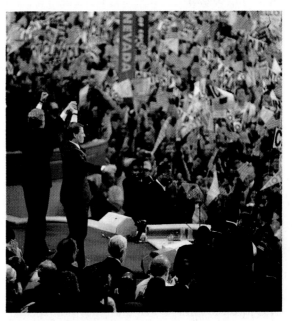

▲ **Presidential and Vice-Presidential Nominees**   Bill Clinton and his running mate, Al Gore, enjoy acclaim in New York City in 1992. At left, George Bush and his vice-presidential nominee, J. Danforth Quayle, are joined by their wives as they accept the cheers of delegates at the 1992 Republican Convention.

several years. Thus, the Republicans picked Barry Goldwater of Arizona in 1964; and the Democrats' most recent nominees have included George McGovern of South Dakota in 1972, Jimmy Carter of Georgia in 1976, and Bill Clinton of Arkansas in 1992.

Neither party has, to this point, seriously considered a woman as its candidate for the presidency—or, until 1984 and the Democratic party's nomination of Geraldine Ferraro, for the vice presidency. Nor has either party yet nominated a member of any minority group for either role. Jesse Jackson, an African American, did show significant strength in the 1988 pre-convention race, eventually losing the Democratic presidential nomination to Michael Dukakis of Massachusetts.

The candidates usually have a pleasant and healthy appearance, seem to be happily married, and have a happy (and exploitable) family. Adlai Stevenson, the Democratic nominee in 1952 and 1956, and Ronald Reagan, the GOP candidate in 1980 and 1984, are the only nominees of one of the major parties ever to have been divorced.

A well-developed speaking ability has always been a major factor of availability in American politics. Of course, being able to project well over television and in other media has become a must in recent decades.

# Section 5 Review

1. **Define:** keynote address, platform
2. (a) What happens at a national convention? (b) What is the major event?
3. What is the general tone of a party platform?
4. Why are incumbent Presidents almost certain to win their party's nomination if they choose to pursue it?

**Critical Thinking**

5. **Recognizing Bias** (p. 19) Consider the concept of availability in presidential politics. (a) In what ways are women and minorities unavailable as candidates? (b) What does this suggest about American politics and voters?

★

# 6 The Election

### Find Out:

- How does the electoral college work today?
- What are the major criticisms of the electoral college?
- What are some of the proposals to revise the presidential selection process?

### Key Term:

electorate

The presidential campaign, the all-out effort to win the votes of the people, begins soon after the conventions. Both candidates' campaign organizations work to present them in the best possible light. Radio and television speeches; "whistle-stop" tours; press conferences and press releases; public rallies; party dinners; newspaper, radio, and television advertisements; stickers and buttons; placards and pamphlets; billboards and matchcovers—all bombard the voters. The candidates pose for hundreds of photographs and shake thousands of hands as each of them tries to convince the people that he is best for the country.

The presidential campaign ends on election day. Millions of voters go to the polls in all 50 States and the District of Columbia. But the President, whoever that is to be, is not actually elected until the presidential electors cast their votes, several weeks later.

In this section, you will focus on the present-day workings of the electoral college, and on several major proposals for its reform.

## The Electoral College Today

Here you come to one of the least understood parts of the American political process. As the people vote in the presidential election, they do not cast a vote directly for one of the contenders for the presidency. Instead, they vote to elect presidential electors.

Remember, the Constitution provides for the election of the President by the electoral college, in which each State has as many electors as it has members of Congress. The Framers expected that the electors would use their own judgment in selecting a President. But today the electors, once chosen, are really just "rubber stamps." They are expected to vote, automatically, for their party's candidates for President and Vice President.

In short, the electors go through the form set out in the Constitution, in order to meet the letter of the Constitution—but their behavior is a far cry from its original intent.

The electors are chosen by popular vote in every State[26] and on the same day everywhere, the Tuesday after the first Monday in November every fourth year. So, in 1996 the presidential election will take place on November 5.

The electors are chosen at-large in every State except Maine.[27] That is, they are chosen on a winner-take-all basis. The presidential candidate—technically, the slate of elector-candidates nominated by his party—receiving the largest popular vote in a State wins all of that State's electoral votes. Today, the names of the individual elector-candidates appear on the ballot in less than a fourth of the States. In most, only the names of the presidential and vice-presidential candidates are listed. They stand as "shorthand" for the elector slates.

The electors meet at their State capitol on the date set by Congress, now the Monday after the

---

[26]The Constitution (Article II, Section 1, Clause 2) says that the electors are to be chosen in each State "in such manner as the legislature thereof may direct." In several States the legislatures themselves chose the electors in the first several elections. By 1832, however, every State except South Carolina had provided for popular election. The electors were picked by the legislature in South Carolina through the elections of 1860. Since then, all presidential electors have been chosen by popular vote in every State, with two exceptions. The State legislatures chose the electors in Florida in 1868 and in Colorado in 1876.

[27]Maine (beginning in 1972) and Nebraska (1992) use the "district plan." In those States, two electors are chosen from the State at large and the others are picked in each of the State's congressional districts. The district plan was used by several States in the first several presidential elections, but every State except South Carolina had provided for the choice of the electors from the State at large by 1832. Since then, the district plan has been used only by Michigan in 1892 and by Maine and Nebraska.

# How to Follow the Election Process

## Electoral College

Presidential electors meet in State capitals on the Monday following the second Wednesday in December to cast their electoral votes, to be officially counted in Washington on January 6. A majority of electoral votes—270 out of 538—is needed for election as President. The winner is sworn in on January 20.

## Election Day

Voters cast their ballots on the Tuesday following the first Monday in November. In choosing between candidates, voters actually pick presidential electors. These electors are expected, though not bound, to cast their votes for a specific candidate.

## National Conventions

Delegates choose the nominee of each major party—with the convention of both major parties held in mid-summer.

## Presidential Primaries

In States with presidential primaries, party's voters select some or all of the national convention delegates and/or express a preference among various contenders for the party's presidential nominee.

## District Conventions

Conventions held in the several congressional districts select some or all of the State's delegates to the party's national convention.

## State Conventions

Convention held at the State level picks some or all of the State's delegates to the party's national convention.

## Local Caucuses

Party voters in local meetings choose delegates to conventions at the congressional district and/or State levels.

## Candidate

Two main paths are taken to win delegates at the national nominating convention of a candidate's party—one in States that choose delegates through primaries, the other in States that choose delegates by party caucuses and conventions.

▲ **Interpreting Charts**   The Framers of the Constitution established the electoral college to allow the most capable citizens in each State to select the President. Is this how the electoral college operates today? Why or why not?

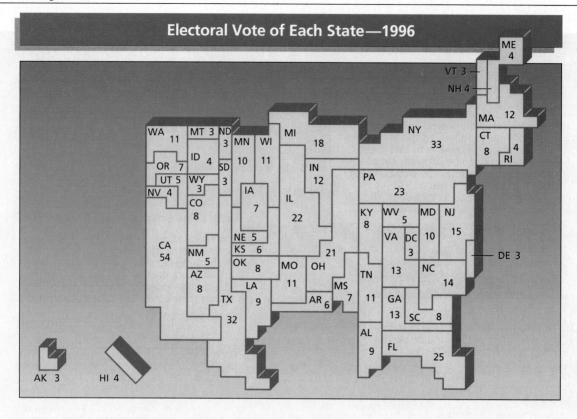

## Electoral Vote of Each State—1996

**Interpreting Maps**   Each State has as many electoral votes as it has members of Congress. Why are those larger States that might be won by either party in an election called "pivotal" States?

second Wednesday in December.[28] There they each cast their electoral votes, one for President and one for Vice President. The ballots of the electors, signed and sealed, are sent by registered mail to the President of the Senate in Washington.

Which party has won a majority of the electoral votes, and who then will be the next President of the United States, is usually known by midnight of election day, more than a month before the electors cast their ballots. But the formal election of the President and Vice President finally takes place on January 6.[29]

On that date, the President of the Senate opens the electoral votes from each State and counts them before a joint session of Congress. The candidate who receives a majority of the electors' votes for President is declared elected, as is the candidate with a majority of the votes for Vice President.

If no one has a majority for President—at least 270 of the 538 electoral votes—the election is thrown into the House of Representatives. This happened in 1800, and again in 1824. The House chooses a President from among the top three candidates in the electoral college. Each State delegation has one vote, and it takes a majority of 26 to elect. If the House fails to choose a President by January 20, the 20th Amendment provides that the newly elected Vice President shall act as President until it does.[30]

If no person receives a majority for Vice President, the Senate decides between the top two

---

[28]Article II, Section I, Clause 4 provides that the date Congress sets "shall be the same throughout the United States." The 12th Amendment provides that the electors "shall meet in their respective States."

[29]Unless that day falls on a Sunday, as it did most recently in 1985 (but will not again until 2013). Then, the ballot-counting is held the following day.

candidates. It takes a majority of the whole Senate to elect. The Senate has had to choose a Vice President only once. It elected Richard M. Johnson in 1837.

## Flaws in the Electoral College

The electoral college system is plagued by three major defects.

**The First Major Defect**   There is the ever-present threat that the winner of the popular vote will not win the presidency. This continuing threat is largely the result of two factors. The most important is the winner-take-all feature of the electoral college system. In each State the winning candidate customarily receives all that State's electoral votes. Thus, in 1992 Bill Clinton won barely 50 percent of the popular vote in New York, but all of that State's 33 electoral votes—even though some 2.2 million New Yorkers voted for Republican George Bush and another 1.1 million for Independent Ross Perot.

The other major culprit here is the way the electoral votes are distributed among the States. Remember, each State has two electors because of its Senate seats, regardless of its population. Because of them, the distribution of electoral votes does not match the facts of population and voter distribution.

Take the extreme case to illustrate this situation: California, the largest State, now has 54 electoral votes, or one for each 551,112 persons, based on its 1990 population of 29,760,021. Alaska has three electoral votes, or one for each 183,348 persons, with its 1990 population of 550,043.

The popular vote winner has, in fact, failed to win the presidency three times: 1824, 1876, and 1888. In 1824, Andrew Jackson won the largest share (a plurality, but not a majority) of the popular votes: 151,174, or 40.3 percent of the total. Jackson's nearest rival, John Quincy Adams, received 113,122 votes, or 30.9 percent. Ninety-nine of the 261 electors then voted for Jackson, again more than any other candidate but far short of a majority. The election thus went to the House and, early in 1825, it elected Adams to the presidency.[31]

In the election of 1876, Republican candidate Rutherford B. Hayes received 4,034,311 popular votes and his Democratic opponent, Samuel J. Tilden, won 4,288,548. Tilden received 184 electoral votes; Hayes won 185 electoral votes and so became President.[32]

In 1888 President Grover Cleveland won 5,534,488 popular votes, 90,596 more than his Republican opponent, Benjamin Harrison. But Harrison received 233 electoral votes to Cleveland's 168, and so became the 23rd President.[33]

The system has not misfired since 1888, but it could have several times—most recently in 1976. As the table on page 344 shows, Jimmy Carter defeated Republican Gerald Ford by only a bare majority of the popular vote. If only a handful of voters in a few States had voted for Ford instead of Carter, Ford would have had a majority of the electoral votes and so kept the

---

[30]The 20th Amendment further provides that "the Congress may by law provide for the case wherein neither a President-elect nor a Vice President-elect shall have qualified" by inauguration day. Congress has done so in the Succession Act of 1947; see Section 2. The Speaker of the House would "act as President . . . until a President or Vice President shall have qualified."

[31]These figures, as most of the popular vote results cited in this book, are drawn from the authoritative *Guide to U.S. Elections*, Congressional Quarterly, Inc., 2nd ed., 1985, and updates of that volume.

[32]The election of 1876 is often called "the Stolen Election." Two conflicting sets of electoral votes were received from Florida (4 votes), Louisiana (8 votes), and South Carolina (7 votes), and the validity of one vote from Oregon was disputed. Congress set up an Electoral Commission with five Senators, five Representatives, and five Supreme Court Justices—to decide the matter. The Commissioners, eight Republicans and seven Democrats, voted on strict party lines, awarding all of the disputed votes, and so the presidency, to Hayes.

[33]To this point, 14 Presidents have been elected although they did not win a majority of the popular vote. You have already read about John Quincy Adams, Hayes, and Benjamin Harrison. The other 11 all were elected with a plurality, but not a majority, of the popular vote. These "minority Presidents": James K. Polk (1844), Zachary Taylor (1848), James Buchanan (1856), Abraham Lincoln (1860), James A. Garfield (1880), Grover Cleveland (1884 and 1892), Woodrow Wilson (1912 and 1916), Harry Truman (1948), John F. Kennedy (1960), Richard Nixon (1968), Bill Clinton (1992).

presidency. Different combinations of several States can be used to play this game, but the simplest one involves Ohio (25 electoral votes) and Wisconsin (11 electoral votes). If only 5,554 of the 2,011,621 Carter votes in Ohio and only 17,623 of the 1,040,232 Carter votes in Wisconsin had gone instead to Ford, Ford would have received 276 electoral votes and won the election.

Several other presidential elections can be used to illustrate the point, as well. In short, the "winner-take-all" factor produces an electoral vote result that is, at best, a distorted reflection of the popular vote. You can see the gap between the percentages of popular and electoral votes in the 1992 figures shown in the table below right.

**The Second Major Defect** Nothing in the Constitution, nor in any federal statute, requires the electors to vote for the candidate favored by the popular vote in their States. Several States do have such laws, but they are of doubtful constitutionality, and none has ever been enforced.

The electors are expected to vote for the candidate who carries their State, and as loyal members of their parties, they almost always do. Thus far, electors have "broken their pledges"—voted for someone other than their party's presidential nominee—on only nine occasions: in 1796, 1820, 1948, 1956, 1960, 1968, 1972, 1976, and 1988. In the most recent case, a West Virginia elector turned her party's ticket upside down; she voted for Lloyd Bentsen for President and Michael Dukakis for Vice President. Bentsen was the Democrats' candidate for Vice President.

In no case has the vote of a "faithless elector" had a bearing on the outcome of a presidential election—but the potential is certainly there.

**The Third Major Defect** In any presidential election, it is possible that the contest will be decided in the House of Representatives. This has happened only twice, as you know, and not since 1824. But in several other elections—especially in 1912, 1924, 1948, and 1968—a strong third-party bid has threatened to make it impossible for either major party candidate to win a majority in the electoral college. Look at the 1968 results in the table on page 345.

George Wallace, the American Independent party candidate, won five States and 46 electoral votes. If Democrat Hubert Humphrey had carried Alaska, Delaware, Missouri, Nevada, and Wisconsin—States where Richard Nixon's margin was thin and in which Wallace had a substantial vote—Nixon's electoral vote would have been 268 and Humphrey's 224. Neither would have had a majority. The House would then have had to decide the election.

Three serious objections can be raised to election by the House. First, the voting in such cases is by States, not by individual members. A small State, such as Alaska or Nevada, would have as much weight as even the most populous States. Second, if the Representatives from a State were so divided that no candidate was favored by a majority of them, the State would lose its vote. Third, the Constitution requires a majority of the States for election in the House—today 26 States. If a strong third-party candidate were

## Popular Vote vs. Electoral Vote, 1976

| 1976 | Popular Vote | % | Electoral Vote | % |
|---|---|---|---|---|
| Carter | 40,825,839 | 50.03 | 297 | 55.2 |
| Ford | 39,147,770 | 47.97 | 240 | 44.6 |
| Others | 1,629,737 | 2.00 | 1 | 0.2 |

▲ **Interpreting Tables** How did the 1976 election point up the possibility for trouble in the electoral college system?

## Popular Vote vs. Electoral Vote, 1992

| 1992 | Popular Vote | % | Electoral Vote | % |
|---|---|---|---|---|
| Clinton | 44,909,326 | 43.0 | 370 | 68.8 |
| Bush | 39,103,882 | 37.4 | 168 | 31.2 |
| Perot | 19,741,657 | 18.9 | — | — |
| Others | 670,149 | 0.6 | — | — |

▲ **Interpreting Tables** How does this table reflect the "winner-take-all" factor in the electoral college system?

involved, there is a real possibility that the House could not make a decision by inauguration day.[34]

## Proposed Reforms

Observers have long recognized the defects in the electoral college system. Constitutional amendments to change the process have been introduced in every term of Congress since 1789. Most of the reforms people have offered fall under three headings: the district plan, the proportional plan, and direct popular election.

**The District Plan** Over time, many have proposed that the electors be chosen in each State as are members of Congress. That is, two electors would be chosen from the State at-large, and they would cast their electoral votes in line with the statewide popular vote result. The other electors would be elected, separately, in each of the State's congressional districts. Their votes would be cast in accord with the popular vote result in their district.[35]

The district plan would do away with the winner-take-all problem in the present system. Its supporters have argued that it would make the electoral vote a more accurate reflection of the popular returns.

The strongest argument against the plan is that it would not eliminate the possibility that the loser of the popular vote could still win the electoral vote. In fact, had it been in effect in 1960, Richard Nixon would have received 278 electoral votes, and he, not John Kennedy, would have won the presidency.

### Popular Vote vs. Electoral Vote, 1968

| 1968 | Popular Vote | % | Electoral Vote | % |
|------|-------------|-----|---------------|------|
| Nixon | 31,785,148 | 43.4 | 301 | 55.9 |
| Humphrey | 31,274,503 | 42.7 | 191 | 35.5 |
| Wallace | 9,901,151 | 13.5 | 46 | 8.6 |
| Others | 242,568 | | — | — |

▲ **Interpreting Tables**  Third party power was a real threat to the Democratic and Republican candidates in 1968. How is this suggested by the table?

Further, the results under the district plan would depend very much on how the congressional districts were drawn in each State. Its use would be yet another motive for gerrymandering.

**The Proportional Plan** Under this arrangement, each presidential candidate would receive the same share of a State's electoral vote as he or she received in the State's popular vote. Thus, if a candidate won 40 percent of the votes cast in a State with 20 electoral votes, he or she would get eight of that State's electoral votes.

Clearly, this plan would cure the winner-take-all problem and eliminate faithless electors. And it would yield an electoral vote count more nearly in line with the popular vote, at least for each State.

The proportional plan would not, however, necessarily produce the same result nationally. Because each of the smaller States is overweighted by its two Senate-based electors, the proportional plan would still make it possible for the loser of the popular vote to win the presidency in the electoral vote. In fact, this would have happened in 1896. William Jennings Bryan would have defeated William McKinley even though McKinley had a comfortable popular vote margin of 596,985 (5.1 percent).[36]

---

[34]In such a case, Section 3 of the 20th Amendment states that "the Vice President-elect shall act as President until a President shall have qualified." If no Vice President-elect is available, the Presidential Succession Act would come into play. Notice that it is even mathematically possible for the minority party in the House to have control of a majority of the individual State delegations. That party could then elect its candidate, even though he or she may have run second or even third in both the popular and the electoral vote contests.

[35]Maine and Nebraska now use the district plan, as noted earlier. Any other State could do so, but it would take a constitutional amendment to make its use mandatory in all States.

[36]In the closest of all the presidential elections, Winfield S. Hancock would have defeated James A. Garfield in 1880, even though Garfield had a popular plurality of only 1,898 votes, 0.0213 percent. On the other hand, there would have been no "Stolen Election" in 1876, and Cleveland would have defeated Harrison in 1888.

Many critics of the plan worry about its effect on the two-party system. Certainly, its adoption would bring an increase in the number and vigor of minor parties. They would no longer need to win entire States in order to get electoral votes. Their candidates would regularly win at least some share of the electoral vote—and the odds that a presidential election would have to go to the House would be increased.[37]

**Direct Popular Election**  The most common and widely supported proposal is the most obvious one: Do away with the electoral college system altogether and allow direct popular election of the President.

The arguments for direct election seem overpowering. The strongest one is that it would support the democratic ideal: Each vote would count equally in the national result. The winner would always be the majority or plurality choice. The dangers and confusions of the present system would be eliminated, replaced by a simple and easily understood process.

Several "practical" obstacles stand in the way of this proposal, however. Because of them, there seems little real chance of its adoption any time soon.[38]

The constitutional amendment process itself is a major stumbling block. First, there are three built-in minority vetoes in the amendment process. Two of them are in Congress, where one-third plus one of the members of either house can block the proposal of an amendment. And, one-fourth plus one of the State legislatures or conventions can defeat an amendment once it is proposed.

Second, the smaller States are greatly overrepresented in the electoral college. They would lose that advantage in a direct election—so, likely, enough Senators, Representatives, or small States would oppose a direct election amendment to kill it.

Some opponents of direct election argue that it would weaken federalism, because the States, as States, would lose their role in the choice of a President.

Others believe that direct election would put too great a load on the election process. They say that because every vote cast in each State would count in the national result, the candidates would have to campaign strenuously in every State. The impact that would have on campaign time, effort, and finance would be huge and, opponents argue, probably unmanageable.[39]

Some say that direct election would spur ballot-box stuffing and other forms of vote fraud. And that, they predict, would lead to lengthy, bitter, highly explosive post-election challenges.

In many States, a State-wide election often hangs on the behavior of some specific group in the **electorate**—the mass of people who actually cast votes in an election. The result depends on how those voters cast their ballots or, even more importantly, on how heavily they do or do not turn out to vote. Thus, for example, the African American vote in Chicago is often decisive in the presidential election in Illinois. But in a direct election these groups would not hold the balance of power, the clout, they now have—so many of them oppose the direct election plan.

Given all this, there seems little real chance that direct election will come to pass any time soon—unless, that is, the electoral college system malfunctions in another presidential election. Then, a direct election amendment would likely be adopted, and quickly.

**The National Bonus Plan**  Another and very different plan has recently surfaced. It is the national bonus plan. At first glance, the plan seems quite complicated and "off the wall." In fact, it is neither.

---

[37]Most of the plan's backers agree that an increase in minor party clout would mean that the popular vote winner would often fail to gain a clear majority of the electoral vote; see the table on page 345. Hence, they would lower the present requirement of a majority of the electoral votes to a plurality of at least 40 percent. If no candidate won 40 percent of the electoral votes, the two frontrunners would face one another in a runoff election.

[38]The House of Representatives did approve a direct election amendment by the necessary two-thirds vote in 1969. The measure was killed by a Senate filibuster in 1970. President Carter championed a similar proposal, but it was rejected by a Senate floor vote in 1979.

[39]In fact, it is possible for a candidate to win the presidency by carrying only the 11 largest States, because they now have a total of 270 electoral votes, exactly the minimum number to win the presidency.

The national bonus plan would keep much of the electoral college system, especially its winner-take-all feature. It would weight that feature in favor of the winner of the popular vote, however.

Under the plan, a national pool of 102 electoral votes would be awarded, automatically, to the winner of the popular vote contest. That is, that bloc of electoral votes would be added to the electoral votes that candidate won in the election. If all those votes added up to a majority of the electoral college—at least 321—that candidate would be declared the winner of the presidency. In the unlikely event that they did not, a runoff election between the two front-runners in the popular vote would then be held.

The advocates of this plan see the electors themselves as unnecessary to it, and so would do away with them. They say that their plan meets all of the major objections to the present system and all of those raised against the other proposals for its reform. They also claim their plan would almost guarantee that the winner of the popular vote would always be the winner of the electoral vote.

To date, the national bonus plan has not attracted much public attention—let alone understanding, interest, or support.

**A Final Word**  Their case is not often heard, but the present electoral college system does have its defenders. They react to the several proposed reforms by raising the various objections to them you have just read. Beyond that they argue that critics exaggerate the "dangers" in the system. Only two elections have ever gone to the House of Representatives and none in nearly 170 years. True, the loser of the popular vote has three times won the presidency, but that has not happened in more than a century.

They also say that the arrangement, whatever its warts, has two major strengths:

(1) It is a known process. Each of the proposed, but untried, reforms may very well have defects that could not be known until they appeared in practice.

(2) It identifies the winner of the presidential election, and it does so quickly and certainly. Even in a close election, the nation does not have to wait for weeks or months to know the outcome.

## VOICES on Government

### On the Presidential Selection Process

**Jimmy Carter,** 39th President of the United States

❝The present system is satisfactory. To abbreviate the [presidential election] season, some evolutionary trend toward regional primaries would be good and is already taking place. The long ordeal sometimes endured by candidates can be beneficial in two ways: It ensures a broader and deeper knowledge of our country, including the smaller states, and it provides a mental, political and physical test of the various would-be Presidents in full view of the American people.❞

## Section 6 Review

1. **Define:** electorate
2. (a) How many electors does each State have, and (b) how are they chosen?
3. What happens if no candidate gets a majority of the electoral vote?
4. What are the three major weaknesses in the electoral college system?
5. Which plan for reform of the electoral college is most widely supported?
6. On what grounds do some defend the present electoral college system?

**Critical Thinking**

7. **Identifying Alternatives** (p. 19) What should be the major goal of the presidential election system? Choose one of the methods discussed in this section, or make up your own.

★

# Testing Conclusions

Testing conclusions means examining a conclusion and determining whether or not it is supported by known facts. As you make the many decisions required of a citizen in a democracy, you will need to test the validity of the conclusions on which those decisions are based. Follow the steps below to practice testing conclusions.

**1. Identify what kind of data you will need to test your conclusion.** In order to test a conclusion, you need facts on which to base your test. Read the conclusion below. (a) What is the subject of the conclusion? (b) What kind of information might enable you to test this conclusion?

**2. Decide what source of information you will use to test your conclusion.** Once you have determined what kind of information you need to test your conclusion, you will need to find an "answer key." Look at information sets A, B, and C in the box below. (a) Will any set provide an answer to the test? (b) Can you use more than one information set?

**3. Test the conclusion by comparing it to the selected information.** Once you have selected your answer key or keys, you can test the conclusion. (a) Does the information set or sets you have chosen support the conclusion? (b) Is more information necessary? (c) Give reasons for each of your answers.

**Conclusion:** **The electoral college system fails to ensure that the choice for President accurately reflects the will of the majority of voters.**

**A**

**Article II, Section 1, Clause 2:** "Each State shall appoint, in such manner as the legislature thereof may direct, a number of Electors, equal to the whole number of Senators and Representatives, to which the State may be entitled in Congress . . . "

**12th Amendment:** "The Electors shall meet in their respective States, and vote by ballot for President and Vice President . . . . the person having the greatest number of [electoral] votes for President shall be the President, if such number be a majority of the whole number of Electors appointed . . . "

**B**

### Electoral Vote for President (Selected Years)

| Year | President Elected and Electoral Vote | | Opponents and Electoral Vote | |
|------|------------------------------------|-----|------------------------------|-----|
| 1824 | John Quincy Adams | 84 | Andrew Jackson<br>Henry Clay<br>William H. Crawford | 99<br>37<br>41 |
| 1876 | Rutherford B. Hayes | 185 | Samuel J. Tilden | 184 |
| 1888 | Benjamin Harrison | 233 | Grover Cleveland | 168 |

**C**

### Popular Vote for President (Selected Years)

| Year | President Elected and Popular Vote | | Opponents and Popular Vote | |
|------|-----------------------------------|---------|----------------------------|---------|
| 1824 | John Quincy Adams | 113,122 | Andrew Jackson<br>Henry Clay<br>William H. Crawford | 151,174<br>46,587<br>44,282 |
| 1876 | Rutherford B. Hayes | 4,034,311 | Samuel J. Tilden | 4,288,548 |
| 1888 | Benjamin Harrison | 5,443,892 | Grover Cleveland | 5,534,488 |

# Chapter-in-Brief

Scan all headings, photographs, charts, and other visuals in the chapter before reading the section summaries below.

## Section 1 The President's Job Description (pp. 315–321)
The President is simultaneously the nation's (1) chief of state, (2) chief executive, (3) chief administrator, (4) chief diplomat, (5) commander in chief, (6) chief legislator, (7) chief of party, and (8) chief citizen. These roles are all closely interrelated; none can be played in isolation from the others.

The Constitution sets out certain formal qualifications for the presidency.

## Section 2 Presidential Succession and the Vice Presidency (pp. 323–326)
Originally, the Constitution was vague about what was to happen if a vacancy in the presidency occurred. The 25th Amendment formalized the practice of making the Vice President the President on the death, resignation, or removal of the President.

Even though the Vice President is "only a heartbeat away from the presidency," the office has long been treated as one of little consequence. No President has made the Vice President a real assistant President.

## Section 3 Presidential Selection: The Framers' Plan (pp. 327–329)
The Framers did not believe that the people were qualified to select a President. So, they developed the complicated electoral college to perform this function.

Electors, chosen in each State, were to be independent agents in the selection of the President. Political parties soon transformed the original scheme, however. Today, the electors are really "rubber stamps" for the popular vote result.

## Section 4 Nominating Presidential Candidates Today (pp. 330–335)
The two major parties have nominated their presidential candidates at national conventions since 1832. Today, more than three-fourths of the delegates to those conventions are chosen in some form of the presidential primary. In some States delegates are picked by caucuses and State or district conventions.

Neither major party has ever been much interested in alternatives to the national convention process.

## Section 5 At the National Convention (pp. 335–339)
Conventions are grand events full of speeches and displays of party enthusiasm. They are held (1) to adopt the party's platform, (2) to nominate its presidential and vice-presidential candidates, and (3) to unify the party behind that ticket for the upcoming campaign.

Each party seeks a candidate who can win, and the nomination of the candidate marks the high point of each convention.

## Section 6 The Election (pp. 340–347)
Voters finally cast presidential ballots in November. However, their votes do not actually elect the President. The voters select presidential electors who in turn choose the President.

The electoral college system is seriously flawed. It is possible that the loser of the popular vote will nonetheless win the presidency—either in the electoral vote or in the House of Representatives.

A number of plans to reform the electoral college system have been offered and debated over the past 200 years. Even the most widely supported of those proposals, direct popular vote, will not likely be adopted in the foreseeable future.

# Chapter Review

## Vocabulary and Key Terms

chief of state (p. 316)
chief executive (p. 316)
chief administrator (p. 316)
chief diplomat (p. 316)
commander in chief (p. 316)
chief legislator (p. 316)

chief of party (p. 316)
chief citizen (p. 316)
presidential succession (p. 324)
presidential elector (p. 327)
electoral college (p. 328)
presidential primary (p. 331)

winner-take-all (p. 332)
keynote address (p. 336)
platform (p. 337)
electorate (p. 346)

**Matching:** *Review the key terms in the list above. If you are not sure of a term's meaning, look up the term and review its definition. Choose a term from the list above that best matches each description.*

1. the group chosen every four years to make the formal selection of the President and Vice President
2. the role in which the President exercises leadership over his or her political party
3. the role in which the President acts as the main architect of the nation's public policies
4. an election at which a party's voters choose delegates to the party's national convention and/or express a preference for candidates for the party's nomination
5. all the people entitled to vote in a given election
6. the role in which the President acts as the head of the government
7. the role in which the President exercises the executive power of the United States

**True or False:** *Determine whether each statement is true or false. If it is true, write "true." If it is false, change the underlined word or words to make the statement true.*

1. As <u>chief executive</u>, the President is the primary architect of the nation's foreign policy.
2. As the <u>chief of state</u>, the President is the leader of the nation's armed forces.

3. In actuality, the <u>electorate</u> casts the votes that officially select the President of the United States.
4. The <u>keynote address</u> is usually delivered by one of the party's best orators and is one of the highlights of a national convention.
5. According to the arrangement for <u>presidential succession</u>, the Vice President is first in line to fill a vacancy in the presidency.

**Word Relationships:** *Replace the underlined definition with the correct term from the list above.*

1. In the past, some presidential primaries were <u>contests in which the winner of the preference vote won the support of all the delegates</u>.
2. As <u>the representative of all the people</u>, the President speaks for the people of the nation and offers important moral leadership.
3. As the <u>head of a large organization that employs nearly three million people</u>, the President leads one of the world's largest governmental machines.
4. The <u>written declaration of the principles and policy decisions</u> of a party is an important product of each national convention.

## Main Ideas

### Section 1 (pp. 315–321)

1. For what reason is it important that the President fulfill each presidential role?

**2.** Describe the historical development of the guidelines for the length of a President's term.

**3.** (a) How much is the President paid? (b) What additional forms of compensation does the President receive?

### Section 2 (pp. 323–326)

**4.** How does the Constitution ensure a smooth transition of power in the event of presidential disability or vacancy?

**5.** How has the Constitution been changed over the course of history to ensure a smooth arrangement for presidential succession in all situations?

**6.** (a) What does the Constitution say about the role of the Vice President? (b) How does this fact relate to the reputation of the office?

**7.** What factors count most in the selection of a Vice President today?

### Section 3 (pp. 327–329)

**8.** Describe the Framers' original plan and intent for the selection of the nation's President.

**9.** How did the rise of parties affect the functioning of the plan developed by the Framers?

**10.** How did the 12th Amendment change the way Presidents and Vice Presidents are selected?

### Section 4 (pp. 330–335)

**11.** What role do political parties play in the nominating process today?

**12.** What are the major purposes of presidential primaries in the nominating process?

**13.** What factors make the current presidential nominating process confusing?

### Section 5 (pp. 335–339)

**14.** For what major purposes do parties hold national conventions?

**15.** What kind of image does a convention hope to present to the voters?

**16.** What factors are most important to a party in the selection of a candidate?

### Section 6 (pp. 340–347)

**17.** How does the way that electors cast their votes today differ from the intent of the Framers?

**18.** On what grounds is the electoral college system criticized?

**19.** What attempts have been made to address these criticisms?

## Critical Thinking

**1. Testing Conclusions** (p. 19)   What kind of information might enable you to test the accuracy of the following conclusion? Conclusion: The presidential nominating process is an important demonstration of this nation's continuing commitment to its basic principles of popular sovereignty and limited government.

**2. Checking Consistency** (p. 19)   The vice presidency is regarded as both highly important and insignificant. Summarize the reasons for these conflicting viewpoints.

## Getting Involved

**1. Writing Your Opinion**   Write a letter to an official of one of the major parties urging him or her to nominate a woman or a minority candidate for the presidency and/or vice presidency. In your letter, explain why you believe such a nomination would be good for the nation. Also explain why such a nomination would be good for the party. After you have completed your first draft, review your arguments to ensure that they are as persuasive as possible. Correct any errors and draft a final copy.

**2. Gathering Information**   If you wanted to study the relationship of popular vote to electoral vote throughout the history of United States' presidential elections, what sources might you use? Check the Government Resources Handbook on page 690 to find possible answers.

# CHAPTER 14

# The Presidency in Action

## Chapter Preview

As one of the benefits of his office, President Clinton receives full use of Air Force One, the presidential jet. The jet has been described as an extension of the Oval Office, where the President works, and a mobile East Wing, where he sleeps. The airplane features 85 telephones, four computers, two copying machines, a conference room, a pressroom with TV monitors, and a television system that can receive eight channels at the same time.

Even when traveling six miles above the earth, the President is never out of touch. Perhaps it was this characteristic of the office that prompted Lyndon B. Johnson to write, "No one can experience with the President of the United States the glory and agony of his office. . . . No one can share the burden of his decisions or the scope of his duties." This chapter is about the scope and growth of those duties and the ways in which they are exercised.

### Before you read this chapter:

- **Describe** several of the President's many jobs and duties.
- **Predict** why President Truman displayed a sign on his desk reading, "The buck stops here."

### As you read, focus on the main objective for each section. Understand:

1. The historic and ongoing debate over the scope of presidential power.
2. The nature and extent of the executive power of the President.
3. The President's diplomatic and military powers.
4. The President's legislative and judicial powers.
5. The functions of the executive agencies and the role of the cabinet.

▲ **Play Ball!** President Clinton helped the Cleveland Indians dedicate their new stadium by throwing out the first ball. Such events are among many that the President must attend, and they often color the public's perception of the man.

# 1 The Changing View of Presidential Power

### Find Out:
- What is the historic and ongoing debate over the proper scope of presidential power?
- In what ways has the power grown over time?

### Key Term:
media

The presidency is often called "the most powerful office in the world." But is this what the Framers had in mind when they created the post in 1787? At Philadelphia, they purposely created a single executive with broad powers. But they also agreed with Thomas Jefferson, who wrote in the Declaration of Independence that "a Tyrant is unfit to be the ruler of a free people." And so, just as purposely, they constructed a "checked" presidency.

In this section, you will consider the forces that have shaped the growth of presidential power over the past 200 years.

Article II of the Constitution begins in the following way:

❝The executive power shall be vested in a President of the United States of America.❞

With those few words, the Framers established the presidency. With them, they laid the basis for the vast power and influence the nation's chief executive has today.

The Constitution does set out several other, and somewhat more specific, grants of presidential power. Thus, as you have read at various points in the book, the President is given the power to command the armed forces, to make treaties, to approve or veto acts of Congress, to send and receive diplomatic representatives, to grant pardons and reprieves, and "to take care that the laws be faithfully executed."[1]

But, notice that the Constitution deals with the powers of the presidency in very sketchy fashion. Article II reads almost as an outline. It has been called "the most loosely drawn chapter" in

---

[1] Most of the specific grants of presidential power are found in Article II, Sections 2 and 3. A few are elsewhere in the Constitution, however, such as the veto power, in Article I, Section 7, Clause 2.

the nation's fundamental law.[2] It does not define "the executive power." The other grants of presidential authority are put in equally broad terms.

Much of the story of the development of the American system of government can be told in terms of the growth of presidential power. A large part of our political history has revolved around a continuing struggle over the meaning of the constitutional phrase "executive power." That struggle has pitted those who have argued for a weaker presidency, subordinate to Congress, against those who have pressed for a stronger, independent chief executive.

That never-ending contest began at the Philadelphia Convention in 1787. At that time, several Framers agreed with Roger Sherman of Connecticut who, according to James Madison's *Notes,*

66 considered the executive magistracy as nothing more than an institution for carrying the will of the legislature into effect, and that the person or persons [occupying the presidency] ought to be appointed by and accountable to the legislature only, which was the depository of the supreme will of the Society. 99

[2] Edward S. Corwin, *The President: Office and Powers* (New York: New York University Press, 1957), 4th ed., page 3.

**Interpreting Political Cartoons**   The cartoon above comments on the growth of presidential power through the years. Who does the cartoonist blame for allowing this expansion to occur?

As you have seen, those who argued for a stronger executive—led by Alexander Hamilton, James Wilson, and James Madison—carried the day. They persuaded the convention to establish a single executive, chosen independently of Congress and with its own distinct field of powers.

## Why Presidential Power Has Grown

Over the course of American history, the champions of a stronger presidency have almost always prevailed. One of the leading reasons they have is the "unity" of the presidency. The office and its powers are held by one person. The President is the single, commanding head of the executive branch. On the other hand, Congress consists of two houses. Both of them must agree on a matter before the Congress can do anything. Moreover, one of those two houses is made up of 100 separately elected members, and the other has 435 members.

Several other factors have worked to strengthen the role and the powers of the presidency. One highly important one has been referred to a number of times: the influence the Presidents themselves have had on the office.

Yet another influence has been pressures from the increasingly complex nature of the nation's social and economic life. As the United States has become more industrialized and technologically centered, the people have demanded that the Federal Government play a larger role in a long list of areas of public concern, such as transportation, labor-management relations, civil rights, health, welfare, communications, education, and environmental protection. And it has been to the presidency that they have most often looked for leadership in these matters.

Another of these closely related factors has been the frequent need for extraordinary and decisive action in times of national emergency— most notably in times of war. The ability of the President—the single, commanding chief executive—to act in such situations has done much to strengthen the executive power.

Congress itself has had a major hand in strengthening the presidency, especially as it has passed the thousands of laws that have been an essential part of the historic growth of the Federal Government. Congress has neither the time nor the technical knowledge to do much more than provide the basic outlines of public policy. It has been forced to delegate substantial authority to the executive branch.

A number of other factors have also fed the growth of the executive power. Among them have been the President's roles as chief legislator, party leader, and chief citizen. Another is the huge amount of staff support a President has. Still another is the unique position from which the President can attract and hold the public's attention, and so gather support for policies and actions. Every recent President, from Franklin Roosevelt to Bill Clinton, has purposely used the **media**—means of communicating with people, such as the press, radio, and television—to that end.

## How Presidents Have Viewed Their Power

What the presidency is at any given time depends, in no small part, on the manner in which the President views the office and exercises its several powers.

Historically, Presidents have held one of two general and contrasting views. The stronger and the more effective of them have taken a broad view of their powers. Theodore Roosevelt defined this position in what he called the stewardship theory:

“My view was that every executive officer . . . in high position, was a steward of the people bound actively and affirmatively to do all he could for the people. . . . I declined to adopt the view that what was imperatively necessary for the Nation could not be done by the President unless he could find some specific authorization to do it. My belief was that it was not only [a President's] right but his duty to do anything that the needs of the Nation demanded unless such action was forbidden by the Constitution or by the laws. . . . I did not usurp power, but I did greatly broaden the use of executive power. In other words, I acted for the public welfare, I acted for the common well-being of all our people, whenever and in whatever manner was necessary, unless prevented by direct constitutional or legislative prohibition.”[3]

Ironically, the strongest presidential statement of the opposing view came from Roosevelt's handpicked successor in the office, William Howard Taft. Looking back upon his presidency, Taft had this to say about Roosevelt's view:

“My judgment is that the view of Mr. Roosevelt, ascribing an undefined residuum of power to the President, is an unsafe doctrine. . . . The true view of the executive function is, as I conceive it, that the President can exercise no power which cannot be fairly and reasonably traced to some specific grant of power or justly implied and included within such express grant . . . Such specific grant must be either in the Federal Constitution or in an act of Congress passed in pursuance thereof. There is no undefined residuum of power which he can exercise because it seems to be in the public interest.”[4]

Recall this point, from Section 1 of the last chapter: The President plays a number of different roles. As you will see in the sections ahead, the presidency can also be described in another quite useful way—by grouping the specific powers of the office under five main headings: the President's executive, diplomatic, military, legislative, and judicial powers.

## Section 1 Review

1. **Define:** media
2. Around what two competing views of "the executive power" can much of the nation's political history be written?
3. What are three reasons for the historical growth of presidential power?
4. Describe the two major and contrasting views of the presidency.

### Critical Thinking

5. **Identifying Assumptions** (p. 19) Read the statement by Theodore Roosevelt on this page. What does Roosevelt assume about the "needs of the Nation"? Explain why you agree or disagree with this assumption.

★

---

[3]*Theodore Roosevelt: An Autobiography* (New York: Macmillan, 1913), page 389.

[4]*Our Chief Magistrate and His Powers* (New York: Columbia University Press, 1916), pages 139–140, 144.

# 2 The President's Executive Powers

**Find Out:**
- What is the scope of the President's executive powers?
- How does the President exercise these powers?

**Key Term:**
executive order

Thomas Jefferson wrote this to a friend in 1789: "The execution of the laws is more important than the making of them." Whether Jefferson was altogether right about that or not, in this section you will see that the President's power to execute the law endows him with an enormous amount of power.

## Executing the Law

As chief executive, the President executes—enforces, administers, carries out—the provisions of federal law. The power to do so rests on two brief constitutional provisions. The first of them is the oath of office the President must take:

❝I do solemnly swear (or affirm), that I will faithfully execute the office of President of the United States, and will, to the best of my ability, preserve, protect, and defend the Constitution of the United States.❞[5]

The other provision is the Constitution's command that "he shall take care that the laws be faithfully executed."[6] The President's power to execute the law covers all federal laws. Their number, and the different subject matters they cover, nearly boggle the mind. The armed forces, social security, civil rights, housing, taxes, environmental pollution, collective bargaining, farm price supports, public health, and immigration—these only begin the list; there are scores of others.

---

[5]Article II, Section 1, Clause 8.
[6]Article II, Section 3; this provision gives the President what is often called the take care power.

The President and the President's subordinates have much to say about the meaning of the law, just as do Congress and the courts. In executing and enforcing law, the executive branch also interprets it. The Constitution requires the President to execute *all* federal laws no matter what the chief executive's own views of any of them may be. But the President may, and does, use some discretion as to how vigorously and in what particular way any given law will be applied in practice.

To look at the point more closely: Many laws that Congress passes are written in fairly broad terms. Congress sets out the basic policies and standards. The specific details, much of the fine print, necessary to the actual, day-to-day administration of the law, are usually left to be worked out in the executive branch.

For example, the immigration laws require that all immigrants seeking permanent admission to this country must be able to "read and understand some dialect or language." But what does this literacy requirement mean in everyday practice? How well must an alien be able to read and write? What words in some language must he or she know, and how many of them? The law does not say. Rather, such answers come from within the executive branch—in this case, from the Immigration and Naturalization Service in the Department of Justice.

## The Ordinance Power

From what has just been said, the President clearly deserves the title of chief administrator as well as chief executive. The job of administering and applying most federal law is the day-to-day work of all of the many departments, bureaus, offices, boards, commissions, councils, and other agencies that make up the huge executive branch of the Federal Government. All of the some three million men and women who staff those agencies are subject to the President's control and direction.

The President has the power to issue executive orders. An **executive order** is a directive, rule, or regulation that has the effect of law. The power to issue these orders, the ordinance power, arises from two sources: the Constitution and acts of Congress.

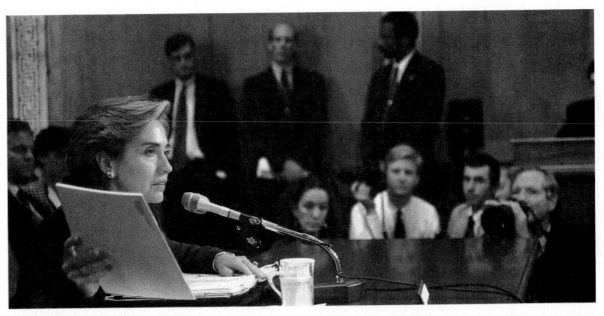

▲ **Appointing Power**   President Clinton appointed his wife, Hillary Rodham Clinton, to head the Health Care Reform Task Force. Here, Mrs. Clinton testifies on health care reform before the Senate Finance Committee.

The Constitution does not mention the ordinance power in so many words, but that power is clearly intended. In granting certain powers to the President, the Constitution obviously anticipates their use. In order to exercise those powers, the President must have the power to issue the necessary orders, as well as the power to implement them. The President must also have the power to authorize his subordinates to issue such orders.[7]

As the number, the scope, and the complexity of governmental problems have grown, Congress has found it necessary to delegate more and more discretion to the President and to presidential subordinates to spell out the policies and programs it has passed. Members of Congress are not, and cannot be expected to be, experts in all of the fields in which they must legislate.

## The Appointing Power

A President cannot hope to succeed without loyal subordinates who support the policies of the President's administration.

The Constitution provides that the President

❝ by and with the advice and consent of the Senate . . . shall appoint ambassadors, other public ministers, and consuls, judges of the Supreme Court, and all other officers of the United States whose appointments are not herein otherwise provided for . . . but the Congress may by law vest the appointment of such inferior officers, as they think proper, in the President alone, in the courts of law, or in the heads of departments. ❞[8]

Acting alone, the President names only a handful of the nearly three million federal civilian employees. Many of that handful fill the top spots in the White House Office, as you will read. With Senate consent, the President names most of the top-ranking officers of the Federal Government. Among them are ambassadors and

---

[7]All executive orders are published in the *Federal Register*, which appears five times a week. At least annually, all orders currently in force are published in the *Code of Federal Regulations*. Both of these publications are issued by the National Archives and Records Administration.

[8]Article II, Section 2, Clause 2. Those whose appointments are "otherwise provided for" are the Vice President, senators, representatives, and presidential electors.

## *Voices on Government*

**Lyndon B. Johnson,**
36th President of the
United States

### On Working with Congress to Execute the Law

"[A] President must be willing to bypass the Congress and take the issue to the people. By instinct and experience, I preferred to work from within, knowing that good legislation is the product not of public rhetoric but of private negotiations and compromise. But sometimes a President has to put Congress' feet to the fire. . . . Sometimes it seemed that the only way to reach the papers and the people was to pick a fight with the Congress, to say mean words and show my temper."

other diplomats; cabinet members and their top aides; the heads of such independent agencies as the Environmental Protection Agency and the National Aeronautics and Space Administration; all federal judges, attorneys, and marshals; and all officers in the armed forces.

When the President makes one of these appointments, the nomination is sent to the Senate where the support of a majority of the senators present and voting is needed for confirmation. As you may recall, the unwritten rule of senatorial courtesy plays an important part in this process. As noted in Chapter 11, Section 4, that rule applies to the choice of those federal officers who serve within a State—a federal district judge or a federal marshal, for example. The rule holds that the Senate will approve only those federal appointees acceptable to the senator or senators of the President's party from the State involved.

The practical effect of this custom, which is closely followed in the Senate, is to place a meaningful part of the President's appointing power in the hands of particular senators.

Of course, not all executive branch employees are chosen by the President and Senate. Well over half of all the federal civilian work force is selected on the basis of competitive civil service examinations. Today, the Office of Personnel Management examines applicants for some two million positions.

### The Removal Power

The power to remove is the other side of the appointment coin, and it is as critically important to presidential success as the power to appoint. Except for mention of the little-used impeachment process,[9] however, the Constitution does not say how or by whom appointed officers may be dismissed, whether for incompetence, for opposition to presidential policies, or for any other cause.

**The Historical Debate** The question was hotly debated in the first session of Congress in 1789. Several members argued that for those offices for which appointment required Senate approval, Senate consent should also be required for removal. They insisted that this restriction on presidential authority was essential to congressional supervision (oversight) of the executive branch. But others argued that the President could not "take care that the laws be faithfully executed" without a free hand to dismiss those who were incompetent or otherwise undesirable.

The latter view prevailed. The 1st Congress gave to the President the power to remove any officer he appointed, except federal judges. Over the years since then, Congress has sometimes tried, with little success, to restrict the President's freedom to dismiss.

One notable instance came in 1867. Locked with Andrew Johnson in the fight over Reconstruction, Congress passed the Tenure of Office Act. The law's plain purpose was to prevent

---

[9]Article II, Section 4; see Chapter 11, Section 4.

President Johnson from removing several top officers in his administration, especially the secretary of war, Edwin M. Stanton. The law provided that any person holding an office by presidential appointment with Senate consent should remain in that office until a successor had been confirmed by the Senate. The President vetoed the bill, charging that it was an unconstitutional invasion of executive authority. The veto, which was overridden, and Stanton's removal sparked the move for Johnson's impeachment. Nevertheless, the law was ignored in practice. It was finally repealed in 1887.

**Removal and the Supreme Court** The question of the President's removal power did not reach the Supreme Court until *Myers* v. *United States,* 1926. In 1876, Congress had passed a law requiring Senate consent before the President could dismiss any first-, second-, or third-class postmaster.

In 1920, without consulting the Senate, President Woodrow Wilson removed Frank Myers as the postmaster at Portland, Oregon. Myers then sued for the salary for the rest of his four-year term. He based his claim on the point that he had been removed in violation of the 1876 law. The Court found the law unconstitutional, however. Its opinion was written by Chief Justice William Howard Taft, himself a former President. The Court held that the power of removal was an essential part of the executive power, clearly necessary to the faithful execution of the laws.

The Supreme Court did place some limits on the President's removal power in 1935, in *Humphrey's Executor* v. *United States.* President Herbert Hoover had appointed William Humphrey to a seven-year term on the Federal Trade Commission (FTC) in 1931. When Franklin D. Roosevelt entered office in 1933, he found Humphrey in sharp disagreement with many of his policies. He asked Humphrey to resign, saying that his administration would be better served with someone else on the FTC. When Humphrey refused, Roosevelt removed him. Humphrey soon died, but his heirs filed a suit for back salary.

The Supreme Court upheld the heirs' claim. It based its decision on the act creating the FTC.

## Presidents on the Presidency

"[The presidency is] a place of splendid misery."
–Thomas Jefferson

"The four most miserable years of my life were my four years in the presidency."
–John Quincy Adams

"Nobody ever left the presidency with less regret."
–Rutherford B. Hayes

"What is there in this place that a man should ever want to get into it!"
–James A. Garfield

"I have had enough of it, Heaven knows! I have had all the honor there is in this place, and have had responsibilities enough to kill any man."
–William McKinley

"I'm glad to be going– this is the loneliest place in the world."
–William H. Taft

"[The presidency is] a prison."
–Warren G. Harding

"The first twelve years are the hardest."
–Franklin D. Roosevelt

"There is no exaltation in the office of the President of the United States—sorrow is the proper word."
–Harry S Truman

"No one can experience with the President of the United States the glory and agony of his office."
–Lyndon B. Johnson

**Interpreting Charts** This chart shows that many Presidents have viewed the presidency as a bittersweet experience. What common theme runs through these quotations?

**Lonely at the Top**   The enormous responsibility shouldered by the chief executive is evident in this famous photograph of President John F. Kennedy alone in the Oval Office.

That law provides that a member of the commission may be removed only for "inefficiency, neglect of duty, or malfeasance in office."[10] The President had given none of these reasons when he removed Humphrey.

The Court further held that Congress does have the power to set the conditions under which a member of the FTC and other such agencies might be removed by the President. It did so because those agencies, the independent regulatory commissions, are not purely executive agencies—a rather complicated point that you will consider in the next chapter.

As a general rule, however, the President may remove those whom the President appoints. Occasionally, the President does have to remove someone; most often, however, what was in fact a dismissal is called a "resignation."

---

[10]*Malfeasance* is wrongful conduct, especially by a public officeholder.

## Section 2 Review

1. **Define:** executive order
2. In what way can the executive branch affect the meaning of a particular law?
3. How is the President the chief administrator as well as the chief executive?
4. In what way does the ordinance power enable the President to exercise the executive powers?
5. (a) What officers does the President appoint? (b) What is the Senate's role in the appointment process?

**Critical Thinking**

6. **Demonstrating Reasoned Judgment** (p. 19) Explain why you agree or disagree with this statement: The unwritten rule of senatorial courtesy contradicts the principle of separation of powers.

★

# 3 The Diplomatic and Military Powers

**Find Out:**

- What is the scope of the President's diplomatic powers? How does the President exercise these powers?
- What is the scope of the President's military powers? How does the President exercise these powers?

**Key Terms:**

treaty, executive agreement, recognition

President John F. Kennedy once described the pressures of the presidency in these words:

66 When I ran for the presidency . . . I knew the country faced serious challenges, but I could not realize—nor could any man who does not bear the burdens of this office—how heavy and constant would be those burdens. 99

When Kennedy made that comment, he had in mind, particularly, the subject of this section: the President's awesome responsibilities as chief diplomat and as commander in chief.

## The Power to Make Treaties

A **treaty** is a formal agreement between two or more sovereign states. The President, usually acting through the secretary of state, negotiates these international agreements. The Senate must give its approval, by a two-thirds vote of the members present, before a treaty made by the President can become effective.[11] Recall, the Constitution makes treaties a part of the "supreme law of the land."

The Framers considered the Senate—with, originally, only 26 members—a suitable council to advise the President in foreign affairs. Secrecy was thought to be necessary and was seen as an impossibility in a body as large as the House.

The two-thirds rule creates the possibility that a relatively small minority in the Senate can kill a treaty. To take one example: In 1919 the Senate rejected the Versailles Treaty, the general peace agreement to end World War I. The treaty included provisions for the League of Nations. Forty-nine senators voted for the pact and 35 against, but the vote was 7 short of the necessary two-thirds. More than once a President has been forced to bow to the views of a few senators in order to get a treaty approved, even when this has meant making concessions opposed by the majority.

At times, a President has had to turn to roundabout methods in order to achieve his goals. When a Senate minority defeated a treaty to annex Texas, President Tyler was able to bring about annexation in 1845 by encouraging passage of a joint resolution—a move that required only a majority vote in each house. In 1898 President McKinley used the same tactic to annex Hawaii, again after a treaty his administration had negotiated had failed to achieve the necessary two-thirds vote in the Senate.

## Executive Agreements

More and more, international agreements, especially the routine ones, are made as executive agreements. **Executive agreements** are pacts between the President and the heads of foreign states, or their subordinates. Unlike treaties, executive agreements do not require Senate consent.

Most executive agreements either flow out of legislation already passed by Congress or out of treaties to which the Senate has agreed. The President can make these executive agreements

---

[11]Contrary to popular belief, the Senate does not ratify treaties. The Constitution requires the Senate's "advice and consent" to a treaty made by the President. Once the Senate has approved a treaty, the President ratifies it by the exchange of formal notifications with the other party or parties to the agreement.

Treaties have the same legal standing as do acts passed by Congress. Congress may repeal (abrogate) a treaty by passing a law contrary to its provisions, and an existing law may be repealed by the terms of a treaty. When a treaty and a statute conflict, the courts consider the latest enacted to be the law (*The Head Money Cases*, 1884). The terms of a treaty cannot conflict with the higher law of the Constitution (*Missouri* v. *Holland*, 1920), but the Supreme Court has never found a treaty provision to be unconstitutional.

▲ **The Art of Diplomacy**   In 1945 President Roosevelt met with King Ibn Saud aboard a cruiser to establish closer relations between Saudi Arabia and the United States. Such negotiations typify a crucial role played by the President.

without any congressional action or approval, however.[12]

Dozens of routine executive agreements are made each year. At times, though, they are extraordinary. For example, in the "Destroyer-Bases Deal" of 1940, the United States gave the British 50 "over-age" destroyers in return for 99-year leases to several island bases extending from Newfoundland to the Caribbean.

## The Power of Recognition

When the President receives the diplomatic representatives of another sovereign state, the President exercises the power of **recognition**. That is, the President, acting for the United States, acknowledges the legal existence of that country and its government. The President indicates that the United States accepts that country as an equal in the family of nations.[13]

Recognition does not mean that one government approves of the character and conduct of another. The United States recognizes several governments about which it has serious misgivings—among the most notable examples of the point today, the People's Republic of China. The facts of life in world politics make relations with these governments necessary.

___

[12]The Supreme Court has held executive agreements to be as binding as treaties and a part of the supreme law of the land, *United States* v. *Belmont*, 1937; *Pink* v. *United States*, 1942.

[13]Sovereign states generally recognize one another through the exchange of diplomatic representatives. Recognition may be carried out in any of several other ways, however. For example, it may be accomplished by proposing to negotiate a treaty, since under international law only sovereign states can make such agreements.

Recognition is often used as a weapon in foreign relations, too. Prompt recognition of a new state or government may do much to guarantee its life. In the same way, the withholding of recognition may seriously affect its continued existence.

President Theodore Roosevelt's quick recognition of the Republic of Panama in 1903 is one of the classic examples of American use of the power as a diplomatic weapon. He recognized the new state less than three days after the Panamanians had begun an American-supported revolt against Colombia, of which Panama had been a part. Roosevelt's quick action guaranteed their success. Similarly, President Truman's recognition of Israel, within 24 hours of its creation in 1948, helped that new state to survive its turbulent beginnings.

The President may show the United States' displeasure with the conduct of another country by asking for the recall of that nation's ambassador or other diplomatic representatives in this country. The official recalled is declared to be *persona non grata*—an unwelcome person. A similar message can be sent by the recalling of an American diplomat from a post in another country. The withdrawal of recognition is the sharpest diplomatic rebuke one government may give to another and has often been a step on the way to war.

## The President's Dominant Role in Military Affairs

The Constitution makes the President the commander in chief of the nation's armed forces.[14] Even though Congress shares the war powers,[15] the President's position in military affairs is as dominant as it is in the field of foreign affairs. In fact, it does not stretch the matter too far to say that the President's powers as commander in chief are almost without limit.

Consider this illustration of the point: In 1907 Theodore Roosevelt sent the Great White Fleet around the world. Several members of Congress objected to the cost and threatened to block the bill to fund the President's project.

To which Roosevelt replied: "Very well, the existing appropriation will carry the Navy halfway around the world and if Congress chooses to leave it on the other side, all right." Congress was forced to give in.

Presidents almost always delegate much of their command authority to military subordinates. They are not required to do so, however. George Washington actually took command of federal troops and led them into Pennsylvania during the Whiskey Rebellion of 1794. Abraham Lincoln often visited the Army of the Potomac and instructed his generals in the field during the Civil War.

Most Presidents have not become so directly involved in military operations. Still, the President always has the final authority over and responsibility for any and all military matters. The most critical decisions are invariably made by the commander in chief. Thus, it was President

**Power of Recognition** The 15 republics of the old Soviet Union became independent states in 1989 and 1990. Today, the United States maintains diplomatic relations with each of these new states.

[14]Article II, Section 2, Clause 1; see also Chapter 17.
[15]Article I, Section 8, Clauses 11–17; see also Chapter 11, Section 2.

Harry Truman who made the fateful decision to use nuclear weapons against Japan in 1945 and so bring World War II to a close.

**Making Undeclared War** Several Presidents have used the armed forces abroad, in combat, without a declaration of war by Congress. In fact, most Presidents have done so, and on no fewer than 200 occasions.

John Adams was the first to do so, in 1798. At his command, the Navy fought and won a number of battles with French warships harassing American merchantmen in the Atlantic and the Caribbean. Thomas Jefferson and then James Madison followed that precedent in the war against the Barbary Coast pirates of North Africa in the early 1800s. Many other foreign adventures occurred throughout the last century and into the present one. The long military conflicts in Korea (from 1950 to 1953) and in Vietnam (from 1965 to 1973) were the largest of those "undeclared wars."

From 1982 to 1984, President Reagan commanded the Marines and Navy to join in an international peacekeeping force in Beirut, Lebanon. An invasion of Grenada in 1983 involved the Army, Navy, and Air Force. Iran's attacks in the Persian Gulf prompted Reagan to order a Navy escort for oil tankers there in 1987 and 1988. The most recent uses of this nation's armed forces in combat abroad came during the Bush Administration. President Bush sent the armed forces into battle twice—first in Panama in late 1989 and then in Kuwait and Iraq in early 1991. Mr. Bush ordered the invasion of Panama to oust that country's dictator, General Manuel Noriega, and to safeguard American interests there, most notably, the Panama Canal.

As the American military buildup continued, Iraqi dictator Saddam Hussein ignored the repeated demands of the United States and the United Nations Security Council that Iraq withdraw from Kuwait. Nearly all of the world community joined in support of those demands.

Finally, on January 16, 1991, American warplanes began a sustained bombing of Iraqi positions in Kuwait and of targets in Iraq itself. British, French, Saudi Arabian, and other air forces also took part in that devastating attack. Then, on February 24th, a massive land offensive was launched, led by American forces.

The ground fighting in the Gulf War lasted less than 100 days. Iraqi troops were driven from Kuwait, and much of southern Iraq was occupied for a brief time by American and allied troops.

Altogether, more than 500,000 Americans saw duty in the Gulf War. Several thousand remain stationed in the region, mostly in Saudi Arabia. President Bush did not seek a declaration of war in 1991, but Congress did pass a joint resolution authorizing the use of American military force in the region at the time.

President Clinton used the threat of this nation's military might to restore democratic government to Haiti in 1994, and, at the same time, to stem the flow of thousands of illegal immigrants from Haiti to the United States. In 1991, a coup led by General Raoul Cédras had deposed President Jean-Bertrand Aristide, the first popularly elected leader in Haiti's history. Faced with the certainty of an invasion by the United States, the Cédras dictatorship collapsed. American troops occupied the country and President Aristide was returned to power.

**Wartime Powers** The President's powers as commander in chief are far greater during a war than they are in more normal times. In fact, presidential wartime authority goes far beyond the traditional military field. Thus, in World War II, for example, Congress gave the President the power to do such things as ration food and gasoline, control wages and prices, and seize and operate certain private industries.

The President may also use the armed forces to keep the domestic peace, as you saw in Chapter 4.[16] When necessary, the President also has the power to call any State's militia, or all of them, into federal service.[17]

**The War Powers Resolution** In today's world, no one can doubt that the President must be able to respond rapidly and effectively to threats to this nation's security. Still, many have long warned of the dangers inherent in the President's power to involve the nation in undeclared wars. They insist that

---

[16]Article IV, Section 4.
[17]Article I, Section 8, Clause 15; Article II, Section 2, Clause 1.

▲ **Power During Crisis**   Thomas Jefferson issued Mediterranean passports, or "sea letters" (inset), in the early 1800s to safeguard American ships from pirates. In 1991 Congress supported President Bush's decision to use force to drive the invading Iraqi forces out of Kuwait.

the Constitution never intended the President to have such power.

The nation's frustrations and growing anguish over the war in Vietnam finally moved Congress to pass the War Powers Resolution of 1973. The act is designed to place close limits on the President's war-making powers. President Nixon vetoed the measure, calling it "both unconstitutional and dangerous to the best interest of our nation." Congress overrode the veto.

The resolution's central provisions require that:

1. Within 48 hours after committing American forces to combat abroad, the President must report to Congress, detailing the circumstances and the scope of his actions.

2. That combat commitment must end within 60 days, unless Congress authorizes a longer period. That 60-day deadline may be extended for as much as 30 days, however, to allow for the safe withdrawal of the American forces involved.

3. Congress may bring an end to the combat commitment at any time, by passing a concurrent resolution to that effect.

The constitutionality of the War Powers Resolution remains in dispute. A determination of the question must await a situation in which Congress demands that its provisions be obeyed but the President refuses to do so.

## Section 3 Review

1. **Define:** treaty, executive agreement, recognition

2. What powers does the President have in foreign affairs?

3. (a) How does the President usually exercise the power of recognition? (b) How can the power of recognition be used as a weapon?

4. (a) What is the President's major military power? (b) What limits are placed on that power?

5. (a) For what purpose was the War Powers Resolution designed? (b) What is the controversy surrounding the resolution?

**Critical Thinking**

6. **Determining Relevance** (p. 19) Framer George Mason said, "The purse and the sword must never be in the same hands." How is this idea reflected in the War Powers Resolution?

★

# 4 The Legislative and Judicial Powers

**Find Out:**

■ What is the scope of the President's legislative and judicial powers?
■ How does the President exercise these powers?

**Key Terms:**

reprieve, pardon, commutation, amnesty

As you know, the Federal Government is built on the principles of the separation of powers and checks and balances. Each branch has formal powers with which it can check, delay, or block actions by the other branches. In this section you will consider the President's constitutional powers in the legislative and the judicial domains.

## The President in the Legislative Field

With his legislative powers—and the skillful playing of his roles as chief of party and chief citizen—the President can have a considerable influence on Congress. The President is in effect, then, the nation's chief legislator.

**Power to Recommend Legislation** The Constitution says that the President

" . . . shall, from time to time, give to the Congress information of the state of the Union, and recommend to their consideration such measures as he shall judge necessary and expedient. . . ."[18]

Soon after the beginning of each congressional session, the President delivers his State of the Union message to Congress. This is followed by the proposed budget and the annual Economic Report. At times, the President also submits special messages on certain subjects to Congress. In all of them the legislators are called on to enact those laws the President thinks are necessary to the welfare of the nation. Many recommendations are shared with the public.

**The Veto Power** The Constitution says that "every bill" and "every order, resolution, or vote to which the concurrence of the Senate and House of Representatives may be necessary (except on a question of adjournment) shall be presented to the President."[19]

As noted in Chapter 12, the Constitution presents the President with four options when the Congress passes a measure. First, the President may sign the bill, thus making it law. Second, the President may veto[20] the bill.

As a third option, the President may allow the bill to become law by not acting on it, neither signing nor vetoing it, within 10 days (not counting Sundays). This rarely happens.

The fourth option, the pocket veto, can be used only at the end of a congressional session. If Congress adjourns within 10 days of sending a bill to the President and the chief executive does not act on it, the measure dies.

The veto power allows the President, the only representative of all the people, to act as a check on Congress. Often, just the threat of a veto is enough to defeat a bill or to bring about changes in the measure.

The historical record of presidential vetoes, and the fact that they are rarely overridden, can be seen in the table on page 367.

Bills must be vetoed in their entirety. The President has no "item veto," as do most State governors; see Chapter 24, Section 2. With that power, specific items can be eliminated from an appropriations measure or an objectionable provision removed from a bill the President might otherwise wish to become law.

On the other hand, some observers worry that the power could be used as a weapon to punish or pressure the President's opponents in Congress by specifically targeting parts of legislation that directly affect them. Nevertheless, every President since Woodrow Wilson has favored a constitutional amendment to add the item veto to the President's arsenal of legislative powers.

---

[18]Article II, Section 3; see also Chapter 12, Section 1.

[19]Article I, Section 7, Clauses 2 and 3. Notice that in practice, joint resolutions proposing constitutional amendments and concurrent resolutions, which do not have the force of law, are not sent to the President.

[20]*Veto,* from the Latin, "I forbid."

## Presidential Vetoes

| President | Regular Vetoes | Pocket Vetoes | Total | Vetoes Overridden |
|---|---|---|---|---|
| Washington (1789–97) | 2 | – | 2 | – |
| Madison (1809–17) | 5 | 2 | 7 | – |
| Monroe (1817–25) | 1 | – | 1 | – |
| Jackson (1829–37) | 5 | 7 | 12 | – |
| Van Buren (1837–41) | – | 1 | 1 | – |
| Tyler (1841–45) | 6 | 4 | 10 | 1 |
| Polk (1845–49) | 2 | 1 | 3 | – |
| Pierce (1853–57) | 9 | – | 9 | 5 |
| Buchanan (1857–61) | 4 | 3 | 7 | – |
| Lincoln (1861–65) | 2 | 5 | 7 | – |
| Johnson (1865–69) | 21 | 8 | 29 | 15 |
| Grant (1869–77) | 45 | 48 | 93 | 4 |
| Hayes (1877–81) | 12 | 1 | 13 | 1 |
| Arthur (1881–85) | 4 | 8 | 12 | 1 |
| Cleveland (1885–89) | 304 | 110 | 414 | 2 |
| Harrison (1889–93) | 19 | 25 | 44 | 1 |
| Cleveland (1893–97) | 42 | 128 | 170 | 5 |
| McKinley (1897–1901) | 6 | 36 | 42 | – |
| Roosevelt (1901–09) | 42 | 40 | 82 | 1 |
| Taft (1909–13) | 30 | 9 | 39 | 1 |
| Wilson (1913–21) | 33 | 11 | 44 | 6 |
| Harding (1921–23) | 5 | 1 | 6 | – |
| Coolidge (1923–29) | 20 | 30 | 50 | 4 |
| Hoover (1929–33) | 21 | 16 | 37 | 3 |
| Roosevelt (1933–45) | 372 | 263 | 635 | 9 |
| Truman (1945–53) | 180 | 70 | 250 | 12 |
| Eisenhower (1953–61) | 73 | 108 | 181 | 2 |
| Kennedy (1961–63) | 12 | 9 | 21 | – |
| Johnson (1963–69) | 16 | 14 | 30 | – |
| Nixon (1969–74) | 26 | 17 | 43 | 5 |
| Ford (1974–77) | 48 | 18 | 66 | 12 |
| Carter (1977–81) | 13 | 18 | 31 | 2 |
| Reagan (1981–89) | 39 | 39 | 78 | 9 |
| Bush (1989–93) | 37 | 9 | 46 | 1 |
| | **1,456** | **1,059** | **2,515** | **102** |

*Source:* Congressional Research Service, Library of Congress. The Presidents not listed vetoed no measures.

▲ Interpreting Tables   Why is the veto power an effective tool in the American system of checks and balances?

**Other Legislative Powers**   Only the President has the authority to call special sessions of Congress, as you read in Chapter 10, Section 1. The President also has the power to adjourn (prorogue) Congress when the Senate and House cannot agree together on an adjournment date—something that has never happened.

## Judicial Powers

The President has the constitutional power to

« . . . grant reprieves and pardons for offences against the United States, except in cases of impeachment. »[21]

---

[21]Article II, Section 2, Clause 1.

A **reprieve** is the postponement of the execution of a sentence. A **pardon** is legal forgiveness of a crime.

The President's power to grant reprieves and pardons is absolute—except in cases of impeachment, where they may never be granted. These powers of clemency—of mercy, leniency—may be used only in cases involving federal offenses, however. The President has no such authority with regard to those who violate State law. As you will read in Chapter 24, Section 2, each State governor generally possesses the powers of clemency.

Presidential pardons are usually granted after a person has been convicted in court. The President may pardon a federal offender before that person is tried, however. In fact, a pardon may be issued even before that person has been formally charged.

Pardons in advance of a trial or charge are rare. The most noteworthy pardon, by far, was granted in 1974. In that year, President Gerald Ford gave "a full, free and absolute pardon unto Richard Nixon for all offenses against the United States which he . . . has committed or may have committed or taken part in during the period from January 20, 1969, through August 9, 1974." Of course, Ford's pardon referred to the series of events that are known today as the Watergate scandal.

To be effective, a pardon must be accepted by the person to whom it is granted. When one is granted before charge or conviction, as in Mr. Nixon's case, its acceptance is regularly seen as an admission of guilt by the person to whom it is given.

The pardoning power includes the power to grant conditional pardons if the conditions are reasonable. It also includes the power of **commutation**—that is, the power to commute (reduce) the length of a sentence or a fine imposed by a court.

The pardoning power also includes the power of **amnesty**—in effect, a general pardon offered to a group of law violators. Thus, in 1893 President Benjamin Harrison issued a proclamation of amnesty forgiving all Mormons who had violated the antipolygamy laws in the federal territories. And in 1977 President Jimmy Carter granted a blanket pardon to Vietnam War draft evaders.

## Section 4 Review

1. **Define:** pardon, amnesty, reprieve, commutation
2. (a) Why does the Constitution give certain legislative powers to the President? (b) What are they?
3. (a) What vote is required for Congress to override a presidential veto? (b) In what way is the threat of a veto at times an important presidential tool?
4. Under what circumstances may a President pardon someone?
5. What is the difference between a pocket veto and an item veto?

**Critical Thinking**

6. **Predicting Consequences** (p. 19) How might (a) the President and (b) a member of Congress answer this question: Would giving the President the item veto have any significant effect on the separation of powers between the two branches?

▲ **Judicial Power of Pardon** Gerald Ford felt compelled to end the "long national nightmare" by granting a pardon to Richard Nixon, who was the first President ever to resign from office.

★

## Should the Government Limit Individual Liberties During Wartime?

### *Korematsu v. United States*, 1944

Japan's attack on Pearl Harbor, Hawaii, on December 7, 1941, prompted widespread fear of a Japanese invasion of the West Coast of the United States. And a great many people were immediately suspicious of the loyalty of the approximately 120,000 persons of Japanese descent living in the States bordering the Pacific Ocean. Of that number, about 70,000 were *Nisei*— that is, native-born American citizens.

On February 19, 1942, President Franklin Roosevelt issued Executive Order No. 9066. That order authorized the military to "prescribe military areas . . . from which any or all persons may be excluded." Executive Order 9066 was intended to help protect the nation from possible acts of espionage and sabotage. Congress soon went even further. It passed a law to provide for the relocation of all persons excluded from any of those military areas; they were to be sent to "war relocation camps," outside the sensitive areas.

On March 2, 1942, the general commanding the Western Defense Command issued the first of a series of orders that identified the entire Pacific Coast as Military Area No. 1 because it was vulnerable to attack and espionage. On March 24 he began to issue orders that excluded all persons of Japanese descent from Military Area No. 1.

Toyosaburo Korematsu, a native-born American citizen, refused to leave his home in San Leandro, across the bay from San Francisco. He was arrested and charged with failure to report for relocation. He was convicted of that charge in federal district court; and that conviction was subsequently upheld in the United States Court of Appeals. At that point, Korematsu appealed to the United States Supreme Court.

*Review the following evidence and arguments presented to the U.S. Supreme Court:*

### Arguments for Korematsu

**1.** Executive Order 9066 denied Korematsu his liberty without due process, in violation of the 5th Amendment.
**2.** Martial law had not been declared in the area; therefore, the President could not give the military power to regulate civilian conduct.
**3.** The exclusion order provided for a race-based classification; the Constitution forbids such arbitrary classifications.

### Arguments for the United States

**1.** The potential for espionage and sabotage justified this denial of liberty to American citizens.
**2.** War had been declared. The President, as commander in chief, had the authority to issue such orders to the military.
**3.** The United States had been attacked by Japan, and it was logical that people of Japanese ancestry were suspect. Race-based prejudice was not involved here.

## Getting Involved

**1. Identify** the constitutional grounds on which each side based its arguments.
**2. Debate** the opposing viewpoints presented in this case.
**3. Predict** how you think the Supreme Court ruled in this case and why. Refer to page 766 in the Supreme Court Glossary to read about the decision. Discuss the impact of the Court's decision on the right of American citizens to equal protection.

# 5 The Executive Office of the President and the Cabinet

**Find Out:**

- For what reason is the Executive Office of the President described as umbrella-like?
- What are some of the key components of the Executive Office?
- How has the cabinet and its current role evolved?
- How are cabinet members selected?

**Key Terms:**

federal budget, cabinet

Thomas Jefferson performed his presidential duties with the help of two aides, one a messenger and the other his secretary. And, like other early Presidents, he paid their salaries out of his own pocket. Indeed, Congress did not provide any money for presidential staff until 1857—when it gave President James Buchanan $2,500 for one clerk.

Things are much different today. You will look at the federal bureaucracy, that huge complex of agencies that makes up the bulk of the executive branch, in the next chapter. But first, you will examine the two agencies that are specifically designed to help the President meet the immense responsibilities of his office today: the Executive Office of the President and the cabinet.

## The Executive Office of the President

Every officer, every employee, and every agency in the executive branch of the Federal Government are legally subordinate to the President. They all exist to help the President—the chief executive—in the exercise of his executive power.

The President's *chief* right arm, however, is the Executive Office of the President (the EOP). The Executive Office of the President is, in fact, an umbrella agency—a complex of several separate agencies staffed by the President's most trusted advisers and assistants.

The EOP was established by Congress in 1939, and it has been reorganized in every administration over the years since then—including the Clinton Administration.

**The White House Office**   The "nerve center" of the Executive Office of the President—in fact, of the entire executive branch—is the White House Office. It houses the President's key personal and political staff. Most of them have offices in one of the two wings on either side of the White House. They occupy most of the crowded West Wing, which the public seldom sees and where the legendary Oval Office and the Cabinet Room are located. Some of them work in the East Wing, where public tours of the White House begin. And still others are housed in the historic Old Executive Office Building, which is adjacent to the West Wing.

The chief of staff to the President directs all of the operations of the White House Office and is among the most influential of all these presidential aides. So, too, is the counselor to the President and a number of senior advisers who are also key members of the Clinton inner circle today.

Several other top officials in the White House Office, assistants and deputy assistants to the President, aid the chief executive in such

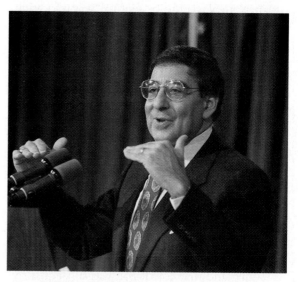

▲ **Budget Briefing**   Chief of Staff Leon Panetta briefs the press. Clinton described the Panetta appointment as part of a drive to "find the highest and best use for talented people of good will" in his administration.

vital areas as foreign policy, defense, the economy, national health carte, political affairs, congressional relations, and contacts with the news media and the public.

The staff of the White House Office also includes such other major presidential aides as the press secretary, the counsel to the President, and the President's physician. The large role that Hillary Rodham Clinton has taken in the current administration is reflected by the fact that one of the assistants to the President serves as chief of staff to the first lady; and one of the several deputy assistants is her press secretary.

Altogether, the staff of the White House Office now numbers some 400 men and women—men and women who, in a very real sense, work for the President.

**The National Security Council** Most of the President's major steps in foreign affairs are taken in close consultation with the National Security Council (NSC). It meets at the President's call, often on short notice, to advise him in all domestic, foreign, and military matters that bear on the nation's security.

The President chairs the Council. Its other members are the Vice President and the secretaries of state and defense. The director of the Central Intelligence Agency (CIA) and the chairman of the Joint Chiefs of Staff also attend its meetings.

The NSC has a small staff of foreign and military policy experts. They work under the direction of the President's assistant for national security affairs, who is often called the President's national security adviser.

The super-secret Central Intelligence Agency does much of its work at the direction of the NSC.

The National Security Council is a staff agency. That is, its job is to advise the President in all matters affecting the nation's security. However, during the Reagan administration in the 1980s, the NSC's staff actually conducted a number of secret operations. The most spectacular of them involved the sale of arms to Iran and the use of some of the proceeds from those sales to aid the Contra rebels in Nicaragua. Congress had prohibited military aid to the Contras, and the disclosure of the NSC's activities produced the Iran-Contra scandal of the mid-1980s.

## The Office of Management and Budget

The Office of Management and Budget (OMB) is the largest and, after the White House Office, the most influential unit in the Executive Office. The OMB is headed by a director who is appointed by the President and confirmed by the Senate. The OMB's major task is the preparation of the federal budget, which the President must submit to Congress in January or February each year.

The budget-making function is far more than a routine bookkeeping chore. It is the preparation of an annual statement of the public policies of the United States expressed as dollars and cents.

The **federal budget** is a financial document, a detailed estimate of receipts and expenditures, an anticipation of federal income and outgo during the coming fiscal year.[23] More than that, it is a work plan for the conduct of government and the execution of public policy.

The many steps by which each fiscal year's budget is built is a lengthy process. In fact, it begins more than a year before the start of the fiscal year for which the budget is intended. In its first stages, each federal agency prepares detailed estimates of its spending needs for the upcoming 12-month period. Those proposals are reviewed by the OMB, usually in a series of budget hearings at which agency officials defend their requests. Following that review, the revised—and usually lowered—spending estimates are fitted into the President's overall program. They become a part of the budget document the chief executive presents to Congress.

The OMB is much more than a budget-making agency. It also monitors the spending of the funds Congress appropriates. That is, it oversees the execution of the budget. The President's close control over the preparation and execution of the budget is a major factor in the President's ability to command the huge executive branch.

Beyond its budget chores, the OMB is a sort of presidential odd-job agency. It makes studies

---

[23]A fiscal year is the 12-month period used by a government and the business world for its record-keeping, budgeting, revenue-collecting, and other financial management purposes. The Federal Government's fiscal year now runs from October 1 through September 30.

of the organization and management of the executive branch and keeps the President up to date on the work of all its agencies. The OMB checks and clears agency stands on all legislative matters to be certain that they agree with the President's own positions. It also helps the President prepare the hundreds of executive orders he must issue and the veto messages he occasionally sends to Congress and does much more to live up to the word *management* in its title.

### The Office of National Drug Control Policy

The Office of National Drug Control Policy is the newest of the major units within the Executive Office. It was established in 1989, and its existence dramatizes the nation's concern over drugs. The office is headed by a director who is appointed by the President, subject to the approval of the Senate.

The news media regularly identify the director as "the nation's drug czar." But, to this point, at least, the office has operated as an advisory and a planning agency. It has two major responsibilities: (1) to prepare an annual national drug control strategy, which the President sends on to Congress; and (2) to coordinate the efforts of the more than 50 federal agencies participating in the war on drugs.

### The Council of Economic Advisers

Three of the country's leading economists, chosen by the President with the consent of the Senate, make up the Council of Economic Advisers. It is the chief executive's major source of information and advice on the state of the nation's economy. The Council also helps the President prepare his annual Economic Report to Congress. That report, together with a presidential message, goes to Capitol Hill in late January or early February each year.

### Other Units in the Executive Office

Several other agencies in the Executive Office house key presidential aides—men and women who give the President the assistance he must have in order to meet his many responsibilities.

THE OFFICE OF POLICY DEVELOPMENT. The President is—and must be—constantly concerned with the nation's domestic affairs, of course. The Office of Policy Development advises him on all matters in that whole and many-sided arena. The Office is headed by the assistant to the President for domestic policy.

THE COUNCIL ON ENVIRONMENTAL QUALITY. The council aids the President in all environmental policy matters and in the writing of the annual "state of the environment" report to Congress. Its basic job is to see that other federal agencies comply with the provisions of the nation's many environmental laws and with the President's environmental policies.

The council's three members are appointed by the President, with the Senate's consent. They are sometimes called upon to act as referees in disputes between or among executive branch agencies—for example, a conflict between the Environmental Protection Agency and one or more agencies in the Departments of the Agriculture, Interior, or Energy.

President Clinton has asked Congress to elevate the Environmental Protection Agency to cabinet status, as the Department of the Environment. If and when that happens, the Council on Environmental Quality is to be abolished.

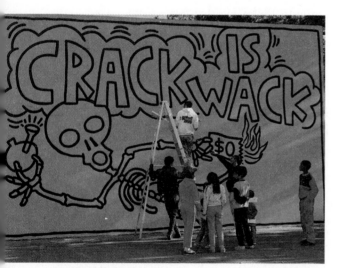

▲ **The War on Drugs**   The campaign against illicit drug use in the United States was supported by the Office of National Drug Control Policy. This street mural by artist Keith Haring graphically communicates its antidrug message.

THE OFFICE OF UNITED STATES TRADE REPRESENTATIVE. This agency advises the chief executive in all matters of foreign trade. The trade representative, appointed by the President and confirmed by the Senate, carries the rank of ambassador and represents the President in foreign trade negotiations.

THE OFFICE OF SCIENCE AND TECHNOLOGY POLICY. The President's major adviser in all scientific, engineering, and other technological matters bearing on national policies and programs is the Office of Science and Technology Policy. Its director, who is chosen by the President and confirmed by the Senate, is drawn from the nation's scientific community.

THE OFFICE OF ADMINISTRATION. This is the general housekeeping agency for all the other units in the Executive Office. It provides them with the many support services they must have in order to do their jobs. The list of those things is almost endless: clerical help, data processing, library services, transportation, and much more.

## The Cabinet

The **cabinet** is an informal advisory body brought together by the President to serve his needs. The Constitution makes no mention of it,[24] nor did Congress create it. Instead, the cabinet is the product of custom and usage.

At its first session in 1789, Congress established four executive posts: secretary of state, secretary of the treasury, secretary of war, and attorney general. By his second term, Washington was regularly seeking the advice of the four outstanding people he had named to those offices: Thomas Jefferson in the Department of State, Alexander Hamilton at the Treasury, Henry Knox in the War Department, and Edmund Randolph, the attorney general. So the cabinet was born.

---

[24]The closest approach to it is in Article II, Section 2, Clause 1, where the President is given the power to "require the opinion, in writing, of the principal officer in each of the executive departments, upon any subject relating to the duties of their respective offices." The cabinet was first mentioned in an act of Congress in 1907, well over a century after its birth.

**The First Cabinet**  The nation's first cabinet included President George Washington (right); Secretary of State Thomas Jefferson (second left); and Secretary of the Treasury Alexander Hamilton (second right).

By tradition, the heads of the now 14 executive departments form the cabinet. Each of the last several Presidents has regularly added a number of other top officials to the group—most notably, the director of the OMB, the trade representative, and the President's chief domestic policy adviser. Every Vice President since Alben Barkley, who served under President Truman (1949–1953), has also been a regular participant at cabinet meetings. Several other major figures are usually there, as well—in particular, the White House chief of staff.

**Choosing Cabinet Members**  The President appoints the head of each of the 14 executive departments. Each of these appointments is subject to confirmation by the Senate, but rejections have been exceedingly rare. The Senate generally respects the personal choice of the President. Of the more than 600 presidential appointments made since 1789, only 12 have been turned down by the Senate.[25]

Many factors influence these presidential choices. Republican Presidents do not often pick Democrats, and vice versa. One or more of a new President's appointees usually come from

---

[25]The most recent rejection occurred in 1989, when the Senate refused to confirm President Bush's selection of John Tower as secretary of defense.

## The President's Cabinet

**Cabinet Post\* (Year Created)**

**Secretary of State** (established 1789)

**Secretary of the Treasury** (established 1789)

**Secretary of Defense** (established 1947)[a]

**Attorney General** (established 1789)

**Secretary of the Interior** (established 1849)

**Secretary of Agriculture** (established 1889)

**Secretary of Commerce** (established 1903)[b]

**Secretary of Labor** (established 1913)

**Secretary of Health and Human Services** (established 1953)[c]

**Secretary of Housing and Urban Development** (established 1965)

**Secretary of Transportation** (established 1967)

**Secretary of Energy** (established 1977)

**Secretary of Education** (established 1979)

**Secretary of Veterans Affairs** (established 1989)

\*The cabinet posts are listed in the order in which each was established. This ranking is followed for formal and ceremonial purposes (protocol) and also is the order in which the cabinet officers rank in the line of presidential succession; see page 323. Note: The Postmaster General, who headed the cabinet-level Post Office Department, was a member of the cabinet from 1829 until Congress replaced the department with an independent agency, the United States Postal Service, in 1971.

[a]Congress created the National Military Establishment as an executive department in 1947. It was renamed the Department of Defense in 1949. Since 1947 it has included the former cabinet-level Departments of War (1789), and the Navy (1798), and the Department of the Air Force (1947). The secretaries of Army, Navy, and Air Force do not hold cabinet rank.

[b]The secretary of commerce was originally the secretary of commerce and labor. The Department of Commerce and Labor, created in 1903, was replaced by the separate Departments of Commerce and of Labor in 1913.

[c]The secretary of health and human services was originally the secretary of health, education, and welfare. The Department of Health, Education, and Welfare was created in 1953. HEW's education functions were transferred to a separate Department of Education in 1979, and HEW was renamed at that time.

**Interpreting Charts** Cabinet posts are listed in the order in which they were established. What does this order tell you about presidential succession?

---

among those who played a major role in the recent presidential campaign.

Of course, professional qualifications and practical experience are also taken into account in the selection of cabinet secretaries. Geography also plays a part. In broad terms, each President tries to give some sectional balance to the cabinet. Thus, the secretary of the interior often comes from the West, where most of the department's work is carried out.

Many interest groups care about who are appointed to head certain departments, and these groups influence some of the choices. Thus, the secretary of agriculture almost always has a background closely related to agriculture. The secretary of the treasury usually comes from the financial community, the secretary of commerce from the ranks of business, and so on.

Gender and race, an appointee's stand on the "hot" issues of the day, management abilities and experience, and other personal characteristics— these and a host of other factors play a part of the decision mix in selecting cabinet members.

### Women and Minorities in the Cabinet

To this point (1995), only 13 women, seven African Americans, and four Hispanics have ever held cabinet posts. Franklin Roosevelt appointed the first woman, Frances T. Perkins, secretary of labor from 1933 to 1945. Lyndon Johnson named the first African American, Robert C. Weaver, as the first secretary of housing and urban development (HUD) in 1966. The Ford cabinet was the first to include both a woman (Carla Hills, secretary of HUD) and an African American (William T. Coleman, secretary of transportation); both were appointed in 1975. Jimmy Carter appointed the first (and so far only) African-American woman to the cabinet; Patricia Roberts Harris was named secretary of HUD in 1977 and then secretary of health and human services (HHS) in 1979. Ronald Reagan appointed the first Hispanic cabinet member; Lauro F. Cavazos became secretary of education in 1988.

President Clinton's cabinet includes three women—Janet Reno (attorney general), Donna Shalala (HHS secretary), and Hazel O'Leary (secretary of energy), two African Americans— Mike Espy (agriculture secretary) and Ron

Brown (secretary of commerce), and two Hispanics—Henry Cisneros (HUD secretary) and Federico Pena (secretary of transportation).

## The Cabinet's Role

Cabinet members have two major jobs. Individually, each is the administrative head of one of the executive departments. Together, they are advisers to the President.

A number of Presidents have given great weight to the cabinet and to its advice; others have given it only a secondary role. The Bush cabinet wielded more power and apparently had more influence with the President than any cabinet since the Eisenhower presidency in the 1950s; and the cabinet plays a prominent role in the Clinton administration. On the other hand, John Kennedy described his cabinet meetings as "a waste of time."

Kennedy's view notwithstanding, most Presidents have held regular cabinet meetings—where reports are made and discussed, and advice is offered to the chief executive. That advice need not be taken, of course. Abraham Lincoln once laid a proposition he favored before his cabinet. Each member opposed it, whereupon Lincoln declared: "Seven nays, one aye: the ayes have it."

William Howard Taft put the role of the cabinet in its proper light years ago:

⟨⟨The Constitution . . . contains no suggestion of a meeting of all of the department heads in consultation over general governmental matters. The Cabinet is a mere creation of the President's will. It exists only by custom. If the President desired to dispense with it, he could do so.⟩⟩[26]

No President has ever gone so far as to suggest eliminating the cabinet. However, several Presidents have leaned on other, unofficial advisory groups, and sometimes more heavily than on the cabinet. Andrew Jackson began the practice when he became President in 1829. Several of his close friends often met with him in the kitchen at the White House and, inevitably, came to be known as the Kitchen Cabinet.

▲ **1966: Noteworthy Cabinet Appointment**
President Lyndon Johnson congratulates Robert C. Weaver, the first African American in the nation's history to be named to a cabinet post.

Franklin Roosevelt's Brain Trust of the 1930s and Harry Truman's cronies in the late 1940s were in the same mold.

# Section 5 Review

1. **Define:** federal budget, cabinet
2. In what way is the Executive Office of the President an umbrella agency?
3. Name the different components of the Executive Office of the President and their roles.
4. (a) How was the cabinet created? (b) Who are its members?
5. What two major jobs do the cabinet members have?

**Critical Thinking**

6. **Identifying Central Issues** (p. 19) In what ways is the budget-making power a major administrative tool for the President?

---

[26]*Our Chief Magistrate and His Powers* (New York: Columbia University Press, 1916), pages 29–30.

★

## *Making Comparisons*

**M**aking comparisons means identifying how different ideas, objects, people, or situations are alike and/or different. Mastering this skill is key to the process of decision making. The decisions you make as a citizen—such as the ones you make in a voting booth, for instance—are among the most important decisions you will make in your life.

For example, making comparisons between different presidential leadership styles can help you decide what kind of leader you want for your President. As you know, the ability to lead is a critically important quality in a President. If a President cannot lead the people and the Congress, his or her administration will be crippled. Follow the steps below to practice making comparisons.

**1. Identify the basis on which you will make the comparison.** Have you ever heard the expression "comparing apples to oranges"? It refers to the impossibility of comparing items that are fundamentally different. Making a comparison is possible only on the basis of a concept or characteristic that each item shares in common. Read each of the statements below. (a) What is the subject of each statement? (b) On what basis can you compare the differing views of each President?

**2. Determine the ways in which each item is alike.** Making comparisons includes finding ways in which two items are the same. (a) Are any of the statements below similar in their views on public opinion? (b) If so, in what ways are they similar?

**3. Determine the ways in which each item is different.** Of course, the other purpose of making comparisons is to identify differences between items. In what ways do each of the statements below differ from one another?

**4. Summarize the comparison between the items.** Once you have identified the similarities and differences between the items, you can complete the comparison. (a) How do the three Presidents quoted below compare in their views of popular opinion and the presidency? (b) In your opinion, which President has the view that is most unlike the others?

### Presidential Leadership Styles

| Harry Truman | Theodore Roosevelt | Woodrow Wilson |
|---|---|---|
| "A man who is influenced by the polls or is afraid to make decisions which may make him unpopular is not a man to represent the welfare of the country." | "I did not 'divine' how the people were going to think; I simply made up my mind what they ought to think, and then did my best to get them to think it." | "If he rightly interprets the national thought and boldly insists upon it, he is irresistible; and the country never feels the zest of action so much as when its President is of such insight and calibre." |

# Chapter-in-Brief

Scan all headings, photographs, charts, and other visuals in the chapter before reading the section summaries below.

## Section 1 The Changing View of Presidential Power (pp. 353–355)
The powers of the President have grown since 1787. The fact that the presidency consists of one person has given the office great stature—and power. Also, as American economic and social life has become more complex, people have looked to the President for more and more leadership.

Historically, the actions of those Presidents who favored a stronger presidential role have helped expand the powers of the office.

## Section 2 The President's Executive Powers (pp. 356–360)
The President is responsible for executing federal laws. But the meaning of many laws is vague, and enforcing them is a matter of interpretation. So, the President enjoys some special powers to help him execute and enforce laws.

The President can issue executive orders, which have the force of law. And the President may appoint subordinates—and dismiss those whom he no longer wants.

## Section 3 The Diplomatic and Military Powers (pp. 361–365)
The President presides over relations with other countries. This duty requires that the President possess certain powers. Thus, only the President may negotiate treaties, and only the President may recognize the existence of foreign countries. The President alone may appoint ambassadors and other diplomatic officers.

Though Congress shares some powers in military affairs, the President is the undisputed leader. For example, though Congress can declare war, a President can—and on 200 occasions has—carried out military action without the consent of Congress. Congress has tried to contain the President's power through the War Powers Resolution, but its success has been limited.

## Section 4 The Legislative and Judicial Powers (pp. 366–368)
As part of the system of checks and balances, the President holds several legislative and judicial powers.

The President may recommend legislation, and he may veto bills passed by Congress. Congress may override a veto, but rarely does so.

In the judicial field, a President may delay the carrying out of a sentence (a reprieve), legally forgive a convicted person (a pardon), lessen a convicted person's sentence (commutation), or offer a general pardon to a group of law violators (amnesty).

## Section 5 The Executive Office of the President and the Cabinet (pp. 370–375)
As the President performs his vital responsibilities, he relies on the assistance and guidance of key advisors and agencies.

The Executive Office of the President acts as the President's "right arm." It includes the White House Office. A key member of this office is the Chief of Staff. Other offices of the Executive Office support the President's foreign policy efforts, the administration of the budget, and numerous other endeavors.

The cabinet is not mentioned in the Constitution. Yet it has played an important role in every administration.

The cabinet has two major roles. Each cabinet member serves as head of an executive department, such as Defense or the Treasury. Collectively, the cabinet serves as an advisory body to the President.

# Chapter Review

## Vocabulary and Key Terms

media (p. 355)★
executive order (p. 356)★
treaty (p. 361)★
executive agreement (p. 361)★

recognition (p. 362)★
reprieve (p. 368)★
pardon (p. 368)★
commutation (p. 368)★

amnesty (p. 368)★
federal budget (p. 371)★
cabinet (p. 373)★

**Matching:** *Review the key terms in the list above. If you are not sure of a term's meaning, look up the term and review its definition. Choose a term from the list above that best matches each description.*

1. the collective term for the press, radio, and television; a powerful tool through which the President attracts and holds public attention
2. a directive, rule, or regulation made by a President and/or the President's subordinates that has the force of law
3. the official postponement of the execution of a sentence in a crime
4. the power to reduce the length of a sentence in a crime
5. a formal agreement made between or among sovereign states

**True or False:** *Determine whether each statement is true or false. If it is true, write "true." If it is false, change the underlined word or words to make the statement true.*

1. A <u>pardon</u> enables the President to release a person from the punishment or legal consequences of a crime.
2. A <u>reprieve</u> is a general pardon issued to a group of law-breakers.
3. An <u>executive agreement</u> has the force of law but does not require the approval of the Senate.
4. An <u>executive order</u> is a pact between the President and the head of a foreign state or the President's subordinates.

**Word Relationships:** *Replace the underlined definition with the correct term from the list above.*

1. Different Presidents have relied on <u>the presidential advisory body composed of heads of the executive departments</u> for different purposes.
2. <u>A formal agreement made between or among sovereign states</u> requires the approval of the Senate.
3. <u>A financial document, a detailed estimate of federal income and outgo in the coming fiscal year</u>, is a carefully drawn plan for the conduct of government.
4. By exercising <u>the exclusive power of the President to establish formal diplomatic relations with foreign states</u>, the President accepts a country as an equal in the family of nations.

## Main Ideas

### Section 1 (pp. 353–355)
1. What were the differing views of the presidency held by the Framers?
2. Which view has prevailed and for what reasons?
3. How have Presidents themselves viewed their powers?

### Section 2 (pp. 356–360)
4. For what reason does the presidential power to execute the law grant the President such power?
5. How do the President's executive responsibilities relate to administrative responsibilities?

6. What is the extent of the President's control over the personnel of the President's administration?
7. For what reason does the President have the ordinance power?

### Section 3 (pp. 361–365)
8. Through what means can the President make agreements on behalf of the country with foreign states?
9. What is the power of recognition and how can the President use it as a diplomatic tool?
10. Describe the President's role in the military affairs of the country.

### Section 4 (pp. 366–368)
11. How do the President's legislative and judicial powers serve the principle of separation of powers?
12. What are the President's primary legislative powers?
13. What are the President's primary judicial powers?

### Section 5 (pp. 370–375)
14. What agencies work directly with the President to give assistance and advice?
15. What responsibilities does the cabinet have that the Executive Office of the President does not?
16. How have Presidents differed in their reliance on the cabinet?

## Critical Thinking
1. **Making Comparisons** (p. 19) Compare the cabinet of today with the first cabinet under President Washington. (a) How are the two alike? (b) How are they different? (c) Why do you think cabinet membership has grown since Washington's first term of office?
2. **Identifying Central Issues** (p. 19) Article II of the Constitution, which covers the powers of the executive, has been called the most loosely drawn chapter in the Constitution. Why might the Framers have created Article II in this way?

3. **Drawing Conclusions** (p. 19) The text cites the unity of the presidency as a key reason for the growth of presidential power. Assuming this is true, what does that fact suggest about the American people's view of political leadership?
4. **Demonstrating Reasoned Judgment** (p. 19) The text states that the President's powers in the field of military affairs is nearly without limit. What are the benefits and drawbacks of this fact?

## Getting Involved

1. **Writing Your Opinion** You have just been elected President of the United States. Write a diary entry in which you explain how you intend to lead the nation in the four years ahead. Open with a statement in which you summarize your beliefs about the proper role of the President in the American political system. Then, explain how you intend to fulfill this role. Write one paragraph each on such topics as your cabinet and Executive Office, your constitutional powers, and your overall view of presidential power. Conclude by expressing what you predict will be your greatest challenge in office. Revise to correct for errors, and draft a final copy.
2. **Class Debate** Hold a class debate on the following topic: *Resolved*, That the Constitution be amended to forbid the President to use the armed forces in combat without a declaration of war by Congress. Choose teams to debate each side of the topic. The rest of the class should evaluate each team's presentation.
3. **Gathering Information** (a) What sources might you consult to learn about how different Presidents have viewed their use of military power? (b) What sources might you use to learn about the historical view of Congress on this issue? Use the Government Resources Handbook on page 690 to identify possible sources.

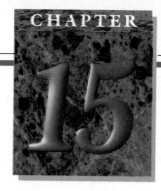

# Government at Work: The Bureaucracy

## Chapter Preview

Bureaucracy. The word is used most often as an insult—a scornful, derogatory, belittling term. It is used that way by those who see government and those who work for it as too powerful, unresponsive, overpaid and underworked, or all of those things. But, as you will see, the word does have another, important and neutral, meaning.

Today, the Federal Government has nearly three million civilian employees, and they will be paid nearly $160 billion this year. What do all of those people do? An almost endless variety of tasks—from collecting taxes to delivering the mail, from investigating airplane crashes to enforcing minimum wage laws, from monitoring air pollution to seeking the causes of cancer, diabetes, and epilepsy, and many, many other things. This chapter is about the federal bureaucracy—about the machinery and the personnel through which the executive branch of the Federal Government operates.

### Before you read this chapter:

- **Describe** two jobs in your community that are part of the federal bureaucracy.
- **Predict** what is meant by the "merit system."

### As you read, focus on the main objective for each section. Understand:

1. The need for and growth of the federal bureaucracy.
2. The organization and functions of the executive departments and the independent agencies.
3. The development of the federal civil service.

**"The greatest monstrosity in America"** So-called by President Truman, this Washington, D.C. building stands as an apt symbol for the massive, complicated—and growing—federal bureaucracy. The building once housed the Defense and State departments, but today is too small even to contain all the President's aides.

# 1 The Federal Bureaucracy

## Find Out:

- In what sense is the Federal Government a bureaucracy?
- What are the various titles given to administrative units?
- How do staff and line agencies differ?

## Key Terms:

bureaucracy, bureaucrat, administration

Think about this for a moment. It is impossible for you to live through a single day without somehow encountering the federal bureaucracy. Federal employees deliver the mail, collect federal taxes, regulate business practices, manage the national forests, conduct American foreign policy, administer social security programs—the list goes on and on.

In this section you will consider the nature and the overall shape of the federal bureaucracy.

## What Is a Bureaucracy?

People often use the word *bureaucracy* to identify any large and complex administrative body.[1] In dictionary terms, a **bureaucracy** is an organization built on three principles.

1. Hierarchical authority. The organization is like a pyramid in structure. Officials and units at the top of the organization have control over those in the middle, who in turn direct those at the bottom.

2. Job specialization. Each person who works for the organization—each **bureaucrat**—has defined duties and responsibilities. There is a specific division of labor.

---

[1]The term is a combination of the French word *bureau*, which originally referred to a desk of a government official and later to the place where an official worked, and the suffix *-cracy*, signifying a type of governmental structure.

3. Formal rules. The organization conducts its operations according to established regulations and procedures.

In short, a bureaucracy is a way of organizing people to do work.[2] Bureaucracies are found in both the public and private sectors. Thus, the United States Army, your school, McDonald's, the Department of Agriculture, and the Roman Catholic Church are all bureaucracies.

## Major Elements of the Federal Bureaucracy

The federal bureaucracy is all of the agencies, people, and procedures through which the Federal Government operates. It is the means by which the government makes and administers public policy—the sum of its decisions and actions. As the chart on the next page shows, nearly all of that bureaucracy is in the executive branch.

The Constitution says little about the organization of the executive branch. It does make the President its chief administrator by giving him the power to "take care that the laws be faithfully executed."[3] But the Constitution makes only the barest mention of the administrative machinery through which the President is to exercise that power.

Article II does suggest executive departments by giving to the President the power to "require the opinion, in writing, of the principal officers in each of the executive departments."[4] And it anticipates two departments in particular, one for military and one for foreign affairs, by making the President the "commander in chief of the army and navy," and by giving him the power to make treaties and to appoint "ambassadors, other public ministers, and consuls."[5]

Beyond those references, the Constitution is silent on the organization of the executive branch. However, the Framers certainly intended for administrative agencies to be created. They understood that no matter how wise the President and the Congress, their decisions still had to be acted upon to be effective. Without an **administration**—the government's many administrators and agencies—even the best policies would amount to so many words.

As the chart on page 383 shows, the executive branch is now made up of three major groups of administrative agencies: (1) the Executive Office of the President, (2) the 14 cabinet departments, and (3) a large number of independent agencies.[6] You read about the Executive Office and its several agencies in Chapter 14. You will look at the other groups shortly.

## The Name Game

The titles given to the many units that make up the executive branch vary a great deal. The name *department* is reserved for agencies of cabinet rank. Beyond that, however, there is little standardized use of titles.

The term *agency* is often used to refer to any governmental body. It is sometimes used to identify a major unit headed by a single administrator of near-cabinet status, such as the Environmental Protection Agency. But the same is true of the title *administration*; for example, the National Aeronautics and Space Administration.

The name *commission* is usually given to agencies charged with the regulation of business activities, such as the Interstate Commerce Commission and the Securities and Exchange Commission. These units are composed of varying numbers of top-ranking officers called commissioners. The same title, however, is given to

---

[2]Some use the words *bureaucracy* and *bureaucrat* in another, less than complimentary sense. Big government has never been popular in this country and, to many Americans, *bureaucracy* is simply another way of saying big government.

[3]Article II, Section 3.

[4]Article II, Section 2, Clause 1. There is also a reference to "heads of departments" in Clause 2, and to "any department or officer" of the government in Article I, Section 8, Clause 18.

---

[5]Article II, Section 2, Clauses 1 and 2.

[6]The chart is adapted from the current edition of the *United States Government Manual*, published each year by the Office of the Federal Register in the National Archives and Records Administration. The *Manual* includes a brief description of every agency in each of the three branches of the Federal Government. Nearly 800 of its now more than 900 pages are devoted to the executive branch.

# The Government of the United States

## THE CONSTITUTION

### LEGISLATIVE

**THE CONGRESS**
Senate          House

Architect of the Capitol
General Accounting Office
Government Printing Office
Library of Congress
United States Botanic Garden
Office of Technology Assessment
Congressional Budget Office
Copyright Royalty Tribunal
United States Tax Court

### EXECUTIVE

**THE PRESIDENT**
**Executive Office of the President**

White House Office
Office of Management and Budget
Council of Economic Advisers
National Security Council
Office of National Drug Control Policy
Office of the United States Trade Representative
Council on Environmental Quality
Office of Science and Technology Policy
Office of Administration
THE VICE PRESIDENT

### JUDICIAL

**THE SUPREME COURT of the United States**

Courts of Appeals
District Courts
Federal Claims Court
Court of Appeals for the Federal Circuit
Court of International Trade
Territorial Courts
Court of Military Appeals
Court of Veterans Appeals
Administrative Office of the United States Courts
Federal Judicial Center

| Department of State | Department of the Treasury | Department of Defense | Department of Justice | Department of the Interior | Department of Agriculture | Department of Commerce |
|---|---|---|---|---|---|---|
| Department of Labor | Department of Health and Human Services | Department of Housing and Urban Development | Department of Transportation | Department of Energy | Department of Education | Department of Veterans Affairs |

### Major Independent Agencies
(Note: Altogether, there are more than 200 independent agencies in the executive branch.)

Central Intelligence Agency
Commission on Civil Rights
Commodity Futures Trading Commission
Consumer Product Safety Commission
Corporation for National and Community Service
Defense Nuclear Facilities Safety Board
Environmental Protection Agency
Equal Employment Opportunity Commission
Export-Import Bank of the U.S.
Farm Credit Administration
Federal Communications Commission
Federal Deposit Insurance Corporation
Federal Election Commission
Federal Emergency Management Agency
Federal Housing Finance Board
Federal Maritime Commission
Federal Mediation and Conciliation Service

Federal Reserve System
Federal Trade Commission
General Services Administration
Interstate Commerce Commission
National Aeronautics and Space Administration
National Labor Relations Board
National Transportation Safety Board
Nuclear Regulatory Commission
Office of Government Ethics
Office of Personnel Management
Securities and Exchange Commission
Selective Service System
Small Business Administration
Social Security Administration
Tennessee Valley Authority
U.S. Arms Control and Disarmament Agency
U.S. Postal Service

▲ Interpreting Charts   The daily workings of government depend on these departments and agencies, which are staffed by nonelected employees. According to this chart, which branch makes up the largest share of the federal bureaucracy?

## What Top Federal Career Employees Like Least and Most About Their Work

### Like Least

Inability to take personnel actions that should be a manager's prerogative (e.g., hiring and discipline)
Inadequate resources (e.g., personnel, budget)
Personal financial sacrifice
"Red tape"
Frustrations in dealing with interest groups and Congress

### Like Most

Challenging assignments
Opportunity to have an impact on policy programs
Opportunity for public service
Opportunity to use and expand one's knowledge and skills
Caliber of colleagues

"Think of it. Presidents come and go, but WE go on forever!"

Reprinted by permission of NEA, Inc.—Berry's World.

**Interpreting Tables and Political Cartoons** From the table you should be able to glean some idea of what the work of civil service employees is like. What criticism does the cartoon level against bureaucrats?

some investigative, advisory, and reporting bodies, including the Civil Rights Commission and the Federal Election Commission.

Either *corporation* or *authority* is the title most often given to agencies headed by a board and a manager, and that conduct business-like activities—for example, the Federal Deposit Insurance Corporation and the Tennessee Valley Authority.

Within each major agency, the same confusing lack of uniformity in the use of names is common. *Bureau* is the name often given to the major elements in a department, but *service, administration, office, branch,* and *division* are often used for the same purpose. This lack of uniformity in agency names can be clearly seen in the chart on page 383.

---

[7]The use of acronyms can sometimes cause problems. When the old Bureau of the Budget was reorganized in 1970, it was also renamed. It is now the Office of Management and Budget (OMB). However, it was for a time slated to be known as the Bureau of Management and Budget (BOMB).

Many federal agencies are often referred to by their initials. The EPA, IRS, FBI, CIA, FCC, and TVA are but a few of the dozens of familiar examples.[7] A few of the federal agencies are also known by nicknames. For example, the Federal National Mortgage Association is often called "Fannie Mae" and the National Railroad Passenger Corporation is better known as Amtrak.

## Staff and Line

The several units that make up any administrative organization can be classified as either staff or line agencies. Staff agencies serve in a support capacity. They aid the chief executive and other administrators by furnishing advice and other assistance in the management of the organization. Line agencies, on the other hand, actually perform the tasks for which the organization exists.

Two illustrations of this distinction are the several agencies that make up the Executive Office of the President and, in contrast, the Environmental Protection Agency. The agencies that make up the Executive Office—the White House Office, the National Security Council, and so on—each exist as staff support to the President. Their primary mission is to assist the President in the exercise of the executive power and in the overall management of the executive branch. They are not operating agencies. That is, they do not actually operate—administer—public programs.

The Environmental Protection Agency (EPA), on the other hand, has a different mission. It is responsible for the day-to-day enforcement of the several federal antipollution laws. The EPA operates "on the line," where "the action" is.

This difference between staff agencies and line agencies can help you find your way through the complexities of the federal bureaucracy. But remember, the distinction between the two can be oversimplified. For example, most line agencies do have staff units to aid them in their line operations. Thus, the EPA's Office of Civil Rights is a staff unit established to insure that the agency's personnel practices do not violate the Federal Government's antidiscrimination policies.

## Section 1 Review

**1. Define:** bureaucracy, bureaucrat, administration

**2.** In which branch of the government is most of the federal bureaucracy located?

**3.** (a) What does the Constitution say about the organization of the executive branch? (b) How did those words contribute to the creation of the federal bureaucracy?

**4.** (a) What terms are most often used in the titles of federal agencies? (b) How does the use of those terms create confusion?

**5.** (a) What are staff agencies and functions? (b) Line agencies and functions?

### Critical Thinking

**6. Demonstrating Reasoned Judgment** (p. 19) Explain how the characteristics of a bureaucracy both help and hurt the effective and efficient administration of government.

★

## 2 The Executive Departments and the Independent Agencies

**Find Out:**
- What are the responsibilities of each of the 14 executive departments?
- For what reasons are the departments composed of so many subagencies?
- What are the three types of independent agencies and what do they do?

**Key Terms:**

independent agencies, quasi-legislative, quasi-judicial

Mario Cuomo, governor of New York from 1983 to 1995, once said, "Democracy is not meant to be efficient, it is meant to be fair." What do you think? Does the demand for fairness offer any possible explanation for why public bureaucracies are sometimes less efficient than private ones?

In this section, you will read about the major components of the federal bureaucracy.

## The Cabinet

Most federal bureaucrats work in one of the 14 cabinet departments. The cabinet departments are also called the executive departments. They are the traditional units of the federal administration, and each is built around a broad field of activity.

The 1st Congress set up three of these departments in 1789: State, Treasury, and War. As the size and the workload of the Federal Government grew, Congress added new departments. Some of the newer departments took over various duties originally assigned to older departments, and they gradually assumed new functions, as well. The Congress also created, and later abolished, a few departments.

The head of each department is known as the secretary, except for the attorney general, who directs the work of the Justice Department. The President names each department head, subject to confirmation by the Senate.

**Census-Taking**    The Census Bureau is within the Commerce Department. Here, census takers gather population data in the mid-1800s (top), 1940, and 1990. The cartoon comments on the fact that the Census Bureau now says that it under-counted the nation's population by some 5.3 million people in 1990. What does the cartoon say about the Bureau's methods?

Together, the department secretaries serve as the members of the President's cabinet, as you saw in the last chapter. Their duties as the chief officers of their own departments generally take most of their time, however. Each of them is the primary link between presidential policy and his or her own department. Of equal importance are each department head's efforts to promote and protect that department with the President, congressional committees, the rest of the bureaucracy, and the public.

An under secretary or deputy secretary and several assistant secretaries aid the secretary in his or her multidimensional role. These officials are also named by the President and confirmed by the Senate. Staff support for the secretary comes from assistants and aides with a wide range of titles in such areas as personnel, planning, legal advice, budgeting, and public relations.

Each department is made up of a number of subunits, both staff and line. As noted earlier, these agencies are known as bureaus, offices, services, divisions, and so on. Each of these agencies is usually further divided into smaller working units. Thus, the Criminal Division in the Department of Justice is composed of many sections—

# Global Awareness

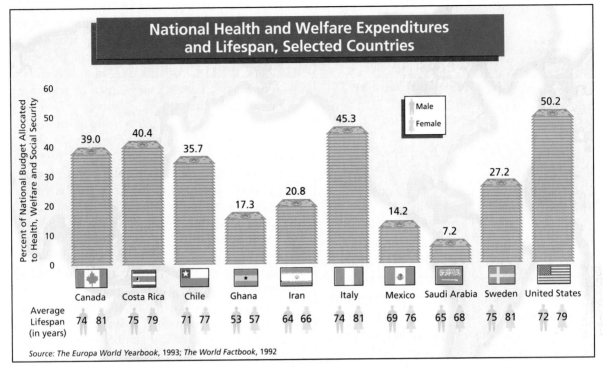

## National Health and Welfare Expenditures and Lifespan, Selected Countries

Percent of National Budget Allocated to Health, Welfare and Social Security

| | Canada | Costa Rica | Chile | Ghana | Iran | Italy | Mexico | Saudi Arabia | Sweden | United States |
|---|---|---|---|---|---|---|---|---|---|---|
| Percent | 39.0 | 40.4 | 35.7 | 17.3 | 20.8 | 45.3 | 14.2 | 7.2 | 27.2 | 50.2 |
| Average Lifespan (in years) Male | 74 | 75 | 71 | 53 | 64 | 74 | 69 | 65 | 75 | 72 |
| Average Lifespan (in years) Female | 81 | 79 | 77 | 57 | 66 | 81 | 76 | 68 | 81 | 79 |

Male
Female

*Source: The Europa World Yearbook, 1993; The World Factbook, 1992*

▲ **Interpreting Graphs** The Department of Health and Human Services is responsible for dispensing health and social security services to the public. How does this graph show the essential relationship between national health budgets and public welfare?

including, for example, the Narcotic and Dangerous Drugs Section and the Fraud Section. About 80 percent of the bureau and office chiefs are career people, not political appointees.

The internal structure of most of the departments is arranged on a geographic basis. That is, each department conducts many of its activities through regional offices that direct the work of agency employees in the field. For example, the Treasury Department's Internal Revenue Service (IRS) is headquartered in Washington. Yet, the IRS carries out most of its tax collection and enforcement work through 7 regional offices, 65 district offices, and some 200 local offices. Altogether, nearly 90 percent of all federal civilian employees work outside the nation's capital.

The 14 executive departments that exist today are listed here followed by the year each was created: the State Department (1789); Department of the Treasury (1789); Depart-

ment of Defense (1949); Department of Justice (1870); Department of the Interior (1849); Department of Agriculture (1889); Department of Commerce (1903); Department of Labor (1913); Department of Health and Human Services (1953); Department of Housing and Urban Development (1965); Department of Transportation (1966); Department of Energy (1977); Department of Education (1979); and Department of Veterans Affairs (1989).

You will find summaries of the work and functions of the executive departments on pages 696–709. The Departments of State and Defense are discussed in further detail in Chapter 17.

## What Are Independent Agencies?

Until the 1880s, nearly all that the Federal Government did was done through the cabinet departments. Since then, however, Congress has

## *VOICES on Government*

**Susan E. Alvarado,**
Board of Governors,
U.S. Postal Service

### On the U.S. Postal Service, an Independent Agency

❝ No other independent agency touches the fabric of American life like the mail delivery system. People across the nation communicate the events of daily life via the mail—from the announcement of births, deaths, and marriages to graduations, birthdays, and holiday greetings. The post office serves as the conduit to help Americans stay connected to one another despite geographic distances.

Today's Postal Service will move into the 21st century as a vital link along the information superhighway by changing to meet the demands of the future. ❞

created a large number of additional agencies— the **independent agencies** located outside of the departments. Today, they number more than 200. Most of the more important ones are listed in the chart on page 383.

Several independent agencies administer programs that are very similar to those of the cabinet departments. The work of the National Aeronautics and Space Administration (NASA), for example, is similar to that of a number of agencies in the Defense Department; and NASA's responsibilities are not very far removed from those of the Department of Transportation.

Neither the size of an independent agency's budget nor the number of its employees provides a good way to distinguish between many of these agencies and the executive departments. Take the newest and largest of them, the Social Security Administration. It became an

independent agency in 1994 and its budget for fiscal year 1995 exceeds $330 billion—more than that of any cabinet department. The Administration now employs more than 64,000 people, and so has more workers and a larger payroll than each of these six cabinet departments: the Departments of Commerce, Education, Energy, Housing and Urban Development, Labor, and State.

The reasons these agencies exist outside of the cabinet departments are nearly as numerous as the agencies themselves. A few major reasons stand out, however. Some agencies have been set up outside of the regular departmental structure because they do not fit well within any department. The General Services Administration (GSA) is a leading example. The GSA is the Federal Government's major housekeeping agency. Its main chores include the construction and operation of public buildings, purchase and distribution of supplies and equipment, management of real property, and a host of similar services to most other federal agencies. The Office of Personnel Management (OPM) is another example. It is the hiring agency for nearly all other federal agencies.

Congress has given some of these agencies an independent status to protect them from the influence of both partisan and pressure politics. The OPM is an example of just such an agency, as are the Social Security Administration and the Federal Election Commission. The point can be turned on its head, also; some agencies are located outside the cabinet departments because that is exactly where certain pressure groups want them. Other federal agencies were born as independents largely by accident. In short, no thought was given to the problems of administrative confusion when they were created. Finally, some agencies are independent because of the peculiar and sensitive nature of their functions. This is especially true of the independent regulatory commissions.

The label *independent agency* is a catchall. Most of these agencies are independent only in the sense that they are not located within any of the 14 cabinet departments. They are not independent of the President and the executive branch. Some are independent in a much more concrete way, however. For most purposes, they do lie outside the executive branch and are largely free of presidential control.

Perhaps the best way to understand all of these independent agencies is to divide them into three main groups: (1) the independent executive agencies, (2) the independent regulatory commissions, and (3) the government corporations.

## The Independent Executive Agencies

This group includes most of the independent agencies. Some are large, with thousands of employees, multimillion-dollar or even billion-dollar budgets, and extremely important public tasks to perform. The GSA, NASA, and the EPA are three examples of larger, independent executive agencies. They are organized much like the cabinet departments—that is, they are headed by a single administrator with subunits operating on a regional basis, and so on. The most important difference between the independent executive agencies and the 14 executive departments is simply that they do not have cabinet status.

Some of the agencies in this group are not administrative and policy giants. They do important work, however, and sometimes attract public notice. The Civil Rights Commission, the Peace Corps, the Federal Election Commission, and the new Corporation for National and Community Service all fall into this category.

Most independent executive agencies operate far from the limelight. They have few employees, small budgets, and almost never attract any attention. The American Battle Monuments Commission, the Citizens' Stamp Advisory Committee, and the Migratory Bird Conservation Commission are typical of the dozens of these seldom seen or heard public bodies.

## The Independent Regulatory Commissions

The independent regulatory commissions stand out among the independent agencies because they are largely beyond the reach of presidential direction and control. There are 11 of these agencies today, each created to regulate, or police, important aspects of the nation's econo-

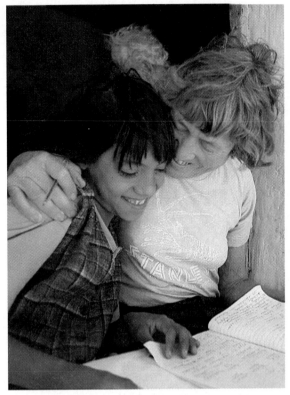

**Peace Corps Volunteer**  This Honduran child is learning English from a member of the Peace Corps, an independent agency that was originally part of the State Department.

my. The vital statistics of the 11 independent regulatory commissions appear in the table on page 390.

The independent regulatory commissions' large measure of independence from the White House comes mainly from the way in which Congress has structured them. Each is headed by a board or commission made up of from five to seven members appointed by the President with Senate consent. However, those officials have terms of such length that it is unlikely a President will gain control over any of these agencies through the appointment process, at least not in a single presidential term.

Several other features of these boards and commissions put them beyond the reach of presidential control. No more than a bare majority of the members of each board or commission may belong to the same political party. Thus, several of those officers must belong to the party out of power. Moreover, the appointed terms of

## The Independent Regulatory Commissions

| Agency, Date Established | Term of Members | Major Functions |
|---|---|---|
| Interstate Commerce Commission (ICC), 1887 | 5 years | Licenses, regulates rates and oversees other aspects of commercial transportation by railroad, highway, and domestic waterway. |
| Board of Governors, Federal Reserve System (the Fed), 1913 | 14 years | Supervises banking system, practices; regulates money supply, use of credit in economy. |
| Federal Trade Commission (FTC), 1914 | 7 years | Enforces antitrust, other laws prohibiting unfair competition, price-fixing, false advertising, other unfair business practices. |
| Securities and Exchange Commission (SEC), 1934 | 5 years | Regulates securities, other financial markets, investment companies, brokers; enforces laws prohibiting fraud, other dishonest investment practices. |
| Federal Communications Commission (FCC), 1934 | 5 years | Regulates radio and television broadcasting, telephone, telegraph, and cable television operations, two-way radio and radio operators, and satellite communications. |
| National Labor Relations Board (NLRB), 1935 | 5 years | Administers federal labor-management relations laws; holds collective bargaining elections; prevents, remedies unfair labor practices. |
| Federal Maritime Commission (FMC), 1936 | 5 years | Regulates waterborne foreign, domestic off-shore commerce of the United States; supervises rates, services. |
| Consumer Product Safety Commission (CPSC), 1972 | 7 years | Sets, enforces safety standards for consumer products; directs recall of unsafe products; conducts safety research, information programs. |
| Nuclear Regulatory Commission (NRC), 1974 | 5 years | Licenses, regulates all civilian nuclear facilities, all civilian uses of nuclear materials.[a] |
| Commodity Futures Trading Commission (CFTC), 1974 | 5 years | Regulates commodity exchanges, brokers, futures trading in agricultural, metal, other commodities. |
| Federal Energy Regulatory Commission (FERC), 1977 | 4 years | Regulates, fixes rates for transportation, sale of natural gas, transportation of oil by pipelines, interstate transmission, sale of electricity.[b] |

[a]These functions performed by the Atomic Energy Commission from 1946 to 1974 (when AEC was abolished); other AEC functions now performed by agencies in the Energy Department.

[b]These functions performed by the Federal Power Commission (created in 1930) until FPC was abolished in 1977. FERC is within the Energy Department, but only for administrative purposes; otherwise is independent (except Energy Secretary may set reasonable deadlines for FERC action in any matter before it). Under terms of National Energy Act of 1978, FERC's authority to regulate natural gas prices ended in 1985.

 **Interpreting Tables**   These commissions are independent of all three branches of government, and thus are exceptions to the separation of powers rule. How do the functions listed on the table show the unique role of the commissions as quasi-judicial and quasi-legislative agencies?

the members are staggered so that the term of only one member on each board or commission expires in any one year. Finally, the President can remove most of these officers only for those causes Congress has specified.[8]

As with the other independent agencies, the regulatory commissions are executive bodies. That is, Congress has given them the power to administer the programs for which they were created. However, unlike those other independent agencies, the regulatory commissions are

---

[8]Recall this point from Chapter 14. The members of five of these bodies (the SEC, FCC, CPSC, NRC, and CFTC) are exceptions. Congress has provided that any of them may be removed at the President's discretion.

**quasi-legislative** and **quasi-judicial** bodies.[9] That is, Congress has given them certain legislative-like and judicial-like powers.

These agencies exercise their quasi-legislative powers when they make rules and regulations. Those rules and regulations have the force of law. They explain the details of the laws Congress has directed these regulatory bodies to enforce. For example, Congress has said the railroads must offer "reasonable service" to the public and charge only "just and reasonable" rates for that service. The Interstate Commerce Commission (ICC) implements those requirements—directs how the railroads are to meet them—by issuing detailed rules and regulations.

The regulatory commissions exercise their quasi-judicial powers when they decide disputes in those fields in which Congress has given them their policing authority. For example, if a railroad asks the ICC for permission to raise its rates for carrying goods between two points, that request is likely to be opposed by the companies that ship those goods. The ICC holds a hearing to determine the merits of each side of the argument. It then makes a decision, much as a court would do. The decisions made by the ICC, and by the other independent regulatory bodies, can be appealed to the United States courts of appeals, as you will see in Chapter 18.

In a sense, Congress has created these agencies to act in its place. Congress could hold hearings and set freight rates, license radio and TV stations and nuclear reactors, check on business practices, and do the many other things it has directed the regulatory commissions to do. But these activities are complex and time-consuming, and they demand constant and expert attention. If Congress did all of this work it would then have no time for its important legislative work.

Note that these regulatory bodies possess all three of the basic governmental powers: executive, legislative, and judicial. They are exceptions to the principle of separation of powers. They should not be grouped with the other independent agencies, as they are in the chart on page 383. Instead, they should somehow be located somewhere between the executive and legislative branches, and between the executive and judicial branches, too.

Several authorities, and most recent Presidents, have urged that at least the administrative functions of the independent regulatory commissions be given to cabinet department agencies. Other serious questions have arisen about these agencies and have prompted proposals to abolish or redesign them. The most troubling questions are these: Have some of the independent regulatory commissions been captured by the special interests they are expected to regulate? Are all of the many and detailed rules made by these agencies really needed? Do some of them have the effect of stifling legitimate competition in the free enterprise system? Do some of them add unreasonably to the costs of doing business and therefore to the prices that consumers must pay?[10]

The regulatory authority of some of these agencies has been decreased in recent years. Ronald Reagan campaigned for the presidency in 1980 promising to cut most federal domestic programs—and, in particular, to reduce the government's regulation of the business community. Indeed, the 1980s came to be known as "the era of deregulation."[11] The Reagan administration pushed hard for a general deregulation of the nation's economic life, and the Bush administration took the same position.

---

[9]The prefix *quasi* is from the Latin, meaning "in a certain sense, resembling, seemingly."

[10]Because Congress sets the basic policies of these regulatory bodies, the major responsibility for answering these questions lies with Congress. It has responded to some of them in recent years. In particular, and especially at the urging of the Reagan administration in the 1980s, it has deregulated much of the nation's transportation industry, giving airlines, truckers, bus companies, railroads, and so on much greater freedom to operate.

[11]Deregulation had in fact begun before Mr. Reagan's first election. In several statutes, Congress had given the nation's transportation industry much greater freedom to operate in the late 1970s; for example, the Airline Deregulation Act of 1978. That law all but eliminated the power of the Civil Aeronautics Board (CAB) to regulate commercial airlines. Instead, the CAB's mission became the promotion of competition in the air transport industry. The law also provided that the CAB was to be abolished by 1985, and it was.

▲ Interpreting Political Art   *Government Bureau* is the title of this eerie painting by George Tooker, which is displayed in the Metropolitan Museum of Art. How does the artist view bureaucracies?

The S&L scandal demonstrates that deregulation has not been altogether successful. When Congress ended restrictions on how savings and loan (S&L) institutions could invest their depositors' savings, many of them put billions of dollars into high-risk business ventures. Bad investments and fraud brought the failure of more than 1,000 S&Ls in the late 1980s and early 1990s.

## The Government Corporations

Several of the independent agencies are government corporations. Like most of the other independent agencies, they are within the executive branch and subject to the President's direction and control. Unlike the other agencies, however, Congress created these agencies to carry out certain business-like activities.

Congress established the first government corporation when it chartered the First Bank of the United States in 1791. Yet government corporations were little used until World War I and the Depression. In both periods Congress set up dozens of corporations to carry out crash programs. Several still exist—among them, the Federal Deposit Insurance Corporation (FDIC), which insures bank deposits, and the Export-Import Bank of the United States (Eximbank), which makes loans to help the export and sale of American goods abroad.

There are over 60 of these government corporations today. Examples of the operations they perform include mail service (the United States Postal Service); the insurance of bank deposits (the FDIC); the management of the assets and liabilities of failed savings and loan institutions (the FDIC and the Resolution Trust Corporation); and the protection of pension benefits (the Pension Benefit Guaranty Corporation).[12]

---

[12]State and local governments maintain many of their own government corporations, most often called *authorities*, to operate airports, turnpikes, seaports, power plants, liquor stores, housing developments, and to conduct many other corporate activities. Of them all, the Port of New York Authority is probably the best known.

The typical government corporation is set up much like a corporation in the private sector. It is run by a board of directors, with a general manager who directs the corporation's operations in line with the policies established by that board. Most government corporations produce income that is plowed back into the business.

There are several striking differences between government and private corporations, however. Congress decides the purpose for which the public agencies exist and the functions they can perform. Their officers are public officers; in fact, all who work for these corporations are public employees. The President selects most of the top officers of government corporations with Senate confirmation. These public agencies get their financing from public monies appropriated by Congress, not from private investors. The Federal Government owns the stock.

The advantage most often claimed for the use of government corporations is their flexibility. It is said that the government corporation, freed from the controls of regular departmental organization, can carry on its activities with the incentive, efficiency, and ability to experiment that make many private concerns successful. Whether or not that claim is valid is open to question. At the very least, it raises this complex issue: Is a public corporation's need for flexibility in its operations compatible with democratic government's requirement that all public agencies be held responsible and accountable to the people?

The degree of independence and flexibility government corporations have varies considerably. In fact, some corporations are not independent at all. They are attached to an executive department. The Commodity Credit Corporation, for example, is the government's major crop-loan and farm-subsidy agency. It is located within the Department of Agriculture, and the secretary of agriculture chairs its seven-member board. The Commodity Credit Corporation carries out most of its functions through a line agency in the Department of Agriculture—the Agricultural Stabilization and Conservation Service—which is also subject to the direct control of the secretary.

Some corporations do have considerable independence, however. The Tennessee Valley Authority (TVA) is a case in point. It operates under a statute in which Congress has given it considerable discretion over its policies and programs. Although its budget is subject to review by the OMB, the President, and then Congress, the TVA has a large say in the uses of the income its several operations produce. It even has its own civil service system.[13]

# Section 2 Review

**1. Define:** independent agencies, quasi-legislative, quasi-judicial
**2.** What are the main responsibilities of the department secretaries?
**3.** What agencies performed the activities of the independent agencies prior to the 1880s?
**4.** (a) For what reasons has Congress created many independent agencies in the executive branch? (b) In what sense are they independent?
**5.** In what ways are the independent regulatory commissions most strikingly different from other independent agencies?
**6.** What major advantage is claimed for the creation of government corporations?

**Critical Thinking**

**7. Making Comparisons** (p. 19) Compare the view put forth by Mario Cuomo in the quote at the beginning of the section with the views of those who support the use of government corporations.

---

[13]The TVA is one of the major illustrations of government in business. It was established by Congress, after years of controversy, in the Tennessee Valley Authority Act of 1933. The act called for the coordinated development and use of the natural resources of a huge area that today includes large parts of Tennessee, Kentucky, Virginia, North Carolina, Georgia, Alabama, and Mississippi.

The TVA has had an extraordinary impact on the Tennessee River Valley and its approximately four million residents. Its operations include electric power development, flood control and navigation work, reforestation, soil conservation, fertilizer production, agricultural research, recreational facilities, and the promotion of industrial growth in the Tennessee River Valley. The TVA's power program is self-supporting. Much of the support for its other activities comes from Congress. Still, it generates considerable revenues from sales of electricity and fertilizer and from its power to issue bonds.

## Realizing a Dream

I have a dream that one day this nation will rise up and live out the true meaning of its creed: We hold these truths to be self-evident, that all men are created equal.

Those now familiar, soul-stirring words were uttered by the Reverend Martin Luther King, Jr., at the Lincoln Memorial in Washington, D.C., on August 28, 1963. Dr. King stood on the steps of the Memorial and spoke to more than 250,000 people. By the tens of thousands, they had come from all over the country to join him in a rally for equal rights for all Americans.

In March of 1989, 12 students from Saguaro High School in Scottsdale, Arizona, visited the Lincoln Memorial with their teacher, John Calvin. When Mr. Calvin reminded them that they were at the site of Dr. King's famous speech, they were amazed that they could find no marker or any other visible commemoration of the historic event.

Back home, the students began a campaign to install a plaque on the steps of the Memorial to mark the spot from which Dr. King had spoken. Soon, dozens of other Saguaro High students joined in the project, and, almost at once, they won the backing of Arizona's potent Congressman Morris Udall and the State's senior United States senator, Dennis DeConcini.

But the students soon encountered a major problem: Federal law prohibits the placing of a memorial of any kind on the site of an existing memorial. Undaunted, the students adapted their project. Now they proposed that the National Park Service establish a museum inside the Memorial, a gallery to portray the history of the Memorial's inception on to the present day.

The students contacted other high schools, in Arizona and throughout the country. They attracted media coverage and gained support from civic groups and local politicians.

Six Saguaro High students went to Washington in the fall of 1990. There they buttonholed members of Congress, met with officials of the Park Service, and presented their project to the National Parks and Public Lands Subcommittee of the House Interior Committee. A month later, the Park Service approved their project. The museum, the Legacy of Lincoln Exhibit, opened at the Memorial in September of 1994.

The exhibit features Dr. King's speech and several other chapters in the history of the Lincoln Memorial—including Marian Anderson's dramatic Easter concert there in 1939 and President Harry Truman's historic announcement of his order to integrate the nation's armed forces in 1948.

A few high school students saw both the need and the chance to make an important statement—and they did so.

## Getting Involved

**1. Identify** a need in your school or community that is similar to the one addressed in this case.

**2. Formulate** a plan for ways that you could convince government officials to listen to your ideas, and identify resources that could be used in your plan.

**3. Predict** any problems or objections you might encounter in putting your plan into action.

# 3 The Civil Service

**Find Out:**
- How did the civil service system begin?
- How did the spoils system work?
- How does the civil service operate today?

**Key Terms:**
spoils system, patronage, register

Some 2.8 million men and women work for the Federal Government today.[14] Only about 300,000 of those federal bureaucrats live and work in the Washington area. Nearly 90 percent of all career federal employees have jobs in regional, field, and local offices scattered throughout the country and around the world.

The President appoints the people who hold the highest ranking jobs in the executive branch. There are only about 2,500 of those positions at the top levels of the Executive Office, the cabinet departments, the independent agencies, and in American embassies and other diplomatic stations.

All of the other jobs in the federal bureaucracy are covered, as you will see in this section, by some aspect of the civil service system.

## Development of the Civil Service

The Constitution says very little about the staffing of the federal bureaucracy. In fact, its only direct reference is in Article II, Section 2, Clause 2. There the Constitution says that the President

❝. . . shall nominate, and, by and with the advice and consent of the Senate, shall appoint ambassadors, other public ministers, and consuls, judges of the Supreme Court, and all other officers of the United States whose

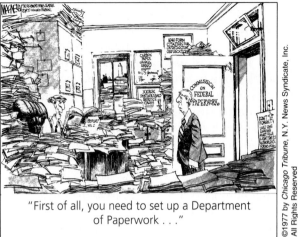

"First of all, you need to set up a Department of Paperwork . . ."

▲ **Interpreting Political Cartoons**  What comment does this cartoon make about the federal bureaucracy?

appointments are not herein otherwise provided for, and which shall be established by law; but the Congress may by law vest the appointment of such inferior officers, as they think proper, in the President alone, in the courts of law, or in the heads of departments. ❞

**The Beginnings**  When he became President in 1789, George Washington knew that the success of the new government would depend in large part on those whom he appointed to office. Those to be chosen, he said, would be "such persons alone . . . as shall be the best qualified." Still, he favored members of his own party, the Federalists. So did his successor, John Adams.

In 1801 Thomas Jefferson found most federal posts filled by men politically and personally opposed to him. He agreed with Washington's standard of fitness for office, but he combined it with another: political acceptability. Jefferson had several hundred Federalists dismissed and replaced by Democratic-Republicans.

**The Spoils System**  By the late 1820s, the number of federal employees had risen above 10,000. When Andrew Jackson became President in 1829, he dismissed over 200 presidential appointees and nearly 2,000 other officeholders. They were replaced by Jacksonian Democrats.

Ever since, Andrew Jackson has been called the father of the **spoils system**—a reference to the the practice of giving offices and other favors of

[14]Another 1.7 million men and women serve in the armed forces; see Chapter 17. Altogether, there are now some 17.5 million civilian public employees in this country. Nearly 4.3 million work for the States, and another 10.5 million work for local governments (including 6.2 million persons employed by school districts). About 2.5 million of those who work for State and local governments are employed on a part-time basis.

government to political supporters and friends.[15] This title is not altogether fair, however. The practice of giving jobs to supporters and friends, also known as **patronage**, was in wide use in politics long before Jackson's presidency.

Jackson saw his appointing policy as democratic. In his first message to Congress, he explained and defended it on four grounds: (1) Since the duties of public office are basically simple, any normally intelligent person can fill such office. (2) There should be a "rotation in office" so that a large number of people can have the privilege of serving in government. (3) Long service in office by any person can lead to both tyranny and inefficiency. (4) The people are entitled to have the party they have placed in power in control of all offices of government, top to bottom.

Whatever Jackson's view, many saw the spoils system as a way to build and hold power. For the next half-century, every change of administration brought a new round of rewards and

---

[15]The phrase comes from a statement made on the floor of the Senate in 1832. Senator William Learned Marcy of New York, defending Jackson's appointment of an ambassador, declared: "To the victor belongs the spoils of the enemy."

punishments. Many posts were filled by political hacks who were ill-equipped for their jobs and interested mainly in enriching themselves or their friends. Inefficiency and even corruption became the order of the day.

**The Movement to Reform**  Able people, in and out of government, pressed for reforms. Congress did create a Civil Service Commission in 1871. But that effort soon died, mainly because Congress failed to give the commission enough money to do a proper job.

A tragedy at last brought about fundamental changes in the hiring and other staffing practices of the Federal Government. In 1881, a deranged and disappointed office-seeker assassinated President James Garfield. The nation was outraged. Congress, pushed hard by Garfield's successor, Chester Arthur, passed the Pendleton Act—the Civil Service Act of 1883.[16]

**The Pendleton Act**  The 1883 law laid the foundation of the present federal civil service. The act's main purpose was to make merit the basis for hiring, promotion, and other personnel actions in the federal work force.

The Pendleton Act set up two categories of employment in the executive branch: the classified

A NICE FAMILY PARTY.

Interpreting Political Cartoons   These cartoons comment on the spoils system, or patronage practices of the kind used by Andrew Jackson. How does the 1872 cartoon (right) illustrate this practice?

and the unclassified service. The act gave the President the key power to decide into which of these categories most federal agencies and their personnel were to be placed. All hiring for the classified service was to be based on merit, determined by "practical" examinations given by an independent agency called the Civil Service Commission.

The Pendleton Act forbade classified employees to take any part in partisan politics. But two of the law's other provisions undercut the law's emphasis on merit, at least to a degree. One provision required that the federal work force was to be made up of men and women from every State, and the number from each State had to bear a close relationship to that State's share of the total population. The other provision was the veterans' preference: All veterans, especially disabled veterans and veterans' widows, received preferred ranking in federal hiring.

At first only about 10 percent of the Federal Government's then 130,000 employees were placed into the classified service. However, the merit system began to grow rapidly when Theodore Roosevelt became President. When Roosevelt left office in 1909, the classified umbrella covered two-thirds of the federal work force, which by then had climbed to 365,000. Today, nearly 90 percent of all the men and women who work for executive branch agencies are in the classified service.[17]

## Civil Service Today

The first goal of civil service reform—doing away with the spoils system—was largely reached in the early part of this century. Gradually, a newer goal emerged: recruiting and keeping the best available people in the federal work force.

On the whole, efforts to reach that goal have succeeded. Most federal employees are hired through competitive examinations; they are paid and promoted on the basis of evaluations by their superiors; and they are largely protected from dismissal for partisan reasons.

Still, the civil service has never been perfect. Critics often claim that not enough attention has been paid to merit in the merit system.

President Jimmy Carter put it this way in 1978:

    **"**The Pendleton Act, . . . the Civil Service Commission and the merit system . . . have served our nation well in fostering the development of a federal work force which is basically honest, competent, and dedicated.

But the system has serious defects. It has become a bureaucratic maze which neglects merit, tolerates poor performance, and mires every personnel action in red tape, delay, and confusion.

Most civil service employees perform with spirit and integrity. Nevertheless, the public suspects that there are too many government workers, that they are underworked, overpaid, and insulated from the consequences of incompetence.

Such sweeping criticisms are unfair; but we must recognize that the only way to restore public confidence in the vast majority who work well is to deal effectively with the few who do not.**"**

**Reorganization** At President Carter's urging, Congress passed the Civil Service Reform Act of 1978. That law made major changes in the civil service system. The Civil Service Commission was replaced by two new independent agencies— the Office of Personnel Management (OPM) and the Merit Systems Protection Board.

The Office of Personnel Management is now the Government's central personnel agency. The OPM is headed by a single director appointed by the President and Senate. The OPM examines and recruits most new federal employees, carries on extensive training programs for career civil

---

[16]The 1880 Republican convention was sharply divided by the civil service question. Its nominee, Garfield, was a strong supporter of reform. To balance the ticket, the Republicans chose Arthur, a leader of the anti-reform faction, as his running mate. President Garfield was shot by Charles J. Guiteau at Washington's Union Station on July 2, 1881; he died 80 days later, on September 19. Garfield had refused Guiteau's request that he be appointed American ambassador to Austria. Garfield's assassination brought a complete change in Arthur's stand; as President he became the leading champion of reform.

---

[17]That is, 90 percent not counting the United States Postal Service and a few other federal agencies. The Postal Service, with almost 710,000 employees, is the largest agency not covered by the civil service system. It is the only federal agency in which employment policies are set by collective bargaining and labor union contracts. The other major agencies not counted in fixing that 90 percent figure are the FBI, CIA, and TVA; each of those agencies has its own merit system.

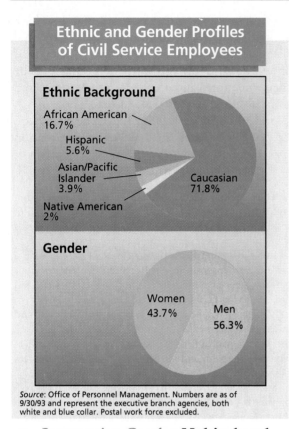

**Ethnic and Gender Profiles of Civil Service Employees**

**Ethnic Background**

African American 16.7%
Hispanic 5.6%
Asian/Pacific Islander 3.9%
Native American 2%
Caucasian 71.8%

**Gender**

Women 43.7%
Men 56.3%

*Source*: Office of Personnel Management. Numbers are as of 9/30/93 and represent the executive branch agencies, both white and blue collar. Postal work force excluded.

▲ Interpreting Graphs: **Multicultural Awareness**  The Civil Service must be nondiscriminatory in its hiring practices. What percentage of its workers are white?

servants, sets position classifications, and manages the salary and other job benefits for some 2.2 million of the people who work for Uncle Sam.

The Merit Systems Protection Board handles the rest of the work once done by the Civil Service Commission. A bipartisan three-member panel picked by the President and Senate, it is the agency that polices and protects the merit principle in the federal bureaucracy.[18]

[18]Another independent agency, the Federal Labor Relations Authority, now handles labor-management relationships in federal employment. It, too, is a bipartisan three-member body appointed by the President and Senate.

[19]The place each applicant for a federal job has on a register is fixed by three factors: (1) time of application, (2) OPM test scores, and (3) veterans' preference points, if any. Nearly half of all federal jobs are now held by veterans, wives of disabled veterans, and unremarried widows of veterans. Some jobs, such as guards and messengers, are reserved especially for veterans.

The Office of Personnel Management can best be described as the central clearinghouse in the federal recruiting, examining, and hiring process. It advertises for employees, gives examinations, and keeps **registers**—lists of those persons who pass its tests.

When there is a job opening in some agency, OPM usually sends it the names of the top three persons on its register for that type of position.[19] If the agency turns down all three, it asks OPM for another set. Many jobs can also be filled by promotion from within an agency or by transfer from another agency. The OPM supervises those processes, too.

## Federal Employees and Party Activists

Federal employees may not strike. Strikes and similar work stoppages are outlawed by the Labor-Management Relations (Taft-Hartley) Act of 1947. Within that framework, federal employees can join any of several labor unions and other groups that promote the interests of government employees.

Federal employees' political activities are also subject to limit. The major statute here is the Hatch Act of 1939. In essence, that law says that classified employees cannot be party activists. However, they can register and vote as they choose. They can belong to a party, make voluntary campaign contributions, take part in—but not organize or lead—partisan rallies. They can also put bumper stickers on their own cars and wear campaign buttons when off duty. And they can take an active part in nonpartisan politics and even be elected to nonpartisan local offices.

But they cannot do such things as run for a partisan office, become an officer in a political organization or a delegate to a party convention, or raise funds for a political party or any of its candidates.

Many see these limits as both unnecessary and unjustifiable limits on their political and civil rights.[20] Those who support the limits say that they prevent the use of federal workers in presidential and congressional campaigns and the possibility that employees' job security might come to depend on party loyalty.

## How to Get a Government Job

**1. Determine what positions are available.** Contact the Federal Job Information Center or the State Employment Security Office serving the area in which you are seeking federal employment to determine what positions are available. You can locate this telephone number in a telephone directory or by calling the Job Information Center in Washington D.C. at (202) 606-2700. You may also check the newspapers, post office, or library for this information.

**2. Determine whether you are qualified for the available position in which you are interested.** The Federal Job Information Center will tell you the specific qualifications required for the position, as well as its grade level (salary) and location. Only qualified applicants are considered, so evaluate your standing carefully. Most civil service jobs require a high school diploma.

**3. Complete the appropriate application form.** The Federal Job Information Center will provide you with the correct form. Application forms vary from position to position, so be sure your application is for the position in which you are interested.

**4. Take the civil service examination.** Some positions require that you take this written exam. The Federal Job Information Center will advise you if this is true in your case. If you pass the exam, your name is included on a list of qualified applicants.

**5. Wait for notification that you will be interviewed.** When a position opens, the top three applicants on the list will be interviewed. Those applicants will be notified by mail. If you are not hired, your name will remain on the list of qualified applicants in the event of a future opening.

▲ Interpreting Charts   The standard steps to getting a job with the government are listed above. After examining these steps, list three probable requirements for a government position.

**Pay and Benefit Issues**  Equal opportunities for career advancement remains a problem in the federal bureaucracy. Although minority groups and women are well represented in most agencies, they tend to be concentrated in lower-level positions. Women, for example, now hold nearly half of all white-collar federal jobs; but they hold less than 10 percent of the highest paid positions.

Congress sets the pay and other job conditions for everyone who works for the Federal Government.[21] At the lower and middle levels, civil service pay compares fairly well with salaries paid in the private sector. Government can never hope to compete dollar for dollar with private industry at the upper levels, however.

---

[20]The Supreme Court has upheld them, however, as reasonable restrictions on 1st Amendment rights. The leading case is *Civil Service Commission* v. *National Association of Letter Carriers, AFL-CIO*, 1973.

[21]Except postal workers; see page 397, note 17.

## Section 3 Review

1. **Define:** spoils system, patronage, register†
2. What standard did George Washington set for federal employment?
3. How did Andrew Jackson defend his version of the spoils system?
4. Describe the features of the Pendleton Act.
5. What is the primary goal of the civil service today?
6. (a) What role does OPM have in the civil service system? (b) The Merit Systems Protection Board?
7. What kinds of political activity are federal workers prohibited from participating in?

### Critical Thinking

8. **Recognizing Cause and Effect** (p. 19) Summarize how the spoils system led to corruption in the government.

★

# How to File a Consumer Complaint

You have just read about the federal bureaucracy and its role in the lives of the American people. Of course, each State has its own bureaucracy, as well. One area in which you can observe your State bureaucracy at work is in the field of consumer affairs.

State governments have become increasingly involved in ensuring the health, safety, and satisfaction of the State's consumers. If you ever lodge a formal complaint against a supplier of a product or service, there is a good chance that you will encounter your State's bureaucracy. Follow the steps below to learn how to file a consumer complaint.

**1. Identify the specific problem you have.** Before you can lodge a complaint, you have to identify specifically the nature of the problem. Ask yourself the following questions: (a) What exactly did you expect the business to supply? (b) How did the business fail to provide that good or service? (c) What do you expect the business to do to solve the problem?

**2. Before making the complaint, make sure that you cannot get satisfaction from the business.** Filing a formal complaint should not be your first step when you experience problems as a consumer. Often, you can receive satisfaction simply by clearly stating your problem and expectations with the appropriate person at the business. Before filing a complaint, make sure you can answer each of the following questions with a "yes": (a) Have you exhausted all your options with that business? For example, have you spoken with a manager or a customer-relations representative? (b) Have you presented your problem calmly and reasonably? (c) Have you made your request in writing (and saved a copy)?

**3. If you are certain that the business will not respond, contact the appropriate consumer agency.** For the most part, individual consumer problems are handled at the State level. To find out where to seek information about lodging a complaint in your State, look in the front section of your telephone book or under your State's name in the white pages. There you will find information about where to call for information about consumer complaints.

**4. Follow the instructions you receive for filing a complaint.** Once you have reached the appropriate organization for your complaint, follow exactly their instructions for filing the complaint. (a) Ask questions about when to expect a response from the agency. (b) Make copies of any letters or paperwork you complete.

**5. Follow up—but give the agency a chance to do its work.** After you file your complaint, give the agency time to do its work. If the agency has not responded in the expected time, follow up with a short letter requesting the status of your complaint. Include a telephone number in your letter to help speed communication.

---

## CONSUMER PROBLEMS (cont)

**Consumer Protection/Consumer Info**

| | |
|---|---|
| Atty Gen Ofc | Bos **727-2200** |
| Consumer Action Center | Bos **482-5772** |
| Exec Ofc Consumer Affairs | Bos **727-7780** |

**Credit Counseling**

| | |
|---|---|
| Consumer Credit Counseling Svc of Eastern MA | Bos **426-6644** |

# Chapter-in-Brief

Scan all headings, photographs, charts, and other visuals in the chapter before reading the section summaries below.

## Section 1 The Federal Bureaucracy (pp. 381–385)
The Federal Government is a bureaucracy; that is, its organization includes hierarchical authority, job specialization, and formalized rules. The federal bureaucracy is the machinery through which the Federal Government makes and administers its public policy.

The bureaucracy consists of numerous administrative agencies. Most of these agencies are in the executive branch and fall into one of three groups: (1) the Executive Office of the President, (2) the 14 cabinet departments, and (3) a large number of independent agencies.

The lack of a uniform system for naming administrative agencies creates confusion. The title department is used exclusively at the cabinet level, but the use of other designations—bureau, service, and so on—follows no consistent pattern.

All administrative organizations are made up of both staff and line units. Staff agencies serve in a support capacity. Line agencies do the work the organization was created to perform.

## Section 2 The Executive Departments and the Independent Agencies (pp. 385–393)
Cabinet departments are the traditional units of federal administration. Today, there are 14 cabinet departments. The head of each department is known as the secretary, except for the attorney general, who heads the Justice Department.

Cabinet secretaries direct the efforts of their departments in line with the policies of the President. A secretary also promotes the department and its programs with Congress, the public, the bureaucracy, and the President.

Each department has a number of staff and line units. In addition, most departments have regional offices outside of Washington.

Until the 1880s, cabinet departments performed most of the work of the Federal Government. Since then, Congress has created numerous independent agencies to perform many administrative functions.

Most independent agencies are independent only in the sense that they are not part of a cabinet department. Some do enjoy significant independence from the executive branch and the President.

Each independent agency falls into one of three groups: (1) the independent executive agencies, (2) the independent regulatory commissions, and (3) the government corporations.

## Section 3 The Civil Service (pp. 395–399)
Today, the federal bureaucracy includes about 3 million employees. Yet the Constitution says little about how these jobs are to be filled. Throughout much of the 1800s, most government posts were filled according to the spoils system. The result was inefficiency and corruption in government.

In 1883, the Pendleton Act laid the foundation for the civil service, the system by which much of the bureaucracy is staffed today. This system attempts to ensure that personnel decisions are based largely on merit.

Today, the civil service system is administered by the Office of Personnel Management, which acts as the government's central personnel agency, and the Merit Systems Protection Board, which polices the merit principle in the federal bureaucracy.

Federal employees cannot strike. And though they are permitted to support, belong to, and make contributions to political parties, they cannot take an activist role in party politics. Equal opportunities for career advancement remains a challenge to the federal bureaucracy.

# Chapter Review

## Vocabulary and Key Terms

bureaucracy (p. 381)
bureaucrat (p. 381)
administration (p. 382)

independent agencies (p. 388)
quasi-legislative (p. 391)
quasi-judicial (p. 391)

spoils system (p. 395)
patronage (p. 396)
registers (p. 398)

**Matching:** *Review the key terms in the list above. If you are not sure of a term's meaning, look up the term and review its definition. Choose a term from the list above that best matches each description.*

1. a government's many administrators and administrative agencies
2. the practice of giving offices and other favors of government to political supporters and friends
3. the lists of the persons who have passed the tests given by the Office of Personnel Management
4. agencies located outside any of the executive departments
5. the term that describes an organization that is built on the principles of hierarchical authority, job specialization, and formalized rules

**True or False:** *Determine whether each statement is true or false. If it is true, write "true." If it is false, change the underlined word or words to make the statement true.*

1. Each person who works in a bureaucracy is known as a _bureaucrat_.
2. The giving of jobs by officeholders to political supporters and friends is known as _patronage_.
3. A _register_ is the name given to a governmental agency that is not part of a cabinet department.

4. Agencies in the executive branch exercise their _quasi-judicial_ function when they formulate regulations.

**Word Relationships:** *Distinguish between words in each pair.*

1. bureaucracy/administration
2. spoils system/patronage
3. quasi-legislative/quasi-judicial

## Main Ideas

### Section 1 (pp. 381–385)

1. How did the different components of the bureaucracy in the Federal Government's executive branch develop?
2. (a) What is the "name game" in the context of the federal bureaucracy? (b) In what sense is it a game?
3. What is the difference between a staff unit and a line unit?
4. Why do many departments have both staff and line units?

### Section 2 (pp. 385–393)

5. In what sense are the cabinet departments of the executive branch the traditional units of federal administration?
6. How are the cabinet departments organized and structured?
7. For what major reasons do the independent agencies exist apart from the cabinet-level departments?

**8.** (a) What are the three types of independent agencies? (b) What are their functions?

## Section 3 (pp. 395–399)

**9.** Briefly describe the standards for staffing the federal bureaucracy that were held by Presidents George Washington and Thomas Jefferson.

**10.** (a) What was the spoils system? (b) What was its effect on the quality of administration of government?

**11.** What was the primary objective of the efforts to reform the country's civil service in the late 1800s?

**12.** (a) What steps do current civil service laws take to ensure that the public work force is free from political influences? (b) What is the controversy over these rules?

## Critical Thinking

**1. Identifying Central Issues** (p. 19)   (a) Is an efficient government always an effective government? (b) What is the proper relationship between efficiency and effectiveness in government? Give support for your answer.

**2. Identifying Assumptions** (p. 19)   Consider the characteristics and role of the independent regulatory agencies that are discussed in Section 2. What is the assumption about the executive branch that underlies the existence of these agencies?

**3. Recognizing Ideologies** (p. 19) Thomas Jefferson once said, "When a man accepts a public trust, he should consider himself a public property." (a) What do you think this statement means? (b) Do you agree or disagree with this statement? (c) What values underlie this statement?

## Getting Involved

**1. Writing Your Opinion**   You are a citizen living in the United States in the 1830s. Write a letter to President Andrew Jackson offering your views on the spoils system. Before you start your letter, determine whether you will argue in favor of or against the spoils system. To what extent does it promote or hinder the democratic process and the smooth operation of government? Identify three reasons why you think the system is good or bad for government. Begin the letter by stating your purpose in writing, including your overall opinion of the spoils system. Then, devote one paragraph each to the three reasons you identified to support your argument. Revise the letter, making sure that each paragraph clearly, persuasively, and respectfully presents your case. Correct any errors and draft a final copy.

**2. Class Debate**   Hold a class debate on one of the following topics: *Resolved,* That the use of government corporations be expanded; *Resolved,* That veterans of the armed forces and their relatives should be denied preference for federal employment in the interest of governmental quality; *Resolved,* That the spoils system practiced by Andrew Jackson fulfilled the principle of representative democracy. Select teams to debate in favor of each side of the issue. The rest of the class should evaluate each team's debate presentation.

**3. Creating a Political Cartoon**   Consider what you have read in Chapter 15 about the federal bureaucracy. Make a political cartoon that illustrates your understanding of the concept of bureaucracy. For example, you might focus on the following ideas: independent regulatory agencies, government corporations, or the name game.

# Financing Government

## Chapter Preview

Did you know that the Federal Government now spends more than $170 million an hour? That's nearly $3 million a minute for every minute of every hour of every day on through the year. Have you ever seen a million dollars, let alone $3 million or $170 million? Not very many people have. But we all know that a million dollars is a lot of money, and $170 million is a great deal more. If someone had enough time to lay out one million dollar bills end-to-end, they would reach more than halfway around the world.

If a million dollars is a lot of money, how much is a billion dollars? The Federal Government now spends more than $4 billion a day, and $120 billion every month. And how about a trillion dollars? As you will read in this chapter, the Federal Government takes in and spends some $1.5 trillion every year. Where does all that money come from, and where does it all go? That, in short, is what this chapter is all about.

### Before you read this chapter:

- **Describe** three types of taxes that you are familiar with.
- **Predict** what most Americans would complain about if there were no taxes.

### As you read, focus on the main objective for each section. Understand:

1. How the Federal Government raises money.
2. Borrowing as a source of government revenue.
3. How the Federal Government spends money and the complex process of preparing the federal budget.

▲ **A Mounting Bill** Concerned students note the latest national debt figure. The bill will no doubt be paid by their generation and those after them. By the end of fiscal year 1995, the figure will likely exceed $4.8 trillion, according to the Office of Management and Budget.

# 1 Where the Money Comes From: Taxes

### Find Out:

- What is the Federal Government's power to tax?
- What kinds of taxes does the Federal Government levy?
- For what purposes may the Federal Government levy taxes?

### Key Terms:

progressive tax, tax return, payroll tax, regressive tax, excise tax, estate tax, gift tax, custom duty

According to Benjamin Franklin's oft-quoted assertion, "in this world nothing is certain but death and taxes." In this section, you will consider the second of Franklin's certainties, taxes—and more specifically, those taxes levied by the Federal Government.[1]

---

[1]On State and local taxes, see Chapter 25.

Next year—during fiscal year 1996, the twelve-month period from October 1, 1995, through September 30, 1996—the Federal Government expects to take in more than $1.4 trillion. And, as you will see, it will almost certainly spend even more than that stupendous sum.

Those mind-boggling numbers tell you that, on average, it now costs every man, woman, and child in this country nearly $6,000 a year to support the activities of the Federal Government. And they should also tell you how important the subject of taxes really is.

### The Power to Tax

The Constitution underscores the cardinal importance of the power to tax by listing it first among the many powers granted to Congress. In Article I, Section 8, Clause 1, the Constitution gives to Congress the power:

❝To lay and collect taxes, duties, imposts and excises, to pay the debts, and provide for the common defense and general welfare of the United States . . . ❞

First and foremost, Congress exercises the taxing power in order to raise money to finance at least most of what it costs to operate the Federal Government. But Congress also levies some taxes for nonrevenue purposes.

## Constitutional Limitations

The power to tax is not an unlimited one. Like all of its other powers, Congress must exercise the taxing power in accord with the Constitution. Thus, for example, Congress cannot levy a tax on church services—for such a levy would violate the provisions of the 1st Amendment.

In more specific terms, the Constitution puts four expressed limits and one very significant implied limit on the power of Congress to tax.

First, taxes must be for public purposes only. That is, the Constitution says that Congress may levy taxes only for public purposes, not for the benefit of some private interest.

The second expressed limit is that export taxes are prohibited. Article I, Section 9, Clause 5 declares that "No tax or duty shall be laid on articles exported from any State." Thus, customs duties can be applied only to imports—on goods brought into the United States. This restriction was written into the Constitution as a part of the Commerce Compromise made by the Framers at Philadelphia in 1787 (see Chapter 2, Section 4).

While Congress cannot tax exports, it can and does prohibit the export of certain items—usually for reasons of national security and acting under its expressed power to regulate foreign commerce.

The third expressed limit is that direct taxes must be equally apportioned. Article I, Section 9, Clause 4 originally provided that:

66 No capitation, or other direct tax, shall be laid, unless in proportion to the census or enumeration hereinbefore directed to be taken. 99

This restriction was a part of the Three-Fifths Compromise the Framers made at the Philadelphia Convention (see Chapter 2, Section 4). In effect, delegates from the northern States insisted that if slaves were to be counted in the populations of the southern States, then those States would have to pay for them.

Recall that a direct tax is one that must be borne by the person upon whom it is levied—as, for example, a tax on land or buildings, which must be paid by the owner of the property; or a capitation tax—a head or poll tax—laid on each person. Other taxes are indirect taxes. That is, they are levies that may be shifted to another for payment—as, for example, the federal tax on liquor. That tax, placed initially on the distiller, is ultimately paid by the person who buys the liquor.

The direct tax restriction means, in effect, that any direct tax that Congress levies must be apportioned among the States according to their populations. Thus, a direct tax that raised $1 billion would have to produce just about $120 million in California and $10 million in Kansas—because California has just about 12 percent of the nation's population and Kansas 1 percent.

Wealth is not evenly distributed among the States, of course. So, a direct tax laid in proportion to population would be grossly unfair; the tax would fall more heavily on the residents of some States than it would on others. As a result, Congress has not imposed a direct tax—except for the income tax—outside the District of Columbia since 1861.

An income tax is a direct tax. But, recall, it may be laid without regard to population because of the 16th Amendment:

66 The Congress shall have power to lay and collect taxes on incomes, from whatever source derived, without apportionment among the several States, and without regard to any census or enumeration. 99

Congress first levied an income tax in 1861, to help finance the Civil War. The tax, which expired in 1873, was later upheld by the Supreme Court, in *Springer* v. *United States*, 1881. A unanimous Court found that income tax to be an indirect rather than a direct tax. But a later income tax law, enacted in 1894, was declared unconstitutional in *Pollock* v. *Farmers' Loan and Trust Co.*, in 1895. There, the Court held that the 1894 law imposed a direct tax that Congress should have apportioned among the several States.

The impossibility of taxing incomes fairly in accord with any plan of apportionment led to the adoption of the 16th Amendment in 1913.

Finally Article I, Section 8, Clause 1 declares that:

"All duties, imposts and excises shall be uniform throughout the United States."

That is, all of the indirect taxes levied by the Federal Government must be laid at the same rate in all parts of the country.

**The Implied Limitation** The Federal Government cannot tax the States or any of their local governments in the exercise of their governmental functions. That is, federal taxes cannot be imposed on those governments when they are doing such things as providing public education, furnishing health care, or building streets and highways. Recall, the Supreme Court laid down that rule in *McCulloch* v. *Maryland* in 1819, when it declared that "the power to tax involves the power to destroy." If the Federal Government could tax the governmental activities of the States or their local units, it could conceivably tax them out of existence and so destroy the federal system.

The Federal Government can and does tax those State and local activities that are of a nongovernmental character, however. Thus, in 1893, South Carolina created a State monopoly to sell liquor, and it claimed that each of its liquor stores was exempt from the federal saloon license tax. But, in *South Carolina* v. *United States*, 1905, the Supreme Court held that the State was liable for the tax—because the sale of liquor is not a necessary or usual governmental activity.

## Current Federal Taxes

Oliver Wendell Holmes once described taxes as "what we pay for civilized society."[2] Society does not appear to be much more civilized today than it was when Justice Holmes made that observation in 1927. But "what we pay" has certainly gone up. In 1927, the Federal Government's tax collections came to, altogether,

less than $3.4 billion. Compare that figure with the figures in the table on page 408.

**The Income Tax** The income tax is the largest source of federal revenue today. It first became the major source in 1917 and 1918. And, except for a few years during the Depression of the 1930s, it has remained so.

Several features suit the income tax to its dominant role. It is a flexible tax; its rates can be adjusted to produce whatever amount of money Congress thinks is necessary. The tax is also easily adapted to the principle of ability to pay. It is a **progressive tax**—that is, the higher the income and the ability to pay, the higher the tax rate. The tax is levied on the earnings of both individuals and corporations.

**The Individual Income Tax** The tax on individuals' incomes regularly produces the largest amount of federal revenue. For fiscal year 1995, the individual income tax is expected to provide more than $600 billion.

The tax is levied on each person's taxable income—one's total income in the previous year minus certain exemptions and deductions. On returns filed in 1995, which covered income that

▲ **Interpreting Political Cartoons** Filing taxes often requires following complicated instructions. According to this cartoon, how effective was the Tax Reform Bill of 1986 in simplifying tax form preparation?

---

[2]In a dissenting opinion in an insurance tax case, *Compania General de Tabacos de Filipinas* v. *Collector of Internal Revenue*, 1927.

| The Federal Government's Income (by major source for selected fiscal years, in billions of dollars) | 1980 | 1985 | 1990 | 1993 | 1994 | 1995 (est.) |
|---|---|---|---|---|---|---|
| Individual income taxes | $244.1 | $334.6 | $466.9 | $509.7 | $542.7 | $603.1 |
| Corporation income taxes | 64.6 | 61.3 | 93.5 | 117.5 | 140.4 | 144.0 |
| Social insurance taxes and contributions | 157.8 | 265.2 | 380.0 | 428.3 | 461.5 | 489.3 |
| Excise taxes | 24.3 | 36.0 | 35.3 | 48.1 | 55.2 | 56.0 |
| Estate and gift taxes | 6.4 | 6.4 | 11.5 | .6 | 15.2 | 14.7 |
| Customs duties | 7.2 | 12.1 | 16.7 | .8 | 20.1 | 22.0 |
| Miscellaneous receipts | 12.7 | 18.5 | 27.3 | 18.2 | 22.1 | 25.4 |
| Total receipts | $517.1 | $734.1 | $1,031.2 | $1,153.2 | $1,257.2 | $1,534.3 |

*Source:* Office of Management and Budget

▲ **Interpreting Tables**   Federal revenues come from several different sources. The monies collected from which of these sources increased by the greatest percentage from 1980 to 1995?

was earned in 1994, each taxpayer had a personal exemption of $2,450, plus another exemption of that amount for each dependent.[3] Deductions are allowed for a number of things, including the costs of some medical care, most State and local taxes (except for sales taxes), interest paid on home mortgages, charitable contributions.

By April 15, all persons who earned taxable income in the preceding calendar year must file **tax returns**—declarations of that income and of the exemptions and deductions claimed. Those returns are filed with the Internal Revenue Service, the IRS. A husband and wife can file a joint return, even if one of them had no income in the previous year. All taxable income received in 1994 was taxed at one of five rates. Couples who filed joint returns paid 15 percent on income up to $38,000, 28 percent on income up to $91,850, 31 percent on income up to $140,000; 36 percent on income up to $250,000;

and 39.6 percent on anything over that amount. Single taxpayers had to pay 15 percent on their incomes up to $22,750, 28 percent up to $55,100, 31 percent up to $115,000, 36 percent up to $250,000, and the top rate of 39.6 percent on anything higher.

Most who pay income taxes do so through withholding—a pay-as-you-go plan. Employers are required to withhold a certain amount from each employee's paycheck and send that money to the IRS. When the employee files a tax return, he or she will receive a refund if more than the tax due has been withheld, or pay an additional amount if not enough has been withheld. Those who have income from sources not subject to withholding must estimate the income tax they will owe and make quarterly payments on that amount through the year.

**The Corporation Income Tax**   Each corporation must pay a tax on its net income—that is, on all of its earnings above the costs of doing business. The corporate tax is the most complicated of all federal taxes because of the many deductions allowed. Nonprofit organizations such as churches and charitable foundations are not subject to the corporation income tax.

---

[3]The personal exemption is adjusted for inflation each year. From 1991 on, the personal exemption amount is reduced for those with higher incomes. For single taxpayers, it begins to decline on taxable income over $100,000, and it disappears altogether on taxable income over $200,000. For married couples who file joint returns, the exemption is phased down on taxable incomes over $150,000 and disappears at $275,000.

"Small Society" by Brickman. Washington Star Syndicate, Inc.

▲ **Interpreting Political Cartoons**   The Internal Revenue Service is responsible for collecting income tax from both individuals and corporations. What does this cartoon reveal about the feedback that the IRS receives?

For 1995, the corporate tax rates run from 15 percent on the first $50,000 of taxable earnings up to a top rate of 34 percent on taxable incomes of more than $15 million.

**Social Insurance Taxes**   The Federal Government collects huge sums to finance three major social welfare programs: (1) the Old-Age, Survivors, and Disability Insurance (OASDI) program—the basic social security program, established by the Social Security Act of 1935; (2) Medicare—health care for the elderly, added to the social security program in 1965; and (3) the unemployment compensation program—benefits paid to jobless workers, a program also established by the Social Security Act in 1935.

OASDI and Medicare are supported by taxes imposed on nearly all employers and their employees, and on self-employed persons. These levies are often called **payroll taxes** because the amounts owed by employees are withheld from their paychecks. To finance OASDI, employees must now (1995) pay a 6.2 percent tax on the first $61,200 of their yearly salaries or wages. Employers must match the OASDI tax paid by each employee. Those persons who are self-employed pay a 12.4 percent tax on the first $61,200 of their annual income.

For Medicare, employees now pay a 1.45 percent tax on all of their annual income. Employers must match the amounts withheld from their employees' paychecks. The self-employed pay a 2.9 percent Medicare tax on their annual incomes.

The unemployment insurance program is a joint federal-State operation, to make payments to workers who lose their jobs for reasons beyond their control. The program now covers most workers in this country. Each State and the District of Columbia, Puerto Rico, and the Virgin Islands has its own unemployment compensation law; and the amount of a worker's weekly benefits, and their duration, is determined by State law.

The unemployment compensation program is financed by a combination of federal and State taxes. The federal tax is now 6.2 percent of the first $7,000 an employer pays to each employee in a year. Each employer is given a credit of up to 5.4 percent against that tax for the unemployment taxes that employer pays to the State—so, usually, the federal tax really amounts to 0.8 percent on the taxable wages.

Notice that these social insurance taxes for OASDI, Medicare, and unemployment compensation are not progressive taxes. They are, instead, **regressive taxes**—taxes levied at a flat rate, without regard to the level of a taxpayer's income or his or her ability to pay them.

The IRS collects the social insurance taxes. The money is then credited to trust accounts maintained by the Treasury, and Congress

**Both Large and Small Contributors** The income tax is collected from both individuals (inset) and huge corporations, like Turner Broadcasting, CNN's parent company.

appropriates funds for the social insurance programs as they are needed.

**Excise Taxes** An **excise tax** is a tax laid on the manufacture, sale, or consumption of goods and/or the performance of services. The Federal Government has imposed and collected them since Congress acquired its taxing power in 1789.

Today, federal excise taxes are imposed on a long list of things, including gasoline, oil, tires, tobacco, liquor, wine, beer, firearms, telephone services, airline tickets, and more. Many excise taxes are often called hidden taxes because they are collected from producers who then figure them into the price that the retail customer finally pays. Some are called luxury taxes because they are levied on goods not usually considered to be necessities. And some excise taxes are known as sin taxes—in particular,

those laid on tobacco products, beer, wine, liquor, and gambling.

**Estate and Gift Taxes** An **estate tax** is a levy imposed on the assets (the estate) of one who dies.[4] A **gift tax** is one imposed on the making of a gift by a living person. Congress first provided for the estate tax in 1916. It added the gift tax in 1932 to plug a loophole in the estate tax—the giving of money or other property before death to avoid the estate tax.

The first $600,000 of an estate is exempt from the federal tax. So, in fact, most estates are not subject to the federal levy. Deductions are allowed for such things as State death taxes and bequests to religious and charitable groups. Anything a husband or wife leaves to the other is taxed, if at all, only when the surviving spouse dies.

Any person may make up to $10,000 in tax-free gifts to any other person in any one year. Gifts that husbands/wives make to one another are not taxed, regardless of value.

The estate and gift taxes are separate federal taxes, but both are levied at the same rates. For 1995, those rates ranged from a minimum of 18 percent on an estate or a gift with a net value of less than $20,000, on up to a maximum of 55 percent on an estate or gift worth more than $3 million.

**Custom Duties** A **custom duty** is a tax laid on goods brought into the United States from abroad. They are also known as tariffs, import duties, or imposts. Congress decides which imports will be dutied and at what rates.[5] Most imports, some 30,000 different items, are dutied; but some are not—for example, Bibles, coffee, bananas, and up to $300 of a tourist's purchases abroad.

---

[4]An inheritance tax is another form of the so-called death tax. It is not levied on the entire net estate but, instead, on each portion inherited by each heir. Most States impose inheritance, not estate, taxes; most States also levy gift taxes.

[5]Since 1922, Congress has authorized the President to raise or lower any tariff by as much as 50 percent. The President can do so by an executive order, issued on the basis of recommendations made by the United States International Trade Commission, which studies the effect of tariffs and imports on the economy.

Custom duties were the major source of income for the Federal Government for more than a century. Now, they produce less than 2 percent of the money the government takes in.

## Taxing for Nonrevenue Purposes

Remember, the power to tax can be, and often is, used for purposes other than the raising of revenue. Usually, that other purpose is to regulate some activity that Congress thinks is harmful or dangerous to the public.

Thus, much of the Federal Government's regulation of narcotics is based on the taxing power. Federal law provides that only those who hold a valid license may legally manufacture, sell, or otherwise deal in those drugs—and licensing is a form of taxation. The government also regulates a number of other things by licensing, including, for example, certain firearms, prospecting on public lands, and the hunting of migratory birds. The federal excise tax on gas-guzzling cars is intended to discourage their purchase.

The Supreme Court first upheld the use of the taxing power for other than revenue purposes in *Veazie Bank* v. *Fenno* in 1869. Congress had established a national paper money system in the midst of the Civil War in 1863. It did so to provide a single, sound currency for the country. Private bank notes, which were also used as paper money, soon interfered with the circulation of the government's new "greenbacks." So, in 1866, Congress composed a 10 percent tax on the issuing of those private notes, and they soon disappeared. In upholding the tax, the Court declared:

❝Having, in the exercise of undisputed constitutional powers, undertaken to provide a currency for the whole country, it cannot be questioned that Congress may, constitutionally, secure the benefits of it to the people by appropriate legislation. ❞

In 1912, Congress used its taxing power to destroy a segment of the domestic match industry. It levied a tax of two cents per hundred on matches made with white or yellow phosphorous—highly poisonous substances that caused serious harm to the workers who produced the matches. Matches made from other substances commonly sold for a penny a hundred, and the two-cent tax drove the phosphorous matches from the market. But Congress cannot use its taxing power in any manner it chooses. As in all other matters, Congress is bound by all of the other provisions of the Constitution.

To illustrate that point, consider several provisions of a 1951 tax law that was aimed at professional gamblers. The law imposed a $50-a-year license tax on bookies, levied other taxes on their activities, and required them to register with and submit detailed reports to the IRS. The law did produce a small amount of income. But its real purpose was to force gamblers into the open and to the attention of State and local police and prosecutors, and to set a federal tax evasion trap for those who failed to comply with the law.

The Supreme Court held the antigambling provisions unconstitutional in *Marchetti* v. *United States*, 1968. The Court did not hold that the taxes had been imposed for some improper purpose. Rather, it held that the tax, registration, and reporting provisions forced gamblers to furnish evidence against themselves—in violation of the 5th Amendment's guarantee against self-incrimination.

## Section 1 Review

1. **Define:** tax return, payroll tax, excise tax, estate tax, gift tax, custom duty
2. What is the major exception to the requirement that direct taxes be levied in proportion to each State's population?
3. What are the two largest income producers for the Federal Government?
4. What is the difference between a progressive and a regressive tax?
5. What is the difference between the rate paid for social insurance taxes by those on payrolls and by those who are self-employed?
6. What limits exist on the power to tax for purposes other than raising revenue?

**Critical Thinking**

7. **Determining Relevance** (p. 19) Explain how you think public opinion might affect and place limits on the government's power to tax.

★

# 2 Nontax Revenues and Borrowing

**Find Out:**

- What are the major sources of nontax revenues in the United States?
- What is the historical purpose of the power to borrow?
- What is the purpose of much of the current borrowing?

**Key Terms:**

deficit, public debt

In *Hamlet*, Shakespeare writes: "Neither a borrower, nor a lender be." That may be good advice in some situations. As you will see in this section, however, it certainly has not been followed by the government of the United States.

## Nontax Revenues

Large sums of money reach the federal treasury from a multitude of nontax sources. As you can see from the table on page 408, these miscellaneous receipts now come to well over $20 billion a year.

These monies come from dozens of places. A large portion comes from the earnings of the Federal Reserve System, mostly in interest charges. The interest on loans made by several other federal agencies, canal tolls, and fees for such items as passports, copyrights, patents, and trademarks also generate large sums. So do the premiums on veterans' life insurance policies, the sale or lease of public lands, the sale of surplus property, and such other things as the fines imposed by the federal courts.

The Treasury Department maintains what it calls the conscience fund for all the money, several thousand dollars a year, that people send in to ease their minds over their past tax-paying mistakes. Another little-known source of nontax money is seigniorage, the profit the United States Mint makes in the production of coins. That profit is the difference between the value of the metals used and the other costs of production and the monetary value of the

▲ **Managing the Country's Money Supply**
Pictured here is a Federal Reserve building in Washington, D.C. There are twelve Federal Reserve banks in this country that supply money to banks throughout the nation.

minted coins. It is a tidy little sum, more than $500 million in most years. The Philatelic Sales Branch of the United States Postal Service sells more than $100 million in mint stamps to collectors each year; and stamp collectors spend untold millions more at local post offices. Most of the stamps they buy are never used on mail.

## Borrowing

Congress has the power "to borrow money on the credit of the United States."[6] Historically, the power to borrow has been viewed as a power that makes it possible for the government to (1) meet the costs of short- and long-term crisis situations and (2) finance large-scale

---

[6]Article I, Section 8, Clause 2.

projects that would not be paid for out of current income. Thus, the Federal Government borrowed huge sums when the United States entered World War I, to combat the Depression of the 1930s, and again during World War II.

In recent decades, the Federal Government has borrowed for yet another reason: deficit financing. Over these years, the government has regularly spent more than it has taken in. That is, it has run up an annual **deficit**—the yearly shortfall between income and outgo; and it has borrowed to make up the difference. Indeed, the Federal Government's financial books have not shown a surplus, more income that outgo, since fiscal year 1969.[7] As the graph on page 414 shows, deficit financing—often called deficit spending—became especially pronounced in the 1980s, and it has continued at a hefty rate in the 1990s.

Congress must authorize any and all federal borrowing. The borrowing itself is done by the Treasury Department, which issues various kinds of securities to investors, principally individuals and banks, investment companies, and other financial institutions. These securities usually take the form of Treasury notes or bills—T-bills—issued for short-term borrowings, or bonds for long-term purposes. They are, in effect, IOUs, promissory notes in which the government agrees to repay a certain sum, with interest, at a certain time.

The government is able to borrow money at lower rates of interest than those paid by private borrowers. This is true largely because investors can find no safer securities than those issued by the United States; if the United States could not pay its debts, no one else would be able to, either. Federal securities are also attractive because the interest they generate cannot be taxed by the States or their local governments.

## The Public Debt

Borrowing produces a debt, of course. The public debt is the result of the Federal Government's borrowing over time. More precisely, the **public debt** is the government's outstanding

Would you support or oppose a constitutional amendment to require a balanced federal budget?

| | Support | Oppose | No Opinion |
|---|---|---|---|
| **Total** | 74% | 19% | 7% |
| **Sex** | | | |
| Men | 77 | 19 | 4 |
| Women | 71 | 18 | 11 |
| **Age** | | | |
| 18–29 | 80 | 18 | 2 |
| 30–49 | 76 | 18 | 6 |
| 50–64 | 75 | 16 | 9 |
| 65 & over | 58 | 23 | 19 |
| **Politics** | | | |
| Republican | 75 | 19 | 6 |
| Democrat | 73 | 17 | 10 |
| Independent | 73 | 20 | 7 |

*Source:* Gallup Poll News Service, February 24, 1994

**Interpreting Tables** Why do you think that persons over 65 are less supportive of a balanced budget amendment than are those in other (younger) age groups?

indebtedness, all of the money borrowed and not yet repaid, plus the accrued interest.[8]

The Federal Government has built up a huge debt over time. As you can see in the table on page 414, the nation's debt doubled in the years 1981 through 1985 because of deficit financing; and it had quadrupled by 1992.

The amounts involved here are absolutely mind-boggling. In 1981, when the debt was approaching $1 trillion, President Ronald Reagan said that he found "such a figure—a trillion dollars—incomprehensible." He then drew this verbal picture: "[I]f you had a stack of $1,000 bills in your hand only four inches high, you would be a millionaire. A trillion dollars would be a stack

[7]In fact, since 1930, the Federal Government has ended only seven fiscal years "in the black"—that is, with a surplus: fiscal years 1947, 1948, 1951, 1956, 1957, 1960, and 1969.

[8]The public debt, often called the national debt, is frequently confused with the government's annual deficits. Notice, however, that each of those deficits amounts to an annual increase in the total of the public debt.

## The Public Debt (at end of selected fiscal years)

| | |
|---|---|
| 1916 (pre-World War I) | $   1.1 billion |
| 1919 (post-World War I) | 25.5 billion |
| 1930 (start of Depression) | 16.2 billion |
| 1940 (decade of Depression) | 43.0 billion |
| 1941 (pre-World War II) | 48.9 billion |
| 1946 (post-World War II) | 269.4 billion |
| 1950 (pre-Korean War) | 256.1 billion |
| 1954 (post-Korean War) | 271.3 billion |
| 1964 (pre-Vietnam War) | 308.1 billion |
| 1974 (post-Vietnam War) | 474.2 billion |
| 1980 ⌉ period of steep | 907.7 billion |
| 1985 ⎬ upturn in | 1.8 trillion |
| 1992 ⌋ deficit financing | 4.0 trillion |
| 1994 | 4.6 trillion |
| 1995 (est.) | 4.8 trillion |

*Source:* Bureau of the Public Debt, Department of the Treasury (1992 estimate by the Office of Management and Budget).

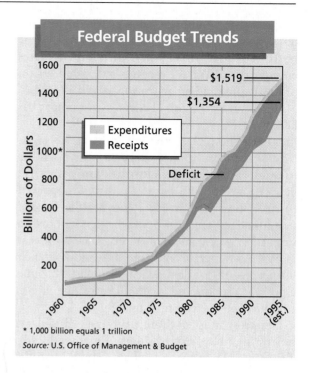

## Federal Budget Trends

* 1,000 billion equals 1 trillion

*Source:* U.S. Office of Management & Budget

**Interpreting Tables and Graphs**   The public debt can be affected by national and world events, as you can see in the table at left. Which recent period saw the greatest growth in deficit spending and, so, in the public debt? Can you think of an explanation for this growth?

67 miles high." Mr. Reagan's stack would have to be nearly 300 miles high to equal the national debt today!

There is no constitutional limit on the amount that may be borrowed, and so there is no constitutional limit on the public debt. Congress has put a statutory ceiling on the debt. But Congress simply adjusts the ceiling upward whenever fiscal realities seem to call for it.

The debt has always been the subject of much controversy; and its rapid rise in recent years has fueled the fire. The annual interest on the debt—the amount that must be paid each year to those from whom the government has borrowed—came to more than $296 billion in 1994; and that figure will approach $300 billion in 1995. That means that about one in five dollars the Federal Government now spends goes just to service the debt.

Most of those who are most concerned about the size of the debt are worried about its impact on future generations of Americans. In short, they believe that today's deficit financing—that

is, today's borrowing to pay for yesterday's and today's spending—is being done at the expense of tomorrow's taxpayers.

## Section 2 Review

1. **Define:** deficit, public debt
2. How much revenue does the government raise through nontax sources?
3. Describe the mechanism by which the Federal Government borrows money.
4. Why is the Federal Government able to borrow money at lower rates of interest than private borrowers?

### Critical Thinking

5. **Predicting Consequences** (p. 19) (a) What would be the consequences of a decision by Congress to bring the practice of deficit spending to an immediate halt? (b) How would the public respond to that step?

★

## Should the Government Subsidize Private School Education?
### Mueller v. Allen, 1983

A Minnesota law allows those who pay that State's individual income tax to deduct the money they pay to provide "tuition, textbooks, and transportation" for their children who attend elementary or secondary schools in the State. Parents can deduct as much as $500 for each dependent child in grades K through 6 and up to $700 per dependent in grades 7 through 12. The law, originally passed in 1955, allows taxpayers to claim the deduction without regard to whether their children attend public or private schools.

In 1981, two Minnesota taxpayers, Van D. Mueller and June Noyes, challenged the constitutionality of the statute. They brought their case before the federal district court in Minneapolis. There, they claimed the law violated the 1st and 14th Amendments' ban on the establishment of religion. They noted that parents with children in public schools pay little or nothing for "tuition, textbooks, and transportation"; so, the law's real benefits go to those who send their children to private schools. Most private schools in Minnesota are parochial, or church-run, schools; therefore, they claimed, the State's law actually provides for the use of public funds to support religion.

Mueller and Noyes lost their case in the district court and carried an appeal to the U.S. Supreme Court.

*Review the following evidence and arguments presented to the United States Supreme Court:*

### Arguments for Mueller

**1.** In effect, the law allows parents to pay parochial school expenses with public tax money, and so it violates the 1st and 14th Amendments' Establishment Clause.

**2.** The law gives an unfair tax advantage to those parents who choose to send their children to private schools.

**3.** The law weakens the State's system of public education by denying to the State tax monies that could be used to support that system. That loss of funds undercuts the quality of the education that can be offered by the public schools.

### Arguments for Allen

**1.** The law does not seek to promote any particular religion; instead, its aim is to promote the education of the children of the State.

**2.** Parents with children in private schools bear an unfair double burden. They must pay the costs of the private schools their children do attend and also pay taxes to support the public schools their children do not attend.

**3.** The people of Minnesota are benefited by the education offered by all of the schools in the State, both public and private.

### Getting Involved

**1. Identify** the constitutional grounds on which each side based its arguments.

**2. Debate** the opposing viewpoints presented in this case.

**3. Predict** how you think the Supreme Court ruled in this case and why. Then refer to the Supreme Court Glossary on page 767 to read about the decision in this case. Discuss the impact of the Court's decision on the future of public education.

# 3 Spending and the Budget

## Find Out:

- What does the Federal Government do with the revenue it collects?
- What is the importance of the federal budget?
- How does the budget process work?

## Key Terms:

entitlement, continuing resolution

The Federal Government will spend more than $1.5 trillion in fiscal year 1995. If you placed 1.5 trillion dollar bills end to end, they would stretch about 140 million miles, just about the distance from the earth to the sun and halfway back.

In this section, you will see how the government spends all that money, and how it plans for that spending, through the budget process.

▲ **Decrease in Military Spending** National budget priorities have changed over the last few years. With the end of the cold war, the nation's armed forces are being down-sized.

## Federal Spending

Look at the table on the next page. As you can see, the newly independent Social Security Administration now spends more money than any other federal agency. Nearly all of Social Security's spending goes for OASDI (Old Age, Survivors, and Disability Insurance) benefit payments and similar entitlement programs. **Entitlements** are benefits that federal law says must be paid to all those who meet the eligibility requirements. OASDI is the largest federal entitlement program today. Others include Medicare, Medicaid, food stamps, unemployment compensation, and veterans' pensions. In effect, the law says that the people who receive benefits paid under those programs are entitled (have a right) to them.

Interest on the public debt is today the second largest object of federal spending. And, stoked by deficit financing, it has consumed a larger and still larger part of the federal budget over the last several years. In the table on page 417, interest on the debt is included in the Treasury Department's spending. For 1994, interest paid on the debt came to $296.3 billion.

Defense expenditures are now decreasing, as you can see in the table. But they still account for the third largest slice of the federal budget—$268.6 billion in 1994. Note that the defense spending figures in the table are somewhat misleading. They do not include the defense-related expenditures of other federal agencies—for example, the extensive nuclear weapons research and development work of the Department of Energy.

**Controllable and Uncontrollable Spending** What the Federal Government spends can be described in terms of controllable and uncontrollable spending. Most specific items in the federal budget are controllable. That is, Congress and the President decide how much will be spent each year on many of the individual expenditures the government makes—for example, on farm subsidies, military equipment, aid to education, and so on. Some spending is uncontrollable, however, such as interest on the debt. That interest is a fixed charge; once the

## Federal Spending, Fiscal Years 1990–1994 (by agency, in billions of dollars)

| Agency | 1990 | 1991 | 1992 | 1993 | 1994 |
|---|---|---|---|---|---|
| Legislative Branch | 2.2 | 2.3 | 2.7 | 2.4 | 2.6 |
| Judicial Branch | 1.6 | 2.0 | 2.3 | 2.6 | 2.7 |
| Executive Office of the President | 0.2 | 0.2 | 0.2 | 0.2 | 0.2 |
| Funds appropriated to the President (Mostly for foreign economic/military aid) | 10.1 | 11.7 | 11.1 | 11.5 | 10.5 |
| Department of Agriculture | 46.0 | 54.1 | 56.4 | 63.1 | 60.8 |
| Department of Commerce | 3.7 | 2.6 | 2.6 | 2.8 | 2.9 |
| Department of Defense—Military | 289.8 | 261.9 | 286.6 | 278.6 | 268.6 |
| Department of Defense—Civil | 25.0 | 26.5 | 28.3 | 29.3 | 30.4 |
| Department of Education | 23.1 | 25.3 | 26.0 | 30.3 | 24.7 |
| Department of Energy | 12.0 | 12.5 | 15.4 | 16.8 | 17.8 |
| Department of Health and Human Services* | 438.7 | 484.4 | 538.7 | 581.1 | 624.7 |
| Department of Housing and Urban Development | 20.2 | 22.8 | 24.5 | 25.2 | 25.8 |
| Department of the Interior | 5.8 | 6.1 | 6.6 | 6.7 | 6.9 |
| Department of Justice | 6.5 | 8.2 | 9.8 | 10.2 | 10.0 |
| Department of Labor | 25.3 | 34.0 | 47.2 | 44.7 | 36.9 |
| Department of State | 4.0 | 4.3 | 5.0 | 5.4 | 5.7 |
| Department of Transportation | 28.6 | 30.5 | 32.5 | 34.5 | 37.3 |
| Department of the Treasury | 255.3 | 276.4 | 293.4 | 298.8 | 307.3 |
| Department of Veterans Affairs | 29.0 | 31.2 | 33.9 | 35.5 | 37.4 |
| Environmental Protection Agency | 5.1 | 5.8 | 5.9 | 5.9 | 5.9 |
| National Aeronautics and Space Administration | 12.4 | 13.9 | 14.0 | 14.3 | 13.7 |
| Office of Personnel Management | 32.0 | 34.8 | 35.6 | 36.8 | 38.6 |
| Resolution Trust Corporation | — | — | -8.9 | -19.2 | 4.1 |
| Other Independent Agencies | 74.4 | 82.3 | 28.6 | 10.2 | 8.5 |
| Deductions (undistributed offsetting receipts) | -99.0 | 110.0 | -117.1 | -119.7 | -123.5 |
| **Total Outlays** | **1,251.8** | **1,323.8** | **1,380.8** | **1,408.0** | **1,460.6** |
| Deficit (Outlays greater than receipts) | -220.4 | -269.5 | -290.3 | -255.3 | -203.4 |

Columns may not add to totals due to rounding. * The Social Security Administration, which accounted for just over half ($313.9 billion) of all HHS spending in 1994 (and a similar proportion in prior years), in 1995 became an independent agency.

*Source:* Financial Management Service, Department of the Treasury

▲ **Interpreting Tables**  Which of the cabinet departments now spends the largest amount of money each year? Which department spends the least?

Federal Government borrows the money, the interest on that loan must be paid when it comes due and at the rate the government promised to pay.

Social security benefits, food stamps, and most other entitlements are also largely uncontrollable because, once Congress has set the standards of eligibility for those programs, it has no control over how many people will then meet those standards. Thus, Congress cannot determine how many people covered by social security will become eligible for retirement benefits. Those expenditures are not completely uncontrollable, however. Congress could redefine eligibility standards, or it could reduce the amount of money each beneficiary is to receive. But, clearly, those actions would be politically difficult.

The Office of Management and Budget estimates that the uncontrollable items in the budget total nearly 80 percent of all current federal spending.

## The Federal Budget

Recall, the Constitution declares that

“No money shall be drawn from the treasury, but in consequence of appropriations made by law. . . .”[9]

Thus, only Congress can provide the money upon which the Federal Government must depend. But it is the President who initiates the spending process by submitting a budget at the beginning of each congressional session.[10] The budget is a hugely important political document. It is the President's work plan for the conduct of government and the execution of public policy.

**The Budget Process** The budgeting process is a joint effort of the President and Congress. The President prepares the budget and submits (proposes) it to Congress. Congress then reacts to the President's proposals, over a period of several months. It usually enacts most of them, usually in some altered form, in appropriations measures.

**The President and the Budget** The process of building the budget is a lengthy one. In fact, that process begins some 18 months before the start of the fiscal year for which it is intended. First, each federal agency prepares detailed estimates of its spending needs for that 12-month period. Each agency submits its spending plans to the Office of Management and Budget, the President's budget-making agency (see Chapter 14, Section 5).

The OMB reviews all of the many agency proposals, often in budget hearings at which agency officials must defend their dollar requests. Following the OMB's review, revised and usually lowered spending plans for all of the agencies in the executive branch are fitted into the President's overall program. They become a part of the budget document the President sends to Capitol Hill.[11]

**Congress and the Budget** Remember that Congress depends upon and works through its standing committees. The President's budget is referred to the Budget Committee in each chamber. There, in both committees, the budget is studied and dissected with the help of the Congressional Budget Office. The CBO is a staff agency, created by Congress in 1974. It provides both houses of Congress and their committees with basic budget and other economic data and analyses. The information that the CBO supplies is independent of the information provided by the OMB, which, recall, is the President's budget agency.

---

[9]Article I, Section 9, Clause 7.

[10]The word *budget* comes from the French *bougette*, meaning a small pouch or bag with its contents. Originally, the budget was the bag in which in the 18th century the British Chancellor of the Exchequer carried financial documents.

---

[11]Congress makes and enacts its own budget. The spending requests for the judicial branch, prepared by the Administrative Office of the United States Courts, are included in the President's budget without OMB review.

# *VOICES on Government*

### On Reducing the Federal Deficit

“We're not cutting the deficit just because experts say it's the thing to do.... We have to cut the deficit because the more we spend paying off the debt, the less tax dollars we have to invest in jobs and education and the future of this country.... We cut the deficit so that our children will be able to buy a home, so that our companies can invest ... in retraining their workers, so that our government can make the kinds of investments we need to be a stronger and smarter and safer nation.... My recommendation makes more than 150 difficult reductions to cut the federal spending by a total of $246 billion.”

**William J. Clinton,**
42nd President of the
United States

**THE WIZARD OF ID**

By permission of Johnny Hart and NAS, Inc.

▲ **Interpreting Political Cartoons** Mayors, governors, and Presidents strive to balance their budgets. According to this cartoon, what is sometimes required to accomplish this task?

The President's budget is also sent to the House and Senate Appropriations Committees.[12] Their subcommittees hold extensive hearings in which they examine agency requests, quiz agency officials, and take testimony from a wide range of interested parties. The two Appropriations Committees fashion measures that later are reported to the floor of each house. Those measures are the bills that actually appropriate the funds on which the government will operate.

The two Budget Committees propose a concurrent resolution on the budget to their respective chambers. That measure, which must be passed by both houses by May 15, sets overall targets for federal receipts and spending in the upcoming fiscal year. The estimates are intended to guide the committees in both houses as they continue to work on the budget.

The two Budget Committees propose a second budget resolution in early September. Congress must pass that resolution by September 15, just two weeks before the beginning of the next fiscal year; it sets binding spending limits for all federal agencies in that upcoming year. No appropriations measure can provide for any spending that exceeds those limits.

Congress passes 13 major appropriations bills each year. Recall, each of these measures must go to the White House for the Presi-

dent's action. Every year, Congress hopes to pass all 13 of the appropriations measures by October 1—that is, by the beginning of the fiscal year. It seldom does so, however, and Congress must then pass emergency spending legislation to avoid a shutdown of those agencies for which appropriations have not yet been signed into law. That legislation takes the form of a **continuing resolution**, a measure that, when signed by the President, allows the affected agencies to continue to function on the basis of the previous year's appropriations.

## Section **3** Review

1. **Define:** entitlement, continuing resolution
2. What are the three most expensive items for which the Federal Government spends money?
3. What is the President's role in the budget-making process?
4. What is the role of the Congress in the budget-making process?
5. (a) Why must Congress pass its appropriations measures by October 1? (b) What happens if it does not?

**Critical Thinking**

6. **Drawing Conclusions** (p. 19) What does the text mean when it says that redefining the eligibility standards for certain entitlement programs would be politically difficult?

---

[12]If the budget includes any tax proposals, they are referred to the House Ways and Means Committee and to the Senate's Finance Committee.

★

# How to File a Tax Return

As you know, the Federal Government requires huge sums of money in order to operate. In addition, State and local governments also require money in order to provide the many services they offer. Governments obtain much of this money by taxing citizens. One important tax that many individuals pay is an income tax. The Federal Government, most States, and many cities require people to pay this type of tax. For this reason, wage earners must file by April 15 a tax return on which they report their incomes from the previous year. This process is called filing a tax return. The steps for filing a federal tax return are outlined below.

**1. Obtain the proper tax forms.** If you have filed a tax return in previous years, you should receive your tax forms in the mail. If you have never filed a return before, you can obtain the forms and instructions at local offices of the Internal Revenue Service, most post offices, and many banks. (a) Look in the phone book under the United States government for the local office of the Internal Revenue Service. (b) Look under your State's and your local government's name to get any State or local forms you need.

**2. Read the instruction booklets.** The booklets that come with the tax forms will answer many of your questions about paying income taxes. They will also help you determine which tax form you will need to fill out. (a) Read the instructions and follow them carefully. (b) Follow the directions for getting help in the instruction booklet.

**3. Collect your W-2 forms.** Each January, you will receive reports from your employer(s) stating the amount of money you earned during the previous year. Usually, these reports are W-2 forms. W-2's report what you were paid, as well as how much money was withheld from your earnings to pay federal, State, and local taxes. W-2's also list FICA withholdings—your contribution to the social security system. The withholdings on your W-2's represent income taxes that you have already paid.

**4. Collect other earnings information.** You may also receive other statements of income. For example, any bank where you earned interest will report those earnings to you. You must also gather information about any income you made, such as tips and cash payments you received, that does not appear on a W-2 form. Remember that no money has been withheld on these earnings.

**5. Complete the form according to the instructions.** (a) Check your arithmetic to be sure you have paid enough tax. (b) Be sure to make copies of your tax return before sending it back to the appropriate agency.

# Chapter-in-Brief

Scan all headings, photographs, charts, and other visuals in the chapter before reading the section summaries below.

**Section 1** **Where the Money Comes From: Taxes (pp. 405–411)** The power to tax is granted to Congress by the Constitution but that power is not unlimited. Congress may levy taxes only for public purposes, not to benefit any private interest. No tax may be applied to any exported articles. Direct taxes must be apportioned among the States according to their populations. Indirect taxes must be uniform in every State. The Federal Government may not tax any governmental function of either State or local governments.

Income taxes levied on individuals and corporations are progressive taxes and are the largest source of federal revenue. Most individuals pay income taxes through withholding from their paychecks. Nonprofit organizations such as churches are not subject to an income tax. Social insurance taxes (payroll taxes) are regressive and pay for three major social welfare programs: Old-Age, Survivors, and Disability Insurance; Medicare; and unemployment compensation. Excise taxes, estate and gift taxes, and customs duties also contribute to federal revenues. Some taxes are used for nonrevenue purposes. Licensing is used for both regulatory purposes and revenue.

**Section 2** **Nontax Revenues and Borrowing (pp. 412–414)** Many nontax sources contribute to the federal treasury: interest on loans made by federal agencies, the "conscience fund," the profit the U.S. Mint makes in the production of coins, and the sale of mint stamps to collectors by the U.S. Postal Service, for example.

The Constitution gives Congress the power to borrow money on the credit of the United States for crisis situations such as war or for large-scale projects. In recent years, the Federal Government has also borrowed for deficit financing and has built up a huge public debt. No constitutional limit exists on the amount of money the Federal Government may borrow. Congress has put a statutory ceiling on the public debt, however, which may be raised whenever the need arises. The current debt will have to be paid by future taxpayers and has always been the subject of much controversy.

**Section 3** **Spending and the Budget (pp. 416–419)** The Federal Government spends the largest amount of money every year for social security and other entitlement programs. Interest on the public debt is now the second largest object of federal spending, followed by defense. Nearly 80 percent of federal spending is uncontrollable—it cannot be reduced.

The executive branch initiates the spending process by submitting a budget to Congress each year. Each federal agency submits a detailed spending plan to the Office of Management and Budget. These become a part of the budget document sent to Congress by the President. In Congress, it is referred to the Budget Committee and the Appropriations Committee in each chamber. Congress reviews the budget, holds hearings, and makes appropriations. Funds cannot be spent until appropriated by Congress. Congress passes 13 major appropriations bills every year, each covering a broad slice of federal spending. Each of these measures must go to the President for approval. Congress must often pass emergency legislation in the form of a continuing resolution. This allows the affected agencies to continue to function on last year's appropriations.

# Chapter Review

## Vocabulary and Key Terms

progressive tax (p. 407)
tax return (p. 408)
payroll tax (p. 409)
regressive tax (p. 409)

excise tax (p. 410)
estate tax (p. 410)
gift tax (p. 410)
customs duty (p. 410)

deficit (p. 413)
public debt (p. 413)
entitlement (p. 416)
continuing resolution
   (p. 419)

**Matching:** *Review the key terms in the list above. If you are not sure of a term's meaning, look up the term and review its definition. Choose a term from the list above that best matches each description.*

1. imposed on the assets of one who dies
2. a tax that falls most heavily on those who are most able to pay
3. the total amount of money owed by the United States, plus all accrued interest
4. payments that federal law says must be paid to all those who meet the eligibility requirements
5. sometimes called tariffs, import duties, or imposts

**True or False:** *Determine whether each statement is true or false. If it is true, write "true." If it is false, change the underlined word or words to make the statement true.*

1. Certain taxes that fall most heavily on those who are least able to pay them are sometimes referred to as <u>progressive taxes</u>.
2. If you were to receive $20,000 as a present from a relative, you would have to pay an <u>estate tax</u>.
3. In recent decades, the United States has been consistently unable to spend less than it takes in; thus, the country runs a yearly <u>public debt</u>.
4. A <u>payroll tax</u> is one in which the amount owed by the individual is withheld from the person's paycheck.

**Word Relationships:** *Replace the underlined definition with the correct term from the list above.*

1. When Congress fails to pass the necessary appropriations by October 1st, they pass a <u>measure that allows affected agencies to continue functioning on the basis of the last year's appropriations</u>.
2. These <u>taxes laid on the manufacture, sale, or consumption of goods and/or the performance of services</u> are sometimes called, luxury, sin, or hidden taxes.
3. Certain items such as bananas and Bibles are exempt from <u>taxes laid on goods brought into the United States from abroad</u>.
4. Wage earners in the United States must file annual <u>declarations of income and exemptions or deductions claimed</u>.

## Main Ideas

### Section 1 (pp. 405–411)

1. What are the four expressed limitations on the Federal Government's power to tax?
2. What is the implied limitation on that power?
3. What are the different taxes by which the Federal Government raises revenue?

**4.** For what purposes besides raising revenue can the Federal Government use its power to levy taxes?

## Section 2 (pp. 412–414)

**5.** List five of the nontax sources of revenue utilized by the Federal Government.

**6.** How does the historical use of borrowing differ from the practice of governmental borrowing in recent decades?

**7.** How has the public debt changed since the 1980s?

**8.** What is the significance of the public debt for future taxpayers?

## Section 3 (pp. 416–419)

**9.** What is the largest item on which the Federal Government spends the money it raises?

**10.** (a) What is the difference between uncontrollable and controllable spending? (b) About what percentage of the annual budget is controllable?

**11.** In what sense is the budget-making process a joint effort of the President and Congress?

**12.** What are the roles of the Budget Committees and the Appropriations Committees?

---

## Critical Thinking

**1. Checking Consistency** (p. 19) Consider the discussion of the purposes for which Congress can levy taxes. Do you think that the Constitution intends for Congress to use its power to tax certain activities as a means of regulating or destroying that activity? Explain your answer.

**2. Predicting Consequences** (p. 19) (a) In your opinion, should the United States seek an amendment to the Constitution requiring a balanced budget? (b) What might be the result of such an amendment?

**3. Testing Conclusions** (p. 19) The text states that "the federal budget is a hugely important political document." Use evidence from the chapter to support and/or explain this statement.

## Getting Involved

**1. Writing Your Opinion** Write a questionnaire you could use to determine people's views on the issue of federal taxes. To begin with, identify what you hope to learn from the survey, and write a statement that explains why you are conducting it. Then, create a list of questions that you hope will produce the kind of information you are looking for. Remember, the questions in your survey must be carefully worded to avoid influencing people's responses. Review each question to ensure that it is presented in a straightforward and unbiased manner. Once you have refined your questions, reread them, correct any errors, and make a final draft.

**2. Cooperative Activity** As a class, consider the table on federal spending on page 417. Work together to create a new budget that reflects the shared priorities of the class. To begin with, list each of the cabinet-level departments that appear on the table. Then, as a group, prioritize these budget items, placing them in order of descending importance. Continue the discussion until a majority of the class agrees on a list. Repeat the process, this time distributing specific funds for each department.

**3. Gathering Information** You are interested in obtaining some information about government finance. Using the Government Resources Handbook that begins on page 690, identify possible sources you could use to (a) find the amount of money the government raised from various revenue sources; (b) read about the budget submitted to Congress by the President; and (c) examine certain figures presented in the two congressional Budget Committees' May 15th budgets.

# Foreign Policy and National Defense

## Chapter Preview

You might find headlines very much like these in your local newspaper today: President to Visit Japan, South Korea. U.S. Bars Entry of IRA Leader. Haiti's Poor Hurt by Sanctions. Israel, Palestinians to Resume Self-Rule Talks. Ukraine Agrees to Ratify Nuclear Arms Pact. Neo-Nazi Candidates Run in German Local Elections. Salvadoran President Denies Death Squad Accusations by U.S. China May Allow Red Cross to Inspect Jails. Somali Gunmen Fire on U.N. Peacekeepers. Stronger Yen Hurts Sale of Japanese Cars. U.S., Other Nations Back Creation of U.N. Human Rights Commission.

Headlines such as these say a great deal about the nature of today's world—and a great deal, too, about the focus of this chapter: the role of the United States in world affairs.

### Before you read this chapter:

- **Describe** three ongoing situations that point up the fact that the post-cold war world is indeed a dangerous place.
- **Predict** the primary goal of United States foreign policy.

### As you read, focus on the main objective of each section. Understand:

1. The historic and continuing goal of America's foreign and defense policies.
2. The foreign and defense policy-making structure.
3. The role of other federal agencies in making and carrying out foreign and defense policies.
4. The major features of American foreign policy, past and present.
5. The purposes of American foreign aid and defense alliances and the role of the United Nations.

▲ **Yugoslav Conflict** As fighting in the former Yugoslavia dragged on through 1995, the United States participated in United Nations-approved air strikes against Serbians in an attempt to bring a halt to the conflict.

# 1 Foreign and Defense Policy: An Overview

## Find Out:

- Why must the United States have a policy for its relationship with the rest of the world?
- What makes up a nation's foreign policy?
- Which officials are primarily responsible for United States foreign policy?

## Key Terms:

isolationism, foreign policy

Do you know where your shoes were made? The odds are that they are not American-made, that they came instead from Mexico or Korea or Italy or somewhere else abroad. What about your shirt or blouse and your pants or skirt? Where were they made? And what about your stereo, compact disc player, television set, watch, umbrella, baseball glove, bicycle?

Those questions, and their answers, ought to begin to suggest to you why the topic of this section is so vitally important to you.

## From Isolationism to Internationalism

Through much of this nation's history, American politics turned largely on questions of domestic concern. For more than 150 years, the American people were chiefly interested in what was happening at home. For most Americans, foreign affairs were matters of little or no concern to them. This country's relationships with countries abroad were largely shaped by a policy of **isolationism**—a purposeful refusal to become generally involved in the affairs of the rest of the world.

The past 50 years have been marked by a profound change in the place of the United States in world affairs, however. That historic shift from isolationism to internationalism brought major changes in American foreign and defense policies. World War II finally convinced the

American people that neither they nor anyone else can live in isolation—that in many ways, whether we like it or not, the world of today is indeed "one world."

That this is one world—that it is, in reality, a "global village"—can be seen most clearly in terms of the nation's security. The well-being of everyone in this country and in fact the very survival of the United States are closely affected by much that happens elsewhere on the globe. If nothing else, the realities of ultra-rapid travel and of instantaneous worldwide communications make that point abundantly clear.

Wars and other political upheavals anywhere on the globe have a decided impact on the interests of the United States—and on the daily lives of every American. Four times in this century the United States has become involved in major wars thousands of miles from its shores; and in several other instances this nation has committed its forces to lesser, but still significant, battles abroad. The nation's security has also been threatened by other events elsewhere on the globe—by the acts of terrorists in Europe and Asia, by racial strife in South Africa, by revolu-

tions in Latin America, Arab-Israeli conflicts in the Middle East, and by many others.

Economic conditions elsewhere also have a direct effect on and in this country. Japanese automobiles, European steel, Arab oil, Brazilian coffee, Italian shoes, and all of the many other things that Americans buy from abroad make that fact an obvious one, every day.

The world of the 1990s cannot be described as "one world" in all respects, however. Relations between the United States and what used to be the Soviet Union have improved remarkably over the past few years, yes: but as you have read, the world remains a dangerous place. Iraq's 1990 invasion of Kuwait and the subsequent Gulf War in 1991 is major proof of that fact. So, too, are the problems the United States has faced in hunger- and strife-torn Somalia, unrest in the former Soviet Union, continuing Arab-Israeli enmities in the Middle East, civil wars in Afghanistan, Morocco, Sri Lanka, the Balkan nations that once were Yugoslavia, and other places, and much more.

Most Americans agree that in such a divided world it is only through policies that are designed to promote and protect the security and well-being of all nations that the security and well-being of the United States, and its citizens, can be assured.

## Foreign Policy: What It Is

Every nation's **foreign policy** is actually many different policies on many different topics. It is made up of all of the stands and actions that a nation takes in every aspect of its relationships with other countries—diplomatic, military, commercial, and all others. To put the point another way, a nation's foreign policy is made up of all of its many foreign policies. In short, it includes everything that that nation's government says and everything that it does in world affairs.

Thus, American foreign policy consists of all of the Federal Government's official statements and all of its actions as it conducts this nation's foreign relations. It involves such matters as treaties and alliances, international trade, the defense budget, foreign economic and military aid, the United Nations, nuclear weapons testing, and disarmament negotiations. It also

**Foreign Policy in Action:** President Clinton and Russian President Boris Yeltsin met in Vancouver, Canada for their first summit meeting. After their talks, both leaders agreed that the United States and Russia had forged a "new democratic partnership."

includes the American position on oil imports, grain exports, immigration, space exploration, fishing rights in the Atlantic and Pacific oceans, cultural exchange programs, economic sanctions, computer technology exports, and a great many other matters.

Some foreign policies remain largely unchanged over time. For example, an insistence on freedom of the seas has been a basic part of American policy from the very earliest years of American history. Other policies are more flexible, subject to change as circumstances change. Thus, only a very few years ago, resisting the ambitions of the Soviet Union was a basic part of American foreign policy. Today, the United States and many of the states that once made up the Soviet Union are seeking and building ever closer political, military, and economic ties with one another.

At times the United States can take the lead in world affairs. It can launch new policies and take initiatives that seek to gain support and heighten America's power and prestige abroad. It has done so on a number of occasions, as you will see later in this chapter—including, for example, the Open Door policy in China at the turn of the last century, the Marshall Plan after World War II, and the forging of the coalition of nations that defeated Iraq in the Persian Gulf War in 1991.

Very often, American policy must be defensive in nature. Leaders must adjust it to meet the actions of some other country. Thus, containment—resisting the spread of Soviet influence—became a basic part of United States foreign policy soon after World War II.

As you will read, this policy of containment began with the Truman Doctrine in 1947, in direct response to the Soviet Union's policy of aggressive expansion in the immediate postwar years; and it was to remain a basic part of American policy until the collapse of the Soviet Union and its communist empire in the late 1980s and early 1990s.

## The President's Responsibilities

The President is both the nation's chief diplomat and the commander in chief of its armed forces. As you have seen, Congress also has significant powers in the fields of foreign and military affairs, especially with its power of the purse, its power to declare war, and in the Senate's role in the treaty-making and the appointment processes.[1] But, as you have also seen, it is the President who dominates those policy fields. Both constitutionally and by tradition, the President bears the major responsibility for both the making and conduct of foreign policy.[2]

The President depends on a number of officials and agencies to meet the immense responsibilities that come with his role as chief diplomat and commander in chief. Recall, you considered the National Security Council, in the Executive Office of the President, in Chapter 14, Section 5. Here, you will look at the other elements of what is often called the foreign policy bureaucracy. You will begin with the Departments of State and Defense, and then encounter several others.

## Section 1 Review

**1. Identify:** isolationism, foreign policy
**2.** Why can the foreign and defense policies of the United States be properly called this country's national security policy?
**3.** (a) In what ways does this nation exist in "one world"? (b) In what ways does it not?
**4.** Of what does a nation's foreign policy consist?
**5.** Who is the commander in chief of the nation's armed forces?

**Critical Thinking**

**6. Distinguishing Fact from Opinion** (p. 19) The text says the world remains a dangerous place. (a) Do you agree with this statement? (b) Why or why not?

★

---

[1]See, especially, Chapter 11, Section 2.
[2]See Chapter 14, Section 3. Recall, the Constitution forbids to the States any role in foreign relations, Article I, Section 10, Clauses 1 and 3.

# 2 The Departments of State and Defense

## Find Out:

- What is the secretary of state's key role in the making and conduct of foreign policy?
- How is the State Department organized?
- What is the key role of the secretary of defense in the making and conduct of national security policy?
- How is the Department of Defense organized?

## Key Terms:

right of legation, ambassador, passport, visa, diplomatic immunity

As Alexander Hamilton noted in *The Federalist* No. 72, the Framers expected that "the actual conduct" of the nation's foreign affairs would be in the hands of "the assistants and deputies of the Chief Magistrate."

As you will see in this section, many of the President's "assistants and deputies" in the field of foreign affairs are in the State Department. In addition, the Department of Defense assists the President in the conduct of military affairs.

▲ **Secretary of State**   Warren Christopher, the highest ranking official in the Clinton cabinet, meets with Israeli leaders during a tour of the Middle East in February 1993. The amount of influence that the secretary of state has on foreign policy is decided by the President.

## The State Department

The State Department, headed by the secretary of state, is the President's right arm in foreign affairs. The secretary is named by the President, subject to confirmation by the Senate. It is to the secretary and to the Department of State that the President looks for advice in both the formulation and conduct of the nation's foreign policy.

The secretary of state ranks first among the members of the President's cabinet. This is true in part because of the importance of the office, but it is especially the case because the Department of State was the first of the now 14 executive departments created by Congress.

The Department of Foreign Affairs, which had first been created in 1781 under the Articles of Confederation, was re-created by Congress in 1789 as the first major unit in the executive branch under the Constitution. Later that same year, its name was changed to the Department of State, and President Washington appointed Thomas Jefferson as the nation's first secretary of state. For 200 years now, 61 other men, many of them quite distinguished, have held that important post.

The duties of the secretary relate almost solely to foreign affairs today: to the making and conduct of policy and to managing the work of the department, its many overseas posts, and its more than 25,000 employees.[3]

Some Presidents have relied heavily on the secretary of state; others have chosen to keep foreign policy more tightly in their own hands. In either case, the secretary has been an important and influential officer in every administration.

## Organization and Key Components

The department is organized along both geographic and functional lines. Some of its

---

[3]The secretary does have some domestic responsibilities. Thus, when Richard Nixon resigned the presidency on August 9, 1974, his formal, legal announcement of that fact had to be submitted to Secretary of State Henry Kissinger. Over the years, the secretary and the department have had (and been relieved of) various domestic functions—including, for example, publishing the nation's laws, issuing patents, and supervising the decennial census.

agencies, such as the Bureau of African Affairs and the Bureau of Near Eastern Affairs, deal with matters involving certain countries or regions of the world. Other agencies have more broadly defined responsibilities, such as the Bureau of Economic and Business Affairs and the Bureau for Refugee Programs. Most of these bureaus are headed by an assistant secretary and include several "offices"—for example, the Passport Office and the Visa Office in the Bureau of Consular Affairs.

**The Foreign Service**   More than 4,200 men and women now represent the United States abroad as members of the Foreign Service.

Under international law[4] every nation has the **right of legation**—the right to send and receive diplomatic representatives. An ancient practice, its roots can be traced back to the Egyptian civilization of 6,000 years ago.

The Second Continental Congress named this nation's first foreign service officer in 1778, when it chose Benjamin Franklin to be America's minister to France.

**Ambassadors**   Today the United States is represented by an ambassador stationed at the capital of each state the United States recognizes.[5] American embassies are found in more than 150 countries around the world today.

The President appoints ambassadors, with Senate consent, and they serve at the President's pleasure. Some of their posts are much desired political plums, and whenever a new President moves into the White House, he typically makes many new appointments. Too often, Presidents have appointed people to ambassadorships and other major diplomatic posts as

**America Abroad**   Jean Kennedy Smith, American ambassador to Ireland, meets that country's prime minister, Albert Reynolds. Ambassador Smith's brother, Senator Ted Kennedy (D., Massachusetts), looks on.

reward for their support—financial and otherwise—of the President's election to office.

President Truman named the first woman as an ambassador, to Denmark, in 1949. President Johnson appointed the first African American (also a woman), as ambassador to Luxembourg in 1965. Today, several women, African Americans, and other minority persons hold high rank in the Foreign Service.

Each American **ambassador** is the personal representative of the President of the United States, and he or she reports to the President through the secretary of state. Each of them must keep the President fully informed of events in the host country, negotiate diplomatic agreements, protect the rights of American citizens abroad, and do whatever else is in the best interests of the United States.[6]

---

[4]International law consists of those rules and principles that guide sovereign states in their dealings with one another and their treatment of foreign nationals (private persons and groups). Its sources include treaties, decisions of international courts, and custom, with treaties being the most important source today.

[5]See page 362. An ambassador's official title is *Ambassador Extraordinary and Plenipotentiary*. When the office is vacant or the ambassador is absent, the post is usually filled by a next-ranking Foreign Service officer in the embassy. That officer, temporarily in charge of embassy affairs, is known as the *chargé d'affaires*.

---

[6]The United States also has some 120 consular offices abroad. There, Foreign Service officers promote American interests in a multitude of ways—e.g., encouraging trade, gathering intelligence data, advising persons who seek to enter this country, and aiding American citizens who are abroad and in need of legal advice or other help.

To carry out these duties effectively, an ambassador must have the closest possible contacts with the leaders of the host country as well as with its people. A well-grounded knowledge of the language, history, customs, and culture of that country is an almost indispensable qualification for the job. To help with their duties, ambassadors have the assistance of a number of skilled advisors.

**Special Diplomats**   Those persons whom the President names to certain other top diplomatic posts also carry the rank of ambassador—for example, the United States representative to the UN and the American member of the North Atlantic Treaty Council; page 448. The President also gives the personal rank of ambassador to those who take on special assignments abroad—for example, representing the United States at an international conference on arms limitations.

**Passports**   A **passport** is a certificate issued by a government to its citizens who travel or live abroad. Passports entitle their holders to the privileges accorded to them by international custom and treaties. Few states will admit persons who do not hold valid passports. Legally, no American citizen may leave the United States without a passport, except for trips to Canada, Mexico, and a few other nearby places.

The State Department's Passport Office now issues some four million passports to American citizens each year. Passports are not the same as visas. A **visa** is a permit to enter another state and must be obtained from the country one wishes to enter. Most visas to enter this country are issued at American consulates abroad.

## Diplomatic Immunity

In international law, every sovereign state is supreme within its own boundaries, and all persons or things found within its territory are subject to its jurisdiction.

As a major exception to that rule of international law, ambassadors are regularly granted **diplomatic immunity**. That is, they are not subject to the laws of the state to which they are accredited. They cannot be arrested, sued, or taxed. Their official residences (embassies) cannot be entered or searched without their consent, and their official communications, papers, and other properties are protected in the same way. All other embassy personnel and their families normally receive this same immunity.

Diplomatic immunity is essential to the ability of every nation to conduct its foreign relations. The practice assumes that diplomats will not abuse their privileged status. If a host government finds a diplomat's conduct unacceptable, that official may be declared *persona non grata* and expelled from the country. The mistreatment of diplomats is a major breach of international law.

Diplomatic immunity is a generally accepted practice. But there are exceptions. The most serious breach in modern times occurred in Iran in late 1979. Militant followers of the Ayatollah Khomeini seized the American embassy in Teheran on November 4 of that year; 52 Americans were taken hostage and held for 444 days. The Iranians finally released the hostages moments after Ronald Reagan became President on January 20, 1981.

## The Defense Department

A nation's military policies are an integral part of its foreign policy. Karl von Clausewitz, the Prussian general and military philosopher, put that point in these oft-quoted words more than 150 years ago: "War is the continuation of political relations by other means."

▲ **Secretary of Defense**   William Perry heads the mighty Defense Department, which boasts over 2.5 million uniformed and civilian employees.

Congress established what is today called the Defense Department in the National Security Act of 1947. It is the present-day successor to two historic cabinet-level agencies: the War Department, created by Congress in 1789, and the Navy Department, created in 1798.[7]

**Civil Control of the Military** The authors of the Constitution understood, absolutely, the importance of the nation's defense. They emphasized that fact clearly in the Preamble, and they underscored it in the body of the Constitution by mentioning defense more frequently than any other governmental function.

The Framers also saw the dangers inherent in military power. They knew that its very existence can pose a threat to free government. For that reason, the Constitution is studded with provisions to keep the military always subject to the control of the nation's civilian authorities.

Thus, the Constitution makes the elected President the commander in chief of the armed forces. To the same end, it gives wide military powers to Congress—that is, to the elected representatives of the people.[8]

The United States has obeyed the principle of civilian control throughout its history. That principle has been a major factor in the making of defense policy, and in the creation and the

"No, no. When I say this new secret weapon can slip past their defenses undetected, I'm not referring to the Russians, I'm referring to Congress."

Drawing by Stevenson; ©1986 The New Yorker Magazine, Inc.

▲ **Interpreting Political Cartoons** The system of checks and balances ensures that the military remains subject to civilian control. How does this cartoonist convey the opinion that this check on the military is necessary?

staffing of the various agencies responsible for the execution of that policy. The point is clearly illustrated by this fact: The National Security Act of 1947 provides that the secretary of defense cannot have served on active duty in any of the armed forces for at least 10 years before being named to that post.

**The Secretary of Defense** The Defense Department is headed by the secretary of defense, who is appointed by the President subject to Senate confirmation. The secretary, who serves at the President's pleasure, has two major responsibilities: (1) as the President's chief aide and adviser in making and carrying out defense policy; and (2) as the operating head of the Defense Department, with its nearly 1.7 million men and women in uniform and more than 900,000 civilian employees.

The secretary's huge domain is often called the Pentagon—because of its massive five-sided headquarters building on the Virginia side of the Potomac River, across from the Capitol. Year in and year out, its operations take a large slice of the federal budget—today, in fact, almost 20 percent of all federal spending. The

---

[7]Congress created the Defense Department in order to unify the nation's armed forces—that is, to bring the then-separate army (including the air force) and the navy under the control of a single cabinet department. The new department was first called the National Military Establishment; Congress gave it its present name in 1949. The secretary of defense has been known by that title from 1947 on.

[8]Recall that the Constitution makes defense a national function and practically excludes the States from that field. Each State does have a militia, which it may use to keep the peace within its own borders. Today the organized portion of the militia is the National Guard. Congress has the power (Article I, Section 8, Clauses 15 and 16) to "provide for calling forth the militia" and to provide for organizing, arming, and disciplining it.

Congress first delegated to the President the power to call the militia into federal service in 1795, and the commander in chief has had that authority ever since. Today the governor of each State is the commander in chief of that State's units of the Army and the Air National Guard, except when the President has ordered those units into federal service.

**Across the River from the Capitol** The Pentagon, which houses the Department of Defense, covers 29 acres and is one of the largest office buildings in the world.

end of the cold war has brought some slight reductions in military spending; still, total outlays for the nation's defense will exceed $260 billion in fiscal year 1995.

**Chief Civilian Aides** The secretary's chief assistant, the deputy secretary, directs the day-to-day operations of the department. There are a number of other civilians at the top levels of the Pentagon. The most important of them are three under secretaries—one who serves as the secretary's chief policy adviser, another in charge of all of the department's research and development programs and its multi-billion dollar purchasing activities, and a third who is responsible for all of the department's personnel matters and all aspects of its military readiness programs. There are also several assistant secretaries, often called ASDs, and the secretaries of the army, the navy, and the air force. All of them are appointed by the President with Senate consent.

**Chief Military Aides** The five members of the Joint Chiefs of Staff serve as the principal military advisers to the secretary, and to the President and the National Security Council, as well. They are the highest ranking uniformed officers in the armed services: the chairman of the Joint Chiefs, the army chief of staff, the

chief of naval operations, the commandant of the Marine Corps, and the air force chief of staff. Each of them is also named by the President, subject to Senate approval.

## The Military Departments

The three military departments—the Departments of the Army, the Navy, and the Air Force—are major units (sub-cabinet departments) within the Department of Defense. Each is headed by a civilian secretary, named by the President and directly responsible to the secretary of defense. The nation's armed forces—the army, the navy, and the air force—operate within that unified structure.[9]

**The Department of the Army** The army is the largest of the armed services, and also the oldest. The American Continental Army, now the United States Army, was established by the Second Continental Congress on June 14, 1775—more than a year before the Declaration of Independence.

The army is essentially a ground-based force, responsible for military operations on land. The army must be ready (1) to defeat any attack on the United States itself and (2) to take swift and forceful action to protect American interests in any other part of the world. It must organize, train, and equip its active duty forces—the Regular Army—and its reserve units—the Army National Guard and the Army Reserve—for those purposes. All of its forces are under the direct command of the army's highest ranking officer, the chief of staff.

The Regular Army is the nation's standing army, the heart of its land forces. There are now some 500,000 men and 40,000 women on active duty in the army—officers and enlisted

---

[9]The United States Marine Corps is a separate branch of the armed forces, but, for organizational purposes, it is located within the Navy Department.

The Coast Guard is also a branch of the armed forces. It is organized as a military service, with a present strength of some 37,000 commissioned officers and enlisted personnel. Since 1967, the Coast Guard has been located in the Department of Transportation. At the President's direction, the Coast Guard becomes a part of the United States Navy.

personnel, professional soldiers, and volunteers. The United States is downsizing the army in the post-cold war environment of the 1990s; its authorized strength is scheduled to drop to some 500,000 in 1996. Women now serve in all of the Regular Army's units and, over recent years, their roles have come to include many combat-related duties in the army and in each of the other armed services, as well.

The army's combat units are made up of soldiers trained and equipped to fight enemy forces. The infantry takes, holds, and defends land areas. The artillery supports the infantry, seeks to destroy enemy concentrations with its heavier guns, and gives antiaircraft cover. The armored cavalry also supports the infantry, using armored vehicles and helicopters to spearhead

assaults and oppose enemy counteroffensives.

The other units of the army provide the many services and supplies for the soldiers in those combat organizations. They could not fight without the help of those other troops: the soldiers of the engineer, quartermaster, signal, ordnance, transportation, chemical, military police, finance, and medical corps.

**The Department of the Navy** The United States Navy was first formed as the Continental Navy—a fledgling naval force formed by the Second Continental Congress on October 13, 1775. From that day to this, its major responsibility has been sea warfare and defense.

The chief of naval operations (CNO) is the navy's highest ranking officer and is responsible

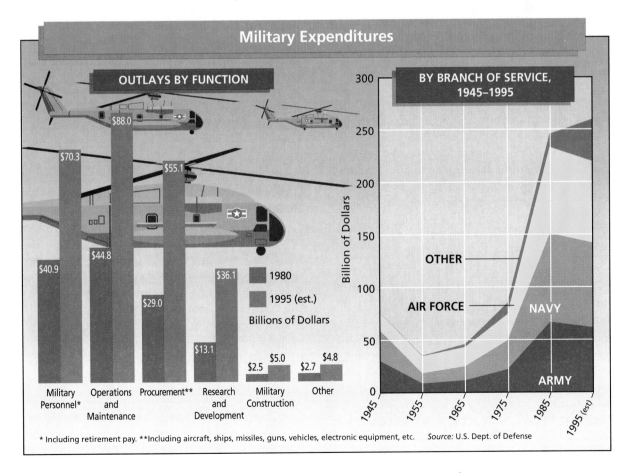

**Military Expenditures**

OUTLAYS BY FUNCTION

$88.0
$70.3
$55.1
$44.8
$40.9
$36.1
$29.0
$13.1
$2.5  $5.0  $2.7  $4.8

■ 1980
■ 1995 (est.)

Billions of Dollars

Military Personnel* | Operations and Maintenance | Procurement** | Research and Development | Military Construction | Other

BY BRANCH OF SERVICE, 1945–1995

Billion of Dollars

300
250
200
150
100
50
0

OTHER
AIR FORCE
NAVY
ARMY

1945  1955  1965  1975  1985  1995 (est.)

* Including retirement pay. **Including aircraft, ships, missiles, guns, vehicles, electronic equipment, etc.    *Source:* U.S. Dept. of Defense

▲ **Interpreting Graphs** How does the growth in military spending in the 1980s compare with its growth in other decades? After examining outlays by function, determine what area of military spending has increased the most since 1980. On what was the increase spent?

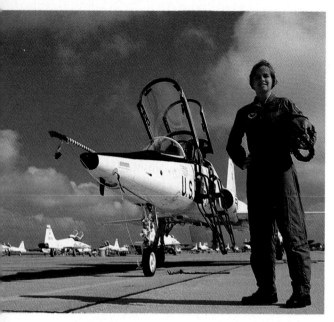

**Fighter Pilot**   In 1993 women became eligible to pilot and serve in combat on fighters and bombers in all four branches of the military. Restrictions on women in certain ground combat jobs still exist.

for its preparations and readiness for war and for its use in combat. Some 470,000 officers and enlisted personnel, including nearly 40,000 women, serve in the navy today; their number is slated to drop to 450,000 in 1996.

The United States Marine Corps was established by the Second Continental Congress on November 10, 1775. Today it operates as a separate armed service, within the Navy Department but not under the control of the chief of naval operations. Its commandant answers directly to the secretary of the navy for the efficiency, readiness, and performance of the corps.

The marines are essentially a combat-ready land force for the navy. They have two major combat missions: (1) to seize or defend land bases from which the ships of the fleet and the navy and marine air arms can operate and (2) to carry out other land operations essential to a naval campaign. Today some 165,000 men and nearly 8,000 women serve in the USMC.

**The Department of the Air Force**   The air force is the youngest of the military services. Congress established the United States Air

Force and made it a separate branch of the armed forces in the National Security Act of 1947. However, its history dates back to 1907, when the army assigned an officer and two enlisted men to a new unit, the Aeronautical Division of the army's Signal Corps. They were ordered to take "charge of all matters pertaining to military ballooning, air machines and all kindred subjects."

Today the USAF is the nation's first line of defense. It has primary responsibility for military air and aerospace operations. In time of war, its major duties are to defend the United States, attack and defeat enemy air, ground, and sea forces, strike military and other war-related targets in enemy territory, and provide transport and combat support for land and naval operations. The air force played a major role in the swift defeat of Iraq during the Persian Gulf War.

The air force now has about 425,000 officers and enlisted personnel, including more than 50,000 women—all under the direct command of the chief of staff of the air force. The authorized strength of the USAF will level out at just over 400,000 in 1996.

# Section 2 Review

**1. Define:** right of legation, ambassador, passport, visa, diplomatic immunity
**2.** What is the secretary of state's first responsibility?
**3.** (a) What is the Foreign Service? (b) What are the principal duties of an ambassador?
**4.** For what reason does the Constitution provide for civilian control of the military?
**5.** What are the two major roles of the secretary of defense?
**6.** Briefly describe the basic military components of the Defense Department.

**Critical Thinking**

**7. Identifying Assumptions** (p. 19) Until recently, women were barred, by law, from all combat roles in the armed forces. What does this suggest about the military's attitude toward women? The view of society at large?

★

# 3 Other Foreign/Defense Policy Agencies

**Find Out:**

- What federal agencies, in addition to the Departments of State and Defense, are involved in making and carrying out foreign and defense policies?
- What roles do these departments play?

**Key Term:**

draft

How many federal agencies, in addition to the Departments of State and Defense, are involved with the nation's foreign affairs? Dozens of them. The Immigration and Naturalization Service deals with those who come here from abroad. The Customs Service combats international smuggling operations. The Public Health Service works with the United Nations and foreign governments to conquer diseases and meet other health problems in many parts of the world. The Coast Guard keeps an iceberg patrol in the North Atlantic to protect the shipping of all nations. . . .

A recitation of this sort could go on and on. But, as you will see, this section deals with those other agencies that are most directly involved in the foreign and defense policy fields.

## The Central Intelligence Agency

The CIA is a key part of the foreign policy establishment. Created by Congress in 1947, the CIA works under the direction of the National Security Council. The "agency," as it is often called, is headed by a director appointed by the President and confirmed by the Senate.

On paper, the CIA has three major tasks: (1) to coordinate the information-gathering activities of all State, Defense, and other federal agencies involved in the areas of foreign affairs and national defense, (2) to analyze and evaluate all data collected by those agencies, and (3) to brief the President and the National Security Council—that is, keep them fully informed of all of that intelligence.

The CIA is far more than a coordinating and reporting body, however. It also conducts its own worldwide intelligence operations. In fact, it is a major "cloak-and-dagger" agency. Much of the information it gathers comes from such more or less open sources as foreign newspapers and other publications, radio broadcasts, travelers, satellite photos, and the like. But a large share of information comes from its own secret, covert activities. Those operations cover the full range of espionage.

The CIA's work is regularly shrouded in deepest secrecy. Even Congress has generally shied away from more than a surface check on its activities. Indeed, the agency's operating funds are disguised in several places in the federal budget each year.

When Congress established the CIA it recognized the need for such an organization in a trouble-filled world—and most agree that that need continues today. But Congress also saw the dangers inherent in a supersecret intelligence agency that operates outside the realm of public scrutiny and knowledge. Therefore, the National Security Act of 1947 expressly denies the CIA the authority to conduct any investigative, surveillance, or other clandestine activities within the United States. The agency has not always obeyed that command, however.

## The United States Information Agency

The United States Information Agency (USIA) is basically a propaganda unit. Its mission is to promote the image of the United States and to sell its policies and its way of life abroad.

The USIA works to sell the United States in a number of ways: by making radio and television broadcasts; distributing publications; producing films and tapes; sponsoring academic exchange programs; organizing cultural exchanges for athletes, artists, and leaders in professional fields such as medicine and politics; and using various other channels. It operates more than 200 libraries, film centers, and other posts in some 130 foreign countries.

The USIA is best known for the Voice of America. The VOA's round-the-clock radio programs are beamed in more than 40 languages to audiences all over the world.

## The National Aeronautics and Space Administration

The modern space age is only some 35 years old. It began on October 4, 1957, when the Soviet Union put its first satellite, *Sputnik I*, in space. The first American satellite, *Explorer I*, was fired into orbit a few months later, on January 31, 1958. From that point on, a great number of space vehicles have been thrust into the heavens by both of the superpowers.

NASA is an independent agency created by Congress in 1958 to handle this nation's space programs. Today, the scope of those programs

▲ **Outer Space** *Atlantis* lifts off from the Kennedy Space Center in Florida. NASA's space shuttle program carries out publicly and privately funded projects and top-secret military missions.

is truly extraordinary. NASA's work now ranges from basic research that focuses on the origin, evolution, and structure of the universe to explorations of outer space and the development of a permanently occupied space station to be deployed sometime in the latter 1990s.

The military importance of NASA's work can hardly be exaggerated, but Congress has ordered the space agency to bend its efforts "to peaceful purposes for the benefit of all humankind," as well. NASA's research and development efforts have opened new frontiers in several fields: in astronomy, physics, and the environmental sciences, in communications, medicine, and weather forecasting, and in many more.

NASA conducts its operations at a number of flight centers, laboratories, and other installations throughout the country. Among the best known are the Kennedy Space Center, at Cape Canaveral in Florida; the Johnson Space Center, near Houston, Texas; the Ames Research Center and the Jet Propulsion Laboratory, both in California; and the Goddard Space Flight Center, at Greenbelt, Maryland.

Over the years, NASA's accomplishments were so many, its programs so successful, that space flights and space probes seemed to become almost routine. Tragedy struck on January 28, 1986, however. The space shuttle *Challenger* exploded moments after liftoff from Cape Canaveral, and all of its seven-member crew died.

NASA appears to have recovered from the disaster to the point where it now tries to launch as many as 10 space vehicles each year, some of them with secret military payloads.

## The United States Arms Control and Disarmament Agency

The ACDA is responsible for American participation in arms limitations and disarmament negotiations with other nuclear powers. Its director also serves as the principal adviser to the President, the National Security Council, and the secretaries of state and defense in all matters dealing with those policy areas.

Much of the agency's work has centered on nuclear test ban and arms limitations talks with the former Soviet Union. Those discussions were held periodically since the late 1950s, most often in Geneva, Switzerland. American-Soviet relations were at best unfriendly and most often hostile well into the late 1980s. Even so, the two superpowers managed to conclude several agreements.

The most recent major U.S.-Soviet arms agreement, the Strategic Arms Reduction Treaty (START), was signed by Presidents Bush and Gorbachev at a summit meeting in Moscow in 1991. That pact obligated both nations to destroy up to half of all their intercontinental ballistic missiles (ICBMs) over the ensuing seven years. The treaty was intended to be a step toward the eventual elimination of all missiles capable of delivering nuclear warheads over long distances.

The United States and the Soviet Union ratified the Intermediate Range Nuclear Force (INF) Treaty in 1988. That agreement called on both nations to eliminate *all* intermediate range missiles—those capable of delivering warheads 300 to 3,400 miles—and this goal had been achieved by 1992.

The successes of the 1980s and early 1990s assumed added importance with the breakup of the Soviet Union in late 1991 and the resulting potential for political turmoil in that region.

## The Selective Service System

Through most of American history, the armed forces have depended on voluntary enlistments to fill their ranks. But from 1940 to 1973, the **draft**—conscription, compulsory military service—was a major source of military manpower. At present, the draft, which is administered by the Selective Service System, exists only on a standby basis.

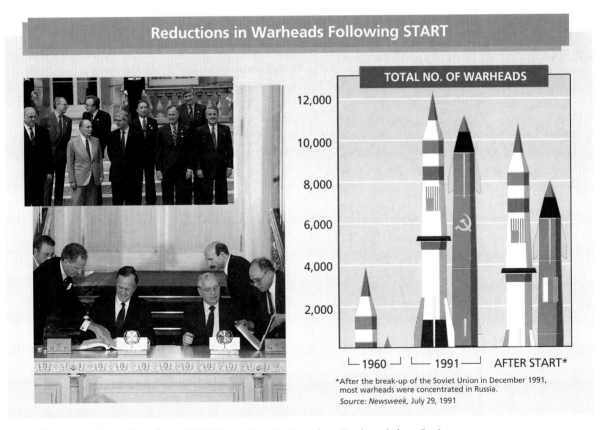

**Reductions in Warheads Following START**

**TOTAL NO. OF WARHEADS**

12,000
10,000
8,000
6,000
4,000
2,000

└ 1960 ┘  └ 1991 ┘  AFTER START*

*After the break-up of the Soviet Union in December 1991, most warheads were concentrated in Russia.

*Source: Newsweek, July 29, 1991*

▲ **Interpreting Graphs** START, ratified by President Bush and then Soviet President Gorbachev in July 1991, is an ambitious plan to phase out both countries' stocks of intercontinental ballistic missiles. World leaders (inset) were briefed on START when Bush visited London the same month. What does the graph show about the build-up of United States/Soviet warheads since 1960?

## How to Register for the Draft

In 1980 the Selective Service System was reinstated. All eligible males must register for military service.

**1. Determine whether you must register.** All male citizens and aliens must register within 30 days after their 18th birthday. Exceptions include those already on active duty with the armed forces and nonimmigrant aliens.

**2. Determine where you should go to register.** You can register for the draft at any United States post office.

**3. Complete a registration form.** The form will ask for such information as your name, address, sex, date of birth, social security number, and current telephone number.

**4. Date and sign the form in the presence of a clerk at the post office.** Be sure to use ink on the form.

▲ **Interpreting Charts** This chart goes through the steps necessary to register for military service. Which major segment of the population is not included in the draft?

Conscription has a long history in this country. Several colonies and later nine States required all able-bodied males to serve in their militia. However, in the 1790s Congress rejected proposals for national compulsory military service.

Both the North and the South did use a limited conscription program in the Civil War. It was not until 1917, however, that a national draft was first used in this country, even in wartime. More than 2.8 million of the 4.7 million men who served in World War I were drafted under the terms of the Selective Service Act of 1917.

The nation's first peacetime draft came with the Selective Service and Training Act of 1940, as World War II raged in Europe. More than 10 million of the 16.3 million Americans in uniform in World War II entered the service under that law.

The World War II draft was ended in 1947. The crises of the postwar period, however, quickly moved Congress to revive the draft with the Selective Service Act of 1948. From 1948 to 1973, nearly 5 million young men were drafted.

Mounting criticisms of compulsory military service, fed by opposition to Vietnam policy, led many Americans to call for an end to the draft in the late 1960s. Fewer than 30,000 men were drafted in 1972, and selective service was suspended in 1973. The draft law is still on the books, however.

The draft law places a military obligation on all males in the United States between the ages of 18 1/2 and 26. Over the years in which the draft operated, it was largely conducted through hundreds of local selective service boards. All young men had to register for service at age 18. The local boards then selected those who were to enter the armed forces.

As of 1980, the registration requirement was back in place. President Carter reactivated it, and his executive order is still in force. All young males are required to sign up soon after they reach their 18th birthday.[10]

## Section 3 Review

**1. Identify:** draft
**2.** Why is it incorrect to view national security policy only in terms of the President and the State and Defense departments?
**3.** What is the primary function of each of these governmental agencies: (a) the USIA? (b) NASA? (c) ACDA?
**4.** What is the status of the selective service system today?

**Critical Thinking**

**5. Checking Consistency** (p. 19) Is the concept of an intelligence agency whose actions can be kept secret from the people consistent with the principle of popular sovereignty?

---

[10]The President's power to order the induction of men into the armed forces expired on June 30, 1973. If the draft is ever to be reactivated, Congress must first renew that presidential authority. Recall that the Supreme Court first upheld the constitutionality of the draft in the *Selective Draft Law Cases* in 1918. The Court also found its all-male features constitutional in *Rostker* v. *Goldberg* in 1981; see page 555.

## Helping Victims of Natural Disasters

On December 7, 1988, a devastating earthquake struck the Soviet Republic of Armenia. In the days following, aftershocks continued to terrify the local population. The official death toll was estimated to be about 40,000; as many as 400,000 Armenian men, women, and children were left homeless amid the twisted rubble of crumbled buildings. The only possible good that could be gleaned from this massive tragedy was the selfless outpouring of aid that flooded into the Soviet Union from around the world.

### International Relief Efforts

As the United States government responded immediately with offers of medicine, medical equipment, doctors, and trained rescue teams, United States citizens of all ages amassed money, clothing, and other supplies under the auspices of the American Red Cross. The Red Cross is an organization whose goal is to relieve human suffering. It has chapters in the United States and in more than 135 countries around the world. Based in Washington, D.C., the work of the American Red Cross depends on more than 10 million volunteers, including students, veterans, and senior citizens. In Glendale, California, a relief group collected $7 million in pledges. Equally significant, students of a school in California sent $800—the money for their school lunches. Relief aid also poured in from churches, synagogues, and colleges, as well as many private organizations.

### A New Era

Two months after the earthquake, an article by Soviet citizen Anna Lerina appeared in *Soviet Life*. Through this medium, she expressed some thoughts and feelings concerning the help that came from American citizens: "For the first time since the Second World War, the Soviet Union accepted humanitarian aid from the government of the United States. The unprecedented bridge of relief aid to Armenia that has spanned thousands of miles and many years of mistrust serves as another confirmation that the United States and the Soviet Union can live in peace and friendship."

By the end of 1991 the Soviet Republic of Armenia was an independent nation. The optimism and words of friendship expressed by the Soviet woman in *Soviet Life* were reinforced when the United States was prompt in officially recognizing Armenian independence. It is one of twelve new republics that marked the demise of the Soviet Union and the beginning of a new world order.

### Getting Involved

**1. Identify** a need in your global or local community similar to the one addressed in this case. Or, identify an organization in your global or local community that helps victims of natural disasters.

**2. Formulate** a plan for organizing volunteer efforts to help remedy this problem and identify resources which could be used in your plan. Or, formulate a plan for the organization you have chosen to help.

**3. Predict** any problems or objections you might encounter in implementing your plan.

# 4 American Foreign Policy: Past and Present

## Find Out:

- What was United States foreign policy for its first 150 years?
- What are the basic elements of American foreign policy today?
- What was the impact of the cold war on American foreign policy?

## Key Terms:

collective security, deterrence, containment

Why should you know as much as you can about history? Let a leading historian answer the question: "History is our social memory. Our memories tell us who we are, where we belong, what has worked and what has not worked, and where we seem to be going."[11]

A complete history of America's foreign relations cannot be told in these pages, of course. But you will find a review of the major themes and highlights of that history here.

## Foreign Policy from Independence Through WWI

As you read in Section 1, American foreign policy was largely built on a policy of isolationism for its first 150 years. At the time, isolationism seemed a wise policy to most Americans. The United States had a great many problems of its own, a huge continent to explore and settle, and two oceans to separate it from the rest of the world. That policy did not demand a complete separation, however. From the first, the United States developed economic and diplomatic ties abroad. In fact, isolationism was, over time, more a statement of America's desire for noninvolvement outside the Western Hemisphere than within it.

---

[11]Robert Kelly, *The Shaping of the American Past* (Englewood Cliffs, New Jersey: Prentice Hall, 1978, 2nd ed., page xxxiii.)

**The Monroe Doctrine**    James Monroe gave the policy of isolationism a wider shape in 1823. In an historic message to Congress, he proclaimed what has been known ever since as the Monroe Doctrine. In his message, President Monroe restated America's intentions to stay out of the affairs of Europe. He also warned the nations of Europe—including Russia, then in control of Alaska—to stay out of the affairs of North and South America. He declared that the United States would look on

❝ any attempt on their part to extend their system to any portion of this hemisphere as dangerous to our peace and safety.❞

At first, most Latin Americans took little notice of the doctrine. They knew that it was really the Royal Navy and British interest in their trade that protected them from European domination. Later, as the United States became more powerful, many Latin Americans came to view the doctrine as a selfish policy designed to protect American interests, not their independence.

**Continental Expansion**    By the Treaty of Paris, which officially ended the Revolutionary War in 1783, the United States held title to all of the territory from the Great Lakes in the north to Spanish Florida in the south and from the Atlantic coast westward to the Mississippi.

The United States began to fill out the continent almost at once. President Jefferson negotiated the Louisiana Purchase in 1803, and at a single stroke, the nation's size was doubled. With the Florida Purchase in 1819, the nation completed its expansion to the south.

Through the second quarter of the 19th century, the United States pursued what most Americans believed was this nation's "Manifest Destiny": the expansion of its boundaries to the Pacific Ocean. Texas was annexed in 1845. The United States obtained the Oregon Country by treaty with Great Britain in 1846. Mexico ceded what today makes up most of the southwestern quarter of the lower 48 states after its defeat in the Mexican War of 1846–1848. The southwestern limits of the United States were rounded out by the Gadsden Purchase in 1853. In 1867 the United States bought Alaska from Russia and so became a colonial power.

**The United States, a World Power** The United States emerged as a first-class power in world politics with the Spanish-American War in 1898. With Spain's decisive defeat, America gained the Philippines and Guam in the Pacific and Puerto Rico in the Caribbean. Cuba became independent, under American protection. Hawaii was also annexed in 1898.

By 1900, the United States had become a colonial power with interests extending across the continent, to Alaska, to the tip of Latin America, and across the Pacific to the Philippines.

**The Good Neighbor Policy** The threat of European intervention, which gave rise to the Monroe Doctrine, declined in the last half of the 19th century. That threat was replaced by problems within the hemisphere. Political instability, revolutions, unpaid foreign debts, and injuries to citizens and property of other countries plagued Central and South America.

Under what came to be known as the Roosevelt Corollary to the Monroe Doctrine, the United States began to police Latin America in the early 1900s. Several times, the marines were used to quell revolutions and other unrest in Nicaragua, Haiti, Cuba, and elsewhere.

In 1903 Panama revolted and became independent of Colombia, with American blessings. In the same year, the United States gained the right to build a canal across the isthmus. In 1917 the Virgin Islands were purchased from Denmark to help guard the canal. These and other steps were resented by many in Latin America. They complained of "the Colossus of the North," of "Yankee imperialism," and of "dollar diplomacy" (and many still do).

This country's Latin American policies took an important turn in the 1930s. Theodore Roosevelt's Corollary was replaced by Franklin Roosevelt's Good Neighbor Policy, a conscious attempt to win friends to the south.

The central provision of the Monroe Doctrine—the warning against foreign encroachments—is now set out in the Inter-American Treaty of Reciprocal Assistance (the Rio Pact) of 1947. Still, the United States is, without question, the dominant power in the Western Hemisphere, and the Monroe Doctrine is still a vital part of American foreign policy. The American

▲ **"Yankee Imperialism"** The Panama Canal, built by the United States as a shorter trade route to the Pacific, opened in 1914. Many Latin American nations resented the presence of the United States in the region.

invasions of Grenada in 1983 and of Panama in 1989 underscored that point.

**The Open Door in China** Historically, American foreign policy interests have centered on Europe and on Latin America. America's involvements in the Far East reach back to the mid-1800s, however. Forty-five years before the United States acquired territory in the far Pacific, the navy's Commodore Matthew Perry had opened Japan to American trade.

By the latter years of the 19th century, America's thriving trade in Asia was seriously threatened. The British, French, Germans, and Japanese were each ready to take slices of the Chinese coast as their own exclusive trading preserves. In 1899 Secretary of State John Hay announced this country's insistence on an Open Door Policy. That doctrine promoted equal trade access for all nations and a demand that China's independence and sovereignty over its own territory be preserved.

The other major powers came to accept the American position, however reluctantly. Relations between the United States and Japan worsened from that point on until the climax at Pearl Harbor in 1941. Over the same period, the United States built increasingly strong ties with China; but those ties were cut when communists won control of the Chinese mainland in 1949. For nearly 30 years, the United States and the People's Republic of China refused to recognize one another.

The realities of world politics finally forced a reshaping of American-Chinese relations in the 1970s. President Nixon made an historic visit to Beijing in 1972, and full-fledged diplomatic ties were reestablished in 1979.

Still, the People's Republic is a totalitarian state, and American policy reflects that fact—though many argue that it does not do so strongly enough. The Chinese government's brutal response to prodemocracy demonstrations by thousands of students in Beijing's Tiananmen Square in 1989 will likely color American-Chinese relations for years to come.

## The Two World Wars

Germany's submarine campaign against American shipping in the North Atlantic forced the United States out of its isolationist cocoon in 1917. America entered World War I "to make the world safe for democracy."

With the defeat of Germany and the Central Powers, however, this nation pulled back from the involvements brought on by the war. The United States refused to join the League of Nations, which had been conceived by President Woodrow Wilson. Briefly, the nation returned to its historical isolationism.

America's commitment to isolationism was finally ended by World War II. The United States became directly involved in the war when the Japanese suddenly attacked Pearl Harbor on December 7, 1941. From that point on, together with the British, the Soviets, the Chinese, and other allies, this country waged an all-out effort to defeat the Axis Powers (Germany, Italy, and Japan). America supplied most of the materials that were essential to victory. Within a short time, the United States was transformed into the world's mightiest military power.

## Foreign Policy from 1945 to Today

World War II led to an historic shift from a position of isolationism to one of internationalism. This nation's foreign policy has been cast in that newer direction for nearly 50 years now. Even so, the overall objective of that policy remains what it has always been: the protection of the security of the United States. The major features of current American foreign policy are all, as you will see, reflections of that overriding goal.

### Peace Through Collective Security

The United States, and most of the rest of a war-weary world, looked to the principle of

**FOOD WILL WIN THE WAR**
You came here seeking Freedom
You must now help to preserve it
**WHEAT is needed for the allies**
Waste nothing
UNITED STATES FOOD ADMINISTRATION

▲ **Poster Art** World War I launched the era of the propaganda poster. What technique does this poster use to convince Americans to save for the war effort?

**collective security** to keep international peace and order after World War II. America hoped to forge a world community in which at least most nations would act together against any nation that threatened the peace.

To that end, the United States took the lead in creating the United Nations in 1945. The organization's charter declares that the UN was formed to promote international cooperation and so "to save succeeding generations from the scourge of war . . . and to maintain international peace and security"; see pages 450–453.

It soon became clear that the future of the world would not be shaped in the UN, however. Rather, international security would depend largely on the nature of the relations between the two superpowers, the United States and the Soviet Union. These relations, never very close, quickly deteriorated—and for the next 40 years American foreign policy was built around that fact.

Relations between the superpowers have improved dramatically in recent years. Still, collective security remains a cornerstone of American policy. The United States has supported the United Nations and other efforts to further international cooperation. And, because the UN did not immediately fulfill the dreams on which it was founded, the United States soon took another path to collective security—a network of regional alliances, as you will see.

The principle of collective security was at work in the 1991 Persian Gulf War, too. The United States led the diplomatic and then the military effort to force Iraq to withdraw from Kuwait—an effort supported by the United Nations and nearly all of its member states.

**Deterrence** The policy of deterrence is another major plank of current American foreign policy. It was begun under President Truman, as the antagonisms between the United States and the Soviet Union grew after World War II. Every President since has maintained it. **Deterrence** is the policy of making America and its allies so militarily strong that its very strength will deter (discourage, prevent) any attack. In short, that policy comes down to this: America's military might is most effective if, in fact, it does not have to be used.

## Resisting Soviet Aggression

One cannot hope to understand either recent or current American foreign policy without a grounding in the long years of the cold war—the more than 40 years in which relations between the two superpowers were at least tense and, more often than not, distinctly hostile.

The United States had planned to work with the Soviet Union, particularly through the UN, to build international cooperation and keep the peace in the postwar world. Those plans were quickly dashed, however.

At the Yalta Conference in early 1945, Soviet Premier Josef Stalin had agreed with President Franklin Roosevelt and British Prime Minister Winston Churchill that "democratic governments" would be established by "free elections" in the liberated countries of Eastern Europe. Instead, the Soviets imposed communist governments on those countries.

As they devoured Eastern Europe, the Soviets also attempted to take over the oil fields of Iran, to the south. At the same time, the Soviets supported communist guerrillas in a civil war in Greece. And, pursuing the historic Russian dream of a "window to the sea," they demanded military and naval bases in Turkey.

### The Truman Doctrine and Containment

The United States began to counter the Soviet Union's aggressive actions in the early months of 1947. The Truman Doctrine marked the first step in that long-standing process. Both Greece and Turkey were in danger of falling under the Soviet Union's control. At President Harry Truman's urgent request, Congress approved a massive program of economic and military aid, and both countries were saved. In his message to Congress, the President declared that it was now

"the policy of the United States to support free peoples who are resisting subjugation by armed minorities or outside pressures. "

The Truman Doctrine soon became part of a broader American plan for dealing with the Soviet Union. From mid-1947 on through the 1980s the United States followed the policy of **containment**. That policy was rooted in the belief that if communism could be contained within its existing boundaries it would collapse under the weight of its internal weaknesses.

The United States and the Soviet Union confronted one another often during the cold war years. Two of those confrontations were of major, near-war proportions: in Berlin in 1948–1949 and in Cuba in 1962. And, during that same time, the United States fought two wars against communist forces in Asia.

**The Berlin Blockade** At the end of World War II, the city of Berlin, surrounded by Soviet-occupied East Germany, was divided into four sectors. One sector, East Berlin, was controlled by the Soviet Union. The other three sectors, comprising West Berlin, were occupied by the United States, Britain, and France.

In 1948 the Soviets tried to force their former allies to withdraw from West Berlin. They clamped a land blockade around the city, stopping the shipment of food and supplies to the western sectors. The United States mounted a massive airlift that kept the city alive until the blockade was lifted, a year and a half after it had begun.

▲ **Executive Action: 1962** Shortly after he ordered the removal of Soviet missiles from Cuba, President Kennedy inspected military installations at Key West, off the Florida coast.

**The Cuban Missile Crisis** The United States and the Soviet Union came perilously close to a nuclear conflict during the Cuban missile crisis in 1962.

Cuba had slipped into the Soviet orbit soon after Fidel Castro gained power there in 1959. By mid-1962, huge quantities of Soviet arms and thousands of Soviet "technicians" had been sent to Cuba. Suddenly, in October, the build-up became unmistakably offensive in character. Aerial photographs revealed the presence of several Soviet missiles capable of nuclear strikes against this country and much of Latin America.

Immediately, President Kennedy ordered a naval blockade of Cuba to prevent the delivery of any more missiles. Cuba and the Soviet Union were warned that the United States would attack Cuba unless the existing Soviet missiles were removed.

After several tense days, the Soviets backed down. Rather than risk all so far from home, they returned the weapons to the Soviet Union.

**The Korean War** The Korean War began on June 25, 1950. South Korea (the UN-sponsored Republic of Korea) was attacked by communist North Korea (the People's Democratic Republic of Korea). Immediately, the UN's Security Council called on all UN members to help South Korea repel the invasion.

The war lasted for more than three years. It pitted the United Nations Command, largely made up of American and South Korean forces, against Soviet-trained and -equipped North Korean and communist Chinese troops. Cease-fire negotiations began in July 1951, but fighting continued until an armistice was signed on July 27, 1953. Final peace terms have never been agreed to.

The long and bitter Korean conflict did not end in a clear-cut UN victory. The war cost the United States 157,530 casualties, including 33,629 combat dead, and more than $20 billion. South Korea's military and civilian casualties ran into the hundreds of thousands, and much of Korea, north and south, was laid to waste.

Still, the invasion was turned back, and the Republic of Korea was saved. Perhaps more importantly, for the first time in history, armed forces fought under an international flag against aggression. There is no telling how far that aggression might have carried had the United States not come to the aid of South Korea.

**The War in Vietnam** In the years following World War II, a Vietnamese nationalist movement, seeking independence from France and made up mostly of communist forces led by Ho Chi Minh, fought and defeated the French in a lengthy conflict. Under truce agreements signed at Geneva in 1954, what had been French Indochina was divided into two zones: a communist-dominated North Vietnam, with its capital in Hanoi, and an anticommunist South Vietnam, based in Saigon.

Almost at once, communist guerrillas (the Viet Cong), supported by North Vietnamese, began a civil war in South Vietnam. The Eisenhower administration responded with economic and then military aid to Saigon. This aid was increased by President Kennedy. But, even with stepped-up U.S. support to South Vietnam, the Viet Cong—and growing numbers of North Vietnamese supplied with mostly Soviet and some Chinese weapons—continued to make major gains.

It was President Johnson who, in early 1965, committed the United States to full-scale war.

By 1968, more than 540,000 Americans were involved in a fierce ground and air conflict.

In 1969, President Nixon began what he called the "Vietnamization" of the war. Over the next four years, American troops were pulled out of combat. Finally, a cease-fire agreement was signed in early 1973, and the last American units were withdrawn. (In spite of the cease-fire, the war between North and South Vietnam went on. By 1975, South Vietnam had been overrun, and the two Vietnams became the Socialist Republic of Vietnam.)

The ill-fated war in Vietnam cost the United States a staggering $165 billion and, irreplaceably, more than 57,000 American lives. In addition, the war caused many to lose faith in the workings of the American political system.

## Détente and the Return to Containment

As the United States withdrew from Vietnam, the Nixon administration embarked on a policy of *détente*. The term is French, meaning "a relaxation of tensions." The policy included a purposeful attempt to improve relations with the Soviet Union and, separately, with China.

▲ **Lest We Forget** Americans were deeply divided by the war in Vietnam. This granite memorial in Washington, D.C., is meant to be a national symbol of healing and forgiveness.

**Global Awareness**

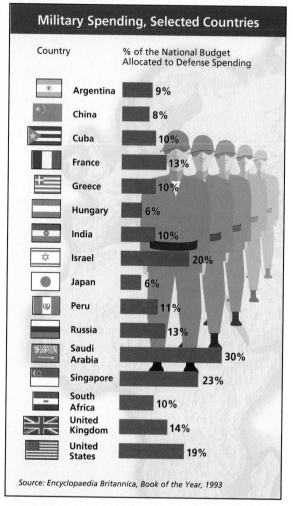

**Military Spending, Selected Countries**

| Country | % of the National Budget Allocated to Defense Spending |
|---|---|
| Argentina | 9% |
| China | 8% |
| Cuba | 10% |
| France | 13% |
| Greece | 10% |
| Hungary | 6% |
| India | 10% |
| Israel | 20% |
| Japan | 6% |
| Peru | 11% |
| Russia | 13% |
| Saudi Arabia | 30% |
| Singapore | 23% |
| South Africa | 10% |
| United Kingdom | 14% |
| United States | 19% |

*Source: Encyclopaedia Britannica, Book of the Year, 1993*

▲ **Interpreting Graphs**   This graph shows the percentage of the national budget allocated to defense spending in various countries. Since the chart lacks political and economic information, can you safely conclude that nations that spend the most for defense are the most militaristic? Why, or why not?

President Nixon flew to Beijing in 1972 to begin a new era in American-Chinese relations. His visit paved the way to further contacts and, finally, to formal diplomatic ties between the United States and the People's Republic.

Less than three months later, Nixon journeyed to Moscow. There, he and Soviet Premier Leonid Brezhnev signed the first Strategic Arms Limitations Talks agreement, SALT. It was a five-year pact in which both sides agreed to a measure of control over their nuclear weapons.

Relations with mainland China have improved fairly steadily since the 1970s. Efforts at détente with the Soviets, however, proved less successful. Moscow continued to apply its expansionist pressures and provided economic and military aid to revolutionary movements around the world.

The short-lived period of détente ended altogether when the Soviets invaded Afghanistan in 1979. From that point, first the Carter and then the Reagan administration placed a renewed emphasis on containing Soviet power.

## The End of the Cold War

Relations between the United States and the Soviet Union improved remarkably after Mikhail Gorbachev gained power in Moscow in 1985. By the 1990s, the cold war had ended.

Presidents Reagan and Gorbachev paved the way to the end of the cold war at four summit conferences. They met first in Geneva in 1985, and then in Reykjavik, Iceland, in 1986, in Washington in 1987, and in Moscow in 1988. Those meetings helped ease longstanding tensions, and they produced a major disarmament pact, the INF Treaty in 1987.

President Bush met with the Soviet leader at Malta in late 1989, in Washington in 1990, and in Washington, London, and Moscow in 1991. Those meetings reaffirmed the friendlier American-Soviet environment. They also produced commitments from both sides to eliminate a portion of their long-range nuclear missiles, to cut stockpiles of chemical weapons, and to reduce the levels of conventional forces.

Clearly, Mikhail Gorbachev deserves a large share of the credit for the fundamental change in the Soviets' approach to world affairs. However, another key factor has been the economic and political chaos that ultimately brought the collapse of the Soviet Union itself in 1991. You will read more about these critical developments in chapters 22 and 23.

The historic fact that the cold war is at long last over can and should be seen in this light: The American policy of containment, first put in place in 1947, finally realized its goal.

## *on Government* VOICES

**General Colin L. Powell,** retired chairman of the Joint Chiefs of Staff

### On United States Foreign Policy in a Changing World

❝Now the task is keeping democracy alive, not fighting and containing communism. Now the task is helping the dozens of democracies that are just being born. Now the task is teaching the basics of government of the people, by the people, and for the people—to the people. Now the task, in the words of the playwright–turned-president [of Czechoslovakia] Vaclav Havel, is to continue 'approaching democracy'—to do so with hundreds of thousands of new recruits. ❞

## Section 4 Review

**1. Define:** collective security, deterrence, containment
**2.** Why did the policy of isolationism make sense to the United States in its early years?
**3.** Briefly trace this nation's policy toward Latin America and the Western Hemisphere.
**4.** What decisive impact did World War II have on the shape of American foreign policy?
**5.** Briefly describe the major political and military events of the cold war.

### Critical Thinking

**6. Testing Conclusions** (p. 19) The text states that "the American policy of containment . . . finally realized its goal." What evidence can you find to support this statement?

★

# 5 Foreign Aid, Defense Alliances, and the United Nations

**Find Out:**
- What are the purposes of foreign aid?
- Why does the United States maintain a network of regional security alliances?
- Why was the United Nations created?
- What are the UN's purposes, organization, and membership?

**Key Terms:**
foreign aid, regional security alliance, UN Security Council

**D**o you know this ancient saying: "Those who help others help themselves"? You will see that that maxim underlies two other and basic elements of present-day American foreign policy: foreign aid and security alliances.

## Foreign Aid

**Foreign aid**—economic and military aid to other countries—has been a basic feature of American foreign policy for more than 50 years now. It began with the Lend-Lease program of the early 1940s, in which the United States gave nearly $50 billion in food, munitions, and other supplies to its allies in World War II. Since then, this country has sent nearly $500 billion in aid to more than 100 countries.

Foreign aid became a part of the containment policy with American aid to Greece and Turkey in 1947. Under the Marshall Plan, named for its author, Secretary of State George C. Marshall, the United States poured some $13.15 billion into 16 nations in Western Europe between 1948 and 1952.

Foreign aid policy has taken several directions over time. Immediately after World War II, American aid was primarily economic in form. Over the years since then, however, military assistance has assumed a large role in aid policy. Until the mid-1950s, Europe received the lion's share of American help. Since then, the largest amounts have gone to nations in Asia and Latin America.

On balance, most aid has been sent to those countries regarded as the most critical to the realization of this country's foreign policy objectives. Over recent years, Israel, Egypt, the Philippines, and various Latin American countries have been the major recipients of American help, both economic and military.

Most foreign aid money must be used to buy American goods and services. So, most of the billions spent for that aid amount to a substantial subsidy to both business and labor in this country. Most of the economic aid programs are administered by the independent Agency for International Development (AID), in close cooperation with the Departments of State and Agriculture. Most military aid is channeled through the Defense Department.

## Security Through Alliances

Over the past four decades, the United States has constructed a network of **regional security alliances** built on mutual defense treaties. In each of those treaties, the United States and the other countries involved have agreed to take collective action to meet aggression in a particular part of the world.

The North Atlantic Treaty, signed in 1949, established NATO, the 16-member North Atlantic Treaty Organization. The alliance was formed to promote the collective defense of Western Europe, particularly against the threat of Soviet aggression. Each member country has agreed that "an armed attack against one or more of them in Europe or in North America shall be considered an attack against them all."[12]

NATO was originally composed of the United States and 11 other countries: Canada, Great Britain, France, Italy, Portugal, the Netherlands,

Belgium, Luxembourg, Denmark, Norway, and Iceland. Greece and Turkey joined the alliance in 1952, West Germany in 1955, and Spain in 1982. When East and West Germany united in 1990, that new state joined NATO.

NATO has been the cornerstone of American foreign policy in Europe ever since its creation. The end of the cold war has not diminished NATO's role. In 1991 the NATO Council reiterated the organization's mission in these words: "To deter and defend against any threat of aggression against the territory of any member state."

**Other Alliances** The Rio Pact, the Inter-American Treaty of Reciprocal Assistance, was signed in 1947. In it, the United States, Canada, and now 32 Latin American countries have agreed "that an armed attack by any state against an American state shall be considered as an attack against all the American states." The treaty pledges those countries to the mutual peaceful settlement of all disputes. In effect, the Rio Pact is a restatement of the Monroe Doctrine.

In addition to NATO and the Rio Pact, the United States is involved with a number of regional security alliances. For example, the ANZUS Pact of 1951 unites Australia, New Zealand, and the United States.

The Japanese Pact also dates from 1951. After six years of American military occupation, the allies of World War II (but not the Soviet Union) signed a peace treaty with Japan. At the same time, the United States and Japan signed a mutual defense treaty. In return for American protection, the United States is permitted to maintain land, sea, and air forces in and about Japan.

The Philippines Pact was also signed in 1951. It, too, is a mutual defense agreement. The pact remains in force, but disagreements over its redrafting prompted the withdrawal of all American military forces from the Philippines in 1992. The Korean Pact, signed in 1953, pledges this country to come to the aid of South Korea should it be attacked again.

The Taiwan Pact was in effect between the United States and Nationalist China from 1954 to 1980. The United States and the People's Republic of China established full diplomatic relations in 1979. At that time, the United States withdrew recognition of the Nationalist

---

[12]In answer to NATO, the Soviets formed the Warsaw Treaty Organization (the Warsaw Pact) in 1955. The Pact created a Moscow-based mutual defense alliance among Albania, Bulgaria, Czechoslovakia, East Germany, Hungary, Poland, Romania, and the Soviet Union. The Warsaw Pact did not survive the collapse of communism in the Soviet Union and Eastern Europe; it was formally dissolved in 1991.

Chinese government; it also served the one-year notice required by the 1954 treaty to abrogate (end) that agreement.

### The United States and the Middle East

The American network of regional alliances is far-reaching. It does not cover all of the globe, however—and most notably today, not the Middle East.

The Middle East is both oil-rich and conflict-ridden. America's foreign policy interests in the region have, for decades, been torn in two quite opposite directions: by its long-standing support of Israel, and by the critical importance of Arab oil.

Israel was established as an independent state by the United Nations in 1948. Carved out of what had been British-controlled Palestine,

Israel has been in near-constant conflict with most of its Arab neighbors ever since.

In spite of its support for Israel, the United States has made considerable efforts to promote friendly relations with most Arab states in the region.

With the active involvement of President Carter, Israel and Egypt negotiated a peace treaty, which became effective in 1979. That agreement, the Camp David Accord, ended more than 30 years of hostilities between those two countries.

New efforts to bring peace to the region were made by the Bush and then the Clinton administrations. Thus far, the most promising result of those renewed efforts has been the signing of a peace accord between Israel and Jordan.

Since the late 1970s, many of America's problems in the Middle East have involved a non-

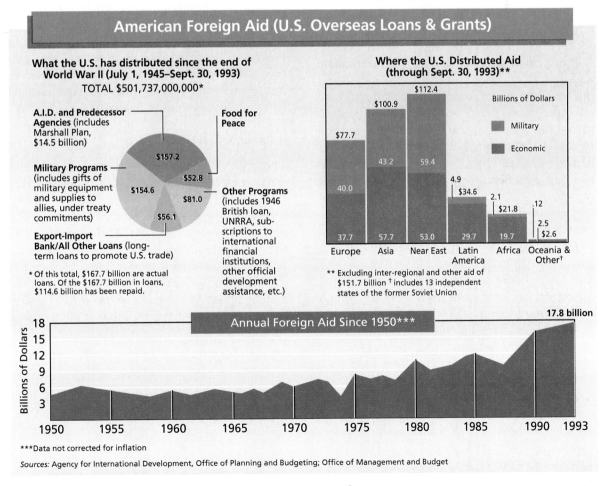

**Interpreting Graphs**   According to the bar graphs above, which region(s) has (have) received the largest share of American foreign aid?

Arab country, Iran—which is fiercely anti-Western, and especially anti-American. Iranian militants seized the American embassy in Teheran in late 1979, and 52 Americans were held hostage for more than a year. Through the 1980s the government of the Ayatollah Ruhollah Khomeini was quite apparently involved in several acts of terrorism in the Middle East and Europe.

In 1988, a UN-sponsored cease-fire halted the Iran–Iraq war. That conflict had begun in 1980, when Iraq's President Saddam Hussein ordered the Iraqi military to attack Iran. The long and bitter struggle threatened world access to Middle East oil—and prompted President Reagan to order the navy to escort oil tankers plying the perilous Persian Gulf in 1987 and 1988.

Saddam Hussein launched another invasion in August of 1990. This time, Iraqi forces overran small, oil-rich Kuwait and threatened the security of America's close ally, Saudi Arabia.

President Bush demanded the immediate withdrawal of Iraqi forces from Kuwait and the restoration of that country's legitimate government. He also ordered a huge deployment of American military might to the Persian Gulf region. That operation was code-named Desert Shield. By early 1991 it brought American troop strength in the Gulf region to more than 500,000—the largest massing of American power since Vietnam.

The American response was backed by most of the world community. A multinational (but mostly American) military force was established. The United Nations Security Council imposed economic sanctions on Iraq, hoping to bring a peaceful resolution to the crisis.

Iraq refused to withdraw from Kuwait, however; and its continued stubbornness finally triggered the Persian Gulf War. That brief conflict, code-named Desert Storm, began in mid-January with sustained air attacks on Iraqi positions. On February 24th, American, British, Saudi, and other allied forces commenced a massive ground attack that in just 100 hours drove Iraq's troops from Kuwait.

When Iraq posed a renewed threat to Kuwait in 1994, President Clinton ordered a new deployment of American forces to the region, to reinforce those that have remained there since the end of the Gulf War.

## The United Nations

The decisive change in American foreign policy that occurred during and immediately after World War II is strikingly illustrated by this country's participation in the United Nations.

The United Nations was formed at the UN Conference on International Organization, which met in San Francisco from April 25 to June 26, 1945. There, the representatives of 51 nations—the victorious allies of World War II—drafted the United Nations Charter. The charter is a treaty among all of the UN's member-states, and it serves as the body's constitution.

The United States became the first nation to ratify the UN Charter. The Senate approved it by an overwhelming vote, 89–2, on July 24, 1945. The charter was then ratified in quick order by the other states that had taken part in the San Francisco Conference. The charter went into force on October 24, 1945, and the UN held its first formal meeting, a session of the General Assembly, in London, on January 10, 1946.

## The UN Charter

The charter is a lengthy document. It opens with an eloquent preamble, which declares that the UN was created "to save succeeding generations from the scourge of war." The body of the document begins in Article I with a statement of the organization's purposes. They are the maintenance of international peace and security, the development of friendly relations between and among all nations, and the promotion of justice and cooperation in the solution of international problems.

**Membership** Today the UN has 179 members. Under the charter, membership is open to those "peace-loving states" that accept the obligations of the charter and are, in the UN's judgment, able and willing to carry out those obligations. New members may be admitted by a two-thirds vote of the General Assembly, upon recommendation by the Security Council.

**Basic Organization** The charter sets forth the complicated structure of the UN, built around six "principal organs": the General Assembly, the Security Council, the Economic and Social Council, the Trusteeship Council, the International Court of Justice, and the Secretariat.

## The General Assembly

The General Assembly has been called "the town meeting of the world." Each of the UN's members has a seat and a vote in the assembly.

The General Assembly meets once a year, normally in September. Most of its sessions are held at the UN's permanent headquarters in New York. Special sessions may be called by the secretary-general, either at the request of the Security Council or a majority of the UN members.

The assembly may take up and debate any matter within the scope of the charter,[13] and it may make whatever recommendation it chooses to the Security Council, the other UN organs, and any member-state. The recommendations it makes to UN members are not legally binding on them. Yet they do carry weight because they have been approved by a significant number of the governments of the world.

The assembly elects the 10 nonpermanent members of the Security Council, the 54 members of the Economic and Social Council, and the elective members of the Trusteeship Council. With the Security Council, the assembly also selects the secretary-general and the 15 judges of the International Court of Justice. The assembly also shares with the Security Council the power to admit, suspend, or expel members. It alone may propose amendments to the charter.

## The Security Council

The **UN Security Council** is made up of 15 members. Five of them—the United States, Britain, France, Russia (the Soviet Union's old seat), and China—are permanent members.[14] The 10 nonpermanent members are chosen by the General Assembly for two-year terms; they

**United Nations** The UN headquarters is located in New York City. The organization was formed in 1945 to work for a more peaceful and secure world for all people.

cannot be immediately reelected. The council meets in continuous session.

The Security Council bears the UN's major responsibility for maintaining international peace. It may take up any matter involving a threat to or a breach of that peace. It may adopt measures ranging from calling on the parties to settle their differences peacefully to placing economic and/or military sanctions on an offending nation. The only time the Security Council has undertaken a military operation against an aggressor came in Korea in 1950. It has provided UN peacekeeping forces in several trouble spots, however—most notably in the Middle East.

On procedural questions—routine matters—decisions of the Security Council can be made by the affirmative vote of any nine members. On the more important matters—substantive

---

[13]Except those matters currently under consideration by the Security Council.

[14]In 1971 the People's Republic of China replaced the Nationalist Chinese regime on Taiwan as a permanent member of the Security Council and acquired China's membership in the UN in all other respects.

# The United Nations

**SECRETARIAT**

**INTERNATIONAL COURT OF JUSTICE**

**TRUSTEESHIP COUNCIL**

**SECURITY COUNCIL**
Military Staff Committee
Peace-Keeping Operations/
Observer Missions

**International Atomic Energy Agency (IAEA)**
(an independent inter-governmental organization sponsored by the UN)

**ECONOMIC & SOCIAL COUNCIL**

**GENERAL ASSEMBLY**

**MAIN COMMITTEES AND SUBSIDIARY ORGANS**
- UN Institute for Training and Research (UNITAR)
- UN Conference on Trade and Development
- UNICEF (UN Children's Fund)
- Office of the UN High Commission for Refugees
- Joint UN/FAO World Food Programme
- UN Development Programme
- UN Environment Programme
- UN University
- UN Special Fund
- World Food Council
- UN Center for Human Settlements (UNCHS) (Habitat)
- UN Relief and Works Agency for Palestine Refugees in the Near East (UNRWA)
- UN Fund for Population Activities (UNFPA)
- UN Industrial Development Organization (UNIDO)

## Specialized Agencies
Functional Commissions
Sessional, Standing, and Ad Hoc Committees
General Agreement on Tariffs and Trade
International Labor Organization (ILO)
Food and Agriculture Organization of the UN (FAO)
UN Educational, Scientific, and Cultural Organization (UNESCO)
World Health Organization (WHO)
International Monetary Fund (IMF)
International Bank for Reconstruction and Development (World Bank)
International Development Association (IDA)
International Finance Corporation (IFC)
International Civil Aviation Organization (ICAO)
Universal Postal Union (UPU)
International Telecommunication Union (ITU)
World Meteorological Organization (WMO)
International Maritime Organization (IMO)
World Intellectual Property Organization (WIPO)
International Fund for Agricultural Development (IFAD)

**Interpreting Charts** This chart shows the principal organs and agencies of the United Nations. The Secretariat, with some 18,000 employees, is the administrative body of the organization. From what you have read, which body within the United Nations has the most power?

questions—at least nine affirmative votes are also needed. But a negative vote by any one of the permanent members is enough to kill any substantive resolution.[15] Because of that veto power, the Security Council is effective only when and if the permanent members are willing to cooperate with one another.

## Other Important UN Bodies

In addition to the General Assembly and Security Council, the UN has several important bodies.

**The Economic and Social Council** The Economic and Social Council is made up of 54 members elected by the General Assembly to three-year terms. The council is responsible to the assembly for carrying out the UN's many economic, cultural, educational, health, and related activities.

**The Trusteeship Council** The UN Charter requires each member to promote the interests and well-being of the peoples of all "non-self-governing territories" as a "sacred trust." The Trusteeship Council sets guidelines for the government of all dependent areas and makes rules for the administration of all UN trust territories.[16]

**The International Court of Justice** The International Court of Justice (ICJ) is the UN's judicial arm.

All members of the UN are automatically parties to the ICJ Statute. Under certain conditions the services of the court are also available to nonmember states. A UN member may agree to accept the court's jurisdiction over cases in which it may be involved either unconditionally or with certain reservations (exceptions that may not conflict with the ICJ Statute).

The ICJ is made up of 15 judges selected for nine-year terms by the General Assembly and the Security Council. It sits in permanent session at The Hague, in the Netherlands. It handles cases brought to it voluntarily by both members and nonmembers of the UN. The ICJ also advises the other UN organs on legal questions arising out of their activities. If any party to a dispute fails to obey a judgment of the court, the other party may take that matter to the Security Council.

**The Secretariat** The Secretariat is the civil service branch of the UN. It is headed by the secretary-general, who is chosen to a five-year term by the General Assembly on the recommendation of the Security Council.

Dr. Boutros Boutros Ghali, an Egyptian, is now the secretary-general. He became the UN's top administrative officer in 1992. In addition to his housekeeping chores, the charter gives him a very important power. He may bring before the Security Council any matter he believes poses a threat to international peace and security.

## Section 5 Review

**1. Define:** foreign aid, regional security alliance, UN Security Council
**2.** What kind of country is generally the recipient of United States foreign aid?
**3.** What regions do the NATO, Rio, and ANZUS pacts cover?
**4.** The United States' interests in the Middle East are torn by what two considerations?
**5.** When, where, and by whom was the UN Charter drafted?
**6.** (a) What are the UN's principal organs? (b) What are the major functions of the General Assembly and the Security Council?

**Critical Thinking**

**7. Making Comparisons** (p. 19) Consider the subject of international alliances. (a) Compare the attitudes of early Americans and the foreign policy makers of today. (b) What factors might have led to this shift in attitude?

---

[15]The veto does not come into play in a situation in which one or more of the permanent members abstains (does not cast a vote). When, on June 25, 1950, the Security Council called on all UN members to aid South Korea to repel the North Korean invasion, the Soviet delegate was boycotting sessions of the Security Council and so was not present to veto that action.

[16]There were 11 of those territories originally—most of them former possessions of the defeated Axis Powers of World War II. There are no trust territories today.

★

# Critical Thinking

## Identifying Alternatives

As a citizen in a democratic society, you will have to make and evaluate a great number and variety of decisions. Some will be simple. Many, however, will be quite complicated. In order to find the best solutions to such problems you must be able to identify alternatives. Mastering this skill will enable you to (1) identify one or more methods to achieve a goal or to solve a problem and (2) recognize the possibility of other goals. Follow the steps below to practice identifying alternatives.

**1. Identify the nature of the problem.** Before you can identify possible solutions to a problem, you must understand exactly what the problem is. Read the paragraph below, describing a foreign policy question faced by the United States. (a) What is the ultimate goal of the United States regarding its military spending? (b) What challenges and questions does the nation face in achieving that goal?

**2. Identify the interests that must be satisfied and/or conditions that must be met. In any conflict or disagreement, a solution must be acceptable to all sides.** Read the passage below again. (a) What is the position of those who favor a cut in military spending? (b) What is the view of those who favor a continuation of military spending at levels similar to those during the cold war?

**3. Identify possible alternatives.** A common technique for identifying alternatives is brainstorming. In a brainstorming session, participants volunteer all sorts of ideas, which are then collected and analyzed. At first some of the ideas may seem odd, and many turn out to be of little value. However, the process often yields unexpected and effective alternatives. Brainstorm ways in which the United States can determine the appropriate level of defense spending. What are some of your ideas?

**4. Test your ideas.** Once you have generated a list of possible alternatives, you should try to eliminate those that will not work. Examine each idea that you brainstormed by answering the following questions: (a) Is this idea likely to accomplish the goal of providing a strong defense for the United States? Why or why not? (b) Will all parties involved in the debate be satisfied? Why or why not?

The end of the cold war has prompted the United States to reevaluate its defense needs. Most American leaders agree that the United States needs a strong defense in order to remain secure. However, there is disagreement about how much money the nation must spend in order to maintain that level of defense. A number of policymakers want to take advantage of the dissolution of the Soviet Union to lower dramatically the nation's defense budget. The resulting so-called peace dividend could then be used to lower the budget deficit and provide more domestic services to the American people. Other analysts insist that in spite of the great changes in the alignment of world military power, the world remains a dangerous place. These leaders point to the Persian Gulf War of 1991 as an example. They insist that the nation continue to invest in its military near the levels of the past in order to ensure the continued ability of the United States to protect its interests around the world.

# Chapter-in-Brief

Scan all headings, photographs, charts, and other visuals in the chapter before reading the section summaries below.

**Section 1** **Foreign and Defense Policy: An Overview (pp. 425–427)** Throughout much of American history, relations with other countries were shaped largely by the policy of isolationism. Today, however, the United States understands that its security is directly linked with that of other nations.

For this reason, governmental leaders carefully shape American foreign policy. The President, as chief diplomat and commander in chief, plays the leading role in foreign and military affairs.

**Section 2** **The Departments of State and Defense (pp. 428–434)** The State Department is the President's right arm in the field of foreign policy. The department is headed by the secretary of state, and it is organized along geographic and functional lines. The department includes the Foreign Service and ambassadors who represent the United States around the world. The State Department also issues passports to American citizens.

The Defense Department assists the President in making and conducting military policy. Its secretary must be a civilian, in keeping with the principle of civilian control of the military.

**Section 3** **Other Foreign/Defense Policy Agencies (pp. 435–438)** Besides the Departments of State and Defense, several agencies are closely involved with foreign policy.

The CIA coordinates the government's intelligence gathering. It also analyzes that data. The United States Information Agency promotes American policy and way of life around the world.

The United States Arms Control and Disarmament Agency is responsible for American participation in arms limitation and disarmament talks. The Selective Service System oversees the draft, which presently exists on a standby basis.

**Section 4** **American Foreign Policy, Past and Present (pp. 441–447)** Isolationism guided American foreign policy for its first 150 years. During that time, the nation expanded; it also promoted such foreign policies as the Monroe Doctrine and the Open Door.

World War I led to a renewed spirit of isolationism in the 1920s and 1930s. World War II put an end to that policy; the war's aftermath saw the beginning of the cold war and the commitment to collective security and deterrence.

During the cold war, the United States pursued containment of communism, particularly through armed conflict in Korea and Vietnam. A period of détente in the 1970s led to better relations with the Soviets and China.

**Section 5** **Foreign Aid, Defense Alliances, and the United Nations (pp. 447–453)** The United States began practicing foreign aid during World War II. Early aid was economic, but military aid has become increasingly important.

Since World War II, the United States has forged a number of regional security alliances. NATO is one example; others include the Rio Pact, ANZUS, the Japanese Pact, the Philippines Pact, the Korean Pact, and the Taiwan Pact.

The United Nations is perhaps the best example of America's full-scale involvement in world affairs. The UN seeks to maintain peace and security, develop friendly relations among nations, and promote justice and cooperation in the solution of international problems.

# Chapter Review

## Vocabulary and Key Terms

isolationism (p. 425)
foreign policy (p. 426)
right of legation (p. 429)
ambassador (p. 429)
passport (p. 430)
visa (p. 430)

diplomatic immunity (p. 430)
draft (p. 437)
collective security (p. 443)
deterrence (p. 443)
containment (p. 443)
foreign aid (p. 447)

regional security
   alliance (p. 448)
UN Security
   Council (p. 451)

**Matching:** *Review the key terms in the list above. If you are not sure of a term's meaning, look up the term and review its definition. Choose a term from the list above that best matches each description.*

1. the right to send and receive diplomatic representatives
2. the rule by which ambassadors are not held subject to the laws of the state to which they are accredited
3. a foreign policy principle based on a world-wide system of security
4. a certificate issued by a government identifying a person as a citizen of a country
5. economic and military aid to foreign countries

**True or False:** *Determine whether each statement is true or false. If it is true, write "true." If it is false, change the underlined word or words to make the statement true.*

1. The <u>right of legation</u> is the means by which the Federal Government requires young men to serve in the military.
2. The personal representative of the United States in foreign states is the <u>ambassador</u>.
3. For its first 150 years, American foreign policy was largely one of <u>diplomatic immunity</u>.
4. The <u>UN Security Council</u> bears a major responsibility for maintaining international peace.

**Word Relationships:** *Distinguish between words in each pair.*

1. passport/visa
2. foreign policy/foreign aid
3. deterrence/containment
4. collective security/regional security alliance

## Main Ideas

### Section 1 (pp. 425–427)

1. Briefly describe the historical attitudes of the United States toward foreign affairs.
2. For what reasons must the United States be concerned about events elsewhere in the world?
3. Which individuals and organizations play major roles in the conduct of foreign policy?

### Section 2 (pp. 428–434)

4. Which two cabinet-level departments are most responsible for the making and conduct of foreign policy?
5. (a) What are the key components of the State Department in the field of foreign policy? (b) What are their functions?
6. What is the main function of the Department of Defense?

### Section 3 (pp. 435–438)

7. List three agencies besides the State Department and the Department of Defense involved with making and/or conducting foreign policy.

8. (a) What is the function of the Central Intelligence Agency? (b) The United States Information Agency?

9. (a) What is the function of the National Aeronautics and Space Administration? (b) The United States Arms Control and Disarmament Agency?

10. Briefly describe the history of the draft in the United States.

## Section 4 (pp. 440–447)

11. Explain the significance of the Monroe Doctrine.

12. Describe two key foreign policy developments of the late 1800s.

13. What two terms describe the broad goals of American foreign policy in the post-World War II era?

14. (a) What was the cold war? (b) What is its status today?

## Section 5 (pp. 447–453)

15. Briefly trace the history of the United States policy of foreign aid.

16. What is the function of the several regional security alliances to which the United States is a party?

17. What, according to the UN charter, are the UN's basic purposes?

18. How does the veto power of the UN's Security Council affect its ability to make policy?

---

## Critical Thinking

1. **Identifying Alternatives** (p. 19) (a) In your opinion, what should be the overall goal of American foreign policy? (b) Which of the principles discussed in this chapter seem most likely to help the United States achieve this goal? Explain your answer.

2. **Recognizing Ideologies** (p. 19) President Dwight Eisenhower once said, " Americans, indeed all free men, remember that in the final choice a soldier's pack is not so heavy a burden as a prisoner's chains." What do you think Eisenhower meant by this comment?

3. **Predicting Consequences** (p. 19) Consider the concept of isolationism discussed in Sections 1 and 4. What would you predict might happen if the United States were again to shape its foreign policy around this principle?

## Getting Involved

1. **Writing Your Opinion** You are a candidate for President of the United States. Write a speech in which you explain to the voters your view of United States foreign policy. Prepare for your speech by reviewing the foreign policy history of the United States. Select those policies and principles that you feel best serve the interests of the country. Begin the speech by stating why you believe the country must have a clearly defined foreign policy. Then, carefully explain each of the principles and policies that you advocate. Remember, the purpose of your speech is to convince voters to support you in the election. So, explain how you believe your policies will benefit the nation. Revise the speech to correct errors, then draft a final copy.

2. **Class Debate** Hold a class debate on one of the following topics: (a) *Resolved,* That the United States should reinstitute compulsory military service for young men and women. (b) *Resolved,* That the United States favor the abolition of the veto power of the permanent members of the United Nations Security Council. Select teams to debate each side of the selected issue. The rest of the class should evaluate each team's presentation.

3. **Creating a Poster** Create a poster to illustrate your understanding of national security. Remember, your poster can include a combination of words and images to communicate your ideas.

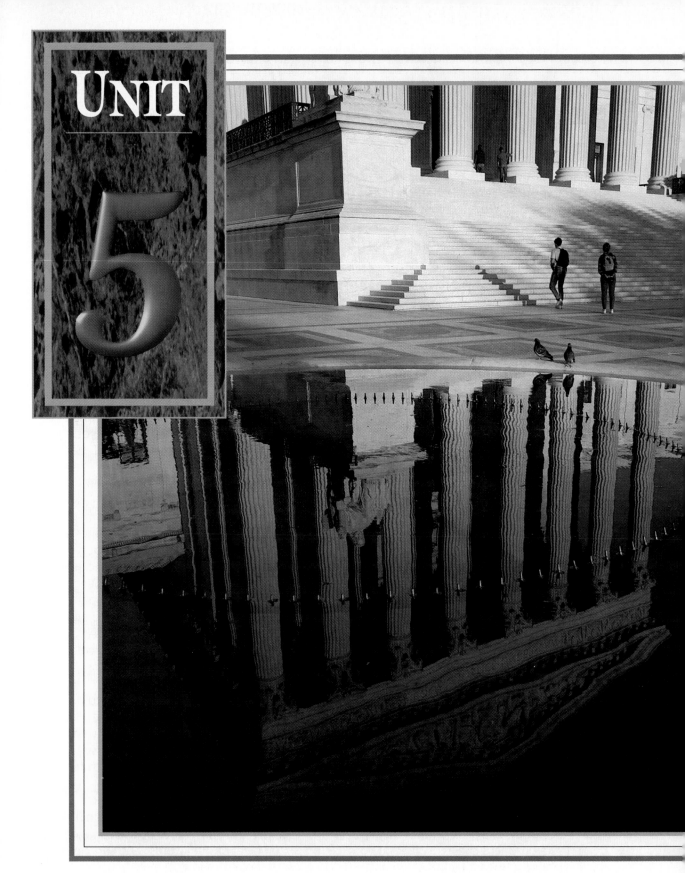

# UNIT
# 5

▲ **The Supreme Court**   "We are very quiet there, but it is the quiet of a storm center. . . ."
—Justice Oliver Wendell Holmes

# The Judicial Branch

I t was the first session of the Supreme Court, and the day was going badly. On February 1, 1790, Chief Justice John Jay and two associate justices arrived at the Royal Exchange Building in New York City and waited for the three remaining justices to arrive. They never showed up. Within a short time it was clear that the Court had little business to conduct. No cases were presented for argument and after ten days the Court adjourned. By contrast, the Supreme Court today schedules to hear about 130 cases of the nearly 6,000 cases that are appealed to it each year. In spite of this and many other changes, tradition dominates the Supreme Court. The marshals still make sure that proper behavior is maintained at all times. Recently, a reporter sitting in the press section draped his arm over the brass rail next to him. A marshal was quickly at his side with the firm but polite request, "No body parts on the brass rail." The room with the brass rail—contained inside the imposing building shown at left—is the meeting place of the topmost level of the judicial branch, which you will study in this unit.

## DID YOU KNOW THAT . . .

- It was not until 1936 that the Supreme Court had its own building. In its early history, the Supreme Court spent a full year convening in a Washington tavern.

- The nation's prison population has more than doubled over the past ten years.

- Only two women have ever served on the Supreme Court, and both sit on the Court today: Sandra Day O'Connor, who has been on the Court since 1981, and Ruth Bader Ginsburg, appointed in 1993.

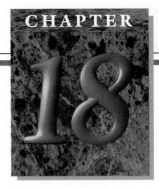

# The Federal Court System

## Chapter Preview

Bankruptcy, personal injury, drug abuse, tax fraud—these are just a few of the most common civil and criminal cases heard in the United States district courts each year. While the Framers of the Constitution may never have imagined all of the types of cases these courts would hear, they did realize that government would be impossible to manage without a judiciary—and so they added Article III to the Constitution. It established the Supreme Court and gave Congress the power to create other, lower federal courts. It is the prime function of the legislative branch to make the law, and of the judicial branch—the system of federal courts and federal judges—to interpret and apply the law. This chapter is about the structure and work of all parts of the federal court system.

### Before you read this chapter:

- **Describe** what the concept of justice means to you.
- **Predict** what might occur if law and the court system did not exist.

### As you read, focus on the main objective for each section. Understand:

1. The basic role of the judiciary in the governmental process.

2. The structure and function of the constitutional courts in the federal court system.

3. The role of the Supreme Court as the nation's highest court, and the significance of judicial review in the American governmental system.

4. The role and jurisdiction of the special courts in the federal court system.

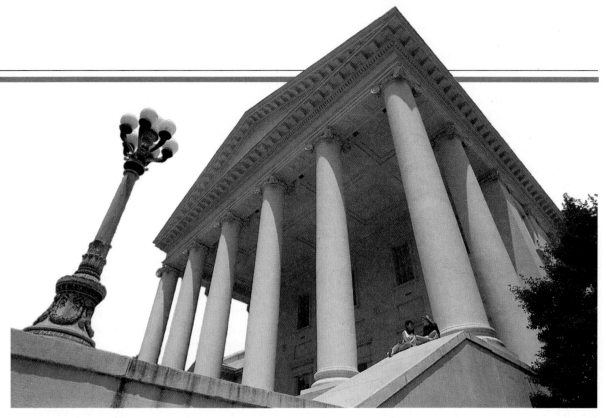

▲ **Richmond, Virginia, Courthouse**   Cases that involve the Constitution or laws of the United States are brought before a federal court rather than a State court.

# 1 The National Judiciary

## Find Out:

- For what reasons was the national court system established?
- On what two bases can the federal courts hear and decide cases?
- What is jurisdiction, and what kinds of jurisdiction do the various federal courts have?
- How are federal judges selected and compensated, and who helps them perform their jobs?

## Key Terms:

jurisdiction, exclusive jurisdiction, concurrent jurisdiction, plaintiff, defendant, original jurisdiction, appellate jurisdiction

Suppose a brand new, bright red sports car is stolen in Chicago. Two days later, the driver is stopped for speeding in Atlanta. Where, now, will he be tried for car theft? In Illinois, where he stole the car? In Georgia, where he was caught? In point of fact, Joe may be on the verge of learning something about the federal court system—and the Dyer Act of 1925, which makes it a federal crime to transport a stolen automobile across a State line.

## The Creation of a National Judiciary

Over the years the Articles of Confederation were in force (1781–1789), there were no national courts, no national judiciary. The laws of the United States were interpreted and applied in the States as each of them chose to do so, and sometimes not at all. Disputes between States and between persons who lived in different States were decided, if at all, by the courts in one of the States involved. Often, decisions by the courts in one State were ignored by the courts in the other States.

Alexander Hamilton spoke to the point in *The Federalist* No. 78. He described "the want of a national judiciary" as a "circumstance that crowns the defects of the Confederation." Arguing the need for a national court system he added:

❝ Laws are dead letters without courts to expound and define their true meaning and operation. ❞

To meet the need, the Framers wrote Article III into the Constitution. It created the national judiciary in a single sentence:

❝ The judicial power of the United States shall be vested in one Supreme Court, and in such inferior courts as the Congress may from time to time ordain and establish. ❞ [1]

**A Dual Court System**   Keep this important point in mind: There are *two* separate court systems in the United States.[2] On one hand, the national judiciary spans the country, with its more than 100 courts. On the other hand, each of the 50 States has its own system of courts. Their numbers run well into the thousands. These State courts hear most of the cases in this country. You will take a look at the States' court systems in Chapter 25.

**Two Kinds of Federal Courts**   The Constitution creates the Supreme Court and leaves to Congress the creation of the inferior courts—the lower federal courts, those beneath the Supreme Court. Over the years, Congress has created two distinct types of federal courts: (1) the constitutional courts and (2) the special courts.

CONSTITUTIONAL COURTS   The constitutional courts are the federal courts that Congress has formed under Article III to exercise "the judicial power of the United States." Together with the Supreme Court, they now include the courts of appeals, the district courts, and the Court of International Trade. The constitutional courts are sometimes called the regular courts, and sometimes Article III courts.

SPECIAL COURTS   The special courts do not exercise the broad "judicial power of the United States." Rather, they have been created by Congress to hear cases arising out of some of the expressed powers given to Congress in Article I. The special courts hear a much narrower range of cases than those that may come before the constitutional courts.

These special courts are sometimes called the legislative courts. Today, they include the Court of Military Appeals, the Court of Veterans Appeals, the Claims Court, the Tax Court, the various territorial courts, and the courts of the District of Columbia. You will read about the unique features of these courts in Section 4. First, however, consider the matter of jurisdiction—the meaning of that term and the jurisdiction of the various federal courts.

## Jurisdiction in the Federal Courts

The constitutional courts hear most of the cases tried in the federal courts. That is, those courts have jurisdiction over most federal cases.

The word **jurisdiction** is defined as the authority of a court to hear and decide a case. The term means, literally, the power "to say the law."

The Constitution gives the federal courts jurisdiction over certain cases. Article III, Section 2 provides that the federal courts may hear a case either because of (1) the subject matter or (2) the parties involved in the case.

**Subject Matter**   In terms of subject matter, the federal courts may hear a case if it deals with:
1. the interpretation and application of a provision in the Constitution or in any federal statute or treaty; or
2. a question of admiralty (matters that arise on the high seas or navigable waters of the United States) or a question of maritime law (matters arising on land but directly relating to the

---

[1]Article III, Section 1. Article I, Section 8, Clause 9 also grants Congress the expressed power "to constitute tribunals inferior to the Supreme Court."

[2]Federalism does not require two separate court systems. Article III provides that Congress "may" establish lower federal courts. At its first session, in 1789, Congress decided to construct a complete set of federal courts to parallel those of the States. In most of the world's other federal systems, the principal courts are those of the states or provinces; typically, the only significant federal court is a national court of last resort, often called the supreme court.

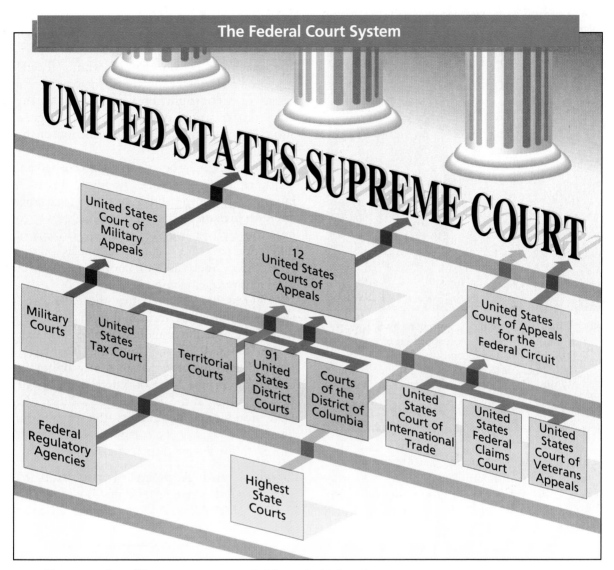

The Federal Court System

**Interpreting Charts** Cases appealed from the highest State courts go directly to the United States Supreme Court. Appeals of decisions by any of the federal regulatory agencies are heard in what courts?

water—for example, a contract to deliver a ship's supplies at dockside).[3]

**Parties** A case comes within the jurisdiction of the federal courts if any of the parties in the case is:

1. the United States or one of its officers or agencies;
2. an ambassador, consul, or other official repre-

sentative of a foreign government;

3. a State suing another State, or a citizen of another State, or a foreign government or one of its subjects;[4]

---

[3]The Framers gave the federal courts exclusive jurisdiction in such cases to ensure national supremacy in the regulation of all waterborne commerce.

[4]Note that the 11th Amendment says that a State may not be sued in the federal courts by a citizen of another State or of a foreign state. A State may be sued without its consent in the federal courts only by the United States, another State, or a foreign state. If a citizen of a State (or of another State or of a foreign state) wants to sue a State, he or she may do so only with that State's consent and only in that State's own courts.

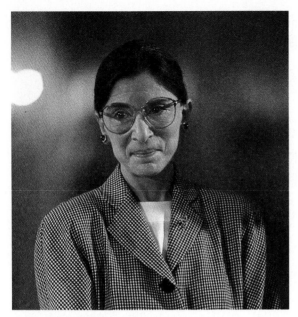

**The 107th Justice** Appointed by President Clinton, Ruth Bader Ginsburg became the 107th justice and second woman to join the Supreme Court. She succeeded Justice Byron White, who retired from the bench in 1993.

4. a citizen of one State suing a citizen of another State;
5. an American citizen suing a foreign government or one of its subjects;
6. a citizen of one State suing a citizen of that same State where both claim land under grants from different States.

Any case falling into any of these categories can be brought in the proper federal court. If a case does not fit into one of these categories, it cannot be heard in a federal court. Remember, most of the cases heard by courts in this country are State, not federal cases.

All of this may seem quite complicated, and it is. But notice that it is a reflection of federalism and, so, of the dual system of courts in this country. Stating the whole point of federal court jurisdiction in another way: All cases that are not heard by the federal courts are within the jurisdiction of the States' courts.

## Exclusive and Concurrent Jurisdiction

In several of the categories of cases just listed, the federal courts have **exclusive jurisdiction**. That is, those cases can be heard only in the federal courts. For example, a case involving an ambassador or some other official of a foreign government cannot be heard in a State court. The trial of a person charged with a federal crime, or a suit involving the infringement of a patent or a copyright, or a case involving any other matter arising out of an act of Congress also falls within the exclusive jurisdiction of the federal courts.

Many cases may be tried in either a federal court or a State court, however. In such instances, the federal and State courts have **concurrent jurisdiction**; they share the power to hear those cases. Disputes involving citizens of different States are common examples of this type of case. Such cases are known in the law as cases in diverse citizenship.[5]

Congress has provided that the federal district courts may hear cases in diverse citizenship only if the amount of money involved in a case is over $50,000. In such cases the **plaintiff**—the one who initiates the suit—may bring the case in the proper State or federal court, as he or she chooses. If the case is brought before the State court, the **defendant**—the party who must defend against the complaint—may have it moved to the federal district court.

## Original and Appellate Jurisdiction

A court in which a case is heard first is said to have **original jurisdiction** over that case. A court that hears a case on appeal from a lower court has **appellate jurisdiction** over that case. The higher court—the appellate court—may uphold, overrule, or in some way modify the decision appealed from the lower court.[6]

In the federal court system, the district courts have only original jurisdiction and the courts of appeals have only appellate jurisdiction. The Supreme Court exercises both original and appellate jurisdiction.

---

[5]The major reason that cases in diverse citizenship may be heard in federal courts is to provide a neutral forum to settle the disputes involved. That reason reflects an early fear that State courts (and their juries) might be prejudiced against "foreigners," residents of other States. There seems little real likelihood of such bias today.

[6]The term appellate comes from the Latin *appellare,* meaning "to speak to, to call upon, to appeal to."

## Appointment of Judges

The manner in which federal judges are chosen, the terms for which they serve, and even the salaries they are paid play a vital part in maintaining the independence of the judicial branch. The Constitution declares that the President

    “ shall nominate, and, by and with the advice and consent of the Senate, shall appoint . . . judges of the Supreme Court. ”[7]

Congress has provided the same procedure for the selection of all other federal judges. So, the President is free to name to the federal bench anyone the Senate will confirm. Recall the very real impact of the unwritten rule of senatorial courtesy here; see Chapter 11, Section 4.

Most federal judges are drawn from the ranks of leading attorneys, legal scholars and law school professors, former members of Congress, and from the State courts. A President's judicial selections are shaped by the same sorts of political considerations as other exercises of the chief executive's appointing power you read about in Chapter 14.

From George Washington's day, Presidents have looked to their own political party in making judicial appointments. Republican Presidents regularly choose Republicans; Democrats usually pick Democrats.

Every President knows that most of the judges he appoints will serve for decades. So, Presidents also regularly look for judges who share their own legal and political outlook—the President's ideology.

The President and his closest political and legal aides, especially the attorney general, take the lead in selecting federal judges, of course. Other major players in the process include influential senators, notably those from the nominee's home State; the legal profession, especially the American Bar Association's Committee on the Federal Judiciary; and various other important personalities in the President's political party.

## Terms and Pay of Judges

Article III, Section 1 reads, in part:

    “ The judges, both of the Supreme and inferior courts, shall hold their offices during good behavior . . . ”

The judges of the constitutional courts are appointed for life—until they resign, retire, or die in office. They may be removed only through the impeachment process. Only 13 federal judges have ever been impeached. Of them, seven were convicted and removed by the Senate, including three in the past few years.[8]

The Constitution's grant of what amounts to life tenure for most judges is intended, and works, to ensure the independence of the federal judiciary.

A few federal judges are not appointed for life. The judges of the Claims Court, the Court of Military Appeals, and the Court of Veterans Appeals are appointed for 15-year terms, and those of the Tax Court for 12 years. Territorial court judges are appointed to 10-year terms. In the District of Columbia, Superior Court judges are chosen for four-year terms; those who sit on the court of appeals are chosen for a period of eight years.

Article III, Section 1 also declares that federal judges

    “ shall, at stated times, receive for their services a compensation which shall not be diminished during their continuance in office. ”

Congress sets the salaries of all federal judges. For their salaries today, see page 478.

---

[7]Article II, Section 2, Clause 2.

[8]The judges removed from office were John Pickering of the district court in New Hampshire, for judicial misconduct and drunkenness, in 1804; West H. Humphreys of the district court in Tennessee, for disloyalty, in 1862; Robert W. Archbald of the old Commerce Court, for improper relations with litigants, in 1913; Halsted L. Ritter of the district court in Florida, on several counts of judicial misconduct, in 1936; Harry E. Claiborne of the district court in Nevada, for filing false income tax returns, in 1986; Alcee Hastings of the district court in Florida, on charges of bribery and false testimony, in 1989; and Walter Nixon of the district court in Mississippi, for perjury, in 1989.

Four judges, impeached by the House, were acquitted in the Senate. Two other district court judges, impeached by the House, resigned and so avoided a Senate trial.

Congress has provided a generous retirement arrangement for federal judges. They may retire at age 70, and if they have served for at least 10 years, receive full salary for the rest of their lives. Or, they may retire at full salary at age 65, after at least 15 years of service. The chief justice may call any retired judge back to temporary duty in a lower federal court at any time.

## Court Officers

Today, federal judges are little involved in the day-to-day administrative operations of the courts over which they preside. Their primary mission is to hear and decide cases. Other judicial personnel provide the support services necessary to permit federal judges to perform that basic task.

Each federal court appoints a clerk who has custody of the seal of the court and keeps a record of the court's proceedings. Deputy clerks, stenographers, bailiffs, and others assist the clerk.

Each of the 91 federal district courts now appoints at least one United States magistrate, an officer of the court who handles a number of legal matters once dealt with by the judges themselves. Federal magistrates serve eight-year terms. They issue warrants of arrest and often hear evidence to decide whether or not a person who has been arrested on a federal charge should be held for action by the grand jury. They also set bail in federal criminal cases, and even have the power to try those who are charged with certain minor offenses.

Each federal judicial district also has at least one bankruptcy judge. These court officers handle bankruptcy cases at the direction of the district court to which they are assigned.[9] There are now altogether 326 bankruptcy judges; they are appointed to 14-year terms by the judges of each of the federal courts of appeals.

The President appoints, subject to Senate confirmation, a United States attorney for each

federal judicial district. The U.S. attorneys and their assistants are responsible for the prosecution of all persons charged with federal crimes and they represent the United States in all civil actions brought by or against the government in their district.

The President and Senate also appoint a United States marshal to serve each district court. Each federal marshal and the marshal's deputies carry out duties much like those handled by a county sheriff and the sheriff's deputies. They make arrests in federal criminal cases, keep accused persons in custody, secure jurors, serve legal papers, keep order in the courtroom, and execute court orders and decisions.

United States attorneys and marshals are each appointed to four-year terms. Although they are officers of the court, they serve under the direction of the attorney general and are officials of the Department of Justice.

## Section 1 Review

1. **Define:** jurisdiction, exclusive jurisdiction, concurrent jurisdiction, plaintiff, defendant, original jurisdiction, appellate jurisdiction
2. For what reasons did the Framers provide for a national judiciary? *to create a national judiciary*
3. What is meant by the phrase "a dual system of courts"? *1 over the whole country + 1 over all 50 states.*
4. What are the two general principles that determine if the federal courts have jurisdiction over cases? *sub. matter + parties*
5. Who appoints federal judges and for what terms? *Pres. w/ senate approval - life term*
6. How may federal judges be removed from office? *impeachment - death, resignment, retirement*
7. Describe the functions of the officers who assist federal judges in the day-to-day operations of their courts. *hear and decide cases.*

### Critical Thinking

8. **Drawing Conclusions** (p. 19) In your opinion, what are the most important qualifications a President should consider in appointing a Supreme Court justice?

---

[9]Recall that bankruptcy is a legal proceeding in which a debtor's assets are distributed among those to whom the bankrupt person, business firm, or other organization owes money. Although some bankruptcy cases are heard in State courts, nearly all of them fall within the jurisdiction of the federal district courts.

★

## Should School Officials Have the Right to Search Your Property?

### *New Jersey* v. *T.L.O.*, 1985

In 1980, a teacher at Piscataway High School in Middlesex County, New Jersey, found T.L.O. and another girl smoking in a lavatory—a place that was by school rule, a nonsmoking area. The two girls were taken to the principal's office, where T.L.O.'s companion did admit that she had been smoking in the restroom. But T.L.O. denied that she had done so; in fact, she claimed that she did not smoke at all.

A vice-principal demanded to see T.L.O.'s purse. Searching through it, he found a pack of cigarettes. He also found rolling papers, a pipe, marijuana, a large wad of dollar bills, and two letters that indicated that T.L.O. was involved in marijuana dealing at the high school.

Both the police and T.L.O.'s mother were then notified of the situation, and T.L.O. was taken to the local police station. There she confessed that she had several times sold marijuana at the school.

In juvenile court, the judge found T.L.O. to be a delinquent, and he sentenced her to a year's probation on the drug-selling charge. On appeal, however, the New Jersey State Supreme Court overturned the juvenile court's action. The State's high court held that (1) the vice-principal's search of T.L.O.'s purse had been conducted in violation of her 4th and 14th Amendment protection against unreasonable searches and seizures, and (2) therefore, the exclusionary rule must be applied to the case—that is, that both the evidence that had been illegally taken from her purse and T.L.O.'s later confession could not be used against her in court.

In response, the State of New Jersey asked the United States Supreme Court to hear its appeal of the case.

*Review the following arguments presented to the U.S. Supreme Court:*

### Arguments for New Jersey

**1.** School officials act for the parents of students. Like parents, they do not need a warrant to make searches or seize evidence.
**2.** School officials must have broad powers to control student conduct, including the powers of search and seizure.
**3.** T.L.O.'s behavior furnished a reasonable basis for the search of her purse; therefore, the exclusionary rule does not apply.

### Arguments for T.L.O.

**1.** Public school officials are employees of the State, not representatives of parents; they have no right to act as parents.
**2.** School officials are public employees and so are obligated to respect every student's rights, including his or her right to privacy.
**3.** The search of T.L.O.'s purse and the seizure of its contents were unreasonable acts, and they led to her confession; therefore, the exclusionary rule does apply.

## Getting Involved

1. **Identify** the constitutional grounds upon which each side based its arguments.
2. **Debate** the opposing viewpoints presented in this case.
3. **Predict** how you think the Supreme Court ruled in this case and why. Then check page 767 of the Supreme Court Glossary. What does this case say about a student's right to privacy?

# 2 The Inferior Courts

**Find Out:**
- Where are most federal cases heard?
- What is the jurisdiction of the federal district court and the courts of appeals?

You know and use a great many words that have more than one meaning. The particular meaning of any of them depends on the context, or the setting, in which you use it. Thus, *pitch* can either be a baseball or a musical term; or it can be used to refer to the setting up of a tent, or to a high-pressure sales talk, or to a number of other things.

So it is with the word *inferior.* Here it describes the lower federal courts, those beneath the Supreme Court.

As you will see in this section, those very important courts handle nearly all of the cases tried in the federal courts.

## The District Courts

The United States district courts are the federal trial courts. Their 632 judges handle some 300,000 cases a year, some 80 percent of the federal caseload.

The district courts were created by Congress in the Judiciary Act of 1789. There are now 91 of them. The 50 States are divided into 89 judicial districts, with one court in each district. There is also a district court in the District of Columbia and another in Puerto Rico. The map on page 470 shows how these districts are distributed across the country.

Each State forms at least one federal judicial district. The larger, more populous States are divided into two or more districts—because of the larger amount of judicial business there, of course. At least two judges are assigned to each district, but many have several. Thus, New York is divided into four judicial districts; and one of those districts, the United States Judicial District for Southern New York, now has 28 judges.

Cases tried in the district courts are most often heard by a single judge. However, certain cases may be heard by a three-judge panel.[10]

**Jurisdiction**   The district courts have original jurisdiction over most cases that are heard in the federal courts.[11] That amounts to another way of saying that these district courts are the principal trial courts in the federal court system.

The district courts hear a wide range of both criminal cases and civil cases.[12] They try cases ranging from bank robbery, kidnapping, and mail fraud to counterfeiting, tax evasion, and narcotics violations. They hear civil cases arising under the bankruptcy, postal, tax, labor relations, public lands, civil rights, and other laws of the United States.

The district courts are the only federal courts that regularly use grand juries to indict defendants and petit juries to try defendants. (You will read about grand and petit juries in more detail in Chapters 20 and 25.)

Most of the decisions made in the 91 federal district courts are final. However, some cases are appealed to the court of appeals in that judicial circuit or, in a few instances, directly to the Supreme Court.

---

[10]Congress has directed that three-judge panels hear certain cases. Chiefly, these are cases that involve congressional districting or State legislative apportionment questions, those arising under the Civil Rights Act of 1964 or the Voting Rights Acts of 1965, 1970, 1975, and 1982, and certain antitrust actions.

[11]The district courts have original jurisdiction over all federal cases except: (1) those few cases that fall within the original jurisdiction of the United States Supreme Court and (2) those cases that are heard by the Court of International Trade or by one of the special courts (see Section 4).

[12]In the federal courts, a criminal case is one in which a defendant is tried for committing some action that Congress has declared by law to be a federal crime, a wrong against the public. A federal civil case involves some noncriminal matter, such as a dispute over the terms of a contract or a claim of patent infringement. The United States is always a party to a federal criminal case, as the prosecutor. Most civil cases involve private parties; but here, too, the United States may be one of the litigants, as either plaintiff or defendant.

## The Courts of Appeals

The courts of appeals were created by Congress in 1891. They were established as "gatekeepers" to relieve the Supreme Court of much of the burden of hearing appeals from the district courts.[13] Those appeals had become so numerous that the Supreme Court was then three years behind its docket—its list of cases to be heard.

There are now 12 courts of appeals in the judicial system. The United States is divided into 11 judicial circuits, with one court of appeals for each of those circuits; there is also one in the District of Columbia. Again, see the map on page 470.

Altogether, 179 circuit judges sit on these appellate courts. In addition, a justice of the Supreme Court is assigned to each of them. Take, for example, the United States Court of Appeals for the Eleventh Circuit. The circuit covers three States: Alabama, Georgia, and Florida. The court is composed of 12 judges, and Justice Anthony Kennedy is also assigned to the circuit. The judges hold sessions in a number of cities within the circuit.

Each of the courts of appeals usually sits in panels of three judges. However, occasionally, to hear an important case a court will sit *en banc*—that is, with all of the judges for that circuit participating.

**Jurisdiction**  The courts of appeals have only appellate jurisdiction. They hear cases on appeal from the lower federal courts. Most often, those appeals come from the district courts within their circuits. But some do come from the United States Tax Court and from the several territorial courts. The courts of appeals also hear appeals from the decisions of several federal regulatory agencies—from such quasi-judicial agencies as the Interstate Commerce Commission, the Nuclear Regulatory Commission, and the Federal Trade Commission.[14]

---

[13]These tribunals were originally known as the circuit courts of appeals. Before 1891, Supreme Court justices "rode circuit" to hear appeals from the district courts. Congress renamed these courts in 1948, but they still are often called the circuit courts.

[14]Recall that the several independent regulatory commissions have both quasi-legislative (rule-making) and quasi-judicial (decision-making) powers; see Chapter 15, pages 390–391.

▲ **Interpreting Political Cartoons**
What does this cartoon reveal about the need for the creation of the courts of appeals in 1891?

The courts of appeals now handle more than 40,000 cases a year. Their decisions are final, unless the Supreme Court chooses to hear appeals taken from them.

## Two Other Constitutional Courts

The Court of International Trade and the Court of Appeals for the Federal Circuit are also constitutional courts.

**The Court of International Trade**  The Trade Court was originally created as the Board of United States General Appraisers in 1890. That body became the Court of Customs in 1926, and Congress restructured and renamed that court in 1980.

The Trade Court now has nine judges, one of whom is its chief judge. It hears civil cases arising out of the tariff and other trade-related laws. The judges of the Trade Court sit in panels of three and often hold trials at such major ports as New Orleans, San Francisco, Boston, and New York.

Appeals from decisions of the Trade Court are taken to the Court of Appeals for the Federal Circuit.

**The Court of Appeals for the Federal Circuit**  Congress created the Court of Appeals for the Federal Circuit in 1982. It established the new tribunal to centralize, and so speed up, the handling of appeals in certain kinds of civil cases.

## Federal Judicial Circuits and Districts

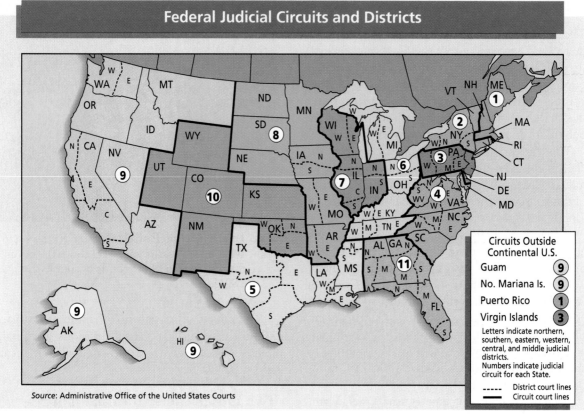

*Source: Administrative Office of the United States Courts*

▲ **Interpreting Maps**   Examine the outlines of the judicial circuits and districts on the map above. How do you think the division of judicial districts was determined?

This court, unlike the 12 other federal courts of appeals, hears cases from all across the country. That is, has a nationwide jurisdiction.

The Court of Appeals for the Federal Circuit hears appeals from several different courts. Many of its cases come from the Trade Court, and others from the Claims Court and the Court of Veterans Appeals, two special courts. It also hears appeals in certain cases—those involving patents, trademarks, or copyrights—decided by any of the 91 district courts around the country. Then, too, it takes cases that arise out of the administrative rulings made by the International Trade Commission, the Patent and Trademark Office in the Department of Commerce, and the Merit Systems Protection Board.

The Court of Appeals for the Federal Circuit has 12 judges. Appeals from their decisions are occasionally carried to the United States Supreme Court.

## Section 2 Review

1. (a) How many federal district courts are there? (b) How many district court judges? *91;632*
2. Over what cases do the district courts have jurisdiction? *criminal & civil*
3. Why were the courts of appeals created? *to relieve Sup. court of burden of appeals*
4. Where do cases that reach the courts of appeals originate? *the district courts in their circuit.*
5. (a) Over what type of cases does the Court of International Trade have jurisdiction? (b) The Court of Appeals for the Federal Circuit? *tariffs & trade related; patents copyrights*

### Critical Thinking

6. **Drawing Conclusions** (p. 19) A significant portion of the federal court system is set up to hear appeals. What does this fact suggest about the nature of law and judicial proceedings?

★

# 3  The Supreme Court

**Find Out:**

- For what reasons is the Supreme Court of the United States often called the High Court?
- Why is judicial review such a key feature of the American system of government?

**Key Terms:**

writ of certiorari, certificate, majority opinion, concurring opinion, dissenting opinion

The eagle, the flag, Uncle Sam—you almost certainly recognize these symbols. They are widely used to represent the United States. You probably also know the symbol for justice—the blindfolded woman holding a balanced scale. She represents what is perhaps this nation's highest goal: equal justice for all. Indeed, those words are chiseled into the marble above the entrance to the Supreme Court building in Washington, D.C.

The Supreme Court of the United States is the only court specifically created in the Constitution.[15] It is made up of the chief justice of the United States, whose office is also established by the Constitution,[16] and eight associate justices.[17] The Framers quite purposely placed the Court on an equal plane with the President and Congress and designed it as the apex, the highest point, of the nation's judicial system. As the highest court in the land, the Supreme Court stands as the court of last resort in all questions of federal law. That is, it is the final authority in any case involving any question arising under the Constitution, an act of Congress, or a treaty of the United States.

---

[15]Article III, Section 1.

[16]Article I, Section 3, Clause 6.

[17]Congress sets the number of associate justices and thus the size of the Supreme Court. The Judiciary Act of 1789 created a Court of six justices, including the chief justice. Its size was reduced to five members in 1801, but increased to seven in 1807, to nine in 1837, and to 10 in 1863. It was reduced to seven in 1866 and raised to its present size in 1869.

## *VOICES on Government*

### On the Function of the Supreme Court

**Sandra Day O'Connor,** Associate Justice of the Supreme Court

"[O]ne of the Supreme Court's most important functions—perhaps the most important function—is to oversee the system-wide elaboration of federal law, with an eye toward creating and preserving uniformity of interpretation. Today, this function is uppermost in the minds of the Justices in exercising the discretion to take cases for review. Indeed, the most commonly enunciated reason for granting review on a case is the need to resolve conflicts among other courts over the interpretation of federal law."

## Judicial Review

As you read in Chapter 3 and elsewhere, most courts in this country, both federal and State, may exercise the critically important power of judicial review. They have the extraordinary power to decide the constitutionality of an act of government, whether executive, legislative, or judicial. The ultimate exercise of that power rests with the Supreme Court of the United States. That single fact makes the Supreme Court the final authority on the meaning of the Constitution.

The Constitution does not in so many words provide for the power of judicial review. Still, there is little room for doubt that the Framers intended that the federal courts—and, in particular, the Supreme Court—should have the power.[18] In *The Federalist* No. 78 Alexander Hamilton wrote:

> ❝The interpretation of the laws is the proper and peculiar province of the courts. A constitution is, in fact, and must be regarded by the judges, as a fundamental law. It therefore belongs to them to ascertain its meaning, as well as the meaning of any particular act proceeding from the legislative body. If there should happen to be an irreconcilable variance between the two, that which has the superior obligation and validity ought, of course, to be preferred; or, in other words, the Constitution ought to be preferred to the statute, the intention of the people to the intention of their agents. ❞

The Court first asserted its power of judicial review in the classic case of *Marbury* v. *Madison* in 1803.[19] The case arose in the aftermath of the stormy elections of 1800. Thomas Jefferson and his Anti-Federalists had won the presidency and control of both houses of Congress. The outgoing Federalists, stung by their defeat, then tried to pack the judiciary with loyal party members. Congress created several new federal judgeships in the early weeks of 1801; President John Adams quickly filled those judgeships with Federalists.

William Marbury had been appointed a justice of the peace for the District of Columbia. The Senate had confirmed his appointment and, late the night of March 3, 1801, the soon-to-be outgoing President Adams had signed his and a number of other new judges' commissions of office. The next day Jefferson became the President—and learned that Marbury's commission, and several others, had not yet been delivered.

Angered by the Federalists' court-packing, Jefferson at once told James Madison, the new secretary of state, not to deliver those commissions to the "midnight justices." William Marbury then went to the Supreme Court, seeking a *writ of mandamus*[20] to force delivery.

Marbury based his suit on a provision of the Judiciary Act of 1789, in which Congress had created the federal court system. That law gave the Supreme Court the right to hear such suits in its *original* jurisdiction (not on appeal from a lower court).

In a unanimous opinion written by Chief Justice John Marshall, the Court refused Marbury's request.[21] It did so because it found the section of the judiciary act on which Marbury had based his case in conflict with the Constitution and, therefore, void. Specifically, it found the statute in conflict with Article III, Section 2, Clause 2, which reads in part:

> ❝In all cases affecting ambassadors, other public ministers and consuls, and those in which a State shall be a party, the Supreme Court shall have original jurisdiction. In all other cases before mentioned, the Supreme Court shall have appellate jurisdiction . . . ❞

The impact of the Court's decision goes far beyond the fate of an obscure individual named William Marbury. In this decision, Chief Justice Marshall claimed for the Court the right to declare acts of Congress unconstitutional, and so laid the foundation for the judicial branch's key role in the development of the American system of government.

Marshall's powerful opinion was based on three propositions. First, the Constitution is, by its own terms, *the* supreme law of the land. Second, all legislative enactments, and all other actions of government, are subordinate to and cannot be allowed to conflict with the supreme law. Third, judges are sworn to enforce the provisions of the Constitution and therefore must refuse to enforce any governmental action they find to be in conflict with it.

---

[18]See Article III, Section 2, setting out the Court's jurisdiction, and Article VI, Section 2, the Supremacy Clause.

[19]It is often mistakenly said that the Court first exercised the power in this case, but, in fact, the Court did so at least as early as *Hylton* v. *United States* in 1798. In that case it upheld the constitutionality of a tax Congress had laid on carriages.

[20]A court order compelling an officer of government to perform an act which that officer has a clear legal duty to perform.

---

[21]Marshall was appointed chief justice by President John Adams, and he took office on January 31, 1801. He served in the post for 34 years, until his death on July 6, 1835. He also served as Adams's secretary of state from May 13, 1800 to March 4, 1801. Thus, he served as secretary of state and as chief justice for more than a month at the end of the Adams administration. What is more, he was the secretary of state who had failed to deliver Marbury's commission in a timely fashion.

**"The Chosen Few"** The members of the High Court pose for their official photograph. From left to right are associate justices Clarence Thomas, Antonin Scalia, Sandra Day O'Connor, Anthony Kennedy, David Souter, Stephen Breyer, John Paul Stevens, Chief Justice William H. Rehnquist, and Ruth Bader Ginsburg.

The Court has used its power of judicial review in thousands of cases since 1803. Usually it has upheld (but sometimes denied) the constitutionality of federal and State actions.

The dramatic and often far-reaching effects of the Supreme Court's exercise of the power of judicial review tends to overshadow much of its other work. Each year it hears dozens of cases in which questions of constitutionality are not raised, but in which federal law still is interpreted and applied. Thus, many of the more important statutes that Congress has passed have been brought to the Supreme Court time and again for decision. So, too, have many of the lesser ones. In interpreting those laws and applying them to specific situations, the Court has had a real impact on both their meaning and their effect.

Remember, too, that the Court has a very large role as the umpire in the federal system, as noted in Chapter 4. It decides those legal disputes that arise between the National Government and the States and those that arise between or among the States.

## Jurisdiction

The Supreme Court has both original and appellate jurisdiction. But most of its cases come on appeal—from the lower federal courts and from the highest State courts.

Article III, Section 2 of the Constitution spells out two classes of cases that may be heard by the High Court in its original jurisdiction: (1) those to which a State is a party and (2) those affecting ambassadors, other public ministers, and consuls.

Congress cannot enlarge on this constitutional grant of original jurisdiction. If Congress could do so, it would in effect be amending the Constitution. But Congress can implement the constitutional provision, and it has done so. It has provided that the Court shall have original *and* exclusive jurisdiction over (1) all controversies between two or more States and (2) all cases brought against ambassadors or other public ministers, but not consuls. The Court may, if it chooses to do so, take original jurisdiction over any other case covered by the broad wording in Article III, Section 2 of the Constitution. But, almost always, those cases are tried in the lower courts. The Supreme Court hears only a very small number of cases in its original jurisdiction—in fact, only a case or two each term.

Article III, Section 2 of the Constitution also gives to Congress the power to set the Court's appellate jurisdiction. Until 1925 the High Court had little control over its caseload; since then, however, Congress has given it an increasingly broad authority to choose the cases it will review. Today, that authority is practically complete.

## How Cases Reach the Court

Some 5,000 to 6,000 cases are now appealed to the Supreme Court each year. Of these, the Court accepts only a few hundred for decision. The Court selects those cases it will hear according to "the rule of four": at least four of its nine justices must agree that a case should be put on the Court's docket.

More than half the cases decided by the Court are disposed of in brief orders. For example, an order may remand (return) a case to a lower court for reconsideration in the light of some other recent and related case decided by the High Court. All told, the Court decides, after hearing arguments and with full opinions, fewer than 100 cases a year.

Most cases reach the Supreme Court by **writ of certiorari** (from the Latin, "to be made more certain"). This writ is an order by the Court directing a lower court to send up the record in a given case for its review.

Either party to a case can petition the Court to issue a writ. But, again, "cert" is granted in only a limited number of instances—typically, only when a petition raises some important constitutional question or a serious problem of statutory interpretation.

When certiorari is denied, the decision of the lower court stands in that particular case. But the denial of cert is not a decision on the merits of a case. All that a denial means is that, for

## Chief Justices of the United States

| Name and Years of Service | State From Which Appointed | President By Whom Appointed | Life Span | Age When Appointed |
|---|---|---|---|---|
| John Jay (1789–1795) | New York | Washington | 1745–1829 | 44 |
| John Rutledge (1795)* | South Carolina | Washington | 1739–1800 | 55 |
| Oliver Ellsworth (1796–1800) | Connecticut | Washington | 1745–1807 | 51 |
| John Marshall (1801–1835) | Virginia | John Adams | 1755–1835 | 46 |
| Roger B. Taney (1836–1864) | Maryland | Jackson | 1777–1864 | 59 |
| Salmon P. Chase (1864–1873) | Ohio | Lincoln | 1808–1873 | 56 |
| Morrison R. Waite (1874–1888) | Ohio | Grant | 1816–1888 | 58 |
| Melville W. Fuller (1888–1910) | Illinois | Cleveland | 1833–1910 | 55 |
| Edward D. White (1910–1921) | Louisiana | Taft | 1845–1921 | 65 |
| William Howard Taft (1921–1930) | Connecticut | Harding | 1857–1930 | 64 |
| Charles Evans Hughes (1930–1941) | New York | Hoover | 1862–1948 | 68 |
| Harlan F. Stone (1941–1946) | New York | F. D. Roosevelt | 1872–1946 | 69 |
| Fred M. Vinson (1946–1953) | Kentucky | Truman | 1890–1953 | 56 |
| Earl Warren (1953–1969) | California | Eisenhower | 1891–1974 | 62 |
| Warren E. Burger (1969–1986) | Washington, D.C. | Nixon | 1907– | 61 |
| William H. Rehnquist (1986– ) | Arizona | Reagan | 1924– | 62 |

*Rutledge was appointed chief justice on July 1, 1795, while Congress was not in session. He presided over the August 1795 term of the Supreme Court, but the Senate rejected his appointment on December 15, 1795.

**Interpreting Tables**   Which of the nation's now 16 Chief Justices held that post for the longest time, and which for the shortest term?

## Justices of the Supreme Court

| Name | State From Which Appointed | President By Whom Appointed | Year of Birth | Year When Appointed |
|------|---------------------------|----------------------------|---------------|---------------------|
| **Chief Justice:** William H. Rehnquist | Arizona | Reagan | 1924 | 1986* |
| **Associate Justices:** John Paul Stevens | Illinois | Ford | 1916 | 1975 |
| Sandra Day O'Connor | Arizona | Reagan | 1930 | 1981 |
| Antonin Scalia | Washington, D.C. | Reagan | 1936 | 1986 |
| Anthony M. Kennedy | California | Reagan | 1935 | 1988 |
| David H. Souter | New Hampshire | Bush | 1939 | 1990 |
| Clarence Thomas | Washington, D.C. | Bush | 1948 | 1991 |
| Ruth Bader Ginsburg | Washington, D.C. | Clinton | 1933 | 1993 |
| Stephen G. Breyer | Massachusetts | Clinton | 1938 | 1994 |

*Originally nominated as an associate justice by President Nixon in 1971.

**Interpreting Tables**    The judicial appointments a President makes have long-term consequences. Which President named the largest number of the current members of the Supreme Court?

whatever reason, four or more justices could not agree that the Supreme Court should accept that case for review.

A few cases do reach the Court in yet another way, by **certificate**. This process is used when a lower court is not clear about the procedure or the rule of law that should apply in a case. The lower court asks the Supreme Court to certify the answer to a specific question in the matter.

Most cases that reach the Court do so from the highest State courts and the federal courts of appeal. A few do come, however, from the federal district courts and a very few from the Court of Military Appeals.

## The Supreme Court at Work

The Court sits from the first Monday in October to sometime the following June or July. Each term is identified by the year in which it began. Thus, the 1995 term begins on October 4, 1995.

**Oral Arguments**    Once the Supreme Court accepts a case, it sets a date on which lawyers on both sides will present oral arguments.

As a rule, the justices consider cases in two-week cycles, from October to early May. They hear oral arguments in several cases for two weeks;

then the justices recess for two weeks, to consider those cases and handle other Court business.

While the Supreme Court is hearing oral arguments, it convenes at 10 A.M. on Mondays, Tuesdays, Wednesdays, and sometimes Thursdays. At those public sessions, the lawyers make their oral arguments. Their presentations are almost always limited to 30 minutes.[22] Most lawyers try to use that half hour to emphasize the major points they made in their written briefs.

**Briefs**    Briefs are written documents filed with the Court before oral argument. They are detailed statements that support one side of a case and are largely built of relevant facts and the citation of previous cases. Many run to hundreds of pages.

The Court may also receive *amicus curiae* (friend of the court) briefs. These are briefs filed by persons or groups who are not actual parties to a case but who nonetheless have a substantial

---

[22]The justices usually listen closely to the lawyers' oral arguments and sometimes interrupt them with questions or requests for information. After 25 minutes of a lawyer's time, a white light comes on at the lectern from which he or she addresses the Court; five minutes later a red light signals the end of that lawyer's presentation, even if he or she is in midsentence.

interest in its outcome. Thus, for example, cases involving such highly charged matters as abortion or affirmative action regularly attract a large number of *amicus* briefs. But, notice, these briefs can be filed only with the Court's permission, or at its request.

**The Solicitor General**    The solicitor general, a principal officer in the Department of Justice, is often called the Federal Government's chief lawyer. The solicitor general represents the United States in all cases to which it is a party in the Supreme Court,[23] and may appear in any federal or State court. He or she decides which cases the government should ask the Supreme Court to review and, also, what position the United States should take in cases before the High Court. The solicitor general often files *amicus* briefs, urging the Federal Government's views in those cases.

**The Conference**    On Wednesdays and Fridays through a term, the justices meet in conference. There, in closest secrecy, they consider the cases in which they have heard oral arguments.[24]

The chief justice presides over the conference. He or she speaks first on each case to be considered, and usually indicates how he or she intends to vote. Then each associate justice summarizes his or her views. Those presentations are made in order of seniority—with the justice most recently named to the Court speaking last. After the justices are "polled," they usually debate the case.

About a third of all the Court's decisions are unanimous, but most find the Court divided. The High Court is sometimes criticized for its split decisions. But, notice, its cases pose very difficult questions. And many also present questions on which lower courts have disagreed. In short, most of the Court's cases are the difficult ones; the easy cases seldom get that far.

**Opinions**    If the chief justice is in the majority on a case, he or she assigns the writing of the Court's opinion. When the chief justice is in the minority, the assignment is handled by the senior associate justice on the majority side.

The Court's opinion is often called the **majority opinion**; officially, it is the Opinion of the Court. It announces the Court's decision in a case and sets out the reasoning on which it is based.[25] Often, one or more of the justices who agree with the Court's decision may write a **concurring opinion**—to make or emphasize a point that was not made in the majority opinion. One or more **dissenting opinions** are often written, too, by those justices who do not agree with the Court's majority decision.

The Court's written opinions are exceedingly valuable. The majority opinions stand as precedents to be followed in similar cases as they arise in the lower courts or reach the Supreme Court. The concurring opinions may bring the Supreme Court to modify its present stand in future cases. Chief Justice Hughes once described dissenting opinions as "an appeal to the brooding spirit of the law, to the intelligence of a future day." On rare occasions, the Supreme Court does reverse itself; the minority opinion of today could become the Court's majority position in the future.

## Section **3** Review

**1. Define:** writ of certiorari, certificate, majority opinion, concurring opinion, dissenting opinion
**2.** (a) Which is the only court created in the Constitution? (b) The only judicial office?
**3.** What is the power of judicial review?
**4.** (a) Over what cases does the Court have original jurisdiction? (b) Exclusive jurisdiction?
**5.** From what courts are cases appealed to the Supreme Court?

**Critical Thinking**

**6. Demonstrating Reasoned Judgment** (p. 19) The chapter says that "easy" cases do not reach the Supreme Court. For what reason do you think this is so?

★

---

[23]The attorney general may argue the government's position before the Supreme Court but rarely does.
[24]At conference, the justices also decide which new cases they will accept for decision.

[25]Most majority opinions, and many concurring and dissenting opinions, run to dozens of pages. Some decisions are accompanied by very brief and unsigned opinions, however. These *per curiam*, or for the court, opinions seldom run more than a paragraph or two and usually dispose of relatively uncomplicated cases.

# 4 The Special Courts

**Find Out:**

- In what ways do the special courts differ from the constitutional courts?

**Key Term:**

redress

Recall that, in the United States, the federal court system is made up of two quite distinct types of courts: (1) the constitutional, or regular courts, at which you have just looked, and (2) the special courts, to which you now turn.

The several special courts in the federal judiciary are those courts that Congress has created to hear only certain cases—cases that involve only a particular few of the many subjects covered by the numerous expressed powers of Congress.

These courts, also known as legislative courts, were not established under Article III, so they do not exercise the broad "judicial power of the United States." Rather, as you will see in this section, each of them has a very narrow jurisdiction.

## The U.S. Federal Claims Court

The United States cannot be sued—by anyone, in any court, for any reason—without its consent. It may be taken to court only in those cases in which Congress has declared that the government is open to suit.[26]

---

[26]The government is shielded from suit by the doctrine of sovereign immunity. It comes from an ancient principle of English public law summed up by the phrase: "The King can do no wrong." The rule is not intended to protect public officials from charges of corruption or any other wrongdoing. Rather, it is intended to prevent government from being hamstrung in its own courts. Congress has long since agreed to a long list of legitimate court actions against the government.

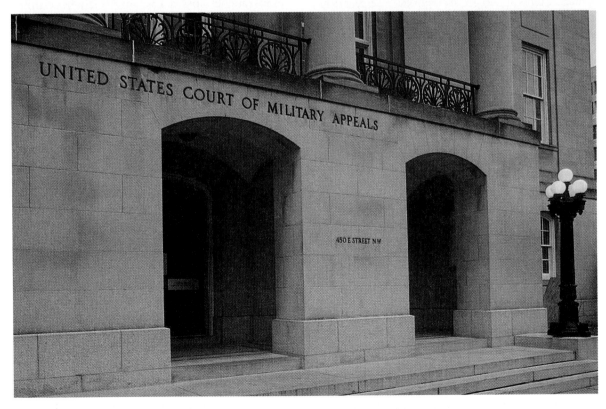

▲ **"GI Supreme Court"** The Court of Military Appeals, located in Washington, D.C., is a special court that reviews the more serious court-martial convictions of members of the armed forces.

## The National Judiciary

| Court | Created | Number of Courts | Number of Judges | Term of Judges | Judges Appointed by[a] | Salary of Judges |
|---|---|---|---|---|---|---|
| District Court | 1789 | 91 | 632 | Life | President | $133,644 |
| Court of Appeals | 1891 | 12 | 179 | Life | President | $141,763 |
| Supreme Court | 1789 | 1 | 9 | Life | President | $164,090[b] |
| Trade Court | 1926 | 1 | 9 | Life | President | $133,644 |
| Court of Appeals for the Federal Circuit | 1982 | 1 | 12 | Life | President | $141,763 |
| Federal Claims Court | 1982 | 1 | 16 | 15 years | President | $133,644 |
| Court of Military Appeals | 1950 | 1 | 5 | 15 years | President | $141,763 |
| Court of Veterans Appeals | 1988 | 1 | 7 | 15 years | President | $133,644 |
| Tax Court | 1969 | 1 | 19 | 12 years | President | $133,644 |

[a]With Senate confirmation    [b]Chief justice receives $171,299.

▲ **Interpreting Tables**   How are (1) the principle of separation of powers and (2) the principle of checks and balances illustrated in this table?

Originally, a person with a claim against the United States could secure **redress**—satisfaction of the claim, payment—only by an act of Congress. In 1855, however, Congress set up the Court of Claims to hear these pleas.[27] Congress restructured the Court of Claims as the United States Claims Court in 1982, and that body became the United States Court of Federal Claims in 1993.

The Claims Court is composed of 16 judges appointed by the President and Senate for 15-year terms. They hold trials—hear claims for damages against the government—throughout the country.[28] Those claims they uphold cannot in fact be paid until Congress appropriates the money, which it does almost as a matter of standard procedure. Appeals from the court's decisions may be carried to the Court of Appeals for the Federal Circuit.

Occasionally, those who lose in the Claims Court still manage to win some compensation.

Some years ago, for example, a Puget Sound mink rancher lost a case in which he claimed that low-flying Navy planes had frightened his animals and caused several of the females to become sterile. He asked $100 per mink. After the rancher lost the case, his congressman introduced a private bill that eventually paid him $10 for each animal.

## The Territorial Courts

Acting under its power to "make all needful rules and regulations respecting the territory . . . belonging to the United States,"[29] Congress has created courts for the nation's territories. Today these courts sit in the Virgin Islands, Guam, and the Northern Marianas and function much as do the local courts in each of the 50 States.

## The Courts of the District of Columbia

Acting under its power "to exercise exclusive legislation in all cases whatsoever, over such District . . .

---

[27]Congress acted under its expressed power to pay the debts of the United States, Article I, Section 8, Clause 1.

[28]Under the Federal Tort Claims Act of 1946, the district courts also have jurisdiction over many claims cases, but only where the amount sought is not more than $10,000.

---

[29]Article IV, Section 3, Clause 2. Two judges hear cases in the territorial court in the Virgin Islands, one in Guam, and one in the Northern Marianas.

as may . . . become the seat of the government of the United States,"[30] Congress has set up a judicial system for the nation's capital. Both the District Court and the Court of Appeals for the District of Columbia hear many local cases as well as those they try as constitutional courts. Congress has also established two local courts, much like the courts in the States: a superior court, which is the general trial court, and a court of appeals.

## The Court of Military Appeals

Acting under its power "to make rules for the government and regulation of the land and naval forces,"[31] Congress created the United States Court of Military Appeals in 1950. The court is a civilian tribunal. Its chief judge and four associate judges are *not* members of the armed forces; they are appointed by the President and Senate to 15-year terms.

The Court of Military Appeals has been called the GI Supreme Court. It reviews the more serious court-martial convictions of members of the armed forces. Appeals from its decisions can be, but almost never are, heard by the Supreme Court. The Court of Military Appeals is, then, the court of last resort in most cases involving offenses against military law.

## The Court of Veterans Appeals

Acting under its power to "constitute tribunals inferior to the Supreme Court,"[32] Congress created the United States Court of Veterans Appeals in 1988. This newest court in the federal judiciary is composed of a chief judge and up to six associate judges, all appointed by the President and Senate to 15-year terms.

---

[30]Article I, Section 8, Clause 17.

[31]Article I, Section 8, Clause 14. This provision, and the 5th Amendment, allows Congress to regulate the conduct of members of the armed forces under a separate, noncivilian code of military law. The present-day system of military justice has developed over a period of more than 200 years, since the Revolutionary War. Today, the Uniform Code of Military Justice, passed by Congress in 1950, and the military justice acts of 1968 and of 1983 are the major statutes designed to meet the special disciplinary needs of the armed forces.

[32]Article I, Section 8, Clause 9.

The court has the power to hear appeals from the decisions of an administrative agency, the Board of Veterans Appeals in the Department of Veterans Affairs. Thus, this court hears cases in which individuals claim that the VA has denied or otherwise mishandled valid claims for veterans' benefits. Appeals from the decisions of the Court of Veterans Appeals can be taken to the Court of Appeals for the Federal Circuit.

## The United States Tax Court

Acting under its constitutionally granted power to tax,[33] Congress established the United States Tax Court in 1969. The Tax Court has 19 judges, one of whom serves as chief judge. Each of these 19 judges is named by the President and the Senate for a 12-year term.

The Tax Court hears civil, but not criminal, cases involving disputes over the application of the tax laws. Most of its cases, then, are generated by the Internal Revenue Service and other Treasury Department agencies. Its decisions may be appealed to the federal courts of appeals.

# Section **4** Review

1. **Define:** redress
2. Which are the special courts in the national judiciary?
3. (a) Over what types of cases do the territorial courts have jurisdiction? (b) The Claims Court? (c) The Court of Veterans Appeals?
4. In what sense is the Court of Military Appeals the court of last resort for most cases involving offenses against military law?

## Critical Thinking

5. **Checking Consistency** (p. 19) The powers of Congress have increased over the years. So, too, has the number of courts in the federal judiciary. How are these two facts related?

★

---

[33]Article I, Section 8, Clause 1.

# Identifying Assumptions

Identifying assumptions means recognizing unstated beliefs that may underlie a statement, action, or event. An assumption is an idea that a person assumes to be true. In reality, an assumption may prove to be either true or false. But before you can determine the accuracy of an assumption, you must be able to identify it.

Newspaper editorial and opinion pieces, such as the one below, frequently contain many assumptions. Follow the steps below to practice identifying assumptions.

**1. Read the selection carefully to determine its topic.** Identify the subject matter of the editorial in question. Answer the following questions: (a) What is the subject of the editorial below? (b) What is the editorial's overall message?

**2. Define the author's opinion and the arguments used to defend it.** Summarize the author's opinion on the subject and the way in which he or she states the argument.

Answer the following question: On what grounds does the author base his or her opinions?

**3. Look for facts that support the author's opinion.** An author will often use factual information to support his or her opinions. Factual information can include statistical data, direct quotations, and any other information that everyone accepts as correct. Answer the following questions: (a) What factual information, if any, does the writer cite in the editorial? (b) Which of the writer's points are supported by facts?

**4. Identify any assumptions used in the author's argument.** When an author presents an opinion as a fact without valid factual information to support it, the author has made an assumption. For each of the arguments presented in the editorial, ask: Is there any factual information to support the opinion?

---

### The *New York Times*
### April 7, 1994

"The shoes are large," President Clinton said yesterday of the retiring Supreme Court Justice Harry Blackmun. "The role that he has filled on this Court is terribly important. I will attempt to appoint someone of genuine stature and largeness of ability and spirit to the Court."

Mr. Clinton first must find a nominee of unquestioned excellence who will secure the Court's ideological balance, someone highly qualified who, like Justice Blackmun, will hold the line on civil rights, civil liberties, abortion, religious liberty and other precious rights that the Reagan and Bush Administrations sought to restrict.

But in seeking candidates of excellence who will protect basic liberties, the President needs to reach beyond the herd of white male candidates who have long been amply represented on the Court. Mr. Clinton has a chance to make the high court look more like the face of America. That would enhance the stature, competence and spirit of the Supreme Court itself. The institution's ability to adjudicate for an increasingly diverse nation will be improved if it has more members who come from more richly diverse communities. . . .

A Supreme Court that looks more like America can do more for justice because it starts by earning more of America's confidence. President Clinton and his judicial talent scouts know this, and should not forget it.

# Chapter-in-Brief

Scan all headings, photographs, charts, and other visuals in the chapter before reading the section summaries below.

## Section 1 The National Judiciary (pp. 461–466)
In reaction to a major flaw in the Articles of Confederation, the Framers included a judiciary in the Constitution. Article III calls for the establishment of a Supreme Court and gives Congress power to set up other courts. These federal courts work alongside the court systems of the 50 States.

The federal system sets up two types of courts: special courts, which hear a narrow range of cases related to the expressed powers of Congress; and constitutional courts. These include the Supreme Court, district courts, courts of appeals, and several others.

The federal courts have jurisdiction over (the power to try and to decide) only certain cases. Their jurisdiction is determined by the subject matter of a case and/or the parties involved in that case. Most cases do not fall within the jurisdiction of the federal courts.

Judges in the federal courts are appointed by the President and confirmed by the Senate. Judges of the constitutional courts are appointed for life (though they can be impeached).

## Section 2 The Inferior Courts (pp. 468–470)
The inferior courts include all constitutional courts below the Supreme Court. The district courts are the federal trial courts and hear about 80 percent of the federal caseload. There are 91 of these courts spread across the country, with at least one in each State. District courts have original jurisdiction over most cases heard in the federal courts.

The courts of appeals have only appellate jurisdiction. This means they can only hear cases on appeal from another court. There are 12 courts of appeals, with 179 judges. Each court is also assigned one of the Supreme Court justices.

There are two other inferior courts: the Court of International Trade and the Court of Appeals for the Federal Circuit.

## Section 3 The Supreme Court (pp. 471–476)
The Supreme Court has the final word on the constitutionality of any issue. The key to the Court's power is its power of judicial review. This means that the Court can determine the constitutionality of an act of government. The Supreme Court claimed this power in the landmark case *Marbury* v. *Madison*.

The Court has appellate jurisdiction and original jurisdiction over specific types of cases. In reality, the Court hears only those few hundred cases that pose complicated or important constitutional questions.

After hearing oral arguments from lawyers in the case and reading their briefs, the justices render opinions. The majority opinion states the majority decision of the court. Justices who agree with that decision but who wish to state other or additional reasons issue concurrent opinions. Justices who disagree issue dissenting opinions.

## Section 4 The Special Courts (pp. 477–479)
Special courts are sometimes called legislative courts. Their job is to hear cases that arise from the exercise by Congress of certain of its expressed powers. For example, Congress has created territorial courts, acting under its constitutional power to govern territories of the United States.

There are also the United States Federal Claims Court, the courts of the District of Columbia, a Court of Military Appeals, a Court of Veterans Affairs, and a United States Tax Court. These courts were established by Congress in the exercise of its various expressed powers.

# Chapter Review

## Vocabulary and Key Terms

- jurisdiction (p. 462)
- exclusive jurisdiction (p. 464)
- concurrent jurisdiction (p. 464)
- plaintiff (p. 464)
- defendant (p. 464)

- original jurisdiction (p. 464)
- appellate jurisdiction (p. 464)
- writ of certiorari (p. 474)
- certificate (p. 475)
- majority opinion (p. 476)

- concurring opinion (p. 476)
- dissenting opinion (p. 476)
- redress (p. 478)

**Matching:** *Review the key terms in the list above. If you are not sure of a term's meaning, look up the term and review its definition. Choose a term from the list above that best matches each description.*

1. the satisfaction of a claim
2. the power of a court to hear a case
3. a written statement by more than half the judges on a court supporting the court's decision
4. an order of the Supreme Court directing a lower court to send the Court the record of a certain case
5. the authority of a court to review the decisions of lower courts

**True or False:** *Determine whether each statement is true or false. If it is true, write "true." If it is false, change the underlined word or words to make the statement true.*

1. A court in which a case is heard for the first time is said to have <u>original jurisdiction</u> over the case.
2. A <u>concurring opinion</u> expresses a judge or judges' disagreement with a court's majority decision.
3. A <u>plaintiff</u> is the person who brings a suit against another party.
4. <u>Certificate</u> is the most common way by which a case reaches the United States Supreme Court.

**Word Relationships:** *Distinguish between the words in each pair.*

1. exclusive jurisdiction/concurrent jurisdiction
2. plaintiff/defendant
3. writ of certiorari/certificate

## Main Ideas

### Section 1 (pp. 461–466)

1. For what reasons was the national judiciary created?
2. Under what circumstances do federal courts have jurisdiction in a case?
3. In what ways does the method of selection, terms, and salaries of judges play a role in preserving the independence of the judicial branch?

### Section 2 (pp. 468–470)

4. What are the inferior courts?
5. What is the role of the inferior courts in the national judiciary?
6. Why can it be said that the United States district courts are the principal trial courts in the federal judiciary?

### Section 3 (pp. 471–476)

7. Why is the Supreme Court's exercise of the power of judicial review so significant, and how did the Court gain that power?
8. What kinds of cases does the Supreme Court hear, and by what means do they get there?

9. What are the Court's opinions and what makes them so important?

**Section 4** (pp. 477–479)
10. What role do the special courts play in the federal court system?
11. What does it mean to say that these courts have a very narrow jurisdiction?
12. Which court would hear a civil case arising out of a person's federal income tax return?

## Critical Thinking

1. **Identifying Alternatives** (p. 19)   Federal judges are always appointed for life. (a) In your opinion, is this the best way to achieve a judiciary that is free from political pressures? (b) What other methods of achieving an independent judiciary can you think of?
2. **Checking Consistency** (p. 19)   Consider the principles of popular sovereignty and majority rule discussed in earlier chapters. Explain why you do or do not think the power of judicial review is consistent with those concepts.
3. **Testing Conclusions** (p. 19)   Woodrow Wilson once described the Supreme Court as "a constitutional convention in continuous session." Find evidence in the chapter to support this view.
4. **Identifying Assumptions** (p. 19)   Chief Justice Warren Burger once suggested that a new level of appellate courts be created just below the Supreme Court to relieve its caseload. What assumption do you think that proposal makes about the cases that reach the Supreme Court?

## Getting Involved

1. **Writing Your Opinion**   You are a newspaper editor in the year 1803. The Supreme Court has just issued its opinion in *Marbury* v. *Madison*. Write a newspaper editorial in which you respond to this decision. Review the case and its outcome by reading page 472. Begin your editorial by telling readers briefly about the facts of the case and explaining the significance of the decision. Then, explain the reasons why you agree or disagree with the decision. Devote one well-written paragraph to each of your ideas. Then, review your first draft to ensure that your editorial forcefully and clearly argues your point. Finally, correct any errors and draft a final copy.
2. **Class Debate**   Hold a debate on the following topic: *Resolved*, That federal judges should be popularly elected, not appointed. Select teams to debate each side of the issue. The rest of the class can evaluate each team's presentation and vote to determine the "winning" side.
3. **Class Activity**   Create a bulletin board display devoted to the federal courts and their activities. Ask each class member to bring in newspaper or magazine articles, political cartoons, or other materials that communicate information about the judicial system. Create separate categories for the Supreme Court, other federal courts, State courts, and local courts.
4. **Creating a Political Cartoon**   Create a political cartoon that illustrates the concept of justice. To get ideas for your cartoon, review what you have read in the chapter about the role of the courts in the American system of government. Recall, your cartoon may use words and pictures to communicate your message.
5. **Creating a Poster**   Create a poster that is a "help wanted" advertisement for a federal judge. Describe the characteristics that you think should be requirements for the position. State the term of office and salary offered.

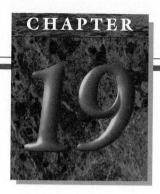

# Civil Liberties: First Amendment Freedoms

## Chapter Preview _____

How much violence—how many murders and how many other criminal acts—have you seen on television? Quite a few, probably. Indeed, one advocacy group, Americans for Responsible Television (ART), says that the typical high school senior today, to this point in his or her life, has seen an astonishing 33,000 murders and some 200,000 other acts of violence on television. Whatever the accuracy of that claim, ART and several other groups insist that government must act to curb the portrayal of violence on television and elsewhere in the entertainment field—in the movies and on compact discs, for example.

What do you think? What, if anything, should government do about violence on television, in the movies, on recordings, and so on? As you compose your answer to that question you must contemplate the central topic of this chapter: freedom of expression.

### Before you read this chapter:

- **Describe** your feelings about the voicing of unpopular views.
- **Predict** what might occur if no limits on free speech existed.

### As you read, focus on the main objective for each section. Understand:

1. The relationship between individual liberties and the concept of limited government.
2. The importance of religious freedom in the United States.
3. The scope of and limits on free speech and free press.
4. The relationship between individual liberties and national security.
5. The limits on the freedoms of assembly and petition.

**Freedom of Religion** Among other rights, every citizen of the United States has the right to worship according to his or her beliefs, without fear of interference from the government.

# 1 The Unalienable Rights

### Find Out:

- For what reasons were individual rights included in the Constitution?
- What factors limit individual rights?
- For what reasons is the Due Process Clause of the 14th Amendment so important?

### Key Terms:

Bill of Rights, civil liberties, civil rights, alien, Due Process Clause

Have you ever heard of Walter Barnette? Probably not. How about Toyosaburo Korematsu? Dollree Mapp? Clarence Earl Gideon? Almost certainly, the same answer: No.

Walter Barnette was a Jehovah's Witness who told his children not to salute the flag or recite the Pledge of Allegiance. Toyosaburo Korematsu was a citizen of the United States interned by the Federal Government during World War II. Dollree Mapp was fined $25 for possessing "lewd and lascivious books." And Clarence Earl Gideon was sentenced to prison for breaking into and entering a poolroom.

You will encounter their names again over the next few pages, for each of them played an important part in the building and protecting of the rights that all Americans hold.

### Rights and Liberties in American Political Thought

A commitment to personal freedom is deeply rooted in America's colonial past. Over centuries, the English people had waged a continuing struggle for individual rights, and the early colonists brought a dedication to that cause with them to America.

Their commitment took root here, and it flourished. The Revolutionary War was fought to preserve and expand the rights of the individual against government. In proclaiming the independence of the new United States, the founders of this country declared:

> 66We hold these truths to be self-evident, that all men are created equal, that they are endowed by their Creator with certain unalienable Rights, that among these are Life, Liberty and the pursuit of Happiness. . . . to secure these rights, Governments are instituted among Men. 99

The Framers of the Constitution repeated that justification for the existence of government in the Preamble to the Constitution.

The Constitution, as it was written at Philadelphia, contained a number of important guarantees—notably in Article I, Sections 9 and 10 and in Article III. Unlike many of the first State constitutions, however, it did not include a general listing of the rights of the people.

The outcry that that omission raised was so strong that several States ratified the Constitution only with the understanding that such a listing be immediately added. The first session of the new Congress met that demand with a series of proposed amendments. Ten of them, the **Bill of Rights**, were ratified by the States and became a part of the Constitution on December 15, 1791. Later amendments, especially the 13th and the 14th, have added to the Constitution's guarantees of personal freedom.

The Constitution guarantees many rights and liberties to the American people. However, there are several points you must understand about the overall shape of those guarantees.

**Civil Rights and Civil Liberties**   The distinction between civil rights and civil liberties is at best murky. Legal scholars often disagree on the matter, and the two terms are quite often used interchangeably. In general, however, **civil liberties** are protections against government. They are guarantees of the safety of persons, opinions, and property from the arbitrary acts of government. Examples of civil liberties include freedom of religion, freedom of speech and press, and the guarantees of fair trial.

The term **civil rights** is sometimes reserved for those positive acts of government that seek to make constitutional guarantees a reality for all people. From this perspective, examples of civil rights would include the prohibitions of discrimination on the basis of race or sex set out in the Civil Rights Act of 1964.

## Individual Rights and the Principle of Limited Government

As you know, government in the United States is limited government. It can do only those things the sovereign people have given it the power to do. The Constitution is filled with examples of this fact. Chief among them are its many guarantees of personal freedom. Each one of those guarantees is either an outright prohibition or a restriction on the power of government to do something.

All governments have and use authority over individuals. The all-important difference between a democratic government and a dictatorial one lies in the extent of that authority. In a dictatorial regime, the government's powers are practically unlimited. The government regularly suppresses dissent, often harshly. In the United States, however, governmental authority is closely limited. As Justice Robert H. Jackson once wrote:

> 66 If there is any fixed star in our constitutional constellation, it is that no official, high or petty, can prescribe what shall be orthodox in politics, nationalism, religion, or any other matter of opinion or force citizens to confess by word or act their faith therein. 99 [1]

## Relativity of Individual Rights

The Constitution guarantees a number of rights. But no one has the right to do as he or she pleases. Rather, all persons have the right to do as they please as long as they do not infringe on the rights of others. Each person's rights are relative to the rights of every other person.

To illustrate the point, everyone in the United States has a right of free speech, but no one enjoys absolute freedom of speech. A person

---

[1]In *West Virginia Board of Education* v. *Barnette,* 1943; see page 497.

found guilty of using obscene language can be punished by a court. So, too, can someone who uses words in a way that causes another person to commit a crime—for example, to riot or to desert the armed forces.

Justice Oliver Wendell Holmes once put the relative nature of each person's rights this way:

❝The most stringent protection of free speech would not protect a man in falsely shouting fire in a theatre and causing a panic.❞[2]

## When Rights Conflict

People usually think of individual rights guarantees in ways that suggest that each of them are to be observed all of the time. In fact, there are many situations in which different rights conflict with one another. Take this celebrated, but not uncommon, example of rights in conflict: free press versus fair trial.

Dr. Samuel Sheppard of Cleveland, Ohio, had been convicted of murdering his wife. His lengthy trial was widely covered in the national media. On appeal, Sheppard claimed that the highly sensational coverage had denied him a fair trial. The Supreme Court agreed. It rejected the free press argument, overturned his conviction, and ordered a new trial, *Sheppard* v. *Maxwell*, 1966.

## Persons to Whom Rights Are Guaranteed

Most constitutional rights are extended to all persons. The Supreme Court has often held that the Constitution's word "persons" covers **aliens**—foreign-born residents, noncitizens—as well as citizens.

Not all rights are given to aliens, however. Thus, the right to travel freely throughout the country is guaranteed to all citizens by the Constitution's two Privileges and Immunities clauses.[3] But aliens can be restricted in this regard.

**Robert Shapiro, Lead Lawyer**   The trial of O.J. Simpson amplified a problem encountered often in our society: Is it possible for a person whose case attracts extensive media coverage to receive a fair trial?

Early in World War II, all persons of Japanese descent living on the Pacific Coast were evacuated—forcibly moved—inland. Some 120,000 persons, two-thirds of them native-born American citizens, were detained in "war relocation camps." Many suffered economic and other hardships. In 1944 the Supreme Court reluctantly upheld the forced evacuation as a reasonable wartime emergency measure.[4] The relocation program has been strongly criticized over the years.

In 1988, the Federal Government admitted that the wartime relocation was unnecessary and unjust. Congress voted to pay $20,000 to each of the internees still alive. It also declared: "On behalf of the nation, the Congress apologizes."

---

[2]In *Schenck* v. *United States*, 1919; see page 506.

[3]Article IV, Section 2, Clause 1 and the 14th Amendment; see page 91. The guarantee does not extend to citizens in jail, on bail, committed to a mental institution, etc.

---

[4]*Korematsu* v. *United States*, 1944; however, on the same day the Court held in *Ex parte Endo* that once the loyalty of any citizen internee had been established, no restriction could be placed on that person's freedom to travel that was not legally imposed on all other citizens.

# Federalism and Individual Rights

Federalism produces this complex pattern of individual rights guarantees:

1. Some rights are guaranteed against the National Government only.
2. Some rights are guaranteed against the States and their local governments only.
3. A great many rights are guaranteed against both the National Government and the States and their local governments.
4. Some rights guaranteed against a State and its local governments arise from the National Constitution while others arise from that State's own constitution.

Over time, the Supreme Court has modified (lessened) some of the impact of federalism here, especially in a long series of decisions involving the 14th Amendment's Due Process Clause. Before you can understand that complicated matter, however, you must grasp this point: The provisions of the Bill of Rights apply against the National Government only—not the States.

**The Scope of the Bill of Rights** Remember, the first 10 amendments were originally intended as restrictions on the new National Government, not on the already existing States. They continue to function that way today.[5]

▲ **Internment Camps** "They say: 'We did it for your protection.' When you protect somebody, you don't aim a gun at the guy you're protecting": the words of a Japanese internee.

Take the 2nd Amendment to make the point here. It reads:

❝A well-regulated militia being necessary to the security of a free state, the right of the people to keep and bear arms shall not be infringed.❞

This restriction applies only to the National Government. The States can and do limit the right to keep and bear arms. They can require the registration of all or of certain guns, forbid the carrying of concealed weapons, and so on.

**The Modifying Effect of the 14th Amendment** Again, the provisions of the Bill of Rights apply against the National Government only. This does *not* mean, however, that the States can deny people their rights.

In part, the States cannot do that because each of their own constitutions contains a bill of rights. Also, they cannot because of the 14th Amendment's **Due Process Clause**. It says:

❝No State shall . . . deprive any person of life, liberty, or property, without due process of law. . . .❞

The Supreme Court has often held that this provision means that no State can deny to any person any right that is "basic or essential to the American concept of ordered liberty."

But what rights are "basic or essential"? In a long series of cases, the Court has ruled that most of the protections set out in the Bill of Rights are also within the meaning of the 14th Amendment, and so are applicable against the States.

This complicated matter can be stated this way: The Supreme Court has "nationalized" the Bill of Rights by holding that most of its protections apply against the States, as a part of the meaning of the 14th Amendment's Due Process Clause.

The Court began this historic process in *Gitlow* v. *New York*, in 1925. That landmark case involved Benjamin Gitlow, a communist, who had been convicted in the State courts of criminal anarchy. On appeal, the Supreme Court

---

[5]The Supreme Court first held that the provisions of the Bill of Rights restrict only the National Government in *Barron* v. *Baltimore*, 1833.

upheld Gitlow's conviction and the State law under which he had been tried. In deciding the case, however, the Court made this crucial point: Freedom of speech and press, which the 1st Amendment says cannot be denied by the National Government, are also "among the fundamental personal rights and liberties protected by the Due Process Clause of the 14th Amendment from impairment by the States."

Soon after *Gitlow*, the Court held each of the 1st Amendment's guarantees to be covered by the 14th Amendment. It struck down State laws involving speech (*Fiske* v. *Kansas*, 1927; *Stromberg* v. *California*, 1931), the press (*Near* v. *Minnesota*, 1931), assembly and petition (*DeJonge* v. *Oregon*, 1937), and religion (*Cantwell* v. *Connecticut*, 1940). In each of those cases, the Court declared a State law unconstitutional as a violation of the 14th Amendment's Due Process Clause.

The Court extended the scope of the 14th Amendment's Due Process Clause even further in several cases in the 1960s—to the point where, today, it covers nearly all of the guarantees set out in the Bill of Rights.

Thus, in *Mapp* v. *Ohio*, 1961, the Court held that the 14th Amendment's Due Process Clause prohibits unreasonable searches and seizures by State and local police. The clause also forbids State and local police the use of evidence gained by such illegal actions.

In later cases, the Court gave the same 14th Amendment coverage to:

—the 8th Amendment's ban on cruel and unusual punishment, in *Robinson* v. *California*, 1962;

—the 6th Amendment's right to counsel, in *Gideon* v. *Wainwright*, 1963;

—the 5th Amendment's ban on self-incrimination, in *Malloy* v. *Hogan*, 1964;

—the 6th Amendment's right of persons accused of crime to confront the witnesses against them, in *Pointer* v. *Texas*, 1965;

—the 6th Amendment's right of persons accused of crime to compel witnesses to testify in their behalf, in *Washington* v. *Texas*, 1967;

—the 6th Amendment's guarantee of a speedy trial, in *Klopfer* v. *North Carolina*, 1967;

—the 6th Amendment's guarantee of trial by jury, in *Duncan* v. *Louisiana*, 1968; and

—the 5th Amendment's ban of double jeopardy, in *Benton* v. *Maryland*, 1969.

## The Role of the 9th Amendment

As you know, the Constitution contains many guarantees of individual rights. But nowhere in the Constitution—and, indeed, nowhere else—will you find a complete catalog of all of the rights held by the American people.

The little-noted 9th Amendment declares that there are rights beyond those set out in so many words in the Constitution:

❝The enumeration in the Constitution of certain rights shall not be construed to deny or disparage others retained by the people.❞

Over the years, the Supreme Court has found that there are, in fact, a number of other rights "retained by the people." For example: The right of a person charged with a crime not to be tried on the basis of evidence gained by an unlawful search or seizure; and the right of a woman to have an abortion without undue interference by government.

## Section 1 Review

1. **Define:** Bill of Rights, civil liberties, civil rights, alien, Due Process Clause
2. According to the Declaration of Independence, governments exist for what reason?
3. How do individual rights guarantees illustrate the principle of limited government?
4. In what sense are individual rights relative to each other?
5. In what sense has the Supreme Court "nationalized" most of the civil rights protections set out in the Bill of Rights?
6. For what reason is it impossible to list all of the rights guaranteed by the Constitution?

**Critical Thinking**

7. **Identifying Assumptions** (p. 19) For what reason do you think the Supreme Court found that the right to a fair trial outweighed freedom of the press in *Sheppard*? Do you agree with this decision?

★

# 2 Freedom of Religion

## Find Out:

- For what reason is freedom of expression vital to democracy?
- To what extent does the Constitution prohibit government establishment of religion?
- To what extent do Americans enjoy free exercise of religion?

## Key Terms:

Establishment Clause, Free Exercise Clause

A century and a half ago, Alexis de Tocqueville came to the United States from France to observe life in the young nation. He later wrote that he had searched for the key to the greatness of America in many places: in its large harbors and deep rivers; in its fertile fields and boundless forests; in its rich mines and vast world commerce; in its public schools and institutions of learning, its democratic legislature, and matchless Constitution. Yet, not until he went into the churches of America, Tocqueville said, did he understand the genius and power of this country.

In this section, you will read about the important—and often controversial—guarantees of religious freedom found in the Constitution.

## Religion and the Bill of Rights

A free society cannot possibly exist without the rights of free expression—without what has been called a "free trade in ideas."

Freedom of expression is protected in the 1st Amendment:

&&Congress shall make no law respecting an establishment of religion, or prohibiting the free exercise thereof; or abridging the freedom of speech or of the press; or the right of the people peaceably to assemble, and to petition the government for a redress of grievances.&&

And, as you know, the 14th Amendment's Due Process Clause protects these freedoms from the arbitrary acts of States or their local governments.

It is not surprising that the Bill of Rights provides first for the protection of religious liberty.

Religion has always played a large and important role in American life. Many of the early colonists, and many later immigrants, came here to escape persecution for their religious beliefs.

The 1st and 14th amendments set out two guarantees of religious freedom. They prohibit (1) an "establishment of religion" (the Establishment Clause) and (2) any arbitrary interference by government in "the free exercise" of religion (the Free Exercise Clause).[6]

## Separation of Church and State

The **Establishment Clause** sets up, in Thomas Jefferson's words, "a wall of separation between church and state." But just how high is that wall? That question remains a matter of continuing and often heated controversy.

Government has done much to encourage churches and religion in this country. Thus, nearly all property of and contributions to churches and religious sects are free from federal, State, and local taxes. Most public officials take an oath of office in the name of God. Sessions of Congress and of most State legislatures and many city councils open with prayer. The nation's anthem and its coins and currency make reference to God. Clearly, the limits of the Establishment Clause cannot be described in precise terms.

The Supreme Court did not hear its first Establishment Clause case until 1947. A few earlier cases did involve government and religion, but none of them involved a direct consideration of the "wall of separation."

The most important of those earlier cases was *Pierce* v. *Society of Sisters*, 1925. There, the Court held an Oregon compulsory school attendance law unconstitutional. That law required parents to send their children to *public* schools. It was purposely intended to eliminate private, and especially parochial (church-related) schools. In destroying the law, the Court did not reach the Establishment Clause question. Instead, it found

---

[6]Also, Article VI, Section 3 provides that ". . . no religious test shall ever be required as a qualification to any office or public trust under the United States." In *Torcaso* v. *Watkins*, 1961, the Supreme Court held that the 14th Amendment puts the same restriction on the States.

the law to be an unreasonable interference with the liberty of parents to direct the upbringing of their children, and, so, in conflict with the Due Process Clause of the 14th Amendment.

The first direct ruling on the Establishment Clause came in *Everson* v. *Board of Education*, a 1947 case often called the *New Jersey School Bus Case*. There the Court upheld a State law that provided for the public, tax-supported busing of students attending any school in the State, including parochial (church-related) schools. Critics attacked the law as a support of religion in that it relieved parochial schools of the need to pay for busing and so freed their money for religious purposes. The Court disagreed; it found the law to be a safety measure intended to benefit children, no matter what schools they might attend.

Since that decision, the largest number of the Court's Establishment Clause cases have involved religion and education.

**Released Time**  "Released time" programs allow public schools to release students from school time to attend religious classes.

In *McCollum* v. *Board of Education*, 1948, the Court struck down the released time program in Champaign, Illinois, because the program used public facilities for religious purposes. In *Zorach* v. *Clauson*, 1952, however, the Court upheld New York City's released time program because that program required that the religious classes be held in private places.

**Prayers and the Bible**  The Court has now decided six major cases involving the recitation of prayers and the reading of the Bible in public schools.

In *Engel* v. *Vitale*, 1962, the Court outlawed the use, even on a voluntary basis, of a prayer written by the New York State Board of Regents. The "Regents' prayer" read:

❝Almighty God, we acknowledge our dependence upon Thee, and we beg Thy blessings upon us, our parents, our teachers, and our country.❞

The Supreme Court held that

❝The constitutional prohibition against laws respecting an establishment of religion must at least mean that in this country it is no part of the business of government to compose official prayers for any group of the American people to recite as part of a religious program carried on by government.❞

The Supreme Court extended that holding in two 1963 cases. In *Abington School District* v. *Schempp*, it struck down a Pennsylvania law that required that each school day begin with readings from the Bible and a recitation of the Lord's Prayer. In *Murray* v. *Curlett*, the Court erased a similar rule in the city of Baltimore. In both cases the Court found violations of

❝the command of the 1st Amendment that the government maintain strict neutrality, neither aiding nor opposing religion.❞

Since then, the Supreme Court has found these practices to be unconstitutional:

—a Kentucky law that required that copies of the Ten Commandments be posted in all public school classrooms, *Stone* v. *Graham*, 1980.

—Alabama's "moment of silence" law, *Wallace* v. *Jaffree*, 1985. That law provided for a one-minute period of silence, for "meditation or voluntary prayer," at the beginning of each school day.

—the offering of prayer as part of a public school graduation ceremony, in a Rhode Island case, *Lee* v. *Weisman*, 1992.

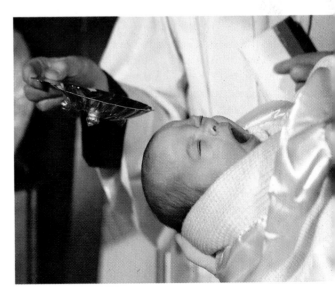

▲ **Freedom of Expression**  Which specific 1st Amendment right is being exercised by the participants in this Catholic baptismal ceremony?

▲ **Bar Mitzvah** The right of Americans to practice religion in their own way is being exercised in this ceremony, which initiates boys into the Jewish religion.

To sum up these rulings, the Court has held that public schools cannot sponsor religious exercises. But it has not held that individuals cannot pray, when and as they choose, in schools, or in any other place. Nor has it held that students cannot study the Bible in a literary or historic frame in the schools.

These rulings have stirred strong criticism. Many individuals and groups have long proposed that the Constitution be amended to allow voluntary prayer in the public schools.

Despite the several decisions here, both organized prayer and Bible readings are found in a great many public school classrooms today.

**Student Religious Groups** Congress has dealt with the matter of prayer in public schools in only one law, the Equal Access Act of 1984. That statute declares that any public high school that receives federal funds—nearly all do—must allow student religious groups to meet in the school on the same terms that it sets for other student organizations.

The Supreme Court upheld the law in *Westside Community Schools* v. *Mergens* in 1990. The case arose at Westside High School in Omaha, Nebraska, in 1985. Bridget Mergens and several other students asked school officials for permission to form a Christian Club at Westside High. They said that membership in their group would be voluntary and open to all students. The Christian Club's main purposes were to permit students to read and discuss the Bible, have fellowship, and pray together.

School officials denied the students' request, mainly on Establishment Clause grounds. The students then took their case to the federal courts, where they finally won their point.

Justice Sandra Day O'Connor delivered the Court's opinion upholding the Equal Access Act. At the core of that opinion, she wrote:

❝Although a school itself may not lead or direct a religious club, a school that permits a student-initiated and student-led religious club to meet after school, just as it permits any other student group to do, does not convey a message of State approval or endorsement of the particular religion.❞

**Evolution** In *Epperson* v. *Arkansas*, 1968, the Court struck down a State law forbidding the teaching of the scientific theory of evolution. The Court held that the Constitution

❝forbids alike the preference of a religious doctrine or the prohibition of theory which is deemed antagonistic to a particular dogma. . . . The State has no legitimate interest in protecting any or all religions from views distasteful to them.❞

The Court found a similar law to be unconstitutional in 1987. In *Edwards* v. *Aguillard*, it voided a 1962 Louisiana law that provided that whenever teachers taught the theory of evolution, they also had to offer instruction in "creation science." The Court held that the law violated the Establishment Clause because its "primary purpose [was] to endorse a particular religious doctrine."

**Seasonal Displays** Many public bodies sponsor celebrations of the holiday season with street

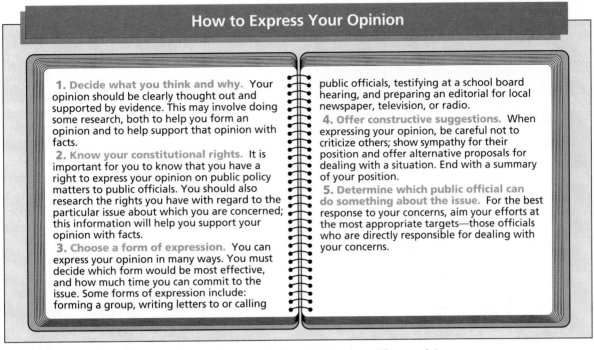

## How to Express Your Opinion

**1. Decide what you think and why.** Your opinion should be clearly thought out and supported by evidence. This may involve doing some research, both to help you form an opinion and to help support that opinion with facts.

**2. Know your constitutional rights.** It is important for you to know that you have a right to express your opinion on public policy matters to public officials. You should also research the rights you have with regard to the particular issue about which you are concerned; this information will help you support your opinion with facts.

**3. Choose a form of expression.** You can express your opinion in many ways. You must decide which form would be most effective, and how much time you can commit to the issue. Some forms of expression include: forming a group, writing letters to or calling

public officials, testifying at a school board hearing, and preparing an editorial for local newspaper, television, or radio.

**4. Offer constructive suggestions.** When expressing your opinion, be careful not to criticize others; show sympathy for their position and offer alternative proposals for dealing with a situation. End with a summary of your position.

**5. Determine which public official can do something about the issue.** For the best response to your concerns, aim your efforts at the most appropriate targets—those officials who are directly responsible for dealing with your concerns.

**Interpreting Charts**   Read the steps outlined in the chart. Then explain why it is important to a democratic society for all people to express their opinions effectively.

---

decorations, programs in public schools, and the like. Can these publicly sponsored observances properly include expressions of religious belief?

In *Lynch* v. *Donnelly*, 1984, the Court held that the city of Pawtucket, Rhode Island, could include the Christian nativity scene in its seasonal display, which also featured nonreligious objects such as candy canes and Santa's sleigh and reindeer. But that ruling left open this question: What about a public display made up *only* of a religious symbol?

The Court faced that question in 1989. In *County of Allegheny* v. *ACLU* it held that the county's seasonal display "endorsed Christian doctrine," and so violated the 1st and 14th amendments. The county had placed a large display celebrating the birth of Jesus on the grand stairway in the county courthouse, with a banner proclaiming "Glory to God in the Highest."

At the same time, however, the Court upheld another holiday display in *Pittsburgh* v. *ACLU*. The city's display consisted of a large Christmas tree, an 18-foot menorah, and a sign declaring the city's dedication to freedom.

**Chaplains in Congress and the State Legislatures**   Daily sessions of both houses of Congress and most of the State legislatures begin with prayer. In Congress, and in many States, a chaplain paid with public funds offers the opening prayer.

The Supreme Court has ruled that this practice, unlike prayers in the public schools, is constitutionally permissible—in a case involving Nebraska's one-house legislature, *Marsh* v. *Chambers*, 1983. The Court rested its distinction between school prayers and legislative prayers on two points. First, prayers have been offered in the nation's legislative bodies "from colonial times through the founding of the Republic and ever since." Second, legislators, unlike schoolchildren, are not "susceptible to religious indoctrination or peer pressure."

**Tax Exemptions**   Every State exempts property of religious organizations used for religious purposes from State and local taxation. The Supreme Court has upheld this practice, *Walz* v. *New York City Tax Commission*, 1970.

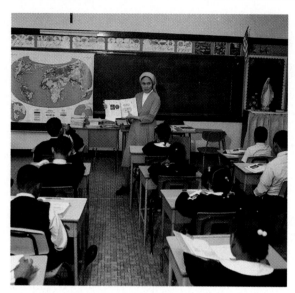

▲ **Separation of Church and State**   Parochial, or religion-affiliated, schools are entitled to federal aid for only secular, or nonreligious, purposes.

A citizen named Walz had challenged the exemption of houses of worship from local property taxes. He argued that these exemptions made property tax bills higher than they would otherwise be, and that the exemptions amounted to a public support of religion.

The Court turned down Walz's plea. It found that those exemptions are evidence only of a State's "benevolent neutrality" toward religion, not support of it. Said the Court, the exemptions "create only a minimal and remote," and therefore permissible, "involvement between church and state."

But the Court has ruled that church-related schools that discriminate on the basis of race can be denied a tax-exempt status under federal law, *Bob Jones University* v. *United States* and *Goldsboro Christian Schools* v. *United States*, 1983. The schools involved in these 1983 cases argued that their racial policies reflected their sincerely held religious beliefs. The Supreme Court granted that point. It said, nevertheless, that the nation's interest in eradicating racial discrimination in education "substantially outweighs whatever burden denial of tax benefits places on [those schools in the] exercise of their religious beliefs."

**State Aid to Parochial Schools**   Most recent Establishment Clause cases have centered on this highly controversial question: What forms of State aid to parochial schools are constitutional?

Several States give help to private schools—including those related to church organizations—for transportation, textbooks, laboratory equipment, standardized testing, and much else.

Those who support that aid argue that parochial schools enroll large numbers of students who would otherwise have to be educated at public expense. They also point to the fact that the Supreme Court has held that parents have a legal right to send their children to those schools (*Pierce* v. *Society of Sisters*). To give that right real meaning, they say, the State must give some aid to parochial schools—to relieve parents of some of the double burden they carry because they must pay taxes to support the public schools their children do not attend. Many advocates also insist that schools run by religious organizations pose no real church-state problems, because, they say, those schools devote most of their time to secular (nonreligious) subjects rather than to sectarian (religious) ones.

Opponents of aid to parochial schools argue that those parents who choose to send children to parochial schools should accept the financial consequences of that choice. Many of them also insist that it is impossible to draw clear lines between secular and sectarian courses in parochial schools. They say that religious beliefs are bound to have an effect on the teaching of non-religious subjects in church-run schools.

**The *Lemon* Test**   The Supreme Court has been picking its way through cases involving State aid laws for several years. In most of them, it now applies a three-pronged standard, the *Lemon* test: (1) The purpose of the aid must be clearly secular, not religious, (2) its primary effect must neither advance nor inhibit religion, and (3) it must avoid an "excessive entanglement of government with religion."

The test stems from *Lemon* v. *Kurtzman*, 1971. There, the Supreme Court held that the Establishment Clause is designed to prevent three main evils: "sponsorship, financial support, and active involvement of the sovereign in religious activity."

In *Lemon*, the Court struck down a Pennsylvania law that provided for reimbursements—financial payments—to private schools to cover their costs for teachers' salaries, textbooks, and other teaching materials in nonreligious courses.

The Court held that the State program was of direct benefit to the parochial schools, and so to the churches sponsoring them. It also found that the program required such close State supervision that it produced an excessive entanglement of government with religion.

A number of State aid programs have passed the *Lemon* test over the past 20 years, and others have failed it. Thus, for example, the Court has allowed the use of public funds to loan textbooks to students in parochial schools, in a case from Pennsylvania, *Meek* v. *Pittinger*, 1975. And it has held that a State can pay church-related schools what it costs them to administer the State's standardized tests, in a New York case, *Committee for Public Education and Religious Liberty* v. *Regan*, 1980. Both textbooks and standardized tests can be evaluated to be sure that they do not promote religion.

But public funds cannot be used to pay for such things as field trips for students at parochial schools, *Wolman* v. *Walter*, 1977. In that Ohio case, the Court said that field trips managed by parochial school teachers present "an unacceptable risk of fostering of religion." Nor can tax monies be used to pay any part of the salaries of parochial school teachers, including those who teach only secular courses, *Grand Rapids School District* v. *Ball*, 1985. The Court said in that Michigan case that while the contents of a book can be checked easily, the way a teacher handles a course cannot.[7]

The Supreme Court struck down a New York law that provided for direct cash payments to parents to reimburse them for the tuition they paid to schools operated by religious organizations, *Committee for Public Education* v. *Nyquist*, 1973. But the Court has upheld a Minnesota tax law that accomplishes the same end, *Mueller* v. *Allen*, 1983. That law gives parents a State income tax deduction for the costs of tuition, textbooks, and transportation. Parents can claim the tax break no matter what schools their children attend. Most public school parents pay little or nothing for these items. Hence, the law is of particular benefit to parents with children in private, mostly parochial, schools. The Court found that the law meets the *Lemon* test, and it also leaned on this point: The deduction is available to all parents with children in school, and they are free to decide which type of school their children attend.

In *Bowen* v. *Kendrick*, 1988, the Court took a more tolerant view of government aid to religion than it has in most recent cases. There, it upheld a controversial federal statute, the Adolescent Family Life Act of 1981. That law provides for grants to both public and private agencies dealing with the problems of adolescent sex and pregnancy. Some of the grants were made to religious groups that oppose abortion, prompting the argument that those groups use federal money to teach religious doctrine. However, the Supreme Court found the law's purpose—curbing "the social and economic problems caused by teenage sexuality, pregnancy, and parenthood"—to be a legitimate one. That some grants pay for counseling that "happens to coincide with the religious views" of some groups does not by itself mean that the federal funds are being used with "a primary effect of advancing religion."

And in a 1993 case from Arizona, *Zobrest* v. *Catalina Foothills School District*, the Court said that the use of public money to provide an interpreter for a deaf student who attends a Catholic high school does not violate the Establishment Clause. The Constitution, said the Court, does not lay down an absolute barrier to the placing of a public employee in a religious school.

But in *Board of Education of Kiryas Joel* v. *Grumet*, 1994, the Court struck down a New York law creating a school district purposely designed to benefit handicapped children in a tight-knit community of Hasidic Jews.

---

[7]The Court has taken a markedly different view toward public aid to church-related colleges and universities. Thus, in *Tilton* v. *Richardson*, 1971, it upheld federal grants for the construction of academic buildings to be used for nonreligious purposes at such institutions. The Court could find no excessive entanglement in these "one-shot" grants.

**The Free Exercise Clause**   This clause upholds the right to freedom of religion; but the law can require Hare Krishna members to limit public handouts of their literature.

## The Free Exercise of Religion

The second part of the constitutional guarantee of religious freedom is set out in the Constitution's **Free Exercise Clause**. That clause guarantees to each person the right to believe whatever that person chooses to believe in matters of religion. It is protected by the 1st and the 14th amendments.

No person has an absolute right to act as he or she chooses, however. The Free Exercise Clause does *not* give one the right to violate the criminal laws, offend public morals, or otherwise threaten the health, welfare, or safety of the community.

The Supreme Court laid down the basic shape of the Free Exercise Clause in the first case it heard on the point, *Reynolds* v. *United States*, 1879. Reynolds, a Mormon, had two wives. That practice—polygamy—was allowed by the teachings of his church; but it was prohibited by a federal law.

Reynolds was tried and convicted under the law. On appeal, he argued that the law violated his constitutional right to the free exercise of his religious beliefs. The Supreme Court disagreed, however. It held that the 1st Amendment does not forbid Congress the power to punish those actions that are "violations of social duties or subversive of good order." To hold otherwise, said the Court

❝ would be to make the professed doctrines of religious belief superior to the law of the land, and in effect permit every citizen to become a law unto himself. ❞

Over the years, the Court has approved many regulations of human conduct in the face of free exercise challenges. For example, it has upheld laws that require the vaccination of school children, *Jacobson* v. *Massachusetts*, 1905; that forbid the use of poisonous snakes in religious rites, *Bunn* v. *North Carolina*, 1949; and so-called blue laws that require businesses to be closed on Sundays, *McGowan* v. *Maryland*, 1961.

A State can require religious groups to have a permit to hold a parade on the public streets, *Cox* v. *New Hampshire*, 1941; and organizations that enlist children to sell religious literature must obey child labor laws, *Prince* v. *Massachusetts*, 1944. The Federal Government can draft those who have religious objections to military service, *Welsh* v. *United States*, 1970.[8] The Air Force can forbid an Orthodox Jew the right to wear his yarmulke—skull cap—while on active duty, *Goldman* v. *Weinberger*, 1986. The U.S. Forest Service can allow private companies to build roads and cut timber in national forests that Native Americans have traditionally used for religious purposes, *Lyng* v. *Northwest Indian Cemetery Protective Association*, 1988. And a State can deny unemployment benefits to a man fired by a private drug counseling group because he used peyote in violation of the State's drug laws—even though he ingested the hallucinogenic drug as part of a ceremony of his Native American Church, *Oregon* v. *Smith*, 1990.

But, over time, the Court has also found many actions by governments to be contrary to

---

[8]The Court has made this ruling many times. *Welsh* is the leading case from the Vietnam War period. There, the Court held that the only persons who could not be drafted were those "whose consciences . . . would give them no rest if they allowed themselves to become part of an instrument of war."

the Free Exercise guarantee. The Court did so for the first time in one of the landmark Due Process cases cited earlier in this chapter, *Cantwell* v. *Connecticut*, 1940. There, the Court struck down a law requiring a license before any person could solicit money for a religious cause.

There are many other cases in that line. Thus, Amish children cannot be forced to attend school beyond the 8th grade, because that sect's centuries-old "self-sufficient agrarian lifestyle essential to their religious faith is threatened by modern education," *Wisconsin* v. *Yoder*, 1972. But the Amish, who take care of their own people, must pay social security taxes, as all other employers do, *United States* v. *Lee*, 1982.

A State cannot forbid ministers to hold elected public offices, *McDaniel* v. *Paty*, 1978. Nor can it deny unemployment compensation benefits to a worker who quit a job because it involved some conflict with his or her religious beliefs, *Sherbert* v. *Verner*, 1963; *Thomas* v. *Indiana*, 1981; *Hobbie* v. *Florida*, 1987; *Frazee* v. *Illinois*, 1989.[9]

The Court has often held that "only those beliefs rooted in religion are protected by the Free Exercise Clause" (*Sherbert* v. *Verner*, 1963). But what beliefs are those "rooted in religion"? Clearly, religions that seem strange or even bizarre to most Americans are as entitled to constitutional protection as are the more traditional ones. To the point, the High Court recently struck down a Florida city's ordinance that outlawed animal sacrifices as part of any church services, *Lukumi Babalu Aye* v. *City of Hialeah*, 1993.

---

[9]Typically, State unemployment compensation laws bar such benefits to those who leave jobs voluntarily and "without good cause in connection with the work." Some bar benefits to those who are fired. In *Sherbert*, to take one example of these cases, a Seventh Day Adventist lost her job in a South Carolina textile mill when she refused to work on Saturdays, her Sabbath. In *Thomas*, a Jehovah's Witness who worked for a machinery company quit after he was transferred from one section of the company that was being closed down to another where gun turrets for tanks were made. He left because, he said, his religious beliefs would not allow him to work on war materials. Note this distinction between these two cases and *Oregon* v. *Smith*, 1990: Smith's conduct involved the violation of a State law.

The Jehovah's Witnesses have carried several important religious freedom cases to the Supreme Court. Perhaps the stormiest of the controversies that sect has stirred arose out of the Witnesses' refusal to salute the flag.

The Witnesses refuse to salute the flag because they see such conduct as a violation of the Bible's commandment against idolatry. In *Minersville School District* v. *Gobitis*, 1940, the Court upheld a Pennsylvania school board regulation requiring students to salute the flag at the beginning of each school day. Gobitis instructed his children not to do so, and the school expelled them. He went to court, basing his case on the constitutional guarantee. He finally lost in the Supreme Court, however. The Court declared that the board's rule was not an infringement of religious liberty. Rather, the Court held that the rule was a lawful attempt to promote patriotism and national unity.

Three years later, the Court reversed that decision. In *West Virginia Board of Education* v. *Barnette*, 1943, it held a compulsory flag-salute law unconstitutional. Justice Robert H. Jackson's words on page 486 are from the Court's powerful opinion in that case. So are these:

    ❝To believe that patriotism will not flourish if patriotic ceremonies are voluntary and spontaneous instead of a compulsory routine is to make an unflattering estimate of the appeal of our institutions to free minds.❞

## Section 2 Review

1. **Define:** Establishment Clause, Free Exercise Clause
2. What does it mean to say that it is unclear how high the wall between church and state is?
3. Over what subjects have most Establishment Clause cases been fought?
4. What is the basic shape of the rights guaranteed by the Free Exercise Clause?

### Critical Thinking

5. **Identifying Central Issues** (p. 19) Some observers feel that Supreme Court decisions such as *Engel* v. *Vitale* and *Murray* v. *Curlett* limit people's free exercise of religion. Do you agree or disagree?

★

## Can Public Schools Ban Political Protests?

### *Tinker v. Des Moines Independent School District,* 1969

In December of 1965, a group of adults and students in Des Moines, Iowa, met to express their opposition to American involvement in the war in Vietnam. They decided to publicize their views in two ways: (1) by wearing black armbands during the holiday season, and (2) by fasting on two days, December 16 and December 31.

The principals of the Des Moines schools soon became aware of the protesters' plans. They met to discuss the matter on December 14 and on the same day announced this policy: Any student wearing an armband to school would be asked to remove it. If the student refused, he or she would be suspended from school. Any student suspended for wearing an armband would not be allowed to return to school until he or she appeared without that symbol.

On December 16, Mary Beth and Christopher Tinker wore black armbands to school. The next day their brother John and some other students did so, too. All were suspended and sent home. They did not return to school until after New Year's Day—that is, until after the end of the period for which they had planned their protest.

The Tinkers and several other students, acting through their parents, went to court. They asked the federal district court in Iowa to issue an injunction—a court order to prevent enforcement of the school district's ban on the wearing of armbands.

The federal district court refused to issue that order, and the federal court of appeals affirmed that decision. The Tinkers, supported by the American Civil Liberties Union, then took their case to the United States Supreme Court.

*Review the following evidence and arguments presented to the Supreme Court:*

### Arguments for Des Moines School District

**1.** No one has an absolute right to freedom of expression. Reasonable limits may be placed on that right.

**2.** The ban on armbands was put in place to avoid disruption of school discipline.

**3.** The orderly atmosphere of the classroom, not the right to wear an armband, is entitled to constitutional protection.

**4.** School is not the appropriate place for a political demonstration. Controversies should be dealt with in classroom discussions, not by distracting protests.

### Arguments for Tinker

**1.** The school district did not ban all political symbols, only black armbands. Such a selective ban is unconstitutional.

**2.** The students who wore armbands did not in fact disrupt school discipline.

**3.** The armbands were worn as symbols of the students' views and so were entitled to constitutional protection.

**4.** Students are as entitled to respect for their rights in school as in any other place.

### Getting Involved

**1. Identify** the constitutional grounds upon which each side based its arguments.

**2. Debate** the opposing viewpoints presented in this case.

**3. Predict** how you think the Supreme Court ruled in this case and why. Then refer to page 769 of the Supreme Court Glossary to read about the decision. What do you think of the Court's decision in this case?

# 3 Freedom of Speech and Press

## Find Out:

- What is the breadth of the guarantees of free speech and free press?
- What are the limits on the guarantees of free speech and free press?

## Key Terms:

libel, slander, shield law, symbolic speech, picketing

Think about this children's verse for a moment: "Sticks and stones may break my bones, but names will never hurt me." That rhyme says, in effect, that acts and words are separate things and that acts can do harm but words cannot.

Is that really true? Certainly not. You know that words can and do have consequences—sometimes powerful consequences. Words, spoken or written, can make you happy, sad, bored, informed, or entertained. They can also expose you to danger, deny you a job, or lead to other serious consequences.

In this section you will read about the Constitution's protection of the vitally important freedom of expression and how the meaning of those freedoms has developed over the course of American history.

## Democracy and Freedom of Expression

The 1st and 14th amendments' protections of free speech and a free press serve two fundamentally important purposes:

1. To guarantee to each person a right of free expression—in the spoken and the written word, and by all other means of communication, as well.
2. To ensure to all persons a full, wide-ranging discussion of public affairs.

That is, the 1st and 14th amendments give to all people the right to have their say and to hear what others have to say. Most often, people think of these great freedoms in terms of that first purpose. The second one is just as important, however.

The American system of government depends on the ability of the people to make sound, reasoned judgments on matters of public concern. Clearly, people can best make such judgments when they know all of the facts in a given matter, *and* can hear all the available interpretations of those facts.

Justice Oliver Wendell Holmes once underscored the importance of that second purpose in these words:

❝ Persecution for the expression of opinions seems to me perfectly logical. If you have no doubt of your premises and want a certain result with all your heart, you naturally express your wishes in law and sweep away all opposition. . . . But when men have realized that time has upset many fighting faiths, they may come to believe even more than they believe the very foundations of their own conduct that the ultimate good desired is better reached by free trade in ideas—that the best test of truth is the power of the thought to get itself accepted in the competition of the market. . . . That at any rate is the theory of our Constitution. ❞ [10]

As you examine the Constitution's 1st and 14th amendments here, keep two other key points in mind:

First, the guarantees of free speech and press are intended to protect the expression of unpopular views. That is because the opinions of the majority need, after all, little or no constitutional protection.

Second, some forms of expression are not protected by the Constitution. No person has an unbridled right of free speech or free press. Many reasonable restrictions can be placed on those rights.

You will see a number of illustrations of this point over the next several pages. For now, recall Justice Holmes's comment about the right to shout "Fire!" in a crowded theater. Or, note this restriction: No person has the right to libel or slander another. **Libel** is the false and malicious use of printed words; **slander** is such use of spoken words. Similarly, the law prohibits the use of

---

[10]Dissenting in *Abrams* v. *United States*, 1919.

obscene words, the printing and distributing of obscene materials, and false advertising.[11]

## Obscenity

The 1st and 14th amendments do not protect obscenity, but in recent years the Court has had to wrestle several times with these questions: What language in printed matter, films, and other materials are, in fact, obscene? What restrictions can be properly placed on such materials?[12]

Today, the leading case is *Miller* v. *California*, 1973. There the Court laid down a three-part test to determine what material is obscene and what is not.

A book, film, recording, or other piece of material is legally obscene if (1) "the average person applying contemporary [local] community standards" finds that the work, taken as a whole, "appeals to the prurient interest"—that is, tends to excite lust; (2) "the work depicts or describes, in a patently offensive way," a form of sexual conduct specifically dealt with in an antiobscenity law; and (3) "the work, taken as a whole, lacks serious literary, artistic, political, or scientific value."

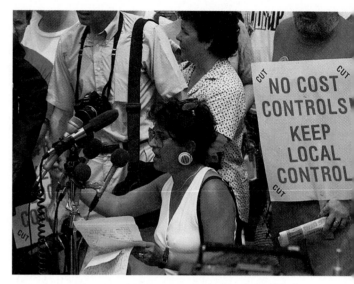

▲ **Freedoms of Speech and Assembly** The 1st and 14th amendments guarantee freedom of expression to everyone in this country.

A sampling of Supreme Court decisions involving local attempts to regulate so-called adult book stores and similar places shows how thorny the problem of obscenity can be. Most of what those stores sell cannot be mailed, sent across State lines, or imported—at least not legally. Still, those shops are usually well-stocked.

The 1st and 14th amendments do not prevent a city from regulating the location of "adult entertainment establishments," *Young* v. *American Mini Theaters*, 1976. A city can decide to bar the location of such places within 1,000 feet of a residential zone, church, park, or school, *City of Renton* v. *Playtimes Theaters, Inc.*, 1986. But a city cannot prohibit live entertainment in any and all commercial establishments, *Schad* v. *Borough of Mount Ephraim*, 1981 (a case that involved nude dancing in adult book stores).

The Supreme Court has upheld a State law that makes it a crime to possess or view child pornography, including films. In *Osborne* v. *Ohio*, 1990, the Court ruled that the State has a compelling interest in protecting the physical and the psychological well-being of minors and in the destruction of the market in which they are exploited.

---

[11]Libel and slander involve the use of words, maliciously—with vicious purpose—to injure a person's character or reputation or expose that person to public contempt, ridicule, or hatred. Truth is generally an absolute defense against a libel or slander claim. The law is less protective of public officials, however. In *New York Times* v. *Sullivan*, 1964, the Supreme Court held that public officials cannot recover damages for a published criticism, even if exaggerated or false, unless "the statement was made with actual malice—that is with knowledge that it was false or with reckless disregard of whether it was false or not." Several later decisions have extended that ruling to cover "public figures" and even private individuals who have become involved in newsworthy events. Those public figures cannot win damages even for an "intentional infliction of emotional distress," *Hustler Magazine* v. *Falwell*, 1988.

[12]Congress passed the first of a series of laws to keep obscene matter from the mails in 1872. The current law was upheld by the Court in *Roth* v. *United States*, 1957. The law excludes "every obscene, lewd, lascivious, or filthy" piece of material. The Court found the law a proper exercise of the postal power (Article I, Section 8, Clause 7), and so not prohibited by the 1st Amendment. *Roth* marked the Court's first attempt to find an adequate definition of obscenity.

Businesses that offer "dial-a-porn" services have sprung up around the country in the past few years. Congress and several State legislatures have moved against these services.

The federal law, passed in 1988, made it a crime for any person to use a telephone to send any "obscene or indecent" communication for a commercial purpose. The Supreme Court destroyed the statute, however, in *Sable Communications* v. *FCC* in 1989. A unanimous Court held that only "obscene" calls—and not those that are merely "indecent"—can be outlawed under the 1st Amendment.

## Prior Restraint

The Constitution allows government to punish some utterances, *after* they are made. But, with almost no exceptions, government cannot place any prior restraint on spoken or written words. That is, except in the most extreme situations, government cannot curb ideas before they are expressed.

*Near* v. *Minnesota*, 1931, is a leading case in point. The Supreme Court struck down a State law that prohibited the publication of any "malicious, scandalous, and defamatory" periodical. Acting under that law, a local court had issued an order forbidding the publication of the *Saturday Press*. The Minneapolis paper had printed several articles charging public corruption and attacking "grafters" and "Jewish gangsters." The Court held that the guarantee of a free press does not allow a prior restraint on publication, except in such extreme cases as wartime, or when a publication is obscene or incites readers to violence. The Court said that even "miscreant purveyors of scandal" and anti-Semitism have a constitutional protection against prior restraint.

The Constitution does not forbid any and all forms of prior censorship, but "a prior restraint on expression comes to this Court with a 'heavy presumption' against its constitutionality," *Nebraska Press Association* v. *Stuart*, 1976.[15] The Court has used that general rule several times—

for example, in the famous Pentagon Papers Case, *New York Times* v. *United States*, 1971.

In that case, several newspapers had obtained copies of a set of classified documents. The documents, widely known as the Pentagon Papers, were officially titled *History of U.S. Decision-Making Process on Viet Nam Policy*. They had been stolen from the Defense Department and then leaked to the press. The government sought a court order to bar their publication, but the Court held that the government had not shown that printing the documents would endanger the nation's security, and so had not overcome the "heavy presumption" against prior censorship.

The few prior restraints the Court has approved include regulations prohibiting the distribution of political literature on military bases without the approval of military authorities, *Greer* v. *Spock*, 1976; a CIA rule that agents must agree never to publish anything about the agency without the CIA's permission, *Snepp* v. *United States*, 1980; a federal prison rule that allows officials to prevent an inmate from receiving publications considered "detrimental to the security, good order, or discipline" of the prison, *Thornburgh* v. *Abbott*, 1989.

The Court has recently said that public school officials have a broad power to censor school newspapers, plays, and other "school-sponsored expressive activities." In *Hazelwood School District* v. *Kuhlmeier*, 1988, it held that "educators do not offend the 1st Amendment by exercising editorial control over the style and content of student speech in school-sponsored expressive activities so long as their actions are reasonably related to legitimate pedagogical [teaching] concerns."

## Confidentiality

Can news reporters be forced to testify before a grand jury, in court, or before a legislative committee, and there be required to name their sources and reveal other confidential information?

Many reporters and news organizations insist that they must have the right to refuse to testify, the right to protect their sources. They argue that without this right they cannot assure confidentiality to their sources. Unless they can

---

[15]In this case a judge had ordered the media not to report certain details of a murder trial. The Court held the judge's gag order to be unconstitutional.

**Federally Regulated** Television and radio are subject to more federal regulation than other media, on the grounds that the airwaves they use are public property.

do that, reporters say, many sources will not give them information they need to keep the public informed.

Both State and federal courts have generally rejected the news media argument. In recent years several reporters have refused to obey court orders directing them to give information. As a consequence, a number of reporters have gone to jail, testifying to the importance of these issues.

In the leading case, *Branzburg* v. *Hayes*, 1972, the Supreme Court held that reporters, "like other citizens, [must] respond to relevant questions put to them in the course of a valid grand jury investigation or criminal trial." If the media are to receive any special exemptions, said the Court, the exemptions must come from Congress and the State legislatures.

To date, Congress has not acted on the Court's suggestion. However, some 30 States have passed so-called **shield laws**. These laws give reporters some protection against having to disclose their sources or reveal other confidential information in legal proceedings in those States.

## Motion Pictures

The Supreme Court took its first look at motion pictures early in the history of the movie industry. In 1915, in *Mutual Film Corporation* v. *Ohio*, the Court upheld a State law that barred the showing of any film that was not of a "moral, educational, or harmless and amusing character." The Court declared that "the exhibition of moving pictures is a business, pure and simple," and "not . . . part of the press of the country." With that decision, nearly every State and thousands of communities set up movie review—really movie censorship—programs.

The Court reversed itself in 1952, however. In *Burstyn* v. *Wilson*, a New York censorship case, it found that "liberty of expression by means of motion pictures is guaranteed by the 1st and 14th amendments."

Movie censorship is not necessarily unconstitutional, however. A State or local government can ban an obscene film, but only under a law that provides for a prompt judicial hearing. At that hearing that government must show that the picture in question is in fact obscene, *Teitel Film Corporation* v. *Cusack*, 1968.

Very few of the once common local movie review boards still exist. Most movie-goers now depend on the film industry's own rating system and on the comments of movie critics on television and in newspapers and magazines.

## Radio and Television

Both radio and television broadcasting are subject to extensive federal regulation. Most of this regulation is based on the often-amended Federal Communications Act of 1934, which is administered by the Federal Communications Commission. As the Supreme Court has described the situation: "Of all forms of communication, it is broadcasting that has received the most limited 1st Amendment protection," *Red Lion Broadcasting Co.* v. *FCC*, 1969.

The Court has several times upheld this wide-ranging federal regulation as a proper exercise of the commerce power. Unlike newspapers and other print media, radio and television use the public's property—the public airwaves—to broadcast their materials. They have no right to do so without the public's permission—that is, without a proper license, *National Broadcasting Co.* v. *United States*, 1943.

The Court has regularly rejected the argument that the 1st Amendment prohibits such regulations. Instead, it has taken the view that the regulation implements the constitutional guarantee. It has held that there is no "unabridgeable 1st Amendment right to broadcast comparable to the right of every individual to speak, write, or publish." However, "this is not to say that the 1st Amendment is irrelevant to broadcasting. But . . . it is the right of the viewers and the listeners, not the right of the broadcasters, which is paramount."[16]

Congress has forbidden the FCC to censor the content of programs before they are broadcast. But the FCC can prohibit the use of indecent language, and it can take violations of the ban into account when a station applies for the renewal of its operating license, *FCC* v. *Pacifica Foundation*, 1978. The FCC has refused applications for renewal of licenses due to past use of objectionable practices. And Congress itself cannot prohibit the broadcasting of editorials by public radio and television stations, *FCC* v. *League of Women Voters of California*, 1984.

In several recent decisions, the Supreme Court has given the growing cable television industry broader 1st Amendment freedoms than those enjoyed by traditional television. A 1987 case, *Wilkinson* v. *Jones*, is fairly typical. There, the Court held that the States cannot regulate "indecent" cable programming. It reached that

---

[16]*Red Lion Broadcasting Co.* v. *FCC*, 1969, in which the Court upheld the fairness doctrine, an FCC rule in effect until its repeal by the commission in 1987. The rule provided that broadcasters had to air opposing viewpoints, not just one side, on important issues.

The FCC still enforces the equal time doctrine, set out in the Communications Act. The law's equal time provision means that if, for example, a television network makes air time available to one candidate for a public office, it must offer equal time to all other candidates for that office. Most of those who have opposed the fairness doctrine also oppose this rule and urge Congress to repeal it.

## VOICES *on Government*

### To the Press, on Freedom of the Press

❝The press . . . has the power to inform, but that implies the power to distort. You have the power to instruct, but that implies the power to mislead. . . . You can lead our society toward a more mature and discriminating understanding of the process by which we choose our leaders, make our rules, and construct our values. Or you can encourage people to despise our systems and avoid participating in them. You can teach our children a taste for violence, encourage a fascination with perversity and inflicted pain. Or you can show them a beauty they have not known. . . . You can make us all wiser, fuller, surer, sweeter than we are. Or you can do less. And worse. And one of the miracles of this democracy is that you are free to make all the choices.❞

**Mario M. Cuomo,**
governor of New York,
1983–1995

decision by striking down a Utah law that prohibited the cable broadcast of any sexually explicit or other "indecent material" between the hours of 7 A.M. and midnight.

## Symbolic Speech

People also communicate ideas by conduct—by the way a person does some particular thing. Thus, a person can say something with a facial expression or a shrug of the shoulders, or by carrying a sign or wearing an arm band. This mode of expression—expression by conduct—is known as **symbolic speech**.

Clearly, not all conduct amounts to symbolic speech. If it did, murder or robbery or any other crime could be excused on grounds that the person who committed the act meant to say something by doing so.

But, just as clearly, some conduct does express opinion. Take picketing in a labor dispute as an example. **Picketing** involves patrolling of a business site by workers who are on strike. By their conduct, picketers attempt to inform the public of the controversy, and to persuade others not to deal with the firm involved. Picketing is, then, a form of expression. If peaceful, it is protected by the 1st and 14th amendments.[17]

Generally, the Supreme Court has been sympathetic to the symbolic speech argument. But it has not given blanket 1st Amendment protection to that means of expression. As a sampling, note these cases:

*United States* v. *O'Brien*, 1968, involved four young men who had burned their draft cards to protest the war in Vietnam. A court convicted them of violating a federal law that makes that act a crime. O'Brien appealed, arguing that the 1st Amendment protects "all modes of communication of ideas by conduct." The Supreme Court disagreed. Said the Court: "We cannot accept the view that an apparently limitless variety of conduct can be labeled 'speech' whenever the person engaging in the conduct intends thereby to express an idea."

The Court also held that acts of dissent by conduct can be punished if: (1) the object of the protest—here, the war and the draft—is within the constitutional powers of the government; (2) whatever restriction is placed on expression is no greater than necessary in the circumstances; and (3) the government's real interest in the matter is not to squelch dissent.

Using that test, the court has denied some claims of symbolic speech. Thus, for example, it

held that a policeman does not have a constitutional right to protest a department dress code by growing long hair—even if he believes that to be "a means of expressing his attitude and lifestyle"—because a government has a reasonable stake in requiring a "similarity of garb and appearance" among its police officers, *Kelley* v. *Johnson*, 1976. And the Court upheld a National Park Service regulation under which a group of protesters was not allowed to sleep overnight in Lafayette Park near the White House, *Clark* v. *Community for Creative Non-Violence*, 1984.

*Tinker* v. *Des Moines School District*, 1969, on the other hand, is one of several cases in which the Court has come down on the side of symbolic speech. A small group of students in the Des Moines public schools had worn black armbands to publicize their opposition to the war in Vietnam. The school suspended them for it. The Court ruled that school officials had overstepped their authority and violated the Constitution. Said the Court: "It can hardly be argued that either students or teachers shed their constitutional rights to freedom of speech or expression at the schoolhouse gate."[18]

Campaign contributions are "a symbolic expression of support" for candidates, so the making of those contributions is entitled to constitutional protection, *Buckley* v. *Valeo*, 1976. Both federal and State laws regulate campaign contributions, but the fact that in politics "money is speech" greatly complicates that whole matter of campaign finance regulation (see Chapter 7).

Burning the American flag as an act of political protest is expressive conduct protected by the 1st and 14th amendments—so a sharply divided Court has twice held. In *Texas* v. *Johnson*, 1989, a 5–4 majority ruled that State authorities had violated a protester's rights when they prosecuted him under a law that forbids the "desecration of a venerated object." Johnson had set fire to

---

[17]The leading case on the point is *Thornhill* v. *Alabama*, 1940. There, the Court struck down a State law that made it a crime for one to loiter about or picket a place of business in order to influence others not to trade or work there. But picketing that is "set in a background of violence" can be prevented. Even peaceful picketing can be restricted if it is conducted for some illegal purpose, for example, to force someone to do something that is itself illegal.

[18]Do not read too much into this, however, for the Court added, it "has repeatedly affirmed the comprehensive authority of the States and of school authorities, consistent with fundamental constitutional safeguards, to prescribe and control conduct in the schools." The fact that in *Tinker* the students' conduct did not produce any substantial disruption of normal school activities was an important factor in the Court's decision.

an American flag during an anti-Reagan demonstration at the Republican National Convention in Dallas in 1984. Said the Court:

> ❝If there is a bedrock principle underlying the 1st Amendment, it is that the government may not prohibit the expression of an idea simply because society finds the idea itself offensive. . . . We do not consecrate the flag by punishing its desecration, for in doing so we dilute the freedom that this cherished emblem represents.❞

The Court's decision in *Johnson* set off a firestorm of criticism around the country and prompted Congress to pass the Flag Protection Act of 1989. It, too, was struck down by the Court, 5 to 4, in *United States* v. *Eichman* in 1990—on the same grounds as those set out a year earlier in *Johnson*.

## Commercial Speech

Commercial speech is speech for business purposes—mostly, advertising. Until fairly recently, it was generally thought that the 1st and 14th amendments did not protect such speech. In *Bigelow* v. *Virginia*, 1975, however, the Supreme Court held unconstitutional a State law that prohibited the newspaper advertising of abortion services. And in 1976 it struck down another Virginia law forbidding the advertisement of prescription drug prices, *Virginia State Board of Pharmacy* v. *Virginia Citizens Consumer Council*.

Not all commercial speech is protected, however. Thus, government can and does prohibit false and misleading advertisements, and the advertising of illegal goods or services.

In fact, government can even forbid advertising that is neither false nor misleading. Thus, in 1970 Congress banned cigarette ads on radio and television, and in 1986 it extended the ban to include chewing tobacco and snuff. The tobacco industry did not challenge the constitutionality of either of those actions.

In most of its commercial speech cases the Court has struck down some arbitrary restriction on advertising. For example, in *Carey* v. *Population Services International*, 1977, it voided a New York law forbidding the advertisement of contraceptives. A more recent case involved certified public accountants. In *Edenfield* v. *Fane*, 1993, the Court struck down a rule made by Florida's Board of Accountancy. That public agency had barred any CPA practicing in Florida from any "direct, in-person, uninvited solicitation" to gain new clients. The Court found that what the Board had prohibited was clearly commercial speech covered by the 1st and 14th amendments' protection.

One of the Court's first commercial speech cases had a peculiar twist to it. In *Wooley* v. *Maynard*, 1977, the Court held that a State cannot force its citizens to act as "mobile billboards"—not, at least, when the words used conflict with their religious or moral beliefs. The Maynards, who were Jehovah's Witnesses, objected to the New Hampshire State motto on their automobile license plates. The words *Live Free or Die* clashed with their belief in everlasting life, and so they covered those words with tape. For this, Maynard was arrested three times. On appeal, the Supreme Court sided with Maynard.

## Section 3 Review

**1. Define:** libel, slander, shield law, symbolic speech, picketing

**2.** For what reason does the Constitution guarantee freedom of expression?

**3.** The rights of free speech and press are especially intended to protect the expression of what views?

**4.** When can government impose a prior restraint on expression?

**5.** Is obscenity entitled to constitutional protections?

**6.** What special protections of freedom of expression do many news reporters enjoy?

**7.** What is the extent of government regulation of movies, radio, and television?

**8.** What are the constitutional protections of (a) symbolic speech? (b) commercial speech?

**Critical Thinking**

**9. Identifying Central Issues** (p. 19) Is American society better or worse off for allowing even those who promote racist and sexist views to express their beliefs?

★

# 4 Freedom of Expression and National Security

## Find Out:

- How do protection of civil rights and the demands of national security conflict?
- How has government tried to settle that conflict?

## Key Terms:

espionage, sabotage, treason, sedition

For several years in the early 1950s, Senator Joseph McCarthy waged an intense battle to rid the United States Government of what he claimed was communist infiltration. McCarthy found no real evidence of subversion. However, his smear tactics and wild accusations did manage to destroy the reputations and lives of dozens of innocent people.

Eventually, McCarthy was exposed and denounced for his actions. His story, however, touches on an important dilemma facing the American political system: Government has a right to protect itself against domestic threats to the nation's security. But how far can government go when it tries to accomplish that goal? In this section, you will focus on that dilemma.

## Punishable Acts

Clearly, government can punish espionage, sabotage, and treason. These are forms of conduct. **Espionage** is the practice of spying for a foreign power. **Sabotage** involves an act of destruction intended to hinder a nation's war or defense effort. **Treason** is defined in the Constitution in Article III, Section 3. It can consist only in levying war against the nation or supporting its enemies.

Sedition presents a much more delicate problem, for it involves the use of spoken or written words. **Sedition** is the incitement of resistance to lawful authority. It does not necessarily involve acts of violence or betrayal.

## The Alien and Sedition Acts

Congress first acted to curb opposition to government in the Alien and Sedition Acts of 1798.[19] Those laws gave the President power to deport undesirable aliens and made "any false, scandalous, and malicious" criticism of the government a crime. The acts were intended to stifle the opponents of John Adams and the Federalists.

The Alien and Sedition Acts were undoubtedly unconstitutional, but they were never tested in the courts. Some 25 persons paid fines or went to jail for violating them. The acts expired before President Jefferson took office and, in 1801, he pardoned those sentenced under the acts.

## Seditious Acts in Wartime

Congress passed another sedition law during World War I, as part of the Espionage Act of 1917. That law made it a crime to encourage disloyalty, interfere with the draft, obstruct recruiting, incite insubordination in the armed forces, or hinder the sale of government bonds. The act also made it a crime to "willfully utter, print, write, or publish any disloyal, profane, scurrilous, or abusive language about the form of government of the United States."

More than 2,000 persons were convicted for violating the Espionage Act. The constitutionality of the law was tested and upheld several times. The most important of those tests came in *Schenck* v. *United States*, 1919.

Charles Schenck, an officer of the Socialist party, had been found guilty of obstructing the war effort. He had sent fiery leaflets to some 15,000 men who had been drafted, urging them to resist the call to military service.

The Supreme Court upheld Schenck's conviction. The case is particularly noteworthy because the Court's opinion, written by Justice

---

[19]This is the collective title given to a number of different laws passed by Congress at the time. Violations were punishable by a maximum fine of $2,000 and two years in prison. The first person convicted under the acts was Matthew Lyon, a member of Congress from Vermont. He had accused President Adams of "a continual grasp for power—an unbounded thirst for ridiculous pomp, foolish adulation and selfish avarice."

Oliver Wendell Holmes, established the "clear and present danger" rule.

❝Words can be weapons. . . . The question in every case is whether the words used are used in such circumstances and are of such nature as to create a clear and present danger that they will bring about the substantive evils that Congress has a right to prevent.❞

In short, the rule says that words can be outlawed, and those who utter them can be punished when the words they use trigger an immediate danger that criminal acts will follow.

## Sedition in Peacetime

In 1940, however, Congress passed a new sedition law, the Smith Act, and made it applicable in peacetime. Congress later passed two other such statutes: the Internal Security (McCarran) Act of 1950 and the Communist Control Act of 1954.

The Smith Act makes it unlawful for any person to teach or advocate the violent overthrow of government in the United States or to organize or knowingly be a member of any group with such an aim. It also forbids conspiring with others to commit any of those acts.

The Court first upheld the Smith Act in *Dennis* v. *United States* in 1951. Eleven leaders of the Communist party had been convicted of advocating the overthrow of the Federal Government. On appeal, they argued that the law violated the 1st Amendment's guarantees of freedom of speech and press. They also claimed that no act of theirs constituted a clear and present danger to this country. The Court disagreed, and modified Justice Holmes's doctrine as it did so:

❝An attempt to overthrow the government by force, even though doomed from the outset because of inadequate numbers or power of the revolutionists, is a sufficient evil for Congress to prevent. . . .❞

The Court modified that holding in several later cases, however. In *Yates* v. *United States*, 1957, for example, the Court overturned the Smith Act convictions of several party leaders. It held: Merely to urge someone to *believe* something, in contrast to urging that person to *do* something, cannot be made illegal.

The result of *Yates* and other Smith Act cases was this: The Court upheld the constitutionality

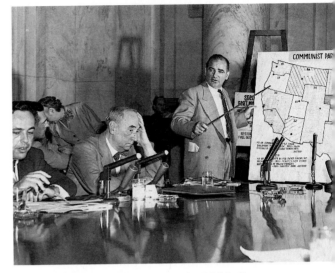

**Trial by Accusation** In the 1950s Senator Joseph McCarthy's unjust accusations of "un-American" beliefs or activities created a climate of fear across the country.

of the law, but construed its provisions so that enforcement was practically impossible.

The McCarran Act proved to be an even less effective sedition law. It required every "communist-front" and "communist-action" organization to register with the attorney general. The act also created the Subversive Activities Control Board to decide which groups were subject to the law.

The Board first ordered the Communist party to register in 1953, and the Supreme Court held that it could be forced to do so, *Communist Party* v. *SACB*, 1961. It never actually did, however, largely because any person who came forward to register the party could then be charged as a "knowing member" under the Smith Act. In 1965 the Court held that to force someone into this position would contradict the 5th Amendment's guarantee against self-incrimination, *Albertson* v. *SACB*, 1965.[20]

The Court further limited the effectiveness of the McCarran Act by holding other parts of it to be unconstitutional. The net effect of the Court's response was to leave it a hollow shell.

---

[20]The decision left the SACB with no real functions to perform. It finally passed out of existence when Congress stopped funding it in 1973.

The Communist Control Act declares the Communist party in this country to be "a conspiracy to overthrow the Government of the United States." The act's goal was to outlaw the party and keep its candidates off the ballot in any election. The law was never enforced.

Two factors have made the matter of internal subversion much less prominent today than it was a few years ago. One is the overall ineffectiveness of the sedition laws. The other is that U.S.-Soviet relations are today remarkably different from what they were in the cold war period.

Not all applications of the clear and present danger rule have centered on members of the Communist party. Take *Brandenburg* v. *Ohio*, 1969, as a leading case in point.

Clarence Brandenburg, a Ku Klux Klan leader in Ohio, had been punished for violating the State's criminal syndicalism law. He had organized a rally where, standing in front of a burning cross, he had addressed a group of men, most of them hooded and some of them armed. Brandenburg shouted: "We are not a revengent organization, but if our President, our Congress, our Supreme Court continues to suppress the white, Caucasian race, it's possible that there might have to be some revengence taken." For those remarks an Ohio court sentenced Brandenburg to ten years in prison.

The Supreme Court reversed that conviction. It held that although Brandenburg had urged others to break the law, his remarks had produced no likelihood of "imminent lawless action."

## Section 4 Review

**1. Define:** espionage, sabotage, treason, sedition
**2.** What were the Alien and Sedition Acts, and what became of them?
**3.** What is the clear and present danger rule?
**4.** What became of the Smith Act, McCarran Act, and the Communist Control Act?

**Critical Thinking**

**5. Checking Consistency** (p. 19) Should American society limit those who seek revolution, given the revolutionary history of this country?

★

# 5 Freedom of Assembly and Petition

**Find Out:**

- For what reasons are there limits on the freedoms of assembly and of petition?

A noisy street demonstration by gay rights activists, or by neo-Nazis, or by any number of other groups; a candlelight vigil of opponents of the death penalty; the prolife faithful singing hymns as they picket an abortion clinic; prochoice partisans gathered on the steps of the State capitol . . . These are commonplace events today, and they are also everyday manifestations of freedom of assembly and petition.

In this section, you will examine the shape of that freedom and its importance to you and to all Americans.

## The Constitution's Guarantees

The 1st Amendment guarantees

"... the right of the people peaceably to assemble, and to petition government for a redress of grievances."

The 14th Amendment's Due Process Clause also protects those rights of assembly and petition against actions by the States or their local governments. The Supreme Court first made that holding in *DeJonge* v. *Oregon*, 1937.

A court in Oregon had found Dirk DeJonge guilty of violating Oregon's criminal syndicalism law. The statute prohibited "any unlawful acts" that were intended to bring about "industrial or political change or revolution." DeJonge had helped organize and had spoken at a meeting of the Communist party. For that behavior, a State court sentenced him to seven years in prison.[21]

The Supreme Court reversed DeJonge's conviction, declaring: "Peaceable assembly for lawful discussion cannot be made a crime."

---

[21]Note the close similarities between *DeJonge* and *Brandenburg* v. *Ohio*.

The Constitution protects the right of the people to assemble—to gather with one another—to express their views on public matters. It protects their right to organize—in political parties, pressure groups, and other organizations—to influence public policy. It also protects the people's right to bring their views to the attention of public officials by such varied means as written petitions, letters, or advertisements; lobbying; or parades, marches, or other demonstrations.

But, notice, the 1st and 14th amendments protect the rights of peaceable assembly and petition. The Constitution does not give people the right to incite others to violence, to block a public street, close a school, or otherwise to endanger life, property, or public order.

## Time–Place–Manner Regulations

Government can make and enforce reasonable rules covering the time, place, and manner of assemblies. Thus, the Supreme Court has upheld a city ordinance that prohibits making a noise or causing any other diversion near a school if that action disrupts school activities, *Grayned* v. *City of Rockford*, 1972. It has also upheld a State law that forbids parades near a courthouse when they are intended to influence court proceedings, *Cox* v. *Louisiana*, 1965.

But rules for keeping the public peace must be more than reasonable. They must also be precisely drawn and fairly administered. In *Coates* v. *Cincinnati*, 1971, the Court struck down a city ordinance that made it a crime for "three or more persons to assemble" on a sidewalk or street corner "and there conduct themselves in a manner annoying to persons passing by, or to occupants of adjacent buildings." The Court found the ordinance too vague. It was so loosely drawn that it contained "an obvious invitation to discriminatory enforcement against those whose association together is 'annoying' because their ideas, their lifestyle, or their physical appearance is resented by the majority."

Government's rules must be content neutral. That is, while government can regulate assemblies on the basis of time, place, and manner, it cannot regulate them on the basis of what might be said there. Thus, in *Forsyth County* v. *Nationalist Movement*, 1992, the Court threw out a Georgia county's ordinance that levied a fee of up to $1,000 for public demonstrations. The law was contested by a white supremacist group seeking to protest the creation of a holiday to honor Martin Luther King, Jr. The Court found the ordinance not to be content neutral, particularly because county officials had unlimited power to set the exact fee to be paid by any group.

Notice that the power to control traffic or keep a protest rally from becoming a riot *can* be used as an excuse to prevent speech. The line between crowd control and thought control can be very thin, indeed.

## Demonstrations on Public Property

Over the past several years, most of the Court's freedom of assembly cases have involved organized demonstrations. Demonstrations are, of course, assemblies.

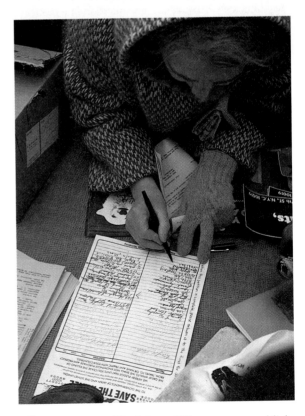

▲ **Freedom of Petition**   When persons publicly solicit signatures or conduct opinion polls, they are exercising rights guaranteed under the 1st and 14th amendments.

Most demonstrations take place in public places—on streets and sidewalks, in parks or public buildings, and so on. Demonstrations take place in these locations because it is the public the demonstrators want to reach.

Demonstrations almost always involve some degree of conflict. Mostly, they are held to protest something, and so a clash of ideas is present. Many times there is also a conflict with the normal use of streets or other public facilities. It is hardly surprising, then, that the tension generated can sometimes rise to a serious level.

Given all this, the Supreme Court has often upheld laws that require advance notice and permits for demonstrations in public places. In an early leading case, *Cox v. New Hampshire*, 1941,[22] it unanimously approved such a law:

‟The authority of a municipality to impose regulations in order to assure the safety and convenience of the people in the use of public highways has never been regarded as inconsistent with civil liberties but rather as one of the means of safeguarding the good order on which they ultimately depend. . . . The question in a particular case is whether the control is exercised so as to deny . . . the right of assembly and the opportunity for the communication of thought and the discussion of public questions. ″

Right-to-demonstrate cases raise many basic and thorny questions. How and to what extent can government regulate demonstrators and their demonstrations? Does the Constitution require that police officers allow an unpopular group to continue to demonstrate when its activities have excited others to violence? When, in the name of public peace and safety, can police properly order demonstrators to disband?

Among these cases, *Gregory v. Chicago*, 1969, remains typical. While under police protection, Dick Gregory and others had marched—singing, chanting, and carrying placards—from city hall to the mayor's home some five miles away. Marching in the streets around the mayor's house, they demanded the firing of the city's school superintendent and an end to de facto segregation in the city's schools.

A crowd of several hundred people, including many residents of the all-white neighborhood quickly gathered. Soon, the bystanders began throwing insults and threats, rocks, eggs, and other objects. The police tried to keep order, but after about an hour, they decided that serious violence was about to break out. At that point, they ordered the demonstrators to leave the area. When Gregory and the others failed to do so, the police arrested them and charged them with disorderly conduct.

The convictions of the demonstrators were unanimously overturned by the High Court. The Court noted that the marchers had done no more than exercise their constitutional rights of assembly and petition. Neighborhood residents and others, not the demonstrators, had caused the disorder. So long as the demonstrators acted peacefully, they could not be punished for disorderly conduct.

Over recent years, the most controversial demonstrations have been those orchestrated by Operation Rescue and other anti-abortion groups. In the main, those groups' efforts have been aimed at discouraging women from seeking the services of abortion clinics; and those efforts have generated many lawsuits. In the most notable case to date, *Madsen* v. *Women's Health Services, Inc.*, 1994, the Supreme Court upheld a Florida judge's order directing protesters not to block access to an abortion clinic. The judge's order had drawn a 36-foot buffer zone around the clinic, and the High Court found that to be a reasonable limit on the demonstrators' activities.

## Right of Assembly and Private Property

What of demonstrations on private property—for example, at shopping centers? The Court has heard only a few cases raising this question. However, at least this much can be said: The rights of assembly and petition do not give people a right to trespass on private property, even if they wish to express political views.

Privately owned shopping centers are not public streets, sidewalks, parks, and other "places of public assembly." Thus, no one has a constitutional right to do such things as hand

---

[22]This is one of the several Jehovah's Witness cases referred to on page 497. Cox and several other Witnesses had violated a State law that required a license to hold a parade or procession on the public streets.

out political leaflets or ask people to sign petitions in those places.

These comments are based on the leading case here, *Lloyd Corporation* v. *Tanner*, 1972. However, since that case the Court has held this: A State supreme court may interpret the provisions of that State's own constitution in such a way as to require the owners of shopping centers to allow the reasonable exercise of the right of petition on their private property. In that event, there is no violation of the property owners' rights under any provision in the federal Constitution, *PruneYard Shopping Center* v. *Robins*, 1980. In that case, several California high school students had set up a card table in the shopping center, passed out pro-Israeli pamphlets, and asked passersby to sign petitions to be sent to the President and Congress.

## Freedom of Association

The guarantees of freedom of assembly and petition include a guarantee of association. That is, those guarantees include the right to associate with others to promote political, economic, and other social causes. That right is not set out in so many words in the Constitution, but the Supreme Court has said "it is beyond doubt that freedom to engage in association for the advancement of beliefs and ideas is an inseparable aspect" of the Constitution's guarantees of free expression, *National Association for the Advancement of Colored People* v. *Alabama*, 1958. Of course, there is no right to gather to pursue illegal ends.

The case just cited is one of the early right to associate cases. There, a State law required the Alabama branch of the NAACP to disclose the names of all its members in that State. When the organization refused a court's order that it do so, it was found in contempt of court and fined $100,000.

The Supreme Court overturned the contempt conviction. It said that it could find no legitimate reason why the State should have the NAACP's membership list.

You have seen some illustration of the guarantee of freedom of expression at work in earlier chapters. Recall, for example, *Tashjian* v. *Republican Party of Connecticut*, a 1986 case noted

"I DON'T WANT YOU PLAYING WITH THAT LITTLE JONES BOY..... WHY, HIS FAMILY DOESN'T EVEN COMPOST!"

© Reprinted with special permission of King Features Syndicate, Inc.

▲ **Interpreting Political Cartoons**
What bias is guiding this parent's decision to limit her son's freedom of association?

on page 162. In that case the Supreme Court held that a State's election laws cannot forbid a political party to allow independents to vote in that party's primary if the party wants to do so.

You will see other illustrations later on. Thus, in Chapter 21 you will consider such cases as *Roberts* v. *United States Jaycees*, 1984 and *Board of Directors of Rotary International* v. *Rotary Club of Duarte*, 1987. In both cases the Supreme Court rejected attempts by an all-male organization to invoke freedom of association as a shield against the admission of women to the club.

## Section 5 Review

1. What does the guarantee of freedom of assembly and petition intend to protect?
2. On what basis can government regulate the rights of assembly and petition?
3. What factors make the right to demonstrate such a thorny issue?
4. For what reason is the right to associate protected by the Constitution?

### Critical Thinking

5. **Identifying Alternatives** (p. 19) What might be an acceptable response to the announcement that a neo-Nazi group was planning a demonstration in your community?

★

# Predicting Consequences

**W**hen you predict consequences, you determine the likely effect of an event or action on the outcome of future events or actions. Predicting consequences is an important skill that enables you to make decisions and choices that are likely to be effective. Of course, no one can be certain about what will happen in the future. However, there are ways to foresee how one set of actions will influence future events or actions. Follow the steps below to practice your skill at predicting consequences.

**1. Have a clear and accurate understanding of the event or action in question.** Your predictions can only be as valid as the information upon which you base them. Read the information below, and answer the following questions: (a) What is the nature of the legal conflict in this hypothetical case? (b) What does the Constitution say about the subject?

**2. Identify and evaluate all possible consequences.** Study the facts below and answer the following questions: (a) What are the possible consequences of the hypothetical case given below? (b) How likely is it that any of these consequences will occur?

**3. Use your knowledge of history.** The pattern of events in the past can be helpful in predicting future outcomes, particularly when strong parallels exist. Read the information about a past Supreme Court decision on this topic. Answer the following questions: (a) How has the Supreme Court ruled in the past on the subject of free exercise of religion? (b) What other facts do you know about this subject and how the courts have responded in the past?

**4. Predict the consequences.** Combine your knowledge of history with your evaluation of the possible consequences to predict the consequences of the hypothetical case below. Answer the following question: (a) How do you expect the sect leader to argue his or her case? (b) How do you expect the courts to respond to the sect leader's arguments?

---

### Hypothetical Case

The leader of a small religious sect is convicted under a State law that outlaws the inhumane treatment of animals. The incident in question occurred during one of the sect's religious observances, which involves the ritual sacrifice of animals.

### Constitutional Background

The 1st Amendment: "Congress shall make no law respecting an establishment of religion, or prohibiting the free exercise thereof, or abridging the freedom of speech, or of the press; or the right of the people peaceably to assemble, and to petition the government for a redress of grievances."

### Past Supreme Court Action

"Laws are made for the government of actions, and while they cannot interfere with mere religious belief and opinions, they may with practices. Suppose one believed that human sacrifices were a necessary part of religious worship, would it be seriously contended that the civil government could not interfere to prevent a sacrifice?"—from *Reynolds* v. *United States*, 1879.

# Chapter-in-Brief

Scan all headings, photographs, charts, and other visuals in the chapter before reading the section summaries below.

**Section 1** **The Unalienable Rights (pp. 485–489)** The Constitution, especially its Bill of Rights, guarantees many rights and liberties to the American people. These guarantees reflect the principle of limited government.

An individual's rights can be exercised only to the extent that they do not limit the rights of others. In cases where individual rights conflict, one right must take precedence.

The Bill of Rights restricts only the National Government. Each State constitution, however, contains its own bill of rights. Also, the 14th Amendment's Due Process Clause "nationalizes" most of the protections of the Bill of Rights.

**Section 2** **Freedom of Religion (pp. 490–497)** Freedom of expression is vital to democracy. One key component of this freedom is the freedom of religion.

Freedom of religion is guaranteed in part by the Establishment Clause. Still, the nature of the wall between church and state has been the subject of many court decisions.

Freedom of religion is also guaranteed by the Free Exercise Clause. This clause protects people's right to believe—though not necessarily to do—whatever they wish regarding religion.

**Section 3** **Freedom of Speech and Press (pp. 499–505)** The 1st and 14th amendments' guarantee of free speech and free press protect people's right to speak and their right to be heard.

There are limits to these rights. Obscene material is not protected, nor is slanderous and libelous speech. Freedom of the press does not allow reporters to withhold certain information from government. Movies and electronic media are also subject to regulation. In most cases, government cannot exercise prior restraint.

Symbolic and commercial speech also enjoy constitutional protection. Yet, government can limit both under certain circumstances.

**Section 4** **Freedom of Expression and National Security (pp. 506–508)** Government must protect itself from internal subversion. Therefore, government can regulate some expression in the interest of national security.

Historically, some government attempts to regulate opposition to the government have proven unworkable. For example, the Alien and Sedition Acts of 1798 and several anti-communist efforts of the cold war era were largely ineffective. However, the Supreme Court has held that government has a right to control speech that creates "a clear and present danger" of violence or harm to public order or national security.

**Section 5** **Freedom of Assembly and Petition (pp. 508–511)** The 1st Amendment guarantees the right to assemble peaceably and to petition for the redress of grievances. Government can reasonably regulate the time, place, and manner of such expression. Those regulations must, however, be "content neutral."

The Court has held that demonstrations targeted at specific private residences can be outlawed. Also, citizens do not generally enjoy the right to assemble on private property.

Freedom of assembly and petition includes a guarantee of association. This means that people are free to to associate with others in order to promote causes of mutual concern.

# Chapter Review

## Vocabulary and Key Terms

Bill of Rights (p. 486)
civil liberties (p. 486)
civil rights (p. 486)
aliens (p. 487)
Due Process Clause (p. 488)
Establishment Clause (p. 490)

Free Exercise Clause (p. 496)
libel (p. 499)
slander (p. 499)
shield laws (p. 502)
symbolic speech (p. 503)

picketing (p. 504)
espionage (p. 506)
sabotage (p. 506)
treason (p. 506)
sedition (p. 506)

**Matching:** *Review the key terms in the list above. If you are not sure of a term's meaning, look up the term and review its definition. Choose a term from the list above that best matches each description.*

1. the part of the Constitution that ensures that no State can deny any right that is "basic or essential to the American concept of ordered liberty"
2. designed to protect reporters in the media from having to reveal their confidential news sources
3. what striking workers do when they patrol outside a business
4. what the first 10 amendments to the Constitution are called
5. the crime of levying war against the United States or giving aid and comfort to the enemy

**True or False:** *Determine whether each statement is true or false. If it is true, write "true." If it is false, change the underlined word or words to make the statement true.*

1. <u>Symbolic speech</u> is the expression of beliefs or ideas by conduct.
2. An <u>alien</u> is one who is not a citizen of the state in which he or she lives.
3. When workers who are on strike patrol a business, they are engaged in a practice called <u>sabotage</u>.

4. That part of the Constitution in which many civil rights and liberties are spelled out is the <u>Free Exercise Clause</u>.

**Word Relationships:** *Distinguish between words in each pair.*

1. libel/slander
2. Free Exercise Clause/Establishment Clause
3. treason/sedition
4. espionage/sabotage
5. civil rights/civil liberties

## Main Ideas

### Section 1 (pp. 485–489)

1. What does it mean to say that the concept of individual freedom is rooted in American colonial history?
2. What does it mean to say that individual rights guaranteed in the Constitution are relative and not absolute?
3. What is the relationship between the 14th Amendment and the Bill of Rights?

### Section 2 (pp. 490–497)

4. Summarize the meaning and impact of the Establishment Clause. How does this clause help guarantee "a free trade in ideas"?
5. Summarize the meaning and impact of the Free Exercise Clause. How does this clause help guarantee a "free trade in ideas"?

**6.** At what point can the government limit a person's exercise of religion?

## Section 3 (pp. 499-505)

**7.** Why does the Constitution seek to guarantee the right of people both to speak and to hear?

**8.** Give three examples of circumstances in which the freedom of speech is not protected under the Constitution.

**9.** What kinds of actions are protected as "speech"?

## Section 4 (pp. 506–508)

**10.** Summarize the conflict between the need for national security and the need for individual rights.

**11.** What is the significance of the "clear and present danger" rule?

**12.** What has been the overall result of the United States' efforts to prevent internal subversion?

## Section 5 (pp. 508–511)

**13.** At what point do people cease to enjoy the right to assemble and petition?

**14.** Briefly describe the nature of the limits a government can place upon assemblies.

**15.** (a) What is the freedom of association? (b) What is the limit on that freedom?

## Critical Thinking

**1. Checking Consistency** (p. 19) The American government places the highest possible value on individual rights. Yet it also protects the rights of the many against the actions of the few. Are these statements consistent? If so, how?

**2. Identifying Assumptions** (p. 19) Consider the concept of "the free marketplace of ideas." (a) What do you think this concept really means? (b) What does this concept suggest about the role and responsibility of citizens in the American democratic society?

**3. Predicting Consequences** (p. 19) (a) Why is it so important that the Constitution

guarantee the rights of people to assemble and associate. (b) What might happen if people could not enjoy this right? (c) How might this right be increased?

## Getting Involved

**1. Writing Your Opinion** You are a Supreme Court justice sitting on a case involving the free exercise of religion. Write an opinion in which you create a test for determining at what point a government can constitutionally restrict a person's free exercise of religion. Begin your opinion by stating the test you have established. Then, explain the reasoning on which you have based the test. Devote one paragraph to each idea that supports your reasoning. Review the paragraphs to be sure they logically and clearly explain why you think your ideas are supported by the Constitution. Revise to correct any errors. Then make a final copy.

**2. Class Debate** Hold a class debate on the following topic: *Resolved*, That the Federal and State governments should be allowed to provide financial assistance to parents with children in parochial schools. Select teams to debate each side of the issue. The rest of the class can evaluate each team's arguments.

**3. Gathering Information** Suppose you were researching the development of the concept of individual rights in American political history. (a) What source might you be able to use to identify the names and citation numbers of some important Supreme Court cases? (b) How might you find the text of the decisions once you have found their citations? Use the Government Resources Handbook that appears on page 690 of your textbook to identify possible sources of this information.

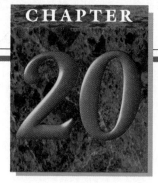

**CHAPTER**

# Civil Liberties: Protecting Individual Freedoms

## Chapter Preview

In 1960, Danny Escobedo was one of the very large number of people in this country who became enmeshed in the criminal justice system. That year, Escobedo was convicted in Chicago, Illinois, of killing his brother-in-law. Whether Escobedo actually fired the shot that killed his brother-in-law or not is unclear; but he most certainly did participate in the crime. Escobedo's conviction, however, was overturned by the United States Supreme Court in 1964, and he "walked."

If a guilty person goes free, if he or she "beats the rap," are the ends of justice served? That question has been debated for centuries, and will continue to be for as long as the American constitutional system lasts. This chapter addresses questions of justice and the Constitution's many protections of individual rights.

### Before you read this chapter:

- **Describe** what you think justice is.
- **Predict** what might occur if safeguards for people accused of crimes did not exist.

### As you read, focus on the main objective for each section. Understand:

1. The concept of due process of law.
2. The rights to freedom and security of the person.
3. The rights of the accused to a fair trial.
4. The constitutional limits on punishments for crime.

▲ **Symbol of Justice** The courts help ensure that, in all that it does, government acts fairly and in accord with established rules in order that individual freedoms are protected.

# 1 Due Process of Law

### Find Out:

- For what reason is there no exact definition of the due process guarantees?
- What is the difference between procedural and substantive due process?

### Key Terms:

due process, police power, search warrant

In Argentina they are called the *desaparecidos*—the disappeared. They are the thousands of Argentinians, most of them young, who were secretly abducted, tortured, and killed by the military in the 1970s and early 1980s. Their crime? They had criticized the government.

Could such a nightmare occur in this country? No? Why not? Because of the deep-rooted American commitment to the concept of due process.

The Constitution includes two Due Process clauses. The 5th Amendment declares that the Federal Government cannot deprive any person of "life, liberty, or property, without due process of law." The 14th Amendment places that same restriction on the States.

## Procedural and Substantive Due Process

It is impossible to define the two due process guarantees in exact and complete terms. Over the years, the Supreme Court has consistently refused to give them an exact definition. Instead, it has relied on finding the meaning of due process on a case-by-case basis. Fundamentally, the constitutional guarantees of **due process** mean this: Government must act fairly and in accord with established rules.

The concept of due process began and developed in English and then in American law as a procedural concept. That is, it developed as a requirement that government must act fairly, using fair procedures.

Fair procedures are of little value, however, if they are used to administer unfair laws. The Supreme Court recognized this fact toward the end of the last century. It began to hold that

## *VOICES on Government*

**Thurgood Marshall,**
deceased Supreme Court justice

### On the Supreme Court and Civil Liberties

❝ Paraphrasing [President] Kennedy, those who wish to assure the continued protection of important civil rights should 'ask not what the Supreme Court alone can do for civil rights; ask what you can do to help the cause of civil rights.'

Today, the answer to that question lies in bringing pressure to bear on all branches of Federal and State governmental units, including the Court, and urging them to undertake the battles for civil liberties that remain to be won. With that goal as our guide, we can go forward together to advance civil rights and liberty rights with the fervor we have shown in the past. ❞

due process requires that both the ways in which government acts *and* the laws under which it acts must be fair. Thus, the Court added the idea of substantive due process to the original notion of procedural due process.

### Examples of Procedural and Substantive Due Process

Any number of cases illustrate these elements of due process. Consider *Rochin* v. *California*, 1952, as an illustration of procedural due process.

Rochin was a suspected narcotics pusher. Acting on a tip, three Los Angeles County deputy sheriffs went to his rooming house. They forced their way into Rochin's room. There the deputies found him sitting on a bed and spotted two capsules on a nightstand. When one of the deputies

asked, "Whose stuff is this?" Rochin popped the capsules into his mouth, and although all three officers jumped him, managed to swallow them.

The deputies took Rochin to a hospital, where his stomach was pumped. The capsules were recovered and found to contain morphine. The State then prosecuted and convicted Rochin for violating the State's narcotics laws.

The Supreme Court held that the deputies had violated the 14th Amendment's guarantee of procedural due process. Said the Court:

❝This is conduct that shocks the conscience. Illegally breaking into the privacy of the petitioner, the struggle to open his mouth and remove what was there, the forcible extraction of his stomach's contents—this course of proceeding by agents of government to obtain evidence is bound to offend even hardened sensibilities. They are methods too close to the rack and the screw. . . . ❞

As an example of substantive due process, take a case considered earlier, *Pierce* v. *Society of Sisters*, 1925. In 1922 Oregon voters had adopted a new compulsory school-attendance law. It required that all persons between the ages of 8 and 16 who had not completed the eighth grade had to attend public schools.

A Roman Catholic order challenged the constitutionality of the law. The Supreme Court ruled that the law violated the 14th Amendment's Due Process Clause.

Note that the Court did not find that the State had enforced the law unfairly. Rather, the Court found fault with the law itself.

**The 14th Amendment and the Bill of Rights** Recall this crucial point from the last chapter: The provisions of the Bill of Rights apply only to actions of the Federal Government. As you read on page 489, the Supreme Court has held that most of those rights are also protected against the actions by the States through the 14th Amendment's Due Process Clause.[1]

Understanding this nationalization of rights is crucial to an understanding of the 14th Amendment's Due Process Clause and the meaning of individual rights in this country.

---

[1]The key 1st Amendment cases were discussed in Chapter 19. You will look at those involving the 4th through the 8th amendments over the next several pages.

## Due Process and the Police Power

In the federal system, the reserved powers of the States include the broad and important **police power**—the power of each State to act to protect and promote the public health, safety, morals, and general welfare.

What a State and its local governments can and cannot do in the exercise of their police power is decided by the courts. They must strike a balance between the needs of society and the rights of individuals to due process.

Any number of cases can illustrate the conflict between the use of a State's police power and the rights of individuals. Take, as an example, a matter often involved in drunk-driving cases.

Every State's laws allow the use of one or more tests to determine whether a person arrested and charged with drunk driving was in fact drunk at the time of the incident.

Does the requirement that a person submit to such a test violate his or her rights under the 14th Amendment? Does the test involve an unconstitutional search for and seizure of evidence? Does it amount to forcing a person to testify against himself or herself—unconstitutional compulsory self-incrimination? Or is the requirement a proper use of the police power?

Time after time, State and federal courts have upheld the right of society to protect itself against drunk drivers and rejected the individual rights' argument.

The leading case is *Schmerber* v. *California*, 1966. The Court found no objection to a situation in which a police officer had directed a doctor to draw blood from a drunk-driving suspect. The Court stressed these points: The blood sample was drawn in accord with accepted medical practice. The officer had reasonable grounds to believe that the suspect was drunk. Further, had the officer taken time to secure a **search warrant**—a court order authorizing a search—the evidence could have disappeared from the suspect's system.

Legislators and judges have often found the public's health, safety, morals, and/or welfare to be of overriding importance. For example:

—To promote health: States can limit the sale of alcoholic beverages and tobacco, make laws to combat pollution, and require the vaccination of school children.

—To promote safety: States can forbid concealed weapons, require the use of seatbelts, and punish drunk drivers.

—To promote morals: States can outlaw gambling, the sale of obscene materials, and the practice of prostitution.

—To promote the general welfare: States can enact compulsory education laws, provide help to the medically needy, and limit the profits of public utilities.

Clearly, no government can use the police power in any unreasonable or unfair way. In short, they cannot violate the 14th Amendment's Due Process Clause. Thus, police officers may not use unnecessary force as they enforce the criminal law. No State may prohibit the operation of private schools. And a city may not ban a street demonstration simply because the mayor opposes the demonstrators' cause.

## Right of Privacy

The constitutional guarantees of due process create a right of privacy. As the Supreme Court defined it in *Stanley* v. *Georgia*, in 1969, the right of privacy is "the right to be free, except in very limited circumstances, from unwanted governmental intrusions into one's privacy."[2]

The Constitution makes no specific mention of the right, but the Supreme Court declared its existence in *Griswold* v. *Connecticut* in 1965. That case centered on a State law that outlawed birth-control counseling and prohibited all use of birth-control devices. The Court held the law to be a violation of the 14th Amendment's Due Process Clause, and noted that the State had no business policing the marital bedroom.

**Abortion** The most controversial applications of the right of privacy have come in cases that raise this question: To what extent can a State limit a woman's right to an abortion?

The leading case is *Roe* v. *Wade*, 1973. There, the Supreme Court struck down a Texas law

---

[2]Recall, *Stanley* involved the possession of obscene materials in one's own home; see page 500. More recently, the Court upheld a Georgia law that provides for the punishment of homosexual conduct in the privacy of one's home, *Bowers* v. *Hardwick*, 1986.

that made abortion a crime except when necessary to save the life of the mother.

In *Roe*, the Court held that the 14th Amendment's right of privacy "encompass[es] a woman's decision whether or not to terminate her pregnancy." More specifically, the Court ruled that (1) during the first trimester of pregnancy (about three months) a State must recognize a woman's right to choose an abortion and cannot interfere with medical judgments in that matter; (2) during the second trimester a State, acting in the interest of women who undergo abortions, can make reasonable regulations about how, when, and where abortions can be performed, but cannot prohibit the procedure; and (3) during the final trimester a State, acting to protect the unborn child, can choose to prohibit all abortions except those necessary to preserve the life or health of the mother.

In several later cases the Court rejected a number of challenges to its basic holding in *Roe*. But as the composition of the Court has changed, so has the Court's position on abortion—and that point can be seen in the Court's decisions in recent cases in the matter.

In *Webster* v. *Reproductive Health Services*, in 1989, the Court upheld two key parts of a Missouri law. Those provisions prohibit abortions, except those to preserve the mother's life or health, (1) in any public hospital or clinic in that State and (2) in any case where the mother is 20 or more weeks pregnant and tests show that the fetus is viable—capable of life outside the mother's body.

In two 1990 cases, the Court said that a State may require a minor (1) to inform at least one parent before she can obtain an abortion, *Ohio* v. *Akron Center for Reproductive Health*, 1990, and (2) to tell both parents of her plans, except in cases where a judge gives permission for an abortion without parental knowledge, *Minnesota* v. *Hodgson*, 1990.

In the most recent case, *Planned Parenthood of Southeastern Pennsylvania* v. *Casey*, 1992, the Court announced this new rule: A State may place reasonable limits on a woman's right to choose an abortion, but those restrictions cannot impose an "undue burden" on her choice of that procedure.

In *Casey*, the Court applied that new standard to Pennsylvania's Abortion Control Act. It upheld sections of that law that say:

1. A woman who seeks an abortion must be given professional counseling intended to persuade her to change her mind;
2. A woman must delay an abortion for at least 24 hours after that counseling;
3. An unmarried female under 18 must have the consent of a parent, or the permission of a judge, before an abortion; and
4. Doctors and clinics must keep detailed records of all abortions they perform.

Those four requirements do not impose an undue burden on a woman; they do not, said the Court, place "a substantial obstacle in the path of a woman seeking an abortion of a nonviable fetus."

But the Court did strike down another key part of the Pennsylvania law. That provision required that a married woman must tell her husband of her plan to have an abortion.

In none of these cases did the Court overturn *Roe* v. *Wade*. But, as you can see, these decisions have made it much more possible for State legislatures to adopt stricter regulation of abortion than was originally the case under *Roe*.

## Section 1 Review

**1. Define:** due process, police power, search warrant
**2.** What is the difference between procedural and substantive due process?
**3.** What is the relationship between the Bill of Rights and the 14th Amendment's Due Process Clause?
**4.** What is a State's police power?
**5.** What is the right to privacy, and from where in the Constitution does it come?

**Critical Thinking**

**6. Checking Consistency** (p. 19) Considering the constitutional right to privacy, do you think it is proper for a State to use its police power to promote morals among its citizens?

★

# 2 Freedom and Security of the Person

**Find Out:**

■ How does the Constitution protect the freedom and security of the person?
■ What is the extent of those protections?

**Key Terms:**

probable cause, exclusionary rule

Few people realize how many different rights the Constitution guarantees to the American people. More than three dozen individual liberties are protected by that document.

As you will see in this section, several of those guarantees protect the right of each person to be free from physical restraint and to be reasonably secure in his or her person and home.

## Slavery and Involuntary Servitude: The 13th Amendment

The 13th Amendment was added to the Constitution in 1865, ending over 200 years of slavery in this country. Section 1 of the amendment declares, "Neither slavery nor involuntary servitude . . . shall exist within the United States, or any place subject to their jurisdiction." Importantly, Section 2 of this amendment gives Congress the expressed power "to enforce this article by appropriate legislation."

Until 1865, each State could decide for itself whether or not to allow slavery. With the 13th Amendment, that power was denied to them, and to the National Government, as well.

**Section 1** As a widespread practice, slavery disappeared more than 125 years ago. There are still occasional cases of it, however. As recently as 1986, in fact, three men were sentenced to prison in Texas for the crime. They had been convicted of holding four drifters at an isolated ranch.

Most cases that have arisen under Section 1 have turned on the question of "involuntary servitude"—that is, forced labor. The Antipeon-

age Act of 1867 makes it a federal crime for any person to hold another in peonage—a condition in which a person is bound to work for another in order to fulfill a contract or satisfy a debt.

Several times, the Supreme Court has struck down State laws making it a crime for any person to fail to work after having received money or other benefits by promising to do so.[3]

The 13th Amendment does not forbid *all* forms of involuntary servitude, however. Thus, in 1918 the Court drew a distinction between "involuntary servitude" and "duty" in upholding the constitutionality of the selective service system—the draft.[4] And, those who are convicted of crimes can be forced to work.

**Section 2** Shortly after the Civil War, Congress passed several civil rights laws, based on the 13th Amendment. But in several cases, especially the *Civil Rights Cases*, 1883, the Supreme Court sharply narrowed the scope of federal authority. In effect, the Court held that racial discrimination against African Americans by *private* persons did not place the "badge of slavery" on them nor keep them in servitude.

---

[3]But note, the fact that a person cannot be forced to work in order to satisfy a debt does not relieve that person of the legal obligation to pay the debt.

[4]*Selective Draft Law Cases* (*Arver* v. *United States*), 1918.

**Equal Opportunity in Employment** It is illegal for employers to discriminate on the basis of race, color, sex, religion, or national origin.

Congress soon repealed most of those laws based on the 13th Amendment. Federal enforcement of the few that remained was, at best, unimpressive.

In *Jones* v. *Mayer*, 1968, however, the Supreme Court breathed new life into the 13th Amendment. The case centered on one of the post-Civil War acts Congress had not repealed. Passed in 1866, that almost-forgotten law provided in part:

> ❝All citizens of the United States shall have the same right in every State and Territory, as is enjoyed by white citizens thereof, to inherit, purchase, lease, sell, hold, and convey real and personal property.❞

Jones, an African American, had sued because Mayer had refused to sell him a home, solely because of his race. Mayer contended that the 1866 law was unconstitutional, as it sought to prohibit private racial discrimination.

The Court upheld the law, declaring that the 13th Amendment abolished slavery and gave to Congress the power to abolish "the badges and the incidents of slavery." Said the Court:

> ❝At the very least, the freedom that Congress is empowered to secure under the 13th Amendment includes the freedom to buy whatever a white man can buy, the right to live wherever a white man can live.❞

The Court affirmed that decision in several later cases.[5] For example, in *Runyon* v. *McCrary*, 1976, two private schools had refused to admit two African Americans. The Court found that the schools had violated another provision of the 1866 law:

> ❝All persons . . . shall have the same right in every State and Territory to make and enforce contracts . . . as is enjoyed by white citizens.❞

The Court has also ruled that the Civil Rights Act of 1966 protects all "identifiable groups who are subject to intentional discrimination solely because of their ancestry or ethnic characteristics"—for example, Jews, *Shaare Tefila Congregation* v. *Cobb*, 1987; and Arabs, *St. Francis College* v. *Al-Khazraji*, 1987.

---

[5]While *Jones* v. *Mayer* was before the Court, Congress enacted the Civil Rights (Open Housing) Act of 1968; see Chapter 21, Section 3.

Most recently, however, the Court has backed off a bit. In *Patterson* v. *McLean Credit Union*, 1989, it declared that while the 1866 law does prohibit race discrimination in a contract of employment, any on-the-job discrimination should be handled in accord with the Civil Rights Act of 1964—which is treated in Chapter 21, Section 3.

Still, note this critical point: The Court has now several times held that the 13th Amendment gives Congress significant power to attack "the badges and incidents of slavery."

## Right to Keep and Bear Arms

The 2nd Amendment reads this way:

> ❝A well-regulated militia being necessary to the security of a free state, the right of the people to keep and bear arms shall not be infringed.❞

The 2nd Amendment is widely misunderstood. It was added to the Constitution to protect the right of each State to keep a militia. Its aim was to preserve the concept of the citizen-soldier. It does not guarantee a right to keep and bear arms free from restriction by government.

The only important 2nd Amendment case is *United States* v. *Miller*, 1939. There, the Court upheld a section of the National Firearms Act of 1934. That section makes it a crime to ship sawed-off shotguns, machine guns, or silencers across State lines unless the shipper has registered the weapons with the Treasury Department and paid a $200 tax. The Court said that it could find no reasonable link between the sawed-off shotgun and "the preservation . . . of a well-regulated militia."

The Court has never found the 2nd Amendment to be within the meaning of the 14th Amendment's Due Process Clause. Thus, each of the States can limit the right to keep and bear arms—and all of them do, in various ways.

## Security of Home and Person

In several provisions, the Constitution insists that government cannot arbitrarily violate the home or the person of any American citizen.

**The 3rd Amendment** This Amendment forbids the quartering of soldiers in private homes in time of peace. It also prohibits the practice in time of war except "in a manner to be prescribed by law." The guarantee was added to prevent what had been British practice in colonial days.

The amendment has had almost no importance since its adoption, however. It has never been the subject of a Supreme Court case.

**The 4th Amendment** The 4th Amendment also grew out of colonial practice. It was designed to prevent the use of writs of assistance—blanket search warrants with which British customs officials had invaded private homes to search for smuggled goods.

Unlike the 3rd Amendment, the 4th has proved a highly important guarantee. It reads:

❝The right of the people to be secure in their persons, houses, papers, and effects, against unreasonable searches and seizures, shall not be violated; and no warrants shall issue, but upon probable cause, supported by oath or affirmation, and particularly describing the place to be searched, and the persons or things to be seized.❞

Each State constitution has a similar provision. The guarantee also applies to the States through the 14th Amendment's Due Process Clause.

The general rule laid down by the 4th Amendment is this: Police officers have no general right to search for evidence or to seize either evidence or persons. Except in particular circumstances, they must have a proper warrant obtained with **probable cause**—that is, reasonable grounds.

The Supreme Court has often said that police need a search warrant whenever the person targeted by the search has "a reasonable expectation of privacy." The particular place is not that important, for the Constitution "protects people—and not simply 'areas'—against unreasonable searches and seizures." The Court first made that important point in *Katz* v. *United States*, 1967.

Again, there are many situations in which police do not need a warrant. They do not, for example, when evidence is "in plain view." Thus, the Court recently upheld a search in which officers, equipped with a warrant to search a home for stolen jewelry, found illegal weapons in plain view and seized them, *Horton*

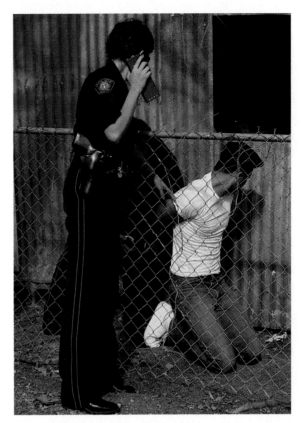

▲ **Probable Cause** Police can arrest a person in a public place without a warrant provided they have probable cause to believe that person is about to commit or has committed a crime.

v. *California*, 1990. As one more example: The Court recently endorsed the warrantless search of plastic garbage bags left at the curb, in *California* v. *Greenwood*, 1988. There is, said the Court, no "reasonable expectation of privacy" in the garbage one puts out to be hauled away.

Take a widely noted case to illustrate the line between warrantless searches that are lawful and those that are not. In *Michigan* v. *Tyler*, 1978, the Court set aside the arson convictions of two furniture dealers. Much of the evidence against them had come from two separate sets of warrantless searches. The first searches were made as the fire department fought a blaze in their store and immediately thereafter. The other searches were conducted some weeks later.

The Court found that a burning building presents an emergency situation, one in which a warrantless entry is clearly reasonable. But the

Court also held that the later searches, made well after the emergency, and also made without warrants, violated the 4th and 14th amendments.

An arrest is the seizure of a person. When officers make a lawful arrest of a person, they do not need a warrant to search "the area within which he might gain possession of a weapon or destructible evidence."[6]

In fact, most arrests take place without a warrant. Police can arrest a person in a public place without one, provided they have probable cause to believe that that person has committed or is about to commit a crime.[7]

When, exactly, does the 4th Amendment protection come into play? The Court has several times held that that point is reached "only when the officer, by means of physical force or show of authority, has in some way restrained the liberty of a citizen," *Terry* v. *Ohio*, 1968. Thus, the driver of a stolen car was "seized" when deputies blocked his escape by placing an 18-wheel tractor-trailer across both lanes of a two-lane highway, *Brower* v. *Inyo County*, 1989.

**Automobiles**   The Court has long had difficulty applying the 4th Amendment to automobiles. It has several times held that an officer needs no warrant to search an automobile, a boat, an airplane, or some other vehicle when there is probable cause to believe that it is involved in illegal activities—because such a "movable scene of crime" could disappear while a warrant was being sought.[8] The Court has also recently held that police can stop automobiles at roadside checkpoints to examine drivers and passengers for signs of intoxication—even when they have no evidence to indicate that the occupants of a particular car have been drinking, *Michigan* v. *Sitz*, 1990.

The court overturned a long string of automobile-search cases in 1991. Prior to that date, it had held in several cases that a warrant was generally needed to search a glove compartment, a paper bag, a piece of luggage, or other "closed container" in an automobile. But in *California* v. *Acevedo*, 1991, the Court set out what it called "one clear-cut rule to govern automobile searches": Whenever police lawfully stop a car, they do not need a warrant to search anything in that vehicle that they have reason to believe holds evidence of a crime.

**The Exclusionary Rule**   If an unlawful search or seizure does occur, what use can be made of the evidence that is found? If that "tainted evidence" can be used in court, then the 4th Amendment offers no real protection to a person accused of crime.

To meet that problem posed by that issue, the Supreme Court adopted, and is still refining, the **exclusionary rule**. At base, the rule is this: Evidence gained as the result of an illegal act by police cannot be used against the person from whom it was seized.

The rule was first laid down in *Weeks* v. *United States*, 1914. The Court held that evidence obtained illegally by federal officers cannot be used in the federal courts.

The exclusionary rule was extended to cover the States by the Supreme Court's historic decision in *Mapp* v. *Ohio*, 1961 (see page 489). There, police officers had entered Mapp's home without a warrant. They said they were looking for evidence of illegal gambling. They found no gambling evidence, but their very thorough search did turn up some dirty books. Mapp was convicted of possession of obscene materials and sentenced to jail. The Supreme Court found that the evidence against her had been found and seized without a proper warrant.

The exclusionary rule was intended to put teeth into the 4th Amendment, and it has. The rule says to police: As you enforce the law, obey the law. Critics of the rule note that the rule enables some persons who are clearly guilty to go free. Why, they often ask, should criminals be able "to beat the rap" on "a technicality"?

---

[6]The present rule, quoted here, was first laid down in *Chimel* v. *California*, 1969.

[7]A person arrested without a warrant must be brought promptly before a judge for a probable cause hearing. In *County of Riverside* v. *McLaughlin*, 1991, the Court held that "promptly" means within 48 hours.

[8]In an early leading case on the point, *Carroll* v. *United States*, 1925, the Court emphasized that "where the securing of a warrant is reasonably practicable it must be used. . . . In cases where seizure is impossible except without a warrant, the seizing officer acts unlawfully and at his peril unless he can show the court probable cause."

Of late, the High Court has been narrowing the scope of the rule.[9] It has done so most notably in three recent cases. First, it found an "inevitable discovery" exception to the rule, in *Nix* v. *Williams* in 1984. There the Court held that tainted evidence can be used if that evidence "ultimately or inevitably would have been discovered by lawful means."

Then, in another 1984 case, *United States* v. *Leon*, the Court found a "good faith" exception to the rule. There, federal agents in Los Angeles had used what they thought was a proper warrant to seize illicit drugs. Their warrant was later shown to be faulty, however. The Court upheld their actions nonetheless. It said: "When an officer acting with objective good faith has obtained a search warrant . . . and acted within its scope . . . there is nothing to deter."

The Court has also given police room for "honest mistakes." In *Maryland* v. *Garrison*, 1987, it allowed the use of evidence seized in the mistaken search of an apartment in Baltimore. Officers had a warrant to search for drugs in an apartment on the third floor of a building. Not realizing that there were two apartments there, they entered, searched, and found drugs in the apartment for which they did not have a warrant.

The Federal Government's drug testing programs involve searches of persons, and so they are covered by the 4th Amendment. To date, the Court has upheld two of those programs. In both instances it found that carefully drawn tests are a reasonable response to the drug problem, and they can be conducted without either warrants or even any indication of drug use by those who must take them. The first case, *Skinner* v. *Railway Labor Executives Association*, 1989, involved the Federal Railway Administration's requirement that workers take

▲ **Interpreting Political Art** An untitled painting by Hank Virgona shows a court in session. What impression of a courtroom does this painting give you?

drug tests after a major accident. The other case, *National Treasury Employees Union* v. *Von Raab*, 1989, centered on a Customs Service rule mandating drug tests for all employees who carry firearms.

**Wiretapping** Law-enforcement agents now frequently use wiretapping and other sophisticated means of "bugging."

In its first wiretapping case, in 1928, the Supreme Court held that intercepting telephone conversations without a warrant was not an unreasonable search or seizure. In 1967 it reversed that decision, however.

The earlier case, *Olmstead* v. *United States*, 1928, involved a large ring of bootleggers. Federal agents had tapped Olmstead's telephone calls over several months. That bugging produced a mass of evidence that authorities presented in court to convict him and others in the ring. The Supreme Court upheld their convictions. It found that there had been no "actual physical invasion"

[9]For example, the Court has held that the rule does not apply to federal grand jury proceedings, *United States* v. *Calandra*, 1974. Thus, tainted evidence that cannot be used at a person's trial could nonetheless be presented to the grand jury—the body that indicted that person and so caused the trial. The Court has also held that evidence against a defendant that was gained by an illegal search of another person's property can be used in a criminal trial, *United States* v. *Payner*, 1980.

of Olmstead's home or office; the agents had tapped the lines outside those places.[10]

The Supreme Court expressly overruled *Olmstead* in *Katz* v. *United States*, 1967. Katz had been found guilty of transmitting betting information across State lines from a public phone booth in Los Angeles to his contacts in Boston and Miami. Much of the evidence against him came from an electronic bug FBI agents had placed on the outside of the booth. The Supreme Court reversed the conviction and overruled *Olmstead*. It held that the 4th Amendment protects persons and not just places. Though Katz was in a public, glass-enclosed booth, he was entitled to make a private call. Said the Court:

❝What a person knowingly exposes to the public, even in his own home or office, is not a subject of 4th Amendment protection. . . . But what he seeks to preserve as private, even in an area accessible to the public, may be constitutionally protected.❞

The Court went on to say, however, that the 4th Amendment could be satisfied in such situations if police officers have a proper warrant before they install a listening device.

Congress reacted to *Katz* in a number of sections in the Omnibus Crime Control Act of 1968. They make it illegal for any unauthorized person to tap telephone wires or use electronic bugging devices or sell those devices in interstate commerce.

The 1968 law does allow federal and State police agencies to search for and seize evidence by electronic means under close court control. If officers can show probable cause, a federal or State judge can issue a warrant for a bugging operation.[11]

When it passed the 1968 law, Congress carefully avoided this knotty question: Does the President, acting under the inherent power to protect the nation against foreign attack and internal subversion, have the power to order the bugging of suspected foreign agents or domestic subversives without a warrant? For many years, several Presidents had used the FBI, the CIA, and other federal police agencies in just that way.

The Supreme Court has since ruled that the President has no such power in cases of domestic subversion, *United States* v. *United States District Court*, 1972. In the Foreign Intelligence Surveillance Act of 1978, Congress, for the first time, required a warrant even for the wiretapping or other electronic bugging of foreign agents in this country.[12]

# Section 2 Review

1. **Define:** probable cause, exclusionary rule
2. For what reason does the 13th Amendment not forbid all forms of involuntary servitude?
3. In what sense has the Supreme Court "breathed new life" into the 13th Amendment?
4. What is the true purpose of the 2nd Amendment?
5. In what sense is the 3rd Amendment of so little importance?
6. What is the basic purpose of the 4th Amendment?
7. (a) What is the exclusionary rule? (b) In what ways has the Supreme Court been narrowing the rule in recent years?

## Critical Thinking

8. **Expressing Problems Clearly** (p. 19) Discuss whether or not you feel that people who have clearly committed crimes should be able to go free if their rights are violated during arrest or trial.

★

---

[10]In a vigorous dissent, Justice Oliver Wendell Holmes was strongly critical of "such dirty business"—federal agents acting without a warrant. He wrote: "For my part I think it is a less evil that some criminals should escape than that the government should play such an ignoble part."

[11]In certain "emergency" situations, especially those involving national security or organized crime, the attorney general can authorize bugging operations by federal agents for up to 48 hours without a judge's approval—that is, without a warrant. Agents must seek a warrant during that period, however.

---

[12]The 1978 law set up a special federal court, the Foreign Intelligence Surveillance Court, with the power to issue such warrants.

The law allows only one exception to its warrant requirement: The National Security Agency, the Defense Department's top-secret code-making and code-breaking agency, does not need a warrant to eavesdrop on the electronic communications of foreign governments.

## Do Defendants Have a Right to Appointed Counsel?

### *Gideon* v. *Wainwright*, 1963

Clarence Earl Gideon was arrested by Bay Harbor, Florida, police late one night in June, 1961. He had broken into a pool room, and he was charged with breaking and entering to commit a misdemeanor. That crime, a felony in Florida law, was punishable by a fine of not more than $500 and/or up to five years in prison.

Gideon was indigent—destitute, broke. At trial, he pleaded not guilty and asked that an attorney be appointed to represent him. But the judge denied that request; Gideon was told that the State of Florida provided appointed counsel for defendants only in capital cases—that is, cases that could result in a sentence of death.

So, Gideon acted as his own attorney— and he lost the case. The jury convicted him, and the judge sentenced him to five years in the State penitentiary.

After unsuccessful appeals in the Florida courts, Gideon sent a handwritten petition to the U.S. Supreme Court. He asked that his conviction be reversed because he had been denied counsel at his Florida trial.

The Supreme Court agreed to hear Gideon's case, and it appointed an attorney to represent him. The Court took his case in large part because it wanted to reexamine one of its earlier decisions, *Betts* v. *Brady,* 1942. There, the Court had held that the 14th Amendment's Due Process Clause did not incorporate the 6th Amendment's right to counsel except in cases where "special circumstances" indicated that, without counsel, there would be "a denial of fundamental fairness, shocking to the universal sense of justice."

*Review the following evidence and arguments presented to the U.S. Supreme Court:*

### Arguments for Gideon

**1.** The right to be represented by counsel is central to the concept of a fair trial.
**2.** The 14th Amendment's Due Process Clause should be interpreted to include within its meaning the guarantee of the right to counsel in all criminal cases.
**3.** The ruling in *Betts* v. *Brady* was too narrow and should be overturned.

### Arguments for Wainwright

**1.** The 14th Amendment should not be read to require the State to provide counsel for indigent persons who are accused of relatively insignificant crimes.

**2.** *Betts* v. *Brady* should not be overruled. That action would impose a huge financial burden on every State, requiring them to furnish counsel in untold thousands of cases.

**3.** Gideon received a fair trial, and there were no "special circumstances" in his case that would warrant court-appointed counsel.

## Getting Involved

**1. Identify** the constitutional grounds on which each side based its arguments.
**2. Debate** the opposing viewpoints presented in this case.
**3. Predict** how you think the Supreme Court ruled in this case and why. Then refer to the Supreme Court Glossary on page 764 to read about the decision in the case. Discuss the impact of the Court's decision on the judicial system, the rights of the accused, and the individual States.

# 3 Rights of the Accused

**Find Out:**

- What protections does the Constitution set out for persons accused of crime?
- What constitutes a fair trial?

**Key Terms:**

writ of habeas corpus, bill of attainder, ex post facto law, grand jury, indictment, presentment, information, double jeopardy, bench trial, Miranda Rule

Think about this statement for a moment: "It is better that ten guilty persons go free than that one innocent person be punished." That maxim expresses one of the bedrock principles of the American legal system.

Of course, society *must* punish criminals in order to preserve itself. However, the law intends that any person who is suspected or accused of a crime must be presumed to be innocent—until that person is proved guilty by fair and lawful means.

## Habeas Corpus

The **writ of habeas corpus**, sometimes called the writ of liberty, is intended to prevent unjust arrests and imprisonments.[13] It is a court order directed to an officer holding a prisoner. It commands that the prisoner be brought before the court and that the officer show cause—explain, with good reason—why the prisoner should not be released.

The right to seek a writ of habeas corpus is protected against the National Government in Article I, Section 9 of the Constitution. That right is guaranteed against the States in each of their own constitutions.

The right to the writ cannot be suspended, says the Constitution, "unless when in cases of rebellion or invasion the public safety may

---

[13]The phrase *habeas corpus* comes from the Latin, meaning "you should have the body," and those are the opening words of the writ.

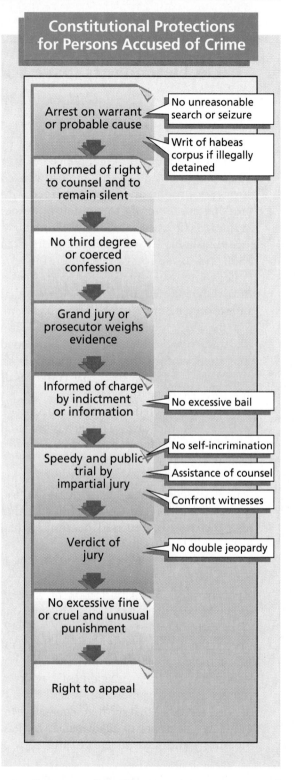

**Constitutional Protections for Persons Accused of Crime**

- Arrest on warrant or probable cause
  - No unreasonable search or seizure
  - Writ of habeas corpus if illegally detained
- Informed of right to counsel and to remain silent
- No third degree or coerced confession
- Grand jury or prosecutor weighs evidence
- Informed of charge by indictment or information
  - No excessive bail
- Speedy and public trial by impartial jury
  - No self-incrimination
  - Assistance of counsel
  - Confront witnesses
- Verdict of jury
  - No double jeopardy
- No excessive fine or cruel and unusual punishment
- Right to appeal

▲ **Interpreting Charts** Any person accused of a crime is presumed innocent until proven guilty. What protections does the Constitution extend to those who are convicted of a crime?

require it." In *Ex parte Milligan*, 1866, the Supreme Court ruled that neither the President nor Congress can legally suspend the writ in those places where there is no actual fighting nor the likelihood of any.[14]

The right to the writ has been suspended only once since the Civil War, in Hawaii during World War II; and the Supreme Court later ruled that action illegal.

## Bills of Attainder

A **bill of attainder** is a legislative act that inflicts punishment without a court trial. Neither Congress nor the States can pass such measures.[15]

The ban on bills of attainder is both a protection of individual freedom and a part of the system of separation of powers. A legislative body can pass laws that define crime and set the penalties for violation of those laws. But it cannot decide that a person is guilty of a crime and then impose a punishment on that person.

The Supreme Court has held that the prohibition is aimed at all legislative acts that apply "to named individuals or to easily ascertainable members of a group in such a way as to inflict punishment on them without a judicial trial," *United States* v. *Lovett*, 1946. The "punishment" may include the loss of a privilege.

*United States* v. *Brown*, 1965, is one of the few cases in which the Court has struck down a law as a bill of attainder. There it overturned a provision of the Landrum-Griffin Act of 1959 that made it a federal crime for a member of the Communist party to serve as an officer of a labor union.

## Ex Post Facto Laws

An **ex post facto law** has three features. It is (1) a criminal law, one defining a crime or providing for its punishment; (2) applied to an act committed before its passage; and (3) a law that works to the disadvantage of the accused. Neither Congress nor the State legislatures may pass such laws.[16]

For example, a law making it a crime to sell marijuana cannot be applied to one who sold it before that law was passed. Or, a law that changed the penalty for murder from life in prison to death could not be applied to a person who committed a murder before the punishment was changed.

Retroactive civil laws are *not* forbidden. Thus, a law raising income tax rates could be passed in November and applied to income earned through the whole year.

## Grand Jury

The 5th Amendment also provides that:

> ❝No person shall be held to answer for a capital, or otherwise infamous, crime, unless on a presentment or indictment of a grand jury. . . . ❞

The **grand jury** is the formal device by which a person can be accused of a serious crime.[17] In federal cases, it is a body of from 16 to 23 persons drawn from the area of the federal district court that it serves. The votes of at least 12 of the grand jurors are needed to return an indictment or to make a presentment. An **indictment** is a formal complaint laid before a grand jury by the prosecutor. It charges the accused with one or more crimes. If the grand jury finds that there is enough evidence for a trial, it returns a "true bill of indictment." The accused is then held for prosecution. If the grand jury does not make such a finding, the charge is dropped.

---

[14]President Lincoln suspended the writ in 1861. His order covered various parts of the country, including several areas in which war was not then being waged. Chief Justice Roger B. Taney, sitting as a circuit judge, held Lincoln's action unconstitutional. Congress then passed the Habeas Corpus Act of 1863, giving the President the power to suspend the writ when and where, in his judgment, that action was necessary. Note that *Ex parte Milligan* arose after the enactment of the 1863 law.

[15]Article I, Sections 9 and 10.

---

[16]Article I, Sections 9 and 10. The phrase *ex post facto* is from the Latin, meaning "after the fact."

[17]The 5th Amendment provides that the guarantee of grand jury does not extend "to cases arising in the land or naval forces." The conduct of members of the armed forces is regulated under a code of military law enacted by Congress.

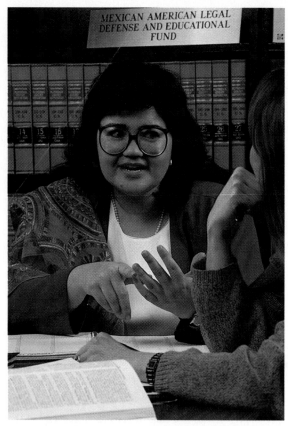

▲ **The Right to Counsel** The 6th Amendment right to be represented by a lawyer is a vital part of the right to fair trial.

A **presentment** is a formal accusation brought by the grand jury on its own motion, rather than that of the prosecutor. It is little used in federal courts.

A grand jury's proceedings are not a trial, and since unfair harm could come if they were public, its sessions are secret. They are also one-sided—in the law, *ex parte.* That is, only the prosecution, not the defense, is present.

The 5th Amendment's grand jury provision is the only part of the Bill of Rights relating to criminal prosecution that the Supreme Court has not brought within the coverage of the 14th Amendment's Due Process Clause.

The right to grand jury is intended as a protection against overzealous prosecutors. Its critics say that it is too time-consuming, too expensive, and too likely to follow the dictates of the prosecutor. In most States today, most criminal charges are not brought by grand jury indictment. They are brought, instead, by an **information**—an affidavit in which the prosecutor swears that there is enough evidence to justify a trial; see Chapter 25, pages 675–676.

## Double Jeopardy

The 5th Amendment's guarantee against double jeopardy is the first of several protections in the Bill of Rights especially intended to ensure fair trial in the federal courts.[18] Fair trials are guaranteed in State courts by each State's own constitution and by the 14th Amendment's Due Process Clause.

The 5th Amendment says in part that no person can be "twice put in jeopardy of life or limb." Today, this prohibition against **double jeopardy** means that once a person has been tried for a crime, he or she cannot be tried again for that same crime.

A person can violate both a federal *and* a State law in a single act—for example, by selling narcotics. That person can then be tried for the federal crime in a federal court and for the State crime in a State court. A single act can also result in the commission of several crimes. A person who breaks into a store, steals liquor, and sells it, can be tried for illegal entry, theft, and selling liquor without a license.

In a trial in which a jury cannot agree on a verdict, there is no jeopardy. It is as though no trial had been held, and the accused can be tried again. Nor is double jeopardy involved when a case is appealed to a higher court.[19] Recall that the Supreme Court has held that the 5th Amendment's ban on double jeopardy applies against the States through the 14th Amendment, *Benton* v. *Maryland,* 1969.

---

[18]See the 5th, 6th, 7th, and 8th amendments and also Article III, Section 2, Clause 3. The practice of excluding evidence obtained in violation of the 4th Amendment is also intended to guarantee a fair trial.

[19]The Organized Crime Control Act of 1970 allows federal prosecutors to appeal sentences they believe to be too lenient. The Supreme Court has held that such appeals do not violate the double jeopardy guarantee, *United States* v. *Di Francesco,* 1980.

## Speedy and Public Trial

The 6th Amendment commands:

❝In all criminal prosecutions, the accused shall enjoy the right to a speedy and public trial. . . .❞

**Speedy Trial** The guarantee of a speedy trial is meant to ensure that government will try a person accused of crime in a reasonable time, without undue delay. But how long a delay is too long? The Supreme Court has long recognized that no two cases are the same, and each must be looked at on its own merits.[20]

The Speedy Trial Act of 1974 says that the time between a person's arrest and the beginning of his or her federal criminal trial cannot be more than 100 days. The law does allow for some exceptions, however—in a case where the defendant must undergo extensive mental tests, for example, or when the defendant or a key witness is ill.

**Public Trial** The 6th Amendment says that a speedy trial must also be a public trial. The right to be tried in public is also part of the 14th Amendment's guarantee of procedural due process.

A trial must not be *too* speedy or *too* public, however. The Supreme Court threw out an Arkansas murder conviction in 1923 on just those grounds. The trial had taken only 45 minutes, and it had been held in a courtroom packed by a threatening mob.

Within reason, a judge can limit both the number and the kinds of spectators who may be present at a trial. Those who seek to disrupt a courtroom can be barred from it. A judge can order a courtroom cleared when the expected testimony may be embarrassing to a witness or to someone else not a party to the case.

Many of the questions about how public a trial should be involve the media. As noted in Chapter 19, the guarantees of fair trial and of free press often come into conflict in the courts. On the one hand: "A trial courtroom is a public place where the people generally—and representatives of the media—have a right to be present," *Richmond Newspapers, Inc.* v. *Virginia*, 1980. On the other hand, the Court has ruled, "Trial judges must take strong measures to ensure that the balance is never weighted against the accused," *Sheppard* v. *Maxwell*, 1966.

Champions of the public's right to know hold that the courts must allow the broadest possible press coverage. The Supreme Court has often held, however, that the media have only the same right as the general public to be present in a courtroom. The right to a public trial belongs to the defendant, not to the media.

What of televised trials? Television cameras are barred from all federal courtrooms. Most do allow some form of in-court television. Does the televising of a criminal trial violate a defendant's rights?

An early major case on the point was *Estes* v. *Texas*, 1965. The Court held that the radio and television reporting of Estes' case, which had been allowed from within the courtroom and over his objections, had been so disruptive that it denied Estes a fair trial.

Most recently, the Court held in *Chandler* v. *Florida*, 1981, that there is nothing in the Constitution to prevent a State from allowing the televising of a criminal trial—so long as steps are taken to avoid too much publicity and protect the defendant's rights.

## Trial by Jury

The 6th Amendment also says that a person accused of a federal crime must be tried "by an impartial jury."[21] This guarantee reinforces an earlier one set out in the Constitution, in Article III, Section 2. The right to trial by jury is also

---

[20]In a leading case, *Barker* v. *Wingo*, 1972, the Court listed four criteria for determining if a delay has violated the constitutional protection; the length of the delay, the reasons for it, whether the delay has in fact harmed the defendant, and whether the defendant asked for a prompt trial.

[21]The amendment adds that the members of the jury must be drawn from "the State and district wherein the crime shall have been committed, which district shall have been previously ascertained by law." This clause gives the defendant any benefit there might be in having a court and jury familiar with the people and problems of the area. A defendant may ask to be tried in another place—seek a "change of venue"—on grounds that the people of the locality are so prejudiced in the case that an impartial jury cannot be drawn. The judge must decide whether or not a change of venue is justified.

## How to Serve on a Jury

The following instructions are given to jurors before a trial begins. Judges also instruct jurors on the specific points of law that pertain to the case they are hearing.

**1. Give careful attention to the testimony and evidence presented during the trial.** Make decisions based only on these pieces of information.

**2. Do not be influenced by either sympathy for or against the defendant or the government.**

**3. Follow the law as it is explained whether or not you agree with the law.**

**4. Do not single out or disregard any of the court's instructions on the law.**

**5. Remember that the defendant is presumed by the law to be innocent.** The government has the burden of prov-

ing a defendant guilty beyond a reasonable doubt. If it fails to do so, then the verdict must be "not guilty."

**6. Keep an open mind and do not form or state any opinion about the case one way or the other until you have heard all the evidence and have heard the closing arguments of the lawyers and the judge's instructions on the applicable law.**

**7. During the trial do not discuss the case in any manner with other members of the jury or with anyone else.** Do not permit anyone to attempt to discuss it with you or in your presence. Avoid reading any newspaper articles that might be published about the case once the trial has begun. Avoid listening to or observing any broadcast news program on either television or radio.

*Source: Manual of Model Criminal Jury Instructions for the District Courts of the Eighth Circuit.*

▲ **Interpreting Charts**  Why do you think jurors are told not to read newspaper articles or listen to or watch any news programs once the trial has begun?

binding on the States through the 14th Amendment's Due Process Clause, *Duncan* v. *Louisiana*, 1968.[22]

The trial jury is often called the petit jury—*petit*, from the French word for small. You will read more about the trial jury in the State judicial system in Chapter 25. For now, however, note these points.

A defendant may waive the right to a jury trial. But he or she can do that only if the judge is satisfied that the defendant is fully aware of his or her rights and understands what that action means. In fact, a judge can order a jury trial even when a defendant does not want one,

*One Lot Emerald Cut Stones and One Ring* v. *United States*, 1972. If a defendant waives the right, a **bench trial** is held. That is, a judge alone hears the case.

In federal practice a jury is made up of 12 persons. Several States now provide for smaller juries, however, often with six members. A federal jury can convict only by unanimous vote. Most of the States follow the same rule.[23]

In a long series of cases, dating from *Strauder* v. *West Virginia*, 1880, the Supreme Court has held that a jury must be "drawn from a fair

---

[22]More precisely, in *Duncan* the Court held that the 14th Amendment's Due Process Clause guarantees trial by jury for those persons accused of "serious" crimes; in *Baldwin* v. *New York*, 1970, it defined those crimes as offenses for which imprisonment for more than six months is possible.

[23]The 14th Amendment does not say that there cannot be juries of fewer than 12 persons, *Williams* v. *Florida*, 1970, but it does not allow juries of less than six members, *Ballew* v. *Georgia*, 1978. Nor does it prevent a State from providing for a conviction on a less than unanimous jury vote, *Apodaca* v. *Oregon*, 1972. But if a jury has only six members, it may convict only by a unanimous vote, *Burch* v. *Louisiana*, 1979.

## the small society
### by Bill Yates

**Interpreting Political Cartoons** What comment does the cartoon make about jury service as an obligation of citizenship?

cross section of the community." A person is denied the right to an impartial jury if he or she is tried by a jury from which members of any groups "playing major roles in the community" have been excluded, *Taylor* v. *Louisiana*, 1975.

In short, no person can be kept off a jury on such grounds as race, color, religion, national origin, or sex. As the Court put it in its most recent decision on the point: Both the 5th and the 14th Amendments mean that jury service cannot be determined by "the pigmentation of skin, the accident of birth, or the choice of religion," *Georgia* v. *McCollum*, 1992.

### Right to an Adequate Defense

Every person accused of crime has the right to offer the best possible defense that circumstances will allow. The 6th Amendment says that a defendant has the right (1) "to be informed of the nature and cause of the accusation," (2) "to be confronted with the witnesses against him" and question them in open court, (3) "to have compulsory process for obtaining witnesses in his favor," and (4) "to have the assistance of counsel for his defence."

These key safeguards apply in the federal courts. Still, if a State fails to honor any of them, the accused can appeal a conviction on grounds that the 14th Amendment's Due Process Clause has been violated. Recall from page 489, the Supreme Court protected the right to counsel in *Gideon* v. *Wainwright*, 1963; the right of confrontation in *Pointer* v. *Texas*, 1965; and the right

to call witnesses in *Washington* v. *Texas*, 1967.

These guarantees are intended to prevent the cards from being stacked in favor of the prosecution. One of the leading right-to-counsel cases, *Escobedo* v. *Illinois*, 1964, illustrates this point.

Danny Escobedo was picked up by Chicago police for questioning in the death of his brother-in-law. On the way to the police station, and then while he was being questioned there, he asked several times to see his lawyer. The police denied these requests—even though his lawyer was in the station and was trying to see him, and the police knew he was there. Through a long night of questioning, Escobedo made several damaging statements. Prosecutors later used those statements in court as a major part of the evidence that led to his murder conviction.

The Supreme Court ordered Escobedo freed from prison four years later. It held that he had been improperly denied his right to counsel.

In *Gideon* v. *Wainwright*, 1963, the Court held that an attorney must be furnished to a defendant who cannot afford one. In many places, a judge still assigns a lawyer from the local community, or a private legal aid association provides counsel. Since *Gideon*, however, a growing number of States, and many local governments, have established tax-supported public defender offices. In 1970 Congress authorized the appointment of federal public defenders or, as an alternative, the creation of community legal service organizations financed by federal grants.

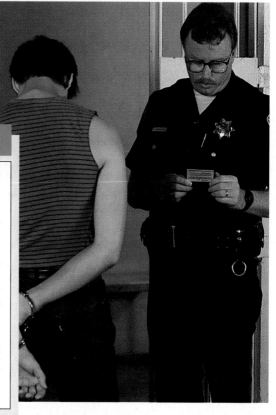

## Reading of Rights to the Accused

Before asking you any questions, it is my duty to advise you of your rights:

1. You have the right to remain silent;

2. If you choose to speak, anything you say may be used against you in a court of law or other proceeding;

3. You have the right to consult with a lawyer before answering any questions and you may have a lawyer present with you during questioning;

4. If you cannot afford a lawyer and you want one, a lawyer will be provided for you by the Commonwealth without cost to you;

5. Do you understand what I have told you?

6. You may also waive the right to counsel and your right to remain silent and you may answer any question or make any statement you wish. If you decide to answer questions you may stop at any time to consult with a lawyer.

▲ **"You Have the Right to Remain Silent"**  Once a person knowingly waives his Miranda rights, police may question him until and unless he unambiguously (clearly, forthrightly) asks for an attorney, *Davis* v. *United States,* 1994.

## Self-Incrimination

The guarantee against self-incrimination is among the protections set out in the 5th Amendment—which declares that no person can be

❝ compelled in any criminal case to be a witness against himself.❞

This protection must be honored in both the federal and State courts, *Malloy* v. *Hogan,* 1964.

In a criminal case, the burden of proof is always on the prosecution. The defendant does not have to prove his or her innocence. The ban on self-incrimination prevents the prosecution from shifting the burden of proof to the defendant.

The language of the 5th Amendment suggests that the guarantee applies only to criminal cases. In fact, it covers *any* governmental proceeding in which a person is legally compelled to answer any question that could lead to a criminal charge.

The courts, not the individuals who claim it, decide when the right can be properly invoked. If the plea of self-incrimination is pushed too far, a person can be held in contempt of court.

The privilege against self-incrimination is a personal right. One can claim it only for himself or herself.[24] It cannot be invoked in someone else's behalf; a person *can* be forced to "rat" on another.

The privilege does not protect a person from being fingerprinted or photographed, submitting a handwriting sample, or appearing in a police lineup, or taking a blood test. And the slurred nature of the answers a drunk-driving suspect gave to questions asked by the arresting

---

[24]With this major exception: A husband cannot be forced to testify against his wife, or a wife against her husband, *Trammel* v. *United States,* 1980.

officer can properly be used as evidence at the suspect's trial, *Pennsylvania* v. *Muniz*, 1990.

A person cannot be forced to confess to a crime under duress—that is, as a result of torture or other physical or psychological pressure. In *Ashcraft* v. *Tennessee*, 1944, for example, the Supreme Court threw out the conviction of a man accused of hiring another to murder his wife. The confession on which his conviction rested had been secured only after some 36 hours of continuous, threatening interrogation. The questioning was conducted by officers who worked in shifts because, they said, they became so tired they had to rest.

The gulf between what the Constitution says and what goes on in some police stations can be wide, indeed. For that reason, the Supreme Court has come down hard in many cases involving the protection against self-incrimination and the right to counsel.

Recall, for example, the Court's decision in *Escobedo* v. *Illinois*. In a truly historic decision two years later, *Miranda* v. *Arizona*, 1966, the Court refined that holding. A mentally retarded man, Ernesto Miranda, had been convicted of kidnapping and rape. Ten days after the crime, the victim picked him out of a police lineup. After two hours of questioning, during which the police did not tell him of his rights, he confessed. The Supreme Court struck down his conviction. More importantly, the Court said that, from that point on, it would not uphold convictions in any cases in which suspects had not been told of their constitutional rights before police questioning. It thus laid down what has since come to be called the **Miranda Rule**. Under the rule, before police may question suspects, those persons must be read the rights that appear next to the photo on the previous page.

The Miranda Rule has been in force for more than 25 years now, and the Supreme Court is still refining it, case by case. Most often, the rule has been strictly enforced.

There are a very few situations to which, reasonably, the rule does not apply. For example, in *Illinois* v. *Perkins*, 1990, the Supreme Court held that an undercover police officer, posing as a prisoner in a jail, did not have to give his cellmate a Miranda warning before prompting him to talk about a murder.[25]

Many police officials, and others, criticize the Miranda Rule. They see it as a serious obstacle to effective law enforcement. Many of them say that it "puts criminals back on the streets." Others applaud it, however. They hold that criminal law enforcement is most effective when it depends on independently secured evidence.

# Section 3 Review

1. **Define:** writ of habeas corpus, bill of attainder, ex post facto law, grand jury, indictment, presentment, information, double jeopardy, bench trial, Miranda Rule
2. Under what circumstances can the right to a writ of habeas corpus be suspended?
3. On what two bases are bills of attainder forbidden?
4. What is the basic function of a grand jury?
5. What are the limits on the Constitution's guarantee of a speedy and public trial?
6. What guarantees does the Constitution make about the make-up of juries in federal trials?
7. What are the 6th Amendment guarantees of the right to an adequate defense?
8. For what reason is compulsory self-incrimination forbidden?

## Critical Thinking

9. **Identifying Assumptions** (p. 19) Consider the statement, "It is better that ten guilty persons go free than one innocent person be punished." What does this statement suggest about the relationship between individual rights and society?

---

[25]In *Berkemer* v. *McCarty*, 1984, the Court held that the rule does not apply to routine traffic stops, where a motorist "most likely will be allowed to continue on his way." But once a person is placed "in custody," the rule must be observed "regardless of the nature or severity of the offense" involved.

# 4 Rights of the Accused: Punishment

## Find Out:

- How does the Constitution set limits on punishments for crime?
- For what reason does the Constitution define the crime of treason?

## Key Term:

bail

Once more, think about the statement, "It is better that ten guilty persons go free than one innocent person be punished." Now how do you feel about it?

What about those persons who are guilty and are convicted, and so do not go free? How should they be treated? As you see in this section, the Constitution provides its most specific answers to that question in the 8th Amendment. And here you will also look at treason, at the nature of that singular crime and its punishment.

## Excessive Bail, Fines

The 8th Amendment says, in part:

“Excessive bail shall not be required, nor excessive fines imposed. . . . ”

Each of the State constitutions sets out similar restrictions. The general rule here is that the bail or fine in a case must bear a reasonable relationship to the seriousness of the crime involved.

**Bail** is a sum of money that the accused may be required to post (deposit with the court) as a guarantee that he or she will appear in court at the proper time. The use of bail is justified on two grounds: (1) A person should not be jailed until his or her guilt is established; and (2) a defendant is better able to prepare for trial outside of a jail.

But, note, the Constitution does not say that all persons accused of crime are automatically entitled to bail. Rather, the guarantee is that, in those cases where bail is set, the amount of that bail will not be excessive.[26]

The leading case on bail in the federal courts is *Stack* v. *Boyle*, 1951. There the Court ruled that "bail set at a figure higher than the amount reasonably calculated" to insure a defendant's appearance at a trial "is 'excessive' under the 8th Amendment."

**Preventive Detention**  In 1984 Congress provided for the "preventive detention" of some persons accused of committing federal crimes. Under the law, federal judges can order that an accused felon be held, without bail, when there is good reason to believe that that person will commit yet another serious crime before trial.

Critics of the law claim that preventive detention really amounts to punishment before trial; and, they say, it undercuts the presumption of innocence to which defendants are entitled.

The Supreme Court upheld the 1984 law, 6–3, in *United States* v. *Salerno*, 1987. The majority rejected the argument that preventive detention is punishment. Rather, it found the practice a legitimate response to a "pressing societal problem." More than half the States have recently adopted preventive detention laws.

## Cruel and Unusual Punishment

The 8th Amendment also forbids "cruel and unusual punishment." The 14th Amendment extends that prohibition against the States, *Robinson* v. *California*, 1962. Each State constitution contains a similar provision.

The Supreme Court decided its first cruel and unusual case over 100 years ago. In *Wilkerson* v. *Utah*, 1879, a territorial court had sentenced a convicted murderer to death by a firing squad. The Court held that that punishment was not forbidden by the Constitution. The

---

[26]A defendant can appeal the denial of release on bail or the amount of the bail. Bail is usually set in accord with the charge and the reputation and resources of the accused. Those with little or no income often have trouble raising bail; so, the federal and most State courts release many defendants "on their own recognizance," *i.e.*, on their honor. Failure to appear for trial, "jumping bail," is itself a punishable crime.

kinds of penalties the Constitution intended to prevent, said the Court, were such barbaric tortures as burning at the stake, crucifixion, drawing and quartering, "and all others in the same line of unnecessary cruelty."

Since then, the Court has heard only a handful of cruel and unusual cases—except for those relating to capital punishment, as you will see. More often than not, the Court has rejected the cruel and unusual punishment claim.[27]

*Louisiana* v. *Resweber*, 1947, is typical. There the Court found that it was not unconstitutional to subject a convicted murderer to a second electrocution after the chair had failed to work properly on the first occasion.

*Rummel* v. *Estelle*, 1980, is another example. There a Texas court had imposed a mandatory life sentence on a "three-time loser"—even though the three crimes of which the individual had been convicted were all petty and nonviolent, and had altogether involved a small amount of money—less than $230.

However, the Court has held some punishments to be cruel and unusual. Thus, in *Robinson* v. *California*, 1962, the Supreme Court held that a State law that defined narcotics addiction as a crime to be punished, rather than an illness to be treated, violated the 8th and 14th amendments.[28] And, to take another example, in *Estelle* v. *Gamble*, 1976, it ruled that a Texas prison

---

[27]The prohibition of cruel and unusual punishment is limited to criminal matters. It does not forbid paddling or similar punishments in the public schools, *Ingraham* v. *Wright*, 1977.

[28]But, notice, that does not mean that buying, selling, or possessing narcotics cannot be made a crime. Such criminal laws are designed to punish persons for their behavior, not for being ill.

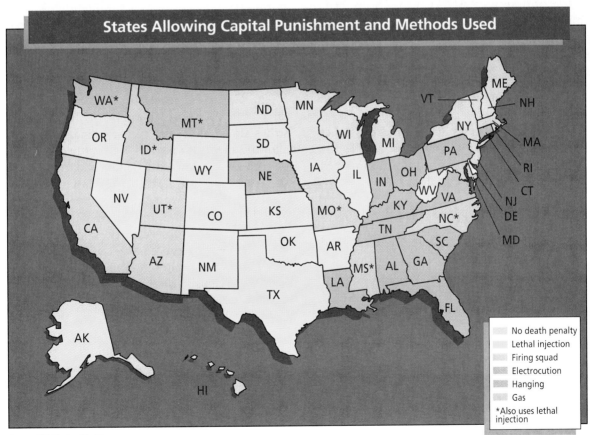

## States Allowing Capital Punishment and Methods Used

No death penalty
Lethal injection
Firing squad
Electrocution
Hanging
Gas
*Also uses lethal injection

Source: U.S. Dept. of Justice

▲ **Interpreting Maps**   Most States allow the use of capital punishment. Why do you think some States, such as Nevada, Illinois, and Texas, use lethal injection rather than one of the other methods?

**Global Awareness**

| Use of Capital Punishment, Selected Countries | | | |
|---|---|---|---|
| Country | Does the law allow for capital punishment? | Some of the offenses punishable by death | Number of executions in 1992 |
| Algeria | yes | treason, spying, armed robbery, arson (total of 30 offenses) | none |
| Canada | yes (for military offenses) | mutiny and offenses committed in the presence of an enemy | none |
| Egypt | yes | premeditated murder, arson when death results, accomplice to murder, causing the death of a child, rape | 5 |
| Ireland | yes | capital murder, treason, certain military offenses | none |
| Japan | yes | murder, intentional damage to inhabited structures, crimes against the state | none |
| Thailand | yes | premeditated murder, the murder of an official on government business and murder of a king. Death penalty is optional for robbery, rape, kidnapping, arson, and bombing. Children under age 15 and the king cannot be sentenced to death. | none |
| United States | yes (in 36 states) | for death resulting from aircraft hijacking, first degree murder, espionage and desertion when committed in wartime | 31 |

*Source:* Amnesty International Report, 1993

▲ **Interpreting Charts: Multicultural Awareness**   Why do the laws of most countries reserve the death penalty for those persons who have been convicted of the most vicious or abhorrent of crimes?

inmate could not properly be denied needed medical care.

But again most cases have gone the other way. Thus, in *Rhodes* v. *Chapman,* 1981, the Court held that putting two prisoners in a cell built for one is not cruel and unusual.

## Capital Punishment

Is the death penalty cruel and unusual and therefore unconstitutional? For years the Supreme Court was reluctant to face that highly charged issue. In fact, it did not give a direct answer to that question until 1976.[29]

---

[29]The phrase "capital punishment" comes from the Latin *caput,* meaning "head"; in many cultures, the historically preferred method for executing criminals was beheading (decapitation).

The Court avoided a direct ruling on the constitutionality of capital punishment laws in several cases before 1972. Thus, it did hold that neither death by firing squad (*Wilkerson* v. *Utah*) nor by a second electrocution (*Louisiana* v. *Resweber*) is unconstitutional. But in neither of those cases, nor in others, did it deal with the question of the death penalty as such.

The Court did meet the issue more or less directly in *Furman* v. *Georgia,* 1972. There it struck down all of the then existing State laws allowing the death penalty, but *not* because that penalty as such was cruel and unusual. Rather, the Court voided those laws because they gave too much discretion to judges or juries in deciding whether or not to impose the death penalty. The Court noted that of all those persons convicted of capital crimes, only "a random few," most of them African American or poor or both, were "capriciously selected" for execution.

Since that decision, 36 States have passed new capital punishment laws. At first, those laws took one of two forms: Several States removed all discretion from the sentencing process. They made the death penalty mandatory for certain crimes, such as the killing of a police officer or murder done while committing rape, kidnap, or arson. Other States provided for a two-stage process in capital cases: a trial first to settle the issue of guilt or innocence; then a second hearing to decide whether the circumstances justify a sentence of death.

The Supreme Court has considered scores of challenges to those newer laws. It found the mandatory death penalty laws to be unconstitutional. They were "unduly harsh and rigidly unworkable," and simply attempts to "paper over" the decision in *Furman,* said the Court in *Woodson* v. *North Carolina,* 1976. But the two-stage approach to capital punishment is constitutional. In *Gregg* v. *Georgia,* 1976, the Court held, for the first time, that the "punishment of death does not invariably violate the Constitution." It ruled that well-drawn two-stage laws can practically eliminate "the risk that [the death penalty] will be inflicted in an arbitrary or capricious manner."

A State can impose the death penalty only for "crimes resulting in the death of the victim," *Coker* v. *Georgia,* 1977; and a capital punishment law "must allow for whatever mitigating circumstances" may be present in a case, *Roberts* v. *Louisiana,* 1977.

Opponents of the death penalty continue to appeal cases to the Court, but to no real avail. The sum of the Court's many decisions in those cases over the past fifteen years is this: The death penalty, fairly applied, is acceptable under the Constitution.

Death penalty cases raise many difficult questions. That point can be seen in these recent cases, each of them decided by a divided Court. In *Ford* v. *Wainwright,* 1986, it ruled that a person who is insane at the time set for his execution cannot be put to death. In *Thompson* v. *Oklahoma,* 1988, the Court held that the 8th and 14th amendments prohibit the execution of a man for a murder he committed when he was 15 years old. But, a year later, the Court allowed the execution of a man for a murder he had committed at age 16, *Wilkins* v. *Missouri,* 1989; and it came to the same decision in *Stanford* v. *Kentucky,* 1989, where the murderer's age was 17.

Most recently, the Court has ruled that, in deciding whether a death penalty should be imposed or not, a jury can consider the impact the murderer's crime has had on the victim's family, *Payne* v. *Tennessee,* 1991.

## Treason

Treason against the United States is the only crime that is defined in the Constitution. The Framers provided a specific definition of the crime because they knew that the charge of treason is a favorite weapon in the hands of tyrants.

Treason, says Article III, Section 3, can consist of only two things: either (1) levying war against the United States or (2) "adhering to their enemies, giving them aid and comfort." No person can be convicted of the crime "unless on the testimony of two witnesses to the same overt act, or on confession in open court."

The law of treason covers all American citizens, at home or abroad, and all permanent resident aliens. Congress has established the death penalty as the maximum penalty for treason against the United States, but no person has ever been executed for the crime.

Note that a person can commit treason only in wartime. But Congress has also made it a crime, in either peace- or wartime, to commit espionage or sabotage, to attempt to overthrow the government by force, or to conspire to do any of these things.

Most of the State constitutions also provide for treason. John Brown was hanged as a traitor to Virginia after his raid on Harpers Ferry in 1859. He is believed to be the only person ever to be executed for treason against a State.

## Section 4 Review

1. **Define:** bail
2. What constitutes "excessive" bail?
3. (a) What punishments does the Constitution prohibit? (b) What is the Supreme Court's view of capital punishment?
4. For what reason is treason specifically defined by the Constitution?

### Critical Thinking

5. **Demonstrating Reasoned Judgment** (p. 19) Based on what you have read, what is the point at which a punishment becomes "unnecessarily" cruel?

★

# Formulating Questions

Experts on creativity maintain that the quality of one's creativity depends on the quality of one's questions. The same can be said about the quality of thinking critically.

Formulating questions means creating questions that lead to a deeper understanding of an issue. Being able to formulate good questions enables you to discover new information through inquiry. Good questions also can help you sharpen your understanding of a topic—even questions you might fear will be dismissed as not being worth asking. Follow these steps to practice formulating good questions.

**1. Identify the topic.** Try to identify the main idea of the piece of information you are considering. By finding the main idea, you can narrow down your area of inquiry and formulate questions that get at the heart of the matter. Read the selection below and answer the following questions: (a) What is the topic of the dispute described below? (b) What are the two opposing views?

**2. Locate the important details.** Consider information that you already have on the subject. Then you will be able to identify the questions you will need to ask. Answer the following questions: (a) What factual information does each side use to support its argument? (b) What opinions does each side use to support its argument?

**3. Keep in mind these basic questions: Who? What? When? Where? Why? How?** These six questions serve as the foundation of any inquiry into a topic. How can you use these questions to gain a deeper understanding of the information below?

**4. Determine what else you need to know about the topic, and formulate your questions.** Once you understand the topic, you can formulate the questions that will enable you to gather more information. Answer the following questions: (a) What would you want to know about the ordinance supporters' argument before you supported gun control? (b) What would you want to know about the opponents before you supported their view?

---

Local officials have introduced an ordinance that outlaws the private possession, use, or sale of all handguns in the city. The only exception would be those handguns kept in gun collections or used only for target-shooting purposes.

Most people who support the ordinance have argued that its adoption would help to reduce violent crime in the city. They have built much of their case on the FBI's crime reports, which show that firearms are now used to commit more than 11,000 murders, 200,000 aggravated assaults, and 180,000 robberies in this country every year. Supporters also point to thousands of accidental deaths and injuries that occur every year because of the careless handling of firearms.

Opponents of the ordinance cite the Constitution's 2nd Amendment and what they insist is the Constitution's guarantee of their right to keep and bear arms. Opponents also insist that the ordinance aims at the wrong target. Guns don't kill people, they say, people do. They also point out that criminals will always be able to get guns, and that outlawing handguns will only make it more difficult for innocent people to defend themselves. The opponents also make use of FBI statistics, pointing out that the average person can expect to live well over 20,000 years before being murdered.

# Chapter-in-Brief

Scan all headings, photographs, charts, and other visuals in the chapter before reading the section summaries below.

## Section 1 Due Process of Law (pp. 517–520)

The 5th and 14th amendments guarantee that government cannot deprive a person of "life, liberty, or property, without due process of law." The meaning of due process has developed along two lines: procedural and substantive. Procedural due process means that government must act according to fair procedures. Substantive due process means that laws and policies must be fair.

The government does have the power to protect and promote public health, safety, morals, and general welfare. The exercise of this police power can lead to conflicts with the rights of individuals.

The guarantee of due process has led to the creation of a right of privacy. The most controversial applications of the right of privacy have come in cases involving the question of abortion.

## Section 2 Freedom and Security of the Person (pp. 521–526)

The Constitution guarantees more than three dozen individual liberties. Among them are those intended to guarantee security of the person.

The 13th Amendment was added to the Constitution in 1865 in order to end slavery. This amendment has also enabled Congress and the Courts to destroy the "badges and incidents of slavery," as well.

The 3rd and 4th amendments aim to make people "secure in their persons, houses, papers, and effects." This includes the guarantee against unreasonable searches and seizures.

The 2nd Amendment guarantees people the right to keep and bear arms. However, government does have the power to restrict the right.

## Section 3 Rights of the Accused (pp. 528–535)

The Constitution sets out several guarantees for persons accused of crime. These include the right to seek a writ of habeas corpus, which aims at preventing unjust arrests and imprisonments. The Constitution also prohibits bills of attainder, which are legislative acts that inflict punishment without court trials. In addition, Congress and the States are prohibited from passing ex post facto laws.

The Federal and State governments guarantee all who are accused of crime a fair trial. No person, for example, can be exposed to double jeopardy.

The Federal Government guarantees that those accused of a serious federal crime will not face charges unless indicted by a grand jury. This right, however, is not guaranteed against the States by the 14th Amendment.

Accused persons are guaranteed the right to a speedy and public trial. The accused also have the right to a trial by jury. And, they have the right to an adequate defense. This means that the accused must be allowed access to a lawyer. In addition, the accused cannot be made to testify against themselves.

## Section 4 Rights of the Accused: Punishment (pp. 536–539)

According to the federal and State constitutions, the accused must not face excessive bail or fines. This prohibition is based on the concept that the accused are innocent until proven guilty.

The Constitution also includes a prohibition against cruel and unusual punishment. The Supreme Court, however, has consistently held that the death penalty is constitutional if it is fairly applied.

Treason is the only crime specifically defined in the Constitution because the Framers wanted to prevent tyrants from using the charge of treason to punish political opponents.

# Chapter Review

## Vocabulary and Key Terms

due process (p. 517)
police power (p. 519)
search warrant (p. 519)
probable cause (p. 523)
exclusionary rule (p. 524)

writ of habeas corpus (p. 528)
bill of attainder (p. 529)
ex post facto law (p. 529)
grand jury (p. 529)
indictment (p. 529)

presentment (p. 530)
information (p. 530)
double jeopardy (p. 530)
bench trial (p. 532)
Miranda Rule (p. 535)
bail (p. 536)

**Matching:** *Review the key terms in the list above. If you are not sure of a term's meaning, look up the term and review its definition. Choose a term from the list above that best matches each description.*

1. a group convened by a court to determine whether or not there is enough evidence against a person to justify a trial
2. a constitutional guarantee that a government will not deprive any person of life, liberty, or property by any unfair, arbitrary, or unreasonable action
3. trial a second time for a crime of which the accused was acquitted in the first trial
4. the power of a government to act to ensure the overall welfare of a society
5. a trial without a jury

**True or False:** *Determine whether each statement is true or false. If it is true, write "true." If it is false, change the underlined word or words to make the statement true.*

1. An <u>ex post facto law</u> is one applied to acts performed before the law was passed.
2. A legislative act that inflicts punishment upon a person or group without a trial is a <u>Miranda Rule</u>.
3. A listing of the rights of which suspects must be advised before police questioning is called <u>information</u>.
4. When a person is tried twice for the same crime, he or she may have been exposed to <u>double jeopardy</u>.
5. An indictment is a formal finding by a <u>grand jury</u> that there is sufficient evidence to warrant a trial.
6. Police generally need a <u>search warrant</u> in order to search someone's house.

**Word Relationships:** *Three of the terms in each of the following sets of terms are related. Choose the term that does not belong and explain why it does not belong.*

1. (a) writ of habeas corpus (b) excessive bail (c) ex post facto law (d) bill of attainder
2. (a) indictment (b) presentment (c) information (d) Miranda Rule
3. (a) search warrant (b) exclusionary rule (c) Miranda Rule (d) police power

## Main Ideas

### Section 1 (pp. 517–520)

1. Along what two lines has the Supreme Court developed the meaning of due process?
2. For what reasons is it necessary to have both substantive and procedural due process?
3. Describe the relationship between the States' police power and due process of law.
4. From what part of the Constitution does the right of privacy stem?

## Section 2 (pp. 521–526)

**5.** (a) What was the aim of the 13th Amendment? (b) How have Congress and the courts changed in their view of this amendment in the last 25 years?

**6.** In what sense is the 2nd Amendment misunderstood?

**7.** What is the aim of the 4th Amendment?

**8.** How does the exclusionary rule help protect citizens?

## Section 3 (pp. 528–535)

**9.** (a) What are crimes? (b) Why must they be punished?

**10.** (a) For what reason does the Constitution protect the rights of those accused of crime? (b) In what ways does the Constitution protect the rights of those accused of crime?

**11.** What are the key constitutional guarantees of a fair trial?

**12.** (a) What guarantees and rules exist to ensure the accused the right not to incriminate themselves? (b) What guarantees exist to ensure the accused an adequate defense?

## Section 4 (pp. 536–539)

**13.** What are the key constitutional guarantees regarding punishment of the guilty?

**14.** Under what circumstances has the Supreme Court found death penalty laws to be unconstitutional?

**15.** For what reason is treason the only crime defined in the Constitution?

## Critical Thinking

**1. Recognizing Ideologies** (p. 19) Summarize the belief that underlies the power of the States to exercise their police power, even at the expense of certain individual rights.

**2. Identifying Assumptions** (p. 19) What assumptions underlie the existence of the Miranda Rule and the specific provisions included in it?

**3. Checking Consistency** (p. 19) Recall that Congress passed a law by which the accused can be held without bail when there is reason to believe the person will commit a crime. In your opinion, does this law violate the principle of presumed innocence until proven guilty?

## Getting Involved

**1. Writing Your Opinion** Create a survey designed to gauge citizens' opinions of the Constitution's civil liberties protections. Begin by listing the different rights discussed in this chapter; for example, due process and the right against self-incrimination. Next, note some of the more controversial aspects of these rights; for example, the fact that evidence gathered illegally cannot be used against a person. Write an introduction to your survey explaining why you are interested in people's opinions on this topic. Then create a list of questions designed to gather those opinions. Revise your questions to ensure that they do not convey your own bias on the issues under consideration. Correct any errors, then make a final draft.

**2. Cooperative Activity** Work as a class to create a quiz game called "Civil Rights and Liberties." Have each member of the class write a list of five questions and answers involving some aspect of civil rights and liberties. For example, one question could ask whether or not it is constitutional for police to stop cars randomly to check for drunk drivers. Then, decide as a class on the rules for the game. Encourage students to add more questions to the game as ideas occur to them.

**3. Creating a Political Advertisement** Create an advertisement that illustrates your view of one of the issues discussed in this chapter. Your ad can express support or opposition to your chosen constitutional principle or interpretation.

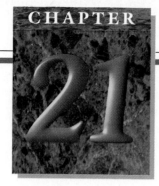

# Civil Rights: Equal Justice Under Law

## Chapter Preview

A tall, well-dressed man stood outside of the suburban post office. While reading his mail, he was confronted by a throng of police officers who forced him at gunpoint to lie face down on the pavement. Was he, as suspected, the gunman who robbed a local bank three days before?

The man in this true story was Dee Brown—a Boston Celtics rookie guard who is African American. The suburb was mostly white Wellesley, Massachusetts. It turned out that the only characteristic Brown had in common with the bank robber was the color of his skin. Brown, who has since accepted the apologies of Wellesley police and residents, believes the only reason the incident was newsworthy was not that it was unique, but that it happened to a professional athlete. As you can see from this example, the American democratic system has not yet succeeded in extending the guarantees of fair and equal treatment to all persons in the United States. This chapter is about equality as a continuing goal in that democratic ideal.

### Before you read this chapter:

- **Describe** two actions or policies that you think are discriminatory.
- **Predict** the meaning of "equal justice under the law."

### As you read, focus on the main objective for each section. Understand:

1. The multicultural character of the United States' population.
2. The constitutional guarantees of equality before the law.
3. The civil rights laws passed by Congress over 30 years.
4. How American citizenship is acquired.

▲ **Still Making Good on the Promise** This principal has succeeded in her career despite the fact that women and Native Americans, among others, are often discriminated against in our society. Many positive steps have been taken in recent years to right this imbalance.

# 1 Diversity and Discrimination in American Society

**Find Out:**

- How has the makeup of the American population changed over the course of its history?
- What is the historical record of the United States' treatment of minority groups?
- What is the historical record of the United States' treatment of women?

**Key Terms:**

reservation, refugee

Do you know the word *heterogeneous*? It is a compound of two Greek words: *heteros*, meaning other or different, and *genos*, meaning race, family, or kind. As any good dictionary will tell you, something that is heterogeneous is made up of a mix of several ingredients.

As you will see in this section, "We the People of the United States" are a heterogeneous lot—and are becoming more so, year to year.

## A Heterogeneous Population

The population of the United States is predominantly white. It is today and, as you can see in the table on page 547, it has been historically. The first census in 1790 reported that there were 3.929 million people living in this country and that four out of every five of them were white. As the nation's population grew over the decades, so, too, did the proportion of the American people who were white—that is, until recently.

Today, the ethnic composition of the population is strikingly different from what it was only a generation ago. Immigrants have arrived in near-record numbers every year since the mid-1960s; and, over that period, the nation's African-American, Hispanic-American, and Asian-American populations have grown at rates several times that of whites.

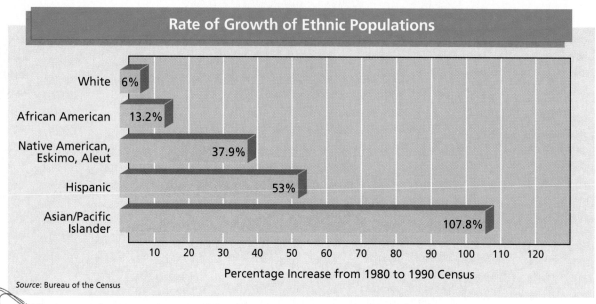

## Rate of Growth of Ethnic Populations

White — 6%
African American — 13.2%
Native American, Eskimo, Aleut — 37.9%
Hispanic — 53%
Asian/Pacific Islander — 107.8%

Percentage Increase from 1980 to 1990 Census

*Source:* Bureau of the Census

**Interpreting Graphs: Multicultural Awareness**  While the population in the United States remains predominantly white, this table shows that the rate of growth of that group is by far the slowest. What does this suggest about the future population of the United States?

Females are more numerous in the population than males—and they have been for nearly half a century now.

As a result of these changes in the American population, the United States is more heterogeneous than ever before in its history. That fact is likely to have a profound effect on the American social, political, and economic landscape.

## Discrimination

As you will see in this chapter, white Americans have been historically reluctant to yield to non-white Americans a full and equal place in the social, economic, and political life of this nation. Over time, the principal targets of that ethnic prejudice have been African Americans, Native Americans, Asian Americans, and Hispanic Americans. The white-male-dominated power structure has also been slow to recognize the claims of women to a full and equal place in American society.

**African Americans**  Much of what you will read in these pages focuses on discrimination against African Americans for three reasons:

(1) African Americans constitute by far the largest minority group in the United States. They number more than 30 million today—more than 12 percent of all the American people.

(2) African Americans have been the victims of consistently and deliberately unjust treatment for a longer period of time than perhaps any other group of Americans.[1] It took a civil war to end more than 200 years of slavery in this country. As you have read, slavery was finally abolished by the 13th Amendment in 1865, but the Civil War and the ratification of that amendment did not bring an end to widespread racial discrimination in the United States.

(3) Most of the gains that the nation has made in translating the Constitution's guarantees of equality into a reality for all persons have come out of efforts made by and on behalf of African Americans. You have already encountered a number of illustrations of this point. Recall, for example, the struggles of Martin Luther King, Jr. and others that resulted in the

---

[1]Slavery began in what was to become the United States in 1619; in June of that year, 20 Africans were sold to white settlers at Jamestown.

## The Ethnic Composition of the Population, 1790-1990 (in thousands)

| Census | White | % | African American | % | Native American[1] | Asian American[2] | Hispanic Origin[3] | % |
|--------|-------|-----|-----------------|------|----------|----------|----------|-----|
| 1790 | 3,172 | 80.7 | 757 | 19.3 | * | * | * | * |
| 1800 | 4,306 | 81.0 | 1,002 | 19.0 | * | * | * | * |
| 1850 | 19,553 | 84.3 | 3,639 | 15.7 | * | * | * | * |
| 1890 | 55,101 | 87.5 | 7,489 | 11.9 | 248 | 110 | * | * |
| 1900 | 66,809 | 87.9 | 8,834 | 11.6 | 237 | 114 | * | * |
| 1940 | 118,215 | 89.8 | 12,866 | 9.8 | 334 | 204 | * | * |
| 1950 | 135,150 | 89.3 | 15,045 | 9.9 | 343 | 259 | * | * |
| 1960 | 158,832 | 88.6 | 18,872 | 10.5 | 524 | 702 | * | * |
| 1970 | 178,098 | 87.6 | 22,581 | 11.1 | 793 | 1,026 | * | * |
| 1980 | 194,713 | 85.9 | 26,683 | 11.8 | 1,420 | 3,729 | 14,609 | 6.4 |
| 1990 | 209,491 | 84.3 | 29,986 | 12.1 | 1,959 | 7,274 | 22,354 | 9.0 |

*Not Available.
[1]Includes Alaska Natives, 1960 and later.
[2]Includes Pacific Islanders.
[3]Persons of Hispanic origin may be of any race.
*Source:* Bureau of the Census

▲ **Interpreting Tables: Multicultural Awareness** This table shows that minority populations are increasing at higher rates than the majority population. According to the table, which group is growing the fastest?

Civil Rights Act of 1964 and then the Voting Rights Act of 1965; see Chapter 6, Section 3.

Of course this is not to say that other groups of Americans have not also suffered the effects of discrimination. Clearly, they have.

**Native Americans** White settlers first began to arrive in America in large numbers in the early middle years of the 17th century. At the time, some one million Native Americans were living in territory that was to become the United States.[2] By 1900, however, their number had fallen to less than 250,000. Diseases brought by white settlers had decimated those first Americans. So, too, did the succession of military campaigns that accompanied the westward expansion of the United States. To quote one historian, "'The only good Indian' is a dead Indian' is not simply a hackneyed expression from cowboy movies. It was part of the strategy of westward expansion, as settlers and U. S. troops alike mercilessly drove the eastern Indians from their ancestral lands to the Great Plains, then took those lands too."[3] Today, nearly two million Native Americans live in this country, about a third of them on or near **reservations**—areas of public land set aside by a government for use by a Native-American group.

Like African Americans, Native Americans have been the victims of overbearing discrimination. The consequences of that bias have been truly appalling, and they remain all too evident today. The life expectancy of the more than one million Native Americans living on reservations in the 1990s is 10 years less than the national average, and their infant mortality rate is three times that for white Americans.

[2]Most authorities estimate that there were some 8 to 10 million Native Americans living in all of North and South America in the mid-1600s.

[3]Thomas E. Patterson, *The American Democracy* (New York: McGraw Hill, 1990), page 153.

**Asian Americans** The story of white America's mistreatment of Asians is a lengthy one, too. Chinese laborers were the first Asians to come to the United States in large numbers. They were brought here in the 1850s to 1860s as contract laborers to work in the mines and build railroads in the West. Many white Americans, both native-born and immigrants, resented the competition of "coolie labor," and their resentments were frequently expressed in violence toward Asians.

As you will see on page 565, Congress passed the Chinese Exclusion Act in 1882; as a result of this and other government actions, only a very small number of Chinese, Japanese, and other Asians were permitted to enter the United States for more than 80 years. Early in World War II, the Federal Government ordered the evacuation of all persons of Japanese descent

from the Pacific Coast. Some 120,000 people, two-thirds of them native-born American citizens, were forcibly removed to inland "war relocation camps"; see Chapter 19, Section 1.

Congress made dramatic changes in American immigration policies in 1965 and, since then, more than three million Asian immigrants have come to this country—mostly from the Philippines, China, Korea, Vietnam, and India.

Today, the Asian-American population approaches 7.5 million; and, as you can see in the table on page 546, it is one of the nation's fastest growing minority groups. By the year 2000, the Asian-American component of the population will likely exceed 12 million. Most Asian Americans now live on the West Coast.

**Hispanic Americans** Hispanic Americans are those nearly 23 million people in this country who have a Spanish-speaking background; many prefer to be called Latinos. Hispanics may be of any race; they "are among the world's most complex groupings of human beings. [The largest number] are white, millions . . . are mestizo, nearly half a million in the United States are black or mulatto."[4] Hispanics now constitute the second largest minority group of Americans, and they could replace African Americans as the largest such group by the year 2000.

Hispanic Americans can generally be divided into four main groups:

(1) MEXICAN AMERICANS More than half of all Hispanics in the United States, at least 12 million persons, were either born in Mexico or trace their ancestry there. Those who were born in this country of Mexican parents are often called Chicanos.

(2) PUERTO RICANS Another large group of Hispanics have come to the mainland from their native Puerto Rico. There are now some three million Puerto Ricans in the population.

(3) CUBAN AMERICANS The Hispanic population also includes approximately one million

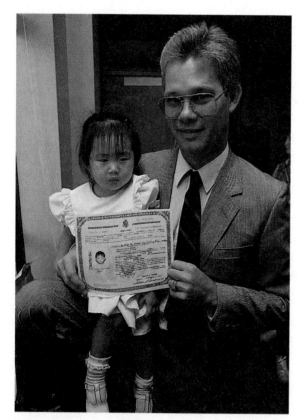

▲ **The American Dream: Multicultural Awareness** After a naturalization ceremony a proud father holds his adopted Korean daughter, a new citizen of the United States.

[4]The Bilateral Commission on the Future of United States–Mexican Relations, *The Challenge of Interdependence* (Bethesda: University Press of America, 1989), page 99. A mestizo is a person with both Spanish or Portuguese and Native-American ancestry. A mulatto is a person with African and white ancestry.

Cuban Americans. They are mostly persons who fled the Castro dictatorship in Cuba and their descendants.

(4) CENTRAL AND SOUTH AMERICANS The fourth major subgroup of Hispanic Americans came here from Central and South America, most as refugees. A **refugee** is one who leaves his or her home to seek refuge from war, persecution, or some other danger. More than three million persons have emigrated to the United States from countries south of Mexico over the past 25 years; they have come in the largest numbers from Nicaragua, El Salvador, and Chile.

## Discrimination Against Women

Unlike the several ethnic groups described here, women are not a minority in the United States. They are, in fact, a majority group. Still, traditionally in American law and public policy, women have not enjoyed the same rights as men—including, in many instances, men who were themselves the target of virulent discrimination. Women have, instead, been treated as less than equal in a great many matters—including, for example, property rights, education, and employment opportunities.

Those who fought and finally won the long struggle for women's suffrage believed that, with the vote, women would soon achieve other basic rights. That assumption proved to be false. Although more than 51 percent of the population is female, women have held only a fraction of one percent of the nation's top public offices since 1789. Even today, women hold little more than 10 percent (57) of the 535 seats in Congress and only 20 percent (some 1,500) of the 7,461 seats in the 50 State legislatures; and only one of the 50 State governors today is a woman. To the same point, fewer than 20 percent of the nation's doctors, lawyers, and college professors are women.

It is illegal to pay women less than men for the same work. The Equal Pay Act of 1963 requires employers to pay men and women the same wages if they perform the same jobs in the same establishment under the same working conditions. The Civil Rights Act of 1964 also prohibits job discrimination based on sex. Yet, 30 years after Congress passed those laws, work-

ing women earn, on the average, only about 70 cents for every dollar earned by working men. See the table on page 555.

Women earn less than men for a number of reasons—including the fact that the male work force is, over all, better educated and has more job experience than the female work force. (Note that these factors themselves can often be traced to discrimination.) But the primary reason is that until quite recently only a fairly narrow range of jobs were open to most women. Even now, more than three-fourths of all jobs held by women are in low-paying clerical and service occupations. The Bureau of Labor Statistics reports that 99 percent of all secretaries today are women; so too are 98 percent of all child-care workers, 96 percent of all nurses, 88 percent of all waiters, 87 percent of all health technicians, and 81 percent of all bank tellers. Efforts in behalf of equal rights for women have gained significant ground in recent years, as you will see. But, recall, that ground has not included the passage of an Equal Rights Amendment to the Constitution.

## Section 1 Review

1. **Define:** reservation, refugee
2. In what way has the composition of the American population changed over the course of United States history?
3. Which group has dominated political and social life in the United States since its beginnings?
4. Who have been the traditional targets of prejudice in America?
5. In what sense are women an unusual group among those who have suffered discrimination?

**Critical Thinking**

6. **Checking Consistency** (p. 19) Consider what you have read about minority groups in this country. How do these facts measure up to the ideals for human freedom expressed in documents such as the Declaration of Independence and the Constitution?

★

# 2 Equality Before the Law

**Find Out:**

- In what sense does the Constitution guarantee equality of all persons?
- On what grounds can government draw distinctions between groups of people?
- On what grounds is government forbidden from drawing distinctions between groups?

**Key Terms:**

segregation, Jim Crow law, separate-but-equal doctrine, de jure segregation, de facto segregation

Have you read George Orwell's classic, *Animal Farm*? Even if you have not, you may have heard its most celebrated line: "All animals are equal, but some animals are more equal than others." In this section, you will examine the Constitution's guarantees of equality—and, as you do, you might keep that Orwellian aphorism in mind.

## The Equal Protection Clause

Nothing can make people equal in a literal sense. Individuals differ in strength, intelligence, height, and countless other ways. But the democratic ideal demands that, insofar as government is concerned, all persons must be treated alike.

The equality of all persons—so boldly set out in the Declaration of Independence—is not proclaimed in so many words in the Constitution. Still, that concept pervades the document.

The closest approach to a literal statement of equality is to be found in the 14th Amendment's Equal Protection Clause. It declares:

❝No State shall . . . deny to any person within its jurisdiction the equal protection of the laws.❞

The clause was originally intended to benefit those individuals newly freed from slavery. Over time, it has acquired a broader meaning. Today, the Due Process Clause forbids States and their local governments to draw unreasonable distinctions between classes of persons. The Supreme Court has often held that the 5th Amendment's Due Process Clause puts the same restriction on the Federal Government.

**Reasonable Classification**    Government must have the power to draw distinctions between persons and groups. That is, the States can and do discriminate. Thus, those who rob banks fall into a special class and are subject to special treatment by the law. Or, the State can prohibit marriage by those under a certain age. These are reasonable discriminations.

The States cannot discriminate unreasonably. For example, every State now levies a sales tax on cigarettes—and so taxes smokers. But no State can tax only blonde smokers. Nor, for example, may a State make women eligible for alimony in divorce actions but provide that men are not, *Orr* v. *Orr*, in 1979.

Over time, the Supreme Court has rejected many equal protection challenges to the actions of State and local governments. More often

## VOICES on Government

**Larry Echohawk,**
attorney general of Idaho, 1991–1995

### On Equal Protection Under the Law

❝At 14, my father— a Pawnee Indian—was taken from his family's Oklahoma reservation and sent to boarding school. There he was forced . . . [to shun] his native language, disavow his culture. For people of color sixty years ago, equal protection was a largely empty promise. For me, it's been more. I went to school, succeeded in law, entered public service—while maintaining my cultural heritage. But . . . as long as our legal system is less than color-blind, 'equal protection' will be less than a reality.❞

than not, it has found that what those governments have done is, in fact, constitutional.[5] The Court's most recent Equal Protection Clause case provides an example. In *Gregory* v. *Ashcroft*, 1991, the Court upheld a provision in the Missouri constitution that sets a mandatory retirement age for State judges but not for other top officeholders.

**The Rational Basis Test**   The Supreme Court most often decides equal protection cases by applying a standard known as the rational basis test. This test asks: Does the classification in question bear a reasonable relationship to the achievement of some proper governmental purpose?

A California case, *Michael M.* v. *Superior Court*, 1981, illustrates that test. California law says that a man who has sexual relations with a girl under 18 to whom he is not married can be prosecuted for statutory rape; but the girl cannot be charged with that crime, even if she is a willing partner. The Court found the law to bear a reasonable relationship to the achievement of a proper public end: preventing teenage pregnancies.

**The Strict Scrutiny Test**   The Supreme Court imposes a more demanding standard in some equal protection cases, however. This is especially true when a law or some other action deals with (1) such "fundamental rights" as the right to vote, the right to travel between the States, or the rights guaranteed in the 1st Amendment; or (2) such "suspect classifications" as those based on race, sex, or national origins.

In these instances, the Court has said that a law must meet a higher standard than the rational basis test. This standard is called the strict scrutiny test. The State must be able to show that some "compelling governmental interest" justifies the distinctions it has drawn between classes of people. The alimony case cited a moment ago, *Orr* v. *Orr*, involved the use of that stricter test. The Alabama law that made only women eligible for alimony was held

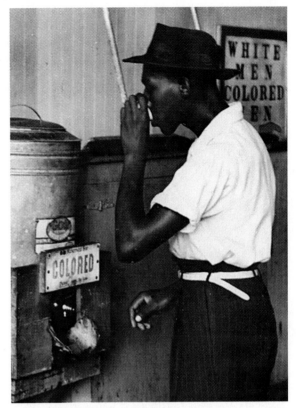

▲ **Separate, But Not Equal**   The goal of the civil rights movement of the 1960s was to show the need for legislation that made racial segregation and discrimination unlawful in public places, employment, housing, and voting.

unconstitutional, as a denial of equal protection, because the law's distinction between men and women did not serve a compelling governmental interest.

## Segregation in America

Beginning in the late 1800s, nearly half of the States passed a number of racial segregation laws. **Segregation** means the isolation and separation of one group from another. Most of those were **Jim Crow laws** aimed at African Americans. Some of them were drawn to affect other groups, as well—especially Mexican Americans, people of Asian descent, and Native Americans. These laws required segregation by race in the use of both public and private facilities: streetcars, schools, parks and playgrounds, hotels and restaurants, even public drinking fountains.

---

[5]The Court has voided a number of those actions, however—for example, too-lengthy residence requirements for voting purposes; see pages 132–133.

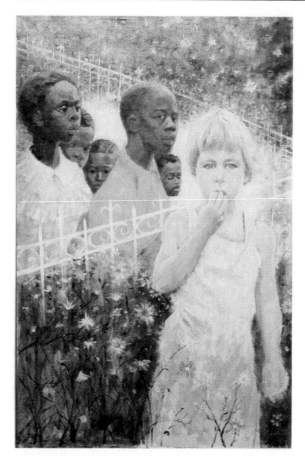

**Interpreting Political Art**   *The White Fence* by Ernest Crichlow symbolizes the barriers of prejudice that separate African-American children from opportunities that are available to white children. The flowers surrounding the white child represent those opportunities.

**The Separate-but-Equal Doctrine**   In 1896, the Supreme Court provided a constitutional basis for these many segregation laws: the **separate-but-equal doctrine**. In *Plessy* v. *Ferguson* it upheld a Louisiana law requiring the segregation of whites and African Americans in rail coaches. It held that the law did not violate the Equal Protection Clause because the separate facilities for African Americans were equal to those for whites.

The separate-but-equal doctrine stood for nearly 60 years. Indeed, until the late 1930s, little real effort was made by the courts or any other arm of government even to see that the separate accommodations for African Americans were, in fact, equal to those reserved to whites.

***Brown* v. *Board of Education of Topeka,* 1954**   The Supreme Court began to chip away at the separate-but-equal doctrine in the late 1930s and the 1940s. It did so for the first time in *Missouri ex rel. Gaines* v. *Canada* in 1938. Lloyd Gaines, an African American, was denied admission to the law school at the all-white University of Missouri. Gaines was fully qualified for admission—except that he was an African American. However, the State did offer to pay his tuition at a public law school in any of four neighboring States.

The Supreme Court held that the separate-but-equal doctrine left the State of Missouri with but two choices here: It could either (1) admit Gaines to the State's law school or (2) establish a separate-but-equal one for him. The State gave in and admitted Gaines rather than build a separate-but-equal law school.

Over the next several years the Supreme Court took an increasingly stern attitude toward the doctrine's requirement of equal facilities. In a number of cases it insisted on equality in fact—that is, in terms of quality—between separate facilities. Finally, in an historic decision in 1954, the Court reversed *Plessy* v. *Ferguson*. In *Brown* v. *Board of Education of Topeka*, it struck down the laws of four States requiring or allowing separate public schools for white and African-American students.[6]

Unanimously, the Supreme Court held that segregation by race in public education is unconstitutional:

❝Does segregation of children in public schools solely on the basis of race, even though the physical facilities and other "tangible" factors may be equal, deprive the children of the minority group of equal educational opportunities? We believe that it does.

. . . To separate them from others of similar age and qualifications solely because of their race generates a feeling of inferiority as to their status in the community that may affect their hearts and minds in a way unlikely ever to be undone. . . . We conclude that in the field of public education the doctrine of "separate but equal" has no place. Separate educational facilities are inherently unequal.❞

---

[6]Kansas, Delaware, South Carolina, and Virginia. On the same day, it also struck down racially segregated public schools in the District of Columbia, under the 5th Amendment, *Bolling* v. *Sharpe*, 1954.

The Court in 1955 directed the States to make "a prompt and reasonable start" and to end segregation "with all deliberate speed."

A "reasonable start" was made in several places: Baltimore, Louisville, St. Louis, Washington, D.C., and elsewhere. In most of the Deep South, however, what came to be known as "massive resistance" soon developed. State legislatures passed laws to block integration. Most were clearly unconstitutional; but the process of attacking them in the federal courts was costly and slow. Many school boards also worked to bar progress.

The pace of desegregation quickened after Congress passed the Civil Rights Act of 1964. That act forbids the use of federal funds to aid any State or local activity in which racial segregation is practiced. It directed the Justice Department to file suits to prompt desegregation actions.

The Supreme Court itself pushed that pace along in 1969. In a case from Mississippi, *Alexander* v. *Holmes County Board of Education*, it ruled that, after 15 years, the time for "all deliberate speed" had finally run out. Said a unanimous Court: "The continued operation of segregated schools under a standard allowing for 'all deliberate speed' . . . is no longer constitutionally permissible."

**De Jure and De Facto Segregation**  By fall 1970, school systems with **de jure segregation**—segregation by law, with legal sanction— had been abolished. That is not to say that desegregation itself had been fully accomplished. The process of achieving a complete integration of the country's schools still continues more than 35 years after the Court's decision in *Brown*.[7]

Many recent integration controversies have come in places where the schools have never been segregated by law. They have occurred, instead, in communities in which de facto segregation has long been present, and continues.

---

[7]Some States, several school districts, and many parents and private groups have sought to avoid integrated schools through established or, often, newly created private schools. See the Court's rulings in two 1983 cases, *Bob Jones University* v. *United States* and *Goldsboro Christian Schools* v. *United States* (page 494) and *Runyan* v. *McCrary*, 1976 (page 522).

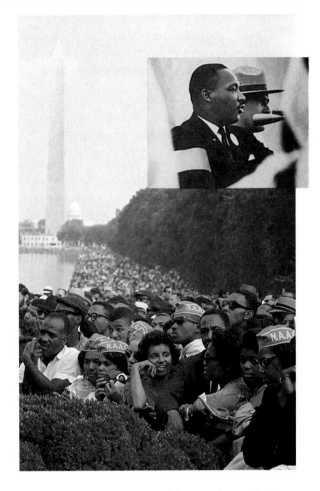

▲ **"I Have A Dream"**  Thousands marched on the Capitol in 1963 to support Martin Luther King, Jr.'s plea for stronger civil rights laws.

**De facto segregation** is segregation in fact, even though no law requires it. Housing patterns have most often been its major cause. The concentration of African Americans in certain sections of cities inevitably led to local school systems in which some schools are largely African American. That condition is apparent in many northern as well as southern communities.

Efforts to desegregate those school systems have taken several forms. School district lines have been redrawn, pupil assignment programs have been put in place, and the busing of students out of racially segregated neighborhoods has been tried. These efforts have often brought strong protests in many places and violence in some.

The Supreme Court first sanctioned busing in a North Carolina case, *Swann* v. *Charlotte-Mecklenburg Board of Education*, 1971. There it held that "desegregation plans cannot be limited to walk-in schools." Since then, busing has been used to try to increase the racial mix in many school districts across the country—in some by court order, in others voluntarily.

**Segregation in Other Fields**    This nation has not yet achieved a complete integration of the public schools. Legally enforced racial segregation in all other areas of life has been eliminated, however. Governments and courts have repealed and struck down many discriminatory State laws and local ordinances.

The Supreme Court has found segregation by race to be as unconstitutional in other areas as it is in public education. Thus, for example, it has held that the Equal Protection Clause forbids segregated public swimming pools or other recreational facilities, *Dawson* v. *Baltimore*, 1955. It has made the same holding with regard to such things as local transportation, *Gayle* v. *Browder*, 1956, and State prisons and local jails, *Lee* v. *Washington*, 1968. The High Court struck down all State miscegenation laws—laws that forbid interracial marriages—in *Loving* v. *Virginia*, 1967. Most recently, it has held that race cannot be the basis upon which a child custody decision is based, *Palmore* v. *Sidoti*, 1984.

## Classification by Sex

In its many civil rights provisions, the Constitution speaks of "the people," "persons," and "citizens." Nowhere does it make its guarantees only to "men" or separately to "women." The only reference to sex is in the 19th Amendment, which forbids denial of the right to vote "on account of sex."

Gender has long been used as a basis of classification in the law, however. Most often, society and the courts viewed those laws that treated men and women differently as necessary to the protection of "the weaker sex." Over the years, the Supreme Court read that view into the 14th Amendment. It did not find *any* sex-based classification to be unconstitutional until as recently as 1971.

In the first case to challenge sex discrimination, *Bradwell* v. *Illinois*, 1873, the Court upheld a State law barring women from the practice of law. In that case, Justice Joseph P. Bradley wrote:

“The civil law, as well as nature itself, has always recognized a wide difference in the respective spheres and destinies of man and woman. Man is, or should be, woman's protector and defender. The natural and proper timidity and delicacy of the female sex evidently unfits it for many of the occupations of civil life.”

Even as late as 1961, in *Hoyt* v. *Florida*, the Court could find no constitutional fault with a law that required men to serve on juries but gave women the choice of serving or not.

Matters are far different today. As you have read, the Court now takes a very close look at cases involving claims of sex discrimination. Thus, in 1971, in *Reed* v. *Reed*, it struck down an Idaho law that gave fathers preference over mothers in the administration of their children's estates.

Since then, the Supreme Court has found a number of sex-based distinctions to be unconstitutional. You have already encountered some of them—for example, *Taylor* v. *Louisiana*, 1975, holding that the Equal Protection Clause forbids the States to exclude women from jury service; see Chapter 20, Section 3. As other examples, it has also struck down: an Oklahoma law that prohibited the sale of beer to males under 21 and to females under 18, *Craig* v. *Boren*, 1976; an Arizona rule permitting public employee retirement plans providing for smaller pensions for women than for men who paid the same premiums during their working years, *Arizona Governing Committee* v. *Norris*, 1983.

In the same vein, the Supreme Court has upheld a California law that prohibits community service clubs from excluding women from membership, *Rotary International* v. *Rotary Club of Duarte*, 1987, and a New York City ordinance that forbids sex discrimination in any place of public accommodation, including large private membership clubs used by their members for business purposes, *New York State Club Association, Inc.* v. *City of New York*, 1988.

The Court's present attitude was put this way by Justice William Brennan in *Frontiero* v. *Richardson*, 1973:

## Median Earnings of Men and Women*

$40,381

$31,413

$29,284

$26,766

$21,987

$21,179

$18,648

$13,760

9th to 12th grade (no diploma)

High school graduate

Some college (no degree)

4 years of college (Bachelor's degree)

*Median earnings of fulltime, year-round American workers, age 25 and over, 1992.
*Source:* Census Bureau

▲ **Interpreting Graphs**  What does this graph show about equality in the workplace a full one hundred years after the women's suffrage movement began?

❝There can be no doubt that our nation has had a long and unfortunate history of sex discrimination. Traditionally, such discrimination was rationalized by an attitude of 'romantic paternalism' which, in practical effect, put women, not on a pedestal, but in a cage.❞[8]

But not all sex-based distinctions are unconstitutional. The Supreme Court has upheld some of them in several cases. You saw one example of this in *Michael M.* v. *Superior Court*,

1981. And the court has held there was no denial of equal protection in:

—a Florida law that gives an extra property tax exemption to widows, but not to widowers, *Kahn* v. *Shevin*, 1974.

—an Alabama law forbidding women to serve as prison guards in all-male penitentiaries, *Dothard* v. *Rawlinson*, 1977.

—the federal selective service law that requires only men to register for the draft, and also its provisions that exclude women from any future draft, *Rostker* v. *Goldberg*, 1981.

In effect, these cases say this: Classification by sex is not in and of itself unconstitutional. However, laws that treat men and women differently will not be upheld by the courts unless (1) they are intended to serve an "important governmental objective" and (2) they are "substantially related" to achieving that goal.

Thus, in upholding the all-male draft, the Court found that Congress did in fact have such an important governmental objective: to raise and support armies and, if necessary, to do so by "a draft of combat troops." "Since women are excluded from combat," said the Supreme Court, "they may properly be excluded from the draft."

## Section 2 Review

1. **Define:** segregation, Jim Crow law, separate-but-equal doctrine
2. The Equal Protection Clause forbids what kinds of discrimination by the States?
3. What was the significance of the Supreme Court's decision in *Plessy* v. *Ferguson*?
4. What did the Court hold in *Brown* v. *Board of Education of Topeka*?
5. What is the difference between de jure and de facto segregation?
6. Does the Constitution forbid laws that treat men and women differently?

### Critical Thinking

7. **Drawing Conclusions** (p. 19) (a) In your opinion, which would be harder to combat, de facto or de jure segregation? (b) Why?

---

[8]In this case the Court for the first time struck down a federal law providing for sex-based discrimination, as a violation of the 5th Amendment's Due Process Clause. That law gave various housing, medical, and other allowances to a serviceman for his wife and other dependents, but it made those same allowances available to a servicewoman only if her husband was dependent on her for more than half of his support.

★

# 3 Federal Civil Rights Laws

## Find Out

- What did Congress do to ensure civil rights between the 1870s and 1950s? What has Congress done in the last 30 years?
- How has the Federal Government sought to overcome the effects of past discrimination?
- How has the Supreme Court responded to affirmative action?

## Key Terms:

affirmative action, quota, reverse discrimination

You may have heard this oft-made argument: "You can't legislate morality." That is, racism, sexism, and other forms of discrimination cannot be eliminated merely with laws.

Martin Luther King, Jr., replied to that contention this way: "Laws," he said, "may not change the heart, but they can restrain the heartless."

As you will see, Congress has several times agreed with Dr. King—as it has enacted a number of civil rights laws over the past 30 years.

## Civil Rights: Reconstruction to Today

From the 1870s to the late 1950s, Congress did not pass a single piece of meaningful civil rights legislation. There were several reasons for that sorry fact. First, through that period the nation's predominantly white population was generally unaware and little concerned with the plight of African Americans, Native Americans, or other nonwhites in this country. Secondly, southern white Democrats, bolstered by such devices as the seniority system and the filibuster, held many of the most strategic posts in Congress.

That historic logjam was broken in 1957— very largely as a result of the pressures brought to bear by the civil rights movement led by Dr. King.[9] Beginning in that year, Congress has passed a number of civil rights laws—notably,

▲ **Equality in the Workplace** The Americans with Disabilities Act of 1990 prohibits discrimination based on disability in employment, public services, and public accommodations.

the Civil Rights Acts of 1957, 1960, 1964, and 1968 and the Voting Rights Acts of 1965, 1970, 1975, and 1982. The 1957 and 1960 laws set up modest safeguards for the right to vote.[10] In Chapter 6 you considered those two statutes, together with the related provisions of the Civil Rights Act of 1964 and the much stronger Voting Rights Act of 1965.

**The Civil Rights Act of 1964** The 1964 law is the most far-reaching of these statutes. It passed after the longest debate in the Senate's history (83 days), and only after the Senate had invoked cloture to kill a filibuster.

Beyond its voting rights provisions, the 1964 law outlaws discrimination in a number of areas of American life. With its several later amendments, the law's major sections now:

---

[9]See Chapter 6, Section 3.

[10]The 1957 law created the U.S. Civil Rights Commission. The commission is an independent eight-member agency that is supposed to monitor the enforcement of the various civil rights laws, investigate cases of alleged discrimination and report its findings to the President, Congress, and the public. The commission was very active in the 1960s and 1970s.

(1) provide that no person may be denied access to or refused service in various "public accommodations" because of race, color, religion, or national origin (Title II).[11]

(2) prohibit discrimination against any person on grounds of race, color, religion, national origin, sex, or physical disability in any program that receives any federal funding; require the cut-off of federal funds to any program that practices such discrimination (Title VI).

(3) forbid employers and labor unions to discriminate against any person on grounds of race, color, religion, sex, physical disability, or age (40 to 65) in job-related matters (Title VII).[12]

**The Civil Rights Act of 1968**  The Civil Rights Act of 1968 is often called the Open Housing Act. With minor exceptions, it forbids anyone to refuse to sell or rent a dwelling to any person on grounds of race, color, religion, national origin, sex, or disability, or to a family with children. Until Congress amended the law, the major burden for its enforcement was placed on those persons who claimed to be the victims of housing discrimination. Congress finally strengthened the law in 1988, by allowing the Justice Department to bring criminal charges against those who violate its terms.

## Affirmative Action

These several civil rights statutes all come down to this: Discriminatory practices based on such factors as race, color, national origin, or sex are illegal. But what about the present and continuing effects of past discrimination? Consider, for example, the African American who, for no reason of his or her own making, did not get a decent education and so today

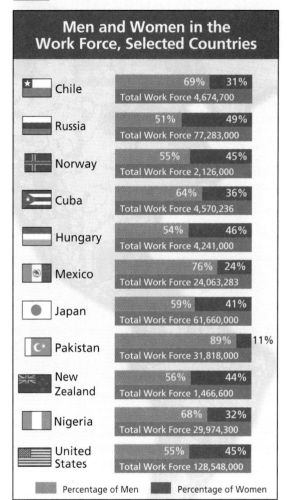

## Global Awareness

### Men and Women in the Work Force, Selected Countries

| Country | Percentage of Men | Percentage of Women | Total Work Force |
|---|---|---|---|
| Chile | 69% | 31% | 4,674,700 |
| Russia | 51% | 49% | 77,283,000 |
| Norway | 55% | 45% | 2,126,000 |
| Cuba | 64% | 36% | 4,570,236 |
| Hungary | 54% | 46% | 4,241,000 |
| Mexico | 76% | 24% | 24,063,283 |
| Japan | 59% | 41% | 61,660,000 |
| Pakistan | 89% | 11% | 31,818,000 |
| New Zealand | 56% | 44% | 1,466,600 |
| Nigeria | 68% | 32% | 29,974,300 |
| United States | 55% | 45% | 128,548,000 |

*Source:* The Europa World Yearbook, 1993.

▲ **Interpreting Graphs: Multicultural Awareness**   This graph gives statistics on the percentage of men and women in the work force in selected countries. Which two countries employ the lowest percentages of women? The highest?

cannot get a decent job. Of what real help to that person are all of those laws that make illegal today what was done years ago?

So far, the Federal Government's chief answer to this troubling question has been a policy of **affirmative action**. That policy requires that most employers take positive steps (affirmative action) to remedy the effects of past discriminations.

---

[11]Congress based this section of the law on its commerce power; see Chapter 11, Section 2. Title II covers those places in which lodgings are offered to transient guests and those where a significant portion of the items sold have moved in interstate commerce. The Supreme Court upheld Title II and the use of the Commerce Clause as a basis for civil rights legislation in *Heart of Atlanta Motel, Inc.* v. *United States,* 1964.

[12]The 1964 law also created the Equal Employment Opportunity Commission. The five-member EEOC's major charge is the enforcement of Title VII.

## Measuring the National Mood on Race-Related Questions

Do you believe that because of past discrimination against African-American people, qualified African Americans should receive preference over equally qualified white Americans in such matters as getting into college or getting jobs?

|            | African Americans | White Americans |
|------------|-------------------|-----------------|
| Should     | 48%               | 19%             |
| Should not | 42%               | 72%             |

Can fairness in education, hiring, and promotion be accomplished without quotas?

|     | African Americans | White Americans |
|-----|-------------------|-----------------|
| Yes | 26%               | 59%             |
| No  | 61%               | 29%             |

Which categories apply to you?

|                                          | African Americans | White Americans |
|------------------------------------------|-------------------|-----------------|
| Worked with many members of another race | 84%               | 51%             |
| Worked for a boss of another race        | 92%               | 47%             |

*Source:* The Newsweek Poll ©1991, *Newsweek*, Inc.

▲ **Interpreting Tables: Multicultural Awareness**   After comparing the ways African and white Americans view their positions today, suggest two possible ways to improve racial equality in America.

The policy applies to all the agencies of the Federal Government, to all the States and their local governments, and to all those private employers who sell goods or services to any agency of the Federal Government.[13]

To illustrate the policy, take the case of a company that does business with the Federal Government. That private business must adopt an affirmative action plan designed to make its work force reflect the general makeup of the population in its locale. The company's program must also include steps to correct or prevent inequalities in such matters as pay, promotions, and fringe benefits. For many employers this has meant that they must hire and/or promote more workers with minority backgrounds and more females. Such rules requiring certain numbers of jobs or promotions for certain groups are called **quotas**.

**Reverse Discrimination?**   Affirmative action programs necessarily involve race-based and/or sex-based classifications. Are programs such as these constitutional?

Critics of the policy say that affirmative action amounts to **reverse discrimination**—discrimination against the majority group. It demands that preference be given to females and/or nonwhites, solely on the basis of sex or race. Critics insist that the Constitution requires that all public policies be "color blind."

**The Bakke Case**   The Supreme Court has been wrestling with affirmative action cases for more than a dozen years now. The Court's first major case, *Regents of the University of California* v. *Bakke*, was decided in 1978. Allan Bakke, a white male, had been denied admission to the university's medical school at Davis. The school had set aside 16 of the 100 seats in each year's entering class for nonwhite students. He sued, charging the university with reverse discrimination and, so, a violation of the 14th Amendment's Equal Protection Clause. By a 5–4 majority the Court held that Bakke had been denied equal protection and should be admitted to the medical school.

A differently composed 5–4 majority made the really important ruling in the case, however: Although the Constitution does not allow race to be used as the *only* factor in the making of affirmative action decisions, both the Constitution and the 1964 Civil Rights Act do allow its use as one among several factors in such situations.

**The Weber Case**   The Court has upheld quotas in some cases, especially where longstanding and flagrant discrimination was involved.

In *United Steelworkers* v. *Weber*, 1979, the Kaiser Aluminum Company had created train-

---

[13]The Federal Government began to demand the adoption of affirmative action programs in 1965. Some programs are simply plans that call for the wide advertisement of job openings. Most, however, establish guidelines and timetables to overcome past discriminations.

Affirmative action programs were very actively supported and enforced by the Federal Government from the early 1960s to 1981. Its efforts were much less aggressive from 1981 to 1993; but that earlier level of support has now been renewed.

ing programs, intended especially to increase the number of skilled African Americans in its work force. Trainees were chosen on the basis of race and seniority. Brian Weber, a white worker, was rejected for training three times. Each time, however, a number of African Americans with less seniority were picked.

Weber went to court. The Court found that the training programs, although built on quotas, did not violate the 1964 law—which, it said, Congress had purposely designed to "overcome manifest racial imbalances."

*Fullilove* v. *Klutznick*, 1980, was another case in which the Court upheld quotas. That case centered on a law Congress had passed that provided $4 billion in grants to State and local governments for public works projects. It also contained a "minority set-aside" provision, requiring that at least 10 percent of each grant had to be set aside for minority-owned businesses.

A white contractor challenged the set-asides. He argued that they were quotas and therefore unconstitutional—because they did not give white contractors an equal chance to compete for all of the available funds.

The Court held the law to be a permissible attempt to overcome the effects of blatant and longstanding bias in the construction industry.

Note, however, that quotas can be used in only the most extreme situations. Thus, the Court rejected a city's minority set-aside policy in *Richmond* v. *Croson*, 1989. There the Court held, 6–3, that the city of Richmond, Virginia, had not shown that its ordinance was justified by past discrimination. Therefore, it had denied white contractors their right to equal protection.

*Johnson* v. *Transportation Agency of Santa Clara County*, 1987, marked the first time the Court decided a case of preferential treatment on the basis of sex. By a 6–3 vote, the justices held that neither the Equal Protection Clause nor Title VII of the 1964 law forbids the promotion of a woman rather than a man, even though he had scored higher on a qualifying interview than she did. The case arose in California, when a woman was promoted to a job that until then had always been held by a man.

**Recent Developments** The current Supreme Court's increasingly conservative bent is evident in some of its more recent affirmative action decisions. Thus, for example, in *Wards Cove Packing Co.* v. *Atonio*, 1989, the Court made it more difficult for those who charge discrimination to prove their point. There, a group of nonwhite cannery workers in Alaska produced statistical evidence showing a longstanding pattern of employment practices by which their cannery company channeled nonwhites into low-paying jobs while whites received the much more desirable positions.

But the Court ruled against them. It held, 5–4, that such statistical evidence was not an adequate proof of race discrimination. Instead, said the majority, Title VII requires that those who claim discrimination in employment must be able to show that the conditions they challenge are not the result of some legitimate "business necessity."

The Court's holding in *Wards Cove* was pointedly rejected by an act of Congress in 1991. In effect, Congress said that the Court had misread Title VII. The new law declares that Title VII means this: Any business practice that results in the unequal treatment of female or minority employees is permissible only if the employer can show that that practice is based on some legitimate business necessity. Note that in *Wards Cove* it was the employees' responsibility to show that the action did not serve a legitimate business necessity.

# Section 3 Review

1. **Define:** affirmative action, quota, reverse discrimination
2. During what time period was most of the nation's civil rights legislation passed?
3. What are the major provisions of the Civil Rights Act of 1964?
4. What is the significance of the *Bakke* case?
5. Under what circumstances has the Supreme Court allowed quotas?

**Critical Thinking**
6. **Identifying Central Issues** (p. 19) In your opinion, is it society's responsibility to rectify the harm suffered by a group of people as a result of discrimination in the past?

★

# Debating Key Issues

## Should Universities Have the Right to Use Admissions Quotas?
### *Regents of the University of California* v. *Bakke*, 1978

In 1973, at age 37, Allan Bakke decided that he wanted to go to medical school. He was at the time a NASA engineer, with two degrees in engineering.

Bakke, who is white, applied for admission to the Medical School of the University of California at Davis. His application was rejected, however, principally because he missed the school's filing deadline. He applied again, early in 1974; but that application was also rejected.

At the time, the Medical School's admissions policy set aside 16 of 100 places in each year's entering class for "disadvantaged" applicants. This policy was purposely designed to attract ethnic minority students to the school and so to the medical profession.

Bakke went to court when he discovered this fact: Several applicants, with entrance exam scores, scholastic averages, and other qualifications lower than his, had been admitted to the Medical School in both 1973 and 1974, most of them under the set-aside policy.

The superior court of Yolo County agreed with Bakke that the school's admissions policy violated the equal protection guarantees of both the California and the Federal Constitutions. The trial court refused to order his admission to the Medical School, however; it found that Bakke had failed to prove that he would have been admitted to the school had there been no set-aside program.

On appeal, the California Supreme Court also held the Medical School's admissions program unconstitutional, and it ordered the school to admit Bakke to its next entering class. The Regents of the University of California then carried the case to the United States Supreme Court.

*Review the following arguments presented to the United States Supreme Court.*

### Arguments for Bakke

**1.** The refusal to admit Bakke violates the 14th Amendment's Equal Protection Clause because that action (1) was based on a policy built on racial quotas and (2) amounted to reverse discrimination.

**2.** The school's admission policy also violates Title VI of the Civil Rights Act of 1964, which forbids race-based discrimination in programs receiving federal financial aid.

### Arguments for Regents of the University of California

**1.** People of certain minority backgrounds are disadvantaged from the day they are born and so must be afforded greater protection under the 14th Amendment.

**2.** The Civil Rights Act of 1964 intends to overcome the effects of past discrimination and so should protect minority students who might otherwise be displaced by whites.

## Getting Involved

**1. Identify** the constitutional grounds on which each side based its arguments.

**2. Debate** the opposing viewpoints presented in this case. Predict how you think the Supreme Court ruled and why. Refer to the Supreme Court Glossary on page 768 to read the decision in this case.

**3. Discuss** the impact of the Court's decision in this case on minority rights and advancement in the future.

# 4 American Citizenship

**Find Out:**
- How can American citizenship be acquired?
- What is the immigration policy of the United States?
- What is the undocumented alien problem?

**Key Terms:**

citizen, jus soli, jus sanguinis, naturalization, alien, expatriation, denaturalization, deportation

Are you an American **citizen**—one who owes allegiance to the state and is entitled to its protection? Very likely you are; more than 90 percent of all the people who live in this country are citizens of the United States. In addition, many of those who are not citizens are actively seeking citizenship.

In this section, you will examine the issue of United States citizenship—what it is, how it is acquired, and who may acquire it.

## The Question of Citizenship

As it was originally written, the Constitution mentioned both "citizens of the United States" and "citizens of the States." It did not define either of those phrases, however. Through much of America's early history it was generally agreed that national citizenship followed that of the States.

The coming of the Civil War and the adoption of the 13th Amendment in 1865 raised the need for a constitutional definition, however.[14] That need was finally met by the 14th Amendment in 1868. The amendment begins with these words:

❝All persons born or naturalized in the United States, and subject to the jurisdiction thereof, are citizens of the United States and of the State wherein they reside.❞

---

[14]In the *Dred Scott* case (*Scott* v. *Sandford*) in 1857, the Supreme Court had ruled that neither the States nor the National Government had the power to confer citizenship on African Americans—slave or free. The dispute over that issue was one of the several causes of the Civil War.

Thus, the 14th Amendment declares that a person can become an American citizen either by birth or by naturalization. The chart on page 563 summarizes the means of acquiring American citizenship.

## Citizenship by Birth

More than 225 million Americans—more than 90 percent of all of us—are American citizens because we were born in the United States. Another several million are also citizens by birth, even though they were born abroad. Citizenship by birth is determined by either (1) **jus soli**—the law of the soil, where born, or (2) **jus sanguinis**—the law of the blood, to whom born.

**Jus Soli**  The 14th Amendment confers citizenship according to the location of a person's birth: "All persons born . . . in the United States . . . " By law, Congress has defined the United States to include, for purposes of citizenship, the 50 States, the District of Columbia, Puerto Rico, Guam, the Virgin Islands, and the Northern Mariana Islands. It includes, as well, all American embassies and all American public vessels anywhere in the world.[15]

**Jus Sanguinis**  A child born abroad can become an American citizen at birth under certain circumstances. The child must be born to at least one parent who is a citizen and who has at some time lived in the United States.

The 14th Amendment does not provide for jus sanguinis, but Congress has included it as a part of American citizenship law since 1790. The constitutionality of the rule has never been challenged. But if it were, it would almost certainly be upheld—if for no other reason than because of its longstanding history.

---

[15]United States embassies are, in effect, parts of the United States. A public vessel is any ship or aircraft operated by any agency of the government.

Until 1924, Native Americans born to tribal members living on reservations were not considered citizens. They were instead wards, persons under the legal guardianship, of the government. In that year, however, Congress granted citizenship to all Native Americans who did not already possess it.

## How to Apply for Naturalization

**1. File an Application.** You must be 18 years of age and have lived in the United States for at least five continuous years to file an application for naturalization. The application consists of Application Form N-400, a fingerprint card, and a Biographic Information form. These materials can be acquired at your nearest office of the Immigration and Naturalization Service or from a social service agency in your community. Fill out these forms according to the instructions, then file them with the office of the Immigration and Naturalization Service with jurisdiction over your residence. Three unsigned photographs (described in the application form) must also be submitted.

**2. Take the Examination on the Application.** You will be informed by the Immigration and Naturalization Service when and where to appear for the examination. During this examination, the examiner will ask questions pertaining to United States history and government. If found eligible by the examiner, you then will be assisted in filing the legal petition for naturalization. At this time, you will be requested to pay a fee to the clerk of the naturalization court.

**3. Appear Before the Court for the Final Hearing.** At this hearing, the naturalization examiner will inform the judge that you have been found qualified and should be made a citizen. If you have been notified that you are not eligible for naturalization, you may appear at the final hearing, with or without an attorney, and request naturalization before the judge. The judge will listen to your arguments regarding your fitness for citizenship and decide whether to grant citizenship. When the court decides that you should be made a citizen, you will take an oath of allegiance to the United States. In doing so, you give up allegiance to any foreign country and promise to support and defend the Constitution and laws of the United States.

▲ **Interpreting Charts**  This chart outlines the qualifications necessary to become a citizen of the United States. Why do you think the examination is oral, rather than written?

## Citizenship by Naturalization

**Naturalization** is the legal process by which a person becomes a citizen of another country at some time after birth. Congress has the exclusive power to grant naturalization. No State may do so.[16] The naturalization process may be either an individual or a collective one.

**Individual Naturalization**  The process is most often an individual one, conducted by a court. More than 250,000 **aliens**—citizens or nationals of a foreign state living in this country—now become naturalized American citizens each year.

As a general rule, any person who has come to the United States as an immigrant, that is, an alien legally admitted as a permanent resident, can be naturalized. More specifically, current law provides that a person who wants to become a naturalized citizen must:

—have entered the United States legally, lived here for at least five years and in some State for at least three months, and be at least 18 years old.[17]

—file a petition for naturalization with the clerk of a federal district court or of a state court of record.

—be literate in the English language.

—be "of good moral character," "attached to the principles of the Constitution," and "well disposed to the good order and happiness of the United States."

—have "a knowledge and understanding of the fundamentals of the history, and the principles and form of government, of the United States."

---

[16]Article I, Section 8, Clause 4.

[17]The residence requirements are eased somewhat for the alien husbands, wives, and children of citizens and for present and former members of the armed forces. Also, the naturalization of both parents—one parent, if the other is dead or divorced—automatically naturalizes their children under 16 years of age if the children are living permanently in the United States.

—take an oath or affirmation in which he or she absolutely renounces any allegiance to any foreign power and promises to "support and defend the Constitution and laws of the United States against all enemies, foreign and domestic."[18]

The Immigration and Naturalization Service (INS) in the Department of Justice investigates

---

[18]In an oath a person swears to something and binds that pledge with the words "so help me God." Those whose beliefs will not allow them to invoke a supreme being in that way may instead make an affirmation (a legally binding pledge that does not refer to a supreme being).

In the oath or affirmation the citizen-to-be also promises to "bear arms in behalf of the United States" if required to do so by law. However, those whose religious beliefs will not allow them to do so may promise to serve as noncombatants in the armed forces or perform some work of national importance under civilian direction.

each applicant. An INS examiner then reports to the judge of the court in which the petition for naturalization was filed. If the judge is satisfied, the oath or affirmation is administered in open court, and the new citizen receives a certificate of naturalization.

**Collective Naturalization**  At various times in American history an entire group of persons has been naturalized en masse. This has most often happened when the United States has acquired new territory. As the table on this page indicates, those living in the areas involved were naturalized by a treaty or by an act or a joint resolution passed by Congress. The largest single instance of collective naturalization came with the ratification of the 14th Amendment, however. The most recent instance occurred in 1977, when Congress gave citizenship to the more than 16,000 native-born residents of the Northern Mariana Islands.

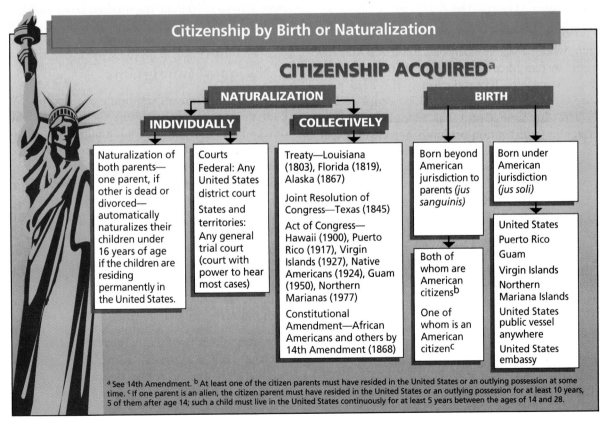

**Citizenship by Birth or Naturalization**

**CITIZENSHIP ACQUIRED**[a]

**NATURALIZATION**

**INDIVIDUALLY**

Naturalization of both parents—one parent, if other is dead or divorced—automatically naturalizes their children under 16 years of age if the children are residing permanently in the United States.

Courts
Federal: Any United States district court

States and territories: Any general trial court (court with power to hear most cases)

**COLLECTIVELY**

Treaty—Louisiana (1803), Florida (1819), Alaska (1867)

Joint Resolution of Congress—Texas (1845)

Act of Congress—Hawaii (1900), Puerto Rico (1917), Virgin Islands (1927), Native Americans (1924), Guam (1950), Northern Marianas (1977)

Constitutional Amendment—African Americans and others by 14th Amendment (1868)

**BIRTH**

Born beyond American jurisdiction to parents (*jus sanguinis*)

Both of whom are American citizens[b]

One of whom is an American citizen[c]

Born under American jurisdiction (*jus soli*)

United States
Puerto Rico
Guam
Virgin Islands
Northern Mariana Islands
United States public vessel anywhere
United States embassy

[a] See 14th Amendment. [b] At least one of the citizen parents must have resided in the United States or an outlying possession at some time. [c] If one parent is an alien, the citizen parent must have resided in the United States or an outlying possession for at least 10 years, 5 of them after age 14; such a child must live in the United States continuously for at least 5 years between the ages of 14 and 28.

▲ **Interpreting Charts: Multicultural Awareness**  Most Americans acquire citizenship by birth. After examining the chart, name at least two other means of acquiring citizenship.

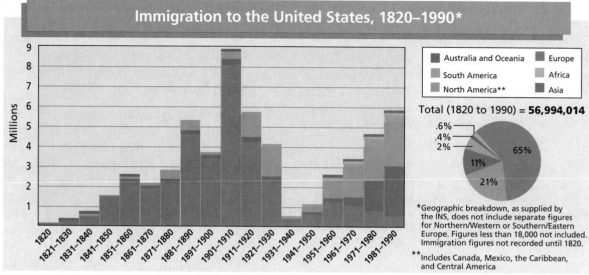

## Immigration to the United States, 1820–1990*

*Legend:*
- Australia and Oceania
- South America
- North America**
- Europe
- Africa
- Asia

Total (1820 to 1990) = **56,994,014**

.6%
.4%
2%
11%
21%
65%

*Geographic breakdown, as supplied by the INS, does not include separate figures for Northern/Western or Southern/Eastern Europe. Figures less than 18,000 not included. Immigration figures not recorded until 1820.

**Includes Canada, Mexico, the Caribbean, and Central America

*Source:* Dept. of Justice, Immigration and Naturalization Service

▲ **Interpreting Graphs: Multicultural Awareness** The graph shows that, until the 1970s, Europeans dominated United States immigration figures. Which two groups are the largest now?

## Loss of Citizenship

Although it rarely happens, every American citizen, whether native-born or naturalized, has the right to renounce—voluntarily abandon—his or her citizenship. **Expatriation** is the legal process by which a loss of citizenship occurs.

The Supreme Court has several times held that the Constitution prohibits automatic expatriation. That is, Congress cannot provide for the involuntary loss of a person's citizenship for something he or she has done—for example, committing a crime, voting in a foreign election, or serving in the armed forces of another country.[19]

Naturalized citizens can lose their citizenship involuntarily, however. That is, they can be denaturalized. But this process—**denaturalization**—can occur only by court order and only after it has been shown that the person became a citizen by fraud or deception.

A person cannot gain nor lose American citizenship by marriage. The only significant effect

that marriage has on the matter is to shorten the time required for the naturalization of an alien who marries an American citizen.

## A Nation of Immigrants

We are a nation of immigrants. Except for Native Americans—and even they may be the descendants of earlier immigrants—all of us have come here from abroad or are descended from those who did.

There were only some 2.5 million persons in the United States in 1776. Since then, the population has grown a hundredfold, to over 250 million people today. That extraordinary population growth has come from two sources: natural increase—births—and immigration. As the graph on this page shows, more than 55 million immigrants have come here since 1820, when such figures were first recorded.

**The Regulation of Immigration** Congress has the exclusive power to regulate immigration—that is, the power to decide who may be admitted to the United States and under what conditions.[20]

The United States made no serious attempt to regulate immigration for more than a century after independence. As long as land was plenti-

---

[19]A person convicted of a federal or a State crime may lose some of the privileges of citizenship, however, either temporarily or permanently—for example, the right to travel freely or to vote or hold public office.

ful and rapidly expanding industry demanded more and more workers, immigration was encouraged.

By 1890, however, the open frontier was a thing of the past, and labor was no longer in short supply. Then, too, the major source of immigration had shifted. Until the 1880s most immigrants had come from the countries of northern and western Europe. The "new immigration" from the 1880s onward came mostly from southern and eastern Europe—and included peoples against whom there was considerable prejudice.

Congress placed the first major restrictions on immigration with the passage of the Chinese Exclusion Act in 1882. At the same time, it barred the entry of convicts, "lunatics," paupers, and others likely to become public charges. Over the next several years a long list of "undesirables" was added to the law. Thus, contract laborers were excluded in 1885, immoral persons and anarchists in 1903, and illiterates in 1917. By 1920 more than 30 groups were denied admission on grounds of various personal traits.

The tide of newcomers continued to mount, however. In the 10 years from 1905 through 1914 an average of more than a million persons—most of them from southern and eastern Europe—came to this country.

Congress responded to the many pressures for tighter regulation by adding quantitative limits (numerical ceilings) to the qualitative restrictions (personal characteristics) already in place. The Immigration Acts of 1921 and 1924 and the National Origins Act of 1929 established a national origins quota system. Each

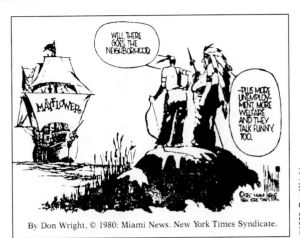

By Don Wright, © 1980: Miami News. New York Times Syndicate.

©1980, Don Wright.

▲ **Interpreting Political Cartoons:**
**Multicultural Awareness** Newcomers are greeted with suspicion by most cultures. Why is this cartoon particularly pointed?

country in Europe was assigned a quota—a limit on the number of immigrants who could enter the United States from that country each year. The quotas were purposely drawn to favor northern and western Europe. The quota system was not applied to the Western Hemisphere, but immigration from Asia, Africa, and elsewhere was generally prohibited.

In 1952 Congress passed yet another basic law, the Immigration and Nationality Act. That statute modified the quota system to cover every country outside the Western Hemisphere.

Congress finally eliminated the country-based quota system in the Immigration Act of 1965. That law provided that as many as 270,000 immigrants could enter the United States each year—without regard to race, nationality, or country of origin. The 1965 law did establish a special preference for one group of immigrants in particular, however: the immediate relatives of American citizens or of aliens legally residing in this country.

**Present Immigration Policies** Today, the Immigration Act of 1990, which became effective on October 1, 1991, is the basic law governing the admission of aliens to the United States. Like its predecessors, it was adopted only after years of intense debate, and many of

---

[20]The power to control the nation's borders is an inherent power of the United States, and that power includes the control of immigration. On the inherent powers, see Chapter 4, Section 1. In an early leading case on the point, the Supreme Court upheld the constitutionality of the Chinese Exclusion Act of 1882. That law generally barred Chinese from entering this country. The Court ruled that the power of the United States to "exclude aliens from its territory . . . is not open to controversy," *Chae Chan Ping* v. *United States*, 1889. The States have no power in the field, *The Passenger Cases*, 1849.

▲ **South of the Border** An Immigration and Naturalization Service officer patrols the Mexican border, on the watch for people entering the country illegally.

its provisions are certain to be the subject of continuing controversy.

The new law provides for a substantial increase in the number of immigrants who may enter the United States each year. As many as 700,000 are to be admitted in 1992, in 1993, and in 1994. The annual limit is set at 675,000 for 1995 and beyond.

The current law continues the family-preference policy first put in place in 1965; at least a third of those persons admitted under its terms are to be the close relatives of American citizens or resident aliens. Those immigrants who have occupational talents in short supply in the United States—notably, highly skilled researchers, engineers, and scientists—also receive special preference.

Only those aliens who can qualify for citizenship can be admitted as immigrants. The law's list of "excludable aliens"—those barred because of some personal characteristic—is extensive. Among those excluded are, for example, criminals, persons with communicable diseases, drug abusers and addicts, illiterates, and

mentally disturbed persons who might pose a threat to the safety of others.

**Deportation** Most of the civil rights set out in the Constitution are guaranteed to "persons." That term covers aliens as well as citizens. In one important respect, however, the status of aliens is altogether unlike that of citizens: Aliens may be subject to **deportation**—that is, a legal process in which aliens are legally required to leave the United States.[21]

Congress has provided that an alien may be deported on any one of several grounds. The most common today is illegal entry. Hundreds of thousands of aliens who enter with false papers, sneak in by ship or plane, or slip across the border at night are caught each year—most of them by the Border Patrol, the police arm of the Immigration and Naturalization Service. Conviction of any serious crime, federal or State, usually leads to a deportation order by the INS. In recent years several thousand aliens have been expelled on the basis of their criminal records, especially narcotics violators.

## Undocumented Aliens

No one knows just how many undocumented aliens there are in the United States today. The Census Bureau has put their number at somewhere between three and a half and five million, and the INS at four to six million. Some authorities believe that the actual figure is at least twice those estimates.

However many there are, the number of undocumented aliens is increasing by at least half

---

[21]The Supreme Court has long held that the United States has the same almost-unlimited power to deport aliens as it has to exclude them. In an early major case, the Court ruled that (1) deportation is an inherent power, arising out of the sovereignty of the United States, and (2) deportation is not criminal punishment, and so does not require a criminal trial, *Fong Yue Ting* v. *United States*, 1893. Those major points remain basic to American law. Because deportation is a civil, not a criminal matter, several constitutional safeguards (for example, with regard to bail and ex post facto laws) do not apply. As but one illustration of this: In *Immigration and Naturalization Service* v. *Lopez-Mendoza*, 1984, the Court held that illegally seized evidence, which under the exclusionary rule cannot be used in a criminal trial, can be used at a deportation hearing.

a million a year, according to the INS. Most of these undocumented persons enter the country by slipping across the Mexican or Canadian border, usually at night. Some come with forged papers. Many are aliens who entered legally, as nonimmigrants, but have now overstayed their legal welcomes.[22]

Once here, most undocumented aliens find it fairly easy to become "invisible," especially in larger cities, and the understaffed INS finds it very difficult to locate them. Even so, immigration officials have apprehended more than a million undocumented aliens in each of the last several years. Nearly all are sent home. Most go voluntarily, but some leave only as the result of formal deportation proceedings.

The presence of so many undocumented persons has raised a number of difficult problems. Those problems have grown worse over the past several years and, until recently, not much had been done to meet them.

Take, as one illustration of those many problems, this: Until 1987, it was not illegal to hire undocumented aliens. As a result approximately 3.5 million persons who now hold jobs in this country came here illegally. Some employers were more than willing to hire undocumented aliens—because many of them are willing to work for substandard wages and under substandard conditions. Hundreds of thousands of undocumented aliens have taken jobs on farms, often as laborers; thousands more have become janitors and dishwashers, or seamstresses in sweatshops, or found other menial work. The increase in population has also added stress to the public schools and welfare services of several States—most notably California, Arizona, New Mexico, Texas, and Florida.

Many groups—labor, farm, business, religious, ethnic, civil rights, and others—have been troubled and divided by the problem of undocumented aliens. Finally, after wrestling with the issue for years, Congress passed the Immigration Reform and Control Act of 1986.

In its major provisions, that statute (1) offered a legalized status—amnesty—to many undocumented aliens and (2) made it unlawful for anyone to hire undocumented aliens.

The law's amnesty program was in effect for one year. From mid-1987 to mid-1988, those who could show that they entered this country before January 1, 1982, and had lived here "in an unlawful status" since then, could ask to have their stay legalized. Those who applied successfully became temporary legal residents. After 18 months (by late 1989/early 1990) they could become permanent residents and, eventually, naturalized American citizens.[23] More than 1.75 million aliens took advantage of the law's amnesty provisions.

By law, all prospective employees must now verify their citizenship. An employer who knowingly hires undocumented aliens can be fined from $250 to as much as $10,000 for each offense and, in the case of repeat offenders, can be jailed for as long as six months.

## Section 4 Review

**1. Define:** citizen, jus soli, jus sanguinis, naturalization, alien, expatriation, denaturalization, deportation
**2.** By what two ways can a person become an American citizen?
**3.** How are individuals naturalized?
**4.** How may a person lose citizenship?
**5.** For what reasons can a person be deported?
**6.** What has Congress recently done about the undocumented aliens issue?

### Critical Thinking

**7. Drawing Conclusions** (p. 19) Why do you think the current immigration law gives special preference to immigrants who have certain occupations?

★

---

[22]Well over half of all undocumented aliens have come from Mexico; most of the others come from other Latin American countries and from Asia. A majority of the Mexicans stay here only four to six months a year, working on farms or in other seasonal jobs. Most other illegal aliens hope to remain permanently.

---

[23]The law also provides temporary resident status for up to 350,000 aliens who can show that they have lived in the United States for at least three years and that they worked in American agriculture for at least 90 days in each of those years.

# Demonstrating Reasoned Judgment

Demonstrating reasoned judgment means presenting evidence or reasoning that supports a given opinion or statement. It means being able to use your reasoning abilities to help formulate a final judgment or reach a conclusion about a piece of information.

The statement on this page about minority rights is followed by nine points of evidence that relate directly or indirectly to the statement. Use the steps below to practice using reasoned judgment about the statement and evidence.

**1. Determine the main message of the statement.** Before you can make an evaluation of a particular piece of information, you must make sure that you understand that information. Read the statement. (a) What is the statement's conclusion about the effectiveness of the 14th Amendment? (b) What is the statement's conclusion about civil rights today?

**2. Summarize the meaning of each piece of evidence.** Analyze the evidence to determine how each piece relates to the statement in question. (a) Which pieces of evidence relate directly to the subject of advances in civil rights for African Americans? (b) Which pieces relate indirectly to the topic of civil rights? (c) Which pieces provide no information about civil rights?

**3. Identify the relationship of each piece of evidence to the statement.** Consider how each piece of evidence relates to the statement. (a) In your opinion, does the evidence support the statement? (b) Based on this evidence, do you agree or disagree with the statement? (c) What additional information might you like to have to aid you in making your judgment?

**Statement:**

Despite the passage of the 14th Amendment in 1868, which guaranteed African Americans equal protection under the law, many parts of the nation instituted laws that effectively placed African Americans in an inferior status socially, politically, and educationally. Fortunately, this history of injustice toward minority groups is finally being addressed. Since the mid-1950s, this nation has made significant progress in the battle for civil rights for all citizens.

**Evidence:**

**1.** The United States armed forces were desegregated in 1948.

**2.** In 1896 the Supreme Court decided that communities could provide separate-but-equal facilities for white people and African Americans.

**3.** The United States Supreme Court declared public school segregation unconstitutional in 1954.

**4.** Between 1970 and 1990, the number of African-American elected officials in the South rose from over 500 to over 4,000.

**5.** Martin Luther King, Jr., was assassinated in Memphis, Tennessee, in 1968.

**6.** Integrated professional sports teams were first allowed to compete in Georgia in 1966.

**7.** The Civil Rights Act of 1964 was passed by the United States Congress.

**8.** In the 1960s, African Americans in many communities were unable to register to vote.

**9.** More than 28 million African Americans live in the United States.

# Chapter-in-Brief

Scan all headings, photographs, charts, and other visuals in the chapter before reading the section summaries below.

## Section 1 Diversity and Discrimination in American Society (pp. 545–549)
The United States' population is largely white. Yet in recent decades, the populations of certain minority groups have grown significantly.

Historically, white America has been reluctant to yield an equal place in society to minority groups. For example, African Americans have been the subject of unjust treatment throughout much of the nation's history. Native Americans, Hispanic Americans, and Asian Americans also have suffered discrimination.

Women, though a majority of the population, have traditionally been denied the rights enjoyed by men. These inequities are still evident, especially in the workplace.

## Section 2 Equality Before the Law (pp. 550–555)
The 5th and 14th amendments forbid government the power to draw unreasonable distinctions between classes of people. Reasonable classifications are permissible, however. If a government-made classification is challenged, the courts will determine its constitutionality via the rational basis test or, in some cases, the strict scrutiny test.

Historically, many States passed racial segregation laws. The Supreme Court allowed these laws with the separate-but-equal doctrine. The Court reversed itself in 1954, when it found in *Brown* v. *Board of Education of Topeka* that separate was inherently unequal. Since that time, the Court has found segregation in many areas unconstitutional.

The Court also has held that classifications based on gender are unconstitutional unless they can pass the strict scrutiny and rational basis tests.

## Section 3 Federal Civil Rights Laws (pp. 556–559)
Congress enacted the first in a series of civil rights laws with its passage of the Civil Rights Act of 1957. The most far-reaching of the later acts, which include civil rights acts in 1960 and 1968, is the Civil Rights Act of 1964. All of the legislation comes down to this fact: Discriminatory practices based on race, color, sex, or national origin are illegal.

The Federal Government has used affirmative action to overcome the effects of discrimination. This has been widely criticized by those who feel that it is reverse discrimination. But the Supreme Court has found that affirmative action is constitutional as long as race or gender is not the only factor in the decision and as long as evidence of longstanding and flagrant discrimination exists.

## Section 4 American Citizenship (pp. 561–567)
According to the Constitution, there are two ways to become an American citizen. Those who are born in the United States, or to a parent who is a citizen and who has lived in the United States, become citizens at birth. Others can become citizens through naturalization.

Citizens can choose to renounce their citizenship. And naturalized citizens who acquired citizenship by deception or fraud can be denaturalized.

Since the late 1800s, United States policy consisted of setting quotas for immigration from different nations. Today, the nation has no quotas, but it does have a ceiling on the number of immigrants it allows.

In 1986, Congress passed legislation to address the issue of undocumented aliens. The law offered amnesty to certain undocumented aliens and made it illegal for employers to hire undocumented aliens.

# Chapter Review

## Vocabulary and Key Terms

reservation (p. 547)
refugee (p. 549)
segregation (p. 551)
Jim Crow law (p. 551)
separate-but-equal
    doctrine (p. 552)
de jure segregation (p. 553)

de facto segregation (p. 553)
affirmative action (p. 557)
quota (p. 558)
reverse discrimination (p. 558)
citizen (p. 561)
*jus sanguinis* (p. 561)

*jus soli* (p. 561)
naturalization (p. 562)
alien (p. 562)
expatriation (p. 564)
denaturalization (p. 564)
deported (p. 566)

---

**Matching:** *Review the key terms in the list above. If you are not sure of a term's meaning, look up the term and review its definition. Choose a term from the list above that best matches each description.*

1. a person who leaves his or her home in order to escape the dangers of war, political persecution, or other causes
2. the law of the soil; a means by which one acquires citizenship
3. laws that required separate facilities for African Americans and whites
4. an act by which one forfeits citizenship
5. segregation as a result of laws

**True or False:** *Determine whether each statement is true or false. If it is true, write "true." If it is false, change the underlined word or words to make the statement true.*

1. The separation or isolation of one group from another is called <u>segregation</u>.
2. One who owes allegiance to a state and is entitled to protection by it is a <u>refugee</u>.
3. According to the concept of <u>*jus sanguinis,*</u> a person born to a parent who is an American citizen becomes a citizen him- or herself.
4. Many Native Americans today live on <u>reservations</u>.
5. The Supreme Court's decision in *Plessy* v. *Ferguson* established <u>affirmative action</u>.

**Word Relationships:** *Three of the terms in each of the following sets of terms are related. Choose the term that does not belong and explain why it does not belong.*

1. (a) Jim Crow law (b) de facto segregation (c) de jure segregation (d) separate-but-equal doctrine
2. (a) alien (b) reverse discrimination (c) affirmative action (d) quota
3. (a) naturalization (b) expatriation (c) deportation (d) denaturalization

## Main Ideas

### Section 1 (pp. 545–549)

1. What does it mean to say that the population of the United States is heterogeneous?
2. Briefly describe the trends in the composition of the population over the course of U.S. history.
3. Briefly describe the historical treatment of minority groups in the United States.
4. In what respect do women as a group resemble minority groups?

### Section 2 (pp. 550–555)

5. What kind of equality does the Constitution guarantee?
6. According to the Supreme Court, what standards must laws that discriminate between groups meet?

7. Briefly describe the history of racial segregation from the late 1800s to today.

8. Briefly describe the history of the Supreme Court's view of classifications based on gender.

### Section 3 (pp. 556–559)

9. Briefly describe the history of civil rights legislation between the 1870s and today.

10. (a) What was the major piece of civil rights legislation during the 1960s? (b) What are its major features?

11. Summarize the reasoning behind affirmative action programs. What is the main criticism of these programs?

12. Under what circumstances have affirmative action programs generally been allowed by the courts?

### Section 4 (pp. 561–567)

13. Describe the means by which people can become citizens of the United States.

14. Describe the means by which people can lose citizenship.

15. Briefly describe immigration in the United States today.

## Critical Thinking

1. **Making Comparisons** (p. 19) Recall what you read in Section 2 regarding the Supreme Court's attitude toward women. How has this attitude changed between the 1800s and today? How has society's attitude changed?

2. **Expressing Problems Clearly** (p. 19) Consider the doctrine of separate-but-equal. (a) Do you think it is possible for facilities that are segregated on the basis of race or gender to be truly equal? (b) Why or why not?

3. **Identifying Alternatives** (p. 19) Consider the process by which aliens can become naturalized United States citizens. (a) In your opinion, should this process be easier or more difficult? (b) What standards should be added or removed?

## Getting Involved

1. **Writing Your Opinion** You are to give a speech before the United Nations on the value of diversity in the American population. Before you begin writing, brainstorm a list of the benefits this nation has received as a result of its diverse population. Open your speech with a statement that expresses your opinion on the topic. Then devote one paragraph to each of the benefits you identified in your list. Conclude with a statement in which you express your hopes for the future relations between the many peoples who make up American society. Review each paragraph to ensure that your ideas are stated positively and persuasively. Correct any errors and make a final draft.

2. **Cooperative Activity** Work as a class to create a package of proposed amendments and/or legislation to address the questions of civil rights raised in this chapter. Begin by holding a class discussion to generate a list of topics for the proposed amendments and legislation. Then divide into teams to create the wording for each proposed measure. When each team has completed its work, discuss as a class the strengths and weaknesses of each idea. Then have each team incorporate the comments of the class into a final draft. Finally, collect all the proposed measures in a single civil rights package.

3. **Class Debate** Hold a classroom debate on the following topic: *Resolved,* That United States immigration policy should set no limit to the numbers of immigrants. Select teams to debate each side of this issue. The rest of the class can evaluate each team's response.

4. **Creating a Political Cartoon** Create a cartoon to illustrate one of the concepts discussed in this chapter, such as affirmative action, separate but equal, or some other idea. Remember that you can use a combination of words and images in your cartoon.

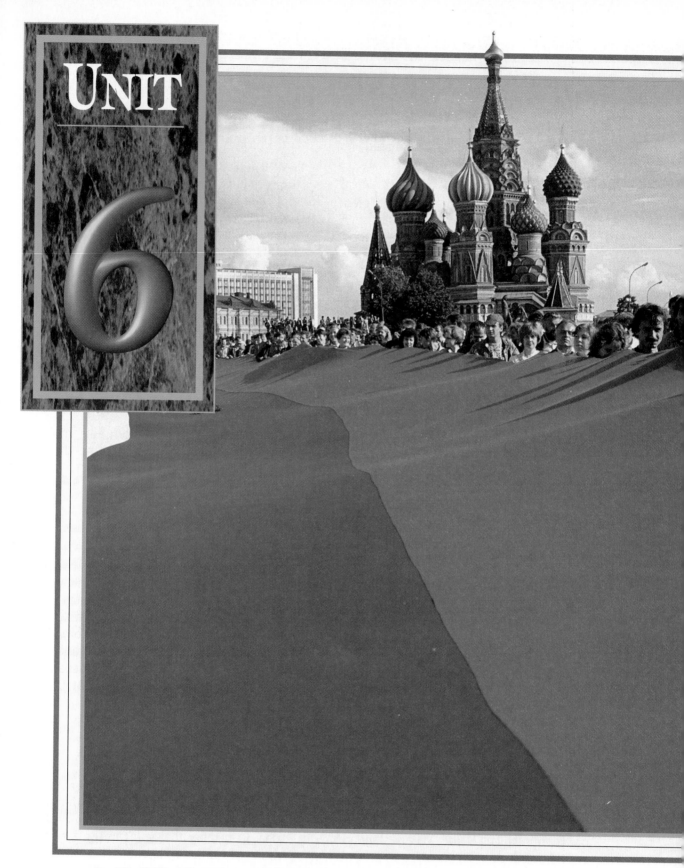

# UNIT 6

**The Will of the People** Citizens of the new state of Russia display a giant Russian flag to celebrate the end of Soviet communist rule.

# Comparative Political and Economic Systems

O n July 4, 1776, the new United States announced its independence. It proclaimed, ". . . [I]t is the Right of the People to . . . institute new Government, laying its foundations on such principles and organizing its power in such form, as to them shall seem most likely to effect their Safety and Happiness." This bold Declaration that people are the source of political power set the United States apart from every other government of its time.

Today, this concept known as popular sovereignty has spread throughout the world. In the 1990s, people in various parts of the world established almost thirty new states and changed the governments of many others. Among the new governments were many once organized along the principles of communism. In the two chapters of this unit, you will examine some of the different political and economic systems that people have formed to secure their safety and happiness.

## DID YOU KNOW THAT . . .

- Experts estimate that in the year 2100 the world's three most populous countries will be India, China, and Nigeria.

- Iraq spends six times more on its military than on health and education.

- Japan and Ireland have the lowest reported rate of murders in industrialized countries—fewer than 1 murder per 100,000 people.

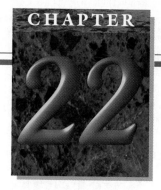

# Comparative Political Systems

## Chapter Preview

For almost 75 years the leaders of the Soviet Union told the world that their Communist system of government was superior to all others. In December 1991, however, the people of the Soviet Union voted their country out of existence. In its place they formed 15 independent, sovereign countries—including the world's largest state, Russia. Each of these states then set out to determine what political system would best serve its needs.

The 15 "new" states are not new at all. Their traditions and histories are ancient; they have merely reclaimed the right to govern themselves in their own ways. Ironically, as the Soviet Union broke up, its western neighbors in the European Community worked toward greater union—each grappling to maintain national identities within that union. In this chapter, you will learn about other similarities and differences in four of the world's political systems.

### Before you read this chapter:

- **Describe** the meaning of national identity.
- **Predict** the role of national identity in the former Soviet Union and the European Community by the year 2000.

### As you read, focus on the main objective for each section. Understand:

1. The British Parliamentary system of government.
2. The characteristics of Japan's constitutional monarchy.
3. The characteristics of Mexico's system of government.
4. The history, break-up, and future of the former Soviet Union.

▲ **Momentous Changes in the Former Soviet Union**   The Ukrainian people in this photograph are taking part in a religious ceremony. By December of 1991, this former Soviet republic had announced its independence.

# 1 Great Britain

### Find Out:

- How are the British and American governments different and alike?
- What is the role of tradition and the unwritten constitution in British government?

### Key Terms:

monarchy, by-election, coalition, minister, shadow cabinet

**B**ritish government is democratic government. So, too, is American government; its roots are buried deep in English political and social history. Yet there are important differences between the two systems of government. Most of those differences grow out of this fundamentally important point: Unlike government in the United States, government in Great Britain[1] is unitary and parliamentary in form and rests upon an unwritten constitution.

---

[1]Great Britain is, officially, the United Kingdom of Great Britain and Northern Ireland. It contains four principal parts: England, with 80 percent of the population and more than half of the land area; Wales, conquered by England in the 13th century; Scotland, joined to England and Wales by the Act of Union that created the United Kingdom in 1707; and Northern Ireland, which became part of the United Kingdom in 1800.

## The Unwritten Constitution

Actually, it is not strictly true to say that the British constitution is entirely unwritten. Parts of the constitution can be found in books and charters. However, no single document serves as the British constitution.

The written part of the British constitution includes historic charters, acts of Parliament, and innumerable court decisions. The unwritten part derives from customs and usages—practices that have gained acceptance over time. The written parts are called the law of the constitution, and the unwritten parts are called the conventions of the constitution.

**The Law of the Constitution**  Many historic documents figure in Britain's written constitution. Perhaps the best known is the Magna Carta of 1215. Others include the Petition of Right of 1628 and the Bill of Rights of 1689. (See Chapter 2, Section 1.) Each of those documents was a landmark in the centuries-long struggle to limit the powers of the English monarch and advance the concept of due process of law.

Certain acts of Parliament also form a basic part of the British constitution. One example of these is the Representation of the People Act of 1969. That act lowered the voting age in all British elections from 21 to 18. In the United States, you will recall, such a change required a formal amendment to the Constitution.[2]

Finally, court decisions are another part of the law of the constitution. Centuries of court decisions have created a body of legal rules covering nearly every aspect of human conduct. Such decisions make up the common law. (See Chapter 25, Section 3 for a discussion of the common law in the American judicial system.)

**The Conventions of the Constitution**  The truly unwritten part of the British constitution consists of the customs and practices of British politics. For example, no document says that Parliament must hold a new session each year. It just does. There are no written rules giving the lower house of Parliament the power to force the government to resign. That feature of British government developed over hundreds of years and is now a matter of custom.

**Continuity and Change**  With its open-ended constitution, Britain has a flexible set of rules that is always evolving and open to change. A majority vote in Parliament can easily remove an old provision of the constitution or add a new one. The flexibility of this system can be very useful. But without the delays and safeguards that a system such as the American system would impose, there is always the danger of ill-considered and hasty action that might fundamentally alter the people's rights.

## The Monarchy

In contrast to such republics as the United States and France, Britain has a hereditary ruler; so Great Britain is a **monarchy**. Its monarch bears the title of queen or king. While English monarchs once ruled with absolute power, their role has dwindled, and they are now little more than figureheads.[3] Because her powers and duties are controlled by Britain's unwritten constitution, Elizabeth II, Britain's queen since 1952, is known as a constitutional monarch.

In formal terms, all acts of the British government are performed in the name of the queen. As you will read shortly, however, the real power of government is exercised by the prime minister and other high officials.[4] The queen does appoint the prime minister, but her choice is subject to the approval of the House of Commons. So, traditionally, she chooses the leader of the majority party in that house to be prime

---

[2]The 26th Amendment, effective in 1971.

[3]Most present-day monarchs, especially in industrial democracies like Sweden, Norway, and Japan, are also figureheads. In the developing world, however, the monarchs of such nations as Saudi Arabia and Morocco still wield considerable power.

[4]The individual who symbolizes a nation's sovereignty is called the head of state, and the individual who directs the government, the head of government. In the United States, the President is both head of state and head of government. In Britain, the queen is head of state, and the prime minister is head of government.

minister. She has no power to dismiss the prime minister and no veto over acts of Parliament.

Today's British monarch reigns but does not rule. Nonetheless, the queen stands as a living symbol of the British state, as a focus of loyalty and pride. Periodic proposals to do away with the monarchy bring an outpouring of support for "our dear queen," although recently a movement for the queen to be required to pay taxes has been gaining support.

## Parliament

Parliament is the central institution of British government. It holds both the legislative and the executive powers of the nation—powers that in the United States are divided between separate and independent branches of government. By its legislative power, Parliament passes Britain's laws. By its executive power, it chooses some of its members (the prime minister and the cabinet) to administer the departments of government and run the nation's affairs. In the British system, as in all parliamentary systems, government is built on the fusion of powers. The government's legislative and executive authority is fused—combined—in Parliament and the prime minister and cabinet.

Parliament is bicameral; its two houses are the House of Lords and the House of Commons. Of the two, the House of Commons is by far the more powerful body.

**The House of Lords** The upper chamber, the House of Lords, is a predominantly aristocratic body of more than 1,100 members. More than 750 of its members have inherited their positions. They hold noble titles—such as duke, marquess, earl, viscount, and baron—and are known as the hereditary peers. The other members are appointed for life by the queen. They include two archbishops and 24 bishops of the Church of England, law lords (eminent judges), and some 350 life peers. The life peers are persons who have been honored for their careers in science, literature, the arts, politics, or business. Attendance at sessions of the Lords rarely exceeds 200.

The House of Lords holds no real power over legislation. If it rejects a bill passed by the

▲ **"Trooping the Color"** This term describes the annual troop inspection led by Queen Elizabeth II of Great Britain. With no voice in government, the monarch is a symbol of British history and traditions.

House of Commons, the Commons has only to approve the bill a second time, and it becomes law. The Lords can merely delay but not block a bill's passage.[5] The upper house can also amend a bill and return it to the lower house. The lower house can—and usually does—remove the amendment by a simple majority vote.

Clearly, the House of Lords does not fit the pattern of a representative democracy. Various critics have urged that it be abolished—a deed that the House of Commons could readily accomplish by passing a law. Defenders of the upper house argue that it plays a useful role, however. By delaying passage of a controversial bill, they say, it may allow tempers to cool and

---

[5]The upper house has 30 days to act on a money bill and one year to act on other bills.

give the lower house more time to weigh the full effects of a bill.

Besides its legislative role, the House of Lords does perform an important judicial function. Its nine law lords serve as the final court of appeals in both civil and criminal cases in the British court system. It is important to note that the British courts and judges, including the law lords, do not possess the power of judicial review. They cannot overrule a law or an act of government, even if they believe that it violates the constitution.

**The House of Commons** The lower house, known familiarly as the Commons, is a representative body. Its 651 members are called MPs, which stands for member of parliament. All are popularly elected from single-member districts, or constituencies, that are roughly equal in population. Currently, there are 524 constituencies in England, 38 in Wales, 72 in Scotland, and 17 in Northern Ireland.

A general election—one in which all seats in the Commons are at stake—takes place at least once every five years. Election dates are not firmly fixed. If an MP dies or resigns, a special election called a **by-election** is held in that MP's constituency to choose a replacement.[6]

The Commons meets in a small, rectangular chamber within the majestic building of Parliament. The high-ceilinged House chamber was originally designed for just 350 members. It is, quite literally, a political arena. The members of rival parties sit on facing rows of benches, talk-ing and sometimes hooting at one another.[7] An open space occupies much of the center of the chamber, with a raised chair at one end for the presiding officer (known as the speaker).[8] Leading members of the major parties sit on the front rows of benches. Those who occupy the remaining rows are known as backbenchers.

The majority party largely controls the work of the Commons. While any MP can introduce a bill, most measures are in fact offered by the prime minister and the cabinet. The prime minister and cabinet head the executive arm of British government. They form what, in the British and other parliamentary systems, is regularly called "the government"—what, in the United States, is referred to as the administration.

Up to 10 standing committees consider bills and prepare them for final consideration by the full chamber. Committees in the Commons are generalists; any committee may consider any bill. Their main task is to put measures in proper form for final floor consideration. All bills sent to committee must be reported to the floor, where a party-line vote generally follows the will of the government.

**The Prime Minister** The prime minister, although formally appointed by the queen, is in fact responsible to the House of Commons. When a single party holds a majority in the Commons, as usually happens, that party's leader becomes prime minister. If no single party holds a majority, a coalition must be formed. In this sense, a **coalition** is a temporary alliance of parties for the purpose of forming a government. Two or more parties must agree on a common choice for prime minister and on a joint slate of cabinet members.[9]

**The Cabinet** The prime minister selects the members of the cabinet. Most cabinet members, or **ministers**, are members of the House of Commons. A few may sit in the House of Lords.

---

[6]The Conservative party won their fourth straight general election in April, 1992. This has not occurred since the early 19th century. Conservatives were victorious in 336 constituencies, giving them 42 percent of the seats; compared to 271 (34 percent) for the Labour party, 20 seats (18 percent) for the Liberal Democrats, and 24 seats (6 percent) for other parties and independents. The 21 seat majority was their smallest since the Conservatives took control of the government in 1979. With Great Britain experiencing its longest economic recession since the 1930s, the Conservative majority lost two more seats in subsequent by-elections.

[7]MPs often heckle their rivals, loudly.

[8]The speaker is always a member of the House of Commons and is chosen by it. As an MP, the speaker must win reelection to the House of Commons at each general election—but the speaker always runs unopposed in those elections.

[9]Britain's last coalition government served during World War II, from 1940 to 1945. It was headed by Prime Minister Winston Churchill, a Conservative. Britain is the only parliamentary democracy in Europe that has not had a coalition government since World War II.

Collectively, the prime minister and the cabinet provide political leadership, both in the making and the carrying out of public policy. Individually, cabinet ministers head the various executive departments. One minister serves as foreign secretary—responsible for foreign affairs. Another serves as chancellor of the exchequer—responsible for finance. All told there are about 20 ministers, each with his or her own department and functions. The size of the cabinet varies from time to time, depending on the wishes of the prime minister.

The cabinet is accountable to the House of Commons. An almost daily feature of parliamentary sessions is question time, when cabinet ministers appear in the Commons to answer questions about their area of responsibility. Any MP may ask a question about any relevant subject.

The opposition parties appoint their own teams of potential cabinet members. Each of these opposition MPs shadows, or watches, one particular member of the cabinet. If an opposition party should succeed in gaining a majority, its so-called **shadow cabinet** would then be ready to run the government.

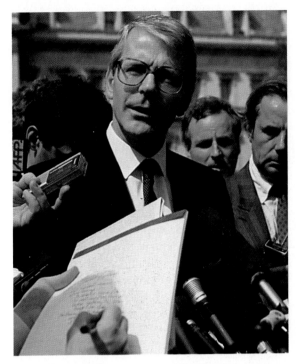

**John Major** Margaret Thatcher's successor as British prime minister leads a country with an important position in world affairs.

## Calling Elections

Britain has no fixed date for holding elections. A general election must be held at least once every five years, but one can take place at any time within that period.

The prime minister decides when a general election will occur. As a rule, elections are called at a time when conditions seem to favor the government and its candidates. If in fact they do, the prime minister's party will likely increase its majority or at the least preserve its control of the House of Commons. If they do not, the other major party may take over the government.

Occasionally, an election is triggered by quite different circumstances: when the government falls, as the result of losing the confidence, or support, of the House of Commons. Normally, a government with a clear majority of seats in the Commons has little trouble keeping that support. But the opposition can cut into the government's majority by winning a series of by-elections. Or, rarely, some majority party

MPs may become upset with their party and vote against the government.

The government is acknowledged to have lost Parliament's support if it is defeated on some critical issue in the House of Commons. When the government loses such a vote, the government falls, and the prime minister asks the queen to dissolve Parliament—end its session—and call a new general election.

In rarer instances, changes within the majority party can lead to changes in the government. This is clearly illustrated by the Conservative party infighting that led to Prime Minister Margaret Thatcher's resignation in November 1990. In the face of harsh criticism from within her Conservative party, several Conservative MPs mounted a strong challenge to her leadership. Mrs. Thatcher resigned, thus ending a period of over 11 years as the government's leader. John Major, her chancellor of the exchequer, won the balloting held by the Conservative party members of Parliament to become the party leader and the youngest prime minister in this century.

In this way, the Conservatives retained control of the government without losing a vote of confidence or risking their seats in a general election. Most of the policies that cost Margaret Thatcher her position were gradually reversed by the new government headed by John Major.

This basic feature of British parliamentary government—the ability to change governments in these ways—has great significance. It means that a prime minister who becomes either ineffective or unpopular can be put out of office before his or her actions can cause serious damage to the political system. Clearly, this feature avoids a problem sometimes found in the American system of presidential government: continuing conflict, even deadlock, between the executive and the legislative branches. But, just as clearly, the British arrangement does not allow for any system of checks and balances between those two branches.

▲ **Local Government in England** The less-populated villages dotting the English countryside are run by elected county councils.

## The Party System

Because British voters do not elect candidates for nationwide office, the focus of elections in Great Britain is more localized than in the United States. While two major parties have dominated British politics in recent decades, the local focus makes it easier for smaller parties to exist. These may represent positions on specific issues or narrow ideological stands, or they may promote the interests of nationalist groups in Wales, Scotland, and Northern Ireland. Their existence can force the major parties to address these interests, or, if a party can get seats in the House of Commons, might even force a coalition to form by denying a larger party an outright majority.

The two big British political parties are the Conservative party and the Labour party. The Conservative party draws its main support from middle- and upper-class Britons. It tends to favor private economic initiatives and the traditions of the British class system. On the other hand the Labour party appeals largely to working-class voters. It tends to favor government involvement in the economic system and a more socially equal society. In the past it has preached doctrinaire socialism. Under the current leadership of Tony Blair, however, the Labour party has moderated this approach and moved toward the mainstream of public opinion.

Another significant political party, the Social and Liberal Democratic party—popularly called "the Democrats"—also has a fairly broad base of support today. The Democrats are a centrist group that emerged in 1988, out of a merger of two older parties in British politics: (1) the Liberal party, one of the nation's two major parties until it was displaced by Labour in the 1920s, and (2) the Social Democratic party, a splinter group that broke away from the Labour party in 1981.

British parties are more highly organized and centrally directed than the major parties in American politics. High levels of party loyalty and party discipline characterize the British party system. Voter behavior clearly reflects that point. Voters in the constituencies regularly vote for candidates for the House of Commons on the basis of their party labels, not their individual qualifications.

## Local Government

Recall that Britain has a unitary form of government (see Chapter 1, Section 2). Governmental power is centralized, or held at the national level. There is no division of powers by which some powers are vested in a national government while others belong to regional or local governments, as in the American federal system.

All local governments in Great Britain are creations of Parliament. To whatever extent those governments can deliver services or do anything else, it is only because the central government has created them, given them powers, and provided the financial means to carry them out.

The structure of local government in Britain depends on population density. In more heavily settled metropolitan areas, local government is centered in popularly elected district councils. In the shire counties, elected county councils are the principal institutions of local government.

The members of the local council are chosen by the voters in their district or county for four-year terms. Each council selects its chairperson from among its own members. In districts with enough population to be a borough or a town, the chairperson of the district council is known as the mayor; in larger cities, he or she is the lord mayor (even if the office is held by a woman).

## Section 1 Review

1. **Define:** monarchy, by-election, coalition, minister, shadow cabinet
2. (a) In what sense does Britain have an unwritten constitution? (b) Describe the law of the constitution and the conventions of the constitution.
3. What is the essential role of the queen in British government today?
4. Cite three major differences between (a) the British Parliament and the U.S. Congress, and (b) the prime minister and the President.

### Critical Thinking

5. **Making Comparisons** (p. 19) What is the major difference between the British and American two-party systems?

★

# 2 Japan

**Find Out:**

- What are the characteristics of Japan's parliamentary monarchy?
- In what ways is Japan's government centrally controlled?

**Key Terms:**

National Diet, prefecture, multi-seat district, consensus, dissolution

You are likely familiar with Japan as the efficient manufacturer and marketer of consumer electronics, automobiles, and video games. It is less likely that you are aware of the island nation's[10] consciously chosen path to political and technological modernization.

In this section, you will read about the government of Japan, which like Great Britain's, is a parliamentary democracy.

## Japanese Government Before World War II

According to legend, the Japanese state was founded by the Emperor Jimmu in 660 B.C., but records indicate that it began to emerge about 1,000 years later, in the 4th century A.D. During the next 1,500 years, the country developed a political system in which territories were ruled by nobles (*daimyo*) backed by large families who owed only nominal loyalty to the imperial ruler living in the ancient city of Kyoto. Contacts with foreigners during that time were highly restricted.[11]

---

[10]Japan includes more than 2,000 islands. Its four main islands—Honshu, Hokkaido, Kyushu, and Shikoku—hold 98 percent of its land area and most of its 125 million people.

[11]Dutch and Portuguese traders had some contacts with the Japanese in the 16th and 17th centuries. The country was not opened to any meaningful Western contacts until 1853, however, when a U.S. naval squadron made a polite but firm visit. Japan and the United States concluded a commercial treaty the following year, and the Japanese then negotiated similar agreements with other Western powers.

**Yesterday and Today**   Japan's countryside remains much the same as it was in the days of the *daimyo*, Emperor Meiji, and the *samurai*, but 80 percent of Japan's population lives in crowded cities like Tokyo (right).

Japan freed itself in 1868 from the rule of a repressive military dictator, ending centuries of feudalism. An oligarchy of nobles backed by the legitimacy of Emperor Meiji then began a series of rapid changes. They openly studied and adopted Western forms, and rapidly pushed the country from isolation on the edge of Asia to an important position among the modern industrial nations.

As its industry grew and rights of suffrage spread to more of the population, the nation sought to secure the requirements for continued growth through the conquest of eastern Asia. The close partnership of the dominant political and economic elites gave rise to a form of fascism and militarism that pushed the Japanese into war with the United States, resulting in Japan's defeat at the end of World War II.

Japan was occupied by the United States for nearly seven years following the war, from 1945 to 1952. The occupation forces rewrote the country's old constitution and removed over 200,000 people from the top ranks of the military, the bureaucracy, and the major business conglomerates. The nation's remarkable postwar economic recovery was begun during the occupation and so, too, was the development of its present political system. Today, Japan is the leading democracy and the leading economic power in the largely undemocratic non-Western world.

## The Constitution

The rewritten Constitution of 1947 made the government into a more effective parliamentary system. Suffrage was given to all citizens over the age of 20. The parliament, or **National Diet**, was formed with two, fully elected chambers. The larger, more powerful House of Representatives became the body from which the prime minister and cabinet were to be selected.

Unlike the British system, the judiciary has independent powers, and the Japanese Supreme Court can rule on the constitutionality of legislation. The powers of local government were increased and the top positions were made elective. The constitution contains quite an extensive listing of basic freedoms—in effect, a bill of rights.

Also part of the constitution is a unique anti-military clause. The clause says that the Japanese people "forever renounce war as a sovereign right of the nation." It adds: "Land, sea, and air forces, as well as other war potential, will never be maintained."

United States officials insisted on the clause because they feared a revival of Japanese militarism. Later, they began to see Japan as an ally in the cold war. With encouragement from the United States, Japanese leaders since 1954 have given the clause a broad interpretation. They say that it rules out an army, a navy, and an air force, but not a so-called self-defense force. Thus, Japan has rebuilt its three military arms, calling them "ground, maritime, and air self-defense forces."

Also under the constitution, the Japanese emperor serves as the symbol of the state and the unity of the people. But, the emperor has no power to govern.

## The National Diet

Under its constitution, Japan's National Diet is considered the highest organ of state power. The Diet contains an upper house, called the House of Councilors, and a lower house, called the House of Representatives. As in Britain, the lower house wields the greater power.

The prime minister and at least half of all Japan's cabinet ministers must be members of the Diet. Usually the prime minister comes from the lower house.

**House of Councilors**  The House of Councilors has prestige but little power. Its 252 members sit for six years, in staggered terms. Three-fifths of the members are elected from districts that are based on Japan's **prefectures**—the 47 political subdivisions into which Japan is divided. The remaining two-fifths of the seats are elected by the nation as a whole. Because it has fewer responsibilities than the lower house, the House of Councilors tends to serve an essentially deliberative, advisory role.

**House of Representatives**  The House of Representatives has many important powers. It makes, and can also break, the prime minister. By a vote of no confidence, the House can force the prime minister either to resign or to dissolve the House of Representatives and call an early election. In addition, the lower house has full power to make treaties, raise funds, and make appropriations. On other matters, bills must be passed by both the lower and upper houses. But the lower house can override a negative vote in the upper house by passing a bill for a second time, by a two-thirds majority.

There are now 500 seats in the lower house. The country is divided into 300 single-member districts, and the voters in each of those relatively small constituencies choose one house member. The nation is also divided into 11 **multi-seat districts**, with voters in each electoral district choosing more than one representative. The voters in those much larger constituencies fill the other 200 seats. Representatives serve for four years—or less, if the house is dissolved and new elections are held.

**Consensus Politics**  The atmosphere in both houses of the National Diet is sedate compared to that in the legislative bodies in Britain and the United States. Japanese society places great stress on avoiding confrontation. Therefore, politicians seek to reach **consensus**—broad agreement—on issues. A political majority tries to avoid pushing through a bill against strong opposition. Nearly all of the more important measures enacted by the Diet are first introduced by the government.

## Prime Minister and Cabinet

The prime minister and the cabinet perform the executive functions of government in the Japanese governmental system. The cabinet members serve as heads of major departments.

## Japan's Annual GDP*

| Year | Percent Change in GDP* from Previous Year |
|------|-------------------------------------------|
| 1980 | 3.6% |
| 1985 | 5.0% |
| 1990 | 4.8% |
| 1991 | 4.0% |
| 1992 | 1.3% |
| 1993 | −0.5% |
| 1994 | 0.5% |
| 1995 | 2.3% |

*GDP, gross domestic product, is the total market value of all goods and services produced within a country during a given period, usually a year. Minus sign indicates decline.

*Source: Statistical Abstract of the United States.*

▲ **Interpreting Tables** Japan's bureaucracy, especially its Ministry of Trade and Industry, has played a large part in the country's economic success. Based on the table, what appears to have occurred in the Japanese economy during the early 1990s? How does this compare with the United States economy during the same time period?

Those members of the cabinet who are not members of Parliament are usually borrowed from the bureaucracy, an important part of the political system of which you will read shortly.

Voting to choose a prime minister takes place within the party and usually along party or factional lines. (Some parties are divided into factions.) The prime minister thus represents the majority party or a majority coalition within the House of Representatives.

The prime minister appoints the members of the cabinet. Membership in the cabinet is considered a great honor, and appointment may be a reward for faithful service to the prime minister. Under a system known as collective responsibility, cabinet members are considered to act as a group. A member who is for some reason unable to support a cabinet decision usually resigns from office.

The prime minister has the power to dissolve the House of Representatives, but not the House of Councilors. This step, called **dissolution**, leads to immediate elections in which voters select a new House.

## The Bureaucracy

The large Japanese bureaucracy, or civil service, enjoys unusual respect within Japanese society. It also wields great power. Top members of the bureaucracy are technocrats, or experts in technical and administrative affairs. They include many of the leading graduates of the nation's top universities, who compete to win civil service positions. Jobs in the bureaucracy do not pay as well as many private sector jobs do, and most of them demand long hours, as well. Still, those jobs are highly prized by Japanese who want to serve the public and/or seek the prestige of civil service rank.

Japan's vast bureaucracy developed under the old imperial oligarchy, before World War II, as a succession of emperors sought to modernize the nation as rapidly as possible. The bureaucracy undertook many tasks in that era—in the economic as well as administrative arena. Today, it plays a key role in Japan's economy. The Ministry of Trade and Industry helps coordinate the plans and strategies of dozens of large Japanese firms. The close relationship between the public and the private sectors of Japanese society is a key reason why Japan has been able to build one of the world's most dynamic capitalist economies.

## The Party System

Japan has a multi-party system. Until quite recently, that system was regularly dominated by one of its several parties, the Liberal Democratic party (LDP). Despite that word "liberal" in its title, the LDP is a party of the right and follows generally conservative policies. From its formation in 1955 on to 1993, the LDP furnished all of Japan's prime ministers, although at times it had to rule in coalition with another party.

A series of bribery and other scandals rocked the LDP in the late 1980s and early 1990s, and the government of Prime Minister Kiichi Miyazawa lost a vote of confidence in the House of Representatives in June of 1993. In the general election campaign that followed, many younger members of the LDP, who had pressed for reforms that the older leadership of the party would not accept, left the LDP. They either formed new parties or joined other, established groups. Chief among the groups to which they turned were the newly created Japan Renewal party (JRP) and New Japan party (JNP) and the established *Komeito* (Clean Government) party.

In the general election, which was held in July of 1993, the LDP won 223 seats in the Diet's lower house—far short of the majority needed to control that body. The Japan Socialist party (JSP), which draws most of its strength from the nation's large labor unions, won 70 seats. The JRP elected 55 of its candidates, the Komeito 51, and the JNP 35. The other seats were split among a number of other minor parties and 30 independent candidates.

A seven-party coalition, which the LDP refused to join, formed a new government in August of 1993. That very shaky partnership struggled through several months of chaos, and two prime ministers, before it fell in early 1994.

The present government emerged out of yet another coalition formed in June of 1994. It is headed by Japan's first socialist prime minister, Tomiichi Murayama, and is mostly a fragile partnership among unlikely bedfellows: the LDP, the Socialists, and a handful of independent members of the House of Representatives.

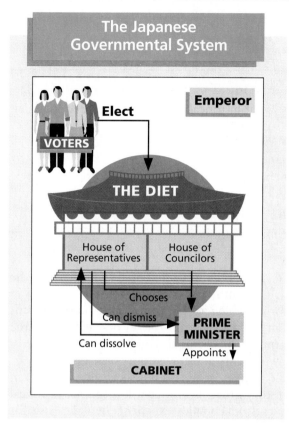

▲ **Interpreting Charts** Japan has a constitutional monarchy. In what way does this chart indicate that the emperor has no real power?

## The Courts

Japan has an independent judicial system patterned on the American model—with trial courts at the local level, several intermediate appellate courts, and a Supreme Court. The courts hold the power of judicial review—the power to determine the constitutionality of laws passed by the Diet.

The Supreme Court has seldom struck down an act of the Diet. It has three times found the apportionment of seats in the Diet to be unconstitutional, however. By the Court's reckoning, votes cast in many lightly populated rural districts were worth four to five times as much as votes cast in many densely populated urban districts. It was to those decisions that the Diet responded in 1994, by providing that 200 of the 500 seats in its lower house were to be filled by proportional representation.

# Section 2 Review

1. **Define:** National Diet, prefecture, multi-seat district, consensus, dissolution
2. What is one similarity and one difference between the Japanese constitution and the United States Constitution?
3. What exclusive powers does the Japanese House of Representatives hold?
4. What is collective responsibility?
5. What role does the bureaucracy play in the Japanese economy?

**Critical Thinking**

6. **Recognizing Cause and Effect** (p. 19) In what ways is World War II the most significant event in modern Japanese political history?

★

# 3 Mexico

**Find Out:**

- What historical events led to the development of the Mexican system of government?
- What is the structure of Mexico's federal government?
- How does the dominance of a single political party affect government in Mexico?

**Key Term:**

nationalization

Mexico, the United States' neighbor to the south, has a political system that is, in form, influenced by its modeling on the American political system. But in operation, it is the product of a unique combination of Mexico's own history and the cultural makeup of its people. While Americans tend to think of Mexican history in terms of only a few specific historical events, its complex experience sets the basis for the system that exists today.

## Mexico's Early Political History

The first evidence of important civilization in Mexico dates back to 1200 B.C. But Mexico is most commonly associated with the rich and complex Aztec civilization that gave way to Spanish colonialism in 1521 after Cortés defeated the Aztec emperor Cuauhtemoc in the battle of Tenochtitlán. During the next three centuries Spanish territorial claims expanded into North and South America. However, constant border disputes with England, France, and the newly independent United States seriously reduced Spain's area of domination by the early 19th century.

**Independence from Spain** Meanwhile, generations of Spaniards in Mexico intermixed with the native peoples, giving rise to a colonial elite with its own unique mestizo culture. Because of the decline of the Spanish empire and the conflicts over succession to the Spanish throne that followed, the Mexicans were able to declare their independence from Spain in 1821, establishing a monarchy with an elected emperor.

The Mexican monarchy lasted only two years before General Antonio López de Santa Anna deposed the emperor and set up a democratic republic with a constitution adopted in 1824. However, this republic was democratic only in the narrowest sense since most of the population, especially the Native Americans, could not participate.

Mexico's first constitution set the framework for dealing with several key issues and questions in the Mexican system: Should there be a centralized or federal government? How much power should a single political leader have? How could Mexico remain independent from its powerful neighbor to the north and other major world powers?

Over the next 100 years these issues appeared, disappeared, and reappeared with regularity in Mexican politics. Mexico experienced dictatorships and reform movements, one of which led to a revised constitution in 1857. There were periods of foreign invasion and interference as well as internal wars and revolution. Yet throughout this century of conflict, democratic reformers were able to gain political power at crucial times. The reformers reasserted the principles of Mexican independence and constitutional representative government.

In the early years of the 20th century, significant changes based on democratic principles occurred when a reform movement called the Regeneration Group and a leader named Venustiano Carranza sparked a revolution. They removed the dictatorship of Porfirio Diaz and oversaw the writing of the Constitution of 1917.

**The Constitution of 1917** The Mexican Constitution of 1917 was in many respects an updating of the document written in 1857. In fact, many of the features of the constitutions of 1824 and 1857 were included in the new document. The new constitution, however, created a system in which the government played a more active role in promoting the quality of Mexican social, economic, and cultural life. The rights of previously excluded portions of the population are also specified.

▲ **Interpreting Political Art: Multicultural Awareness** This mural, painted by Mexican artist Diego Rivera in 1927, shows Mexican peasants planting the seeds that led to the country's 1910 revolution.

## Mexico's Three Branches of Government

Like the United States, the Mexican Constitution sets up three independent branches of government—the executive led by the president, the legislature composed of two houses, and the judicial.

**The President** The president is the chief executive and is directly elected to a six-year term. The president has the power to appoint a cabinet and the attorney general, the top leadership of the

military, and the judges of the federal courts. The president also has the power to propose constitutional amendments, which must be approved by two-thirds of the Congress and a majority of the state legislatures.

An important feature of the executive office is the constitutional rule preventing the president from being elected to successive terms. The intent of the rule is to prevent the possibility of a popular leader becoming a forceful dictator by continual reelection. While presidents cannot remain in office indefinitely, they do have considerably more power than a simple description of constitutional details suggests. This power comes from certain unique features of the Mexican political party system that you will read about in the pages ahead.

**The Congress** The Mexican Congress is a bicameral body with a Senate and a Chamber of Deputies.

There are 64 senators, two from each of the 31 Mexican states and two from the Federal District, which includes Mexico City. Senators are elected to six-year terms. The senators' terms are staggered so that half are elected at the time of the presidential election and half at a mid-term election three years later.

The Chamber of Deputies has 500 members. The deputies are elected to three-year terms

and they cannot be reelected. Three hundred of the deputies are directly elected from districts of approximately 200,000 people. The rest of the seats are filled from the ranks of the various political parties based on the percentage of the total vote each receives in the national election. Thus, the Chamber of Deputies is elected on a mixed system of direct and proportional representation.[12]

The Congress meets from September 1 to December 31 each year. When it is not in session, a permanent committee of 15 deputies and 14 senators serves to approve presidential actions. Overall, because of their short sessions and the term limitations that produce a high rate of turnover, the Mexican Congress has far less power in governing the country than does the United States Congress.

**The Court System** The Mexican judicial system is very similar to that in the United States. Although appointed by the political leadership, the judiciary is independent. Two systems of courts—the state and the federal—operate within Mexico's federal system. Each has its own separate jurisdiction.

The federal court system contains layers of circuit courts with federal district courts below. At the top is the Mexican Supreme Court. These courts have the power to judge cases that bear on federal law. In addition, they decide on constitutional issues. Each state court system has civil and criminal courts that are overseen by a Superior Court of Justice.

## Political Parties

The Mexican national identity and independence from foreign domination are important ongoing themes in its national politics. These themes are woven throughout the country's his-

▲ **National Palace, Mexico City** Mexico's three branches of government mirror those in the United States. This building contains the presidential and other executive offices of the Mexican government.

[12]The proportional representation system was added to the constitution in 1963 in order to promote the existence of opposition parties. This maintains the democratic nature of the Mexican system. Each registered political party getting a minimum of 2.5 percent of the national vote is entitled to one seat in the Chamber of Deputies for every 1/2 percent it received, to a maximum of 20 seats.

tory—in its precolonial past, the revolution against Spain, and the **nationalization**—governmental acquisition of private industry for public use—of the oil industry in 1938.

Although the Mexican party system is a multiparty system, like the Japanese arrangement, it has been dominated for decades by one powerful and successful force: the Institutional Revolutionary party (PRI). The PRI has controlled the government and politics of Mexico for more than 65 years. Its domination has been so complete that its presidential candidate has won every election since the party was first organized in 1929.

In 1928 General Alvaro Obregon was elected to succeed Plutarco Elias Calles as president. But Obregon, who had been President from 1920 to 1924, was assassinated before he could take office again. The turmoil surrounding that event persuaded President Calles to remain in office and, in 1929, he and other leaders of the day formed the National Revolutionary party (PRN). That group became the PRI in 1946.

The PRI began to take its present shape in the mid-1930s, under the leadership of President Lazaro Cardenas del Rio. Cardenas, who became president in 1934, presided over an extensive redistribution of land to the peasantry and, in 1938, he restructured the PRN on the basis of four major groups in Mexican society: the peasants, organized labor, the military, and the popular sector (the middle class and professionals). In 1938 Cardenas also nationalized—seized—the assets of all United States oil companies in Mexico—thus ensuring his place as a hero of Mexican nationalism.

The overall shape of the PRI in the years since Cardenas—and that means, then, the overall shape of Mexican politics over the past fifty years, has been away from the party's traditional labor base toward business and the popular sector.

The PRI's dominant role in Mexican politics was seriously threatened in the 1980s. The government had borrowed heavily from foreign lenders in the 1970s, on the expectation that oil prices would remain at their then-high levels. When oil prices declined sharply worldwide, the nation was plunged into economic chaos. Debt problems led to severe cutbacks in government

▲ **Mexican Pride** President Ernesto Zedillo, a member of the PRI, hails the public from Zocalo Plaza in Mexico City.

programs. Prices soared and investment capital fled the country.

The political consequences of that economic calamity were apparent in the elections of 1988. Although economic conditions had begun to improve, the PRI made its worst showing ever. Its presidential candidate, Carlos Salinas de Gortari, did win, and the party kept its solid hold on both houses of Congress. But its electoral margins were narrow—and it is generally agreed that many of the claims of election fraud were valid.

President Salinas pursued broad-based economic, social, and electoral reforms during his six-year term. He also negotiated the North American Free Trade Agreement (NAFTA) with the United States and Canada. That pact, ratified in 1993, has already produced a marked increase in trade between the United States and Mexico.

The most recent national elections, held in 1994, were monitored by thousands of foreign observers and were comparatively fraud-free. The PRI's presidential candidate, Ernesto Zedilla Ponce de Leon, won just over 50 percent of the total vote. The conservative National Action party (PAN) took nearly 27 percent of the vote and the leftist Democratic Revolutionary party (PDR) 17 percent. The PRI also won 278 of the 300 races for seats in the House of Deputies and all of the 32 Senate contests on the ballot. After the election, the remaining 200 seats in the lower house were distributed—divided according to their respective percentages of all of the votes cast—among, altogether, nine political parties.

The growing strength of the opposition to the PRI and the spreading appeal of the National Action party make it almost certain that the era of near-complete domination by the PRI is nearly over. But, at least for now, that party remains in firm control of Mexican government and politics, at the state and local levels as well as nationally.

## Local Government

Mexico is divided into 31 states and one Federal District of Mexico City. Each state is an autonomous unit with its own constitution. The state governments are headed by governors who are elected by direct popular election every six years. Each state also has a unicameral legislature with two classes of members who are directly elected. The deputies, like those at the national level, serve for three-year terms. The state senators serve for four-year terms.

Within the states, Mexico's political and economic organization is based on the principal of free municipalities. Thus, local government in Mexico is more like the United States than in highly centralized governmental systems such as Great Britain and France.

### How to Obtain a U.S. Passport

**1. Complete a passport application form.** You can pick up and submit this application at federal passport agencies, many local courthouses, and authorized post offices. (For the nearest federal passport agency, check the Federal Government listings in the telephone book under "State Department.")

**2. Submit the application form.** Include the following items:

- Proof of citizenship
  This can be in the form of:
  a) a previous US passport
  b) a certified birth certificate
  c) a naturalization certificate
- Two forms of current identification, one of which must bear your photograph or physical description, signature, and show an issue or expiration date.
- Two photographs, which must have been taken within the last six months, and must measure 2"x 2". The photo must be a full face shot with a plain white background.

**3. Pay the passport fee.** The following fees are applicable as of December, 1991:

- Under age 18: $40 (valid for five years)
- Over age 18: $65 (valid for ten years)

**4. Wait for your application to be processed.** The processing time for passport applications varies. You should apply for your passport well in advance of your proposed travel date.

▲ **Interpreting Charts**   Follow the steps given above on how to obtain an American passport. Identify two reasons why a person might not be eligible for a passport.

## Section 3 Review

1. **Define:** nationalization
2. What type of events did Mexico experience in its first century after gaining independence from Spain?
3. In what ways are the three branches of Mexican government similar to those in the United States?
4. How does the political control of the PRI affect the balance of power between the executive branch and the legislative branch of government?

**Critical Thinking**

5. **Drawing Conclusions** (p. 19) (a) Can a country where one political party remains in continuing power truly be called democratic? (b) Use the examples of Japan and Mexico to support your answer.

★

## Supporting Human Rights

They can be so basic as to be necessary, such as the right to shelter and food. They can be denied by governments that are totalitarian dictatorships, that practice torture, that imprison people for their beliefs. "They" are human rights.

Although there are many ways of campaigning for human rights, each effort begins the same way—with an awareness of even one small aspect of this broad issue. It is awareness—and inspiration—that is the theme of the Reebok Human Rights Awards, presented annually by the Massachusetts-based sports shoe manufacturer, Reebok International, Ltd.

At the fourth annual awards ceremony in Boston in 1991, Reebok's chairman described the awards as "a way of combining a passion for young people and a commitment for human rights." The chairman introduced the keynote speaker, Jimmy Carter, as "the president who will be remembered for human rights."

Special awards were presented posthumously to the parents of three men who died within minutes of each other on the streets of Moscow in August 1991. What tragic chain of events links Dmitri Alexandrovich Komar, 22; Ilya Maratovich Krichevsky, 28; and Vladimir Alexandrovich Usov, 37, in the spirit of human rights?

For four tense days that August, the Soviet Union's hard road to democracy was gravely threatened when a hard-line group deposed leader Mikhail Gorbachev and refused to allow Russian President Boris Yeltsin and other officials to leave the parliament building in Moscow.

When tanks loyal to the junta converged outside the building, a human barrier formed in a spirit of solidarity with Yeltsin and the parliament under siege. Komar, a decorated veteran, entered one of the tanks in an attempt to persuade the crew to stop threatening civilians. He was shot and dragged behind the tank until Usov tried to free his body. Usov was shot for this act of courage. When a horrified spectator, Krichevsky, screamed at the tank crew to stop the violence, he was shot as well.

The unarmed victims were strangers in life, but are joined in death by their brave commitment to human rights. On receiving the Reebok award on Usov's behalf, his father said: "Each of our children made a statement and gave their lives for humanity."

The Reebok award recipients come from many parts of the world. Besides the young Russians, the 1991 honorees included 11-year-old Ashley Black of Marlboro, New Jersey, who led a petition drive to stop video games "that teach hate and bigotry"; and 24-year-old Carlos Toledo of Guatemala for his work in Covenant House, an organization that works to protect and shelter street children.

### Getting Involved

**1. Identify** a human rights abuse in your local community or the global arena. If you need to do research, your local library would be an ideal place. There, you could consult your local newspaper, various daily papers and news magazines, and books on the subject.

**2. Formulate** a plan for organizing volunteer efforts to help remedy this problem and identify resources that could be used in your plan.

**3. Predict** any problems or objections you might encounter in implementing your plan.

# 4 The Russian Federation and the End of the Soviet Union

**Find Out:**

- How did the reforms of Mikhail Gorbachev lead to the end of Soviet communist government?
- How did the role of the Communist party change in Soviet politics?
- How was the former Soviet government organized?

**Key Terms:**

*perestroika*, *glasnost*, purge, Supreme Soviet, interim government, Politburo

In August 1991 Soviet President Mikhail Gorbachev was vacationing in the Crimea when a group of Communist party leaders placed him under arrest. These party leaders

▲ **Freedom Fighters: Moscow**   A hard-line military coup, intending to remove the existing Soviet government, lasted just four days in August 1991.

objected to the democratic reforms that Gorbachev had begun in the communist government of the Soviet Union. They wanted a return to the policies of the old Soviet communist government. When the Soviet public heard of the attempted coup, protesters took to the streets, and popularly elected office holders, Russian Republic President Boris Yeltsin prominent among them, denounced this coup d'etat. The world anxiously awaited what would happen next. After several tense and uncertain days, the conspirators surrendered. Their coup had failed.

In the aftermath, extraordinary changes began occurring in this once monolithic political system. Gorbachev, whom some accused of conspiring with the coup's leadership, was politically weakened and had to fight for power with Yeltsin and other parliamentary opponents over the nation's future course. Boris Yeltsin became the major proponent of a sweeping, radical economic reform plan. And in November 1991, the parliament granted him complete control over the implementation of his plan. As leader of the largest, most dominant republic in the Soviet Union, and with this mandate from parliament, Yeltsin's power overshadowed that of Gorbachev. In recognition of that reality, the man whose bold efforts brought previously unimaginable changes in the communist superpower resigned on December 25, and within hours the Soviet Union was disbanded.

What emerged was a loose confederation of 10 of the 15 former Soviet republics[14], calling itself the Commonwealth of Independent States (CIS). While each republic retained the sovereignty associated with an independent country, they intended to work together in certain trade and military interests. But after several meetings to resolve differences, the attempted dominance by the Russian Republic in conflict with the determined nationalism of the other members effectively destroyed the grouping which had been so much a part of world affairs for seventy years.

## The Changing Soviet Government

There were three distinct periods of Soviet government: (1) a totalitarian communist dictatorship,

(2) a reform-minded communist government attempting to become more open and less repressive, and (3) the dissolution of the Soviet Union and the emergence of the Russian Republic moving rapidly toward a political democracy with a market economy.

The first period of Soviet government began with the communist revolution of 1917 and the emergence of the Communist party of the Soviet Union (the CPSU), which ruled the country with an iron fist.

The second period, which began in the mid-1980s, followed Mikhail Gorbachev's leadership. His program of *perestroika*, the restructuring of political and economic life, attempted the fundamental alteration of the political system. The many and far-reaching changes that he put in place were illustrated by *glasnost*, the policy of "openness" that included the government's expanded tolerance of dissent and freedom of expression. But the many and often far-reaching changes that Gorbachev initiated appeared to have embodied incompatible goals—establishing a democratic and open system of government while preserving the communist system. Gorbachev's program of trying to nurture political and economic reforms while preserving the Communist party and the Soviet bureaucracy and the elites they supported may have been impossible from the start.

The third period of Soviet government began with the failed coup of August 1991 and continues today in the internal politics of the Republic of Russia following the dissolution of the Soviet Union. Whether Boris Yeltsin is successful in reforming the Russian political and economic system is a key question in the world today.

No one can forecast the eventual outcome of the struggles in Russia, but examining the Soviet system as it existed and as it is changing will help you to understand two powerful lessons about government: No political system is immune from change or collapse; and political change is rarely a straight, smooth, or easy path.

<hr />

[14]The former Soviet republic of Georgia never officially joined the new commonwealth, and Azerbaijan voted against joining in late 1992. The Baltic republics of Estonia, Lithuania, and Latvia had declared their independence earlier in 1991.

" GORBACHEV'S GOING TOO FAST! "

By permission of Doug Marlette and Creators Syndicate.

▲ **Interpreting Political Cartoons**  Soviet President Gorbachev's mission was to undo the legacy of Marxist-Leninism, or communism. What does the cartoon say about this policy?

## A Political History of the Soviet Union

The Soviet Union—once known officially as the Union of Soviet Socialist Republics—was the world's largest country in area. In the immediate aftermath of the 1991 coup, it still occupied one-sixth of all of the land surface of the earth.

The Soviet Union was the modern successor to the czarist Russian empire, which began to emerge in the 15th century and was formally established by Peter the Great in 1721. The Russian empire was ruled by a succession of tyrannical czars.

Heavy losses in the Russo-Japanese War of 1904–1905 and then in World War I began the collapse of czarist rule, and the empire was destroyed in the first of two revolutions in 1917. In March, scattered, spreading strikes and riots forced Czar Nicholas II to quit his office. Out of that first revolution came a short-lived attempt at democratic government. However, that government was overthrown on November 7, 1917—and out of that second coup, led by Vladimir Ilyich Lenin, the Communist party came to power.

Until 1991, the Soviet Union was composed of 15 regional units, the constituent republics, each of them inhabited by a major nationality group. The largest and most important of the constituent republics was the Russian Soviet Federal Socialist Republic—the RSFSR or, simply, Russia. It included more than 70 percent of the land area of the Soviet Union and contained more than half its population.[15]

**Lenin** Lenin was the architect of what became the Soviet Union. He began the task of transforming an ancient, tradition-bound, underdeveloped country into the world's first communist state. Lenin constructed a complex government with several layers of elected soviets, or councils. There were soviets at the factory level, farm level, city level, and regional and national levels. Despite that elaborate and representative structure, major policy decisions were made at the top by the Communist party leadership and passed down through the soviets.

**Stalin** Lenin's death in 1924 prompted a fierce struggle for power among his topmost lieutenants, and out of that conflict Josef Stalin emerged as the new Soviet leader.[16] Stalin consolidated his power over the next several years in a series of **purges**—the ruthless elimination of rivals and other dissidents.[17] By the mid-1930s Stalin had become, for all practical purposes, a dictator.

Under Stalin, the Soviet dictatorship began an intensive industrialization program and forced collectivization of the nation's agriculture. Farmers, workers, and others who resisted were imprisoned, shot, or sent to forced labor camps. At the appalling cost of millions of lives, Stalin was able to build the Soviet Union into a major industrial and military power.

---

[15]Ethnic Russians, who live mainly in the RSFSR, dominated the political and cultural life of the Soviet Union. But the nation contained millions of non-Russian peoples. The Soviet Union was made up of more than 100 distinct ethnic groups, speaking at least 100 different languages.

[16]Stalin was born Iosif Vissarionovich Dzhugashvili in 1879. He served as one of Lenin's closest aides and adopted the name Stalin (man of steel) some time before the revolution.

[17]Technically, a "purge" is a purification. Stalin "purified" the party and government by having his rivals—and millions of other dissidents—jailed, exiled, or executed in the 1930s and 1940s.

World War II brought a severe test of Stalin's leadership. Nazi Germany invaded the Soviet Union in mid-1941 and quickly seized control of most of European Russia. The Soviets suffered enormous casualties; at least 20 million Soviet citizens were killed during World War II. Finally, by early 1945, with the help of huge amounts of American aid, Soviet armies drove the Germans out of Eastern Europe.

At war's end, the Soviet Union was in control of all of Eastern Europe; and it had become one of the world's two superpowers, rivaling the United States in military power. Immediately, Stalin began the rebuilding of the nation's war-torn industry and agriculture. He also launched the aggressive foreign policy actions that soon brought on the cold war.

**Soviet Leaders After Stalin** Josef Stalin died in 1953, and Nikita Khrushchev became the leader of the Soviet Union. Under him the country began the process of "de-Stalinization." The levels of brutality and repression that had stained the Stalin era were diminished.

Khrushchev and later leaders did not hold the kind of absolute power that Stalin had. However, the person holding the positions of party chairman and Soviet premier exerted considerable control over Soviet society.

## Gorbachev

Mikhail S. Gorbachev took control of the CPSU in 1985. From his first days in power, he pushed *perestroika*—his plan for the economic and political restructuring of the Soviet Union.

Like many others both within and outside his country, Gorbachev had long been aware of a number of major problems in the Soviet system. Among the most troublesome were:

— a rigid, inflexible government, burdened by slow-moving processes and an unresponsive bureaucracy.

— foreign and domestic policies too deeply rooted in the past and too tightly controlled by a small group of aging leaders.

— a stagnant economy plagued by widespread shortages of food, housing, and other consumer goods and by outmoded, inefficient, and unproductive workplaces.

— tension among the various ethnic groups, each having a base within one of the republics, for greater national autonomy.

Originally, Gorbachev saw *perestroika* as a policy for changing the economy. His early efforts at economic reform made little headway, however—mostly because of (1) opposition from entrenched bureaucracies in the party and the government and (2) the apathetic reactions of an unconvinced Soviet people. So, the general secretary concluded, political reform had to come first.[18]

In 1988 Gorbachev put several proposals for major change in the Soviet political system before the party's central committee. He then submitted those same proposals to the **Supreme Soviet**, the national legislature. His reforms were promptly adopted by the party and the Supreme Soviet.

**The Consequences of Reform**   The Soviet Union's influence over its communist neighbors declined markedly as the reforms of *perestroika* and *glasnost* progressed. In the late 1980s it watched as Solidarity, a democratic workers' movement, unseated Poland's communist government and as other Eastern-bloc countries that had once been directly under Moscow's control made overtures to the West.

In the closing months of 1989 a wave of independence swelled across Eastern Europe, sweeping aside even the most hardline communist governments such as East Germany and Romania. National independence movements in the Baltic Soviet republics of Lithuania, Latvia, and Estonia strengthened as the democratization of Eastern Europe took hold. By the middle of 1990, the large and powerful republics of Russia, Ukraine, and Byelorussia, joined by the Baltic republics and several smaller republics, had declared independence from the Soviet central authority. The newly elected president of the Russian Republic, Boris Yeltsin, further challenged the government and Gorbachev's leadership by resigning from the Communist party and having the laws of the Russian Republic declared sovereign over its population and territory.

---

[18]The economic aspects of *perestroika* are discussed in the next chapter.

### The Effect of the End of Communism on Soviet Youth

**Natalie Koulik,** a student in Richmond, Virginia, and a native of St. Petersburg in Russia.

"As a teen-ager, I was forced to join Komsomol, the Young Communist League. In the old days, I would not have passed my college entrance examinations if I had not been a member of the league. Only three years ago campus life at universities was controlled by Komsomol. But the Party has lost the support of Russian youth; its membership has plummeted from 100 percent to 10 percent. . . . *Glasnost* and *perestroika* inspired Russian youth to break from Communist party control."

Events had moved beyond Gorbachev's control. He wavered between siding with the hardline communists, who wanted reforms to stop, and supporting even more reforms. At the same time the political and economic foundation of the Soviet Union was falling apart.

**The End of the Communist State**   The failed coup of August 1991 followed. Communist party leaders took the majority of the blame for this attack on the democratic movement, and party activities were even suspended for a brief time. Gorbachev returned to Moscow, but his power was severely undercut. With Yeltsin's collaboration Gorbachev called an unscheduled session of the legislature in September 1991 to present proposals for an **interim government**—a new, transitional government. The legislature approved the proposals. An interim government was then set up awaiting the outcome of negotiations among the republics and between the republics and the central Soviet government.

The interim government agreed to the departure of the three Baltic republics (Latvia, Estonia, and Lithuania) from the union. And, when the remaining 12 republics insisted that they wanted an end to the old Soviet Union, the interim government dissolved itself and stepped down from power.

The features of the government of the former Soviet Union—its constitution, the role of the Communist party, and its formal structure—will now be examined.

## The Soviet Constitution

The details of the old Soviet communist system were set out in the constitution of the Soviet Union. The most recent version of that document was adopted in 1977.

**The 1977 Constitution**   In form, this document was similar to the constitutions of Western democracies—at least in the sense that it set out the structure and powers of Soviet government. It was not, however, a fundamental law nor was it a charter intended to limit government and the exercise of political power. The Western concept of constitutionalism was foreign to Soviet communist thought and practice.[19]

Like Western constitutions, the Soviet document contained several civil rights provisions. But Soviet citizens were not guaranteed such basic rights as those of free speech, press, and association in the way they are secured, for example, by the American Bill of Rights. The Soviet constitution declared the existence of those rights, but it also declared that "The exercise by citizens of rights and freedoms must not injure the interests of society and the state."

The constitution could be amended in fairly easy fashion, by a simple majority vote in the legislature. In recent years it had become top-heavy with many amendments prompted by the many Gorbachev reforms.

**After the Coup**   In September 1991, in the aftermath of the failed coup against Gorbachev's government, the old constitution was heavily modified. In addition, a Declaration of Human Rights and Freedoms was approved.

Articles of this document stated: "The freedom of the individual, his or her honor and dignity are of supreme value in our society." No group, party, or state interests can be placed above the interests of the individual. The protection of "human freedoms as supreme social values" is the obligation of all agencies of the state. Other articles of the document guaranteed freedom of speech, freedom of conscience and religion, the right to peaceful assembly, and the right to form political parties and unions independent of the government.

▲ **President of the Russian Republic**   Boris Yeltsin's support of independence for the Soviet republics triumphed over Gorbachev's insistence on maintaining the Soviet Union.

---

[19]To this point at least, the Soviet Union has been ruled by people, not by any written law. But there seems to be a new spirit of reliance on laws.

## The Role of the Communist Party

Since the revolution of October 1917, the CPSU played a commanding role in the Soviet political system. Indeed, through more than 73 years, from the revolution on to 1990, the CPSU was the only political party in the Soviet Union. No other parties were allowed, and the communists' monopoly position was reinforced by the constitution. It declared the CPSU to be "the leading and directing force in Soviet society, the nucleus of its political system and of state and public organizations."

**Before the Coup**  The CPSU was an elite party, composed of some 19 million specially chosen people. Those party members made up about nine percent of the Soviet Union's adult population.

The CPSU was organized like a giant pyramid. At the bottom were some 400,000 primary party organizations (once called cells), each headed by a party committee. The party hierarchy extended upward from the primary party organization, throughout the country. It followed a pattern known as parallel organization: The party's structure paralleled that of government in each of the 15 constituent republics; each layer of government—local, regional, republic, national—had its corresponding layer of party organization. Thus, at every level, party officials were able to oversee the work of the government.

At the top of the pyramid were the most important elements of the party's structure, the Central Committee of the CPSU, the Politburo, and the general secretary. The Central Committee of the CPSU was responsible for the party's affairs. It assembled once every six months—usually just before its governmental counterpart, the Supreme Soviet, met. Thus, Gorbachev's proposals for a new governmental structure in 1990 were first presented to the Central Committee.

The Central Committee elected the much smaller **Politburo**—the body that in fact ran the CPSU. The general secretary was the head of the Politburo. He presided over its meetings and his post allowed him to gain and exercise wide power. For most of the post-Stalin era,

the general secretary also held the top post in the government.

The Politburo (political bureau) was a full-time decision-making body. Its members were the experienced, the powerful, and until very recently the elderly, heads of the party. Most of them also held key posts in the government—although the structure of the party was formally separate from that of the government. It was within this group that the coup against Gorbachev was plotted.

Before the attempted coup in August 1991, there were several indications that the party had lost at least some of its long-held power. First, the constitutional article guaranteeing the power of the CPSU was repealed in 1990, and a number of smaller political parties emerged within the Soviet Union. Second, Mikhail Gorbachev, clearly the most visible symbol of the Soviet political system, began to regularly present himself as the head of state, the president of the Soviet Union, rather than as the head of the party.

**After the Coup**  Being a small, elite party with clearly identifiable offices, the CPSU was easily targeted and disbanded after the coup failed. Its assets were confiscated in several republics and localities. The once-privileged party officials suddenly faced unemployment. Statues of the party's founder, Lenin, were toppled; and the city of Leningrad became St. Petersburg (its old name under the czars).

The initial reaction against the CPSU moderated. Its existence, like that of other political parties, was guaranteed under the Declaration of Human Rights and Freedoms. The deep distrust of communism remains, however, and it appears that the CPSU will never have the power it once held.

## The Government

The old totalitarian communist system in the Soviet Union allowed citizens to vote for members of the legislature. However, voters did not make choices. Generally, only one candidate ran for each office, and this candidate was either a CPSU member or a vocal supporter of the party.

# Global Awareness

The Human Suffering Index rates living conditions in 141 countries against ten indicators of human welfare. The ten indicators are:

- Life expectancy
- Daily calorie supply
- Clean drinking water
- Infant immunization
- Secondary school enrollment
- GNP per capita
- Rate of inflation
- Communications technology
- Political freedom
- Civil rights

*Because most of the data are from official government sources, countries may receive artificially enhanced scores if governments tend to overstate the extent of their social service programs.*

*The index is based on a 1992 index compiled by Population Crisis Committee, 1120 19th Street, NW, Washington, D.C.

## The Human Suffering Index*

*The countries are listed from highest to lowest in terms of human suffering. Annual population increase is included because often those countries with high human suffering scores have high rates of population growth.*

| Annual Population Increase (%) | Country | Human Suffering Index | Annual Population Increase (%) | Country | Human Suffering Index |
|---|---|---|---|---|---|
| 2.9 | Somalia | 92 | 2.3 | Venezuela | 51 |
| 2.9 | Haiti | 89 | 3.4 | Saudi Arabia | 44 |
| 2.9 | Ethiopia | 85 | 0.5 | Yugoslavia | 44 |
| 2.3 | Vietnam | 76 | 1.2 | Argentina | 39 |
| 3.8 | Kenya | 75 | 1.1 | Cuba | 38 |
| 2.8 | Nigeria | 70 | 0.5 | Poland | 33 |
| 2.4 | Bangladesh | 68 | 3.0 | Kuwait | 28 |
| 3.0 | Pakistan | 67 | 0.2 | Czechoslovakia | 25 |
| 2.7 | Iraq | 65 | 1.6 | Israel | 21 |
| 2.0 | India | 63 | 0.2 | United Kingdom | 16 |
| 2.3 | Peru | 63 | 0.1 | Italy | 12 |
| 1.4 | China | 61 | 0.3 | Sweden | 11 |
| 2.7 | South Africa | 61 | 0.9 | New Zealand | 8 |
| 2.9 | Egypt | 59 | 0.3 | Japan | 7 |
| 1.5 | Sri Lanka | 58 | 0.4 | France | 7 |
| 2.7 | Botswana | 57 | 0.3 | Switzerland | 3 |
| 2.3 | Mexico | 53 | 0.7 | Canada | 3 |

*Source: World Eagle, November 1992*

 **Interpreting Charts:  Multicultural Awareness**   Note the correlation in this chart between high human suffering and high rates of population growth. What factors might cause this correlation? Are there any exceptions to this generalization in the chart? What are they?

**The Legislature**   Under communist control, the Supreme Soviet was a kind of puppet theater, assembled for a few days each year to rubber-stamp the decrees of the CPSU.

Gorbachev's reforms altered the national legislature so that it was composed of two elements: the large Congress of People's Deputies and the smaller Supreme Soviet. Two-thirds of the 2,250 members of the Congress of People's Deputies were elected by the voters in districts throughout the country. The election of those deputies in 1989 marked the first time that competitive, multi-candidate elections had been held in the Soviet Union in more than 70 years.[20] The major job of the Congress of People's Deputies was that of choosing, from among its own members, the members of the Supreme Soviet, the other legislative chamber.

From 1989 to 1991, this Supreme Soviet met in spring and fall sessions, each lasting for three to four months. It operated under rules that allowed the introduction and debate of competing legislative proposals. It had several important powers—notably, to make laws, to approve the national budget, to confirm or reject the appointments of top government officials, and to declare war. And, importantly, it elected the president of the Soviet Union.

**The Executive**   Gorbachev's restructuring of Soviet government in 1989 produced a new

---

[20]Even so, those elections were hardly democratic in the Western sense. The complex nominating process was very largely controlled by the CPSU; nine out of 10 of all of the candidates were party members. There was only one candidate on the ballot in 384 of the 1,500 districts.

office, that of president of the Soviet Union elected by the Supreme Soviet. In early 1990, Gorbachev proposed the creation of a more Western-style presidency in which the presidency was to be filled by a direct vote of the Soviet people. Such an election had not taken place when the coup occurred.

As president, Gorbachev held the executive power of Soviet government. He appointed the other top officers of the government, set the lawmaking agenda for the Supreme Soviet, headed the defense establishment, and was responsible for the making and conduct of Soviet foreign policy.

The president had the power to veto any measure passed by the Supreme Soviet; but that body could override a presidential veto by a two-thirds majority in each of its chambers.

**After the Coup**   Russian president Yeltsin emerged as the strongest voice for political and economic change in the uncertain situation following the failed coup. Arguing that his own economic plan to save the rapidly faltering Soviet economy (see Chapter 23) required extraordinary measures, Yeltsin sought the power to rule by decree. The Congress of People's Deputies granted those powers in November 1991 intending them to remain in effect until December 1992. Thus enabled, Yeltsin had the power to by-pass parliamentary review of his actions and direct the economy as he saw fit. If the CPD or Supreme Soviet passed contrary legislation, Yeltsin could ignore it. He further had the power to postpone elections at all levels while the powers were in force, could himself appoint local and regional officials, and even veto local or regional legislation.

Strangely, the structure of the government was still based on the old Soviet Constitution of 1977 as modified in 1991 with a parliament made up of members elected during the old communist era. The relative powers of the president and the parliament had never been clearly described in the constitution or by the historical precedent of actual working relationships because the issue was never in question under the past dictatorial regimes. When Yeltsin sought to extend his powers of rule by decree as they expired, his opponents refused. This led to

a protracted power struggle between president and parliament. The impasse became so great that the president felt forced to dissolve the parliament in September 1993 and call for new elections the following December.

The parliamentary hardliners responded by declaring that Yeltsin was no longer president and appointed the vice-president to fill the vacated post. They also refused to leave the Russian parliament building, called "the White House" because of its white marble exterior. After several weeks of stalemate, armed hardline supporters finally provoked the military to aid Yeltsin, evicting those occupying the parliament building by force.

Once again the future evolution of the Russian democracy appears uncertain. The Russian people seem to support President Yeltsin in his struggle against the remnants of the past. But whether the military leadership or even Yeltsin himself will remain committed to democracy is in question. It is evident that the process of change begun under Gorbachev and accelerated by Boris Yeltsin will not be completed for years to come.

## Section 4 Review

1. **Define:** *perestroika, glasnost*, purge, Supreme Soviet, interim government, Politburo
2. Describe the three distinct periods of recent Soviet government.
3. What were the roles of Lenin and Stalin in creating the Soviet communist state?
4. What major problems was Gorbachev attempting to correct with the introduction of *perestroika*?
5. How did the Declaration of Human Rights and Freedoms differ from the old Soviet constitution?
6. How has the role of the CPSU changed in the Soviet Union?

**Critical Thinking**

7. **Identifying Central Issues** (p. 19) How was the process of democratization in the Soviet Union incompatible with the one-party communist state?

## Recognizing Ideologies

Recognizing ideologies means identifying underlying beliefs from actions or statements. This skill helps you to understand the basic reasons why people or governments act the way they do. By recognizing ideologies, you will be better able to establish a framework for understanding other people and for participating fully and effectively in society. Follow the steps below to practice this skill.

**1. Know what an ideology is.** An ideology is the body of ideas and beliefs on which a political, economic, or social system is based. Read the passage below, which comes from the Declaration of Independence. (a) What kind of system does the passage seem to be discussing—political, social, or economic? (b) On what do you base this conclusion?

**2. Identify the basic ideas contained in an action or statement.** Part of the skill of recognizing ideologies means being able to identify the broad themes that underlie any set of stated ideas. It is by piecing together and interpreting these broad themes that you are ultimately able to recognize the ideology present in a statement or action. Read the excerpt below again. (a) What is your understanding of the phrase "all men are created equal"? (b) What do you think the phrase "deriving their just powers from the consent of the governed" means? (c) What other broad concepts or ideas can you identify in the passage? (d) How would you summarize the ideology of the piece?

**3. Consider the possible consequences of the ideology.** Historically, some ideologies have been used as a basis for enslaving or oppressing a people. Other ideologies have formed the foundation of productive and successful political, economic, or social systems. It is therefore important to be able to evaluate the positive and negative potential behind any ideology you encounter. Read again the passage below, and answer the following questions. (a) What is your evaluation of the ideology presented in the statement below? (b) What are some of the positive aspects of the ideology stated there? (c) What evidence can you find from your knowledge of United States history to test whether or not the United States has lived up to this ideology through its actions and politics?

> "We hold these truths to be self-evident, that all men are created equal, that they are endowed by their Creator with certain unalienable Rights, that among these are Life, Liberty and the pursuit of Happiness. That to secure these rights, Governments are instituted among Men, deriving their just powers from the consent of the governed; That whenever any Form of Government becomes destructive of these ends it is the Right of the People to alter or to abolish it, and to institute new Government, laying its foundation on such principles and organizing its powers in such form, as to them shall seem most likely to effect their Safety and Happiness."
>
> —The Declaration of Independence

# Chapter-in-Brief

Scan all headings, photographs, charts, and other visuals in the chapter before reading the section summaries below.

## Section 1 Great Britain (pp. 575–581)

Great Britain has a unitary government based on an unwritten constitution.

The monarch is the head of state who reigns but does not rule. Instead, the bicameral Parliament holds the legislative and executive powers. Most of this power is centered in the popularly elected House of Commons; the House of Lords has little authority, although its nine law lords do have judicial functions.

The prime minister and cabinet are members of Parliament who are chosen by Parliament from among the ranks of the majority party. If the prime minister loses the support of Parliament, his or her administration—the government—falls, and new elections are held.

## Section 2 Japan (pp. 581–585)

Throughout much of its centuries-long history, Japan's was a feudal society. However, more Western and democratic forms began to emerge in the late 1800s.

Japan's constitution of 1947 was written largely at the direction of American occupation authorities after World War II; it contains a unique antimilitary provision. The elected national legislature, the Diet, is bicameral. Most legislative power lies in the House of Representatives; the House of Councilors has little authority. The prime minister and cabinet are chosen by and are responsible to the House of Representatives. These officials are elected from the ranks of the majority party or coalition.

Japan's bureaucracy holds a unique position of prestige and power. It works closely with Japanese industry to coordinate policy.

## Section 3 Mexico (pp. 586–590)

An advanced civilization has existed in Mexico at least since the time of the Aztec empire. However, Spanish colonization destroyed that civilization.

Mexican independence came in 1821. Today, Mexican government is based on the Constitution of 1917. While its format is democratic, the government has been controlled by one party (PRI) for more than 60 years. Mexico's president can serve only one six-year term, but can handpick a successor.

The legislature is bicameral, but neither house is very powerful. The judiciary is independent and shares many of the same features of the United States court system.

Mexico's is a federal government, and state and local government have considerable autonomy.

## Section 4 The Former Soviet Union (pp. 592–599)

Soviet government was a dictatorship for more than 70 years. It has undergone broad and ongoing change since Mikhail Gorbachev gained power in 1985. A failed coup in the summer of 1991 introduced an element of crisis and uncertainty that makes the political situation in the nation very unstable.

Before the coup, the Soviet constitution was similar in form to Western-style constitutions. However, it did little to limit government or the ironclad control of the Communist party.

After the coup, a modified constitution, together with a Declaration of Human Rights and Freedoms, was approved. The role of the once dominant Communist party is uncertain but certainly diminished.

Under Gorbachev, Soviet government had been moving toward democracy. In January 1992, a Commonwealth of Independent States broke up the Union. Russian President Yeltsin struggles against remnants of his country's Communist past, continuing the difficult process of change.

# Chapter Review

## Vocabulary and Key Terms

monarchy (p. 576)
by-election (p. 578)
coalition (p. 578)
minister (p. 578)
shadow cabinet (p. 579)
National Diet (p. 582)

prefecture (p. 583)
multi-seat district (p. 583)
consensus (p. 583)
dissolution (p. 584)
nationalization (p. 589)
*perestroika* (p. 593)

*glasnost* (p. 593)
purges (p. 594)
Supreme Soviet (p. 595)
interim government
   (p. 596)
Politburo (p. 597)

**Matching:** *Review the key terms in the list above. If you are not sure of a term's meaning, look up the term and review its definition. Choose a term from the list above that best matches each description.*

1. Stalin's elimination of rivals and other dissidents
2. agreement among groups with varying interests
3. a transitional government intended to operate for a limited period of time
4. an electoral unit in which several people are elected to the same office
5. Japan's legislature

**True or False:** *Determine whether each statement is true or false. If it is true, write "true." If it is false, change the underlined word or words to make the statement true.*

1. <u>Nationalization</u> involves the takeover of private industries by the government.
2. A <u>by-election</u> is held to fill a vacant seat in Britain's House of Commons.
3. When the prime minister of Japan dissolves the House of Representatives, it is called <u>coalition</u>.
4. In parliamentary systems, a <u>minister</u> of several parties may take control in the absence of a majority party.
5. Gorbachev's program for restructuring the Soviet economy is known as <u>prefecture</u>.

**Word Relationships:** *Distinguish between words in each pair.*

1. *perestroika/glasnost*
2. prefecture/multi-seat district
3. shadow cabinet/National Diet
4. monarchy/minister

## Main Ideas

### Section 1 (pp. 575–581)

1. In what way is Great Britain's constitution different than the United States Constitution?
2. What is the role of the monarchy in the British government?
3. Briefly describe the organization of Britain's Parliament.
4. How are Britain's prime minister and cabinet members chosen?

### Section 2 (pp. 581–585)

5. Briefly describe Japan's government before World War II.
6. (a) What is the antimilitary clause of Japan's constitution? (b) Why is it a part of their constitution?
7. (a) Briefly describe the organization of the National Diet. (b) How are the prime minister and cabinet chosen?
8. What are some unusual characteristics of the Japanese bureaucracy?

## Section 3 (pp. 586–590)

**9.** Briefly describe Mexico's political history up to 1821.

**10.** Briefly describe Mexico's first 100 years of independence.

**11.** Briefly describe the three branches of government set up under the Constitution of 1917.

**12.** What is the special role of PRI in the Mexican political system?

## Section 4 (pp. 592–599)

**13.** How did the Soviet government change over the course of its brief history?

**14.** Briefly describe Gorbachev's plans for *perestroika*.

**15.** What happened in the Soviet Union in the years following Gorbachev's ascent to political power?

**16.** (a) Briefly describe the anticipated future role of the Communist party. (b) Briefly describe the form of government that exists in the former Soviet Union.

## Critical Thinking

**1. Recognizing Ideologies** (p. 19) What does the close cooperation between industry and the government suggest about the Japanese political and economic system? Would you support a similar system in the United States?

**2. Making Comparisons** (p. 19) Consider the practice of *tapadismo*, the handpicking of presidential successors practiced by the PRI in Mexico. (a) In what way is the selection of Republican and Democratic presidential candidates similar to the practice in Mexico? (b) In what ways is it different?

**3. Testing Conclusions** (p. 19) Recall the text's statement that Gorbachev's original goals of introducing democracy while at the same time preserving the communist system were possibly incompatible. What evidence can you find in the chapter to support that statement?

**4. Formulating Questions** (p. 19) What questions could you ask to discover why Great Britain retains its constitutional monarchy?

# Getting Involved

**1. Writing Your Opinion** You are a citizen of the Soviet Union. It is the fall of 1991, just after the failed coup. Write a diary entry about your hopes for the future of your nation. Begin your entry by recounting the main events leading up to and including the coup. Then discuss your feelings about such issues as the fate of the Communist party, the possible breakaway of the republics that once made up the Soviet Union, your own personal future, and how the current disorder might affect you. As you write, keep in mind that you are writing from the point of view of a Soviet citizen living in a time of uncertainty. Revise your entry to correct any errors, and then make a final draft.

**2. Cooperative Activity** Hold a class constitutional convention in which you outline a new constitution. For this constitution, draw on the best characteristics of the governments discussed in the chapter. Begin by creating four teams to identify the strengths and weaknesses of each of the governments. Each group should consider such factors as the relationship between legislative and executive, the role and power of the parties, and the court system. Have each team present its findings to the class. Then, debate as a class which features you would like in your constitution, and hold brief votes to settle any disputes.

**3. Gathering Information** You are interested in finding out some basic information about a foreign country's governmental system. Use the Government Resources Handbook on page 690 to identify some sources you could use to find this information.

# Comparative Economic Systems

## Chapter Preview

On December 7, 1991, ceremonies at Pearl Harbor, Hawaii, marked the Japanese attack that plunged the United States into World War II. Robert Reinhold, reporting for the *New York Times*, wrote: "The ceremonies . . . spoke volumes about the complex relationship that has since developed with Japan. The aged veterans who returned to the scene of their youthful terror . . . carried Japanese cameras, and the television monitors watched were made in Japan by Sony and Panasonic." In the postwar era, Reinhold's words reminded us, Japan's economy grew faster than any other in the world.

Today, the tiny island nation is a capitalistic model of efficiency and superior quality products. This chapter is about the ways in which economic life varies greatly from one country to another—the different ways that goods and services are produced, distributed, and consumed.

### Before you read this chapter:

- **Describe** three ways that economics plays a part in your life.
- **Predict** how a country's political structure affects its economic success.

### As you read, focus on the main objective for each section. Understand:

1. The fundamental principles of a free market system.

2. The nature of socialist political and economic thought.

3. The history and end of Soviet communism.

▲ **Fueling the Economy** Industry, whether large, like this airplane factory in France, or small, has a sizeable impact on a nation's economy. The structure of the economy, in turn, affects whether the nation's industry is owned privately or publicly.

# 1 Capitalism

**Find Out:**

- On what fundamental principle is capitalism based?
- What are the main characteristics of a free enterprise system?
- What are the basic types of business organizations?

**Key Terms:**

capital, capitalist, free enterprise system, entrepreneur, laws of supply and demand, monopoly

You have confronted these questions several times in this book: What are the functions a government ought to undertake? What should it have the power to do? What should it not be allowed to do? Certainly these questions can be asked of just about all areas of human activity, but they are raised most significantly in the realm of economic affairs.

Questions of politics and of economics are, in fact, inseparable. The most important economic questions faced by a nation are clearly political questions, as well. For example: What social services should a government provide? How should goods and services be distributed and exchanged within a nation? What types of income or property ought to be taxed?

In this section, you will examine how the system called capitalism responds to those questions.

## Private Ownership of Productive Property

Capitalism, the economic system found in the United States, Japan, and Germany, to name a few prominent examples, is based on private ownership of productive property. Productive property is different from personal property, such as your toothbrush and your stereo. Personal property is typically privately owned under all the world's major economic systems. Productive property can be things such as a worker's tools, a farmer's fields, or a factory's machines. It can also take the form of original ideas, such as those in computer software, music, or inventions. These items are called productive since their use can produce other objects of economic value, income, or money.

What is distinctive about capitalism is that private individuals and companies own most of the productive property. They decide how their property is used, and the benefits of what it produces also become their property.

**Four Factors of Production**    Four types of resources are especially important for any nation's economy. These basic resources are known as factors of production. One factor of production is land. Land can be put to a variety of economic uses for agriculture, mining, and forestry. A second factor of production is a human resource—labor. Men and women who work in mines, factories, offices, hospitals, and other places all provide labor that is an essential part of a nation's economy. Management, which is a special type of skilled labor, is a third factor of production. Management is the labor involved in organizing the other factors of production and making businesses run efficiently.

The fourth factor of production is **capital**—the wealth, be it money, factories, or machinery—that is used to produce goods and services. Capital has to be made before it can be used. In other words, capital is a product of the economy that is then put back into the economy to make more products.

**The Role of the Capitalist**    Someone who owns capital and puts it to productive use is called a **capitalist**. The term is most often applied to people who own large businesses or factories. Capitalists, using their privately owned productive property, create and expand industries, make investments in new technologies, and engage in activities that create jobs and contribute to the high standard of living for which modern capitalistic societies are admired. The United States economy is called capitalistic because it depends on the energy and drive of thousands of individual capitalists.

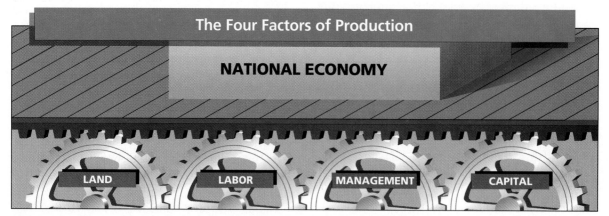

**Interpreting Graphics**    The four factors of production work together to keep an economy moving forward. According to what you have read, what is the role of the capitalist in a capitalistic economic system?

Drawing by Dan Fradon; ©1990 *The New Yorker Magazine, Inc.*

▲ **Interpreting Political Cartoons**   The move to a free market system does not bring instant wealth to a country. What does this cartoon suggest about the difficulties of such an adjustment?

## The Free Enterprise System

A capitalistic economy is sometimes referred to as a **free enterprise system**. In such a system, individuals are free to start and run their own businesses—their own enterprises. They are also free to dissolve those businesses. Free enterprise systems have five noteworthy characteristics.

**Private Ownership**   In a free enterprise system, most of the means of production are privately rather than publicly owned. The owners are sometimes individuals. Often, however, they are groups of people who share ownership of a company.

**Guarantees for Property Rights**   A free enterprise system can work only when property rights are guaranteed. In the United States, the 5th and 14th amendments to the Constitution declare that no person may "be deprived of life, liberty, or property without due process of law." The Constitution also requires that "just compensation" be paid to owners when private property is taken for public use.

**Decentralized Decision Making**   Under capitalism, basic decisions about what to produce and how to produce it are left to private decision makers. Public officials do not order factories to produce products. Thus, if existing companies cannot meet the demand for a product, an enterprising capitalist might see a chance to make some money by starting up a new company. A person who takes the initiative and risk of starting or expanding a business is called an **entrepreneur**—an enterpriser.

**Competition**   Because people are generally free to enter a new business at any time, a number of companies usually offer the same product or service. Companies must compete against one another for customers. Competition among multiple sellers helps to hold down prices and keep quality high, since customers are likely to buy from the company with the best product at the lowest price. Competition thus promotes efficiency since the producer has the incentive to keep costs low.

Under competitive conditions, the laws of supply and demand determine prices. Supply is the quantity of goods or services for sale. Demand is the desire of potential buyers for those goods and services. According to the **laws of supply and demand**, when supplies become more plentiful, prices tend to drop. As supplies become limited, prices tend to rise. By the same token, if demand drops—that is, if there are few buyers—sellers will probably lower their prices in order to make a sale. If demand rises, sellers can raise prices.

Competition does not always work smoothly. Sometimes a single business becomes so successful that all of its rivals go out of business. A firm that is the only source of a product or service is called a **monopoly**. Monopolies can be very powerful in the marketplace. Practically speaking, they can charge as much as they want for a product. Since there is no other supplier of that good or service, the consumer must pay up or do without.

Political leaders in the United States decided late in the nineteenth century that monopolies were dangerous. American leaders were especially concerned about a type of monopoly called a trust.[1] The Federal Department of Justice has a division that analyzes business activities to determine if competition within an industry is threatened. It can, for example, stop the sale of a company if that sale might result in the elimination of competitive conditions in the marketplace.

---

[1] A device by which several corporations in the same line of business combine to eliminate competition and regulate prices. The Sherman Antitrust Act of 1890 remains the basic law against monopolies today. It prohibits "every contract, combination in the form of a trust or otherwise, or conspiracy in restraint of trade or commerce among the several States, or with foreign nations."

▲ **Interpreting Political Cartoons**   Healthy economies require a fine balance between supply and demand. What does this cartoon suggest about the Soviet Union's economy in the early 1990s?

**Freedom of Choice**   A fifth characteristic of free enterprise is that consumers, entrepreneurs, and workers enjoy freedom of choice. Consumers can choose from a variety of products and services. Entrepreneurs can switch from one business to another. Workers can quit their jobs and take new ones. However, federal and State governments do place restrictions on freedom of choice. For example, the government prohibits the sale of products deemed hazardous to people's health or safety.

## Laissez-Faire Theory

Early capitalist philosophers believed that, if only government did not interfere, the free enterprise system could work automatically. Adam Smith presented the classic expression of that view in *The Wealth of Nations*, in 1776. Smith claimed that when all individuals are free to pursue their own private interests, an "invisible hand" works to promote the general welfare. In short, Smith preached laissez-faire capitalism.[2]

Laissez-faire theory holds that government should play only a very limited, hands-off role in society. Governmental activity should be confined to: (1) foreign relations and national defense, (2) the maintenance of police and courts to protect private property and the health, safety, and morals of the people, and (3) those few other functions that cannot be performed by private enterprise at a profit. Properly, government's role in economic affairs should be restricted to functions intended to promote and protect the free play of competition and the operation of the laws of supply and demand.

Laissez-faire capitalism never in fact operated in this country. But it is clear that the concept had, and still has, a profound effect on the structure of the American economic system.

## A Mixed Economy

Although the American economic system is essentially private in character, government has always played a large part in it. So, economists usually describe the American system as a

▲ **An "Invisible Hand" at Work**   Laissez-faire theory holds that government should not interfere with business. Yet business has often been charged with exerting undue influence on the United States government.

mixed economy—one in which private enterprise and governmental participation coexist.[3]

Many aspects of American economic life are regulated by government at every level. For example, the government prohibits trusts, protects the environment, and ensures the quality of food.

Many aspects of American economic life are promoted by government, as well. For example, the government constructs public roads and highways, provides such services as the postal system, the census, and weather reports, and offers many kinds of subsidies and loan programs.

The United States economy is also mixed in another sense: Government conducts some enterprises that might well be operated privately. Here, too, you can find examples at every level of government: public education, the postal system, various forms of transportation, and water and power systems.

---

[2]The term *laissez faire* comes from a French idiom meaning "to let alone."

[3]Recall, for example, the various powers of Congress discussed in Chapter 11. You will also read about the many powers of the State and local governments in Chapter 24.

# VOICES *on Government*

**Kathleen Feldstein,**
economist and columnist

**Martin Feldstein,**
former chief of the Council of Economic Advisers

### On the Importance of Savings to a Capitalist Economy

❝The funds that private individuals put into savings accounts or money market funds or bonds provide the source of business borrowing. For businesses to invest in new plants and equipment or in training programs or in research and development, they must be able to borrow. And if they can't borrow enough from Americans, they will turn to foreign investors. That is exactly the pattern that is evolving now. . . . Yet far from being understood, this phenomenon is stirring up latent fears of foreigners and renewed protectionist sympathy. The sad fact is that without foreign investment there would be very little capital available for our economy to grow.❞

## Three Kinds of Business Organization

While the United States economy contains a number of gigantic companies with thousands of employees and with plants all over the world, most businesses in the United States are relatively small. Some 80 percent of businesses employ fewer than 20 people.

There are three basic types of business organizations—sole proprietorships, partnerships, and corporations. Each has its advantages and disadvantages.

Businesses owned by a single individual are sole proprietorships. Typical of businesses in this category might be a beauty shop, a garage, or a doctor's practice. A major advantage of sole proprietorships is that decisions can be made quickly, by the single owner. A major disadvantage is that the owner is personally liable for debts the business might build up.

Businesses owned by two or more individuals, called partners, are partnerships. An advantage is that a partnership can draw on the resources of more than one person for capital to start or expand the business. A disadvantage is that partnerships end if a partner leaves or dies.

Unlike partnerships, corporations have many owners, called shareholders.[4] A corporation might continue indefinitely because a shareholder's death does not affect the legal status of the corporation. In other words, the corporation exists as its own legal entity, independent from the existence of any stockholders.

Corporations can draw their capital from hundreds and even thousands of investors, thus enabling them to finance such costly projects as putting an earth satellite in orbit or building an oil pipeline. Shareholders are responsible only for the amount of money they have invested. If the business fails, they might lose that amount, but no more. The shareholders have limited liability, and are not held responsible for any debts the corporation might have.

One disadvantage of corporations is that their income is taxed twice. First, the corporation pays a tax on its profits. Then, individual shareholders pay a tax on their dividends.

## Profit and Loss

What drives the capitalist economy? The best answer, most often, is profit.

To understand what profit is, you must first understand the idea of investment. An investment is a sum of money, or capital, that is put

---

[4]A share is a fraction of ownership in the corporation.

## Top Purchasers and Suppliers of U.S. Exports and Imports

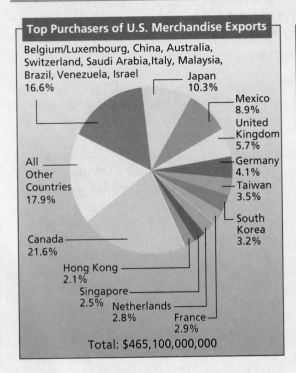

### Top Purchasers of U.S. Merchandise Exports

Belgium/Luxembourg, China, Australia, Switzerland, Saudi Arabia, Italy, Malaysia, Brazil, Venezuela, Israel
16.6%

Japan 10.3%

Mexico 8.9%

United Kingdom 5.7%

Germany 4.1%

Taiwan 3.5%

South Korea 3.2%

France 2.9%

Netherlands 2.8%

Singapore 2.5%

Hong Kong 2.1%

Canada 21.6%

All Other Countries 17.9%

Total: $465,100,000,000

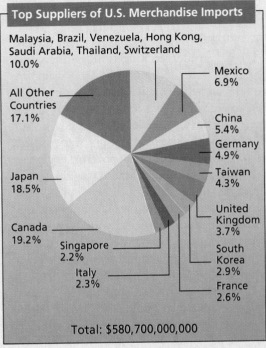

### Top Suppliers of U.S. Merchandise Imports

Malaysia, Brazil, Venezuela, Hong Kong, Saudi Arabia, Thailand, Switzerland
10.0%

All Other Countries 17.1%

Mexico 6.9%

China 5.4%

Germany 4.9%

Taiwan 4.3%

United Kingdom 3.7%

South Korea 2.9%

France 2.6%

Italy 2.3%

Singapore 2.2%

Japan 18.5%

Canada 19.2%

Total: $580,700,000,000

*Source*: U.S. Dept. of Commerce, International Trade Administration, Office of Trade and Investment Analysis, *1993 U.S. Foreign Trade Highlights.*

▲ **Interpreting Graphs: Multicultural Awareness** The United States economy does not exist in isolation but is linked with the economies of many other countries. Which country conducts the most trade with the United States?

into a business enterprise. For example, if you buy a car to start a business delivering groceries, what you pay for the car is an investment. The profit will be the amount of money earned from the business, after having subtracted the costs associated with earning that money—in this case, the purchase of the car and the costs of operating it, plus whatever you pay yourself. If earnings are less than the costs, the business has not made a profit; instead, it has taken a loss.

Taking risks and making investments, therefore, are an essential part of the capitalist system. Every year, many businesses fail for lack of profit. Businesses that survive tend to be those that have learned to make the most efficient use of the factors of production.

## Section 1 Review

1. **Define:** capital, capitalist, free enterprise system, entrepreneur, laws of supply and demand, monopoly
2. Who controls most of the productive property in a capitalist economy?
3. What are the five characteristics of a free enterprise system?
4. What are the three basic business types in the United States?

**Critical Thinking**

5. **Understanding Cause and Effect** (p. 19) Explain how competition promotes efficiency.

★

# What You Can Do

## Working to End World Hunger

When Mary Varilla, a high school student in Ridgefield, Connecticut, saw footage of an Ethiopian famine on television news reports in 1984, she became deeply concerned. She introduced the subject in a global issues discussion group at her school. After listening to Mary, others in the group shared her concern. Together, they decided that they wanted to do something to help victims of the famine. The group began by sponsoring school assemblies to educate students about world hunger. At these assemblies, students learned that the fight to end world hunger takes place on two fronts. Money raised through fund-raising and donations serves to provide emergency relief to those in immediate need. More importantly, money is also raised to help implement programs designed to prevent poverty and starvation in the future.

Mary and her group launched their fund-raising effort by soliciting support from local businesses, churches, synagogues, and other schools. The group's first joint project, a townwide walk-a-thon, attracted 2,000 participants and raised $60,000. After consulting with an experienced relief organization, they chose to send the money to Yifat Na Timuga, a poor, malaria-plagued town in Ethiopia in need of funds for three building projects already under way: a well to provide the town with clean water, homes for orphaned children, and a grain storage house.

### Seeing the Results

By 1987, donations to Mary's group had slowed to a trickle. Many people questioned what their donations had accomplished, if anything. Mary and four of her classmates decided to find out for themselves. That summer, they embarked on a trip to Yifat Na Timuga to see the projects that they helped sponsor. The American teenagers were gratified by what they saw. A recently completed catch basin supplied the village with safe water for drinking, washing, and irrigation. They learned that people who had previously left the village were able to return because of the improved sanitary conditions. Children who before had to spend their days walking long distances to obtain clean water now had the time to attend school. The students also visited the orphanages that they helped to fund and enjoyed a challenging game of volleyball with a group of teens there.

Thousands of American teens have joined in the fight against hunger by educating those around them, raising funds, and working in relief projects. For some, the desire to stamp out hunger may become a lifetime commitment and a career goal. For others, the experience may simply be one chance to do some good. But by becoming active in fund-raising and service projects, students can make a difference—at home and around the world.

## Getting Involved

**1. Identify** a need in your school, local, or global community similar to the one addressed in this case.

**2. Formulate** a plan for how you might organize volunteer efforts to help remedy this problem and identify resources that could be used in your plan.

**3. Predict** any problems you might encounter in implementing your idea. Also predict how you might solve those problems.

# 2 Socialism

## Find Out:

- What are the historic roots of socialism?
- How are market economies different from command economies?
- What are the principal arguments for and against socialism?

## Key Terms:

proletariat, bourgeoisie, welfare state, market economy, command economy

You know that in the United States, all people are entitled to equal protection under the law. Of course, this political equality is not the same as economic equality. As you have read, America's capitalistic system enables some to achieve greater financial rewards than others.

There is, however, an economic system that seeks to equitably distribute wealth through society. This section is about that system.

## What Is Socialism?

Socialism is an economic and a political philosophy based on the idea that the benefits of economic activity—wealth—should be equitably distributed throughout a society. This fairness is achieved through the principle of collective—that is, public—ownership of the most important means by which goods and services are produced and distributed.

Socialism rejects the concepts of private ownership, individualism, and competition for profit that lie at the heart of capitalistic thought and practice. Instead, socialists emphasize cooperation and social responsibility in order to achieve this more equitable distribution of both income and opportunity. Political equality is not enough, they say. Real equality can come only when extreme differences in wealth across the population are reduced, and the public controls the centers of economic power in a society.

The roots of socialism lie deep in history. Almost from the beginning there have been those who have dreamed of a society built on

socialist doctrine. Most earlier socialists foresaw a collective economy that would arise out of and then be managed by voluntary private action. With few exceptions, they believed that they could reach their goals without governmental action—and, so, early socialist doctrine is often called "private socialism."

## The Industrial Revolution

Present-day socialism developed in large part as a reaction to the poverty and other miseries that accompanied the Industrial Revolution.

The Industrial Revolution occurred as the Western world moved from an agricultural to an industrial economy. It appeared most distinctly

### How to Convert Foreign Currency to Dollars

**1. Determine the exchange rate.** Telephone your local bank to find out the exchange rate for the currency of the country in which you are interested. For example, the exchange rate for British pounds may be $1.40. This means you can buy one British pound for $1.40. If you divide one dollar by the British value ($1.00 ÷ $1.40), you can determine how many pounds your U.S. dollar will buy (0.70 pound).

**2. Multiply by the exchange rate to determine how much U.S. money you can get for your foreign currency.** For example, if you have 10 pounds left when you leave Great Britain, you will get 10 x $1.40, or $14.00 of U.S. currency.

**3. Practice converting currency for other countries.** If you arrive in Mexico City with $100, and you determine that the exchange rate is .0026 dollars to the peso or 380 pesos for each dollar, how many pesos can you get for your $100? (38,000 pesos) If you have 1000 pesos left when you leave Mexico, how many dollars should you expect to get? ($2.60)

▲ **Interpreting Charts**  The exchange rate between various currencies can change from day to day. In step 2, what would you get if the pound was worth $1.50 when you left Great Britain?

in Great Britain in the late 18th century and spread generally through Western Europe and to the United States in the 19th century. It was marked by rapid urbanization and the growth of large-scale manufacturing.

Many observers of 19th-century British factories and factory towns were appalled by the conditions they found. Men and women often worked 14- to 16-hour days—usually in filthy, noisy, and unsafe conditions. Small children regularly worked alongside their parents, for even less pay. Most factory workers and their families lived in dank, crowded, and unhealthful slums.

Those and other adverse effects of the Industrial Revolution led many to seek social and economic reforms. And those conditions led some to argue for much more radical change.

**Karl Marx** Clearly, Karl Marx (1818-1883), the father of modern-day socialism, was the most significant critic of capitalism to emerge in the

▲ **Nationalization and Socialism** In socialist economies such as Sweden's, key transportation and communications industries may be nationalized. Other businesses, such as this Swedish auto manufacturer, remain in private hands.

19th century. Much of his work and most of his extensive writings were done in collaboration with Friedrich Engels (1820-1895). Together, Marx and Engels wrote *The Communist Manifesto* in 1848—"to do for history," as Engels later said, "what Darwin's theory has done for biology."

Marx believed that capitalism was fatally flawed. The **proletariat**—the workers—were being so badly abused by the **bourgeoisie**—the capitalists—that they were certain to rise up and overthrow the capitalistic system. You will read more about Marx and his ideas in the next section.

**Socialists and Communists** A powerful socialist movement took shape among European workers and thinkers during the middle and late 19th century. Almost all socialists accepted Marx's criticism of capitalism. But the movement was deeply split by the question of how best to achieve socialism. Some argued that a socialist society could come only out of a "violent and bloody revolution." Over time, those who took that view came to be called communists. Others argued that socialism could be attained by peaceful means, through the democratic process. Today, the terms *socialism* and *socialist* are usually used to identify those evolutionary socialists.

The British Labour party and the major "social democratic" parties of Western Europe are leading examples of that brand of socialism. At various times in recent history, these parties have controlled their governments and have instituted many socialist programs through democratic means.

## Characteristics of Socialist Economies

Countries that have socialist governments typically enact one or more of the following measures to achieve the aims of socialist philosophy.

**Nationalization** Organizing enterprises under governmental control—often by taking over privately owned industries—is called nationalization. Recall that in the last chapter you read about nationalization in Mexico in the 1930s. In democratic countries such as Britain, the government might nationalize enterprises, paying the former owners what it calculates to be a fair price. In some countries, however, governments have nationalized industries without paying any compensation.

Nationalization sometimes, but rarely, includes all businesses in a country. Typically, nationalization is selective. Socialist governments usually want to control the country's most important industries, but they may allow many types of businesses to remain in private hands. Also, socialist countries might want certain important industries that are based upon newly emerging technologies to remain private since individual initiative and entrepreneurial risk-taking are very important during the early phases of a business.

A goal of many socialist governments is to give each company's workers a say in deciding how the company is run. Sweden's Social Democratic party, for example, has a plan for gradually transferring ownership of private companies to their workers. Elected worker representatives now sit on many companies' boards of directors.

## Public Services and the Welfare State

Socialists stress the goal of assuring that everyone in a society is decently housed and fed. Stated another way, socialists aim to guarantee the public welfare by providing for the equal distribution of necessities and services. Public services are considered to be government's responsibility. One of the earliest to implement such ideas was Britain's Liberal government, which adopted pensions, health insurance, and unemployment insurance between 1908 and 1911. Other countries' programs may range from free university education to free housing for the poor.

Countries that provide extensive social services at little or no cost to the users are called **welfare states**. In such countries, medical and dental services may be provided free or for a small charge. People who lose their jobs or who are physically unable to work receive government payments that are nearly as high as their former wages. All people above retirement age receive government pensions. Parents may receive government payments for each child until the child reaches the age of 18.

**Taxation**  All governments, capitalistic or socialist, get their funds from taxation. But because social welfare services are quite expensive, taxes in socialist countries tend to be high. It is not uncommon for taxes to take 50 or 60

▲ **Health Care for All**  Many social services—including medical care—are provided to citizens of Canada by their government. Canadians also receive education and other services.

percent of an individual's total income. Socialists tend to place most of the burden on the upper and middle classes, consistent with their philosophy of achieving a more equal distribution of wealth. Tax rates can amount to 90 percent of a wealthy person's income.

**The Command Economy**  Economies can be divided into two broad categories, depending on how basic decisions are made. Under capitalism, as you have seen, the government's role is a limited one. Key decisions are made by thousands of private individuals and companies through the give and take of the marketplace. For that reason, capitalistic economies are called **market economies**.

Under socialism, and also communism, decision making is much more centralized. Public bodies can plan how an economy will develop over a period of years. Governments set targets for production. They guide investment into specific industries. In theory, therefore, governments can direct the economy along desired paths. Thus, socialist and communist economies are called **command economies**.

A document called the five-year plan plays a key role in many command economies. The plan is a blueprint showing how leaders want the economy to develop over the next five years. (You will read about the use of five-year plans in the former Soviet Union in the next section.) Making a five-

Hi looser

year plan is an intricate process drawing on experts from many areas of national life. The purpose is to set economic goals for the future and to plan how to achieve those goals most efficiently.

## Socialism in Developing Countries

Socialism has won a large following in developing countries. There, public ownership and centralized planning are widespread.

One reason for socialism's appeal is that most developing countries are starting from scratch at building industry. Such countries have no tradition of locally controlled, large-scale industry. Large industries that do exist often are owned by foreign interests—firms that have a base in one country and holdings in many others. By nationalizing a foreign-owned company and placing local people in charge, a political leader can win broad public support.

Socialism also appeals to leaders who want to mobilize an entire nation behind a program of industrial growth. Through central planning, leaders can channel investment into the parts of the economy they think are most essential.

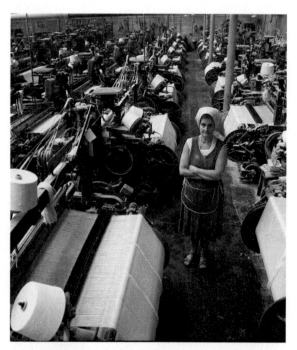

▲ **Birthplace of an Ideology**    The Industrial Revolution that so horrified Karl Marx began in Great Britain's textile mills. This is one of Britain's textile mills today.

Often, however, guided growth of this sort requires painful sacrifices by a nation's people. High taxes skim off a large part of people's income. The government may devote so much attention to one or two basic industries that the production of consumer goods or food may be neglected. Then public unrest may develop.

Political instability is a persistent problem in developing nations. It is one reason for the tendency of socialist and other governments in such nations to turn to authoritarian methods. Few developing nations have succeeded in establishing the democratic versions of socialism that are found in parts of the industrial world.

## Major Criticisms of Socialism

Both capitalistic and socialist economies have their strengths and their weaknesses. For supporters of capitalism, it is easy to see weaknesses in the theory and practice of socialism. For supporters of socialism, on the other hand, it is capitalism that is riddled with faults.

Critics say socialist countries have a tendency to develop too many layers of bureaucracy. They say this complicates decision making and has a deadening effect on individual initiative. As a result, critics say, socialist economies are slower to take advantage of new technologies.

In the eyes of socialism's critics, the smooth running of an economy is too complex to be directed by central planners. Too many unpredictable events are involved, they claim. Too many clashing interests are at stake. For all its faults, the invisible hand of the market economy works more efficiently than the visible hand of the command economy, say socialism's critics.

Another criticism is that socialism deprives people of the freedom to decide for themselves how to use their income. Most of a person's income goes to taxes. Since earners get to keep only a part of their earnings, they have little incentive to work harder and earn more. Why work hard when your basic needs will be taken care of anyway? So ask socialism's critics.

In response, socialists point to the inequalities of wealth and power that exist under capitalism. Socialists argue that socialism evens out inequalities and thus is morally superior to capitalism. In their view, socialism makes political democra-

Global Awareness

## Food Prices and Average Weekly Incomes for Selected Cities (Current Prices in U.S. Dollars)

| | Brasilia | London | Madrid | Mexico City | Pretoria | Seoul | Tokyo | Washington D.C. |
|---|---|---|---|---|---|---|---|---|
| Sirloin Steak (1 kg*) | 3.24 | 13.10 | 15.03 | 6.40 | 5.92 | 26.43 | 56.45 | 9.06 |
| Whole Broilers (1 kg) | 1.47 | 2.89 | 3.75 | 2.24 | 2.33 | 2.67 | 6.85 | 1.68 |
| Large Eggs (1 doz) | 0.69 | 2.07 | 2.01 | 1.13 | 1.13 | 1.96 | 1.63 | 0.99 |
| Cheddar Cheese (1 kg) | 3.41 | 6.20 | 11.29 | 7.36 | 5.90 | 14.42 | 16.86 | 7.72 |
| Milk (1 liter**) | 0.67 | 0.73 | 0.86 | 0.53 | 0.85 | 1.43 | 1.60 | 0.67 |
| Butter (1 kg) | 2.39 | 3.87 | 8.05 | 3.46 | 4.26 | 9.02 | 10.67 | 3.86 |
| Apples (1 kg) | 1.76 | 1.67 | 1.61 | 1.29 | 1.28 | 2.70 | 3.35 | 1.54 |
| Flour (1 kg) | 0.55 | 0.73 | 0.93 | 0.49 | 0.80 | 0.48 | 1.56 | 0.51 |
| Rice (1 kg) | 0.61 | 1.45 | 2.08 | 1.01 | 1.17 | 1.88 | 2.99 | 1.00 |
| Sugar (1 kg) | 0.53 | .94 | 1.16 | 0.60 | 0.79 | 0.80 | 2.04 | 0.95 |
| Coffee (1 kg) | 3.67 | 8.70 | 6.25 | 4.80 | 9.79 | 8.17 | 28.63 | 5.42 |
| Potatoes (1 kg) | .69 | 0.60 | 0.51 | 1.25 | 0.64 | 1.38 | 2.66 | 0.77 |
| Average Weekly Income | $59 | $317 | $227 | $61 | $55 | $106 | $495 | $424 |

*1 kg is equal to 2.205 pounds.
**1 liter is equal to 1.057 quarts.
*Source:* U.S. Department of Agriculture. Foreign Agriculture Service, *Agricultural Trade Highlights*, January 1993

▲ **Interpreting Tables: Multicultural Awareness** The world's economies are closely related, yet they still differ greatly. How do the prices paid in the United States compare with those paid elsewhere?

cy work more smoothly by supplementing it with economic democracy.

Defenders of socialism also argue that it gives workers and ordinary citizens more control over their daily lives. Under capitalism, they say, a company's management can abruptly decide to close a factory that is no longer making money. The company has no obligation to ask its workers' opinions, even though such a decision can throw thousands out of work and disrupt an entire community. This could not happen under socialism, the argument goes. Workers and community leaders would sit on the company's board. They would help decide what was best for the entire work force and community—not just for the company's shareholders.

## Section 2 Review

1. **Define:** proletariat, bourgeoisie, welfare state, market economy, command economy
2. How does socialism differ from capitalism?
3. What part did the Industrial Revolution play in the birth of modern socialism?
4. State two criticisms of socialism and two criticisms of capitalism.

### Critical Thinking

5. **Making Comparisons** (p. 19) How might a socialist and capitalist government differ in their treatment of the problem of unemployment?

 ★

# 3 Communism

**Find Out:**

- What are the basic concepts of Marx's communist theory?
- How was communist theory put into action in the Soviet Union?
- How did Gorbachev's economic reforms lead to the collapse of communism in the former Soviet Union?

**Key Terms:**

five-year plan, collectivization

What is *communism*? From the mid-1940s on to the early 1990s, much of American foreign policy was aimed at countering the influence of communism in the world. Yet, even today, many Americans do not have a very clear understanding of that doctrine.

Communism as it is known in today's world was born in Europe in the middle of the last century.[5] It is a political, economic, and social theory built by Karl Marx and then, especially in the Soviet Union, by Vladimir Lenin and Josef Stalin.[6]

## Karl Marx's Communist Theory

Communism is often called a collective ideology. That is, it is a theory that calls for the collective, or state, ownership of all land and other productive property. As you have read, its basic concepts were first set out in *The Communist Manifesto*, written in 1848 by Karl Marx and Friedrich Engels. This political document condemned the

---

[5]The word *communism* comes from the Latin *communis*, meaning "common, belonging to all." The idea of communal property dates back at least to the early Greeks. In the fourth century B.C., Plato proposed a system of communal property in *The Republic*.

[6]Stalin, and other communists in the Soviet Union and elsewhere, frequently referred to the ideology as Marxist-Leninism. Marx originally used the term *scientific socialism* to distinguish his thought from older and less extreme forms of socialism. In later years, Marx came to prefer the term *communism*.

misery and the exploitations of the Industrial Revolution in Europe, and it called upon oppressed workers across the continent to free themselves from "capitalist enslavement." The pamphlet ended with this rallying cry:

❝The proletarians have nothing to lose but their chains. They have a world to win. Workingmen of all countries, unite!❞

In his major work, *Das Kapital* (first published in 1867), Marx analyzed the development and workings of capitalism from its historical roots. It presented Marx's view of capitalism based on four closely related concepts: (1) his theory of history, (2) the theory of value and capitalist accumulation, (3) his view of the nature of the state, and (4) the dictatorship of the proletariat.

Based on his ideology, Marx envisioned communism as a "free, classless society"—a society in which all social classes would vanish and all property would be owned by all people in common. There would be no exploitation of labor and no unemployment. Goods would be produced in abundance, and they would be available to all according to need. People would be happy to work hard, pleased to contribute their best for the benefit of all.

**The Marxian View of History**  To Marx, all of human history has been a story of class struggle—of conflict among social classes competing for the control of labor and of productive property. In that view, there have always been two major and opposing classes in society—one an oppressor class and the other an oppressed class. Thus, in the Middle Ages the contending classes were the nobility and their serfs. In the modern world it is the bourgeoisie who keep the proletariat in submission.

Marx's doctrine held that the conflict between the classes would become so intense in the modern era that a revolt of the masses and the downfall of the bourgeoisie would be inevitable. The communists' political role was that of speeding up these revolutionary processes, by violence if need be.

**The Labor Theory of Value**  In the communist view, the value of every commodity is set by the amount of socially useful labor put into it. In short, labor creates all value. A pair of shoes or a rebuilt engine is each worth so much because it takes that much labor to produce it. Because the laborer made the shoes or rebuilt the engine, the communist argues that the laborer should receive that value in full.

Marxists reject the free enterprise notions of competition and profit. Competition, they say, forces the capitalist to drive workers' wages down to the lowest possible point. Profits are condemned as "surplus value," wrung from the grinding toil of the masses.

### The Nature of the State

Marx saw the state and its government as the instrument of the dominant class in society—a tool by which the capitalists maintained their power and privileged position. Other social institutions were also seen as playing a role in enforcing capitalist control over the masses. Thus, Marx described religion as "the opiate of the people." Religious beliefs, he wrote, are a drug fed to the masses, a hoax through which they are persuaded to tolerate their harsh lot in this life in the hope that someday they will gain what Marx called a "fictional afterlife."

### The Dictatorship of the Proletariat

Marx did not believe that the final form of communist society would appear immediately upon the overthrow of the bourgeoisie. He saw the need for a transitional phase during which the state would represent and enforce the interest of the masses. This was called, in Marx's terminology, the "dictatorship of the proletariat"—a period of authoritarian rule through which society must pass on the way to the goal of a classless society. He argued that once the goal of classlessness was realized, the need for the state and its government would disappear.

Marx also expected that the bonds of common interest between workers in different countries would be so strong that they would overshadow national identities and national loyalties. Thus, for example, he thought that French and German factory workers would come together on the basis of their shared economic situation—and so nationalism, a major cause of European wars, would be eliminated with the establishment of communism.

## Communism in the Soviet Union

Marx was convinced that the world's most advanced industrialized countries, with their large working-class populations, were ripe for revolution. In particular, Marx expected that workers' revolutions would occur in France, Germany, and Great Britain, and then in the United States. But, that revolution actually occurred in the largely agricultural Russia in 1917; and with that upheaval came the creation of the world's first communist state.[7]

---

[7]In his later years, Marx did recognize the possibility that his theories might first be tested in practice in Russia.

Lenin also took the Russia-first view, in the early 1900s. He thought that less advanced countries, with their comparatively small industrial populations, offered certain advantages to a revolutionary movement—notably, the effectiveness with which workers could be organized and controlled.

▲ **The First Marxist** Karl Marx was an ardent critic of the capitalist system. He anticipated a violent rejection of capitalist ideals by the workers of the world.

▲  **Farming Under Communism**    Contrary to Marx's original expectation, communism first took root in largely agricultural Russia, not in the industrialized centers of Europe.

Marx's analysis of capitalism did not provide a real blueprint—or anything close to one—for the formation of a communist society. This left the leaders of the Russian communist revolution with the task of interpreting his ideas for clues on what was to be done.

**Communism Under Lenin**    In November 1917, Lenin and his followers seized power in Russia, established a communist government, and began at once their attempt to create their vision of a communist society. The new government ordered the nationalization of all banks and large businesses, and it moved to create workers' councils (soviets) in every enterprise to manage them. Outside the cities, Lenin encouraged the peasants to seize whatever land they could.

Lenin's government was immediately torn by civil war—three years of brutal conflict in which several groups challenged communist rule. Lenin, using both military force and terror on a broad scale, was able to defeat his foes, who were divided and poorly led. But by 1921

conditions had become extremely grave throughout the country. Peasant revolts had broken out in several places, and the threat of famine was widespread.

Lenin realized that the attempt to create an instant communist society had failed, and in 1921 he introduced the New Economic Policy, NEP. The NEP was a clear compromise between socialist principles and capitalism that was intended to revive agricultural production and promote manufacturing. The government continued to control what Lenin called the "commanding heights"—heavy industry, banking, foreign trade, wholesale commerce, and transportation. But private ownership of rural land and trade for profit were allowed to flourish. Said Lenin: "If we cannot go to communism directly, we shall zigzag to it through socialism."

By the time Lenin died in 1924, the Soviet Union had become a one-party state. All opposition to communism had been banned, and the communists had taken control of all of the country's social, political, and economic institutions.

**Communism Under Stalin** Lenin's death prompted a fierce struggle for power among his chief aides. Josef Stalin defeated his several rivals one by one, and he gained complete control of the Communist party and the government of the Soviet Union by 1928. For the next 25 years, Stalin ruled with an iron fist. As you have read, the Soviet economy and its influence abroad grew rapidly—but at a huge cost in human life and personal freedom.

Under Stalin, the 1930s were dominated by two major economic programs: the forced collectivization of Soviet agriculture and the rapid industrialization of the country's economy.

The NEP was ended in 1928. Stalin and others feared that its successes meant that free enterprise was gaining a foothold in the Soviet Union; and they also thought that steel and other heavy industries had received too little attention by the NEP. In its place came centralized economic planning for the entire country and the First Five-Year Plan.

**The Five-Year Plans** The **five-year plans** marked the first attempt by any society to combine large-scale centralized planning with the public ownership of the means of production as the basis for a nation's economic advancement. The First Five-Year Plan ran from 1928 to 1933.

The plan was dominated by two major goals: (1) **collectivization**—the combining of millions of small peasant farms into giant collective, government-controlled farms, called *kolkhozy*, and (2) huge production increases in the nation's chemical, petroleum, machine tool, construction, steel, and other heavy industries.

Stalin ordered the creation of the *kolkhozy* in 1929. There was great resistance from the largest, most prosperous landholders whose numbers had grown under the NEP. They killed their livestock and destroyed farmland as an act of resistance. Party zealots from the cities invaded the rural areas, killing hundreds of thousands of peasant families and sending many more to labor camps in Siberia and Central Asia.

The First Five-Year Plan also aimed at bringing a greatly expanded industrial capacity to the Soviet Union. That goal was also emphasized in the Second and Third Five-Year plans.[8] By concentrating Soviet resources on the development of heavy industry, Stalin hoped to end the nation's economic backwardness and reduce its military vulnerability. The success of the collectivization of agriculture also depended on industrialization—because the farmers needed a source of farm machinery and gasoline.

The first three five-year plans were at least partial successes. The Soviet Union achieved rapid, if uneven, industrialization, but the need for consumer goods and urban services was ignored. Many products had to be rationed; housing shortages became common; and sewers, water systems, and other needs lagged behind a dramatic growth in urban population.

To spur greater production, Stalin also gave economic rewards and other incentives to party officials, bureaucrats, and factory managers. People with special talents—writers, artists, musicians, and athletes, for example—were also rewarded. Thus, Stalin created an elite class in the Soviet Union, a class that owed its privileged status to the Communist party and the state—and he also corrupted the Marxian ideal of the economic and social equality of all.

## The Gorbachev Reforms

When Mikhail Gorbachev gained power in the Soviet Union in 1985, he inherited an economic system largely unchanged from the one built from 1928 to 1953 by Josef Stalin. It was an economic system directed by a totalitarian dictatorship. It was a very rigid command system driven by five-year plans created by central planners.

Gorbachev's first statements as leader of the Communist party pledged the continuation of the old policies. However, he acknowledged that rapid economic improvement was the government's most important goal. The ending of the Eleventh Five-Year Plan that year was marked by declining economic growth and worker output, which Gorbachev blamed on poor organization, complacency, and irresponsibility.

---

[8]The First Five-Year Plan, launched in 1928, was declared completed in 1932, nine months ahead of schedule. The second plan ran from 1932 to 1937 and the third from 1937 until it was interrupted by the German invasion of the Soviet Union in 1941.

**New Economic Policies**  Several months later, Gorbachev abruptly broke with the past, criticizing a draft of the Twelfth Five-Year Plan for not putting enough emphasis on capital reinvestment in existing factories and not addressing consumer demand. He blamed previous leaders for not changing the shape of Soviet economic activity.

Gorbachev proposed instead a program that covered not only the period of the next plan, but also the two that followed until the year 2000. Thus he articulated the economic aspects of *perestroika*, his plan for the reorganization of the Soviet system. To show his seriousness he ousted the chairman of the central planning commission who had served for 20 years.

Gorbachev's plan for "radical reform" included more authority for local farm and factory managers, a more flexible pricing system, tying salaries to performance, and allowing enterprises to distribute production above planned levels "as they saw fit." In 1987, the "Law of Individual Labor Activity" was passed, permitting private profit-making activities in 40 categories. It even allowed state workers to quit their jobs to pursue these personal opportunities.

Further details of economic *perestroika* even included competition among state enterprises for contracts; self-financing of operations, which would allow the reduction of state subsidies; and the application of "full-scale profit and loss accounting." The proposals were approved by the party Central Committee in June 1987 and by the Supreme Soviet four days later.

In 1988 an official publication of the Communist party predicted the merging of socialism and capitalism in the Soviet Union.[9] It observed, "We cannot ignore the experience of mankind as a whole, including the nonsocialist world."

**Political Changes**  Three years of bold proposals could not undo more than 60 years of entrenched bureaucracy. This, coupled with such events as a terrible nuclear accident at Chernobyl, poor harvests, growing unrest in the republics, and the crumbling of its bloc of Eastern European allies, produced a failing economy by the beginning of 1990. Gorbachev was still in power, but his foundation was weak.

The Communist party was split into factions. One faction, the liberals, wanted the immediate shift to free market capitalism. The other group, the conservatives, wanted a slower transition. The conservatives feared that too swift a move would create severe unemployment and soaring prices, which would lead to social disorder. The liberals countered with the argument that "property in the hands of each individual is a guarantee of the stability of society."

Debate over the various reform plans raged for nearly seven months in 1990. A compromise "President's Plan" was finally adopted in October. It was less radical than the liberals wanted but much more radical than the conservative faction was willing to accept.

One month later, the first stock exchange in Soviet history was founded in Moscow, with the participation of 187 enterprises and banks. The

▲ **Power Struggle**  Narrowly surviving a parliamentary vote to impeach him, Russian President Boris Yeltsin continues to face opposition from hard-line communists.

---

[9]The statement, from *Pravda*, was made by Vadim Medvedev, the official Communist party ideologist.

foremost symbol of American capitalism, the New York Stock Exchange, provided technical assistance for the Soviets.

**Remaking the Russian Economy** It is clear that the transition from a communist economy to a free market system and the movement toward democratic government that you read about in the previous chapter are closely linked. Much of Gorbachev's performance prior to the coup in August 1991 was judged by the progress of his economic plan. And the decision to grant Russian President Boris Yeltsin the power to rule by decree was based on his plan to accelerate the restructuring of the economy.

The economic plan that Yeltsin instituted was radical. Its first phase called for the lifting of all price controls by the end of 1991, the privatization of all small and medium-sized farms and factories, the creation of a convertible currency, and basing trade with other former Soviet republics on hard currency exchange rather than on subsidies, as was previously the case.

The second phase of Yeltsin's plan came only six months later. It emphasized the privatization of larger businesses and gaining control over the high rates of inflation that had been climbing since prices were deregulated.

The scale of these actions was unprecedented and the results have been uneven. Although more than 40,000 smaller enterprises were put into private ownership in the first fifteen months of the plan, production has remained sluggish; inflation has driven consumer prices beyond the means of most citizens; and the exchange value of the ruble has fallen drastically. In addition, the crime rate—particularly crimes against property—has soared in many Russian cities.

Thus far, no one has publicly called for a return to the old communist system. Conservatives would like to slow the pace of economic restructuring to ensure that social welfare needs can be met and to alleviate the poverty that some Russians are experiencing. Yeltsin and the radical reformers insist that Russia's short-term pain will be outweighed by the future benefits of a free market economy. As an economic system and as a repressive political system, communism remains a major force in today's world.

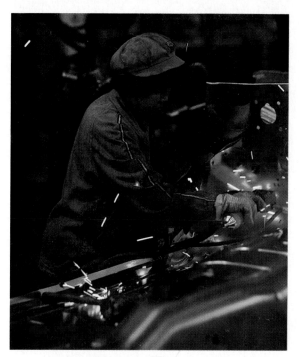

**Bastion of Communism** Though communism appears to be on the decline around the world, fully one-fifth of the planet's population lives and works under the communist government of China.

The island nation of Cuba, off Florida's coast, and China, the world's most populous nation, still stand as examples of communist states.

# Section 3 Review

1. **Define**: five-year plan, collectivization
2. On what four closely related concepts did Marx build communist ideology?
3. (a) Where did Marx believe the first communist societies would appear? (b) Why?
4. How well did Soviet communism follow the socialist ideal of economic and social equality?
5. What were the differing views of liberals and conservatives about Gorbachev's reforms?

**Critical Thinking**

6. **Drawing Conclusions** (p. 19) Recall the statement on page 623: "Property in the hands of each individual is a guarantee of the stability of society." What do you think this statement means?

★

# How to Start a Small Business

Since 80 percent of the nation's businesses employ fewer than 20 people, it should come as no surprise that the Federal Government's Small Business Administration (SBA) maintains that small businesses form the backbone of the country's economy. Successful small businesses help create new markets and jobs that spark economic growth for the entire nation. Follow the steps below to learn about starting a small business.

**1. Know the risks.** It is essential for anyone considering starting a business to be fully aware of the risks involved. Approximately three out of four new small businesses fail within a short period of time, often resulting in financial loss for the owner. To begin with, a small business must have a solid, marketable product—without it, no amount of money or planning can ensure success.

**2. Contact the SBA.** The SBA issues a wide variety of helpful publications and offers counseling, training programs, and financial assistance. A first step for anyone interested in opening a new business is to call the SBA or to write a letter stating his

or her business plans. How could you use the Government Resources Handbook on page 690 to find the number and address of the SBA?

**3. Ensure sufficient financing.** Raising capital—the money needed to operate a business—is a basic task required in all successful business ventures. However, it can be a difficult and frustrating process. There are several sources available, and a business owner must consider the various options before making a decision. Some of these sources may be personal savings, friends and relatives, banks and credit unions. The SBA also offers a variety of loan programs. To be successful in obtaining loans, a person must be prepared to explain how much money is needed, why it is needed, and when it can be paid back.

**4. Have a thorough knowledge of the business.** For example, if a person is interested in opening a plumbing supply shop, it is essential that he or she know everything there is to know about the plumbing business. It is important also to know what kind of business information is available, where to get it, and how to use it. A few key sources of information include: the SBA District Office, the Small Business Development Center (SBDC), and the Small Business Institute (SBI). What might happen to a business person who does not know his or her business thoroughly?

**5. Research the market.** Having a good product and having the proper financing mean little if there is no demand for the product. The organizations mentioned in Step 4 can provide assistance in determining the best methods for recognizing customer needs and for creating a plan for developing potential customers.

# Chapter-in-Brief

Scan all headings, photographs, charts, and other visuals in the chapter before reading the summaries below.

## Section 1  Capitalism (pp. 605–611)

Capitalism is based on private ownership of productive property. Private individuals and companies decide how their property is used, and they own the benefits that their property creates. Those who own capital and put it to productive use are called capitalists.

A capitalistic economy is often called a free enterprise system. Such systems are characterized by: (1) private ownership of property, (2) the guarantee of property rights, (3) decentralized decision making, (4) competition, and (5) freedom of choice.

According to the laissez-faire theory, a capitalistic system works best with minimum interference from government. However, the United States Government plays a significant role in the American economy.

There are three kinds of business organizations—sole proprietorships, partnerships, and corporations. No matter what the kind of business, the driving force is generally profit. In a capitalist economy, operating a business includes the potential of earning a profit—or of losing money.

## Section 2  Socialism (pp. 613–617)

Socialism is an economic and political philosophy based on the idea that the benefits of economic activity should be equitably distributed.

Socialism developed in part as a reaction to the Industrial Revolution. Karl Marx was the key critic of capitalism. Those who believed that Marx's ideal could be achieved through democratic means came to be known as socialists.

Socialist economies often have nationalized industries. They also aim to guarantee social welfare through the equal distribution of necessities and services. In order to provide this level of service, taxes in socialist countries tend to be high.

Socialism is appealing to many developing nations. However, the costs and sacrifices required under such a system are difficult for such societies to bear.

In a socialist system, economic decision making is centralized. For this reason, such economies are called command economies. However, many critics feel that such central planning of a complex economy is impossible. Others criticize socialism because it denies individuals the right to decide how to use their incomes. Defenders of socialism say that capitalism leads to its own inefficiencies and inequities.

## Section 3  Communism (pp. 618–623)

Communism calls for collective ownership of productive property. Its basic concepts came from Marx and *The Communist Manifesto*.

In spite of Marx's expectation that the workers' revolution would begin in industrialized Europe, it first took place in largely agricultural Russia. Led by Lenin, communists took control of what would become the Soviet Union. Later, under Stalin, the central government took complete control of the economy.

Stalin's system remained intact until the arrival of Gorbachev in 1985. Gorbachev introduced elements into the economy such as private property and even a stock exchange. Yet persistent problems in the economy and political structure helped produce dissatisfaction from both liberals and conservatives. One manifestation of this unrest was the failed 1991 coup. The results of Russian President Boris Yeltsin's radical economic reforms have been uneven. Neither side in the economic debate has called for a return to communism.

Communism remains a force in places such as Cuba and China.

# Chapter Review

## Vocabulary and Key Terms

capital (p. 606)
capitalist (p. 606)
free enterprise system (p. 607)
entrepreneur (p. 607)
laws of supply and
   demand (p. 608)

monopoly (p. 608)
proletariat (p. 614)
bourgeoisie (p. 614)
welfare state (p. 615)
market economy (p. 615)

command economy
   (p. 615)
five-year plan (p. 621)
collectivization (p. 621)

**Matching:** *Review the key terms in the list above. If you are not sure of a term's meaning, look up the term and review its definition. Choose a term from the list above that best matches each description.*

1. a firm that is the only source of a product or service
2. in Marxist terms, the capitalists
3. an economic system in which individuals are free to start and run their own businesses
4. a government that assumes the role of promoter of citizen welfare through programs sponsored by the government
5. economic system in which the government directs the economy along a government-determined path

**True or False:** *Determine whether each statement is true or false. If it is true, write "true." If it is false, change the underlined word or words to make the statement true.*

1. Marx believed that the <u>bourgeoisie</u> would one day rise up and overthrow the capitalistic system.
2. An economy in which the economic decisions are made by thousands of private individuals and companies is called a <u>market economy</u>.
3. <u>Capital</u> consists of the wealth used to produce goods and services.

4. Under competitive conditions, the <u>free enterprise system</u> determines prices as a function of the quantity of goods available and customer need for those goods.
5. The <u>five-year plans</u> represented the first attempt by a society to combine large-scale centralized economic planning with public ownership of the means of production.

**Word Relationships:** *Replace the underlined definition with the correct term from the list above.*

1. Countries with socialist governments are sometimes referred to as <u>governments that provide citizens with extensive social services such as medical and dental care</u>.
2. <u>Someone who owns capital and puts it to productive use</u> creates and expands industries, invests in new technologies, and engages in activities that create jobs.
3. If existing companies do not see and meet demand, an <u>individual who takes the initiative of starting or expanding a business</u> may do so.
4. Socialist and communist economies are sometimes called <u>those in which governments can direct the economy along the desired path</u>.
5. Stalin's First Five-Year Plan included the goal of <u>the combining of millions of small peasant farms</u>.

## Main Ideas

### Section 1 (pp. 605–611)

1. What is the most distinctive characteristic of capitalism?
2. What are the hallmarks of a free enterprise system?
3. (a) Briefly describe the laissez-faire theory. (b) Why is it incorrect to call American capitalism laissez-faire capitalism?
4. Briefly describe the role of profit and loss in a capitalist system.

### Section 2 (pp. 613–617)

5. Briefly describe Karl Marx's basic ideas about the capitalist system.
6. Briefly describe the meaning of the term *socialism*.
7. What are three characteristics commonly found in socialist countries?
8. What are the major criticisms of socialism?

### Section 3 (pp. 618–623)

9. Briefly describe Marx's view of history and the labor theory of value.
10. Briefly describe communism under Lenin and Stalin.
11. Briefly describe the overall approach advocated by Gorbachev when he first assumed power in 1985.
12. What was the dispute between liberals and conservatives over Gorbachev's reforms?

## Critical Thinking

1. **Formulating Questions** (p. 19)   Create a list of questions you could use to evaluate the strengths and weaknesses of the capitalist system as it exists in the United States.
2. **Expressing Problems Clearly** (p. 19) Communist theory has always insisted on this guiding principle: "From each according to his ability, to each according to his need." Do you think that this principle represents a positive ideal? Explain your answer.
3. **Identifying Assumptions** (p. 19)   Consider the common criticism of socialism on the grounds that it kills individual initiative.

(a) What assumption about initiative underlies this criticism? (b) Is this assumption valid? Why or why not?

## Getting Involved

1. **Writing Your Opinion**   You are a newspaper editor in a country that operates under a command economy. Write a newspaper editorial in which you offer your opinion on the benefits and/or drawbacks of such a system. Review the characteristics of command economies as discussed in Sections 2 and 3. Consider the impact of such systems on individuals and on the country as a whole. Identify three arguments to support your general views on the benefits and drawbacks of a command economy. Begin the editorial by stating your overall opinion on the subject. Then, present your three arguments in a logical and orderly manner, devoting one paragraph to each. Remember, the purpose of an editorial is to communicate your opinion, so as you revise your first draft, make sure your arguments are as persuasive and clear as possible. Correct any errors, then draft a final copy.

2. **Class Debate**   Hold a class debate on the following topic: *Resolved*, That the United States should more strictly observe the laissez-faire theory as put forward by Adam Smith. Select teams to debate each side of this topic. The rest of the class should evaluate each team's presentation.

3. **Gathering Information**   Suppose you are interested in finding out some basic economic information about the United States, such as its gross national product, the per capita income, and other basic economic indicators. You would also like to compare these statistics with those of other leading countries. Use the Government Resources Handbook on page 690 to identify sources you might use to find this information.

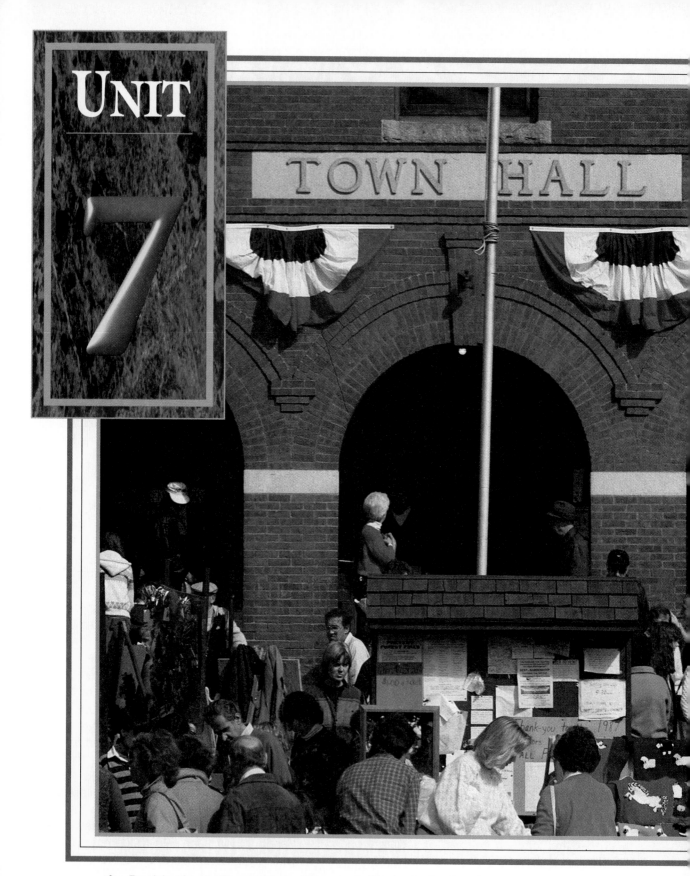

**UNIT**

**7**

▲ **Participation in Government** The town hall is the focal point of many community activities for these New Hampshire townspeople.

# Participating in State and Local Government

In March 1991, at the venerable age of 97, Ernest W. Hibbard attended the annual town meeting in Hadley, Massachusetts. That fact taken by itself is in no way remarkable. New England town meetings may very well be the best exemplification of pure democracy in America. On town meeting day, any citizen may attend, speak on any question, and if old enough, vote. Mr. Hibbard was well acquainted with the process. He went to his first town meeting as a boy of 12. It was 1906, and the meeting was held in the afternoon when Ernest was scheduled to be in school. His father believed, however, that the boy would benefit more from attending town meeting than from his classes. Although he was too young to vote that day, the meeting must have made quite an impression on him: Ernest Hibbard didn't miss a single town meeting in the next 86 years— and his attendance serves as an enduring example of participation in government.

## DID YOU KNOW THAT . . .

- Besides traditional law-enforcement activities such as crime investigation, patrol, and traffic enforcement, 50 percent of local police agencies have primary responsibility for animal control.

- A law still on the books in Oak Park, Illinois, prohibits roosters from crowing before 6 A.M.

- An old Virginia law makes it illegal to take a bath without a doctor's permission.

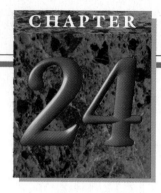

# Organization of State and Local Government

## Chapter Preview

Look at the front page of this morning's newspaper. Watch the news programs on network TV this evening. Almost certainly, you will find that their major stories deal with events at the national and the international levels: Something the President has just said or done. A controversial measure in the Senate, an upcoming vote in the House of Representatives. An important decision by the Supreme Court. A critical situation in the Middle East or in the Balkans or somewhere else in the world.

The fact that the major news media almost always feature matters of national and of international concern can blind us to this very significant point: Most of what government in this country does is done by the States and by their thousands of local governments. In this chapter, and the next one, you will look at all of those "other" governments in the United States—at their overall shapes and at what they do and how they do it.

### Before you read this chapter:

- **Describe** what you know about the governor of your State.
- **Predict** what might occur if the Federal Government took over all the functions of State governments.

### As you read, focus on the main objective for each section. Understand:

1. The structure, organization, and powers of State legislatures.
2. The overall shape of the office of governor.
3. The structure of local governments as creations of the State.
4. The governments of American cities.

▲ **Governors Hear Health Plan**  President Clinton had the attention of the governors of all fifty States when he explained his planned health-care reform proposals at the 1993 meeting of the National Governor's Association.

# 1 The State Legislatures

### Find Out:

- What is a State constitution?
- What basic governmental functions does each State legislature perform?
- How are the State legislatures organized?

### Key Terms:

initiative, referendum

The basic features of government at both the national and State levels in the United States are remarkably similar. At both levels the governmental structure is set out in a constitution that provides for legislative, executive, and judicial branches.

As you will see in this section, each State's constitution is that State's fundamental law. And, each State constitution establishes a legislative body that is, in effect, the powerhouse of that State's government.

## The State Constitutions

Each State has a written constitution. That fact is, in itself, significant. From its very beginnings, American government has been based on written constitutions. In fact, the United States has sometimes been called "a land of constitutions."

The American experience with such documents dates from 1606 when King James I granted a charter to the Virginia Company. That act led to the settlement at Jamestown in the following year and, with it, the first government in British North America. Each of the other English colonies was established and governed on the basis of a written charter.

Since the first State constitutions were written in 1776, the States have drafted and approved nearly 150 of them. In a very real sense, each of the present-day State constitutions is a link in a chain of written documents that now stretches over nearly 400 years of American history.

A State constitution is that State's fundamental law. It sets out the way in which the government of that State is organized, and it distributes power among the various branches

## VOICES *on Government*

### On Serving as a Legislator

**Brynhild Haugland,**
farmer and Republican
State legislator for North
Dakota, 1939 to 1990

❝No party [Democratic or Republican] has a monopoly on good people or good ideas. . . . There were 24 women in the legislature last year, but I have been the lone woman in some sessions. Still, no doors have ever been closed to me. The only limiting factor here is ability. . . . We are on the threshold of great change in this state, the nation and the world. Legislating is an ongoing process. . . . Most any good thing can be accomplished eventually if you aren't particular who gets the credit.❞

of State government. It authorizes the exercise of power of government and puts limits on the exercise of governmental power. A State's constitution is superior to any and all other forms of State and local law within that State.

But remember this, too: Each State's constitution is subordinate to the United States Constitution; see Article VI, Section 2. No provision in any State constitution may conflict with any provision in any form of federal law.

## The Legislature: Structure and Size

In every State, the legislature is the lawmaking branch of State government. Its basic function goes to the heart of democratic government: It is responsible for translating the public will into the State's public policy.

What is commonly called the legislature is officially known by that title in just over half the States. In several others, however, the constitution calls the legislature the General Assembly, and in a few the Legislative Assembly or the General Court.

Forty-nine of the 50 State legislatures are bicameral. The upper house is called the Senate in all States. The lower house is referred to as the House of Representatives in most, though some States call it the Assembly, General Assembly, or House of Delegates. Nebraska, the only State with a one-house legislature, calls its single chamber the Unicameral Legislature.

**Size** There is no exact figure for the ideal size of a legislative body. Two basic considerations are important, however. First, a legislature, and each of its houses, should not be so large as to hamper the orderly conduct of the people's business. Second, it should not be so small that the many views and interests within the State cannot be adequately represented. The upper house in most States has from 30 to 50 members. There are only 20 seats in Alaska's senate, however, and but 21 in the upper house in both Nevada and Delaware. Minnesota now has the largest upper house, with 67 members.

The lower house usually ranges between 100 and 150 members. However, only 40 members sit in the lower chamber in Alaska, 41 in Delaware, and 42 in Nevada. At the other extreme, Pennsylvania has 203 seats in its house, and New Hampshire has an almost incredible 400.

## The State Legislators

You might find it surprising that the details of service in each of the 50 State legislatures are so much alike. However, all the States share traditions of government that help explain these similarities.

**Qualifications** Every State's constitution sets out certain requirements—of age, citizenship, and residence—for membership in the legislature. For example, most States require representatives to be at least 21 and senators to be 25. These qualifications do vary from State to State but, on the whole, they are not very difficult to meet.

The realities of politics place still other qualifications on those who seek seats in their State legislatures. These qualifications, though informal, are even harder to meet than the formal ones. They have to do with a candidate's vote-getting abilities, and they are based on such characteristics as occupation, name familiarity, party identification, race, religion, national origin, and the like.

**Election** Voters voting in popular elections select the legislators in every State. Nearly everywhere, candidates for the legislature are nominated at party primaries, and opposing candidates face one another in a partisan general election. Legislative nominees are picked by conventions in only a few States—Delaware, for example. In only one State, Nebraska, are the candidates nominated in nonpartisan primaries. There the opposing candidates are not identified by party in the general election, either.

In most States the lawmakers are elected in November of even-numbered years. In four States—Mississippi, New Jersey, Virginia, and Louisiana—legislative elections are held in the odd-numbered years in the hope of separating State and local issues from national politics.

**Terms** Legislators serve either two-year or four-year terms. Senators are usually elected for longer terms than are their colleagues in the lower house. The rate of turnover in legislative seats is fairly high. In a given year, more than one-fourth of the 7,461 State legislators around the country are serving their first terms in office.

**Compensation** Far too often, capable men and women refuse to run for seats in State legislatures because of the financial sacrifices that such service entails. Salaries are generally too low, although most States provide some sort of additional allowances to help ease the financial burden of serving as a legislator.

Oregon provides a fairly typical example of the compensation offered to legislators by States. The basic salary is now $1,092 a month, or $26,208 for the biennium, a two-year period. In addition, each member receives an expense allowance: $75 for each day of the leg-

### How to Make Decisions

**1. Decide What Your Options Are.** Make a list of every option you can choose. For example, perhaps you are trying to decide between doing your homework or going to a movie with a friend.

**2. Determine the Possible Outcomes of Each Option.** Often, more than one outcome is possible as the result of a decision. List the various outcomes under each option. For example, if you do your homework you will be prepared for class, you will learn more, and so on. If you go to the movie, you will have a chance to visit with your friend and relax.

**3. Assign a Value to Each Outcome.** This is sometimes called assigning payoffs. All payoffs for each outcome should be in the same units. For example, dollars, time saved, lives saved, and so on. Doing your homework should help you get a better grade in the course. Going to a movie should have its own educational benefits and be enjoyable.

**4. Make Your Decision.** Compare the values of each outcome and the likelihood of achieving the value. For example, the likelihood that doing your homework will help you get a better grade may be 75% and the likelihood that going to a movie will be educational and enjoyable may be 95%. Based on this and the above information, decide which option to pursue.

▲ **Interpreting Charts** Making choices—voting, making decisions—is one of the key responsibilities of a legislator. What outcomes of those decisions must legislators consider before they vote on an issue (Step 2)?

islative session, which usually lasts for about 180 days, and for each day he or she attends interim committee meetings (meetings held between sessions). Each member also has an expense allowance of up to $550 for each month in which the legislature is not in session. The total compensation per member, including both salary and allowances, comes to only some $29,000 a year.

**Legislative Sessions** Forty-two State legislatures now hold annual sessions, and the California legislature meets in a continuous two-year session. Only Arkansas, Kentucky, Montana,

Nevada, North Dakota, Oregon, and Texas still meet on an every-other-year (biennial) basis.

Most States have turned to annual sessions only in the past decade or so, as it has become increasingly apparent that legislators cannot handle the legislative workload by meeting every other year for a few months. As a general rule, regular sessions, whether annual or biennial, are becoming longer and longer. All 50 governors, and just over half of the State legislatures too, can call special sessions to allow the lawmaking body to take up urgent matters for consideration between its regularly scheduled meetings.

## Powers of the Legislature

Identifying those powers that belong to a State legislature is a complicated matter. In each State the legislature has all of those powers (1) that the State constitution does not grant exclusively to the executive or judicial branches of the State's government or its local units, and (2) that neither the State constitution nor the United States Constitution denies to the legislature.

**Legislative Powers** State legislatures can pass any law that does not conflict with federal law or with any part of that State's constitution. Therefore, it is impossible to list all the powers of the State legislatures. However, most State constitutions do list several of the legislature's more important powers. Those most often mentioned include the powers to tax, spend, borrow, establish courts, define crimes and provide for their punishment, regulate commercial activities, and maintain public schools.

Every legislature's powers include the vital "police power"—the State's power to protect and promote the public health, safety, morals, and welfare. This broad power is the basis of thousands of State laws, including those that require vaccinations and prohibit the ownership of dangerous weapons, for example. You read about the police power in Chapter 20, Section 1.

**Nonlegislative Powers** All 50 State legislatures possess certain nonlegislative powers in addition to those they exercise in making law.

EXECUTIVE POWERS Some of a legislature's powers are executive in nature. For example, the governor's power to appoint certain officials is subject to approval by the legislature, or at least the upper house. In some States the legislature itself appoints certain executive officeholders. Thus, the secretary of state is chosen by the legislature in Maine, New Hampshire, and Tennessee.

JUDICIAL POWERS Each State legislature also has certain judicial powers. The chief illustration is the

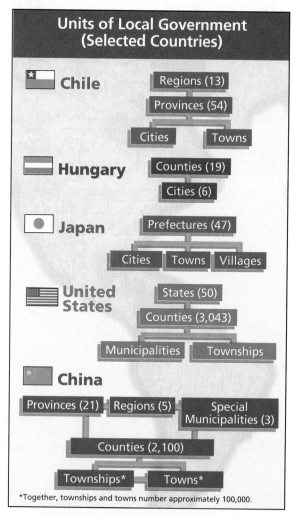

## Global Awareness

**Units of Local Government (Selected Countries)**

**Chile**
- Regions (13)
- Provinces (54)
- Cities
- Towns

**Hungary**
- Counties (19)
- Cities (6)

**Japan**
- Prefectures (47)
- Cities
- Towns
- Villages

**United States**
- States (50)
- Counties (3,043)
- Municipalities
- Townships

**China**
- Provinces (21)
- Regions (5)
- Special Municipalities (3)
- Counties (2,100)
- Townships*
- Towns*

*Together, townships and towns number approximately 100,000.

▲ **Interpreting Charts** Which country has the least hierarchical government structure?

power of impeachment. In every State except Oregon, the legislature can remove any State executive officer or judge through that process.

Each legislature also has judicial powers with regard to its own members. Thus, disputes about the election or the qualifications of a member-elect are usually decided by the house involved in the matter. Then, too, because legislators themselves are not subject to impeachment (although in 16 States they can be recalled by voters), each chamber has the power to discipline any of its members, and in extreme cases even to expel them.

CONSTITUENT POWERS State legislatures play a role in constitution-making and the constitutional amendment process. Since this does not involve the making of statutes, this function—the constituent power—is a nonlegislative one.

## Organization of the Legislature

In general terms, each State legislature is organized in much the same manner as Congress.

**The Presiding Officers** Those who preside over the sessions of the nation's 99 State legislative chambers are almost always powerful political figures—in the legislature itself and elsewhere in State politics.

The lower house in each of the 49 bicameral legislatures elects its own presiding officer, known everywhere as the speaker.

The senate chooses its own presiding officer in 22 States. In the other 28 States, the lieutenant governor serves as the president of the senate. Where the lieutenant governor does preside, the senate selects a president *pro tempore* to serve when the lieutenant governor is absent.[1]

Except for the lieutenant governors, each of these presiding officers is chosen by a vote of the full membership in his or her legislative chamber. In fact those who fill leadership posts are usually picked by the majority party's caucus just before the legislature starts a new session.

▲ **Women in State Government** Pennsylvania State representative Rosita Youngblood serves on the Urban Affairs Committee and is interested in creating safe and affordable housing for the people of her district.

The chief duties of those presiding officers center on the conduct of the legislature's floor business—and these duties are a major source of their power. The presiding officers refer bills to committee, recognize members who seek the floor, and interpret and apply the rules of their chamber to its proceedings.

Unlike the Speaker of the House in Congress, the speaker in nearly every State appoints the chairperson and other members of each house committee. The senate's president or president *pro tem* has the same power in just over half the States. The presiding officers regularly use the power to name committees as they use their other powers: to reward their friends, punish their enemies, and otherwise work their influence on the legislature.

**The Committee System** The committee system in State legislatures works much as it does in Congress. Much of the work of the legislature is done by committee members when

---

[1]The term *pro tempore* means "temporary." In practice this officer's title is generally shortened to president *pro tem.*

they sort out those bills that will reach the floor and when they inform the full chamber on measures they have handled.

The standing committees in each house are generally set up by subject matter, such as committees on highways, education, and so on. A bill may be amended or even very largely rewritten in committee or, as often happens, ignored altogether.[2] Joint committees—permanent groups made up of members of both houses—are being used increasingly in the State legislatures. These committees can produce substantial savings of legislative time and effort.

## The Legislative Process

The major steps in the legislative process in a typical State legislature are much like those in Congress. You can review the legislative process in Congress by studying the diagram of the legislative process that appears on page 305, Chapter 12.

Legally, only a member may introduce a bill in either house in any of the State legislatures. So, in the strictest sense, legislators themselves are the source of all measures introduced. In broader terms, however, the lawmakers are the real source, the authors, of only a relative handful of bills.

A large number of bills come from public sources, from officers and agencies of State and local government. Every governor has a legislative program of some sort—and often an extensive and ambitious one.

Many bills are born in other public places too. Take, for example, a measure to increase the maximum penalty for some crime. That bill might be proposed by the attorney general. A bill to give cities a larger share of the money raised by the State's gasoline tax might be initiated in a city council or in some city manager's office.

Bills also come from a wide range of private sources. In fact, the largest single source for proposed legislation in the States appears to be interest groups. As you may remember from Chapter 9, those groups and their lobbyists have one overriding purpose: to influence public policy to benefit their own special interests. Of course, some bills do originate with private individuals—business people, farmers, labor union members, and other citizens—who, for one reason or another, think that "there ought to be a law . . ."

## Direct Legislation

Several States allow voters to take a direct part in the lawmaking process through the initiative and the referendum.

**The Initiative**  Through the **initiative** process, voters can propose by petition constitutional amendments in 17 States. In 21 States voters can use the initiative to initiate ordinary statutes, as well. Among these 21 States, the initiative takes two quite different forms: the more common direct initiative and the little-used indirect initiative.

In both the direct and indirect initiative, a certain number of qualified voters must sign initiative petitions to propose a law. The key difference between them lies in what happens to the proposed measure once enough valid signatures have been collected.

Where the direct initiative is used, the measure goes directly to the ballot, usually at the next general election. If the voters approve the measure, it becomes law. If not, it dies.

In the indirect initiative, the proposal goes first to the legislature. That body may pass it, making it a law. If it does not, the measure then goes to the voters. The number of voters who must sign petitions to initiate a statute varies from State to State.

**The Referendum**  A **referendum** is a process in which a legislative measure is referred to the State's voters for final approval or rejection. Three different forms of the referendum are now used among the States: mandatory, optional, and popular.

---

[2]The "pigeonholing" of bills is as well known in the States as it is in Congress; see page 298. In fact, in most States one of the standing committees in each house is regularly the "graveyard committee," a body to which bills are sent to be buried. The judiciary committee, to which bills may be referred "on grounds of doubtful constitutionality," often fills this role. A vivid illustration of a graveyard committee existed for several years in the lower house in landlocked Oklahoma: the Committee on Deep Sea Navigation.

The mandatory referendum is involved whenever the legislature is required to refer a measure to the voters. Thus, in every State except Delaware, the legislature must submit proposed amendments to the constitution to the electorate. In several States some other measures also must go to the voters for final action—for example, measures to borrow funds.

An optional referendum measure is one that the legislature refers to the voters voluntarily. Such measures are rare. When one does appear on a State's ballot, it usually involves a "hot potato" question—that is, one lawmakers would rather not take direct responsibility for deciding themselves.

The popular referendum is the form most often connected with the idea of direct legislation. Under the popular referendum, the people may demand via a petition that a measure passed by the legislature be referred to them for final action. Most attempts to use the popular referendum in fact fail. Usually the opponents of a particular measure simply cannot gather the required number of signatures for their petitions to force a popular vote on the matter.

## Section **1** Review

1. **Define:** initiative, referendum
2. How do each of the State constitutions fit within the scheme of federalism?
3. Name a few typical characteristics that are among the most important qualifications for the office of State legislator.
4. What are two judicial powers of State legislatures?
5. What is the difference between a direct and an indirect initiative?
6. What are the three types of referendum found among the states?

### Critical Thinking

7. **Making Comparisons** (p. 19) Consider what you know about Congress and the State legislatures. (a) In what areas are they most alike? (b) In what areas are they the most different?

★

## 2 The Governor and State Administration

### Find Out:

■ What are the structural details of the typical governorship—its qualifications, selection, term, succession, and compensation?
■ What are the governor's executive, legislative, and judicial powers?
■ What are the titles and functions of the officers who share executive authority with the governor?

### Key Terms:

item veto, pardon, commute, reprieve, parole

In colonial America, it was the actions of the royal governors that inspired much of the resentment that fueled the Revolution. That attitude was carried over into the first State constitutions, in which the new State governors had little real authority.

In each of the 50 States, the office of governor has changed a great deal since those early days. In this section, you will explore the governorship today.

### The Governorship

The governor is the principal executive officer in each of the 50 States. He or she is always a central figure in State politics and is often a well-known national personality, as well. Indeed, the governorships have produced several Presidents and many members of both houses of Congress.

**Selecting the Governor**   As in the case of candidates for the State legislator, candidates for the governorship must meet both formal and informal requirements. Thousands of persons in every State could fulfill the formal requirements, which include American citizenship, a minimum age (usually 25 or 30), and residence in the State.

The informal qualifications, however, are more difficult to meet. Any person who wants

**Massachusetts Governor**   William Weld serves a four-year term. Shortly after taking office, Weld was already fielding questions on his thoughts on making a run for the White House in the next presidential election.

to be governor—or hold any other elected office, for that matter—must first satisfy certain political requirements. The candidate must be "available" and have those characteristics that will win the votes of the party's nominators and those of the voters in the general election. Exactly what, in particular, those characteristics are varies from State to State, and even from election to election. Race, sex, religion, personality, name familiarity, party membership, experience, stands on the issues, the ability to use television effectively—these and several other factors are all a part of the mix.[3]

**Selection**   In every State the governor is chosen by popular vote. In all but five States—Arizona, Georgia, Louisiana, Mississippi, and Vermont—only a plurality is needed for election. The major parties' gubernatorial candidates are usually picked in primaries. Nearly half the States now provide for the joint election of the governor and lieutenant governor. In those States, each party's candidates for those offices run as a team, and the voter casts one vote to fill both posts.

**Term**   The one-year gubernatorial term disappeared long ago. Governors are elected to four-year terms nearly everywhere today. Only three States—New Hampshire, Rhode Island, and Vermont—now provide for two-year terms.

More than half of the States now place some limit on the number of terms a governor may serve. Kentucky and Virginia have what amounts to a one-term limit; they forbid the governor to succeed himself/herself in office. In most of the other States that cap gubernatorial tenure, the limit is now two terms.

Those governors who run for another term most often make it. Over time, just about two-thirds of them have won the new term.

**Succession**   Occasionally, a governor dies in office. Every so often, one resigns in midterm—to become a United States senator or to accept a presidential appointment, for example. No matter what the cause of the vacancy, the State constitution provides for a successor. In 43 States the lieutenant governor is first in the line of succession. In Maine, New Hampshire, New Jersey, and West Virginia, the president of the senate succeeds. In Arizona, Oregon, and Wyoming the office passes to the secretary of state.

---

[3]All told, some 2,400 persons have ever served as governors of the various States. Of that number, only 13 have been women. Twelve women have been elected to a governorship; only one of them is now in office: Governor Christine Todd Whitman of New Jersey, who was chosen in 1993. Her 11 elected predecessors: Nellie Ross (Wyoming, 1925–1927), Miriam Ferguson (Texas, 1925–1927, 1933–1935), Lurleen Wallace (Alabama, 1967–1968), Ella Grasso (Connecticut, 1975–1980), Dixy Lee Ray (Washington, 1977–1981), Martha Layne Collins (Kentucky, 1983–1987), Madeleine Kunin (Vermont, 1985–1991), Kay Orr (Nebraska, 1987–1991), Joan Finney (Kansas, 1991–1995), Ann Richards (Texas, 1991–1995), and Barbara Roberts (Oregon, 1991–1995). Also, Rose Mofford (who had been secretary of state) succeeded to the governorship in Arizona in 1988, after that State's legislature impeached and removed Governor Evan Mecham; Governor Mofford served until 1991. At present there is but one woman governor, Republican Christine Whitman of New Jersey.

**Removal** The governor may be removed from office by the impeachment process in every State except Oregon. Only five governors have been ousted since Reconstruction, and only one—Arizona's Evan Mecham in 1988—has suffered that fate in the last 60 years.

The voters in 16 States have the power to recall the governor. This has happened only once, however—to Governor Lynn J. Frazier of North Dakota, in 1921. Removal did not keep him out of public office long: He was elected to the United States Senate the very next year.

**Compensation** A glance at the table on this page will show that gubernatorial salaries now average about $90,000 a year. The spread is fairly wide among the States, however, ranging from just over $55,000 in Montana to a high of $130,000 in New Jersey and New York. Most States also provide the governor with an official residence, generally called the governor's mansion, and a more or less generous expense account.

## The Governor's Executive Powers

Recall, the Federal Constitution makes the President *the* executive in the National Government. The State constitutions, on the other hand, regularly describe the governor as the State's *chief* executive—and the distinction here is a critical one.

Only a part of that authority is held by the governor, who is in fact only a "first among equals." Yet, whatever the realities of the distribution of power may be, it is the governor to whom the people look for leadership in State affairs and hold responsible for the condition of the State. The governor is given a number of specific powers with which to accomplish that job.

**Appointment and Removal** A leading test of any administrator is his or her ability to select loyal and able assistants. Two major factors work against the governor's effectiveness here, however. First, of course, is the existence of other elected executives in State government. The people choose them and the governor cannot remove them.

| Terms and Salaries of Governors | | |
|---|---|---|
| **State** | **Term in Years** | **Annual Salary\*** |
| Alabama | 4 | $81,522 |
| Alaska | 4 | $81,648 |
| Arizona | 4 | $75,000 |
| Arkansas | 4 | $60,000 |
| California | 4 | $120,000 |
| Colorado | 4 | $70,000 |
| Connecticut | 4 | $78,000 |
| Delaware | 4 | $95,000 |
| Florida | 4 | $101,764 |
| Georgia | 4 | $98,166 |
| Hawaii | 4 | $94,780 |
| Idaho | 4 | $85,000 |
| Illinois | 4 | $105,788 |
| Indiana | 4 | $77,200 |
| Iowa | 4 | $76,700 |
| Kansas | 4 | $77,623 |
| Kentucky | 4 | $83,000 |
| Louisiana | 4 | $73,440 |
| Maine | 4 | $70,000 |
| Maryland | 4 | $120,000 |
| Massachusetts | 4 | $75,000 |
| Michigan | 4 | $112,025 |
| Minnesota | 4 | $109,053 |
| Mississippi | 4 | $75,600 |
| Missouri | 4 | $94,564 |
| Montana | 4 | $55,288 |
| Nebraska | 4 | $65,000 |
| Nevada | 4 | $90,000 |
| New Hampshire | 2 | $86,235 |
| New Jersey | 4 | $130,000 |
| New Mexico | 4 | $90,000 |
| New York | 4 | $130,000 |
| North Carolina | 4 | $97,600 |
| North Dakota | 4 | $68,284 |
| Ohio | 4 | $115,763 |
| Oklahoma | 4 | $70,000 |
| Oregon | 4 | $80,000 |
| Pennsylvania | 4 | $105,000 |
| Rhode Island | 2 | $69,900 |
| South Carolina | 4 | $106,077 |
| South Dakota | 4 | $79,875 |
| Tennessee | 4 | $85,000 |
| Texas | 4 | $99,000 |
| Utah | 4 | $110,000 |
| Vermont | 2 | $80,725 |
| Virginia | 4 | $101,861 |
| Washington | 4 | $121,000 |
| West Virginia | 4 | $72,000 |
| Wisconsin | 4 | $92,283 |
| Wyoming | 4 | $70,000 |

\*The governor is furnished an official residence in every State except Arizona, Massachusetts, Rhode Island, and Vermont. *Sources:* State constitutions and statutes and information furnished by appropriate State officials.

▲ **Interpreting Tables** Does there seem to be any correlation between a State's population and the governor's salary?

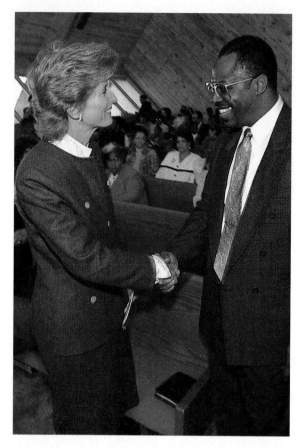

**At the State's Helm** Christine Todd Whitman became the governor of New Jersey in 1994. Whitman is now the only woman in the country to hold the office of governor.

Second, the State's constitution and statutes place restrictions on the governor's power to hire and fire. In most States the constitution requires that most of the governor's major appointees be confirmed by the State senate. Moreover, the legislature often sets qualifications that must be met by those appointed to the offices it has created by statute. In a vigorous two-party State, for example, the law often requires that not more than a certain number of the members of each board or commission be from the same political party. Thus, a governor must appoint some members of the opposing party to posts in his or her administration.

Consider one more example: The law often requires that those persons the governor appoints to any of the State's professional licensing boards must themselves be licensed to practice in the particular field that that board regulates. Thus, only licensed realtors can be appointed to the real estate board; only licensed physicians can serve on the board of medical examiners; and so on.

In spite of these restrictions, the governor has the authority to fill many important posts. How a governor exercises this power is a key to his or her success.

**Supervisory Powers** The governor is empowered to supervise the work of thousands of men and women who staff the State's executive branch. But here again, the governor's authority in this field is often limited by the constitution and statutes of the State. Many State agencies are subject to the governor's direct control, but many are not. The governor's powers of persuasion and ability to operate through such informal channels as party leadership and appeals to the public can also make a significant difference in his or her ability to supervise the executive branch.

**The Budget** In most States the governor prepares the annual or biennial budget that goes to the legislature. The legislature may make changes in the governor's financial plan, of course. It may appropriate this or that amount, or nothing, for this agency and that program, as it chooses. But the governor's budget recommendations carry a great deal of weight.

The governor's budget-making power is an effective tool for controlling State administration. Although unable to appoint or remove the head of a certain agency, for example, the governor can use the budget-making power to affect that agency's programs. So the governor can have a real impact on the attitudes and behavior of many officials.

**Military Powers** Every State constitution makes the governor the commander in chief of the State militia—in effect, of the State's units of the National Guard. Governors may find it necessary to call out the National Guard to deal with such emergencies as prison riots or to aid in relief and prevent looting after a flood or some other natural disaster.[4]

## The Governor's Legislative Powers

The State's principal executive officer has important formal legislative powers. These powers, together with the governor's own political clout, often make the governor in effect the State's chief legislator.

**The Message Power**  The message power is really the power to recommend legislation. A strong governor can do much with it. A governor's program for legislative action is given to the lawmakers in a yearly State of the State address, in the budget, and in several special messages.

**Special Sessions**  The governor in every State has the power to call the legislature into special sessions. On occasion, a governor has persuaded reluctant legislators to pass a bill by threatening to call them back in a special session if they adjourn the regular session without having done so.

**The Veto Power**  Except for North Carolina, the governor in every State has the power to veto measures passed by the legislature. This power, as well as the threat to use it, is often the most potent power the governor has in influencing the work of the legislature.

In 43 States the governor's veto power includes the **item veto**. That is, the governor may veto one or more items in a bill without rejecting the entire measure. The power is most often, but not always, restricted to items in appropriations bills. The item veto is regularly used to cancel inappropriate or unaffordable legislative appropriations.

The vote needed to override a governor's veto varies by State, but two-thirds of the full membership in each house is most common. In actual practice, less than 5 percent of all measures passed by the State legislatures are rejected by governors. However, when the veto power is used, it is quite effective. Less than 10 percent of all vetoes are overridden.

## The Governor's Judicial Powers

In every State the governor has several judicial powers. Most of them are powers of executive clemency—powers of mercy that may be shown toward those convicted of crime.[5] For example, by the power to **pardon**, a governor may release a person from the legal consequences of a crime. In most States, a pardon may be full or conditional, and it can be granted only after conviction.

With the power to **commute**, a governor may reduce the sentence imposed by a court. Thus a death sentence may be commuted to life imprisonment. The power to **reprieve** postpones the execution of a sentence. The power to **parole** allows the release of a prisoner short of the completion of the term to which he or she was originally sentenced.

The governor may have some or all of these powers. However, they are often shared with one or more boards. For example, a governor may share the pardoning or parole power with a board of pardons and/or a parole board.

## Other Executive Officers

As you have already seen, in nearly every State the governor must share the control of his or her administration with a number of other elected officials. In most States, these offices are filled by popular election. The individuals who fill them must have a variety of different qualifications for these jobs.

**The Lieutenant Governor**  The formal duties of the lieutenant governor are much like those of the Vice President at the national level—that is, there is little to do. He or she succeeds to the governorship if there is a vacancy in the office and presides over the senate in most States. Nevertheless, seven States

---

[4]In a national emergency, the National Guard may be called into federal service by the President. All of the States' National Guard units were federalized in 1940 and served as part of the nation's armed forces in World War II. Many units also saw combat duty in both Korea and Vietnam. A number were also called up in 1990, to serve during Operation Desert Shield. National Guard units are not often called into federal service in domestic crisis situations, however.

---

[5]An extradition request from another State also puts the governor in a judicial role.

seem to get along quite well without a lieutenant governor.

**The Secretary of State**   The office of secretary of state exists everywhere but in Alaska, Hawaii, and Utah. The secretary of state is the State's chief clerk and record-keeper. He or she has charge of a great variety of public documents, records the official acts of the governor and the legislature, and usually administers the election laws. As with most of these other elected executives, the secretary of state has little real discretionary power or authority.

**The Treasurer**   The treasurer is the custodian of State funds, often the State's chief tax collector, and regularly the State's paymaster.

▲ **Lawyer for the State of Alaska**   Alaska's attorney general, Charles E. Cole, was appointed by the governor and approved by a majority of the State legislature.

The treasurer's major job is to make payments out of the State treasury. Most of those payments go to meet the many agency payrolls of the State and to pay the bills for the various goods or services supplied to the State by its many suppliers.

**The Attorney General**   The attorney general is the State's lawyer. He or she acts as the legal adviser to State officers and agencies as they perform their official functions, represents the State in court, and oversees the work of local prosecutors as they try cases on behalf of the State.

Much of the power of the office centers on the attorney general's formal written interpretations of constitutional and statutory law. These interpretations, called opinions, are issued to answer questions raised by the governor, other executive officers, legislators, and local officials regarding the lawfulness of their actions or proposed actions. In most States these opinions have the force of law unless successfully challenged in court.

## Section 2 Review

1. **Define:** item veto, pardon, commute, reprieve, parole
2. Describe four circumstances under which a successor may take the place of a governor before that governor's usual term of office comes to an end.
3. List two ways in which a State legislature may place limits upon a governor's power to appoint officials.
4. What is the significance of the item veto to the legislative process at the State level?
5. What are the duties of the typical lieutenant governor?

**Critical Thinking**

6. **Checking Consistency** (p. 19) The governor is not only the State's principal executive officer, but is often the State's chief legislator also. (a) Explain how this is so. (b) Does this arrangement violate the principle of separation of powers?

★

# 3 Counties, Towns, Townships, and Special Districts

## Find Out:

- What are the major elements of county governments?
- How are towns and townships governed?
- What are the reasons behind the creation of special districts?

## Key Terms:

county, parish, borough, township, special district

Washington has the White House, and your State has its own impressive capitol. These structures serve as functioning and symbolic centers for the Federal and State governments. In most communities, however, local government has no grand dome or stately mansion. Government in these places is visible mainly in the form of the day-to-day services that keep communities going.

In spite of its humble appearance, local government is vitally important in the lives of every American. As one measure of that fact, recall what you read earlier: Of the 86,743 units of government across the nation, 86,692 of these units are at the local level.

All local governments in the United States are creations of the States. Whether they are providing services, regulating activities, collecting taxes, or doing anything else, local governments can only act because the State has established them and permits them to. In this section, you will read about these units and about the complicated pattern of local government in the United States.

## The Counties

The 3,043 counties cover nearly all of the United States. A **county** is a major unit of local government. Organized county governments are found in all States except Connecticut and Rhode Island. In Louisiana what are known elsewhere as counties are called **parishes**, and in Alaska they are known as **boroughs**. In addition to Connecticut and Rhode Island, there are

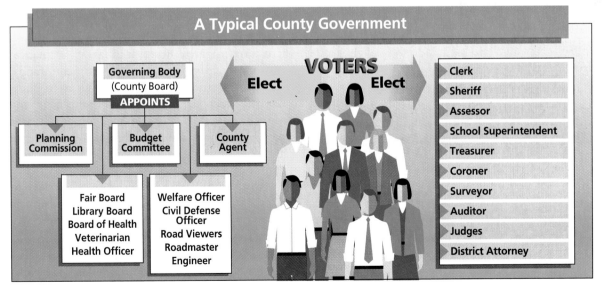

**A Typical County Government**

Governing Body (County Board) — **APPOINTS**

Planning Commission

Budget Committee

County Agent

Fair Board
Library Board
Board of Health
Veterinarian
Health Officer

Welfare Officer
Civil Defense Officer
Road Viewers
Roadmaster
Engineer

**VOTERS**  Elect  Elect

Clerk
Sheriff
Assessor
School Superintendent
Treasurer
Coroner
Surveyor
Auditor
Judges
District Attorney

▲ **Interpreting Graphics** In many States, the county board has both executive and legislative powers. Yet the board's executive power usually is shared with other elected officials. Why might such an arrangement cause confusion?

several places across the country where no organized county government exists. About 10 percent of the nation's population lives in those areas today.

The function of counties varies from region to region. Counties serve almost solely as judicial districts in the New England States. There, towns carry out most of the functions undertaken by counties elsewhere. Counties and townships share the functions of rural local government from New York and New Jersey west to the Dakotas, Nebraska, and Kansas. In the South and the West, counties are the major units of government in rural areas.

In terms of area, San Bernardino County in southern California is the largest in the United States. San Bernardino County covers 20,102 square miles. Kalawao County in Hawaii is the smallest, covering only 14 square miles. There is a marked variation in the area covered by each of the several counties within each State, too.

Counties also vary widely in terms of population. Nearly 9 million people now live in Los Angeles County in California. At the other end of the scale, only 107 residents were counted in Loving County, in western Texas, in the 1990 census. Most counties—in fact 75 percent of them—serve populations of fewer than 50,000.

## Common Elements of County Governments

The structures of county government differ, often considerably. But, as you can see from the chart on page 643, they typically have four major elements: a governing body, elected officials, a number of boards, and appointed bureaucrats.

**The Governing Body** The governing body of the county is often called the county board. It is known by at least 20 other names among the States—for example: the board of commissioners, board of supervisors, police jury, fiscal court, county court, and board of chosen freeholders.

The members of the board, whatever its title, are almost always popularly elected. They are usually chosen from districts in the county rather than on an at-large basis. Terms of office run from one to eight years, but four-year terms are the most common.

Generally, county boards can be grouped into two types: boards of commissioners and boards of supervisors. The board of commissioners is the smaller and more common type. Found everywhere in the South and West, the board is also well known elsewhere. It most often has three or five members, but some have seven or more. The members, usually called commissioners, are elected only to these bodies. As a rule, they hold no other public office.

The board of supervisors is typically a much larger body, having an average of about 15 members but sometimes running to as many as 80 or more. The supervisors are elected from each of the several townships in the county, as in New York, Nebraska, and Wisconsin. Each supervisor is usually an officer of his or her township as well as a member of the countywide governing body.

The powers held by the county governing bodies are detailed in the State constitution and acts of the State legislature. However restricted they may be, the powers of these boards are generally both executive and legislative, despite the American tradition of separation of powers.

County governments' most important legislative powers are those dealing with finance. County boards levy taxes, appropriate funds, and incur limited debts. They also have a number of lesser legislative powers, many in the regulatory field. For example, county boards pass health and zoning ordinances and control amusement places found outside incorporated communities.

Most county boards carry out a number of administrative functions. They supervise the road program and manage county property such as the courthouse, jails, hospitals, parks, and the like. County boards are often responsible for the administration of welfare programs and the conduct of elections. They also appoint certain county officers, deputies, and assistants of many kinds, as well as most other county employees. In addition, they fix the salaries of most of those who work for the county.

As you will see, most of these governing bodies share their executive powers with other elected boards and officials. As a result, efficiency, economy, and accountability are often almost impossible to achieve.

**Elected Officials**  A number of officials with countywide jurisdiction are separately elected. These other officers, and their principal duties, are most likely to include:

—The sheriff, who keeps the jail, furnishes police protection in rural areas, carries out the orders of the local courts, and is often the tax collector.

—The clerk, who registers and records such documents as deeds, mortgages, birth and marriage certificates, and divorce decrees. The county clerk often administers elections within the county, and acts as secretary to the county board and as clerk of the local courts.[6]

—The assessor, who appraises (sets the value of) all of the taxable property in the county.

—The treasurer, who keeps county funds and makes authorized payments from these funds.

—The auditor, who keeps financial records and authorizes payments to meet county obligations.

—The district attorney, who is the prosecuting attorney, carries out criminal investigations, and prosecutes those who break the law.

—The superintendent of schools, who is responsible for the administration of all or many of the public elementary and secondary schools in the county.

—The coroner, who investigates violent deaths and certifies the causes of deaths unattended by a physician.

Many other county officers are often elected. They include a surveyor, who surveys land and sets boundary lines; an engineer, who supervises the building of county roads, bridges, drains, and other improvements; and one or more judges of local courts.

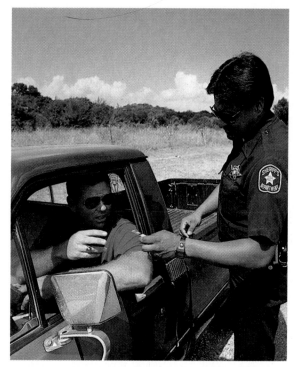

◢ **Covering All the Bases**  A county sheriff has a wide range of law enforcement responsibilities. Here, one of the sheriff's officers checks a motorist's driver's license.

**Boards or Commissions**  These bodies, whose members are also sometimes elected, have authority over a number of county functions. They commonly include a fair board, a library board, a planning commission, a hospital board, a board of road viewers, a board of health, and, sometimes, a civil service commission. Members of the county board often serve *ex officio*—because of their office—on one or more of these other agencies.

**County Bureaucracy**  Counties now employ approximately 2 million men and women. They, of course, do the day-to-day work of each of the nation's 3,043 counties.

## Functions of Counties

Because counties are creations of the State, they are responsible for the administration of State laws and such county laws as the State's constitution and legislature allow them to make.

---

[6]In several States a separate officer known as the recorder or the register of deeds has custody of those documents dealing with property transactions.

**Inmates at Work in County Jail** One function of county government is to manage county jails—an increasingly difficult task with the nation's jails becoming more and more crowded.

Historically, counties have been institutions of rural government. Most counties remain rurally oriented today. Though there is some difference from State to State, their major functions reflect their rural character. The most common ones are to keep the peace and maintain jails and other correctional facilities; assess property for tax purposes; collect taxes and spend county funds; build and repair roads, bridges, drains, and other such public works; and maintain schools. Counties record deeds, mortgages, marriage licenses, and other documents; issue licenses for such things as hunting, fishing, and marriage; administer elections; care for the poor; and protect the health of the people who live in the county.

Many counties have taken on other functions as they have become more urbanized. Two-thirds of the people in the United States today live within the boundaries of 375 of the nation's 3,043 counties. Several of these more heavily populated counties now offer many of the public services and facilities that are usually found in cities. They do such things as provide water and sewer service; have professionally trained police, fire, and medical units; and operate airports and mass transit systems. Some also enforce zoning and other land-use regulations, and many have built and operate auditoriums, sports stadiums, golf courses, and other recreational facilities.

## Towns and Townships

The town or township is found as a separate unit of local government in nearly half the States. Although little known in the South or the West, it is found through the region stretching from New England to the Middle West. [7]

**The New England Town** In New England, the town is a major unit of local government. Except for just a few cities, each of the six States in the region is divided into towns. Each town generally includes all of the rural and the urban areas within its boundaries. The town is the unit that delivers most of those services that are the responsibility of cities and counties elsewhere in the country.

The roots of the New England town reach back to colonial beginnings. The Pilgrims landed at Plymouth Rock in 1620 as an organized congregation. They quickly set up a close-knit community in which their church and their government were almost one. Other Puritan congregations followed the Pilgrims' pattern. The desire to be near the church, the real or imagined threat from Native Americans, the severe climate, and the fact that the land was not suited to large farms or plantations led the settlers to form tight little communities. Their settlements were soon known as towns, as in England.[8]

At least in form, much of town government today is little changed from colonial times. The

---

[7]The term *town* is used in some States as the legal designation for smaller urban places; it is also sometimes used as another word for township. *Township* is also a federal public lands survey term, used to identify geographic units (often called congressional townships), each having exactly 36 square miles (36 sections).

[8]When a clan in England or in Northern Europe settled in a particular place, it usually built a wall around it. In Old English, the wall was a *tun*. In time the space within the wall became known as the *tun*, and then the town. As the New England towns grew in number and in population, it became necessary to survey their boundaries. The small and irregular shapes that resulted were called "townships" (town shapes). The suffix *ship* comes from the Old English word *scip*, meaning "shape."

main feature is the town meeting, long praised as the ideal vehicle of direct democracy. The town meeting is an assembly open to all the town's eligible voters. It meets yearly, and sometimes more often, to levy taxes, make spending and other policy decisions, and elect officers for the next year.

Between town meetings the board of selectmen/selectwomen, chosen at the annual meeting, manages the town's business. Typically, the board is a three-member body and has responsibilities for such things as roads, schools, care of the poor, sanitation, and so on. Other officers regularly selected at the annual meeting include the town clerk, a tax assessor, a tax collector, a constable, road commissioners, and school board members.

The ideal of direct democracy is still alive in many smaller New England towns. It has given way, however, to the pressures of time, population, and the complexities of public problems in many of the larger towns. There, representative government has largely replaced it. The officers of the town are often elected before the yearly gathering. Many of the decisions once made by the assembled voters are now made by the selectmen and -women. In recent years several towns have gone to a town manager system for the day-to-day administration of local affairs.

**Townships** Outside of New England, **townships** are found as units of local government in those States bounded by New York and New Jersey on the east and the Dakotas, Nebraska, and Kansas on the west. In none of those States do the townships blanket the State, however. Where they are found, townships are mostly county subdivisions.

In New York, New Jersey, and Pennsylvania, townships were formed as areas were settled and the people needed the services of local government. As a result, the township maps of those States often resemble crazy-quilts. But from Ohio westward, township lines are more regular. They mostly follow the lines drawn in federal public land surveys, and many are perfect squares.

About half of these States provide for annual township meetings, like those held in New England towns. Otherwise, most townships have much the same governmental mechanisms. The governing body is a three-member or five-member board, generally called the board of trustees or board of supervisors. Often, its members are popularly elected for two-year or four-year terms. In many places, however, the board's members serve because they hold other elected township offices, such as supervisor, clerk, and treasurer. There is often an assessor, a constable, a justice of the peace, and a body of road commissioners.

Unlike in New England, a municipality within a township, especially one of large size, usually exists as a separate governmental entity. Thus, township functions tend to be rural, involving such matters as roads, cemeteries, noxious weed control, drainage, and minor law enforcement. In some States, however, the township is also the basic unit of public school administration.

Many believe that townships have outlived their usefulness. More than half the States get along without them, suggesting that they are not indispensable. Many rural townships have been abolished in the past few decades, the victims of declining populations, improvements in transportation, and a host of other factors.

Some of the more densely populated townships appear to have brighter futures than their country cousins, however. This seems especially true in the suburban areas around some larger cities. Some States, like Pennsylvania, now allow townships to exercise many of the powers and furnish many of the services once reserved to cities.

## Special Districts

There are now thousands of special districts across the country. A **special district** is an independent unit created to perform one or more related governmental functions at the local level. These districts are found in almost mind-boggling variety and in every State.

The school districts are by far the most widely found examples. Including them, there are more than 47,000 special districts today. The first of these districts was created by New York in 1812 for school purposes. By the 1950s, there were more than 50,000 school districts. Reorganizations have cut that number to less than 15,000 today.

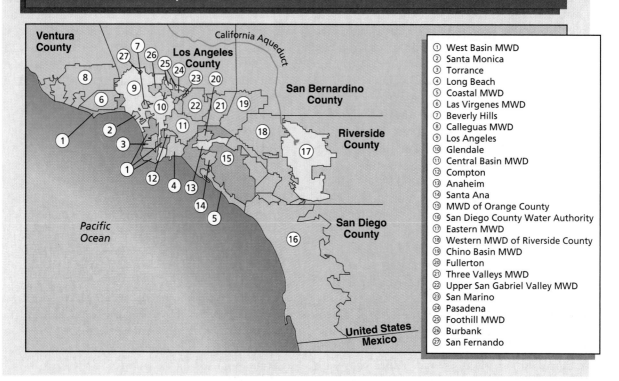

## The Metropolitan Water District of Southern California

Ventura County

California Aqueduct

Los Angeles County

San Bernardino County

Riverside County

San Diego County

Pacific Ocean

United States
Mexico

① West Basin MWD
② Santa Monica
③ Torrance
④ Long Beach
⑤ Coastal MWD
⑥ Las Virgenes MWD
⑦ Beverly Hills
⑧ Calleguas MWD
⑨ Los Angeles
⑩ Glendale
⑪ Central Basin MWD
⑫ Compton
⑬ Anaheim
⑭ Santa Ana
⑮ MWD of Orange County
⑯ San Diego County Water Authority
⑰ Eastern MWD
⑱ Western MWD of Riverside County
⑲ Chino Basin MWD
⑳ Fullerton
㉑ Three Valleys MWD
㉒ Upper San Gabriel Valley MWD
㉓ San Marino
㉔ Pasadena
㉕ Foothill MWD
㉖ Burbank
㉗ San Fernando

▲ **Interpreting Maps**   The metropolitan water district of southern California is made up of 27 member agencies from six counties. This special district has been called one of the most powerful government agencies in the State. What is the largest member agency in the MWD?

Most of the other special districts, which serve a wide range of purposes, have been created since the Depression of the 1930s, and their numbers are still growing. They are found most often, but by no means always, in rural and suburban areas. Many special districts have been created to provide water, sewage, or electrical service; to furnish fire, police, or sanitation protection; and to build and maintain bridges, airports, swimming pools, libraries, or parks. For example, fire protection might be provided in some out-of-the-way locale by setting up a special district. Others have been created for such purposes as soil conservation, housing, slum clearance, public transportation, irrigation, or reforestation. There are even, in many places, special districts for dog control or mosquito or other insect pest control purposes.

## Section 3 Review

1. **Define:** county, parish, borough, township, special district
2. What are two major types of county boards?
3. What factors make county government generally inefficient?
4. List three elected officials commonly found in county government.
5. What is a town meeting?
6. Describe the history of school districts in the United States.

### Critical Thinking

7. **Identifying Assumptions** (p. 19) Consider the idea of the New England town meeting. What does this method of town government assume about the citizens of the town?

★

## Should the Government Require Students to Salute the Flag?

### *West Virginia Board of Education* v. *Barnette*, 1943

Early in World War II, the West Virginia legislature passed a law that required all of the State's public schools to offer classes in history, civics, and the Constitution in order to perpetuate "the ideals, principles, and spirit of Americanism." The State's Board of Education also directed all public school students and teachers to take part in a flag-salute ceremony every school day. Any student who refused to salute the flag was to be expelled from school until he/she agreed to obey the salute requirement. Until then the student was "unlawfully absent," and his/her parents were subject to a fine.

Walter Barnette, and a number of other of the Jehovah's Witnesses with children in the State's public schools, filed suit in federal district court to prevent the enforcement of the Board's rule. They argued that the Board's edict violated their 1st and 14th amendment rights to the free exercise of their religious beliefs. To obey the rule, they said, would be to violate the doctrine forbidding the worship of "any graven (human-made) image."

The trial court ruled in Barnette's favor. It found the flag-salute rule to be an unconstitutional infringement of religious freedom. The State Board appealed that decision to the United States Supreme Court.

*Review the following evidence and arguments presented to the Supreme Court:*

### Arguments for the Board

**1.** The Constitution's 1st and 14th amendments do not guarantee to anyone an absolute right to do as that person pleases. In this instance, those provisions do not guarantee to school children a right to refuse to salute the American flag.

**2.** The Board's rule is intended to promote good citizenship, patriotism, and national unity. Because it does those things, it is a legitimate part of the State's public school program and should be upheld.

### Arguments for Barnette

**1.** The Board's compulsory flag-salute rule is a clear violation of the 1st and 14th amendments' protection of religious beliefs. The Constitution intends, most especially, to protect those religious views that are not shared by a majority of the American people.

**2.** The Board's rule is based on a false premise. In a free society, patriotism will flourish without compulsion. The free exercise of religious beliefs is a far more powerful affirmation of patriotism than is a symbolic, coerced salute.

### Getting Involved

**1. Identify** the constitutional grounds on which each side based its arguments.

**2. Debate** the opposing viewpoints presented in this case.

**3. Predict** how you think the Supreme Court ruled in this case and why. Then turn to the Supreme Court Glossary on page 770 to read about the decision.

**4. Discuss** the impact of the Court's decision on other personal freedoms. Under what circumstances, if any, should the government place limits on individual freedom?

# 4 Cities and Metropolitan Areas

**Find Out:**

- What are the various forms of city government?
- Why are city planning and zoning vital?
- Why has population shifted so dramatically from cities to suburbs?

**Key Terms:**

mayor-council government, strong-mayor government, weak-mayor government, commission form, council-manager form, zoning, metropolitan area

How times have changed. In 1790, a mere five percent of the nation's population lived in the nation's few cities. Today, America's cities and their surrounding communities are home to nearly four of every five persons.[9]

In this section, you will read about the government of American cities and their surrounding communities.

## Forms of City Government

Although there are variations from city to city, each city has either (1) a mayor-council, (2) a commission, or (3) a council-manager form of government.

**The Mayor-Council Form**  The **mayor-council government** is the oldest and still the

---

[9]Depending on local custom and State law, municipalities may be known as cities, towns, boroughs, or villages. The use and meaning of these terms vary among the States. The larger municipalities are known everywhere as cities, and the usual practice is to use that title only for those communities with a significant population.

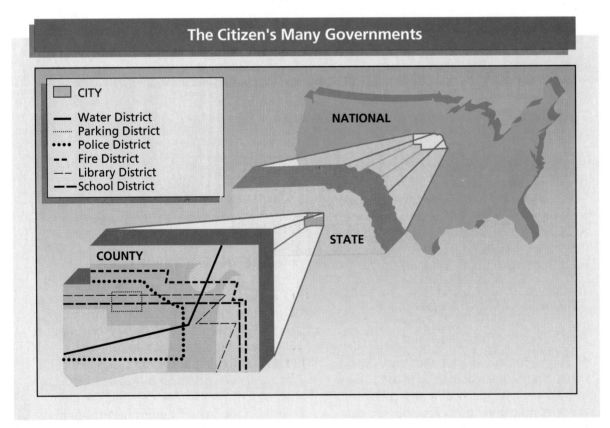

## The Citizen's Many Governments

CITY
— Water District
······· Parking District
•••• Police District
-- Fire District
— — Library District
——School District

NATIONAL

STATE

COUNTY

▲ **Interpreting Maps**   Many units of local government exist in this country. What is the chain of command from national government to the district level?

**Mayor-Council Form of Government**

**Strong Mayor-Council Plan**

**V O T E R S**
**ELECT**

VETO POWER

Municipal Judges

Mayor (chief executive)

City Council (legislative body)

**APPOINTS**

Police
Fire
Public Works
Civil Service
Public Welfare & Health Assessments
Utilities & Transportation

Makes policy

Carry out policy

**Weak Mayor-Council Plan**

**V O T E R S**
**ELECT**

Mayor (chief executive)

Acts must be approved by council

City Council (legislative body) and Other Elected Officials

**APPOINTS**

Police
Fire
Public Works
Civil Service
Public Welfare & Health Assessments
Utilities & Transportation

Make policy

Carry out policy

▲ **Interpreting Graphics** Compare and contrast the mayor-council plans above. What prevents a mayor of a city governed under a weak mayor-council plan from having greater power?

most widely used type of city government. It features an elected mayor as the chief executive and an elected council as its legislative body.

The council is almost always unicameral. In fact, Everett, Massachusetts, is the only city in the United States that has a two-chambered council today. The typical council has five, seven, or nine members, but some larger cities have more. New York now has the largest council, with 51 members.

The members of the council are popularly elected everywhere. Terms of office run from one to as many as six years, but four-year terms are the most common. Council members are now most often elected from the city at-large, and that is the trend. Many cities, including several larger ones, however, choose their council members from wards (districts) within the city.

A move to nonpartisan city government began in the early 1900s. Its champions believed that (1) political parties were a major source for corruption in city government and (2) partisan contests at the Statewide and national levels have little to do with municipal problems and local issues. Today, less than a third of all cities still run their elections on a partisan basis.

Generally the mayor is also elected by the voters. In some places, however, the office is filled by appointment by the council from among its own members. The mayor presides at council meetings, usually may vote only to break a tie, and may recommend and usually veto ordinances. In most cities the veto can be overridden by the council.

Mayor-council governments are often described as either of the strong-mayor type, or the weak-mayor type, depending on the powers given to the mayor. This classification is useful for purposes of description. However, it blurs the importance of informal power in city politics.

In a **strong-mayor government**, the mayor heads the city's administration, usually has the power to hire and fire employees, and prepares the budget. Typically, the mayor is otherwise able to exercise strong leadership in the making of city policy and the running of its affairs.

In a **weak-mayor government**, the mayor has much less formal power. Executive duties are shared with such other elected officials as the clerk, treasurer, city engineer, police chief, and council members. Powers of appointment, removal, and budget are shared with the council or exercised by that body alone; the mayor seldom has a veto power.

Most mayor-council cities operate under the weak-mayor rather than the strong-mayor plan. But the latter form is generally found in larger cities.

The success of the mayor-council form depends in very large measure on the power, ability, and influence of the mayor. In weak-mayor cities, responsibility for action or inaction is hard to fix.

The strong-mayor plan helps to solve the problems of leadership and responsibility. Still, it has three large weaknesses. First, it depends very heavily on the capacities of the mayor. As you have seen in the case of other elected officials, political and administrative talents are not often combined in the same person.

Second, a major dispute between the mayor and the council can stall the workings of city government. This is another way of saying that the mayor-council form incorporates the principles of separation of powers and checks and balances—with all their benefits and drawbacks.

Third, the mayor-council form is quite complicated and so is often little understood by the average citizen.

**The Commission Form**  Only a few American cities now have a commission form of government.[10] The largest of these are Portland, Oregon; Mobile, Alabama; and Jackson, Mississippi.

The **commission form** is simple. Three to nine, but usually five, commissioners are

---

[10]The commission form was born in Galveston, Texas, in 1901. A tidal wave had swept the island city the year before, killing 7,000 persons and laying much of it to waste. The old mayor-council regime was too incompetent and corrupt to cope with the emergency. The Texas legislature gave Galveston a new charter, providing for five commissioners to make and enforce the law in the stricken city. Intended to be temporary, the arrangement proved so effective that it soon spread to other Texas cities and then elsewhere in the country. Its popularity has waned, however. In 1960 Galveston's voters approved a new city charter providing for council-manager government.

**Commission Form of Government**

VOTERS

ELECT

COMMISSIONERS
(Act as a city council)

EACH HEADS A DEPARTMENT
(Executive powers)

LEGISLATIVE POWERS

Pass ordinances
Control purse strings

Police   Fire   Public Works   Public Welfare   Finance

(Carry out policy)

▲ **Interpreting Graphics**  This form of government is one of the most uncomplicated systems for a city or town. Does a system of checks and balances exist in the commission form of government? Why or why not?

popularly elected. Together, they form the city council, pass ordinances, and control the purse strings. Individually, they head the different departments of city government—police, fire, public works, finance, parks, and so on. Thus, both legislative and executive powers are centered in one body.

Depending on the city, either the voters or the commissioners themselves choose one of the commissioners to serve as the mayor. Like the other commissioners, the mayor heads one of the city's departments. He or she also presides at council meetings and represents the city on ceremonial occasions. The mayor generally has no more authority than the other commissioners and rarely has the veto power.

The commissioners are usually elected for two-year or four-year terms, and almost always from the city at-large and on nonpartisan ballots. Unlike their counterparts in mayor-council and council-manager cities, they regularly serve as full-time officers.

The commission form has three chief defects. First, the lack of a single chief executive (or, the presence of several chiefs among equals) makes it difficult to fix responsibility. This also means that the city generally has no effective political leadership.

Second, there is a built-in tendency toward "empire-building," in which each commissioner tries to draw as much of the city's money and influence as possible to his or her own department.

Finally, there is a lack of coordination at the topmost levels of policymaking and administration. Each commissioner is likely to equate the citywide public good with the peculiar interests and functions of his or her department.

**The Council-Manager Form**  The **council-manager form** is a modification of the mayor-council form. It features (1) a strong council, of usually five or seven members, elected at-large on a nonpartisan ballot, (2) a weak mayor, chosen by the voters, and (3) a manager, the city's chief administrative officer, named by the council.

The council is the city's policy-making body. The manager carries out the policies the council makes and is directly responsible to that body for the efficient administration of the city. The manager serves at the council's pleasure and may be dismissed by the council at any time and for any reason.

Today, most city managers are professionally trained career administrators. As chief administrator, the manager directs the work of all city

**Council-Manager Form of Government**

VOTERS — ELECT → COUNCIL (Makes policy) — EMPLOYS → MANAGER (Chief Administrator)

MAYOR

ADMINISTERS → Police  Fire  Public Works  Public Welfare  Finance (Carry out policy)

▲ **Interpreting Graphics**  In the council-manager form of government, a professional manager sees that necessary services are performed for the residents of the city. What keeps the actions of a manager from becoming strictly politically motivated?

departments and has the power to hire and fire all city employees. The manager also prepares the budget for council consideration, and then controls the spending of the funds the council appropriates.

The council-manager plan has the backing of nearly every student of municipal affairs, and its use has spread widely. It is now found in more than 8,000 communities, including a majority of all of those cities with populations between 25,000 and 250,000.

The council-manager plan has three major advantages over either the mayor-council or the commission forms of city government. First, it is simple in form. Second, it is clear who has the responsibility for policy, on the one hand, and for its application, on the other. Third, it relies on highly trained experts who are skilled in modern techniques of budgeting, planning, computerization, and other administrative tools.

Some critics of the plan hold that it is undemocratic because the chief executive is not elected. Others say that it does not offer strong political leadership. This is a particular shortcoming, they argue, in larger cities, where the population is often quite diverse and its interests are competitive.

## Municipal Functions

A city exists primarily to provide services to those who live within its boundaries.

Consider just a few of the many things that most or all cities do: provide police and fire protection; build and maintain streets, sidewalks, bridges, street lighting systems, parks and playgrounds, swimming pools, golf courses, libraries, hospitals, schools, correctional institutions, day-care centers, airports, public markets, parking facilities, auditoriums, and sports arenas. They furnish such public health and sanitation services as sewers and waste-water treatment, garbage collection and disposal, and disease prevention and eradication programs. Cities operate water, gas, light, and transportation systems. They regulate traffic; building practices; air, water, and noise pollution; and public utilities.

Many cities build and manage public housing projects, clear slums, provide summer youth

camps, build and operate docks and other harbor facilities, and maintain tourist attractions.

## City Planning

With few exceptions, most American cities developed haphazardly, without a plan, and with no eye to the future. The results of this shortsightedness can be seen almost everywhere. The most obvious, and damaging, examples can be seen in what is often called the core area or the inner city, the older and usually overcrowded central sections of larger cities.

Industrial plants were placed anywhere their owners chose to build them. Rail lines were run through the heart of the community. Towering buildings shut out the sunlight from the too-narrow streets below. Main roads were laid out too close together and sometimes too far apart. Schools, police and fire stations, and other public buildings were squeezed onto cheap land or

▲ **City Hall in Dallas, Texas**  Dallas is one of the largest cities in the United States with a council-manager government.

put where the political organization could make a profit. Examples are endless.

**Planning Growth**  Fortunately, many cities have seen the need to create order out of their random growth. Most have established some sort of planning agency, usually a planning commission, supported by a trained professional staff. A number of factors have prompted this step. The need to correct past mistakes has often been an absolutely compelling one, of course. Then, too, many cities have recognized the advantages that can result, and the pitfalls that can be avoided, through well-planned and orderly development. Importantly, cities have been spurred on by the Federal Government. Most federal grant and loan programs require that cities that seek aid must first have a master plan as a guide to future growth.

Washington, D.C., is one of the few cities in the nation that has been a planned city from its beginning. Its basic plan was approved by Congress before a single building was erected in 1790. The original plan has been followed fairly closely through the years. The National Capitol Planning Commission guides the city's development today.

**City Zoning**  The practice of dividing a city into a number of districts, or zones, and regulating the uses to which property in each of them may be put, is called **zoning**. Generally, a zoning ordinance places each parcel of land in the city into one of three zones: residential, commercial, or industrial. Each of these is then divided into subzones. For example, each or several residential zones may be broken down into several areas. One may be just for single-family residences. Another may allow both one-family and two-family dwellings. In still another, apartment houses and other multifamily units may be allowed.[11]

---

[11]Most zoning ordinances also prescribe limits on the height and area of buildings, determine how much of a lot may be occupied by a structure, and set out several other such restrictions on land use. They often have "set-back" requirements, which state that structures must be placed at least a certain distance from the street and from other property lines.

"The zoning commission would like to point out an irregularity!"

▲ **Interpreting Political Cartoons**
Zoning relates to the overall plan for a city's development. What is one of the roles of the zoning commission, according to this cartoon?

Zoning is really a phase of city planning—and an important means for assuring orderly growth. Zoning still meets opposition from many who object to this interference with their right to use their property as they choose. Even so, nearly every city of any size in the United States is zoned today. The city of Houston, where zoning was turned down twice by popular vote, remained the only major exception until the early 1990s, when the city council finally decided to adopt zoning.

Zoning ordinances must be reasonable. Remember that the 14th Amendment prohibits any State, and thus its cities, from depriving any person of life, liberty, or property without due process of law. Each of the 50 State constitutions contains a similar provision.

Clearly, zoning does deprive a person of the right to use his or her property for certain purposes. Thus, if an area is zoned only for single-family dwellings, one cannot build an apartment house or a service station on his or her property in that zone. Zoning can also reduce the value of a particular piece of property—for example, a choice corner lot may be much more valuable with a drive-in restaurant on the property than a house.[12]

While zoning may at times deprive a person of liberty or property, the key question always is this: Does it do so without due process? That is, does it do so unreasonably?

The question of reasonableness is one for the courts to decide. The Supreme Court first upheld zoning as a proper use of the police power in *Euclid* v. *Amber Realty Co.*, 1926, a case involving an ordinance enacted by the city council of Euclid, Ohio.

## Suburbanitis and Metropolitan Areas

The growth and sprawl of urban areas have raised many problems for cities, as well as for residents of the suburbs that surround those cities.

**Suburbanitis**  Most larger cities, and many smaller ones, suffer from what has been called "suburbanitis." Today, nearly 115 million Americans—more than 45 percent of the population—live in suburbs.

The nation's suburbs began to grow at a rapid rate in the years immediately after World War II—in the late 1940s, and then on through the 1950s and 1960s. The suburban growth rate slowed somewhat in the 1970s, but it rebounded in the 1980s and on into the 1990s—especially around the Sun Belt cities of the South and West.

This dramatic shift in population can be explained on several grounds. Many quite understandable desires have helped to bring it about, including needs for more room; cheaper land; less smoke, dirt, noise, and congestion; and greater privacy. Suburban growth has sharpened a great many problems for core cities. As many of

the better-educated, high-income families have moved out, they have taken their civic, financial, and social resources with them. They have left behind a central city, which in contrast to its suburbs has much higher percentages of older persons, low-income families, and minorities. The cities also have more older buildings and substandard housing, more unemployment, and higher crime rates. Inevitably, both the need for and the stress on city services have multiplied.

**Metropolitan Areas**  Suburbanites face their share of problems too. Water supply, sewage disposal, police and fire protection, transportation, and traffic control are only some of them. Duplication of such functions by city and suburb or by city and county can be wasteful and dangerous. More than one fire has burned on while neighboring fire departments quibbled over which of them was responsible for fighting it.

Attempts to meet the needs of **metropolitan areas**—that is, of the cities and the areas around them—have taken several forms. Over the years, annexation has been the standard means. Outlying

▲ **Interpreting Political Cartoons**
The current "suburbanitis" plague has created many problems, caused by thousands of people living in the suburbs and working in the city. What does this cartoon say about commuting to work?

---

[12]However, nonconforming uses in existence before a zoning ordinance is passed are almost always allowed to continue. Most ordinances give the city council the right to grant exceptions, called variances, in cases where property owners might suffer undue hardships.

areas have simply been brought within a city's boundaries. But many suburbanites resist annexation. Cities, too, have often been slow to take on the burdens involved.

Another approach involves the creation of special districts, which you have already studied. The best known and most common are school districts, but there are now more than 29,000 sanitary, water, fire protection, and other special districts across the country. Many of them have been created especially to meet the problems of heavily populated urban areas. Their boundaries frequently cut across county and city lines to include the entire metropolitan area, and they are often called metropolitan districts.

These metropolitan districts are generally set up for a single purpose; for example, for park development, as in the Cleveland Metropolitan Park Development District. There is no reason why a district's authority cannot be expanded to cover other functions, however. The Metropolitan District Commission (MDC), created by Massachusetts, until 1992 had its own police department and controlled park development for the city of Boston and neighboring communities. The MDC also had a number of planning functions in the district as a whole. Boston has only about a third of the district's population; the balance lives within 40 other municipalities.

Yet another approach to the challenges facing metropolitan areas is increasing the authority of counties. Among local governments around the country, counties are generally the largest in area and are most likely to include those places demanding new and increased services.

The functions of many urban counties have grown in recent years, as you have already seen. Dade County (Miami), Florida, has undertaken the nation's most ambitious approach to metropolitan problems. In 1957 its voters approved the first home rule charter designed "to create a metropolitan government." Under it, a countywide metropolitan government (Metro) is responsible for areawide functions. These include fire and police protection; an integrated water, sewer, and drainage system; zoning; expressway construction; and the like. Miami and the other 26 cities within the county continue to perform the strictly local functions and services.

▲ **Metropolitan Government in Florida**
An officer of the Dade County metropolitan government is one of the participants in this ambitious countywide system, which includes Miami and 26 other cities.

## Section 4 Review

1. **Define:** mayor-council government, strong-mayor government, weak-mayor government, commission form, council-manager form, zoning, metropolitan area
2. What are the three major forms of city government?
3. Cite three examples of municipal functions.
4. Why did city planning become so necessary?
5. How has the growth of the suburbs affected central or core cities?
6. What is the purpose of a metropolitan district?

**Critical Thinking**

7. **Testing Conclusions** (p. 19) Based on what you have read in this section, do you agree or disagree with this statement: Citizens prefer to have a single leader whom they can look to for leadership and hold responsible for errors.

★

# *How to Write to Your Legislators*

**M**ost elected officials pay close attention to mail from their constituents. Senator Phil Gramm (R., Texas) says that, after years in Congress, "I am more convinced than ever of the wisdom of the 'average' citizen and the value of his advice." Every day, your representatives receive dozens to hundreds of letters from "the folks back home," and all of them must be answered. The volume of constituent mail has become so great that handling it now takes a large amount of staff time. The use of computer-driven personalized form letters enables legislators to respond quickly and has eased the burden considerably.

Former Congressman Morris Udall (D., Arizona) suggests several guidelines for writing an effective letter. Use the following steps when writing to your lawmakers.

**1. Address your letter properly.** You can send your letter to Washington or to your State representative's or senator's local office. The proper addresses in Washington, D.C., are:

Representative _____

House Office Building
Washington, D.C. 20515

or:

Senator _____

Senate Office Building
Washington, D.C. 20510

Answer these questions: (a) How would you locate your State representatives' and senators' local offices? (b) Why do those offices exist?

**2. Make sure the letter is timely.** Most members of Congress say that letters that deal with public policy matters, and especially views on pending legislation, are the most welcome. Do not wait until a bill is out of committee or has passed the House (or Senate). Also, do not try to instruct your lawmaker on every issue. Answer the question: Why might it be best to write a lawmaker before the matter in question has gotten out of committee or passed one of the two houses?

**3. Identify the bill or issue that prompts your letter.** It is preferable to mention the bill or issue in the first paragraph and to be as specific as you can. Give the bill number, or mention its popular title—for example, the Minimum Wage Bill or the S&L Bailout Bill. Answer the question: What is the best way to learn your legislator's stand on a bill or issue?

**4. Give the reasons for the stand you take. Be specific and constructive.** Do not make threats or promises or berate your lawmaker, and do not pretend to wield vast political influence. Such an approach is unnecessary and ineffective. Former Senator Stephen M. Young (D., Ohio) sometimes replied to abrasive letters with notes like this one, "I'm sending you a letter received this morning, evidently from some crackpot who signed your name." Answer the question: Why might it be more effective to try to use reason than threats when communicating with lawmakers?

**5. State other purposes clearly and briefly.** Many constituents write seeking information on everything from how to obtain a passport to the best ways to prune and fertilize roses. Many others ask for help—with everything from untangling a problem with the Social Security Administration to a mother's plea that her soldier son be stationed somewhere closer to home. (a) Why is it important to be brief and to the point when writing legislators? (b) What might happen if all legislators were regularly expected to respond to such types of questions and requests?

★

# Chapter-in-Brief

Scan all headings, photographs, charts, and other visuals in the chapter before reading the section summaries below.

## Section 1 The State Legislatures (pp. 631–637)
Each State's constitution is that State's fundamental law. State legislators are popularly elected, serve similar terms, and meet similar qualifications.

Each legislature has certain nonlegislative powers. These powers are similar to the nonlegislative powers of Congress. One difference is that some State legislatures have the power to appoint certain executive officers.

Legislative activity in the States also resembles that of Congress. Presiding officers exert a strong influence, and much of the work takes place in committees. One key difference is that many States allow voters to take a direct part in lawmaking through the initiative and referendum.

## Section 2 The Governor and State Administration (pp. 637–642)
The governor is the principal executive officer in all 50 States. He or she is popularly elected everywhere, usually to four-year terms.

Governors share their executive authority with such other offices as lieutenant governor, attorney general, and secretary of state, and treasurer. Nevertheless, governors tend to be the persons to whom voters look for leadership.

A governor's powers regularly include the power to appoint and remove certain officials, and the power to supervise employees. Governors also prepare the budget.

Governors also possess legislative powers, such as the message power and the power to call legislative sessions. Another key legislative power is the veto power.

## Section 3 Counties, Towns, Townships, and Special Districts (pp. 643–648)
All local governments are creations of the States. Nearly every government in the United States is a local government.

Counties or their equivalent exist in all but two States. Their functions vary depending on the region. Counties also vary in their structures, which generally include county boards, plus elected officials such as sheriffs, clerks, and others.

As a unit of government, towns and townships are found in about half the States. Towns are the major unit of government in New England. Townships are subdivisions of counties, and they tend to have primarily rural functions.

There are many special districts in every State. These units are used to provide a wide variety of services, including education, water and sewage, police and fire, and airport and park services.

## Section 4 Cities and Metropolitan Areas (pp. 650–657)
Cities exist to provide services to their citizens. As a means of fulfilling that task, city governments take one of three forms: (1) mayor-council, (2) commission, or (3) council-manager. The mayor-council form is the most popular, and it has two major variations—the strong mayor type and the weak mayor type.

Historically, cities often grew up haphazardly. Today, however, many cities have established some sort of planning agency. Zoning is another method cities use to manage growth and change.

Recent population shifts from many cities to the suburbs has left cities with fewer resources to deal with growing problems. One response has been the organization of metropolitan districts to provide services to entire metropolitan areas.

# Chapter Review

## Vocabulary and Key Terms

initiative (p. 636)
referendum (p. 636)
item veto (p. 641)
pardon (p. 641)
commute (p. 641)
reprieve (p. 641)
parole (p. 641)
county (p. 643)

parish (p. 643)
borough (p. 643)
township (p. 647)
special district (p. 647)
mayor-council government
   (p. 651)
strong-mayor government
   (p. 652)

weak-mayor
   government (p. 652)
commission form (p. 652)
council-manager form
   (p. 653)
zoning (p. 655)
metropolitan area (p. 656)

**Matching:** *Review the key terms in the list above. If you are not sure of a term's meaning, look up the term and review its definition. Choose a term from the list above that best matches each description.*

1. a governor's power to reject certain provisions of measures passed by the legislature
2. a modification of the mayor-council form of government featuring a strong council, a weak mayor, and a manager who is the city's chief administrative officer
3. the power of a governor to reduce the sentence imposed by a court
4. the major unit of local government in most States outside of New England
5. a form of city government consisting of three to nine popularly elected commissioners who form the city council

**True or False:** *Determine whether each statement is true or false. If it is true, write "true." If it is false, change the underlined word or words to make the statement true.*

1. What are known as counties in most other States are called <u>boroughs</u> in Alaska.
2. Cities and the areas around them are known as <u>special districts</u>.

3. In a <u>mayor-council government</u>, the mayor heads the city administration, can hire and fire many employees, prepares the budget, and generally exercises strong leadership.
4. In a number of States, citizens can propose constitutional amendments or statutes via the <u>referendum</u>.
5. <u>Reprieve</u> means the release of a prisoner before the completion of his or her sentence.

**Word Relationships:** *Three of the terms in each of the following sets of terms are related. Choose the term that does not belong and explain why it does not belong.*

1. (a) township (b) zoning (c) county (d) parish
2. (a) referendum (b) pardon (c) reprieve (d) commute
3. (a) mayor-council government (b) weak-mayor government (c) commission form (d) special district
4. (a) initiative (b) parole (c) item veto (d) referendum

## Main Ideas

**Section 1** (pp. 631–637)
1. Briefly describe the notable features of the State legislatures, their organization, and structure.

2. Briefly describe the general characteristics of the job of State legislator.
3. What is direct legislation?

## Section 2 (pp. 637–642)

4. In what general ways are State governors similar to the President?
5. In what general ways are most governorships different from the presidency?
6. Why is it significant that many executive department officials are elected?

## Section 3 (pp. 643–648)

7. How are local governments created?
8. What are the major forms of local government in the United States?
9. In what ways does the function of counties vary from region to region?
10. What are the most common types of special districts?

## Section 4 (pp. 650–657)

11. (a) What are the basic forms of city government? (b) What variations exist of the mayor-council form?
12. (a) Briefly describe how most cities in the United States developed. (b) How have cities responded to growth?
13. Briefly describe the phenomenon and impact of "suburbanitis."
14. What are some of the issues that led to the creation of metropolitan districts?

## Critical Thinking

1. **Recognizing Ideologies** (p. 19)   Recall that many States have provisions for the initiative or referendum. What does the existence of these methods of direct legislation suggest about the role of the people in government?
2. **Making Comparisons** (p. 19)   You read that many governors share executive power with several other elected officials. In your opinion, is effective government served by distributing power among several officials?
3. **Drawing Conclusions** (p. 19)   Different regions of the country rely on different

means of local government. (a) Explain how differences from region to region might affect the selection of a form of government. (b) How might the form of local government affect the democratic process?

## Getting Involved

1. **Writing Your Opinion**   You are a legislator in a State that is considering adding initiative and referendum to your State constitution. Write a speech in which you argue in favor of or against the initiative and referendum. Begin by stating your feelings on the topic. Then, write one paragraph for each of the reasons you do or do not support the proposed change. Remember that your speech should aim to persuade other lawmakers to support your position. It should also appeal to the voters. Revise your first draft to ensure that your arguments are clearly presented and politically sound. Correct any errors, then draft a final copy.

2. **Cooperative Activity**   Work as a class to create a development plan for a new city. Begin by brainstorming a list of the features an ideal city should seek to develop. Select five items on which everyone agrees. These five items will then be translated into a written city plan. To create this plan, divide the class into five groups, and assign each group one of the items. The groups should then create a written guideline for implementing their items. Ask the class to offer suggestions and improvements for each guideline.

3. **Creating a Poster**   Consider what you have read in this chapter about local government. Create a poster that illustrates your understanding of the place of local government in the American political system. Your poster should use a combination of words and pictures to communicate its message.

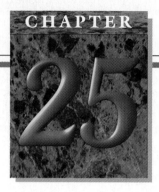

**CHAPTER**

# State and Local Government in Action

## Chapter Preview

In 1845 Henry David Thoreau built a sparse, one-room cabin in the lush, green woods surrounding Walden Pond in Concord, Massachusetts. He lived there alone for more than two years, writing his book *Walden, or Life in the Woods*. Over the years, the historic site has been threatened by a growing suburbia—by people using the site for swimming, hiking, and picnicking, for example, and most recently, by the desire of developers to build an office and condominium complex within a stone's throw of the pond. Almost immediately, strong opinions emerged on both sides of the controversy. Naturalists, who wished to conserve the history and beauty of the site, locked horns with those who saw the economic rewards development would bring.

The debate has raged now for several years over how this land should be used: development, recreation, or preservation? In this chapter you will see how the many functions of State government play a role in the outcome of these types of questions.

### Before you read this chapter:

- **Describe** three services that States provide for their citizens.
- **Predict** how States obtain the revenue to provide these services.

### As you read, focus on the main objective for each section. Understand:

1. The many services provided by States for their citizens.
2. The major sources of State and local government revenues.
3. The different kinds of law applied by State courts.
4. The overall organization of the State court systems.

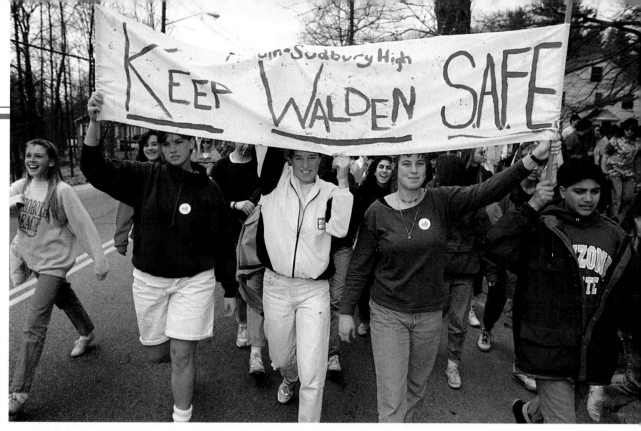

▲ **Getting Involved** This group of teenagers is marching to show their support for saving Walden Woods in Concord, Massachusetts, from development. State and local governments debate many issues that concern teenagers, who often decide to get involved in influencing the outcome of those debates.

# 1 Providing Important Services

### Find Out:

- What are some of the many services provided by the States?
- What factors help to influence a State's economy and budget?

### Key Term:

urbanization

You may have noticed while reading the last chapter and other points in this book how similar the State governments are in form to the Federal Government. For example, each has three branches of government, all but one have bicameral legislatures, each has its own constitution, and so on. Given these similarities, it is easy to overlook the many unique

features and functions of your own State government, and the many services it provides to its citizens.

In this section, you will read about State governments and their important role in the day-to-day lives of their citizens.

## What State Governments Do

Over the course of this book, you have read many times about the key role of the States in the American federal system. Recall that there was a widespread distrust among the Framers of a strong, central government, and so they created a system in which the States held many important powers. As you read in Chapter 4, Section 1, the Constitution reserves to the States all those powers not expressly delegated to Congress and not specifically denied to the States. These reserved powers are broad—in fact, they are too numerous to list here. In addition, the exercise of these powers varies greatly from one State to the next. Again, that fact

## How to Volunteer

**1. Choose a volunteer organization that reflects your interests.** Start by listing two or three of your interests. Next, do research to match one of your interests with a volunteer organization. You can do this by contacting your local government. Many cities keep directories of local volunteer organizations. Or you might talk with your parents, teachers, guidance counselors, friends, and neighbors. For example, suppose your interests include reading, pursuing a career in health care, and being outdoors. Your research might put you in touch with a tutoring organization, a hospital volunteer program, or a conservation group.

**2. Determine how much time you can spend on volunteer work each week or month.** Because American society depends heavily on volunteer help, your commitment is essential. Decide before you volunteer how often you can realistically expect to be able to work outside your regular activities. Be sure to let the person who is organizing the volunteer work know from the start what your time commitment is, and remember—even a minimal time commitment will probably mean a great deal to the individual or organization that you are helping.

**3. Decide whether you will need a means of transportation.** Is the organization or home at which you will volunteer within walking distance? If not, can someone at the organization or your parents give you a ride? Can you make use of public transportation?

▲ **Interpreting Charts** Read these suggestions on how to be a good volunteer. Why do you think thoughtful research is emphasized in Step 1?

reflects the conscious aim of the Framers and the federal system they created.

Along with the powers reserved to the States come some important responsibilities. Like the Federal Government, State governments generally aim to fulfill the lofty purposes set forward in the preamble to the Constitution; that is, they seek to "establish justice, ensure domestic tranquility, provide for the common defense, promote the general welfare, and secure the blessings of liberty . . . "

You have already read about one of the ways that State governments perform their function. They establish local governments of all types. As you read in Chapter 24, these various local units provide a great many services to those who live within their borders.

States also take a direct role in providing services to the people of the State. The services they provide fall into a number of broad categories.

**Education** The education of the State's residents is one of the most important responsibilities that the States have taken upon themselves. It is also the most expensive entry in every State budget, representing about one-third of overall State expenditures. The cost of providing education has risen sharply in recent decades and continues to increase year to year.

As you have read, the education of schoolchildren at the primary and secondary levels is, to a significant degree, a responsibility of local governments. As you will read shortly, local taxes, especially property taxes, provide a significant proportion of the funding for primary and secondary schools.

Of course, the States do provide some financial assistance to their local governments for the purposes of education. The level of this aid varies from State to State—and widely. Some States contribute well over half of the cost of educating primary and secondary students. Other States contribute a fraction of that amount. In addition, the States set guidelines in order to maintain high quality in the schools. For example, State laws set minimum qualifications for teachers, establish curricula and screen the quality of educational materials, establish the minimum length for the school year, and much more.

At the college and university levels, the States play a major role. States understand that the ability to provide highly trained college graduates is a key to the success of businesses in the State—and to the decisions of other businesses to locate there. Every State has its own public higher education system, and in some States that system is extensive, including several universities, technical universities, and community colleges. California's system is the largest such system in the nation. The University of California alone has nine campuses, and California State University has 19. In addition, the State has an extensive system of community

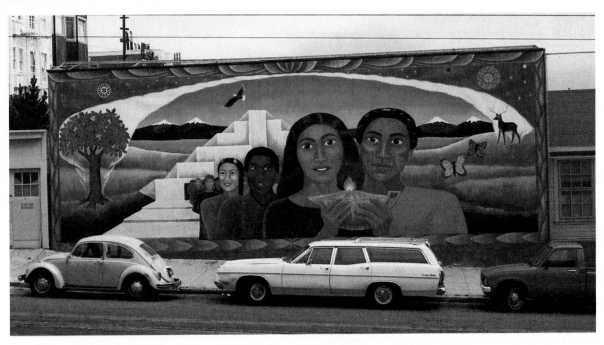

▲ **Interpreting Political Art: Multicultural Awareness** This mural is painted on the side of a high school in San Francisco. The lamp of learning in the mural represents the high value placed on education by the community.

colleges—colleges that offer two–, rather than four–year, programs of study.

Education at State universities and colleges is generally much less expensive than that obtained at private institutions. On average, tuition at four-year public colleges and universities is about one-fifth that of private four-year institutions. Nevertheless, many State universities, such as the University of California (Berkeley) and the University of Michigan (Ann Arbor), are included among the ranks of the world's finest institutions.

**Public Welfare** The States take an active role in promoting the health and welfare of their citizens. States pursue this goal by a variety of means.

Most States fund ambitious public health programs. States operate public hospitals and offer direct care to millions of citizens. They immunize children against dangerous childhood diseases—measles and mumps, for example. With the Federal Government, the States administer such programs as Medicaid, Medicare, and Aid to Families with Dependent Children. In addition, States have many similar programs of their own to care for their needy.

Recent soaring costs in the health-care industry have placed a great strain on many States' ability to care for their people. Many governors, State legislators, mayors, and other public officials are among the leading advocates of some sort of national health-insurance plan.

Beyond the direct provision of health care, States do much to ensure the public health and welfare. State efforts to protect the environment are one such example; many enforce stringent antipollution laws. States also inspect factories and other workplaces to protect worker health and safety. And, they license health-care practitioners to ensure quality care. (Licensing also serves another purpose—that of providing revenue to the States.) Again, the list of services in this area goes on and on.

**Public Safety** The first State police outfit was the legendary Texas Rangers, established in 1835. Today, every State maintains a police force to preserve law and order. A State's police are perhaps most visible as they patrol the State's roads and highways. However, State law-enforcement forces perform many other vital

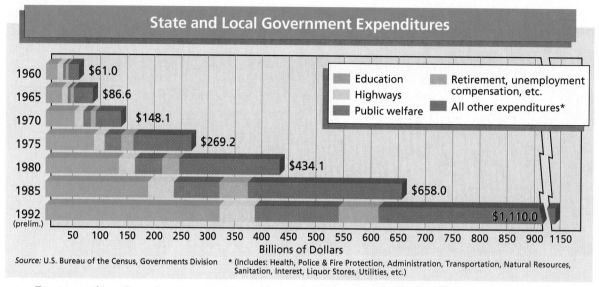

**State and Local Government Expenditures**

| Year | Amount |
|------|--------|
| 1960 | $61.0 |
| 1965 | $86.6 |
| 1970 | $148.1 |
| 1975 | $269.2 |
| 1980 | $434.1 |
| 1985 | $658.0 |
| 1992 (prelim.) | $1,110.0 |

Legend:
- Education
- Highways
- Public welfare
- Retirement, unemployment compensation, etc.
- All other expenditures*

Billions of Dollars: 50 100 150 200 250 300 350 400 450 500 550 600 650 700 750 800 850 900 1150

*Source:* U.S. Bureau of the Census, Governments Division    * (Includes: Health, Police & Fire Protection, Administration, Transportation, Natural Resources, Sanitation, Interest, Liquor Stores, Utilities, etc.)

**Interpreting Graphs**    This graph breaks down the various expenditures for which State and local governments are responsible. Over time, which expense has increased the most?

services. Depending on the State, they may function as the primary police force in many rural communities. The State police departments also offer a centralized file for fingerprints and other information, and they provide training and many other services in support of local law-enforcement agencies.

Each State has its own corrections system for those who are convicted of committing State crimes. Thus States operate prisons, penitentiaries, and a variety of other facilities, including reformatories specifically designed for juvenile offenders.

**Highways**    Building and maintaining the roads and highways of the State is an enormous job, and it regularly ranks second or third in each State's budget in terms of spending.

Again, the Federal Government is a partner with the States in the funding of many highways. However, a great many roadways are built solely with State funds, not with money from the Federal Government.

Once the roads are built, States must maintain them. The States also look after the physical safety of the roads and make repairs as needed. You have already read about the role of the State police in ensuring the safety of drivers on the road. In addition, States license drivers to ensure their competence. They set speed limits.

And, in many States, the State requires the periodic inspection of vehicles to ensure their safety.

**Other Services**    As noted earlier, the many services that the States provide to their citizens are too numerous to be listed here. You have just read about some of the more obvious ones. But no less important are such functions as the setting aside of public lands for conservation and recreation; the regulation of businesses and the commerce they conduct within the State; the protection of consumers from a variety of dangers and inconveniences; and many, many more.

## Differences Among the States

If you have ever traveled around the United States, you know that the variety in the geography and in the people is truly amazing. That variety has made this nation rich in every sense of that word. The variety found among the States also helps to explain some of the differences in what, and how much, the different States provide to their citizens.

One key characteristic that influences State budgets is the degree to which the State is urbanized. **Urbanization** is defined as the percentage of the population of a State living in cities of more than 250,000 people or in suburbs of cities with more than 50,000. The budgets of those States that have a high percentage of their population living in urbanized areas—States such as California and New Jersey—tend to reflect the special challenges of governing urbanized communities. For example, the management of roads and traffic is more complicated in urban areas, and thus requires more money to achieve.

Similarly, less urbanized States, such as Vermont and West Virginia, have budgets that reflect their own special needs.

Another factor influencing State budgets is the physical geography of a State. Again, a look at the map on page 712 will confirm what you already know: Each State is different in its size, shape, and physical features. Such issues as location relative to major national and world markets, energy supplies, natural resources, and agricultural resources help shape the State's economy and its budget. Thus, each State government considers its own needs, its own strengths, and its own future as it produces its operating plans. These budgets can differ widely in their size and shape, depending in large part on where that State is located.

## Section 1 Review

1. **Define:** urbanization
2. In general, what is the most expensive item in the budgets of the States?
3. What are some of the ways in which States try to protect their citizens' health, welfare, and safety?
4. What are three factors that can influence the shape of an individual State's budget and the services it provides?

**Critical Thinking**

5. **Recognizing Cause and Effect** (p. 19) Briefly explain how the unique physical features of a State might influence the shaping of a State's budget and the services it provides.

---

# 2 Financing State Government

**Find Out:**
- What are the powers of the State and local governments to tax?
- What are the different types of State and local revenue?
- What is the State budget and how is it made?

**Key Terms:**

sales tax, regressive tax, income tax, progressive tax, property tax, assessment, inheritance tax, estate tax

You know by now that government is an expensive proposition, and it is becoming more so from year to year. Altogether, the 50 States and their thousands of local governments now take in and spend well over one trillion dollars a year.

In this section, you will read about how the State and local governments get their money, and how they decide how to spend it.

## Raising Revenue at the State and Local Level

The States now take in nearly $500 billion in taxes, and all their local units collect more than $300 billion. In addition, the 50 States and their local governments also receive $500 billion or so from a number of nontax sources. Recall that taxes are charges made to raise money for public purposes.

The power to tax is one of the major powers reserved to each of the States. In the strictly legal sense, then, it is limited only by those restrictions imposed by the Federal Constitution and by its own fundamental law.[1]

**Federal Limitations** The Federal Constitution places only a few restrictions on State and local taxing powers.

INTERSTATE AND FOREIGN COMMERCE As you have already seen, the Constitution forbids the States the power to "lay any imposts or duties on imports or exports" and "any duty of tonnage."[2] In effect, the States are here prohibited from taxing interstate and foreign commerce. The Supreme Court has often held that because the Constitution gives to Congress the power to regulate that trade, the States are generally forbidden to do so.

THE NATIONAL GOVERNMENT AND ITS AGENCIES Ever since the Supreme Court's decision in *McCulloch* v. *Maryland*, 1819, the States have been forbidden to tax the Federal Government or any of its agencies or functions. They are forbidden to do so because, as Chief Justice Marshall put it in *McCulloch*: "The power to tax involves the power to destroy."

THE 14TH AMENDMENT The Due Process and Equal Protection clauses place limits on the power to tax at the State and local levels. Essentially, the Due Process Clause requires that taxes be (1) imposed and administered fairly, (2) not so heavy as to actually confiscate property, and (3) imposed only for public purposes.

The Equal Protection Clause forbids the making of unreasonable classifications for taxing purposes such as those based on race, religion, nationality, political party membership, or similarly unreasonable factors.

**State Constitutional Limitations** Each State's constitution limits the taxing powers of that State and also those of its local governments. For example, most State constitutions exempt the properties of churches, private schools, museums, cemeteries, and the like from taxation. Many set maximum tax rates, and some prohibit certain kinds of taxes.

## Types of State and Local Revenue

Beyond the limits just noted, a State can levy taxes as it chooses. The legislature decides what taxes the State will levy, and at what rates. It also decides what taxes the local units can levy.[3]

**The Sales Tax** The sales tax is the most productive source of income among the 50 States today. It accounts for just about a third of all tax monies the States collect each year.

A **sales tax** is a tax placed on the sale of various commodities; it is paid by the purchaser. It may be either general or selective in form. A general sales tax is one applied to the sale of most commodities. A selective sales tax is one placed only on the sale of certain commodities, such as cigarettes, liquor, or gasoline.

Today, 45 States levy a general sales tax.[4] The rates range among the States from a low of 3 percent in Colorado and Wyoming to a high of 8 percent in Connecticut.

Every State now levies a selective sales tax on gasoline and other motor fuels, alcoholic beverages, insurance policies, and cigarettes. Most States also have additional selective sales taxes.

There are two major reasons why the sales tax is so widely used. First, it is relatively easy to collect. Second, it is a fairly dependable revenue producer. But notice that it is a **regressive tax**—one that is the same for all people and not geared to the ability to pay. Therefore, it falls most heavily on those with lower incomes.

**The Income Tax** The **income tax**, levied on the income of individuals and/or corporations, yields almost a third of State tax revenues today. Forty-three States levy an individual income tax; 45 have some form of corporate income tax.[5]

The individual income tax is usually a **progressive tax**—that is, the higher the income, the higher the tax rate. The rates vary among the States, from 1 or 2 percent on lower incomes in most States to 10 percent or more on the highest incomes in some States.

The corporate income tax rates are most often uniform, a certain fixed percentage of income. Only a few States set the rates on a graduated—progressive—basis. The progressive

---

[2]Article I, Section 10, Clauses 2 and 3.

[3]A State constitution sometimes grants certain taxing powers directly to local governments, but this is not at all common.

[4]All except Alaska, Delaware, Montana, New Hampshire, and Oregon. Each of these States does impose various selective sales taxes, however.

[5]Nevada, South Dakota, Texas, Washington, and Wyoming levy neither type of income tax. Alaska and Florida impose only the corporate tax.

income tax is held by many to be the fairest form of taxation, especially because it may be closely geared to the ability to pay.

**The Property Tax**  The **property tax** is the chief source of income for local governments today. It accounts for approximately 80 percent of all of their tax receipts.

A government levies the property tax on (1) real property—land, buildings, and improvements that go with the property if sold, or (2) personal property—either tangible or intangible. Tangible personal property includes all movable wealth that is visible and the value of which can be easily assessed, such as television sets, automobiles, and air conditioners. Examples of intangible personal property include such things as stocks, bonds, mortgages and bank accounts. Because one can hide intangibles from the tax assessor, many States do not tax them. In others, they are taxed at a lower rate than tangible personal property.

The process of determining the value of the property to be taxed is known as **assessment**. The task is usually carried out by an elected county, township, or city assessor.

Several arguments support the property tax. Because government protects property—and often enhances its value—property can properly be required to contribute to the support of government. It is also a dependable source of revenue.

Similarly, there are some major criticisms of the property tax. For one, the tax is not geared to the ability to pay. Although the amount of real property one owns may have been a fair measure of one's wealth in earlier history, it is not today. Second, it is all but impossible to assess all taxable property on a fair and equal basis.

**Inheritance or Estate Taxes**  Every State except Nevada levies inheritance or estate taxes, so-called "death taxes." An **inheritance tax** is one levied on the beneficiary's share of an estate, and an **estate tax** is one levied directly on the full estate itself.

**Business Taxes**  A wide variety of business taxes, in addition to the corporate income tax, are important sources of revenue in most States.

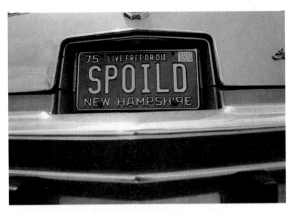

▲ **Live Free or Die**  New Hampshire's State motto is reflected in the absence of a sales tax in that State.

Over half the States impose severance taxes. These are taxes placed on the removal of such natural resources as timber, oil, gas, minerals, and fish from the land or water.

Every State has several different license taxes. These are fees that permit persons to engage in a business, occupation, or activity that is otherwise unlawful. All States require that corporations be licensed to do business in the State. Certain kinds of businesses—chain stores, amusement parks, bars and taverns, and transportation lines—must also have an additional license to operate. Then, too, most or all States require the licensing of doctors, lawyers, dentists, morticians, barbers, hairdressers, plumbers, engineers, electricians, and many others.

Nearly half the States have levies known as documentary and stock transfer taxes. These are charges made on the recording, registering, and transfer of such documents as mortgages, deeds, and securities. Some States also impose capital stock taxes, which are levied on the total assessed value of the shares of stock issued by a business concern.

**Other Taxes**  State and/or local governments impose a number of other taxes. More than half the States levy amusement taxes—usually on the tickets of admission to theaters, sports events, circuses, and the like. Payroll taxes produce huge sums—in all, well over $100 billion among the States today. But money produced by these taxes is held in trust

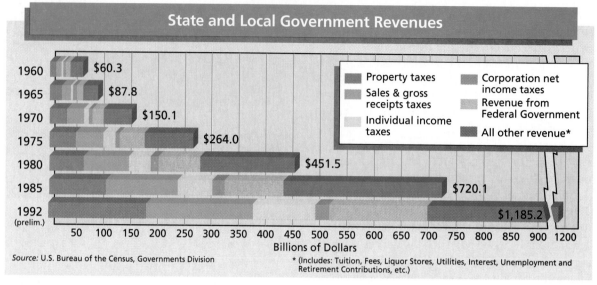

**State and Local Government Revenues**

| Year | | |
|---|---|---|
| 1960 | | $60.3 |
| 1965 | | $87.8 |
| 1970 | | $150.1 |
| 1975 | | $264.0 |
| 1980 | | $451.5 |
| 1985 | | $720.1 |
| 1992 (prelim.) | | $1,185.2 |

Legend:
- Property taxes
- Sales & gross receipts taxes
- Individual income taxes
- Corporation net income taxes
- Revenue from Federal Government
- All other revenue*

50 100 150 200 250 300 350 400 450 500 550 600 650 700 750 800 850 900 1200
Billions of Dollars

*Source:* U.S. Bureau of the Census, Governments Division

* (Includes: Tuition, Fees, Liquor Stores, Utilities, Interest, Unemployment and Retirement Contributions, etc.)

▲ **Interpreting Graphs** After examining the growth of State and local government finances, compare this graph to the graph on page 666. In which years have expenditures of State and local governments exceeded revenues?

funds for such social welfare programs as unemployment compensation, accident insurance, and retirement programs.

All States levy license taxes for other than business purposes too, such as those for motor vehicles and motor vehicle operators, and hunting, fishing, and marriage licenses.

## Nontax Receipts

State and local governments now take in over $500 billion a year from a wide range of nontax sources. A large portion of that huge amount comes from the Federal Government each year.

Each of the States and many of their local governments make money from a number of different publicly operated business enterprises. Toll bridges and toll roads are found in many parts of the country; several States are in the ferry business. North Dakota markets a flour sold under the brand-name "Dakota-Maid" and is also in the commercial banking business. California operates a short railway line in San Francisco.

Eighteen States are in the liquor-dispensing business, selling it through State-operated stores.[6] Many cities own and operate their water, electric power, and bus transportation systems.

Other nontax sources include court fines, the sale or leasing of public lands, interest from such sources as loans, investments, and late tax payments, and much else.

Several States have relaxed their once-strict antigambling laws, hoping to attract dollars, jobs, and tourists. State-run lotteries now make close to $10 billion a year for 33 States.[7]

## Borrowing

States and their local governments often must borrow money for unusually large undertakings, such as public buildings or toll bridges and

---

[6]Alabama, Idaho, Iowa, Maine, Michigan, Mississippi, Montana, New Hampshire, North Carolina, Ohio, Oregon, Pennsylvania, Utah, Vermont, Virginia, Washington, West Virginia, Wyoming. North Carolina's stores are operated by the counties; Wyoming's liquor monopoly operates only at the wholesale level.

[7]Arizona, California, Colorado, Connecticut, Delaware, Florida, Idaho, Illinois, Indiana, Iowa, Kansas, Kentucky, Louisiana, Maine, Maryland, Massachusetts, Michigan, Minnesota, Missouri, Montana, New Hampshire, New Jersey, New York, Ohio, Oregon, Pennsylvania, Rhode Island, South Dakota, Vermont, Virginia, Washington, West Virginia, Wisconsin.

highways, that cannot be paid for out of current income. That borrowing is most often done by issuing bonds, much as the Federal Government does. Generally, State and local bonds are fairly easy to market because the interest from them is not taxed by any level of government.

Many State and local governments have, in times past, had to default on their debts. Thus, most State constitutions now place detailed limits on the power to borrow.

## The State Budget

In Chapter 16, Section 3, you read that a budget is a financial plan, a plan for the control and use of public money, personnel, and property. It is also a political document, a statement of public policy.

Forty-seven States have now adopted the executive budget. That is, they have given the governor two vital powers: (1) the power to prepare the State budget, and (2) the authority to administer the funds the legislature has appropriated. In most States the governor has the help of a budget agency, appointed by and answering to the governor.[8]

The basic steps in the budget process are much the same at the State and local levels as they are at the federal level:

1. Each agency prepares estimates of its needs and expenditures in the upcoming fiscal period.
2. Those estimates are reviewed by an executive budget agency.
3. The revised estimates and supporting information are brought together in a budget for the governor to present to the legislature.
4. The budget is considered, the necessary funds are appropriated, and any necessary revenue measures are passed by the legislature.
5. The execution of the budget approved by the legislature is supervised by the governor.
6. The execution of the budget is given an independent check, the postaudit.

---

[8]Responsibility for the preparation of the budget is shared by the governor and the legislature in the other three States: Mississippi, South Carolina, and Texas.

## VOICES *on Government*

### On Budget Reductions

❝Reducing the budget will not be easy, but the 'Let's Have It All' decade of the 1980s is over. A lot of jurisdictions in this country are going through a 'downsizing' process. . . . It is time for a strong dose of financial discipline

**Sharon Pratt Dixon,** mayor of Washington, D.C., 1991–1995

and an honest deal for our citizens. Enough is enough. Necessity may have to be the mother of invention. One way or another, this government is going to provide a dollar's worth of services for a dollar's worth of taxes. We can accept nothing less.❞

## Section 2 Review

1. **Define:** sales tax, regressive tax, income tax, progressive tax, property tax, assessment, inheritance tax, estate tax
2. What restrictions does the Federal Constitution place on the taxing powers of the States?
3. What are the main forms of State taxes to which individuals are subject?
4. What are the main State taxes to which businesses are subject?
5. What are the other sources of State revenue?

### Critical Thinking

6. **Expressing Problems Clearly** (p. 19) In your opinion, should a tax be applied at the same rate to all people, or should those who have more be expected to pay at a higher rate?

★

# 3 In the Courtroom

**Find Out:**

- What kinds of law are applied in State courts?
- What are the functions of a grand jury?
- What is a petit jury and how does it function?

**Key Terms:**

common law, precedent, criminal law, civil law, petit jury

The principal function of the State courts is to decide disputes between private persons and between private persons and government. And, because nearly all of them can exercise the power of judicial review, they act as potent checks on the conduct of all of the other agencies of both State and local government.

In this section, you will read about the laws that are applied in State courts and about one of the ways those courts decide matters of the law.

## Kinds of Law Applied in State Courts

The law—the code of conduct by which society is governed—is made up of several different forms,[9] including:

CONSTITUTIONAL LAW   As you have read, the highest form of law in this country is based on the provisions of the United States Constitution and the State constitution, and judicial interpretations of them.

STATUTORY LAW   This form of law consists of the law—statutes—enacted by legislative bodies, including the United States Congress, the State legislature, the people (through the initiative or referendum), and city councils and other local legislative bodies.

ADMINISTRATIVE LAW   This form of law is composed of the rules, orders, and regulations that are issued by federal, State, or local executive officers, acting under proper constitutional and/or statutory authority.

COMMON LAW   The common law makes up a large part of the law of each State except Louisiana.[10] **Common law** is unwritten, judge-made law that has developed over centuries from those generally accepted ideas of right and wrong that have gained judicial recognition. State courts apply common law except when it is in conflict with written law.

The common law originated in England. It developed as judges followed **precedent** and abided by earlier court decisions—that is, as they applied the rule of *stare decisis,* "let the decision stand."[11] Most legal disputes in American courts are fought out very largely over the application of precedents.

EQUITY   This is a branch of the law that supplements common law. Whereas the common law applies to or provides a remedy for matters *after* they have happened, equity seeks to stop wrongs before they occur.

To illustrate this point, suppose your neighbors plan to add a room to their house. You think that a part of the planned addition will be on your land, and you know that it will destroy your rose garden. You can prevent the construction by getting an injunction.

## Criminal and Civil Law

You have probably heard reference to criminal law and civil law. These are two other bases by which the law is commonly classified.

**Criminal Law**   That portion of the law that defines public wrongs—offenses against the

---

[9]In its overall sense, the term *law* may be defined as the whole body of "rules and principles of conduct which the governing power in a community recognizes as those which it will enforce or sanction, and according to which it will regulate, limit, or protect the conduct of its members"; *Bouvier's Law Dictionary*, 3rd revision, vol. II, pp. 1875–76.

[10]Because of the early French influence, Louisiana's legal system is largely based on French legal concepts, derived from Roman law. The common law has worked its way into Louisiana law, however.

[11]American courts generally follow the rule. A decision, once made, becomes a precedent—a guide to be followed in all later, similar cases, unless compelling reasons call for its abandonment and the setting of a new precedent.

public order—and provides for their punishment is the **criminal law**. A criminal case is one brought by the State against a person accused of committing a crime. The State as the prosecution is always a party in a criminal case.

Crimes are of two kinds: felonies and misdemeanors. A felony is the greater crime and may be punished by a heavy fine and/or imprisonment or even death. A misdemeanor is the lesser offense, punishable by a small fine and/or a short jail term.

**Civil Law**   The **civil law** is that portion of the law relating to human conduct, to disputes between private parties, and to disputes between private parties and government not covered by criminal law. Civil cases in the legal system are usually referred to as suits and often lead to the award of money or a fine. Civil law can involve a wide range of issues, including divorce and custody disputes, torts—private wrongs against a person or property—and contracts.

## The Jury System

A jury is a body of persons selected according to law who hear evidence and decide questions of fact in a court case. There are two basic types of juries in the American legal system: (1) the grand jury and (2) the petit jury.

The grand jury is used only in criminal proceedings. The petit jury is the trial jury, and it is used in both civil and criminal cases.

**The Grand Jury**   The grand jury has from six to 23 persons, depending on the State. Where larger juries are used, generally at least 12 jurors must agree that an accused person is probably guilty before a formal accusation is made. Similarly, with smaller juries, an extraordinary majority is needed to indict, or bring the formal charge.

When a grand jury is impaneled, or selected, the judge instructs the jurors to find a true bill of indictment against any and all persons whom the prosecuting attorney brings to their attention and who they think are probably guilty. The judge also instructs them to bring a presentment, or accusation, against any persons whom they, of their own knowledge, believe have violated the State's criminal laws.

"Your honor, the jury finds the defendant weakly developed as a central character, overshadowed by the principal witness, unconvincingly portrayed as a victim of society, and guilty as charged."

*Drawing by Cheney; ©1988 The New Yorker Magazine, Inc.*

▲ **Interpreting Political Cartoons**
The drama of the courtroom has sometimes been portrayed in movies and books. What does this cartoon say about the potential drama in the justice system?

The grand jury meets in secret. To preside over its sessions, either the judge appoints or the jurors select one of their number to serve as the foreman or -woman. The prosecuting attorney presents witnesses and evidence against persons suspected of crime. The jurors may question those witnesses and summon others to testify against a suspect.

After receiving the evidence and hearing witnesses, the grand jury deliberates, with only the jurors themselves present. With the completion of their review, they move to the courtroom where their report, including any indictments they may have returned, is read in their presence.

The grand jury is expensive, cumbersome, and time-consuming. Hence, most of the States today depend more heavily on a much simpler process of accusation: the information.

An information is a formal charge filed by the prosecutor, without the action of a grand jury. The information is now used for most minor offenses. More than half the States now use it in most of the more serious cases, as well. The use of the information has much to recommend it. It is far less costly and time-consuming. Then, too, since grand juries most often follow the prosecutor's recommendations, many argue that a grand jury is really unnecessary.

**The Petit Jury** As you have seen, the **petit jury** is the trial jury. It hears the evidence in a case and decides the disputed facts. The number of trial jurors may vary. As it developed in England, the jury consisted of "12 men good and true." Although 12 is still the usual number, a lesser number, often six, now fills jury boxes in several States. Today, women everywhere are qualified to serve on juries.

In over a third of the States, jury verdicts need not be unanimous in civil and minor criminal cases. Rather, some extraordinary majority is needed. If a jury cannot agree on a verdict (a so-called hung jury), either another trial with a new jury takes place or the matter is dropped.

Misdemeanor cases and civil proceedings in which only minor sums are involved are often heard without a jury. In several States even the most serious of crimes may be heard without a jury—if the accused, fully informed of his or her rights, waives the right to trial by jury.

**Selection of Jurors** Jurors are picked in more or less the same way in most States. Periodically, some county official[12] or special jury commissioners prepare a list of persons eligible for jury service. Depending on the State, the lists are drawn from the poll books, the county tax rolls, motor vehicle and drivers license lists, and even public utility and telephone company billings.

The sheriff serves each person with a court order, a writ of *venire facias,* meaning "you must come." Persons under 18 and those over 70 years of age, illiterates, the ill, and criminals are commonly excluded. In many States those in occupations vital to the public interest—physicians, druggists, teachers, firefighters, and the like—are also excused.

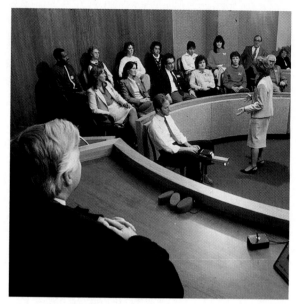

▲ **Trial by Jury** Jurors have decided the guilt or innocence of their peers since ancient times. In the United States, jury duty is an obligation of citizenship.

As with the grand jury, the States are moving away from the use of the trial jury. The greater time and cost of jury trials are leading reasons. The competence of the average jury and the impulses that may lead it to a verdict are often questioned, as well.

## Section 3 Review

**1. Define:** common law, precedent, criminal law, civil law, petit jury
**2.** What are four kinds of law that State courts apply?
**3.** (a) How did common law originate? (b) What makes precedents a key part of common law?
**4.** What is the primary duty of a grand jury?
**5.** (a) What is an indictment? (b) A presentment? (c) An information?

**Critical Thinking**

**6. Drawing Conclusions** (p. 19) In your opinion, would justice be better served by relying more or less on juries? Explain your answer.

---

[12]Most often it is the clerk of the court, the sheriff, or the county governing body, and sometimes the presiding judge, and in New England, officers of the town.

★

# What You Can Do

## Volunteering for Community Service

When you think of citizenship participation, what comes to mind? The first thing you might think of is voting. While there is no doubt that casting a ballot ranks as an important means of citizenship participation, there is another way to participate as a citizen—and you don't need to be of voting age. Volunteering for community service is a means of citizenship participation available to everyone, whether or not they are eligible to vote.

There are countless ways to work as a community volunteer. Volunteers work in hospitals, schools, nursing homes, and shelters, just to name a few places. They visit shut-ins, build playground equipment, read books to children at libraries—the list goes on and on. The citizenship chart on page 664 outlines steps that help you decide where and how to volunteer. For now, read on to learn about a high school student whose volunteer work made a difference in Oak Park, Illinois.

Whitney Heidenrich, a student at Oak Park and River Forest High School, decided to help children who are victims of abuse, neglect, or abandonment. Through her school service club, she became a volunteer "big sister" at the Hephzibah Children's Association Shelter in Oak Park. The shelter offers temporary care to area children suffering from abuse, neglect, or abandonment; tries to reunite children with their parents; or, in severe cases, helps them find foster or adopted families. After completing specialized training, Whitney and 40 other students made a commitment to spend at least one hour a week with a child at the shelter.

Whitney was paired up with a ten-year-old girl who described herself this way: "Some kids don't have families to care for them and give them clothes and things to eat. One of them is me." After her mother died, the girl's father remarried. Her father and stepmother, she said, "just didn't want me." While the shelter worked to find her a new family, she counted on regular visits from 17-year-old Whitney.

Whether it's helping with homework, reading books, baking cookies, playing video games, or just talking quietly together, Hephzibah's volunteer siblings are an important part of the lives of their little "brothers" and "sisters." Whitney said this about the arrangement: "I feel I'm someone she can talk to. I think she needs that. It's just that much more attention she gets."

The volunteer siblings think they get as much from the program as they give. Every month, they meet with staff members of the shelter to discuss treatment methods for child abuse. And, like Whitney, they get the satisfaction that comes from knowing their efforts make a difference.

## Getting Involved

**1. Identify** a need in your community similar to the one addressed in this case. You might start by doing research at your local library or by calling your local government to inquire about children's shelters. Or, identify any need in your community that might benefit from volunteer service.

**2. Formulate** a plan for how you might organize volunteer efforts to help remedy this problem and identify resources which could be used in your plan.

**3. Predict** any problems you might encounter in implementing your plan. How might you solve them in order to carry out your plan?

# 4 The Courts and Their Judges

**Find Out:**
- How are State court systems organized?
- What are the methods by which judges are selected in the various States?

**Key Term:**
appellate jurisdiction

They deal with everything from traffic tickets to murder, from disputes over nickels and dimes to settlements involving millions. They are the State courts and the judges who sit in them. In this section, you will read about the way these courts are organized.

## Organization of State Court Systems

Each of the State constitutions creates a court system for that State, and most of them leave the many details of its organization to the legislature. The following are some of the common features of those State and local court systems.

**Justices of the Peace** Justices of the peace—JPs—stand on the lowest rung of the State judicial ladder. They preside over what are commonly called justice courts.

JPs are almost always popularly elected. Mostly, JPs try misdemeanors—cases involving such petty offenses as traffic violations, disturbing the peace, public drunkenness, and the like. They can almost never settle civil disputes involving more than a few hundred dollars. They do issue certain kinds of warrants, hold preliminary hearings, and often perform marriages.[13]

---

[13]Recall, a warrant is a court order authorizing, or making legal, some official action, for example, a search warrant or an arrest warrant. A preliminary hearing is generally the first step in a major criminal prosecution. There the judge decides if the evidence is in fact enough to hold that person—bind that person over—for action by the grand jury or the prosecutor.

**Magistrates' Courts** Magistrates are the city cousins of JPs. For the most part, magistrates handle those minor civil complaints and misdemeanor cases that arise in an urban setting. They preside over what are generally called magistrates' courts or, in some places, police courts. Those courts are much like the justice courts, with just about the same jurisdiction. Magistrates, like JPs, are usually popularly elected and for short terms.

**Municipal Courts** Municipal courts are found in most of the nation's larger cities and many of its middle-sized and small ones. The jurisdiction of municipal courts is citywide. They can often hear civil cases involving several thousands of dollars as well as the usual run of misdemeanors. Many municipal courts are organized into divisions, which hear cases of a given kind, for example, civil, criminal, small claims, traffic, and probate divisions.

Consider the small claims division, often called the small claims court. Many people cannot afford the costs of suing for the collection of a small debt.

Small claims courts are designed for just such situations. In them, a person can bring a claim for little or no cost. The proceedings are usually informal, and the judge often handles the matter without attorneys for either side.

**Juvenile Courts** Individuals under 18 years of age are generally not subject to the justice of the courts in which adults are tried. Minors who are arrested for some offense or otherwise come to the attention of the police or other authorities may appear in juvenile courts.

The juvenile justice system is designed to address the special needs and problems of young people. This system generally emphasizes rehabilitation more than punishment. However, under certain circumstances juvenile courts do refer certain offenders to an adult criminal court for trial.

**General Trial Courts** Most of the more important civil and criminal cases heard in the United States are heard in the States' general trial courts.

Each State is divided into a number of judicial districts, or circuits, each generally covering one or

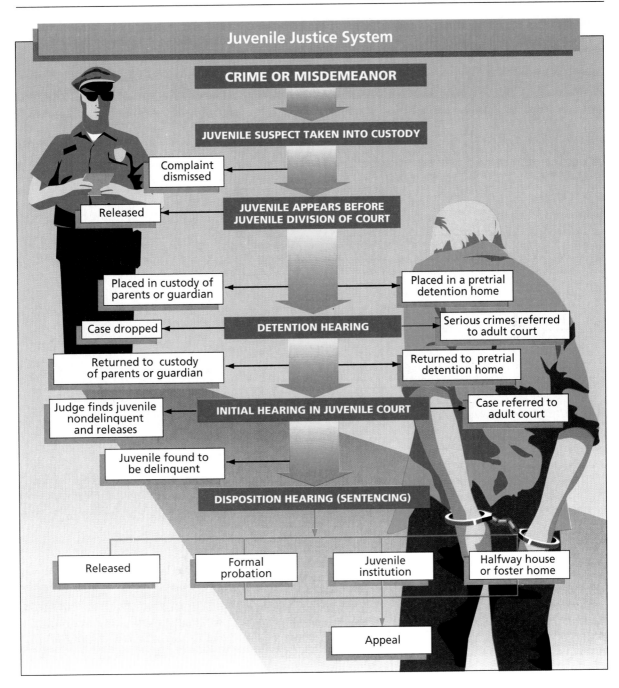

Juvenile Justice System

**CRIME OR MISDEMEANOR**

**JUVENILE SUSPECT TAKEN INTO CUSTODY**

Complaint dismissed

**JUVENILE APPEARS BEFORE JUVENILE DIVISION OF COURT**

Released

Placed in custody of parents or guardian

Placed in a pretrial detention home

**DETENTION HEARING**

Case dropped

Serious crimes referred to adult court

Returned to custody of parents or guardian

Returned to pretrial detention home

**INITIAL HEARING IN JUVENILE COURT**

Judge finds juvenile nondelinquent and releases

Case referred to adult court

Juvenile found to be delinquent

**DISPOSITION HEARING (SENTENCING)**

Released

Formal probation

Juvenile institution

Halfway house or foster home

Appeal

**Interpreting Charts**   Delinquency is conduct that is out of step with accepted social behavior or is against the law. How does the chart show that the justice system makes every effort to rehabilitate, rather than to punish, juvenile offenders?

more counties. For each district there is a general trial court, known variously as district, circuit, chancery, county, or superior courts, or courts of common pleas. Most legal actions brought under State law are begun in these courts.

These general trial courts are courts of "first instance." That is, they exercise original jurisdiction over most of the cases they hear. When cases do come to them on appeal from some lower court, a trial *de novo* (a new trial, as

# Global Awareness

## Crime Rates and Police Protection, Selected Countries

| Country | Total* | Offenses Reported to the Police Per 100,000 People | | | | Population per Police Officer** |
| | | Personal | | Property | | |
| | | Murder | Assault | Burglary | Automobile theft | |
|---------|--------|--------|---------|----------|------------------|---------------------------------|
| Australia | 6,773 | 4.5 | 369.6 | 1,962.8 | 770.6 | 450 |
| Finland | 9,631 | 0.6 | 47.2 | 1,432.6 | 364.8 | 640 |
| Hungary | 3,287 | 3.1 | 66.0 | 742.9 | 77.6 | 710 |
| Kenya | 364 | 4.2 | 57.3 | 63.5 | 6.6 | 1,500 |
| Jordan | 625 | 1.9 | 13.6 | 44.4 | 12.3 | 630 |
| Kuwait | 695 | 6.6 | 25.8 | 66.8 | 17.1 | 80 |
| Japan | 1,397 | 1.0 | 15.7 | 184.3 | 27.6 | 480 |
| Peru | 474 | 12.0 | 8.9 | 243.7 | — | 730 |
| Canada | 11,442.6 | 5.7 | 134.3 | 1,331.7 | 382.7 | 8,640 |
| Thailand | 1,449 | 9.5 | 21.8 | 25.0 | 4.2 | 530 |
| United States | 5,820 | 9.4 | 424.1 | 1,235.9 | 657.8 | 345 |

*Figure for total offenses reported includes crimes other than those listed in the table.
**Includes full-time, paid professionals performing domestic security functions. Includes administrative staff but excludes clerical employees.

*Source:* Encyclopaedia Britannica, *1994 Book of the Year.*

▲ **Interpreting Charts: Multicultural Awareness**   Which country has the most people per police officer? The least? What correlation can you find between these figures and the amount of crime in a country?

---

though the case had not been heard before) is usually held.

The trial court is seldom limited as to the kinds of cases it may hear. Although its decision on the facts in a case is usually final, disputes over questions of law may be carried to a higher court.

In the more heavily populated districts of some States, cases involving such matters as the settlement of estates or the affairs of minors are heard in separate trial courts. Where they are found, these tribunals are often called surrogate, probate, or orphans' courts.

**Intermediate Appellate Courts**   All but a few States now have one or more intermediate appellate courts. They are courts of appeal that stand between the trial courts and the State's

supreme court. These appellate courts serve to ease the burden of the high court.

Like the trial courts, the appellate courts have different names among the States, but they are most often called the court of appeals.[14] Most work of these courts involves the review of cases decided in the trial courts. That is, these appeals courts exercise mostly **appellate jurisdiction**. Their original jurisdiction, where it exists, is limited to a few specific kinds of cases—election disputes, for example. In exercising their appellate

---

[14]In New York the general trial court is called the supreme court; the intermediate appellate court is the appellate division of the supreme court; the State's highest court is known as the Court of Appeals.

jurisdiction, these courts do not hold trials. Rather, they hear oral arguments from attorneys, study the briefs—written arguments—that attorneys submit, and review the record of the case in the lower court.

Ordinarily, an appellate court does not concern itself with the facts in a case. Rather, its decision turns on whether the law was correctly interpreted and applied in the court below. Its decision may be reviewed by the State's high court, but its disposition of a case is usually final.

**The State Supreme Court** The State's supreme court is the highest court in its judicial system.[15] Its major function is to review the decisions of lower courts in those cases that are appealed to it.

The size of each State supreme court is fixed by each State constitution. In most States five or seven justices sit on the high bench.

The justices, including a chief justice, are appointed by the governor in 23 States. They are selected by the legislature in four States, and by the voters in the other 23.

The State supreme court is the court of last resort in the State's judicial system. It has the final say in all matters of State law. But, remember, many cases also raise questions of federal law. So, some State supreme court decisions may be reviewed by the United States Supreme Court. In fact, however, not very many of them are.[16] Recall, an appeal from a State's high court will be heard in the federal Supreme Court only if (1) a "federal question"—some matter of federal law—is involved in the case and (2) the Supreme Court agrees to hear that appeal.

In short, most State supreme court decisions are final. The oft-heard claim "I'll fight this case all the way to the United States Supreme Court" is almost always just so much hot air.[17]

## Unified Court Systems

The typical State court system is organized geographically rather than by types of cases. Thus, the general trial courts are most often organized so that each hears those cases arising within its own district, circuit, or county, no matter what the subject matter may be.

In these map-based systems, a judge must hear cases in nearly all areas of the law. A backlog of cases can and often does build up in some courts while judges sit with little to do in others. Moreover, uneven interpretations and applications of the law may and sometimes do occur from one part of the State to another.

To overcome these difficulties, a number of States have begun to abandon geographical organization in recent years. They have turned, instead, to a unified court system, one that is organized on a functional, or case-type, basis.

In a completely unified court system, there is technically only one court for the entire State. It is presided over (administered by) a chief judge or judicial council. There are a number of levels within the single court, such as supreme, intermediate appellate, and general trial sections. At each level within each section, divisions are established to hear cases in certain specialized or heavy caseload areas of the law—criminal, juvenile, family relations, and other areas that need special attention.

In such an arrangement, a judge can be assigned to that section or division to which his or her talents and interests seem best suited. To relieve overcrowded dockets, judges may be moved from one section or division to another.

---

[15]The State's highest court is known by that title in 45 States. But in Maine and Massachusetts it is called the Supreme Judicial Court; in Maryland and New York, the Court of Appeals; and in West Virginia, the Supreme Court of Appeals. Two States actually have two high courts. In Oklahoma and in Texas, the Supreme Court is the highest court in civil cases, and a separate Court of Criminal Appeals is the court of last resort in criminal cases.

[16]However, you did look at several such cases in Chapters 19, 20, and 21, most especially cases involving the 14th Amendment's Due Process and Equal Protection clauses.

---

[17]State law regularly gives its lower courts final jurisdiction over many types of minor cases. That is, review cannot be sought in a higher State court. In those cases, the lower court is the State's court of last resort. If any review is to be had, it can be only in the United States Supreme Court. Such reviews are extremely rare.

## Minority and Women Judges*, Selected States

| State | Minorities | Women |
|---|---|---|
| Hawaii | 70.5% | 11.5% |
| New Mexico | 25.0% | 12.5% |
| California | 13.5% | 10.5% |
| Maryland | 9.8% | 7.9% |
| Michigan | 8.9% | 8.3% |
| Texas | 8.5% | 6.2% |
| New York | 7.4% | 9.7% |
| North Carolina | 7.2% | 5.0% |
| Illinois | 6.2% | 4.3% |
| Colorado | 5.6% | 11.3% |
| Delaware | 5.3% | 19.1% |
| Connecticut | 5.1% | 8.0% |
| Virginia | 4.8% | 2.3% |
| Florida | 4.6% | 7.8% |
| New Jersey | 4.6% | 6.5% |
| Washington | 4.5% | 13.0% |
| Nevada | 4.5% | 7.7% |
| Pennsylvania | 4.4% | 4.0% |
| Alabama | 4.3% | 6.0% |
| Alaska | 3.9% | 21.0% |
| Georgia | 3.2% | 4.1% |
| West Virginia | 3.1% | 3.1% |
| Minnesota | 2.7% | 7.8% |
| Utah | 2.4% | 6.0% |
| Ohio | 2.4% | 4.2% |
| Idaho | 2.4% | 2.4% |
| Louisiana | 2.2% | 4.7% |
| Rhode Island | 2.1% | 10.6% |
| Missouri | 1.8% | 5.3% |
| Mississippi | 1.8% | 2.7% |
| Indiana | 1.4% | 6.0% |
| Kansas | 1.3% | 11.6% |
| Oklahoma | 0.8% | 9.3% |
| Nebraska | 0.8% | 3.4% |
| Montana | 0.0% | 14.3% |
| Maine | 0.0% | 10.6% |
| Wyoming | 0.0% | 7.3% |
| North Dakota | 0.0% | 5.3% |
| Arkansas | 0.0% | 3.6% |
| New Hampshire | 0.0% | 2.7% |
| South Dakota | 0.0% | 2.5% |
| **Federal Judiciary** | **10.5%** | **7.4%** |

*Minorities and females have been found to be better represented in those states that appoint, rather than elect, judges.

*Source:* Reprinted from *U.S. News & World Report*, January 20, 1986. Copyright 1986 U.S. News & World Report.

▲ **Interpreting Tables: Multicultural Awareness**  Women first began to win equal rights in the western States, some say because women played such a large role in settling the frontier. Does this table reflect a progressive attitude toward women in the western States?

# Selection of Judges

More than 15,000 judges sit in the State and local courts today. They are most often chosen in one of three ways: by (1) popular election, (2) appointment by the governor, or (3) appointment by the legislature.

Popular election is by far the most widely used method by which judges are picked around the country. The voters choose about three-fourths of all judges sitting in American courts today.

In fact, in 11 States popular election is the only method by which judges are chosen. In most of the other States, most or at least some judges are also chosen at the polls. About half of all judicial elections are nonpartisan contests today.[18]

Selection by the legislature is the least commonly used of the three major methods. The legislature now chooses all or at least most judges in only four States: Connecticut, Rhode Island, South Carolina, and Virginia.

The governor appoints nearly a fourth of all State judges today. In three States—Delaware, Massachusetts, and New Hampshire—all judges are named by the governor. In several other States, the governor has the power to appoint all or many of them, but under a Missouri Plan arrangement, as you will see in just a moment.

**How Should Judges Be Selected?**  Most people believe that judges should be independent, that they should "stay out of politics." Whatever method of selection is used, then, should be designed with that goal in mind.

Nearly all authorities agree that selection by the legislature is the most political of all the methods of choice—and few favor it. So, the question is really: Which is better, popular election of judges or appointment by the governor?

Those who agree on popular election generally make the democratic argument. Because judges "say the law," interpret and apply it, they should be chosen by and answer directly to the people. Some also argue that the concept of

[18]Except that vacancies caused by deaths or by midterm resignations are usually filled by appointments made by the governor. The 12 States are Arkansas, Kentucky, Louisiana, Minnesota, Montana, Nevada, North Carolina, North Dakota, Pennsylvania, West Virginia, and Wisconsin.

"We all make mistakes, as Your Honor knows, having been twice reprimanded by the New York State Commission on Judicial Conduct."

DRAWING BY STEVENSON; ©1981 *The New Yorker Magazine, Inc.*

▲ **Interpreting Political Cartoons**
The manner of selecting judges varies from State to State. Do you think this cartoonist would favor popular election or appointment of judges?

separation of powers is undercut if the executive (the governor) has the power to name the members of the judicial branch.

Those who favor appointment by the governor argue that the judicial function should be carried out only by those who are well qualified. Proponents of executive appointment insist it is the best way to ensure that those who preside in courts will have the qualities most needed in that role: absolute honesty and integrity, fairness, and the necessary training and ability in the law.

Popular election is both widely used and widely supported. Moves to abandon it have been strongly opposed by party organizations. So, most moves to revise the method of judicial selection have kept at least some element of voter choice.

**The Missouri Plan**  For nearly 70 years now, the American Bar Association (ABA) has sponsored an approach that combines the election and appointment processes. Because its adoption in Missouri in 1940 involved much

political drama, and so attracted wide attention, the method is often called the Missouri Plan.

Missouri's version of the plan is more or less typical of its shape in those other States where it is now used. The governor appoints the seven justices of the State's supreme court, the 32 judges of the court of appeals, and all judges who sit in certain of the State's trial courts. The governor must make each appointment from a panel, or list, of three names recommended by a judicial nominating commission. The commission is made up of a sitting judge, several members of the bar, and private citizens.

Each judge named by the governor then serves until the first general election after he or she has been in office for at least a year. The judge's name then appears on the ballot, without opposition. The voters decide whether or not that judge should be kept in office.

If the vote is favorable, the judge then serves a regular term—six years for a trial court judge and 12 years for one who sits on a higher court in Missouri. Thereafter, the judge may seek further terms in future retain-reject elections. Should the voters reject a sitting judge, the process begins again. In nearly half the States, some form of the Missouri Plan is now used for selecting at least some judges.

## Section 4 Review

1. **Define:** appellate jurisdiction
2. What courts are frequently found at the lowest, most local level in a State's court system?
3. Why do nearly all States now have intermediate appellate courts?
4. What is the primary function of each State's supreme court?
5. What three methods are used to select State judges?
6. Why is the Missouri Plan so favored by nearly all students of judicial administration?

**Critical Thinking**

7. **Identifying Alternatives** (p. 19) Consider the role and function of judges in the State courts. In your opinion, what would be the best way to select quality judges?

★

# How to File a Claim in Small Claims Court

Small claims courts are usually city or county courts designed to resolve claims involving small amounts of money. The maximum value of a small claim varies depending on where you live, but can range up to $5,000. No lawyers are necessary to bring a claim in small claims court, which makes the court easier and less expensive for the public to use. Follow the steps below to learn how to file a claim in small claims court.

**1. Obtain an application form.** To find out where the small claims court in your area is located, consult a local telephone directory. The information section at the front of the directory may include information about the small claims court in your area. Or, look under the name of your city or county for a listing of the courthouse. Once you have found the number of the court, ask for a small claims court application form.

**2. Consider mediation.** In some locations, mediation services are available as an alternative to small claims court. Mediation is a process in which a mediator assists two parties in finding their own resolution to their dispute without going to court. Your small claims application form may include information about mediation. If you are interested in this service, follow the directions on the form. Why might mediation be a good alternative to going to court?

**3. Complete and return the application form.** If you decide to follow through with your claim, complete the application form. Be sure to include all the requested information, and be as thorough and clear as possible in your responses. Though you do not need to hire a lawyer, filing a small claim will involve a small fee, usually around $10. The completed form and payment may be mailed or delivered in person to the clerk-magistrate's office where you are filing your claim. Why do you think it is important to fill out the forms completely and accurately?

**4. Prepare for the trial.** Your success at small claims court will depend on your presentation before the judge who will hear your case. In order to make a good presentation, it is important to prepare for your day in court. Bring to court any and all witnesses, checks, bills, photographs, or copies of letters that will help you prove your case. Both sides will have an opportunity to present their version of the dispute. When—and only when—the judge asks you to speak, make your presentation calmly and politely. Notice of the judge's decision will either be given or sent to each side. Why do you think it is important to make your case calmly and politely?

# Chapter-in-Brief

Scan all headings, photographs, charts, and other visuals in the chapter before reading the section summaries below.

## Section 1  Providing Important Services (pp. 663–667)
The federal system is one in which the States have many important powers and provide many important services.

States provide services directly to citizens. For example, States spend the largest portion of their budgets on education. Their most direct involvement is in higher education.

States are directly involved in the promotion of public health and welfare. In cooperation with the Federal Government and on their own, States administer a variety of programs. They also protect public safety, build and maintain roadways, protect the environment, and more.

Differences in the geography of the States lead to differences in each State's budget. Factors such as availability of resources and location have a powerful impact on the local economy.

## Section 2  Financing State Government (pp. 667–671)
State and local governments rely on a variety of methods to raise revenues. Most States—and a number of local governments—have general and/or selective sales taxes. These taxes are solid revenue producers, but they are regressive.

Other widely used taxes include the income tax, the property tax, and a variety of business taxes. In addition, State and local governments raise funds by running businesses and State lotteries. They also rely on borrowing.

The State budget is the means by which States plan the control and use of State money. Most States use the executive budget.

## Section 3  In the Courtroom (pp. 672–674)
State courts apply several forms of law, including constitutional law, statutory law, administrative law, common law, and equity law. Law is also classified as either criminal or civil.

A jury is a body of persons selected to hear evidence and decide questions of fact in a court case. Grand juries decide whether or not there is enough evidence to justify a formal accusation against a person. Petit juries hear evidence and decide the disputed facts.

Jurors are picked from among the State's citizens. Many States are deemphasizing the use of both grand juries and trial juries. Among the criticisms of juries is their cost and their competence. However, the system has a long and honorable place in the development of American law.

## Section 4  The Courts and Their Judges (pp. 676–681)
Each State constitution creates its own court system. There are, however, many common features among the States. For example, many State systems include justices of the peace and magistrates' courts. Municipal and juvenile courts are also common.

Most important civil and criminal cases heard in United States courts are heard in the States' general trial courts. All but a few States now have one or more intermediate appellate courts. The highest court in a State's judicial system is the State's supreme court.

Many States are moving to a unified court system. These systems abandon the geographic organization of the courts in favor of organization on a functional, or case-type, basis.

Judges in State and local courts are chosen by either (1) popular election, (2) appointment by the governor, or (3) appointment by the legislature. Popular election is the most widely used form.

One method used for selecting judges in a growing number of States is the so-called Missouri Plan, which combines appointment by the governor and popular election.

# Chapter Review

## Vocabulary and Key Terms

urbanization (p. 666)
sales tax (p. 668)
regressive tax (p. 668)
income tax (p. 668)
progressive tax (p. 668)
property tax (p. 669)

assessment (p. 669)
inheritance tax (p. 669)
estate tax (p. 669)
common law (p. 672)
precedent (p. 672)
criminal law (p. 673)

civil law (p. 673)
petit jury (p. 674)
appellate jurisdiction
 (p. 678)

**Matching:** *Review the key terms in the list above. If you are not sure of a term's meaning, look up the term and review its definition. Choose a term from the list above that best matches each description.*

1. a tax on individual and corporate income
2. what is levied on a beneficiary's share of an estate
3. the body of law that defines public wrongs and provides for their punishment
4. previous court decisions that serve as the basis for later cases
5. what is levied on tangible and intangible personal wealth and on land and buildings

**True or False:** *Determine whether each statement is true or false. If it is true, write "true." If it is false, change the underlined word or words to make the statement true.*

1. <u>Common law</u> is that which relates to disputes between private persons.
2. An <u>inheritance tax</u> is levied directly on the estate of a person.
3. A tax that is based upon a person's ability to pay is called a <u>progressive tax</u>.
4. The tax paid by the purchaser upon the sale of a commodity is a <u>sales tax</u>.
5. The <u>petit jury</u> often consists of 12 people, and it hears the evidence and decides questions of fact in a case.

**Word Relationships:** *Replace the underlined definition with the correct term from the list above.*

1. Much of the law applied in the State courts is based on <u>that body of law made up of generally accepted standards of rights and wrongs</u>.
2. State appellate courts have <u>the authority to review the decisions of inferior courts</u>.
3. Local governments must conduct <u>the process of determining the value of property for purposes of taxation</u> in order to determine property taxes.
4. The sales tax is criticized for being <u>a tax levied at a flat rate so that it falls most heavily on those least able to pay</u>.
5. One factor that impacts the budget of a government is <u>the percentage of people living in cities of a certain size</u>.

## Main Ideas

### Section 1 (pp. 663–667)

1. Briefly describe the major categories of services that States provide to their citizens.
2. What is the most costly of these services?
3. What kinds of differences exist among the States that influence the shapes of their budgets?

## Section 2 (pp. 667–671)

**4.** What are the general limits of a State's power to tax?

**5.** List the major categories of taxes that exist at the State and local level.

**6.** What are the main sources of nontax revenue available to the States?

**7.** In what sense is the State budget "more than bookkeeping entries and dollar signs"?

## Section 3 (pp. 672–674)

**8.** What kinds of law applied in State courts are discussed in Section 3?

**9.** What is the difference between civil and criminal law?

**10.** (a) What is the role of the grand jury in the State court system? (b) What is the role of the petit jury?

**11.** How are jurors selected?

## Section 4 (pp. 676–681)

**12.** Briefly describe the types of courts found in the typical State judicial system.

**13.** What are unified court systems?

**14.** How are judges selected at the State level today?

**15.** What are the main features of the Missouri Plan for selecting judges?

---

## Critical Thinking

**1. Formulating Questions** (p. 19) State and local governments spend the largest share of their budgets on education, highways, public welfare, and retirement and unemployment compensation for workers. Write a list of questions you could use to explore whether or not you agree with these spending priorities.

**2. Making Comparisons** (p. 19) Review the concepts of regressive and progressive taxes discussed in Section 2. (a) Which of these kinds of taxes do you think is most fair? (b) Explain your reasoning.

**3. Expressing Problems Clearly** (p. 19) In your opinion, what should be the characteristics required of all judges in the State judicial system?

## Getting Involved

**1. Writing Your Opinion** Recall what you have read in Section 4 about criticisms of the grand jury and petit jury in the State judicial systems. Write a letter to the governor in which you argue for or against the continued use of such juries. To help organize your thoughts, create a chart in which you list the pros and cons of grand juries and petit juries. Once you have decided on a position, begin by explaining your purpose in writing and stating your overall position on the matter. Then, explain in separate paragraphs the different reasons for your position. If you advocate an alternative or improvement to the jury system, be sure to include it. Revise to correct errors and to ensure the clarity of your letter, then draft a final copy.

**2. Cooperative Activity** Hold a class committee hearing to decide how to distribute $6 billion in State funds among several competing interests. First, assign teams of two or three individuals to represent four interests: (1) education, (2) highways, (3) public welfare, and (4) public safety. Each team will attempt to persuade the committee to approve its request for $2 billion. Allow each team time to prepare and deliver a brief presentation to the class explaining why they require the funding. (For purposes of the activity, assume that $2 billion represents an appropriate request from each department.) After each team has finished, discuss as a class how to divide the $6 billion among the groups. Submit various proposals to a class vote. The plan that receives the most votes wins.

**3. Gathering Information** Using the Government Resources Handbook on page 690, identify possible sources you could use to find out about the amount of tax revenue and the kinds of taxes collected in your State.

# STOP THE PRESSES

*Bury me on my face; for in a little while everything will be turned upside down.*

—DIOGENES

On this and the following pages you will find a number of changes and corrections which could not be included in the main body of the text.

## Electoral Politics

### Campaign Finance

■ FOR YEARS NOW, MEANINGFUL CAMPAIGN finance reform has been stalled in Congress—chiefly because most members of both parties in both houses have balked at the idea of giving up the campaign funding advantages that incumbent members of Congress regularly enjoy. Dramatic changes may be in the offing, however.

For the first time in more than a decade, a bipartisan campaign finance reform bill was introduced, in nearly identical form, in both houses in late 1995—and the measure has gained significant support, within and outside of Congress. The proposed legislation is built around four major points:

—*Voluntary campaign spending limits.* Spending caps would be based on the voting age population of each State and congressional district. (Recall that the Supreme Court has held that mandatory spending limits violate the 1st Amendment, *Buckley* v. *Valeo*, 1976.) The need for some kind of limits is underscored by the continuing escalation of campaign costs. The Federal Election Commission has reported that congressional candidates raised a record $740 million for their 1994 races and spent a record $724 million on those contests. Nearly $44.4 million was spent on a single 1994 Senate contest in California.

—*Free and reduced-rate television.* Those candidates who agree to abide by the voluntary spending limits would receive blocs of air time for their campaigns.

—*Restriction on PACs.* Political action committees would be abolished altogether or, alternatively, their ability to contribute to campaigns would be severely restricted.

—*Elimination of soft money.* The huge soft-money loophole in existing federal campaign finance regulation would be plugged—by an outright prohibition of all soft-money contributions.

In 1995, and again in 1996, each person who filed a federal income tax return could opt to assign $3 of his or her tax payment ($6 on a joint return) to the Presidential Election Campaign Fund—to pay for public funding of various aspects of the presidential election process.

The Federal Election Commission provided $12,024,000 to each of the two major parties to finance the planning and conduct of their national conventions in 1996. Also, according to the FEC's projections:

—Each contender for the Republican and the Democratic presidential nomination in 1996 who qualifies for public funding will be limited to spending just over $30 million on his or her pre-convention campaign—and so will be eligible to receive as much as $15 million from the FEC.

—The Republican and Democratic presidential nominees each can receive FEC grants of just over $60 million to finance their general election campaigns—and, if they choose to accept the public funds, will be limited to spending no more than that amount on their campaigns. *Pages 173–179.*

### Presidential Primaries

■ SOME FORM OF THE PRESIDENTIAL PRIMARY WAS in place in 41 States in 1996. In most of those States, State law requires both major parties to hold a primary. In some of them, however, the law gives each major party a choice: it may stage a primary or it may, instead, rely on the caucus process to select its national convention delegates. So, in some States only one of the major parties actually held a presidential primary in 1996—only the Republicans (not the Democrats) in Arizona, Idaho, Louisiana, Michigan, North Dakota, South Carolina, Texas, and Washington, and only the Democrats in Montana.

The nine States in which both of the major parties picked their convention delegates by caucus in 1996 were Alaska, Hawaii, Iowa, Minnesota, Missouri, Nevada, Utah, Virginia, and Wyoming.

For 1996, the Republicans chose 1,984 delegates to meet in their national convention in San Diego. The Democrats sent 4,295 delegates to their meeting in Chicago. *Pages 165, 330–334.*

# Congress

## Term Limits

■ THE SUPREME COURT HAS HELD THAT NO State can place any limit on the number of terms to which any person may be elected to either house of Congress. The Court has also held that Congress does not have the power to enact a term-limits statute; the only way congressional term limits can be imposed is through an amendment to the Constitution. The High Court made those rulings in two cases from Arkansas, *U.S. Term Limits, Inc.* v. *Thornton* and *Bryant* v. *Hill,* 1995.

Speaking for the Court's 5–4 majority, Justice John Paul Stevens declared that "neither Congress nor the States possess the power to supplement the exclusive qualifications [of age, citizenship, and residence] set forth" in the Constitution.

The dissenting justices argued that nothing in the Constitution explicitly prohibits any State from setting additional qualifications, including term limits, for those candidates who seek to represent them in Congress. "The Constitution is simply silent on this question," wrote Justice Clarence Thomas.

The House defeated a proposed term-limits amendment in 1995 by a vote of 227 to 204—sixty-one votes short of the two-thirds needed for passage. Proponents of terms limits have redoubled their efforts to persuade Congress, and both houses will likely consider the matter again in 1996.

The Court's decision in the Arkansas cases does not disturb the power of any State to set limits on the number of terms or years to which a person may be elected to any State or local office. *Pages 60–63, 239, 245.*

## Gifts, Other Favors

■ THE SENATE HAS ADOPTED NEW RULES TO CURB the value of gifts and other favors that senators receive from lobbyists and special interests. As of January 1, 1996, senators may no longer accept such things as expense-paid trips to the Super Bowl, free skiing junkets to Vail, or golf outings in Palm Springs. Now, each senator is subject to a $100 limit on the value of gifts he or she can accept from any one source in any year. Although a lobbyist can still do such things as take a senator to lunch or present him or her with tickets to an athletic or other entertainment event, the value of such gifts cannot exceed $50 per instance and cannot total more than $100 in a calendar year.

Similar restrictions are under consideration in the House and may be adopted some time in 1996. *Pages 251–253.*

## The Commerce Power

■ IN *U.S.* v. *Lopez,* 1995, THE SUPREME COURT declared the Gun-Free School Zones Act of 1990 unconstitutional. That law, passed by Congress under its authority to regulate interstate commerce, had made it a federal crime for any person to possess a firearm within or immediately near any school in the United States.

Alfonso Lopez, then a senior at Edison High School in San Antonio, Texas, was convicted of violating the law. Lopez had arrived at school one morning in 1992 carrying a concealed .38 caliber handgun and five bullets. A federal district judge sentenced him to six months in prison and two years of supervised release.

The Supreme Court overturned Lopez's conviction: The Gun-Free School Zones Act "neither regulates a commercial activity nor contains a requirement that possession in any way be connected to interstate commerce. We hold that the Act exceeds the authority of Congress 'to regulate Commerce . . . among the several States. . . .' "

*Lopez* marked the first time in sixty years that the Court had struck down a federal law on grounds that Congress had overstepped the limits on its commerce power. *Pages 65–67, 264–266, 473–475.*

## Committee Chairs

■ BOTH HOUSES HAVE NOW PLACED A SIX-YEAR limit on the length of time that any member can serve as the chairperson of a standing committee. In the House, the new limit became effective with the beginning of the 104th Congress, in January of 1995. The Senate's restriction will go into force with the start of the next term of Congress—that is, in January 1997. *Pages 287–290.*

# Civil Rights and Civil Liberties

## Affirmative Action

■ THE SUPREME COURT'S 5–4 DECISION IN *Adarand Constructors, Inc.* v. *Pena*, 1995, marks a major departure from the High Court's previous rulings in affirmative action cases. Until *Adarand,* the Court had regularly accepted affirmative action laws, regulations, and programs as "benign"—that is, mild but necessary—instances of "race-conscious policy-making." Now, however, in *Adarand,* the Court has held that whenever government provides for any preferential treatment based on race, that action is almost always unconstitutional, even when the action is intended to benefit minority groups suffering from past injustices.

"The Constitution protects persons, not groups," wrote Justice Sandra Day O'Connor for the Court's majority. "Whenever the government treats any person unequally because of his or her race, that person has suffered an injury that falls squarely within the language and spirit of the Constitution's guarantee of equal treatment."

The Court did leave a small window open for the conduct of some affirmative action programs by government. Such programs can be used by government, it said, but only when they are "narrowly tailored" to overcome specific, clearly provable cases of discrimination.

*Adarand* arose out of a Federal Highway Administration policy based on a 1987 act of Congress. Under that policy, the federal road agency gave bonuses to federal highway contractors if 10 percent or more of their construction work was subcontracted to "socially and economically disadvantaged" businesses, including those owned by racial minorities.

Adarand Constructors, Inc., a white-owned Colorado company, sued the government, arguing that the FHA's policy amounted to race-based discrimination. The lower federal courts ruled against the firm, basing their decisions on previous Supreme Court cases, and Adarand took its appeal from those decisions to the Supreme Court. *Pages 557–559.*

## The Establishment Clause

■ THE SUPREME COURT DECIDED TWO important church-state cases in 1995, both centering on the expression of religious views:

—In *Rosenberger* v. *University of Virginia*, it approved, for the first time, the direct public subsidization of a private religious activity. The Court ruled 5–4 that the University of Virginia, a public school, violated the free-speech rights of the student members of a campus Christian group when it refused to pay for the printing of that group's newspaper but did pay for the publications of a wide range of other (nonreligious) student organizations.

—The Court came to a similar conclusion in *Capitol Square Review and Advisory Board* v. *Pinette*. There, it held 7–2 that the State of Ohio had violated the free-speech rights of members of the Ku Klux Klan by refusing to allow the Klan to erect a cross in a public park near the State capitol in Columbus at Christmas time. The Klan sought to put the cross in Capitol Square, a 10-acre plaza around the Ohio state house. For well over 100 years, the square has been used as a public forum—a place for gatherings, speeches, and other events to promote many different causes, both secular and religious.

## Freedom of Speech

■ IN *McIntyre* v. *Ohio*, 1995, THE HIGH COURT struck down a State law that prohibited the circulation of political leaflets, fliers, brochures, and similar campaign materials that do not carry a sponsor's name and address. The Court's ruling destroyed the similar statutes of nearly all of the other States.

The Ohio law was invoked when the late Margaret McIntyre of Columbus was fined $100 for distributing an unsigned flier opposing a local school tax. The Ohio Supreme Court upheld her conviction, calling the law a "minor requirement" justified by the need to prevent fraud and libel. But, writing for the United State Supreme Court's 7–2 majority, Justice John Paul Stevens declared: "Under our Constitution, anonymous pamphleteering is not a pernicious, fraudulent practice, but an honorable tradition of advocacy and dissent. Anonymity is a shield from the tyranny of the majority. . . . The speech in which Mrs. McIntyre engaged—handing out leaflets in the advocacy of a politically controversial viewpoint—

is the essence of 1st Amendment expression." *Pages 499–505.*

## Federal Spending and Income

■ FIGURES FOR 1995 AND 1996 show that the Social Security Administration still spends more money than any other federal agency, followed by interest on the public debt (included in the Treasury Department's spending). The largest amount of revenue still comes from the individual income tax. According to the Bureau of the Public Debt, at the beginning of fiscal year 1996, the public debt totaled $4,884,604,986,450.

| Federal Spending, Fiscal Year 1995 | | | |
|---|---|---|---|
| (By agency, in billions of dollars) | | | |
| Legislative Branch | $2.6 | Department of Labor | 32.2 |
| The Judiciary | 2.9 | Department of State | 5.3 |
| Executive Office of the President | 0.2 | Department of Transportation | 38.8 |
| Funds appropriated to the President | 11.2 | Department of the Treasury | 348.4 |
| (Mostly for foreign economic/military aid) | | Department of Veterans Affairs | 37.8 |
| Department of Agriculture | 56.7 | Environmental Protection Agency | 6.3 |
| Department of Commerce | 3.4 | National Aeronautics and | |
| Department of Defense—Military | 259.6 | Space Administration | 13.4 |
| Department of Defense—Civil | 31.7 | Office of Personnel Management | 41.3 |
| Department of Education | 31.3 | Social Security Administration | 362.2 |
| Department of Energy | 17.6 | Resolution Trust Corporation | -10.6 |
| Department of Health and Human | | Other Independent Agencies | 9.5 |
| Services | 303.1 | Deductions | |
| Department of Housing and | | (Undistributed offsetting receipts) | -137.6 |
| Urban Development | 29.0 | **Total Outlays** | **$1,514.4** |
| Department of the Interior | 7.4 | Deficit | |
| Department of Justice | 10.8 | (Outlays greater than receipts) | -163.8 |

*Source:* Financial Management Service, Department of the Treasury

| The Federal Government's Income | | |
|---|---|---|
| [By major source, for fiscal year 1995 (actual) and 1996 (estimated)] | | |
| | **1995 Actual** | **1996 Estimated** |
| Individual Income Taxes | $590.2 | $623.4 |
| Corporation Income Taxes | 157.1 | 157.4 |
| Social Insurance Taxes and Contributions | 484.5 | 509.3 |
| Excise Taxes | 57.5 | 57.2 |
| Estate and Gift Taxes | 14.8 | 16.8 |
| Customs Duties | 19.3 | 22.3 |
| Miscellaneous Receipts | 27.3 | 29.0 |
| **Total Receipts** | **$1,350.6** | **$1,415.5** |

*Source:* Office of Management and Budget; Financial Management Service, Department of the Treasury

# GOVERNMENT RESOURCES HANDBOOK

## Public and Private Resources

James Madison directed these words to the Americans of his day—and they are just as telling in our time as they were in his:

"A people who mean to be their own governors must arm themselves with the power that knowledge gives."

As a citizen, you have a great many obligations—and not the least of them is the duty to inform yourself, the obligation to know as much as you possibly can about American government and politics. Granted, the field of American government and politics is vast, and it is also very complex. But here, as with any other subject, you just recognize this: The fact that there is so much to know is not an excuse for knowing nothing.

Remember, from Chapter 8, the point that most Americans learn most of what they know about public affairs from television. Television is both an important and a useful source of information—and so, too, are radio and newspapers. But the people who depend solely on those sources can have only a very imperfect picture of the political world. Those media focus mostly on the sensational and the newsworthy, and so they provide only a part of the whole picture. They are not, and they do not intend to be, of much help to you in finding answers to such questions as these: What is the power of judicial review, and why is it important? How can you discover how your senators and representatives in Congress have voted on particular measures? What were the principle issues in the elections of 1836 and of 1932, and why were those elections so critical in he development of the American political system? Why is Congress and all but one of the 50 State legislatures bicameral, and why is that important?

Fortunately, there are a great many other sources—both public and private—to which you can turn to discover a great deal about the subject of American government and politics. These several pages are intended to guide you to those sources.

## Government Publications

Nearly all federal agencies publish pamphlets and reports to describe their work and to provide general or specialized information to the public. Most of them will supply a list of available publications. (The addresses of the public information offices of the principal federal agencies are cited in the *United States Government Manual*; see below.) Some of these publications can be obtained from the particular agencies on request. Many of them are available at a nominal price from the Superintendent of Documents, Government Printing Office, Washington, D.C. 20402.

Most of the many publications produced by federal agencies—including congressional committee hearings and reports—can be found in any of the more than 1,000 depository libraries across the country. A depository library is one to which the Government Printing Office regularly sends copies of the materials it publishes. There are also more than 8,500 public libraries in the United States, and many hundreds of other more specialized and private libraries that contain the most useful of the government's publications.

The Government Printing Office publishes three very useful catalogs. Two of them are free, available from the GPO on request: (1) *U. S. Government Books*, which lists hundreds of the GPO's best-selling titles, and (2) *New Books*, a bimonthly listing of all of the government's books that have become available from the GPO in the preceding two months. The third one, the *Monthly Catalog of U.S. Government Publications*, is sent to subscribers at a nominal charge. It is a comprehensive listing of all federal agency publications currently for sale by the GPO. The Government Printing Office also maintains retail outlets, GPO Bookstores, in 22 major cities around the country. Each of them can be found in the telephone book for the particular locale.

The following are among the most useful of all government publications, and you should have access to them, in your school's library or another one nearby.

**United States Government Manual.** Published annually by the National Archives and Records Administration. The *Manual* describes the creation, organization, and work of every unit in the executive, legislative, and judicial branches of the Federal Government. It also contains up-to-date organization charts and lists persons holding upper-level government posts.

**Congressional Directory.** Published once every two years with an annual supplement by the congressional Joint Committee on Printing, the *Directory* contains some of the material found in the *Government Manual*, but focuses on the legislative branch. It includes autobiographical sketches of all members of Congress, lists congressional committees and committee assignments, identifies office and committee staff personnel, tabulates statistics for recent congressional elections, and reprints the map of each congressional district.

**Statistical Abstract of the United States.** Published annually by the Census Bureau in the Department of Commerce. The *Abstract* is an extensive and comprehensive compilation of recent and current statistical data on virtually every aspect of American economic, social, and political life. Its hundreds of charts, graphs, and tables cover such topics as population, immigration, public finance, and law enforcement. (Your librarian can also point you to many other useful items published by the Census Bureau.)

**Congressional Record.** Published for every day that Congress is in session, and bound and indexed annually by the congressional Joint Committee on Printing. The *Record* contains everything that is said (and much that is not) and reports all the actions taken on the floor in either house. A twice-monthly *Congressional Record Index* contains the same information. (Each member of Congress has an allotment of subscriptions of the *Record,* to be mailed to whomever he or she chooses. Your local or school librarian might wish to contact your member of Congress to see about obtaining a copy.)

**Weekly Compilation of Presidential Documents.** Published every Monday by the White House. It reprints the President's public messages, speeches, and other statements; the text of press conferences; and a checklist of bill signings, appointments, and White House press releases.

**Historical Statistics of the United States, Colonial Times to 1970.** This volume, first published in 1976 by the Bureau of the Census, is a supplement to the annual *Statistical Abstract.* It takes much of the data reported in the annual publications and reports the information on an historical basis.

**Budget of the United States Government.** Published annually by the Office of Management and Budget. The budget document provides a summary of the budget for the year, special analyses of the budget, historical tables, organization charts of the United States Government, and details of new policy initiatives.

**State Manual, or Blue Book.** Published once every year or two, usually by each State's office of the secretary of state, it often contains the text of the State's constitution, brief descriptions of State and local governmental structure and agencies, recent election results, lists of State and local officials, and much historical, descriptive, and other data about the State.

**The Book of the States.** Published every two years by the Council of State Governments. It contains a wealth of factual and comparative data on the organization, procedures, and major functions of State governments and several essays on current developments in State government and politics.

## Guides and Indexes

Several privately published guides to printed materials will help you find information in a variety of publications. Guides are published monthly, quarterly, or annually, and most are available in a public library.

In addition to these printed publications, many libraries now have computers that access guides which are updated on a weekly or daily basis. On-line computer services, which allow someone to locate (and possibly retrieve) a publication or item of information while sitting at a computer terminal, are also available to individuals and schools. These on-line computer services are worth investigating as new storage and retrieval systems make these services more available and useful to the public.

**Books in Print.** This book is a continuing list of all hardbound books, new and old, that are published in the United States and currently available. The books are indexed by author, title, publisher, and ISBN.

**Paperbound Books in Print.** This is a continuing catalog of all paperback books published and currently available in the United States.

**Readers' Guide to Periodical Literature.** The *Periodical Guide* contains an index of all articles appearing in most magazines and other periodicals of any significant circulation in the country.

**The Public Affairs Information Service.** This index provides a continuing listing by subject of current books, pamphlets, periodical articles, government documents, and other library materials on a broad range of topics in public affairs.

**The Social Science Index.** This index is a more specialized, academically oriented catalog of periodical articles in the social sciences. You will find listings of articles on political science, public administration, economics, and criminology in addition to the other social sciences.

Most major (and many smaller) newspapers publish indexes to their daily editions, typically on a bi-weekly or monthly and annual basis. The *New York Times Index* and the *Wall Street Journal Index* are outstanding examples of this kind of very valuable research tool and can be found in larger libraries.

## General Reference Works

Many general reference works will prove very useful to an understanding of American government and politics. A few of the important works published by governmental agencies are listed on the previous page. The list of works published by private sources is extremely long and grows yearly. Here are several books that you will likely be able to find in your school or local library. Most of these books are revised and updated on a regular basis.

*The American Political Dictionary* by Jack Plano and Milton Greenberg. (Published by Holt, Rinehart and Winston)

*Safire's Political Dictionary* by William Safire. (Published by Random House)

*Encyclopedia of American History,* edited by Richard B. Morris and Henry Steele Commager. (Published by Harper & Row)

*The Encyclopedia of the American Constitution,* edited by Leonard W. Levy, Kenneth L. Karst, and Dennis J. Mahoney. (Published by Macmillan, 4 volumes)

*History of U.S. Political Parties* by Arthur M. Schlesinger, Jr. (Published by Bowker, 4 volumes)

*Documents of American History,* edited by Henry Steele Commager and Milton Cantor. (Published by Prentice Hall, 2 volumes)

*Summaries of Leading Cases on the Constitution* by Paul Bartholomew and Joseph Menez. (Published by Littlefield, Adams)

*Politics in America: Members of Congress in Washington and at Home,* edited by Alan Ehrenhalt. (Published by Congressional Quarterly Press)

Several publications by *Congressional Quarterly* are cited at various points in this textbook. Among the several excellent reference works published by *Congressional Quarterly* are these volumes:

*Congressional Quarterly's Guide to U.S. Elections.* This book is a massive collection of returns for all House and Senate elections since 1914, all gubernatorial elections since 1788, and all presidential elections and national nominating conventions.

*Congressional Quarterly's Guide to Congress.* This is a comprehensive study of the origins, history, power, and procedures of the nation's lawmaking body.

*Congressional Quarterly's Guide to the United States Supreme Court.* This guide is one of the most extensive compilations of information ever published about the Court, its members, history, and the cases it has decided.

*Congressional Quarterly's Guide to the Presidency.* This guide provides in-depth information about the presidency and the executive agencies.

*Washington Information Directory.* This book provides information about all the Political Action Committees and political organizations that have offices in Washington.

## Almanacs

Almanacs are handy reference tools that contain a wealth of up-to-date information on a variety of topics. Most almanacs give you ready access to data about politics, the economy, population, history, and other areas of vital information. Because almanacs are inexpensive, one-volume books that are published annually, you should easily be able to find a current edition in a library or bookstore, or even in your classroom. Some of the best-known almanacs are listed below.

**The World Almanac and Book of Facts.** This general almanac contains close to 1,000 pages and 10,000 listings, most of which are useful to students of American government. The book contains separate sections with the previous year in review, time lines on world and American history, and listings for each State in the Union and each country in the world.

**Information Please Almanac.** Much like *The World Almanac* in size and scope, this almanac also contains special consumer features on such issues as drug abuse, taxes, first aid, science, law enforcement, etc.

**The Universal Almanac.** This new almanac features larger, easier-to-read type than most other almanacs. It also incorporates more graphics than other almanacs. The larger-than-average international section is very useful for comparative government statistics.

**The Statesman's Year-Book.** Published for over 125 years, this specialized British almanac features close to 1700 pages of information about the countries of the world. Entries are listed by country and include information about the history, population, geography, climate, government, defense, international relations, economy, energy, natural resources, industry, trade, communications, religion, education, and social welfare of a nation.

**The Almanac of American Politics.** More expensive and more specialized than the other almanacs, this reference work is devoted exclusively to information about the 535 members of the United States Congress. This almanac describes each congressional district and gives detailed information about its representative, including his or her voting record on key issues.

**Encyclopaedia Britannica, Book of the Year.** This volume is not strictly an almanac; it is the yearly supplement to the encyclopedia. However, the last few hundred pages contain up-to-date statistical information about all the countries of the world, similar to the information you would find in an almanac.

## Periodicals

A vast amount of basic information can be found in the news stories, feature articles, and commentaries in magazines and other periodicals. To locate articles, use one of the references or guides listed.

Many periodicals—such as *Time, Newsweek,* or *U.S. News & World Report*—provide general news coverage. However, keep in mind that many periodicals reflect a strong liberal or conservative perspective on their coverage of current events. For example, the *National Review* has a conservative bent and *The New Republic* offers a contrasting liberal perspective.

Most libraries will carry at least several of these well-respected magazines:

*American Heritage*
*The Atlantic*
*Business Week*
*Commentary*
*Common Cause Magazine*
*Congressional Digest*
*Congressional Quarterly Weekly Report*
*Forbes*
*Fortune*
*Harper's*
*Insight*
*National Civic Review*
*National Journal*
*National Review*
*Nation's Business*
*The New Republic*
*Newsweek*
*Public Opinion*
*Senior Scholastic*
*Time*
*U.S. News & World Report*
*World Press Review*

A number of more specialized scholarly journals are also available in many libraries. The following are among the most useful for students of American government:

*American Journal of Political Science*
*The American Political Science Review*
*The Annals of the American Academy of Political
   and Social Sciences*
*Foreign Affairs*
*Foreign Policy*
*Journal of International Affairs*
*The Journal of Politics*
*Public Administration Review*
*Public Opinion Quarterly*
*Publius: The Journal of Federalism*
*State Government*

## Private Organizations

A large number of private organizations publish informative pamphlets and other materials on American government and politics, focusing especially on various public policy questions. To find the names and addresses of an organization, see *The Encyclopedia of Associations,* a reference work published yearly that is a guide to national and international organizations.

A sampling of some of the most prominent organizations are listed below:

The American Federation of Labor and Congress of Industrial Organizations (AFL-CIO), 815 16th Street, NW, Washington, D.C. 20006

The American Enterprise Institute for Public Policy Research, 1150 17th Street, NW, Washington, D.C. 20036

Chamber of Commerce of the United States, 1615 H Street, NW, Washington, D.C. 20062

The Committee for Economic Development, 477 Madison Avenue, New York, NY 10022

Common Cause, 2030 M Street, NW, Washington, D.C. 20036

The Democratic National Committee, 430 S. Capitol Street, SE, Washington, D.C. 20003

The Foreign Policy Association, 729 7th Avenue, New York, NY 10019

The League of Women Voters of the United States, 1730 M Street, NW, Washington, D.C. 20036

The National Association for the Advancement of Colored People (NAACP), 4805 Mt. Hope Drive, Baltimore, MD 21215

The National Municipal League, 47 E. 68th Street, New York, NY 10021

The Republican National Committee, 310 1st Street, SE, Washington, D.C. 20003

# Books

This unit-by-unit listing is not intended as an exhaustive bibliography. It is, instead, a sampling of many recently published volumes useful to the study of American government.

## Unit 1

Caplan, Richard and John Feiffer (eds.) *State of the Union, 1994.* Westview, 1994.

Cuomo, Mario M. and Harold Holzer (eds.) *Lincoln on Democracy: An Anthology.* HarperCollins, 1994.

Ebenstein, William and Alan O. *Introduction to Political Thinkers.* Harcourt, Brace, 1993.

Elkins, Stanley and Eric McKittrick. *The Age of Federalism: The Early American Republic, 1788–1800.* Oxford, 1993.

Isaak, Robert. *American Political Thinking: Readings from the Political Origins to the 21st Century.* Harcourt, Brace, 1994.

Klosko, George. *History of Political Theory: An Introduction.* Harcourt Brace, 1994.

Lawson, Kay. *The Human Polity: A Comparative Introduction to Political Science.* Houghton Mifflin, 3rd ed., 1993.

Miroff, Bruce. *Icons of Democracy.* Basic Books, 1993.

O'Toole, Laurence J., Jr. *American Intergovernmental Relations.* CQ Press, 2nd ed., 1992.

Peltason, J. W. *Understanding the Constitution.* Harcourt Brace, 13th ed., 1994.

## Unit 2

Ansolabehere, Stephen *et al. The Media Game: American Politics in the Television Age.* Macmillan, 1993.

Clawson, Dan *et al. Money Talks: Corporate PACs and Political Influence.* Basic Books, 1993.

Crotty, William (ed.) *America's Choice: The Election of 1992.* Dushkin, 1993.

Flanigan, William H. and Nancy H. Zingale. *Political Behavior of the American Electorate.* CQ Press, 8th ed., 1994.

Gruber, Doris A. *Media Power in Politics.* CQ Press, 3rd ed., 1994.

Maisel, L. Sandy and William G. Slade (eds.) *Parties and Politics in American History.* Garland, 1995.

Matalin, Mary and James Carville. *All's Fair: Love, War, and Running for President.* Simon & Schuster, 1994.

Nelson, Michael (ed.) *The Elections of 1992.* CQ Press, 1993.

Richardson, Jeremy T. *Pressure Groups.* Oxford, 1993.

Rosenstone, Steven J. and John M. Hansen. *Mobilization, Participation and Democracy in America.* Macmillan, 1993.

Uslaner, Eric N. (ed.) *American Political Parties: A Reader.* Peacock, 1993.

## Unit 3

Dodd, Lawrence C. and Bruce I Oppenheimer. *Congress Reconsidered.* CQ Press, 5th ed., 1993.

Harris, Fred R. *Deadlock or Decision: The U.S. Senate and the Rise of National Parties.* Oxford, 1993.

Paul S. Herrnson. *Congressional Elections: Campaigning at Home and in Washington.* Congressional Quarterly, 1994.

Thomas Kazee. *Who Runs for Congress?* Congressional Quarterly, 1994.

Keefe, William J. and Morris Ogul. *The American Legislative Process: Congress and the States.* Prentice Hall, 8th ed., 1993.

LeLoup, Lance T. and Steven A. Shull. *Congress and the President.* Wadsworth, 1993.

Mann, Thomas E. and Norman J. Ornstein (eds.) *Congress, the Press, and the Public.* Brookings, 1994.

Olson, David M. *Democratic Legislative Institutions: A Comparative View.* Sharpe, 1994.

Schneier, Edward and Bertram Gross. *Congress Today.* St. Martin's, 1993.

Schudson, Michael. *Watergate in American Memory: How We Remember, Forget, and Reconstruct the Past.* Basic Books, 1993.

## Unit 4

Abramson, Paul R. et al. *Change and Continuity in the 1992 Elections.* Congressional Quarterly, 1994.

Briggs, Philip J. *Making Foreign Policy.* Bowman and Littlefield, 1995.

Denton, Robert E., Jr. *The 1992 Presidential Campaign: A Communications Perspective.* Praeger, 1994.

Halle, Lewis J. *The Cold War as History.* HarperCollins, 1994.

Kegley, Charles W., Jr. and Eugene R. Wittkopf. *The Future of American Foreign Policy.* St. Martin's Press, 2nd ed., 1994.

Meier, Kenneth J. *Politics and the Bureaucracy.* Brooks/Cole, 3rd ed., 1993.

Milkis, Sidney M. and Michael Nelson. *The American Presidency: Origins and Development, 1776–1993.* CQ Press, 2nd ed., 1994.

Papp, Daniel S. *Contemporary International Relations*. Macmillan, 1994.

Pfiffner, James P. *The Modern Presidency*. St. Martin's, 1994.

Riggs, Robert E. and Jack C. Plano. *The United Nations*. Wadsworth, 2nd ed., 1994.

Rosati, Jerel A. *The Politics of United States Foreign Policy*. Harcourt Brace, 1994.

Schulzinger, Robert D. *American Diplomacy in the Twentieth Century*. Oxford, 2nd ed., 1994.

Snow, Donald M. and Dennis M. Drew. *From Lexington to Desert Storm: War and Politics in the American Experience*. Sharpe, 1993.

Spanier, John W. and Eric M. Uslaner. *American Foreign Policy Making*. Macmillan, 1994.

## UNIT 5

Abraham, Henry and Barbara Perry. *Freedom and the Court: Civil Rights and Liberties in the United States*. Oxford, 1994.

_____, *The Judicial Process*. Oxford, 6th ed., 1993.

Barnum, David G. *The Supreme Court in American Democracy*. St. Martin's, 1993.

Colaiaco, Joseph A. *Martin Luther King, Jr.* St. Martin's, 1993.

Cushman, Clare. *The Supreme Court Justices: Illustrated Biographies, 1789–1993*. CQ Press, 1993.

Hall, Kermit L. (ed.) *The Oxford Companion to the Supreme Court of the United States*. Oxford, 1992.

Hentoff, Nat. *Free Speech for Me—But Not for Thee*. HarperCollins, 1993.

Levy, Peter B. *Let Freedom Ring: A Documentary History of the Modern Civil Rights Movement*. Praeger, 1992.

Licht, Robert A. (ed.) *The Framers and Fundamental Rights*. AEI Press, 1992.

McGlen, Nancy E. and Karen O'Connor. *Women, Politics, and American Society*. Prentice Hall, 1995.

O'Brien, David M. *Storm Center: The Supreme Court in American Politics*. Norton, 3rd ed., 1993.

Schrecker, Ellen. *The Age of McCarthyism: A Brief History with Documents*. St. Martin's, 1994.

Witt, Linda *et al. Running as a Woman: Gender and Power in American Politics*. The Free Press, 1994.

## UNIT 6

Adonis, Andrew. *Parliament Today*. St. Martin's, 2nd ed., 1993.

Calvert, Peter and Susan. *Latin America in the Twentieth Century*. St. Martin's, 2nd ed., 1993.

Camp, Robert A. *Politics in Mexico*. Oxford, 1993.

Curtis, Michael (ed.) *Introduction to Comparative Politics*. HarperCollins, 3rd ed., 1993.

Hauss, Charles. *Comparative Politics: Domestic Responses to Global Challenges*. West, 1994.

Kort, Michael. *The Soviet Colossus: The Rise and Fall of the USSR*. Sharpe, 3rd ed., 1993.

Magstadt, Thomas M. *Nations and Governments: Comparative Politics in Regional Perspective*. St. Martin's Press, 2nd ed., 1994.

Meny, Yves and Andrew Knapp. *Government and Politics in Western Europe*. Oxford, 1993.

Rasmussen, Jorgen S. *The British Political Process*. Wadsworth, 1993.

Rywkin, Michael. *Moscow's Last Empire*. Sharpe, 1994.

Skidmore, Max J. *Ideologies: Politics in Action*. Harcourt, Brace, 2nd ed., 1993.

Soe, Christian (ed.) *Comparative Politics, 95–96*, Dushkin, 1995.

## UNIT 7

Berman, David. *State and Local Politics*. Brown & Benchmark, 7th ed., 1994.

Beyle, Thad (ed.) *State Government: CQ's Guide to Current Issues and Activities, 1995–1996*. CQ Press, 1995.

Bonsignore, John J. *et al. Before the Law: An Introduction to the Legal Process*. Houghton Mifflin, 2nd ed., 1994.

Bowman, Ann O'M. and Richard C. Kearney. *State and Local Government*. Houghton Mifflin, 2nd ed., 1993.

Dye, Thomas R. *Politics in States and Communities*. Prentice Hall, 8th ed., 1994.

Friedman, Lawrence M. *Crime and Punishment in American History*. Basic Books, 1993.

Saffel, David C. *State and Local Government: Politics and Public Policies*. McGraw Hill, 5th ed., 1993.

Stinebrickner, Bruce (ed.) *State and Local Government*. Dushkin, 1995.

Straayer, John A. *et al. State and Local Politics*. St. Martin's Press, 1994.

# The Executive Departments: Principal Agencies and Functions*

## Department of State

Established: 1789

Head: Secretary of State

Employees, 1993: 26,425

The State Department's primary objective is to promote the long-range security and well-being of the United States. Its major functions include advising the

* The agencies listed on these pages are the major units in the 14 cabinet departments. For information on other agencies in each of them, see *The Government Manual.* Source for employees per department: Office of Personnel Management.

President in forming and executing foreign policy, negotiating treaties and agreements with foreign nations, speaking for the United States in the United Nations and other international organizations, and representing the United States at more than 800 international conferences each year.

**Bureau of Economic and Business Affairs.** Designs and carries out policy regarding foreign economic matters, including resources and food, energy issues, trade, international finance and development, and aviation and maritime affairs.

**Regional Bureaus.** Responsible for U.S. foreign affairs activities in five geographic regions: the Bureaus of African Affairs, European and Canadian Affairs, East Asian and Pacific Affairs, Inter-American Affairs, and Near Eastern and South Asian Affairs.

**Bureau of Public Affairs.** Provides information on foreign policy to the American people through conferences, briefings, and speaking and media engagements. This bureau also produces and distributes publications, videotapes, and films on U.S. foreign policy.

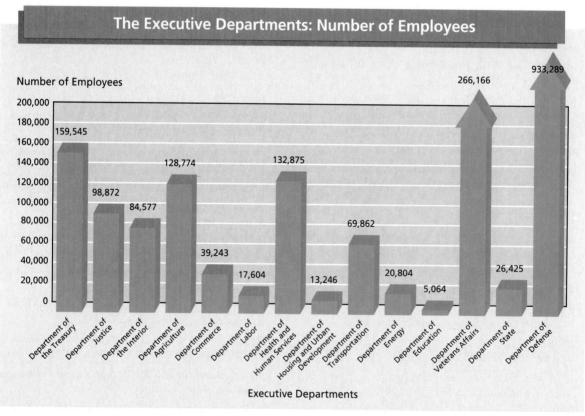

**The Executive Departments: Number of Employees**

Number of Employees

- Department of the Treasury: 159,545
- Department of Justice: 98,872
- Department of the Interior: 84,577
- Department of Agriculture: 128,774
- Department of Commerce: 39,243
- Department of Labor: 17,604
- Department of Health and Human Services: 132,875
- Department of Housing and Urban Development: 13,246
- Department of Transportation: 69,862
- Department of Energy: 20,804
- Department of Education: 5,064
- Department of Veterans Affairs: 266,166
- Department of State: 26,425
- Department of Defense: 933,289

Executive Departments

As you can see, the number of men and women who work for the several cabinet departments ranges from little more than 5,000 in one of them to nearly a million in another.

**Bureau of Intelligence and Research.** Coordinates and analyzes the output of the department's intelligence gathering activities, and those of other government agencies.

**Bureau of Consular Affairs.** Issues 4 million passports to American citizens each year, through its Passport Office; also responsible for granting visas to foreigners and for the protection of American citizens abroad.

**Bureau of Politico-Military Affairs.** Develops policy and provides direction on issues that affect U.S. security policies, military assistance, nuclear policy, and arms control matters.

**Office of the Chief of Protocol.** Advises the President, the Vice President, and the secretary of state and other agencies on matters of diplomatic procedure according to international laws and customs; responsible for coordinating visits of foreign officials and conducting ceremonial functions and public events.

**United States Foreign Service.** Staffs and maintains American embassies, consulates, missions, and other diplomatic stations throughout the world.

**Bureau of Diplomatic Security.** Provides protection for department personnel here and abroad and maintains the security of American embassies and other diplomatic stations abroad.

**Bureau of International Organization Affairs.** Responsible for American participation in international organizations and conferences.

**Bureau for Refugee Programs.** Administers U.S. refugee programs abroad, in cooperation with other federal agencies, foreign governments, international organizations, and private groups.

**Bureau of Human Rights and Humanitarian Affairs.** Responsible for implementing U.S. policy relating to the observance of human rights throughout the world; monitors the behavior of other governments in human rights matters.

## Department of the Treasury

Established: 1789

Head: Secretary of the Treasury

Employees, 1993: 159,545

The Treasury Department is the Federal Government's leading financial agency. Its major functions include the collection of tax revenue and customs duties, borrowing and the management of the public debt, criminal law enforcement (notably tax evasion, smuggling, and counterfeiting), accounting for public monies, the manufacture of coins and currency, and the supervision of national banks.

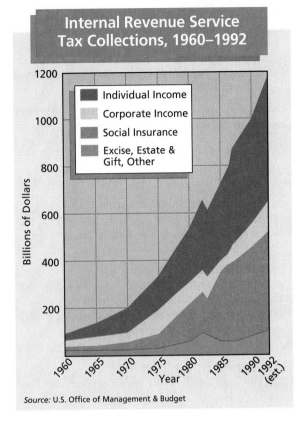

**Internal Revenue Service Tax Collections, 1960–1992**

Source: U.S. Office of Management & Budget

The income tax became the largest source of federal revenue in 1917–1918 and, except for a few years during the Depression of the 1930s, it has remained so ever since.

**Internal Revenue Service.** Administers, enforces most federal tax laws; collects nearly all federal taxes (including, especially, personal and corporate income, social security, excise, estate, and gift taxes).

**United States Customs Service.** Administers, enforces customs laws; collects duties on imports; combats smuggling and other illegal practices in international trade.

**Bureau of the Public Debt**. Supervises most federal borrowing; manages the public debt.

**Bureau of Alcohol, Tobacco, and Firearms.** Administers and enforces federal laws governing firearms and explosives, and those covering the production, use, and distribution of alcohol and tobacco products.

**Financial Management Service.** Government's central bookkeeper and principal financial reporting agency.

**Bureau of Engraving and Printing.** Designs, engraves, prints all currency (paper money), treasury bonds and notes, postage stamps, food coupons, and similar financial items issued by the Federal Government.

**United States Mint.** Manufactures all U.S. coins; holds stocks of gold and silver; operates mints in San Francisco, California; Philadelphia, Pennsylvania; Denver, Colorado; and West Point, New York; the assay office in San Francisco, California; and the bullion depository in Fort Knox, Kentucky.

**Office of the Comptroller of the Currency.** Headed by the comptroller of the currency; administers federal banking laws and generally supervises the operations of some 3,600 national banks; directs staff of more than 2,000 bank examiners to assure the soundness of the operations and financial condition of all national banks.

**Office of Thrift Supervision.** Monitors and regulates the approximately 2,600 savings and loan institutions covered by Savings Association Insurance Fund (SAIF), which insures deposits in S & L's.

**United States Secret Service.** Protects the President and Vice President, the members of their immediate families, former Presidents and their wives or widows, presidential and vice-presidential candidates, and visiting heads of foreign states; enforces laws against counterfeiting.

# Department of Justice

Established: 1870

Head: Attorney General

Employees, 1993: 98,872

The Department of Justice is the nation's largest law firm. Among its major responsibilities, it furnishes legal advice to the President and heads of the other executive departments; represents the United States in court; enforces most federal criminal laws; enforces federal civil rights, antitrust, public lands, immigration and naturalization laws, and supervises the federal penal system.

**Solicitor General.** Represents the United States in the Supreme Court; decides which lower court decisions the Federal Government should appeal to the High Court and the position the United States should take in these cases.

**Antitrust Division.** Handles court cases involving violations of antitrust laws, other federal statutes covering illegal business practices.

**Environment and Natural Resources Division.** Handles most civil (noncriminal) cases involving public lands and natural resources, wildlife resources, Native American lands and claims; prosecutes civil and criminal cases arising out of federal environmental protection laws.

**Tax Division.** Handles civil and criminal cases arising out of the tax laws; often acts as in-court attorney for the Internal Revenue Service.

**Civil Rights Division.** Handles both civil and criminal cases involving acts of discrimination prohibited by the various federal civil rights laws.

**Civil Division.** Handles most civil cases to which the United States is a party (all civil cases not handled by one of the other divisions).

**Criminal Division.** Handles most court cases involving federal crimes (all criminal cases not handled by one of the other divisions).

**Immigration and Naturalization Service.** Administers and enforces the immigration laws (involving aliens who seek to enter or remain in the United States) and the naturalization laws (relating to aliens who seek citizenship).

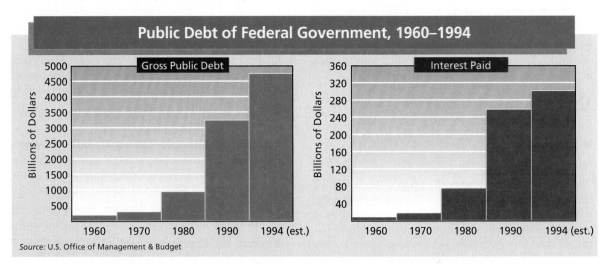

**Public Debt of Federal Government, 1960–1994**

Source: U.S. Office of Management & Budget

▲ The Constitution (Article I, Section 8, Clause 2) gives Congress the power "to borrow money on the credit of the United States." Those few words provide the basis on which the government borrows hundreds of billions of dollars every year.

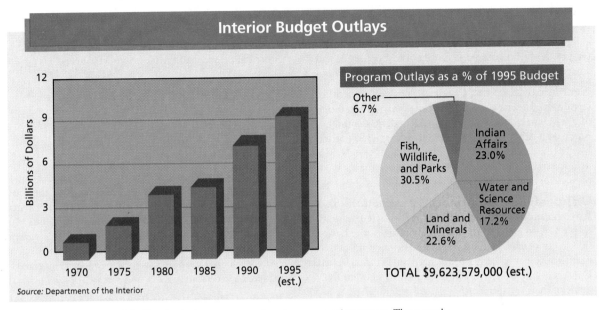

## Interior Budget Outlays

**Billions of Dollars** (left chart): 1970, 1975, 1980, 1985, 1990, 1995 (est.)

*Source:* Department of the Interior

**Program Outlays as a % of 1995 Budget**

- Other 6.7%
- Indian Affairs 23.0%
- Fish, Wildlife, and Parks 30.5%
- Water and Science Resources 17.2%
- Land and Minerals 22.6%

TOTAL $9,623,579,000 (est.)

The Department of the Interior is the government's major conservation agency. These graphs show the amount of money spent by this department since 1970 (left) and the breakdown of the department's budget for 1995 by agency.

**United States Marshals Service.** The oldest federal law enforcement agency; its nearly 3,000 officers protect federal courts, execute federal court orders, arrest most federal fugitives, operate the Witness Security Program, and respond to such emergency situations as terrorist incidents.

**Federal Bureau of Investigation.** Principal investigative arm of the Justice Department; handles all violations of federal law except those specifically assigned to another federal law enforcement agency; gathers and reports facts, locates witnesses, compiles evidence in those cases.

**Drug Enforcement Administration.** Administers and enforces laws relating to controlled substances (principally narcotics and dangerous drugs).

**Bureau of Prisons.** Operates the federal penal system (including six penitentiaries and more than 70 correctional institutions, prison camps, detention centers, medical centers, and other jail facilities).

## Department of the Interior

Established: 1849

Head: Secretary of the Interior

Employees, 1993: 84,577

The Interior Department is the Federal Government's major conservation agency. Its principal work involves the management of more than 500 million acres of public lands; conservation, development, and use of mineral, water, fish, and wildlife resources; reclamation of arid lands; operation of federal hydroelectric power facilities; administration of the national parks system; and responsibility for Native American reservations.

**Bureau of Land Management.** Controls, manages some 270 million acres of public lands (located chiefly in the West and Alaska); manages timber, oil, gas, minerals, rangeland, recreation, and other resources of those lands; leases public lands for such purposes as grazing and the commercial development of oil, gas, minerals, and other resources.

**Minerals Management Service.** Leases the offshore (outer continental shelf) lands for oil, gas, and other resource development.

**Bureau of Reclamation.** Builds, operates water projects to reclaim arid and semiarid lands in the western States; most projects are multipurpose. That is, in addition to water conservation, storage, and irrigation, they serve such other purposes as hydroelectric power generation, flood control, municipal and industrial water supply, navigation, and outdoor recreation.

**National Park Service.** Administers the more than 360 units of the National Park System (including national parks, national monuments, scenic rivers, lakeshores and seashores, recreation areas, and historic sites); plays host to more than 300 million tourist visits each year.

**United States Fish and Wildlife Service.** Responsible for protecting and increasing the nation's fish and wildlife resources; maintains more than 450 wildlife refuges, 70 fish hatcheries, a number of laboratories, and a nationwide network of wildlife law enforcement agents.

**Geological Survey.** Conducts surveys and other research to describe (map) the geography and geology of the United States and to locate oil, gas, mineral, water, and other natural resources; studies such natural hazards as earthquakes, volcanoes, and floods. Its detailed maps and reports now cover more than half of the land area of the United States.

**Office of Surface Mining Reclamation and Enforcement.** Administers and enforces federal laws to protect people and the environment from the harmful effects of coal mining; regulates stripmining activities; works to reclaim abandoned mines and mined lands; aids the States in the development and enforcement of their own similar regulatory programs.

**Bureau of Mines.** Conducts research and issues factual reports on mining techniques, mine health and safety, environmental pollution, the recycling of solid wastes, and nearly all other phases of mining activity in this country.

**Bureau of Indian Affairs.** Administers educational, public health, and other social assistance and economic development programs for the nation's Native American and Alaskan Native population, especially the approximately 600,000 Native Americans who now live on or near some 260 reservations.

**Office for Territorial and International Affairs.** Works to promote the economic, social, and political development of the territories of the Virgin Islands, Guam, American Samoa, and the Northern Marianas.

# Department of Agriculture

Established: 1889

Head: Secretary of Agriculture

Employees, 1993: 128, 774

The Department of Agriculture reflects this fundamentally important point: the nation's farms produce the food upon which all of us must depend, and they also produce a goodly share of the raw materials essential to the nation's manufacturing industries. The USDA's several agencies have wide-ranging responsibilities in the areas of agricultural conservation and rural development, marketing, credit, crop stabilization, and research and education.

**Farmers Home Administration.** Makes low-interest, long-term loans to farmers, ranchers, and farm groups unable to get credit at reasonable terms from other (private) lenders; also guarantees loans from private lenders. Most FHA loans are made for the purchase, enlargement, improvement, or operation of family-sized farms.

**Rural Electrification Administration.** Makes low-interest, long-term loans to farm cooperatives and other rural-based nonprofit groups to provide electric power and/or telephone service to people in rural areas; also guarantees loans from private lenders.

**Agricultural Budget Outlays***

Billions of dollars: 60, 45, 30, 15, 0 — 1970, 1975, 1980, 1985, 1990, 1995 (est.)

*Based on President's budget, not actual congressional appropriations.
*Source:* Department of Agriculture

Program Outlays as a % of 1995 Budget

Research/Statistical Services 2.9%
Commodity Credit Corp. 16.0%
Food Assistance 62.8%
Forest and Soil Conservation 10.3%
Rural Development 3.3%
All Other 4.7%

TOTAL $61,300,000,000

Outlays by the Department of Agriculture have increased nearly seven times since 1970 (left). The food assistance program takes the largest share of these funds (62.8 percent).

**Agricultural Cooperative Service.** Helps farmers to form and run cooperatives, especially to market their crops and to purchase farm supplies.

**Agricultural Marketing Service.** Aids farmers to market their products; issues daily reports on crop conditions, demands, prices, and other local and national market data, through press, radio, television; enforces several laws that prohibit fraud and other deceptive market practices.

**Animal and Plant Health Inspection Service.** Conducts inspections and may impose quarantines to prevent, control, or eradicate animal and plant pests and diseases; regulates the manufacture and sale of chemical and other products used to control such pests and diseases; administers laws for humane treatment of livestock and circus, zoo, and laboratory animals.

**Food and Nutrition Service.** Administers the food stamp program (coupons for low-income persons and families to increase their food purchasing power); provides grants and/or foodstuffs for other food assistance programs (most notably, the National School Lunch Program).

**Food Safety and Inspection Service.** Inspects poultry and meat processing plants and grades their products under federal laws that set safety, quality, and label standards.

**Federal Grain Inspection Service.** Weighs and inspects all grain exports from the United States; oversees State and private inspection of grain marketed within the country.

**Agricultural Stabilization and Conservation Service.** Administers several price support, commodity loan, and subsidy payment programs to "stabilize" (maintain, bolster) farm incomes and market prices for certain crops.

**Commodity Credit Corporation.** Holds (stores) crops purchased or accepted as payments of loans under the various programs administered by the ASCS; reduces surplus crop holdings (mostly by donations to federal, State, and private welfare agencies and programs).

**Federal Crop Insurance Corporation.** Offers (sells directly) and contracts with private companies to provide insurance to producers of most widely grown crops, to protect them against unavoidable losses from such causes as weather, insects, and diseases.

**Agricultural Research Service.** Conducts basic and applied research programs; makes grants to support research at State agricultural experiment stations and land-grant universities; provides financial support for

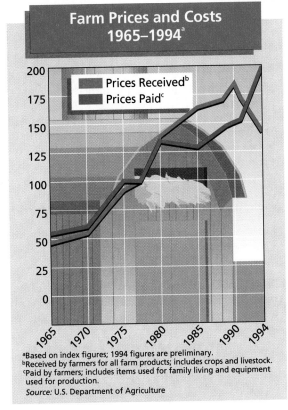

**Farm Prices and Costs 1965–1994[a]**

[Legend:]
Prices Received[b]
Prices Paid[c]

[a]Based on index figures; 1994 figures are preliminary.
[b]Received by farmers for all farm products; includes crops and livestock.
[c]Paid by farmers; includes items used for family living and equipment used for production.
*Source:* U.S. Department of Agriculture

The graph above shows the increasing disparity between prices received by farmers for their goods and prices paid by farmers for their operating expenses.

the Extension Service (which operates through land-grant universities and county extension agents, to promote "beyond-the-classroom" education and other farm-related activities, especially in rural areas); administers grants and other financial aid for higher education in food and agricultural sciences, veterinary medicine.

**Forest Service.** Manages the national forest system (155 national forests, 20 national grasslands, and 8 land use projects on 191 million acres in 44 States, the Virgin Islands and Puerto Rico); sells timber and issues oil, gas, mineral, grazing leases; provides outdoor recreation facilities and protects scenic areas and wildlife habitat; makes grants for forestry research.

**Soil Conservation Service.** Directs and/or provides financial and other assistance for a broad range of soil conservation, watershed protection, and related programs; promotes the creation of and gives technical help to local soil conservation districts (which now number about 3,000 and cover more than 90 percent of the nation's farms and farmlands).

# Department of Commerce

Established: 1903

Head: Secretary of Commerce

Employees, 1993: 39,243

Many of the Federal Government's programs to promote business and the overall well-being of the nation's economy are centered in the Commerce Department. Its several agencies are charged with this broad mission: to promote international trade, spur the nation's economic growth, and encourage technological advancement.

**Bureau of the Census.** Takes a census of the nation's population every 10 years (as required by the Constitution); collects, analyzes, and publishes other statistical data about the people and the economy of the nation.

**National Institute of Standards and Technology.** Formerly, the National Bureau of Standards; maintains the uniform standards of all weights and measures that, by law, can be used in the United States; conducts advanced scientific and other experimental research and testing; provides scientific/technological services to government, private industry.

**Patent and Trademark Office.** Issues more than 100,000 patents a year (patents of invention, good for 17 years; patents of design, good for 14 years; and plant patents, good for 17 years); registers more than 80,000 trademarks each year (good for 10 years and renewable).

**National Oceanic and Atmospheric Administration.** Operates the National Weather Service, which forecasts and reports weather conditions; makes satellite observations of weather and other features of the earth's environment; conducts oceanic, atmospheric, seismological and other environmental research; publishes nautical and aeronautical maps, charts, and other reports; administers the Sea Grant program (grants for marine research, education).

**United States Travel and Tourism Administration.** Works with the travel industry, here and abroad, to attract tourists and other foreign visitors to this country.

**National Telecommunications and Information Service.** Central federal service for machine processable data files and computer software in engineering, medical, and other scientific and technical fields.

**Minority Business Development Agency.** Promotes and coordinates federal and other public and private efforts to help organize and strengthen businesses owned and operated by members of minority groups; furnishes management and technical assistance to minority firms.

**Bureau of Economic Analysis.** Collects and analyzes data to provide a detailed picture of the structure, condition, and prospects of the nation's economy; reports on the gross national product (the GDP, the total annual national output of goods and services, measured in dollar terms).

**International Trade Administration.** Promotes American interests in foreign trade, enforces federal laws to protect American industry against unfair foreign competition, maintains a network of Foreign Commercial Service offices to report on business conditions and investment opportunities abroad, and conducts trade fairs and operates trade centers in other countries.

**Bureau of Export Administration.** Enforces laws that control the export of products, materials, and technology for reasons of national security.

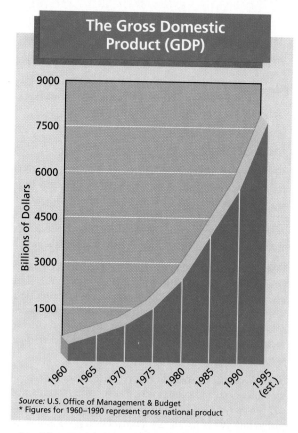

**The Gross Domestic Product (GDP)**

Billions of Dollars

9000
7500
6000
4500
3000
1500

1960  1965  1970  1975  1980  1985  1990  1995 (est.)

Source: U.S. Office of Management & Budget
* Figures for 1960–1990 represent gross national product

The GDP, the total annual national output of goods and services, has been the primary measure of United States production since December 1960.

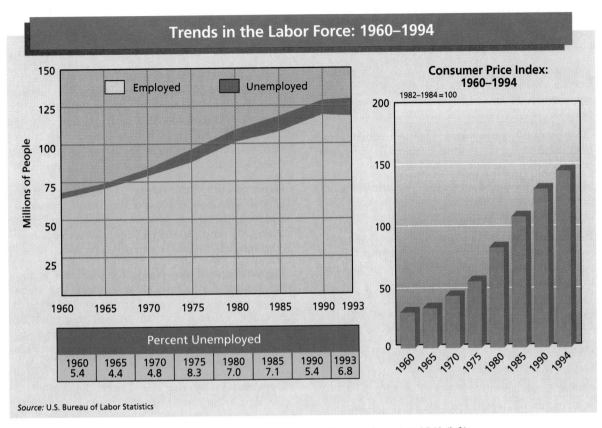

## Trends in the Labor Force: 1960–1994

Millions of People — Employed / Unemployed

### Percent Unemployed

| | 1960 | 1965 | 1970 | 1975 | 1980 | 1985 | 1990 | 1993 |
|---|---|---|---|---|---|---|---|---|
| | 5.4 | 4.4 | 4.8 | 8.3 | 7.0 | 7.1 | 5.4 | 6.8 |

### Consumer Price Index: 1960–1994
1982–1984 = 100

*Source:* U.S. Bureau of Labor Statistics

These graphs show the number of employed and unemployed in the labor force since 1960 (left) as well as the consumer price index, which is based on average prices paid for day-to-day items such as food, clothing, shelter, transportation, fuels, drugs, and other goods and services.

## Department of Labor

Established: 1913

Head: Secretary of Labor

Employees, 1993: 17,604

For more than 75 years now, the Labor Department's job has been the one Congress first assigned to it in 1913: "to foster, promote, and develop the welfare of the wage earners of the United States, to improve their working conditions, and to advance their opportunities for profitable employment."

**Employment and Training Administration.** An umbrella agency: through the United States Employment Service, aids the States to operate a system of local employment offices; through the Federal Unemployment Insurance Service, supervises the States' administration of their unemployment compensation programs (largely financed by a federal tax on employers); through the Office of Job Training Programs, makes grants for and administers job training, work experience, and public ser-

vice employment programs; through the Bureau of Apprenticeship and Training, works to improve the standards of apprenticeship and training for skilled jobs.

**Employment Standards Administration.** An umbrella agency: through the Wage and Hour Division, enforces federal minimum wage and maximum hours laws; through the Office of Federal Contract Compliance Programs, enforces laws prohibiting discrimination in employment on all federally supported construction projects; through the Office of Workers' Compensation Programs, administers laws providing injury and accident benefits for federal employees.

**Office of the American Workplace.** An umbrella agency: through the Office of Labor-Management Programs, offers technical and information assistance to employers, unions, and other groups involved in the collective bargaining arena; through the Office of Labor-Management Standards, administers various federal laws intended to safeguard the interests of union members by regulating the internal procedures and finances of labor unions.

**Pension and Welfare Benefits Administration.** Enforces federal laws regulating conduct of private pension, welfare plans.

**Veterans' Employment and Training Service.** Works with the VA and other public and private agencies to ensure the reemployment and other work benefit rights of veterans.

**Occupational Safety and Health Administration.** Enforces federal laws that set minimum safety and health standards in most work situations.

**Mine Safety and Health Administration.** Enforces federal laws setting minimum safety and health standards for mining operations.

**Bureau of Labor Statistics.** Collects, analyzes, and publishes data on employment, unemployment, hours of work, wages, prices, productivity, and several other topics in the field of labor economics.

## Department of Defense

Established: 1949

Head: Secretary of Defense

Civilian Employees, 1993: 933,289

The Department of Defense is responsible for providing the military forces needed to prevent war and protect the security of our country. The major elements of these forces are the army, navy, Marine Corps, and air force, consisting of about 1.6 million men and women

on active duty. DOD's huge civilian workforce provides various support services for the armed forces, at the Pentagon and at military installations in this country and abroad.

**Joint Chiefs of Staff.** The principal military advisers to the President, the National Security Council, and the secretary of defense. Headed by the Chairman of the Joint Chiefs; other members are the Army's Chief of Staff, the Air Force Chief of Staff, the Chief of Naval Operations, and the Commandant of the Marine Corps.

**Department of the Army.** The army is essentially a ground-based force, responsible for military operations on land; organizes, trains, and equips active duty and reserve forces to defend the United States and accomplish any other missions that may be assigned to the army.

**Department of the Navy.** The primary mission of the Department of the Navy, including its Marine Corps component, is to protect the United States by effectively carrying out war at sea. Responsibilities include seizing or defending advanced naval bases; supporting, as required, all other military forces; and maintaining freedom of the seas.

**Department of the Air Force.** Responsible for providing an air force that is capable of preserving the peace and security of the United States internationally and in space.

**Service Academies.** The United States Military Academy (West Point, New York), the United States Air

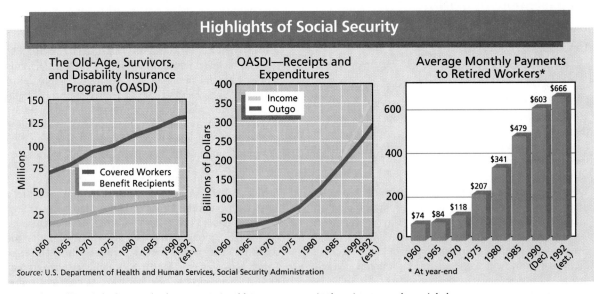

## Highlights of Social Security

**The Old-Age, Survivors, and Disability Insurance Program (OASDI)**

— Covered Workers
— Benefit Recipients

**OASDI—Receipts and Expenditures**

— Income
— Outgo

**Average Monthly Payments to Retired Workers***

$74, $84, $118, $207, $341, $479, $603, $666

*Source:* U.S. Department of Health and Human Services, Social Security Administration

* At year-end

According to the bar graph, the average monthly payment to a single retiree more than tripled from 1975 to 1992.

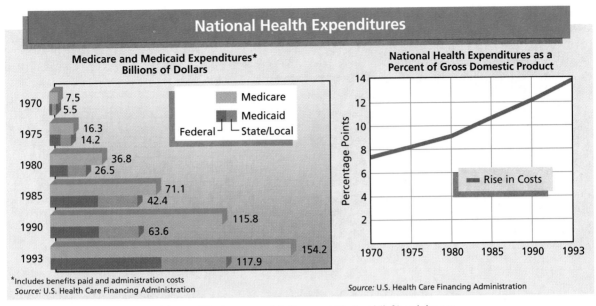

## National Health Expenditures

### Medicare and Medicaid Expenditures*
### Billions of Dollars

- Medicare
- Medicaid
- Federal — State/Local

| Year | Medicare | Medicaid |
|------|----------|----------|
| 1970 | 7.5 | 5.5 |
| 1975 | 16.3 | 14.2 |
| 1980 | 36.8 | 26.5 |
| 1985 | 71.1 | 42.4 |
| 1990 | 115.8 | 63.6 |
| 1993 | 154.2 | 117.9 |

*Includes benefits paid and administration costs
*Source:* U.S. Health Care Financing Administration

### National Health Expenditures as a Percent of Gross Domestic Product

— Rise in Costs

*Source:* U.S. Health Care Financing Administration

These graphs show the breakdown of funds spent on Medicare and Medicaid (left) and the percentage of the GDP taken by health expenditures. According to the line graph, national health expenditures as a percent of GDP nearly doubled between 1970 and 1993.

Force Academy (Colorado Springs, Colorado), and the United States Naval Academy (Annapolis, Maryland) all offer theoretical and practical officer training as well as a four-year comprehensive college education.

**Department of Defense Agencies.** Various defense agencies established for specific purposes include:

- National Security Agency
- Defense Information Systems Agency
- Defense Investigative Service
- Defense Mapping Agency

# Department of Health and Human Services

Established: 1953

Head: Secretary of Health and Human Services

Employees, 1993: 132,875

The Department of Health and Human Services administers several welfare, public assistance, and public health programs and also has a number of research, educational, and regulatory functions in those areas. HHS has described itself as "a department of people serving people, from newborn infants to our most elderly citizens."

**Administration on Aging.** Advises the secretary and all federal agencies on the characteristics and needs of older Americans; makes grants, gives other support to State and local government programs that provide social services for older Americans.

**Substance Abuse and Mental Health Services Administration.** Makes grants to State and local governments for the prevention and treatment of (1) alcohol and other drug abuses and (2) mental illnesses.

**Public Health Service.** An umbrella agency: through the Centers for Disease Control, conducts research and treatment programs for the prevention and control of communicable and other diseases; through the Food and Drug Administration, conducts research and administers federal laws that prohibit the manufacture, shipment, or sale of impure and unsafe foods, drugs, cosmetics, medical devices, and other items; through the Bureau of Health Resources Development, makes grants to strengthen State, local, and private nonprofit hospital and other health care facilities and programs; funds centers to train health professionals serving AIDS patients; provides medical and other health care services to certain groups (e.g., Coast Guard personnel and their dependents, federal prisoners, Native Americans); through the National Institutes of Health, makes grants to support medical research and operates several research institutes (e.g., the National Cancer Institute, the National Institute of Allergy and Infectious Diseases, and the National Institute of Environmental Health Sciences).

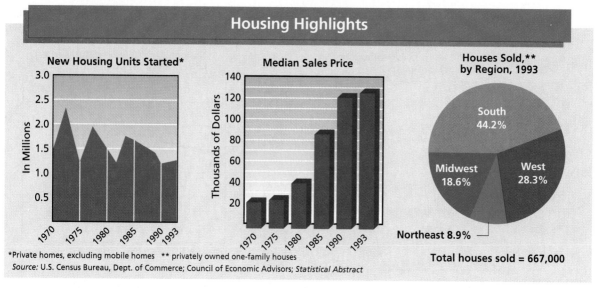

## Housing Highlights

**New Housing Units Started***

*In Millions*

3.0
2.5
2.0
1.5
1.0
0.5

1970 1975 1980 1985 1990 1993

**Median Sales Price**

*Thousands of Dollars*

140
120
100
80
60
40
20

1970 1975 1980 1985 1990 1993

**Houses Sold,** **
**by Region, 1993**

South 44.2%
West 28.3%
Midwest 18.6%
Northeast 8.9%

*Private homes, excluding mobile homes   ** privately owned one-family houses

*Source:* U.S. Census Bureau, Dept. of Commerce; Council of Economic Advisors; *Statistical Abstract*

Total houses sold = 667,000

Housing statistics such as those above often are used as indicators of an economy's overall health. The major portion of most families' incomes goes to housing, which now costs more than six times what it did in 1970.

**Social Security Administration.** Administers several major elements of the social security program, especially: (1) the Old-Age, Survivors, and Disability Insurance (OASDI) program—under which compulsory payroll taxes paid by employers, employees, and the self-employed finance payments (pensions and other benefits) to persons covered under the program when they retire or become permanently disabled and to their dependents or survivors; (2) the Supplemental Security Income (SSI) program—which gives direct federal assistance (payments) to needy aged, blind, and disabled persons. *Note:* The SSA became an independent agency in 1994.

**Health Care Financing Administration.** Administers two other major elements of the social security program: (1) Medicare—a health insurance program for most elderly persons (those over 65 who receive OASDI benefits), to help pay at least most of their hospital, medical, and other health care bills (financed by a combination of compulsory payroll taxes and optional monthly fees); and (2) Medicaid—a federal grant program, to help the States pay the health care bills of more than 30 million Americans—mostly needy children and the needy blind, elderly, and disabled.

**Administration for Children and Families.** Manages the other major element of the social security program: Aid to Families with Dependent Children (AFDC)—under which federal grants help the States give financial assistance to children who lack adequate parental support; administers federal laws that require States to enforce child support obligations of absent parents.

## Department of Housing and Urban Development**

Established: 1965

Head: Secretary of Housing and Urban Development

Employees, 1993: 13,426

The Department of Housing and Urban Development is the principal federal agency concerned with the nation's housing needs and with the development and rehabilitation of its urban communities. HUD conducts a number of insurance, rent subsidy, and grant programs.

**Assistant Secretary for Community Planning and Development.** Administers several grant programs to aid State and local government efforts to improve housing conditions in urban areas (e.g., water, sewer, and slum clearance projects; rehabilitation of residential housing units; rental assistance for low-income families).

**Assistant Secretary for Housing (Federal Housing Commissioner).** Administers several programs, including: (1) mortgage insurance programs—the Federal Government guarantees loans made by private lenders (mortgages) for the purchase of private housing (mostly

---

**HUD and two other departments (Energy and Education) are not organized in quite the same way as the other Cabinet departments. Most of their functions and programs are administered directly by a number of assistant secretaries (rather than by several bureaus, services, or similar line agencies).

single-family residences and such multifamily units as apartment houses and condominiums); (2) loan programs—to help public and private borrowers finance housing projects for the elderly (e.g., nursing homes) and people with disabilities; (3) the Rent Supplement Program—in which HUD pays a portion of the rents of low-income families.

**Assistant Secretary for Public and Indian Housing.** Administers several programs, including: (1) public housing programs in which loans, subsidies, and other aid are given to local agencies to build and operate public housing projects (mostly for low-income families); and (2) housing programs for Native Americans—to provide low-income public housing, and promote private home ownership on and near reservations.

# Department of Transportation

Established: 1966

Head: Secretary of Transportation

Employees, 1993: 69,862

Most of the Federal Government's activities relating to the movement of persons and goods by ground, water, or air are located in the Department of Transportation. DOT's several agencies conduct a number of promotional and regulatory programs covering matters ranging from highway construction to offshore maritime safety to commercial air traffic.

**United States Coast Guard.** Enforces federal maritime laws (laws relating to the high seas and the navigable waters of the United States—e.g., smuggling, ship safety, port security, and spillage, pollution, and other marine environmental protection statutes); maintains ships and other vessels, aircraft, and communications facilities, especially for search and rescue operations; operates an extensive network of aids to navigation (e.g., lighthouses, buoys, icebreakers, radio and other electronic devices); operates the U.S. Coast Guard Academy (at New London, Connecticut).

**Federal Aviation Administration.** Enforces federal laws regulating air commerce (including, for example, aircraft safety, pilot licensing, and air traffic), operates an extensive network of aids to air navigation (e.g., air traffic control towers and centers, radio and other electronic communications facilities), makes grants for the construction and improvement of public airports, and conducts a wide range of aviation-related research projects.

**Federal Highway Administration.** Administers several grant programs to aid State and local construction and maintenance of highways and other roads (including the 42,500-mile interstate highway system); makes grants for such other purposes as highway safety (e.g., traffic signs and signals, projects to eliminate traffic hazards) and beautification; enforces federal highway safety laws (e.g., laws regulating the movement of such dangerous cargoes as

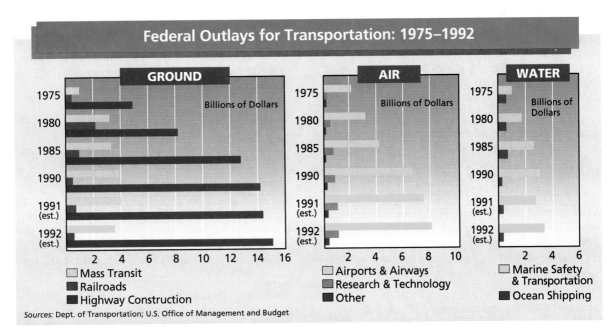

**Federal Outlays for Transportation: 1975–1992**

**GROUND**

Billions of Dollars

1975, 1980, 1985, 1990, 1991 (est.), 1992 (est.)

2  4  6  8  10  12  14  16

□ Mass Transit
■ Railroads
■ Highway Construction

**AIR**

Billions of Dollars

1975, 1980, 1985, 1990, 1991 (est.), 1992 (est.)

2  4  6  8  10

□ Airports & Airways
■ Research & Technology
■ Other

**WATER**

Billions of Dollars

1975, 1980, 1985, 1990, 1991 (est.), 1992 (est.)

2  4  6

□ Marine Safety & Transportation
■ Ocean Shipping

*Sources:* Dept. of Transportation; U.S. Office of Management and Budget

As the first graph shows, federal outlays for railroads peaked in the early 1980s and have decreased since that time. The graphs also show outlays for air and water transportation.

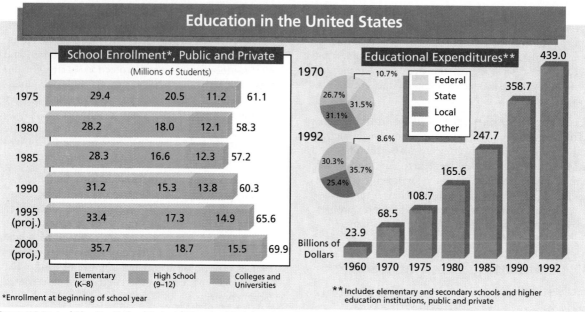

**Education in the United States**

**School Enrollment*, Public and Private**
(Millions of Students)

| Year | Elementary (K–8) | High School (9–12) | Colleges and Universities | Total |
|------|------|------|------|------|
| 1975 | 29.4 | 20.5 | 11.2 | 61.1 |
| 1980 | 28.2 | 18.0 | 12.1 | 58.3 |
| 1985 | 28.3 | 16.6 | 12.3 | 57.2 |
| 1990 | 31.2 | 15.3 | 13.8 | 60.3 |
| 1995 (proj.) | 33.4 | 17.3 | 14.9 | 65.6 |
| 2000 (proj.) | 35.7 | 18.7 | 15.5 | 69.9 |

*Enrollment at beginning of school year

**Educational Expenditures****

1970: Federal 10.7%, State 31.5%, Local 31.1%, Other 26.7%

1992: Federal 8.6%, State 35.7%, Local 25.4%, Other 30.3%

Billions of Dollars:
- 1960: 23.9
- 1970: 68.5
- 1975: 108.7
- 1980: 165.6
- 1985: 247.7
- 1990: 358.7
- 1992: 439.0

** Includes elementary and secondary schools and higher education institutions, public and private

*Source:* U.S. Dept. of Education, National Center for Educational Statistics; *Digest of Education Statistics*

As shown on the graph at left, enrollment in colleges and universities has increased steadily since 1975. In 1992, as the pie graph shows, State governments paid the largest share of the cost of education; the category "Other," which includes such things as donations from private individuals, is surprisingly close behind.

explosives and hazardous wastes); builds and maintains roads in such federal areas as national parks, national forests, and Native American reservations; conducts research on a wide range of highway-related matters.

**National Highway Traffic Safety Administration.** Enforces federal motor vehicle safety laws, makes grants to support State and local motor vehicle safety and accident-prevention programs (including driver training), and conducts research on matters relating to motor vehicle safety.

**Federal Railroad Administration.** Enforces federal rail safety laws, gives financial and other aid to certain railroads (especially those in financial difficulty), and conducts research on most phases of rail transportation.

**Federal Transit Administration.** Administers several grant and loan programs to help State and local governments develop and operate bus, rail, and other mass transit systems in urban areas; conducts research covering most phases of urban mass transportation and its operational efficiency.

**Maritime Administration.** Promotes development and operations of the nation's merchant marine, subsidizes shipbuilding and certain ship operating costs (to counter foreign competition), conducts research

programs to improve the merchant marine, and trains officers for the merchant marine (at the U.S. Merchant Marine Academy, at Kings Point, New York).

**Saint Lawrence Seaway Development Corporation.** Operates that part of the Seaway within the United States (the American side of the stretch between Montreal and Lake Erie), sets and collects tolls and otherwise works in close cooperation with the St. Lawrence Seaway Authority of Canada.

## Department of Energy

Established: 1977

Head: Secretary of Energy

Employees, 1993: 20,804

The functions of the Department of Energy reflect the critical importance of the development, use, and conservation of the nation's energy resources. DOE's several agencies focus on such matters as high-technology research, nuclear weapons programs, the marketing of federal power, energy conservation, and much more.

**Assistant Secretary, Fossil Energy.** Directs research and development programs involving fossil fuels—coal, petroleum, and gas (e.g., study and demonstration projects relating to mining, drilling, and other methods of fuel extraction); manages the

Strategic Petroleum Reserve and other petroleum storage projects.

**Office of Nuclear Energy.** Directs research and development programs involving fission energy (e.g., projects relating to nuclear reactor development and the disposal of reactor wastes).

**Assistant Secretary, Defense Programs.** Directs nuclear weapons research, development, testing, and production programs.

**Assistant Secretary, Energy Efficiency and Renewable Energy.** Directs research and development programs designed to promote more efficient uses (conservation) of energy and to increase the production and use of solar, wind, tidal, and other energy from renewable sources; makes grants to support State and local efforts in those areas (e.g., local projects to weatherize housing).

**Energy Information Administration.** Collects, analyzes, and publishes a broad range of data relating to energy (e.g., information on energy resources, production, and consumption).

**Economic Regulatory Administration.** Enforces laws regulating aspects of energy production, sale, and use (e.g., laws regulating drilling on leased federal lands, placing controls on fossil fuel exports, requiring increased industrial use of coal in place of oil and natural gas).

**Bonneville Power Administration.** Markets electric power generated by the vast network of federal multipurpose dams (constructed and operated by the Army Corps of Engineers and Interior's Bureau of Reclamation) in the Pacific Northwest. (Smaller-scale operations are conducted in four other regions.)

## Department of Education

Established: 1979

Head: Secretary of Education

Employees, 1993: 5,064

Nearly 60 million Americans attend school. The Department of Education administers a number of programs designed to aid the States and their local units in the field of public education.

**Office of Special Education and Rehabilitative Services.** Makes grants for research and to support teacher training and other State and local programs for the education of children with disabilities and for rehabilitation programs for those children.

**Office of Postsecondary Education.** Administers several grant programs to support and expand instructional and other educational services and facilities in colleges, universities, and similar institutions; administers several different types of student grant and loan programs.

**Office of Vocational and Adult Education.** Administers grants and other programs to support and expand State and local efforts in vocational training and adult education.

**Office of Elementary and Secondary Education.** Administers grant programs to support a variety of State and local efforts in preschool, elementary, and secondary education, including grants to local school districts for Native American and migrant education and for drug-free schools.

**Office of Educational Research and Improvement.** Directs research and administers grant programs to support State and local school efforts in a wide range of instructional service and resource areas (e.g., basic skills, library and laboratory resources, and education on health, abuse of alcohol and other drugs).

## Department of Veterans Affairs

Established: 1989

Head: Secretary of Veterans Affairs

Employees, 1993: 266,166

The Department of Veterans Affairs reflects a historic concern for the welfare of those men and women who have served in the nation's armed forces. Today, the Department operates a number of programs that make a broad range of benefits available to more than 27 million veterans and their dependents.

**Veterans Health Administration.** Provides hospital, nursing home, domiciliary care, outpatient medical and dental care to eligible veterans; operates 171 hospitals, more than 300 clinics and other facilities in this country and in the Philippines.

**Veterans Benefits Administration.** Provides pensions and other compensations for service-connected (and many nonservice-connected) disabilities; administers vocational rehabilitation, job training, and other educational assistance programs; administers veterans' home-loan guarantee and life insurance programs.

**National Cemetery System.** Maintains more than 100 cemeteries for veterans around the country; provides headstones and markers for graves of veterans.

| State | Capital | Population (in thousands) | | | Area in Square Miles | % Land Federally Owned | Population per sq. mi. |
|---|---|---|---|---|---|---|---|
| | | 1990 | 1980 | % Change | | | |
| **United States** | **Washington, D.C.** | **248,710** | **226,546** | **+9.8** | **3,787,425** | **29.2** | **70.3** |
| Alabama | Montgomery | 4,041 | 3,894 | +3.8 | 52,423 | 1.7 | 79.6 |
| Alaska | Juneau | 550 | 402 | +36.9 | 656,424 | 81.1 | 1.0 |
| Arizona | Phoenix | 3,665 | 2,718 | +34.8 | 114,006 | 43.3 | 32.3 |
| Arkansas | Little Rock | 2,351 | 2,286 | +2.8 | 53,182 | 10.2 | 45.1 |
| California | Sacramento | 29,760 | 23,668 | +25.7 | 163,707 | 60.9 | 190.8 |
| Colorado | Denver | 3,294 | 2,890 | +14.0 | 104,100 | 34.1 | 31.8 |
| Connecticut | Hartford | 3,287 | 3,108 | +5.8 | 5,544 | 0.4 | 678.4 |
| Delaware | Dover | 666 | 594 | +12.1 | 2,489 | 2.4 | 340.8 |
| Florida | Tallahassee | 12,938 | 9,746 | +32.7 | 65,758 | 9.7 | 239.6 |
| Georgia | Atlanta | 6,478 | 5,463 | +18.6 | 59,441 | 6.1 | 111.9 |
| Hawaii | Honolulu | 1,108 | 965 | +14.9 | 10,392 | 16.5 | 172.9 |
| Idaho | Boise | 1,007 | 944 | +6.7 | 83,574 | 62.6 | 12.2 |
| Illinois | Springfield | 11,431 | 11,427 | 0.0 | 57,918 | 1.4 | 205.6 |
| Indiana | Indianapolis | 5,544 | 5,490 | +1.0 | 36,420 | 2.0 | 154.6 |
| Iowa | Des Moines | 2,777 | 2,914 | -4.7 | 56,276 | 0.4 | 49.7 |
| Kansas | Topeka | 2,478 | 2,364 | +4.8 | 82,282 | 1.3 | 30.3 |
| Kentucky | Frankfort | 3,685 | 3,661 | +0.7 | 40,411 | 5.5 | 92.8 |
| Louisiana | Baton Rouge | 4,220 | 4,206 | +0.3 | 51,843 | 22.6 | 96.9 |
| Maine | Augusta | 1,228 | 1,125 | +9.2 | 35,387 | 0.8 | 39.8 |
| Maryland | Annapolis | 4,781 | 4,217 | +13.4 | 12,407 | 3.1 | 489.2 |
| Massachusetts | Boston | 6,016 | 5,737 | +4.9 | 10,555 | 1.6 | 767.6 |
| Michigan | Lansing | 9,295 | 9,262 | +0.4 | 96,810 | 9.8 | 163.6 |
| Minnesota | St. Paul | 4,375 | 4,076 | +7.3 | 86,943 | 4.7 | 55.0 |
| Mississippi | Jackson | 2,573 | 2,521 | +2.1 | 48,434 | 5.5 | 54.9 |
| Missouri | Jefferson City | 5,117 | 4,917 | +4.1 | 69,709 | 4.6 | 74.3 |
| Montana | Helena | 799 | 787 | +1.6 | 147,046 | 27.7 | 5.5 |
| Nebraska | Lincoln | 1,578 | 1,570 | +0.5 | 77,358 | 1.5 | 20.5 |
| Nevada | Carson City | 1,202 | 800 | +50.1 | 110,567 | 82.3 | 10.9 |
| New Hampshire | Concord | 1,109 | 921 | +20.5 | 9,351 | 13.1 | 123.7 |
| New Jersey | Trenton | 7,730 | 7,365 | +5.0 | 8,722 | 2.8 | 1,042.9 |
| New Mexico | Santa Fe | 1,515 | 1,303 | +16.3 | 121,598 | 33.1 | 12.5 |
| New York | Albany | 17,990 | 17,558 | +2.5 | 54,475 | 0.7 | 381.0 |
| North Carolina | Raleigh | 6,629 | 5,882 | +12.7 | 53,821 | 7.1 | 136.1 |
| North Dakota | Bismarck | 639 | 653 | -2.1 | 70,704 | 4.4 | 9.3 |
| Ohio | Columbus | 10,847 | 10,798 | +0.5 | 44,828 | 1.2 | 264.9 |
| Oklahoma | Oklahoma City | 3,146 | 3,025 | +4.0 | 69,903 | 2.0 | 45.8 |
| Oregon | Salem | 2,842 | 2,633 | +7.9 | 98,386 | 48.2 | 29.6 |
| Pennsylvania | Harrisburg | 11,882 | 11,864 | +0.1 | 46,058 | 2.2 | 265.1 |
| Rhode Island | Providence | 1,003 | 947 | +5.9 | 1,545 | 0.7 | 960.3 |
| South Carolina | Columbia | 3,487 | 3,122 | +11.7 | 32,007 | 2.2 | 115.8 |
| South Dakota | Pierre | 696 | 691 | +.8 | 77,121 | 5.6 | 9.2 |
| Tennessee | Nashville | 4,877 | 4,591 | +6.2 | 42,146 | 4.9 | 118.3 |
| Texas | Austin | 16,987 | 14,229 | +19.4 | 268,601 | 1.7 | 64.9 |
| Utah | Salt Lake City | 1,723 | 1,461 | +17.9 | 84,904 | 63.8 | 21.0 |
| Vermont | Montpelier | 563 | 511 | +10.0 | 9,615 | 6.0 | 60.8 |
| Virginia | Richmond | 6,187 | 5,347 | +15.7 | 42,769 | 7.5 | 156.3 |
| Washington | Olympia | 4,867 | 4,132 | +17.8 | 71,303 | 29.0 | 73.1 |
| West Virginia | Charleston | 1,793 | 1,950 | -8.0 | 24,231 | 13.6 | 74.5 |
| Wisconsin | Madison | 4,892 | 4,706 | +4.0 | 65,503 | 5.4 | 90.1 |
| Wyoming | Cheyenne | 454 | 470 | -3.4 | 97,818 | 48.8 | 4.7 |
| Washington, D.C | | 607 | 638 | -4.9 | 68 | 27.8 | 9,882.8 |

*All data for 1990, except 1980 population figures and 1992 election figures.
Sources: Bureau of the Census; Congressional Quarterly

## The United States: A Statistical Profile

| State | % Urban | African American (in thousands) | Hispanic Origin† (in thousands) | % Foreign Born | Bill Clinton (Democrat) | % | George Bush (Republican) | % | Ross Perot (Independent) | % |
|---|---|---|---|---|---|---|---|---|---|---|
| **United States** | **75.2** | **29,986** | **22,354** | **7.9** | **44,908,233** | **43** | **39,102,282** | **38** | **19,741,048** | **19** |
| Alabama | 60.4 | 1,021 | 25 | 1.1 | 690,080 | 41 | 804,283 | 48 | 183,109 | 11 |
| Alaska | 67.5 | 22 | 18 | 4.5 | 78,294 | 32 | 102,000 | 41 | 73,481 | 27 |
| Arizona | 87.5 | 111 | 688 | 7.6 | 543,050 | 37 | 572,086 | 39 | 353,741 | 24 |
| Arkansas | 53.5 | 374 | 20 | 1.1 | 505,823 | 54 | 337,324 | 36 | 99,132 | 11 |
| California | 92.6 | 2,209 | 7,688 | 21.7 | 5,121,325 | 47 | 3,630,575 | 32 | 2,296,006 | 21 |
| Colorado | 82.4 | 133 | 424 | 4.3 | 629,681 | 40 | 562,850 | 36 | 366,010 | 23 |
| Connecticut | 79.1 | 274 | 213 | 8.5 | 682,318 | 42 | 578,313 | 36 | 348,771 | 22 |
| Delaware | 73.0 | 112 | 16 | 3.3 | 126,054 | 44 | 102,313 | 36 | 59,213 | 21 |
| Florida | 84.8 | 1,760 | 1,574 | 2.7 | 2,071,651 | 39 | 2,171,781 | 41 | 1,052,481 | 20 |
| Georgia | 63.2 | 1,747 | 109 | 12.9 | 1,008,966 | 44 | 995,252 | 43 | 309,657 | 13 |
| Hawaii | 89.0 | 27 | 81 | 14.7 | 179,310 | 49 | 136,822 | 37 | 53,003 | 14 |
| Idaho | 57.4 | 3 | 53 | 2.9 | 137,013 | 29 | 202,645 | 43 | 130,395 | 28 |
| Illinois | 84.6 | 1,694 | 904 | 8.3 | 2,453,350 | 48 | 1,734,096 | 35 | 840,515 | 17 |
| Indiana | 64.9 | 432 | 99 | 1.7 | 848,420 | 37 | 989,375 | 43 | 455,934 | 20 |
| Iowa | 60.6 | 48 | 33 | 1.6 | 586,353 | 44 | 504,891 | 38 | 253,468 | 19 |
| Kansas | 69.1 | 143 | 94 | 2.5 | 390,434 | 34 | 449,951 | 39 | 312,358 | 27 |
| Kentucky | 51.8 | 263 | 22 | 0.9 | 655,104 | 45 | 617,178 | 42 | 203,944 | 14 |
| Louisiana | 68.1 | 1,299 | 93 | 2.1 | 815,971 | 46 | 733,386 | 42 | 211,478 | 12 |
| Maine | 44.6 | 5 | 7 | 3.0 | 263,420 | 39 | 206,504 | 30 | 206,820 | 30 |
| Maryland | 81.3 | 1,190 | 125 | 6.6 | 988,571 | 50 | 707,094 | 36 | 281,414 | 14 |
| Massachusetts | 84.3 | 300 | 288 | 9.5 | 1,318,639 | 48 | 805,039 | 29 | 630,731 | 23 |
| Michigan | 70.5 | 1,292 | 202 | 3.8 | 1,871,182 | 44 | 1,554,940 | 37 | 824,813 | 19 |
| Minnesota | 69.9 | 95 | 54 | 2.6 | 1,020,997 | 44 | 747,841 | 32 | 562,508 | 24 |
| Mississippi | 47.1 | 915 | 16 | 0.8 | 400,258 | 41 | 487,793 | 50 | 85,626 | 9 |
| Missouri | 68.7 | 548 | 62 | 1.6 | 1,053,873 | 44 | 811,159 | 34 | 518,741 | 22 |
| Montana | 52.5 | 2 | 12 | 1.7 | 154,507 | 38 | 144,207 | 36 | 107,225 | 26 |
| Nebraska | 66.1 | 57 | 37 | 1.8 | 216,864 | 30 | 343,678 | 47 | 174,104 | 24 |
| Nevada | 88.3 | 79 | 124 | 8.7 | 189,148 | 38 | 175,828 | 35 | 132,580 | 26 |
| New Hampshire | 51.0 | 7 | 11 | 3.7 | 209,040 | 39 | 202,484 | 38 | 121,337 | 23 |
| New Jersey | 89.4 | 1,037 | 740 | 12.5 | 1,436,206 | 43 | 1,356,865 | 41 | 521,829 | 16 |
| New Mexico | 73.0 | 30 | 579 | 15.9 | 261,617 | 46 | 212,824 | 38 | 91,895 | 16 |
| New York | 84.3 | 2,859 | 2,214 | 5.3 | 3,444,450 | 50 | 2,346,649 | 34 | 1,090,721 | 16 |
| North Carolina | 50.4 | 1,456 | 77 | 1.7 | 1,114,042 | 43 | 1,134,681 | 44 | 357,864 | 14 |
| North Dakota | 53.3 | 4 | 5 | 1.5 | 99,168 | 32 | 138,244 | 44 | 71,084 | 23 |
| Ohio | 74.1 | 1,155 | 140 | 2.4 | 1,984,919 | 40 | 1,894,246 | 39 | 1,036,403 | 21 |
| Oklahoma | 67.7 | 234 | 86 | 2.1 | 473,066 | 34 | 592,929 | 43 | 319,878 | 23 |
| Oregon | 70.5 | 46 | 113 | 4.9 | 621,314 | 43 | 475,757 | 32 | 354,091 | 25 |
| Pennsylvania | 68.9 | 1,090 | 213 | 3.1 | 2,239,164 | 45 | 1,791,841 | 36 | 902,667 | 18 |
| Rhode Island | 86.0 | 39 | 46 | 9.5 | 213,299 | 48 | 131,601 | 29 | 105,045 | 23 |
| South Carolina | 54.6 | 1,040 | 31 | 1.4 | 479,514 | 40 | 577,507 | 48 | 138,872 | 12 |
| South Dakota | 50.0 | 3 | 5 | 1.1 | 124,888 | 37 | 136,718 | 41 | 73,295 | 22 |
| Tennessee | 60.9 | 778 | 33 | 1.2 | 933,521 | 47 | 841,300 | 43 | 199,968 | 10 |
| Texas | 80.3 | 2,022 | 4,340 | 9.0 | 2,281,815 | 37 | 2,496,071 | 40 | 1,354,781 | 22 |
| Utah | 87.0 | 12 | 85 | 3.4 | 183,429 | 26 | 322,632 | 45 | 203,400 | 29 |
| Vermont | 32.2 | 2 | 4 | 3.1 | 133,592 | 46 | 88,122 | 31 | 65,991 | 23 |
| Virginia | 69.4 | 1,163 | 160 | 5.0 | 1,038,650 | 41 | 1,150,517 | 45 | 348,639 | 14 |
| Washington | 76.4 | 150 | 215 | 6.6 | 993,037 | 44 | 731,234 | 32 | 541,780 | 24 |
| West Virginia | 36.1 | 56 | 8 | 0.9 | 331,001 | 49 | 241,974 | 36 | 108,829 | 16 |
| Wisconsin | 65.7 | 39 | 93 | 2.5 | 1,041,066 | 41 | 930,855 | 37 | 544,479 | 22 |
| Wyoming | 65.0 | 4 | 26 | 1.7 | 68,160 | 34 | 79,347 | 40 | 51,263 | 26 |
| Washington, D.C. | 100.0 | 400 | 33 | 9.7 | 192,619 | 86 | 20,698 | 9 | 9,681 | 4 |

† Persons of Hispanic origin may be of any race.

CANADA

Winnipeg

L. Superior

Duluth

MINNESOTA

Minneapolis
St. Paul

WISCONSIN

Green Bay

Madison

Milwaukee

IOWA

Sioux City

Des Moines

Kansas City
Jefferson
City
St. Louis

MISSOURI

Tulsa

OMA

Fort Smith

ARKANSAS

Little Rock

Red R.

Dallas

Shreveport

LOUISIANA

Beaumont

Houston

New Orleans

Baton Rouge

GULF OF MEXICO

Sault Ste. Marie

MICHIGAN

L. Michigan

Grand
Rapids

Flint

Lansing

Detroit

Chicago

Gary
Fort Wayne

Peoria

ILLINOIS

Springfield

Evansville

Louisville

KENTUCKY

Nashville

Memphis

Chattanooga

TENNESSEE

MISSISSIPPI

Meridian

Jackson

Montgomery

ALABAMA

Birmingham

Columbus

Mobile

Tallahassee

L. Huron

Toronto

L. Ontario

Rochester

Hamilton

Buffalo

Syracuse

L. Erie

Erie

Cleveland

Toledo

Akron

OHIO

Columbus

Dayton
Cincinnati

Indianapolis

INDIANA

Ohio R.

Frankfort

WEST
VIRGINIA

Huntington

Charleston

Knoxville

NORTH CAROLINA

Charlotte

SOUTH
CAROLINA

Columbia

Atlanta

Columbus

GEORGIA

Savannah

Charleston

Jacksonville

FLORIDA

Tampa

Miami

Key West

Quebec

St. Lawrence R.

Montreal

Ottawa

MAINE

Augusta

Burlington

Portland

VT. N.H.

Montpelier

Concord

Manchester

Boston

Albany

MASS.

Worcester
Providence

Hartford

CONN. R.I.

New Haven

NEW YORK

Scranton

PENNSYLVANIA

Newark

New York

Harrisburg

Trenton

Pittsburgh

NEW JERSEY

Philadelphia

Baltimore

Wilmington

Dover

Washington,
D.C.

Annapolis

DELAWARE

MARYLAND

Richmond

VIRGINIA

Norfolk

Raleigh

Fredericton

St. John

ATLANTIC OCEAN

40°

30°

BAHAMAS

Straits of Florida

Havana

CUBA

80°

# United States
## Political

0        1000 Miles

0    1000 Kilometers

# World Data Bank

The tables and graphs in this World Data Bank provide you with an opportunity to compare the governments, economies, and certain qualities of life for selected countries. Similar comparisons are found in the Global Awareness charts on the following pages in your textbook:

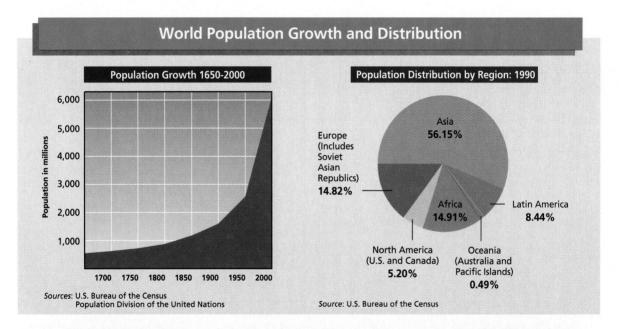

## World Population Growth and Distribution

### Population Growth 1650-2000

Population in millions: 1,000–6,000 (years 1700–2000)

*Sources:* U.S. Bureau of the Census
Population Division of the United Nations

### Population Distribution by Region: 1990

Asia 56.15%
Europe (Includes Soviet Asian Republics) 14.82%
Africa 14.91%
Latin America 8.44%
North America (U.S. and Canada) 5.20%
Oceania (Australia and Pacific Islands) 0.49%

*Source:* U.S. Bureau of the Census

## Education in Selected Countries

| COUNTRY | % of Children in Age Group in Primary Schools | % of Children in Age Group in Secondary Schools | % of Population over Age 25 with Some College | % of Government Budget Spent on Education | % of Population over Age 25 that Is Literate |
|---|---|---|---|---|---|
| United States | 97 | 90 | 32.2 | 7.5 | 95.5 |
| Algeria | 88 | 45 | 0.3 | 6.1 | 44.7 |
| Brazil | 82 | 15 | 5.0 | 3.3 | 79.3 |
| Cameroon | 75 | 15 | 0.3 | 2.6 | 55.2 |
| Cuba | 95 | 69 | 5.9 | 6.3 | 96.0 |
| Japan | 100 | 96 | 14.3 | 5.1 | 100.0 |
| Nepal | 56 | 18 | 6.8 | 3.0 | 20.7 |
| Poland | 99 | 73 | 5.7 | 3.8 | 99.2 |
| Sweden | 96 | 81 | 15.4 | 7.6 | 100.0 |

## World Population Density

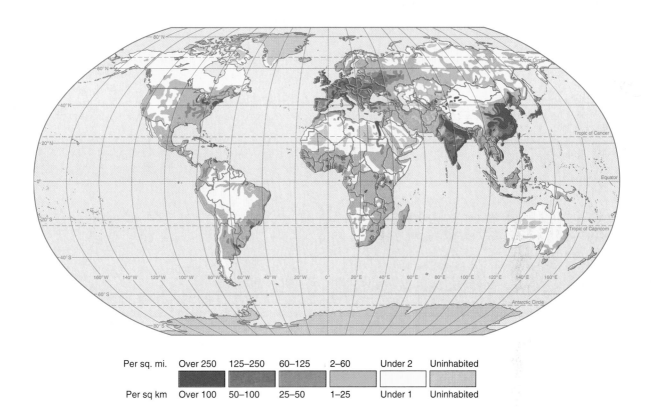

| Per sq. mi. | Over 250 | 125–250 | 60–125 | 2–60 | Under 2 | Uninhabited |
|---|---|---|---|---|---|---|
| Per sq km | Over 100 | 50–100 | 25–50 | 1–25 | Under 1 | Uninhabited |

## Economic and Health Statistics for Selected Countries: 1989[1]

| COUNTRY | Per Capita GNP | Life Expectancy at Birth (Female) | Infant Mortality Rate[2] | Average Daily Calorie Consumption |
|---|---|---|---|---|
| United States | $ 17,592 | 79 | 9.1 | 3,642 |
| Argentina | $ 2,134 | 74 | 32.0 | 3,191 |
| Canada | $ 19,020 | 80 | 7.3 | 3,425 |
| China | $ 360 | 70 | 33.0 | 2,628 |
| India | $ 350 | 58 | 91.0 | 2,204 |
| Japan | $ 15,030 | 82 | 5.0 | 2,858 |
| Mexico | $ 2,373 | 73 | 42.0 | 3,148 |
| United Kingdom | $ 14,535 | 78 | 13.3 | 3,218 |
| Zaire | $ 260 | 54 | 107.0 | 2,160 |

[1] The year 1989 is used because this is the most recent year for which data is available for all countries.
[2] Number of deaths before age one per 1,000 live births.

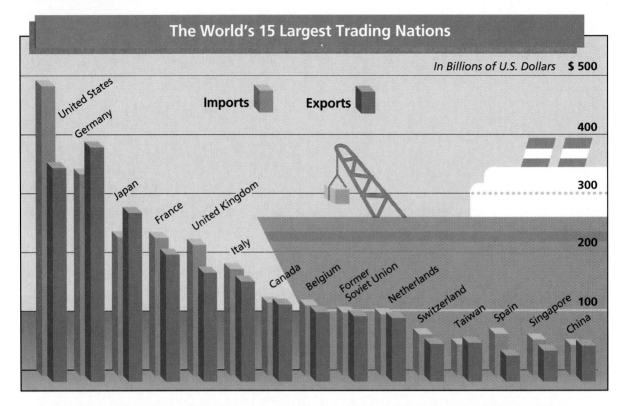

## The World's 15 Largest Trading Nations

*In Billions of U.S. Dollars*    $ 500

Imports    Exports

400

300

200

100

United States
Germany
Japan
France
United Kingdom
Italy
Canada
Belgium
Former Soviet Union
Netherlands
Switzerland
Taiwan
Spain
Singapore
China

## Major United States Trading Partners: 1990

*In Millions of U.S. Dollars*    $ 100,000

Exports to U.S.    Imports from U.S.

$ 80,000

$ 60,000

$ 40,000

$ 20,000

Canada
Japan
Mexico
United Kingdom
Germany
South Korea
France
Netherlands
Taiwan

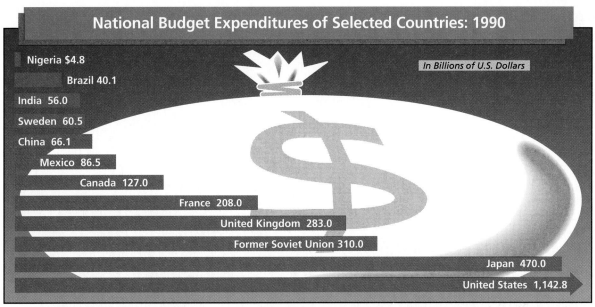

## National Budget Expenditures of Selected Countries: 1990

*In Billions of U.S. Dollars*

- Nigeria $4.8
- Brazil 40.1
- India 56.0
- Sweden 60.5
- China 66.1
- Mexico 86.5
- Canada 127.0
- France 208.0
- United Kingdom 283.0
- Former Soviet Union 310.0
- Japan 470.0
- United States 1,142.8

*Source:* The World Almanac and Book of Facts, 1992

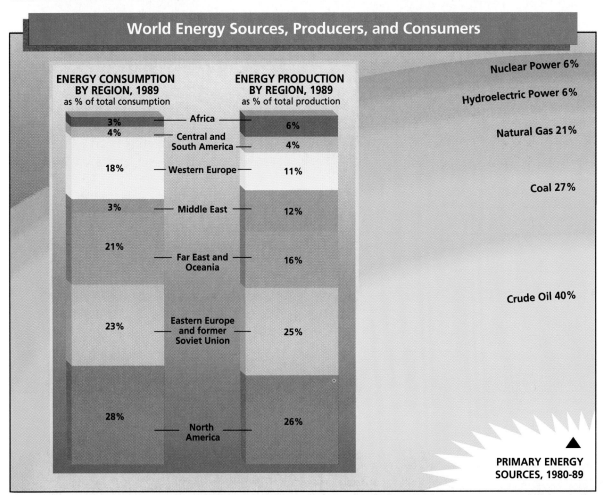

## World Energy Sources, Producers, and Consumers

**ENERGY CONSUMPTION BY REGION, 1989**
as % of total consumption

**ENERGY PRODUCTION BY REGION, 1989**
as % of total production

| Region | Consumption | Production |
|---|---|---|
| Africa | 3% | 6% |
| Central and South America | 4% | 4% |
| Western Europe | 18% | 11% |
| Middle East | 3% | 12% |
| Far East and Oceania | 21% | 16% |
| Eastern Europe and former Soviet Union | 23% | 25% |
| North America | 28% | 26% |

Nuclear Power 6%

Hydroelectric Power 6%

Natural Gas 21%

Coal 27%

Crude Oil 40%

**PRIMARY ENERGY SOURCES, 1980-89**

718

# World Political

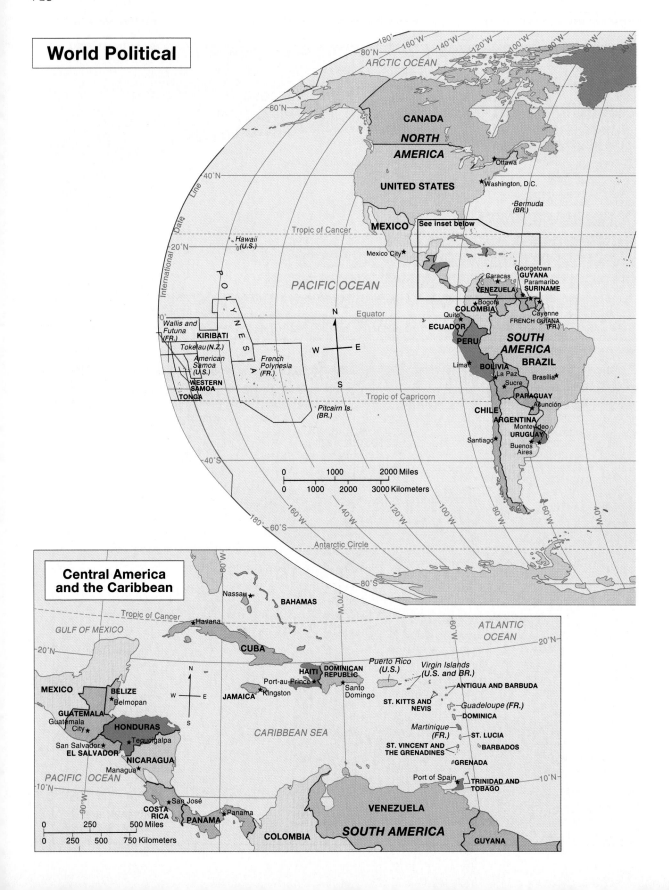

ARCTIC OCEAN

**CANADA**

*NORTH AMERICA*

**UNITED STATES**

★Ottawa

★Washington, D.C.

·Bermuda (BR.)

Tropic of Cancer

**MEXICO**

20°N

*Hawaii (U.S.)*

Mexico City★

PACIFIC OCEAN

Equator

N

W E

S

International Date Line

P O L Y N E S I A

*Wallis and Futuna (FR.)*

**KIRIBATI**

*Tokelau (N.Z.)*

*American Samoa (U.S.)*

*French Polynesia (FR.)*

**WESTERN SAMOA**

**TONGA**

Tropic of Capricorn

*Pitcairn Is. (BR.)*

Georgetown **GUYANA**
Paramaribo
Caracas★ **SURINAME**
**VENEZUELA**
Bogotá·
**COLOMBIA**
Quito★ Cayenne
FRENCH GUIANA (FR.)
**ECUADOR**
**PERU** *SOUTH AMERICA*
**BRAZIL**
Lima★ **BOLIVIA**
La Paz·
Sucre★ Brasília★
**PARAGUAY**
Asunción·
**CHILE** **ARGENTINA**
Montevideo·
**URUGUAY**
Santiago★ Buenos Aires

0   1000   2000 Miles
0  1000  2000  3000 Kilometers

Antarctic Circle

---

# Central America and the Caribbean

Tropic of Cancer

GULF OF MEXICO

Nassau★

**BAHAMAS**

★Havana

20°N

**CUBA**

**MEXICO**

**BELIZE**
★Belmopan

N
W E
S

ATLANTIC OCEAN

20°N

**HAITI** **DOMINICAN REPUBLIC**
*Puerto Rico (U.S.)*
*Virgin Islands (U.S. and BR.)*
Port-au-Prince★
**JAMAICA** ★Kingston
Santo Domingo
**ANTIGUA AND BARBUDA**
**ST. KITTS AND NEVIS**
·Guadeloupe (FR.)
·DOMINICA
*Martinique (FR.)*
·ST. LUCIA
**ST. VINCENT AND THE GRENADINES**
·BARBADOS
·GRENADA

**GUATEMALA**
Guatemala City★
**HONDURAS**
·Tegucigalpa
San Salvador★
**EL SALVADOR**
**NICARAGUA**
Managua★

CARIBBEAN SEA

PACIFIC OCEAN

San José★
**COSTA RICA**
**PANAMA** ★Panama

Port of Spain★ **TRINIDAD AND TOBAGO**

10°N

**VENEZUELA**

**COLOMBIA**

*SOUTH AMERICA*

**GUYANA**

0   250   500 Miles
0  250  500  750 Kilometers

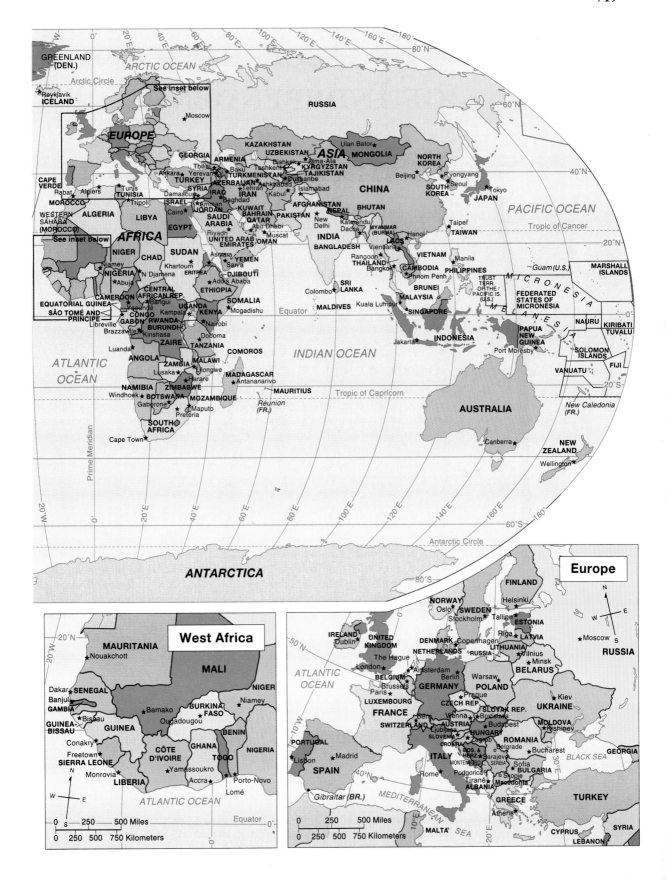

# THE DECLARATION OF INDEPENDENCE

*In Congress, July 4, 1776*

THE UNANIMOUS DECLARATION OF THE THIRTEEN UNITED STATES OF AMERICA

When in the Course of human events, it becomes necessary for one people to dissolve the political bands which have connected them with another, and to assume among the powers of the earth, the separate and equal station to which the Laws of nature and of Nature's God entitle them, a decent respect to the opinions of mankind requires that they should declare the causes which impel them to the separation.

The opening paragraph of the Declaration describes the basic purpose of the document: to set out the reasons why the former colonists declared their independence.

## THE POLITICAL THEORY OF THE DECLARATION

We hold these truths to be self-evident, that all men are created equal, that they are endowed by their Creator with certain unalienable Rights, that among these are Life, Liberty and the pursuit of Happiness. That to secure these rights, Governments are instituted among Men, deriving their just powers from the consent of the governed; That whenever any Form of Government becomes destructive of these ends it is the Right of the People to alter or to abolish it, and to institute new Government, laying its foundation on such principles and organizing its powers in such form, as to them shall seem most likely to effect their Safety and Happiness. Prudence, indeed, will dictate that Governments long established should not be changed for light and transient causes; and accordingly all experience hath shown, that mankind are more disposed to suffer, while evils are sufferable, than to right themselves by abolishing the forms to which they are accustomed. But when a long train of abuses and usurpations, pursuing invariably the same Objects evinces a design to reduce them under absolute Despotism, it is their right, it is their duty, to throw off such Government, and to provide new Guards for their future security.

The Declaration was written by a five-member committee appointed by the Second Continental Congress on June 11, 1776. The document was very largely the work of Thomas Jefferson, who chaired the committee. Its other members (John Adams, Benjamin Franklin, Roger Sherman, and Robert Livingston) made minor changes in Jefferson's original draft before the final version was reported to Congress. Jefferson drew heavily from the ideas of English philosopher John Locke to declare these "self-evident" truths: the equality of all men; the natural rights of men, granted to them by God; the principle of limited government; government only by the consent of the governed; and the right to rebel against tyrannical government.

## THE "INJURIES AND USURPATIONS"

Such has been the patient sufferance of these Colonies; and such is now the necessity which constrains them to alter their former Systems of Government. The history of the present King of Great Britain is a history of repeated injuries and usurpations, all having in direct object the establishment of an absolute Tyranny over these States. To prove this, let Facts be submitted to a candid world.

He has refused his Assent to Laws, the most wholesome and necessary for the public good.

He has forbidden his Governors to pass Laws of immediate and pressing importance, unless suspended in their operation till his Assent should be obtained; and when so suspended, he has utterly neglected to attend to them.

He has refused to pass other Laws for the accommodation of large districts of people, unless those people would relinquish the right of Representation in the Legislature, a right inestimable to them and formidable to tyrants only.

He has called together legislative bodies at places unusual, uncomfortable, and distant from the depository of their public records, for the sole purpose of fatiguing them into compliance with his measures.

He has dissolved Representative Houses repeatedly, for opposing with manly firmness his invasions on the rights of the people.

He has refused for a long time, after such dissolutions, to cause others to be elected; whereby the Legislative powers, incapable of Annihilation, have returned to the People at large for their exercise; the State remaining in the mean time exposed to all the dangers of invasions from without, and convulsions within.

He has endeavored to prevent the population of these States; for that purpose obstructing the Laws for Naturalization of Foreigners; refusing to pass others to encourage their migration hither, and raising the conditions of new Appropriations of Lands.

He has obstructed the Administration of Justice, by refusing his Assent to Laws for establishing Judiciary powers.

He has made Judges dependent on his Will alone for the tenure of their offices, and the amount and payment of their salaries.

He has erected a multitude of New Offices, and sent hither swarms of Officers to harass our people and eat out their substance.

He has kept among us in time of peace, Standing Armies, without the Consent of our legislatures.

He has affected to render the Military independent of, and superior to, the Civil Power.

He has combined with others to subject us to a jurisdiction foreign to our constitutions, and unacknowledged by our laws; giving his Assent to their Acts of pretended Legislation:

For quartering large bodies of armed troops among us;

For protecting them, by a mock Trial, from punishment for any Murders which they should commit on the Inhabitants of these States;

For cutting off our Trade with all parts of the world;

For imposing taxes on us without our Consent;

For depriving us, in many cases, of the benefits of Trial by Jury;

For transporting us beyond Seas, to be tried for pretended offenses;

For abolishing the free System of English Laws in a neighboring Province, establishing therein an Arbitrary government, and enlarging its Boundaries, so as to render it at once an example and fit instrument for introducing the same absolute rule into these Colonies;

For taking away our Charters, abolishing our most valuable Laws, and altering, fundamentally, the Forms of our Governments;

For suspending our own Legislatures, and declaring themselves invested with Power to legislate for us in all cases whatsoever.

He has abdicated Government here, by declaring us out of his Protection, and waging War against us.

He has plundered our seas, ravaged our Coasts, burned our towns, and destroyed the lives of our people.

He is at this time transporting large Armies of foreign Mercenaries to complete the works of death, desolation and tyranny, already begun with circumstances of Cruelty and perfidy scarcely paralleled in the most barbarous ages, and totally unworthy the Head of a civilized nation.

He has constrained our fellow Citizens taken Captive on the high Seas to bear Arms against their Country, to become the executioners of their friends and Brethren, or to fall themselves by their Hands.

He has excited domestic insurrections amongst us, and has endeavored to bring on the inhabitants of our frontiers the merciless Indian Savages whose known rule of warfare is an undistinguished destruction of all ages, sexes, and conditions.

In every stage of these Oppressions We have Petitioned for Redress in the most humble terms. Our repeated Petitions have been answered only by repeated injury. A Prince whose character is thus marked by every act which may define a Tyrant, is unfit to be the ruler of a free people.

Nor have We been wanting in attentions to our British brethren. We have warned them from time to time of attempts by their legislature to extend an unwarrantable jurisdiction over us. We have reminded them of the circumstances of our emigration and settlement here. We have appealed to their native justice and magnanimity, and we have conjured them by the ties of our common kindred to disavow these usurpations, which, would inevitably interrupt our connections and correspondence. They too have been deaf to the voice of justice and of consanguinity. We must, therefore, acquiesce in the necessity, which denounces our Separation, and hold them, as we hold the rest of mankind, Enemies in War, in Peace Friends.—

The body of the Declaration sets out the long list of grievances felt by the colonists and cites their repeated but unsuccessful attempts to redress them by peaceful means.

### THE FORMAL PROCLAMATION OF INDEPENDENCE

We, therefore, the Representatives of the United States of America, in General Congress, Assembled, appealing to the Supreme Judge of the world for the rectitude of our intentions, do, in the Name, and by the Authority of the good People of these Colonies, solemnly publish and declare, That these United Colonies are, and of right ought to be Free and Independent States; that they are Absolved from all Allegiance to the British Crown, and that all political connection between them and the State of Great Britain, is and ought to be totally dissolved, and that as Free and Independent States, they have full Power to levy War, conclude Peace, contract Alliances, establish Commerce, and to do all other Acts and Things which Independent States may of right do. And for the support of this Declaration, with a firm reliance on the protection of Divine Providence, we mutually pledge to each other our Lives, our Fortunes and our sacred Honor.

The final paragraph of the Declaration makes the formal pronouncement of independence from Great Britain, and claims for the United States all of the rights to which an independent nation is entitled.

JOHN HANCOCK
President of the
Continental Congress
1775–1777

NEW HAMPSHIRE
*Josiah Bartlett*
*William Whipple*
*Matthew Thornton*

MASSACHUSETTS BAY
*Samuel Adams*
*John Adams*
*Robert Treat Paine*
*Elbridge Gerry*

RHODE ISLAND
*Stephan Hopkins*
*William Ellery*

CONNECTICUT
*Roger Sherman*
*Samuel Huntington*
*William Williams*
*Oliver Wolcott*

NEW YORK
*William Floyd*
*Philip Livingston*
*Francis Lewis*
*Lewis Morris*

NEW JERSEY
*Richard Stockton*
*John Witherspoon*
*Francis Hopkinson*
*John Hart*
*Abraham Clark*

DELAWARE
*Caesar Rodney*
*George Read*
*Thomas M'Kean*

MARYLAND
*Samuel Chase*
*William Paca*
*Thomas Stone*
*Charles Carroll*
*of Carrollton*

VIRGINIA
*George Wythe*
*Richard Henry Lee*
*Thomas Jefferson*
*Benjamin Harrison*
*Thomas Nelson, Jr.*
*Francis Lightfoot Lee*
*Carter Braxton*

PENNSYLVANIA
*Robert Morris*
*Benjamin Rush*
*Benjamin Franklin*
*John Morton*
*George Clymer*
*James Smith*
*George Taylor*
*James Wilson*
*George Ross*

NORTH CAROLINA
*William Hooper*
*Joseph Hewes*
*John Penn*

SOUTH CAROLINA
*Edward Rutledge*
*Thomas Heyward, Jr.*
*Thomas Lynch, Jr.*
*Arthur Middleton*

GEORGIA
*Button Gwinnett*
*Lyman Hall*
*George Walton*

# AN OUTLINE OF THE CONSTITUTION OF THE UNITED STATES

❝ The American Constitution is the most wonderful work ever struck off at a given time by the brain and purpose of man. ❞

—William E. Gladstone

# THE CONSTITUTION OF THE UNITED STATES

## PREAMBLE

We the People of the United States, in Order to form a more perfect Union, establish Justice, insure domestic Tranquility, provide for the common defence, promote the general Welfare, and secure the Blessings of Liberty to ourselves and our Posterity, do ordain and establish this Constitution for the United States of America.

The Preamble states the broad purposes the Constitution is intended to serve—to establish a government that provides for greater cooperation among the States, ensures justice and peace, provides for defense against foreign enemies, promotes the general well-being of the people, and secures liberty now and in the future. The phrase *We the People* emphasizes the twin concepts of popular sovereignty and of representative government.

## Article I

### LEGISLATIVE DEPARTMENT

**Section 1.** *Legislative Power; The Congress*

All legislative powers herein granted shall be vested in a Congress of the United States, which shall consist of a Senate and House of Representatives.

SECTION 1. LEGISLATIVE POWER, CONGRESS Congress, the nation's lawmaking body, is bicameral in form; that is, it is composed of two houses: the Senate and the House of Representatives. The Framers of the Constitution purposely separated the lawmaking power from the power to enforce the laws (Article II, the Executive Branch) and the power to interpret them (Article III, the Judicial Branch). This system of separation of powers is supplemented by a system of checks and balances; that is, in several provisions the Constitution gives to each of the three branches various powers with which it may check, restrain, the actions of the other two branches.

**Section 2.** *House of Representatives*

1. The House of Representatives shall be composed of members chosen every second year by the people of the several States, and the electors in each State shall have the qualifications requisite for electors of the most numerous branch of the State legislature.

CLAUSE 1. ELECTION Electors means voters. Members of the House of Representatives are elected every two years. Each State must permit the same persons to vote for United States representatives as it permits to vote for the members of the larger house of its own legislature. The 17th Amendment (1913) extends this requirement to the qualification of voters for United States senators.

2. No person shall be a Representative who shall not have attained to the age of twenty-five years, and been seven years a citizen of the United States, and who shall not, when elected, be an inhabitant of that State in which he shall be chosen.

CLAUSE 2. QUALIFICATIONS A member of the House of Representatives must be at least 25 years old, an American citizen for seven years, and a resident of the State he or she represents. In addition, political custom requires that a representative also reside in the district from which he or she is elected.

3. Representatives ~~and direct taxes~~* shall be apportioned among the several States which may be included within this Union, according to their respective numbers, ~~which shall be determined by adding to the whole number of free persons, including those bound to service for a term of years and excluding Indians not taxed, three fifths of all other persons~~. The actual enumeration shall be made within three years after the first meeting of the Congress of the United States, and within every subsequent term of ten years, in such manner as they shall by law direct. The number of Representatives shall not exceed one for every thirty thousand, but each State shall have at least one Representative; and, until such enumeration shall be made, the State of New Hampshire shall be entitled to choose three, Massachusetts eight, Rhode Island and Providence Plantations one, Connecticut five, New York six, New Jersey four, Pennsylvania eight, Delaware one, Maryland six, Virginia ten, North Carolina five, South Carolina five, and Georgia three.

CLAUSE 3. APPORTIONMENT The number of representatives each State is entitled to is based on its population, which is counted every 10 years in the census. Congress reapportions the seats among the States after each census. In the Reapportionment Act of 1929, Congress fixed the permanent size of the House at 435 members with each State having at least one representative. Today there is one House seat for approximately every 575,000 persons in the population.

---

*The black lines indicate portions of the Constitution altered by subsequent amendments to the document.

The words "three-fifths of all other persons" referred to slaves and reflected the Three-Fifths Compromise reached by the Framers at Philadelphia in 1787; the phrase was made obsolete, was in effect repealed, by the 13th Amendment in 1865.

4. When vacancies happen in the representation from any State, the executive authority thereof shall issue writs of election to fill such vacancies.

CLAUSE 4. VACANCIES The executive authority refers to the governor of a State. If a member leaves office or dies before the expiration of his or her term, the governor is to call a special election to fill the vacancy.

5. The House of Representatives shall choose their Speaker and other officers; and shall have the sole power of impeachment.

CLAUSE 5. OFFICERS; IMPEACHMENT The House elects a Speaker, customarily chosen from the majority party in the House. Impeachment means accusation. The House has the exclusive power to impeach, or accuse, civil officers; the Senate (Article I, Section 3, Clause 6) has the exclusive power to try those impeached by the House.

## Section 3. *Senate*

1. The Senate of the United States shall be composed of two Senators from each State ~~chosen by the legislature thereof~~ for six years; and each Senator shall have one vote.

CLAUSE 1. COMPOSITION, ELECTION, TERM Each State has two senators. Each serves for six years and has one vote. Orginally, senators were not elected directly by the people, but by each State's legislature. The 17th Amendment, added in 1913, provides for the popular election of senators.

2. Immediately after they shall be assembled in consequences of the first election, they shall be divided, as equally as may be, into three classes. The seats of the Senators of the first class shall be vacated at the expiration of the second year; of the second class, at the expiration of the fourth year; and of the third class, at the expiration of the sixth year; so that one-third may be chosen every second year~~; and if vacancies happen by resignation, or otherwise, during the recess of the legislature of any State, the execution thereof may make temporary appointments until the next meeting of the legislature, which shall then fill such vacancies~~.

CLAUSE 2. CLASSIFICATION The senators elected in 1788 were divided into three groups so that the Senate could become a "continuing body." Only one-third of the Senate's seats are up for election every two years.

The 17th Amendment provides that a Senate vacancy is to be filled at a special election called by the governor; State law may also permit the governor to appoint a successor to serve until that election is held.

3. No person shall be a Senator who shall not have attained to the age of thirty years, and been nine years a citizen of the United States, who shall not, when elected, be an inhabitant of that State for which he shall be chosen.

CLAUSE 3. QUALIFICATIONS A senator must be at least 30 years old, a citizen for at least nine years, and a resident of the State from which elected.

4. The Vice President of the United States shall be President of the Senate, but shall have no vote, unless they be equally divided.

CLAUSE 4. PRESIDING OFFICER The Vice President presides over the Senate, but may vote only to break a tie.

5. The Senate shall choose their other officers, and also a President pro tempore, in the absence of the Vice President, or when he shall exercise the office of President of the United States.

CLAUSE 5. OTHER OFFICERS The Senate chooses its own officers, including someone to preside when the Vice President is not there. That senator is called the Senate's president pro tempore.

6. The Senate shall have the sole power to try all impeachments. When sitting for that purpose, they shall be on oath or affirmation. When the President of the United States is tried, the Chief Justice shall preside; and no person shall be convicted without the concurrence of two-thirds of the members present.

CLAUSE 6. IMPEACHMENT TRIALS The Senate conducts the trials of those officials impeached by the House. The Vice President presides unless the President is on trial, in which case the chief justice of the United States takes charge of the proceedings. To convict an official two-thirds of the members present must vote a guilty verdict.

No President has ever been convicted. In 1868 the House impeached President Andrew Johnson but the Senate acquitted him of the charges by one vote. In 1974 the Judiciary Committee of the House of Representatives recommended to the House that President Richard M. Nixon be impeached, but he resigned from office before further action could be taken.

7. Judgment in cases of impeachment shall not extend further than to removal from office, and disqualification to hold and enjoy any office of honor, trust, or profit under the United States; but the party convicted shall, nevertheless, be liable and subject to indictment, trial, judgment, and punishment, according to law.

CLAUSE 7. PENALTY ON CONVICTION The only punishment allowed for an official who is convicted in an impeachment case is removal from office and disqualification from holding any other federal office. However, the convicted official may still be tried in a regular court of law for the same offense.

## Section 4. *Elections and Meetings*

1. The times, places, and manner of holding elections for Senators and Representatives, shall be prescribed in each State by the legislature thereof: but the Congress may at any time, by law, make or alter such regulations, except as to the places of choosing Senators.

CLAUSE 1. ELECTION In 1842 Congress required that representatives be elected from districts within each State with more than one seat in the House. The districts in each State are drawn by that State's legislature. Seven States now have only one seat in the House: Alaska, Delaware, Montana, North Dakota, South Dakota, Vermont, and Wyoming. The 1842 law also directed that representatives be elected in each State on the same day: the Tuesday after the first Monday in November of every even-numbered year. In 1914 Congress also set that same date for the election of senators.

2. The Congress shall assemble at least once in every year, and such meeting shall be on the first Monday in December, unless they shall by law appoint a different day.

CLAUSE 2. SESSIONS Congress must meet at least once a year. The 20th Amendment (1933) changed the opening date to January 3.

## Section 5. *Legislative Proceedings*

1. Each House shall be the judge of the elections, returns, and qualifications of its own members, and a majority of each shall constitute a quorum to do business; but a smaller number may adjourn from day to day, and may be authorized to compel the attendance of absent members, in such manner, and under such penalties, as each House may provide.

CLAUSE 1. ADMISSION OF MEMBERS; QUORUM In 1969 the Supreme Court held that the House cannot exclude any member-elect who satisfies the qualifications set out in Article I, Section 2, Clause 2.

A majority in the House (218 members) or Senate (51) constitutes a quorum. In practice, both houses often proceed with less than a quorum present. However, any member may raise a point of order (demand a "quorum call"). If a roll call then reveals less than a majority of the members present, that chamber must either adjourn or the sergeant at arms must be ordered to round up absent members.

2. Each House may determine the rules of its proceedings, punish its members for disorderly behavior, and, with the concurrence of two-thirds, expel a member.

CLAUSE 2. RULES Each house has adopted detailed rules to guide its proceedings. Each house may discipline members for unacceptable conduct; expulsion requires a two-thirds vote.

3. Each House shall keep a journal of its proceedings, and, from time to time, publish the same, excepting such parts as may, in their judgment, require secrecy; and the yeas and nays of the members of either House, on any question, shall, at the desire of one-fifth of those present, be entered on the journal.

CLAUSE 3. RECORD Each house must keep and publish a record of its meetings. The *Congressional Record* is published for every day that either house of Congress is in session, and provides a written record of all that is said and done on the floor of each house each session.

4. Neither House, during the session of Congress, shall, without the consent of the other, adjourn for more than three days, nor to any other place than that in which the two Houses shall be sitting.

CLAUSE 4. ADJOURNMENT Once in session, neither house may suspend (recess) its work for more than three days without the approval of the other house. Both houses must always meet in the same location.

## Section 6. *Compensation, Immunities, and Disabilities of Members*

1. The Senators and Representatives shall receive a compensation for their services, to be ascertained by law, and paid out of the treasury of the United States. They shall, in all cases, except treason, felony, and breach of the peace, be privileged from arrest during their attendance at the session of their respective Houses, and in going to, and returning from, the same; and for any speech or debate in either House, they shall not be questioned in any other place.

CLAUSE 1. SALARIES; IMMUNITIES Each house sets its members' salaries, paid by the United States; the 27th Amendment (1992) modified this pay-setting power. This provision establishes "legislative immunity." The purpose of this immunity is to allow members to speak and debate freely in Congress itself. Treason is strictly defined in Article III, Section 3. A felony is any serious crime. A breach of the peace is any indictable offense less than treason or a felony; this exemption from arrest is of little real importance today.

2. No Senator or Representative shall, during the time for which he was elected, be appointed to any civil office under the authority of the United States, which shall have been created, or the emoluments whereof shall have been increased during such time; and no person, holding any office under the United States, shall be a member of either House during his continuance in office.

CLAUSE 2. RESTRICTIONS ON OFFICE HOLDING No sitting member of either house may be appointed to an office in the executive or in the judicial branch if that position was created or its salary was increased during that member's current elected term. The second part of this clause—forbidding any person serving in either the executive or the judicial branch from also serving in Congress—reinforces the principle of separation of powers.

## Section 7. *Revenue Bills, President's Veto*

1. All bills for raising revenue shall originate in the House of Representatives, but the Senate may propose or concur with amendments as on other bills.

CLAUSE 1. REVENUE BILLS All bills that raise money must originate in the House. However, the Senate has the power to amend any revenue bill sent to it from the lower house.

2. Every bill which shall have passed the House of Representatives and the Senate, shall, before it become a law, be presented to the President of the United

States; if he approve, he shall sign it, but if not, he shall return it, with his objections, to that House in which it shall have originated, who shall enter the objections at large on their journal, and proceed to reconsider it. If, after such reconsideration, two-thirds of the House shall agree to pass the bill, it shall be sent, together with the objections, to the other House, by which it shall likewise be reconsidered, and, if approved by two-thirds of that House, it shall become a law: But in all such cases the votes of both Houses shall be determined by yeas and nays, and the names of the persons voting for and against the bill shall be entered on the journal of each House respectively. If any bill shall not be returned by the President within ten days (Sunday excepted) after it shall have been presented to him, the same shall be a law, in like manner as if he had signed it, unless the Congress, by their adjournment, prevent its return, in which case it shall not be a law.

CLAUSE 2. ENACTMENT OF LAWS; VETO Once both houses have passed a bill, it must be sent to the President. The President may (1) sign the bill, thus making it law; (2) veto (reject) the bill, whereupon it must be returned to the house in which it originated; or (3) allow the bill to become law without signature, by not acting upon it within 10 days of its receipt from Congress, not counting Sundays. The President has a fourth option at the end of a congressional session: If he does not act on a measure within 10 days, and Congress adjourns during that period, the bill dies; the "pocket veto" has been applied to it. A presidential veto may be overridden by a two-thirds vote in each house.

3. Every order, resolution, or vote, to which the concurrence of the Senate and House of Representatives may be necessary (except on a question of adjournment), shall be presented to the President of the United States; and before the same shall take effect, shall be approved by him, or, being disapproved by him, shall be repassed by two-thirds of the Senate and House of Representatives, according to the rules and limitations prescribed in the case of a bill.

CLAUSE 3. OTHER MEASURES This clause refers to joint resolutions, measures Congress often passes to deal with unusual, temporary, or ceremonial matters. A joint resolution passed by Congress and signed by the President has the force of law, just as a bill does. As a matter of custom, a joint resolution proposing an amendment to the Constitution is not submitted to the President for signature or veto. Concurrent and simple resolutions do not have the force of law and, therefore, are not submitted to the President.

### Section 8. *Powers of Congress*

The Congress shall have power

1. To lay and collect taxes, duties, imposts and excises, to pay the debts, and provide for the common defence and general welfare of the United States; but all duties, imposts and excises, shall be uniform throughout the United States;

CLAUSE 1. The 18 separate clauses in this section set out 27 of the many expressed powers the Constitution grants to Congress. In this clause Congress is given the power to levy and provide for the collection of various kinds of taxes, in order to finance the operations of the government. All federal taxes must be levied at the same rates throughout the country.

2. To borrow money on the credit of the United States;

CLAUSE 2. Congress has power to borrow money to help finance the government. Federal borrowing is most often done through the sale of bonds on which interest is paid. The Constitution does not limit the amount the government may borrow.

3. To regulate commerce with foreign nations, and among the several States, and with the Indian tribes;

CLAUSE 3. This clause, the Commerce Clause, gives Congress the power to regulate both foreign and interstate trade. Much of what Congress does, it does on the basis of its commerce power.

4. To establish an uniform rule of naturalization, and uniform laws on the subject of bankruptcies, throughout the United States;

CLAUSE 4. Congress has the exclusive power to determine how aliens may become citizens of the United States. Congress may also pass laws relating to bankruptcy.

5. To coin money, regulate the value thereof, and of foreign coin, and fix the standard of weights and measures;

CLAUSE 5. Congress has the power to establish and require the use of uniform gauges of time, distance, weight, volume, area, and the like.

6. To provide for the punishment of counterfeiting the securities and current coin of the United States;

CLAUSE 6. Congress has the power to make it a federal crime to falsify the coins, paper money, bonds, stamps, and the like of the United States.

7. To establish post offices and post roads;

CLAUSE 7. Congress has the postal power, the power to provide for and regulate the transportation and delivery of mail; "post offices" are those buildings and other places where mail is deposited for dispatch; "post roads" include all routes over or upon which mail is carried.

8. To promote the progress of science and useful arts, by securing, for limited times, to authors and inventors, the exclusive right to their respective writings and discoveries;

CLAUSE 8. Congress has the power to provide for copyrights and patents. A copyright gives an author or composer the exclusive right to control the reproduction, publication, and sale of literary, musical, or other creative work. A patent gives a person the exclusive right to control the manufacture or sale of his or her invention.

9. To constitute tribunals inferior to the Supreme Court;

CLAUSE 9. Congress has the power to create the lower federal courts, all of the several federal courts that function beneath the Supreme Court.

10. To define and punish piracies and felonies, committed on the high seas, and offences against the law of nations;

CLAUSE 10. Congress has the power to prohibit, as a federal crime: (1) certain acts committed outside the territorial jurisdiction of the United States, and (2) the commission within the United States of any wrong against any nation with which we are at peace.

11. To declare war, grant letters of marque and reprisal, and make rules concerning captures on land and water;

CLAUSE 11. Only Congress can declare war. However, the President, as commander in chief of the armed forces (Article II, Section 2, Clause 1), can make war without such a formal declaration. Letters of marque and reprisal are (were) commissions authorizing private persons to outfit vessels (privateers) to capture and destroy enemy ships in time of war; they are forbidden in international law by the Declaration of Paris of 1856, and the United States has honored the ban since the Civil War.

12. To raise and support armies; but no appropriation of money to that use shall be for a longer term than two years;

13. To provide and maintain a navy;

CLAUSES 12 and 13. Congress has the power to provide for and maintain the nation's armed forces. It established the air force as an independent element of the armed forces in 1947, an exercise of its inherent powers in foreign relations and national defense. The two-year limit on spending for the army insures civilian control of the military.

14. To make rules for the government and regulation of the land and naval forces;

CLAUSE 14. Today these rules are set out in a lengthy, oft-amended law, the Uniform Code of Military Justice, passed by Congress in 1950.

15. To provide for calling forth the militia to execute the laws of the Union, suppress insurrections, and repel invasions;

16. To provide for organizing, arming, and disciplining the militia, and for governing such part of them as may be employed in the service of the United States, reserving to the States respectively the appointment of the officers, and the authority of training the militia, according to the discipline prescribed by Congress;

CLAUSES 15 and 16. In the National Defense Act of 1916, Congress made each State's militia (volunteer army) a part of the National Guard. Today, Congress and the States cooperate in its maintenance. Ordinarily, each State's National Guard is under the command of that State's governor; but Congress has given the Presi-

dent the power to call any or all of those units into federal service when necessary.

17. To exercise exclusive legislation in all cases whatsoever, over such district (not exceeding ten miles square) as may, by cession of particular States, and the acceptance of Congress, become the seat of the Government of the United States, and to exercise like authority over all places, purchased by the consent of the legislature of the State in which the same shall be, for the erection of forts, magazines, arsenals, dockyards, and other needful buildings; and

CLAUSE 17. In 1791 Congress accepted land grants from Maryland and Virginia and established the District of Columbia for the nation's capital. Assuming Virginia's grant would never be needed, Congress returned it in 1846. Today, the elected government of the District's 69 square miles operates under the authority of Congress. Congress also has the power to acquire other lands from the States for various federal purposes.

18. To make all laws which shall be necessary and proper for carrying into execution the foregoing powers, and all other powers vested by this Constitution in the Government of the United States, or in any department or officer thereof.

CLAUSE 18. This is the Necessary and Proper Clause, also often called the Elastic Clause. It is the constitutional basis for the many and far-reaching implied powers of the Federal Government.

### Section 9.  *Powers Denied to Congress*

1. The migration or importation of such persons as any of the States now existing shall think proper to admit, shall not be prohibited by the Congress prior to the year one thousand eight hundred and eight; but a tax or duty may be imposed on such importation, not exceeding ten dollars for each person.

CLAUSE 1. "Such persons" referred to slaves. This provision was part of the Commerce Compromise, one of the bargains struck in the writing of the Constitution. Congress outlawed the slave trade in 1808.

2. The privilege of the writ of habeas corpus shall not be suspended, unless when, in cases of rebellion or invasion, the public safety may require it.

CLAUSE 2. A writ of habeas corpus, the "great writ of liberty," is a court order directing a sheriff, warden, or other public officer, or a private person, who is detaining another to "produce the body" of the one being held in order that the legality of the detention may be determined by the court.

3. No bill of attainder or *ex post facto* law shall be passed.

CLAUSE 3. A bill of attainder is a legislative act that inflicts punishment without a judicial trial. See Article I, Section 10, and Article III, Section 3, Clause 2. An *ex post facto* law is any criminal law that operates retroactively to the disadvantage of the accused. See Article I, Section 10.

4. No capitation, ~~or other direct tax~~, shall be laid, unless in proportion to the census or enumeration hereinbefore directed to be taken.

CLAUSE 4. A capitation tax is literally a "head tax," a tax levied on each person in the population. A direct tax is one paid directly to the government by the taxpayer—for example, an income or a property tax; an indirect tax is one paid to another private party who then pays it to the government—for example, a sales tax. This provision was modified by the 16th Amendment (1913), giving Congress the power to levy "taxes on incomes, from whatever source derived."

5. No tax or duty shall be laid on articles exported from any State.

CLAUSE 5. This provision was a part of the Commerce Compromise made by the Framers in 1787. Congress has the power to tax imported goods, however.

6. No preference shall be given by any regulation of commerce or revenue to the ports of one State over those of another, nor shall vessels bound to, or from, one State, be obliged to enter, clear, or pay duties, in another.

CLAUSE 6. All ports within the United States must be treated alike by Congress as it exercises its taxing and commerce powers. Congress cannot tax goods sent by water from one State to another, nor may it give the ports of one State any legal advantage over those of another.

7. No money shall be drawn from the treasury, but in consequence of appropriations made by law; and a regular statement and account of the receipts and expenditures of all public money shall be published from time to time.

CLAUSE 7. This clause gives Congress its vastly important "power of the purse," a major check on presidential power. Federal money can be spent only in those amounts and for those purposes expressly authorized by an act of Congress. All federal income and spending must be accounted for, regularly and publicly.

8. No title of nobility shall be granted by the United States; and no person holding any office of profit or trust under them shall, without the consent of the Congress, accept of any present, emolument, office, or title, of any kind whatever, from any king, prince, or foreign state.

CLAUSE 8. This provision, preventing the establishment of a nobility, reflects the principle that "all men are created equal." It was also intended to discourage foreign attempts to bribe or otherwise corrupt officers of the government.

### Section 10. *Powers Denied to the States*

1. No State shall enter into any treaty, alliance, or confederation; grant letters of marque and reprisal; coin money; emit bills of credit; make anything but gold and silver coin a tender in payment of debts; pass any bill of attainder, *ex post facto* law, or law impairing the obligations of contracts, or grant any title of nobility.

CLAUSE 1. The States are not sovereign governments and so cannot make agreements or otherwise negotiate with foreign states; the power to conduct foreign relations is an exclusive power of the National Government. The power to coin money is also an exclusive power of the National Government. Several powers forbidden to the National Government are here also forbidden to the States.

2. No State shall, without the consent of the Congress, lay any imposts or duties on imports or exports, except what may be absolutely necessary for executing its inspection laws; and the net produce of all duties and imposts, laid by any State on imports or exports, shall be for the use of the treasury of the United States; and all such laws shall be subject to the revision and control of the Congress.

CLAUSE 2. This provision relates to foreign, not interstate, commerce. Only Congress, not the States, can tax imports; and the States are, like Congress, forbidden the power to tax exports.

3. No State shall, without the consent of Congress, lay any duty of tonnage, keep troops, or ships of war, in time of peace, enter into any agreement or compact with another State, or with a foreign power, or engage in war, unless actually invaded, or in such imminent danger as will not admit of delay.

CLAUSE 3. A duty of tonnage is a tax laid on ships according to their cargo capacity. Each State has a constitutional right to provide for and maintain a militia; but no State may keep a standing army or navy. The several restrictions here prevent the States from assuming powers that the Constitution elsewhere grants to the National Government.

## Article II

### EXECUTIVE DEPARTMENT

**Section 1.** *President and Vice President*

1. The executive power shall be vested in a President of the United States of America. He shall hold his office during the term of four years, and together with the Vice President, chosen for the same term, be elected as follows:

CLAUSE 1. EXECUTIVE POWER, TERM This clause gives to the President the very broad "executive power," the power to enforce the laws and otherwise administer the public policies of the United States. It also sets the length of the presidential (and vice-presidential) term of office; see the 22nd Amendment (1951), which places a limit on presidential (but not vice-presidential) tenure.

2. Each State shall appoint, in such manner as the legislature thereof may direct, a number of Electors, equal to the whole number of Senators and Representatives, to which the State may be entitled in the Congress; but no Senator or Representative, or person holding an office of trust or profit, under the United States, shall be appointed an Elector.

CLAUSE 2. ELECTORAL COLLEGE This clause establishes the "electoral college," although the Constitution does not use that term. It is a body of presidential electors chosen in each State, and it selects the President and

Vice President every four years. The number of electors chosen in each State equals the number of senators and representatives that State has in Congress.

3. ~~The Electors shall meet in their respective States, and vote by ballot for two persons, of whom one, at least, shall not be an inhabitant of the same State with themselves. And they shall make a list of all the persons voted for, and of the number of votes for each; which list they shall sign and certify, and transmit, sealed, to the seat of the Government of the United States, directed to the President of the Senate. The President of the Senate shall, in the presence of the Senate and House of Representatives, open all the certificates, and the votes shall then be counted. The person having the greatest number of votes shall be the President, if such number be a majority of the whole number of Electors appointed; and if there be more than one, who have such majority, and have an equal number of votes, then, the House of Representatives shall immediately choose, by ballot, one of them for President; and if no person have a majority, then, from the five highest on the list, the said House shall, in like manner, choose the President. But in choosing the President, the votes shall be taken by States, the representation from each State having one vote; a quorum for this purpose shall consist of a member or members from two-thirds of the States, and a majority of all the States shall be necessary to a choice. In every case, after the choice of the President, the person having the greatest number of votes of the Electors shall be the Vice President. But if there should remain two or more who have equal votes, the Senate shall choose from them, by ballot, the Vice President.~~

CLAUSE 3. ELECTION OF PRESIDENT AND VICE PRESIDENT This clause was replaced by the 12th Amendment in 1804.

4. The Congress may determine the time of choosing the Electors, and the day on which they shall give their votes; which day shall be the same throughout the United States.

CLAUSE 4. DATE Congress has set the date for the choosing of electors as the Tuesday after the first Monday in November every fourth year, and for the casting of electoral votes as the Monday after the second Wednesday in December of that year.

5. No person, except a natural-born citizen, or a citizen of the United States at the time of the adoption of this Constitution, shall be eligible to the office of President; neither shall any person be eligible to that office, who shall not have attained to the age of thirty-five years, and been fourteen years a resident within the United States.

CLAUSE 5. QUALIFICATIONS The President must have been born a citizen of the United States, be at least 35 years old, and have been a resident of the United States for at least 14 years.

6. ~~In case of the removal of the president from office, or of his death, resignation, or inability to discharge the~~ ~~powers and duties of the said office, the same shall devolve on the Vice President~~, and the Congress may by law provide for the case of removal, death, resignation or inability, both of the President and Vice President, declaring what officer shall then act as President, and such officer shall act accordingly, until the disability be removed, or a President shall be elected.

CLAUSE 6. VACANCY This clause was modified by the 25th Amendment (1967), which provides expressly for the succession of the Vice President, for the filling of a vacancy in the Vice Presidency, and for the determination of presidential inability.

7. The President shall, at stated times, receive for his services a compensation, which shall neither be increased nor diminished during the period for which he shall have been elected, and he shall not receive, within that period, any other emolument from the United States, or any of them.

CLAUSE 7. COMPENSATION The President now receives a salary of $200,000 and a taxable expense account of $50,000 a year. Those amounts cannot be changed during a presidential term; thus, Congress cannot use the President's compensation as a bargaining tool to influence executive decisions. The phrase "any other emolument" means, in effect, any valuable gift; it does not mean that the President cannot be provided with such benefits of office as the White House, extensive staff assistance, and much else.

8. Before he enter on the execution of his office, he shall take the following oath or affirmation:

"I do solemnly swear (or affirm), that I will faithfully execute the office of President of the United States, and will, to the best of my ability, preserve, protect, and defend the Constitution of the United States."

CLAUSE 8. OATH OF OFFICE The chief justice of the United States regularly administers this oath or affirmation, but any judicial officer may do so. Thus, Calvin Coolidge was sworn into office in 1923 by his father, a justice of the peace in Vermont.

**Section 2.** *President's Powers and Duties*

1. The President shall be Commander in Chief of the army and navy of the United States, and of the militia of the several States, when called into the actual service of the United States; he may require the opinion, in writing, of the principal officer in each of the executive departments upon any subject relating to the duties of their respective offices, and he shall have power to grant reprieves and pardons for offences against the United States, except in cases of impeachment.

CLAUSE 1. MILITARY, CIVIL POWERS The President, a civilian, heads the nation's armed forces, a key element in the Constitution's insistence on civilian control of the military. The President's power to "require the opinion, in writing" provides the constitutional basis for the cabinet. The President's power to grant reprieves and pardons, the power of clemency, extends only to federal cases.

2. He shall have power, by and with the advice and consent of the Senate, to make treaties, provided two-thirds of the Senators present concur; and he shall nominate, and, by and with the advice and consent of the Senate, shall appoint ambassadors, other public ministers, and consuls, judges of the Supreme Court, and all other officers of the United States whose appointments are not herein otherwise provided for, and which shall be established by law; but the Congress may by law vest the appointment of such inferior officers, as they think proper, in the President alone, in the courts of law, or in the heads of departments.

CLAUSE 2. TREATIES, APPOINTMENTS The President has the sole power to make treaties; to become effective, a treaty must be approved by a two-thirds vote in the Senate. In practice, the President can also make executive agreements with foreign governments; these pacts, which are frequently made and usually deal with routine matters, do not require Senate consent. The President appoints the principal officers of the executive branch and all federal judges; the "inferior officers" are those who hold lesser posts.

3. The President shall have power to fill up all vacancies that may happen during the recess of the Senate, by granting commissions which shall expire at the end of their next session.

CLAUSE 3. RECESS APPOINTMENTS When the Senate is not in session, appointments that require Senate consent can be made by the President on a temporary basis, as "recess appointments."

### Section 3. *President's Powers and Duties*

He shall, from time to time, give to the Congress information of the state of the Union, and recommend to their consideration such measures as he shall judge necessary and expedient; he may, on extraordinary occasions, convene both Houses, or either of them, and in case of disagreement between them, with respect to the time of adjournment, he may adjourn them to such time as he shall think proper; he shall receive ambassadors and other public ministers; he shall take care that the laws be faithfully executed, and shall commission all the officers of the United States.

The President delivers a State of the Union Message to Congress soon after that body convenes each year. That message is delivered to the nation's lawmakers and, importantly, to the American people, as well. It is shortly followed by the proposed federal budget and an economic report; and the President may send special messages to Congress at any time. In all of these communications, Congress is urged to take those actions the Chief Executive finds to be in the national interest. The President also has the power: to call special sessions of Congress; to adjourn Congress if its two houses cannot agree for that purpose; to receive the diplomatic representatives of other governments; to insure the proper execution of all federal laws; and to empower federal officers to hold their posts and perform their duties.

### Section 4. *Impeachment*

The President, Vice President, and all civil officers of the United States, shall be removed from office on impeachment for, and conviction of, treason, bribery, or other high crimes and misdemeanors.

The Constitution outlines the impeachment process in Article I, Section 2, Clause 5 and in Section 3, Clauses 6 and 7.

## Article III

### JUDICIAL DEPARTMENT

### Section 1. *Courts, Terms of Office*

The judicial power of the United States shall be vested in one Supreme Court, and in such inferior courts as the Congress may from time to time ordain and establish. The judges, both of the Supreme and inferior courts, shall hold their offices during good behavior, and shall, at stated times, receive for their services a compensation which shall not be diminished during their continuance in office.

The judicial power conferred here is the power of federal courts to hear and decide cases, disputes between the government and individuals and between private persons (parties). The Constitution creates only the Supreme Court of the United States; it gives to Congress the power to establish other, lower federal courts (Article I, Section 8, Clause 9) and to fix the size of the Supreme Court. The words "during good behavior" mean, in effect, for life.

### Section 2. *Jurisdiction*

1. The judicial power shall extend to all cases, in law and equity, arising under this Constitution, the laws of the United States, and treaties made, or which shall be made, under their authority; to all cases affecting ambassadors, other public ministers, and consuls; to all cases of admiralty and maritime jurisdiction; to controversies to which the United States shall be a party; to controversies between two or more States, ~~between a State and a citizen of another State~~, between citizens of different States, between citizens of the same State claiming lands under grants of different States, ~~and between a State, or the citizens thereof, and foreign states, citizens, or subjects~~.

CLAUSE 1. CASES TO BE HEARD This clause sets out the jurisdiction of the federal courts; that is, it identifies those cases that may be tried in those courts. The federal courts can hear and decide—have jurisdiction over—a case depending on either the subject matter or the parties involved in that case. The jurisdiction of the federal courts in cases involving States was substantially restricted by the 11th Amendment in 1795.

2. In all cases affecting ambassadors, other public ministers and consuls, and those in which a State shall be a party, the Supreme Court shall have original jurisdiction. In all the other cases before mentioned, the

Supreme Court shall have appellate jurisdiction, both as to law and fact, with such exceptions and under such regulations as the Congress shall make.

CLAUSE 2. SUPREME COURT JURISDICTION Original jurisdiction refers to the power of a court to hear a case in the first instance, not on appeal from a lower court. Appellate jurisdiction refers to a court's power to hear a case on appeal from a lower court, from the court in which the case was originally tried. This clause gives the Supreme Court both original and appellate jurisdiction. However, nearly all of the cases the High Court hears are brought to it on appeal from the lower federal courts and the highest State courts.

3. The trial of all crimes, except in cases of impeachment, shall be by jury; and such trial shall be held in the State where the said crimes shall have been committed; but when not committed within any State the trial shall be at such place or places as the Congress may by law have directed.

CLAUSE 3. JURY TRIAL IN CRIMINAL CASES A person accused of a federal crime is guaranteed the right to trial by jury in a federal court in the State where the crime was committed; see the 5th and 6th amendments. The right to trial by jury in serious criminal cases in the State courts is guaranteed by the 6th and 14th amendments.

### Section 3. *Treason*

1. Treason against the United States shall consist only in levying war against them, or in adhering to their enemies, giving them aid and comfort. No person shall be convicted of treason unless on the testimony of two witnesses to the same overt act, or on confession in open court.

CLAUSE 1. DEFINITION Treason is the only crime defined in the Constitution. The Framers intended the very specific definition here to prevent the loose use of the charge of treason—for example, against persons who criticize the government. Treason can be committed only in time of war and only by a citizen or a resident alien.

2. The Congress shall have power to declare the punishment of treason, but no attainder of treason shall work corruption of blood, or forfeiture except during the life of the person attainted.

CLAUSE 2. PUNISHMENT Congress has provided that the punishment that a federal court may impose on a convicted traitor may range from a minimum of five years in prison and/or a $10,000 fine to a maximum of death; no person convicted of treason has ever been executed by the United States. No legal punishment can be imposed on the family or descendants of a convicted traitor. Congress has also made it a crime for any person (in either peace or wartime) to commit espionage or sabotage, to attempt to overthrow the government by force, or to conspire to do any of these things.

### Article IV

### RELATIONS AMONG STATES

### Section 1. *Full Faith and Credit*

Full faith and credit shall be given in each State to the public acts, records, and judicial proceedings of every other State. And the Congress may, by general laws, prescribe the manner in which such acts, records, and proceedings shall be proved, and the effect thereof.

Each State must respect—recognize the validity of—the laws, public records, and court decisions of every other State.

### Section 2. *Privileges and Immunities of Citizens*

1. The citizens of each State shall be entitled to all privileges and immunities of citizens in the several States.

CLAUSE 1. RESIDENTS OF OTHER STATES In effect, this clause means that no State may discriminate against the residents of other States; that is, a State's laws cannot draw unreasonable distinctions between its own residents and those of any of the other States. See Section 1 of the 14th Amendment.

2. A person charged in any State with treason, felony, or other crime, who shall flee from justice, and be found in another State, shall, on demand of the executive authority of the State from which he fled, be delivered up, to be removed to the State having jurisdiction of the crime.

CLAUSE 2. EXTRADITION The process of returning a fugitive to another State is known as "interstate rendition" or, more commonly, "extradition." Usually, that process works routinely; some extradition requests are contested however—especially in cases with racial or political overtones. A governor may refuse to extradite a fugitive; but the federal courts can compel an unwilling governor to obey this constitutional command.

3. No person held to service or labor in one State, under the laws therof, escaping into another, shall, in consequence of any law or regulation therein, be discharged from service or labor, but shall be delivered up on claim of the party to whom such service or labor may be due.

CLAUSE 3. FUGITIVE SLAVES This clause was nullified by the 13th Amendment, which abolished slavery in 1865.

### Section 3. *New States; Territories*

1. New States may be admitted by the Congress into this Union; but no new State shall be formed or erected within the jurisdiction of any other State, nor any State be formed by the junction of two or more States, or parts of States, without the consent of the legislatures of the States concerned as well as of the Congress.

CLAUSE 1. NEW STATES ONLY Congress can admit new States to the Union. A new State may not be created by taking territory from an existing State without the consent of that State's legislature.

Congress has admitted 37 States since the original 13 formed the Union. Five States—Vermont, Kentucky, Tennessee, Maine, and West Virginia—were created from parts of existing States. Texas was an independent republic before admission. California was admitted after being ceded to the United States by Mexico. Each of the other 30 States entered the Union only after a period of time as an organized territory of the United States.

2. The Congress shall have power to dispose of and make all needful rules and regulations respecting the territory or other property belonging to the United States; and nothing in this Constitution shall be so construed as to prejudice any claims of the United States, or of any particular State.

CLAUSE 2. TERRITORY, PROPERTY Congress has the power to make laws concerning the territories, other public lands, and all other property of the United States.

## Section 4. *Protection Afforded to States by the Nation*

The United States shall guarantee to every State in this Union a republican form of government, and shall protect each of them against invasion; and on application of the legislature, or of the executive (when the legislature cannot be convened), against domestic violence.

The Constitution does not define "a republican form of government," but the phrase is generally understood to mean a representative government. The Federal Government must also defend each State against attacks from outside its border and, at the request of a State's legislature or its governor, aid its efforts to put down internal disorders.

## Article V
### PROVISIONS FOR AMENDMENT

The Congress, whenever two-thirds of both Houses shall deem it necessary, shall propose amendments to this Constitution, or, on the application of the legislatures of two-thirds of the several States, shall call a convention for proposing amendments, which, in either case, shall be valid, to all intents and purposes, as part of this Constitution, when ratified by the legislatures of three-fourths of the several States, or by conventions in three-fourths thereof, as the one or the other mode of ratification may be proposed by the Congress; provided ~~that no amendment which may be made prior to the year one thousand eight hundred and eight shall in any manner affect the first and fourth clauses in the ninth section of the first Article; and~~ that no State, without its consent, shall be deprived of its equal suffrage in the Senate.

This section provides for the methods by which formal changes can be made in the Constitution. An amendment may be proposed in one of two ways: by a two-

thirds vote in each house of Congress, or by a national convention called by Congress at the request of two-thirds of the State legislatures. A proposed amendment may be ratified in one of two ways: by three-fourths of the State legislatures, or by three-fourths of the States in conventions called for that purpose. Congress has the power to determine the method by which a proposed amendment may be ratified. The amendment process cannot be used to deny any State its equal representation in the United States Senate. To this point, 27 amendments have been adopted. To date, all of the amendments except the 21st Amendment were proposed by Congress and ratified by the State legislatures. Only the 21st Amendment was ratified by the convention method.

## Article VI
### NATIONAL DEBTS, SUPREMACY OF NATIONAL LAW, OATH

### Section 1. *Validity of Debts*

All debts contracted and engagements entered into, before the adoption of this Constitution, shall be as valid against the United States under this Constitution, as under the Confederation.

Congress had borrowed large sums of money during the Revolution and later during the Critical Period of the 1780s. This provision, a pledge that the new government would honor those debts, did much to create confidence in that government.

### Section 2. *Supremacy of National Law*

This Constitution, and the laws of the United States which shall be made in pursuance thereof, and all treaties made, or which shall be made, under the authority of the United States, shall be the supreme law of the land; and the judges in every State shall be bound thereby, anything in the constitution or laws of any State to the contrary notwithstanding.

This section sets out the Supremacy Clause, a specific declaration of the supremacy of federal law over any and all forms of State law. No State, including its local governments, may make or enforce any law that conflicts with any provision in the Constitution, an act of Congress, a treaty, or an order, rule, or regulation properly issued by the President or his subordinates in the executive branch.

### Section 3. *Oaths of Office*

The Senators and Representatives before mentioned, and the members of the several State legislatures, and all executive and judicial officers, both of the United States and of the several States, shall be bound, by oath or affirmation, to support this Constitution; but no religious test shall ever be required as a qualification to any office or public trust under the United States.

This provision reinforces the Supremacy Clause; all public officers, at every level in the United States, owe their first allegiance to the Constitution of the United States. No religious qualification can be imposed as a condition for holding any public office.

## Article VII
### RATIFICATION OF CONSTITUTION

The ratification of the conventions of nine States shall be sufficient for the establishment of this Constitution between the States so ratifying the same.

The proposed Constitution was signed by George Washington and 37 of his fellow Framers on September 17, 1787. (George Read of Delaware signed for himself and also for his absent colleague, John Dickinson.)

Done in Convention, by the unanimous consent of the States present, the seventeenth day of September, in the year of our Lord one thousand seven hundred and eighty-seven, and of the Independence of the United States of America the twelfth. *In Witness* whereof, we have hereunto subscribed our names.

Attest: William Jackson,
SECRETARY

George Washington, PRESIDENT AND DEPUTY FROM VIRGINIA

**NEW HAMPSHIRE**
John Langdon
Nicholas Gilman

**MASSACHUSETTS**
Nathaniel Gorham
Rufus King

**CONNECTICUT**
William Samuel Johnson
Roger Sherman

**NEW YORK**
Alexander Hamilton

**NEW JERSEY**
William Livingston
David Brearley
William Paterson
Jonathan Dayton

**PENNSYLVANIA**
Benjamin Franklin
Thomas Mifflin
Robert Morris
George Clymer
Thomas Fitzsimons
Jared Ingersoll
James Wilson
Gouverneur Morris

**DELAWARE**
George Read
Gunning Bedford, Jr.
John Dickinson
Richard Bassett
Jacob Broom

**MARYLAND**
James McHenry
Dan of St. Thomas Jennifer
Daniel Carroll

**VIRGINIA**
John Blair
James Madison, Jr.

**NORTH CAROLINA**
William Blount
Richard Dobbs Spaight
Hugh Williamson

**SOUTH CAROLINA**
John Rutledge
Charles Cotesworth Pinckney
Charles Pinckney
Pierce Butler

**GEORGIA**
William Few
Abraham Baldwin

## AMENDMENTS

The first 10 amendments, the Bill of Rights, were each proposed by Congress on September 25, 1789, and ratified by the necessary three-fourths of the States on December 15, 1791. These amendments were originally intended to restrict the National Government—not the States. However, the Supreme Court has several times held that most of their provisions also apply to the States, through the 14th Amendment's Due Process Clause.

### 1ST AMENDMENT. *Freedom of Religion, Speech, Press, Assembly, and Petition*

Congress shall make no law respecting an establishment of religion, or prohibiting the free exercise thereof, or abridging the freedom of speech, or of the press; or the right of the people peaceably to assemble, and to petition the government for a redress of grievances.

The 1st AMENDMENT sets out five basic liberties: The guarantee of freedom of religion is both a protection of religious thought and practice and a command of separation of church and state. The guarantees of freedom of speech and press assure to all persons a right to speak, publish, and otherwise express their views. The guarantees of the rights of assembly and petition protect the right to join with others in public meetings, political parties, pressure groups, and other associations to discuss public affairs and influence public policy. None of these rights is guaranteed in absolute terms, however; like all other civil rights guarantees, each of them may be exercised only with regard to the rights of all other persons.

### 2ND AMENDMENT. *Bearing Arms*

A well-regulated militia being necessary to the security of a free state, the right of the people to keep and bear arms shall not be infringed.

Each State has the right to maintain a militia, a volunteer armed force for its own protection; however, both the

National Government and the States can and do regulate the possession and use of firearms by private persons.

### 3RD AMENDMENT. *Quartering of Troops*

No soldier shall, in time of peace, be quartered in any house, without the consent of the owner; nor, in time of war, but in a manner to be prescribed by law.

This amendment was intended to prevent what had been common British practice in the colonial period; see the Declaration of Independence. This provision is of virtually no importance today.

### 4TH AMENDMENT. *Searches and Seizures*

The right of the people to be secure in their persons, houses, papers, and effects, against unreasonable searches and seizures, shall not be violated; and no warrants shall issue, but upon probable cause, supported by oath or affirmation, and particularly describing the place to be searched and the persons or things to be seized.

The basic rule laid down by the 4th Amendment is this: Police officers have no general right to search for or seize evidence or seize (arrest) persons. Except in particular circumstances, they must have a proper warrant (a court order) obtained with probable cause (on reasonable grounds). This guarantee is reinforced by the exclusionary rule, developed by the Supreme Court: Evidence gained as the result of an unlawful search or seizure cannot be used at the court trial of the person from whom it was seized.

### 5TH AMENDMENT. *Criminal Proceedings; Due Process; Eminent Domain*

No person shall be held to answer for a capital, or otherwise infamous, crime, unless on a presentment or indictment of a grand jury, except in cases arising in the land or naval forces, or in the militia, when in actual service, in time of war, or public danger; nor shall any person be subject, for the same offence, to be twice put in jeopardy of life or limb; nor shall be compelled, in any criminal case, to be a witness against himself; nor be deprived of life, liberty, or property, without due process of law; nor shall private property be taken for public use, without just compensation.

A person can be tried for a serious federal crime only if he or she has been indicted (charged, accused of that crime) by a grand jury. No one may be subjected to double jeopardy—that is, tried twice for the same crime. All persons are protected against self-incrimination; no person can be legally compelled to answer any question in any governmental proceeding if that answer could lead to that person's prosecution. The 5th Amendment's Due Process Clause prohibits unfair, arbitrary actions by the Federal Government; a like prohibition is set out against the States in the 14th Amendment. Government may take private property for a legitimate public purpose; but when it exercises that power of eminent domain, it must pay a fair price for the property seized.

### 6TH AMENDMENT. *Criminal Proceedings*

In all criminal prosecutions, the accused shall enjoy the right to a speedy and public trial, by an impartial jury of the State and district wherein the crime shall have been committed, which district shall have been previously ascertained by law; and to be informed of the nature and cause of the accusation; to be confronted with the witnesses against him; to have compulsory process for obtaining witnesses in his favor; and to have the assistance of counsel for his defence.

A person accused of crime has the right to be tried in court without undue delay and by an impartial jury; see Article III, Section 2, Clause 3. The defendant must be informed of the charge upon which he or she is to be tried, has the right to cross-examine hostile witnesses, and has the right to require the testimony of favorable witnesses. The defendant also has the right to be represented by an attorney at every stage in the criminal process.

### 7TH AMENDMENT. *Civil Trials*

In suits at common law, where the value in controversy shall exceed twenty dollars, the right of trial by jury shall be preserved; and no fact, tried by a jury, shall be otherwise re-examined in any court of the United States than according to the rules of the common law.

This amendment applies only to civil cases heard in federal courts. A civil case does not involve criminal matters; it is a dispute between private parties or between the government and a private party. The right to trial by jury is guaranteed in any civil case in a federal court if the amount of money involved in that case exceeds $20 (most cases today involve a much larger sum); that right may be waived (relinquished, put aside) if both parties agree to a bench trial (a trial by a judge, without a jury).

### 8TH AMENDMENT. *Punishment for Crimes*

Excessive bail shall not be required, nor excessive fines imposed, nor cruel and unusual punishment inflicted.

Bail is the sum of money that a person accused of crime may be required to post (deposit with the court) as a guarantee that he or she will appear in court at the proper time. The amount of bail required and/or a fine imposed as punishment must bear a reasonable relationship to the seriousness of the crime involved in the case. The prohibition of cruel and unusual punishment forbids any punishment judged to be too harsh, too severe for the crime for which it is imposed.

### 9TH AMENDMENT. *Unenumerated Rights*

The enumeration in the Constitution of certain rights shall not be construed to deny or disparage others retained by the people.

The fact that the Constitution sets out many civil rights guarantees, expressly provides for many protections against government, does not mean that there are not other rights also held by the people.

#### 10TH AMENDMENT. *Powers Reserved to the States*

The powers not delegated to the United States by the Constitution, nor prohibited by it to the States, are reserved to the States respectively, or to the people.

This amendment identifies the area of power that may be exercised by the States. All of those powers the Constitution does not grant to the National Government, and at the same time does not forbid to the States, belong to each of the States, or to the people of each State.

#### 11TH AMENDMENT. *Suits against States*

The judicial power of the United States shall not be construed to extend to any suit in law or equity, commenced or prosecuted against one of the United States by citizens of another State or by citizens or subjects of any foreign state.

Proposed by Congress March 4, 1794; ratified February 7, 1795, but official announcement of the ratification was delayed until January 8, 1798. This amendment repealed part of Article III, Section 2, Clause 1. No State may be sued in a federal court by a resident of another State or of a foreign country; the Supreme Court has long held that this provision also means that a State cannot be sued in a federal court by a foreign country or, more importantly, even by one of its own residents.

#### 12TH AMENDMENT. *Election of President and Vice President*

The Electors shall meet in their respective States, and vote by ballot for President and Vice President, one of whom, at least, shall not be an inhabitant of the same State with themselves; they shall name in their ballots the person voted for as President, and in distinct ballots the person voted for as Vice President; and they shall make distinct lists of all persons voted for as President, and of all persons voted for as Vice President, and of the number of votes for each, which lists they shall sign, and certify, and transmit, sealed, to the seat of the Government of the United States, directed to the President of the Senate; the President of the Senate shall, in the presence of the Senate and the House of Representatives, open all the certificates, and the votes shall then be counted; the person having the greatest number of votes for President shall be the President, if such number be a majority of the whole number of Electors appointed; and if no person have such a majority, then, from the persons having the highest numbers, not exceeding three, on the list of those voted for as President, the House of Representatives shall choose immediately, by ballot, the President. But in choosing the President, the votes shall be taken by States, the representation from each State having one vote; a quorum for this purpose shall consist of a member or members from two-thirds of the States, and a majority of all the States shall be necessary to a choice. And if the House of Representatives shall not choose a President, whenever the right of choice shall devolve upon them, before the fourth day of March next following, then the Vice President shall act as President, as in case of death, or other constitutional disability, of the President. The person having the greatest number of votes as Vice President, shall be the Vice President, if such number be a majority of the whole number of Electors appointed; and if no person have a majority, then, from the two highest numbers on the list, the Senate shall choose the Vice President; a quorum for the purpose shall consist of two-thirds of the whole number of Senators; a majority of the whole number shall be necessary to a choice. But no person constitutionally ineligible to the office of President shall be eligible to that of Vice-President of the United States.

Proposed by Congress December 9, 1803; ratified June 15, 1804. This amendment replaced Article II, Section 1, Clause 3. Originally, each elector cast two ballots, each for a different person for President. The person with the largest number of electoral votes, provided that number was a majority of the electors, was to become President; the person with the second highest number was to become Vice President. This arrangement produced an electoral vote tie between Thomas Jefferson and Aaron Burr in 1800; the House finally chose Jefferson as President in 1801. The 12th Amendment separated the balloting for President and Vice President; each elector now casts one ballot for someone as President and a second ballot for another person as Vice President. Note that the 20th Amendment changed the date set here (March 4) to January 20, and that the 23rd Amendment (1961) provides for electors from the District of Columbia. This amendment also provides that the Vice President must meet the same qualifications as those set out for the President in Article II, Section 1, Clause 5.

#### 13TH AMENDMENT. *Slavery and Involuntary Servitude*

SECTION 1. Neither slavery nor involuntary servitude, except as a punishment for crime, whereof the party shall have been duly convicted, shall exist within the United States, or any place subject to their jurisdiction.

SECTION 2. Congress shall have power to enforce this article by appropriate legislation.

Proposed by Congress January 31, 1865; ratified December 6, 1865. This amendment forbids slavery in the United States and in any area under its control. It also forbids other forms of forced labor, except punishments for crime; but some forms of compulsory service are not prohibited—for example, service on juries or in the armed forces. Section 2 gives to Congress the power to carry out the provisions of Section 1 of this amendment.

**14TH AMENDMENT.** *Rights of Citizens*

SECTION 1. All persons born or naturalized in the United States, and subject to the jurisdiction thereof, are citizens of the United States and of the State wherein they reside. No State shall make or enforce any law which shall abridge the privileges or immunities of citizens of the United States; nor shall any State deprive any person of life, liberty, or property, without due process of law, nor deny to any person within its jurisdiction the equal protection of the laws.

Proposed by Congress June 13, 1866; ratified July 9, 1868. Section 1 defines citizenship. It provides for the acquisition of United States citizenship by birth or by naturalization. Citizenship at birth is determined according to the principle of *jus soli*—"the law of the soil," where born; naturalization is the legal process by which one acquires a new citizenship at some time after birth. Under certain circumstances, citizenship can also be gained at birth abroad, according to the principle of *jus sanguinis*—"the law of the blood," to whom born. This section also contains two major civil rights provisions: the Due Process Clause forbids a State (and its local governments) to act in any unfair or arbitrary way; the Equal Protection Clause forbids a State (and its local governments) to discriminate against, draw unreasonable distinctions between, persons.

Most of the rights set out against the National Government in the first eight amendments have been extended against the States (and their local governments) through Supreme Court decisions involving the 14th Amendment's Due Process Clause.

SECTION 2. Representatives shall be apportioned among the several States according to their respective numbers, counting the whole number of persons in each State, excluding Indians not taxed. But when the right to vote at any election for the choice of electors for President and Vice President of the United States, Representatives in Congress, the executive and judicial officers of a State, or the members of the legislature thereof, is denied to any of the male inhabitants of such State, being twenty-one years of age and citizens of the United States, or in any way abridged, except for participation in rebellion or other crime, the basis of representation therein shall be reduced in the proportion which the number of such male citizens shall bear to the whole number of male citizens twenty-one years of age in such State.

The first sentence here replaced Article I, Section 2, Clause 3, the Three-Fifths Compromise provision. Essentially, all persons in the United States are counted in each decennial census, the basis for the distribution of House seats. The balance of this section has never been enforced and is generally thought to be obsolete.

SECTION 3. No person shall be a Senator or Representative in Congress, or elector of President and Vice President, or hold any office, civil or military, under the United States, or under any State, who, having previously taken an oath, as a member of Congress, or as an officer of the United States, or as a member of any State legislature, or as an executive or judicial officer of any State, to support the Constitution of the United States, shall have engaged in insurrection or rebellion against the same, or given aid or comfort to the enemies thereof. But Congress may, by a vote of two-thirds of each House, remove such disability.

This section limited the President's power to pardon those persons who had led the Confederacy during the Civil War. Congress finally removed this disability in 1898.

SECTION 4. The validity of the public debt of the United States, authorized by law, including debts incurred for payment of pensions and bounties for services in suppressing insurrection or rebellion, shall not be questioned. But neither the United States nor any State shall assume or pay any debt or obligation incurred in aid of insurrection or rebellion against the United States, or any claim for the loss or emancipation of any slave, but all such debts, obligations, and claims shall be held illegal and void.

Section 4 also dealt with matters directly related to the Civil War. It reaffirmed the public debt of the United States; but it invalidated, prohibited payment of, any debt contracted by the Confederate States and also prohibited any compensation of former slave owners.

SECTION 5. The Congress shall have power to enforce, by appropriate legislation, the provisions of this article.

**15TH AMENDMENT.** *Right to Vote—Race, Color, Servitude*

SECTION 1. The right of citizens of the United States to vote shall not be denied or abridged by the United States or by any State on account of race, color, or previous condition of servitude.

SECTION 2. The Congress shall have power to enforce this article by appropriate legislation.

Proposed by Congress February 26, 1869; ratified February 3, 1870. The immediate purpose of this amendment was to guarantee to newly freed slaves their right to vote. It has a much broader application today.

**16TH AMENDMENT.** *Income Tax*

The Congress shall have power to lay and collect taxes on incomes, from whatever source derived, without apportionment among the several States, and without regard to any census or enumeration.

Proposed by Congress July 12, 1909; ratified February 3, 1913. This amendment modified two provisions in Article I: Section 2, Clause 3, and Section 9, Clause 4. It gives to Congress the power to levy an income tax, a direct tax, without regard to the populations of any of the States.

## 17TH AMENDMENT. *Popular Election of Senators*

The Senate of the United States shall be composed of two Senators from each State, elected by the people thereof, for six years; and each Senator shall have one vote. The electors in each State shall have the qualifications requisite for electors of the most numerous branch of the State legislatures.

When vacancies happen in the representation of any State in the Senate, the executive authority of such State shall issue writs of election to fill such vacancies: Provided, That the legislature of any State may empower the executive thereof to make temporary appointment until the people fill the vacancies by election as the legislature may direct.

This Amendment shall not be so construed as to affect the election or term of any Senator chosen before it becomes valid as part of the Constitution.

Proposed by Congress May 13, 1912; ratified April 8, 1913. This amendment repealed those portions of Article I, Section 3, Clauses 1 and 2 relating to the election of senators. Senators are now elected by the voters in each State. If a vacancy occurs, the governor of the State involved must call an election to fill the seat; the governor may appoint a senator to serve until the next election, if the State's legislature has authorized that step.

## 18TH AMENDMENT. *Prohibition of Intoxicating Liquors*

SECTION 1. After one year from the ratification of this article the manufacture, sale or transportation of intoxicating liquors within, the importation thereof into, or the exportation thereof from the United States and all territory subject to the jurisdiction thereof for beverage purposes is hereby prohibited.

SECTION 2. The Congress and the several States shall have concurrent power to enforce this article by appropriate legislation.

SECTION 3. This article shall be inoperative unless it shall have been ratified as an Amendment to the Constitution by the legislatures of the several States, as provided in the Constitution, within seven years of the date of the submission hereof to the States by Congress.

Proposed by Congress December 18, 1917; ratified January 16, 1919. This amendment outlawed the making, selling, transporting, importing, or exporting of alcoholic beverages in the United States. It was repealed in its entirety by the 21st Amendment in 1933.

## 19TH AMENDMENT. *Equal Suffrage—Sex*

The right of citizens of the United States to vote shall not be denied or abridged by the United States or by any State on account of sex.

Congress shall have power to enforce this article by appropriate legislation.

Proposed by Congress June 4, 1919; ratified August 18, 1920. No person can be denied the right to vote in any election in the United States on account of his or her sex.

## 20TH AMENDMENT. *Commencement of Terms; Sessions of Congress; Death or Disqualification of President-Elect*

SECTION 1. The terms of the President and Vice President shall end at noon on the 20th day of January, and the terms of Senators and Representatives at noon on the 3d day of January, of the years in which such terms would have ended if this article had not been ratified; and the terms of their successors shall then begin.

SECTION 2. The Congress shall assemble at least once in every year, and such meeting shall begin at noon on the 3d day of January, unless they shall by law appoint a different day.

Proposed by Congress March 2, 1932; ratified January 23, 1933. The provisions of Sections 1 and 2 relating to Congress modified Article I, Section 4, Clause 2, and those provisions relating to the President, the 12th Amendment. The date on which the President and Vice President now take office was moved from March 4 to January 20. Similarly, the members of Congress now begin their terms on January 3. The 20th Amendment is sometimes called the "Lame Duck Amendment" because it shortened the period of time a member of Congress who was defeated for reelection (a "lame duck") remains in office.

SECTION 3. If, at the time fixed for the beginning of the term of the President, the President-elect shall have died, the Vice President-elect shall become President. If a President shall not have been chosen before the time fixed for the beginning of his term, or if the President-elect shall have failed to qualify, then the Vice President-elect shall act as President until a President shall have qualified; and the Congress may by law provide for the case wherein neither a President-elect nor a Vice President-elect shall have qualified, declaring who shall then act as President, or the manner in which one who is to act shall be selected, and such person shall act accordingly until a President or Vice President shall have qualified.

This section deals with certain possibilities that were not covered by the presidential selection provisions of either Article II or the 12th Amendment. To this point, none of these situations has occurred. Note that there is neither a President-elect nor a Vice President-elect until the electoral votes have been counted by Congress, or, if the electoral college cannot decide the matter, the House has chosen a President or the Senate has chosen a Vice President.

SECTION 4. The Congress may by law provide for the case of the death of any of the persons from whom the House of Representatives may choose a President whenever the right of choice shall have devolved upon them, and for the case of the death of any of the persons from whom the Senate may choose a Vice President whenever the right of choice shall have devolved upon them.

Congress has not in fact ever passed such a law. See Section 2 of the 25th Amendment, regarding a vacancy in the vice presidency; that provision could some day have an impact here.

SECTION 5. Sections 1 and 2 shall take effect on the 15th day of October following the ratification of this article.

SECTION 6. This article shall be inoperative unless it shall have been ratified as an Amendment to the Constitution by the legislatures of three fourths of the several States within seven years from the date of its submission.

Section 5 set the date on which this amendment came into force. Section 6 placed a time limit on the ratification process; note that a similar provision was written into the 18th, 21st, and 22nd amendments.

### 21ST AMENDMENT. *Repeal of 18th Amendment*

SECTION 1. The eighteenth article of Amendment to the Constitution of the United States is hereby repealed.

SECTION 2. The transportation or importation into any State, Territory, or possession of the United States for delivery or use therein of intoxicating liquors, in violation of the laws thereof, is hereby prohibited.

SECTION 3. This article shall be inoperative unless it shall have been ratified as an Amendment to the Constitution by conventions in the several States, as provided in the Constitution, within seven years from the date of the submission hereof to the States by the Congress.

Proposed by Congress February 20, 1933; ratified December 5, 1933. This amendment repealed all of the 18th Amendment. Section 2 modifies the scope of the Federal Government's commerce power set out in Article I, Section 8, Clause 3; it gives to each State the power to regulate the transportation or importation and the distribution or use of intoxicating liquors in ways that would be unconstitutional in the case of any other commodity. The 21st Amendment is the only amendment Congress has thus far submitted to the States for ratification by conventions.

### 22ND AMENDMENT. *Presidential Tenure*

SECTION 1. No person shall be elected to the office of the President more than twice, and no person who has held the office of President, or acted as President, for more than two years of a term to which some other person was elected President shall be elected to the office of the President more than once. But this Article shall not apply to any person holding the office of President when this Article was proposed by the Congress, and shall not prevent any person who may

be holding the office of President, or acting as President, during the term within which this Article becomes operative from holding the office of President or acting as President during the remainder of such term.

SECTION 2. This article shall be inoperative unless it shall have been ratified as an Amendment to the Constitution by the legislatures of three fourths of the several states within seven years from the date of its submission to the States by the Congress.

Proposed by Congress March 24, 1947; ratified February 27, 1951. This amendment modified Article II, Section I, Clause 1. It stipulates that no President may serve more than two elected terms. But a President who has succeeded to the office beyond the midpoint in a term to which another President was originally elected may serve for more than eight years. In any case, however, a President may not serve more than 10 years. Prior to Franklin Roosevelt, who was elected to four terms, no President had served more than two full terms in office.

### 23RD AMENDMENT. *Presidential Electors for the District of Columbia*

SECTION 1. The District constituting the seat of Government of the United States shall appoint in such manner as the Congress may direct:

A number of electors of President and Vice President equal to the whole number of Senators and Representatives in Congress to which the District would be entitled if it were a State, but in no event more than the least populous State; they shall be considered, for the purposes of the election of President and Vice President, to be electors appointed by a State; and they shall meet in the District and perform such duties as provided by the twelfth article of Amendment.

SECTION 2. The Congress shall have power to enforce this article by appropriate legislation.

Proposed by Congress June 16, 1960; ratified March 29, 1961. This amendment modified Article II, Section I, Clause 2 and the 12th Amendment. It included the voters of the District of Columbia in the presidential electorate; and provides that the District is to have the same number of electors as the least populous State—three electors—but no more than that number.

### 24TH AMENDMENT. *Right to Vote in Federal Elections—Tax Payment*

SECTION 1. The right of citizens of the United States to vote in any primary or other election for President or Vice President, for electors for President or Vice President, or for Senator or Representative in Congress, shall not be denied or abridged by the United States or any State by reason of failure to pay any poll tax or other tax.

SECTION 2. The Congress shall have power to enforce this article by appropriate legislation.

Proposed by Congress September 14, 1962; ratified January 23, 1964. This amendment outlawed the payment of any tax as a condition for taking part in the nomination or election of any federal officeholder.

### 25TH AMENDMENT. *Presidential Succession, Vice Presidential Vacancy, Presidential Inability*

SECTION 1. In case of the removal of the President from office or of his death or resignation, the Vice President shall become President.

Proposed by Congress July 6, 1965; ratified February 10, 1967. Section 1 revised the imprecise provision on presidential succession in Article II, Section 1, Clause 6. It wrote into the Constitution the precedent set by Vice President John Tyler, who became President on the death of William Henry Harrison in 1841.

SECTION 2. Whenever there is a vacancy in the office of the Vice President, the President shall nominate a Vice President who shall take office upon confirmation by a majority vote of both Houses of Congress.

This section provides for the filling of a vacancy in the office of Vice President. Prior to its adoption, the office had been vacant on 16 occasions and had remained unfilled for the remainder of each term involved. When Spiro Agnew resigned the office in 1973, President Nixon selected Gerald Ford in accord with this provision; and, when President Nixon resigned in 1974, Gerald Ford became President and then chose Nelson Rockefeller as Vice President.

SECTION 3. Whenever the President transmits to the President *pro tempore* of the Senate and the Speaker of the House of Representatives his written declaration that he is unable to discharge the powers and duties of his office, and until he transmits to them a written declaration to the contrary, such powers and duties shall be discharged by the Vice President as Acting President.

This section created a procedure for determining if a President is so incapacitated that he cannot perform the powers and duties of his office.

SECTION 4. Whenever the Vice President and a majority of either the principal officers of the executive departments or of such other body as Congress may by law provide, transmit to the President *pro tempore* of the Senate and the Speaker of the House of Representatives their written declaration that the President is unable to discharge the powers and duties of his office, the Vice President shall immediately assume the powers and duties of the office as Acting President.

Thereafter, when the President transmits to the President *pro tempore* of the Senate and the Speaker of the House of Representatives his written declaration that no inability exists, he shall resume the powers and duties of his office unless the Vice President and a majority of either the principal officers of the executive department or of such other body as Congress may by law provide, transmit within four days to the President *pro tempore* of the Senate and the Speaker of the House of Representatives their written declaration that the President is unable to discharge the powers and duties of his office. Thereupon Congress shall decide the issue, assembling within forty-eight hours for that purpose if not in session. If the Congress, within twenty-one days after receipt of the latter written declaration, or, if Congress is not in session, within twenty-one days after Congress is required to assemble, determines by two-thirds vote of both Houses that the President is unable to discharge the powers and duties of his office, the Vice President shall continue to discharge the same as Acting President; otherwise, the President shall resume the powers and duties of his office.

This section deals with the circumstance in which a President will not be able to determine the fact of incapacity. To this point, Congress has not established the "such other body" referred to here. This section contains the only typographical error in the Constitution; in its second paragraph, the word "department" should in fact read "departments."

### 26TH AMENDMENT. *Right to Vote—Age*

SECTION 1. The right of citizens of the United States, who are eighteen years of age or older, to vote shall not be denied or abridged by the United States or by any State on account of age.

SECTION 2. The Congress shall have the power to enforce this article by appropriate legislation.

Proposed by Congress March 23, 1971; ratified July 1, 1971. This amendment provides that the minimum age for voting in any election in the United States cannot be more than 18 years. (A State may set a minimum voting age of less than 18, however.)

### 27TH AMENDMENT. *Congressional Pay*

No law varying the compensation for the services of the Senators and Representatives, shall take effect, until an election of Representatives shall have intervened.

Proposed by Congress September 25, 1789; ratified May 18, 1992. This amendment modified Article I, Section 6, Clause 1. It limits Congress' power to fix the salaries of its members—by delaying the effectiveness of any increase in that pay until after the next regular congressional election.

# HISTORICAL DOCUMENTS

## The Code of Hammurabi

The code of Hammurabi, believed to date before 1750 B.C., is a series of laws decreed by Hammurabi, the ruler of the city of Babylon when that ancient city was at the peak of its power. Inscribed on stone columns over seven feet high, these laws were intended to inform the people of what they could and could not do. They were written down and codified so that judges and administrators would have a uniform set of rules to follow in deciding disputes and imposing penalties for crimes. The Code consists of 280 sections that deal with such matters as land tenure, property rights, trade and commerce, family relations, and the administration of justice. Selected sections of the Code are excerpted below:

■ If a man practice (robbery) and be captured, that man shall be put to death. . . .

■ If a man has come forward in a lawsuit for the witnessing of false things, and has not proved the thing that he said, if that lawsuit is a capital case, that man shall be put to death. If he came forward for witnessing about corn or silver, he shall bear the penalty (which applies to) that case.

■ If a man has concealed in his house a lost slave or slave-girl belonging to the Palace or to a subject, and has not brought him (or her) out at the proclamation of the Crier, the owner of the house shall be put to death.

■ If a fire has broken out in a man's house, and a man who has gone to extinguish it has cast his eye on the property of the owner of the house and has taken the property of the owner of the house, that man shall be thrown into the fire.

■ If a man is subject to a debt bearing interest, and Adad (the Weather-god) has saturated his field or a high flood has carried (its crop) away, or because of lack of water he has not produced corn in that field, in that year he shall not return any corn to (his) creditor. He shall . . . not pay interest for that year.

■ If a man has donated field, orchard or house to his favourite heir and has written a sealed document for him (confirming this), after the father has gone to his doom, when the brothers share he (the favorite heir) shall take the gift that his father gave him, and apart from that they shall share equally in the property of the paternal estate.

■ If an artisan has taken a child for bringing up, and has taught him his manual skill, (the child) shall not be (re)claimed. If he has not taught him his manual skill, that pupil may return to his father's house.

■ If a man aid a male or female slave . . . to escape from the city gates, he shall be put to death . . . .

■ If a man be in debt and sell his wife, son, or daughter, or bind them over to service, for three years they shall work in the house of the purchaser or master; in the fourth year they shall be given their freedom. . . .

■ If a builder has made a house for a man but has not made his work strong, so that the house he made falls down and causes the death of the owner of the house, that builder shall be put to death. If it causes the death of the son of the owner of the house, they shall kill the son of the builder.

■ If a man would put away [divorce] his wife who has not borne him children, he shall give her money to the amount of her marriage settlement and he shall make good to her the dowry which she brought from her father's house and then he may put her away.

■ If a son has struck his father, they shall cut off his hand.

■ If a man has destroyed the eye of a man of the "gentleman" class, they shall destroy his eye. If he has broken a gentleman's bone, they shall break his bone. If he has destroyed the eye of a commoner or broken a bone of a commoner, he shall pay one mina (about $300) of silver. If he has destroyed the eye of a gentleman's slave, he shall pay half the slave's price.

■ If a gentleman's slave strikes the cheek of a man of the "gentleman" class, they shall cut off (the slave's) ear.

■ If a gentleman strikes a gentleman in a free fight and inflicts an injury on him, that man shall swear "I did not strike him deliberately," and he shall pay the surgeon.

# The Magna Carta

The Magna Carta (Great Charter) was wrested from King John by several barons of the realm, at Runnymede in 1215. One of the great documents of liberty, the Magna Carta rested on the feudal principle that the king and nobles had mutual contractual obligations. Its provisions limited the power of the crown and firmly planted the principle that the king, like other Englishmen, is subject to law. It became a symbol of political liberty and the foundation of constitutional government. Here are excerpts from 13 of its 63 articles:

1. That the English church shall be free, and shall have her rights entire, and her liberties inviolate; and we will that it be thus observed; and our will is that it be observed in good faith by our heirs forever.

2. We also have granted to all the freemen of our kingdom, for us and for our heirs forever, all the underwritten liberties, to be had and holden by them and their heirs, of us and our heirs forever. . . .

12. No scutage or aid shall be imposed in our kingdom, unless by the general council of our kingdom; except for ransoming our person, making our eldest son a knight and once for marrying our eldest daughter; and for these there shall be paid no more than a reasonable aid.

14. And for holding the general council of the kingdom concerning the assessment of aids, except in the three cases aforesaid, and for the assessing of scutage, we shall cause to be summoned the archbishops, bishops, abbots, earls, and greater barons of the realm, singly by our letters. And furthermore, we shall cause to be summoned generally, by our sheriffs and bailiffs all others who hold of us in chief, for a certain day, that is to say, forty days before their meeting at least, and to a certain place. And in all letters of such summons we will declare the cause of such summons. And summons being thus made, the business shall proceed on the day appointed, according to the advice of such as shall be present, although all that were summoned come not.

15. We will not in the future grant to any one that he may take aid of his own free tenants, except to ransom his body, and to make his eldest son a knight, and once to marry his eldest daughter; and for this there shall be paid only a reasonable aid. . . .

36. Nothing from henceforth shall be given or taken for a writ of inquisition of life or limb, but it shall be granted freely, and not denied. . . .

39. No freeman shall be taken or imprisoned, or diseised [deprived], or outlawed, or banished, or in any way destroyed, nor will we pass upon him, nor will we send upon him, unless by the lawful judgment of his peers, or by the law of the land.

40. We will sell to no man, we will not deny to any man, either justice or right.

41. All merchants shall have safe and secure conduct to go out of, and to come into, England, and to stay there and to pass as well by land as by water, for buying and selling by the ancient and allowed customs, without any unjust tolls, except in time of war, or when they are of any nation at war with us. . . .

42. It shall be lawful, for the time to come, for any one to go out of our kingdom and return safely and securely by land or by water, saving his allegiance to us (unless in time of war, by some short space, for the common benefit of the realm).

60. All the aforesaid customs and liberties, which we have granted to be holden in our kingdom, as much as it belongs to us, all people of our kingdom, as well clergy as laity, shall observe, as far as they are concerned, towards their dependents.

61. And whereas, for the honor of God and the amendment of our kingdom, and for the better quieting the discord that has arisen between us and our barons, we have granted all these things aforesaid. Willing to render them firm and lasting, we do give and grant our subjects the underwritten security, namely, that the barons may choose five and twenty barons of the kingdom, whom they think convenient, who shall take care, with all their might, to hold and observe, and cause to be observed, the peace and liberties we have granted them, and by this our present Charter confirmed. . . .

63. . . . It is also sworn, as well on our part as on the part of the barons, that all the things aforesaid shall be observed in good faith, and without evil duplicity. Given under our hand, in the presence of the witnesses above named, and many others, in the meadow called Runnymede, between Windsor and Staines, the 15th day of June, in the 17th year of our reign.

# Madison's *Notes*: Debate of June 6 on the Virginia Plan

James Madison's *Notes* enable readers today to gain a glimpse of the debates that took place behind closed doors at the Constitutional Convention held in Philadelphia in the summer of 1787. Excerpted here are portions of Madison's *Notes* on the debate of June 6 on the Virginia Plan's call for a bicameral (two house) legislature.

MR. PINCKNEY [S.C.], according to previous notice and rule obtained, moved "that the first branch of the national legislature be elected by the state legislatures, and not by the people," contending that the people were less fit judges in such a case, and that the legislatures would be less likely to promote the adoption of the new government if they were to be excluded from all share in it.

MR. RUTLEDGE [S.C.] seconded the motion.

MR. GERRY [MASS.]: Much depends on the mode of election. In England the people will probably lose their liberty from the smallness of the proportion having a right of suffrage. Our danger arises from the opposite extreme; hence in Massachusetts the worst men get into the legislature. Several members of that body had lately been convicted of infamous crimes. Men of indigence, ignorance, and baseness spare no pains, however dirty, to carry their point against men who are superior to the artifices practised. He was not disposed to run into extremes. He was as much principled as ever against aristocracy and monarchy. It was necessary, on the one hand, that the people should appoint one branch of the government in order to inspire them with the necessary confidence. . . . His idea was that the people should nominate certain persons in certain districts, out of whom the state legislatures should make the appointment.

MR. WILSON [PA.]: He wished for vigor in the government, but he wished that vigorous authority to flow immediately from the legitimate source of all authority. The government ought to possess not only, first, the *force* but, second, the *mind or sense* of the people at large. The legislature ought to be the most exact transcript of the whole society. Representation is made necessary only because it is impossible for the people to act collectively. . . .

MR. SHERMAN [CONN.]: If it were in view to abolish the state governments, the elections ought to be by the people. If the state governments are to be continued, it is necessary, in order to preserve harmony between the national and state governments, that the elections to the former should be made by the latter. The right of participating in the national government would be sufficiently secured to the people by their election of the state legislatures. The objects of the Union, he thought, were few: (1) defense against foreign danger; (2) against internal disputes and a resort to force; (3) treaties with foreign nations; (4) regulating foreign commerce and drawing revenue from it. These, and perhaps a few lesser objects, alone rendered a confederation of the states necessary. All other matters, civil and criminal, would be much better in the hands of the states. . . .

COLONEL MASON [VA.]: Under the existing Confederacy, Congress represent the *states,* not the *people* of the states; their acts operate on the *states,* not on the individuals. The case will be changed in the new plan of government. The people will be represented; they ought therefore to choose the representatives. The requisites in actual representation are that the representatives should sympathize with their constituents, should think as they think and feel as they feel, and that, for these purposes, [they] should even be residents among them. Much, he said, had been alleged against democratic elections. He admitted that much might be said; but it was to be considered that no government was free from imperfections and evils and that improper elections, in many instances, were inseparable from republican governments. . . .

MR. MADISON [VA.] considered an election of one branch, at least, of the legislature by the people immediately as a clear principle of free government, and that this mode, under proper regulations, had the additional advantage of securing better representatives as well as of avoiding too great an agency of the state governments in the general one. He differed from the member from Connecticut (Mr. Sherman) in thinking the objects mentioned to be all the principal ones that required a national government. Those were certainly important and necessary objects; but he combined with them the necessity of providing more effectually for the security of private rights and the steady dispensation of justice.

Interferences with these were evils which had more, perhaps, than anything else produced this Convention. Was it to be supposed that republican liberty could long exist under the abuses of it practised in some of the states? . . .

All civilized societies would be divided into different sects, factions, and interests, as they happened to consist of rich and poor, debtors and creditors, the landed, the manufacturing, the commercial interests, the inhabitants of this district or that district, the followers of this political leader or that political leader, the disciples of this religious sect or that religious sect. In all cases where a majority are united by a common interest or passion, the rights of the minority are in danger. What motives are to restrain them? . . .

Conscience, the only remaining tie, is known to be inadequate in individuals; in large numbers, little is to be expected from it. . . .

What has been the source of those unjust laws complained of among ourselves? Has it not been the real or supposed interest of the major number? Debtors have defrauded their creditors. The landed interest has borne hard on the mercantile interest. The holders of one species of property have thrown a disproportion of taxes on the holders of another species.

The lesson we are to draw from the whole is that where a majority are united by a common sentiment, and have an opportunity, the rights of the minor party become insecure. In a republican government the majority, if united, have always an opportunity. . . .

MR. DICKINSON [DEL.] considered it as essential that one branch of the legislature should be drawn immediately from the people and as expedient that the other should be chosen by the legislatures of the states. This combination of the state governments with the national government was as politic as it was unavoidable. In the formation of the Senate, we ought to carry it through such a refining process as will assimilate it as near as may be to the House of Lords in England. He repeated his warm eulogiums on the British constitution. He was for a strong national government but for leaving the states a considerable agency in the system. The objection against making the former dependent on the latter might be obviated by giving to the Senate an authority permanent and irrevocable for three, five, or seven years. Being thus independent, they will speak and decide with becoming freedom.

MR. READ [DEL.]: Too much attachment is betrayed to the state governments. We must look beyond their continuance. A national government must soon of necessity swallow all of them up. They will soon be reduced to the mere office of electing the national Senate. He was against patching up the old federal system; he hoped the idea would be dismissed. It would be like putting new cloth on an old garment. The Confederation was founded on temporary principles. It cannot last; it cannot be amended. If we do not establish a good government on new principles, we must either go to ruin or have the work to do over again. . . .

MR. PIERCE [GA.] was for an election by the people as to the first branch and by the states as to the second branch, by which means the citizens of the states would be represented both *individually* and *collectively*.

GENERAL PINCKNEY wished to have a good national government and at the same time to leave a considerable share of power in the states. An election of either branch by the people, scattered as they are in many states, particularly in South Carolina, was totally impracticable. He differed from gentlemen who thought that a choice by the people would be a better guard against bad measures than by the legislatures. . . .

The state legislatures also, he said, would be more jealous and more ready to thwart the national government if excluded from a participation in it. The idea of abolishing these legislatures would never go down.

MR. WILSON would not have spoken again but for what had fallen from Mr. Read; namely, that the idea of preserving the state governments ought to be abandoned. He saw no incompatibility between the national and state governments, provided the latter were restrained to certain local purposes; nor any probability of their being devoured by the former. . . .

On the question for electing the first branch by the state legislatures as moved by Mr. Pinckney, it was negatived.

# *The Federalist* No. 10
# (James Madison)

One of the 26 essays believed to have been written by James Madison, the tenth of *The Federalist* papers presents Madison's observations on dealing with the "mischiefs of factions" and the advantages of a republican (representative) form of government over that of a pure democracy. This essay was first published on November 23, 1787.

Among the numerous advantages promised by a well-constructed Union, none deserves to be more accurately developed than its tendency to break and control the violence of faction. The friend of popular governments never finds himself so much alarmed for their character and fate as when he contemplates their propensity to this dangerous vice. He will not fail, therefore, to set a due value on any plan which, without violating the principles to which he is attached, provides a proper cure for it. The instability, injustice, and confusion introduced into the public councils have, in truth, been the mortal diseases under which popular governments have everywhere perished; as they continue to be the favorite and fruitful topics from which the adversaries to liberty derive their most specious declamations.

The valuable improvements made by the American constitutions on the popular models, both ancient and modern, cannot certainly be too much admired; but it would be an unwarrantable partiality to contend that they have as effectually obviated the danger on this side, as was wished and expected. Complaints are everywhere heard from our most considerate and virtuous citizens, equally the friends of public and private faith, and of public and personal liberty, that our governments are too unstable, that the public good is disregarded in the conflicts of rival parties, and that measures are too often decided, not according to the rules of justice and the rights of the minor party, but by the superior force of an interested and overbearing majority. However anxiously we may wish that these complaints had no foundation, the evidence of known facts will not permit us to deny that they are in some degree true.

It will be found, indeed, on a candid review of our situation, that some of the distresses under which we labor have been erroneously charged on the operation of our governments; but it will be found, at the same time, that other causes will not alone account for many of our heaviest misfortunes; and, particularly, for that prevailing and increasing distrust of public engagements, and alarm for private rights, which are echoed from one end of the continent to the other. These must be chiefly, if not wholly, effects of the unsteadiness and injustice with which a factious spirit has tainted our public administrations.

By a faction, I understand a number of citizens, whether amounting to a majority or minority of the whole, who are united and actuated by some common impulse of passion, or of interest, adverse to the rights of other citizens, or to the permanent and aggregate interests of the community.

There are two methods of curing the mischiefs of faction: the one, by removing its causes; the other, by controlling its effects.

There are again two methods of removing the causes of faction: the one, by destroying the liberty which is essential to its existence; the other, by giving to every citizen the same opinions, the same passions, and the same interests.

It could never be more truly said than of the first remedy that it was worse than the disease. Liberty is to faction what air is to fire, an ailment without which it instantly expires. But it could not be less folly to abolish liberty, which is essential to political life, because it nourishes faction, than it would be to wish the annihilation of air, which is essential to animal life, because it imparts to fire its destructive agency.

The second expedient is as impracticable as the first would be unwise. As long as the reason of man continues fallible, and he is at liberty to exercise it, different opinions will be formed. As long as the connection subsists between his reason and his self-love, his opinions and his passions will have a reciprocal influence on each other; and the former will be objects to which the latter will attach themselves. The diversity in the faculties of men, from which the rights of property originate, is not less an insuperable obstacle to a uniformity of interests. The protection of these faculties is the first object of government. From the protection of different and unequal faculties of acquiring property, the possession of different degrees and kinds of property immediately results; and from the influence of these on the sentiments and views of the respective proprietors ensues a division of the society into different interests and parties.

The latent causes of faction are thus sown in the nature of man; and we see them everywhere brought into different degrees of activity, according to the different circumstances of civil society. A zeal for different opinions concerning religion, concerning government, and many other points, as well of speculation as of practice; an attachment of different leaders ambitiously contending for preeminence and power; or to persons of other descriptions whose fortunes have been interesting to the human passions, have, in turn, divided mankind into parties, inflamed them with mutual animosity, and rendered them much more disposed to vex and oppress each other than to cooperate for their common good. So strong is this propensity of mankind to fall into mutual animosities that, where no substantial occasion presents itself, the most frivolous and fanciful distinctions have been sufficient to kindle their unfriendly passions and excite their most violent conflicts. But the most common and durable source of factions has been the various and unequal distribution of property.

Those who hold and those who are without property have ever formed distinct interests in society. Those who are creditors and those who are debtors fall under a like discrimination. A landed interest, a manufacturing interest, a mercantile interest, a moneyed interest, with many lesser interests, grow up of necessity in civilized nations and divide them into different classes, actuated by different sentiments and views. The regulation of these various and interfering interests forms the principal task of modern legislation and involves the spirit of party and faction in the necessary and ordinary operations of the government.

No man is allowed to be a judge in his own cause, because his interest would certainly bias his judgment and, not improbably, corrupt his integrity. With equal, nay, with greater reason, a body of men are unfit to be both judges and parties at the same time; yet what are many of the most important acts of legislation but so many judicial determinations, not indeed concerning the rights of single persons, but concerning the rights of large bodies of citizens? And what are the different classes of legislators but advocates and parties to the causes which they determine? Is a law proposed concerning private debts? It is a question to which the creditors are parties on one side and the debtors on the other. Justice ought to hold the balance between them. Yet the parties are, and must be, themselves the judges; and the most numerous party or, in other words, the most powerful faction must be expected to prevail.

Shall domestic manufactures be encouraged, and in what degree, by restrictions on foreign manufactures? [These] are questions which would be differently decided by the landed and the manufacturing classes, and probably by neither with a sole regard to justice and the public good. The apportionment of taxes on the various descriptions of property is an act which seems to require the most exact impartiality; yet there is, perhaps, no legislative act in which greater opportunity and temptation are given to a predominant party to trample on the rules of justice. Every shilling with which they overburden the inferior number is a shilling saved to their own pockets.

It is in vain to say that enlightened statesmen will be able to adjust these clashing interests and render them all subservient to the public good. Enlightened statesmen will not always be at the helm. Nor, in many cases, can such an adjustment be made at all without taking into view indirect and remote considerations, which will rarely prevail over the immediate interest which one party may find in disregarding the rights of another or the good of the whole. The inference to which we are brought is that the *causes* of faction cannot be removed and that relief is only to be sought in the means of controlling its *effects*.

If a faction consists of less than a majority, relief is supplied by the republican principle, which enables the majority to defeat its sinister views by regular vote. It may clog the administration, it may convulse the society; but it will be unable to execute and mask its violence under the forms of the Constitution. When a majority is included in a faction, the form of popular government, on the other hand, enables it to sacrifice to its ruling passion or interest both the public good and the rights of other citizens. To secure the public good and private rights against the danger of such a faction, and at the same time to preserve the spirit and the form of popular government, is then the great object to which our inquiries are directed. Let me add that it is the great desideratum by which this form of government can be rescued from the opprobrium under which it has so long labored and be recommended to the esteem and adoption of mankind.

By what means is this object attainable? Evidently by one of two only. Either the existence of the same passion or interest in a majority at the same time must be prevented, or the majority, having such coexistent passion or interest, must be rendered, by their number and local situation, unable to concert and carry into effect schemes of oppression. If the impulse and the opportunity be suffered to coincide, we well know that neither moral nor religious motives can be relied on as an adequate control. They are not found to be such on the injustice and violence of individuals and lose their efficacy in proportion to the number combined together, that is, in proportion as their efficacy becomes needful.

From this view of the subject it may be concluded that a pure democracy, by which I mean a society consisting of a small number of citizens who assemble and administer the government in person, can admit of no cure for the mischiefs of faction. A common passion or interest will, in almost every case, be felt by a majority of the whole; a communication and concert result from the form of government itself; and there is nothing to check the inducements to sacrifice the weaker party or an obnoxious individual. Hence it is that such democracies have ever been spectacles of turbulence and contention; have ever been found incompatible with personal security or the rights of property; and have in general been as short in their lives as they have been violent in their deaths. Theoretic politicians, who have patronized this species of government, have erroneously supposed that by reducing mankind to a perfect equality in their political rights, they would, at the same time, be perfectly equalized and assimilated in their possessions, their opinions, and their passions.

A republic, by which I mean a government in which the scheme of representation takes place, opens a different prospect and promises the cure for which we are seeking. Let us examine the points in which it varies from pure democracy, and we shall comprehend both the nature of the cure and the efficacy which it must derive from the Union.

The two great points of difference between a democracy and a republic are: first, the delegation of the government, in the latter, to a small number of citizens elected by the rest; secondly, the greater number of citizens, and greater sphere of country, over which the latter may be extended.

The effect of the first difference is, on the one hand, to refine and enlarge the public views by passing them through the medium of a chosen body of citizens, whose wisdom may best discern the true interest of their country, and whose patriotism and love of justice will be least likely to sacrifice it to temporary or partial considerations. Under such a regulation, it may well happen that the public voice, pronounced by the representatives of the people, will be more consonant to the public good than if pronounced by the people themselves, convened for the purpose. On the other hand, the effect may be inverted. Men of factious tempers, of local prejudices, or of sinister designs may, by intrigue, by corruption, or by other means, first obtain the suffrages, and then betray the interests of the people. The question resulting is, whether small or extensive republics are more favorable to the election of proper guardians of the public weal; and it is clearly decided in favor of the latter by two obvious considerations:

In the first place, it is to be remarked that, however small the republic may be, the representatives must be raised to a certain number, in order to guard against the cabals of a few; and that, however large it may be, they must be limited to a certain number, in order to guard against the confusion of a multitude. Hence, the number of representatives in the two cases not being in proportion to that of the two constituents, and being proportionally greater in the small republic, it follows that, if the proportion of fit characters be not less in the large than in the small republic, the former will present a greater option, and consequently a greater probability of a fit choice.

In the next place, as each representative will be chosen by a greater number of citizens in the large than in the small republic, it will be more difficult for unworthy candidates to practice with success the vicious arts by which elections are too often carried; and the suffrages of the people being more free, will be more likely to center in men who possess the most attractive merit and the most diffusive and established character.

It must be confessed that in this, as in most other cases, there is a mean, on both sides of which inconveniences will be found to lie. By enlarging too much the number of electors, you render the representative too little acquainted with all their local circumstances and lesser interests; as by reducing it too much, you render him unduly attached to these and too little fit to comprehend and pursue great and national objects. The federal Constitution forms a happy combination in this respect: the great and aggregate interests being referred to the national, the local and particular to the state legislatures.

The other point of difference is the greater number of citizens and extent of territory which may be brought within the compass of republican than of democratic government; and it is this circumstance principally which renders factious combinations less to be dreaded in the former than in the latter. The smaller the society, the fewer probably will be the distinct parties and interests composing it; the fewer the distinct parties and interests, the more frequently will a majority be found of the same party; and the smaller the number of individuals composing a majority, and the smaller the compass within which they are placed, the more easily will they concert and execute their plans of oppression. Extend the sphere and you take in a greater variety of parties and interests; you make it less probable that a majority of the whole will have a common motive to invade the rights of other citizens; or if such a common motive exists, it will be more difficult for all who feel it to discover their own strength and to act in unison with each other. Besides other impediments, it may be remarked that, where there is a consciousness of unjust or dishonorable purposes, communication is always checked by distrust in proportion to the number whose concurrence is necessary.

Hence, it clearly appears that the same advantage which a republic has over a democracy, in controlling the effects of factions, is enjoyed by a large over a small republic—is enjoyed by the Union over the states composing it. Does the advantage consist in the substitution of representatives whose enlightened views and virtuous sentiments render them superior to local prejudices and to schemes of injustice? It will not be denied that the representation of the Union will be most likely to possess these requisite endowments. Does it consist in the greater security afforded by a greater variety of parties, against the event of any one party being able to outnumber and oppress the rest? In an equal degree does the increased variety of parties comprised within the Union increase this security? Does it, in fine, consist in the greater obstacles opposed to the concert and accomplishment of the secret wishes of an unjust and interested majority? Here, again, the extent of the Union gives it the most palpable advantage.

The influence of factious leaders may kindle a flame within their particular states but will be unable to spread a general conflagration through the other states. A religious sect may degenerate into a political faction in a part of the Confederacy; but the variety of sects dispersed over the entire face of it must secure the national councils against any danger from that source. A rage for paper money, for an abolition of debts, for an equal division of property, or for any other improper or wicked project will be less apt to pervade the whole body of the Union than a particular member of it; in the same proportion as such a malady is more likely to taint a particular county or district than an entire state.

In the extent, and proper structure of the Union, therefore, we behold a republican remedy for the diseases most incident to republican government. And according to the degree of pleasure and pride we feel in being republicans, ought to be our zeal in cherishing the spirit and supporting the character of Federalists.

# *The Federalist* No. 51
## (James Madison)

To what expedient, then, shall we finally resort, for maintaining in practice the necessary partition of power among the several departments as laid down in the Constitution? The only answer that can be given is that as all these exterior provisions are found to be inadequate the defect must be supplied, by so contriving the interior structure of the government as that its several constituent parts may, by their mutual relations, be the means of keeping each other in their proper places. Without presuming to undertake a full development of this important idea, I will hazard a few general observations which may perhaps place it in a clearer light, and enable us to form a more correct judgment of the principles and structure of the government planned by the convention.

In order to lay a due foundation for that separate and distinct exercise of the different powers of government, which to a certain extent is admitted on all hands to be essential to the preservation of liberty, it is evident that each department should have a will of its own; and consequently should be so constituted that the members of each should have as little agency as possible in the appointment of the members of the others. Were this principle rigorously adhered to, it would require that all the appointments for the supreme executive, legislative, and judiciary magistracies should be drawn from the same fountain of authority, the people, through channels having no communication whatever with one another. Perhaps such a plan of constructing the several departments would be less difficult in practice than it may in contemplation appear. Some difficulties, however, and some additional expense would attend the execution of it. Some deviations, therefore, from the principle must be admitted. In the constitution of the judiciary department in particular, it might be inexpedient to insist rigorously on the principle; first, because peculiar qualifications being essential in the members, the primary consideration ought to be to select that mode of choice which best secures these qualifications; second, because the permanent tenure by which the appointments are held in that department must soon destroy all sense of dependence on the authority conferring them.

It is equally evident that the members of each department should be as little dependent as possible on those of the others for the emoluments annexed to their offices. Were the executive magistrate, or the judges, not independent of the legislature in this particular, their independence in every other would be merely nominal.

But the great security against a gradual concentration of the several powers in the same department consists in giving to those who administer each department the necessary constitutional means and personal motives to resist encroachments of the others. The provision for defense must in this, as in all other cases, be made commensurate to the danger of attack. Ambition must be made to counteract ambition. The interest of the man must be connected with the constitutional rights of the place. It may be a reflection on human nature that such devices should be necessary to control the abuses of government. But what is government itself but the greatest of all reflections on human nature? If men were angels, no government would be necessary. If angels were to govern men, neither external nor internal controls on government would be necessary. In framing a government which is to be administered by men over men, the great difficulty lies in this: You must first enable the government to control the governed; and in the next place, oblige it to control itself. A dependence on the people is, no doubt, the primary control on the government; but experience has taught mankind the necessity of auxiliary precautions.

This policy of supplying, by opposite and rival interests, the defect of better motives might be traced through the whole system of human affairs, private as well as public. We see it particularly displayed in all the subordinate distributions of power; where the constant aim is to divide and arrange the several offices in such a manner as that each may be a check on the other—that the private interest of every individual may be a sentinel over the public rights. These inventions of prudence cannot be less requisite in the distribution of the supreme powers of the State.

But it is not possible to give to each department an equal power of self-defense. In republican government, the legislative authority necessarily predominates. The remedy for this inconveniency is to divide the legislature into different branches; and to render them, by different modes of election, and different principles of action, as little connected with each other as the nature of their common functions and their common dependence on the society will admit. It may even be necessary to guard against dangerous encroachments by still further precautions. As the weight of the legislative authority requires that it should be thus divided, the weakness of the executive may require, on the other hand, that it should be fortified. An absolute negative on the legislature appears, at first view, to be the natural defense with which the executive magistrate should be armed. But perhaps it would be neither altogether safe nor alone sufficient. On ordinary occasions it might not be exerted with the requisite firmness, and on extraordinary occasions it might be perfidiously abused. May not this defect of an absolute negative be supplied by some qualified connection between this weaker department and the weaker branch of the stronger department, by which the latter may be led to support the constitutional rights of the former, without being too much detached from the rights of its own department?

If the principles on which these observations are founded be just, as I persuade myself they are, and they be applied as a criterion to the several State constitutions, and to the federal Constitution, it will be found that if the latter does not perfectly correspond with them, the former are infinitely less able to bear such a test.

There are, moreover, two considerations particularly applicable to the federal system of America, which place that system in a very interesting point of view.

*First.* In a single republic, all the power surrendered by the people is submitted to the administration of a single government; and the usurpations are guarded against by a division of the government into distinct and separate departments. In the compound republic of America, the power surrendered by the people is first divided between two distinct governments, and then the portion allotted to each subdivided among distinct and separate departments. Hence a double security arises to the rights of the people. The different governments will control each other, at the same time that each will be controlled by itself.

*Second.* It is of great importance in a republic not only to guard the society against the oppression of its rulers, but to guard one part of the society against the injustice of the other part. Different interests necessarily exist in different classes of citizens. If a majority be united by a common interest, the rights of the minority will be insecure. There are but two methods of providing against this evil: The one by creating a will in the community independent of the majority—that is, of the society itself; the other, by comprehending in the society so many separate descriptions of citizens as will render an unjust combination of a majority of the whole very improbable, if not impracticable. The first method prevails in all governments possessing an hereditary or self appointed authority. This, at best, is but a precarious security; because a power independent of the society may as well espouse the unjust views of the major as the rightful interests of the minor party, and may possibly be turned against both parties. The second method will be exemplified in the federal republic of the United States. While all authority in it will be derived from and dependent on the society, the society itself will be broken into so many parts, interests, and classes of citizens, that the rights of individuals, or of the minority, will be in little danger from interested combinations of the majority. In a free government the security for civil rights must be the same as that for religious rights. It consists in the one case in the multiplicity of interests, and in the other in the multiplicity of sects. The degree of security in both cases will depend on the number of interests and sects; and this may be presumed to depend on the extent of country and number of people comprehended under the same government. This view of the subject must particularly recommend a proper federal system to all the sincere and considerate friends of republican government, since it shows that in exact proportion as the territory of the Union may be formed into more circumscribed Confederacies, or States, oppressive combinations of a majority will be facilitated: the best security, under the republican forms, for the rights of every class of citizens, will be diminished; and consequently, the stability and independence of some member of the government, the only other security, must be proportionally increased. Justice is the end of government. It is the end of civil society. It ever has been and ever will be pursued until it be obtained, or until liberty be lost in the pursuit. In a society under the forms of which the stronger faction can readily unite and oppress the weaker, anarchy may as truly be said to reign as in a state of nature, where the weaker individual is not secured against the violence of the stronger: And as, in the latter state, even the stronger individuals are prompted, by the uncertainty of their condition to submit to a government which may protect the weak as well as themselves. So, in the former state, will the more powerful factions or parties be gradually induced, by a like motive, to wish for a government which will protect all parties, the weaker as well as the more powerful. It can be little doubted that if the State of Rhode Island was separated from the Confederacy and left to itself, the insecurity of rights under the popular form of government within such narrow limits would be displayed by such reiterated oppressions of factious majorities that some power altogether independent of the people would soon be called for by the voice of the very factions whose misrule had proved the necessity of it. In the extended republic of the United States, and among the great variety of interests, parties, and sects which it embraces, a coalition of a majority of the whole society could seldom take place on any other principles than those of justice and the general good; and there being thus less danger to a minor from the will of the major party, there must be less pretext, also, to provide for the security of the former, by introducing into the government a will not dependent on the latter; or, in other words, a will independent of the society itself. It is no less certain that it is important, notwithstanding the contrary opinions which have been entertained, that the larger the society, provided it lie within a practicable sphere, the more duly capable it will be of self-government. And happily for the *republican cause*, the practicable sphere may be carried to a very great extent by a judicious modification and mixture of the *federal principle*.

# *The Federalist* No. 78
## (Alexander Hamilton)

We proceed now to an examination of the judiciary department of the proposed government. In unfolding the defects of the existing Confederation, the utility and necessity of a federal judicature have been clearly pointed out. It is the less necessary to recapitulate the considerations there urged as the propriety of the institution in the abstract is not disputed; the only questions which have been raised being relative to the manner of constituting it, and to its extent. To these points, therefore, our observations shall be confined.

The manner of constituting it seems to embrace these several objects: 1st. The mode of appointing the judges. 2nd. The tenure by which they are to hold their places. 3rd. The partition of the judiciary authority between different courts and their relations to each other.

*First*. As to the mode of appointing the judges: this is the same with that of appointing the officers of the Union in general and has been so fully discussed in the two last numbers that nothing can be said here which would not be useless repetition.

*Second*. As to the tenure by which the judges are to hold their places: this chiefly concerns their duration in office, the provisions for their support, the precautions for their responsibility.

According to the plan of the convention, all judges who may be appointed by the United States are to hold their offices *during good behavior*, which is conformable to the most approved of the State constitutions, and among the rest, to that of this State. Its propriety having been drawn into question by the adversaries of that plan is no light symptom of the rage for objection which disorders their imaginations and judgments. The standard of good behavior for the continuance in office of the judicial magistracy is certainly one of the most valuable of the modern improvements in the practice of government. In a monarchy it is an excellent barrier to the despotism of the prince; in a republic it is a no less excellent barrier to the encroachments and oppressions of the representative body. And it is the best expedient which can be devised in any government to secure a steady, upright, and impartial administration of the laws.

Whoever attentively considers the different departments of power must perceive that, in a government in which they are separated from each other, the judiciary, from the nature of its functions, will always be the least dangerous to the political rights of the Constitution; because it will be least in a capacity to annoy or injure them. The executive not only dispenses the honors but holds the sword of the community. The legislature not only commands the purse but prescribes the rules by which the duties and rights of every citizen are to be regulated. The judiciary, on the contrary, has no influence over either the sword or the purse; no direction either of the strength or of the wealth of the society, and can take no active resolution whatever. It may truly be said to have neither FORCE nor WILL but merely judgment; and must ultimately depend upon the aid of the executive arm even for the efficacy of its judgments.

This simple view of the matter suggests several important consequences. It proves incontestably that the judiciary is beyond comparison the weakest of the three departments of power; that it can never attack with success either of the other two; and that all possible care is requisite to enable it to defend itself against their attacks. It equally proves that though individual oppression may now and then proceed from the courts of justice, the general liberty of the people can never be endangered from that quarter; I mean so long as the judiciary remains truly distinct from both the legislature and the executive. For I agree that "there is no liberty if the power of judging be not separated from the legislative and executive powers." And it proves, in the last place, that as liberty can have nothing to fear from the judiciary alone, but would have everything to fear from its union with either of the other departments; that as all the effects of such a union must ensue from a dependence of the former on the latter, notwithstanding a nominal and apparent separation; that as, from the natural feebleness of the judiciary, it is in continual jeopardy of being overpowered, awed, or influenced by its coordinate branches; and that as nothing can contribute so much to its firmness and independence as permanency in office, this quality may therefore be justly regarded as an indispensable ingredient in its constitution, and, in a great measure, as the citadel of the public justice and the public security.

The complete independence of the courts of justice is peculiarly essential in a limited Constitution. By a limited Constitution, I understand one which contains certain specified exceptions to the legislative authority; such, for instance, as that it shall pass no bills of attainder, no *ex post facto* laws, and the like. Limitations of this kind can be preserved in practice no other way than through the medium of courts of justice, whose duty it must be to declare all acts contrary to the manifest tenor of the Constitution void. Without this, all the reservations of particular rights or privileges would amount to nothing.

Some perplexity respecting the rights of the courts to pronounce legislative acts void, because contrary to the Constitution, has arisen from an imagination that the doctrine would imply a superiority of the judiciary to the legislative power. It is urged that the authority which can declare the acts of another void must necessarily be superior to the one whose acts may be declared void. As this doctrine is of great importance in all the American constitutions, a brief discussion of the grounds on which it rests cannot be unacceptable.

There is no position which depends on clearer principles than that every act of a delegated authority, contrary to the tenor of the commission under which it is exercised, is void. No legislative act, therefore, contrary to the Constitution, can be valid. To deny this would be to affirm that the deputy is greater than his principal; that the servant is above his master; that the representatives of the people are superior to the people themselves; that men acting by virtue of powers may do not only what their powers do not authorize, but what they forbid.

If it be said that the legislative body are themselves the constitutional judges of their own powers and that the construction they put upon them is conclusive upon the other departments, it may be answered that this cannot be the natural presumption where it is not to be collected from any particular provisions in the Constitution. It is not otherwise to be supposed that the Constitution could intend to enable the representatives of the people to substitute their *will* to that of their constituents. It is far more rational to suppose that the courts were designed to be an intermediate body between the people and the legislature in order, among other things, to keep the latter within the limits assigned to their authority. The interpretation of the laws is the proper and peculiar province of the courts. A constitution is, in fact, and must be regarded by the judges as, a fundamental law. It therefore belongs to them to ascertain its meaning as well as the meaning of any particular act proceeding from the legislative body. If there should happen to be an irreconcilable variance between the two, that which has the superior obligation and validity ought, of course, to be preferred; or, in other words, the Constitution ought to be preferred to the statute, the intention of the people to the intention of their agents.

Nor does this conclusion by any means suppose a superiority of the judicial to the legislative power. It only supposes that the power of the people is superior to both, and that where the will of the legislature, declared in its statutes, stands in opposition to that of the people, declared in the Constitution, the judges ought to be governed by the latter rather than the former. They ought to regulate their decisions by the fundamental laws rather than by those which are not fundamental.

This exercise of judicial discretion in determining between two contradictory laws is exemplified in a familiar instance. It not uncommonly happens that there are two statutes existing at one time, clashing in whole or in part with each other and neither of them containing any repealing clause or expression. In such a case, it is the province of the courts to liquidate and fix their meaning and operation. So far as they can, by any fair construction, be reconciled to each other, reason and law conspire to dictate that this should be done; where this is impracticable, it becomes a matter of necessity to give effect to one in exclusion of the other. The rule which has obtained in the courts for determining their relative validity is that the last in order of time shall be preferred to the first. But this is a mere rule of construction, not derived from any positive law but from the nature and reason of the thing. It is a rule not enjoined upon the courts by legislative provision but adopted by themselves, as consonant to truth and propriety, for the direction of their conduct as interpreters of the law. They thought it reasonable that between the interfering acts of an *equal* authority that which was the last indication of its will should have the preference.

But in regard to the interfering acts of a superior and subordinate authority of an original and derivative power, the nature and reason of the thing indicate the converse of that rule as proper to be followed. They teach us that the prior act of a superior ought to be preferred to the subsequent act of an inferior and subordinate authority; and that accordingly, whenever a particular statute contravenes the Constitution, it will be the duty of the judicial tribunals to adhere to the latter and disregard the former.

It can be of no weight to say that the courts, on the pretense of a repugnancy, may substitute their own pleasure to the constitutional intentions of the legislature. This might as well happen in the case of two contradictory statutes; or it might as well happen in every adjudication upon any single statute. The courts must declare the sense of the law; and if they should be disposed to exercise WILL instead of JUDGMENT, the consequence would equally be the substitution of their pleasure to that of the legislative body. The observation, if it prove anything, would prove that there ought to be no judges distinct from that body.

If, then, the courts of justice are to be considered as the bulwarks of a limited Constitution against legislative encroachments, this consideration will afford a strong argument for the permanent tenure of judicial offices, since nothing will contribute so much as this to that independent spirit in the judges which must be essential to the faithful performance of so arduous a duty.

This independence of the judges is equally requisite to guard the Constitution and the rights of individuals from the effects of those ill humors which the arts of designing men, or the influence of particular conjunctures, sometimes disseminate among the people themselves, and which, though they speedily give place to better information, and more deliberate reflection, have a tendency, in the meantime, to occasion dangerous innovations in the government, and serious oppressions of the minor party in the community. Though I trust the friends of the proposed Constitution will never concur with its enemies in questioning that fundamental principle of Republican government which admits the right of the people to alter or abolish the established Constitution whenever they find it inconsistent with their happiness; yet it is not to be inferred from this principle that the representatives of the people, whenever a momentary inclination happens to lay hold of a majority of their constituents incompatible with the provisions in the existing Constitution would, on that account, be justifiable in a violation of those provisions; or that the courts would be under a greater obligation to connive at infractions in this shape than when they had proceeded wholly from the cabals of the representative body. Until the people have, by some solemn and authoritative act, annulled or changed the established form, it is binding upon themselves collectively, as well as individually; and no presumption, or even knowledge of their sentiments, can warrant their representatives in a departure from it prior to such an act. But it is easy to see that it would require an uncommon portion of fortitude in the judges to do their duty as faithful guardians of the Constitution, where legislative invasions of it had been instigated by the major voice of the community.

But it is not with a view to infractions of the Constitution only that the independence of the judges may be an essential safeguard against the effects of occasional ill humors in the society. These sometimes extend no farther than to the injury of the private rights of particular classes of citizens, by unjust and partial laws. Here also the firmness of the judicial magistracy is of vast importance in mitigating the severity and confining the operation of such laws. It not only serves to moderate the immediate mischiefs of those which may have been passed but it operates as a check upon the legislative body in passing them; who, perceiving that obstacles to the success of iniquitous intention are to be expected from the scruples of the courts, are in a manner compelled, by the very motives of the injustice they mediate, to qualify their attempts. This is a circumstance calculated to have more influence upon the character of our governments than but few may be aware of. The benefits of the integrity and moderation of the judiciary have already been felt in more States than one; and though they may have displeased those whose sinister expectations they may have disappointed, they must have commanded the esteem and applause of all the virtuous and disinterested. Considerate men of every description ought to prize whatever will tend to beget or fortify that temper in the courts; as no man can be sure that he may not be tomorrow the victim of a spirit of injustice, by which he may be a gainer today. And every man must now feel that the inevitable tendency of such a spirit is to sap the foundations of public and private confidence and to introduce in its stead universal distrust and distress.

That inflexible and uniform adherence to the rights of the Constitution, and of individuals, which we perceive to be indispensable in the courts of justice, can certainly not be expected from judges who hold their offices by a temporary commission. Periodical appointments, however regulated, or by whomsoever made, would, in some way or other, be fatal to their necessary independence. If the power of making them was committed either to the executive or legislature there would be danger of an improper complaisance to the branch which possessed it; if to both, there would be an unwillingness to hazard the displeasure of either; if to the people, or to persons chosen by them for the special purpose, there would be too great a disposition to consult popularity to justify a reliance that nothing would be consulted but the Constitution and the laws.

There is yet a further and a weighty reason for the permanency of the judicial offices which is deducible from the nature of the qualifications they require. It has been frequently remarked with great propriety that a voluminous code of laws is one of the inconveniences necessarily connected with the advantages of a free government. To avoid an arbitrary discretion in the courts, it is indispensable that they should be bound down by strict rules and precedents which serve to define and point out their duty in every particular case that comes before them; and it will readily be conceived from the variety of controversies which grow out of the folly and wickedness of mankind that the records of those precedents must unavoidably swell to a very considerable bulk and must demand long and laborious study to acquire a competent knowledge of them. Hence it is that there can be but few men in the society who will have sufficient skill in the laws to qualify them for the stations of judges. And making the proper deductions for the ordinary depravity of human nature, the number must be still smaller of those who unite the requisite integrity with the requisite knowledge. These considerations apprise us that the government can have no great option between fit characters; and that a temporary duration in office which would naturally discourage such characters from quitting a lucrative line of practice to accept a seat on the bench would have a tendency to throw the administration of justice into hands less able and less well qualified to conduct it with utility and dignity. In the present circumstances of this country and in those in which it is likely to be for a long time to come, the disadvantages on this score would be greater than they may at first sight appear; but it must be confessed that they are far inferior to those which present themselves under the other aspects of the subject.

Upon the whole, there can be no room to doubt that the convention acted wisely in copying from the models of those constitutions which have established *good behavior* as the tenure of their judicial offices, in point of duration; and that so far from being blamable on this account, their plan would have been inexcusably defective if it had wanted this important feature of good government. The experience of Great Britain affords an illustrious comment on the excellence of the institution.

# Anti-Federalist Responses: Arguments Against the Adoption of the Constitution

When the Constitutional Convention of 1787 produced the new Constitution, many thoughtful, patriotic people from all over the country opposed its adoption. These Anti-Federalists, as they were known, had a number of objections to the Constitution. Five of their most significant objections were these: (1) The new Constitution was a document written by and for the primary benefit of a wealthy and powerful aristocracy. (2) The Constitution lacked a bill of rights. (3) The Constitutional Convention was not authorized to do anything but amend the Articles of Confederation; therefore, the Constitution was an illegal document. (4) States would be wholly subordinate to the new National Government and lose their sovereignty. (5) The powers given to the new United States Government were so extensive as to lead inevitably to tyranny and despotism. The following documents provide a sampling of Anti-Federalist arguments.

## Richard Henry Lee

Lee from Virginia wrote the best-known Anti-Federalist essays of the time, "Letters from the Federal Farmer to the Republican." These excerpts are from these letters written in October 1787.

The present moment discovers a new face in our affairs. Our object has been all along to reform our federal system and to strengthen our governments—to establish peace, order, and justice in the community—but a new object now presents. The plan of government now proposed is evidently calculated totally to change, in time, our condition as a people. Instead of being thirteen republics under a federal head, it is clearly designed to make us one consolidated government. . . . This consolidation of the states has been the object of several men in this country for some time past. Whether such a change can ever be effected, in any manner; whether it can be effected without convulsions and civil wars; whether such a change will not totally destroy the liberties of this country, time only can determine. . . .

The Confederation was formed when great confidence was placed in the voluntary exertions of individuals and of the respective states; and the framers of it, to guard against usurpation, so limited and checked the powers that, in many respects, they are inadequate to the exigencies of the Union. We find, therefore, members of Congress urging alterations in the federal system almost as soon as it was adopted. . . .

We expected too much from the return of peace, and, of course, we have been disappointed. Our governments have been new and unsettled; and several legislature, [by their actions] . . . have given just cause of uneasiness. . . .

The conduct of several legislatures touching paper-money and tender laws has prepared many honest men for changes in government, which otherwise they would not have thought of—when by the evils, on the one hand, and by the secret instigations of artful men, on the other, the minds of men were become sufficiently uneasy, a bold step was taken, which is usually followed by a revolution or a civil war. A general convention for mere commercial purposes was moved for—the authors of this measure saw that the people's attention was turned solely to the amendment of the federal system; and that, had the idea of a total change been started, probably no state would have appointed members to the Convention. The idea of destroying, ultimately, the state government and forming one consolidated system could not have been admitted. A convention, therefore, merely for vesting in Congress power to regulate trade was proposed. . . .

The plan proposed appears to be partly federal, but principally, however, calculated ultimately to make the states one consolidated government.

The first interesting question therefore suggested is how far the states can be consolidated into one entire government on free principles. In considering this question, extensive objects are to be taken into view, and important changes in the forms of government to be carefully attended to in all their consequences. The happiness of the people at large must be the great object with every honest statesman, and he will direct every movement to this point. If we are so situated as a people as not to be able to enjoy equal happiness and advantages under one government, the consolidation of the states cannot be admitted.

\* \* \*

There are certain unalienable and fundamental rights, which in forming the social compact ought to be explicitly ascertained and fixed. A free and enlightened people, in forming this compact, will not resign all their rights to those who govern, and they will fix limits [a bill of rights] to their legislators and rulers, which will soon be plainly seen by those who are governed, as well as by those who govern; and the latter will know they cannot be passed unperceived by the former and without giving a general alarm. These rights should be made the basis of every constitution; and if a people be so situated, or have such different opinions, that they cannot agree in ascertaining and fixing them, it is a very strong argument against their attempting to form one entire society, to live under one system of laws only.

* * *

It may also be worthy our examination how far the provision for amending this plan, when it shall be adopted, is of any importance. No measures can be taken toward amendments unless two-thirds of the Congress, or two-thirds of the legislature of the several states, shall agree. While power is in the hands of the people, or democratic part of the community, more especially as at present, it is easy, according to the general course of human affairs, for the few influential men in the community to obtain conventions, alterations in government, and to persuade the common people that they may change for the better, and to get from them a part of the power. But when power is once transferred from the many to the few, all changes become extremely difficult; the government in this case being beneficial to the few, they will be exceedingly artful and adroit in preventing any measures which may lead to a change; and nothing will produce it but great exertions and severe struggles on the part of the common people. Every man of reflection must see that the change now proposed is a transfer of power from the many to the few, and the probability is the artful and ever active aristocracy will prevent all peaceful measures for changes, unless when they shall discover some favorable moment to increase their own influence.

* * *

It is true there may be danger in delay; but there is danger in adopting the system in its present form. And I see the danger in either case will arise principally from the conduct and views of two very unprincipled parties in the United States—two fires, between which the honest and substantial people have long found themselves situated. One party is composed of little insurgents, men in debt, who want no law and who want a share of the property of others—these are called levelers, Shayites, etc. The other party is composed of a few but more dangerous men, with their servile dependents; these avariciously grasp at all power and property. You may discover in all the actions of these men an evident dislike to free and equal government, and they will go systematically to work to change, essentially, the forms of government in this country—these are called aristocrats. . . .

. . . The fact is, these aristocrats support and hasten the adoption of the proposed Constitution merely because they think it is a stepping-stone to their favorite object. I think I am well-founded in this idea; I think the general politics of these men support it, as well as the common observation among them that the proffered plan is the best that can be got at present; it will do for a few years, and lead to something better. . . .

## Luther Martin

Martin, the leading Anti-Federalist from Maryland, attended the Constitutional Convention as a delegate. In this excerpt from a speech before the Maryland State legislature on November 29, 1787, he defends his decision to leave the Convention before its work was finished.

It was the states as states, by their representatives in Congress, that formed the Articles of Confederation; it was the states as states, by their legislatures, who ratified those Articles; and it was there established and provided that the states as states (that is, by their legislatures) should agree to any alterations that should hereafter be proposed in the federal government, before they should be binding; and any alterations agreed to in any other manner cannot release the states from the obligation they are under to each other by virtue of the original Articles of Confederation. The people of the different states never made any objection to the manner in which the Articles of Confederation were formed or ratified, or to the mode by which alterations were to be made in that government—with the rights of their respective states they wished not to interfere. Nor do I believe the people, in their individual capacity, would ever have expected or desired to have been appealed to on the present occasion, in violation of the rights of their respective states, if the favorers of the proposed Constitution, imagining they had a better chance of forcing it to be adopted by a hasty appeal to the people at large (who could not be so good judges of the dangerous consequence), had not insisted upon this mode . . . .

It was also my opinion that, upon principles of sound policy, the agreement or disagreement to the proposed system ought to have been by the state legislatures; in which case, let the event have been what it would, there would have been but little prospect of the public peace being disturbed thereby; whereas the attempt to force down this system, although Congress and the respective state legislatures should disapprove, by appealing to the people and to procure its establishment in a manner totally unconstitutional, has a tendency to set the state governments and their subjects at variance with each other, to lessen the obligations of government, to weaken the bands of society, to introduce anarchy and confusion, and to light the torch of discord and civil war throughout this continent. All these considerations weighed with me most forcibly against giving my assent to the mode by which it is resolved that this system is to be ratified, and were urged by me in opposition to the measure.

. . . [A] great portion of that time which ought to have been devoted calmly and impartially to consider what alterations in our federal government would be most likely to procure and preserve the happiness of the Union was employed in a violent struggle on the one side to obtain all power and dominion in their own hands, and on the other to prevent it; and that the aggrandizement of particular states, and particular individuals, appears to have been much more the subject sought after than the welfare of our country . . . .

When I took my seat in the Convention, I found them attempting to bring forward a system which, I was sure, never had entered into the contemplation of those I had the honor to represent, and which, upon the fullest consideration, I considered not only injurious to the interest and rights of this state but also incompatible with the political happiness and freedom of the states in general. From that time until my business compelled me to leave the Convention, I gave it every possible opposition, in every stage of its progression. I opposed the system there with the same explicit frankness with which I have here given you a history of our proceedings, an account of my own conduct, which in a particular manner I consider you as having a right to know. While there, I endeavored to act as became a freeman and the delegate of a free state. Should my conduct obtain the approbation of those who appointed me, I will not deny it would afford me satisfaction; but to me that approbation was at most no more than a secondary consideration—my first was to deserve it. Left to myself to act according to the best of my discretion, my conduct should have been the same had I been even sure your censure would have been my only reward, since I hold it sacredly my duty to dash the cup of poison, if possible, from the hand of a state or an individual, however anxious the one or the other might be to swallow it . . . .

## William Findley, Robert Whitehill, and John Smilie

Findley, Whitehill, and Smilie—who were delegates to the Pennsylvania State convention—believed that they and other opponents of the Constitution were prevented from expressing their views because of the political maneuverings of the Federalists. This excerpt is from "The Address and Reasons of Dissent of the Minority of the Convention of the State of Pennsylvania to their Constituents," which the three men published in the *Pennsylvania Packet and Daily Advertiser* on December 18, 1787.

The Continental Convention met in the city of Philadelphia at the time appointed. It was composed of some men of excellent character; of others who were more remarkable for their ambition and cunning than their patriotism; and of some who had been opponents to the independence of the United States. The delegates from Pennsylvania were, six of them, uniform and decided opponents to the constitution of the commonwealth

[the Articles of Confederation]. The convention sat upward of four months. The doors were kept shut, and the members brought under the most solemn engagements of secrecy. Some of those who opposed their going so far beyond their powers, retired, hopeless, from the convention; others had the firmness to refuse signing the plan altogether; and many who did sign it, did it not as a system they wholly approved but as the best that could be then obtained; and notwithstanding the time spent on this subject, it is agreed on all hands to be a work of haste and accommodation. . . .

Our objections are comprised under three general heads of dissent, viz.:

We dissent, first, because it is the opinion of the most celebrated writers on government, and confirmed by uniform experience, that a very extensive territory cannot be governed on the principles of freedom otherwise than by a confederation of republics, possessing all the powers of internal government but united in the management of their general and foreign concerns. . . .

We dissent, secondly, because the powers vested in Congress by this Constitution must necessarily annihilate and absorb the legislative, executive, and judicial powers of the several states, and produce from their ruins one consolidated government, which from the nature of things will be *an iron-handed despotism*, as nothing short of the supremacy of despotic sway could connect and govern these United States under one government.

As the truth of this position is of such decisive importance, it ought to be fully investigated, and if it is founded, to be clearly ascertained; for, should it be demonstrated that the powers vested by this Constitution in Congress will have such an effect as necessarily to produce one consolidated government, the question then will be reduced to this short issue, viz.: whether satiated with the blessings of liberty, whether repenting of the folly of so recently asserting their unalienable rights against foreign despots at the expense of so much blood and treasure, and such painful and arduous struggles, the people of America are now willing to resign every privilege of freemen, and submit to the dominion of an absolute government that will embrace all America in one chain of despotism; or whether they will, with virtuous indignation, spurn at the shackles prepared for them, and confirm their liberties by a conduct becoming freemen. . . .

We dissent, thirdly, because if it were practicable to govern so extensive a territory as these United States include, on the plan of a consolidated government, consistent with the principles of liberty and the happiness of the people, yet the construction of this Constitution is not calculated to attain the object; for independent of the nature of the case, it would of itself necessarily produce a despotism, and that not by the usual gradations but with the celerity that has hitherto only attended revolutions effected by the sword.

To establish the truth of this position, a cursory investigation of the principles and form of this Constitution will suffice.

The first consideration that this review suggests is the omission of a Bill of Rights ascertaining and fundamentally establishing those unalienable and personal rights of men, without the full, free, and secure enjoyment of which there can be no liberty, and over which it is not necessary for a good government to have the control—the principal of which are the rights of conscience, personal liberty by the clear and unequivocal establishment of the writ of habeas corpus, jury trial in criminal and civil cases, by an impartial jury of the vicinage or county, with the common law proceedings for the safety of the accused in criminal prosecutions; and the liberty of the press, that scourge of tyrants, and the grand bulwark of every other liberty and privilege. The stipulations heretofore made in favor of them in the state constitutions are entirely superseded by this Constitution. . . .

## Anonymous

*This excerpt is from an essay that appeared in the* Boston Gazette and the Country Journal *on November 26, 1787. Its anonymous author used the misleading pen name, "A Federalist."*

I am pleased to see a spirit of inquiry burst the band of constraint upon the subject of the new plan for consolidating the governments of the United States as recommended by the late Convention. If it is suitable to the genius and habits of the citizens of these states, it will bear the strictest scrutiny. The people are the grand inquest who have a right to judge of its merits. The hideous demon of aristocracy has hitherto had so much influence as to bar the channels of investigation, preclude the people from inquiry, and extinguish every spark of liberal information of its qualities.

. . . Those furious zealots who are for cramming it [the Constitution] down the throats of the people without allowing them either time or opportunity to scan or weigh it in the balance of their understandings bear the same marks in their features as those who have been long wishing to erect an aristocracy in this commonwealth. Their menacing cry is for a rigid government; it matters little to them of what kind, provided it answers that description.

As the plan now offered comes something near their wishes, and is the most consonant to their views of any they can hope for, they come boldly forward and demand its adoption. They brand with infamy every man who is not as determined and zealous in its favor as themselves. They cry aloud the whole must be swallowed or none at all, thinking thereby to preclude any amendment; they are afraid of having it abated of its present rigid aspect. They have striven to overawe or seduce printers to stifle and obstruct a free discussion, and have endeavored to hasten it to a decision before the people can duly reflect upon its properties.

In order to deceive them, they incessantly declare that none can discover any defect in the system but bankrupts who wish no government, and officers of the present government who fear to lose a part of their power. These zealous partisans may injure their own cause, and endanger the public tranquility by impeding a proper inquiry; the people may suspect the whole to be a dangerous plan, from such covered and designing schemes to enforce it upon them. Compulsive or treacherous measures to establish any government whatever will always excite jealousy among a free people. Better remain single and alone than blindly adopt whatever a few individuals shall demand, be they ever so wise. I had rather be a free citizen of the small republic of Massachusetts than an oppressed subject of the great American empire. Let all act understandingly or not at all. . . .

It will first be allowed that many undesigning citizens may wish its adoption from the best motives, but these are modest and silent when compared to the greater number who endeavor to suppress all attempts for investigation. These violent partisans are for having the people gulp down the gilded pill blindfolded, whole and without any qualification whatever. These consist generally of the noble order of Cincinnatus, holders of public securities, men of great wealth and expectations of public office, bankers and lawyers. These, with their train of dependents, form the aristocratic combination. The lawyers in particular keep up an incessant declamation for its adoption; like greedy gudgeons they long to satiate their voracious stomachs with the golden bait. The numerous tribunals to be erected by the new plan of consolidated empire will find employment for ten times their present numbers; these are the loaves and fishes for which they hunger. They will probably find it suited to their habits, if not to the habits of the people. . . .

# Articles of Confederation

In force from March 1, 1781 to March 4, 1789

To all to whom these Presents shall come, we the undersigned Delegates of the States affixed to our Names send greeting. Whereas the Delegates of the United States of America in Congress assembled did on the fifteenth day of November in the Year of our Lord One Thousand Seven Hundred and Seventy seven, and in the Second Year of the Independence of America agree to certain articles of Confederation an perpetual Union between tne States of Newhampshire, Massachusetts-bay, Rhode-island and Providence Plantations, Connecticut, New York, New Jersey, Pennsylvania, Delaware, Maryland, Virginia, North-Carolina, South-Carolina and Georgia in the Words following, viz. "Articles of Confederation and perpetual Union between the states of Newhampshire, Massachusetts-bay, Rhode-island and Providence Plantations, Connecticut, New-York, New-Jersey, Pennsylvania, Delaware, Maryland, Virginia, North-Carolina, South-Carolina and Georgia.

[ART. I.] The Stile of this confederacy shall be "The United States of America."

[ART. II.] Each state retains its sovereignty, freedom and independence, and every Power, Jurisdiction and right, which is not by this confederation expressly delegated to the United States, in Congress assembled.

[ART. III.] The said states hereby severally enter into a firm league of friendship with each other, for their common defence, the security of their Liberties, and their mutual and general welfare, binding themselves to assist each other, against all force offered to, or attacks made upon them, or any of them, on account of religion, sovereignty, trade, or any other pretence whatever.

[ART. IV.] The better to secure and perpetuate mutual friendship and intercourse among the people of the different states in this union, the free inhabitants of each of these states, paupers, vagabonds and fugitives from Justice excepted, shall be entitled to all privileges and immunities of free citizens in the several states; and the people of each state shall have free ingress and regress to and from any other state, and shall enjoy therein all the privileges of trade and commerce, subject to the same duties, impositions and restrictions as the inhabitants thereof respectively, provided that such restriction shall not extend so far as to prevent the removal of property imported into any state, to any other state of which the Owner is an inhabitant; provided also that no imposition, duties or restriction shall be laid by any state, on the property of the united states, or either of them.

If any Person guilty of, or charged with treason, felony, or other high misdemeanor in any state, shall flee from Justice, and be found in any of the united states, he shall upon demand of the Governor or executive power, of the state from which he fled, be delivered up and removed to the state having jurisdiction of his offence.

Full faith and credit shall be given in each of these states to the records, acts and judicial proceedings of the courts and magistrates of every other state.

[ART. V.] For the more convenient management of the general interests of the united states, delegates shall be annually appointed in such manner as the legislature of each state shall direct, to meet in Congress on the first Monday in November, in every year, with a power reserved to each state, to recall its delegates, or any of them, at any time within the year, and to send others in their stead, for the remainder of the Year.

No state shall be represented in Congress by less than two, nor by more than seven Members; and no person shall be capable of being a delegate for more than three years in any term of six years; nor shall any person, being a delegate, be capable of holding any office under the united states, for which he, or another for his benefit receives any salary, fees or emolument of any kind.

Each state shall maintain its own delegates in a meeting of the states, and while they act as members of the committee of the states.

In determining questions in the united states, in Congress assembled, each state shall have one vote.

Freedom of speech and debate in Congress shall not be impeached or questioned in any Court, or place out of Congress, and the members of congress shall be protected in their persons from arrests and imprisonments, during the time of their going to and from, and attendance on congress, except for treason, felony, or breach of the peace.

[ART. VI.] No state without the Consent of the united states in congress assembled, shall send any embassy to, or receive any embassy from, or enter into any conference, agreement, or alliance or treaty with any King, prince or state; nor shall any person holding any office of profit or trust under the united states, or any of them, accept of any present, emolument, office or title of any kind whatever from any king, prince or foreign state; nor shall the united states in congress assembled, or any of them, grant any title of nobility.

No two or more states shall enter into any treaty, confederation or alliance whatever between them, without the consent of the united states in congress assembled, specifying accurately the purposes for which the same is to be entered into, and how long it shall continue.

No state shall lay any imposts or duties, which may interfere with any stipulations in treaties, entered into by the united states in congress assembled, with any king, prince or state, in pursuance of any treaties already proposed by congress, to the courts of France and Spain.

No vessels of war shall be kept up in time of peace by any state, except such number only, as shall be deemed necessary by the united states in congress assembled, for the defence of such state, or its trade; nor shall any body of forces be kept up by any state, in time of peace, except such number only, as in the judgment of the united states, in congress assembled, shall be deemed requisite to garrison the forts necessary for the defence of such state; but every state shall always keep up a well regulated and disciplined militia, sufficiently armed and accounted, and shall provide and constantly have ready for use, in public stores, a due number of field pieces and tents, and a proper quantity of arms, ammunition and camp equipage.

No state shall engage in any war without the consent of the united states in congress assembled, unless such state be actually invaded by enemies, or shall have received certain advice of a resolution being formed by some nation of Indians to invade such state and the danger is so imminent as not to admit of a delay, till the united states in congress assembled can be consulted: nor shall any state grant commissions to any ships or vessels of war, nor letters of marque or reprisal, except it be after a declaration of war by the united states in congress assembled, and then only against the kingdom or state and the subjects thereof, against which war has been so declared, and under such regulations as shall be established by the united states in congress assembled, unless such state be infested by pirates, in which case vessels of war may be fitted out for that occasion, and kept so long as the danger shall continue, or until the united states in congress assembled shall determine otherwise.

[ART. VII.] When land-forces are raised by any state for the common defence, all officers of or under the rank of colonel, shall be appointed by the legislature of each state respectively by whom such forces shall be raised, or in such manner as such state shall direct, and all vacancies shall be filled up by the state which first made the appointment.

[ART. VIII.] All charges of war, and all other expences that shall be incurred for the common defence or general welfare, and allowed by the united states in congress assembled, shall be defrayed out of a common treasury, which shall be supplied by the several states, in proportion to the value of all land within each state, granted to or surveyed for any Person, as such land and the buildings and improvements thereon shall be estimated according to such mode as the united states in congress assembled, shall from time to time direct and appoint. The taxes for paying that proportion shall be laid and levied by the authority and direction of the legislatures of the several states within the time agreed upon by the united states in congress assembled.

[ART. IX.] The united states in congress assembled, shall have the sole and exclusive right and power of determining on peace and war, except in the cases mentioned in the sixth article—of sending and receiving ambassadors—entering into treaties and alliances, provided that no treaty of commerce shall be made whereby the legislative power of the respective states shall be restrained from imposing such imposts and duties on foreigners, as their own people are subjected to, or from prohibiting the exportation or importation of any species of goods or commodities whatsoever—of establishing rules for deciding in all cases, what captures on land or water shall be legal, and in what manner prizes taken by land or naval forces in the service of the united states shall be divided or appropriated.—of granting letters of marque and reprisal in times of peace—appointing courts for the trial of piracies and felonies committed on the high seas and establishing courts for receiving and determining finally appeals in all cases of captures, provided that no member of congress shall be appointed a judge of any of the said courts.

The united states in congress assembled shall also be the last resort on appeal in all disputes and differences now subsisting or that hereafter may arise between two or more states concerning boundary, jurisdiction or any other cause whatever; which authority shall always be exercised in the manner following. Whenever the legislative or executive authority or lawful agent of any state in controversy with another shall present a petition to congress stating the matter in question and praying for a hearing, notice thereof shall be given by order of congress to the legislative or executive authority of the other state in controversy, and a day assigned for the appearance of the parties by their lawful agents, who shall then be directed to appoint by joint consent, commissioners or judges to constitute a court for hearing and determining the matter in question: but if they cannot agree, congress shall name three persons out of each of the united states, and from the list of such persons each party shall alternately strike out one, the petitioners beginning, until the number shall be reduced to thirteen; and from that number not less than seven, nor more than nine names as congress shall direct, shall in the presence of congress be drawn out by lot, and the persons whose names shall be so drawn or any five of them, shall be commissioners or judges, to hear and finally determine the controversy, so always as a major part of the judges who shall hear the cause shall agree in the determination: and if either party shall neglect to attend at the day appointed, without shewing reasons, which congress shall judge sufficient, or being present shall refuse to strike, the congress shall proceed to nominate three persons out of each state, and the secretary of congress shall strike in behalf of such party absent or refusing; and the judgment and sentence of the court to be appointed, in the manner before prescribed, shall be final and conclusive; and if any of the parties shall refuse to submit to the authority of such court, or to appear to defend their claim or cause, the court shall nevertheless proceed to pronounce sentence, or judgment, which shall in like manner be final and decisive, the judgment or sentence and other proceedings being in either case transmitted to congress, and lodged among the acts of congress for the security of the parties concerned: provided that every commissioner, before he sits in judgment, shall take an oath to be administered by one of the judges of the supreme or superior court of the state, where the cause shall be tried, "well and truly to hear and determine the matter in question, according to the best of his judgment, without favour, affection or hope of reward:" provided also that no state shall be deprived of territory for the benefit of the united states.

All controversies concerning the private right of soil claimed under different grants of two or more states, whose jurisdictions as they may respect such lands, and the states which passed such grants are adjusted, the said grants or either of them being at the same time claimed to have originated antecedent to such settlement of jurisdiction, shall on the petition of either party to the congress of the united states, be finally determined as near as may be in the same manner as is before prescribed for deciding disputes respecting territorial jurisdiction between different states.

The united states in congress assembled shall also have the sole and exclusive right and power of regulating the alloy and value of coin struck by their own authority, or by that of the respective states—fixing the standard of weights and measures throughout the united states.—regulating the trade and managing all affairs with the Indians, not members of any of the states, provided that the legislative right of any state within its own limits be not infringed or violated—establishing and regulating post-offices from one state to another, throughout all the united states, and exacting such postage on the papers passing thro' the same as may be requisite to defray the expences of the said office—appointing all officers of the land forces, in the service of the united states, excepting regimental officers.—appointing all the officers of the naval forces, and commissioning all officers whatever in the service of the united states—making rules for the government and regulation of the said land and naval forces, and directing their operations.

The united states in congress assembled shall have authority to appoint a committee, to sit in the recess of congress, to be denominated "A Committee of the States," and to consist of one delegate from each state; and to appoint such other committees and civil officers as may be necessary for managing the general affairs of the united states under their direction—to appoint one of their number to preside, provided that no person be allowed to serve in the office of president more than one year in any term of three years; to ascertain the necessary sums of Money to be raised for the service of the united states, and to appropriate and apply the same for defraying the public expences—to borrow money, or emit bills on the credit of the united states, transmitting every half year to the respective states an account of the sums of money so borrowed or emitted,—to build and equip a navy—to agree upon the number of land forces, and to make requisitions from each state for its quota, in proportion to the number of white inhabitants in such state; which requisition shall be binding, and thereupon the legislature of each state shall appoint the regimental officers, raise the men and cloath, arm and equip them in a soldier like manner, at the expence of the united states, and the officers and men so cloathed, armed and equipped shall march to the place appointed, and within the time agreed on by the united states in congress assembled: But if the united states in congress assembled shall, on consideration of circumstances judge proper that any state should not raise men, or should raise a smaller number than its quota, and that any other state should raise a greater number of men than the quota thereof, such extra number shall be raised, officered, cloathed, armed and equipped in the same manner as the quota of such state, unless the legislature of such state shall judge that such extra number cannot be safely spared out of the same, in which case they shall raise officer, cloath, arm and equip as many of such extra number as they judge can be safely spared. And the officers and men so cloathed, armed and equipped, shall march to the place appointed, and within the time agreed on by the united states in congress assembled.

The united states in congress assembled shall never engage in a war, nor grant letters of marque and reprisal in time of peace, nor enter into any treaties or alliances, nor coin money, nor regulate the value thereof, nor ascertain the sums and expences necessary for the defence and welfare of the united states, or any of them, nor emit bills, nor borrow money on the credit of the united states, nor appropriate money, nor agree upon the number of vessels of war, to be built or purchased, or the number of land or sea forces to be raised, nor appoint a commander in chief of the army or navy, unless nine states assent to the same: nor shall a question on any other point, except for adjourning from day to day be determined, unless by the votes of a majority of the united states in congress assembled.

The congress of the united states shall have power to adjourn to any time within the year, and to any place within the united states, so that no period of adjournment be for a longer duration than the space of six Months, and shall publish the Journal of their proceedings monthly, except such parts thereof relating to treaties, alliances or military operations as in their judgment require secrecy; and the yeas and nays of the delegates of each state on any question shall be entered on the Journal, when it is desired by any delegate; and the delegates of a state, or any of them, at his or their request shall be furnished with a transcript of the said Journal, except such parts as are above excepted, to lay before the legislatures of the several states.

[Art. X.] The committee of the states, or any nine of them, shall be authorised to execute, in the recess of congress, such of the powers of congress as the united states in congress assembled, by the consent of nine states, shall from time to time think expedient to vest them with; provided that no power be delegated to the said committee, for the exercise of which, by the articles of confederation, the voice of nine states in the congress of the united states assembled is requisite.

[ART. XI.] Canada acceding to this confederation, and joining in the measures of the united states, shall be admitted into, and entitled to all the advantages of this union: but no other colony shall be admitted into the same, unless such admission be agreed to by nine states.

[ART. XII.] All bills of credit emitted, monies borrowed and debts contracted by, or under the authority of congress, before the assembling of the united states, in pursuance of the present confederation, shall be deemed and considered as a charge against the united states, for payment and satisfaction whereof the said united states, and the public faith are hereby solemnly pledged.

[ART. XIII.] Every state shall abide by the determinations of the united states in congress assembled, on all questions which by this confederation are submitted to them. And the Articles of this confederation shall be inviolably observed by every state, and the union shall be perpetual; nor shall any alteration at any time hereafter be made in any of them; unless such alteration be agreed to in a congress of the united states, and be afterwards confirmed by the legislatures of every state.

And whereas it hath pleased the Great Governor of the World to incline the hearts of the legislatures we respectively represent in congress, to approve of, and to authorize us to ratify the said articles of confederation and perpetual union. Know ye that we the undersigned delegates, by virtue of the power and authority to us given for that purpose, do by these presents, in the name and in behalf of our respective constituents, fully and entirely ratify and confirm each and every of the said articles of confederation and perpetual union, and all and singular the matters and things therein contained: And we do further solemnly plight and engage the faith of our respective constituents, that they shall abide by the determinations of the united states in congress assembled, on all questions, which by the said confederation are submitted to them. And that the articles thereof shall be inviolably observed by the states we respectively represent, and that the union shall be perpetual. In Witness whereof we have hereunto set our hands in Congress. Done at Philadelphia in the state of Pennsylvania the ninth Day of July in the Year of our Lord one Thousand seven Hundred and Seventy-eight, and in the third year of the independence of America.

JOSIAH BARTLETT
JOHN WENTWORTH Jun[r]
August 8th 1778
On the part & behalf of
the State of New Hampshire

JOHN HANCOCK
SAMUEL ADAMS
ELBRIDGE GERRY
FRANCIS DANA
JAMES LOVELL
SAMUEL HOLTEN
On the part and behalf of
the State of Massachusetts Bay

WILLIAM ELLERY
HENRY MARCHANT
JOHN COLLINS
On the part and behalf
of the State of Rhode-Island
and Providence Plantations

ROGER SHERMAN
SAMUEL HUNTINGTON
OLIVER WOLCOTT
TITUS HOSMER
ANDREW ADAMS
On the part and behalf of
the State of Connecticut

JA[S] DUANE
FRA[S] LEWIS
W[M] DUER.
GOUV MORRIS
On the Part and Behalf of
the State of New York

JNO WITHERSPOON
NATH[L] SCUDDER
On the Part and in Behalf of
the State of New Jersey.
Nov[r] 26, 1778.—

ROB[T] MORRIS
DANIEL ROBERDEAU
JON[A] BAYARD SMITH.
WILLIAM CLINGAN
JOSEPH REED
22[d] July 1778
On the part and behalf of
the State of Pennsylvania

THO M:KEAN
Feby 12 1779
JOHN DICKINSON
May 5th 1779
NICHOLAS VAN DYKE,
On the part & behalf of
the State of Delaware

JOHN HANSON
March 1 1781
DANIEL CARROLL d[o]
On the part and behalf
of the State of Maryland

RICHARD HENRY LEE
JOHN BANISTER
THOMAS ADAMS
JN[O] HARVIE
FRANCIS LIGHTFOOT LEE
On the Part and Behalf of
the State of Virginia

JOHN PENN
July 21st 1778
CORN[S] HARNETT
JN[O] WILLIAMS
On the part and Behalf
of the State of N[o] Carolina

HENRY LAURENS
WILLIAM HENRY DRAYTON
JN[O] MATHEWS
RICH[D] HUTSON.
THO[S] HEYWARD Jun[r]
On the part & behalf of
the State of South-Carolina

JN[O] WALTON
24th July 1778
EDW[D] TELFAIR.
EDW[D] LANGWORTHY
On the part and behalf of
the State of Georgia

# The Emancipation Proclamation

Issued by President Abraham Lincoln on January 1, 1863.

Whereas on the 22d day of September, A.D. 1862, a proclamation was issued by the President of the United States, containing, among other things, the following, to wit:

"That on the 1st day of January, A.D. 1863, all persons held as slaves within any State or designated part of a State the people whereof shall then be in rebellion against the United States shall be then, thenceforward, and forever free; and the Executive Government of the United States, including the military and naval authority thereof, will recognize and maintain the freedom of such persons and will do no act or acts to repress such persons, or any of them, in any efforts they may make for their actual freedom.

"That the executive will on the 1st day of January aforesaid, by proclamation, designate the States and parts of States, if any, in which the people thereof, respectively, shall then be in rebellion against the United States; and the fact that any State or the people thereof shall on that day be in good faith represented in the Congress of the United States by members chosen thereto at elections wherein a majority of the qualified voters of such States shall have participated shall, in the absence of strong countervailing testimony, be deemed conclusive evidence that such State and the people thereof are not then in rebellion against the United States."

Now, therefore, I, Abraham Lincoln, President of the United States, by virtue of the power in me vested as Commander-in-Chief of the Army and Navy of the United States in time of actual armed rebellion against the authority and government of the United States, and as a fit and necessary war measure for suppressing said rebellion, do, on this 1st day of January, A.D. 1863, and in accordance with my purpose so to do, publicly proclaimed for the full period of one hundred days from the first day above mentioned, order and designate as the States and parts of States wherein the people thereof, respectively, are this day in rebellion against the United States the following, to wit:

Arkansas, Texas, Louisiana (except the parishes of St. Bernard, Plaquemines, Jefferson, St. John, St. Charles, St. James, Ascension, Assumption, Terrebonne, Lafourche, St. Mary, St. Martin, and Orleans, including the city of New Orleans), Mississippi, Alabama, Florida, Georgia, South Carolina, North Carolina, and Virginia (except the forty-eight counties designated as West Virginia, and also the counties of Berkeley, Accomac, Northhampton, Elizabeth City, York, Princess Anne, and Norfolk, including the cities of Norfolk and Portsmouth), and which excepted parts are for the present left precisely as if this proclamation were not issued.

And by virtue of the power and for the purpose aforesaid, I do order and declare that all persons held as slaves within said designated States and parts of States are, and henceforward shall be, free; and that the Executive Government of the United States, including the military and naval authorities thereof, will recognize and maintain the freedom of said persons.

And I hereby enjoin upon the people so declared to be free to abstain from all violence, unless in necessary self-defense; and I recommend to them that, in all cases when allowed, they labor faithfully for reasonable wages.

And I further declare and make known that such persons of suitable condition will be received into the armed service of the United States to garrison forts, positions, stations, and other places, and to man vessels of all sorts in said service.

And upon this act, sincerely believed to be an act of justice, warranted by the Constitution upon military necessity, I invoke the considerate judgment of mankind and the gracious favor of Almighty God.

# SUPREME COURT GLOSSARY

Cases discussed in "Debating Key Issues" appear without constitutional references.

### *Baker* v. *Carr,* 1962
(14th Amendment, Equal Protection Clause) Rapid population growth in Nashville and reluctance of the rural-dominated Tennessee legislature to redraw State legislature districts led Mayor Baker of Nashville to ask for federal court help. The federal district court refused to enter the "political thicket" of State legislature redistricting and the case was appealed. The Court directed a trial to be held in a Tennessee federal court. The case led to the 1964 *Westberry* decision, which created the "one man, one vote" equal representation concept.

### *Bethel School District #403* v. *Fraser,* 1986
(1st Amendment, freedom of speech) A high school student gave a sexually suggestive political speech at a high school assembly to elect student officers. The school administration strongly disciplined the student, Fraser, who argued that school rules unfairly limited his freedom of political speech. Fraser's view was upheld in State court. Oregon appealed to the Supreme Court, which found that "It does not follow, however, that simply because the use of an offensive form of expression may not be prohibited to adults making what the speaker considers a political point, the same latitude must be permitted to children in a public school."

### *Betts* v. *Brady,* 1942
(6th and 14th amendments, due process) A Maryland man named Betts was unable to pay for an attorney but was denied court-appointed counsel under Maryland law. Defending himself, he was found guilty. When he appealed, the Court further developed the "special circumstances" rule it had begun in 1932, saying that although "right to counsel" was not absolutely guaranteed by the 6th Amendment in State court trials, there were some "special circumstances" where counsel was required. The Court preferred, over the next 20 years, to review the "right to counsel" cases on a case-by-case basis. Overturned by *Gideon*, 1963.

### *Bob Jones University* v. *United States,* 1983
(14th Amendment in conflict with 1st Amendment) Bob Jones University, a private school, denied admission to applicants in an interracial marriage or who "espouse" interracial marriage or dating. The Internal Revenue Service then denied tax exempt status to the school because of racial discrimination. The university appealed, claiming that their policy was based on the Bible. The Court upheld the IRS ruling, stating that ". . . Government has a fundamental overriding interest in eradicating racial discrimination in education."

### *Brown* v. *Board of Education of Topeka,* 1954
(14th Amendment, Equal Protection Clause) Probably no 20th century Supreme Court decision so deeply stirred and changed life in the United States as *Brown*. A 10-year-old Topeka girl was not permitted to attend her neighborhood school because she was an African American. The Court heard arguments about whether segregation itself was a violation of the Equal Protection Clause and found that it was, commenting that "in the field of public education the doctrine of 'separate but equal' has no place. . . . Segregation is a denial of the equal protection of the laws." The decision overturned *Plessy*, 1896.

### *California* v. *Greenwood,* 1988
(4th Amendment, illegal evidence) Acting on a tip that Billy Greenwood was selling narcotics, police examined trash bags that had been picked up from Greenwood's house. Items associated with drug use were found in the garbage and were listed in the application for a search warrant. The subsequent search revealed further evidence that was used in a trial to obtain a conviction. When Greenwood appealed the "warrantless search," the Court said that garbage bags left in the street are accessible to "animals, children, scavengers, snoops, and other members of the public." Greenwood could not reasonably have expected that the contents of the garbage would remain private. The evidence was admissible.

### *The Civil Rights Cases,* 1883
(14th Amendment, Equal Protection Clause) The Civil Rights Acts of 1875 included punishments for businesses that practiced discrimination. The Court ruled on a number of cases involving the Acts in 1883, finding that the Constitution, "while prohibiting discrimination by governments, made no provisions . . . for acts of racial discrimination by private individuals." The decision limited the impact of the Equal Protection Clause, giving tacit approval for segregation in the private sector.

### *Dennis* v. *United States,* 1951
(1st Amendment, freedom of speech) The Smith Act of 1940 made it a crime for any person to work for the violent overthrow of the United States in peacetime or war. Eleven Communist party leaders, including Dennis, had been convicted of violating the Smith Act, and they appealed. The Court upheld the Act. Much modified by later decisions, the Dennis case focused on anti-government speech as an area of controversy.

### *Dred Scott* v. *Sandford*, 1857

(6th Amendment, individual rights) This decision upheld property rights over human rights by saying that Dred Scott, a slave, could not become a free man just because he had traveled in "free soil" States with his master. A badly divided nation was further fragmented by the decision. "Free soil" federal laws and the Missouri Compromise line of 1820 were held unconstitutional because they deprived a slave owner of the right to his "property" without just compensation. This narrow reading of the Constitution, a landmark case of the Court, was most clearly stated by Chief Justice Roger B. Taney, a States' rights advocate.

### *Edwards* v. *South Carolina*, 1963

(1st Amendment, freedom of speech and assembly) A group of mostly African-American civil rights activists held a rally at the South Carolina State Capitol, protesting segregation. A hostile crowd gathered and the rally leaders were arrested and convicted for "breach of the peace." The Court overturned the convictions, saying that "The Fourteenth Amendment does not permit a State to make criminal the peaceful expression of unpopular views."

### *Engel* v. *Vitale*, 1962

(1st Amendment, Establishment Clause) The State Board of Regents of New York required the recitation of a 22-word nonsectarian prayer at the beginning of each school day. A group of parents filed suit against the required prayer, claiming it violated their 1st Amendment rights. The Court found New York's action to be unconstitutional, observing, "There can be no doubt that . . . religious beliefs [are] embodied in the Regent's prayer."

### *Escobedo* v. *Illinois*, 1964

(6th Amendment, right to counsel) In a case involving a murder confession by a person known to Chicago-area police and who was not afforded counsel while under interrogation, the Court extended the "exclusionary rule" to illegal confessions in State court proceedings. Carefully defining an "Escobedo Rule," the Court said, "where . . . the investigation is no longer a general inquiry . . . but has begun to focus on a particular suspect . . . (and where) the suspect has been taken into custody . . . the suspect has requested . . . his lawyer, and the police have not . . . warned him of his right to remain silent, the accused has been denied . . . counsel in violation of the Sixth Amendment."

### *Everson* v. *Board of Education*, 1947

(1st Amendment, Establishment Clause) In a case known as "the New Jersey School Bus Case," the Court considered the use of public funds for the operation of school buses in New Jersey, including buses carrying students to parochial schools. The Court permitted New Jersey to continue the payments, saying that the aid to children was not governmental support for religion. The decision, however, strongly stated that the wall separating church and state must be kept "high and impregnable." This was a clear incorporation of 1st Amendment limits on States.

### *Ex Parte Milligan*, 1866

(Article II, executive powers) An Indiana man was arrested, treated as a prisoner of war, and imprisoned by a military court during the Civil War under presidential order. He claimed that his rights to a fair trial were interfered with and that military courts had no authority outside of "conquered territory." He was released because "the Constitution . . . is a law for rulers and people, equally in war and peace, and covers . . . all . . . men, at all times, and under all circumstances." The Court held that presidential powers to suspend the writ of *habeas corpus* in time of war did not extend to creating another court system run by the military.

### *Feiner* v. *New York*, 1951

Decision: The Court upheld the disorderly conduct conviction of Feiner, observing that "it is one thing to say that the police cannot be used as an instrument of suppression of unpopular views, and another to say that . . . they are powerless to prevent a breach of the peace." Free speech, therefore, may be limited when a clear and present danger exists. (See "Debating Key Issues" feature on page 137.)

### *Furman* v. *Georgia*, 1972

(8th Amendment, capital punishment) Three different death penalty cases, including *Furman*, raised the question of racial imbalances in the use of death sentences by State courts. Furman had been convicted and sentenced to death in Georgia. In deciding to overturn existing State death-penalty laws, the Court noted that there was an "apparent arbitrariness of the use of the sentence. . . ." Many States rewrote their death-penalty statutes and these were generally upheld in *Gregg* v. *Georgia*, 1976.

### *Gibbons* v. *Ogden*, 1824

(Article I, Section 8, Commerce Clause) This decision involved a careful examination of the power of Congress to "regulate interstate commerce." Aaron Ogden's exclusive New York ferry license gave him the right to operate steamboats to and from New York. He said that Thomas Gibbon's federal "coasting license" did not include "landing rights" in New York City. Federal and State regulation of commerce conflicted. The Court strengthened the power of the United States to regulate any interstate business relationship. Federal regulation of television, pipelines, and banking are all based on *Gibbons*.

### *Gideon* v. *Wainwright*, 1963

Decision: Gideon won a new trial and was found not guilty with the help of a court-appointed attorney. The "Gideon Rule" upheld the 6th Amendment's guarantee of counsel for all poor persons facing a felony charge, a further incorporation of Bill of Rights guarantees into State constitutions. (See "Debating Key Issues" feature on page 527.)

## *Gitlow* v. *New York*, 1925

(1st Amendment, freedom of speech) For the first time, the Court considered whether the 1st and 14th amendments had influence on State laws. The case, involving "criminal anarchy" under New York law, was the first consideration of what came to be known as the "incorporation" doctrine, under which, it was argued, the provisions of the 1st Amendment were "incorporated" by the 14th Amendment. Although New York law was not overruled in the case, the decision clearly indicated that the Supreme Court could make such a ruling. Another important incorporation case is *Powell* v. *Alabama*, 1932.

## *Gregg* v. *Georgia*, 1976

Decision: The Court upheld the Georgia death sentence, finding that it did not violate the cruel and unusual punishment clause of the 8th Amendment. The Court stated for the first time that "punishment of death does not invariably violate the Constitution." (See "Debating Key Issues" feature on page 64.)

## *Griswold* v. *Connecticut*, 1965

(14th Amendment, Due Process Clause) A Connecticut law forbade the use of "any drug, medicinal article, or instrument for the purpose of preventing conception." Griswold, director of Planned Parenthood in New Haven, was arrested for counseling married persons and after conviction, appealed. The Court overturned the Connecticut law, saying that "various guarantees (of the Constitution) create zones of privacy . . ." and questioning, ". . . would we allow the police to search the sacred precincts of marital bedrooms . . . ?" The decision is significant for raising for more careful inspection the concept of "unenumerated rights" in the 9th Amendment, later central to *Roe*, 1973.

## *Hazelwood School District* v. *Kuhlmeier*, 1988

Decision: The Court upheld the principal's action because the school official acted as the publisher of the newspaper. "1st Amendment rights of students . . . are not automatically coextensive with the rights of adults in other settings. . . ." School officials had full control over school-sponsored activities "so long as their actions are reasonably related to legitimate pedagogical concerns. . . ." (See "Debating Key Issues" feature on page 39.)

## *Heart of Atlanta Motel, Inc.* v. *United States*, 1964

Decision: The Court upheld the law, saying, "If it is interstate commerce that feels the pinch, it does not matter how 'local' the operation which applies the squeeze. . . . The power of Congress to promote interstate commerce also includes the power to regulate the local incidents thereof, including local activities . . . which have a substantial and harmful effect upon that commerce." Segregation by race of private facilities engaged in interstate commerce was found unconstitutional. (See "Debating Key Issues" feature on page 274.)

## *In Re Gault*, 1966

(14th Amendment, Due Process Clause) Prior to the Gault case, proceedings against juvenile offenders were generally handled as "family law," not "criminal law" and provided few due process guarantees. Gerald Gault was assigned to six years in a State juvenile detention facility for an alleged obscene phone call. He was not provided counsel and not permitted to confront or cross-examine the principal witness. The Court overturned the juvenile proceedings and required that States provide juveniles "some of the due process guarantees of adults," including a right to a phone call, to counsel, to cross-examine, to confront their accuser, and to be advised of their right to silence.

## *Island Trees School District* v. *Pico*, 1982

(1st Amendment, freedom of speech) A number of books were removed by the school board from the library at Island Trees High School, New York. When a group of students sued to have the books returned, the case reached the Supreme Court. The Court reversed the decision of the school board, saying that though school boards "possess significant discretion to determine the content of their school libraries . . . that discretion may not be exercised in a narrowly partisan or political manner."

## *Katz* v. *United States*, 1967

(4th Amendment, electronic surveillance) The Court reversed *Olmstead*, 1928, in this decision about wiretapping. Arrested for illegal gambling after using a public phone to transmit information about betting, Katz claimed that the electronic bug, used without a warrant, was a violation of his 4th Amendment rights. The Court expanded the protections of the 4th Amendment, observing that persons, not just property, are protected against illegal searches. Whatever a citizen "seeks to preserve as private, even in an area accessible to the public, may be constitutionally protected."

## *Korematsu* v. *United States*, 1944

Decision: The Court upheld the military order, noting that "pressing public necessity [World War II] may sometimes justify the existence of restrictions which curtail the civil rights of a single racial group . . ." but added that "racial antagonism never can . . . [justify such restrictions]." Only Japanese Americans were interned during World War II. (See "Debating Key Issues" feature on page 369.)

## *Lemon* v. *Kurzman*, 1971

(1st Amendment, Establishment Clause) In overturning State laws regarding aid to church-supported schools in this and a similar Rhode Island case, the Court created the *Lemon* test limiting ". . . excessive government entanglement with religion." The Court noted that any State law about aid to religion must meet three criteria: (1) purpose of the aid must be clearly secular, not religious, (2) its primary effect must neither advance nor inhibit religion, and (3) it must avoid "excessive entanglement of government with religion."

## *Mapp* v. *Ohio*, 1961

(4th and 14th amendments, illegal evidence and Due Process Clause) Admitting evidence gained by illegal searches was permitted by some State constitutions before *Mapp*. Cleveland police raided Ms. Mapp's home without a warrant and found obscene materials. She appealed her conviction, saying that the 4th and 14th amendments protected her against improper police behavior. The Court agreed, extending "exclusionary rule" protections to citizens in State courts, saying that the prohibition against unreasonable searches would be "meaningless" unless evidence gained in such searches was "excluded." This case further developed the concept of "incorporation" begun in *Gitlow*, 1925.

## *Marbury* v. *Madison*, 1803

(Article III, judicial powers) Chief Justice Marshall established "judicial review" as a power of the Supreme Court. After defeat in the 1800 election, President Adams appointed many Federalists to the federal courts, but the commissions were not delivered. New Secretary of State James Madison refused to deliver them. Marbury sued in the Supreme Court. The Court declared a portion of the Judiciary Act of 1789 unconstitutional, thereby declaring the Court's power to find acts of Congress unconstitutional.

## *Massachusetts* v. *Sheppard*, 1984

(4th Amendment, illegal evidence) A search in Massachusetts was based on a warrant issued on an improper form. Sheppard argued that the search was illegal and the evidence was inadmissible under *Mapp*, 1962. Massachusetts argued that the police acted in "good faith," believing that the warrant was correct. The Court agreed with Massachusetts, noting that the exclusionary rule should not be applied when the officer conducting the search had acted with the reasonable belief that he was following proper procedures. This was the first of several exceptions to the Exclusionary Rule handed down by the Court in the 1980s, including *Nix*, 1984, and *United States* v. *Leon*, 1984.

## *McCulloch* v. *Maryland*, 1819

(Article I, Section 8, Necessary and Proper Clause) Called the "Bank of the United States" case. A Maryland law required federally chartered banks to use only a special paper to print money, which amounted to a tax. William McCulloch, the cashier of the Baltimore branch of the bank, refused to use the paper, claiming that States could not tax the Federal Government. The Court declared the Maryland law unconstitutional, commenting ". . . the power to tax implies the power to destroy."

## *Miller* v. *California*, 1973

(1st Amendment, freedom of the press) In *Miller*, the Court upheld a stringent application of California obscenity law by Newport Beach, California, and attempted to define what is obscene. The "Miller Rule" included three criteria: (1) That the average person would, applying contemporary community standards, find that the work appealed to the prurient interest; (2) that the work depicts or describes, in an offensive way, sexual conduct defined by State law; and (3) that "the work, taken as a whole, lacks serious literary, artistic, political or scientific value. . . ."

## *Miranda* v. *Arizona*, 1966

(5th, 6th, and 14th amendments, rights of the accused) Arrested for kidnapping and sexual assault, Ernesto Miranda signed a confession including a statement that he had "full knowledge of [his] legal rights. . . ." After conviction, he appealed, claiming that without counsel and without warnings, the confession was illegally gained. The Court agreed with Miranda that "he must be warned prior to any questioning that he has the right to remain silent, that anything he says can be used against him in a court of law, that he has a right to . . . an attorney and that if he cannot afford an attorney one will be appointed for him. . . ." Although later modified by *Nix*, 1984, and other cases, *Miranda* firmly upheld citizen rights to fair trial in State courts.

## *Cruzan* v. *Director, Missouri Dept. of Health*, 1990

(9th Amendment, right to die) A Missouri woman was in a coma from an automobile accident in 1983. Her family, facing astronomical medical bills and deciding that "her life had ended in 1987," directed the health care providers to end intravenous feeding. The State of Missouri opposed the family's decision. The family went to court and the Supreme Court ruled that States could require "clear and convincing" evidence that Cruzan would have wanted to die, although the Court did not require other States to meet the Missouri standard. Following the ruling, another hearing was held in Missouri at which "clear and convincing evidence" was presented to a judge. The intravenous feeding was ended and Cruzan died on December 26, 1990.

## *Mueller* v. *Allen*, 1983

Decision: The Court upheld the law, stating that it met the *Lemon* test (*Lemon*, 1972), and that the deduction was available to all parents with children in school. Although it was of greater benefit to parents of children in private schools, each parent had the choice of which school their children attended. (See "Debating Key Issues" feature on page 415.)

## *New Jersey* v. *T.L.O.*, 1985

Decision: The court set a new standard for searches in schools in this case, stating that the school had a "legitimate need to maintain an environment in which learning can take place," and that to do this "requires some easing of the restrictions to which searches by public authorities are ordinarily subject. . . ." The Court thus created a "reasonable suspicion" rule for school searches, a change from the "probable cause" requirement in the wider society. (See "Debating Key Issues" feature on page 467.)

### New York Times v. United States, 1971

Decision: The Court cited the 1st Amendment guarantee of a free press and refused to uphold the injunction against publication, observing that it is the obligation of the government to prove that actual harm to the nation's security would be caused by the publication. The decision limited "prior restraint" of the press. (See "Debating Key Issues" feature on page 197.)

### Nix v. Williams, 1984

(4th Amendment, illegal evidence) A man was convicted of murdering a 10-year-old girl after he led officers to the body. He had been arrested, but not advised of his rights, in a distant city, and in transit, he had conversed with a police officer. Williams agreed that the child should have a proper burial and directed the officer to the body. Later, on appeal, Williams's attorneys argued that the body should not be admitted as evidence because the questioning was illegal. The Court disagreed, observing that search parties were within two and one-half miles of the body. "Evidence otherwise excluded may be admissible when it would have been discovered anyway." The decision was one of several "exceptions to the exclusionary rule" handed down by the Court in the 1980s.

### Olmstead v. United States, 1928

(4th Amendment, electronic surveillance) Olmstead was engaged in the illegal sale of alcohol. Much of the evidence against him was gained through a wiretap made without a warrant. Olmstead argued that he had "a reasonable expectation of privacy," and that the *Weeks* decision of 1914 should be applied to exclude the evidence gained by the wiretap. The Court disagreed, saying that Olmstead intended "to project his voice to those quite outside . . . and that . . . nothing tangible was taken." Reversed by subsequent decisions, this case contains the first usage of the concept of "reasonable expectation of privacy" that would mark later 4th Amendment decisions.

### Plessy v. Ferguson, 1896

(14th Amendment, Equal Protection Clause) A Louisiana law required separate seating for white and African-American citizens on public railroads, a form of segregation. Herman Plessy argued that his right to "equal protection of the laws" was violated. The Court held that segregation was permitted if facilities were equal. The Court interpreted the 14th Amendment as "not intended to give Negroes social equality but only political and civil equality. . . ." The Louisiana law was seen as a "reasonable exercise of (State) police power . . ." Segregated public facilities were permitted until *Plessy* was overturned by the *Brown* v. *Board of Education* case of 1954.

### Powell v. Alabama, 1932

(6th Amendment, right to counsel) The case involved the "Scottsboro Boys," seven "young negro men" accused of sexual assault. This case was a landmark in the development of a "fundamentals of fairness" doctrine of the Court over the next 40 years. The Scottsboro boys were quickly prosecuted without the benefit of counsel and sentenced to death. The Court overturned the decision, stating that poor people facing the death penalty in State courts must be provided counsel, and commenting, ". . . there are certain principles of Justice which adhere to the very idea of free government, which no [State] may disregard." The case was another step toward incorporation of the Bill of Rights into State constitutions.

### Regents of the University of California v. Bakke, 1978

Decision: The Court ruled narrowly, providing an admission for Bakke, but not overturning "affirmative action," preferring to take discrimination questions on a case-by-case basis. (See "Debating Key Issues" feature on page 560.)

### Reynolds v. United States, 1878

(1st Amendment, Free Exercise Clause) Called the "Mormon Case," this decision involved George Reynolds, an "old order" Mormon with multiple wives. An anti-Mormon law forbidding bigamy was passed by Congress, and Reynolds was prosecuted. He claimed that his religious belief overrode federal laws and that the law was unconstitutional. The Court ruled that "freedom of religion means freedom to hold an opinion or belief, but not to take action . . . subversive to good order."

### Roe v. Wade, 1973

(9th Amendment, right to privacy) A Texas woman challenged a State law forbidding the artificial termination of a pregnancy, saying that she "had a fundamental right to privacy." The Court upheld a woman's right to choose in this case, noting that the State's "important and legitimate interest in protecting the potentiality of human life" became "compelling" at the end of the first trimester, and that before then ". . . the attending physician, in consultation with his patient, is free to determine, without regulation by the State, that . . . the patient's pregnancy should be terminated." The decision struck down State regulation of abortion in the first three months of pregnancy and was modified by *Webster*, 1989.

### Rostker v. Goldberg, 1981

Decision: The Court did not support the challenge, observing that "the purpose of registration was to prepare for draft of combat troops" and that "Congress and the Executive have decided that women should not serve in combat." Since the matter of using women in combat had received considerable attention in Congress, with debates, hearings, and committee actions, the Court agreed that Congress did not act unthinkingly or reflexively. (See "Debating Key Issues" feature on page 295.)

### Roth v. United States, 1957

(1st Amendment, freedom of the press) A New York man named Roth operated a business that used the mail to invite people to buy materials considered obscene by postal inspectors. The Court, in its first consideration of censorship of obscenity, created the "prevailing community standards" rule, which required a consideration of the work as a whole. In its decision, the Court defined as obscene that which offended "the average person, applying contemporary community standards." In a case decided the same day, the Court applied the same "test" to State obscenity laws.

### *Schenck* v. *United States,* 1919

(1st Amendment, freedom of speech) Charles Schenck was an officer of an antiwar political group who was arrested for alleged violations of the Espionage Act of 1917, which made active opposition to the war a crime. He had urged thousands of young men called to service by the draft act to resist and to avoid induction. The Court limited free speech in time of war, stating that Schenck's words, under the circumstances, presented a "clear and present danger. . . ." Although later decisions modified the decision, the Schenck case created a precedent that 1st Amendment guarantees were not absolute.

### *School District of Abington Township, Pennsylvania* v. *Schempp,* 1963

(1st Amendment, Establishment Clause) A Pennsylvania State law required reading from the Bible each day at school as an all-school activity. Some parents objected and sought legal remedy. When the case reached the Court, it agreed with the parents, saying that the Establishment Clause and Free Exercise Clause both forbade States from engaging in religious activity. The Court created a rule holding that if the purpose and effect of a law "is the advancement or inhibition of religion," it "exceeds the scope of legislative power."

### *Sheppard* v. *Maxwell,* 1966

(14th Amendment, Due Process Clause) Dr. Samuel Sheppard was convicted of murdering his wife in a trial widely covered by national news media. Sheppard appealed his conviction, claiming that the pretrial publicity had made it impossible to get a fair trial. The Court rejected arguments about "press freedom," overturned his conviction, and ordered a new trial. As a result of the Sheppard decision, some judges have issued "gag" orders limiting pretrial publicity.

### *South Dakota* v. *Dole,* 1986

Decision: The Court upheld the right of the National Government to limit highway funds to States that did not qualify under the rules of "entitlement." All States that wished to continue to receive full federal highway aid were required to raise the legal age to purchase and consume alcohol to 21 years. In recent years the Federal Government has attached similar strings to federal aid in a number of instances, including mandating maximum speed limits on interstate highways. (See "Debating Key Issues" feature on page 87.)

### *Tennessee Valley Authority* v. *Hiram G. Hill, Jr., et al.,* 1978

Decision: The Court found the injunction against TVA's completion of the nearly finished dam, which the interior secretary found would harm an endangered fish species, to be proper to prevent violation of the Endangered Species Act. (See "Debating Key Issues" feature on page 221.)

### *Texas* v. *Johnson,* 1989

(1st Amendment, freedom of speech) Dousing with kerosene and burning a U.S. flag taken from the flagpole at the 1984 Republican National Convention in Dallas, Gregory Johnson led a protest against national policies outside the convention center. He was arrested and convicted under a Texas law prohibiting the desecration of the Texas and United States flags. Johnson's conviction was overturned in the highest criminal court in Texas, and the State appealed. The Court ruled the Texas law placed an unconstitutional limit on "freedom of expression," noting that ". . . nothing in our precedents suggests that a state may foster its own view of the flag by prohibiting expressive conduct relating to it."

### *Thompson* v. *Oklahoma,* 1988

(8th Amendment, capital punishment) An Oklahoma youth was 15 years old when he committed a capital murder. At age 16 he was sentenced to death for the slaying. In hearing an appeal of the case, the Court overturned the death sentence, holding that "[t]he Eighth and Fourteenth Amendments prohibit the execution of a person who was under 16 years of age at the time of his or her offense." A death penalty was cruel and unusual punishment for a 15 year old.

### *Tinker* v. *Des Moines Public Schools,* 1969

Decision: The Court agreed with the Tinkers, upholding students' 1st Amendment rights, noting that students do not abandon their civil rights "at the schoolhouse gate . . ." and that the wearing of black armbands was ". . . silent, passive expression of opinion. . . ." Schools would need to show evidence of the possibility of "substantial disruption" before free speech could be limited at school. (See "Debating Key Issues" feature on page 498.)

### *United States* v. *Nixon,* 1974

Decision: The Court overruled the President and ordered him to surrender the tapes, thereby limiting executive privilege. The President's "generalized interest in confidentiality . . ." was subordinate to "the fundamental demands of due process of law in the fair administration of criminal justice." (See "Debating Key Issues" feature on page 322.)

### *Walz* v. *Tax Commission of the City of New York,* 1970

(1st Amendment, Establishment Clause) State and local governments routinely exempt church property from taxes. Walz claimed that such exemptions were a "support of religion," a subsidy by government. The Court disagreed, noting that such exemptions were just an example of a "benevolent neutrality" between government and churches, not a support of religion. Governments must avoid taxing churches, because taxation would give government a "control" over religion, prohibited by the "wall of separation of church and state" noted in *Everson*, 1947.

### Webster v. Reproductive Health Services, 1989

(9th Amendment, right to privacy) A 1986 Missouri law stated that (1) life began at conception, (2) unborn children have rights, (3) public funds could not be used for abortions not necessary to save the life of the mother, and (4) public funds could not be used for abortion counseling. Health care providers in Missouri filed suit, challenging the law, claiming it was in conflict with *Roe*, 1973, and intruded into "privacy questions." A 5-4 Court upheld the Missouri law, stating that the people of Missouri, through their legislature, could put limits on the use of public funds. The *Webster* decision narrowed the protection of *Roe*.

### Weeks v. United States, 1914

(4th Amendment, illegal evidence) A search without proper warrant was made in San Francisco and evidence was used by a postal inspector to prosecute Mr. Weeks. Weeks claimed that the evidence was gained by an illegal search, and thus was inadmissible. The Court agreed, applying for the first time an "exclusionary rule" for illegally gained evidence in federal courts. The decision stated ". . . if letters and private documents can thus be seized and used as evidence . . . his right to be secure against such searches . . . is of no value, and . . . might as well be stricken from the Constitution." See also *Mapp* v. *Ohio*, 1961; *Massachusetts* v. *Sheppard*, 1984; and *Nix* v. *Williams*, 1984.

### West Virginia Board of Education v. Barnette, 1943

Decision: The Court held that a compulsory flag salute violated the 1st Amendment's exercise of religion clause and was, therefore, unconstitutional. ". . . no official, high or petty, can prescribe what shall be orthodox in politics, nationalism, religion, or other matters of opinion. . . ." (See "Debating Key Issues" feature on page 649.)

### Westside Community Schools v. Mergens, 1990

(1st Amendment, Establishment Clause) A request by Bridget Mergens to form a student Christian religious group at school was denied by an Omaha high school principal. Mergens took legal action, claiming that a 1984 federal law required "equal access" for student religious groups. The Court ordered the school to permit the club, stating, "a high school does not have to permit any extracurricular activities, but when it does, the school is bound by the . . . Act of 1984. Allowing students to meet on campus and discuss religion is constitutional because it does not amount to a 'State sponsorship of a religion.'"

### Wilkins v. Missouri, 1989

(8th Amendment, capital punishment) A 16-year-old abused juvenile runaway in Missouri robbed a convenience store and stabbed the attendant several times, stating that "a dead person can't talk." He was sentenced to death. The Court decided that the death penalty for a 16 year old did not constitute "cruel and unusual punishment," commenting that "we discern neither a historical nor a modern societal consensus forbidding the imposition of capital punishment on any person who murders at 16 or 17 years of age." With *Thompson*, 1988, this case clearly sets the age of 16 as the minimum age for the imposition of capital punishment.

### Wisconsin v. Yoder, 1972

(1st Amendment, Free Exercise Clause) Members of the Amish religious sect in Wisconsin objected to sending their children to public schools after the eighth grade, claiming that such exposure of the children to another culture would endanger the group's self-sufficient agrarian lifestyle essential to their religious faith. The Court agreed with the Amish, while noting that the Court must move carefully to weigh the State's "legitimate social concern when faced with religious claim for exemption from generally applicable educational requirements."

# GLOSSARY

Number(s) after each definition refer to page(s) where the term is defined.

**Act of admission**   A congressional act admitting a United States territory into the Union as a State. p. 83

**Administration**   The officials and agencies of the executive branch that carry out public policies. p. 382

**Affirmative action**   Policy that requires that both public and private organizations take positive steps to overcome the effects of past discrimination. p. 557

**Albany Plan of Union**   Plan put forward by Benjamin Franklin in 1754 that aimed at uniting the 13 colonies for trade, military, and other purposes; never enacted. p. 32

**Alien**   One who is not a citizen (or national) of the state in which he/she lives. pp. 487, 562

**Ambassador**   A personal representative appointed by the head of a nation to represent that nation in matters of diplomacy. p. 429

**Amendment**   A change in, or addition to, a constitution or a law. p. 60

**Amnesty**   A general pardon offered to a group of law violators. p. 368

**Anarchy**   The total absence of government. p. 17

**Anti-Federalists**   Those persons who opposed the adoption of the Constitution in 1787–1788. p. 47

**Appellate jurisdiction**   Authority of a court to review decisions of inferior (lower) courts; see original jurisdiction. pp. 464, 678

**Apportionment**   Distribution of seats in a legislative body among electoral districts. p. 238

**Articles of Confederation**   Document by which the first U.S. government was established after the American Revolution; allowed few important powers to the central government. p. 36

**Assessment**   The process of determining the value of property for purposes of taxation. p. 669

**At-large**   Election of an officeholder by the voters of an entire governmental unit (e.g., a State or county) rather than by the voters of a district, a subdivision of that area. p. 241

**Bail**   Money the accused may be required to post (deposit with the court) as a guarantee that he/she will appear in court at the proper time. p. 536

**Ballot**   Device by which a voter registers a choice in an election. p. 168

**Bankruptcy**   Court action to release a person or corporation from unpaid debts. p. 267

**Bench trial**   A trial held without a jury; civil or criminal proceeding at which the judge decides questions of fact as well as questions of law. p. 532

**Bicameral**   An adjective, describing a legislative body composed of two houses. p. 28

**Bill**   A proposal presented to a legislative body for possible enactment as a law. p. 297

**Bill of attainder**   Legislative act that inflicts punishment upon a person or group without a trial. p. 529

**Bill of Rights**   First 10 amendments to the Constitution. pp. 62, 486

**Blanket primary**   A nominating election in which voters may switch from one party's primary to another on an office-to-office basis; see direct primary. p. 162

**Block grant**   One type of federal grants-in-aid; block-grant monies are to be used in some particular but broadly defined area of public policy (e.g., education or highways); see grants-in-aid. p. 85

**Borough**   A major unit of local government in Alaska, similar to counties in other States; also in some States a small town, village. p. 643

**Bourgeoisie**   In Marxist terms, the social class of the capitalists. p. 614

**Boycott**   Refusal to buy or sell an opponent's goods in order to influence his/her behavior. p. 32

**Bureaucracy**   Any large, complex administrative structure; a hierarchical organization with job specialization and complex rules. p. 381

**Bureaucrat**   Person with defined responsibilities in a bureaucracy. p. 381

**By-election**   A special election held to fill a vacant seat in Britain's House of Commons. p. 578

**Cabinet**   Presidential advisory body, traditionally composed of the heads of the executive departments and other officers the President may choose. p. 373

**Capital**   Wealth used to produce goods and services. p. 606

**Capitalist**   One who controls and uses the capital by which goods and services are produced under a free enterprise system; see free enterprise. p. 606

**Caucus**   A meeting of a group of like-minded persons to select the candidates they will support in an election; see party caucus. p. 158

**Certificate**   A method of putting a case before the Supreme Court; used when a lower court is not clear about the procedure or the rule of law that should apply in a case and asks the Supreme Court to certify the answer to a specific question. p. 475

**Certiorari, writ of**   Order issued by a higher court directing a lower court to send up the record of a case for its review. p. 474

**Checks and balances**   System of overlapping the powers of the legislative, executive, and judicial branches, to permit each branch to check the actions of the others; see separation of powers. p. 57

**Chief administrator**   Term for the President as head of the administration of the Federal Government. p. 316

**Chief citizen** Term for the President as the representative of the people, working for the public interest. p. 316

**Chief diplomat** Term for the President as the main architect of foreign policy and spokesperson to other countries. p. 316

**Chief executive** Term for the President as vested with the executive power of the United States. p. 316

**Chief legislator** Term for the President as architect of public policy and the one who sets the agenda for Congress. p. 316

**Chief of party** Term for the President as the leader of his or her political party. p. 316

**Chief of state** Term for the President as the head of the government of the United States, symbol of all the people of the nation. p. 316

**Citizen** One who owes allegiance to a state and is entitled to its protection. p. 561

**Civil law** That body of law relating to human conduct, including disputes between private persons and between private persons and government, not covered by criminal law. p. 673

**Civil liberties** Guarantees of the safety of persons, opinions, and property from the arbitrary acts of government. p. 486

**Civil rights** Refers to positive acts of government that seek to make constitutional guarantees a reality for all; e.g., prohibition of discrimination. p. 486

**Closed primary** Form of the direct primary in which only declared party members may vote; see open primary, direct primary. p. 162

**Cloture** Procedure that may be used to limit or end floor debate in a legislative body. p. 306

**Coalition** A union of persons or groups of diverse interests; an alliance of parties for the purpose of forming a government. pp. 100, 578

**Coattail effect** Influence that a popular candidate for a top office (e.g., President or governor) can have on the voters' support of other candidates of his/her party on the same ballot. p. 167

**Collective security** Basic purpose of the U.N. and a major goal of American foreign policy, to create a system in which participating nations agree to take joint action to meet any threat to or attack on another member. p. 443

**Collectivization** Stalin's plan of combining small peasant farms. p. 621

**Command economy** Economic system in which the government directs the economy. p. 615

**Commander in chief** Term for the President as commander of the nation's armed forces. p. 316

**Commerce and Slave Trade Compromise** An agreement during the Constitutional Convention of 1787 protecting the interests of slaveholders by forbidding Congress the power to tax the export of goods from any State, and, for 20 years, the power to act on the slave trade. p. 44

**Commerce power** Exclusive power of Congress to regulate interstate and foreign trade. p. 264

**Commission form** Form of city government in which elected commissioners serve collectively as the city council and separately as heads of the city's administrative department. p. 652

**Committee chairman** Member who heads a standing committee in a legislative body. p. 289

**Committee of the Whole** A committee that consists of an entire legislative body; used for a procedure in which a legislative body expedites its business by resolving itself into a committee of itself. p. 301

**Common law** That body of law made up of generally accepted standards of rights and wrongs developed over centuries by judicial decisions rather than in written statutes. p. 672

**Commutation** The power to reduce (commute) the length of a sentence or fine for a crime. pp. 368, 641

**Compromise** The process of reconciling competing views and interests in order to find the position most acceptable to the largest number. p. 17

**Concurrent jurisdiction** Power shared by federal and state courts to hear certain cases. p. 464

**Concurrent powers** Powers held by the National Government and the States in the federal system. p. 78

**Concurrent resolution** Measure passed by both houses of a legislature that does not have the force of law nor require the chief executive's approval; often used to express the legislature's opinion or for internal rules or housekeeping. p. 297

**Concurring opinion** Written explanation of the views of one or more judges who support a decision reached by a majority of the court but disagree with the grounds for that decision. p. 476

**Confederation** Form of government in which an alliance of independent states creates a central government of very limited power; the member states have supreme authority over all matters except in those few areas in which they have expressly delegated power to the central government. p. 11

**Conference committee** Temporary joint committee created to reconcile any differences between the two houses' versions of a bill. p. 294

**Connecticut Compromise** Agreement during the Constitutional Convention that Congress should be composed of a Senate, in which the States would be represented equally, and a House, in which representation would be based upon a State's population. p. 43

**Consensus** General agreement among various groups on fundamental matters. p. 583

**Constituents** All persons represented by a legislator or other elected officeholder. p. 250

**Constitution** Body of fundamental law, setting out the basic principles, structures, processes, and functions of a government and placing limits upon its actions; may be written or unwritten. p. 35

**Constitutionalism** Basic principle that government and those who govern are bound by the fundamental law; the rule of law; see limited government. p. 56

**Containment** Basic feature of American foreign policy since World War II, to contain Soviet communism within its own boundaries as a way to reduce its influence and force its eventual collapse. p. 443

**Continuing resolution** Measure that, when signed by the President, allows an agency to function on the basis of appropriations made the prior year. p. 419

**Continuous body** Governing unit such as the Senate whose seats are never all up for election at the same time. p. 246

**Copyright** The exclusive, legal right of a person to reproduce, publish, or sell his or her own literary, musical, or artistic creations. p. 268

**Council-manager form** Form of city government with an elected council as the policy-making body and an appointed administrator responsible to the council for the running of the city's government. p. 653

**County** A major unit of local government in most States; created by the State; principal powers lie in the fields of law enforcement, roads, schools, welfare. p. 643

**Criminal law** That body of law that defines crimes and provides for their punishment. p. 673

**Custom duty** Tax (tariff) on goods brought into the United States. p. 410

**De facto segregation** Segregation that exists "in fact," not as a result of laws or governmental actions; see de jure segregation, segregation. p. 553

**Defendant** In a civil suit, the person against whom a court action is brought by the plaintiff; in a criminal case, the person charged with the crime. p. 464

**Deficit** Yearly shortfall between revenue and spending. p. 413

**De jure segregation** Segregation that exists as a result of some law or governmental action; see de facto segregation, segregation. p. 553

**Delegated powers** Those powers (expressed, implied, inherent) granted to the National Government by the Constitution. p. 75

**Democracy** System of government in which supreme authority rests with the people; see direct democracy, representative democracy. p. 13

**Denaturalization** Court revocation of naturalized citizenship through due process of law. p. 564

**Deportation** Legal process in which aliens are legally required to leave the United States. p. 566

**Deterrence** Basic feature of American foreign policy; to maintain massive military strength in order to prevent any attack upon this country or its allies. p. 443

**Dictatorship** Form of government in which those who rule cannot be held responsible to the will of the people. p. 12

**Diplomatic immunity** Practice in international law under which ambassadors and other diplomatic officials have special privileges and are not subject to the laws of the state to which they are accredited. p. 430

**Direct democracy** A democratic system of government in which the people participate directly in decision making. p. 13

**Direct primary** The most widely used method of making nominations in American politics; an intra-party nominating election at which those who vote choose a party's candidates to run in the general election; see closed primary, open primary. p. 161

**Direct tax** A tax that must be paid by the person on whom it is levied; see indirect tax. p. 262

**Discharge petition** A procedure to bring a bill to the floor of the legislative body when a committee has refused to report it. p. 298

**Dissenting opinion** Written explanation of the views of one or more judges who disagree with (dissent from) a decision reached by a majority of the court; see majority opinion. p. 476

**Dissolution** Act of dissolving a governing body such as a house of representatives. p. 584

**Division of powers** Basic principle of federalism; the constitutional provisions by which governmental powers are divided on a geographic basis (in the United States, between the National Government and the States). p. 74

**Double jeopardy** Trial a second time for a crime of which the accused was acquitted in a first trial; prohibited by the 5th and 14th amendments. p. 530

**Draft** Process by which people enter compulsory service in the military. p. 437

**Due process/Due Process Clause** Constitutional guarantee, set out in the 5th and 14th amendments to the National Constitution and in every State's constitution, that government will not deprive any person of life, liberty, or property by any unfair, arbitrary, or unreasonable action, and that government must act in accord with established rules. pp. 488, 517

**Economic protest parties** Political parties rooted in periods of economic discontent. p. 115

**Electoral college** Group of persons (presidential electors) chosen in each State and the District of Columbia every four years who make a formal selection of the President and Vice President. p. 328

**Electorate** All of the persons entitled to vote in a given election. pp. 112, 130, 346

**Eminent domain** Power of a government to take private property for a public use. p. 270

**Enabling act** A congressional act that allows the people of a United States territory to prepare a constitution as a step toward admission as a State in the Union. p. 83

**English Bill of Rights** Drawn up by Parliament in 1689 to prevent abuse of power by English monarchs; forms the basis for much in American government and politics today. p. 27

**Entitlement** Benefits that federal law says must be paid to those persons who meet the eligibility requirements set for those payments. p. 416

**Entrepreneur** A person who organizes, operates, and assumes the risks of a business enterprise. p. 607

**Espionage** Spying for a foreign power. p. 506

**Establishment Clause** Part of the 1st Amendment prohibiting either the establishment of a religion or the sanctioning of an existing religion by the government. p. 490.

**Estate tax** A tax levied directly on the estate of a deceased person; see inheritance tax. pp. 410, 669

**Excise tax** Tax levied on the production, transportation, sale, or consumption of goods or services. p. 410

**Exclusionary rule**   Evidence gained by illegal or unreasonable means cannot be used at the court trial of the person from whom it was seized; based upon Supreme Court interpretation of the 4th and 14th amendments. p. 524

**Exclusive jurisdiction**   Power of the federal courts alone to hear certain cases. p. 464

**Exclusive powers**   Most of the delegated powers; those held by the National Government alone (exclusively) in the federal system. p. 78

**Executive agreement**   Pact made by the President with the head of a foreign state; a binding international agreement with the force of law but which (unlike a treaty) does not require Senate consent. pp. 66, 361

**Executive order**   Rules, regulations issued by a chief executive or his/her subordinates, based upon either constitutional or statutory authority and having the force of law. p. 356

**Expatriation**   Act by which one renounces (forfeits, gives up) citizenship. p. 564

**Ex post facto law**   Criminal law applied retroactively to the disadvantage of the accused; prohibited by the Constitution. p. 529

**Expressed powers**   Those delegated powers of the National Government that are given to it in so many words by the Constitution; also sometimes called the "enumerated powers." p. 75

**Extradition**   Legal process by which a fugitive from justice in one State is returned (extradited) to it from another State. p. 90

**Federal budget**   Detailed estimate of federal income and outgo during the coming fiscal year, and a work plan for the execution of public policy. p. 371

**Federal Government, Federalism**   Form of government with governmental powers divided between a central government and several regional governments; this geographically based division of powers is made by an authority superior to both the central and the regional governments. In the United States, the division of powers between the National Government and the 50 States is made by the Constitution. pp. 10, 59, 74

**Federalists**   Those persons who supported the adoption of the Constitution in 1787–1788. p. 47

**Filibuster**   Various tactics (usually prolonged floor debate) aimed at defeating a bill in a legislative body by preventing a final vote on it; often associated with the U.S. Senate; see cloture. p. 304

**Five-year plan**   Attempt to combine large-scale centralized planning with the public ownership of the means of production as the basis for a nation's economic advancement; used in Soviet Union. p. 621

**Floor leader**   Members of the House and Senate picked to carry out party decisions and steer legislative action to meet party goals. p. 286

**Foreign aid**   Economic and military aid to other countries as a means of fulfilling foreign policy goals. p. 447

**Foreign policy**   The actions and stands that a nation takes in every aspect of its relationships with other countries; everything a nation's government says and does in world affairs. p. 426

**Formal amendment**   A modification in the Constitution brought about through one of four methods set forth in the Constitution. p. 60

**Franchise**   Suffrage, the right to vote. p. 129

**Framers**   The group who came together in 1787 to draft the Constitution of the United States. p. 40

**Free enterprise system**   An economic system based on private ownership, individual initiative, profit, and competition; see capitalist, private enterprise. p. 607

**Free Exercise Clause**   Part of the 1st Amendment guaranteeing to each person the right to believe whatever that person chooses in matters of religion. p. 496

**Full Faith and Credit**   Constitution's requirement (Article IV, Section 1) that each State accept (honor the validity of, give full faith and credit to) the public acts, records, and judicial proceedings of every other State. p. 89

**General election**   Regularly scheduled election at which the voters choose public officeholders. p. 158

**Gerrymandering**   The drawing of electoral district lines to the advantage of a party or group. pp. 138, 242

**Gift tax**   Tax imposed on the making of a gift by a living person. p. 410

***Glasnost***   Policy of openness in the former Soviet Union, including government's expanded tolerance of dissent and freedom of expression. p. 593

**Government**   That complex of offices, personnel, and processes by which a state is ruled, by which its public policies are made and enforced. p. 3

**Grand jury**   Body of 12 to 23 persons convened by a court to decide whether or not there is enough evidence to justify bringing a person to trial; see indictment, information, presentment, petit jury. p. 529

**Grants-in-aid program**   Financial aid granted by one government to another (e.g., by the National Government to the States), with the funds available subject to certain conditions and to be used for certain purposes; see block grants. p. 84

**Grass roots**   Of or from the common people, the average voter; used to describe opinion and pressure on public policy. p. 226

**Habeas corpus, writ of**   Court order that a prisoner be brought before the court and that the detaining officer show cause why the prisoner should not be released; designed to prevent illegal arrests and unlawful imprisonments. p. 528

**Ideological party**   Political party based on a particular set of beliefs, a comprehensive view of social, economic, and political matters. p. 114

**Impeachment**   Formal charge (accusation of misconduct) brought against a public official by the lower house in a legislative body; trial, and removal upon conviction, occurs in the upper house. p. 276

**Implied powers**   Those delegated powers of the National Government implied by (inferred from) the expressed powers; those "necessary and proper" to carry out the expressed powers; see delegated powers, expressed powers. p. 75

**Income tax**   A tax levied on individual and corporate income. p. 668

**Independent**   Voter who does not identify with or regularly support a particular party. p. 150

**Independent agency**   Agency created by Congress outside of the cabinet departments. p. 388

**Indictment**   Accusation by a grand jury; a formal finding by that body that there is sufficient evidence against a named person to warrant his/her criminal trial. p. 529

**Indirect tax**   A tax levied on one party but passed on to another for payment. pp. 263, 650

**Informal amendment**   A change made in the Constitution not by actual written amendment, but by the experience of government under the Constitution; the methods include: (1) legislation passed by Congress; (2) actions taken by the President; (3) decisions of the Supreme Court; (4) the activities of political parties; and (5) custom. p. 65

**Information**   Formal charge of crime brought against a named person by the prosecutor directly, rather than by a grand jury; see indictment. p. 530

**Inherent powers**   Those delegated powers of the National Government that belong to it because it is the national government of a sovereign state. p. 75

**Inheritance tax**   A "death tax" levied on the beneficiary's share of an estate; see estate tax. p. 670

**Initiative**   Petition process by which a certain percentage of voters can put a proposed constitutional amendment or statute on the ballot for popular approval or rejection. p. 636

**Injunction**   Court order that requires or forbids some specific action. p. 139

**Interest group**   Private organization that tries to influence public policy. pp. 190, 211

**Interim government**   Government set up to serve during the transition from a previous government. p. 596

**Interstate compact**   Formal agreement between or among States, authorized by the Constitution (Article I, Section 10). p. 88

**Isolationism**   Basic part of American foreign policy until World War II; a policy of refusing to become generally involved in world affairs. p. 425

**Item veto**   Power held by 43 State governors (but not the President) to eliminate (veto) one or more provisions (items) in a bill without rejecting the entire measure; see veto. p. 641

**Jim Crow law**   Law to isolate and separate one group of people from another on the basis of race. p. 551

**Joint committee**   Legislative committee composed of members of both houses. p. 294

**Joint resolution**   Legislative measure that must be passed by both houses and approved by the chief executive to become effective; similar to a bill, with the force of law, and often used for unusual or temporary purposes. p. 297

**Judicial review**   Power of the courts to determine the constitutionality of the actions of the legislative and executive branches of government. p. 58

**Jurisdiction**   Power of a court to try and decide a case. p. 462

**Jus sanguinis**   Acquisition of American citizenship at birth, because of the citizenship of one or both parents; the "law of the blood," to whom born. p. 561

**Jus soli**   Acquisition of American citizenship at birth, because of birth in the United States; the "law of the soil," where born. p. 561

**Keynote address**   Speech given at a party convention to set the tone for the convention and the campaign to come. p. 336

**Labor union**   Organization of workers who share the same type of job or who work in the same industry; see interest group. p. 216

**Legal tender**   Any kind of money that a creditor must by law accept in payment for debts. p. 266

**Libel**   Publication of statements that wrongfully damage another's reputation; see slander. p. 499

**Liberal constructionist**   One who believes that the provisions of the Constitution, and in particular those granting power to government, are to be construed in broad terms. p. 260

**Limited government**   Basic principle of the American system of government; that government is limited in what it may do, and each individual has certain rights that government cannot take away; see constitutionalism, popular sovereignty. pp. 26, 56

**Literacy**   Ability to read and write; tests of literacy once used in several States to prevent voting by certain groups. p. 135

**Lobbying**   Activities of an agent (lobbyist) for a pressure group, usually to influence public policy. p. 224

**Magna Carta**   The Great Charter establishing the principle that the power of the monarchy was not absolute in England; forced upon the king by his barons in 1215, and protecting such fundamental rights as trial by jury. p. 27

**Majority opinion**   Written statement by a majority of the judges of a court in support of a decision made by that court. p. 476

**Major party**   A dominant party in a governmental system (e.g., the Republicans and Democrats in American politics); see minor party. p. 99

**Mandate**   The instructions or commands a constituency gives to its elected officials concerning policies. p. 190

**Market economy**   Economic system in which the government's role is a limited one and key decisions are made by private individuals and companies through the give and take of the marketplace. p. 615

**Mass media**   Those means of communication that reach large audiences, especially television, newspapers, radio, and magazines. p. 198

**Mayor-council government** The most common form of city government in this country, featuring an elected mayor as chief executive and an elected council as the legislative body. p. 650

**Media** Means of communicating with people, such as the press, radio, and television. p. 355

**Medium** A means of transmitting information; the singular form of *media*. p. 198

**Metropolitan area** Term for the large cities and the surrounding separate (but economically and socially integrated) communities. p. 656

**Minister** Cabinet member in a parliamentary government. p. 578

**Minor party** One of the less widely supported political parties in a governmental system; see major party. p. 102

**Miranda rule** A listing of the Constitutional rights that suspects must be advised of before police questioning: (1) they have a right to remain silent; (2) anything they say may be used against them in court; (3) they have a right to an attorney before questioning begins; (4) an attorney will be appointed for them by the court if they cannot afford one; (5) they may bring the questioning to an end at any time. p. 535

**Monarchy** Government with an hereditary ruler. p. 576

**Monopoly** A firm that is the only source of a product or service. p. 608

**Multi-seat district** Electoral districts in which voters choose more than one representative. p. 583

**Multiparty system** Political system in which three or more major parties compete for public offices; see one-party, two-party system. p. 105

**National Diet** Japanese parliament. p. 582

**Nationalization** Governmental acquisition of private industry for public use. p. 589

**Naturalization** Legal process by which a person born a citizen of one country becomes a citizen of another. p. 562

**Necessary and Proper Clause** Part of the Constitution that gives Congress the power to make all laws "necessary and proper" for executing its powers; has been used to expand greatly congressional power. p. 271

**New Jersey Plan** An alternative to the Virginia Plan offered at the Constitutional Convention of 1787, differing chiefly in the matter of how states should be represented in Congress. p. 43

**Nomination** Process of selecting (naming) candidates for office. pp. 158, 230

**One-party system** Political system in which only one party exists, or in which only one party has a reasonable chance of winning elections. p. 105

**Open primary** Form of the direct primary in which any qualified voter may participate without regard to his/her party allegiance. p. 162

**Opinion leader** Any person who has a more than usual influence on the views of others. p. 188

**Original jurisdiction** Power to hear a case first, before any other court. p. 464

**Oversight function** Review by legislative committees of the policies and programs of the executive branch. p. 250

**Pardon** Release from the punishment or legal consequences of a crime, by the President (in a federal case) or a governor (in a State case). pp. 368, 641

**Parish** The Louisiana term for counties. p. 643

**Parliamentary government** Form of government in which the executive leadership (usually, a prime minister and cabinet) is chosen by and responsible to the legislature (parliament), as well as being members of the legislature, as in Great Britain. p. 11

**Parole** Release of a prisoner short of the completion of the term of a sentence. p. 641

**Party caucus** A meeting of party leaders and/or members to conduct party business. p. 287

**Party identification** Person's sense of attachment, loyalty to a political party. p. 149

**Passport** Certificate issued by a government, identifying a person as a citizen of a country and authorizing that person to travel, live abroad. p. 430

**Patent** A license issued to an inventor granting the exclusive right to manufacture and sell his or her invention for a limited period of time. p. 269

**Patronage** Practice of giving government jobs to supporters and friends; see spoils system. p. 396

**Payroll tax** Tax levied on employers and their employees, and on self-employed persons. p. 409

*Perestroika* In the former Soviet Union, policy to restructure political and economic life. p. 593

**Petit jury** Body of (usually) 12 persons who hear the evidence and decide questions of fact in a court case; see trial jury, grand jury. p. 674

**Petition of Right** Challenged the idea of the divine right of kings, declaring in 1628 in England that even a monarch must obey the law of the land. p. 27

**Picketing** Patrolling of a business site by workers on strike; an attempt to inform the public and to persuade others not to deal with the employer involved. p. 504

**Plaintiff** In civil law, the party who brings a suit or some other legal action against another (the defendant) in court. p. 464

**Platform** Written declaration of the principles and policy positions of a political party, usually adopted at that party's convention. p. 337

**Pluralistic society** One consisting of several distinct cultures and groups. p. 104

**Plurality** In an election, at least one more vote than that received by any other candidate; a plurality may or may not be a majority of the total vote. p. 103

**Pocket veto** Type of veto a chief executive may use after a legislature has adjourned; it is applied when the chief executive does not formally sign or reject a bill within the time period allowed to do so; see veto. p. 307

**Police power** Power of a State to act to protect and promote the public health, safety, morals, and welfare. p. 519

**Politburo**   The highest policy-making committee of the Communist party in the former Soviet Union. p. 597

**Political action committee (PAC)**   Political arm of a special interest group that seeks to influence elections and public policy decisions. p. 174

**Political efficacy**   Influence or effectiveness in politics and the workings of government. p. 142

**Political party**   Organized group that seeks to control government through the winning of elections and the holding of public office. p. 99

**Political socialization**   Complex process by which individuals acquire their political attitudes and opinions. p. 145

**Polling place**   Particular location where those voters who live in a particular area (see precinct) vote in an election. p. 167

**Poll tax**   Tax (now unconstitutional) paid in some States before a person was allowed to vote. p. 136

**Popular sovereignty**   Basic principle of the American system of government; that the people are the only source of any and all governmental power, that government must be conducted with the consent of the governed. pp. 35, 55

**Precedent**   Previous court decisions that influence the ruling of later and similar cases. p. 672

**Precinct**   The smallest unit of election administration; a local voting district. pp. 122, 167

**Prefecture**   Political subdivision into which Japan is divided. p. 583

**Presentment**   Formal accusation of crime brought by a grand jury of its own motion. p. 530

**Presidential electors**   The persons elected by the voters to represent them in making a formal selection of the President and Vice President. p. 327

**Presidential government**   Form of government characterized by a separation of powers between independent and coequal executive and legislative branches, as in the United States. p. 11

**Presidential primary**   Election at which a party's voters (1) choose some or all of a State party organization's delegates to that party's national convention, and/or (2) express a preference among various contenders for the party's presidential nomination. p. 331

**Presidential succession**   Manner in which a vacancy in the presidency is to be filled. p. 324

**President of the Senate**   The presiding officer of a senate: in Congress, the Vice President of the United States; in a State's legislature, either the lieutenant governor or a senator. p. 286

**President *pro tempore***   The member of the United States Senate, or of the upper house of a State's legislature, chosen to preside in the absence of the president of the Senate. p. 286

**Probable cause**   Reasonable ground, a good basis for the belief that something is true—e.g., that a crime has been committed. p. 523

**Progressive tax**   Any tax in which each step in the rate schedule is geared to the taxpayer's ability to pay (e.g., an income tax); see regressive tax. pp. 407, 668

**Proletariat**   In Marxist terms, the workers in a capitalist system. p. 614

**Propaganda**   A technique of persuasion, aimed at influencing public opinion to create a particular popular belief. p. 223

**Property tax**   A tax levied on (1) real property (land and buildings), or (2) personal property (tangible and intangible personal wealth); see assessment. p. 669

**Public affairs**   Events and issues that concern the people at large. p. 213

**Public debt**   All of the money borrowed by the government over the years and not yet repaid, plus the accrued interest on that money. p. 413

**Public-interest group**   An organization that seeks to influence public policies on behalf of the "public good," as distinguished from those groups that serve a private interest; see interest group. p. 220

**Public opinion**   Those attitudes shared by a significant number of persons on matters of government and politics; expressed group attitudes. p. 186

**Public opinion poll**   A formal survey of public attitudes. p. 191

**Public policy**   All of those things a government decides to do. pp. 3, 211

**Purge**   Ruthless elimination of rivals and dissidents as practiced by Stalin. p. 594

**Quasi-legislative, quasi-judicial**   Ability of government bodies with certain executive (administrative) functions to exercise certain rule-making and decision-making powers (e.g., the several federal independent regulatory commissions). p. 391

**Quorum**   Least number of members who must be present for a legislative body to conduct business. p. 301

**Quota**   Rules requiring certain numbers of jobs or promotions for certain groups. p. 558

**Quota sample**   In scientific polling, a group chosen to be interviewed in which the members of each of several groups are included in proportion to their percentage in the total population; see random sample, sample. p. 193

**Random sample**   In scientific polling, a sample to be interviewed drawn such that each member of the population has an equal chance to be included in it; see quota sample, sample. p. 192

**Ratification**   Formal approval, final consent to the effectiveness of a constitution, constitutional amendment, or treaty. p. 36

**Reapportionment**   Redistribution of political representation on the basis of population changes, usually after a census; see apportionment. p. 239

**Recognition**   The exclusive power of a President to recognize, establish formal diplomatic relations with, foreign states. p. 362

**Redress**   Satisfaction of a claim brought in court. p. 478

**Referendum**   Process in which a measure passed by a legislature is submitted (referred) to the voters for final approval or rejection. p. 636

**Refugee** One who leaves his or her home to seek refuge from war, persecution, or other danger. p. 549

**Regional security alliance** Defensive alliance formed by negotiating a mutual defense treaty with countries that agree to take collective action to meet aggression in various parts of the world. p. 448

**Register** List of viable job candidates maintained by the Office of Personnel Management in the federal recruiting and hiring process. p. 398

**Registration** Procedure of voter identification, intended to prevent fraudulent voting; also known as enrollment. p. 134

**Regressive tax** Any tax levied at a flat rate, i.e., falls most heavily on those least able to pay it (e.g., a sales tax); see progressive tax. pp. 409, 668

**Representative democracy** A system of government in which a small group of persons chosen by the people to act as their representatives expresses the popular will. p. 13

**Representative government** System of government in which public policies are made by officials who are selected by the voters and held accountable to them in periodic elections; see democracy. p. 27

**Reprieve** An official postponement of execution of a sentence; see pardon. pp. 368, 641

**Reservation** Areas of public land set aside by a government for use by a Native-American group. p. 547

**Reserved powers** Those powers held by the States in the American federal system. p. 77

**Resolution** Measure relating to the internal business of one house in a legislature, or expressing that chamber's opinion on some matter, without the force of law; see concurrent resolution, joint resolution. p. 297

**Reverse discrimination** A description of affirmative action by critics of that policy; holds that giving preference to females and/or nonwhites discriminates against members of the majority group; see affirmative action. p. 558

**Rider** Provision, unlikely to pass on its own merit, added to an important bill certain to pass so that it will "ride" through the legislative process. p. 297

**Right of legation** The right of a nation to send and receive diplomatic representatives. p. 429

**Rule of law** See constitutionalism. p. 56

**Runoff primary** A second primary, involving the two front-runners in the first contest; held where election law requires a majority vote for nomination. p. 163

**Sabotage** Destructive act intended to hinder a nation's war or defense effort. p. 506

**Sales tax** A tax paid by the purchaser on the sale of commodities; the single most important source of income among the States. p. 668

**Sample** In scientific polling, a small number of people chosen as a representative cross-section of the total population to be surveyed; see quota sample, random sample. p. 192

**Search warrant** Court order authorizing a search of a suspect's property or person. p. 519

**Sedition** Spoken, written, or other action promoting resistance to lawful authority; especially advocating the violent overthrow of a government. p. 506

**Segregation** Separation or isolation of a racial or other group from the rest of the population in education or other areas of public or private activity. p. 551

**Select committee** Legislative committee created for a limited time and for some specific purpose; also known as special committee. p. 293

**Seniority rule** Unwritten rule in both houses of Congress, that the top posts in each chamber will (with rare exception) be held by "ranking members," i.e., those with the longest records of service; applied most strictly to committee chairmanships. p. 289

**Separate-but-equal doctrine** Long held by the Supreme Court, that the 14th Amendment's Equal Protection Clause did not forbid racial segregation so long as the separate facilities for African Americans were equal to those provided for whites; overturned in *Brown* v. *Board of Education of Topeka*, 1954. p. 552

**Separation of powers** Basic principle of the American system of government, that the executive, legislative, and judicial powers are divided among three independent and coequal branches of government; see checks and balances. pp. 56, 541

**Session** The regular period of time during which a legislative body conducts business. p. 237

**Shadow cabinet** In a parliamentary system, leading members of the opposition who are likely to be cabinet ministers should their party win a majority at the next election. p. 579

**Shield law** Law found in some States designed to protect reporters against being forced to disclose confidential news sources. p. 502

**Single-interest group** Political action committee that concentrates effort on one issue. p. 224

**Single-issue party** Political party that concentrates on a single public policy issue. p. 115

**Single-member district** Electoral district from which one person is chosen by the voters for each office on the ballot; see at-large. pp. 103, 241

**Slander** Speech that wrongfully damages a person's reputation; see libel. p. 499

**Sound bite** Short, sharply focused television news report. p. 204

**Sovereignty** Supreme, absolute power of a state within its own territory. p. 4

**Speaker of the House** The presiding officer of the House of Representatives, chosen by and from the majority party in the House. p. 285

**Special district** Local unit of government, created to perform (usually) a single public function in a locale (e.g., a school or library district). p. 667

**Special session** An extraordinary session of a legislative body. p. 238

**Splinter party** Political party that has split away from one of the major parties. p. 115

**Split-ticket voting** Voting for candidates of more than one party in the same election; see straight-ticket voting. pp. 122, 150

**Spoils system** Practice of awarding government jobs, contracts, and other favors to friends and supporters; see patronage. p. 395

**Standing committee** Permanent committee in a legislative body to which bills in a specified subject-matter area are referred; see select committee. p. 290

**State** A body of people, living in a defined territory, organized under a government and having the power to make and enforce law without the consent of any higher authority. p. 4

**Straight-ticket voting** Voting for the candidates of one party in an election; see split-ticket voting. p. 149

**Straw vote** Unscientific measurement of public opinion; usually asking the same question of a large number of people. p. 191

**Strict constructionist** One who advocates a narrow interpretation of the Constitution's provisions, in particular those granting power to government. p. 260

**Strong-mayor government** Variety of mayor-council form of city government, featuring a mayor with broad executive powers (e.g., to hire and fire, to prepare budget, to veto ordinances). p. 652

**Subcommittee** Division of existing committee that is formed to address specific issues. p. 298

**Suffrage** Right to vote. p. 129

**Supply and demand, laws of** A basic feature of a capitalistic economy; when supplies of goods, services become plentiful, prices tend to drop; when supplies become scarcer, prices tend to rise. p. 608

**Supreme Soviet** National legislature of the former Soviet Union. p. 595

**Symbolic speech** Expression of beliefs, ideas by conduct rather than in speech or print. p. 503

**Tax return** Declaration of taxable income and the exemptions and deductions claimed; filed with the Internal Revenue Service. p. 408.

**Term** The specified length of time served by elected officials in their elected offices. p. 237

**Three-fifths Compromise** An agreement at the Constitutional Convention of 1787 that slaves should be counted as three-fifths of a person for purposes of determining the population of a state. p. 44

**Township** A term used for a subdivision of a county in many States; see county. p. 647

**Trade association** Interest group representing a segment of the business community. p. 216

**Treason** Crime of disloyalty which, says the Constitution, "shall consist only in levying war against (the United States), or in adhering to their enemies, giving them aid and comfort"; can be committed only in wartime. p. 506

**Treaty** Formal agreement made between or among sovereign states. p. 361

**Two-party system** Political system in which the candidates of only two (major) parties have a reasonable chance of winning elections; see multiparty, one-party system. p. 102

**UN Security Council** United Nations council bearing the UN's major responsibility for maintaining international peace. p. 451

**Unconstitutional** Contrary to constitutional provisions and so invalid. p. 59

**Unicameral** An adjective describing a legislative body with one chamber; see bicameral. p. 29

**Unitary government** Form of government in which all of the powers of the government are held by a single agency, as in Great Britain; local governments are completely subordinate to and have only those powers given to them by the central government. p. 10

**Urbanization** Percentage of population of a State living in cities of more than 2,500 people or in suburbs of cities with more than 50,000. p. 666

**Veto** Chief executive's power to reject a bill passed by a legislature; literally (Latin) "I forbid"; see item veto, pocket veto. p. 307

**Veto power** A constitutional power that enables the President (or a governor) to return legislation to the Congress (or the State legislature) unsigned with reasons for his objection; see pocket veto. pp. 307, 587

**Virginia Plan** Offered at the Constitutional Convention; called for a bicameral legislature in which representation in both houses would be based on population or financial support for the central government. p. 42

**Visa** A permit to enter another state, obtained from the country one wishes to enter. p. 430

**Ward** Local unit of party organization; also, a district within a city for city council elections. p. 122

**Weak-mayor government** Variety of mayor-council form of city government, featuring a mayor with little real power. p. 652

**Welfare state** A government that assumes the role of promoter of citizen welfare through programs sponsored by the government. p. 615

**Whip** Assistants to the floor leaders, responsible for monitoring and marshalling votes. p. 287

**Winner-take-all** An almost obsolete system whereby the presidential aspirant who won the preference vote in a primary automatically won the support of all the delegates chosen in the primary. p. 332

**Zoning** Practice of dividing a city or other unit of government into districts (zones) and regulating by law (a zoning ordinance) the uses of land in each of them. p. 655

# INDEX

**Note:** Entries with a page number followed by an *(n)* denote reference to a footnote on that page; those followed by a *(p)* denote a photo.

# ACKNOWLEDGMENTS

**PICTURE RESEARCH:** Toni Michaels
**EDITORIAL SERVICES:** Dotti Marshall, Marisa Sibio Shuff
**DESIGN SERVICES:** Sara Shelton
**PRODUCTION:** Angelo Rauseo

**COVER PHOTO (front/back):** Anestis Diakopoulos/Stock Boston
**TITLE PAGE: Page i**, President Clinton, ©Ira Wyman/Sygma, Bob Dole, Joint Committee on Printing, Newt Gingrich, ©Terry Ashe/Gamma-Liaison, **ii,iii**, Comstock

**TABLE OF CONTENTS: Page viii**, Malcolm Linton/Black Star, **ix**, Mark Antman/The Image Works **x**, Owen Franken/Stock Boston; **xiii**, Sovfoto/Eastfoto.

**BACKGROUND PHOTO OF AMERICAN FLAG appearing once in each chapter:** Scott Slobodian/TSW

## UNIT 1

**Page 1** ©Cliff Feulner/The Image Bank; **3**, ©Tannenbaum/Sygma; **6**, By permission of Johnny Hart and Creators Syndicate, Inc.; **8**, "Unveiling of the Statue of Liberty." Quilt by Katherine Westphal, 1964. National Museum of American Art - Smithsonian Institution. Gift of the Artist. Photo: Art Resource.; **11**, ©John Running/Stock Boston; **13**, ©Yivo Institute for Jewish Research; **16**, ©Alan Carey/The Image Works; **18**, Courtesy, Mexican American Legal Defense Educational Fund; **25**, ©Bob Daemmrich/The Image Works; **27,29** ©The Granger Collection; **31**, ©Library of Congress; **33**, "Washington Studying the Plans of Battle" (Night Scene) by Dunsmore. Courtesy The Fraunces Tavern Museum, NYC; **34L**, ©Independence National Historic Park Collection; **34R**, ©Bettmann Archive; **38**, ©The Granger Collection; **40**, ©Louis Goldman/Photo Researchers; **41**, ©The Granger Collection; **43**, ©Burr Shafer; **46**, ©Independence National Historic Park; **49C**, ©The Library Company of Philadelphia; **49L**, ©The Bettman Archive; **49R**, ©The Granger Collection; **55**, ©Robert Llewellyn; **57**, ©Bettmann; **62**, ©The Granger Collection; **66L**, ©Bettmann Archive; **66R**, ©Bettmann Archive; **67**, Collection of Bill McClenaghan; **67**, ©The Granger Collection; **73**, ©Gail Shumway/FPG; `©Liederman/Rothco; **81**, ©P. Jones Griffiths/Magnum Photos; **84**, ©Rob Crandall/Picture Group; **85**, ©Bob Daemmrich/The Image Works; **88**, ©John Running/Stock Boston; **91**, ©Vanessa Vick/Photo Researchers.

## UNIT 2

**Pages 96-97**, ©Les Stone/Sygma; **99**, ©Bob Daemmrich/Stock Boston; **101**, The Museum of American Political Life, University of Hartford, West Hartford, CT.; **103**, ©Arthur Grace/Sygma; **104**, Collection of Bill McClenaghan; **106L**, ©Cynthia Johnson/Gamma Liaison; **106R**, Dunagin's People by Ralph Dunagin. Reprinted with special permission of NAS, Inc.; **112**, The Museum of American Political Life, University of Hartford, West Hartford, CT.; **120L**, ©Trippett/Sipa Press; **120R**, ©AP/Wide World Photos; **121R**, ©AP/Wide World Photos; **121L**, ©Joe Traver/Gamma Liaison; **124**, ©1984 by Herblock in the Washington Post.; **129**, ©Peter Blakely/Picture Group; **130L**, ©The Granger Collection; **130R**, ©Library of Congress; **134**, Taylor/Albuquerque Tribune, N.M./Rothco; **135**, ©Ernst Haas/Magnum; **139**, ©UPI/Bettmann Newsphotos; **140**, ©Paul Conklin; **142**, ROB ROGERS reprinted by permission of UFS, Inc.; **150L**, ©Bob Daemmrich/The Image Works; **150R**, ©Bob Daemmrich/Stock Boston; **151**, AUTH copyright 1986 The Philadelphia Inquirer. Reprinted with permission of UNIVERSAL PRESS SYNDICATE. All rights reserved.; **157**, ©Ellis Vener/Woodfin Camp & Associates; **159**, ©The Granger Collection; **160**, The Museum of American Political Life, University of Hartford, West Hartford, CT.; **161**, The Museum of American Political Life, University of Hartford, West Hartford, CT.; **163**, Dunagin's People by Ralph Dunagin. Reprinted with special permission of NAS, Inc.; **164**, ©Frank Siteman/The Picture Cube; **165**, ©Gerry Gropp/Sipa Press; **167**, ©AP/Wide World Photos; **168**, File Photo.; **169L**, Indiana State Election Committee; **169R**, Massachusetts State Election Committee; **170B**, ©Charles Gupton/Stock Boston; **170C**, "©Reprinted with special permission of King Features Syndicate, Inc."; **170T**, ©Mary Heaton; **173**, ©1988 by HERBLOCK in the Washington Post.; **176**, ©Bob Daemmrich ; **179**, ©Leed/Rothco Syndication; **185**, ©Ira Wyman/Sygma; **186**, "©Reprinted with special permission of King Features Syndicate, Inc."; **187**, ©Gabe Kirchheimer/Black Star; **190**, ©Bob Daemmrich/Stock Boston; **191**, File Photo; **192**, By permission of Mike Luckovich and Creators Syndicate.; **193**, ©Bettmann Newsphotos; **195**, ©Ellis Herwig/The Picture Cube; **196**, ©Bettmann Newsphotos; **200**, ©Laima Druskis/Stock Boston; **201**, ©Stephen Frisch/Stock Boston; **203**, ©Huston Westover/F-Stop Pictures; **204**, "©Reprinted with special permission of King Features Syndicate, Inc."; **211**, ©Bob Daemmrich/Stock Boston; **212**, ©Dennis Brack/Black Star; **214**, ©P.F. Gero/Sygma; **217L**, ©Paul Conklin; **217R**, ©Gary Sigman/Black Star; **219L**, ©Luana George/Black Star; **219R**, ©Joe Cempa/Black Star; **220**, "©Reprinted with special permission of King Features Syndicate, Inc."; **222**, ©Mark Antman/The Image Works; **225**, ©Robert Trippett/Sipa Press.

## UNIT 3

**Pages 232-233**, Courtesy, the Supreme Court Historical Society, photograph Ralph D. Jones; **235**, Joint Committee on Printing; **237**, OLIPHANT copyright 1990 UNIVERSAL PRESS SYNDICATE. Reprinted with permission. All rights reserved.; **242**, ©The Granger Collection; **243**, ©Steve Magnuson; **245**, Courtesy,Barbara Mikulski; **246**, Library of Congress; **249**, Library of Congress; **254**, Prentice Hall File Photo; **259**, ©Wally McNamee/Sygma; **260T**, Courtesy Norman Y. Mineta; **260BR**, ©J. Pat Carter/Gamma Liaison; **260BL**, "©Reprinted with special permission of King Features Syndicate, Inc."; **263**, ©C.P. Houston, Houston Chronicle; **265**, ©Holt Confer/The Image Works; **266B**, ©Patrick Aventurier/Gamma Liaison; **266T**, ©The Granger Collection; **267**, ©Les Stone/Sygma; **269**, The Senate. (1935). William Gropper. Oil on Canvas, 25 1/8 x 33 1/8" (63.8 x 84.2 cm). Collection, The Museum of Modern Art, New York. Gift of A. Conger Goodyear; **275**, ©Dennis Brack/Black Star; **277**, Collection of Bill McClenaghan; **283**, ©Rick Friedman/Black Star; **285**, ©Dennis Brack/Black Star; **285** inset, ©The Bettmann Archive; **286**, ©Terry Ashe/Gamma Liaison; **287**, "©Reprinted with special permission of King Features Syndi-